Federal Finances					Size of Government as a Share of GDP	
	Federal Budget Totals (Billions of Dollars)			National Debt		Federal, State, and Local Government	
Year	Fiscal Year Outlays	Fiscal Year Receipts	Surplus (+) or Deficit (−)	Billions of Dollars	As a Percent of GDP	Expenditures (Percent of GDP)	Purchases of Goods & Services (% of GDP)
1959	92.1	79.2	−12.8	287.5	58.5	23.0	22.1
1960	92.2	92.5	0.3	290.5	56.1	23.1	21.5
1961	97.7	94.4	−3.3	292.6	55.1	24.0	22.2
1962	106.8	99.7	−7.1	302.9	53.4	24.1	22.5
1963	111.3	106.6	−4.8	310.3	51.9	24.1	22.3
1964	118.5	112.6	−5.9	316.1	49.4	23.7	21.8
1965	118.2	116.8	−1.4	322.3	46.9	23.4	21.3
1966	134.5	130.8	−3.7	328.5	43.6	24.2	22.0
1967	157.5	148.8	−8.6	340.4	41.9	26.1	23.3
1968	178.1	153.0	−25.2	368.7	42.5	26.8	23.3
1969	183.6	186.9	3.2	365.8	38.6	26.9	22.8
1970	195.6	192.8	−2.8	380.9	37.8	28.3	22.8
1971	210.2	187.1	−23.0	408.2	37.9	28.7	22.2
1972	230.7	207.3	−23.4	435.9	37.0	28.5	21.7
1973	245.7	230.8	−14.9	466.3	35.7	28.0	20.8
1974	269.4	263.2	−6.1	483.9	33.6	29.3	21.6
1975	332.3	279.1	−53.2	541.9	34.9	31.6	22.2
1976	371.8	298.1	−73.7	629.0	36.3	30.6	21.2
1977	409.2	355.6	−53.7	706.4	35.8	29.9	20.6
1978	458.7	399.6	−59.2	776.6	35.1	28.7	20.0
1979	504.0	463.3	−40.7	829.5	33.2	28.4	19.8
1980	590.9	517.1	−73.8	909.1	33.4	30.2	20.6
1981	678.2	599.3	−79.0	994.8	32.6	30.6	20.3
1982	745.8	617.8	−128.0	1,137.3	35.4	32.5	21.1
1983	808.4	600.6	−207.8	1,371.7	40.1	32.4	20.9
1984	851.9	666.5	−185.4	1,564.7	41.0	31.1	20.4
1985	946.4	734.1	−212.3	1,817.5	44.3	31.4	20.9
1986	990.5	769.2	−221.2	2,120.6	48.5	31.6	21.2
1987	1,004.1	854.4	−149.8	2,346.1	50.9	31.4	21.2
1988	1,064.5	909.3	−155.2	2,601.3	52.5	30.7	20.4
1989	1,143.7	991.2	−152.5	2,868.0	53.6	30.5	20.1
1990	1,253.2	1,032.0	−221.2	3,206.6	56.4	31.4	20.5
1991	1,324.4	1,055.0	−269.4	3,598.5	61.4	32.1	20.7
1992	1,381.7	1,091.3	−290.4	4,002.1	65.1	33.1	20.2
1993	1,409.4	1,154.4	−255.0	4,351.4	67.2	32.7	19.6
1994	1,461.7	1,258.6	−203.1	4,643.7	67.8	31.9	18.9
1995	1,515.7	1,351.8	−163.9	4,921.0	68.4	31.8	18.7
1996	1,560.5	1,453.1	−107.5	5,181.9	68.6	31.3	18.3
1997	1,601.2	1,579.3	−21.9	5,369.7	67.2	30.5	17.9
1998	1,652.6	1,721.8	69.2	5,478.7	65.2	29.8	17.5

Sources: *Economic Report of the President,* 1999, and *Survey of Current Business,* March 1999.

Ninth Edition

MACROECONOMICS

Private and Public Choice

Ninth Edition

James D. Gwartney
Florida State University

Richard L. Stroup
Montana State University

Russell S. Sobel
West Virginia University

THE DRYDEN PRESS
A DIVISION OF HARCOURT COLLEGE PUBLISHERS
Fort Worth Philadelphia San Diego New York Orlando Austin San Antonio
Toronto Montreal London Sydney Tokyo

Publisher	MIKE ROCHE
Acquisitions Editor	GARY NELSON
Market Strategist	DEBBIE K. ANDERSON
Developmental Editor	AMY RAY
Project Editor	LAURA J. HANNA
Art Director	BURL SLOAN
Production Manager	LOIS WEST

Cover image: © The Stock Market

ISBN: 0-03-021289-8

Library of Congress Catalog Card Number: 99-64604

Address for Domestic Orders
The Dryden Press, 6277 Sea Harbor Drive, Orlando, FL 32887-6777
800-782-4479

Address for International Orders
International Customer Service
The Dryden Press, 6277 Sea Harbor Drive, Orlando, FL 32887-6777
407-345-3800
(fax) 407-345-4060
(e-mail) hbintl@harcourtbrace.com

Address for Editorial Correspondence
The Dryden Press, 301 Commerce Street, Suite 3700, Fort Worth, TX 76102

Web Site Address
http://www.hbcollege.com

Printed in the United States of America

9 0 1 2 3 4 5 6 7 8 048 9 8 7 6 5 4 3 2 1

The Dryden Press
Harcourt College Publishers

THE DRYDEN PRESS SERIES IN ECONOMICS

Baldani, Bradfield, and Turner
Mathematical Economics

Baumol and Blinder
Economics: Principles and Policy
Eighth Edition
(also available in Micro and Macro paperbacks)

Baumol, Panzar, and Willig
Contestable Markets and the Theory of Industry Structure
Revised Edition

Breit and Elzinga
The Antitrust Casebook: Milestones in Economic Regulation
Third Edition

Brue
The Evolution of Economic Thought
Sixth Edition

Callan and Thomas
Environmental Economics and Management: Theory, Policy, and Applications
Second Edition

Edgmand, Moomaw, and Olson
Economics and Contemporary Issues
Fourth Edition

Gardner
Comparative Economic Systems
Second Edition

Gwartney, Stroup, and Sobel
Economics: Private and Public Choice
Ninth Edition
(also available in Micro and Macro paperbacks)

Gwartney and Stroup
Introduction to Economics: The Wealth and Poverty of Nations

Hess and Ross
Economic Development: Theories, Evidence, and Policies

Hirschey and Pappas
Fundamentals of Managerial Economics
Sixth Edition

Hirschey
Managerial Economics
Revised Edition

Hyman
Public Finance: A Contemporary Application of Theory to Policy
Sixth Edition

Kahn
The Economic Approach to Environmental and Natural Resources
Second Edition

Kaserman and Mayo
Government and Business: The Economics of Antitrust and Regulation

Kaufman
The Economics of Labor Markets
Fifth Edition

Kennett and Lieberman
The Road to Capitalism: The Economic Transformation of Eastern Europe and the Former Soviet Union

Kreinin
International Economics: A Policy Approach
Eighth Edition

Mankiw
Principles of Economics
(also available in Micro and Macro paperbacks)

Nicholson
Intermediate Microeconomics and Its Application
Seventh Edition

Nicholson
Microeconomic Theory: Basic Principles and Extensions
Seventh Edition

Ramanathan
Introductory Econometrics with Applications
Fourth Edition

Rukstad
Corporate Decision Making in the World Economy: Company Case Studies

Rukstad
Macroeconomic Decision Making in the World Economy: Text and Cases
Third Edition

Samuelson and Marks
Managerial Economics
Third Edition

Santerre and Neun
Health Economics: Theories, Insights, and Industry Studies
Revised Edition

Scarth
Macroeconomics: An Introduction to Advanced Methods

Sexton
Exploring Economics: Pathways to Problem Solving
(also available in Micro and Macro paperbacks)

Stockman
Introduction to Economics
Second Edition
(also available in Micro and Macro paperbacks)

Walton and Rockoff
History of the American Economy
Eighth Edition

Welch and Welch
Economics: Theory and Practice
Sixth Edition

Yarbrough and Yarbrough
The World Economy: Trade and Finance
Fifth Edition

PREFACE

We are dogmatic about some things. *We believe that a course on economics principles should focus on the power and relevance of the economic way of thinking.* It is this belief and corresponding writing approach that have made *Economics: Private and Public Choice* one of Harcourt College Publishing's most solid and enduring texts—a cornerstone of its economics program for more than 25 years. With the eighth edition having sold more copies than any prior edition, our commitment to this approach is strengthened.

While models, formulas, and mechanical exercises can be helpful, they should be viewed as tools. In a principles course, they are secondary to the development of the economic way of thinking. Throughout this text, we integrate applications and real-world data in an effort to make the basic concepts of economics come alive for the reader. The book's exercises, testing questions, and even the PowerPoint package developed for this edition are designed to encourage and promote economic reasoning.

The study of economics does not have to be either difficult or "watered down." *Economics: Private and Public Choice* is a comprehensive text, rich in detail. But it is written with the student in mind. We have avoided abstractions and mechanical exercises that stress obscure details rather than basic concepts. The primary objective of our writing style is clarity. We have worked hard to make the material as clear as possible. Examples, illustrations, and visual aides are used to reinforce basic concepts. Simplicity, however, is not substituted for depth. Rather, our aim is to highlight the power, accessibility, and relevance of economic concepts.

This is an exciting time to study economics. More than ever before, the world is characterized by dynamic change, instant communication, and interaction between people in different nations. New products and technologies are constantly replacing the old ways of doing things. In fact, sometimes new products become obsolete just a few years after they are introduced. How will these developments affect your life? What will the U.S. economy be like ten or twenty years from now? Why has the U.S. economy experienced persistent growth during the last 16 years? Why do some countries prosper while others regress? As we proceed, we will use the tools of economics to address these and many other important issues that affect us so dramatically.

CHANGES IN THE NINTH EDITION

A noteworthy change with this edition is the inclusion of new coauthor Russell S. Sobel of West Virginia University. For the better part of a decade, Professor Sobel has contributed significantly to the development and improvement of both *Economics: Private and Public Choice* and its ancillary package. We are convinced that his contributions will continue for many years to come.

To the text itself, we have made a number of structural changes that make this edition more flexible and user-friendly. Additionally, the supplements for this edition—both print and electronic—have been markedly improved. (Please review the "Supplementary Materials" section later in this preface to learn about these exciting new enhancements.) Important changes to the textbook follow.

Division into "Core" Chapters and "Special Topic" Applications

The core chapters found in this edition cover all of the material taught in most principles courses and they are presented in the usual manner. Examples and data from the real world are used to reinforce the analysis. In addition, the final part of the text (Applications and Special Topics), contains a number of short features on high-profile topics. The applications are crisp and clearly focused—about one-third the length of a chapter. They are designed for coverage in a single class period. These features provide a solid foundation for discussing important topics such as the stock market, the future of social security, the impact of unions, welfare reform, natural resources, and environment protection. Instructors stressing applications may choose to build their course around Parts 1 and 2, plus the final part, "Applications and Special Topics." Others may want to use several of the applications to buttress various points as they progress through the core material, or they may want to combine the applications and chapters for the purpose of teaching a survey course. Still others—particularly those teaching honors classes—may want to use the applications as the focal point for special projects or classroom debates. The format of this edition provides each instructor with maximum flexibility. Directly following this preface, you will find some sample course outlines with suggestions for the integration of these applications.

A More Visual Textbook

Today's students read less, but they are better prepared to learn from the superior visual aides and technologies that we can now offer them. Accordingly, we have reduced the number of words in this edition by about 10 percent—taking care to not omit important material or oversimplify the analysis. Illustrative graphics, diagrams, pictures, cartoons, and other visual aides are frequently used to highlight the content and reinforce important points. An example of this is the feature on "Facts and Figures of Government" between Chapters 5 and 6. Rather than using 8 to 10 text pages to present this material as in the last edition, the ninth edition uses graphs and pictures with brief descriptions to illustrate the major points. You will notice that the part openers in the text have also been given special treatment. Each is a photo/graphical montage intended to pique the student's curiosity about the material that follows. You will notice that the end-of-chapter summary paragraphs have been rewritten into point-by-point "key topic" lists. The new format helps students immediately recognize the most important aspects of each chapter, making for easier student review.

More Supply and Demand

Following Chapter 3 on supply, demand, and the market process, we have added a new chapter on applications and extension of the supply and demand model. Instructors tell us that they are using supply and demand more and more to address topics of interest to students. This is precisely what Chapter 4 does. Fun topics integrated into this chapter include black markets, illegal drug trade, rent controls, the minimum wage, actual versus statutory tax incidence, and the Laffer curve.

The Role of Government and Collective Choice

While Chapters 3 and 4 focus on markets, Chapters 5 and 6 analyze the functions and operations of government. These two chapters focus on the protective role of government, why governments are often involved in the provision of public goods, and how the political process actually works. This material consolidates four chapters from the last edition. Regardless of the emphasis placed on the public choice approach, we believe that Chapters 5 and 6 add an important dimension to an economics course. This material will enliven a principles course, while enhancing student understanding of the real world and some of its imperfections. Taken together, the four chapters in Part 2 provide a solid foundation for the topics covered throughout the remainder of the text.

Core Macro

As in the past, our approach to macro highlights the role of and interaction among markets. In this edition, the foreign exchange market is explicitly included in the initial development of the aggregate demand/aggregate supply model. This approach makes it easier to visualize both (a) the role of exchange rates in the coordination of trade and capital flows and (b) the impact of trade and capital flows on the major macroeconomic markets. Chapter 15 on economic stabilization has been extensively revised. The importance of economic growth is stressed throughout the macro section. Chapter 16 focuses on current debates in growth theory while highlighting the importance of institutions and policies that most economists agree influence growth. Both inputs (labor and capital) and a positive political environment (secure property rights, predictable regulatory structure, monetary and price stability, and the openness of an economy) are stressed as being key to long-term economic growth.

ORGANIZATIONAL FEATURES

We have employed several organizational features designed to make the presentation both more interesting and more understandable.

1. **Myths of Economics.** In a series of boxed articles, commonly held fallacies of economic reasoning are dispelled. Each myth is followed by a concise explanation of why it is incorrect, and each one is presented within a chapter containing closely related material.
2. **Applications and Measures in Economics.** The application boxed features apply economic theory to real-world issues and controversies. The measures explain how important economic indicators such as the unemployment rate and the index of leading indicators are assembled.
3. **Chapter Focus Questions and Closing "Key Point" Summaries.** Each chapter begins with several questions that summarize the focus of the chapter. Following the end of each chapter is a Key Points section that provides the student with a concise statement of the material (chapter learning objectives). Reviewing the focus questions and these concise "key points" will help the student better understand the material and integrate it into the broader economic picture.
4. **Key Terms.** The terminology of economics is often confusing to introductory students. Key terms are introduced in the text in bold type; simultaneously, each term is defined in the margin opposite the first reference to the term. A glossary containing the key terms also appears at the end of the book.
5. **Critical Analysis Questions.** Each chapter concludes with a set of discussion questions and problems designed to test the student's ability to analyze economic issues and to apply economic theory to real-world events. Appendix B at the end of the text contains suggested answers for approximately half of the critical analysis questions. We think these answers, illustrating the power of economics, will interest students and will help them develop the economic way of thinking.

SUPPLEMENTARY MATERIALS

***Wall Street Journal* Edition.** Instructors can enhance the real-life applications in the text by ordering *The Wall Street Journal* Edition of the textbook instead of the regular textbook. This special edition of the textbook is the same as the standard edition but includes a discounted 20-week *Wall Street Journal* subscription for students. Professors get a free subscription when 10 or more of their students order the *Journal. The Wall Street Journal* provides a nice tie-in with the text, since new examples of economic principles can be found in each day's paper. Students can activate their subscriptions by simply completing and mailing the business reply card found in the back of the book. Instructors interested in finding out more about this program can contact their sales representative or simply call 800-782-4479. This option is available for both the hardcover version of the book and paperback splits.

Coursebooks

The Coursebooks for this edition were prepared by coauthor Professor Russell Sobel and are now available not in two, but three versions, covering all three courses: economics, microeconomics, and macroeconomics. The Coursebooks are more than study guides. Each includes numerous multiple-choice, true/false, and discussion questions permitting students to self-test their knowledge of each chapter. Answers and short explanations for most questions are provided in the back of the Coursebooks. Each chapter also contains problem and project exercises designed to improve the student's knowledge of the mechanics. A set of short readings chosen to supplement the classroom teaching of important topics is also included. Like the textbook, the Coursebooks are designed to help students develop the economic way of thinking.

EconActive Student-Learning CD ROM

Our new EconActive student-learning CD is html-based and very easy to use. Students will navigate through the software as effortlessly as they do a website. The CD ROM contains chapter-review sections, automatically graded practice quizzes, "cyberproblems" that launch to the worldwide web, and more. It also includes interactive graphs, and graphing problems where students are required to give the correct answers by graphing the solutions. They are then given feedback when they draw the wrong solution. Like the Coursebook, the EconActive CD ROM is designed to help students develop the economic way of thinking within a multimedia environment.

Test Banks

The Test Banks for the ninth edition were prepared by David MacPherson of Florida State University. The two Test Banks contain approximately 7,000 questions—multiple-choice and short answer—most of which have been class tested. Within each chapter, the questions correspond to the major subheadings of the text. The first ten questions of each chapter are suitable for use as a comprehensive quiz covering the material of the chapter.

Computerized Test Banks

The computerized Test Banks for this edition have been enhanced significantly. EXAMaster99 includes a more intuitive graphic interface, increased test sizes of up to 500 questions, the capacity to create up to 99 versions of any one test, on-line testing and grade-book keeping, and many more features. The new software is now available on CD ROM in Windows and Macintosh formats. A more detailed explanation of the enhancements of EXAMaster99 can be found at the front of the Instructor's Manual accompanying this text.

PowerPoint CD-ROM

Prepared by David MacPherson, Chuck Skipton, and James Gwartney, we believe our PowerPoint presentation is the best you will find in the principles market. The new package provides chapter-by-chapter lecture notes with fully animated slides of the textbook's exhibits. The dynamic slides and accompanying captions make it easy for instructors to present (and students to follow) sequential changes. The dynamic graphics are also used to highlight various relationships among economic variables. In order to facilitate discussion and interaction, questions designed to help students develop the economic way of thinking are strategically located throughout each chapter. We have used the material in our own classes and can assure you that students find this method of presentation both enjoyable and helpful. As the graphics are built step-by-step, the accompanying dialogue guides the student through the underlying economic analysis. Economic principles are developed rather than merely portrayed. This makes it so much easier to visualize relationships.

Instructions explaining how professors can easily add, delete, and modify slides in order to tailor-make the presentation to their liking are included with the PowerPoint CD-ROM. If instructors want to make the PowerPoint presentation available to students, they can place it on their web site (or the site for their course). It is also available on the web site for this text at **www.dryden.com/econ/gwartney** and on the EconActive Student-Learning CD ROM. The PowerPoint package also includes self-test quizzes covering the major concepts of each chapter. This is a powerful teaching tool that will both attract student interest and enrich the learning process.

PowerPoint Lecture Notes

For years, we have encouraged students to think rather than focus on note-taking in our classes. It was a hard sell—many feel uncomfortable if they are not developing a set of notes. This booklet contains the PowerPoint slides (both the notes and graphics), along with space for additional note-taking next to each slide. This supplement permits students to focus on the classroom activities while providing them with confidence that they have an excellent set of notes for future reference. Professors who choose to customize their PowerPoint presentations and would like to do the same with their accompanying customized printed lecture notes can do so via Harcourt's custom publishing program. Visit **www.harcourtcollege.com/custom** for more information. Once at the Website, you can locate your area's custom publishing representative by clicking the "Contact Us" icon.

Web-Based Course Management Software

Harcourt now offers instructors html-based software to help them build web-based learning sites for their students. This software can be utilized by nontechnical users to create entire web-based courses, or simply to post office hours or supplementary course materials for students. Instructors can design websites that provide a full array of educational tools, including communications with their students, web testing, student grade tracking with access control, database collaboration and searching, and more. It is free of charge to adopters. For more information, call Harcourt's customer service line at 800-237-2665, or visit our home page at **www.harcourtcollege.com.**

Web Site

Resources for instructors and students, including the PowerPoint slides and Instructor's Manual, can be found at **www.dryden.com/econ/gwartney.** Students will find there chapter-by-chapter links to economic Internet sites, automatically graded practice quizzes, PowerPoint slides for their review, sample chapters from the study guide and EconActive CD ROM, and other resources. Career listings for students, leading economic-indicator information, and an economic URL database can be found at **www.dryden.com.** Because the Internet has become so integral to learning and to our lives, you will notice bound into this book a quick Internet reference card listing important URLs. We hope you and your students find it useful and tear it out for your reference.

Instructor's Manual with Classroom Games

The Instructor's Manual was also prepared by David MacPherson. Instructions and information on how to use and modify the PowerPoint material is contained in the front of the manual. Also included at the front of the manual is information on the enhancements to the new EXAMaster99 testing software. The remainder of the manual is divided into three parts. The first part is a detailed outline of each chapter in lecture-note form. It is designed to help instructors organize and structure their current lecture notes according to the format of the ninth edition. Instructors can easily prepare a detailed, personalized set of notes by revising the computerized form of the notes. The second part of the Instructor's Manual contains teaching tips, sources of supplementary materials, and other helpful information. Part 3 provides instructors with in-class games designed to illustrate and enliven important economic concepts. Contributed in part by Professor Charles Stull of Kalamazoo College, the games are an enormously popular feature with instructors. We hope you will try them. We believe you will find them extremely useful for classroom learning.

Instructor's CD ROM

For the first time, the instructor's supplements accompanying this textbook are now conveniently available on one CD ROM. Included on the CD ROM are the PowerPoint slides, Instructor's Manual, and Test Banks. The CD ROM also displays a navigation bar, allowing professors to easily search among the microeconomics and macroeconomics versions of the supplements.

Color Transparencies

Color transparencies of the major exhibits of the ninth edition have been prepared for use with overhead projectors. They are available to adopters upon request in sets for microeconomics and macroeconomics.

Harcourt College Publishing will provide complimentary supplements or supplement packages to those adopters qualified under our adoption policy. Please contact your sales representative to learn how you may qualify. If as an adopter or potential user you receive supplements you do not need, please return them to your sales representative or send them to:

Attn: Returns Department
Troy Warehouse
465 South Lincoln Drive
Troy, MO 63379

ACKNOWLEDGMENTS

A project of this type is a team effort. Several people contributed substantially to the development of this edition.

We would like to express our appreciation to David MacPherson, who prepared both the Test Banks and Instructor's Manual for this edition. He also directed the development of the PowerPoint slides and assisted us in numerous other ways. We are also indebted to Chuck Skipton who put in numerous hours programming the animation for the PowerPoint slides. Together MacPherson and Skipton have developed what we believe to be the very best PowerPoint materials accompanying a principles text.

In the past, Woody Studenmund of Occidental College prepared the Coursebook and Gary Galles of Pepperdine University coauthored the Instructor's Manual. Both of these supplements still bear the imprint of their contribution. Through the years, numerous people have supplied us with quality questions for the Test Banks. We would like to acknowledge specifically the contributions of J. J. Bethune, University of Tennessee—Martin; Edward Bierhanzl, Florida A&M University; Tim Sass, Florida State University; and Woody Studenmund. Both Amy Gwartney and Kathy Makinen helped with the proofing and provided assistance in several other areas.

We have often revised material in light of suggestions made by reviewers, users, friends, and even a few competitors. In this regard, we would like to express our appreciation to the following people for their contributions to recent editions: Robert N. Baird, Case Western Reserve University; Fred Beebe, Long Beach Community College; John W. Dodge, Jr., University of Sioux Falls; Charles J. Ellard, University of Texas—Pan American; T. Windsor Fields, James Madison University; Joseph Fuhrig, Golden Gate University; Ralph C. Gamble, Jr., Fort Hays State University; Joseph D. Greene, Augusta College; Anthony L. Ostrosky, Illinois State University; Robert C. Rencher, Jr., Liberty University; Torsten Schmidt, University of New Hampshire; Paul M. Taube, University of Texas—Pan American; Donna Thompson, Brookdale Community College; Roger Trenary, Kansas State University.

Many people made important contributions to the ninth edition by providing us with insightful feedback and astute reviews. Their comments enabled us to write a superior ninth edition. We are indebted to them: Douglas Agbetsiafa, Indiana University, South Bend; James C.W. Ahiakpor, California State University, Hayward; Ali T. Akarca, University of Illinois at Chicago; Stephen A. Baker, Capital University; Alana Bhatia, University of Colorado at Boulder; Edward J. Bierhanzl, Florida A&M University; Charles A. Booth, University of Alabama at Birmingham; Ford J. Brown, University of Minnesota—Morris; Dennis Brennen, Harper College; James Bryan, Manhattanville College; Darcy R. Carr, Coastal Carolina University; Mike Cohick, Collin County Community College; David S. Collins, Virginia Highlands Community College; Jim F. Couch, University of North Alabama; Steven R. Cunningham, University of Connecticut; George W. Dollar, Clearwater Christian College; Jeff Edwards, Collin County Community College; Robert C. Eyler, Sonoma State University; James R. Fain, Oklahoma State University; Kathryn Finn, Western Washington University; Andrew W. Foshee, McNeese State University; Marsha Goldfarb, University of Maryland Baltimore County; David Harris, Northwood University; Ronald Helgens, Golden Gate University; Robert E. Herman, Nassau Community College/SUNY; William D. Hermann, Golden Gate University, San Francisco; Brad Hobbs, Florida Gulf Coast University; Woodrow W. Hughes, Jr., Converse College; Rob H. Kamery, Christian Brothers University; Frederic R. Kolb, University of Wisconsin, Eau Claire; Barbara Kouskoulas, Lawrence Technological University; David W.

Kreutzer, James Madison University; George Kuljurgis, Oakland University; Randy W. LaHote, Washtenaw Community College; Tsung-Hui Lai, Liberty University; Bob Lawson, Capital University; Don R. Leet, California State University, Fresno; George P. Lephardt, Milwaukee School of Engineering; Joe LeVesque, Northwood University; G. Dirk Mateer, Grove City College; John McArthur, Wofford College; Ed Mills, Kendell College; David M. Mitchell, Oklahoma State University; Hadley T. Mitchell, Taylor University; Glen A. Moots, Northwood University; John R. Neal, Lake-Sumter Community College; Lloyd Orr, Indiana University, Bloomington; Judd W. Patton, Bellevue College; Robert Reinke, University of South Dakota; Robert C. Rencher, Jr., Liberty University; Dan Rickman, Oklahoma State University; Karin L. Russell, Keiser College; Lewis F. Schlossinger, Community College of Aurora; Thomas W. Secrest, USC Coastal Carolina; Ben S. Shippen, Jr., Mercer University; Charles D. Skipton, Florida State University; Ken Somppi, Southern Union State Community College; William A. Steiden, Jefferson Community College; Richard D.C. Trainer, Warsaw School of Economics; Scott Ward, East Texas Baptist University; Tom Lee Waterston, Northwood University; Jim Wharton, Northwood University; Janice Yee, Wartburg College; and Anthony Zambelli, Cuyamaca College.

We are also indebted to the excellent team of professionals at Harcourt College Publishers: Gary Nelson, acquisitions editor, for his help and support of our efforts; Amy Ray, associate editor, who managed the project and performed countless other tasks for us; Laura Hanna, senior project editor, for orchestrating the copyediting, proofreading, and indexing; Burl Sloan, senior art director, who designed the book; Lois West, senior production manager, who kept it on schedule; Linda Blundell, art and literary rights editor, who helped us locate and obtain permissions for the many photos; and Debbie Anderson, product manager, who worked hard to market the book. Finally, we would like to acknowledge the assistance of Amy Gwartney, Jane Shaw Stroup, and Terri Sobel for their encouragement throughout the project. Without their contributions, we would have been unable to meet the demands and deadlines of this project.

A NOTE TO STUDENTS

This text contains several features that we think will help you maximize (a good economic term) the returns derived from your study effort. Our past experience indicates that awareness of the following points will help you to use the book more effectively.

➤ Each chapter begins with a series of focus questions that communicate the central issues of the chapter. Before you read the chapter, briefly think about the focus questions, why they are important, and how they relate to the material of prior chapters.

➤ The textbook is organized in the form of an outline. The headings within the text (highlighted with a color background) are the major points of the outline. Minor headings are subpoints under the major headings. In addition, important subpoints within sections are often set off and numbered. Bold italicized type is used to highlight material that is particularly important. Sometimes thumbnail sketches are included to help the reader better organize important points. Careful use of the headings, highlighted material, and the thumbnail sketches will help you master the material.

➤ A "Key Points" summary appears at the end of each chapter. Use the summary as a checklist to determine whether you understand the major points of the chapter.

➤ A review of the exhibits and illustrative pictures will also provide you with a summary of the key points of each chapter. The accompanying legend briefly describes the content and analysis of each feature.

➤ The key terms introduced in each chapter are defined in the margins. As you study the chapter, go over the marginal definition of each key term as it is introduced. Later, you may also find it useful to review the marginal definitions. If you have forgotten the meaning of a term introduced earlier, consult the glossary at the end of the book.

➤ The boxed features provide additional depth on various topics without disrupting the flow of the text. In general, the topics of the boxed features have been chosen because of their relevance as an application of the theory or because of past student interest in the topic. Reading the boxed features will supplement the text and enhance your understanding of important economic concepts.

➤ The critical analysis questions at the end of each chapter are intended to test your understanding of the economic way of thinking. Solving these questions and problems will greatly enhance your knowledge of the material. Answers to approximately half of these questions are provided in Appendix B.

If you need more practice, be sure to obtain a Coursebook and solve the questions and problems for each chapter. The Coursebook also contains the answers to the multiple-choice questions and a brief explanation of why an answer is correct (and other choices incorrect). In most cases, if you master the concepts of the test items in the Coursebook, you will do well on the quizzes and examinations of your instructor. For extra help utilizing multimedia tools, obtain a copy of the book's EconActive Student-Learning CD ROM or go to **www.dryden.com/econ/gwartney**, where you will find practice quizzes and PowerPoint reviews of each chapter. If your bookstore doesn't carry the Coursebook or the EconActive CD ROM, you can order them by calling 800-782-4479.

APPLICATION GUIDE

APPLICATION: A check (✓) indicates that the application would go well with or immediately following the chapter.

CHAPTER NUMBER	APPLICATION NUMBER 1	2	3	4	5
1					
2					
3					
4					✓
5	✓			✓	
6	✓			✓	
7					
8	✓				
9	✓				
10					
11					
12		✓			
13					
14					
15	✓	✓	✓	✓	✓
16	✓				✓
17					
18					

CONTENTS IN BRIEF

PART 5 *Applications and Special Topics* 489

Relationship between MAIN EDITION AND MACRO/MICRO EDITIONS

MICRO	MACRO	FULL-LENGTH TEXT	
Part 1	**Part 1**	**Part 1**	**The Economic Way of Thinking — An Introduction**
1	1	1	The Economic Approach
2	2	2	Some Tools of the Economist
Part 2	**Part 2**	**Part 2**	**Markets and Government**
3	3	3	Supply, Demand, and the Market Process
4	4	4	Supply and Demand: Applications and Extensions
5	5	5	The Economic Role of Government
6	6	6	The Economics of Collective Decision Making
	Part 3	**Part 3**	**Core Macroeconomics**
	7	7	Taking the Nation's Economic Pulse
	8	8	Economic Fluctuations, Unemployment, and Inflation
	9	9	An Introduction to Basic Macroeconomic Markets
	10	10	Working with our Basic Aggregate Demand/Aggregate Supply Model
	11	11	Keynesian Foundations of Modern Macroeconomics
	12	12	Fiscal Policy
	13	13	Money and the Banking System
	14	14	Modern Macroeconomics: Monetary Policy
	15	15	Stabilization Policy, Output, and Employment
	16	16	Economic Growth
Part 4	**Part 4**	**Part 4**	**International Economics**
16	17	17	Gaining from International Trade
17	18	18	International Finance and the Foreign Exchange Market
Part 3		**Part 5**	**Core Microeconomics**
7		19	Demand and Consumer Choice
8		20	Costs and the Supply of Goods
9		21	Price Takers and the Competitive Process
10		22	Price-Searcher Markets with Low Entry Barriers
11		23	Price-Searcher Markets with High Entry Barriers
12		24	The Supply of and Demand for Productive Resources
13		25	Earnings, Productivity, and the Job Market
14		26	Investment, the Capital Market, and the Wealth of Nations
15		27	Income Inequality and Poverty
Part 5	**Part 5**	**Part 6**	**Applications and Special Topics**
1	1	1	Labor Markets and Unemployment Rates: A Cross-Country Analysis
	2	2	How Do Budget Deficits and the National Debt Affect Future Generations?
	3	3	The Phillips Curve: Is there a Tradeoff Between Inflation and Unemployment?
2	4	4	Social Security: The Nature of the Problem and the Alternatives for Dealing with It
3	5	5	The Stock Market: What Does it Do and How Has it Performed?
4		6	How Does Government Regulation Affect Your Life?
5		7	Income Inequality, Transfers, and the Role of Government
6		8	Do Labor Unions Increase the Wages of Workers?
7		9	Natural Resources and the Future
8		10	Economics and the Environment

TABLE OF CONTENTS

The economic way of thinking

Economics is about how people choose. The choices we make influence our lives and those of others. Your future will be influenced by the choices you make with regard to education, job opportunities, savings, and investment. We live in a dynamic world. Changes in technology, demographics, communications, and transportation are constantly altering the attractiveness of various options and the opportunities availal to us.

Think for a moment about how the lives of Ame cans have changed and are changing in three area (1) population composition, (2) the workforce, and (3) teraction with people in other countries.

THE WALL STREET JOURNAL
MONEY & INVESTING
Life is a series of choices with regard to how
we earn, spend, save and invest.

ABY BOOMERS AND DEMOGRAPHIC CHANGES

; following the Second World War, there crease in the number of births. As a re- -third of Americans were age 15 years 960 (see Exhibit I-A). The baby boomers orime working-age years of life. Com- he percentage of Americans 40 to 55 risen sharply, while the share of population under 15 years of age has declined substantially. During the next several decades, there will be still more change. By 2025, the proportion of the population age 65 and over will soar to 18.7 percent, more than twice the figure for 1960. Meanwhile, both the young and prime-age workers will decline as a share of the population.

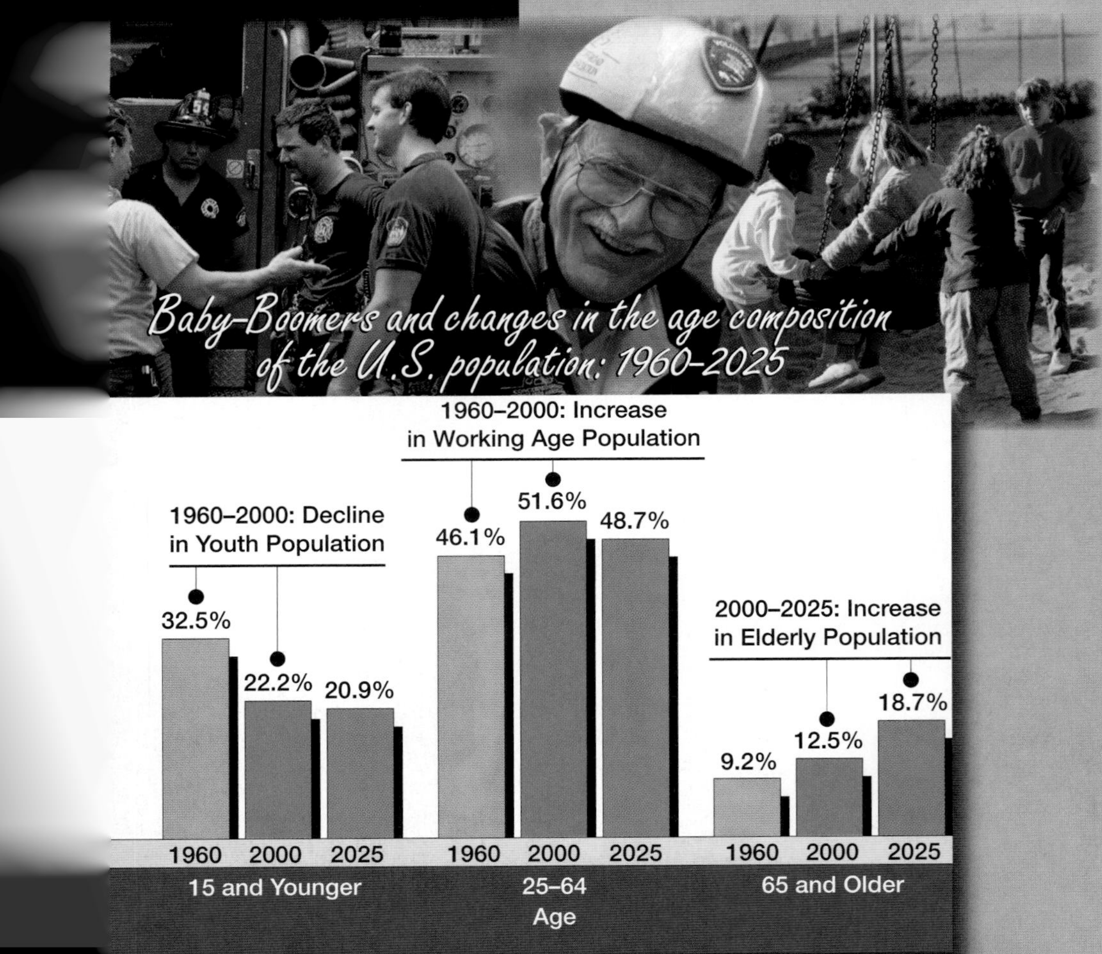

EXHIBIT I-A

SOURCES: Statistical Abstract of the United States *(various years).*

WOMEN AND COLLEGE GRADUATES ARE AN INCREASING SHARE OF THE LABOR FORCE

Since 1950 the labor force has seen a huge influx of women, particularly married women. Today, women comprise 46.2 percent of the labor force, up from 29.6 percent in 1950 (see Exhibit I-B). The proportion of workers with a college degree creased substantially. As Exhibit I-B s graduates now comprise 28.5 percent of up from 6.2 in 1950 and 14.1 in 1970.

SOURCES: Statistical Abstract of the United States *(various years) and* Employment and Training Report of the President *(1979). Note the 1950 figure is for persons age 25 years and older.*

EXHIBIT I-B

INCREASINGLY, WE ARE INVOLVED IN A GLOBAL ECONOMY

is shrinking. In recent decades, trans- and communication costs have fallen ıcreasingly, Americans are buying, invest- and even working abroad. At the same time, foreigners are more likely to do these same things in the United States. As a share of the economy, the size of the international trade sector (exports plus imports) has tripled since 1960 and doubled since 1980.

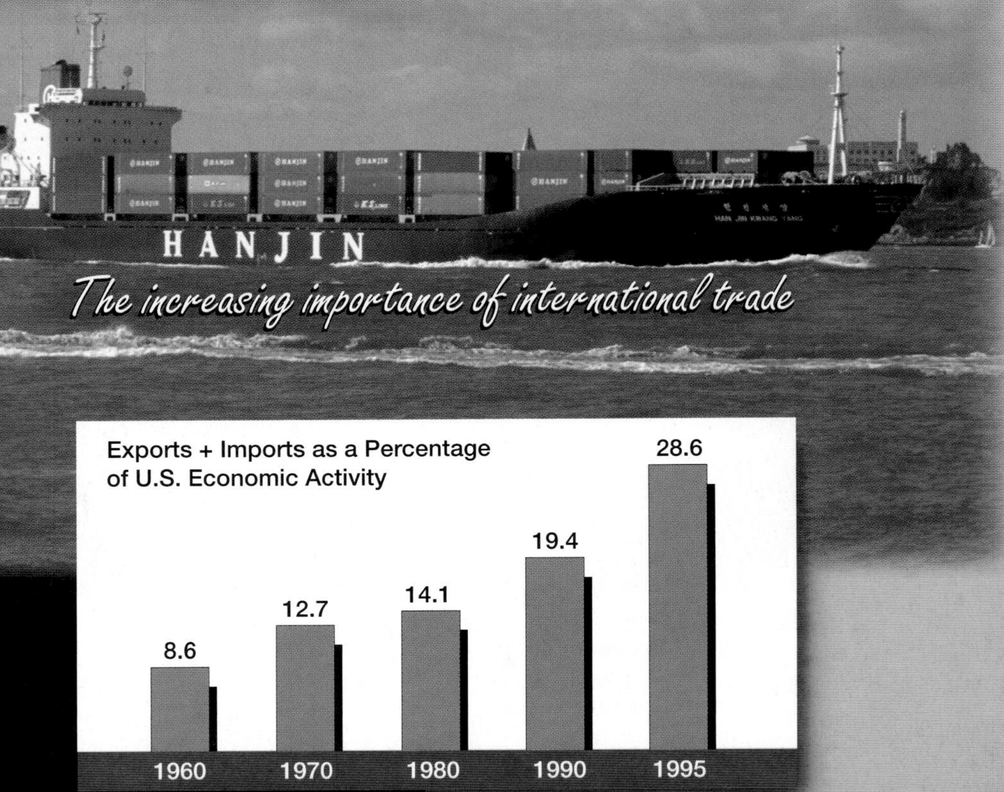

EXHIBIT 1-C

SOURCE: Economic Report of the President: 1998, *table B-2.*

GNIFICANCE OF OUR CHANGING ECONOMY

in the number of elderly Americans, more d college grads in the workforce, and the f economic activity: How will these mega- ce your job opportunities and quality of life? The tools of economics can enhance your understanding of these factors and numerous others that will affect your life. The economic way of thinking will help you make better choices in our dynamic world.

CHAPTER 1

[Economics] is not a body of concrete truth, but an engine for the discovery of concrete truth.

Alfred Marshall[1]

The Economic Approach

CHAPTER FOCUS

- Why is scarcity a key economic concept, even in an affluent economy?
- How does scarcity differ from poverty? Why does scarcity necessitate rationing and cause competition?
- What are the basic principles underlying the economic way of thinking? What is different about the way economists look at choices and human decision making?
- What is the difference between positive and normative economics?

[1]Alfred Marshall, *The Present Position of Economics* (1885), p. 25.

Now is an exciting time to study economics. Recent political campaigns in the United States have centered on such economic issues as budget deficits, the structure and level of taxes, and social security reform. The market economies of Western Europe are struggling to develop a single, integrated economy with a common currency and legal structure. Several countries of Eastern Europe and the former Soviet Union are continuing their struggle to move from socialist central planning toward market-directed economies. Several Asian nations are trying to recover from recent financial difficulties and regain the prosperity they achieved throughout most of the 1980s and 1990s. Latin American and African leaders are searching for economic prescriptions that will generate prosperity and upgrade living standards.

Simultaneously, economies around the world are becoming more and more interrelated. Many of the goods at your favorite shopping mall are produced, at least in part, by people who speak a different language and live in a country far from your own. Similarly, many Americans work for companies that market their products in Europe, Japan, Latin America, or Africa. The pension funds of American workers commonly own stocks from around the world. Ownership shares of American companies are traded not only in New York City but also on stock exchanges in London, Tokyo, and throughout the world.

How will our current economic policies and rapidly changing world affect the economic status of Americans? What impact will the globalization of our economy have on our living standards, lifestyles, and future opportunities? This book will help you better understand the world in which you live. This is not to imply that economics provides easy answers for problems. As Alfred Marshall stated more than a century ago, economics is a discovery process—a way of thinking—rather than a "body of concrete truth" (see chapter opening quote). Our goals are to present the tools of economics and illustrate how the economic way of thinking can enhance your understanding of our rapidly changing world.

WHAT IS ECONOMICS ABOUT?

[Economics is] the science which studies human behavior as a relationship between ends and scarce means which have alternative uses.

Lionel Robbins[2]

Economics is about people and the choices they make. The unit of analysis in economics is the individual. Of course, individuals group together to form collective organizations, such as corporations, labor unions, and governments. Individual choices, however, still underlie and direct these organizations. Thus, even when we study collective

[2]Lionel Robbins, *An Essay on the Nature and Significance of Economic Science* (1932).

organizations, we will focus on the ways in which their operation is affected by the choices of individuals.

Scarcity and Choice

Would you like some new clothes, a nicer car, and a larger apartment? How about better grades and more time to watch television, go skiing, and travel abroad? Most of us would like more of all these goods. The human desire for goods is virtually unlimited. We cannot, however, have more of everything. Both individually and collectively we face a constraint called **scarcity.** Goods are scarce because people's desire for things is far greater than what is freely available from nature. Because scarcity prevents us from having as much as we would like of **economic goods,** we are forced to choose from a restricted set of potential alternatives. **Choice,** the act of selecting among alternatives, is the logical consequence of scarcity. These two—*scarcity* and *choice*—are the basic ingredients of an economic topic.

Scarcity
Fundamental concept of economics that indicates that a good is less freely available than consumers would like.

Economic good
A good that is scarce. The desire for economic goods exceeds the amount that is freely available from nature.

Choice
The act of selecting among alternatives.

Resource
An input used to produce economic goods. Land, labor, skills, natural resources, and capital are examples. Our history is a record of our struggle to transform available, but limited, resources into things that we would like to have—economic goods.

Resources are inputs used to produce goods and services. In essence, they are tools that we can use to battle scarcity. There are three general categories of resources. First, there are human resources—the productive knowledge, skill, and strength of human beings. Second, there are physical resources—things like tools, machines, and buildings that enhance our ability to produce goods. Economists often use the term *capital* when referring to these human-made resources. Third, there are natural resources—things like land, mineral deposits, oceans, and rivers. The ingenuity of humans is often required in order to make these natural resources useful in production. For example, until recently the yew tree was considered a "trash tree," having no value. Then, scientists discovered that the tree produces taxol, a substance that could be used to fight cancer. Human knowledge and ingenuity made yew trees a valuable resource. Natural resources are important, but recognizing the best ways to produce goods, and which goods to produce under changing circumstances, is as important as the existence of the resources themselves.

Exhibit 1–1 provides a listing of the various categories of both desired goods and the limited resources that might be utilized to produce them. Put simply, the basic economic problem concerns how we can best use the limited resources to produce the desired goods. With the passage of time, investment activities—the development of better tools and improved knowledge, for example—can increase the availability of resources; but more investment requires the sacrifice of additional current consumption. If we use more of today's resources to produce education and skill enhancement, more tools and machines, or more factories, then fewer resources will be available to produce goods for consumption right now. Economics is about trade-offs.

During the past 250 years, we have loosened the grip of scarcity a little. Think for a moment what life was like in 1750. People all over the world struggled 50, 60, and 70 hours a week to obtain the basic necessities of life—food, clothing, and shelter. Manual labor was the major source of energy. Animals provided the means of transportation. Tools and machines were primitive by today's standards. As the English philosopher Thomas Hobbes stated in the 17th century, life was "solitary, poor, nasty, brutish, and short."[3]

Throughout much of South America, Africa, and Asia, economic conditions continue to make life difficult. In North America, Western Europe, Oceania, and some parts of Asia, however, substantial economic progress has been made. Of course, scarcity is still a fact of life in these areas, too; the desire for goods and services still far

[3]Thomas Hobbes, *Leviathan* (1651) Part I, Chapter 13.

History is a record of our struggle to transform available, but limited, resources into things that we would like to have—economic goods.

EXHIBIT 1-1

A GENERAL LISTING OF DESIRED ECONOMIC GOODS AND LIMITED RESOURCES

Economic Goods	Limited Resources
Food (bread, milk, meat, eggs, vegetables, coffee, etc.)	Land (various degrees of fertility)
Clothing (shirts, pants, blouses, shoes, socks, coats, sweaters, etc.)	Natural resources (rivers, trees, minerals, oceans, etc.)
Household goods (tables, chairs, rugs, beds, dressers, television sets, etc.)	Machines and other human-made physical resources
Education	Nonhuman animal resources
National defense	Technology (physical and scientific "recipes" of history)
Leisure time	Human resources (the knowledge, skill, and talent of individual human beings)
Entertainment	
Clean air	
Pleasant environment (trees, lakes, rivers, open spaces, etc.)	
Pleasant working conditions	

outstrips the ability of people to produce them. But from a material standpoint, life is more comfortable. As diet and health care have improved, so has life expectancy. Modern energy sources, means of transportation, appliances, and recreational opportunities have reduced physical hardship and the drudgery of life in North America and other wealthy parts of the world. In these areas, a typical family might worry about financing a summer vacation, obtaining a better home computer or an additional car, and providing for the children's college education. Subsistence levels of food, shelter, and clothing are taken for granted.

It is important to note that scarcity and poverty are not the same thing. Poverty implies some basic level of need, either in absolute or relative terms. Absence of poverty means that the basic level has been attained. In contrast, the absence of scarcity would imply that we have as much of all goods as we would like. Both individuals and countries may win the battle against poverty—people may achieve income levels that allow them to satisfy a basic level of need. But it is painfully obvious that we will not triumph over scarcity. Even in the wealthiest of countries, productive capabilities cannot keep pace with material desires. People always want more goods for themselves and others they care about; societies always want more and better medical care, schooling, and national defense than can be produced with available resources.

Rationing
An allocation of a limited supply of a good or resource to users who would like to have more of it. Various criteria, including charging a price, can be utilized to allocate the limited supply. When price performs the rationing function, the good or resource is allocated to those willing to give up the most "other things" in order to obtain ownership rights.

Scarcity Necessitates Rationing

When a good (or resource) is scarce, some criterion must be set up for deciding who will receive the good (or resource) and who will do without it. Scarcity makes **rationing** a necessity.

Several possible criteria could be used in rationing a limited amount of a good among citizens who would like to have more of it. The rationing criterion chosen will influence human behavior. If the criterion were first-come, first-served, goods would be allocated to those who were fastest at getting in line or to those who were most willing to wait in line. If beauty were used, goods would be allocated to those who were thought to be most beautiful. The political process might determine allocations, and goods would be distributed on the basis of political status and ability to manipulate the political process to personal advantage. In a market setting, price is used to ration things; goods and resources are allocated to those willing to pay the highest prices. One thing is certain: Scarcity means that methods must be established to decide who gets the limited amount of available goods and resources.

Competition Results from Scarcity

Competition is a natural outgrowth of scarcity and the desire of human beings to improve their conditions. Competition exists in every economy and every society. It exists both when goods are allocated by price in markets and when they are allocated by other means—political decision making, for example.

Moreover, the rationing criterion will influence which competitive techniques will be used. When the rationing criterion is price, individuals will engage in income-generating activities that enhance their ability to pay the price. The market system encourages individuals to provide goods and services to others in exchange for income. In turn, the income will permit them to procure more scarce goods.

A different rationing criterion will encourage other types of behavior. When the appearance of sincerity, broad knowledge, fairness, good judgment, and a positive television image are important, as they are in the rationing of elected political positions, people will use resources to project these qualities. They will hire makeup artists, public relations experts, and advertising agencies to help them compete. We can change the form of competition, but no society has been able to eliminate it, because no society has been able to eliminate scarcity and the resulting need for rationing. When people who want more scarce goods seek to meet the criteria established to ration those goods, competition occurs.

THE ECONOMIC WAY OF THINKING

It [economics] is a method rather than a doctrine, an apparatus of the mind, a technique of thinking which helps its possessor to draw correct conclusions.

John Maynard Keynes[4]

One does not have to spend much time around economists to recognize that there is an "economic way of thinking." Admittedly, economists, like others, differ widely in their ideological views. A news commentator once remarked that "any half-dozen economists will normally come up with about six different policy prescriptions." Yet, in spite of their philosophical differences, the approach of economists covers a common ground.

---

[4]John Maynard Keynes (1883–1946) was an English economist whose writings during the 1920s and 1930s exerted an enormous impact on both economic theory and policy. Keynes established the terminology and the economic framework that are still widely used when economists study problems of unemployment and inflation.

Reprinted by permission: Tribune Media Services.

Economic theory
A set of definitions, postulates, and principles assembled in a manner that makes clear the "cause-and-effect" relationships of economic data.

That common ground is **economic theory,** developed from basic postulates of human behavior. Economic theory, like a road map or a guidebook, establishes reference points indicating what to look for, and how economic issues are interrelated. To a large degree, the basic economic principles are merely common sense. When applied consistently, however, these commonsense concepts can provide interesting and powerful insights.

Eight Guideposts to Economic Thinking

The economic way of thinking requires the incorporation of certain guidelines—some would say the building blocks of basic economic theory—into one's thought process. Once these guidelines are incorporated, we believe that economics can be a relatively easy subject to master. Students who have difficulty with economics have almost always failed to assimilate these principles. We will outline and discuss eight principles that characterize the economic way of thinking and that are essential to understanding the economic approach.

1. The Use of Scarce Resources to Produce a Good Is Always Costly. Economists sometimes refer to this as "There Ain't No Such Thing As A Free Lunch," or the "TANSTAAFL" principle. The use of resources to produce one good diverts the resources from the production of other goods that are also desired. No option is free of cost. The highest valued alternative that must be sacrificed is the **opportunity cost** of the option. For example, if you use one hour of your scarce time to study economics, you will have one hour less time to watch television, read magazines, sleep, work at a job, or study other subjects. Time spent working at a job, or even time spent sleeping, might be viewed as your highest valued option forgone. The cost of an action is always the highest valued option given up in order to choose the action.

Opportunity cost
The highest valued alternative that must be sacrificed as a result of choosing among alternatives.

It is important to recognize that the "scarce resources have a cost" concept is true regardless of who pays for the good or service produced. In many countries, various kinds of schooling are provided free of charge *to students.* However, provision of the schooling is not free *to the community.* The scarce resources (for example, buildings, equipment, and skills of teachers) used to produce the schooling could have been used instead to produce more recreation, entertainment, housing, or other goods. The cost of the schooling is the highest valued option that must now be given up because the resources required for its production were instead used to produce the schooling.

By now the central point should be obvious. Economic thinking recognizes that the use of a scarce resource always involves a cost. The use of more resources to do one thing implies fewer resources with which to achieve other objectives. In the next chapter we will look more closely at this key concept and some of its implications.

2. Individuals Choose Purposefully; They Try to Get the Most From Their Limited Resources. Recognizing the restrictions imposed by the limited resources available to them (income, time, talent, and so on), individuals will try to select those options that best advance their personal objectives. They will not deliberately waste their valuable resources. In turn, the objectives or preferences of individuals are revealed by the choices they make. **Economizing behavior** results directly from purposeful (rational) decision making. Economizing individuals will seek to accomplish an objective at the least possible cost to themselves. When choosing among things that yield equal benefit, an economizer will select the cheapest option. For example, if a pizza, a lobster dinner, and a sirloin steak are expected to yield identical benefits (including the enjoyment of eating them!), economizing behavior implies that the cheapest of the three alternatives, probably the pizza, will be chosen. In the same way, when choosing among alternatives of equal cost, economizing decision makers will select the option that yields the greatest benefit. If the price of several dinner specials are equal, for example, economizers will choose the one they like the best—the one that provides them the most benefit.

Economizing behavior
Choosing with the objective of gaining a specific benefit at the least possible cost. A corollary of economizing behavior implies that, when choosing among items of equal cost, individuals will choose the option that yields the greatest benefit.

Purposeful choosing implies that decision makers have some basis for their evaluation of alternatives. Economists refer to this evaluation as **utility**—the benefit or satisfaction that an individual expects from the choice of a specific alternative. The utility of an alternative is highly subjective, often differing widely from person to person. The steak dinner that delights one person may be repulsive to another (a vegetarian, for example).

Utility
The benefit or satisfaction expected from a choice or course of action.

OUTSTANDING ECONOMIST

The Importance of Adam Smith, the Father of Economics

Economics is a relatively young science. The foundation of economics was laid in 1776, when Adam Smith (1723–1790) published *An Inquiry Into the Nature and Causes of the Wealth of Nations.* Smith presented what at that time was a revolutionary view. He argued that the wealth of a nation did not lie in gold and silver, but rather in the goods and services produced and consumed by people. According to Smith, coordination, order, and efficiency would result without the planning and direction of a central authority.

Adam Smith was a lecturer at the University of Glasgow, in his native Scotland. Morals and ethics actually were his concern before economics. His first book was *The Theory of Moral Sentiments.* For Smith, self-interest and sympathy for others were complementary. However, he did not believe that charity alone could provide the essentials for a good life. He stressed that free exchange and competitive markets would harness self-interest as a creative force. Directed by the "invisible hand" of market prices, individuals *pursuing their own interests* would be encouraged to produce the goods and supply the resources that others value most highly (relative to costs).

Ideas have consequences. Smith's ideas greatly influenced not only Europeans but also those who mapped out the structure of the U.S. government. Since then, the effectiveness of the "invisible hand" of the market has become accepted as critical to the prosperity of nations.[1]

---

[1]For an excellent biographical sketch of Adam Smith, used to prepare this feature, see David Henderson, ed., *The Fortune Encyclopedia of Economics* (New York: Warner Books, 1993), pp. 836–838.

THE FAMILY CIRCUS®
By Bil Keane
3-25
Copyright 1988 Cowles Syndicate, Inc
"Everybody wants to be sick.
I'm using M&M's for pills."

3. Incentives Matter—Choice Is Influenced in a Predictable Way by Changes in Economic Incentives. This guidepost to clear economic thinking might be called the basic postulate of all economics. *As the personal benefits from choosing an option increase, other things constant, a person will be more likely to choose that option. In contrast, as the personal costs associated with the choice of an item increase, the individual will be less likely to choose that option.* For a group, this basic economic postulate suggests that making an option more attractive will cause more people to choose it. In contrast, as the cost of a selection to the members of a group increases, fewer of them will make this selection.

This basic postulate of economics is a powerful tool because its application is so widespread. Incentives affect behavior in virtually all aspects of our lives, ranging from market decisions about what to buy to political choices concerning for whom to vote. If beef prices rise, making beef consumption more expensive relative to other goods, the basic postulate indicates that consumers will be less likely to choose it. As a result, less beef will be consumed at the higher price. Similarly, the "incentives matter" postulate indicates that a voter will be less likely to support candidates favoring higher taxes to provide goods the voter finds unattractive.

To show its broad scope, we can apply this basic postulate of economics to the examination process. If a classroom instructor makes it more costly to cheat, students will be less likely to do so. There will be little cheating on a closely monitored, individualized essay examination. Why? Because it is difficult (that is, costly) to cheat on such an exam. Suppose, however, that an instructor gives an objective "take-home" exam, basing students' course grades entirely on the results. Among the same group of students, more will be likely to cheat because the benefits of doing so will be great and the risk (cost) minimal. (The boxed feature "Incentives Matter" gives yet another application of this principle.)

Marginal
Term used to describe the effects of a change in the current situation. For example, the marginal cost is the cost of producing an additional unit of a product, given the producer's current facility and production rate.

4. Economic Thinking Is Marginal Thinking. Fundamental to economic reasoning and economizing behavior are the effects of decisions made to change the status quo. Economists describe such decisions as **marginal.** Marginal choices always involve the

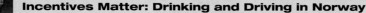

APPLICATIONS IN ECONOMICS

Incentives Matter: Drinking and Driving in Norway

How generally can we apply the "incentives matter" principle? Do differences in incentives influence, for example, the incidence of drinking and driving? Consider the case of Norway, the country that has the toughest drunk-driving laws in the Western world.[1] Drinking a single can of beer before driving can put a first offender in jail for a minimum sentence of three weeks. These drivers generally lose their licenses for up to two years and often get stiff fines as well. Repeat offenders are treated even more harshly. These laws are far more draconian than those of the United States. Surveys indicate that:

1. One out of three Norwegians arrives at parties in a taxi, while nearly all Americans drive their own cars.
2. One out of ten Norwegian partygoers spends the night at the host's home; Americans seldom do.
3. In Norway, 78 percent of drivers totally avoid drinking at parties, compared to only 17 percent of American drivers.

Norwegians do like to drink, though they consume only half as much alcohol as Americans. The strong incentives built into Norwegian law, however, clearly make a difference. Once again, incentives do matter, and matter in a big way.

[1]The information in this feature is from L. Erik Calonius, "Just a Bottle of Beer Can Land a Motorist in Prison in Norway," *Wall Street Journal,* August 16, 1985, p. 1.

effects of net additions to or subtractions from the current conditions. In fact, the word *additional* is often used as a substitute for *marginal.* For example, we might ask, "What is the marginal (or additional) cost of producing one more unit?"

Marginal decisions may involve large or small changes. The "one more unit" could be a new factory or a new stapler. It is marginal because it involves additional costs and additional benefits. Given the current situation, what marginal benefits (additional sales revenues, for example) can be expected from the new factory, and what will be the marginal cost of constructing it? The answers to these questions will determine whether building the new factory is a good decision.

It is important to distinguish between *average* and *marginal.* A manufacturer's current average cost of producing a specific automobile (total cost divided by total number of the cars produced to date) may be $20,000, but the marginal cost of producing an additional automobile (or an additional 1,000 automobiles) might be much lower, say, $5,000 per car. Costs associated with research, testing, design, molds, heavy equipment, and similar factors of production must be incurred whether the manufacturer is going to produce 1,000 units, 10,000 units, or 100,000 units. Such costs will clearly contribute to the average cost of an automobile. However, since these activities have already been undertaken to produce the manufacturer's current output level, the cost of producing additional units (automobiles) will change them very little. Thus, the marginal cost of

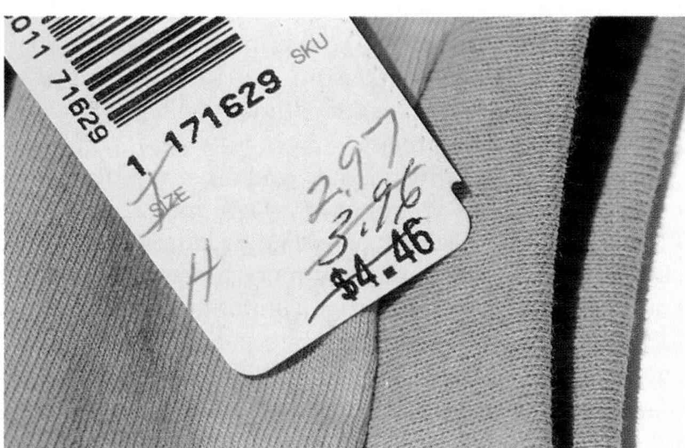

Why do store owners reduce their prices on various items? Do they believe that consumers respond to incentives?

additional units may be substantially less than the average cost. Should production be expanded or reduced? That choice should be based on marginal costs, which indicate the *change* in total cost due to the decision, rather than the current average cost.

We often confront decisions involving a possible change from the current situation. The *marginal benefits* and *marginal costs* associated with the choice will determine the wisdom of our decisions. What happens at the margin is therefore an important element of the economic way of thinking.

5. Although Information Can Help Us Make Better Choices, Its Acquisition Is Costly. Thus we will almost always make choices based on limited knowledge. Information that will help us make better choices is valuable. Like other resources, however, it is also scarce and therefore costly to acquire. As a result, individuals will economize on their search for information just as they economize on the use of other scarce resources. For example, when purchasing a pair of jeans, you may check price and evaluate quality at several different stores. At some point, though, you will decide that additional shopping—that is, acquisition of additional information—is simply not worth the trouble. You will make a choice based on the limited knowledge that you already possess.

The process is similar when individuals search for a restaurant, a new car, or a roommate. They will seek to acquire some information, but at some point, they will decide that the expected benefit derived from still more information is simply not worth the cost. When differences among the alternatives are important to the decision maker, more time and effort will be spent to make a better individual decision. Even then, limited knowledge and resulting uncertainty about the outcome characterize the decision-making process.

6. Economic Actions Often Generate Secondary Effects in Addition to Their Immediate Effects. Failure to consider these secondary effects is the most common source of economic error. Frederic Bastiat, a nineteenth-century French economist, stated that the difference between a good and a bad economist is that the bad economist considers only the immediate, visible effects, whereas the good economist is also aware of the **secondary effects,** effects that result from the initial policy, but that may be seen or felt only with the passage of time.

Secondary effects
Economic consequences of an economic change that are not immediately identifiable but are felt only with the passage of time.

Perhaps a simple example involving both immediate and secondary effects will help us grasp this point. The immediate effect of an aspirin is a bitter taste in one's mouth. The secondary effect, which is not immediately observable, is relief from a headache. The immediate effect of drinking six quarts of beer might be a warm, jolly feeling. The secondary effect is likely to be a sluggish feeling the next morning, and perhaps a pounding headache.

In economics, the immediate, short-term effects that are highly visible are often quite different from the long-term effects. Changes in economic policy often alter the structure of incentives, which indirectly affects how much people work, earn, invest, and conserve for the future. But the impact of the secondary effects is often observable only after the passage of time—and even then only to those who know what to look for in evaluating them.

Consider tariffs, quotas, and other restrictions that limit imports. Proponents of such restrictions argue that they will increase employment; indeed, at first they do. If, for example, the supply of foreign-produced automobiles to the U.S. market were restricted, Americans would buy more American-made automobiles, increasing output and employment in the domestic auto industry. These would be the immediate, easily identified effects. But consider the secondary effects. The restrictions would also reduce supply to the domestic market and increase the price of both foreign- and American-made automobiles. As a result of the higher prices, many auto consumers would pay more for automobiles and thus be forced to curtail their purchases of food, clothing,

Reprinted with special permission of King Features Syndicate.

recreation, and literally thousands of other items. These reductions in spending would mean less output and employment in those areas. There would also be a secondary effect on sales to foreigners. Since foreigners would be selling fewer automobiles to Americans, they would acquire fewer dollars with which to buy American-made goods. U.S. exports, therefore, would fall as a result of the restrictions on automobile imports.

Once the secondary effects are considered, the net impact on employment of the import restrictions is no longer obvious. Although restrictions may increase employment in the auto industry, they will reduce employment in other industries, particularly export industries. Primarily, they will reshuffle employment rather than increase it. As this example illustrates, consideration of secondary effects is an important ingredient of the economic way of thinking.

7. The Value of a Good or Service Is Subjective. Preferences differ, sometimes dramatically, between individuals. How much is a ticket to see tonight's performance of the Bolshoi Ballet worth? Some would be willing to pay a very high price, while others might prefer to stay home and avoid the ballet performance, even if tickets were free! Circumstances can change from day to day, even for a given individual. Alice, a ballet fan who usually would value the ticket at more than its price of $50, is invited to a party, and suddenly becomes uninterested in the ballet tonight. Now what is the ticket worth? If she knows a friend who would give her $20 for the ticket, it is worth at least that much. If she advertises on a bulletin board and gets $40 for it, a higher value is created. But if someone who doesn't know of the ticket would have paid even more, then a potential trade that would have created even more value is missed. If tonight's performance is sold out, perhaps someone in town would be willing to pay $70! One thing is certain: The value of the ticket depends on several things, including who uses it and under what circumstances.

Seldom will one individual know how others would value an item. Consider how difficult it often is to know what would make a good gift, even for a close friend or family member! So, arranging trades, or otherwise moving items to higher-valued users and uses, is not a simple task. The entrepreneurial individual, who knows how to locate the right buyers and arranges for the goods to flow to higher-valued uses, can create huge increases in value from existing resources. In fact, encouragement of individuals to (a) move goods toward those who value them most and (b) combine resources into goods that individuals value more highly than the resources required for their production is a vitally important source of economic progress. As we proceed, we will investigate this issue in detail.

8. The Test of a Theory Is Its Ability to Predict. Economic thinking is **scientific thinking.** The proof of the pudding is in the eating. The usefulness of an economic theory is proved by its ability to predict the future consequences of economic action. Economists develop economic theory from scientific thinking, using basic postulates to

Scientific thinking
Development of a theory from basic postulates and the testing of the implications of that theory as to their consistency with events in the real world. Good theories are consistent with and help explain real-world events. Theories that are inconsistent with the real world are invalid and must be rejected.

analyze how incentives will affect decision makers, and comparing the analysis against events in the real world. If the events in the real world are consistent with a theory, we say that the theory has *predictive value* and is therefore valid.

If it is impossible to test the theoretical relationships of a discipline, the discipline does not qualify as a science. Because economics deals with human beings, who can think and respond in a variety of ways, can economic theories really be tested? The answer to this question is yes, if, on average, human beings respond in predictable and consistent ways to certain changes in economic conditions. The economist believes that this is the case even though not all individuals will respond in a specified manner. Economists usually do not try to predict the behavior of a specific individual; instead, they focus on the general behavior of a large number of individuals.

In the 1950s, economists began to do laboratory experiments to test economic theories. Individuals were brought into laboratories to see how they would act in buying and selling situations, under differing rules. For example, small but concrete cash rewards were given to individuals who, when an auction was conducted among them, were able to sell at high prices and to buy at low prices, thus approximating real-world market incentives. These experiments have verified many of the important propositions of economic theory.

Laboratory experiments, however, cannot duplicate all real economic interactions. How can we test economic theory when controlled experiments are not feasible? This is a problem, but economics is no different from astronomy in this respect. Astronomers can use theories tested in physics laboratories, but they must also deal with the world as it is. They cannot change the course of the stars or planets to see what impact the change would have on the gravitational pull of the earth. Similarly, economists cannot arbitrarily change the prices of cars or unskilled labor services in real markets, just to observe the effects on quantities purchased or levels of employment in the real world outside the laboratory. However, economic conditions (for example, prices, production costs, technology, and transportation costs), like the location of the planets, do change from time to time. As actual conditions change, an economic theory can be tested by comparing its predictions with real-world outcomes. Just as the universe is the main laboratory of the astronomer, the real economic world is often the laboratory of the economist.

POSITIVE AND NORMATIVE ECONOMICS

> ***A positive science may be defined as a body of systematized knowledge concerning what is; a normative or regulative science is a body of systematized knowledge relating to criteria of what ought to be, and concerned therefore with the ideal as distinguished from the actual.***
>
> *John Neville Keynes*[5]

Economics as a social science is concerned with predicting or determining the impact of changes in economic variables on the actions of human beings. Scientific economics, commonly referred to as **positive economics,** attempts to determine "what is." Positive economic statements postulate a relationship that is potentially verifiable or refutable. For example: "If the price of gasoline were higher, people would buy less." Or, "As the money supply increases, the price level will go up." We can statistically investigate (and estimate) the relationship between gasoline prices and gallons sold,

Positive economics
The scientific study of "what is" among economic relationships.

[5]John Neville Keynes, *The Scope and Method of Political Economy,* 4th ed. (1917), pp. 34–35.

or between the supply of money and the general price level. We can analyze the facts to determine the correctness of a statement about positive economics.

Normative economics involves the advocacy of specific policy alternatives, because it uses ethical or value judgments as well as knowledge of positive economics. Normative economic statements concern "what ought to be," given the preferences and philosophical views of the advocate. Value judgments may be the source of disagreement about normative economic matters. Two persons may differ on a policy matter because one is a socialist and the other a libertarian, because one wants cheaper food while the other favors organic farming, or even because one values wilderness highly while the other wants more improved campsites that can be easily reached by roads. They may agree as to the expected outcome of altering an economic variable (that is, the positive economics of an issue), but disagree as to whether that outcome is desirable.

Normative economics
Judgments about "what ought to be" in economic matters. Normative economic views cannot be proved false, because they are based on value judgments.

In contrast with positive economic statements, normative economic statements can neither be confirmed nor proven false through scientific testing. "Business firms should not maximize profits." "The use of pesticides on food to be sold in stores should not be allowed." "More of our national forests should be set aside for wilderness." These normative statements cannot be scientifically tested because their validity rests on value judgments.

Normative economic views can sometimes influence our attitude toward positive economic analysis. When we agree with the objectives of a policy, it is easy to overlook warnings of potential problems implied by positive economics. Although positive economics does not tell us which policy is best, it can provide knowledge that will help reduce the likelihood of false expectations. Desired objectives are not the same as workable solutions. The actual effects of policy alternatives often differ dramatically from the objectives of their proponents. A new law forcing employers to pay all employees at least $12 per hour might be intended to help low-skill workers, but the resulting decline in the number of workers employed (and increase in the number unemployed) would be disastrous despite the good intentions. Proponents of such a law, of course, would not want to believe the economic analysis that predicted the unfortunate outcome.

The task of the professional economist is to expand our knowledge of how the real world operates, both in the private and the public sectors. If we do not fully understand the implications, including the secondary effects, of alternative actions, we will not be able to choose intelligently. Yet, it is not always easy to use economic thinking to isolate the impact of a change in an economic variable or a change in policy. Let us consider some of the potential pitfalls to avoid in economic thinking.

PITFALLS TO AVOID IN ECONOMIC THINKING

VIOLATION OF THE CETERIS PARIBUS CONDITION

Economists often preface their statements with the words **ceteris paribus,** a term from Latin meaning "other things constant." "Other things constant, an increase in the price of housing will cause buyers to reduce their purchases." Unfortunately for the economic researcher, we live in a dynamic world. Other things seldom remain constant. For example, as the price of housing rises, the income of consumers may also be increasing. Each of these factors—higher housing prices and an expansion in consumer income—will have an impact on housing purchases. In fact, we would generally expect them to have opposite effects: higher prices reducing housing purchases but the rise in consumer income increasing the demand for housing. The task of sorting out the specific effects of two or more variables when all are changing at the same time is difficult,

Ceteris paribus
A Latin term meaning "other things constant," used when the effect of one change is being described, recognizing that if other things changed, they also could affect the result. Economists often describe the effects of one change, knowing that in the real world, other things might change and have their effects, too.

though with a strong grip on economic theory, some ingenuity, and enough data, it can often be done. In fact, the major portion of the day-to-day work of many professional economists consists of statistical research.

Association Is Not Causation

In economics, causation is very important, and statistical association alone cannot establish causation. Perhaps an extreme example will illustrate the point. Suppose that each November a witch doctor performs a voodoo dance designed to arouse the cold-weather gods of winter, and that soon after the dance is performed, the weather in fact begins to turn cold. The witch doctor's dance is associated with the arrival of winter, but does it cause the arrival of winter? Most of us would answer in the negative, even though the two are linked statistically.

Unfortunately, cause-and-effect relationships in economics are not always self-evident. For example, it is sometimes difficult to know whether a rise in income has caused people to buy more or, conversely, whether an increase in people's willingness to buy more has created more business and caused incomes to rise. Similarly, economists sometimes argue whether rising money wages are a cause or an effect of inflation. Economic theory, if rooted to the basic postulates, can often help to determine the source of causation, even though competing theories may sometimes suggest differing directions of causation.

Fallacy of Composition

What is true for the individual (or subcomponent) may not be true for the group (or the whole). If you stand up for an exciting play during a football game, you will be better able to see. But what happens if everyone stands up at the same time? What benefits the individual does not necessarily benefit the group as a whole. When everyone stands up, the view for individual spectators fails to improve; it may even become worse.

Fallacy of composition
Erroneous view that what is true for the individual (or the part) will also be true for the group (or the whole).

People who argue that what is true for the part is also true for the whole may be mistaken because of the **fallacy of composition.** Consider an example from economics. If you have an extra $10,000 in your bank account, you will be better off. But, what if everyone suddenly has an additional $10,000? This increase in the money supply will result in higher prices, as people with more money bid against one another for the existing supply of goods. Without an increase in the availability (or production) of scarce economic goods, the additional money will not make anyone better off. What is true for the individual can be misleading and is often fallacious when applied to the entire economy.

Microeconomics
The branch of economics that focuses on how human behavior affects the conduct of affairs within narrowly defined units, such as individual households or business firms.

Macroeconomics
The branch of economics that focuses on how human behavior affects outcomes in highly aggregated markets, such as the markets for labor or consumer products.

Potential error associated with the fallacy of composition highlights the importance of considering both a micro view and a macro view in the study of economics. Because individual decision makers are the moving force behind all economic action, the foundations of economics are clearly rooted in a micro view. **Microeconomics** focuses on the decision making of consumers, producers, and resource suppliers operating in a narrowly defined market, such as that for a specific good or resource.

As we have seen, however, what is true for a small unit may not be true in the aggregate. **Macroeconomics** focuses on how the aggregation of individual micro-units affects our analysis. Like microeconomics, it is concerned with incentives, prices, and output. Macroeconomics, however, aggregates markets, lumping all 100 million households in this country together to study such topics as consumption spending, saving, and employment. Similarly, the nation's 20 million business firms are lumped together in "the business sector."

What factors determine the level of aggregate output, the rate of inflation, the amount of unemployment, and interest rates? These are macroeconomic questions. In

MYTHS OF ECONOMICS

"Economic analysis assumes people act only out of selfish motives. It rejects the humanitarian side of humankind."

Probably because economics focuses on efforts of individuals to satisfy material desires, casual observers often argue that its relevance hinges on selfishness. This view is false. People are motivated by a variety of goals, some humanitarian and some selfish. The basic postulate of economics applies to both. As an action becomes more costly, both the altruist and the selfish egotist will be less likely to choose it. Similarly, when the cost of an option declines, both will be more likely to choose it. Changes in benefits and cost will influence the choices of both. For example, both the altruist and the egotist will be more likely to attempt the rescue of a small child in a three-foot swimming pool than in the rapid currents approaching Niagara Falls. Similarly, both are more likely to give a needy person their hand-me-downs rather than their best clothes.

Sometimes people confuse a focus on narrow goals with selfishness. The two are not the same thing. Many people, humanitarians as well as egotists, focus on a narrow set of objectives. For example, the late Mother Teresa focused on a narrow goal—the improvement in the material and spiritual well-being of the indigent and the sick of Calcutta. Her tireless work in this area was legendary. The late John Muir's love of wilderness and his focus on its eternal protection for all humankind was also legendary. The goals of both Mother Teresa and John Muir were noble and altruistic rather than narrowly selfish. The same could be said of passionate advocates for cancer research, education, historic preservation, the arts, aid to underprivileged children, and a thousand other worthy causes. Advocates in all these areas argue passionately for additional funding and support of their mission at the expense of the "missions" of others. Even without selfishness, the narrow focus of individuals with different primary goals will assure strong competition for scarce resources, economizing behavior, and predictable responses to changes in incentives.

short, macroeconomics examines the forest rather than the individual trees. As we move from the micro components to a macro view of the whole, it is important that we beware of the fallacy of composition.

ECONOMICS AS A CAREER

If you find yourself doing well in this course, and find economics an interesting field of study, you may want to think about majoring in economics. Graduating with a major in economics provides a variety of choices. Many students go on to graduate school in economics, business, public administration, or law. Graduate M.B.A. and law programs find economics majors particularly attractive because of their strong analytical skills.

A graduate degree (a master's or doctorate) in economics is typically required to pursue a career as a professional economist. About one-half of all professional economists are employed by colleges and universities as teachers and researchers. Professional economists also work for the government or private businesses. Most major corporations have a staff of economists to advise them in business decisions, while governments employ economists to analyze the impact of policy alternatives. The federal government has a Council of Economic Advisers whose purpose is to provide the president with analyses of how the activities of the government influence the economy. The chairmanship of the Council of Economic Advisers is a cabinet-level position.

Students who major in economics, but who do not pursue graduate school, have many job opportunities. Because economics is a way of thinking, knowledge of economics is a valuable decision-making tool on almost any job. Undergraduate majors in economics typically work in business, government service, banking, or insurance. There are even increasing opportunities for persons with only undergraduate economics majors to teach economics at the high school level.

The average salary offer for a beginning economics graduate is comparable to those with finance and accounting majors, and is generally higher than for management or marketing. Professional economists with graduate degrees in economics who work for private business average approximately $70,000 per year, and those who choose to work as teachers and researchers at colleges and universities earn approximately $60,000 annually. Although salaries vary substantially, the point is that a career in economics can be rewarding both personally and financially. If you are interested in learning more about a major in economics, and the job opportunities available for economics majors, you might visit your school's career center or speak with your school's undergraduate advisor in economics.

Even if you choose not to major in economics, you will find that your economics courses will broaden your horizons and increase your ability to understand and analyze what is going on around you in the world of politics, business, and human relations. Economics is a social science, often overlapping with the fields of political science, sociology, and psychology. Because the economic way of thinking is so useful in making sense of the abundance of available economic observations and data, and because there is ample opportunity for productive research using economic science in the real world, economics has sometimes been called the "queen of the social sciences." Reflecting the scientific nature of economics, the Swedish Academy of Science in 1969 instituted the Nobel Prize in economic science. The men and women of genius in economics take their place alongside those in physics, chemistry, physiology and medicine, peace, and literature.

LOOKING *Ahead*

The primary purpose of this book is to encourage you to develop the economic way of thinking so that you can separate sound reasoning from economic nonsense. Once you have developed the economic way of thinking, economics will be relatively easy. Using the economic way of thinking can also be fun. Moreover, it will help you become a better citizen. It will give you a different and fascinating perspective on what motivates people, why they act the way they do, and why their actions sometimes go against the best interest of the community or nation. It will also give you some valuable insight into how people's actions can be rechanneled for the benefit of the community at large.

KEY POINTS

➤ Scarcity and choice are the two essential ingredients of an economic topic. Goods are scarce because desire for them far outstrips their availability from nature. Scarcity forces us to choose among available alternatives.

➤ Every society will have to devise some method of rationing the scarce resources among competing uses. Competition is a natural outgrowth of the need to ration scarce goods.

➤ Scarcity and poverty are not the same thing. Absence of poverty implies that some basic level of need has been met. An absence of scarcity would imply that all our desires for goods were fully satisfied. We may someday eliminate poverty, but scarcity will always be with us.

➤ Economics is a way of thinking that emphasizes eight points:

1. Among economic goods, there are no free lunches. The use of scarce resources to produce a good is always costly.

2. Individuals make decisions purposefully, always seeking to choose the option they expect to be most consistent with their personal goals.

3. Incentives matter. The likelihood of people choosing an option increases as personal benefits rise and personal costs decline.

4. Economic reasoning focuses on the impact of marginal changes; decisions will be based on marginal costs and marginal benefits (utility).

5. Since information is scarce, uncertainty is a fact of life.

6. In addition to their initial impact, economic events often generate secondary effects that may be felt only with the passage of time.

7. The value of a good or service is subjective and varies with individual preferences and circumstances.

8. The test of an economic theory is its ability to predict and to explain events in the real world.

➤ Economic science is positive; it attempts to explain the actual consequences of economic actions. Normative economics goes further, applying value judgments to make suggestions about what "ought to be."

➤ Microeconomics focuses on narrowly defined units, while macroeconomics is concerned with highly aggregated units. When shifting focus from micro- to macrounits, one must beware of the fallacy of composition.

➤ The origin of economics as a systematic method of analysis dates to the publication of *The Wealth of Nations* by Adam Smith in 1776. Smith believed a market economy would bring individual self-interest and the public interest into harmony.

CRITICAL ANALYSIS QUESTIONS

1. Indicate how each of the following changes would influence the incentive of a decision maker to undertake the action described.

   a. A reduction in the temperature from 80° to 50° on one's decision to go swimming.
   b. A change in the meeting time of the introductory economics course from 11:00 A.M. to 7:30 A.M. on one's decision to attend the lectures.
   c. A reduction in the number of exam questions that relate directly to the text on the student's decision to read the text.
   d. An increase in the price of beef on one's decision to have steak.
   e. An increase in the rental price of apartments on one's decision to build additional housing units.

*2. "The government should provide such goods as health care, education, and highways because it can provide them free." Is this statement true or false? Explain your answer.

3. Is the following disagreement between Senator Dogooder and Senator Donothing positive or normative? Explain.

Senator Dogooder: I favor an increase in the minimum wage because it would help the unskilled worker.

Senator Donothing: I oppose an increase in the minimum wage because it would cause the unemployment rate among the young and unskilled to rise.

*4. Some groups in the United States have asked for an increase in the personal income tax exemption provided to parents for each dependent child. According to the basic postulate of economics, how would this change affect the birth rate?

*5. "The economic way of thinking stresses that good intentions lead to sound policy." Is this statement true or false? Explain your answer.

6. Economic theory postulates that self-interest is a powerful motivation for action. Does this imply that people are selfish and greedy? Do self-interest and selfishness mean the same thing?

*7. Congress and government agencies often make laws to help protect the safety of product consumers. New cars, for example, are required to have many safety features before they can be sold in the United States. These rules do indeed provide added safety for buyers, although they also add to the cost and price of the new vehicles. But can you think of secondary effects of the laws that tend to undercut or reduce the intended effect of increasing auto safety?

*8. "Individuals who economize are missing the point of life. Money is not so important that it should rule the way we live." Evaluate this statement.

*9. "Positive economics cannot tell us which agricultural policy is better, so it is useless to policymakers." Evaluate this statement.

*10. "I examined the statistics for our basketball team's wins last year and found that, when the third team played more, the winning margin increased. If the coach played the third team more, we would win by a bigger margin." Evaluate this statement.

---

*Asterisk denotes questions for which answers are given in Appendix B.

ADDENDUM

Understanding Graphs

Economists often use graphs to illustrate economic relations. Graphs are like pictures. They are visual aids that can communicate valuable information in a small amount of space. A picture may be worth a thousand words, but only to a person who understands the picture (and the graph).

This addendum illustrates the use of simple graphs as a way to communicate. Many students, particularly those with some mathematics background, are already familiar with this material, and can safely ignore it. This addendum is for those who need to be assured that they can understand graphic illustrations of economic concepts.

The Simple Bar Graph

A simple bar graph helps us to visualize comparative relationships and to understand them better. It is particularly useful for illustrating how an economic indicator varies among countries, among time periods, or under alternative economic conditions.

Exhibit 1A–1 is a bar graph illustrating economic data. The table in part a presents data on the income per person in 1997 for several countries. Part b uses a bar graph to illustrate the same data. The horizontal scale of the graph indicates the total income per person in 1997. A bar is made indicating the income level (see the dollar scale on the *x*-axis) of each country. The length of each bar is in proportion to the per person income of the country. Thus, the length of the bars provides a visual illustration of how per capita income varies across the countries. For example, the extremely short bar for Nigeria shows immediately that income per person there is only a small fraction of the comparable income figure for the United States, Switzerland, Japan, and several other countries.

Linear Graphic Presentation

Economists often want to illustrate variations in economic variables with the passage of time. A linear graph with time on the horizontal axis and an economic variable on the vertical axis is a useful tool to indicate variations over time. **Exhibit 1A–2** illustrates a simple linear graph of changes in consumer prices (the inflation rate) in the United States between 1960 and 1997. The table of the exhibit presents data on the percentage change in consumer prices for each year. Beginning with 1960, the horizontal axis indicates the time period (year). The inflation rate is plotted vertically above each year. Of course, the height of the plot (line) indicates the inflation rate during that year. For example, in 1975 the inflation rate was 6.9 percent. This point is plotted at the 6.9 percent vertical distance directly above the year 1975. In 1976 the inflation rate fell to 4.9 percent. Thus, the vertical plot of the 1976 inflation rate is lower than that for 1975. The inflation rate for each year (part a) is plotted at the corresponding height directly above the year. The linear graph is simply a line connecting the points plotted for each of the years 1960 through 1997.

The linear graph is a visual aid to understanding what happens to the inflation rate during the period. As the graph shows, the inflation rate rose sharply between 1967 and 1969, in 1973–1974, and again in 1977–1979. It was substantially higher during the 1970s than in the early 1960s or the mid-1980s. Although the linear graph does not communicate any information not in the table, it does make it easier to see the pattern of the data. Thus, economists often use simple graphics rather than tables to communicate information.

Direct and Inverse Relationships

Economic logic often suggests that two variables are linked in a specific way. Suppose an investigation reveals that, other things constant, farmers supply more wheat as the price of wheat increases. **Exhibit 1A–3** presents hypothetical data on the relationship between the price of wheat and the quantity supplied by farmers, first in tabular form (part a) and then as a simple two-dimensional graph (part b). Suppose we measure the quantity of wheat supplied by farmers on the *x*-axis (the horizontal axis) and the price of wheat on the *y*-axis (the vertical axis). Points indicating the value of *x* (quantity supplied) at alternative values of *y* (price of wheat) can then be plotted. The line (or curve) linking the points illustrates the relationship between the price of wheat and the amount supplied by farmers.

In the case of price and quantity supplied of wheat, the two variables are directly related. When the *y*-variable increases, so does the *x*-variable. When two variables are directly related, the graph illustrating the linkage between the two will slope upward to the right (as in the case of *SS* in part b).

Sometimes the *x*-variable and the *y*-variable are inversely related. A decline in the *y*-variable is associated with an increase in the *x*-variable. Therefore, a curve picturing the inverse relationship between *x* and *y* slopes downward to the right. **Exhibit 1A–4** illustrates this case. As the data of the table indicate, consumers purchase less as the price of wheat increases. Measuring the price of wheat on the *y*-axis (by convention, economists always place price on the *y*-axis) and the quantity of wheat purchased on the *x*-axis, the relationship between these two variables can also be illustrated graphically. If the price of

EXHIBIT 1A-1

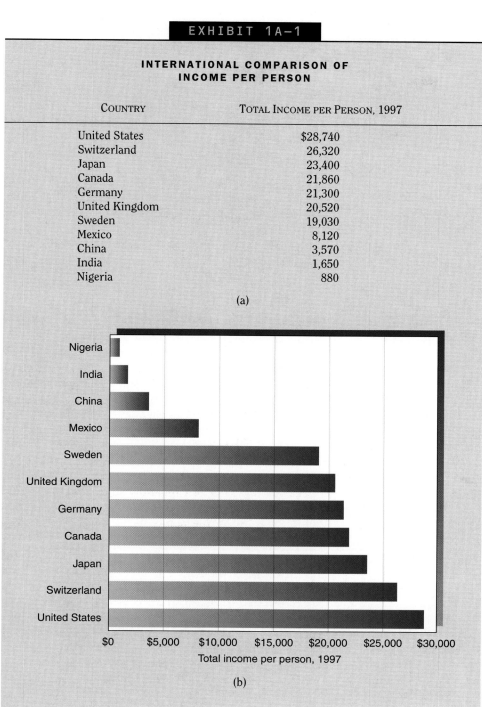

INTERNATIONAL COMPARISON OF INCOME PER PERSON

Country	Total Income per Person, 1997
United States	$28,740
Switzerland	26,320
Japan	23,400
Canada	21,860
Germany	21,300
United Kingdom	20,520
Sweden	19,030
Mexico	8,120
China	3,570
India	1,650
Nigeria	880

(a)

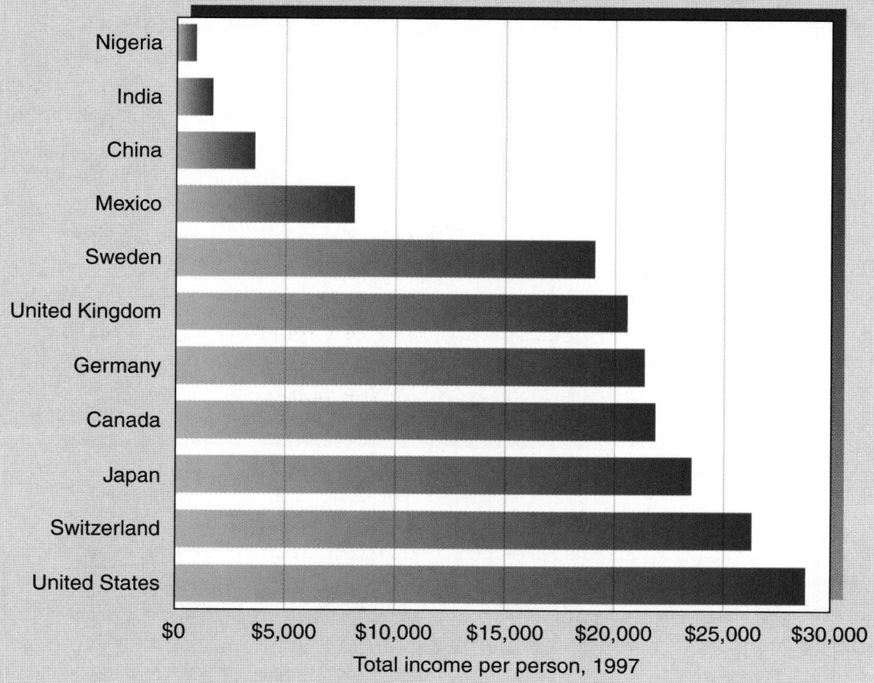

(b)

SOURCE: The World Bank, World Development Report, 1998/99, *Table 1. The income comparisons were derived by the purchasing power parity method.*

wheat were $5 per bushel, only 60 million bushels would be purchased by consumers. As the price declines to $4 per bushel, annual consumption increases to 75 million bushels. At still lower prices, the quantity purchased by consumers will expand to larger and larger amounts. As part b illustrates, the inverse relationship between price and quantity of wheat purchased generates a curve that slopes downward to the right.

The tabular data (a) of the inflation rate are presented in graphic form in (b).

SOURCE: Economic Report of the President, 1991, *Table B-61; and* Economic Report of the President, 1998, *Table B-63.*

EXHIBIT 1A-2

CHANGES IN LEVEL OF PRICES IN UNITED STATES, 1960–1997

Year	Percent Change in Consumer Prices	Year	Percent Change in Consumer Prices
1960	1.4	1979	13.3
1961	0.7	1980	12.5
1962	1.3	1981	8.9
1963	1.6	1982	3.8
1964	1.0	1983	3.8
1965	1.9	1984	3.9
1966	3.5	1985	3.8
1967	3.0	1986	1.1
1968	4.7	1987	4.4
1969	6.2	1988	4.4
1970	5.6	1989	4.6
1971	3.3	1990	6.1
1972	3.4	1991	3.1
1973	8.7	1992	2.9
1974	12.3	1993	2.7
1975	6.9	1994	2.7
1976	4.9	1995	2.5
1977	6.7	1996	3.3
1978	9.0	1997	1.7

(a)

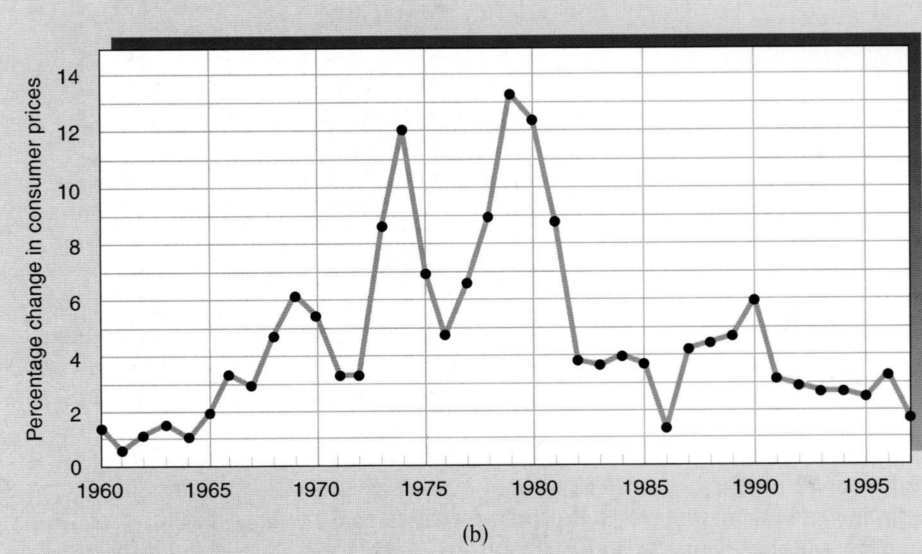

(b)

EXHIBIT 1A–3

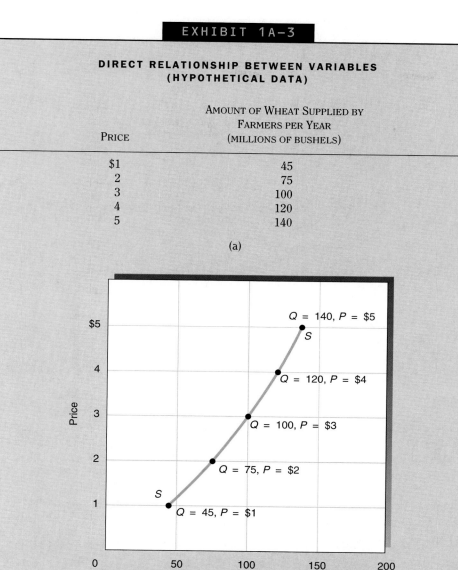

DIRECT RELATIONSHIP BETWEEN VARIABLES (HYPOTHETICAL DATA)

PRICE	AMOUNT OF WHEAT SUPPLIED BY FARMERS PER YEAR (MILLIONS OF BUSHELS)
$1	45
2	75
3	100
4	120
5	140

(a)

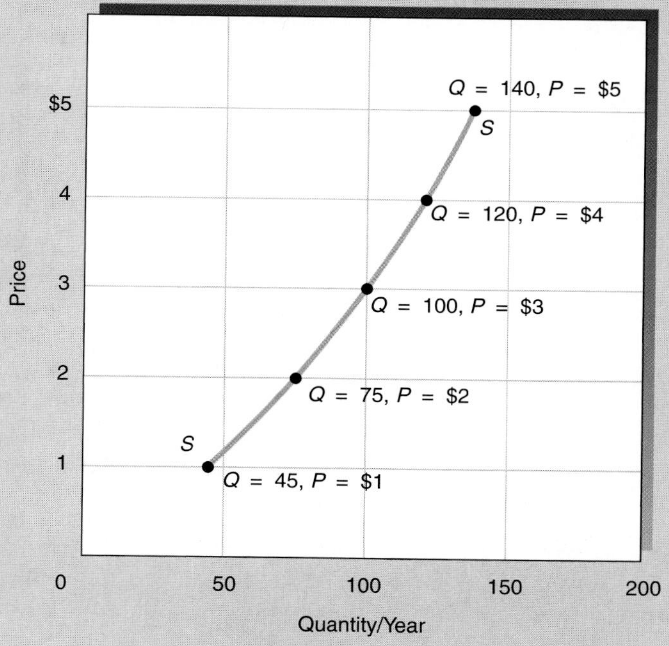

(b)

As the table (a) indicates, farmers are willing to supply more wheat at a higher price. Thus, there is a direct relation between the price of wheat and the quantity supplied. When the x- *and* y- *variables are directly related, a curve mapping the relationship between the two will slope upward to the right like* SS.

Complex Relationships

Sometimes the initial relationship between the x- and y-variables will change. **Exhibit 1A–5** illustrates more complex relations of this type. Part a shows the typical relationship between annual earnings and age. As a young person gets work experience and develops skills, earnings usually expand. Thus, initially, age and annual earnings are directly related; annual earnings increase with age. However, beyond a certain age (approximately age 55), annual earnings generally decline as workers approach retirement. As a result, the initial direct relationship between age and earnings changes to an inverse relation. When this is the case, annual income expands to a maximum (at age 55) and then begins to decline with years of age.

Part b illustrates an initial inverse relation that later changes to a direct relationship. Consider the impact of travel speed on gasoline consumption per mile. At low speeds, the automobile engine will not be used efficiently.

As the table (a) shows, consumers will demand (purchase) more wheat as the price declines. Thus, there is an inverse relationship between the price of wheat and the quantity demanded. When the x- and y-variables are inversely related, a curve showing the relationship between the two will slope downward to the right like DD.

EXHIBIT 1A-4

INVERSE RELATIONSHIP BETWEEN VARIABLES (HYPOTHETICAL DATA)

PRICE	AMOUNT OF WHEAT DEMANDED BY CONSUMERS PER YEAR (MILLIONS OF BUSHELS)
$1	170
2	130
3	100
4	75
5	60

(a)

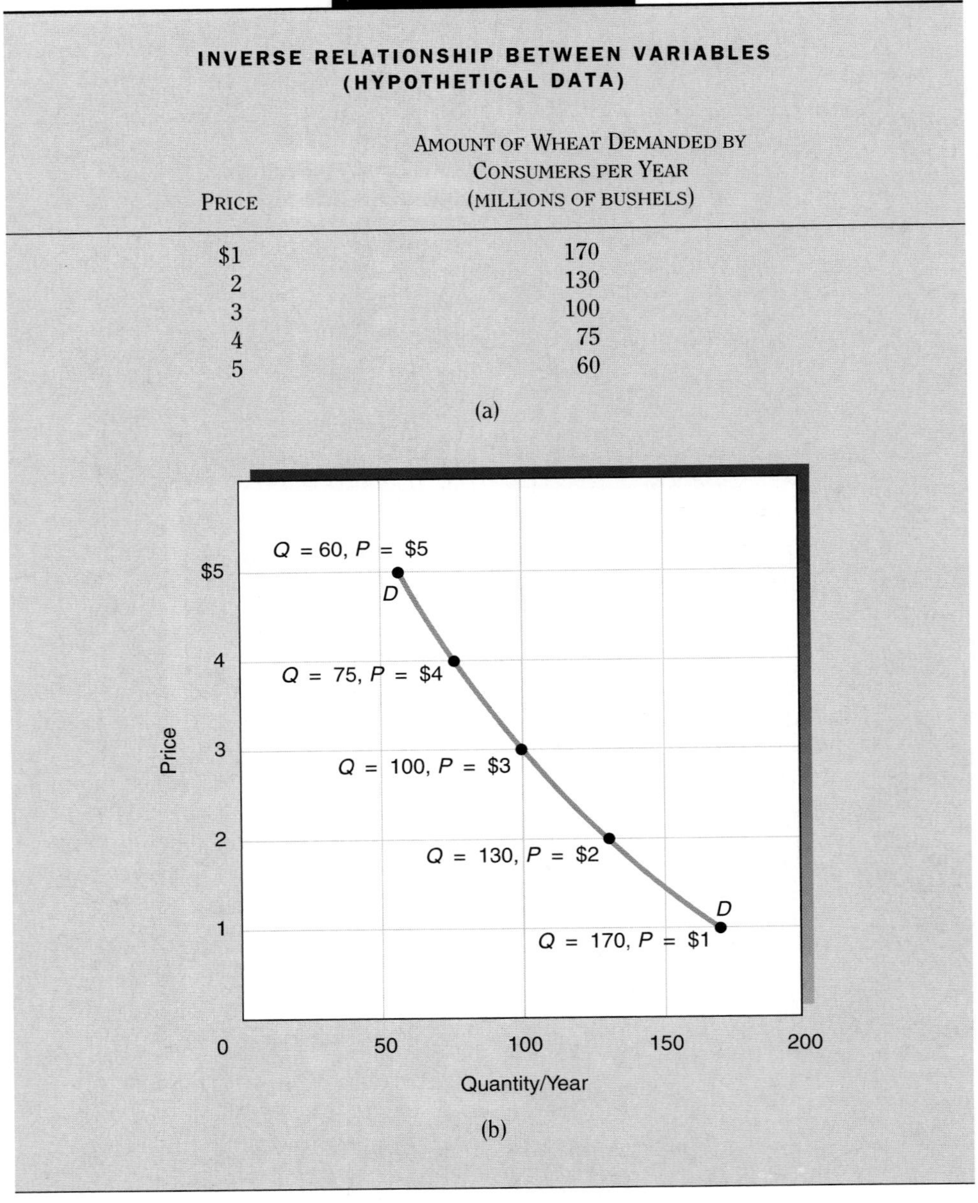

(b)

As speed increases from 5 mph to 10 mph and on to a speed of 40 mph, gasoline consumption per mile declines. In this range, there is an inverse relationship between speed of travel (x) and gasoline consumption per mile (y). However, as speed increases beyond 40 mph, air resistance increases and more gasoline per mile is required to maintain the additional speed. At very high speeds, gasoline consumption per mile increases substantially with speed of travel. Thus, gasoline consumption per mile reaches a minimum, and a direct relationship between the x- and y-variables describes the relationship beyond that point (40 mph).

Slope of a Straight Line

In economics, we are often interested in how much the y-variable changes in response to a change in the x-variable. The slope of the line or curve reveals this information. Mathematically, the slope of a line or curve is equal to the change in the y-variable divided by the change in the x-variable.

EXHIBIT 1A–5

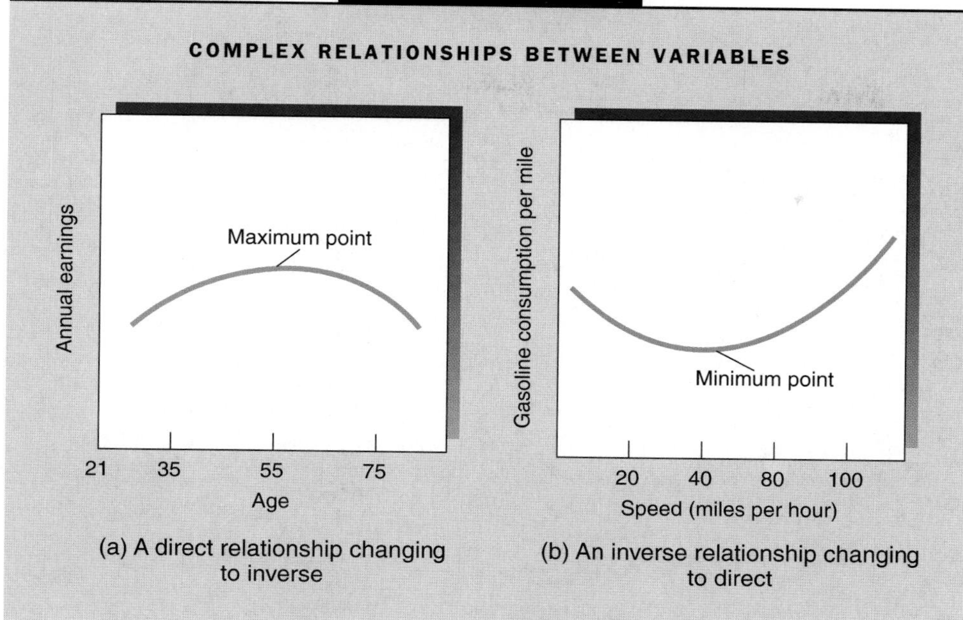

(a) A direct relationship changing to inverse

(b) An inverse relationship changing to direct

At first, an increase in age (and work experience) leads to a higher income, but later earnings decline as the worker approaches retirement (a). Thus, age and annual income are initially directly related but at approximately age 55 an inverse relationship emerges. Part (b) illustrates the relationship between travel speed and gasoline consumption per mile. Initially, gasoline consumption per mile declines as speed increases (an inverse relationship), but as speed increases above 40 mph, gasoline consumption per mile increases with the speed of travel (direct relationship).

Exhibit 1A–6 illustrates the calculation of the slope for a straight line. The exhibit shows how the daily earnings (y-variable) of a worker change with hours worked (the x-variable). The wage rate of the worker is $10 per hour, so when 1 hour is worked, earnings are equal to $10. For 2 hours of work, earnings jump to $20, and so on. A 1-hour change in hours worked leads to a $10 change in earnings. Thus, the slope of the line ($\Delta y/\Delta x$) is equal to 10. (The symbol Δ means "change in.") In the case of a straight line, the change in y, per unit change in x, is equal for all points on the line. Thus, the slope of a straight line is constant for all points along the line.

Exhibit 1A–6 illustrates a case in which a direct relation exists between the x- and y-variables. For an inverse relation, the y-variable decreases as the x-variable increases. So, when x and y are inversely related, the slope of the line will be negative.

Slope of a Curve

In contrast with a straight line, the slope of a curve is different at each point along the curve. The slope of a curve at a specific point is equal to the slope of a line tangent to the curve at the point, meaning a line that just touches the curve.

Exhibit 1A–7 illustrates how the slope of a curve at a specific point is determined. First, consider the slope of the curve at point A. A line tangent to the curve at point A indicates that y changes by one unit when x changes by two units at point A. Thus, the slope ($\Delta y/\Delta x$) of the curve at A is equal to 0.5.

Now consider the slope of the curve at point B. The line tangent to the curve at B indicates that y changes by two units for each one unit change in x at point B. Thus, at B the slope ($\Delta y/\Delta x$) is equal to 2. At point B, a change in the x-variable leads to a much larger change in y than was true at point A. The greater slope of the curve at B reflects this greater change in y per unit change in x at B relative to A.

Graphs Are Not a Substitute for Economic Thinking

By now you should have a fairly good understanding of how to read a graph. If you still feel uncomfortable with graphs, try drawing (graphing) the relationship between several things with which you are familiar. If you work, try graphing the relationship between your hours worked (x-axis) and your weekly earnings (y-axis). Exhibit 1A–6 could guide you with this exercise. Can you graph the relationship between the price of gasoline and your expenditures on gasoline? Graphing these simple relationships will give you greater confidence in your ability to grasp more complex economic relationships presented in graphs.

This text uses only simple graphs. Thus, there is no reason for you to be intimidated. Graphs look much more complex than they really are. In fact, they are nothing more than a simple device to communicate information

EXHIBIT 1A-6

SLOPE OF A STRAIGHT LINE

The slope of a line is equal to the change in y divided by the change in x. The line opposite illustrates the case in which daily earnings increase by $10 per hour worked. Thus, the slope of the earnings function is 10 ($10 ÷ 1 hr). For a straight line, the slope is constant at each point on the line.

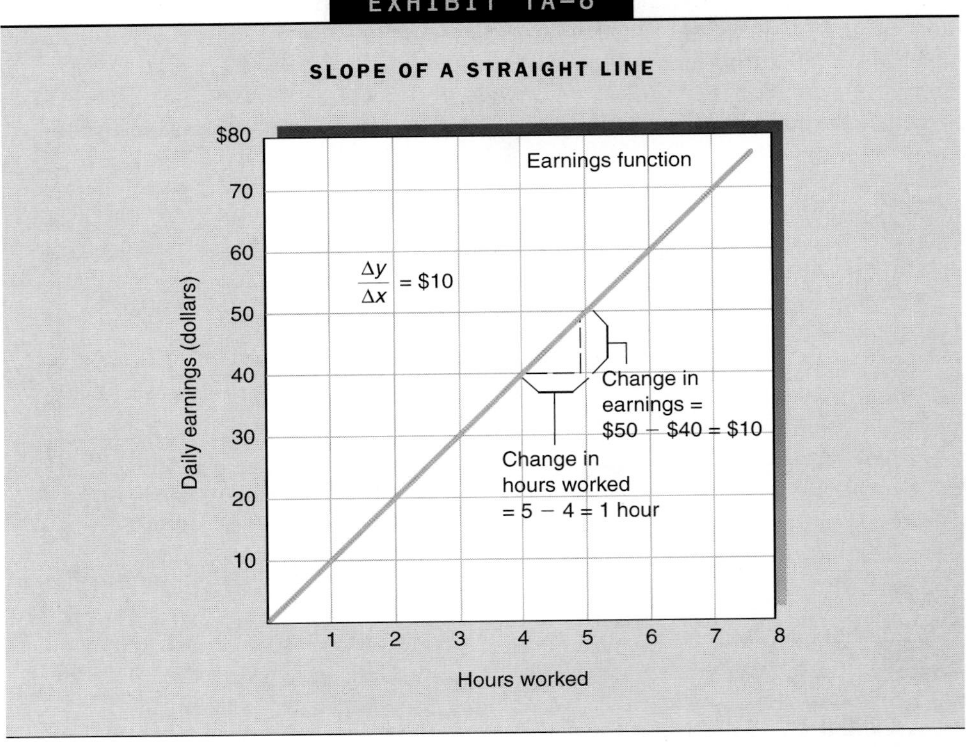

EXHIBIT 1A-7

SLOPE OF A NONLINEAR CURVE

The slope of a curve at any point is equal to the slope of the straight line tangent to the curve at the point. As the lines tangent to the curve at points A and B illustrate, the slope of a curve will change from point to point along the curve.

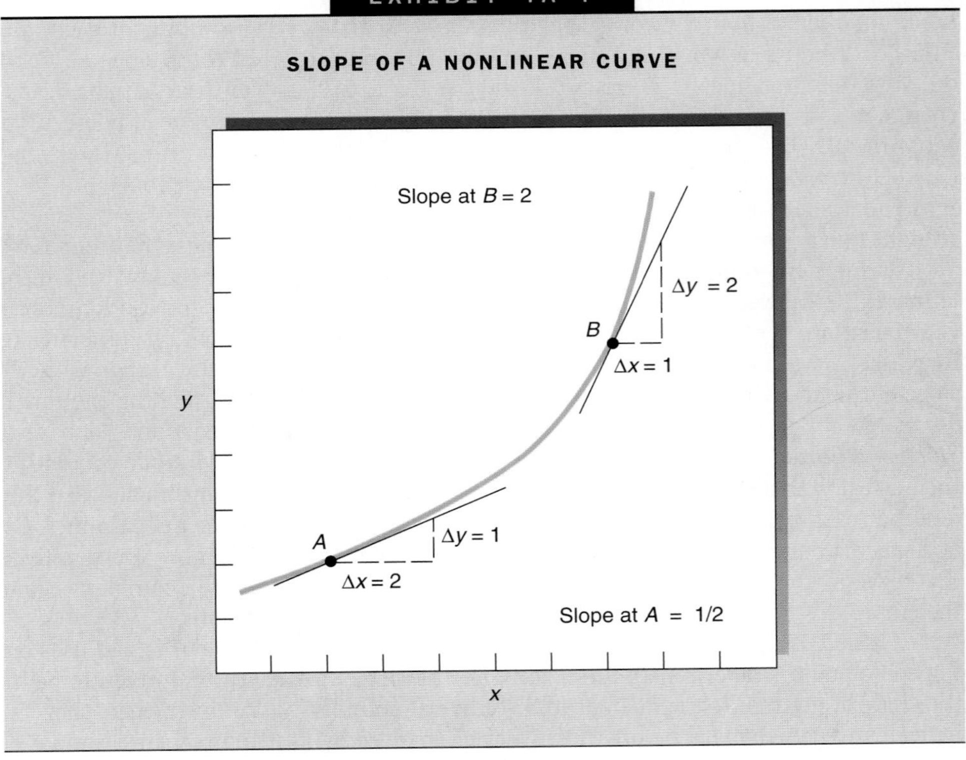

quickly and concisely. Nothing can be communicated with a graph that cannot be communicated verbally.

Most important, graphs are not a substitute for economic thinking. Although a graph may illustrate that two variables are related, it tells us nothing about the cause-and-effect relationship between the variables. To determine probable cause and effect, we must rely on economic theory. Thus, the economic way of thinking, not graphs, is the power station of economic analysis.

CHAPTER 2

The key insight of Adam Smith's Wealth of Nations is misleadingly simple: if an exchange between two parties is voluntary, it will not take place unless both believe they will benefit from it. Most economic fallacies derive from the neglect of this simple insight, from the tendency to assume that there is a fixed pie, that one party can gain only at the expense of another.

Milton and Rose Friedman[1]

Some Tools of the Economist

CHAPTER FOCUS

- What is opportunity cost? Why do economists place so much emphasis on it?
- Why do people engage in exchange?
- How does private ownership affect the use of resources? Will private owners pay any attention to the desires of others?
- What does a production-possibilities curve demonstrate?
- What are sources of gains from trade? How does trade influence our modern living standards?
- What are the two major methods of economic organization? How do they differ?

[1]Milton and Rose Friedman, *Free To Choose* (Harcourt Brace, 1990), p. 13.

In the preceding chapter, you were introduced to the economic way of thinking. We will now begin to apply that approach. This chapter focuses on four topics: opportunity cost, trade, property rights, and the potential output level of an economy. These seemingly diverse topics are in fact highly interrelated. The opportunity cost of goods determines which ones it makes sense for an individual or a nation to produce and which should be acquired through trade. In turn, the structure of both trade and property rights will influence the level of output. We will begin by taking a closer look at the concept of opportunity cost.

WHAT SHALL WE GIVE UP?

Scarcity calls the tune in economics. We cannot have as much of everything as we would like. Most of us would like to have more time for leisure, recreation, vacations, hobbies, education, and skill development. We would also like to have more wealth, a larger savings account, and more consumable goods. However, all these things are scarce, in the sense that they are limited. Our efforts to get more of one will conflict with our efforts to get more of the others.

OPPORTUNITY COST

An unpleasant fact of economics is that the choice to do one thing is, at the same time, a choice not to do something else. Your choice to spend time reading this book is a choice not to spend the time playing tennis, listening to a math lecture, or attending a party. These things must be given up because of your decision to read. As we indicated in Chapter 1, the highest valued alternative sacrificed in order to choose an option is the opportunity cost of that choice.[2]

Costs are subjective. (So are benefits. After all, a cost is a sacrificed benefit!) A cost exists in the mind of the decision maker. It is based on expectation—the expected value of the forgone alternative. Cost can never be directly measured by someone other than the decision maker because only the decision maker can place a value on what is given up.[3] Others, including experts and elected officials, who try to choose for the individual (or group of individuals), face an exceedingly difficult information problem. Individuals differ in the trade-offs they prefer to make, and those preferences change with time and circumstances. Only individuals are in a position to properly evaluate options for themselves, and to decide whether a specific trade-off is a good thing for them, in their specific circumstances of time and place.

---

[2]See also David Henderson, "Opportunity Cost," in *The Fortune Encyclopedia of Economics,* ed. David Henderson (New York: Warner Books, Inc., 1993), pp. 44–45.

[3]See James M. Buchanan, *Cost and Choice* (Chicago: Markham, 1969), for an analysis of the relationship between cost and choice.

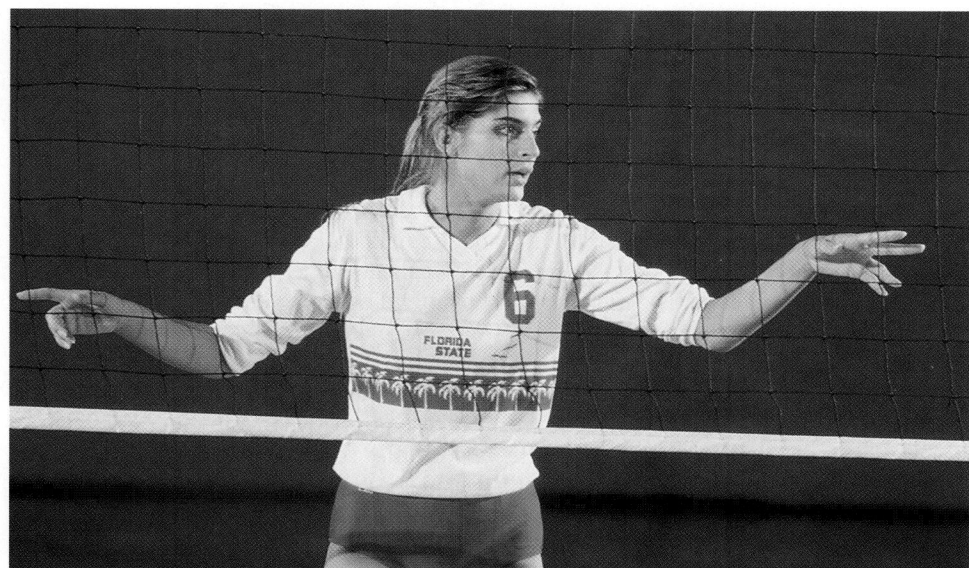

Gabrielle Reece understands opportunity cost. A star volleyball player at Florida State University, she forfeited her $4,500 scholarship (the NCAA prohibits outside employment by scholarship athletes) in order to embark on a six month modeling tour following her freshman year. After an appearance on the cover of Vogue, *her modeling opportunities soared. Even though she was both a good student and super volleyball player, she left school prior to graduation. Given her potential earnings as a model, the opportunity cost of school was simply too great.*

Cost, however, often has a monetary component that enables us to approximate its value. For example, the cost of attending a ballet (or a football game) is the highest valued opportunity lost as a result of (1) the time necessary to attend and (2) the purchasing power—the money—necessary to obtain a ticket. The monetary component is, of course, objective and can be measured. So long as individuals are paying the money price in voluntary exchange, it represents for them opportunity costs. When *nonmonetary* considerations are relatively unimportant, the monetary component will approximate the total cost of an option. We should notice, though, that to a buyer (or to one who refuses to sell), the item is probably worth more than the market price. However, to a seller (or one who does not buy), the item is worth less than the market price.

Opportunity Cost and the Real World

Is real-world decision making influenced by opportunity cost? Remember, the basic economic postulate states that an option is more likely to be chosen when its cost to the decision maker is less. So economic theory does tell us that differences (or changes) in opportunity cost will influence decisions. Recognizing opportunity costs can help us to understand decisions—those made by college students, for example.

Consider your own decision to attend college. Your opportunity cost of going to college is the value of the next best alternative, which could be measured as the salary you would earn if you had chosen to work rather than go to college. Every year you stay in college, you give up what you could have earned by working that year. Changes in the opportunity cost of going to college will affect the choices of potential students. Suppose, for example, that you received a job offer today for $250,000 per year as an athlete or an entertainer, but the job would require so much travel that school would be impossible. Would this change in the opportunity cost of going to college affect your continuation in school? For many students it would; such a large increase in the cost of remaining in school would cause many students to leave. (See feature on Gabrielle Reece above.) It is clear that one of the most important costs of attending college is the value of the next best alternative: the opportunity cost.

Even when their parents pay all the monetary expenses of their college education, some students are surprised to learn that they are actually incurring more of the total cost of going to college than their parents. For example, the average monetary cost (tuition, room and board, books, and so forth) for a resident student attending a public four-year college is about $10,000 per year. Even if the student's next best alternative was working at a job that paid only $15,000 per year, then over a four-year college career, he or she will incur $60,000 of the cost of college in the form of forgone earnings, while the parents will incur only about $40,000 of the cost.[4]

Now consider another decision made by college students—whether to attend a particular meeting of class. The monetary cost of attending a class (bus fare or parking and gasoline, and so on) remains fairly constant from day to day. Why then do students choose to attend class on some days and not on others? Even though the monetary cost is fairly constant, the opportunity cost—the highest valued alternative given up—can change dramatically from day to day. Some days the next best alternative to attending class may be sleeping in or watching TV. Other days, the opportunity cost may be substantially larger, perhaps the value of attending a big football game, getting an early start on a holiday break, or having additional study time for a crucial exam in another class. As options like this increase the cost of attending class, more students will decide not to attend.

Failure to consider opportunity cost often leads to unwise decision making. Suppose that your community builds a beautiful new civic center. The mayor, speaking at the dedication ceremony, tells the world that the center will improve the quality of life in your community. People who understand the concept of opportunity cost may question this view. If the center had not been built, the resources might have funded contruction of a new hospital, improvements to the educational system, or housing for low-income families. Will the civic center contribute more to the well-being of the people in your community than these other facilities? If so, it was a wise investment. If not, however, your community will be worse off than it might have been if decision makers had chosen a higher-valued project (that must now be forgone).

TRADE CREATES VALUE

We learned in the preceding chapter that preferences are subjective, they are known only to the individual, and they differ among individuals. That is why the value of an item can vary greatly from one person to another. In turn, this means that simply trading—rearranging goods and services among people to get them to higher-valued uses and users—can create value. In our Chapter 1 example, the value to Alice of a ticket to attend the Bolshoi Ballet performance was zero once she received the party invitation, but the value to other individuals had not declined. Suppose Jim, who bought it at the advertised price of $40, actually valued it at $55. An unforeseen change in Alice's schedule had destroyed the value of the performance that evening for her, but trading (selling) the ticket to Jim created $40 in value for her, and it netted $15 in value for Jim—the $55 value he placed on the performance minus the $40 he gave to Alice. The performance remained the same, and the seats available remained the same, but trade had created value just as surely as if an additional seat had been made available.

It is wrong to assume that a particular good or service has a fixed value just because it exists.[5] As the example of the ballet ticket illustrates, the value of goods and

---

[4]From the standpoint of the family's total economic cost of sending a child to college, some of the monetary costs, such as room and board, are not costs of choosing to go to college. The cost of living does have to be covered, but it would be incurred whether or not the student went to college.

[5]An illuminating discussion of this subject, termed the "physical fallacy," is found in Thomas Sowell, *Knowledge and Decisions* (New York: Basic Books, 1980), pp. 67–72.

OUTSTANDING ECONOMIST

Thomas Sowell (1930–)

Thomas Sowell, a senior fellow at the Hoover Institution, recognizes the critical importance of the institutions—the "rules of the game"—that shape human interactions. His book, *Knowledge and Decisions,* stresses the difficulty of obtaining knowledge and explores the way different institutional arrangements provide different kinds and amounts of scarce information.

services generally depends on who uses them, and on circumstances, such as when and where they are used, as well as on the physical characteristics. This explains why trades can make existing goods more valuable simply by getting them to the people who value them more.

Transaction Costs—A Barrier to Trade

Unfortunately, Alice did not know about Andrew, another ballet fan, who would have been willing to pay $60 for the ticket. Andrew lives off campus and failed to see the bulletin board ad, so the potential for another $5 increase in value failed to materialize. But if Jim and Andrew happen to meet before the show and the topic of the ballet comes up, the additional $5 in value for the ticket might be created by another transaction: Jim trading the ticket to Andrew. Such a transaction is unlikely, because getting together requires either good luck or costly measures, such as searching bulletin boards. Of course, new and cheaper marketing methods, such as electronic online bulletin boards, can reduce the cost and increase the frequency of value-creating trades. Still, not every trade that could potentially create value will be discovered and made.

Although exchange creates value, it is also costly. The costs of the time, effort, and other resources necessary to search out, negotiate, and conclude an exchange are called **transaction costs.** *Transaction costs reduce our ability to produce gains from potential trades.*

Transaction costs
The time, effort, and other resources needed to search out, negotiate, and consummate an exchange.

Because of transaction costs, we should not expect all potentially valuable trades to take place, any more than we expect all useful knowledge to be learned, all safety measures to be taken, or all potential "A" grades to be earned. Frequent fliers know that if they never miss a flight, they are probably spending too much time waiting in airports. Similarly, the seller of a car, a house, or a ballet ticket knows that to find that one person in the world who would be willing to pay the most money is not worth the enormous effort required to locate that buyer. Information is costly. That is one reason that perfection in exchange, as in most things we do, is seldom reached.

Middleman as Cost Reducer

Because gains from exchange are facilitated by information, some people, called **middlemen,** specialize in providing information at a lower cost, and in arranging trades. Middlemen are generally not very popular; many think that they just add to the buyer's expense without performing a useful function. Once we recognize that transaction costs deter gains from trade, the real contribution of middlemen is obvious: They provide services that reduce the cost of transactions and thereby promote the realization of additional gains from trade. The auto dealer, for example, can help both the

Middleman
A person who buys and sells, or who arranges trades. A middleman reduces transaction costs.

manufacturer and the buyer. By keeping an inventory of autos, and by hiring knowledgeable salespeople, the dealer lowers the cost for the car shopper to learn about the many cars offered, and how each car looks, performs, and "feels." (Since preferences are subjective and not objectively known to others, the reports of other users may not fully inform the potential buyer.) Car buyers also like to know that the local dealer will honor the warranty and provide parts and service for the car. The car maker, by using the dealer as a middleman, is able to concentrate on designing and making cars, leaving to middlemen—that is, dealers—the tasks of marketing and servicing.

Grocers also provide middleman services. Each of us could avoid the grocer by dealing with farmers and other food producers directly. If we did, though, transaction costs would be high and it would be more difficult to squeeze the tomatoes! Alternatively, we could form consumer cooperatives, banding together to eliminate the middleman, using our own warehouses and our own volunteer labor to order, receive, display, redistribute, and collect payment for the food. In fact, some cooperatives like this do exist, but most people prefer instead to pay the grocer to provide all these middleman services.

Stockbrokers, publishers of the Yellow Pages, and merchants of all sorts are middlemen—specialists in selling, guaranteeing, and servicing the items traded. For a fee, they reduce transaction costs both for the shopper and for the seller. By making exchange cheaper and more convenient, middlemen cause more efficient trades to happen. In so doing, they themselves create value.

THE IMPORTANCE OF PROPERTY RIGHTS

[A] private property regime makes people responsible for their own actions in the realm of material goods. Such a system therefore ensures that people experience the consequences of their own acts. Property sets up fences, but it also surrounds us with mirrors, reflecting back upon us the consequences of our own behavior.

Tom Bethell[6]

Property rights
The right to use, control, and obtain the benefits from a good or service.

Private property rights
Property rights that are exclusively held by an owner, or group of owners, and that can be transferred to others at the owner's discretion.

The buyer of an apple, a CD, a television set, or an automobile generally takes the item home. The buyer of a steamship or an office building, though, may never touch it. When exchange occurs, it is really the rights—the **property rights**—to the item that change hands.

Private property rights involve three things: (1) the right to exclusive use, (2) legal protection against invaders—those who would seek to use or abuse the property without the owner's permission, and (3) the right to transfer to (exchange with) another. Private owners cannot do anything they want with their property. Most significantly, they cannot use their property in a manner that invades or infringes on the property of another. For example, I cannot throw the hammer that I own through the television set that you own. If I did, I would be violating your property right to your television. The same is true if I operate a factory that harms you or your land by spewing air pollution.[7] Because an owner has the right to control the use of property, the owner also must accept responsibility for the outcomes of that control.

[6]Tom Bethell, *The Noblest Triumph* (New York: St. Martin's Press, 1998), p. 10.

[7]For a detailed explanation of how property rights protect the environment, with several real-world examples, see Roger E. Meiners and Bruce Yandle, *The Common Law: How It Protects the Environment* (Bozeman, Mont.: PERC, 1998), available online at <www.perc.org>.

As Tom Bethell (see quotation at left) points out, powerful incentive effects follow from private ownership of goods and resources. The following four factors are particularly important.

1. *Private owners can gain by employing their resources in ways that are beneficial to others.* And they bear the opportunity cost of ignoring the wishes of others. If someone values an asset more than its current owner, the current owner can gain by paying heed to the wishes of others. For example, suppose Ed owns a car that others would also like to have. What incentive is there for Ed to pay attention to the desires of the others? If Ed values the car at $4,000, he can gain by selling it at any price in excess of that amount. If transaction costs are low (search is relatively cheap), Ed may well gain by searching for people (potential buyers) who value the car more than he does. Suppose that a potential buyer makes Ed an offer of $4,500 for the car. Turning down this offer will cost Ed a potential net gain of $500. If Ed fails to consider the desires of others, he may penalize potential buyers, but he will also be hurting himself. Thus, when cars and other goods are privately owned and easily transferable, potential buyers and sellers have a strong incentive to search out mutually advantageous trades. After all, if they find such a trade, only the buyer and seller have to approve the deal in order to realize the mutual gain.

As a second example, suppose Ed owns a house and will be out of town all summer. Will the house stay vacant, or will Ed let someone else use it during those months? We don't know, but we do know that Ed can rent the house to someone else if he chooses, and that if he does not, he will incur the opportunity cost—the rental payments he could get, minus any damages, added upkeep, and transaction costs. Even if he is unwilling to rent the house, ownership of the private property rights again faces Ed with the opportunity costs of not renting it out, thereby providing him with a strong incentive to consider the wishes of others regarding the use of his property.

How about the owners of investment properties and businesses—do they have an incentive to heed the desires of others? Consider the owner of an apartment complex near your campus. The owner may not care much for swimming pools, workout facilities, study desks, or green areas, for example. Nonetheless, private ownership provides the owner with a strong incentive to provide these items if students and other potential customers value them enough to cover the cost of their provision. Why? The owner will be able to lease the apartment units for more if they include amenities that are highly valued by others. Investment property owners have a strong incentive to consider the desires of others.

2. *The private owner has a strong incentive to care for and properly manage what he or she owns.* Will Ed change the oil in his car? Will he take care to see that the seats do not get torn? Probably so, since being careless about these things would reduce the car's value, both to him and to any future owner. The car and its value—the sale price if he sells it—belong just to Ed, so he would bear the burden of a decline in the car's value if the oil ran low and ruined the engine, or if the seats were torn. Similarly, he would capture the value of an expenditure that improves the car, such as providing a new paint job. As the owner, Ed has both the authority and the incentive to protect the car against harm or neglect, and even to enhance its value. Private property rights concentrates the owner's interest and attention, providing a strong incentive for good stewardship.

"Their house looks so nice. They must be getting ready to sell it."

From the *Wall Street Journal*—permission, Cartoon Features Syndicate.

The incentive for good care and management by the individual extends also to private investments that yield income. The owner of a hotel does not want to neglect electrical or plumbing problems, if taking care of them now avoids large repair costs due to electrical fires or water leaks. The wealth of the owner, in the form of the value of hotel ownership, is a hostage to the owner's good management. Poor management will reduce the hotel's value, and thus the owner's personal wealth. Again, ownership concentrates the owner's interest and attention on good management of the asset owned.

3. ***The private owner has an incentive to conserve for the future if the property's value is expected to rise.*** Suppose our man Ed owns a case of very good red wine, which is only two years old. Age will improve it substantially if he puts it in his cellar for another five years. Will he do so? Well, if he does not, he will personally bear the consequences. He (and presumably his friends) will drink wine sooner, but they will sacrifice quality. Also, Ed will forgo the chance to sell the wine later for much more than its current worth. The opportunity cost of drinking the wine now is its unavailability later, for drinking or for sale. Ed bears that cost. Private property rights assure that Ed has the authority to preserve the wine, and that he gains the benefits if he does so. If the greater quality is expected to be worth the wait, then Ed can capture the benefits of not drinking the wine "before its time."

In a similar way, if Ed owns land, or a house, or a factory, he has a strong incentive to bear costs now, if necessary, to preserve the asset's value. His wealth is tied up in its value, which reflects nothing more than the net benefits that will be available to the owner in the future. So Ed's wealth depends on his willingness and ability to look ahead, maintain, and conserve those things that will be highly valued in the future.

4. ***With private property rights, the property owner is accountable for damage to others through misuse of the property. Private ownership links responsibility with the right of control.*** Ed, the car owner, has a right to drive his car, but he has no right to drive in a drunken or reckless way that injures Alice. A chemical company has control over its products, but, exactly for that reason, it is legally liable for damages if it mishandles the chemicals. Courts of law recognize and enforce the authority granted by ownership, but they also enforce the responsibility that goes with that authority. Once again, property rights hold accountable the person (owner) with authority over property, concentrating the owner's attention on avoiding the cost of liability for damage done.

Private Ownership and Markets

The incentives provided by the private ownership of property are very useful. As we will discuss in more detail later, private ownership and competitive markets provide the foundation for cooperative behavior among individuals. They provide each individual, however selfish or narrow-minded, with both the information and the incentive to engage in productive activities and cooperate with others. *When private property rights are protected and enforced, permission of the owner is required for the use of a resource. Put another way, if you want to use a good or resource, you must either buy or lease it from the owner. This means that each of us faces the cost of using scarce resources.* Furthermore, when their actions are directed by market price signals, private owners have a strong incentive to consider the desires of others and to use and develop their resources in ways that are valued highly by others. The resulting market exchanges generate what F. A. Hayek, the 1974 Nobel laureate in economics, called the "extended order." Hayek used this expression to describe the tendency of markets to direct individuals from throughout the world to cooperate with each other in mutually beneficial ways despite the fact that they do not know each other, and that they often have vastly different backgrounds, lifestyles, and cultural values.

When apartments and other investment properties are owned privately, the owner has a strong incentive to provide amenities that others value highly relative to their cost.

In contrast, in a community that does not recognize private ownership rights, whoever has the power or the political authority can simply take command of an item, ignoring the wishes of both the person in possession and other potential users. Without private property rights, other methods must be found to provide the incentives for good stewardship of property, and for proper concern for others by the users of property. For example, if the owners of a factory are not held responsible for damages their pollutants impose on the person and property of others, then other measures may be needed to control polluting behavior. We will return to this issue in Chapter 5 and in other sections of the book.

PRODUCTION POSSIBILITIES CURVE

The resources of every individual are limited. Purposeful decision making and economizing behavior imply that individuals seek to get the most from their limited resources. They do not deliberately waste resources.

The nature of the economizing problem can be made more clear with the use of a conceptual tool, the production possibilities diagram. A **production possibilities curve** from this diagram reveals the maximum amount of any two products that can be produced from a fixed set of resources, and the possible trade-offs in production between them.

Production possibilities curve
A curve that outlines all possible combinations of total output that could be produced, assuming (1) the utilization of a fixed amount of productive resources, (2) full and efficient use of those resources, and (3) a specific state of technical knowledge. The slope of the curve indicates the rate at which one product can be traded off to produce more of the other.

Exhibit 2–1 illustrates the production possibilities curve for Susan, an intelligent economics major. This curve indicates the combinations of English and economics grades that she thinks she can earn if she spends a total of 10 hours per week studying for the two subjects. Currently she is choosing the material to study in each course that she expects will help her grade the most, for the time spent, and she is allocating 5 hours of study time to each course. She expects that this amount of time, carefully spent on each course, will allow her to earn a B grade in both, indicated at point *T*. But if she took some time away from studying one of the two subjects and spent it studying the other, she could raise her grade in the course receiving more time. If she

EXHIBIT 2–1

PRODUCTION POSSIBILITIES CURVE FOR SUSAN'S GRADES IN ENGLISH AND ECONOMICS (10 HOURS OF STUDY)

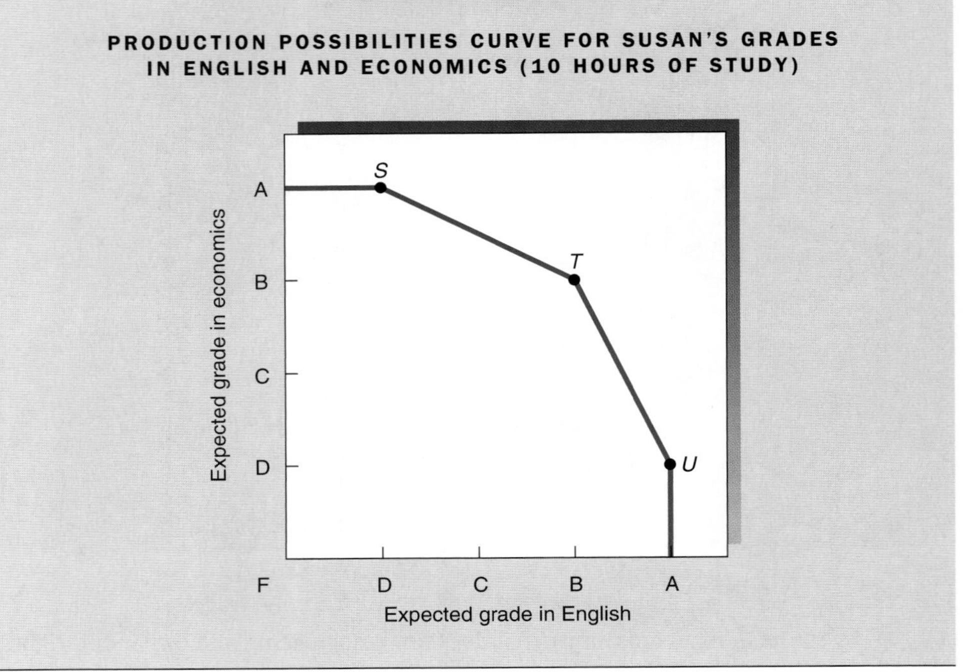

The production possibilities for Susan, in terms of grades, are illustrated for 10 hours of total study time. If Susan studied 10 hours per week in these two classes, she could attain (1) a D in English and an A in economics (point S*), (2) a B in English and a B in economics (point* T*), or (3) a D in economics and an A in English. [Note: Spending even more of her 10 hours on economics than at point* S*, moving along the curve to the left, would decrease her English grade toward an F, but could not improve her A in economics. Similarly, spending more time on English than at point* U*, moving her downward on the curve from there, would decrease her economics grade toward an F, but could not increase her A in English, so we assume that Susan will not choose to spend time on these parts of her production possibilities curve.] Could Susan move the entire curve outward, making higher grades in both? Yes, if she were willing to apply more rescources, perhaps by giving up some leisure or her job.*

spent more hours on economics and fewer on English, for example, her expected economics grade would rise as a result, while her English grade would fall.

Susan's production possibilities curve indicates that the additional study time required to raise her economics grade by one letter, to an A (point *S*), would require giving up two grades in her English class, not just one grade, reducing her English grade to a D. As she shifts more time away from English, she gives up some time that would have been spent studying the most important (grade-increasing) material. In contrast, as she reallocates more and more study time to economics, much of that time is spent studying additional material that is likely to be a little less helpful in producing grade points than the material chosen at point *T*. The curve is flatter to the left of point *T*, and steeper to the right, showing that, as Susan takes more and more of her resources (time, in this case) from one course and puts it into the other, she must give up greater and greater amounts of productivity in the course getting fewer resources.

Of course, Susan could study more economics *without* giving up her English study time, if she gave up some leisure, or study time for other courses, or her part-time job in the campus bookstore. If she gave up leisure or her job to add to the 10 hours of study time for economics and English, the entire *STU* portion of the curve in Exhibit 2–1 would shift outward. She could get better grades in both classes by devoting more of her scarce time to studying for both of them.

Can the production possibilities concept be applied to the entire economy? The answer is yes. We can grow more soybeans if we grow less corn, since both can be grown on the same land. Beefing up the military requires the use of resources that otherwise could be used to produce nonmilitary goods. When scarce resources are being used efficiently, more of one thing requires the sacrifice of others.

Exhibit 2–2 shows a production possibilities curve for an economy producing only two goods: food and clothing. The curve is convex, or bowed out from the origin,

EXHIBIT 2-2

CONCEPT OF PRODUCTION POSSIBILITIES CURVE FOR AN ECONOMY

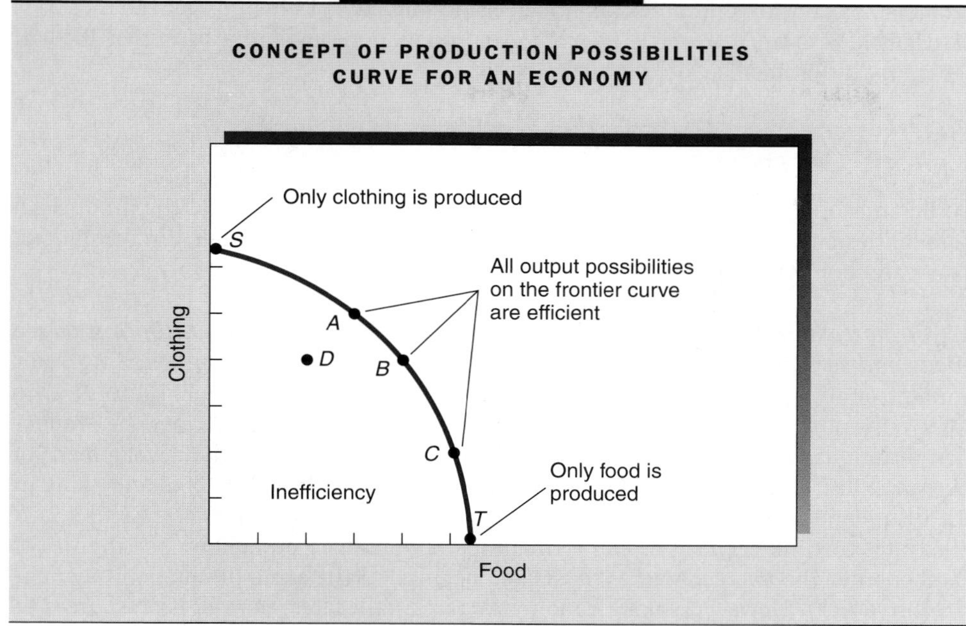

When an economy is using its limited resources efficiently, production of more clothing requires the economy to give up some other goods—food in this simple example. With time, a technological discovery, expansion of the economy's resource base, or improvement in its economic organization could make it possible to produce more of both, shifting the production possibilities curve outward.

Or the citizens of the economy might decide to give up some leisure for more of both goods. These factors aside, limited resources will constrain the production possibilities of an economy.

just as Susan's was in the previous exhibit. Why? Resources are not equally well suited to produce food and clothing. Consider an economy that is using all its resources to produce clothing. At that point (*S*), food production can be expanded by transferring those resources that are best suited for production of food (and least suitable for clothing production) from clothing to food production. Since the resources transferred are chosen to be those that are highly productive in food and not very productive in clothing, in this range the opportunity cost (clothing forgone) of producing additional food is low. However, as more and more resources are devoted to food production, and successively larger amounts of food are produced (moving from *S* to *A* to *B* and so on), the opportunity cost of food will rise. This results because as more and more food is produced, additional food output can be achieved only by using resources that are less and less suitable for the production of food relative to clothing. Thus, as food output is expanded, successively larger amounts of clothing must be forgone per unit of additional food.

What restricts the ability of an economy, once resources are fully utilized, from producing more of everything? The same constraint that kept Susan from making a higher grade in both English and economics—lack of resources. There will be various maximum combinations of goods that an economy will be able to produce when:

1. It uses some fixed quantity of resources.
2. The resources are used efficiently.
3. The level of technology is constant.

When these three conditions are met, the economy will be at the edge of its production possibilities frontier (points such as *A*, *B*, and *C* in Exhibit 2–2). Producing more of one good, such as clothing, will necessitate less production of other goods (for example, food).

When the resources of an economy are used inefficiently, the economy is operating at a point inside the production possibilities curve—point *D*, for example. Why might this happen? It happens if the economy is not properly solving the economizing problem. A major function of economic decision making is to help us get the most out of available resources, to move us out to the production possibilities frontier. We will return to this problem again and again.

Shifting the Production Possibilities Curve Outward

Could an economy ever have more of all goods? In other words, could the production possibilities curve be shifted outward? The answer is yes, under certain circumstances. There are four major possibilities.

Capital formation
The production of buildings, machinery, tools, and other equipment that will enhance the ability of future economic participants to produce. The term can also be applied to efforts to upgrade the knowledge and skill of workers and thereby increase their ability to produce in the future.

1. *An increase in the economy's resource base would expand our ability to produce goods and services.* If we had more and better resources, we could produce a greater amount of all goods. Many resources are human-made. If we were willing to give up some current consumption, we could invest more of today's resources into the production of long-lasting physical structures, machines, education, and the development of human skills. This **capital formation** would provide us with better tools and skills in the future and thereby increase our ability to produce goods and services. **Exhibit 2–3** illustrates the link between capital formation and the future production possibilities of an economy. The two economies illustrated begin with the same production possibilities curve (*RS*). However, since Economy A (part a) allocates more of its resources to investment than does Economy B, A's production possibilities curve shifts outward with the passage of time by a greater amount. The growth rate of A—the expansion rate of the economy's ability to produce goods—is enhanced because the economy allocates a larger share of its output to investment. Of course, more investment in machines and human skills requires a reduction in current consumption.

Here we illustrate two economies that initially confront identical production possibilities curves (RS). The economy illustrated on the left allocates a larger share of its output to investment (I_a, compared to I_b for the economy on the right). As a result, the production possibilities of the high-investment economy will tend to shift outward by a larger amount than will be true for the low-investment economy.

EXHIBIT 2–3

INVESTMENT AND PRODUCTION POSSIBILITIES IN FUTURE

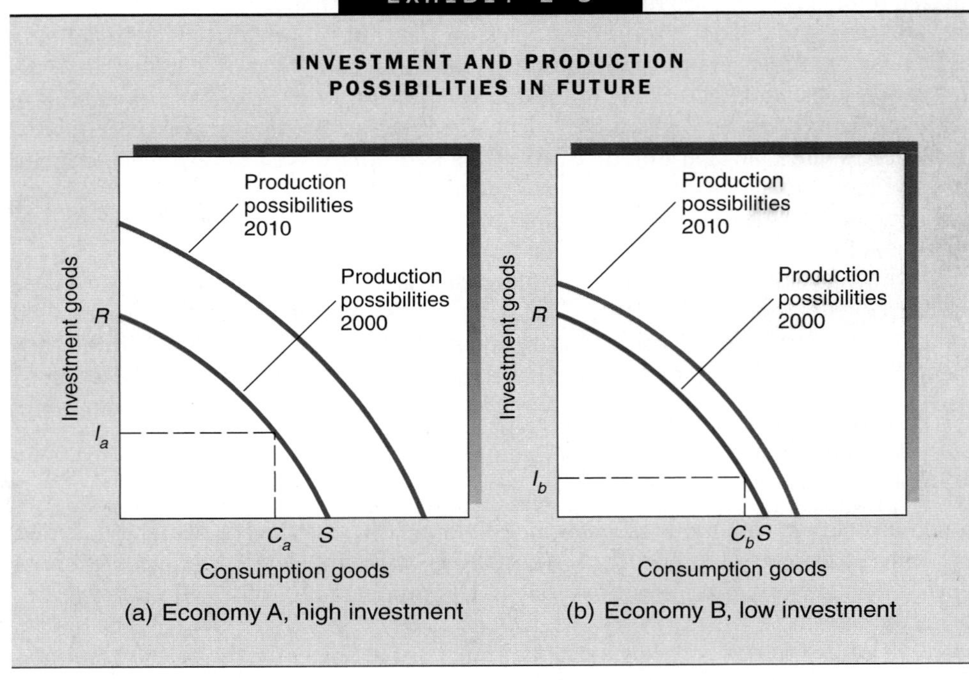

(a) Economy A, high investment

(b) Economy B, low investment

2. *Advancements in technology can expand the economy's production possibilities.* **Technology** determines the maximum physical output obtainable from any particular set of resource inputs. New technology can make it possible to get more from our given base of resources.[8] An important form of technological change is **invention**—the use of science and engineering to create new products or processes. In recent years, for example, inventions have allowed us to develop photographs faster and cheaper, get more oil from existing fields, and send information instantly and cheaply by satellite. Such technological advances increase our production possibilities, shifting the entire curve outward.

Technology
The technological knowledge available at any given time. The level of technology establishes the relationship between inputs and the maximum output they can generate.

Invention
The creation of a new product or process, often facilitated by the knowledge of engineering and scientific relationships.

An economy can also benefit from technology change through **innovation**—the practical and effective adoption of new techniques. Such innovation is commonly carried out by an **entrepreneur**—one who seeks profit by introducing new products or improved techniques to satisfy consumers at a lower cost.[9] To prosper, an entrepreneur must undertake projects that convert and rearrange resources in a manner that will increase their value, thus expanding our production possibilities. Perhaps a few examples will illustrate the importance of this point.

Innovation
The successful introduction and adoption of a new product or process; the economic application of inventions and marketing techniques.

Entrepreneur
A profit-seeking decision maker who decides which projects to undertake and how they should be undertaken. A successful entrepreneur's actions will increase the value of resources.

One entrepreneur, Henry Ford, changed car-making technology by pioneering the assembly line. With the same amount of labor and materials, Ford made more cars, more cheaply. Another entrepreneur, the late Ray Kroc, purchased a hamburger restaurant from Richard McDonald and went on to build the world's largest hamburger chain. In addition to a popular restaurant menu, Kroc provided information to potential customers. By carefully designing a limited menu that could be prepared according to strict formulas, setting up a training school (Hamburger University, outside Chicago) for managers, and providing a program for regular inspection of restaurants, he could guarantee uniformity (known products and quality level) to each customer. Once the McDonald's reputation spread, hungry people knew what to expect at the "golden arches" without even having to enter the restaurant.

Another type of entrepreneur takes inventions produced by others and applies them more effectively. Steven Jobs, cofounder of the Apple Computer Corporation, is an example. He and his firm used the new computer technology to create personal and small-business computers, and pioneered the "user-friendly" software needed by most of us to use such machines. Selling the combination helped make computers useful to millions of people, both at home and on the job, and brought the new technology within their financial reach. Other entrepreneurs subsequently developed hardware and software that has greatly enhanced the usefulness of the personal computer, time and again increasing our ability to find, process, and utilize information, thus further expanding our production possibilities.

3. *An improvement in the rules under which the economy functions can increase output.* The legal system of a country influences the ability of people to cooperate with one another and produce desired goods. Changes in legal institutions that

---

[8]Without modern technical knowledge, it would be impossible to produce the vast array of goods and services responsible for our standard of living. Thomas Sowell makes this point clear when he notes: "The cavemen had the same natural resources at their disposal as we have today, and the difference between their standard of living and ours is a difference between the knowledge they could bring to bear on those resources and the knowledge used today." See Thomas Sowell, *Knowledge and Decisions* (New York: Basic Books, 1980), p. 47.

[9]This French word literally means "one who undertakes." The entrepreneur is the person who is ultimately responsible. Of course, this responsibility may be shared with others (partners or stockholders, for example) or it may be partially delegated to technical experts. Nevertheless, the success or failure of the entrepreneur is dependent on the outcome of the choices he or she makes.

promote social cooperation and enhance the incentive of people to produce will shift the production possibilities curve outward.

Historically, legal innovations have been an important source of economic progress. During the eighteenth century, a system of patents provided inventors with a private property right to their ideas. At about the same time, the recognition of the corporation as a legal entity reduced the cost of forming large firms that were often required for the mass production of manufactured goods. Both of these legal changes improved economic organization and thereby accelerated the growth of output (that is, shifted the production possibilities curve outward more rapidly) in Europe and North America.

Sometimes governments, perhaps as the result of ignorance or prejudice, adopt legal institutions that reduce production possibilities. Laws that restrict or prohibit trade among various groups provide an illustration. For example, the laws of several southern states prohibited the employment of African Americans in certain occupations, and restricted other economic exchanges between blacks and whites for almost 100 years following the Civil War. This legislation was not only harmful to African Americans, it retarded progress and reduced the production possibilities of these states.

The recent experience of Russia illustrates the importance of economic institutions. Following the collapse of communism, Russia was unable to develop legal institutions capable of protecting property rights and enforcing contracts. The absence of these institutions not only retarded investment and gains from trade, but also led to inefficient use of resources and movement of capital to other places where property rights were more secure. Therefore, even though Russia has a well-educated labor force and abundant natural resources, its economic performance has been abysmal. The weak legal structure and insecurity of ownership rights are important elements underlying the economic struggles of Russia.

4. ***By working harder and giving up current leisure, we could increase our production of goods and services.*** Strictly speaking, this is not an expansion in the production frontier because leisure is also a good. We are giving up some of that good to have more of other things.

The work effort of individuals depends not only on their personal preferences but also on public policy. For example, high tax rates may induce individuals to reduce their work time. The basic economic postulate implies that, as high tax rates reduce the personal payoff from working (and earning taxable income), individuals will shift more of their time to other, untaxed activities, including the consumption of leisure, moving the production possibilities curve for market goods inward. (Recall, from Exhibit 2–1, how Susan's production possibilities for grades would shift *outward* if she changed from 10 hours of study per week to more than 10 hours. The reverse would occur if she were to reduce study time below 10 hours.) Any reduction in market work time due to higher taxes not only reduces output directly, but is likely also to reduce the gains from the division of labor, as more people do more work for themselves because doing so is untaxed. We turn now to look at why such a reduction is important.

DIVISION OF LABOR, SPECIALIZATION, AND PRODUCTION POSSIBILITIES

In a modern economy, individuals do not produce most of the items they consume. Instead, we sell our labor services (usually agreeing to do specified productive work) and use the income we get in exchange to buy what we want.

Gains from the Division of Labor and Adoption of Mass Production Processes

Specialization, exchange, and the **division of labor** often allow us to produce far more goods and services through cooperative effort than we could if each household produced its own food, clothing, shelter, transportation, and other desired goods. The most famous example in economics was given over 200 years ago by Adam Smith. Observing the operation of a pin manufacturer, Smith noted that specialization and division of labor permitted far more output. When each worker specialized in a productive function, ten workers were able to produce 48,000 pins per day, or 4,800 pins per worker. Without specialization and division of labor, Smith doubted an individual worker could produce even 20 pins per day.[10]

Division of labor
A method that breaks down the production of a commodity into a series of specific tasks, each performed by a different worker.

The division of labor separates production tasks into a series of related operations. Each worker performs one or a few out of perhaps hundreds of tasks necessary to produce a commodity. There are several reasons why the division of labor often leads to enormous gains in output per worker. First, specialization permits individuals to take advantage of their existing abilities and skills. (Put another way, specialization permits an economy to take advantage of the fact that individuals have different skills.) Different types of work can be assigned to those individuals who are able to accomplish them most efficiently. Second, a worker who specializes in just one narrow area becomes more experienced and more skilled in that task with the passage of time. Third, and perhaps most important, the division of labor lets us adopt complex, large-scale production techniques unthinkable for an individual household. As our knowledge of technology and the potential of machinery expands, capital-intensive production procedures and the division of labor permit us to attain living standards undreamed of just a few decades ago.

Gains from Specialization and Comparative Advantage

Economizing means getting the most out of our available resources. How can this be accomplished? How can we reach our production possibilities curve and achieve the maximum value from our productive activities? To answer these questions, we must understand a basic truth known as the **law of comparative advantage,** which lies at the heart of economizing behavior for any economy. ***Initially developed in the early 1800s by the great English economist David Ricardo, the law of comparative advantage states that the total output of a group of individuals, an entire economy, or a group of nations will be greatest when the output of each good is produced by the person (or firm) with the lowest opportunity cost.***

Law of comparative advantage
A principle that states that individuals, firms, regions, or nations can gain by specializing in the production of goods that they produce cheaply (that is, at a low opportunity cost) and exchanging those goods for other desired goods for which they are high-opportunity-cost producers.

Once one thinks about it, the law of comparative advantage is almost common sense. It simply means that if we want to get a job done (something produced) with the smallest sacrifice, each of us should specialize in that part of the job that we do best, comparatively speaking. If we are going to get the most out of our resources, products must be produced by the low-opportunity-cost producers. If someone else is willing to supply us with a good at a lower cost than we can produce it ourselves, we will be better off to trade for it and use our resources to produce more of the things for which we are a low-cost producer. Failure to have activities carried out by the low-opportunity-cost producers means that we are not economizing—we are getting less than the potential output from our resources.

[10]See Adam Smith, *An Inquiry into the Nature and Causes of the Wealth of Nations* (1776; Cannan's ed., Chicago: University of Chicago Press, 1976), pp. 7–16, for additional detail on the importance of the division of labor.

The principle of comparative advantage is universal. It is just as valid in socialist countries as it is in capitalist countries. It is just as applicable to trade among individuals as it is to trade among nations. Consider the situation of an attorney who can type 120 words per minute. The attorney is trying to decide whether to hire a secretary, who types only 60 words per minute, to complete some legal documents. If the lawyer does the typing job, it will take four hours; if a secretary is hired, the typing job will take eight hours. At first glance, we might think that the cost of the typing is less if the lawyer does it (4 hours) than if the secretary does it (8 hours). Certainly, the lawyer can do the job more quickly than the prospective employee. The *cost* of her time, though, is the $50 per hour she can earn when working as a lawyer, while the typist's time is worth just $7 per hour.

Although she is a fast typist, the attorney is still a high-opportunity-cost producer of typing service. If she types the documents, the job will cost $200, the opportunity cost of four hours of lost time as a lawyer. Alternatively, the cost of having the documents typed by the typist is only $56 (eight hours of typing service at $7 per hour). The lawyer's comparative advantage thus lies in practicing law. She will increase her own productivity, and gain income accordingly, by hiring the typist rather than personally performing the task.

Division of Labor, Specialization, and Exchange

It is difficult to exaggerate the gains derived from division of labor, specialization, and exchange in accordance with the law of comparative advantage. These factors are the primary source of our modern standard of living. Can you imagine the difficulty involved in producing your own housing, clothing, and food, to say nothing of radios,

Trade channels goods to those who value them most and permits us to achieve a larger output as the result of specialization, division of labor, and use of mass production techniques. These factors underlie our modern living standards.

MYTHS OF ECONOMICS

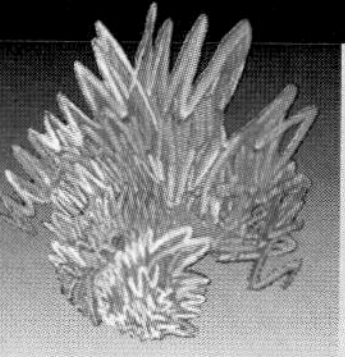

"In exchange, when someone gains, someone else must lose."

People tend to think of making, building, and creating things as productive activities. Agriculture and manufacturing are like this. They create something genuinely new, something that was not there before. On the other hand, trade—the mere exchanging of one thing for another—does not create new material items. Therefore, some conclude that it is a zero-sum game in which one person's gain is necessarily a loss to another. A closer look at the motivation for trade helps us see through this popular fallacy. Exchange is based on the mutual expectation of gain. If both parties did not expect the trade to improve their well-being, they would not agree to the trade. Because trade is mutually advantageous, it must be a positive-sum productive activity.

There are three major reasons why trade is a positive-sum activity. ***First, trade channels goods and services to those who value them most.*** It is easy to think of material things as wealth, but material things are not wealth until they are in the hands of someone who values them. The preferences, knowledge, and goals of people vary widely. A good that is virtually worthless to one may be a precious gem to another. For example, a highly technical book on electronics that is of no value to an art collector may be worth several hundred dollars to an engineer. Similarly, a painting that is unappreciated by an engineer may be of great value to an art collector. Therefore, a voluntary exchange that moves the electronics book to the engineer and the painting to the art collector will increase the value of both goods. Thus, transactions that channel goods and resources toward those who value them most create wealth for both the trading partners and the nation.

Second, exchange permits trading partners to gain from a larger total output as the result of specialization in those areas where they have a comparative advantage. A group of individuals, regions, or nations will be able to produce a larger joint output when each specializes in those productive activities that it does best. In turn, the larger total output allows both trading parties to gain when they produce those goods they can provide at a low cost and use the revenue generated from their sale to purchase desired products that they could produce only at a high cost. For example, exchange permits a skilled carpenter to concentrate on building house frames, while contracting for electrical and plumbing services from others who have comparative advantages in those areas. Similarly, trade permits a country such as Canada to specialize in the production of wheat, while Brazil specializes in coffee. Because the joint output of the two countries is enlarged as the result of this specialization, both can gain from the exchange of Canadian wheat for Brazilian coffee.

Third, voluntary exchange makes it possible for individuals to produce more goods through division of labor and adoption of mass production methods. In the absence of exchange, productive activity would be limited to the individual household. Self-provision and small-scale production would be the rule. Exchange permits business firms to sell their output over a broad market area, so they can plan for large outputs and adopt complex large-scale production processes. Using such mass production procedures often leads to a more efficient utilization of both labor and machinery and enormous increases in output per worker. Without exchanges, these gains could not be achieved.

television sets, dishwashers, automobiles, and telephone services? Yet, most families in North America, Western Europe, Japan, and Australia enjoy all these conveniences. They are able to do so largely because their economies are organized in such a way that individuals can cooperate, specialize, and trade, thereby reaping the benefits of the enormous increases in output—both in quantity and diversity—thus produced.

Gains from trade are a key to economic progress. Human-made obstacles that retard exchange also retard the realization of gains from specialization, comparative advantage, and division of labor. Countries that impose such trade barriers fail to realize their full potential. (See the "Myths of Economics" box concerning gains from trade.)

Personal Motivation, Specialization, and Exchange

Economic thinking implies that people will choose an alternative only if they expect that it will provide benefits (utility) in excess of opportunity costs. Purposeful decision makers will be motivated by the pursuit of personal gain. They will never knowingly choose an alternative when they expect the opportunity cost to exceed the benefits. To do so would be to sacrifice the preferred course of action. That simply would not make sense.

When an individual's interests, aptitudes, abilities, and skills make it possible to gain by exchanging low-opportunity-cost goods for those things that could be produced only at a high opportunity cost, pursuit of the potential gain will motivate the individual to trade precisely in this manner. If free exchange is allowed, people will not have to be ordered to perform the "right" job. In a market setting, the incomes of people will be higher if they produce and sell items for which they have a comparative advantage (items they can produce cheaply). Similarly, they will promote their own interests by buying goods that others can produce more cheaply.

ECONOMIC ORGANIZATION

Every economy must answer three basic questions: (1) What will be produced? (2) How will goods be produced? and (3) For whom will they be produced? These questions are highly interrelated. Throughout, we will consider how alternative forms of economic organization address these three questions.

As we have stressed in this chapter, the availability of most goods we enjoy—our food, clothing, housing, medical services, and so on—reflects cooperative efforts by numerous people, most of whom we have never met. This cooperation does not occur automatically. Economic organization and institutions influence both the type and degree of cooperation.

Two Methods of Economic Organization: Markets and Political Planning

There are two broad ways that an economy can be organized: markets and government (or political) planning. Let us briefly consider each.

Market organization
A method of organization that allows unregulated prices and the decentralized decisions of private property owners to resolve the basic economic problems of consumption, production, and distribution.

Capitalism
An economic system based on private ownership of productive resources and allocation of goods according to the signals provided by market prices.

Market Organization. Private ownership, voluntary contracts (often these contracts are verbal), and reliance upon market prices are the distinguishing features of market organization, or **capitalism,** as it is sometime called.[11] In market economies, people have private ownership rights to productive assets, as well as to consumption goods and their own labor services. Private parties are permitted to buy and sell ownership rights at mutually acceptable prices in unregulated markets. Government plays the limited role of a rule maker and neutral referee. The rule maker role involves the development of a legal structure that recognizes, defines, and protects private ownership rights, enforces contracts, and protects people from violence and fraud. But the government is not an active player in the economy; ideally, the political process avoids modifying market outcomes or favoring some participants at the expense of others. For example, the government does not prevent sellers from undertaking price reductions and quality improvements to compete with other sellers. Nor does it prevent buyers from offering higher prices to bid products or productive resources away from others. No legal restraints (for example, government licensing) limit potential buyers or sellers from producing, selling, or buying in the marketplace. Under market organization, there is no central planning authority. The three basic economic questions are answered through market coordination of the decentralized choices of buyers and sellers.

[11]*Capitalism* is a term coined by Karl Marx.

Political Planning. The major alternative to market organization is **collective decision making,** the use of political organization and government planning to allocate resources. An economic system in which the government owns the income-producing assets (machines, buildings, and land) and directly determines what goods they will produce is called **socialism.** Alternatively, the government may maintain private ownership in name, but use taxes, subsidies, and regulations to resolve the basic economic questions. In either instance, political rather than market forces direct the economy. In both cases, government officials and planning boards hand down decisions to expand or contract the output of education, medical services, automobiles, electricity, steel, consumer durables, and thousands of other commodities. This is not to say that the preferences of individuals have no importance. If the government officials and central planners are influenced by the democratic process, they have to consider how their actions will influence their election prospects. Otherwise, like the firm in a market economy that produces a product that consumers do not want, their tenure of service is likely to be a short one.

Collective decision making
The method of organization that relies on public-sector decision making (voting, political bargaining, lobbying, and so on) to resolve basic issues.

Socialism
A system of economic organization in which (1) the ownership and control of the basic means of production rest with the state, and (2) resource allocation is determined by centralized planning rather than by market forces.

Exit and Voice: Two Methods of Sending Messages

Individual choice provides the foundation for economic analysis. Individuals have two major methods of sending messages and thereby influencing market and political decision makers. First and most directly, they have a **voice**—they can communicate complaints, desires, and suggestions to decision makers. Second, individuals can **exit,** or withdraw from an economic relationship with another person or organization. The individual's voice will generally be more persuasive if exit is also available.

Voice
The ability to communicate complaints, desires and suggestions to decision makers who may be private buyers or sellers, or may be decision makers in government.

Exit
The ability to withdraw from an economic relationship with another person or organization.

The exit option is generally much easier to exercise in a market setting. If you are a dissatisfied customer—if you are unhappy with a retail store, an automobile manufacturer, or a local restaurant—what do you generally do? Some may write a letter of complaint (the voice option), but most of us simply take our business elsewhere (the exit option). The exit option provides us with a relatively easy way of dealing with poor service, shoddy products, and high prices. It is the primary way that customers communicate with business firms.

The exit option is also an effective method of sending a message to corporate managers and labor union leaders. For example, if a stockholder is unhappy with the corporate strategy of a firm, the voice strategy—writing company officers or voicing dissatisfaction at the annual stockholder meeting—is an option. But the exit option, the selling of one's stock, is likely to be both less costly and more effective. When a substantial number of fellow stockholders agree and also sell their stock, the price of the stock will fall and the likelihood of a management shake-up or change of direction will almost certainly increase.

The exit option is generally more difficult to use in a system of political planning than in a market system. This is particularly true at the national level, where an exit message can only be sent by moving to another country. While exit is a more feasible option at the local government level—for example, it may be possible to move from one school district to another at a low cost—even here it is generally more costly to choose the exit option than is true in a market setting. Voice is generally the primary means of sending messages to government officials. In a democratic setting, competitive political parties are present, discussion is encouraged, and the right to speak out is recognized and protected. The vote is another form of voice, but as we will see later, the incentive structure often reduces its potency.

In summary, the exit choice is the primary method of communication among participants in the marketplace. This option is generally limited in the political arena.

Thus, individuals have to rely mostly on voice when sending messages to political decision makers. How will this difference in the importance of the exit option as a method of communication influence the allocation of resources and operation of the two sectors? This question will be dealt with as we analyze the operation of the two sectors in subsequent chapters.

LOOKING *Ahead*

The next two chapters present an overview of the market sector, with real-world applications of the supply and demand model of market behavior. Chapters 5 and 6 focus on how the public sector—the democratic collective decision-making process—functions. The tools of economics can be used to analyze the operation of and allocation of resources in both the market and political sectors.

We think this approach is important, fruitful, and exciting. How does the market sector really work? What does economics say about which activities should be handled by government? What types of economic policies are politically attractive to democratically elected officials? Why is sound economic policy sometimes in conflict with good politics? All these questions will be tackled in the next four chapters.

KEY POINTS

➤ The highest valued activity sacrificed in making a choice is the opportunity cost of the choice; differences (or changes) in opportunity costs help explain human behavior.

➤ Mutual gain is the foundation of trade.

➤ Transaction costs—the time, effort, and other resources necessary to search out, negotiate, and conclude an exchange—are an obstacle to the realization of gains from trade.

➤ Private property rights provide strong incentives for owners to use their resources in ways that benefit others.

➤ The production possibilities curve reveals the maximum combination of any two products that can be produced with a fixed quantity of resources and constant level of technology.

➤ With the passage of time, the production possibilities curve of an economy can be shifted outward through (1) investment, (2) technological advances, (3) improved institutions, and (4) greater work effort (the forgoing of leisure).

➤ The joint output of individuals, regions, or nations will be maximized when goods are exchanged between parties in accordance with the law of comparative advantage.

➤ Voluntary exchange channels goods toward those who value them most and permits us to realize gains from specialization, division of labor, mass production, and cooperative effort among individuals. These elements underlie our modern living standards.

➤ The two basic methods of making economic decisions are the market mechanism and public-sector decision making; in each, the decisions of individuals using voice and exit strategies will influence the result.

➤ The tools of economics are general; they are applicable to choices that influence both market- and public-sector decisions.

CRITICAL ANALYSIS QUESTIONS

1. "If Jones trades $5,000 to Smith for a used car, the items exchanged must be of equal value." Is this statement true, false, or uncertain?

*2. Economists often argue that wage rates reflect productivity. Yet, the wages of house painters have increased nearly as rapidly as the national average, even though these workers use approximately the same methods that were applied 50 years ago. Can you explain why the wages of painters have risen substantially even though their productivity has changed so little?

3. It takes one hour to travel from New York City to Washington, D.C., by air, but it takes five hours by bus. If the air fare is $110 and the bus fare is $70, which would be cheaper for someone whose opportunity cost of travel time is $6 per hour? For someone whose opportunity cost is $10 per hour? $14 per hour?

*4. "People in business get ahead by exploiting the needs of their consumers. The gains of business are at the expense of suffering imposed on their customers." Evaluate this statement from the producer of a prime-time television program.

5. With regard to the use of resources, what is the objective of the entrepreneur? What is the major function of the middleman? Is the middleman an entrepreneur?

6. If you have a private ownership right to something, what does this mean? Does private ownership give you the right to do anything you want with the things that you own? Explain. How does private ownership influence the incentive of individuals to (a) take care of things, (b) conserve resources for the future, and (c) develop and modify things in ways that are objectionable to others? Explain.

7. What is the law of comparative advantage? According to the law of comparative advantage, what should be the distinguishing characteristics of the goods that a nation produces? What should be the distinguishing characteristics of the goods that the nation imports? How will international trade of this type influence the level of production and living standard of the populace? Explain.

*8. Does a 60-year-old tree farmer have an incentive to plant and care for Douglas fir trees that will not reach optimal cutting size for another 50 years?

*9. What forms of competition does a private-property, market-directed economy authorize? What forms does it prohibit?

10. What are the three major sources of gains from trade? Why is exchange important to the prosperity of a nation? How do physical obstacles (such as rivers, mountains, and bad roads) that increase transaction costs influence gains from trade and the prosperity of a nation? How do human-made obstacles (for example, tariffs, quotas, and legal restrictions limiting trade) that increase transaction costs influence gains from trade and prosperity?

*11. "Really good agricultural land should not be developed for housing. Food is far more important." Evaluate this statement.

*12. In many states, the resale of tickets to sporting events at prices above the original purchase price ("ticket scalping") is prohibited. Who is helped and who is hurt by such prohibitions? Can you think of ways ticket owners who want to sell might get around the prohibition? Do you think it would be a good idea to extend the resale prohibition to other things—automobiles, books, works of art, or stock shares, for example? Why or why not?

13. "When you're dealing with questions related to human life, economic costs are irrelevant." Evaluate this statement made by a congressman.

14. Consider the questions below:

a. Do you think that your work effort is influenced by whether there is a close link between personal output and personal compensation (reward)? Explain.

b. Suppose the grades in your class were going to be determined by a random draw at the end of the course. How would this influence your study habits?

c. How would your study habits be influenced if everyone in the class were going to be given an A grade? How about if grades were based entirely on examinations composed of the multiple-choice questions in the coursebook for this textbook?

d. Do you think the total output of goods in the United States is affected by the close link between productive contribution and individual reward? Why or why not?

---

*Asterisk denotes questions for which answers are given in Appendix B.

PART 2

Markets and governments

There are two primary methods of allocating scarce resources among alternative uses: markets and governments.

VISUALIZING MARKET ALLOCATION

Exhibit II-A provides a visual representation of how markets allocate resources toward the production of products (goods and services). Business firms purchase resources, such as materials, labor services, tools, and machines, from households in exchange for income (bottom of diagram). Firms incur costs as the resources are bid away from their alternative uses. Businesses transform the resources into products, such as shoes, automobiles, food products, and medical services, and supply them to households in exchange for revenues (top of diagram). Whether a product is produced depends on sales revenue relative to production costs. *In a market economy, business firms will continue to supply a good or service only if the revenues from the sale of the product are sufficient to cover the cost of the resources required for its production.*

EXHIBIT II-A

VISUALIZING ALLOCATION THROUGH GOVERNMENT

As Exhibit II-B illustrates, allocation through government involves a more complex three-sided exhange. In a democratic political setting, a legislative ody levies taxes on voter-citizens and these revenues re subdivided into budgets, which are allocated to govrnment bureaus and agencies. In turn, the bureaus and gencies use the funds from their budgets to supply oods, services, and income transfers to voter-citizens. he legislative body is like a board of directors elected y the citizens. The competitive pressure to be elected rovides legislators with a strong incentive to cater to the views of voters. In turn, a voter will be more likely to support a legislator if the value of the goods, services, and transfers received by the citizen (link between bureau and citizen) is large relative to the citizen's tax liability (link between voter and legislator). *Goods, services, and income transfers will tend to be supplied through government if, and only if, a majority of the legislators perceive that the provision will enhance their electoral prospects—in other words, the likelihood they will win the next election.*

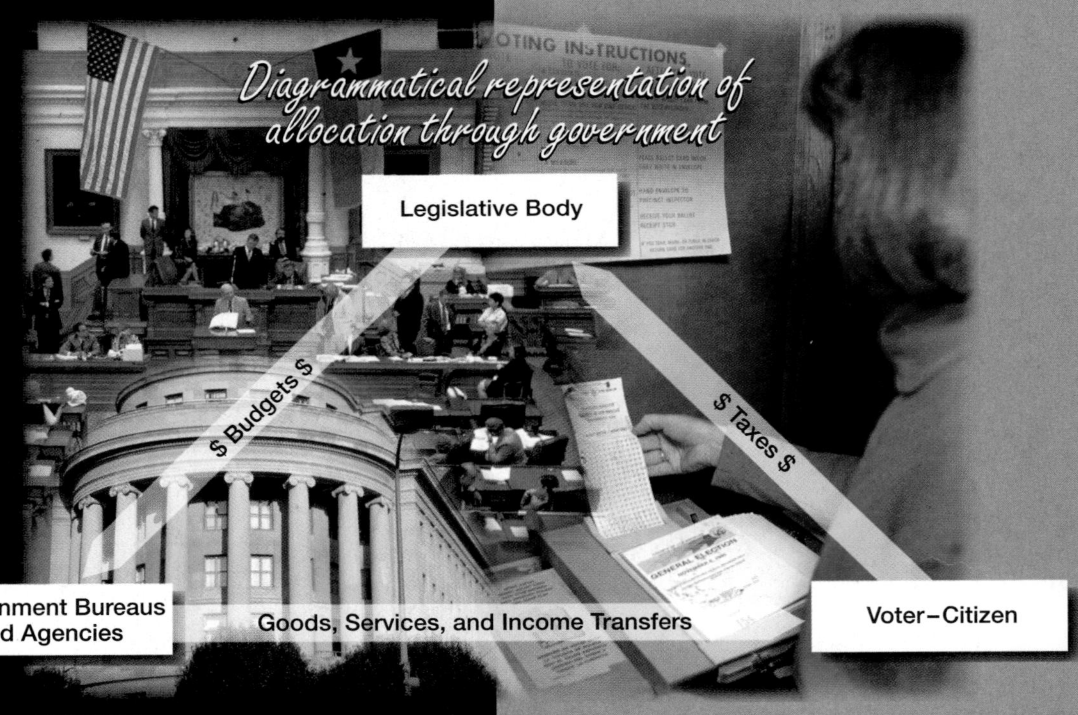

EXHIBIT II-B

SIGNIFICANCE OF ECONOMIC THEORY

Economics has a great deal to say about how both markets and governments allocate scarce resources. It provides insights concerning the conditions under which each will likely work well (and when each will likely work poorly). The next four chapters will focus on this topic.

CHAPTER 3

I am convinced that if it [the market system] were the result of deliberate human design, and if the people guided by the price changes understood that their decisions have significance far beyond their immediate aim, this mechanism would have been acclaimed as one of the greatest triumphs of the human mind.

Friedrich Hayek, Nobel Laureate[1]

From the point of view of physics, it is a miracle that [seven million New Yorkers are fed each day] without any control mechanism other than sheer capitalism.

John H. Holland, scientist, Santa Fe Institute

Supply, Demand, and the Market Process

CHAPTER FOCUS

- What are the laws of demand and supply?
- How do consumers decide whether to purchase a good? How do producers decide whether to supply it?
- How do buyers and sellers respond to changes in the price of a good?
- What are profits and losses? What must a firm do in order to make a profit?
- How is the market price of a good determined?
- How do markets adjust to changes in demand? How do they adjust to changes in supply?
- What is the "invisible hand" principle?

[1]Friedrich Hayek, "The Use of Knowledge in Society," *American Economic Review* 35 (September 1945), pp. 519–530.

To those who study art, the Mona Lisa is much more than a famous painting of a woman. Looking beyond the overall picture, they see and appreciate the brush strokes, colors, and techniques embodied in the painting. Similarly, studying economics can help you to gain an appreciation for the details behind many things from your everyday life. On your last visit to the grocery store, you probably noticed the fruit and vegetable section. Next time, take a moment to ponder how potatoes from Idaho, oranges from Florida, apples from Washington, bananas from Honduras, kiwi fruit from New Zealand, and other items from around the world got to your local grocery store. Literally thousands of different individuals, *working independently,* were involved in the process. Their actions were coordinated such that the quantity of each good was just about right for your local community. Furthermore, the goods, including those transported great distances, were both fresh and reasonably priced.

How does all this happen? The short answer is, "It is the result of market prices, and the incentives and coordination that flow from them." To the economist, the operation of markets—including the local grocery market—is analogous to the brush strokes and techniques underlying a beautiful painting. Reflecting on this point, Professor Hayek speculates that if the market system had been deliberately designed, it would be "acclaimed as one of the greatest triumphs of the human mind." Similarly, computer scientist John H. Holland argues that, from the viewpoint of physics, the feeding of millions of New Yorkers "day after day with very few shortages or surpluses" is a miraculous feat.

Amazingly, markets coordinate the actions of millions of individuals *without* central planning. There is no individual, political authority, or central planning committee in charge. Considering that there are over 260 million Americans with widely varying skills and desires, and roughly 7 million businesses producing a vast array of

The produce section of your local grocery store is a great place to see economics in action. Literally millions of individuals from around the world have been involved in the process of getting these goods to the shelves in just the right quantities. Market prices underlie this feat.

products ranging from diamond rings to toilet paper, the coordination derived from markets is an awesome achievement.

This chapter focuses on supply, demand, and the determination of market prices. For now, we will analyze the operation of competitive markets—that is, markets with rival sellers (and buyers) without restrictions limiting potential rivals from entering and competing in the market. We will also assume that the property rights to both resources and goods are well defined. Later, we will consider what happens when these conditions are absent.

When you sell a car through a classified newspaper ad, as the seller you have in mind a minimum price you will accept for your car. A potential buyer, on the other hand, has in mind a maximum price he or she will pay for the car. If the potential buyer's maximum price is greater than your minimum price, mutual gains from trade are possible. As this simple example shows, the desires and incentives of both buyers and sellers underlie the operation of markets and the determination of prices. We will begin with the demand (buyer's) side, then turn to the supply (seller's) side of the market.

CONSUMER CHOICE AND LAW OF DEMAND

Our desire for goods is far greater than our income. Even high-income consumers are unable to purchase everything they would like. We all must make choices as consumers. Seeking as much satisfaction (value) as possible from our limited income, we choose those alternatives that are expected to enhance our welfare the most, relative to their cost. Clearly, prices influence our decisions. As the price of a good increases, we are required to give up more of *other* goods if we buy at the more expensive price. Thus, we might say that as the price of a good rises, its opportunity cost increases (in terms of other goods forgone).

The basic postulate of economics says that incentives matter: An increase in the cost of an alternative reduces the likelihood that it will be chosen. A straightforward application suggests that consumers will purchase fewer units of a good in response to an increase in its price. ***The* law of demand *states that there is an inverse relationship between the price of a good and the quantity of it that consumers are willing to purchase. As the price of a good rises, consumers buy less of it, and, as the price falls, consumers buy more.***

Law of demand
A principle that states there is an inverse relationship between the price of a good and the amount of it buyers are willing to purchase. As the price of a product increases, other things constant, consumers will purchase less of the product.

Substitutes
Products that serve similar purposes. They are related such that an increase in the price of one will cause an increase in demand for the other (for example, hamburgers and tacos, butter and margarine, Chevrolets and Fords).

The availability of **substitutes**—goods that perform similar functions—underlies the negative relationship between price and quantity purchased. No single good is absolutely essential (see Myths of Economics box); each good can be replaced by other goods. Margarine can be substituted for butter. Wood, aluminum, bricks, and glass can take the place of steel. Going to the movies, playing tennis, watching television, and going to a football game are substitute forms of entertainment. When the price of a good increases, people turn to substitute products and economize on their use of the more expensive good. Prices really do matter.

MARKET DEMAND SCHEDULE

Exhibit 3–1 shows a hypothetical demand schedule for cellular telephones with differing prices and the quantities that consumers would demand at each price.[2] Here, price

[2]These data are actual prices (adjusted to 1994 dollars) and quantities annually for 1988 to 1994 taken from *Statistical Abstract of the United States: 1995* (Washington, D.C.: U.S. Bureau of the Census, 1995). *If we could assume that other demand determinants (income, prices of related goods, etc.) had remained constant,* then this hypothetical demand schedule would be accurate for that time period. Because it is possible that some of these other factors changed, we treat the numbers as hypothetical, depicting alternative prices and quantities *at a given time.* Since 1995, there have been additional price reductions.

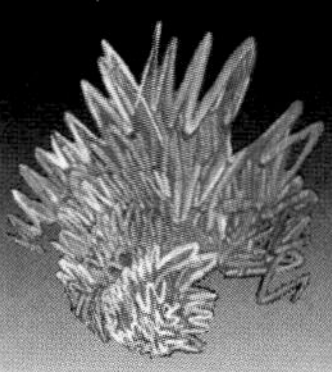

MYTHS OF ECONOMICS

"The Demand Curve for Some Goods Is Vertical, Because Fixed Amounts of Them Are Needed for Consumption."

Noneconomists often ignore the impact of price and make statements implying that, for some goods, there is a fixed amount that must be available for consumption. "During the next five years the United States will need 30 million barrels of oil." "Next year the United States will need 20,000 more physicians." Have you ever heard popular commentators make statements like these, implying that the demand for some commodity is vertical?

Two points should be recognized when evaluating such statements. ***First, we live in a world of substitutes.*** There are alternative ways of satisfying needs. For example, a fax, an e-mail, or a telephone call is a substitute for a letter. Sometimes the substitutes are seemingly unrelated. For example, reading, staying home and watching television, and picnicking in the backyard are substitutes for gasoline used for a Sunday drive. In varying degrees, there are substitutes for everything.

Second, since scarcity and limited income restrict our options, each of us will have to forgo many things that we "need"—or at least think we need. Given our limited income, purchasing them would mean that we would have to give up other things that we value more highly and therefore apparently need more urgently. The concept of need changes with differences in income, preferences, and cultural factors. In affluent countries, families are thought to need at least one bathroom with hot and cold running water, a sink, a toilet, and a bathtub or shower. Yet the typical family in many poorer countries would perceive such a bathroom to be a luxury.

There are substitutes for everything, and price influences the amount "needed" of each good. Thus, the vertical demand curve, like the unicorn, is a myth.

is measured as the average monthly cost, and quantity demanded is the number of subscribers to cellular phone service. In the table, when the price of cellular phone service is $123 per month, just over 2 million consumers subscribe. As the price falls to $107, the quantity rises to 3.5 million; when the price falls to $56 per month, the quantity of subscribers increases to 24.1 million.

Exhibit 3–1 also provides a graphic presentation of the law of demand called the *demand curve.* When representing the demand schedule graphically, economists measure price on the vertical, or y-axis, and the amount demanded on the horizontal, or x-axis. Because of the inverse relationship between price and amount purchased, the demand curve will slope downward to the right.

Read horizontally, the demand curve shows how much of a particular good consumers will buy at a given price. Read vertically, the demand curve also reveals important information about consumer preferences—their valuation of goods. ***The height of the demand curve at any quantity shows the maximum price that consumers are willing to pay for that additional unit.*** If consumers value an additional unit of a product highly, they will be willing to pay a large amount (a high price) for it. Conversely, if their valuation of an additional unit of the good is low, they will be willing to pay only a small amount for it.

Because the amount a consumer is willing to pay for a good is directly related to the good's value to the consumer, the demand curve indicates the marginal benefit consumers receive from additional units. When viewed in this manner, the demand curve reveals that as consumers have more and more of a product, they will value additional units less and less.

Consumer Surplus

Previously, we indicated that voluntary exchange makes both the buyer and seller better off. The demand curve can be used to illustrate the gains of the consumers. Suppose that you value a particular good at $50, but you are able to purchase it for only $30.

EXHIBIT 3–1

LAW OF DEMAND

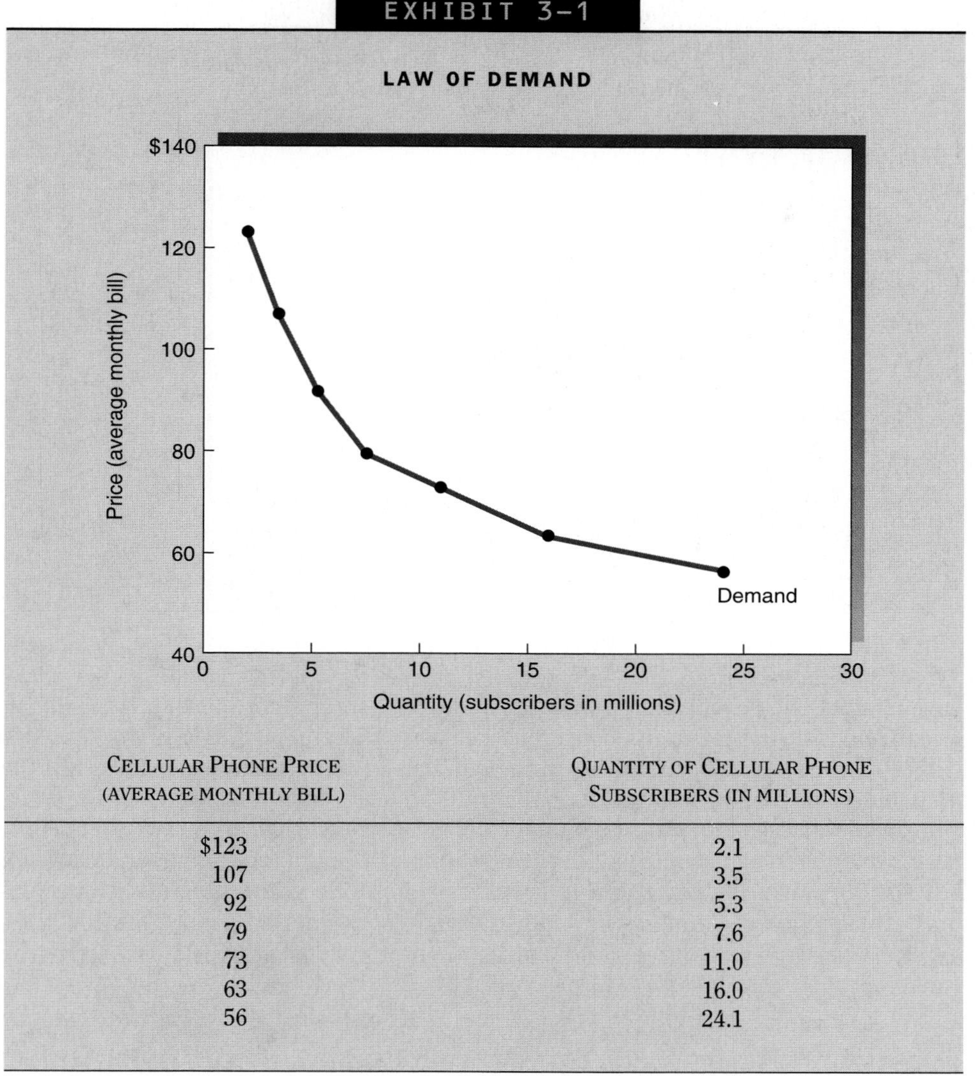

CELLULAR PHONE PRICE (AVERAGE MONTHLY BILL)	QUANTITY OF CELLULAR PHONE SUBSCRIBERS (IN MILLIONS)
$123	2.1
107	3.5
92	5.3
79	7.6
73	11.0
63	16.0
56	24.1

As the table indicates, the number of people subscribing to cellular phone service (just like the consumption of other products) is inversely related to price. The data from the table are plotted as a demand schedule in the graph. The inverse relation between price and amount demanded reflects the fact that consumers will substitute away from a good as it becomes more expensive.

Your net gain from buying the good is $20. Economists call this net gain of buyers **consumer surplus.** In effect, consumer surplus is the difference between the amount that consumers would be willing to pay and the amount they actually pay for each unit of a good. **Exhibit 3–2** illustrates the measurement of consumer surplus. The height of the demand curve measures how much the various buyers value each unit of the good, while the price indicates the amount they actually pay. The difference between these two—the area under the demand curve but above the price paid—is a measure of consumer surplus. The size of the consumer surplus is affected by the market price. A reduction in the market price will lead to an expansion in quantity purchased and a larger consumer surplus. Conversely, a higher market price will reduce the amount purchased and shrink the surplus (net gain) of consumers.

Consumer surplus
The difference between the maximum price consumers are willing to pay and the price they actually pay. It is the net gain derived by the buyers of the good.

In aggregate, the total value (area under the demand curve) to consumers of the units purchased may be far greater than the amount they pay. When additional units are available at a low price, the marginal value of a good may be quite low, even though its total value to consumers is exceedingly high. For example, this

Consumer surplus is the area below the demand curve but above the actual price paid. This area represents the net gains to buyers from market exchange.

EXHIBIT 3–2

CONSUMER SURPLUS

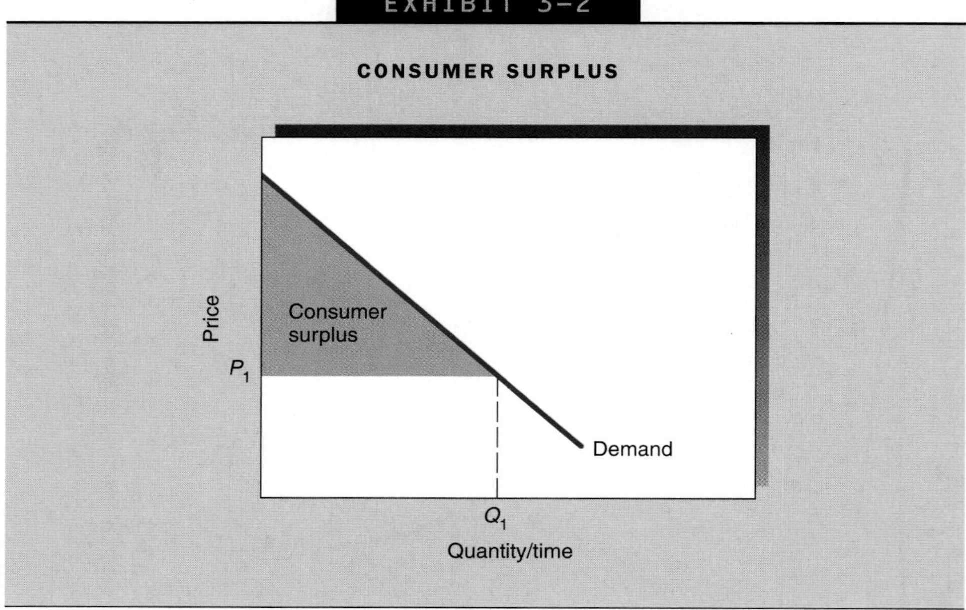

is generally the case with water. Of course, water is essential for life and the value derived from the first few units consumed per day will be exceedingly high. The consumer surplus derived from these units will also be large when water is plentifully available at a low price. As more and more units are consumed, however, the *marginal* value of even something as important as water will fall to a low level. Thus, when water is cheap, people will use it not only for drinking, cleaning, and cooking, but also for washing cars, watering lawns, flushing toilets, and keeping fish aquariums. Thus, while consumers will tend to expand consumption until price and *marginal value* are equal, price reveals little about the *total value* derived from the consumption of a good.

Responsiveness of Quantity Demanded to Price: Elastic and Inelastic Demand Curves

As we previously noted, the availability of substitutes is the main reason why the demand curve for a good slopes downward. Some goods, however, are much easier to substitute away from than others. As the price of tacos rises, most consumers find hamburgers a reasonable substitute. Because of the ease of substitutability, the quantity demanded of tacos is quite sensitive to a change in their price. Economists would say that the demand for tacos is relatively *elastic* because a small price change will cause a rather large change in the amount purchased. Alternatively, such goods as gasoline and electricity have fewer good substitutes. When their prices rise, it is harder for consumers to easily substitute away from these products. When good substitutes are unavailable, even a large price change may not cause much of a change in the quantity demanded. Economists would say that the demand for such goods is relatively *inelastic*.

Graphically, this different degree of responsiveness is reflected in the steepness of the demand curve, as is shown in **Exhibit 3–3**. The flatter demand curve (D_1, left frame) is for a product—tacos—for which the quantity demanded is highly responsive

EXHIBIT 3-3

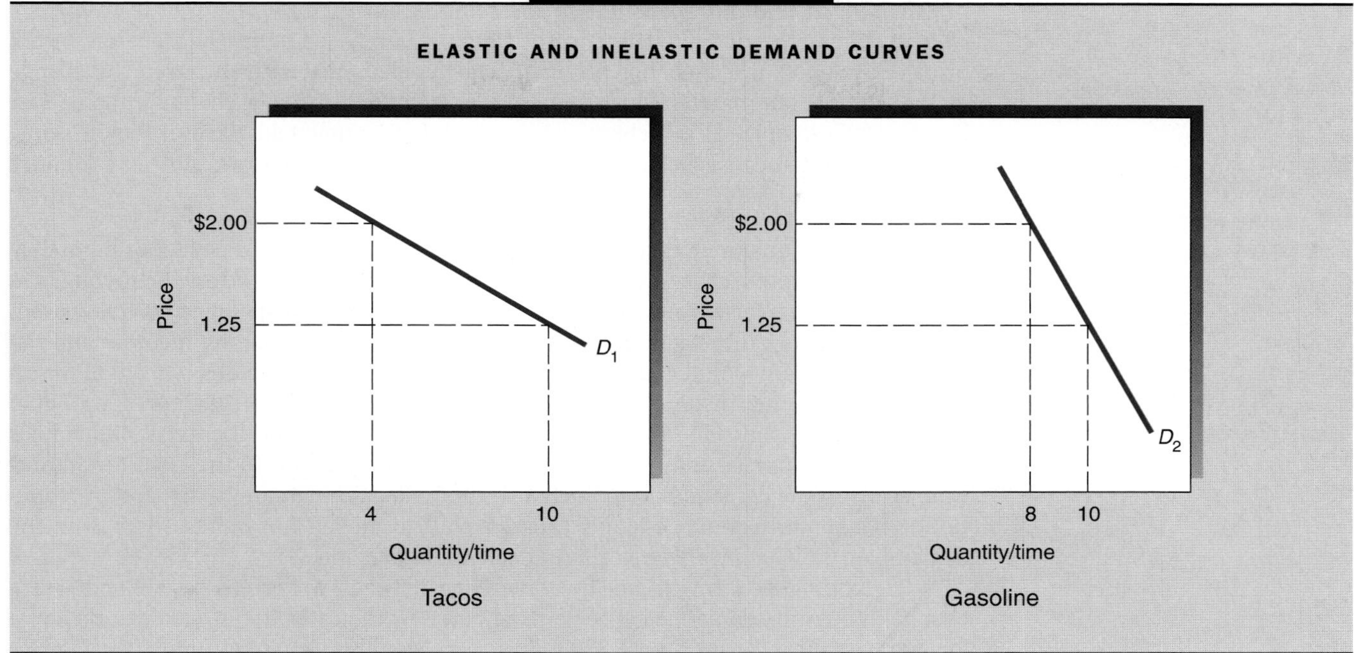

The responsiveness of consumer purchases to a change in price is reflected in the steepness of the demand curve. The flatter demand curve (D_1*) for tacos shows a higher degree of responsiveness and is called relatively elastic, while the steeper demand curve (*D_2*) for gasoline shows a lower degree of responsiveness and is called relatively inelastic.*

to a change in price. As the price increases from $1.25 to $2.00, the quantity demanded falls sharply from 10 to 4 units. The steeper demand curve (D_2, right frame) is for a product—gasoline—where the quantity purchased is much less responsive to a change in price. For gasoline, an increase in price from $1.25 to $2.00 results in only a small reduction in the quantity purchased (from 10 to 8). An economist would say that the flatter demand curve D_1 was relatively elastic, while the steeper demand curve D_2 was relatively inelastic. The availability of substitutes is the main determinant of whether the demand curve is relatively elastic or inelastic.

CHANGES IN DEMAND VERSUS CHANGES IN QUANTITY DEMANDED

The demand curve isolates the impact of price on the amount of a product purchased. Economists refer to a change in the quantity of a good purchased that occurs in response to a price change as a "change in *quantity demanded.*" A change in quantity demanded is a movement along a demand curve from one point to another. Changes in factors like income and the prices of closely related goods will also influence the decision of consumers. If one of these other factors changes, the entire demand curve will shift inwards or outwards. Economists refer to such shifts in the demand curve as a "change in *demand.*"

Failure to distinguish between a change in demand and a change in quantity demanded is one of the most common mistakes made by beginning economics

students.[3] ***A change in demand is a shift in the entire demand curve. A change in quantity demanded is a movement along the same demand curve in response to a price change.*** In essence, if the change in the amount purchased is due to a change in the price of the good, it is a change in quantity demanded. Alternatively, when the change in the amount purchased is due to *anything other than price* (a change in consumer income, for example), it is a change in demand. Let us now take a closer look at some of the factors that cause a change in demand—an inward or outward shift in the entire demand curve.

1. Changes in Consumer Income. An increase in consumer income makes it possible for consumers to purchase more goods. If you were to win the lottery, or if your boss were to give you a raise, you would respond by increasing your spending on many products. Alternatively, if the economy were to go into a recession, falling incomes and rising unemployment would cause consumers to reduce their purchases of many items. A change in consumer income will result in consumers buying more or less of a product *at all possible prices for the product.* When consumer income increases, individuals will generally purchase more of a good. This is shown by a shift to the right (or an outward shift) in the demand curve. Such a shift is called an increase in demand. A reduction in consumer income generally causes a shift to the left (or an inward shift) in the demand curve, which would be called a decrease in demand.

Exhibit 3–4 highlights the difference between a change in demand and a change in quantity demanded. The demand curve D_1 indicates the initial demand curve for compact discs. At a price of \$30, consumers would purchase Q_1 units. If the price declined to \$10, there would be an increase in *quantity demanded* from Q_1 to Q_3. Arrow A indicates the change in *quantity demanded*—a movement along the original

Arrow A *indicates a change in* quantity demanded, *a movement along the demand curve* D_1, *in response to a change in the price of compact discs. The* B *arrows illustrate a change in* demand, *a shift of the entire curve, in this case due to an increase in consumer income.*

EXHIBIT 3–4

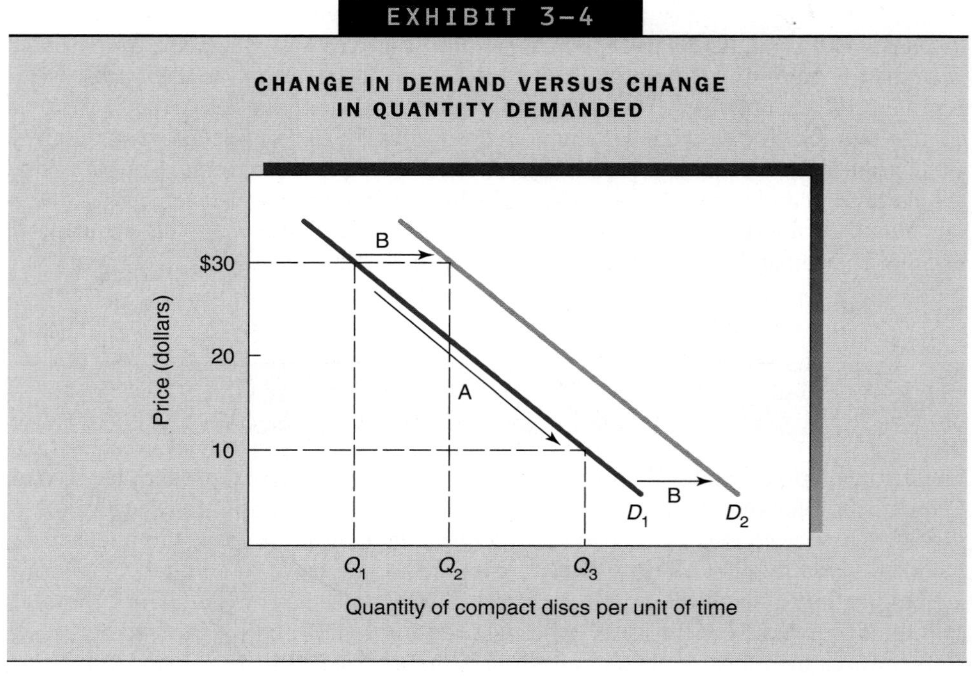

[3]Questions designed to test the ability of students to make this distinction are favorites of many economics instructors. A word to the wise should be sufficient.

EXHIBIT 3–5

A DECREASE IN DEMAND

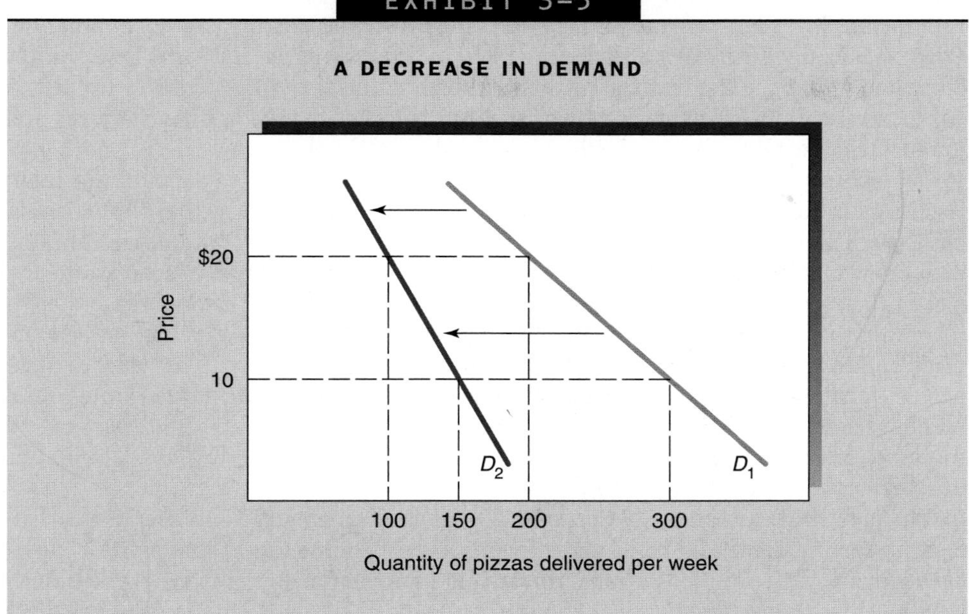

When students go home for the summer, the demand for pizza delivery in college towns decreases. A decrease in demand is a leftward shift in the entire demand curve. Fewer pizzas are demanded at every price.

demand curve D_1. Now, alternatively suppose that there is an increase in consumer income. The *demand* for compact discs would increase from D_1 to D_2. As indicated by the B arrows, the entire demand curve would shift. At the higher income level, consumers would be willing to purchase more compact disks than before. This is true at a price of $30, at $20, at $10, and at every other price. The increase in income leads to an increase in *demand*—a shift in the entire curve. Alternatively, a decrease in consumer income would have led to a decrease in demand—the demand curve would have shifted in the opposite direction (for example, from D_2 inward to D_1).

2. Changes in the Number of Consumers in the Market. Businesses that sell products in college towns are greatly saddened when summer arrives. As you might expect, the demand for many items—from pizza delivery to beer—falls during the summer. **Exhibit 3–5** shows how the falling number of consumers in the market caused by students going home for the summer affects the demand for pizza delivery. With fewer customers, the demand curve shifts inward from D_1 to D_2. There is a decrease in demand; pizza stores will sell fewer pizzas than before regardless of what price they were originally charging. Had their original price been $20, then demand would have fallen from 200 pizzas per week to only 100. Alternatively, had their original price been $10, then demand would have fallen from 300 pizzas to 150. When fall arrives and the students come back to town, there will be an increase in demand, restoring the curve to near its original position. As cities grow and shrink, and as international markets open for domestic firms, changes in the number of consumers have an effect on the demand curves for many products.

3. Changes in the Price of a Related Good. Changes in prices of closely related products also influence the choices of consumers. Related goods may be either substitutes or complements. When two products perform similar functions or fulfill similar needs, they are generally *substitutes.* Economists define goods as substitutes when there is a direct relationship between the price of one and the demand for the other (an increase in the price of one increases demand for the other). For example, margarine is a substitute for butter. If the price of butter rises, it will increase the demand for margarine. Consumers substitute margarine for the more expensive butter. Similarly, lower butter prices would reduce the demand for margarine, shifting the entire curve to the left. A substitute relationship exists between beef and chicken, pencils and pens, apples and oranges, coffee and tea, and so forth.

Other closely related products are consumed jointly, so the demands for them are linked together in a positive way. Examples of goods that "go together," so to speak, could be bread and peanut butter, CDs and CD players, or tents and other camping equipment. For these combinations of goods, called **complements,** a decrease in the price of one will not only increase its quantity demanded, it will also increase the demand for the other. With complements, there is an inverse relationship between the price of one and the demand for the other. For example, lower prices for videocassette players during the 1980s increased the demand for videocassette tapes. Similarly, if hamburger is on sale this week at the grocery store, the store can also expect to sell more hamburger buns, even if the price of buns is unchanged.

Complements
Products that are usually consumed jointly (for example, peanut butter and jelly). They are related such that a decrease in the price of one will cause an increase in demand for the other.

4. Changes in Expectations. Consumers' expectations about the future also can affect the current demand for a product. If consumers begin to expect that a major hurricane will strike their area, the current demand for such goods as batteries and canned food will rise. Expectations about the future direction of the economy can also affect current demand. If consumers become pessimistic about the economy, they might start spending less, causing the current demand for goods to fall. Of perhaps most importance is how a change in the expected future price of a good affects the current demand. When consumers expect the future price of a product to rise, their current demand for it will increase. "Buy now, before the price goes up." On the other hand, consumers will delay a purchase if they expect the item to decrease in price. No doubt you have heard someone say, "I'll wait until it goes on sale." When consumers expect the price to be lower in the near future, they will reduce their current demand for the product.

5. Demographic Changes. The demand for many products is strongly influenced by the demographic composition of the market. An increase in the size of the elderly population during the past decade increased the demand for medical care, retirement housing, and vacation travel, shifting the demand for these goods to the right. During the 1980s, population in the 15–24 age grouping fell by more than 5 million. Because young people are a major part of the U.S. market for jeans, the demand for jeans declined. Sales, which had topped 500 million pairs in 1980, fell to less than 400 million pairs in 1989.[4]

6. Changes in Consumer Tastes and Preferences. Why do preferences change? Preferences change because people learn and change. Consider how consumers responded in the 1980s to new medical information linking certain fats and oils to heart disease. They purchased less of such products as whole milk, butter, and beef, which were thought to be dangerous, and increased their demand for such goods as olive oil and canola oil, thought to be much more "heart-healthy." Sales of olive oil doubled between 1984 and 1989, while canola oil sales doubled between 1988 and 1990. Consumption of butterfat fell at the same time. By 1995, Americans ate 25 percent less beef than they

[4]These figures are from Suzanne Tregarthen, "Market for Jeans Shrinks," *The Margin* 6, no. 3 (January–February 1991), p. 28.

THUMBNAIL SKETCH

This factor increases (decreases) the quantity demanded of a good:

1. A decrease (increase) in the price of the good

These factors increase (decrease) the demand for a good:

1. A rise (fall) in consumer income
2. An increase (decline) in the number of consumers in the market

3a. A rise (fall) in the price of a substitute good
3b. A fall (rise) in the price of a complementary good
4. A rise (fall) in the expected future price of the good
5. Demographic changes: Population increases (decreases) in age groups with strong demand for a good
6. Preferences: Increased (reduced) consumer desires for the good

had in 1970. As consumers became more aware of the health implications of their diet, their preferences changed, shifting the demand for various foods. Trends in clothing, toys, collectables, and in the types of leisure activities that are popular cause continuous changes in the demand for products. Firms may even try to increase the demand for their own products through advertising and information brochures targeted at changing consumer tastes.

The **Thumbnail Sketch** above summarizes the major factors that cause a change in *demand*—a shift of the entire demand curve—and points out that *quantity demanded* (but not demand) will change in response to a change in the price of a good.

PRODUCER CHOICE AND LAW OF SUPPLY

We have now completed the examination of demand and will shift our focus to the supply side of the market. How does the market process determine the amount of each good that will be produced and supplied to the market? We cannot answer this question properly unless we understand the factors that influence the choices of those who supply goods, the producers of goods and services. Often using the business firm, producers:

1. organize productive inputs and resources, such as land, labor, capital, natural resources, and intermediate goods;
2. transform and combine these factors of production into goods and services; and
3. sell the final products to consumers for a price.

Production involves the conversion of resources into commodities and services. Producers will have to purchase the necessary resources at prices that are determined by market forces. Predictably, owners will only supply resources at prices that are at least equal to what they could earn elsewhere. Stated another way, each resource employed has to be bid away from all other uses; its owner will have to be paid its opportunity cost. ***The sum of the producer's cost of employing each resource required to produce the good will equal the product's* opportunity cost of production.**

Opportunity cost of production
The total economic cost of producing a good or service. The cost component includes the opportunity cost of all resources, including those owned by the firm. The opportunity cost is equal to the value of the production of other goods sacrificed as the result of producing the good.

There is an important difference between the opportunity cost of production and standard accounting measures of a firm's cost. Accountants generally do not count the cost of such assets as buildings, equipment, and financial resources *owned by the firm.* These assets have alternative uses and, therefore, costs are incurred when they are used to produce a good. Unless these costs are covered, the resources will eventually be employed in other ways. For now, it is sufficient to think of this cost of employing assets owned by the firm as a normal return (or "normal profit rate") that these assets could earn if employed in another way. For example, the millions of dollars worth of capital, buildings, and equipment held by a shirt manufacturer could also be used in other ways. For one thing, the firm's operating funds could be drawing interest at a bank. If the interest rate was 10%, a firm with $100,000 worth of operating capital could place these funds in a bank (or mutual fund) and earn $10,000 in interest income per year. This income forgone because the funds are tied up running the business is an opportunity cost.

Firms will not remain in business for long unless they are able to cover the cost of all resources employed, including the opportunity cost of resources owned by the firm. Typically, economists will use some measure of an average or normal rate of return as an indicator of the employment cost of assets owned by the firm.

Role of Profits and Losses

Profit
An excess of sales revenue relative to the opportunity cost of production. The cost component includes the opportunity cost of all resources, including those owned by the firm. Therefore, profit accrues only when the value of the good produced is greater than the value of other goods that could have been produced with those same resources.

Business decision makers have a strong incentive to undertake activities that generate **profit,** revenues greater than cost. If an activity is to be profitable, the revenue derived from the sale of the product must exceed the cost of employing the resources required for its production. The opportunity cost of producing a good indicates the value of other goods that might have been produced with the same resources. For example, if the opportunity cost of producing a pair of jeans is $30, this means that the resources used to produce the jeans could have been used to produce other items worth $30 to consumers (perhaps a denim backpack). If consumers are willing to pay more than $30 for the jeans, producing them increases the value of the resources. ***Firms that use resources to supply goods and services for which consumers are willing to pay more than the opportunity cost of the resources will make a profit. The willingness of consumers to pay a price greater than a good's opportunity cost indicates that they value the good more than other things that could have been produced with the same resources.*** Viewed from this perspective, profit is a residual "income reward" earned by entrepreneurs that increase the value of resources.

Loss
Deficit of sales revenue relative to the opportunity cost of production. Losses are a penalty imposed on those who misuse resources in lower-valued uses as judged by buyers in the market.

Sometimes decision makers use resources unwisely. When resources are employed to produce a good or service that has less value to consumers than other things that might have been produced, losses are incurred. **Loss** results because the sales revenue derived from the project is insufficient to cover the opportunity cost of the resources. Losses indicate that the firm has reduced the value of the resources. It would have been better if the resources had been used to produce other things. In a market economy, losses will eventually cause firms to go out of business and the resources will be directed toward other things that are valued more highly.

Profits and losses play a very important role in a market economy. They determine which firms and products will expand and survive, and which will contract and be driven from the market. In 1996, nearly 800,000 new businesses were incorporated in the United States. During the same year, more than 70,000 businesses failed. Although the business failure rate was only 90 out of every 10,000 firms, many more firms incurred losses. Some were taken over by new owners. Marketing studies indicate that only about 55 to 65 percent of the new products introduced are still on the market five years later.[5] Firms come and go at a rapid rate. Business failures are not necessarily bad. To the contrary—as our preceding discussion highlights, losses and business failures direct resources that are being used unwisely toward productive activities that are more highly valued.

Losses are capable of disciplining even the largest of firms. For example, in 1987, General Motors launched the Cadillac Allanté as a $54,700 coupe that would

---

[5]See "Flops," the *Business Week* cover story, August 16, 1993, pp. 76–82, for a history and explanation of new-product failures in the United States.

appeal to car buyers shifting their demands to European cars in that price range. But the car did not have the qualities consumers wanted at that price. It never sold even half of the 7,000 cars per year that General Motors planned. In 1993, the Allanté went out of production.

Supply and the Entrepreneur

Entrepreneurs undertake production organization, deciding what to produce and how to produce it. The business of the entrepreneur is to figure out which projects will be profitable, and then to convince a corporation, a banker, or individual investors to invest the resources needed to give the new idea a chance. Since the profitability of a project is affected by the price consumers are willing to pay for a product, the price of resources required to produce it, and the cost of alternative production processes, successful entrepreneurs must either be knowledgeable in each of these areas or be able to obtain the advice of others who have such knowledge. Being an entrepreneur means taking on the risk of failure.

To prosper, business entrepreneurs must convert and rearrange resources in a manner that will increase their value. An individual who purchases 100 acres of raw land, puts in a street and a sewage-disposal system, divides the plot into one-acre lots, and sells them for 50 percent more than the opportunity cost of all resources used is clearly an entrepreneur. This entrepreneur "profits" because the value of the resources has been increased. Sometimes entrepreneurial activity is less complex. For example, a 15-year-old who purchases a power mower and sells lawn service to the neighbors is also an entrepreneur seeking to profit by increasing the value of resources—his time and equipment. In a market economy, profit is the reward to the entrepreneur who discovers and acts upon an opportunity to produce a good or service that is valued more highly than the resources required for its production. Profit also creates an incentive for rival entrepreneurs to enter the market and further expand the production of the good for consumers.

Market Supply Schedule

How will producer-entrepreneurs respond to a change in product price? Other things constant, a higher price will increase the producer's incentive to supply the good. New entrepreneurs, seeking personal gain, will enter the market and begin supplying the product. Established producers will expand the scale of their operations, leading to an additional expansion in output. Higher prices will induce producers to supply a greater amount. ***The* law of supply *states that there is direct relationship between the price of a product and the amount of it that will be supplied. As the price of a product increases, producers will be willing to supply more. Correspondingly they will supply less, if the price declines.***

Law of supply
A principle that states there is a direct relationship between the price of a good and the amount of it offered for sale. As the price of a product increases, other things constant, producers will increase the amount of the product supplied to the market.

Like the law of demand, the law of supply reflects the basic economic postulate that incentives matter. Higher prices increase the reward entrepreneurs receive from selling their product. When it becomes more profitable, they will be willing to supply more. Conversely, as the price of the good falls, so does the profitability, and thus the incentive to supply the good. Just think about how many hours of tutoring services you would supply for different prices. Would you be willing to supply more hours of work at a wage of $50 per hour than at $5 per hour? The law of supply suggests that you would, and producers of other goods and services are no different.

Exhibit 3–6 provides a graphic presentation of the law of supply called the *supply curve.* Because of the direct relationship between price and the amount offered for sale by suppliers, the supply curve will slope upward to the right. Read horizontally, the supply curve shows how much of a particular good producers are willing to

As the price of a product increases, other things constant, *producers will increase the amount of the product supplied to the market.*

EXHIBIT 3–6

SUPPLY CURVE

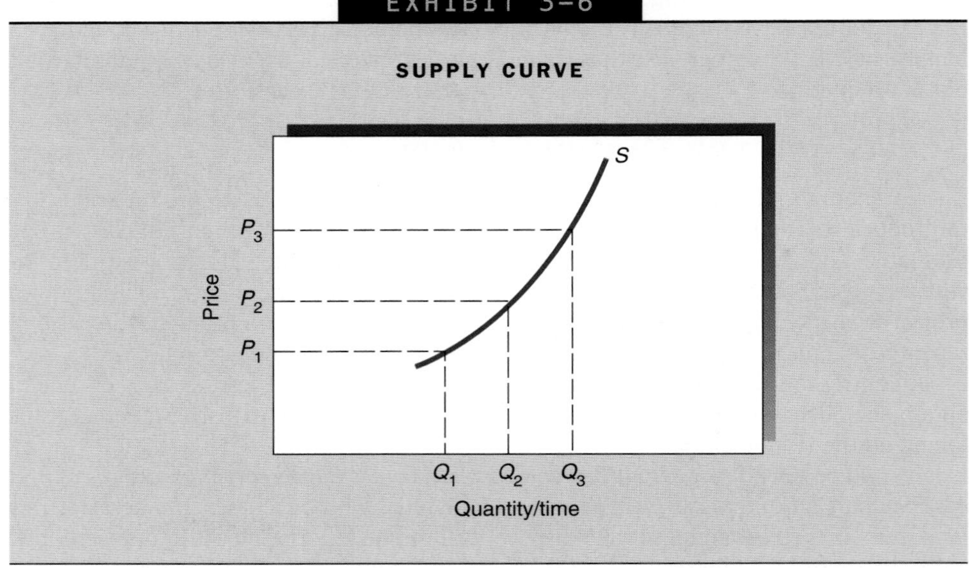

produce and sell at a given price. Read vertically, the supply curve reveals important information about the cost of production. ***The height of the supply curve indicates both (1) the minimum price necessary to induce producers to supply that additional unit and (2) the opportunity cost of producing the additional unit of the good.*** These are both measured by the height because the minimum price required to induce a supplier to sell a unit is precisely the marginal cost of producing it. Just as the demand curve can also be used as a marginal benefit curve, the supply curve can also be used as a marginal cost curve.

Producer Surplus

Producer surplus
The difference between the minimum supply price and the actual sales price. It measures the net gains to producers and resource suppliers from market trade. It is not the same as profit.

We previously used the demand curve to illustrate consumer surplus, the net gains of buyers from market exchange. The supply curve can be used in a similar manner to derive the net gains of producers and resource suppliers. The height of the supply curve shows both the marginal cost of providing various quantities of a good and the minimum price required to induce suppliers to produce these quantities. As the shaded area of **Exhibit 3–7** shows, the net gain of suppliers from the production and exchange of a good is the difference between the market price and the height of the supply curve. This net gain is called **producer surplus.** Suppose that you are a musician and that you would be willing to perform a two-hour concert for $50. If a promoter offers to pay you $200 to perform the concert, you will accept, and receive $150 more than your minimum price. This $150 represents your producer surplus.

It is important to note that producer surplus represents the gains that accrue to all parties that contribute resources used to produce the good. Producer surplus is fundamentally different from profit. Remember, profit is a return that accrues to the owners of the firm when sales revenues exceed the *total* cost of production. The supply curve reflects *marginal* costs (not total or average) of producing various quantities. As production of a good is expanded, the prices of the resources required to produce the good may rise. If so, the rising resource prices generate gains for resource suppliers and these gains are an integral part of producer surplus. In contrast, the higher

EXHIBIT 3-7

PRODUCER SURPLUS

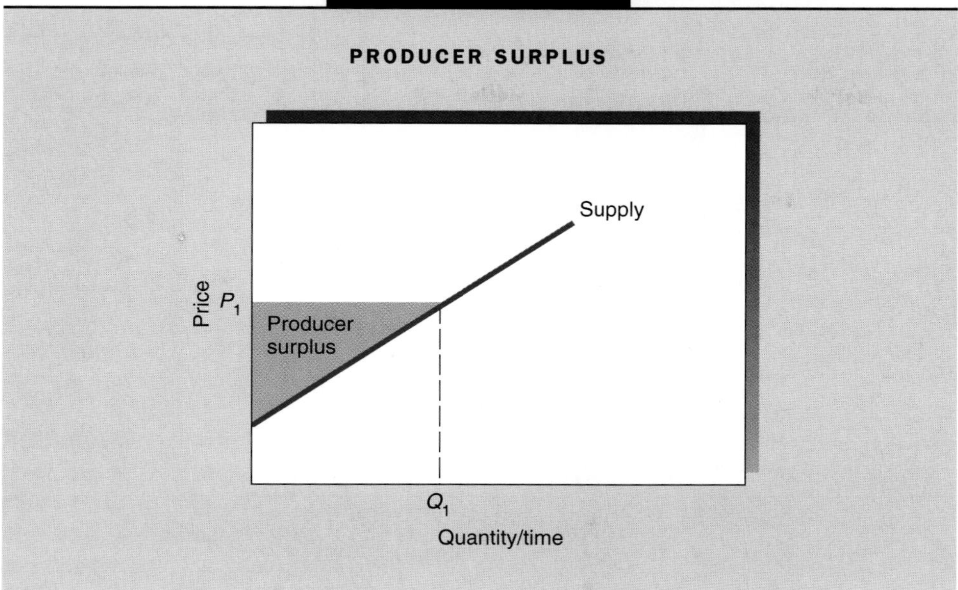

Producer surplus is the area above the supply curve but below the actual sales price. This area represents the net gains to producers and resource suppliers from production and exchange.

resource prices increase the costs of firms producing the good, and thereby reduce their profit. Profit accrues to the owners of the firm, while producer surplus encompasses the net gains derived by all resource owners that help to produce the good, including those employed by or selling resources to the firm.

RESPONSIVENESS OF QUANTITY SUPPLIED TO PRICE: ELASTIC AND INELASTIC SUPPLY CURVES

As in the case of demand, the responsiveness of quantity supplied to a change in price will differ among goods. For some goods, a change in price will lead to a relatively large change in quantity supplied. This will be true when producers can obtain additional resources with only a small increase in their price. When this is the case, the supply curve will be relatively flat. Economists would say that the supply curve is elastic. When quantity supplied is not very responsive to a change in price, supply is said to be inelastic. **Exhibit** 3–8 shows both relatively elastic and inelastic supply curves. The flatter supply curve (S_1, on the left) is relatively elastic, while supply curve S_2 (right frame) is relatively inelastic. In the case of the relatively elastic supply curve S_1, an increase in

OUTSTANDING ECONOMIST

Alfred Marshall (1842–1924)

The most influential economist of his era, Marshall introduced many of the concepts and tools that form the core of modern microeconomics, including the short run, the long run, and equilibrium.

EXHIBIT 3-8

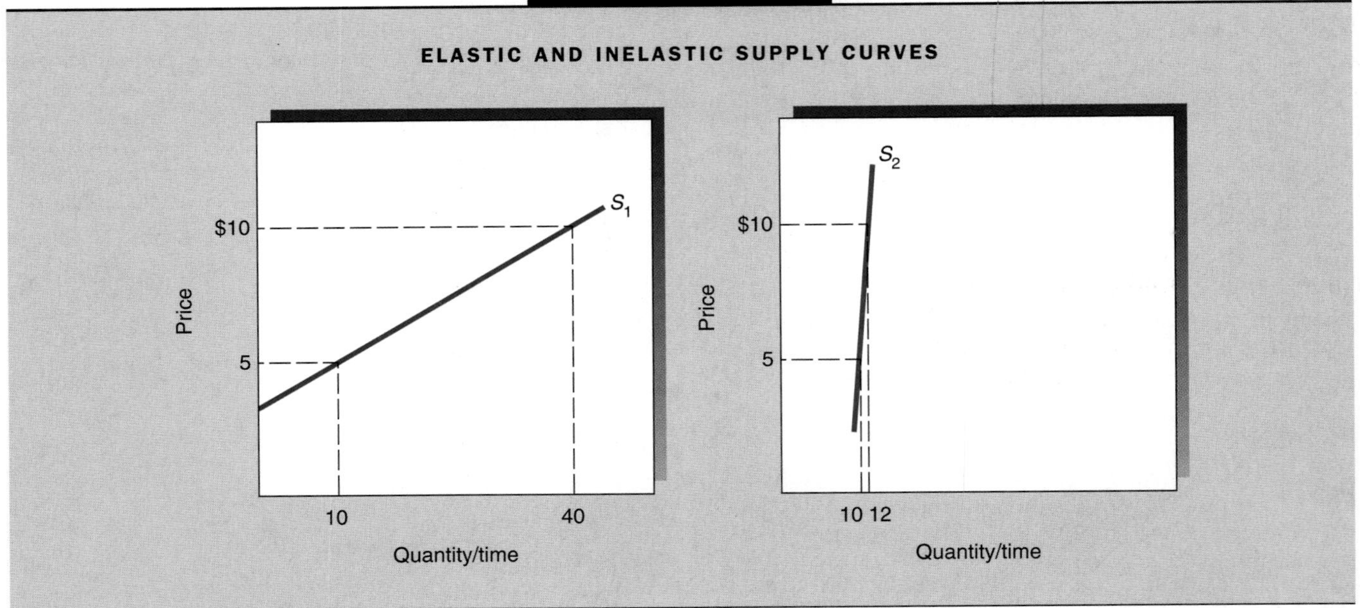

The responsiveness of producer supply to a change in price is reflected in the steepness of the supply curve. The flatter supply curve (S_1) shows a higher degree of responsiveness and is called relatively elastic, while the steeper supply curve (S_2) shows a lower degree of responsiveness and is called relatively inelastic.

price from $5 to $10 leads to an increase in the quantity supplied from 10 units to 40 units. For the inelastic supply curve S_2, the same increase in price leads to an increase in quantity supplied from 10 units to only 12 units. The more inelastic supply, the smaller the output response to a change in price.

Short run
A time period of insufficient length to permit decision makers to adjust fully to a change in market conditions. For example, in the short run, producers will have time to increase output by using more labor and raw materials, but they will not have time to expand the size of their plants or to install additional heavy equipment.

Long run
A time period of sufficient length to enable decision makers to adjust fully to a market change.

The responsiveness of supply to a change in price is affected by time. The great English economist Alfred Marshall introduced the concepts of *short run* and *long run* in order to highlight this point. In the **short run,** firms do not have enough time to build a new plant or expand the size of their current one. Producers are stuck with their existing facility in the short run; they can increase output only by using that facility more intensely. As a result, the immediate supply response to a price change will be limited. Thus, the supply curve for many goods will be relatively inelastic (like the right frame of Exhibit 3–8) in the short run.

The **long run** is a time period lengthy enough for existing firms to alter the size of their plant and for new firms to enter (or exit) the market. Predictably, the change in quantity supplied in response to a change in the price of a good will be greater in the long run than in the short run. Compared to the short run, the supply curve in the long run will be much more elastic (like the left frame of Exhibit 3–8).

CHANGES IN SUPPLY VERSUS CHANGES IN QUANTITY SUPPLIED

As with demand, it is important to distinguish between a change in *quantity supplied* and a change in *supply.* When sellers alter the number of units supplied in response to a change in price, this movement along the same supply curve is referred to as a "change in *quantity supplied.*"

As we previously discussed, profit-seeking entrepreneurs will produce a good only if the sales price of the good is expected to exceed its opportunity cost. Therefore, changes that affect the opportunity cost of supplying a good will also influence the amount of it that producers are willing to supply. These "other factors," such as the price of resources and level of technology, are held constant when drawing a supply curve. Changes in these other factors that influence the opportunity cost of providing the product will shift the entire supply curve for the good. This shift in the entire supply curve is referred to as a "change in *supply*." Factors that increase the opportunity cost of providing a good will discourage production and decrease supply (shift the entire curve inward to the left). Similarly, changes that decrease the opportunity cost of producers will increase supply (shift the entire curve outward to the right).

Let us now take a closer look at the primary factors that will cause a change in supply, a shift in the entire curve to either the right or the left.

1. Changes in Resource Prices. How will an increase in the price of a resource, such as the wages of workers or the materials used to produce a product, affect the supply of the good? There are two ways to view the effects of changing resource prices. First, higher resource prices will increase the cost of production, reducing the profitability of firms buying the resources to supply the good. The higher cost will induce firms to cut back their output. With time, some may even be driven out of business. As **Exhibit 3–9** illustrates, the higher resource prices and increased opportunity cost will reduce the supply of the good, causing a shift to the left in the supply curve from S_1 to S_2. A second way to view the effect of a change in resource prices is to remember that the height of the supply curve measures the marginal cost of production. Thus higher production costs can be thought of as shifting the supply curve upward, showing that the cost of producing each and every unit has now gone up. We would encourage you, however, to think of an increase in supply as a shift to the right and a decrease as a shift to the left. When remembered this way, decreases in both supply and demand are shown by a shift to the left, while increases in both are shifts to the right.

EXHIBIT 3–9

A DECREASE IN SUPPLY

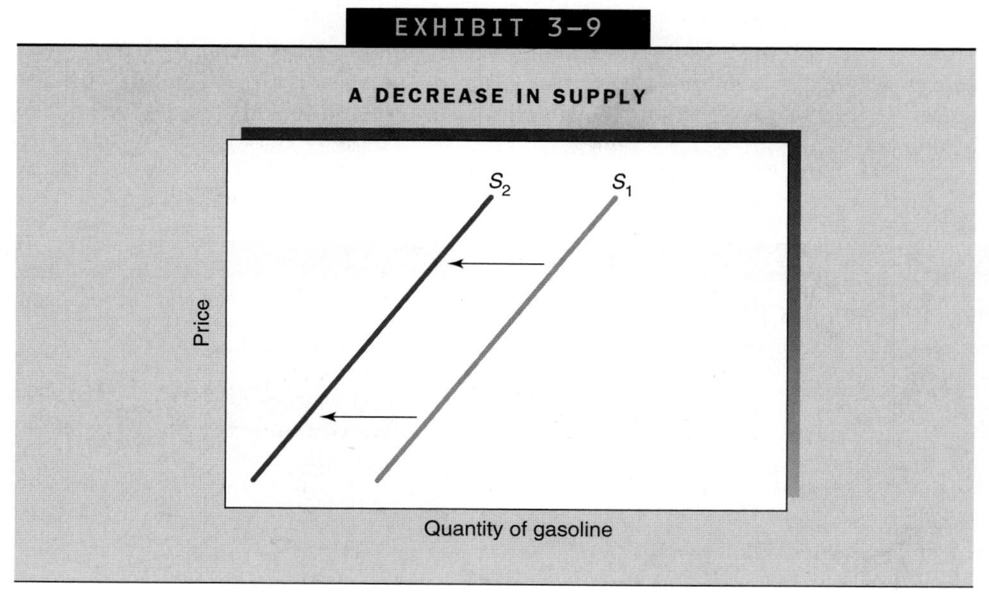

Crude oil is a resource used to produce gasoline. When the price of crude oil rises, it increases the cost of producing gasoline and results in a decrease in the supply of gasoline.

Suppose that the price of a resource used to produce a good falls. How will this affect the supply of the good? Lower resource prices will reduce the cost of producing the good. Suppliers will respond with a larger output, causing the supply curve to shift outward to the right.

2. Changes in Technology. Like lower resource prices, technological improvements—the discovery of new, lower-cost production techniques—reduce production costs, and thereby increase supply (shift the curve to the right). Technological advances have in fact affected the cost of almost everything. Before the invention of the printing press, books had to be handwritten. Just imagine the massive reduction in cost and increase in the supply of books caused by this single invention. Technologically improved farm machinery has reduced cost and vastly expanded the supply of agricultural products through the years. Recent technological improvements in the production of computer chips have drastically reduced the cost of producing such electronic products as calculators, VCRs, microwave ovens, and compact disc players. Robotics have reduced the cost of airplanes, automobiles, and several other types of machinery.

3. Elements of Nature and Political Disruptions. Natural disasters and changing political conditions may also alter supply, sometimes dramatically. During some years, highly favorable weather can lead to higher yields and "bumper crops," increasing the supply of various agricultural products. At other times, droughts may reduce yields, reducing supply. War and political unrest in Iran exerted a major impact on the supply of oil in the late 1970s, as did the invasion of Kuwait by Iraq in 1990. Such factors as these will reduce supply.

4. Changes in Taxes. If the government increases the taxes on the sellers of a product, the result will be the same as any other increase in the cost of doing business. The added tax to be paid by sellers will reduce their willingness to sell at any given price. At each price, only those units for which the price covers all opportunity costs, including the tax, will be offered for sale. For example, the Superfund law placed a special tax on petroleum producers based on petroleum output (not on the producer's past or present pollution level). That raised the cost of producing petroleum products, decreasing the supply of those products.

The accompanying **Thumbnail Sketch** summarizes the major factors that cause a change in *supply*—a shift of the entire supply curve—and points out that *quantity supplied* (but not supply) will change in response to a change in the price of a good.

THUMBNAIL SKETCH

Factors That Cause Changes in Supply and Quantity Supplied

This factor increases (decreases) the quantity supplied of a good:

1. An increase (decrease) in the price of the good

These factors increase (decrease) the supply of a good:

1. A fall (rise) in the price of a resource used in producing the good
2. A technological change allowing cheaper production of the good
3. Favorable weather (bad weather or a disruption in supply due to political factors or war)
4. A reduction (increase) in the taxes imposed on the producers of the good

HOW MARKET PRICES ARE DETERMINED: SUPPLY AND DEMAND INTERACT

Consumer-buyers and producer-sellers make decisions independent of each other, but markets coordinate their choices and influence their actions. To the economist, a **market** is not a physical location, but an abstract concept that encompasses the forces generated by the buying and selling decisions of economic participants. A market may be quite narrow (for example, the market for grade A jumbo eggs), or it may be quite broad when it is useful to aggregate diverse goods into a single market, such as the market for all "consumer goods." There is also a wide range of sophistication among markets. The New York Stock Exchange is a highly computerized market in which, each weekday, buyers and sellers, who seldom formally meet, exchange shares of corporate ownership worth billions of dollars. In contrast, the neighborhood market for lawn-mowing services, or tutoring in economics, may be highly informal, since it brings together buyers and sellers primarily by word of mouth.

Market
An abstract concept that encompasses the trading arrangements of buyers and sellers that underlie the forces of supply and demand.

Equilibrium *is a state in which conflicting forces are in balance. When a market is in equilibrium, the decisions of consumers and producers are brought into harmony with one another. In equilibrium, it will be possible for both buyers and sellers to realize their choices simultaneously.* What could bring these diverse interests into harmony? We will see the answer is market prices.

Equilibrium
A state of balance between conflicting forces, such as supply and demand.

MARKET EQUILIBRIUM

As Exhibit 3–1 illustrates, a higher price will reduce the amount of a good demanded by consumers. On the other hand, Exhibit 3–7 shows that a higher price will increase the amount of a good supplied by producers. The market price of a commodity will tend to change in a direction that will bring into balance the quantity of a good desired by consumers with the quantity supplied by producers. That is, price will tend to move toward equilibrium. If the price is too high, the quantity supplied will exceed the quantity demanded. Producers will be unable to sell as much as they would like unless they reduce their price. Alternatively, if the price is too low, the quantity demanded will exceed the quantity supplied. Some consumers will be unable to get as much as they would like, unless they are willing to pay a higher price. Thus, there will be a tendency for the price in a market to move toward the price that brings the quantity demanded by consumers into balance with the quantity supplied by producers.

Exhibit 3–10 illustrates supply and demand curves in the market for oversize playing cards. At a high price—$12, for example—card producers will plan to supply 600 decks of the cards per month, whereas consumers will choose to purchase only 450. An excess supply of 150 decks (distance *ab* in the graph) will result. Production exceeds sales, pushing the inventories of producers upward. To reduce undesired inventories, some producers of the oversized cards will cut their price in order to increase their sales. Other firms will have to lower their price also, or sell even fewer decks. The lower price will make production of the cards less attractive to producers. Some producers may go out of business, while others will reduce their output. How low will the price go? When it has declined to $10, the quantity supplied by producers and the quantity demanded by consumers will be in balance at 550 decks per month. At this price ($10), the choices of buyers and sellers are brought into harmony. The amount that producers are willing to supply just equals the amount that consumers want to purchase.

What will happen if the price per deck is lower—$8, for example? The amount demanded by consumers (650 units) will exceed the amount supplied by producers (500

The table indicates the supply and demand conditions for oversized playing cards. These conditions are also illustrated by the graph. When the price exceeds $10, an excess supply is present, which places downward pressure on price. In contrast, when the price is less than $10, an excess demand results, which causes the price to rise. Thus, the market price will tend toward $10, at which point supply and demand will be in balance.

EXHIBIT 3-10

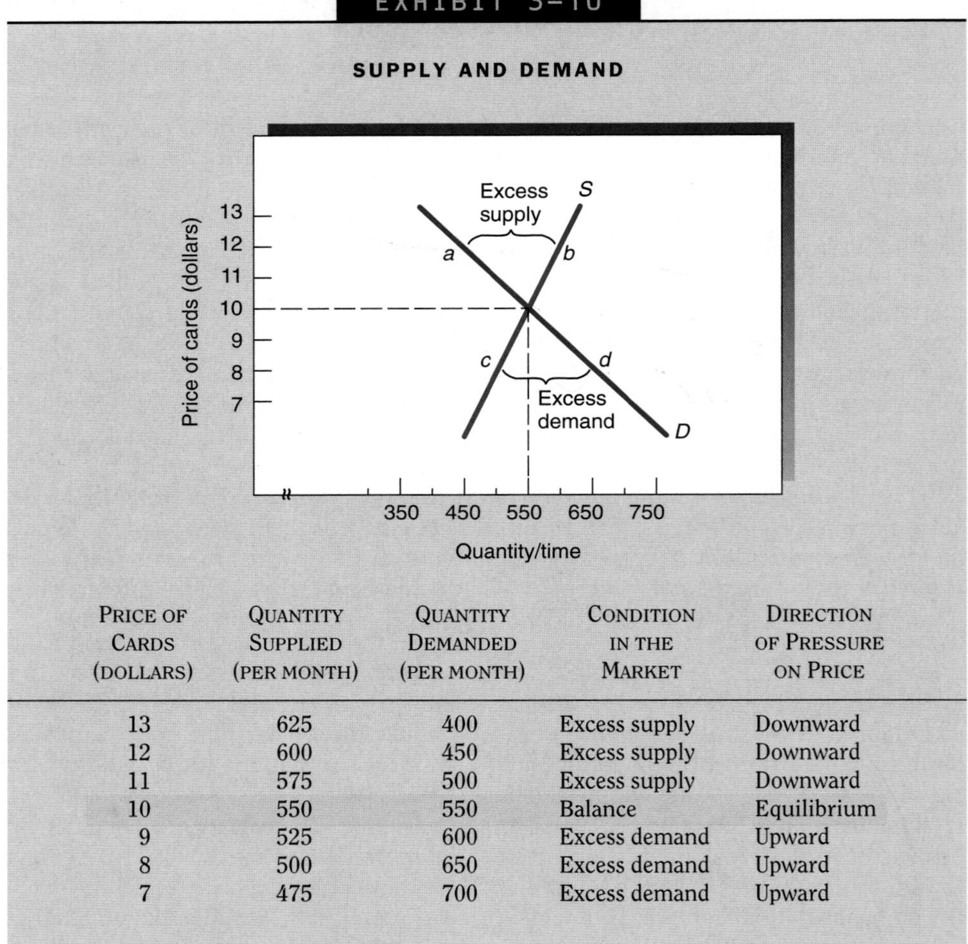

PRICE OF CARDS (DOLLARS)	QUANTITY SUPPLIED (PER MONTH)	QUANTITY DEMANDED (PER MONTH)	CONDITION IN THE MARKET	DIRECTION OF PRESSURE ON PRICE
13	625	400	Excess supply	Downward
12	600	450	Excess supply	Downward
11	575	500	Excess supply	Downward
10	550	550	Balance	Equilibrium
9	525	600	Excess demand	Upward
8	500	650	Excess demand	Upward
7	475	700	Excess demand	Upward

units). An excess demand of 150 units (*cd* in the graph) will be present. Some consumers who are unable to purchase the cards at $8 per unit because of the inadequate supply would be willing to pay a higher price. Recognizing this fact, producers will raise their price. As the price increases to $10, producers will expand their output and consumers will cut down on their consumption. At the $10 price, equilibrium will be restored.

People have a tendency to think of consumers wanting lower prices and producers wanting higher prices. Although true, price changes frequently work in exactly the opposite direction. When a local store has an excess supply of a particular item, how does it get rid of it? By having a sale or somehow otherwise lowering its price (a "blue-light special"). Firms often lower their prices in order to get rid of excess supply. On the other hand, excess demand is solved by consumers bidding up prices. Children's toys around Christmas provide a perfect example. When first introduced, both the Cabbage Patch Doll and the Tickle-Me-Elmo stuffed animal were immediate successes. The firms producing these products had not anticipated the overwhelming demand for their products. Soon every child wanted one of these dolls for Christmas. Lines of parents were forming outside stores before they even opened. Only the first few in line would be able to get the dolls before the store would quickly run out (a sure sign that the store had set the price below equilibrium). Out in the parking lots, and in the classified ads, parents were offering up to $100 or more for these items. If stores were not going to set the prices right, parents in these informal markets would. These examples show that rising prices are often the result of consumers bidding up prices when excess demand is present.

Efficiency and Market Equilibrium

When a market reaches equilibrium all the gains from trade have been fully realized; **economic efficiency** is present. This criterion is important because economists often use it as a standard with which to judge outcomes under alternative circumstances. The central idea of efficiency is a cost versus benefit comparison. Undertaking an economic action will be efficient only if it generates more benefits than costs. On the other hand, undertaking an action that generates more costs than benefits is inefficient. For a market to satisfy the criterion of economic efficiency, all trades that generate more benefits than costs need to be undertaken. In addition, economic efficiency requires that no trades creating more costs than benefits be undertaken.

Economic efficiency
A market meets the criterion of economic efficiency if all the gains from trade have been realized. An action is consistent with efficiency only if it creates more benefits than costs. With well-defined property rights and competition, market equilibrium is efficient.

A closer look at the way in which markets work can help us to understand the concept of efficiency. The supply curve reflects producers' opportunity costs. Each point along the supply curve indicates the minimum price for which the units of a good could be produced without a loss to the seller. On the other side of the market, each point along the demand curve indicates the consumer's valuation of an extra unit of the good—the maximum amount the consumer is willing to pay for the extra unit. Any time the consumer's valuation of a unit (the benefit side) exceeds the producer's minimum supply price (the cost side), producing and selling the unit is consistent with economic efficiency. The trade will result in mutual gain to both parties. When property rights are well defined, and only the buyers and sellers are affected by production and exchange, competitive market forces will automatically guide a market toward an equilibrium level of output that satisfies economic efficiency.

Exhibit 3–11 illustrates why this is true. Suppliers of a good, bicycles in this example, will produce additional units as long as the market price exceeds the production

EXHIBIT 3–11

ECONOMIC EFFICIENCY

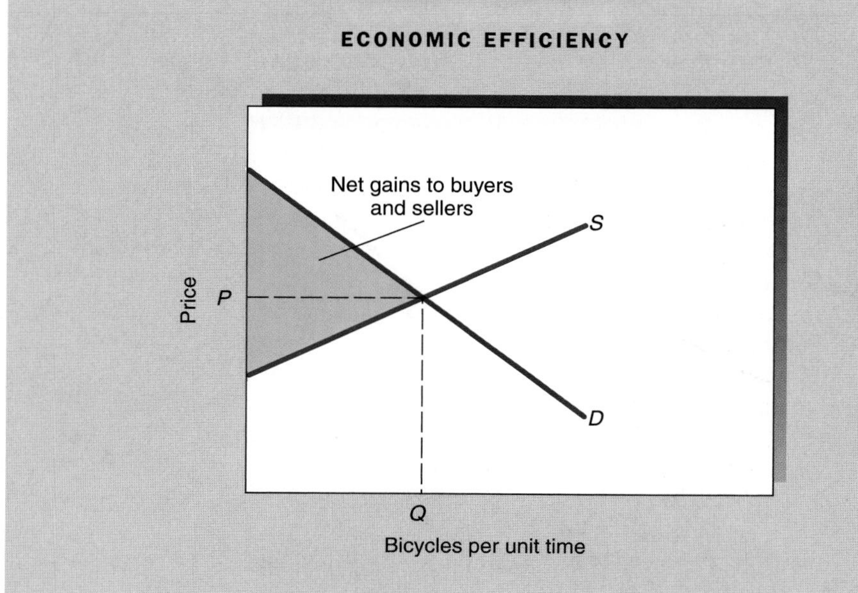

When markets are competitive and property rights are well defined, the equilibrium reached by a market satisfies economic efficiency. All units that create more benefit (the buyer's valuation shown by the height of the demand curve) than cost (opportunity cost of production shown by the height of the supply curve) are produced. This maximizes the total gains from trade, the combined area represented by consumer and producer surplus.

cost. Similarly, consumers will gain from the purchase of additional units as long as their benefits, revealed by the height of the demand curve, exceed the market price. Market forces will result in an equilibrium output level of Q: All units providing benefits to consumers that exceed the costs to suppliers will be produced. Economic efficiency is met because all potential gains from exchange (the shaded area) between consumers and producers are fully realized.

If less than Q bicycles were produced, economic efficiency would be violated and inefficiency would result. This is because the market did not provide all units for which benefits were greater than costs. If more than Q bicycles were produced, inefficiency would also result because units were produced that cost more than the benefits created. With competitive markets, consumers and producers alike will be guided by the pricing system to output level Q, just the right amount from the standpoint of economic efficiency.

HOW MARKETS RESPOND TO CHANGES IN DEMAND AND SUPPLY

How will a market adjust to a change in demand? **Exhibit 3–12** illustrates the market adjustment to an increase in demand. For most of the year, the demand for eggs is primarily for breakfast or the making of other food products. The demand D_1 and supply S indicate the typical conditions throughout most of the year. Typically, the equilibrium price of eggs is P_1. Around Easter time, however, many people purchase extra eggs to decorate or dye with coloring. During the two weeks before Easter, U.S. farmers sell about 600 million more eggs than the average throughout the rest of the year. Thus, at Easter time, there is a sharp increase in demand for eggs (shift from D_1 to D_2 in Exhibit 3–12). This increase in demand for eggs will push their price upward. During the holiday, egg prices are typically about 20 cents higher per dozen. Note that if the price of eggs did not rise, excess demand would be present. At the P_1 price present throughout

EXHIBIT 3–12

MARKET ADJUSTMENT TO INCREASE IN DEMAND

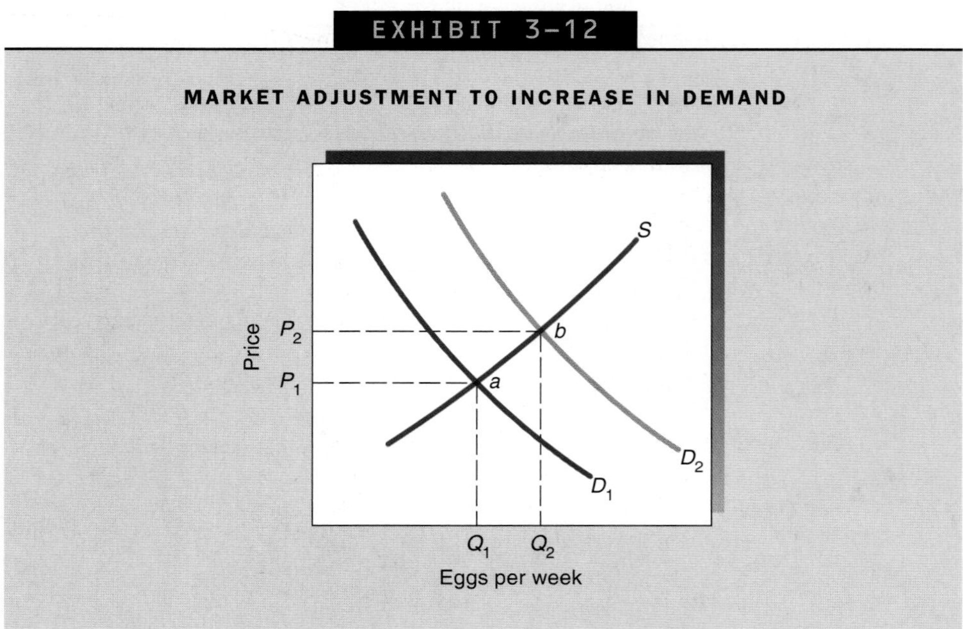

Here we illustrate how the market for eggs adjusts to an increase in demand such as generally occurs around Easter time. Initially (before the Easter season), the market for eggs reflects demand D_1 *and supply* S. *The increase in demand (shift from* D_1 *to* D_2*) pushes price up and leads to a new equilibrium at a higher price (*P_2 *rather than* P_1*) and larger quantity traded (*Q_2*).*

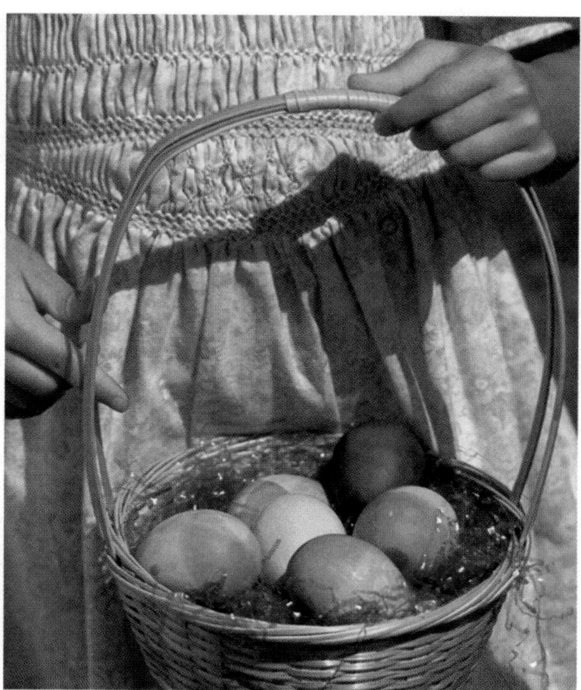

The tradition of coloring and hunting for eggs causes an increase in demand for eggs around Easter. As Exhibit 3-12 illustrates, this leads to higher egg prices and costly actions by producers to supply a larger quantity during this period.

most of the year, consumers at Easter time would want to purchase more than producers were willing to supply. At the higher P_2 price, consumers will moderate their additional purchases and producers will supply a larger quantity (Q_2 rather than Q_1). Because hens lay fewer eggs when they are molting, farmers take costly steps to avoid having the hens molt around Easter. This can be done by changing the quantity and types of feed used, and by changing the brightness of lighting in the birds' sheds. In addition, farmers attempt to build up larger than normal inventories of eggs before Easter. Eggs are typically about two days old when consumers buy them, but can be up to seven days old during Easter.

In a market economy, when the demand for a good increases, its price will rise, which will provide (1) consumers with more incentive to search for substitutes and to moderate their additional purchases and (2) producers with a stronger incentive to supply more of the product. These two forces will keep the quantity demanded and quantity supplied in balance.

When the demand for a product declines, the adjustment process will provide buyers and sellers with just the opposite signals. Take a piece of paper and see if you can show how a decrease in demand will affect a market. If you've done it correctly, a decline in demand (a shift to the left in the demand curve) will lead to a lower price and a lower quantity traded. What's going on in the diagram is that the lower price (caused by lower consumer demand) is reducing the incentive of producers to supply the good. Thus, when consumers no longer want as much of a good, market prices send the signal to producers to cut back on their production. The reduced production allows these resources to be freed up to go into the production of other goods.

How will markets respond to changes in supply? **Exhibit 3-13** uses the example of romaine lettuce to illustrate the market's adjustment to a reduction in supply. Severe rains and flooding in California during the spring and early summer of 1998 destroyed a large portion of the romaine lettuce crop. This reduction in supply (shift from S_1 to S_2)

EXHIBIT 3-13

MARKET ADJUSTMENT TO A DECREASE IN SUPPLY

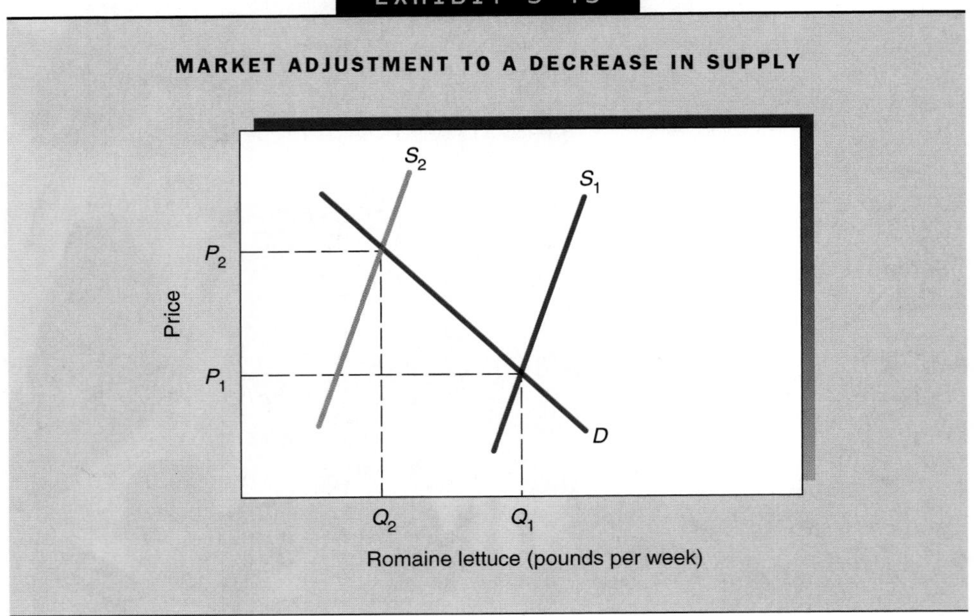

Here, using romaine lettuce as an example, we illustrate how a market adjusts to a decrease in supply. Adverse weather conditions substantially reduced the supply (shift from S_1 to S_2) of romaine during the spring and summer of 1998. The reduction in supply led to an increase in the equilibrium price (from P_1 to P_2) and a reduction in the equilibrium quantity traded (from Q_1 to Q_2).

caused the price of romaine to increase sharply (to P_2). Consumers cut back on their consumption of the now more expensive good. Some switched to substitutes—in this case, probably other varieties of lettuce and leafy vegetables. Producers took extraordinary steps to expand output and replenish the supply. Vegetable farmers shifted from other crops to romaine lettuce. Some greenhouses were even converted to produce romaine lettuce. The higher prices kept the quantity demanded and quantity supplied in balance and provided suppliers with an incentive to expand supply. Eventually, weather patterns returned to normal and the price fell from its temporary high level.

As the lettuce example illustrates, a decrease in supply will lead to higher prices and a reduction in the equilibrium quantity. How would the market adjust to an increase in supply, such as would result from a technological breakthrough or lower resource prices that reduce production cost of a good? Again, try to draw the appropriate supply and demand curves to illustrate this case. If you do it correctly, the graphic will illustrate that an increase in supply (a shift to the right in the supply curve) leads to a lower market price and a larger quantity.

The following **Thumbnail Sketch** summarizes the impact of changes—both increases and decreases—in demand and supply on the equilibrium price and quantity. Sometimes market conditions can be affected by a simultaneous shift in both demand and supply. For example, consumer income might increase at the same time that a technological advance was reducing the cost of producing a good. These two changes will cause demand and supply to increase at the same time. Both curves will shift to the right. The new equilibrium will definitely be at a larger quantity, but the direction of the change in price is indeterminate. Price may either increase or decrease, depending on whether the increase in demand or increase in supply is larger. When both supply and demand shift, either the resulting price (or quantity) will be indeterminate. Which would be indeterminate if an increase in supply and a reduction in demand occurred at the same time? The correct answer is: Price will definitely fall, but the new equilibrium quantity may either increase or decrease. Draw the supply and demand curves for this case and make sure that you understand why.

THUMBNAIL SKETCH

How Changes in Demand and Supply Affect Market Price and Quantity

Changes in Demand

1. An increase in demand (a shift to the right of the demand curve) will cause an increase in both the equilibrium price and quantity.
2. A decrease in demand (a shift to the left of the demand curve) will cause a decrease in both the equilibrium price and quantity.

Changes in Supply

1. An increase in supply (a shift to the right of the supply curve) will cause a decrease in the equilibrium price and an increase in the equilibrium quantity.
2. A decrease in supply (a shift to the left of the supply curve) will cause an increase in the equilibrium price and a decrease in the equilibrium quantity.

TIME AND THE ADJUSTMENT PROCESS

When market prices change, both consumers and producers adjust their behavior to the new structure of incentives. The adjustment process will not be instantaneous, though. Sometimes various signals are sent out by changing market prices and are acted upon only gradually, with the passage of time.

Using gasoline as an example, **Exhibit 3–14** illustrates the role of time as market participants adjust to a decline in supply. During the late 1970s, political turmoil in Iran—an important oil producer—caused a reduction in supply of gasoline, represented by the shift from S_1 to S_2. This led to sharply higher prices for gasoline. Adjusted for inflation, gasoline prices rose from \$0.70 in 1978 to \$1.20 in 1980. *Initially,* consumers responded to rising prices by cutting out some unnecessary trips and leisure driving, and by accelerating more slowly in order to get better gasoline mileage. Adjustments like these allowed consumers to reduce their consumption of gasoline,

EXHIBIT 3–14

TIME, AND ADJUSTMENT TO A REDUCTION IN SUPPLY

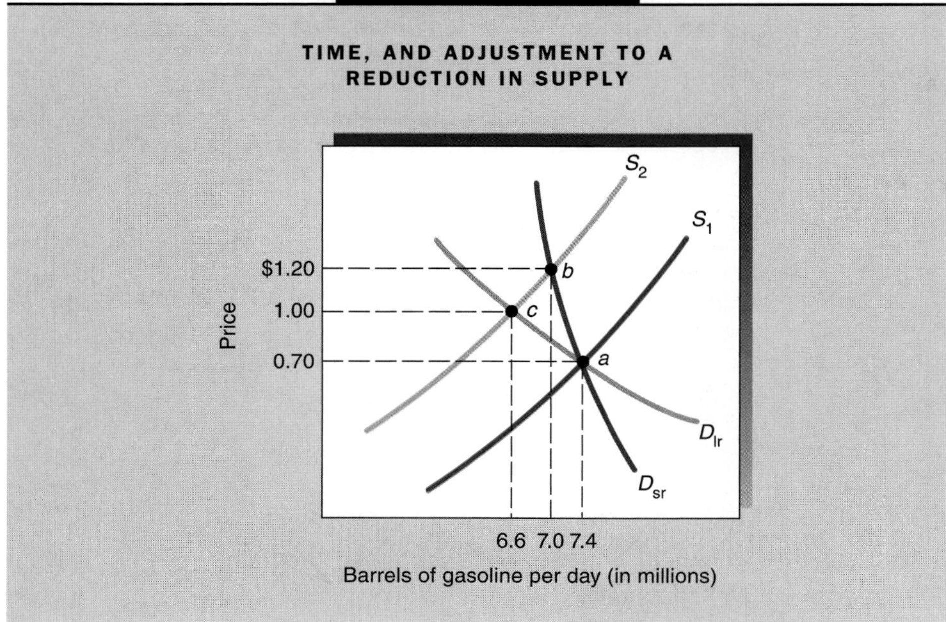

Here we illustrate the adjustment of a market to an unanticipated reduction in supply, such as occurred in the market for gasoline during 1978–1982. Initially, the price of gasoline was 70 cents (equilibrium a*). Supply declined (shifted from* S_1 *to* S_2*) as the result of military conflict and political unrest in the Middle East. In the short run, prices rose sharply to \$1.20, and consumption declined by only a small amount (equilibrium moved from* a *to* b*). In the long run, however, the demand for gasoline was more responsive to the price change. As a result, in the long run the price increase was more moderate (equilibrium moved from* b *to* c*).*

but only by a small amount (from 7.4 million to 7.0 million barrels per day), moving them up D_{sr} from point *a* to point *b*. The demand for gasoline in the short run was relatively inelastic, being not very responsive to the change in price.

Given additional time, however, consumers were able to make other adjustments that influenced their consumption of gasoline. For example, as larger cars that used a lot of gasoline became old and worn out, new car purchases shifted toward smaller cars with better gas mileage. Adjustments like this caused a more price-responsive long-run demand for gasoline. By late 1981, consumption of gasoline had declined to 6.6 million barrels per day, and there was downward pressure on prices.

This adjustment process for gasoline is typical. The consumption response to a price change will usually be smaller in the short run than over a longer period of time. As a result, an unexpected reduction in the supply of a product will generally push the price up more in the short run than in the long run.

Similarly, the adjustments of producers to changing market conditions take time. Suppose that specialized new computer software is developed that causes an increase in demand for notebook computers. How will this change be reflected in the market? **Exhibit 3–15** provides an overview. The increase in demand is shown by the shift from D_1 to D_2. Initially, suppliers of notebook computers see a decline in their inventories as the computers move off their shelves more rapidly. Discounts will be more difficult to find, deliveries to buyers will be slower, and prices will begin to rise as sellers ration their limited supplies among the increased number of buyers. The market price rises from P_1 to P_2.

A few aggressive entrepreneurs in the computer-producing business may quickly expand their production of notebook computers. They increase the quantity supplied quickly, by rush orders of new materials, having employees work overtime, and so on. But since it is costly to expand output quickly, the higher market price (P_2) will lead to only a modest increase in output from Q_1 to Q_2 in the short run. The higher prices and improved profitability, however, will encourage other, more deliberate efforts

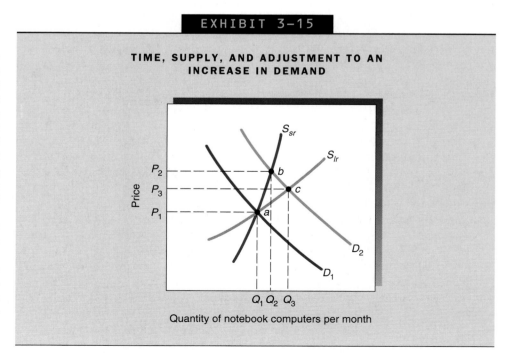

TIME, SUPPLY, AND ADJUSTMENT TO AN INCREASE IN DEMAND

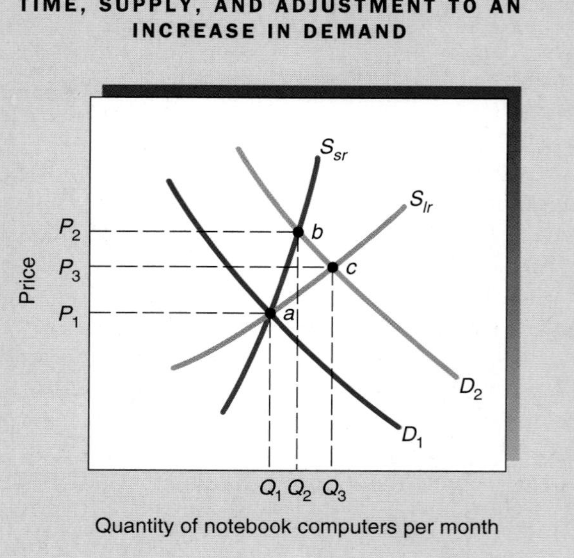

The quantity supplied is generally more responsive to a price change in the long run than in the short run. If the market for notebook computers was initially in equilibrium at P_1 *and* Q_1*, an unexpected increase in demand would push the price of the notebooks up sharply to price* P_2 *(moved from* a *to* b*). Given more time, however, producers will expand output by a larger amount. Therefore, the long-run supply curve will be more responsive to a price change than the short-run curve (*S_{lr} *is flatter than* S_{sr}*). The more responsive supply will place downward pressure on price (moved from* b *to* c*) with the passage of time.*

to supply more notebooks. *With the passage of time,* more resources will be brought into notebook computer production. Some resource prices will have to be bid higher in order to obtain larger quantities. This raises costs, but over time relatively low cost expansion will take place. In the long run the quantity supplied will be more responsive (S_{lr} rather than S_{sr}) and the price increase will be more moderate (P_3 rather than P_2). All these responses will take time, however, even though economists sometimes talk as if the process were instantaneous.

INVISIBLE HAND PRINCIPLE

More than 200 years ago, Adam Smith, the father of economics, stressed that personal self-interest *when directed by the market prices* is a powerful force promoting economic progress. In a famous passage in his *Wealth of Nations,* Smith put it this way:

> Every individual is continually exerting himself to find out the most advantageous employment for whatever capital [income] he can command. It is his own advantage, indeed, and not that of the society which he has in view. But the study of his own advantage naturally, or rather necessarily, leads him to prefer that employment which is most advantageous to society. . . . He intends only his own gain, and he is in this, as in many other cases, led by an invisible hand to promote an end which was not part of his intention. By pursuing his own interest he frequently promotes that of the society more effectually than when he really intends to promote it.[6]

Using the terminology employed by Smith, economists refer to the tendency of competitive markets to direct the actions of self-interested individuals and bring them into harmony with the general welfare (economic progress) as the **invisible hand principle.** Smith's major point was that market prices are able to harness self-interest and put it to work for the benefit of society. Is this really true? Next time you sit down to have a nice dinner, think about all the people who help make it possible. It is unlikely that any of them, from the farmer to the truck driver to the grocer, was motivated by a concern that you have an enjoyable meal. Market prices, however, bring their interest into harmony with yours. Farmers who raise the best beef or turkeys receive higher prices; truck drivers and grocers earn more money if their products are delivered fresh and in good condition; and so on. Let us now take a closer look at how the invisible hand of market prices brings the interests of individuals into harmony with economic progress.

Invisible hand principle
The tendency of market prices to direct individuals pursuing their own interests into productive activities that also promote the economic well-being of the society.

COMMUNICATING INFORMATION TO DECISION MAKERS

Communication of information is one of the most important functions of markets. Markets register information reflecting the choices of consumers, producers, and resource suppliers and tabulate it into a summary statistic called the *market price.* This statistic provides decision makers with valuable information that would be difficult to obtain by any other means. For example, suppose that a drought in Colombia severely reduced the supply of coffee. To ration this reduced supply necessitates that individuals reduce their consumption of coffee. One possibility is to have bulletins on radio and television telling people about the necessity to reduce consumption. However, the information role played by market prices accomplishes this automatically without individuals even knowing about the situation in Colombia. Consumers will see higher

[6]Adam Smith, *An Inquiry into the Nature and Causes of the Wealth of Nations* (New York: Modern Library, 1937), p. 423.

prices for coffee and, even if they have no idea why the prices have changed, they will respond by cutting back on their consumption of coffee.

On the production side, market prices communicate up-to-date information about consumers' valuation of additional units of each commodity. Higher prices signal to producers that the commodity is now more highly valued and encourage producers to expand production. Lower prices signal a reduced desire for the commodity and encourage resources to flow away from the production of such goods into the production of others that are valued more highly relative to their cost. A farmer deciding on the allocation of land between, say, planting corn or green beans would ideally make the decision based upon how intensively consumers want each of the products. Market prices direct the farmer to do just that. When there is a strong demand for corn and therefore its price is relatively high, farmers will plant more corn and fewer green beans. Conversely, if something happened that lowered the demand for and price of corn, farmers will devote less land to corn and more to green beans. Farmers do not need to know how or why consumers decide what to buy. Market prices convey all the information needed for farmers (and other sellers) to make wise decisions.

Market prices also communicate important information about the usage of inputs in the production process. The cost of production, driven by the opportunity cost of resources, tells the business decision maker the relative importance others place on factors of production (for example, skill categories of labor, natural resources, and machinery). A boom in the housing market might cause lumber prices to rise. In turn, furniture makers seeing these higher prices will turn to substitute raw materials such as metal and plastic. Because of market prices, furniture makers will conserve on their usage of lumber, just as if they had known that lumber was now more urgently needed for constructing new housing.

Coordinating Actions of Market Participants

Market prices also coordinate the choices of buyers and sellers, bringing their decisions into line with each other. Excess supply will lead to falling prices, discouraging production and encouraging consumption until the excess supply is eliminated. Alternatively, excess demand will lead to price increases, encouraging consumers to economize on their uses of the good and encouraging suppliers to produce more of it, eliminating the excess demand and bringing the choices of market participants into harmony.

Suppose that farmers produce too few potatoes relative to the desire of consumers. This would lead to higher potato prices. Temporarily, the higher potato prices would discourage consumers from using as many, helping to keep their consumption in balance with the level of production. On the supply side, the higher potato prices would make it more profitable to plant potatoes. In the future, more potatoes will be planted and harvested. Market prices induce responses on both sides of the market in the proper direction to help correct the situation.

The combination of product and resource prices will determine profit (and loss) rates for alternative projects and thereby direct entrepreneurs to undertake the production projects that consumers value most intensely (relative to their cost). If consumers really want more of a good—for example, luxury apartments—the intensity of their demand will lead to a market price that exceeds the opportunity cost of constructing the apartments. The profitable opportunity thus created will soon be discovered by entrepreneurs who will undertake the construction, expanding the availability of the apartments. In contrast, if consumers want less of a good—large cars, for example—the opportunity cost of supplying such cars will exceed the sales revenue from their production, penalizing those who undertake such unprofitable production.

An understanding of the importance of the entrepreneur also sheds light on the market-adjustment process. Since the future is not fully predictable, and information is imperfect, the move toward equilibrium will typically be a groping process. With time, however, successful entrepreneurial activity will be more clearly identified. Successful methods will be copied by other producers. Learning-by-doing and trial-and-error will help producers sort out attractive projects from "losers." The process, though, will never quite be complete. By the time entrepreneurs discover one intensely desired product (or a new, more efficient production technique), change will have occurred elsewhere, creating other unrealized profitable opportunities. The wheels of dynamic change never stop.

Motivating Economic Players

As many leaders of centrally planned economies discovered, people must be motivated to act before production plans can be realized. Market prices establish a reward-penalty (profit-loss) structure that induces participants to work, cooperate with others, use efficient production methods, supply goods that are intensely desired by others, and invest for the future.

No government agency needs to tell business decision makers to use resources wisely (minimize per-unit cost) or to produce those goods intensely desired by consumers. Self-interest and the pursuit of profit will do these jobs. Self-interested entrepreneurs will seek to produce those goods, and only those goods, that consumers value enough to pay a price that is sufficient to cover their costs. Self-interest will also encourage producers to use efficient production methods and adopt cost-saving technologies because lower costs will mean greater profits. Firms that fail to do so, as even giant firms have learned, will be unable to compete successfully in the marketplace.

Similarly, no one has to tell resource suppliers to invest and develop productive resources. Why are many young people willing to undertake the necessary work, stress, late hours of study, and financial cost to acquire a medical or law degree, or an advanced degree in economics, physics, or business administration? Why do others seek to master a skill requiring an apprentice program? Why do individuals save to buy businesses, machines, and other capital assets? The expectation of financial reward is not the only factor, but it is an important stimulus, providing motivation to work, create, develop skills, and supply capital assets to those productive activities most desired by others.

Remember, when you sell something in the market, whether it be a product, a home, or your labor services, the price you will receive is determined by how much other people value what you are selling. To get the most from the sale, you must figure out the best way to provide the most value to potential buyers. The same incentive that motivates sellers to fix up homes before selling them, motivates workers to invest in an education in a field valued by others.

Prices and Market Order

At the beginning of this chapter, we asked you to reflect on why the grocery stores in your local community have approximately the right amount of milk, bread, vegetables, and other goods—an amount sufficiently large that the goods are nearly always available but not so large that spoilage and waste are a problem. We might also reflect on other products. How is it that refrigerators, automobiles, and VCRs, produced at diverse places around the world, are supplied in the U.S. market in approximately the same amount that they are demanded by consumers? The answer is that the invisible hand of market prices directs self-interested individuals into cooperative action and brings their choices into harmony.

The invisible hand principle is difficult for many people to grasp because there is a natural tendency to associate order with central direction. Surely some central authority must be in charge. But this is not the case. ***The pricing system, reflecting the choices of literally millions of consumers, producers, and resource owners, is providing the direction.*** The market process works so automatically that most give little thought to it. They simply take it for granted that the goods most people value will be produced in approximately the quantities that consumers want to purchase.

Perhaps an illustration will enhance your understanding of both the operation and importance of the invisible hand principle. Visualize a busy limited-access highway with four lanes of traffic moving in each direction. No central planning agency assigns lanes and directs traffic. No one tells drivers when to shift to the right, middle, or left lane. Drivers are left to choose for themselves. Nonetheless, they do not all try to drive in the same lane. Why? Drivers are alert for adjustment opportunities that offer personal gain. When traffic in a lane slows due to congestion, some drivers will shift to other lanes and thereby smooth out the flow of traffic among the lanes. Even though central planning is absent, this process of mutual adjustments by the individual drivers results in order and social cooperation. In fact, the degree of social cooperation is generally well beyond what could be achieved if central coordination were attempted—if, for example, each vehicle were assigned a lane. Drivers acting in their own interests and switching to less congested lanes promote the most orderly and quickest flow of traffic for everyone.

Market participation is a lot like driving on the freeway. Success is dependent upon one's ability to act on opportunities. Like the amount of traffic in a lane, profits and losses provide market participants with information concerning the advantages and disadvantages of alternative economic activities. Losses indicate that an economic activity is congested, and, as a result, producers are unable to cover their costs. Successful market participants will shift their resources away from such activities toward other, more valuable uses. Conversely, profits are indicative of an open lane, the opportunity to experience gain if one shifts into an activity where price is currently high relative to per-unit cost. As producers and resource suppliers shift away from activities characterized by congestion and into those characterized by the opportunity for gain (profit), they smooth out economic activity and enhance its flow. Order is the result, even though central planning is absent. This coordination brought about by market prices is precisely what Adam Smith was referring to when he spoke of the "invisible hand" more than 200 years ago.

Qualifications

As we noted at the beginning, the focus of this chapter was the operation of markets where rival firms are free to enter and compete and where property rights are clearly defined and secure. ***The efficiency of market organization is dependent on (1) competitive markets and (2) well-defined private property rights.*** Competition, the great regulator, can protect both buyer and seller. The presence (or possible entry) of independent alternative suppliers protects the consumer against a seller who seeks to charge prices substantially above the cost of production. The existence of alternative resource suppliers protects the producer against a supplier who might otherwise be tempted to withhold a vital resource unless granted exorbitant compensation. The existence of alternative employment opportunities protects the employee from the power of any single employer. Competition can equalize the bargaining power between buyers and sellers.

Understanding the information, coordination, and motivation results of the market mechanism helps us see all the more clearly the importance of property rights, the things actually traded in markets. Property rights force resource users—including users who own the resources—to bear fully the opportunity cost of their actions, and prohibit persons from engaging in destructive forms of competition. When property rights are well defined, secure, and tradeable, suppliers of goods and services will be required to pay resource owners the opportunity cost of each resource employed. They will not be permitted to seize and use scarce resources without compensating the owners—that is, without bidding the resources away from alternative users. Neither will they be permitted to use violence (for example, to attack or invade the property of another) as a means to achieve an economic objective.

LOOKING *Ahead*

Although we incorporated numerous examples designed to enhance your understanding of the supply-and-demand model throughout this chapter, we have only touched the surface. In various modified forms, this model is the central tool of economics. The following chapter will explore several specific applications and extensions of this important model.

KEY POINTS

➤ The law of demand states that there will be an inverse relationship between the price of a good and the amount consumers will want to purchase. The height of the demand curve at any quantity shows the maximum price that consumers are willing to pay for that unit.

➤ The degree of responsiveness of consumer purchases to a change in price is shown by the steepness of the demand curve. The more (less) responsive buyers are to a change in price, the flatter (steeper) the demand curve.

➤ A movement along a demand curve is called a change in quantity demanded. A shift of the entire curve is called a change in demand. A change in *quantity demanded* is caused by a change in the price of the good. A change in *demand* can be caused by several factors, such as a change in consumer income or a change in the price of a closely related good.

➤ The opportunity cost of producing a good is equal to the cost of bidding the resources required for the production of the good away from their alternative uses. Profit indicates that the producer has increased the value of the resources used, while a loss indicates that the producer has reduced the value of the resources.

➤ The law of supply states that there is a direct relationship between the price of a product and the amount supplied. An increase in the price of a product will induce established firms to expand their output and new firms to enter the market.

➤ A change in the price of a good will cause a change in *quantity supplied,* a movement along a single supply curve. A change in *supply* is a shift in the curve caused by other factors, such as a change in the price of resources or a technological improvement.

➤ The responsiveness of supply to a change in price is shown by the steepness of the supply curve. The more willing producers are to alter the quantity supplied in response to a change in price, the more elastic (flatter) the supply curve. The supply curve for most products is more elastic in the long run than in the short run.

➤ Market prices will bring the conflicting forces of supply and demand into balance. There is an automatic tendency for prices to bring about an equilibrium where quantity demanded equals quantity supplied.

➤ Consumer surplus represents the net gain to buyers from market trade, while producer surplus represents the net gain to producers and resource suppliers. In equilibrium, competitive markets maximize these gains, a condition known as economic efficiency.

➤ Changes in the prices of goods are caused by changes in supply and demand. An increase (decrease) in demand will cause prices to rise (fall) and quantity supplied to increase (decline). An increase (decrease) in supply will cause prices to fall (rise) and quantity demanded to expand (decline).

➤ Market prices communicate information, coordinate the actions of buyers and sellers, and provide the incentive structure that motivates decision makers to act. As Adam Smith noted long ago, market prices are generally able to bring the personal self-interest of individuals into harmony with the general welfare (the invisible hand principle). The efficiency of the system is dependent on (1) competitive market conditions and (2) securely defined private property rights.

CRITICAL ANALYSIS QUESTIONS

*1. Which of the following do you think would lead to an increase in the current demand for beef?
a. higher pork prices
b. higher incomes
c. higher prices of feed grains used to feed cattle
d. good weather conditions leading to a bumper (very good) corn crop
e. .an increase in the price of beef

2. What is being held constant when a demand curve for a specific product (like shoes or apples, for example) is constructed? Explain why the demand curve for a product slopes downward to the right.

3. What is the law of supply? How many of the following "goods" do you think conform to the general law of supply? Explain your answer in each case.
a. gasoline
b. cheating on exams
c. political favors from legislators
d. the services of heart specialists
e. children
f. legal divorces
g. the services of a minister

*4. A drought during the summer of 1988 sharply reduced the 1988 output of wheat, corn, soybeans, and hay. Indicate the expected impact of the drought on the following:
a. Prices of feed grains and hay during the summer of 1988
b. Price of cattle during the summer and fall of 1988
c. Price of cattle during the summer and fall of 1989

5. What is being held constant when the supply curve is constructed? Explain why the supply curve slopes upward to the right.

6. Define consumer and producer surplus. What is meant by economic efficiency, and how does it relate to consumer and producer surplus?

7. Recent tax reforms make college tuition partially tax deductible for certain families. This should lead to more people wishing to attend college (a higher demand for a college education). How will this affect tuition prices? How will this affect the cost of college to families who do not qualify for the tax deduction?

*8. "The future of our industrial strength cannot be left to chance. Somebody has to develop notions about which industries are winners and which are losers." Is this statement by a newspaper columnist true? Who is the "somebody"?

9. What role does time play in the market adjustment process? Explain why the response of both consumers and producers to a change in price will be greater in the long run than in the short run.

*10. Production should be for people and not for profit." Answer the following questions concerning this statement:
a. If production is profitable, are people helped or hurt? Explain.
b. Are people helped more if production results in a loss than if it leads to profit? Is there a conflict between production for people and production for profit?

11. What is the opportunity cost of production? What does it tell us about the value of other goods that could have been made with the resources? Within this context, define profit and loss.

*12. Suppose a drought destroyed half the wheat crop in France. What is the expected impact on the market price of wheat in France?

13. **What's Wrong with This Way of Thinking?** "Economists claim that when the price of something goes up, producers bring more of it to the market. But the last year in which the price was really high for oranges, there were not nearly as many oranges as usual. The economists are wrong!"

14. What is the *invisible hand principle?* Does it indicate that "good intentions" are necessary if one's actions are going to be beneficial to others? What are the necessary conditions for the invisible hand to work well? Why are these conditions important?

*15. A popular California winery, and the restaurant on its grounds, can be reached only by a tram with gondola cars, similar to those used at ski resorts. Suppose the owners are charging $3 to winery visitors and restaurant diners alike, but are thinking about providing "free rides" to diners. Explain how this change would affect the following conditions:

a. The demand for dining at the restaurant
b. The price and quantity of meals served at the restaurant

16. **What's Wrong with This Way of Thinking?** "Economists argue that lower prices will necessarily result in less supply. However, there are exceptions to this rule. For example, in 1970, ten-digit electronic calculators sold for $100. By 1995 the price of the same type of calculator had declined to less than $15. Yet business firms produced and sold five times as many calculators in 1995 as in 1970. Lower prices did not result in less production or in a decline in the number of calculators supplied."

---

*Asterisk denotes questions for which answers are given in Appendix B.

CHAPTER 4

The division of labour, from which so many advantages are derived, is not originally the effect of any human wisdom, which foresees and intends that general opulence to which it gives occasion. It is the necessary, though very slow and gradual consequence of a certain propensity in human nature . . . ; the propensity to truck, barter, and exchange one thing for another.

Adam Smith[1]

Nations stumble upon establishments, which are indeed the result of human action, but not the execution of any human design.

Adam Ferguson[2]

Supply and Demand: Applications and Extensions

CHAPTER FOCUS

- Can wage rates, interest rates, and exchange rates be analyzed within the supply and demand framework?
- What happens when prices are set by law above or below the market equilibrium level?
- How do rent controls affect the maintenance and quality of rental housing? How do minimum wage rates influence the job opportunities of low-skilled workers?
- What are "black markets"? How does the lack of a well-structured legal environment affect their operation?
- How does the imposition of a tax affect a market? What determines the distribution of the tax burden between buyers and sellers?
- What is the Laffer curve? What does it indicate about the relationship between tax rates and tax revenues?

---

[1]Adam Smith, *An Inquiry into the Nature and Causes of the Wealth of Nations* (New York: Modern Library, 1937), p. 13.

[2]Adam Ferguson, *An Essay on the History of Civil Society* (London, 1767), p. 187.

Markets are everywhere. They exist in many different forms and degrees of sophistication. In elementary schools, children trade baseball cards; in households, individuals trade chores ("I'll clean the bathroom if you'll clean the kitchen"); on street corners, people buy and sell illegal drugs or tickets to concerts and sporting events; and in the stock market, individuals who have never met exchange shares of corporate stock and other financial assets worth billions of dollars each business day. Even in the nonmarket-based former Soviet Union, black markets were present where individuals bought and sold goods at market-determined prices.

Markets will exist regardless of whether they are legal or illegal, formal or informal. Why? Trading with other individuals is a natural part of human behavior that exists regardless of legal and societal conditions. As Adam Smith put it more than 200 years ago (see quotation, opening of chapter), human beings have a natural propensity "to truck, barter, and exchange one thing for another." We all want to improve our standard of living, and recognize that trading with other individuals is the primary way we can achieve this goal. Whenever and wherever people trade, there is a market. Markets are a result of human action, not of human design, as Adam Ferguson points out.[3]

In the previous chapter we saw how market prices, determined by supply and demand, work through the invisible hand to coordinate the actions of buyers and sellers. In this chapter we explore several important applications and extensions of supply and demand. We will begin by analyzing interest rates, wage rates, and foreign exchange rates within the context of supply and demand. We will then see how several types of government interventions alter the operation of markets.

WAGE RATES, INTEREST RATES, AND EXCHANGE RATES

As Juliet says to Romeo in William Shakespeare's *Romeo and Juliet,* "What's in a name? That which we call a rose by any other name would smell as sweet." In different markets, different names are sometimes used for price. The price of labor is generally referred to as a *wage rate.* The term *interest rate* is used when referring to the price paid by a borrower or received by a lender of loanable funds. The price of one currency in terms of another is called the *exchange rate.* Despite their different names, they are still prices. Therefore, when analyzing these markets, these special names will be measured along the vertical (or *price*) axis of a supply and demand diagram. In some instances, special names for the quantity traded in the market are used as well. In the labor market, the number of workers holding jobs, or the number of hours they work in aggregate, is called *employment* rather than *quantity.* Although the names have been changed, the forces of supply and demand and the workings of price within the market remain the same.

[3]This theme was a focus of much of the work of Nobel Prize–winning economist Friedrich Hayek.

Linkage between Labor and Product Markets

The production process generally involves (a) the purchase of resources—such things as raw materials, labor services, tools, and the services of machines; (b) transformation of these resources into products (goods and services); and (c) the sale of the goods and services in the product market. Business firms are generally utilized to undertake production. Typically, business firms demand resources—labor services and raw materials, for example—while households supply them. Firms demand resources *because* they contribute to the production of goods and services. In turn, households supply them in order to earn income.

Just as in product markets, the demand curve in a **resource market** is typically downward-sloping and the supply curve upward-sloping. An inverse relationship will exist between the amount of a resource demanded and its price because businesses will substitute away from a resource as its price rises. In contrast, there will be a direct relationship between the amount of a resource supplied and its price because a higher price will make it more attractive to provide the resource. As in the case of consumer goods, prices will coordinate the choices of buyers and sellers in resource markets, bringing the quantity demanded into balance with the quantity supplied.

Resource market
Market for inputs used to produce goods and services.

The labor market is a large and important component of the broader resource market. It is important to note that there is not just one market for labor, but rather many labor markets, one for each different skill-experience-occupational category.

The markets for resources and products are closely linked. Changes in one will also alter conditions in the other. Using the labor market for low-skill, inexperienced workers, **Exhibit 4–1** illustrates this point. Reflecting demographic factors, in many areas the supply of youthful, inexperienced workers has declined in recent years. This reduction in supply has pushed the wages of youthful workers upward (increase from $5.25 to $6.50 in Exhibit 4–1a). The higher price of this resource increases the

EXHIBIT 4–1

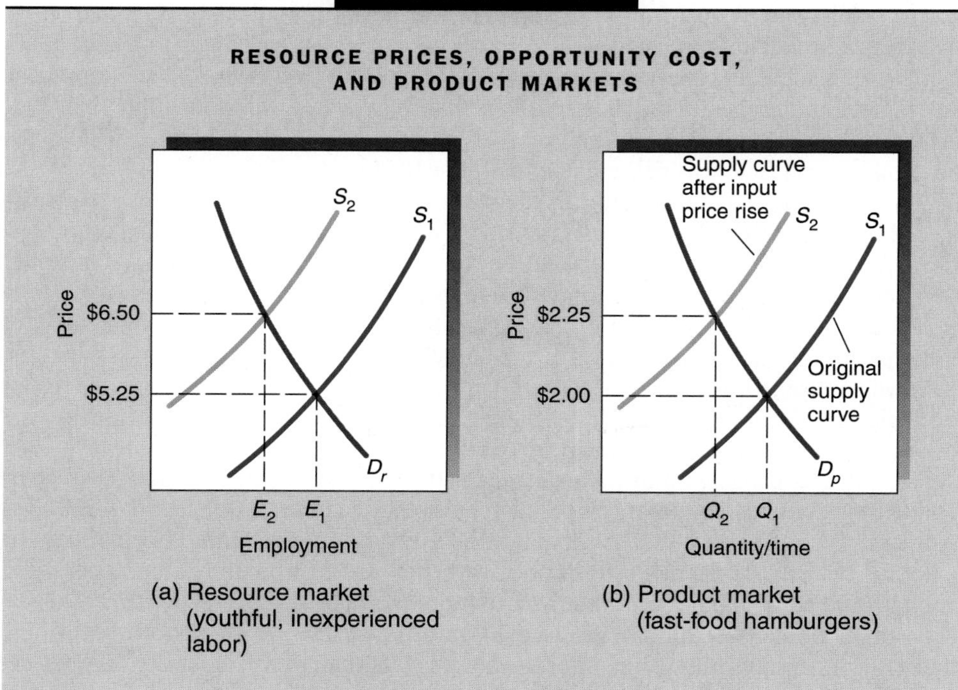

Suppose a reduction in the supply of youthful, inexperienced labor pushes the wage rates of workers hired by fast-food restaurants upward (a). In the product market (b), the higher wage rates will increase the restaurant's opportunity cost, causing a reduction in supply (shift from S_1 *to* S_2*), leading to higher hamburger prices.*

opportunity cost of goods and services the youthful workers help to produce. In turn, the higher cost reduces the supply (shift from S_1 to S_2) of products like hamburgers at McDonald's and other fast-food restaurants, pushing their price upward (Exhibit 4–1b). When the price of a resource increases, it will lead to higher cost, a reduction in supply, and higher prices for the goods and services produced with the resource.

Of course, lower resource prices would exert the opposite effect. A reduction in resource prices will reduce costs and expand the supply (a shift to the right) of consumer goods using the lower-priced resources. The increase in supply will lead to a lower price in the product market.

There is also a close relation between the demand for products and the demand for the resources required for their production. An increase in demand for a consumer good, automobiles for example, will lead to higher auto prices, which will increase the profitability of automakers and provide them with an incentive to expand output. But the expansion in output of automobiles will also increase the demand for and prices of the resources (for example, steel, rubber, plastics, and the labor services of autoworkers) required for the production of automobiles. The higher prices of these resources will cause other industries to conserve on their usage, making it possible for automakers to utilize the additional resources required for the expansion in the output of automobiles.

Of course, the process will work in reverse in the case of a decrease in product demand. A reduction in demand for a product will not only reduce the price of the product but also reduce the demand for and prices of the resources required for its production. As we analyze changes in various markets, we will return to the linkage between product and resource markets again and again.

Loanable Funds Market and the Interest Rate

Loanable funds market
A general term used to describe the broad market that coordinates the borrowing and lending decisions of business firms and households. Commercial banks, savings and loan associations, the stock and bond markets, and insurance companies are important financial institutions in this market.

The **loanable funds market** is highly diverse. Banks, insurance companies, and brokerage firms often act as intermediaries (middlemen) between lenders and borrowers. Bank deposits, bonds, and mutual funds are important financial instruments in this market. In the loanable funds market, borrowers demand the current use of funds in exchange for later repayment, while lenders supply them. As we previously mentioned, the interest rate is the price of loanable funds. To keep things relatively simple, we will assume that there is only a single interest rate. In reality, of course, there is a multitude of interest rates, depending on such factors as risk and length of time the funds are borrowed (or loaned).

The demand and supply curves in this market look like they do in other markets. As part a of **Exhibit 4–2** illustrates, more funds will be borrowed at lower interest rates. A lower interest rate will make it cheaper for households to purchase consumption goods and for businesses to undertake investment projects *during the current period.* Thus, they will borrow more at lower rates, and, as a result, the demand curve for loanable funds will slope downward to the right. On the other hand, lower interest rates will make it less attractive to save (and loan funds). Thus, the supply curve for loanable funds will slope upward to the right, indicating an inverse relationship between the interest rate and the quantity of funds supplied by lenders.

In the loanable funds market, price—the interest rate in this case—will coordinate the actions of borrowers and lenders, just as it coordinates the actions of buyers and sellers in other markets. As Exhibit 4–2a shows, interest rate r_1 will bring the quantity of funds demanded into balance with the quantity supplied. At interest rates greater than r_1, lenders would want to save more than borrowers will demand. This excess supply of loanable funds will place downward pressure on interest rates, pushing them toward equilibrium. If the interest rate was less than r_1, the quantity of funds demanded by borrowers would exceed the quantity supplied by lenders, placing upward

EXHIBIT 4-2

INCREASE IN THE DEMAND FOR LOANABLE FUNDS

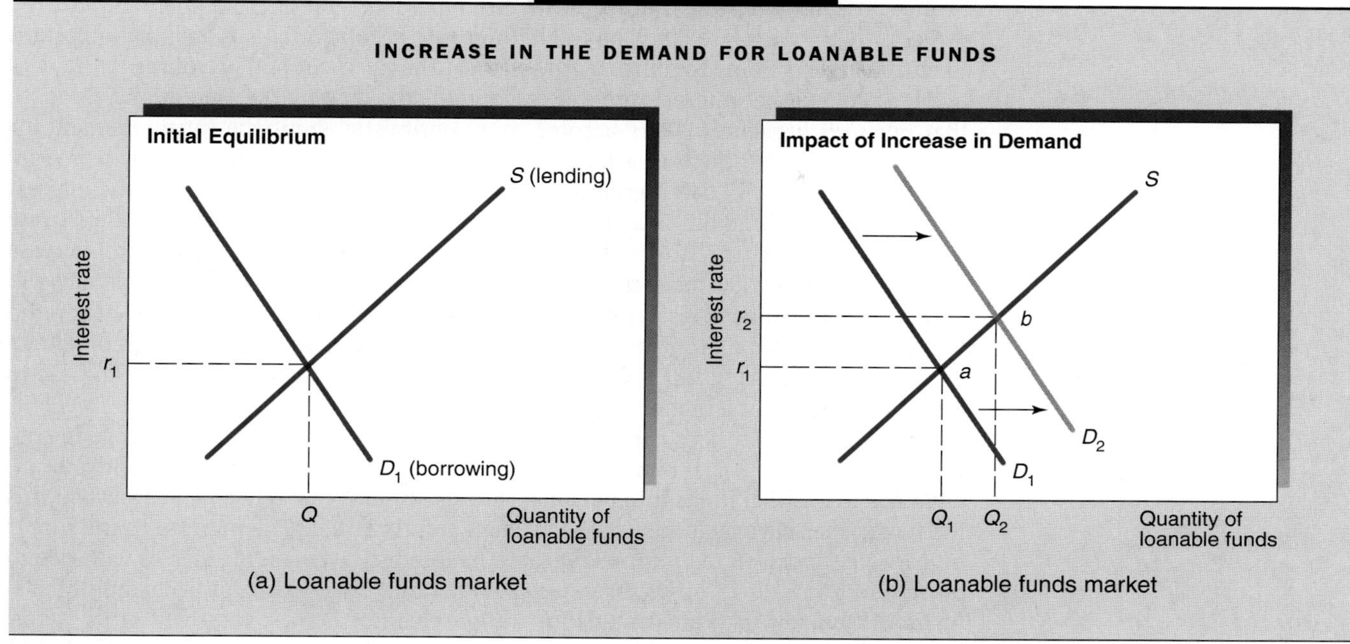

(a) Loanable funds market

(b) Loanable funds market

The interest rates will bring the quantity of loanable funds demanded by borrowers into balance with the quantity supplied by lenders (frame a). An increase in demand for loanable funds will push the interest rate up from r_1 to r_2 (frame b). The higher interest rate will encourage additional savings, making it possible to fund more borrowing.

pressure on the interest rates. Thus, market forces will direct the interest rate toward r_1, the rate that brings the choices of borrowers and lenders into harmony.[4]

The interest rate is vitally important because it connects the price of things today with their price in the future. In essence, it is the price that must be paid for earlier availability. This relative price—the cost of spending today relative to spending in the future—is central to the decision making of both households and businesses. Should you buy a car this year or wait until next year? Should you reduce your current consumption so you can save more? The interest rate helps you evaluate choices like these. An increase in the interest rate will make it more expensive for households to purchase a car, house, vacation, or any other good during the current period rather than waiting until next year or some other time in the future. The interest rate is a primary determinant of how households allocate their income between current consumption of goods and services and savings for future consumption.

The interest rate is also central to the investment choices of business decision makers. At any point in time, there are literally millions of potential investment projects that might be undertaken. However, profit-seeking business decision makers will only want to undertake projects that are expected to yield a rate of return greater than or equal to the interest rate. If a project's rate of return is less than the interest rate, the potential investor would be better off simply putting the funds into a savings account or using them to purchase a bond. The interest rate confronts business

[4]The expectation of inflation will influence the nominal interest rate. This topic will be discussed in a later chapter. For now, when we speak of a change in interest rates, we are referring to a change after adjustment for the effects of inflation.

decision makers with the opportunity cost of funds, providing them with a strong incentive to economize on the use of investment funds and allocate them toward the projects that are expected to yield the highest rate of return. This is a vitally important function if an economy is going to grow and get the most out of its resources.

The market interest rate will respond to changing market conditions. Suppose that business decision makers become more optimistic about the future demand for their product, and therefore seek additional funds to expand the scale of their productive capacity. How will this increase in demand for loanable funds influence the interest rate? As part b of Exhibit 4–2 shows, the stronger demand will push the interest rate up from r_1 to r_2. In turn, the higher interest rate will encourage households to increase their savings (the movement along the supply curve from a to b). The higher rate will also discourage some investors from undertaking marginal projects—ones that are no longer expected to be profitable at the higher rate of interest. This combination of factors—increased saving and reduction in borrowing for marginal projects—will lead to a new equilibrium at a higher interest rate.

Alternatively, let's consider how the market would respond to a change in supply. Suppose that a social security reform is enacted that increases the incentive of individuals to channel funds into personal savings accounts for retirement. How will this inflow of added savings influence the loanable funds market? The increase in the supply of loanable funds will reduce interest rates. As interest rates fall, businesses will wish to borrow more funds in order to undertake additional investment projects, and households will borrow additional funds for the purchase of homes, cars, and other items. The result: At the lower market interest rate, businesses and households will want to borrow the additional savings.

Market for Foreign Exchange

Foreign exchange market
The market in which the currencies of different countries are bought and sold.

The **foreign exchange market** is the market where the currency of one country is traded for the currency of another. Americans demand various foreign currencies so they can buy goods, services, and assets from sellers in these countries. If you were to go on vacation to Mexico, for example, you would want to conduct many transactions in the Mexican currency, the peso. One of your first transactions would be to trade some dollars for pesos in the foreign exchange market. However, even if you purchase a Mexican-made product in the United States, it will generally result in a conversion of dollars to pesos so that the Mexican firm can pay its domestic resource suppliers in pesos.

Although purchases from foreigners underlie the demand for a foreign currency, sales to foreigners give rise to the supply. For example, when an American firm sells lumber to a Japanese purchaser, the Japanese buyer will supply yen to the foreign exchange market in order to acquire the dollars used for the lumber purchase. Thus, the sale of goods, services, and assets to foreigners creates a supply of foreign exchange.

Exchange rate
The price of one unit of foreign currency in terms of the domestic currency. For example, if it takes $1.50 to purchase an English pound, the dollar-pound exchange rate is 1.50.

Using the currency of Guatemala—the quetzal—part a of **Exhibit 4–3** shows how "price," the **exchange rate** between the dollar and the quetzal, is determined in the foreign exchange market. (Note: In order to keep the example simple, we assume that the U.S. and Guatemala only trade with each other.) When the dollar price of the quetzal is low, Guatemalan goods will be cheap for Americans. Therefore, Americans will purchase more Guatemalan goods *and therefore more quetzals* at the lower dollar price of the foreign currency. As a result, the dollar demand for quetzals slopes downward to the right. On the other hand, when the dollar price of the quetzal is high, American-produced goods will be cheap for Guatemalans, which will induce them to buy more American goods. Thus, at the higher dollar price of quetzals, American sales to Guatemalans will be greater. As a result, the supply curve for the quetzal will slope upward to the right. The exchange rate will tend to move toward the equilibrium price

EXHIBIT 4–3

INCREASE IN DEMAND FOR FOREIGN EXCHANGE

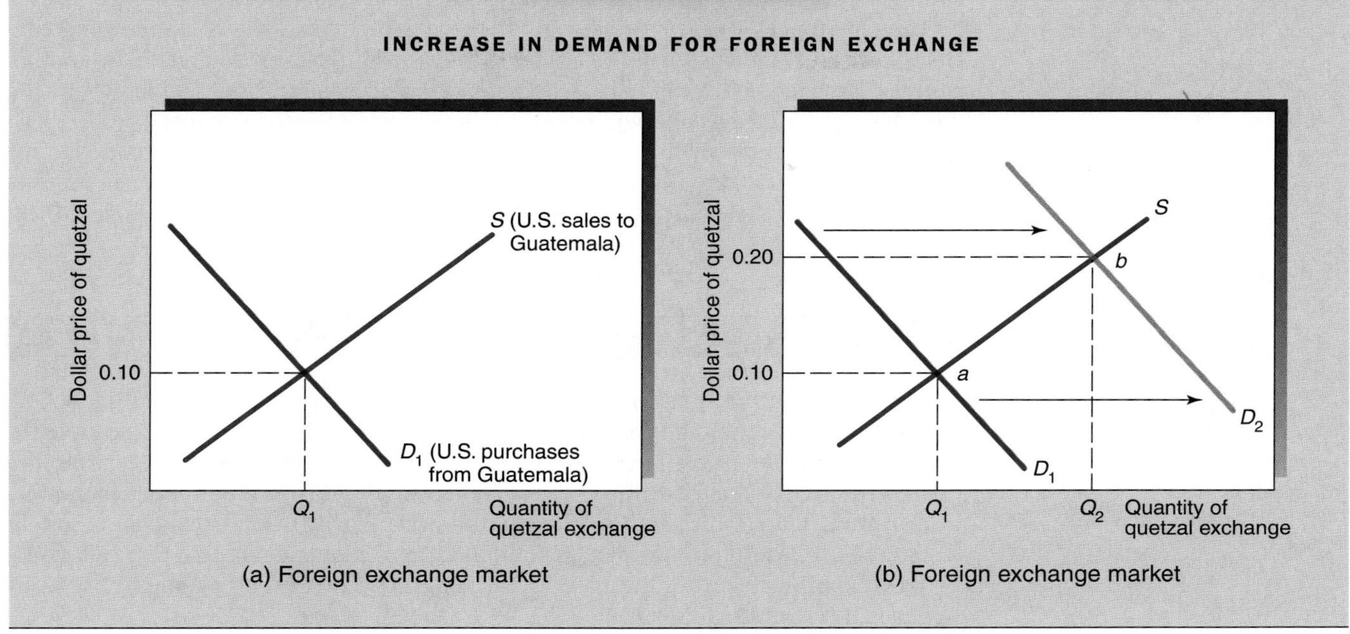

(a) Foreign exchange market

(b) Foreign exchange market

Initially, when the dollar price of the Guatemalan quetzal is $0.10 (10 US cents = 1 quetzal), equilibrium is present in this foreign exchange market (frame a). An increase in the demand of Americans for Guatemalan coffee will also increase the demand for the quetzal. As a result, the dollar price of the quetzal will rise (frame b).

of $0.10 (10 US cents = 1 quetzal), which will bring the quantity demanded of quetzals into equality with the quantity supplied.

Suppose that U.S. citizens suddenly increased their desire for Guatemalan coffee. How will this affect the dollar-quetzal exchange rate? Because every purchase of Guatemalan coffee generates a demand for quetzals, the increase in coffee purchases will increase the demand for quetzals. As part b of Exhibit 4–3 shows, this increase in demand will cause the dollar price of the quetzal to rise to $0.20 (20 cents). How will this affect the cost to a Guatemalan citizen of purchasing a product made in the United States? To answer this, we must first express the exchange rate from the perspective of a Guatemalan citizen. Prior to this change, one quetzal was equal to 10 U.S. cents. Thus, it took 10 quetzals to buy one U.S. dollar. After the dollar price of the quetzal increased to 20 U.S. cents, one U.S. dollar could be purchased for only 5 quetzals. Thus, a U.S.-made product that sells for a price of $100 used to cost the Guatemalan citizen 1,000 quetzals. At the new exchange rate, however, the price of the $100 product has fallen to 500 quetzals. The lower price means that Guatemalan citizens will purchase more American-made products. Thus, the higher U.S. demand for Guatemalan coffee, which results in more imports from Guatemala, will also encourage American exports to Guatemala.

Changes in the exchange rate are vitally important because they alter the prices of all goods, services, and assets that are traded in international markets. They also provide business decision makers with information that will help them compare purchase prices and production costs across countries. Should a business choose to produce output in Mexico, Thailand, the United States, or some other country? Wage rates for most types of labor are likely to be lower in Mexico and Thailand than in the

United States. However, there are several disadvantages of locating a plant in another country. If the good is going to be sold in the United States, transportation costs will probably be higher if it is produced in another country. The risks accompanying contract violations and insecurity of property rights are likely to be greater in another country. Exchange rates will help businesses analyze cost advantages and disadvantages like these. As we proceed, we will return to these topics and related issues.

We have shown how market prices, from wage rates to interest rates to exchange rates, coordinate the actions of buyers and sellers. What would happen if prices were fixed either below or above the market equilibrium? We will now turn to this question.

THE ECONOMICS OF PRICE CONTROLS

Buyers often believe that prices are too high, while sellers complain that they are too low. Unhappy with prices established by market forces, various groups may seek to have the government set the prices of certain products. Government-mandated prices are called **price controls.** They may be either price ceilings, which set a maximum price for a product, or price floors, which impose a minimum price. Fixing prices seems like a simple, straightforward solution. However, do not forget the phenomenon of secondary effects.

Price controls
Government-mandated prices; they may be either greater or less than the market equilibrium price.

PRICE CEILINGS

A **price ceiling** is a legal restriction that prohibits exchanges at prices greater than a designated price—the ceiling price. When imposed below the market equilibrium, the price ceiling will alter the operation of the market. **Exhibit 4–4** illustrates the impact of fixing a price of a product below its equilibrium level. Of course, the price ceiling does result in a lower price than market forces would produce, at least in the short run. At the lower price, however, the quantity that producers are willing to supply decreases,

Price ceiling
A legally established maximum price that sellers may charge for a good or resource.

EXHIBIT 4–4

THE IMPACT OF A PRICE CEILING

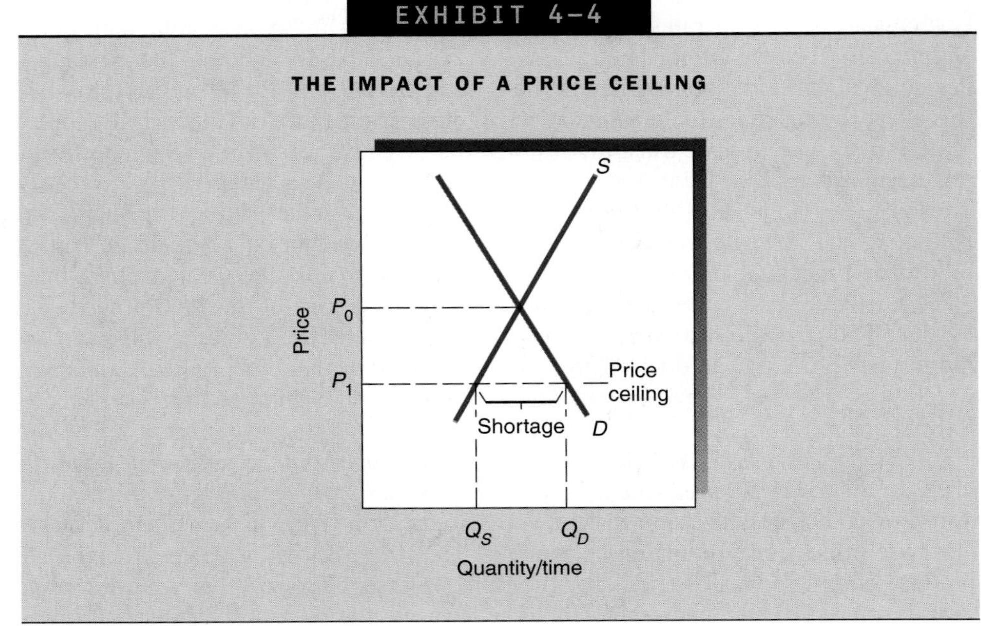

When a price ceiling like P_1 pushes the price of a product (rental housing, for example) below the market equilibrium, a shortage will develop. Because prices are not allowed to direct the market to equilibrium, nonprice elements will become more important. Given the shortage, the nonprice factors will change in ways favorable to sellers.

while the quantity that consumers would like to purchase increases. A **shortage** (Q_D—Q_S) of the good will result, a situation in which the quantity demanded by consumers exceeds the quantity supplied by producers *at the existing price.* After the imposition of the price ceiling, the quantity of the good exchanged declines and the gains from trade fall as well.

Shortage
A condition in which the amount of a good offered for sale by producers is less than the amount demanded by buyers at the existing price. An increase in price would eliminate the shortage.

Normally, the higher price would ration the good to the buyers most willing to pay for it. Because the price ceiling keeps this from happening, other means must be used to allocate the smaller quantity Q_s among consumers seeking to purchase Q_d. Predictably, nonprice factors will become more important in the rationing process. Producers must discriminate on some basis other than willingness to pay as they ration their sales to eager buyers. Sellers will be partial to friends, to buyers who do them favors, and even to buyers who are willing to make illegal "under-the-table" payments. (The accompanying Applications in Economics box, "The Imposition of Price Ceilings during Hurricane Hugo," highlights this point.) Time may also be used as the rationing device, with those willing to wait in line the longest being the ones able to purchase the good. In addition, the below-equilibrium price reduces the incentive of sellers to expand the future supply of the good. With the passage of time, the shortage conditions will worsen. At the lower price, suppliers will direct resources away from production of this commodity and into other, more profitable areas.

What other secondary effects can we expect? ***In the real world, there are two ways that sellers can raise prices. First, they can raise their money price, holding quality constant. Or, second, they can hold the money price constant while reducing the quality of the good.*** (The latter could include a reduction in the size of the product, such as a decline in the size of a candy bar or loaf of bread.) Confronting a price ceiling, sellers will rely on the latter method of raising prices. Rather than do without the good, some buyers will accept the lower-quality product. It is not easy to repeal the laws of supply and demand.

It is important to note that a shortage is not the same as scarcity. ***Scarcity is inescapable.*** Scarcity exists whenever people want more of a good than nature has provided. This means, of course, that almost everything of value is scarce. ***Shortages, on the other hand, are avoidable if prices are permitted to rise.*** A higher, unfixed price (P_0 rather than P_1 in Exhibit 4–4) would stimulate additional production, discourage consumption, and increase the incentive of entrepreneurs to search for and develop substitute goods. This combination of forces would eliminate the shortage.

Rent Control: A Closer Look at a Price Ceiling

Over 200 American cities maintain rent controls, intended to protect residents from high housing prices. Rent controls are a price ceiling. When they push the price of rental housing below the equilibrium level, the amount of rental housing demanded by consumers will exceed the amount landlords will make available. Initially, if the mandated price is only slightly below equilibrium, the impact of rent controls may be barely noticeable. With the passage of time, however, their effects will grow. Inevitably, rent controls will lead to the following results.

1. Shortages and black markets will develop. Since the quantity of housing demanded will exceed the quantity supplied, some persons who value rental housing highly will be unable to find it. Frustrated by the shortage, they will seek methods by which they may induce landlords to rent to them. Some will agree to prepay their rent, including a substantial damage deposit. Others might agree to rent or buy the landlords' furniture at exorbitant prices in order to obtain an apartment. Still others will make under-the-table (black market) payments to secure the cheap housing.

APPLICATIONS IN ECONOMICS

The Imposition of Price Ceilings during Hurricane Hugo

In the fall of 1989 Hurricane Hugo struck the coast of South Carolina, causing massive property damage and widespread power outages lasting for weeks. The lack of electric power meant that gasoline pumps, refrigerators, cash registers, ATM machines, and many other types of electrical equipment did not work. In the hardest hit coastal areas, such as Charleston, the demand for such items as lumber, gasoline, ice, batteries, chain saws, and electric generators increased dramatically. A bag of ice that sold for $1 before the hurricane went up in price to as much as $10, the price of plywood rose to about $200 per sheet, chain saws soared to the $600 range, and gasoline sold for as much as $10.95 per gallon. At these higher prices, individual citizens from other states were renting trucks, buying supplies in their home state, driving them to Charleston, and making enough money to pay for the rental truck and the purchase of the goods and to compensate them for taking time off from their regular jobs.

In response to consumer complaints of "price gouging," the mayor of Charleston signed emergency legislation making it a crime, punishable by up to 30 days in jail and a $200 fine, to sell goods at prices higher than their pre-hurricane levels in the city. The price ceilings kept prices down, but also stopped the flow of goods into the area almost immediately. Shippers of items such as ice would stop outside the harder-hit Charleston area, to avoid the price controls, and sell their goods. Shipments that did make it into the Charleston area were often greeted by long lines of consumers, many of whom would end up without goods after waiting in line for up to five hours. Some of the lucky people who got these items would then drive them back out of the city to sell them at the higher, noncontrolled prices. Shortages became so bad that military guards were required to protect shipments of the goods and maintain order when a shipment did arrive.

The price controls resulted in serious misallocations of resources. Grocery stores could not open because of the lack of electric power; inside the stores, food items were spoiling—thousands of dollars' worth, in some stores. Gasoline pumps require electricity to operate, so, although there was fuel in the underground tanks, there was a shortage of gasoline because of the inability to pump it. Consumers were faced with problems of obtaining money, as ATM machines and banks could not operate without electric power. Hardware stores that sold gasoline-powered electric generators before the hurricane typically had only a few in stock, but suddenly hundreds of businesses and residents wanted to buy them. In the absence of price controls, these generators would have risen to thousands of dollars in price. Individual homeowners would have been outbid by businesses who could have put the generators to use in opening stores and gasoline stations and operating ATM machines. It would have been these uses that could have generated enough revenue to cover the high price of the generators. Individuals who had generators at home would have even found it in their interest to sell them to businesses for the high sum of money involved.

However, the price ceilings prevented prices from allocating these generators to those most willing to pay. Instead, individuals kept their generators, and it was commonplace for hardware store owners who had a few generators on hand to take one home for their family, and then sell the others to their close friends, neighbors, and relatives. In the absence of price rationing, these nonprice factors played a larger role in the allocation process. While these families used the generators for household uses (such as running television sets, lighting, electric razors, and hair dryers), gasoline stations, grocery stores, and banks were closed because of their inability to purchase generators. Thousands of consumers could not get goods they urgently wanted because these businesses were closed. In addition, the flow of new generators into the city effectively ceased, and some were being taken from the city to the less-damaged outlying areas to be sold at higher (noncontrolled) prices. Without price controls, the price of generators would have been bid up to the point where they would be (1) purchased by those who had the most urgent uses for them, and (2) imported into the city fairly rapidly because of the high prices they commanded.

The secondary impacts of the price controls used during Hurricane Hugo in Charleston, South Carolina, highlight the importance of understanding economics and the role of prices in our economy. It is during emergency times such as this, when major reallocations of goods and resources are needed, that reliance on market-determined prices is of most importance. Despite pleas from economists in local newspapers and in the *Wall Street Journal,* the price controls remained in effect, increasing the suffering and retarding the recovery of the areas most severely damaged by the hurricane.[1]

[1]See David N. Leband, "In Hugo's Path, a Man-Made Disaster," *Wall Street Journal,* September 27, 1989, p. A22; and Tim Smith, "Economists Spurn Price Restrictions," *Greenville News,* September 28, 1989, p. C1.

2. The future supply of rental houses will decline. The below-equilibrium price will discourage entrepreneurs from constructing new rental housing units. Private investment will flow elsewhere, since the controls have depressed the rate of return in the rental housing market. In the city of Berkeley, rental units available to students of the University of California reportedly dropped 31 percent in the first five years after the city adopted rent controls in 1978.[5]

3. The quality of rental housing will deteriorate. Economic thinking suggests that there are two ways to raise prices. The nominal price can be increased, quality being held constant. Alternatively, quality can be reduced, while the nominal price is maintained. When landlords are prohibited from adopting the former, they will use the latter. Normal maintenance and repair service will deteriorate. Tenant parking lots will be eliminated (or rented). Eventually, the quality of the rental housing will reflect the controlled price. Cheap housing will be of cheap quality.

4. Nonprice methods of rationing will increase in importance. Because price is no longer allowed to play its normal role, other forms of competition will develop. Prohibited from price rationing, landlords will have to rely more heavily on nonmonetary discriminating devices. They will favor friends, persons of influence, and those with lifestyles similar to their own. In contrast, applicants with many children or unconventional lifestyles, and perhaps racial minorities will find fewer landlords who will rent to them. Since the cost to landlords of discriminating against those with characteristics they do not like has been reduced, such discrimination will become more prevalent in the rationing process.

5. Inefficient use of housing space will result. The tenant in a rent-controlled apartment will think twice before moving. Why? Even though the tenant might want a larger or smaller space or might want to move closer to work, he or she will be less likely to move because it is much more difficult to find a vacancy if rent control ordinances are in effect. Turnover will be lower, and many will find themselves in locations and in apartments not well-suited to their needs. In a college town, apartments will end up being rented too heavily to students whose parents live locally (at the cheaper rent they will be less likely to remain living at home and also their parents will have the best connections to local landlords), while students from farther away, to whom the apartments would be better allocated, will find it harder to find a place to rent.

6. Long-term renters will benefit at the expense of newcomers. People who stay for lengthy periods in the same apartment often pay rents substantially below market value (because the controls restrict rent increases), while newcomers are forced to pay exorbitant prices for units sublet from tenants or for the limited supply of unrestricted units—typically newly constructed and thus temporarily exempted. Distortions and inequities result. A book on housing and the homeless by William Tucker reports several examples, such as "actress Ann Turkel, who paid $2,350 per month for a seven-room, four-and-a-half bathroom duplex on the East Side (of New York City). . . . Identical apartments in the building were subletting for $6,500."[6] Turkel had been spending only two months each year in New York. "Former mayor Edward Koch . . . pays

[5]William Tucker, *The Excluded Americans* (Washington, D.C.: Regnery Gateway, 1990), p. 162. For a more detailed exposition on rent controls, see Walter Block, "Rent Controls," in *Fortune Encyclopedia of Economics,* ed. David Henderson (New York: Warner Books, 1993).

[6]Tucker, *The Excluded Americans,* p. 248.

Rent controls lead to shortages, poor maintenance, and deterioration in the quality of renting housing.

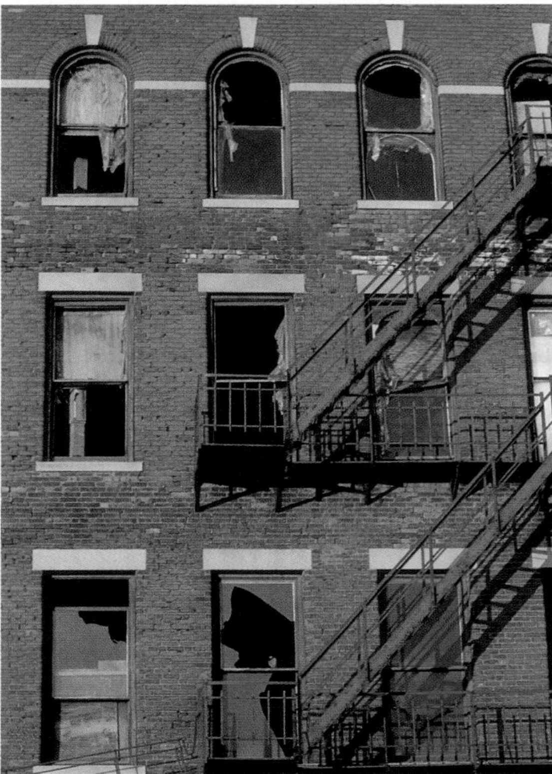

$441.49 a month for a large, one-bedroom apartment . . . that would probably be worth $1,200 in an unregulated market. Koch kept the apartment the entire twelve years he lived in Gracie Mansion (the official mayor's residence)." Tucker uses these and many other such cases to illustrate the distortions brought on by the control of rental prices.

Imposition of rent controls may look like a simple method of dealing with high housing prices. However, the analysis of price ceilings and the experiences where they have been imposed indicate that they cause other problems, including a decline in the supply of rental housing, poor maintenance, and shortages. In the words of Swedish economist Assar Lindbeck: "In many cases rent control appears to be the most efficient technique presently known to destroy a city—except for bombing."[7] Though this may overstate the case somewhat, Lindbeck's point is well taken.

Price Floors

Price floor
A legally established minimum price that buyers must pay for a good or resource.

Surplus
A condition in which the amount of a good offered for sale by producers is greater than the amount that buyers will purchase at the existing price. A decline in price would eliminate the surplus.

While price ceilings set a maximum price, **price floors** establish a minimum price that can legally be charged. **Exhibit 4–5** illustrates the case of a price floor, which fixes the price of a good or resource above the market equilibrium level. At the higher price, sellers will want to bring a larger amount to the market, while buyers will choose to buy less of the good. A **surplus** (Q_S—Q_D) will result. As in the case of the price ceiling, nonprice factors will play a larger role in the rationing process because the price control stifles the normal function of prices. But, because there is a surplus rather than a

[7]Assar Lindbeck, *The Political Economy of the New Left* (New York: Harper and Row, 1972), p. 39.

EXHIBIT 4–5

THE IMPACT OF A PRICE FLOOR

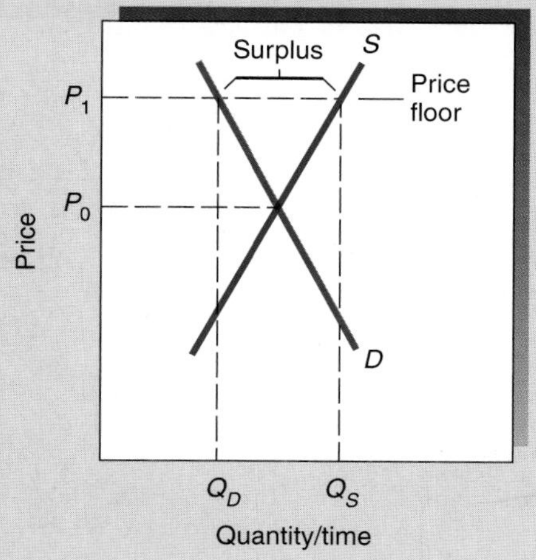

When a price floor like P_1 keeps the price of a good or service above the market equilibrium, a surplus will result. The surplus will cause the nonprice elements of exchange to change in ways favorable to buyers.

shortage, this time it is buyers who will be in a position to be more selective. Buyers can be expected to seek out sellers willing to offer them favors (better service, discounts on other products, or easier credit, for example). Some sellers may be unable to market their product or service. Unsold merchandise and underutilized resources will result.

Note that a surplus does not mean the good is no longer scarce. People still want more of the good than is freely available from nature, even though they desire less *at the current price* than sellers desire to bring to the market. A decline in price would eliminate the surplus but not the scarcity of the item.

Minimum Wage: A Closer Look at a Price Floor

In 1938 Congress passed the Fair Labor Standards Act, which provided for a national **minimum wage** of 25 cents per hour. During the past 50 years, the minimum wage has been increased several times. The current minimum wage is $5.15 per hour.

Minimum wage
Legislation requiring that workers be paid at least the stated minimum hourly rate of pay.

The minimum wage is a price floor. Because most employees in the United States earn wages in excess of the minimum, their employment opportunities are largely unaffected. However, the wages of low-skilled and inexperienced workers will be affected. **Exhibit 4–6** provides a graphic illustration of the direct effect of a $5.15-per-hour minimum wage on the employment opportunities of a group of low-skill workers. Without a minimum wage, the supply of and demand for these low-skill workers would be in balance at a wage rate of $4.00. Because the minimum wage makes low-skill labor service more expensive, employers will substitute machines and more highly skilled workers (whose wages have not been raised by the minimum) for the now more expensive low-skill employees. Fewer low-skill workers will be hired when the minimum wage pushes their wages up. As the wages of low-skill workers are pushed above equilibrium, there will be more unskilled workers looking for jobs than businesses are willing to employ at the minimum wage. Theory indicates that minimum-wage legislation increases the rate of unemployment among low-skill workers. The exceedingly high

EXHIBIT 4-6

EMPLOYMENT AND THE MINIMUM WAGE

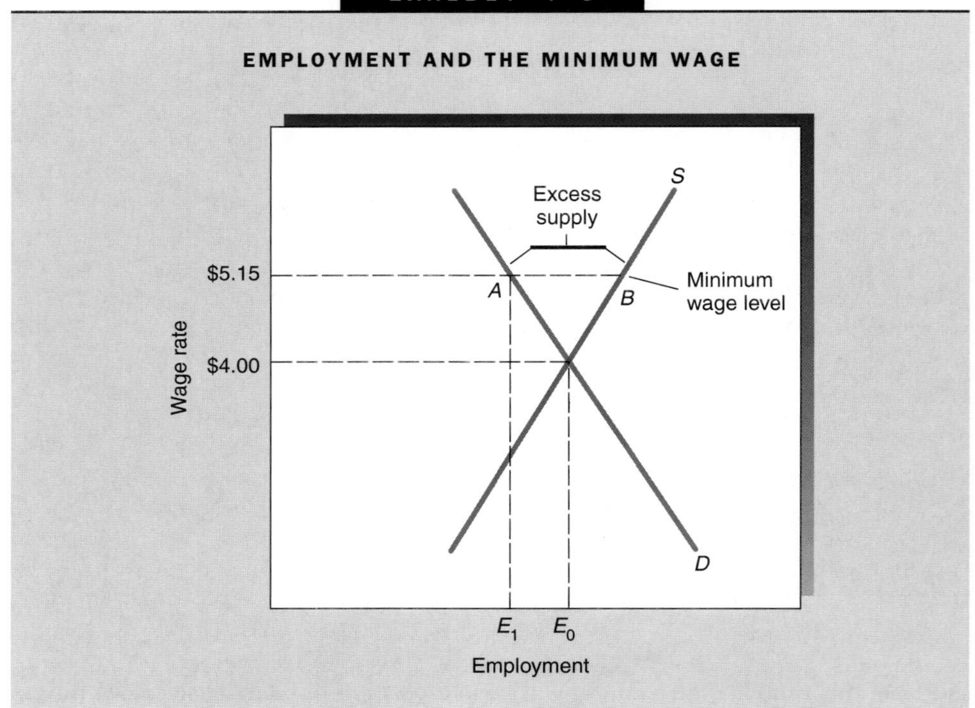

If the market wage of a group of employees were $4.00 per hour, a $5.15-per-hour minimum wage would increase the earnings of persons who were able to maintain employment but would reduce the employment of others (E_0 to E_1), pushing them onto the unemployment rolls or into less-preferred jobs.

unemployment rate of teenagers (one of the most affected groups) is consistent with this view. In the United States, the unemployment rate for teenagers is more than three times the national average, and the rate for black youth has generally exceeded 30 percent in recent years.

When analyzing the effects of the minimum wage, we must not forget that money wages are only one dimension. As we noted in the previous section, a price ceiling will lead to a deterioration in product quality because sellers have little incentive to maintain quality in order to attract buyers. Correspondingly, when a price floor pushes price—remember wage rates are a price—above equilibrium, buyers will have little incentive to offer nonprice terms of trade attractive to sellers. At an above-equilibrium wage, employers will have no trouble hiring low-skill workers. Therefore, they will have little incentive to offer them convenient working hours, training opportunities, continuous employment, and other benefits and nonwage amenities. Predictably, a higher minimum wage will lead to a deterioration of the nonwage attributes of minimum-wage jobs.

The impact of the minimum wage on the opportunity of youthful workers to acquire experience and training is particularly important. Many young, inexperienced workers face a dilemma: They cannot find a job without experience (or skills), but they cannot obtain experience without a job. Low-paying, entry-level jobs can provide workers with experience that will help them move up the job ladder to higher-paying positions. Employment experience obtained at an early age, even on menial tasks, can help one acquire self-confidence, work habits, attitudes, skills, and a reputation for these attributes that will enhance one's value to employers in the future. The minimum wage makes this process more difficult. It also reduces the number of jobs providing low-skill workers with training. Because the minimum wage prohibits the payment of even a temporarily low wage, it is often too costly for employers to offer low-skill workers jobs with training.[8] Not surprisingly, most minimum-wage jobs are dead-end positions with little opportunity for future advancement.[9]

Of course, workers who are able to maintain employment—most likely the better qualified among those with low-skill levels—gain when the minimum wage is increased. Other low-skill workers, particularly those with the lowest prelegislation wage rates and skill levels, will find it more difficult to find employment. How large are the employment reductions of low-skill workers? Studies indicate that a 10 percent increase in the minimum wage reduces the employment of low-skill workers by 1 percent to 3 percent. This relatively small decline in employment is not surprising given the ability of employers to cut training programs and other forms of compensation. Minimum-wage supporters argue that the higher wages for low-skill workers are worth these relatively small reductions in employment and job training opportunities.

The proponents of a higher minimum wage nearly always argue that it will help the poor. The composition of minimum-wage workers should cause one to question its effectiveness as an antipoverty device. Perhaps surprising to some, in 1997 more than half of all the minimum-wage workers were members of a family with an income above the median. Only a small proportion of minimum-wage workers—12 percent in 1997—were sole earners responsible for the support of a family. A majority (53 percent) of the minimum-wage workers were voluntarily working part-time. Approximately one-third (31 percent) were teenagers. The typical minimum-wage worker is a spouse or a teenage member of a household with an income well above the poverty level. Therefore, even if the adverse impacts of a higher minimum wage on employment and nonwage forms of compensation were small, a higher minimum wage would exert little impact on the income of the poor.[10]

BLACK MARKETS AND THE IMPORTANCE OF THE LEGAL STRUCTURE

Not all markets operate within the framework of the law. Some drugs, such as marijuana and cocaine, are illegal. Prostitution is illegal in all states except Nevada. Many states have passed laws making it illegal to sell (and in some cases buy) tickets to concerts and sporting events at prices in excess of the original purchase price. Despite the legal restrictions, when demand is strong and gains from trade are present, markets will develop. Markets that operate outside the legal system, either by selling illegal items or items at illegal prices or terms, are called **black markets.** People may also turn to black markets in order to avoid high taxes and costly regulations. High taxes have created substantial black markets for cigarettes in such countries as England, Italy, Germany, and Canada. Employees in the United States and other countries are sometimes hired "off the books" and paid in unreported cash in order to avoid payroll and income taxes.

Black market
A market that operates outside the legal system, either by selling illegal goods or by selling goods at illegal prices or terms.

---

[8]In order the reduce this obstacle, the Netherlands permits the temporary employment of youthful workers at wage rates that are substantially below the minimum wage of that country.

[9]For evidence that the minimum wage limits training opportunities, see Masanori Hashimoto, "Minimum Wage Effects on Training on the Job," *American Economic Review* 72 (December 1982): 1070–1087; and Charles Brown, "Minimum Wage Laws: Are They Overrated?" *Journal of Economic Perspectives* (summer 1988): 133–145.

[10]See William E. Even and David A. MacPherson, "Consequences of Minimum Wage Indexing," *Contemporary Economic Policy,* 14 (October 1996), for evidence on this point.

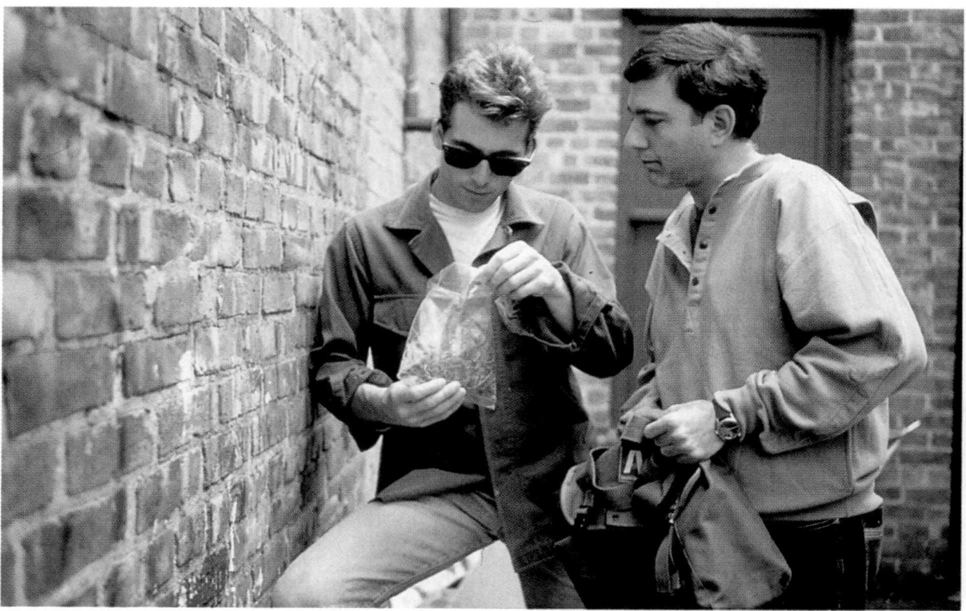

Black markets like those for illegal drugs are characterized by less dependable product quality and greater use of violence as a means of settling disputes between buyers and sellers.

How will black markets work? As in other markets, supply and demand will determine price in black markets. However, because they operate outside the official legal structure, enforcement of contracts and the dependability of quality will be less certain in these markets. Furthermore, participation in black markets involves greater risk, particularly for suppliers. Prices in these markets will have to be high enough to compensate suppliers for the cost of risks they are taking—the threat of arrest, possibility of a fine or jail sentence, and so on. Perhaps most important, there are no legal channels for the peaceful settlement of disputes in black markets. When a buyer or seller fails to deliver, it is the other party who must try to enforce it, usually through the threat of physical force.

Compared to normal markets, black markets are characterized by a higher incidence of defective products, higher profit rates (for those who do not get caught), and greater use of violence. The incidence of phony tickets purchased from street dealers and deaths caused by toxic drugs indicates that the presence of defective goods in these markets is high. Certainly the expensive clothes and automobiles of many drug dealers suggest that monetary profit is relatively high for those who manage to avoid major conflicts with the law. Evidence concerning the use of violence as a means of settling disputes arising from black market transactions is widespread. Illegal drug markets clearly illustrate this point. In New York City during a six-month period in 1988, there were 414 murders, of which 218 were classified as drug-related. Some were committed by persons under the influence of drugs who committed a crime they would not normally have committed. These drug-induced murders accounted for only 29 of the murders, and, of these, 21 were committed by individuals under the influence of alcohol. The remaining 189 murders were all associated with bad trades and competition among dealers in the illegal drug market.

The U.S. experience during the Prohibition era also illustrates the elevated role of violence in markets operating outside the rule of law. When the production and sale of alcohol was illegal during the 1920–1933 Prohibition period, gangsters dominated the alcohol trade, and the murder rate soared to record highs. There were also problems with product quality (such as tainted or highly toxic mixtures) similar to the ones present in modern-day illegal drug markets. When Prohibition was repealed and the market for alcoholic beverages once again began operating within the framework of law, these harmful secondary effects disappeared.

The operation of black markets highlights a point that is often taken for granted: A legal system that provides for secure private property rights, enforcement of contracts, and access to an unbiased court system for the settlement of disputes is vitally important for the smooth operation of markets. While markets will exist in any environment, they can be counted on to function efficiently only within the framework of a structured legal environment. Such an environment is largely absent in black markets; therefore, more fraud, deception, and violence are observed here. The analysis of black markets also provides insights into current conditions in Russia and much of the former Soviet Union. A well-structured legal system is currently absent in these areas. In fact, markets in Russia are quite similar to black markets in Western Europe and North America. So, too, is their operation. Fraud, deception, and the use of violence are widespread, and, from the viewpoint of economic efficiency, the performance of markets in these areas is relatively poor.

THE IMPACT OF A TAX

How do taxes affect market exchanges? When a tax is placed on the sale of a good, who bears the burden? Economists use the term **tax incidence** to indicate how the burden of a tax is *actually* shared between buyers (who pay more for what they purchase) and sellers (who receive less for what they sell). When a tax is imposed, the government can make either the buyer or the seller legally responsible for payment of the tax. The legal assignment is called the *statutory incidence* of the tax. However, the person who writes the check to the government—that is, the person statutorily responsible for the tax—is not always the one who bears the tax burden. The *actual incidence* of a tax may lie elsewhere. If, for example, a tax is placed statutorily on a seller, the seller may increase the price of the product to consumers, in which case the buyers ends up bearing some, or all, of the tax burden.

Tax incidence
The manner in which the burden of a tax is distributed among economic units (consumers, producers, employees, employers, and so on). The actual tax burden does not always fall on those who are statutorily assigned to pay the tax.

To illustrate, **Exhibit 4–7** shows how a $1,000 tax placed on the sale of used cars would affect the market. (In this hypothetical example, we simplify by assuming that all used cars are identical.) Here, the tax has statutorily been placed on the seller. When a tax is imposed on the seller, it shifts the supply curve upward by exactly the amount of the tax, $1,000 in this example. To understand why, remember that the height of the supply curve at a particular quantity shows the minimum price required to cause enough sellers to offer that quantity of cars for sale. Suppose that you were a potential seller, willing to sell your car for any price over $6,000, but unwilling unless you can pocket at least $6,000 from the sale. Because you will have to pay a tax of $1,000 when you sell your car, the minimum price you will accept *from the buyer* must now rise to $7,000 so that after paying the tax, you will retain $6,000. Other potential sellers will be in an identical position. The tax will push the minimum price at which each seller will be willing to supply the good upward by $1,000. Thus, the after-tax supply curve shifts vertically by this amount.

Before the imposition of the tax, used cars sold for a price of $7,000 (at the intersection of the original supply and demand curves shown by point *A*). After the imposition of this tax, the price of used cars will rise to $7,400 (the intersection of the new supply curve that includes the tax, and the demand curve, shown by point *B*). Thus, despite the tax being statutorily imposed on sellers, the higher price shifts some of the tax burden to buyers. A buyer will now pay $400 more for a used car after the imposition of the tax. A seller now receives $7,400 from the sale of a used car, but, after sending the tax of $1,000 to the government, the seller retains only $6,400. This is exactly $600 less

EXHIBIT 4-7

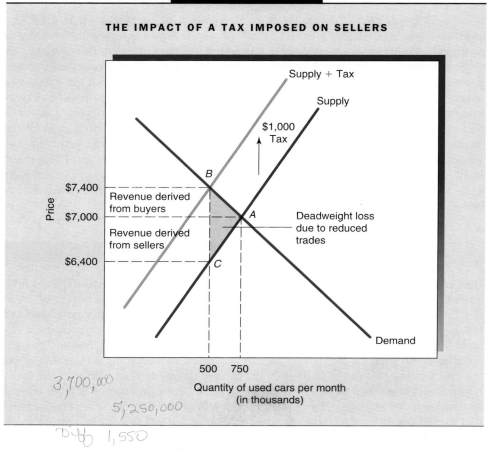

THE IMPACT OF A TAX IMPOSED ON SELLERS

When a $1,000 tax is imposed statutorily on the sellers of used cars, the supply curve shifts vertically upward by the amount of the tax. The price of used cars to buyers rises from $7,000 to $7,400, resulting in buyers bearing $400 of the burden of this tax. The price received by a seller falls from $7,000 to $6,400 ($7,400 minus the $1,000 tax), resulting in sellers bearing $600 of the burden.

than the seller would have received had the tax not been imposed. Because the distance between the supply curves is exactly $1,000, this net price can be found in Exhibit 4-7 by following the vertical line down from the new equilibrium to the original supply curve (point *C*) and over to the price axis. In this case, each $1,000 of tax revenue transferred to the government imposes a burden of $400 on the buyer (in the form of higher used-car prices) and a $600 burden on sellers (in the form of lower net receipts from a car sale).

The tax revenue derived from a tax is equal to the **tax base** (in this case, the number of used cars exchanged) multiplied by the **tax rate.** After the imposition of the tax, the quantity exchanged falls to 500,000 cars per month. In this case, the monthly tax revenue derived from the tax would be $500 million (500,000 cars multiplied by $1,000 tax per car).

Tax base
The level or quantity of the economic activity that is taxed (e.g., gallons of gasoline sold per week). Because they make the activity less attractive, higher tax rates reduce the level of the tax base.

Tax rate
The per-unit amount of the tax or the percentage rate at which the economic activity is taxed.

The Deadweight Loss Accompanying Taxation

Sellers would like to pass the entire tax on to buyers, raising the price by the full amount of the tax, rather than paying any part of it themselves. However, as the price rises, customers respond by purchasing fewer units. Sales decline and sellers must then lower their price toward its pretax level, accepting part of the tax burden themselves in the form of a lower price net of tax. As Exhibit 4–7 shows, the imposition of the $1,000 tax on used cars causes the number of units exchanged to fall from 750,000 to 500,000.

Thus, the imposition of the tax reduces the quantity of units exchanged by 250,000 units. Remember, trade results in mutual gains for both buyers and sellers. The loss of the mutual benefits that would have been derived had the tax not eliminated 250,000 units of exchange also imposes a cost on buyers and sellers. Economists refer to this loss as the **deadweight loss** of taxation. In Exhibit 4–7, the triangle *ABC* measures the size of the deadweight loss. The deadweight loss generates neither revenue for the government nor gains for any other party. It is a burden imposed on buyers and sellers over and above the cost of the revenue transferred to the government. Thus, it is often referred to as the **excess burden of taxation.** It is composed of losses to both buyers (the lost consumer surplus that is the upper part of the triangle *ABC*), and sellers (the lost producer surplus that is the lower part of the triangle *ABC*).

Deadweight loss
A loss of gains from trade resulting from the imposition of a tax. It imposes a burden of taxation over and above the burden associated with the transfer of revenues to the government.

Excess burden of taxation
Another term for deadweight loss. It reflects losses that occur when beneficial activities are forgone because they are taxed.

When a tax is imposed on products currently being produced, the deadweight loss to sellers includes the indirect cost the tax imposes on suppliers of resources to the industry (such as workers). The 1990 luxury boat tax vividly illustrates the potential adverse impact on resource suppliers. Although supporters of the luxury boat tax wanted to shift more of the tax burden toward wealthy yacht purchasers, the actual effects were quite different. As the result of the tax, the sales of luxury boats fell sharply and thousands of workers lost their jobs in the yacht manufacturing industry. Clearly, the boat tax substantially reduced the gains from trade between boat producers and resource suppliers. Thus, the deadweight loss of the tax was quite large. Because of the sharp reduction in luxury boat sales, the tax generated only a meager amount of revenue. This combination—a large deadweight excess burden and meager revenues for the government—eventually led to its repeal.

Actual versus Statutory Incidence

Economic analysis indicates that the actual burden of a tax is independent of whether it is statutorily placed on the buyer or seller. To see this, we must first look at how the market responds to a tax statutorily placed on the buyer. Continuing with the above example, suppose that the government places the $1,000 tax on the buyer of the car, rather than the seller. After making a used-car purchase, the buyer must send a check to the government for $1,000. The imposition of a tax on buyers will shift the demand curve downward by the amount of the tax, as is shown in **Exhibit 4–8**. This is because the height of the demand curve represents the maximum price a buyer is willing to pay

The actual burden of a tax is independent of whether it is imposed on buyers or sellers.

By John Trever, Albuquerque Journal. *Reprinted by permission.*

EXHIBIT 4–8

THE IMPACT OF A TAX IMPOSED ON BUYERS

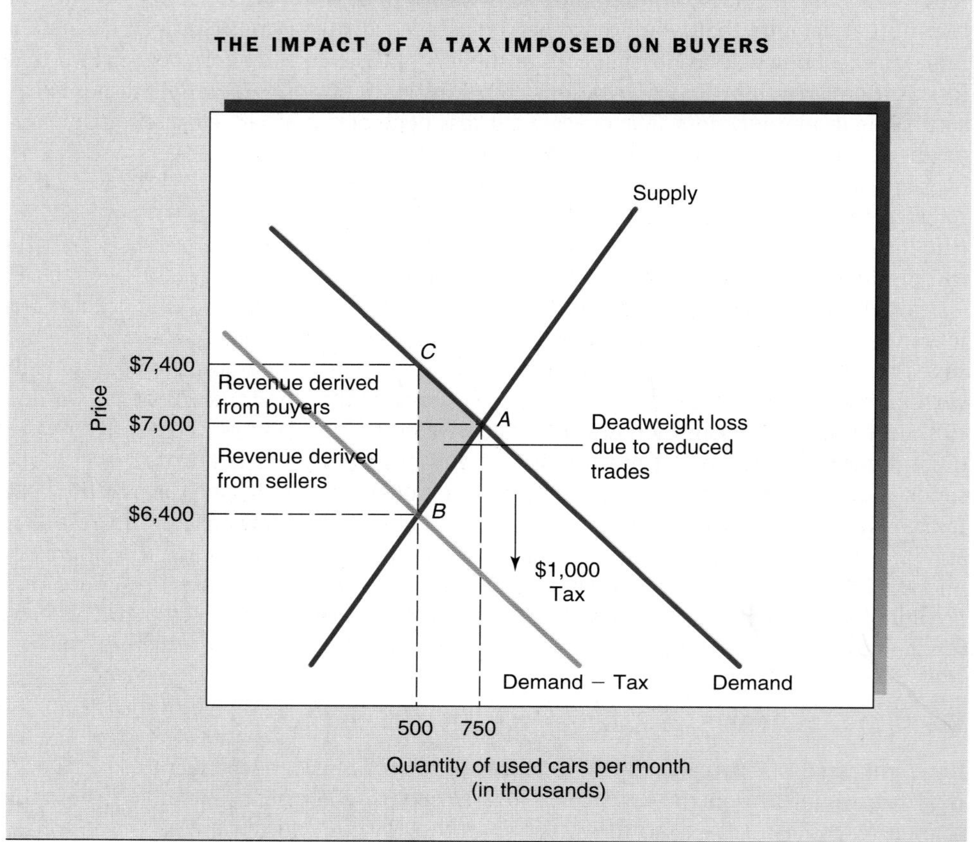

When a $1,000 tax is imposed statutorily on the buyers of used cars, the demand curve shifts vertically downward by the amount of the tax. The price of used cars falls from $7,000 to $6,400, resulting in sellers bearing $600 of the burden. The buyer's total cost of purchasing the car rises from $7,000 to $7,400 ($6,400 plus the $1,000 tax), resulting in buyers bearing $400 of the burden of this tax. The incidence of this tax on used cars is the same regardless of whether it is statutorily imposed on buyers or sellers.

for the car. If a particular buyer is willing and able to pay only $5,000 for a car, the imposition of the $1,000 tax would mean that the most the buyer would be willing to pay *to the seller* was now $4,000. This is because the total cost to the buyer is now the purchase price plus the tax.

As Exhibit 4–8 shows, the price of used cars falls from $7,000 (point *A*) to $6,400 (point *B*) when the tax is statutorily placed on the buyer. Even though the tax is placed on buyers, the resulting reduction in demand causes the price received by sellers to fall by $600. Thus, $600 of the tax is again borne by sellers, just as it was when the tax was placed statutorily on sellers. From the buyer's standpoint, a car now costs $7,400 ($6,400 paid to the seller plus $1,000 in tax to the government). Just as in the case when the tax was imposed on the seller, the buyer now pays $400 more for a used car.

A comparison of Exhibits 4-7 and 4-8 makes it clear that the actual burden of the $1,000 tax is independent of its statutory incidence. In both cases, buyers pay a total price of $7,400 for the car (a $400 increase from the pretax level), and sellers receive $6,400 from the sale (a $600 decrease from the pretax level). Correspondingly, the revenues derived by the government, the number of sales eliminated by the tax, and the size of the deadweight loss are identical regardless of whether the law requires payment of the tax by the sellers or by the buyers.

The equivalence of the actual burden of a tax regardless of its statutory assignment is true for any tax. The 15.3 percent social security payroll tax, for example, is statutorily levied as 7.65 percent on the employee and 7.65 percent on the employer.

The impact is to drive down the net pay received by employees and raise the employers' cost of hiring workers. Economic analysis tells us that the actual burden of this tax will probably differ from its legal assignment. The actual burden imposed on employees and employers, however, will be the same regardless of how the tax is statutorily assigned. Because market prices (here, workers' gross pay) will adjust, the incidence of the tax will be identical regardless of whether the 15.3 percent is levied on employees or on employers or is divided between the two parties.

Elasticity and the Incidence of a Tax

If the actual incidence of a tax is independent of its statutory assignment, what does determine the incidence? The answer: The incidence of a tax depends on the responsiveness of buyers and of sellers to a change in price. When buyers respond to even a small rise in price by leaving this market and buying other things, then they will not be willing to accept a price that is much higher. Similarly, if sellers respond to a small reduction in what they receive by shifting to other areas or going out of business, then they will not be willing to accept a much smaller payment, net of tax. The burden of a tax—its incidence—tends to fall more heavily on whichever side of the market has the least attractive options elsewhere, thus is less sensitive to price changes.

In the preceding chapter, we saw that the steepness of the supply and demand curves reflects the degree of responsiveness to a price change. Relatively inelastic demand or supply curves are steeper (more vertical), indicating less responsiveness to a change in price. Relatively elastic demand or supply curves are flatter (more horizontal), indicating a higher degree of responsiveness to a change in price.

Using gasoline as an example, part a of **Exhibit 4–9** illustrates the impact of a tax when demand is relatively inelastic and supply is relatively elastic. It will not be easy for gasoline consumers to shift—particularly in the short run—to other fuels in response to an increase in the price of gasoline. The inelastic demand reflects this point. When a 20-cent tax is imposed on gasoline, buyers end up paying 15 cents more per gallon ($1.15 instead of $1.00), while the net price of sellers is 5 cents less ($0.95 instead of $1.00). ***When, as in the case of gasoline, demand is relatively inelastic and supply elastic, the primary burden of a tax will fall on buyers.***

In contrast, more of the tax burden will fall on sellers and resource suppliers when demand is relatively elastic and supply inelastic. Using a tax on luxury boats as an example, part b of Exhibit 4–9 illustrates this point. As we mentioned earlier, Congress imposed a tax on the sale of luxury boats in 1990. Later, the tax was repealed because of its adverse impact on sales and employment in the industry. There are many things on which wealthy potential yacht owners can spend their money other than luxury boats *sold in the United States.* For one thing, they can buy a yacht someplace else, perhaps in Mexico, England, or the Bahamas. Or they can spend more time on the golf course, travel to exotic places, or purchase a nicer car or more expensive home. Because there are attractive substitutes, the demand for domestically produced luxury boats is relatively elastic compared to supply. Therefore, when a $25,000 tax is imposed on luxury boats, prices rise by only $5,000 (from $100,000 to $105,000) and output falls substantially (from 10,000 to 5,000). The net price received by sellers falls by $20,000. ***When, as in the case of luxury boats, demand is relatively elastic compared to supply, sellers (including resource suppliers) will bear the larger share of the tax burden.***

Elasticity and the Deadweight Loss

We have seen that elasticities of supply and demand determine how the burden of a tax is distributed between buyer and seller. These elasticities also influence the size of

EXHIBIT 4-9

HOW THE BURDEN OF A TAX DEPENDS ON THE ELASTICITIES OF DEMAND AND SUPPLY

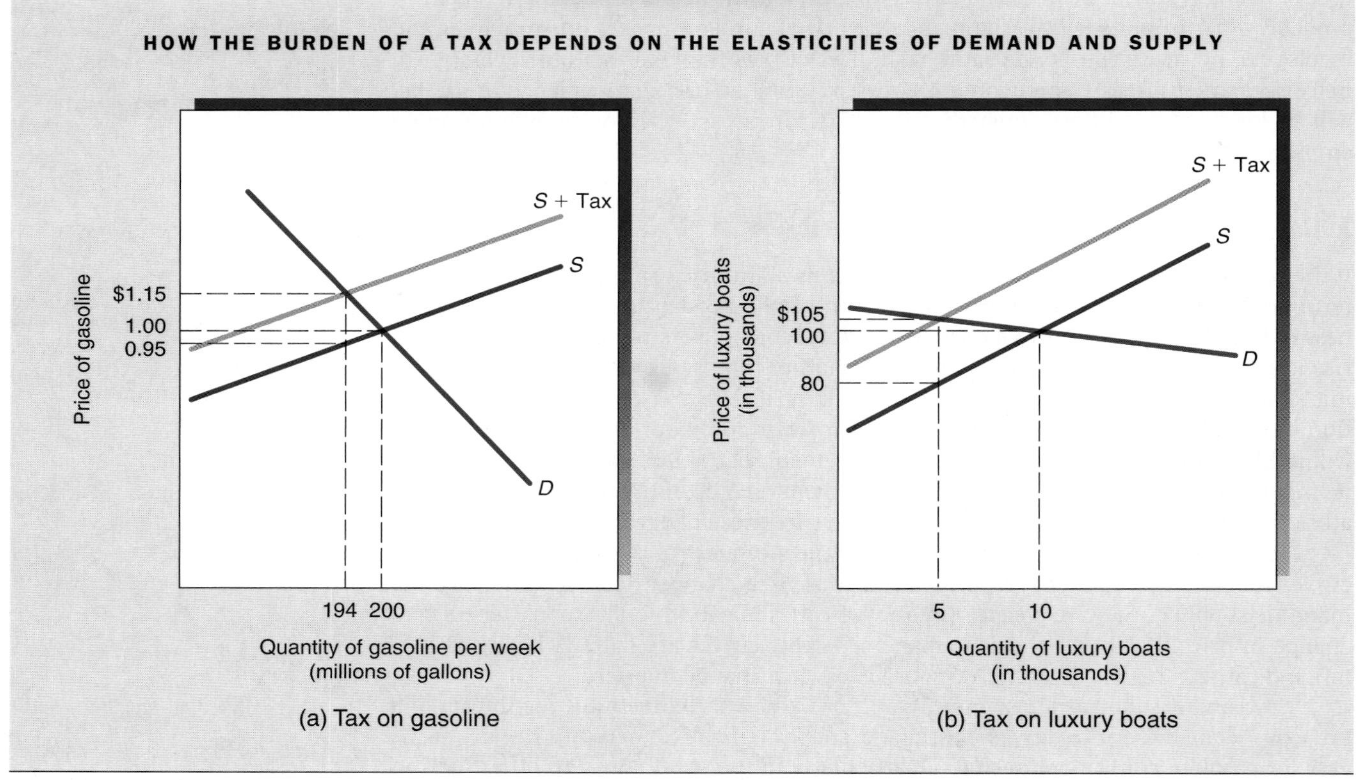

In part a when demand is relatively more inelastic than supply, buyers bear a larger share of the burden of the tax.

In part b when supply is relatively more inelastic than demand, sellers bear a larger share of the tax burden.

the deadweight loss caused by the tax because they determine the total reduction in the quantity of exchange. When either demand or supply is relatively inelastic, fewer trades will be eliminated by imposition of the tax, so the resulting deadweight loss is smaller. From a policy perspective, the excess burden of a tax system will therefore be lower if taxes are levied on goods and services for which either demand or supply is highly inelastic.

TAX RATES, TAX REVENUES, AND THE LAFFER CURVE

Average tax rate (ATR)
Tax liability divided by taxable income. It is the percentage of income paid in taxes.

Progressive tax
A tax in which the average tax rate rises with income. Persons with higher incomes will pay a higher percentage of their income in taxes.

When analyzing the impact of taxation, it is important to distinguish between the average and marginal rates of taxation. The **average tax rate (ATR)** can be expressed as follows:

$$\text{ATR} = \text{Tax liability/Taxable income}$$

For example, if a person's tax liability was $3,000 on an income of $20,000, her average tax rate would be 15 percent ($3,000 divided by $20,000). The average tax rate is simply the percentage of income that is paid in taxes. In the United States, the personal income tax provides the largest single source of government revenue. This tax is particularly important at the federal level. You may have heard reference to the federal income tax being "progressive." A **progressive tax** is defined as a tax in which the average tax rate rises with income. In other words, persons with higher income pay a larger *percentage of their income* in taxes. Alternatively, taxes can be proportional or regressive. A **proportional tax** is one for which the average tax rate is the same across income levels. Here, everyone would pay the same percentage of income in taxes. Finally, a **regressive tax** is one in which the average tax rate falls with income. If someone making $100,000 per year paid $30,000 in taxes (an ATR of 30 percent) while someone making $30,000 per year paid $15,000 in taxes (an ATR of 50 percent), the tax code would be regressive. Note that a regressive tax merely means that the *percentage* paid in taxes declines with income; the actual dollar amount of the tax bill might still be higher for those with larger incomes.

Proportional tax
A tax in which the average tax rate is the same at all income levels. Everyone pays the same percentage of income in taxes.

Regressive tax
A tax in which the average tax rate falls with income. Persons with higher incomes will pay a lower percentage of their income in taxes.

The economic way of thinking stresses that what happens at the margin is of crucial importance in personal decision making. The **marginal tax rate (MTR)** can be expressed as follows:

$$\text{MTR} = \text{Change in tax liability/Change in income}$$

Marginal tax rate (MTR)
Additional tax liability divided by additional taxable income. It is the percentage of an extra dollar of income that must be paid in taxes. It is the marginal tax rate that is relevant in personal decision making.

The MTR reveals both how much of one's *additional* income must be turned over to the tax collector and how much is retained by the individual. For example, when the MTR is 28 percent, $28 of every $100 of additional earnings must be paid in taxes. The individual is permitted to keep only $72 of his or her additional income. The marginal tax rate is vitally important because it affects the incentive to earn additional income. The higher the marginal tax rate, the less incentive individuals have to earn more income.

EXHIBIT 4-10

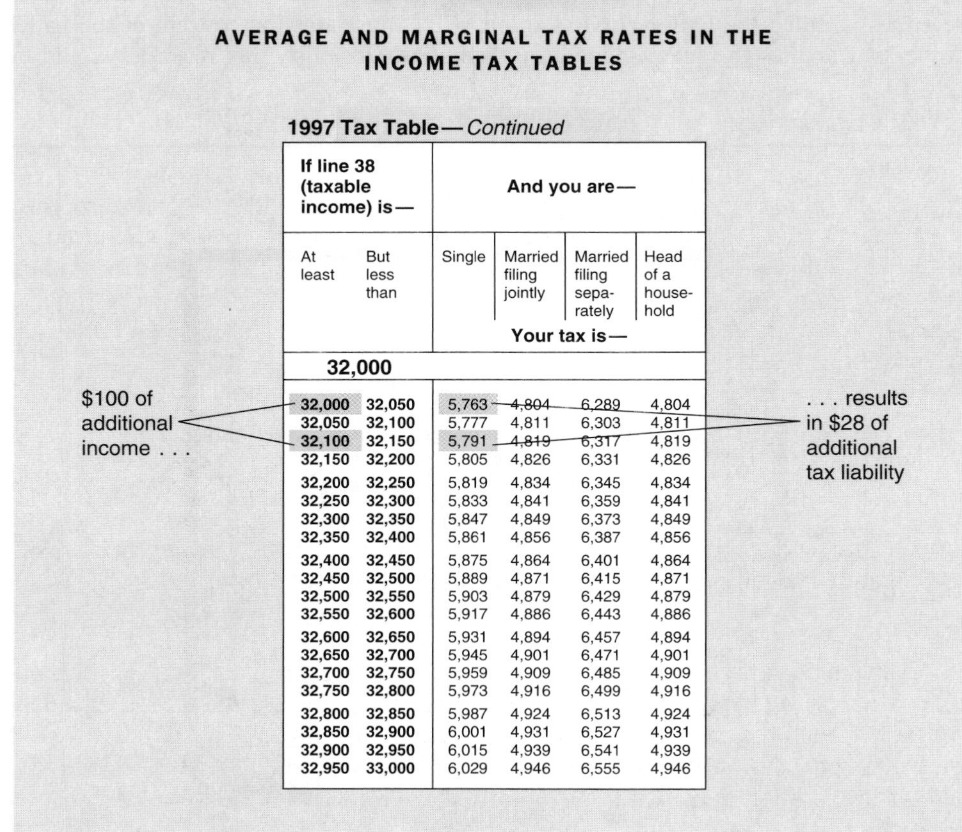

AVERAGE AND MARGINAL TAX RATES IN THE INCOME TAX TABLES

1997 Tax Table—*Continued*

If line 38 (taxable income) is—		And you are—			
At least	But less than	Single	Married filing jointly	Married filing separately	Head of a household
		Your tax is—			
32,000					
32,000	**32,050**	5,763	4,804	6,289	4,804
32,050	**32,100**	5,777	4,811	6,303	4,811
32,100	**32,150**	5,791	4,819	6,317	4,819
32,150	**32,200**	5,805	4,826	6,331	4,826
32,200	**32,250**	5,819	4,834	6,345	4,834
32,250	**32,300**	5,833	4,841	6,359	4,841
32,300	**32,350**	5,847	4,849	6,373	4,849
32,350	**32,400**	5,861	4,856	6,387	4,856
32,400	**32,450**	5,875	4,864	6,401	4,864
32,450	**32,500**	5,889	4,871	6,415	4,871
32,500	**32,550**	5,903	4,879	6,429	4,879
32,550	**32,600**	5,917	4,886	6,443	4,886
32,600	**32,650**	5,931	4,894	6,457	4,894
32,650	**32,700**	5,945	4,901	6,471	4,901
32,700	**32,750**	5,959	4,909	6,485	4,909
32,750	**32,800**	5,973	4,916	6,499	4,916
32,800	**32,850**	5,987	4,924	6,513	4,924
32,850	**32,900**	6,001	4,931	6,527	4,931
32,900	**32,950**	6,015	4,939	6,541	4,939
32,950	**33,000**	6,029	4,946	6,555	4,946

$100 of additional income . . .
. . . results in $28 of additional tax liability

This excerpt from the 1997 federal income tax table shows that in the 28 percent federal marginal income tax bracket, each $100 of additional taxable income (from $32,000 to $32,100) results in tax liability increasing by $28 (from $5,763 to $5,791). Note that the average tax rate for a single taxpayer at $32,000 is about 18 percent ($5,763 ÷ $32,000).

At high marginal rates, spouses will choose to stay home instead of working, and others will choose not to take on second jobs or extra work. **Exhibit 4–10** illustrates the calculation of both the average and marginal tax rates within the framework of the 1997 income tax tables provided to taxpayers.

Generally, a person's income is subject to several taxes, and it is the combined marginal tax rate from all applicable taxes that matters to the individuals in their decision making. For example, in 1997, a married couple with $30,000 in taxable income living in Baltimore, Maryland, would face a 28 percent marginal federal income tax rate, a 7.65 percent marginal social security payroll tax rate, a 5 percent marginal state income tax rate, and a 2.5 percent marginal local income tax rate. If we ignore the relatively small deductions that one tax can generate in calculating certain others, the result is a combined marginal tax rate of 43.15 percent, meaning that an additional $100 of gross income would result in only a $56.85 increase in net take-home income.

Governments generally levy taxes in order to raise revenues. The revenue derived from a tax is equal to the tax base multiplied by the tax rate. As we previously noted, taxes will lower the level of the activity taxed. The basic postulate of economics indicates that when an activity is taxed more heavily, people will choose less of it. The higher the tax rate, the greater the shift away from the activity. If taxpayers can easily escape the tax by altering their behavior (perhaps by shifting to substitutes), the tax base will shrink significantly as rates are increased. This erosion in the tax base in response to higher rates means that an increase in tax rates will generally lead to a less than proportional increase in tax revenues.

Laffer curve
A curve illustrating the relationship between the tax rate and tax revenue. Tax revenue will be low for both very high and very low tax rates. Thus, when tax rates are quite high, a reduction in the tax rate can increase tax revenue.

Economist Arthur Laffer has popularized the idea that, beyond some point, higher tax rates will shrink the tax base so much that tax revenues will decline when tax rates are increased. The curve illustrating the relationship between tax rates and tax revenues is called the **Laffer curve. Exhibit 4–11** illustrates the concept of the Laffer curve as it applies to income-generating activities. Obviously, tax revenues would be

Because taxation affects the amount of the activity being taxed, a change in tax rates will not lead to a proportional change in tax revenues. As the Laffer curve indicates, beyond some point (B), an increase in tax rates may actually cause tax revenues to fall. Because large tax rate increases will lead to only a small expansion in tax revenue as B is approached, there is no presumption that point B is an ideal rate of taxation.

EXHIBIT 4–11

LAFFER CURVE

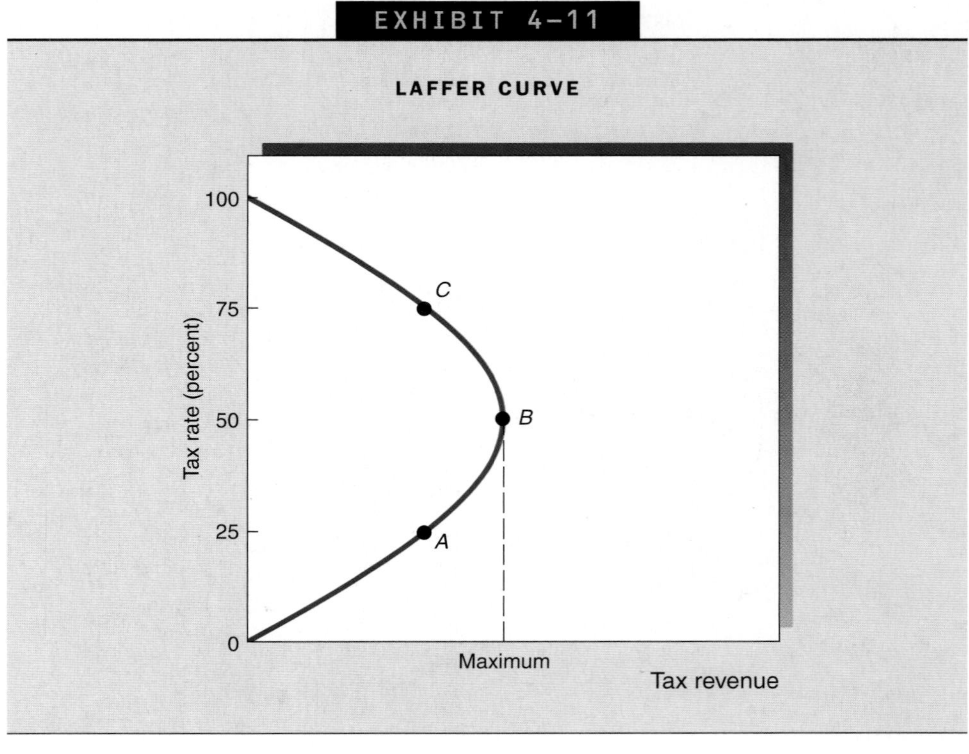

zero if the income tax rate were zero. What is not so obvious is that tax revenues would also be zero (or at least very close to zero) if the tax rate were 100 percent. Confronting a 100 percent tax rate, most individuals would go fishing—or find something else to do rather than engage in taxable productive activity, since the 100 percent tax rate would completely remove the material reward derived from earning taxable income.

As tax rates are reduced from 100 percent, the incentive to work and earn taxable income increases, income expands, and tax revenues rise. Similarly, as tax rates increase from zero, tax revenues expand. Clearly, at some rate greater than zero but less than 100 percent, tax revenues will be maximized (point *B* in Exhibit 4–11). This is not to imply that the tax rate that maximizes revenue is ideal. In fact, as rates are increased and the maximum revenue point (*B*) is approached, relatively large tax rate increases will be necessary to expand tax revenue by even a small amount. In this range, the excess burden of taxation in the form of reductions in gains from trade will be substantial. Thus, ideal tax rates will be lower than the rate that maximizes revenue.

The Laffer curve illustrates that it is important to distinguish between changes in *tax rates* and changes in *tax revenues.* Higher rates will not always lead to more revenue for the government. Similarly, lower rates will not always lead to less revenue. When higher tax rates lead to a substantial shrinkage in the tax base, the higher rates will raise little additional revenue. In extreme cases, revenue may even decline in response to higher tax rates. Correspondingly, tax rates can sometimes be lower without any significant loss of revenue.

It is interesting to view the 1980s within the framework of the Laffer curve. During the eighties there was a sharp reduction in marginal tax rates imposed on those with high incomes. The top marginal rate was reduced from 70 percent at the

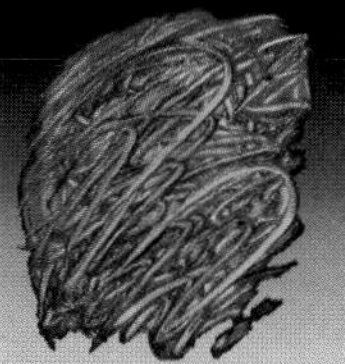

APPLICATIONS IN ECONOMICS

The Laffer Curve and Mountain Climbing Deaths

The Laffer curve is a tool that can be used to illustrate many relationships other than the one between tax rates and tax revenues. Economists J. R. Clark and Dwight Lee have used the Laffer curve framework to analyze the relationship between the safety of mountain climbing and the number of mountain climbing deaths on Mt. McKinley. As the probability of death from the climb fell due to increased government involvement in rescue attempts, the number of people seeking to "conquer the mountain" rose significantly. The increase in the number of climbers dominated the reduction in risk, leading to a Laffer curve–type relationship: An improvement in safety resulted in a *higher* number of total deaths.

Perhaps a numeric example can best illustrate why this might be the case. Assume that if the probability of death from an attempted climb was 90 percent, only 100 persons would attempt to climb the mountain each year, leading to an annual death rate of 90. Now suppose that increased rescue attempts lower this probability of death to 50 percent. Because incentives matter, the increased safety will result in an increase in the number of people attempting to climb the mountain. Suppose that the number of climbers increases from 100 to 200. With 200 climbers and a 50 percent probability of death, the annual number of fatalities would increase to 100, 10 more than before the improvement in safety. Viewing this within the Laffer curve framework, the total number of mountain climbing deaths is lowest both when there is a very high and a very low probability of death. The number of deaths is largest in the middle probability ranges. Thus, making a very risky mountain safer can result in more rather than fewer fatalities.

Besides mountain climbing, these same authors have explored a similar relationship between the average prison sentence length and total prison space occupied. Other authors have explored potential Laffer curve relations between the minimum-wage and the earnings of minimum wage workers and the regulatory costs of the Endangered Species Act on the acres of habitat for endangered species.[1]

[1]See J. R. Clark and Dwight R. Lee, "Too Safe to Be Safe: Some Implications of Short- and Long-Run Rescue Laffer Curves," *Eastern Economic Journal* 23 no. 2 (spring 1997): 127–137; Russell S. Sobel, "Theory and Evidence on the Political Economy of the Minimum Wage," *Journal of Political Economy,* forthcoming; and Richard L. Stroup, "The Endangered Species Act: The Laffer Curve Strikes Again," *The Journal of Private Enterprise,* vol. XIV (special issue 1998): 48–62.

EXHIBIT 4–12

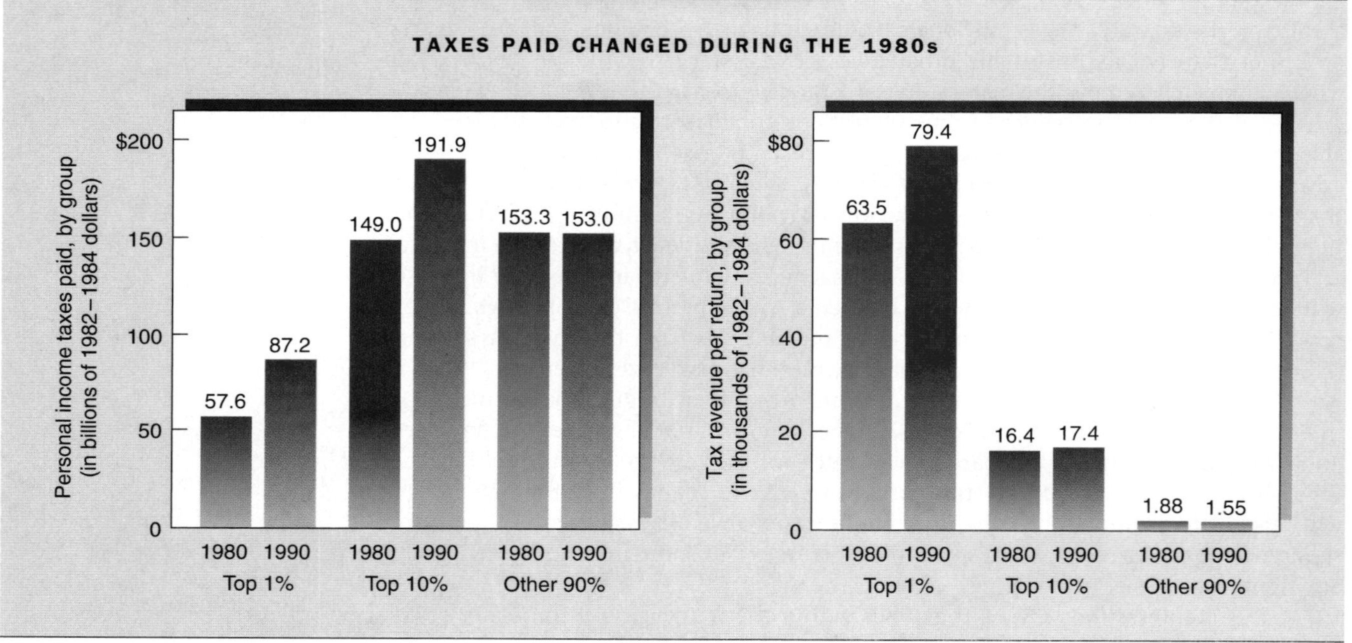

Measured in 1982–1984 dollars, the personal income taxes paid by the top 1 percent and the top 10 percent of income recipients increased between 1980 and 1990, even though their rates were reduced. In contrast, the tax revenue collected from other taxpayers was virtually unchanged during the decade (left frame). Per return, the revenue collected from the top 1 percent and the top 10 percent rose, while the revenue fell for other taxpayers (right frame).

beginning of the decade to 33 percent at the end of the decade. Focusing on this sharp reduction in the top marginal rate, critics charged that the 1980s' tax policies were a bonanza for the rich. When analyzing this view, once again it is important to distinguish between tax rates and tax revenue. Even though the top rates were reduced sharply, both the tax revenue (even after adjustment for inflation) and share of the personal income tax paid by high-income taxpayers rose during the 1980s. As **Exhibit 4–12** illustrates, the real tax revenue (measured in 1982–1984 dollars) collected from the top 1 percent of earners rose from $57.6 billion in 1980 to $87.2 billion in 1990, a whopping increase of 51.4 percent. For the top 10 percent as a whole, real revenue rose from $149.0 billion in 1980 to $191.9 billion in 1990. Meanwhile, the revenue collected from all other taxpayers was virtually unchanged.

Viewed as percentages of total income tax collections, in 1980 the top 1 percent of earners accounted for just over 19 percent of all income tax revenue collected. By 1990 at the lower tax rates, the top 1 percent accounted for more than 25 percent of income tax revenue. The top 10 percent of earners paid just over 49 percent of total income tax liability in 1980 and 55 percent in 1990. Interestingly, the top 10 percent of earners paid more than half of the total income tax liability.

The data from the 1980s are consistent with the Laffer curve. They indicate that in the case of most taxpayers (those in the range near point *A* of Exhibit 4–11), lower tax rates lead to a reduction in the revenue collected from the group. When tax rates are higher (in the range near *B* of Exhibit 4–11), tax rates can be reduced with little or no loss of revenue, and when rates get even higher (in the range near *C* of Exhibit 4–11), lowering tax rates will produce more tax revenue.

LOOKING *Ahead*

The last two chapters have focused on the operation of markets and the role of market prices. At various points, we have stressed the importance of legal structure and secure property rights for the smooth operation of markets. Governmental policies in these and other areas influence both economic efficiency and progress. The next two chapters will focus on the role and operation of government, a topic that is central to understanding the world in which we live.

KEY POINTS

➤ Wage rates, interest rates, and exchange rates are also market prices determined by the forces of supply and demand. In each, these prices play important roles in coordinating the actions of buyers and sellers. Changes in these markets lead to changes in other markets and alter the relative prices of many other goods.

➤ Legally imposed price ceilings result in shortages, while legally imposed price floors will cause surpluses. Both will also cause other harmful secondary effects. Rent controls, for example, will lead to shortages, less investment, poor maintenance, and a deterioration in the quality of rental housing.

➤ The minimum wage is a price floor for unskilled labor. It increases the earnings of some low-skill workers, but also reduces employment and leads to a reduction in training opportunities and a deterioration in the nonwage job benefits available to minimum-wage workers.

➤ Because black markets operate outside the legal system, they are often characterized by deception, fraud, and the use of violence as a means of enforcing contracts. A legal system that provides secure private property rights and unbiased enforcement of contracts enhances the operation of markets.

➤ The division of the actual tax burden between buyers and sellers is determined by the relative elasticities of demand and supply rather than on whom the tax is legally imposed.

➤ In addition to the cost of the tax revenues transferred to the government, taxes will eliminate trades in a market and thereby impose an excess burden or deadweight loss.

➤ Higher tax rates reduce the size of the tax base. The Laffer curve illustrates that when tax rates are quite high, a reduction in the tax rate can result in more tax revenue. The increase in tax revenue obtained from the wealthy as the result of income tax rate reductions during the 1980s is consistent with the Laffer curve.

CRITICAL ANALYSIS QUESTIONS

1. How will a substantial increase in demand for housing affect the wages and employment of carpenters, plumbers, and electricians?

2. Suppose there is a sharp reduction in lumber prices. How will this affect the market for newly constructed housing?

3. Why are nonprice factors, such as product quality, service, and the characteristics of potential trading partners, more important when price ceilings and price floors are imposed than when prices are freely determined?

*4. To be meaningful, a price ceiling must be below the market price. Conversely, a meaningful price floor must be above the market price. What impact will a meaningful price ceiling have on the quantity exchanged? What impact will a meaningful price floor have on the quantity exchanged? Explain.

5. Suppose that college students in your town convinced the town council to enact a law setting the maximum price for rental housing at $100 per month. Will this help or hurt college students who rent housing? In your answer address how this price ceiling will affect (a) the quality of rental housing, (b) the amount of rental housing available, (c) the incentive of landlords to

maintain their property, (d) the amount of racial, gender, and other types of discrimination in the local rental housing market, (e) the ease with which students will be able to find housing, and finally (f) whether a "black market" for housing would develop.

*6. Analyze the impact of an increase in the minimum wage from the current level to $8.00 per hour. How would the following be affected?

a. Employment in skill categories previously earning less than $8 per hour

b. The unemployment rate of teenagers

c. The availability of on-the-job training for low-skill workers

d. The demand for high-skill workers who provide good substitutes for the labor services offered by low-skill workers, who are paid higher wage rates due to the increase in the minimum wage

7. What is a black market? What are some of the main differences in how black markets operate relative to legal markets?

8. How do you think the markets for organ donation and child adoption would be affected if they were made fully legal with a well-functioning price mechanism? What would be the advantages and disadvantages relative to the current system?

9. What is meant by the incidence of a tax? Explain why the statutory and actual incidence of a tax can be different.

10. What conditions must be met for buyers to bear the full burden of a tax? What conditions would cause sellers to bear the full burden? Explain.

*11. What is the nature of the deadweight loss accompanying taxes? Why is it often referred to as an "excess burden" of the tax?

12. The demand and supply curves for unskilled labor in a market are given in the accompanying table.

DEMAND		SUPPLY	
WAGE	QUANTITY DEMANDED	WAGE	QUANTITY SUPPLIED
$6.50	1,000	$6.50	1,900
$6.00	1,200	$6.00	1,800
$5.50	1,400	$5.50	1,700
$5.00	1,600	$5.00	1,600
$4.50	1,800	$4.50	1,500
$4.00	2,000	$4.00	1,400

a. Find the equilibrium wage and number of workers hired.

b. Suppose that a new law is passed requiring employers to pay an unemployment insurance tax of $1.50 per hour for every employee. What happens to the equilibrium wage rate and number of workers hired? How is this tax burden distributed between employers and workers?

c. Now suppose that, rather than being paid by the employers, the tax must be paid by workers. How does this affect the equilibrium wage rate and number of workers hired? How is this tax burden distributed between employers and workers?

d. Does it make a difference who is statutorily liable for the tax?

13. Currently, the social security payroll tax is statutorily imposed at 7.65 percent on the employee and 7.65 percent on the employer. Show this graphically, being careful to distinguish between the total cost to the employer of hiring a worker, the employee's gross wage, and the employee's net wage. Show how the outcome would differ if all 15.3 percent were imposed on the employee or if all 15.3 percent were imposed on the employer.

*14. Suppose that, recognizing that one cannot support a large family at the current minimum wage, Congress passes legislation requiring that businesses employing workers with three or more children pay these employees at least $8.50 per hour. How would this legislation affect the employment level of low-skill workers with three or more children? Do you think some workers with large families might attempt to conceal the fact? Why?

15. "We should impose a 20 percent luxury tax on expensive automobiles (those with a sales price of $50,000 or more) in order to collect more tax revenue from the wealthy." Will the burden of the proposed tax fall primarily on the wealthy? Why or why not?

---

*Asterisk denotes questions for which answers are given in Appendix B.

CHAPTER 5

The principal justification for public policy intervention lies in the frequent and numerous shortcomings of market outcomes.

Charles Wolf[1]

The Economic Role of Government

CHAPTER FOCUS

- What is government?
- How does the nature of decision making in the political and market sectors differ?
- Do taxes measure the opportunity cost of a government?
- Which functions of government are most likely to promote economic well-being?
- Why might markets fail to achieve ideal economic efficiency?

[1]Charles Wolf, Jr., *Markets or Government* (Cambridge: MIT Press, 1988), p. 17.

About two-fifths of U.S. national income is channeled through various government departments and agencies. In addition, about two-fifths of the nation's land is owned by the government. Furthermore, the legal framework set by the government establishes many of the "rules of the game" for the market sector. Government regulation of prices and the use of land, water, and air, along with labor relations and business practices, exerts a major impact on the operation of the economy. Given the size, cost, and influence of government, it is important that we understand what government is, and the reasons that people sometimes turn to it, rather than to the private sector, to get what they want. In this chapter we will examine these issues, focusing in particular on situations in which markets cannot be expected to deliver ideal results.

WHAT IS GOVERNMENT?

At the most basic level, the distinguishing characteristic of government is its monopoly over the legitimate use of force to modify the actions of adults. Most societies allow parents to use force to influence the actions of their children. But with regard to adults, governments possess the exclusive right to use force. No individual or firm has a right to use violence—or the threat of violence—in order to take your wealth. If a business raises its price or performs unsatisfactorily, you always have the right to exit—to take your business elsewhere. But when a government decrees a tax or a new regulation, exit is possible only by moving out of the government's territory. And that is costly, especially when it comes to the national government. Its monopoly on the legitimate use of force to take from its citizens—to tax them and to control their behavior—makes government different from any other form of organization.

Given its unique powers, it is tempting to think of government, particularly democratically elected government, as a tool that can be used to solve all types of problems ranging from inadequate health care to the high cost of housing. Some even argue that government can use income transfers to achieve the "optimal distribution of income."

It is, of course, important to understand alternative actions that might *potentially* lead to outcomes that are more consistent with economic prosperity. But as we will see clearly in the next chapter, government is merely an alternative method of social organization—an institutional process through which individuals collectively make choices and carry out activities. No matter how lofty the rhetoric of political officials, the people (for example, voters, legislators, lobbyists, and bureau managers) who make the choices that determine political outcomes are ordinary mortals, persons with ethical standards, narrow interests, and personal motivations very much like those present in the market sector. Furthermore, government decision makers often confront a reward structure that encourages them to help narrow constituencies at the expense of economic efficiency and activities that are in the interest of all citizens.

Because the incentive structure in the political process generally differs from that of markets, collective outcomes will often differ from market outcomes. For some categories of economic activity, there are reasons to believe that democratic political procedures work quite well. In other instances, there are sound reasons to believe that government allocation will be counterproductive. This chapter and the next will help us understand when—and under what conditions—political decision making is likely to yield positive economic results.

DIFFERENCES AND SIMILARITIES BETWEEN MARKET AND COLLECTIVE ACTION

There is at least one important similarity between the market and the public sectors: The choices of individuals will influence outcomes in both. But there are basic structural differences in the way that individuals exercise their influence. Market transactions are characterized by voluntary exchange coordinated by prices. Only transactions that are voluntarily accepted by both buyer and seller will take place in markets. In contrast, when collective action occurs in a democratic setting, majority rule is the key, either directly or through legislative procedures. Let us take a look at both the differences and similarities between the two sectors.

1. **Competitive behavior is present in both the market and public sectors.** The market sector is sometimes called the "competitive sector," but competitive behavior is present in both sectors. Politicians compete for elective office. Bureau chiefs and agency heads compete for additional taxpayer dollars. Public-sector employees compete for promotions, higher incomes, and additional power, just as they do in the private sector. Lobbyists compete for program funding, for favorable bureaucratic rulings, and for legislation favorable to the interest groups they represent—including both private and government clients. (See Applications in Economics: Perspectives on the Cost of Political Competition.) The nature of the competition and the criteria for success differ between the two sectors, but people compete in both.
2. **Public-sector organization can break the individual consumption-payment link.** In the market, a consumer who wants a commodity must pay the price. In this respect, market and collective action differ in a fundamental way. The government usually does not establish a one-to-one relationship between the individual's payment and receipt of a good. Some individuals receive very large benefits from a government action without any significant impact on their personal tax bill. Others pay substantial taxes while receiving much smaller benefits. In contrast with the market, the amount one pays does not determine the amount one receives in the public sector.
3. **Scarcity imposes the aggregate consumption-payment link in both sectors.** Although the government can break the link between an individual's payment for a good and the right to consume the good, the reality of the ***aggregate consumption–aggregate payment*** link will remain. There are no free lunches. Someone must pay the cost of providing scarce goods, regardless of the sector used to produce (or distribute) them. Free goods provided in the public sector are "free" only to certain individuals. They are certainly not free from the viewpoint of society.
4. **Private-sector action is based on voluntary choice; public-sector action on majority rule.** In the private sector, when two parties engage in trade, they do so voluntarily. Corporations, like Exxon and General Motors, no matter how large or powerful, cannot levy a "tax" on your income or force you to buy their products. Although mutual gain is the foundation for market transactions, the political process generates losers

APPLICATIONS IN ECONOMICS

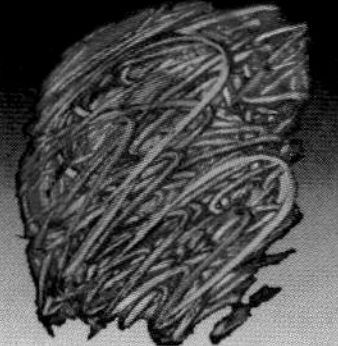

Perspectives on the Cost of Political Competition

We all have our own ideas about how government should be run. Because government is such an extremely important force in our economy and in our lives, individuals and groups try to influence election outcomes by voting, by contributing to political campaigns, and by ringing doorbells, among other activities. In addition, legislative and executive branch decisions can be influenced directly, by lobbying.

Competition for elective office is fierce and campaigns are expensive. In preparation for the 1998 elections, for example, candidates for U.S. House and Senate positions raised $207 million in 1997 alone. In the 1996 presidential race, candidates had spent $237 million through September 1996. Unlike bidders in a market auction, winners and losers alike pay the full costs of the election bid. It is common for lobbying groups to donate to opposing candidates in a close race.

During and after the election, lobbying groups compete for the attention—the ear—of elected officials. In fact, the greatest portion of campaign funds raised by incumbents is not raised at election time; rather, it accrues over their entire term in office. A large campaign contribution may not be able to "buy" a vote, but it certainly enhances the lobbyist's chance to sit down with the elected official to explain the power and the beauty of the contributor's position. In the competitive world of politics, the politician who does not at least listen to helpful "friends of the campaign" is less likely to survive.

Campaign contributions are only the tip of the lobbying iceberg. In Washington, D.C., alone, tens of thousands of individuals, many of them extremely talented, hard-working, and well paid, are dedicated to lobbying Congress and the executive branch of the federal government. Trade associations, for example, have more than 3,000 offices and 80,000 employees in Washington. Of these associations, at least 30 pay their highest officials between $400,000 and $900,000 per year.[1] Another indicator of the enormous amount of time and effort allocated to influencing government is that 65 percent of *Fortune* 200 chief executive officers travel to Washington at least every two weeks, on average. Billions of dollars in budgets, in taxes, and in expenditures required by regulation are at stake. When Congress and the agencies wield such power, competition to obtain the prizes and avoid the penalties naturally results in huge expenditures designed to influence government policy.

[1]The salary range is from Peter H. Stone, "Payday!" *National Journal* (December 17, 1994): 2948–2961. More details on campaign finance can be found in Michael Barone and Grant Ujifusa, *The Almanac of American Politics: 1996* (Washington, D.C.: National Journal, 1995).

as well as winners. If a legislative majority decides on a particular policy, the minority must accept the policy and help pay for it, even if that minority strongly disagrees. If $10 billion is allocated by the legislative branch for the development of a super weapon system (or for welfare programs, health care, or foreign aid), the dissenting minority is required to pay taxes that will help finance the project. Similarly, if government regulators mandate that private parties must provide a wildlife habitat, wetlands, housing at below-market prices, or other goods, both the providers of mandated goods and potential buyers who would like to purchase the same resources for their own use must comply with government orders. When issues are decided in the public sector, those who disagree must, at least temporarily, yield to the view of the current majority.

5. **When collective decisions are made legislatively, voters must choose among candidates who represent a bundle of positions on issues.** On election day, the voter cannot choose the views of Representative Frank Free Lunch on poverty and business welfare and simultaneously choose the views of challenger Amanda Austerity on national defense and tariffs. ***Inability to support a candidate's views on one issue while rejecting that candidate's views on another greatly reduces the voter's power to make preferences count on specific issues.*** Since the average representative is asked to vote on roughly 2,000 different issues during a two-year term, the enormity of the problem is obvious. The situation in a market is quite different. A buyer can purchase some groceries or items of clothing from one store, while choosing related items from different suppliers. There is seldom a bundle purchase problem in markets.

6. **Income and power are distributed differently in the two sectors.** Individuals who supply more highly valued resources in the marketplace have larger incomes. The number of dollar votes available to an individual will reflect his or her abilities, ambitions, skills, perceptiveness, past savings, inheritance, good fortune, and willingness to produce for others, among other things. An unequal distribution of consumer power is the result. In a democratic public sector, ballots call the tune. One citizen, one vote is the rule. But there are other, more powerful ways to deliver votes. An individual might donate money to help a campaign do its work better and capture more votes. Or an individual might provide more direct assistance to the campaign by visiting friends and neighbors, writing letters, or speaking publicly on behalf of the candidate (or party). The political process gives the greatest rewards to those who are best able and most willing to use their time, persuasive skills, organizational abilities, and financial contributions to help politicians get votes. Persons who have more money and skills of this sort—and are willing to spend them in the political arena—can expect to benefit more handsomely from the political process than can individuals who lack these personal resources. In the public sector as in the market, there is an unequal distribution of influence and "income," although the sources of success and influence differ between the two sectors.

THE OPPORTUNITY COST OF GOVERNMENT

Scarcity is inescapable in both the private and the public sectors. People often speak as if taxes are the cost of government. But the cost of any product is what we have to give up in order to produce it—the opportunity cost. Government is no exception. There are three types of cost incurred when an activity is undertaken by the government.

First, there is the opportunity cost of the resources used to produce goods supplied through the public sector. When governments purchase goods and services to provide missiles, education, highways, health care, and other goods, the resources needed must be bid away from private-sector activities. If they were not tied up producing goods provided by government, these resources would be available to produce private-sector goods. Note that this cost is incurred regardless of whether the provision of the public-sector goods is financed by current taxes, by an increase in government debt, or by money creation. This cost can be diminished only by reducing the size of government purchases. And a similar cost is incurred when government does not purchase goods, but orders the provision of goods without payment, or on terms decreed by regulators rather than terms voluntarily agreed upon by trading parties. The fact that government has not paid a market price does not reduce the cost. The Center for the Study of American Business estimated that the cost of complying with federal regulations, on the part of those regulated, was more than $340 billion (approximately $1,250 per person) in 1998. The first and often largest opportunity cost of an item supplied by government is the best alternative use that could have been made of the resources required to provide the good.

Second, there is the cost of resources expended in the collection of taxes and the enforcement of government mandates. Tax laws and regulatory orders must be enforced. Tax returns and formal notices of compliance with regulations must be prepared and monitored. Resources used to prepare, monitor, and enforce tax and regulatory legislation are unavailable for the production of either private- or public-sector goods. In the United States, studies indicate that it takes businesses and individuals approximately 5.5 billion worker-hours (the equivalent of 2.7 million full-time workers) each year just to complete the taxation paperwork. This means that every dollar of tax revenue raised by the government costs taxpayers approximately $1.15.

Finally, there is the excess burden (or deadweight loss) of taxation that we discussed in Chapter 4. Taxes distort incentives. When buyers pay more and sellers receive less due to the payment of a tax, trade and the production of output become less attractive. Trade and output will decline. Individuals will spend less time on productive (but taxed) market activities and more time on tax-avoidance and untaxed activities, such as leisure. Regulation also distorts incentives. When a government agency can mandate the supply of a resource—for example, a tract of land for use as an endangered species habitat—it will tend to allocate more of the "free" resource and less of other resources that it must purchase from its own budget. Regulatory powers, like taxes, distort prices and incentives, thus reducing economic efficiency.

In essence, the cost of government activities is the sum of (1) the opportunity cost of resources used to produce government-supplied goods and services, (2) the cost of tax and regulatory compliance, and (3) the excess-burden cost of taxation and regulation. Thus, government supply of goods and services generally costs the economy a good bit more than either the size of the tax bill or the level of budget expenditures implies.

Who pays the cost of government? Politicians often speak of imposing taxes on "business" as if part of the tax burden could be transferred from individuals to a non-person (business). But business taxes, like all other taxes, are paid by individuals. A corporation or business firm may write the check to the government, but it does not pay the taxes. The business corporation merely collects the money from someone else—from its customers in the form of higher prices, from its suppliers (including employees) in the form of lower wages or prices paid, or from stockholders in the form of lower dividends paid—and transfers the money to the government. The same is true when a firm is forced by government mandate to provide goods. In order for government to provide goods and services, individuals must pay for them.

ECONOMIC EFFICIENCY AND THE ROLE OF GOVERNMENT

Government is a powerful force in the economy. It can produce much that is good. But using government is costly. Why do citizens turn to government? How large should the scope of governmental action be? From an economic viewpoint, what are the proper functions of government?

To address these questions, we need a criterion by which to judge alternative institutional arrangements—that is, market- and public-sector policies. Economists often use the standard of **economic efficiency.** The central idea is straightforward. It simply means that, for any given level of effort (cost), we want to obtain the largest possible benefit. A corollary is that we want to obtain any specific level of benefits with the least possible effort. Economic efficiency simply means getting the most value from the available resources—making the largest pie from the available set of ingredients, so to speak.

Economic efficiency
Economizing behavior. When applied to a community, it implies that (1) an activity should be undertaken if the sum of the benefits to the individuals exceeds the sum of their costs and (2) no activity should be undertaken if the costs borne by the individuals exceed the benefits.

Why efficiency? Economists acknowledge that individuals generally do not have the efficiency of the economy as a primary goal. Rather, each person wants the largest possible "piece of the pie." All might agree that a bigger pie is preferred, however, particularly if each is allowed a larger slice as a result. Thus, efficiency can be in everyone's interest because it makes a larger pie, and, therefore, a larger slice, possible.

What does efficiency mean when applied to the entire economy? Individuals are the final decision makers of an economy, and individuals will bear the costs and reap the benefits of economic activity. When applied to the entire economy, two conditions are necessary for ideal economic efficiency:

Rule 1. ***Undertaking an economic action will be efficient if it produces more benefits than costs for the individuals of the economy.*** Such actions make it possible to improve the well-being of at least some individuals without creating reductions in the welfare of others. Failure to undertake such activities means that potential gain has been forgone.

Rule 2. ***Undertaking an economic action will be inefficient if it produces more costs than benefits to the individuals.*** When an action results in greater total costs than benefits, somebody must be harmed. The benefits that accrue to those who gain are insufficient to compensate for the losses imposed on others. Therefore, when all persons are considered, the net impact of such an action is counterproductive.

Both failure to undertake an efficient action (Rule 1) and the undertaking of inefficient activities (Rule 2) will result in economic inefficiency. The concept of economic efficiency applies to each and every possible income distribution, although a change in income distribution may alter the precise combination of goods and services that is most efficient.[2] Positive economics does not tell us how income should be distributed. Of course, we all have ideas on the subject. Most of us would like to see more income distributed our way. Agreement on what is the best distribution of income is unlikely, but for any particular income distribution, there will be an ideal resource allocation that will be most efficient.

Economic efficiency provides us with a criterion for the evaluation of the scope of government. Of course, this does not completely resolve the issue. Philosophers, economists, and other scholars have debated this issue for centuries. While the debate continues, there is substantial agreement that at least two functions of government are legitimate: (1) protection against invasions by others and (2) provision of goods that cannot easily be provided through markets. These two functions correspond to what Nobel laureate James Buchanan conceptualizes as the protective and productive functions of government.

Protective Function of Government

The most fundamental function of government is the protection of individuals and their property against acts of aggression. As John Locke wrote more than three centuries ago, individuals are constantly threatened by "the invasions of others." Therefore, each individual "is willing to join in society with others, who are already united, or have a mind to unite, for the mutual preservation of their lives, liberties, and estates."[3]

[2]Note to students who may pursue advanced study in economics: Using the concept of efficiency to compare alternative policies typically requires that the analyst estimate costs and benefits that are difficult or impossible to measure. Costs and benefits are the values of opportunities forgone or accepted by individuals, *as evaluated by those individuals.* Then these costs and benefits must be added up across all individuals and compared. But does a dollar's gain for one individual really compensate for a dollar's sacrifice by another? Some economists simply reject the validity of making such comparisons. They say that neither the estimates by the economic analyst of subjectively determined costs and benefits nor the adding up of these costs and benefits across individuals is meaningful. Their case may be valid, but most economists today nevertheless use the concept of efficiency as we present it. No other way to use economic analysis to compare policy alternatives has been found.

[3]John Locke, *Treatise of Civil Government,* 1690 ed. Charles Sherman (New York: Appleton-Century-Crofts, 1937), p. 82.

APPLICATIONS IN ECONOMICS

The Importance of the Protective Function—The Case of Russia

Government does not always protect the rights of those who produce value. It sometimes joins with those seeking to restrict trade or plunder the goods of others. The recent experience of Russia vividly illustrates what happens when the protective function of government is poorly performed. Reporter Andrew Higgins, in a front-page article in *The Wall Street Journal* (October 16, 1998) described how regional officials, or "barons," sought to ban the movement of food out of their domains in order to keep food prices low for their regional constituents. "Eager to keep bread cheap, sausages plentiful and their own interests secure," various regional barons restricted the ability of farm producers to trade with buyers outside of their region. As a result, food prices in Moscow and other large northern cities were substantially higher than in the countryside where the food is produced. Sunflower oil, for example, was selling for 2,000 rubles a ton in one region, while the price was 5,000 rubles in another.

The article describes the plight of Mrs. Irina Radinsya, who stored over 250 tons of rye on her farm, along with barley and a sunflower crop. When she and other farmers tried to move their food 375 miles north to Moscow, where hungry people were willing to pay more, regional police stopped them. Some farmers were refused permission to proceed, and others were required to pay bribes of 150 rubles (about $11.50 at the time) per truck moved out of the region. Far from protecting the property of producers and traders, government officials were restricting trade and seizing property. Under these conditions, less food is produced. Furthermore, some of the harvest rots as farmers seek ways around the artificial trade barriers and the lawless demanding of bribes by government officials.

The protective function of government involves the maintenance of a framework of security and order— an infrastructure of rules within which people can interact peacefully with one another. It also entails the enforcement of rules against theft, fraud, physical harm to one's person and property, and the like. It also involves provision of national defense designed to protect domestic residents against invasion from a foreign power.

It is easy to see the economic importance of this function. When the protective function is performed well, the property of citizens is secure, freedom of exchange is present, and contracts are legally enforceable. With the freedom of exchange and assurance that if they sow (produce), they will be permitted to reap (enjoy the benefits of their output), individuals will move resources toward their highest valued uses. In

The English philosopher John Locke argued that people own themselves and, as a result of this self-ownership, they also own the fruits of their labor. Locke stressed that individuals are not subservient to government. To the contrary, the role of government is to protect the "natural rights" of individuals to their person and property. This view, also reflected in the "unalienable rights" of the American Declaration of Independence, undergirds the protective function of government.

contrast, when property rights are insecure and contracts unenforceable, productive behavior is undermined. Plunder, fraud, and economic chaos result. The recent experience of Russia illustrates this point. (See the accompanying Applications in Economics feature on Russia.)

Productive Function of Government

The nature of some goods makes them difficult to provide through markets. Sometimes it is difficult to establish a one-to-one link between payment for a good and receipt of the good. If this link cannot be established, the incentive of market producers to supply such goods is weak. In addition, high transaction costs—particularly, the cost of monitoring use and collecting fees—can sometimes make it difficult to supply a good through the market. When either of these conditions is present, it may be more efficient for the government to supply the good and use its taxing power to cover the cost.

Of all the productive functions that government can provide, a framework of a stable monetary and financial environment is perhaps the most important. That is so because markets work better within such a framework. Why? If markets are to function well, individuals need to know the value to others of what they are buying or selling. For market prices to convey this information, a stable monetary exchange system must be provided. This is especially true for the many market exchanges that involve a time dimension. Houses, cars, consumer durables, land, buildings, equipment, and many other items are often used and paid for over a period of months or even years. If the purchasing power of the monetary unit, the dollar in the United States, gyrated wildly, previously determined prices would not represent their intended values. Few would want to make transactions involving long-term commitments, due to uncertainty. The smooth functioning of the market would be retarded.

The government's spending and monetary policies exert a powerful influence on economic stability. If properly conducted, these policies contribute to economic stability, full and efficient utilization of resources, and stable prices. However, improper stabilization policies can cause massive unemployment, rapidly rising prices, or both.

Economists are not in complete agreement on the extent to which public policy can stabilize the economy and promote full employment. They often debate the impact of various policy tools. All agree, however, that a stable economic environment is vital to a market economy. (Those pursuing a course in macroeconomics will find both the potential and the limitations of government action as a stabilizing force discussed further in Part Three.)

Thus we can see that government may have a productive role along with its protective role; it may be able to engage in activities that will increase the size of the economic pie.

THE ROLE OF GOVERNMENT AND POTENTIAL SHORTCOMINGS OF THE MARKET

The protective and productive functions of government can be analyzed within the framework of the invisible hand principle. As we previously discussed, the invisible hand of market forces generally provides resource owners and business firms with a strong incentive to undertake projects that create value. Will this always be true? The answer to this question is no. There are four major factors that may undermine the invisible hand and reduce the efficiency of markets: (1) lack of competition, (2) externalities,

(3) public goods, and (4) poorly informed buyers or sellers. We will now consider each of these factors and explain why they may create the potential for productive action through government.

LACK OF COMPETITION

Competition is vital to the proper operation of the pricing mechanism. It is competition among sellers that drives the prices of consumer goods down to the level of their cost. Similarly, competition in markets for productive resources prevents (1) sellers from charging exorbitant prices to producers and (2) buyers from taking advantage of the owners of productive resources. The existence of competing buyers and sellers reduces the power of both to rig the market in their own favor.

Because competition is the enemy of prices higher than costs, sellers have a strong incentive to escape from its pressures. When there are only a few firms in a market, rather than competing, sellers may be able to collude effectively. Efforts in this direction should be expected. Competition is something that is good when the other guy faces it. Individually, each of us would prefer to be loosened from its grip. Students do not like stiff competitors at exam time, when seeking entry to graduate school, or in their social or romantic lives. Similarly, sellers prefer few real competitors.

Exhibit 5–1 illustrates how sellers can gain from collusive action. If a group of sellers could eliminate competition from new entrants to the market, they would be able to raise their prices. The total revenue of sellers is simply the market price multiplied by the quantity sold. The sellers' revenues may well be greater, and their total costs would surely be lower, if the smaller, restricted output Q_2 were sold rather than the competitive output Q_1. The artificially high price P_2 reflects not only resource scarcity, but also a premium due to the reduction in output resulting from collusion among sellers.

If a group of sellers can restrict the entry of competitors and collude to reduce their own output, they can sometimes obtain more total revenue by selling fewer units. Note that the total sales revenue P_2Q_2 for the restricted supply exceeds the sales revenue P_1Q_1 for the competitive supply, in this case. Such behavior reduces the gains from trade, making the market less efficient as a result.

EXHIBIT 5–1

RIGGING THE MARKET

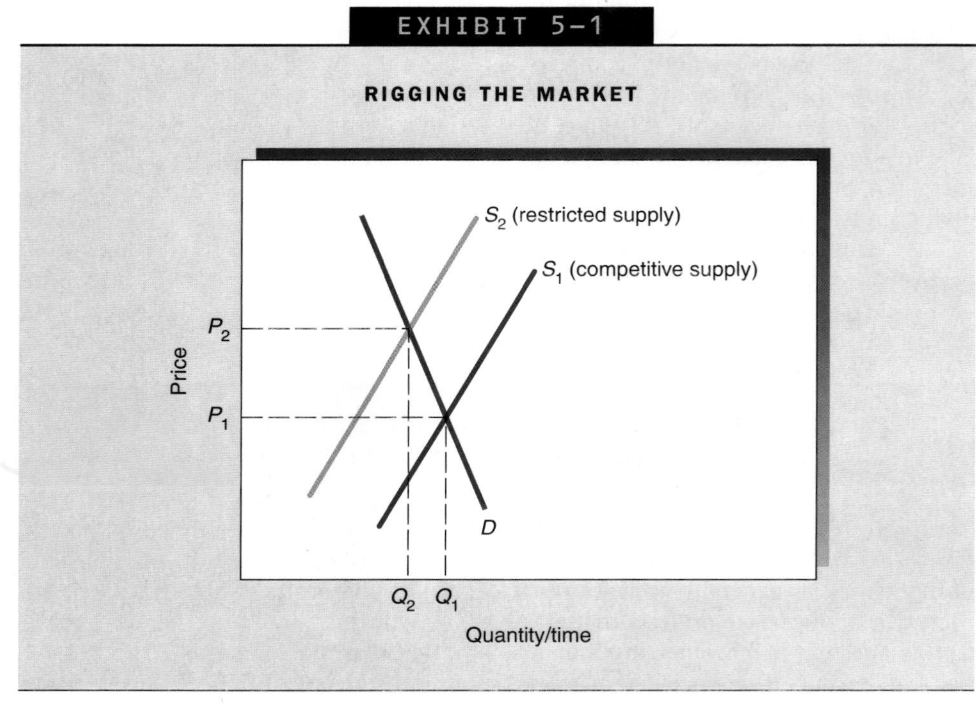

It is in the interest of consumers and the community that output be expanded to Q_1. At output Q_1, all units that are valued more than their cost are produced and sold. Thus, Q_1 is consistent with economic efficiency (Rule 1). It is in the interest of sellers, though, to make the good artificially scarce and raise its price. If sellers could restrict entry into the market and reduce output (to Q_2 for example), they could gain. If this happens, however, inefficiency would result because units valued more than their opportunity cost will not be supplied. There is a potential conflict between the interests of sellers and what is best for the entire community.

What can the government do to ensure that markets are competitive? The first guideline might be borrowed from the medical profession: Do no harm. A productive government will refrain from using its powers to impose licenses, discriminatory taxes, price controls, tariffs, quotas, and other entry and trade restraints that lessen the intensity of competition. Competition is ubiquitous. Without the help of government, sellers will generally find it very difficult to limit the entry of rival firms (including rival producers from other countries) into a market. When entry into a market is costly and there are only a few sellers, collusive behavior is more likely. In an effort to deal with such cases, the United States has enacted a series of antitrust laws, most notably the Sherman Antitrust Act (1890) and the Clayton Act (1914), making it illegal for firms to collude or attempt to monopolize a product market.

For the most part, economists favor the principle of government action to ensure and promote competitive markets. There is considerable debate, however, about the effectiveness of past public policy in this area. Many economists believe that, by and large, antitrust policy has been ineffective. Others stress that government regulatory policies have often been counterproductive by restricting entry, protecting existing producers from potential competitors, and limiting price competition. When government takes these actions, it actually reduces the competitiveness of markets. As we proceed, we will return to this topic and consider it in more detail.

Externalities—Failure to Register Fully Costs and Benefits

When property rights are not fully enforced, the actions of a producer or consumer might harm the property (or the person) of another, because the law fails to force the party doing the harm to bear the cost or to stop the harm. This failure results in spillover effects called **externalities,** actions of an individual or a group that influence the well-being of others without their consent. When spillover effects are present because, for example, the courts have failed to enforce rights against pollution, markets will fail to register the full costs of the resources used to produce a good or service. As a result, the information conveyed by prices is an inaccurate reflection of relative scarcity.

Externalities
The side effects, or spillover effects, of an action that influence the well-being of nonconsenting parties. The nonconsenting parties may be either helped (by external benefits) or harmed (by external costs).

Examples of externalities abound. The steel mill pouring pollution into the air imposes an external cost on surrounding residents. An apartment resident playing loud music may impose a cost on neighbors seeking to study, relax, or sleep. Driving your car during rush hour increases the level of congestion, thereby imposing a cost on other motorists. Similarly, litterbugs, drunk drivers, muggers, and robbers impose unwanted and *unauthorized* costs on others.

The existence of externalities implies the lack of property rights, or a lack of enforcement of those rights. The apartment dweller who is bothered by a neighbor's noise either does not have a right to quiet or is unable to enforce the right. In either case, the maker of the noise is not forced to take into account the resulting discomfort of neighbors. Similarly, each motorist adding his or her car to heavy traffic will not be forced to consider the effects on others, unless there is a highway access fee reflecting the costs of congestion. When enforceable property rights are absent, externalities are a natural occurrence.

Not all externalities result in the imposition of a cost. Sometimes human actions generate benefits for nonparticipating parties. The homeowner who keeps a house in good condition and maintains a neat lawn improves the beauty of the entire community, providing benefits for other community members. A flood-control dam project built by upstream residents for their benefit may also generate gains for those who live downstream. Scientific theories benefit their authors, but the knowledge gained also contributes to the welfare of others who do not help to pay for their development. Again, a lack of enforceable property rights to the created benefit prevents the producer of the good or service generating the positive-valued externalities from reaping the full benefit.

Why do externalities create problems for the market mechanism? **Exhibit 5–2** can help answer this question. With competitive markets in equilibrium, the cost of a good (including the opportunity cost borne by the producer) will be paid by consumers. Unless consumer benefits exceed the opportunity cost of production, the goods will not be produced. What happens, though, when externalities are present?

Suppose that a business firm discharges smoke into the air or sewage into a river. Valuable resources—clean air and pure water—are used essentially for garbage disposal. The polluter may benefit from the garbage removal, but if those downwind or downstream who are harmed cannot successfully sue for damages, neither the firm nor the consumers of its products will pay for these costs. As part a of Exhibit 5–2 shows, the supply curve will understate the opportunity cost of production when these external costs are present. Since the producer has to consider only the cost to the firm and can ignore the costs imposed on secondary parties, supply curve S_1 is present. If the producer had to pay all costs, a smaller supply (S_2) would result.

The actual supply curve S_1 does not register fully the opportunity cost of producing the good. For the producer, the opportunity cost paid is low enough to merit

When external costs are present (a), the output level of a product will exceed the desired amount. Some units (beyond Q_2) will be produced even though their costs exceed the benefits they generate, causing reduced efficiency. In contrast, market output of goods that generate external benefits (b) will be less than the ideal level. Production that could generate more benefits than costs is not undertaken, and a lack of efficiency results.

EXHIBIT 5–2

EXTERNALITIES AND PROBLEMS FOR THE MARKET

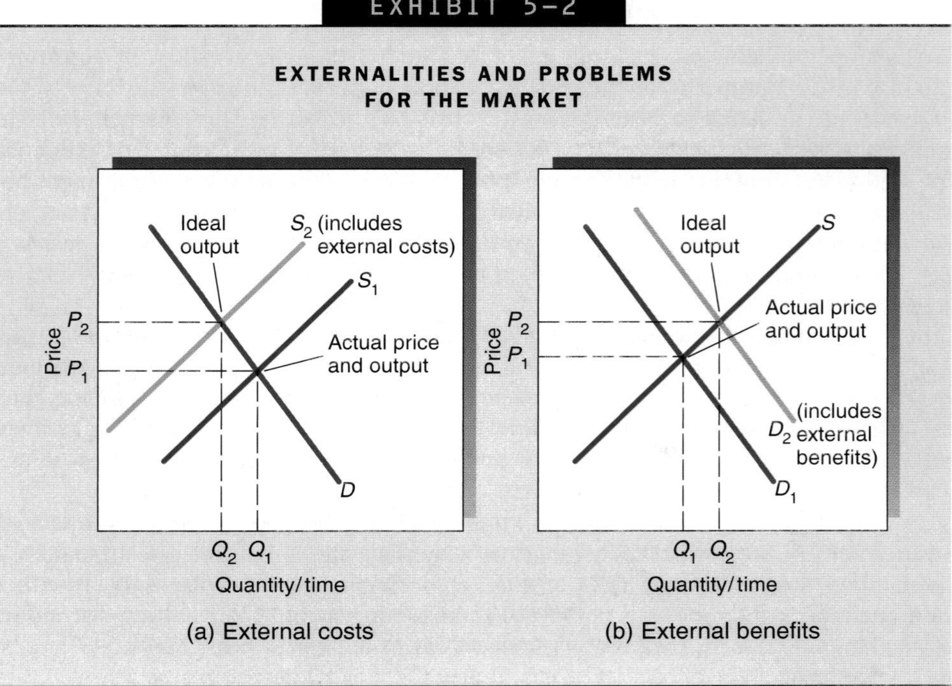

(a) External costs

(b) External benefits

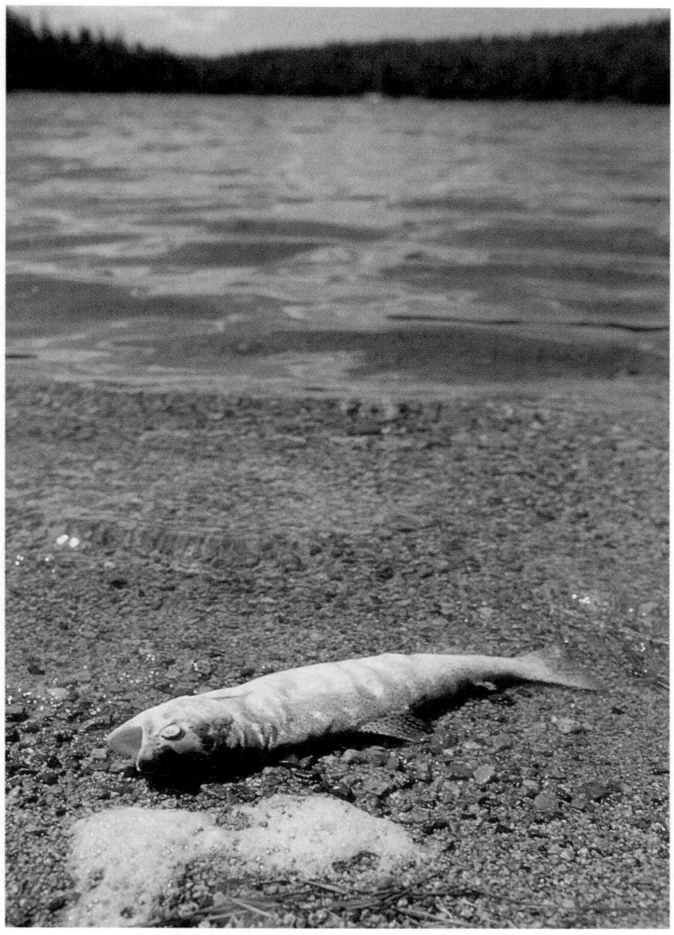

Externalities resulting from poorly defined and enforced property rights underlie the problems of excessive air and water pollution.

expansion in output beyond Q_2 (to Q_1), *even though the buyer's valuation of the additional units is less than their full opportunity cost.* The second efficiency condition, Rule 2, is violated. Inefficiency results because units are produced even though their value is less than their cost. Excessive air and water pollution are side effects. In the total picture, the harm caused by the added pollution outweighs the net benefits derived by buyers and sellers from the production of units beyond Q_2. The economy would have been better off if the units beyond Q_2 had not been produced. To repeat, this problem is caused by the inability or the failure of courts to protect the property rights of those downwind or downstream who are harmed.

As part b of Exhibit 5-2 shows, external benefits often result in opportunities forgone. A good, such as a flower garden in the front yard of a home, may be intended for private consumption. But others also benefit without having to shoulder any of the costs. Under these circumstances, the market demand curve D_1 will not register fully the total benefits, including those received by persons who do not help pay for their cost. Output Q_1 will result. Could the community gain from a greater output of the product? Yes. The demand curve D_2 reflects both the direct benefits to paying consumers and the benefits bestowed on secondary, nonpaying parties. Expansion of output beyond Q_1 to Q_2 would result in a net gain to the community. But because neither producers nor paying consumers can capture the secondary benefits, consumption level Q_1 will result. The potential net gain from the greater output level Q_2 will be lost. Rule 1 of our ideal efficiency criterion is violated. Once again, the failure of property rights enforcement causes the problem. In this case, producers are unable to collect payment from some of those who enjoy the goods or the services they produce.

Market participants can gain if they can figure out a way to capture the external benefits. Sometimes this can be done by expanding the functions of the firm. For example, developers of golf courses in recent years have typically purchased large tracts of land around the planned course *before it is built.* This places them in a position to resell the land at a higher price after the golf course has been completed, and thereby capture what would otherwise be external benefits.

The development of Walt Disney World in Florida provides an interesting case of entrepreneurial ingenuity designed to capture external benefits more fully. When Walt Disney developed Disneyland in California, the market value of the land in the immediate area soared as a result of the increase in demand for services (food, lodging, gasoline, and so on). Because the land in the area was owned by others, the developers of Disneyland were unable to capture these external benefits. However, when Walt Disney World was developed outside of Orlando, Florida, the owners purchased an enormous plot of land, far more than was needed for the amusement park. The value of this land soared, as the demand for hotels, restaurants, and other businesses increased with the development of Disney World. Through the years, the resale of land near the park has provided a major source of revenue for the Disney Corporation. While efforts of this type are helpful, they are unable to overcome fully the problems created by external benefits. Some unrealized potential gains remain, creating the potential for future improvement.

Summarizing, competitive markets will fail to give consumers and producers the correct signals and incentives when property rights are not fully defined and enforced, creating externalities. The market will tend to overallocate resources to the production of goods that impose external costs on nonconsenting parties and underallocate resources to the production of goods with external benefits. Government might be able to alter this situation. For example, it might be able to define and enforce property rights more clearly. Alternatively, it might levy a tax on goods that generate external costs and provide subsidies to activities that generate external benefits. While there is no assurance that government intervention will improve the situation, externalities do create the potential for productive action.

Public Goods—A Potential Problem for the Market

Public goods
Jointly consumed goods that are not diminished when one person enjoys their consumption. When consumed by one person, they are also made available to others. National defense, flood control dams, and scientific theories are all public goods.

Public goods are difficult to provide commercially through the marketplace because there is no way to exclude nonpaying customers. For a good to be considered a public good, it must be (1) *joint-in-consumption* and (2) *nonexcludable.* A good is joint-in-consumption when many individuals can share in the consumption of the same unit of output. A radio broadcast signal, for example, can be shared by everyone within the listening range. When a good is joint-in-consumption, additional consumption by one person does not reduce the amount available to others. If an additional listener turns on her radio, this does not reduce the amount of the signal available for other listeners. Thus, the marginal cost of allowing an additional listener to share in the usage of the good is zero. Most goods do not have this shared consumption characteristic, but are instead rivals-in-consumption. Two individuals cannot simultaneously consume the same pair of jeans, for example. When one person purchases a pair of jeans, there is one less pair available for someone else.

The second characteristic of a public good is that it is nonexcludable. Nonexcludable means that it is impossible (or at least very costly) to exclude nonpaying customers from receipt of the good. Since those who do not pay cannot be excluded, no one has much incentive to help pay for such goods. This creates a problem with **free riders,** persons who receive the benefits of the good without helping to pay for its cost. When a large number of people become free riders, not very much of the public good is produced. This is precisely the problem with market provision in the case of public goods—they will be undersupplied by the market. This will be true even if the good is quite valuable. Suppose national defense were provided entirely through the market. Would you voluntarily help to pay for it? Your contribution would have little impact on the total supply of defense available to each of us, even if you made a large personal contribution. Many citizens, even though they might value defense highly, would become free riders, and few funds would be available for the finance of national defense.

Free rider
One who receives the benefit of a good without contributing to its costs. Public goods and commodities that generate external benefits offer people the opportunity to become free riders.

It is important to note that it is the characteristics of the good, not the sector in which it is produced, that distinguishes a public good. In reality, government produces both public and nonpublic goods, and so do private markets. Many goods provided in the public sector, ranging from medical services and education to mail delivery and trash collection, do not qualify as public goods. In fact, pure public goods are rare. National defense is probably the closest example. Keeping the air in a city clean also qualifies as a public good. Similarly, the actions of a central banking system and the judicial and legal systems could also be classified as public goods.

Just because a good is a public good does not necessarily mean that markets will fail to supply it. When the benefit of producing these goods is high, entrepreneurs will attempt to find innovative ways of overcoming the free rider problem. Radio broadcasts, which have both of the public good characteristics, are still produced well by the private sector. The free rider problem has been overcome through the use of advertising (which generates indirect revenue from listeners), rather than directly charging listeners. Private entrepreneurs have also used such devices as signal encoders for

The Dutch boy has his finger in the dike, to prevent the leak from becoming a torrent and breaking the dike. Will the man help out with a donation, or will he be a free rider?

television broadcasts like HBO, copy protection on videotapes, and tie-in purchases (for example, tying the purchase of a software instruction manual with the purchase of the software itself) to overcome the free rider problem. The marketing of computer software provides an interesting illustration. Since the same software program can be copied without reducing the amount available, and it is costly to prevent consumption by nonpayers, software clearly has public good characteristics. Nonetheless, Bill Gates became the richest man in the world by producing and marketing this public good!

Public goods often cause a breakdown in the harmony between self-interest and the public interest. In spite of the innovative efforts of entrepreneurs, the quantity of a public good supplied strictly through market allocation will often be smaller than the quantity consistent with economic efficiency. This will create the potential for productive public sector action.

Potential Information Problems

In the real world, market choices, like other decisions, are made with incomplete information. Consumers do not have perfect knowledge about the quality of a product, the price of alternative products, or side effects that may result from its use. They may make incorrect decisions, decisions they will later regret, because they do not possess good information.

The reality of imperfect knowledge is not the fault of the market. In fact, the market provides consumers with a strong incentive to acquire information. If they mistakenly purchase a "lemon" product, they will suffer the consequences. Furthermore, sellers have a strong incentive to inform consumers of the benefits of their products, especially in comparison to competing products. However, circumstances will influence the incentive structure confronted by both buyers and sellers.

The consumer's information problem is minimal if the item is purchased regularly. Consider the purchase of soap. There is little cost associated with trying alternative brands. Since soap is a regularly purchased product, trial and error is an economical means of determining which brand is most suitable to one's needs. Soap, like toothpaste, most food products, lawn service, and gasoline, is a **repeat-purchase item.** The consumer can use past experience to good advantage when buying such items.

Repeat-purchase item
An item purchased often by the same buyer.

When dependent on repeat-purchase customers, sellers have a strong incentive to supply consumers with accurate information. Failure to do so would adversely affect future sales. Because future demand is directly related to the satisfaction level of current customers, sellers of repeat-purchase items will want to help their customers make satisfying long-run choices. In this case, there is a harmony of interests between buyers and sellers.

This harmony, however, is not always present. Major problems of conflicting interests, inadequate information, and unhappy customers arise when goods are either (1) difficult to evaluate on inspection and seldom repeatedly purchased from the same producer or (2) potentially capable of serious and lasting harmful side effects that cannot be predicted by a layperson. Under these conditions, human nature being what it is, we would expect some unscrupulous producers to sell low-quality, defective, and even harmful goods.

When customers are unable to distinguish between high-quality and low-quality goods, business entrepreneurs have an incentive to cut costs by reducing quality. Consumers get less for their dollars. Since sellers in this situation are not dependent on repeat customers, those who cut costs by cutting quality may survive and even prosper in the marketplace. ***The probability of customer dissatisfaction is thus increased by the absence of adequate information. Accordingly, the case for an unhampered market mechanism is weakened.***

Consider the consumer's information problem when an automobile is purchased. Are most consumers capable of properly evaluating the safety equipment? Except for a handful of experts, most people are not. Some consumers might individually seek expert advice. And entrepreneurs have sometimes found ingenious ways to benefit from providing consumers with more reliable information. (See the feature on

APPLICATIONS IN ECONOMICS

Information Problems as Profit Opportunities

When consumers can benefit from additional information, entrepreneurs can profit if they find a way to be paid for providing the information. Entrepreneurs are always looking for ways to earn more by providing consumers things for which they are willing to pay. ***Consumers have the incentive to seek good information, even though it is costly. Entrepreneurial publishers and other providers of information help consumers find what they seek by providing expert evaluations of the special characteristics built into complex products.*** For car buyers and computer buyers, for example, publishers market dozens of specialized magazines containing expert analyses and opinions from almost any point of view. Laboratory test results and detailed product evaluations on a wide variety of goods are provided by *Consumer Reports, Consumer Research,* and other publications.

Franchises are another way that entrepreneurs have responded to the need of consumers for more and better information. The tourist traveling through an area for the first time—and very possibly the only time—may find that eating at a franchised food outlet and sleeping at a franchised motel are the cheapest ways to avoid annoying and costly mistakes. The franchiser sets the standards for all firms in the chain and establishes procedures, including continuous inspection, designed to maintain the standards. Franchisers have a strong incentive to maintain their reputation for quality, because if it declines, their ability to sell new franchises is hurt. Even though the tourist may visit a particular establishment only once, the franchise turns that visit into a "repeat purchase," since the reputation of the entire national franchise operation is at stake.

Similarly, the advertising of a brand name nationally develops a reputation that is at stake each time a purchase is made. How much would the Coca-Cola Company pay to avoid the sale of a dangerous bottle of Coke? Surely, it would be a large sum. The company's brand name is worth an estimated $24 billion, and that good name is a hostage to quality control. Because Coke is a household name, any serious quality-control problem would be broadcast worldwide and do enormous financial damage to the firm. Advertising investments play a part, too, helping to build a reputation that consumers know is at stake. The value of the reputation built with the help of advertising is threatened if the firm cheats customers.

Enterprising entrepreneurs have found ways to assure buyers that products meet high standards of quality, even when the producer is small and not so well known. Consider the case of Best Western Motels.[1] Best Western owns no motels; however, building on the franchise idea, it publishes rules and standards with which motel owners must comply if they are to use the Best Western brand name and the reservation service that the company also operates. In order to protect its brand name, Best Western sends out inspectors to see that each Best Western motel in fact meets the standards. Every disappointed customer harms the reputation and reduces the value of the Best Western name, and reduces the willingness of motel owners to pay for use of the name. The standards are designed to keep customers satisfied. Even though each motel owner has only a relatively small operation, renting the Best Western name provides the small operator with the kind of international reputation formerly available only to large firms. In effect, Best Western acts as a regulator of all motels bearing its name. As it does so, it provides both consumers and producers with a market solution to problems resulting from imperfect information.

Another kind of private regulator is Underwriters Laboratories, or UL. It establishes its own standards for safety in electrical equipment. Manufacturers voluntarily submit their equipment to UL and pay the firm to test their products. They do so because if UL certifies that the product meets UL standards, that fact can be advertised, and consumers, knowing the UL reputation, will be more willing to buy the product. Again, the certifying firm, UL in this case, has a strong incentive to certify only those electrical products that do indeed meet their safety standards, because the value of the UL name is at stake. That value depends entirely on the effectiveness of its claims that UL-certified products are safe to use.

As these examples indicate, entrepreneurial measures, such as assuring the quality of a firm or franchise, or otherwise protecting a brand name, can be both expensive and effective. But they cannot guarantee that customers will never be cheated or disappointed after a transaction. We live in a world of imperfect information.

---

[1]This section draws from Randall G. Holcombe and Lora P. Holcombe, "The Market for Regulation," *Journal of Institutional and Theoretical Economics* 142, no. 4 (1986): 684–696.

"Information Problems as Profit Opportunities.") In many cases, however, it may be more efficient to prevent market failure by having the government regulate automobile safety and require certain safety equipment.

As useful and important as are the published evaluations of experts, franchise operations, advertising, brand-name reputations, and private regulatory firms, they cannot solve a kind of information problem that has little to do with product design or manufacture. This is called the **asymmetric-information problem,** and it can make markets themselves, for some products, difficult to operate effectively. ***The problem of asymmetric information arises when either the potential buyer or potential seller has important information that the other side does not have.***

Asymmetric-information problem
A problem arising when either buyers or sellers have important information about the product that is not possessed by the other side in potential transactions.

Think for a moment about buyers trying to avoid "lemons" in the used car market. Sellers know which cars are above average quality and which are below average. Buyers, on the other hand, cannot tell which is which simply by looking at and test-driving them. Thus buyers will be willing to pay no more than what they believe is the average value of all cars on the market. But if better-than-average cars cannot bring better-than-average prices, then fewer of them will be sold in the market, and if below-average cars bring average prices, then more of the below-average cars will be offered. Buyers understand this, so they expect the average car in such a market to be below the average of all existing cars of that age and type. Owners of better cars are reluctant to sell at the low market price and it is hard to make a market for cars of above-average quality when buyers cannot be convinced that they actually are better than average.

Sellers of the better cars have an incentive to provide additional information in order to get a higher price for their superior goods. But how is this done? How can they support their claims about their product being better? The answers differ according to whether the seller is a private owner or a dealership. Car owners can present their records of oil changes and lubrications to show that these services, important to the long-run durability of a car, have been performed on schedule. Dealers, whose mechanics inspect the cars before they are offered for sale, may offer money-back guarantees, or warranties that promise free repairs if needed within a specified time, on the most reliable cars they sell. The other cars they sell will be sold "as is" with no warranty. Sellers of products can even give price guarantees, as some stores do when they advertise that, if the buyer finds a lower price for the same product within a specified period of time, the seller will refund the difference. By offering to bear quality and price risks for buyers, sellers provide credibility to their claims about better products and prices. In other words, they improve the quality of the information offered and reduce the problem of asymmetric information.

The problem of asymmetric information also arises when buyers know more than sellers. Consider the market for health insurance. Buyers know their own health problems better than insurance companies do. Those whose health history and lifestyle threaten greater potential health costs may pay the same as others but later collect more from the insurance company. In contrast, the same insurance at the same price is less attractive to the healthiest people, and fewer of them will buy it. When the company is unable to identify those with the greatest potential health costs and charge them more, it will have to charge its healthier customers a rate that exceeds their expected future insurance claims. But this would drive away even more of the healthier potential buyers, making the situation even worse. As in the case of used cars, asymmetric information reduces the effectiveness of the market. Just as the best used cars may be hard to sell at a price reflecting their full value, so, too, may the healthiest individuals find it hard to find reasonably priced insurance when asymmetric information is present.

What can be done about asymmetric information when buyers have information but sellers do not? Buyers, like sellers, are willing to provide information when it is to their advantage to do so. Insurance buyers with the best health record, who are therefore least likely to have future insurance claims, can often get lower insurance rates by opening their private medical records to the insurance company. Sellers who otherwise have no right to see that information may find it gladly offered by the healthiest buyers when buyers know they will be offered lower insurance prices as a result.

We have discussed many ways in which market participants can reduce the problems they face due to the scarcity and cost of information. These are not totally effective, however. As with imperfect competition, externalities and public goods, poor information remains a problem that keeps markets from reaching their hypothetical ideal.

LOOKING *Ahead*

This chapter focused on the role of government from the standpoint of economic efficiency. Our analysis indicates that government can contribute positively to the prosperity of people through the provision of a legal and monetary environment for the smooth operation of competitive markets. Government may also contribute by providing a limited set of public goods and following policies capable of minimizing problems arising from externalities and poor information.

The potential of government to promote economic efficiency does not necessarily mean that it will. The political process is merely an alternative method of organizing economic activity. There is no assurance that even a democratic government will always "do the right thing." Furthermore, people can be expected to turn to government for reasons other than economic efficiency—pursuit of personal gain through subsidies, income transfers, and regulation of rivals, for example. Political decision making is complex, but the tools of economics can enhance our understanding of how it works. The next chapter will focus on this topic—the operation of government, when it is likely to work well, and when there is reason to expect that it will not work so well.

KEY POINTS

➤ Government has the exclusive right to use coercive force. Individuals and groups compete to influence the use of government's powers to tax, spend, and regulate.

➤ Public-sector organization can take from some and give to others, but scarcity guarantees that someone always pays. Benefits and costs are distributed differently in the public sector, as opposed to the private sector.

➤ Voters face a bundle purchase problem and are unable to vote for some policies favored by one candidate and other policies favored by the candidate's opponent.

➤ To find the cost of government, add the opportunity cost of the resources used to produce goods provided through government, the cost of tax and regulatory compliance, and the excess-burden cost of taxation and regulation. Individuals bear the burden of taxes (and regulations), regardless of whether firms or individuals write the checks to government.

➤ The protective function of government provides a framework in which individuals gain by acting peacefully and constructively. The productive function of government can help people get goods that would not easily be supplied through market transactions.

➤ When markets fail to produce the ideal quantity and mix of outputs, the problems can generally be traced to one of four sources: absence of competition, externalities, public goods, and poor information. Externalities and public goods reflect a lack of fully defined, enforced, and tradeable property rights.

➤ Entrepreneurs in markets have an incentive to find solutions to each market problem, and new solutions are constantly being discovered. But problems remain, and each creates the potential for improvement through government action.

CRITICAL ANALYSIS QUESTIONS

*1. If producers are to be provided with an incentive to produce a good, why is it important for them to be able to prevent nonpaying customers from receiving the good?

2. Explain in your own words what is meant by external costs and external benefits. Why may market allocations be less than ideal when externalities are present?

3. Why are public goods troublesome for markets to allocate efficiently?

*4. Which of the following are public goods?
   (a) an antimissile system surrounding Washington, D.C.
   (b) a fire department
   (c) tennis courts
   (d) Yellowstone National Park
   (e) elementary schools
   Explain, using the definition of a public good.

5. Suppose that Abel builds a factory next to Baker's farm, and air pollution from the factory harms Baker's crops. Is Baker's property right to the land being violated? Is an externality present? What if the pollution invades Baker's home and harms her health? Are her property rights violated? Is an externality present? Explain.

6. English philosopher John Locke argued that the protection of each individual's person and property (acquired without the use of violence, theft, or fraud) was the primary function of government. Why is this protection important to the efficient operation of an economy?

7. "The protective function of government is a key to the success of the market sector in the economy." Is this true or false? Explain.

8. "The traveler, in a market economy, has no chance for a fair deal. Local people may be treated well, but the traveler has no way to know, for example, who offers a good night's lodging at a fair price, if the quality and price are not regulated by government." Is this true or false? Explain.

9. If sellers of toasters were able to organize among themselves, reduce their output, and raise their price, how would economic efficiency be affected? Explain in terms of the impact on the marginal costs to sellers of the last (marginal) units produced, and the marginal benefits to buyers of obtaining the last (marginal) units.

10. (a) Explain why economic inefficiency may result when a producer of copper imposes external costs on growers of alfalfa located downwind from the copper facility.
    (b) In terms of property rights, what must be true if the costs on downwind farmers are external costs?

11. "Elementary education is obviously a public good. After all, it is provided by government." Evaluate this statement.

---

*Asterisk denotes questions for which answers are given in Appendix B.

Special Feature: The Size and Functions of Government—A Graphic and Pictorial Presentation

Chapter 5 has focused on how government might establish a framework for the smooth operation of markets and engage in certain activities—supply public goods and help deal with externalities, for example—that will make it possible to produce more value from the available resources. How do real-world governments fit this model? How have the size and functions of government changed through time? This brief special feature presents data on spending and taxation related to these questions.

GROWTH OF GOVERNMENT

As **Exhibit 5A–1** illustrates, the total government expenditures were only 10.1 percent of GDP in 1929, and most of that was at the state and local levels. (Note: GDP is a measure of the size of the economy. The term will be explained more fully in Chapter 7.) Federal expenditures accounted for only 3 percent of total output in 1929. During the 1930–1970 period, both the size and composition of government changed dramatically. By 1970 total government expenditures had risen to 32.5 percent of the economy, more

EXHIBIT 5A–1

THE GROWTH OF GOVERNMENT EXPENDITURES, 1929–1997

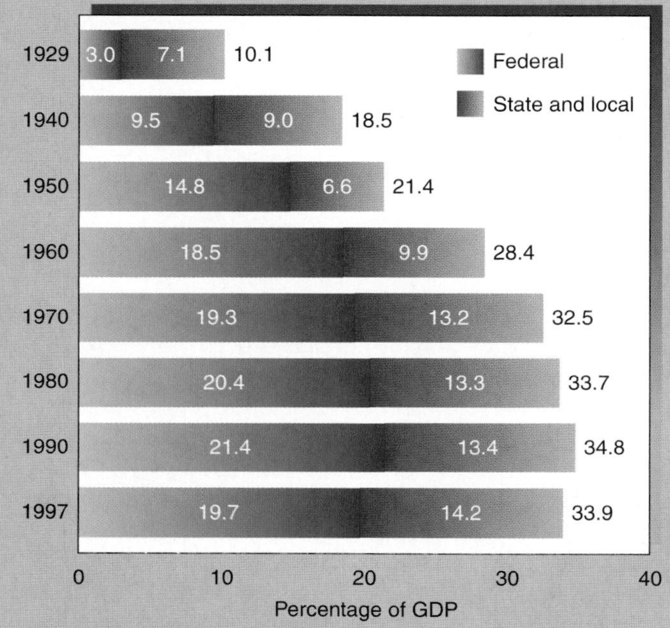

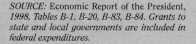

SOURCE: Economic Report of the President, *1998, Tables B-1, B-20, B-83, B-84. Grants to state and local governments are included in federal expenditures.*

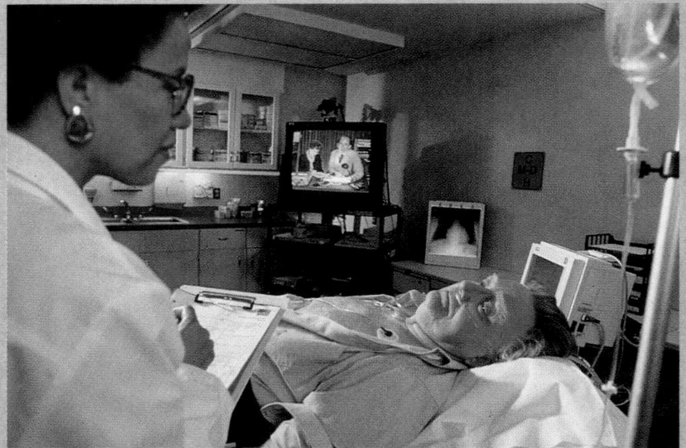

During the past four decades, government spending on defense has declined substantially as a share of the economy, while that for income transfers and health care has increased sharply.

than triple the level of 1929. Most of this growth of government took place at the federal level. *As a share of our economy,* federal expenditures in 1970 were more than six times the level of 1929. Since 1970 the size of government as a proportion of the economy has grown at a much slower rate. ***In 1997 total government expenditures comprised 33.9 percent of GDP, only slightly higher than the figure for 1970.***

SIZE OF GOVERNMENT: UNITED STATES COMPARED TO OTHER COUNTRIES

The size of government varies substantially across countries. As **Exhibit 5A–2** shows, government expenditures constitute 50 percent or more of GDP in Sweden, Denmark, France, Belgium, and Italy. In contrast, government spending amounts to only about one-third of GDP in the United States, Australia, and Japan. In Singapore, South Korea, Thailand, and Hong Kong, the size of government is still smaller.

CHANGING COMPOSITION—LESS SPENDING ON DEFENSE, MORE ON INCOME TRANSFERS AND HEALTH CARE

Government purchases
Current expenditures on consumption and investment goods provided by federal, state, and local governments; they exclude transfer payments.

Transfer payments
Payments to individuals or institutions that are not linked to the current supply of a good or service by the recipient.

It is important to distinguish between (1) government purchases of goods and services and (2) transfer payments. **Government purchases** occur when either consumption or investment goods are supplied through the public sector. Government-supplied consumption goods would include government expenditures on such items as police and fire protection, medical services, and administration. Government investments would include the provision of long-lasting goods, such as highways, jet planes, and buildings. **Transfer payments** are transfers of income from taxpayers to recipients who do not provide current goods and services in exchange for these payments. Simply put, transfer payments take income from some to provide additional income to others. By far, social security is the largest income transfer program. Pensions of retired government employees, along with income transfers to the unemployed, the disabled, and welfare recipients are also included in the income transfer category.

EXHIBIT 5A–2

SIZE OF GOVERNMENT— AN INTERNATIONAL COMPARISON, 1997

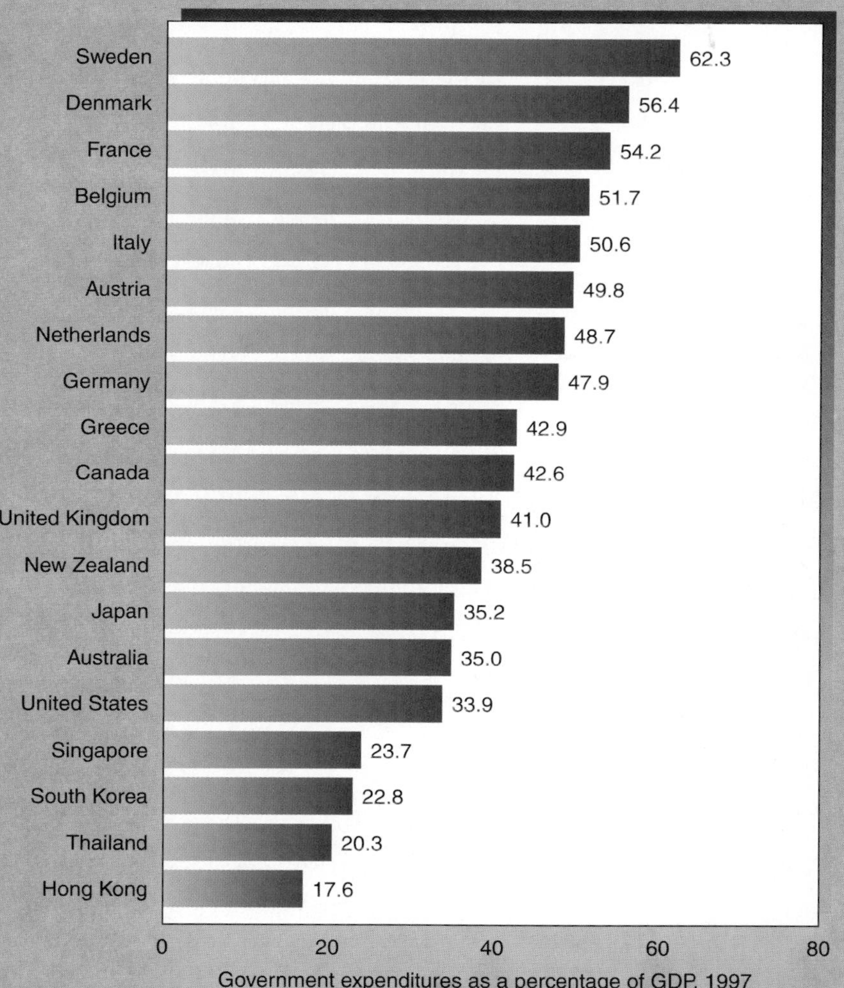

SOURCES: Organization for Economic Cooperation and Development, Economic Outlook, *Dec. 1997;* Economic Report of the President, *1998; and International Monetary Fund,* Government Finance Statistics Yearbook, *1997.*

Even though government spending as a share of the economy in the United States has changed only modestly since 1970, there has been a dramatic shift in the composition of government spending during the past four decades. Spending on defense has fallen as a share of the economy, while expenditures on transfer payments (income transfers) and health care have soared.

As Exhibit 5A–3 shows, in 1960, defense expenditures comprised 10.4 percent of GDP, more than half of the total spending of the federal government. By 1997, defense spending was only 4.3 percent of GDP (and less than 20 percent of the federal budget). In contrast, government expenditures on income transfers rose from 5.6 percent of

EXHIBIT 5A-3

CHANGES IN EXPENDITURES ON DEFENSE, INCOME TRANSFERS, AND HEALTH CARE: 1960–1997

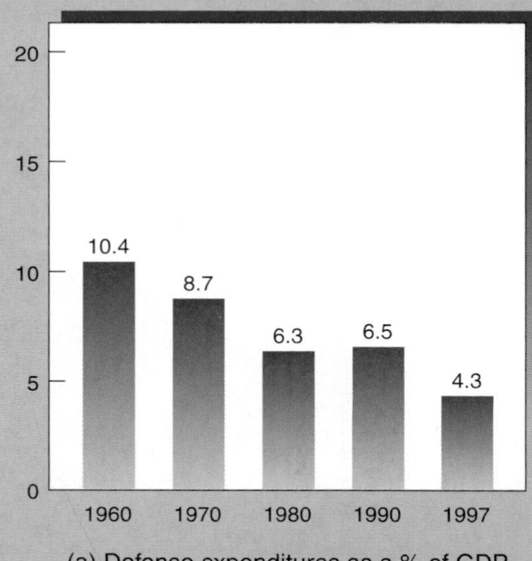

(a) Defense expenditures as a % of GDP

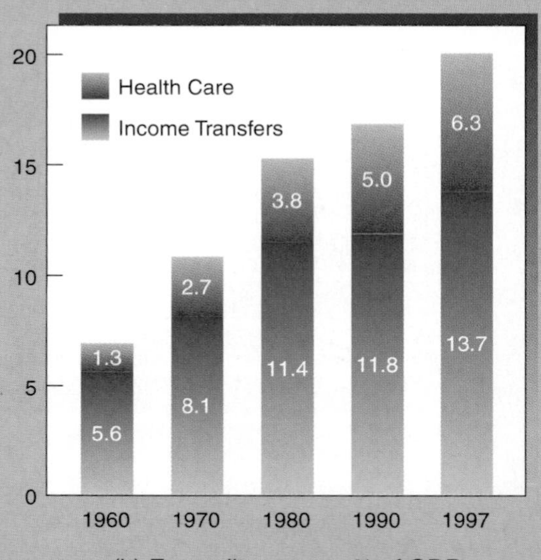

(b) Expenditures as a % of GDP

Note: The 1997 figure for health care expenditures was based on 1996 data.

SOURCES: Economic Report of the President, *1998, Tables B-1 and B-84, and* Health Care Financing Review, *Fall 1997, Table 9, p. 187.*

GDP in 1960 to 13.7 percent in 1997. During this same period, government spending on health care, primarily Medicare for the elderly and Medicaid for those with low incomes, rose from 1.3 percent of GDP in 1960 to 6.3 percent in 1997. Spending on income transfers and health care now constitutes 20 percent of GDP, substantially more than half of total government expenditures.

PRIMARY FUNCTIONS OF GOVERNMENT: FEDERAL COMPARED TO STATE AND LOCAL

Exhibit 5A–4 indicates the primary categories of government spending for both the federal and state and local levels. The figures reveal a great deal about the nature of the federal government in the mid-1990s. As part a of Exhibit 5A–4 shows, federal expenditures for just three things—(1) income transfers (including social security and other income security programs), (2) health care, and (3) net interest on the national debt—accounted for 72 percent of federal spending in 1997. Of course, the federal government is solely responsible for national defense and international affairs, which accounted for an additional 18 percent of the federal budget. This means that expenditures on everything else—the federal courts, national parks, highways, education,

EXHIBIT 5A–4

WHAT GOVERNMENTS BUY

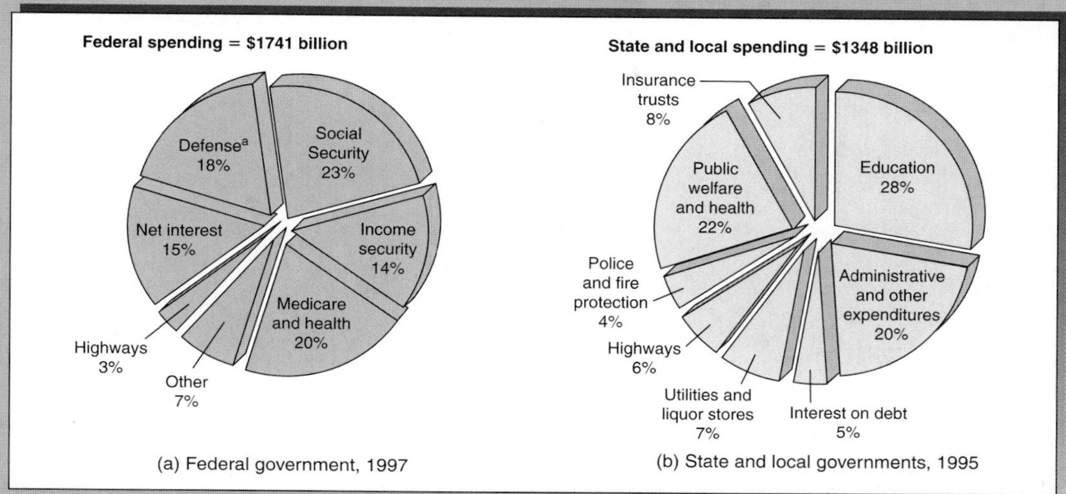

[a]*Including international affairs.*

SOURCES: Economic Report of the President, *1998, Table B-81, and* Statistical Abstract of the United States, *1998, Table 506.*

job training, agriculture, energy, natural resources, federal law enforcement, and numerous other programs—were only 10 percent of the federal budget.

Part b of Exhibit 5A–4 highlights the functional responsibilities of state and local governments. In the United States, public education has traditionally been the responsibility of state and local governments. Education is the largest spending category for state and local governments. Administration, public welfare and health, highways, utilities, insurance trust funds, law enforcement, and fire protection are other major areas of expenditure at the state and local levels.

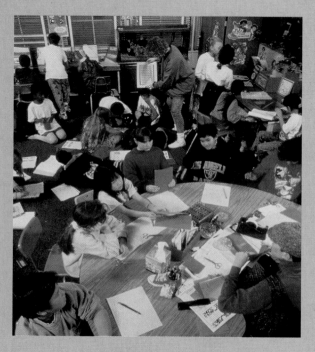

Education constitutes the largest category of spending at the state and local levels of government.

EXHIBIT 5A-5

SOURCES OF GOVERNMENT REVENUE

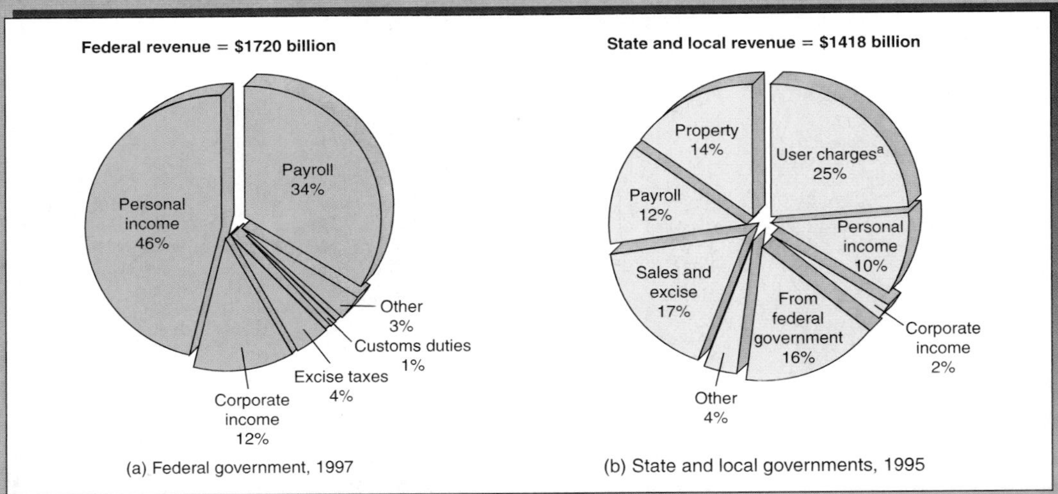

[a] *Revenues from government-operated utilities and liquor stores are included in this category.*

SOURCES: Economic Report of the President, *1998, Table B-81, and* Statistical Abstract of the United States, *1998, Table 506.*

TAXES AND OTHER SOURCES OF GOVERNMENT REVENUES

Exhibit 5A–5 indicates the major revenue sources for both the federal and state and local levels of government. At the federal level, the personal income tax and payroll tax account for 80 percent of federal revenue. At the state and local level, **user charges,** sales taxes, property taxes, and grants from the federal government provide the primary sources of revenue.

User charges
Payments that users (consumers) are required to make if they want to receive certain services provided by the government.

The personal income and payroll taxes account for 80 percent of federal revenue.

CHAPTER 6

[Public choice] analyzes the motives and activities of politicians, civil servants and government officials as people with personal interests that may or may not coincide with the interest of the general public they are supposed to serve. It is an analysis of how people behave in the world as it is.

Arthur Seldon[1]

It does not follow that whenever laissez faire falls short government interference is expedient; since the inevitable drawbacks of the latter may, in any particular case, be worse than the shortcomings of private enterprise.

Harry Sidgwick, 1887[2]

The Economics of Collective Decision Making

CHAPTER FOCUS

- What are the major forces that determine outcomes under representative democracy?
- Can government action be mutually advantageous to all citizens?
- Does democratic decision making lead to economic efficiency? Is there sometimes a conflict between good economics and good politics? Why?
- Why does representative democracy often tax some people in order to provide benefits to others? What types of income transfers are attractive to politicians?
- Can government action sometimes improve on the efficiency of the market? When is it most likely to do so?

[1]Preface to Gordon Tullock, *The Vote Motive* (London: Institute of Economic Affairs, 1976), p. x.

[2] Quoted in Charles Wolf, Jr., *Markets or Government* (Cambridge: MIT Press, 1988), p. 17.

As we stressed in the previous chapter, the economic role of government is pivotal. The government sets the rules of the game. Its performance with regard to the protection of property rights and establishment of a stable monetary environment affects the efficiency of market allocation. Governments may also contribute positively through the efficient production of public goods. In addition to these basic functions, modern governments are also often involved in the operation of enterprises, provision of essentially private goods, regulation, and, most significantly, income transfer activities. (See prior special section, Facts and Figures of Government.)

Given the size and breadth of government economic activity, it is vitally important to understand how it works. Government decisions are collective, or political, decisions. In most industrialized nations, political control is exercised through a representative democracy. In this chapter, we will use the economic way of thinking to study collective decision making and learn more about how a representative democracy functions and what we can expect from it.

AN OVERVIEW OF COLLECTIVE DECISION MAKING

It is important to recognize that government, including one that is controlled democratically, is not a corrective device that will always do the right thing or necessarily undertake policies that promote the general welfare. It is, instead, an alternative method of social organization—an institutional process through which individuals collectively make choices and carry out activities.

Public-choice analysis
The study of decision making as it affects the formation and operation of collective organizations, such as governments. In general, the principles and methodology of economics are applied to political science topics.

Public-choice analysis is a branch of economics that applies the principles and methodology of economics to the operation of the political process. In analyzing the behavior of people in the marketplace, economists develop a logically consistent theory of behavior that can be tested against reality. Public choice applies this same methodology to collective decision making. It develops a logically consistent theory linking individual behavior to political action, analyzes the implications of the theory, and tests them against events in the real world. Since the theory of collective decision making is not as well developed as our theory of market behavior, our conclusions will not be as well defined. During the past 40 years, however, social scientists have made great strides, enhancing our understanding of public sector resource allocation.[3]

Economists use the self-interest postulate to enhance our understanding of decisions in the market. Likewise, public-choice economists apply the self-interest postulate to political decision making. They assume that, just as people are motivated by narrow interests and the desire for personal wealth, power, and prestige in the market sector, so, too, will these factors influence them when they make decisions in the political arena.

---

[3]The contributions of Kenneth Arrow, James Buchanan, Duncan Black, Anthony Downs, Mancur Olson, Robert Tollison, and Gordon Tullock have been particularly important. Public choice is something of a cross between economics and political science. Thus, advanced courses are generally offered in both departments.

OUTSTANDING ECONOMIST

James Buchanan (1919–)

James Buchanan is a key figure in the "public choice revolution." His most famous work, *The Calculus of Consent* (1962), coauthored with Gordon Tullock, argues that unless rules bring the self-interests of the political players into harmony with the wise use of resources, government will go awry.[1] This and related contributions won him the 1986 Nobel Prize in economics.

[1]J. M. Buchanan and G. Tullock, *The Calculus of Consent* (Ann Arbor: University of Michigan Press, 1962).

Closely related to self-interest as a motivator for politicians and bureaucrats are the concepts of survival and expansion. In the private sector, even if some managers are not primarily seeking profits, the profit-making firms are most likely to survive, prosper, and expand; and they are the firms that will be imitated. Similarly, in the public sector, politicians and the bureaucrats they hire must often act in the narrow self-interest of their constituents (and not incidentally in their own career self-interests) if they hope to survive. Those who cooperate most closely with powerful constituency groups will obtain more political clout and have the opportunity to lead larger government agencies.

As we illustrated in Exhibit II-B (Introduction to Part II), the collective decision process can be thought of as a complex interaction among voters, legislators, and bureaucrats. Citizen-voters elect a legislative body, which levies taxes and allocates budgets to various government agencies and bureaus. Directed by legislators, civil servants utilize the funds to supply government services and income transfers to the voters. In a representative democracy, voter support determines the composition of the legislative body, and a majority vote of the legislature is generally required for the passage of taxes, budget allocations, and regulatory activities. Let us take a closer look at the incentive structure confronting the three primary political players—voters, legislators, and bureaucrats—and consider the implications with regard to the operation of the political process.

The Voter-Consumer

How do voters decide whom to support? No doubt many factors influence their decision. Since voters must choose a candidate to represent them on a great many issues, they cannot know in detail how (and how effectively) the candidate will try to influence each issue in the future. Of necessity, the criteria they use must be very general. Which candidate appears to be the most persuasive, so as to represent best the voters back home? Who appears to be honest, sincere, and competent? Most voters do not know the candidates personally, so several such questions may come down to this: Which one presents the best television image?

The self-interest postulate indicates that voters, like market consumers, will ask, "What can you do for me, and for my goals, and how much will it cost me?" The greater the voter's perceived net personal gain from a particular candidate's election, the more likely it is that the voter will favor that candidate. In contrast, the greater the perceived net economic cost imposed on the voter by the positions of a candidate, the less inclined the voter will be to support the candidate. Other things equal, voters will tend to support those candidates whom they believe will provide them the most government services and transfer benefits, net of personal costs.

Unfortunately, rational voters frequently lack the detailed information needed to cast their ballots in a truly knowledgeable fashion. As we discussed in Chapter 5, collective decisions break the direct link between the individual voter's choice and the outcome of the issue. ***Most citizens recognize that their vote is unlikely to determine the outcome of an election. So they have little incentive to spend much effort seeking the information needed to cast an informed ballot. Economists refer to this lack of incentive as the*** **rational ignorance effect.**

Rational ignorance effect
Voter ignorance resulting from the fact that people perceive their individual votes as unlikely to be decisive. Therefore, they rationally have little incentive to seek the information needed to cast an informed vote.

Most voters simply rely on information that is supplied to them freely by candidates (via political advertising) and the mass media, as well as conversations with friends and coworkers. The rational ignorance effect explains why the majority of individuals of voting age cannot accurately identify their congressional representatives, much less identify and understand those representatives' positions on such issues as minimum wage legislation, tariffs, and agricultural policy. The fact that voters acquire scanty information merely indicates that they are responding rationally to economic incentives.

To see in a more personal way why citizens are likely to make better-informed decisions as consumers than as voters, imagine that you are planning to buy a car next week and also to vote for one of two Senate candidates. You have narrowed your choice of a car to either a Ford or a Honda. In the voting booth, you will choose between candidates Smith and Jones. Both the auto purchase and the Senate vote involve complex trade-offs for you. The two cars come with many options, and you must choose among dozens of different combinations; the winning Senate candidate will represent you on hundreds of issues, although you are limited to voting for only one of the two choices.

Which decision will command more of your scarce time for research and thinking about the best choice? Because your choice with regard to the car is decisive, and you must pay for what you choose, an uninformed car purchase could be very costly for you. But if you mistakenly vote for the wrong Senate candidate out of ignorance, the probability is virtually zero that your vote will decide who wins. Because your vote will not swing the election, a mistake or poorly informed choice will have little consequence. It would not be surprising, then, if you spent substantial time considering the car purchase and very little time becoming informed about either the candidates or the political issues at election time. The evidence is consistent with this view. For example, citizens in modern democracies support a great many profitable

Voters, politicians, and bureaucrats are the primary decision makers in the political arena.

auto magazines, while even the very best of the magazines focusing on politics and policy cannot operate without donated funds. Citizens simply will not pay enough for even a single political magazine in the United States to earn a profit.

The fact that one's vote is unlikely to be decisive explains more than lack of information on the part of voters. It also helps to explain why many citizens fail to vote. Even in a presidential election, only about half of all voting-age Americans take the time to register and vote. Given the low probability that one's vote will be decisive, this low voter turnout should not be surprising. The rationality of voters is further indicated by the fact that, when voters perceive that the election is close, voter turnout is larger. A vote in a close election has a greater chance of actually making a difference.

The Politician-Supplier

Public-choice theory postulates that pursuit of votes is the primary stimulus shaping the behavior of political suppliers. In varying degrees, such factors as pursuit of the public interest, compassion for the poor, and the achievement of fame, wealth, and power may influence the behavior of politicians. But regardless of ultimate motivation, the ability of politicians to achieve their objectives is sorely dependent upon their ability to get elected and reelected.

Rationally uninformed voters often must be convinced to "want" a candidate. Voter perceptions may be based on realities, but it is always perceptions, not the realities themselves, that influence decisions. This is true regardless of whether the decisions are private or political. As a result, a candidate's positive attributes must be brought to the attention of the rationally ignorant voters, whose attention is likely to be focused on their jobs, various civic activities, and local sports teams (which are probably more entertaining). An expert staff, sophisticated polling to ferret out which issues and which positions will be favored by voters, and high-quality advertising to shape a favorable image for the candidate are vitally important for a successful campaign. Thus, political campaigns are costly. For example, it is not unusual for an incumbent candidate for the U.S. Senate to spend more than $10 million during the two years prior to each election.

Are we implying that politicians are selfish, caring only for their pocketbooks and reelection chances? The answer is no. When people act in the political sphere, they may genuinely want to help their fellow citizens. Factors other than personal political gain, narrowly defined, may influence their actions. On certain issues, political officials may feel strongly that their position is best for the nation, even though it may not be currently popular. The national interest as perceived by the political supplier may conflict with the position that would be most favorable to reelection prospects. Some politicians may opt for the national interest even when it means political defeat. None of this is inconsistent with an economic view of public choice.

However, the existence of political suicide does not change the fact that most politicians prefer political survival. There is a strong incentive for political suppliers to stake out positions that will increase their vote total in the next election. In fact, competition more or less forces politicians to make decisions in light of political considerations. ***Regardless of ultimate motivation, the ability of politicians to achieve their objectives depends on their ability to get elected and reelected. Just as profits are the lifeblood of the market entrepreneur, votes are the lifeblood of the politician.*** Many factors undoubtedly influence political suppliers. Political competition, however, limits their options. In the same way that neglect of economic profit is the route to market oblivion, neglect of potential votes is the route to political oblivion.

Just as the general does not want his Camp Swampy budget cut, most heads of agencies want expanded budgets to help them do more, and to do it more comfortably.

Civil Servants: Government Bureaucrats as Political Participants

Bureaucratic interests can be an additional factor in politics. The interests of bureaucrats are often complementary with those of special interest groups. The bureaucrats who staff an agency usually want to see their agency's goals furthered, whether the goals are to protect more wilderness, increase the number and the pay of public school teachers, or provide additional subsidized irrigation projects. Like other people, bureaucratic decision makers have narrowly focused interests. Many believe strongly in what they are trying to do. To further those interests usually requires larger budgets for the support of favored constituents' interests. Importantly, the larger budgets also provide bureaucrats with expanded career opportunities. Bureaus, therefore, usually work to expand their programs to deliver benefits to their constituencies who, in turn, work with politicians to expand their bureau budgets and programs.

The political process, which begins with election races and proceeds to legislative decisions and bureaucratic actions, brings about results that please some voters and displease others. In any case, these results help to fuel the next round of activities in the process. The goals of the three major categories of participants—voters, politicians, and bureaucrats—sometimes conflict. Each wants more from the limited supply of resources. But coalitions form among individuals and groups from the three categories, with members of each coalition hoping to enhance their ability to gain more from the government.

WHEN VOTING WORKS WELL

Will voting and representative government provide support for productive projects while rejecting unproductive (and counterproductive) ones? People have a tendency to believe that support by a majority makes a political action productive or legitimate. Perhaps surprising to some, if a government project is really productive, it will always be possible to allocate the project's cost so that *all* voters will gain. **Exhibit 6–1** illustrates this point. Column 1 presents hypothetical data on the distribution of benefits from a government road-construction project. These benefits sum to $40, which exceeds the $25 cost of the road. Because voter benefits exceed costs, the project is indeed productive. If the project's $25 cost were allocated equally among the voters (Plan A), Adams and Chan gain substantially, but Green, Lee, and Diaz will lose. The value of the project to the latter three voters is less than their $5 cost. If the fate of the project were decided by direct majority vote, the project would be defeated by the "no" votes of Green, Lee, and Diaz.

EXHIBIT 6–1

BENEFITS DERIVED BY VOTERS FROM HYPOTHETICAL ROAD CONSTRUCTION PROJECT

Voter	Benefits Received (1)	Tax Payment: Plan A (2)	Tax Payment: Plan B (3)
Adams	$20	$ 5	$12.50
Chan	12	5	7.50
Green	4	5	2.50
Lee	2	5	1.25
Diaz	2	5	1.25
Total	$40	$25	$25.00

In contrast, look what happens if the cost of the project is allocated among voters in proportion to the benefits that they receive (Plan B). Under this arrangement, Adams would pay half ($12.50) of the $25 cost, since he receives half ($20) of the total benefits ($40). The other voters would all pay in proportion to their benefits received. Under this finance plan, all voters would gain from the proposal. Even though the proposal could not muster a majority when the costs were allocated equally among voters, it would be favored by all five voters when they are taxed (or charged) in proportion to the benefits that they receive (Plan B).

This simple illustration highlights an extremely important point about voting and productive projects. ***When voters pay in proportion to benefits received, all voters will gain if the government action is productive (and all will lose if it is unproductive).***[4] When the benefits and costs of voters are closely related, productive government actions will be favored by almost all voters. Correspondingly, if a project is counterproductive—if the costs exceed the benefits generated for voters—it will be opposed by almost all voters. ***Therefore, when voters pay in proportion to benefits received, there is a harmony between good politics and sound economics.***

With public-sector action, however, the link between receipt of and payment for a good can be broken in that the beneficiaries of a proposal may not bear its cost. Public-choice theory indicates that the pattern of benefits and costs among voters will influence the workings of the political process. The benefits from a government action may be either widespread among the general populace or concentrated among a small subgroup (for example, farmers, students, business interests, or members of a labor union). Similarly, the costs may be either widespread or highly concentrated among voters. As **Exhibit 6–2** illustrates, there are four possible patterns of voter benefits and costs: (1) widespread benefits and widespread costs, (2) concentrated benefits and

[4]The principle that productive projects generate the potential for political unanimity was initially articulated by Swedish economist Knut Wicksell in 1896. See Wicksell, "A New Principle of Just Taxation," in *Public Choice and Constitutional Economics,* James Gwartney and Richard Wagner (Greenwich, Connecticut: JAI Press, Inc., 1988). Nobel laureate James Buchanan has stated that Wicksell's work provided him with the insights that led to his large role in the development of modern public-choice theory.

It is useful to vizualize four possible combinations for the distribution of benefits and costs among voters and to consider how the alternative distributions affect the operation of representative government. When the distribution of benefits and costs are both widespread among voters (1) or both concentrated among voters (3), representative government will tend to undertake projects that are productive and reject those that are unproductive. In contrast, when the benefits are concentrated and the costs are widespread (2), representative government is biased toward adoption of counterproductive activity. Finally, when benefits are widespread but the costs concentrated (4), the political process may reject projects that are productive.

EXHIBIT 6-2

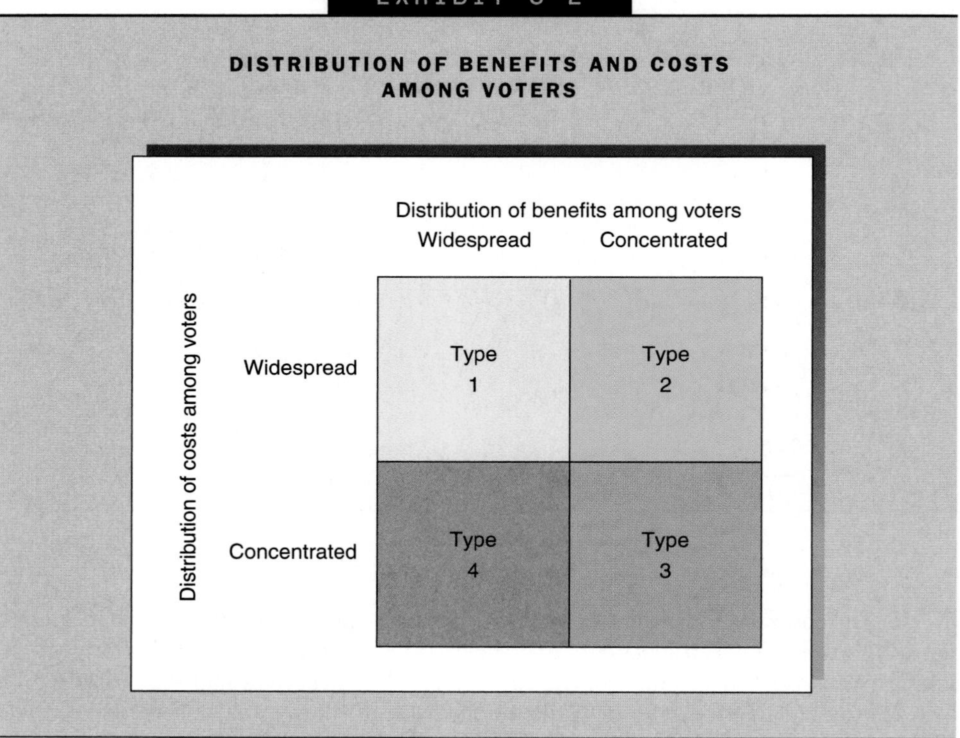

widespread costs, (3) concentrated benefits and concentrated costs, and (4) widespread benefits and concentrated costs.

When both the benefits and costs are widespread among voters (Type 1 issue), essentially everyone benefits and everyone pays. Although the costs of Type 1 measures may not be precisely proportional to benefits, there will be a rough relationship. When Type 1 measures are productive, almost everyone gains more than they pay. There will be little opposition, and political representatives have a strong incentive to support such proposals. In contrast, when Type 1 proposals generate costs in excess of benefits, almost everyone loses, and representatives will confront pressure to oppose such issues. Thus, for Type 1 projects, the political process tends to be consistent with economic efficiency.

Interestingly, the provision of traditional public goods—for example, national defense, a police force and legal system for the protection of persons and property, and stable monetary arrangements to oil the wheels of exchange—best fits Type 1. Nearly everyone pays and nearly everyone benefits from public-sector action of this type.

Similarly, there is reason to believe that the political process will work well for Type 3 measures—those for which both benefits and costs are concentrated on one or more small subgroups. In some cases, the concentrated beneficiaries may pay for the government to provide them a service. This would be the case when user charges finance public services (for example, air safety, electric power, water, sewage) benefiting subgroups of the populace. For these goods, voter-consumers pay roughly in proportion to their consumption of the government-supplied good. Under these circumstances, voter support will provide politicians with an incentive to provide public services that generate value in excess of cost.

Sometimes the subgroup of beneficiaries may differ from the subgroup footing the bill. But even in this case, if the benefits exceed the costs, the concentrated group of beneficiaries will have an incentive to expend more resources supportive of the measure than those harmed by it will expend opposing it. Thus, productive measures will tend to be adopted. Similarly, unproductive measures will tend to be rejected when both the benefits and costs are concentrated.

WHEN VOTING CONFLICTS WITH ECONOMIC EFFICIENCY

Although the political process works well when there is a close relationship between receipt of benefits and payment of costs, the harmony between good politics and sound economics sometimes breaks down. There are four major reasons why unrestrained majority-rule voting may conflict with economic prosperity.

SPECIAL-INTEREST EFFECT

Public-choice analysis indicates that problems will arise when issues of a special-interest nature are financed by general taxation. A **special-interest issue** is one that generates substantial personal benefits for a small number of constituents while imposing a small individual cost on a large number of other voters (Type 2 in Exhibit 6–2). A few gain a great deal individually, while a large number lose a little individually. Examples are not hard to find. The federal government currently spends $75 billion a year on direct subsidies to business. One example is the U.S. Department of Agriculture market promotion program that subsidizes foreign advertising by U.S. corporations selling bakery products, whiskey, and California chardonnay abroad. Measures of this type are special-interest issues. A number of factors combine to make special-interest groups far more powerful in a representative democracy than their numbers would indicate.

Special-interest issue
An issue that generates substantial individual benefits to a small minority while imposing a small individual cost on many other voters. In total, the net cost to the majority might either exceed or fall short of the net benefits to the special-interest group.

It is easy to see how politicians can improve their election prospects by catering to the views of special interests. Since their personal stake is large, members of the interest group (and lobbyists representing their interests) have an incentive to inform themselves and their allies and to let legislators know how strongly they feel about an issue of special importance. Many of them will vote for or against candidates strictly on the basis of whether they support their specific interests. In addition, such interest groups are generally an attractive source of campaign resources, including financial contributions. In contrast, most other voters will care little about a special-interest issue. For the non–special-interest voter, opportunity cost of the time and energy necessary to examine the issue will generally exceed any possible personal gain from a preferrred resolution. Of course, there are many such issues and each would have to be considered separately. Given the costs of information, non–special-interest voters tend to ignore such issues.

If you were a vote-seeking politician, what would you do? Clearly, little gain would be derived from supporting the interest of the largely uninformed and uninterested majority. In contrast, support for the interests of easily identifiable, well-organized groups would generate vocal supporters, campaign workers, and, most important, campaign contributors. ***Predictably, politicians will be led as if by an invisible hand to support legislation that provides concentrated benefits to interest groups at the expense of disorganized groups (such as taxpayers and consumers). This will often be true even if the total community benefit from the special-interest program is less than its cost. Even if the policy is counterproductive, it may still be a political winner.***

The rational ignorance of voters strengthens the power of special interests. Since the cost imposed on individual voters for each specific issue is small, and since the individual is unable to avoid the cost even by becoming informed, voters bearing the cost of special-interest legislation tend to be uninformed on the issue. This will be particularly true if the complexity of the issue makes it difficult for voters to think through how the issue affects their personal welfare. Thus, politicians often make special-interest legislation complex in order to hide the cost imposed on the typical voter.

The ability of the voter to punish politicians for supporting special-interest legislation is further hindered by the fact that many issues are bundled together when the voter chooses between one candidate and another. Even if the voter knows and dislikes the politician's stand on several special-interest issues, the bundling of hundreds of future issues into one candidate choice severely limits the voter's ability to take a stand at the ballot box for or against any particular issue.

Bureaucratic interests can be an additional factor favoring special-interest programs. The interests of bureaucrats are often complementary with those of the interest groups they serve. As we previously discussed, larger budgets to support the interests of bureau constituents also tend to enhance the job opportunities, power, and prestige of those who staff the agency.

Logrolling
The exchange between politicians of political support on one issue for political support on another issue.

Yet another force that strengthens the political clout of special-interest groups is **logrolling,** the practice of trading votes by a representative in order to pass intensely desired legislation. Representative A promises to vote for measures favored by other representatives in exchange for their support of a measure that A strongly favors. With logrolling, legislative bodies often pass a bundle of proposals, each of which would be rejected if voted on separately.

Pork-barrel legislation
A package of spending projects benefiting local areas at federal expense. The projects typically have costs that exceed benefits, but are intensely desired by the residents of the district getting the benefits without having to pay much of the costs.

Relatedly, **pork-barrel legislation** bundles together a set of projects benefiting regional interests (for example, water projects, dredging of harbors, or expenditures on military bases) at the expense of the general taxpayer. As in the case of logrolling, the bundle of pork-barrel projects can often gain approval even if the items by themselves would be seen as counterproductive and would individually be rejected by the legislative assembly.

Exhibit 6–3 provides a numeric illustration of the forces underlying logrolling and pork-barrel legislation. Here we consider the operation of a five-member legislative assembly considering three projects: construction of a post office in District A, dredging of a harbor in District B, and expenditures on a military base in District C. In each case, the project is inefficient—the net cost of the project exceeds the net benefit (by a 12-to-10 ratio). If the projects were voted on separately and the representatives reflected the views of their constituents, each project would lose by a 4-to-1 vote. However, when the projects are bundled together through either logrolling or pork-barrel legislation, Representatives A, B, and C will vote yes. The legislative bundle will pass 3 to 2 even though it is counterproductive (on average, the projects as a bundle reduce the wealth of constituents by $6).[5]

Legislation providing subsidies to electricity consumers in California, Nevada, and Arizona illustrates the relevance of logrolling and pork-barrel legislation. Under legislation passed in 1937, electricity generated by Hoover Dam has been sold to residents in the three surrounding states at rates ranging between 10 percent and 25 percent of the market price. The law providing for the subsidized rates was scheduled to expire in 1987. However, before it did, Congress extended the subsidies for another 30

[5]Logrolling and pork-barrel policies can lead to the adoption of productive measures. However, if a project is productive, there would always be a pattern of finance that would lead to its adoption even if logrolling and pork-barrel policies were absent. Thus, the tendency for logrolling and pork-barrel policies to result in the adoption of inefficient projects is the more significant point.

EXHIBIT 6-3

VOTE TRADING AND PASSING COUNTERPRODUCTIVE LEGISLATION

Voters of District[a]	Net Benefits (+) or Costs (−) to Each Voter in District: Construction of Post Office in A	Dredging Harbor in B	Construction of Military Base in C	Total
A	+$10	−$ 3	−$ 3	+$4
B	−$ 3	+$10	−$ 3	+$4
C	−$ 3	−$ 3	+$10	+$4
D	−$ 3	−$ 3	−$ 3	−$9
E	−$ 3	−$ 3	−$ 3	−$9
Total	−$ 2	−$ 2	−$ 2	−$6

[a]*We assume the districts are of equal size.*

years. The residents of many western states are the recipients of federally subsidized electricity. Every senator west of Missouri voted to continue the subsidized rates for electricity generated by Hoover Dam. In turn, they can expect senators and representatives from California, Arizona, and Nevada to support subsidized electricity rates in their states. In contrast, residents of other states will pay higher taxes so that many residents in western states can enjoy cheap electricity.

A unique form of special-interest lobbying is the monopoly held by Crane & Company for supplying the Bureau of Engraving and Printing with the paper on which U.S. currency is printed. The firm has been the sole supplier of paper for U.S. currency since 1879. Legislation was introduced in 1998 to provide for competition in the bidding, but the Massachusetts Congressional delegation fought off the legislation. Crane is located in Dalton, Massachusetts. The four-year contract is expected to total $400 million.

Why don't representatives oppose measures that force their constituents to pay for projects that benefit others? There is some incentive to do so, but the constituents of any one elected representative can capture only a small portion of the benefits of tax savings from improved efficiency, since they would be spread nationwide among all taxpayers. We would not expect the president of a corporation to devote the firm's resources to projects not primarily benefiting stockholders. Neither should we expect an elected representative to devote political resources to projects such as defeating pork-barrel programs, when the benefits of greater efficiency would not go primarily to that representative's constituents. Instead, each representative has a strong incentive to work for programs whose benefits are concentrated among his or her constituents—especially the organized interest groups that can help the representative be reelected. Heeding such incentives is a survival (reelection) characteristic.

The bottom line is clear: Public-choice analysis indicates that majority voting and representative democracy do not work so well when concentrated interests benefit at the expense of widely dispersed interests. This special-interest bias of the political process helps to explain the presence of many programs that reduce the size of the economic pie.

The analysis is symmetrical. When the benefits of a government action are widespread and the costs highly concentrated (Type 4 of Exhibit 6–2), the concentrated interests will strongly oppose the proposal. Most others will be largely uninformed and uninterested. Once again, politicians will have an incentive to respond to the views of the concentrated interests. Projects of this type will tend to be rejected even when they are productive—that is, when they would generate larger benefits than costs.

Shortsightedness Effect

The complexity of many issues makes it difficult for voters to identify the future benefits and costs. Will a reduction in tariff rates lead to more rapid economic growth? Is global warming a future threat and, if so, what might be done about it? What impact will an increase in the national debt have on future prosperity? These questions are hard to answer. The difficulty of predicting the future results of current policies acts to reinforce the rational ignorance effect. Few voters will seriously research and analyze the implications of complex policy alternatives having impacts mainly in the future. Instead, they rely on current conditions when judging the performance of incumbents. To the voter, the most easily seen indicator of performance is, "How are things now?"

Accordingly, politicians seeking reelection have a strong incentive to support policies that generate current benefits in exchange for future costs, particularly if the future costs will be difficult to identify on election day. Public-sector action will therefore be biased in favor of legislation that offers immediate (and easily identifiable) current benefits in exchange for future costs that are complicated and difficult to identify. Simultaneously, there is a bias against legislation that involves immediate and easily identifiable costs (for example, higher taxes) while yielding future benefits that are complex and difficult to identify. Economists refer to this bias inherent in the collective decision-making process as the **shortsightedness effect.**

Shortsightedness effect
Misallocation of resources that results because public-sector action is biased (1) in favor of proposals yielding clearly defined current benefits in exchange for difficult-to-identify future costs and (2) against proposals with clearly identifiable current costs but yielding less concrete and less obvious future benefits.

The shortsightedness effect is compounded by the lack of tradable property rights—the lack of a capital market—in government enterprises. For comparison with the private sector, consider the problem of choosing programs and strategies for a large corporation, such as General Motors. Its stockholders elect a board of directors to set policy and select professional management leadership. The corporation, like a government, faces complex choices of programs that are difficult for the individual stockholder to understand fully and evaluate. However, when evaluating the business programs and strategy of the corporation, the stockholder has an incentive very different from that of a voter. Why? Any stockholder who senses trouble before others do can sell out before the stock price falls. Similarly, the stockholder (or other observer) who recognizes a good program choice by a firm before others do can profit individually by buying stock in the firm. (Remember our reference to the many profitable auto magazines and the complete lack of profitable political magazines? There are dozens of highly profitable magazines and newsletters for those who follow corporate stocks!)

The choices of informed, quick-to-act stockholders are registered in stock markets and passed on almost instantly. Investor decisions to buy or sell stock cause the stock price to rise or fall, signaling whether trouble or a winning program is forecast by the most attentive buyers and sellers of the stock. A strategy choice or a new program that investors like will quickly be signaled by a rising share price that rewards management choices well ahead of actual changes in profits and losses. No such advanced market signals, complete with incentives, exist in the collective decision-making processes of government. The result is the restriction of the planning horizon of elected officials. ***As a result of the shortsightedness effect, politicians have a strong incentive to promote programs providing easily observable benefits prior to the next***

election, even when the true cost of these programs outweighs the benefits for citizens as a group.

It is easy to think of instances where positive short-term effects have increased the political attractiveness of policies that exert a long-term detrimental impact. For example, budget deficits allow politicians to finance current benefits for constituents with future taxes. This strategy has political attractiveness even though it will probably result in higher interest rates and less capital formation. Rent controls that reduce the current price of rental housing provide another example. As we noted in Chapter 4, the short-term results will be far more positive than the effects in the long run (housing shortages, black markets, and deterioration in the quality of housing).

Rent Seeking

There are two ways individuals can acquire wealth: production and plunder. When individuals produce goods or services and exchange them for income, they not only enrich themselves but they also enhance the wealth of the society. Sometimes the rules—or lack of rule enforcement—also allow people to get ahead by plundering what others have produced. Such activities enrich some at the expense of others, usually after a strenuous political struggle that consumes additional resources and reduces the wealth of the society.

Rent seeking is the term used by economists when referring to actions taken by individuals and groups seeking to use the political process to plunder the wealth of others.[6] The incentive to engage in rent seeking is directly proportional to the ease with which the political process can be used for personal (or interest group) gain at the expense of others. When the effective law of the land makes it difficult to take the property of others or force others to pay for projects favored by you and your interest group, rent seeking is unattractive. Under such circumstances, its benefits are relatively low, and few resources flow into rent-seeking activities. In contrast, when government fails to levy user fees or similar forms of financing to allocate the cost of its projects to the primary beneficiaries, or when it becomes heavily involved in tax-transfer activities, the payoff for rent seeking expands.

Rent seeking
Actions by individuals and interest groups designed to restructure public policy in a manner that will either directly or indirectly redistribute more income to themselves.

Rent seeking—perhaps "favor seeking" would be more descriptive—will also increase when governments become more heavily involved in erecting trade barriers, mandating employment benefits, providing subsidies, fixing prices, and levying discriminatory taxes (taxes unrelated to the provision of public services to the taxpayer). Interests seeking special favors include bureaucratic leaders searching for ways to enlarge their agency budgets and regulatory authority. The narrow interests of government bureaucracies are strongly represented in the political process.

When a government, rather than acting as a neutral force protecting property rights and enforcing contracts, attempts to favor some at the expense of others, counterproductive activities will expand while positive-sum productive activities will shrink. People will spend more time organizing and lobbying politicians and less time producing goods and services. Since fewer resources will be utilized to create wealth (and more utilized in rent-seeking activities), economic progress will be retarded.

Inefficiency of Government Operations

Will government goods and services be produced efficiently? Professional pride, and pride in doing a job well, are likely to be present in the public sector as well as the

[6]See the classic work of Charles K. Rowley, Robert D. Tollison, and Gordon Tullock, *The Political Economy of Rent-Seeking* (Boston: Kluwer Academic Publishers, 1988), for additional details on rent seeking.

private. However, the incentive to operate efficiently differs in the two sectors. In the private sector, there is a strong incentive to produce efficiently because lower costs mean higher profits, and high costs mean losses and even business failure. This index of performance (profit rate) is unavailable in the public sector. Missing also are signals from the capital market. When a corporation announces a strategy or a plan that investors believe to be faulty, the price of the corporation's stock will drop. There is no mechanism similar to the stock market in the public sector. This makes inefficiency more difficult to detect. In addition, direct competition in the form of other firms trying to take an agency's customers is typically absent in the public sector. As a result, bureaucratic leaders are more free to pursue their narrow goals and interests without a strong regard for the control of costs relative to benefits. (See cartoon below.)

While bankruptcy weeds out inefficiency in the private sector, there is no parallel mechanism to eliminate inefficiency in the public sector. In fact, poor performance and failure to achieve objectives are often used as an argument for *increased* funding in the public sector. Furthermore, public-sector managers are seldom in a position to gain personally from measures that reduce costs. The opposite is often true. If an agency fails to spend this year's allocation, its case for a larger budget next year is weakened. Agencies typically go on a spending spree near the end of the budget period if they discover that they have failed to spend all the current year's appropriation.

It is important to note that the argument of internal inefficiency is not based on the assumption that employees of a bureaucratic government are necessarily lazy or incapable. Rather, the emphasis is on the information and incentives under which managers and other workers toil. No individual or relatively small group of individuals has much incentive to ensure economic efficiency. Their performances cannot readily be judged, and, without private ownership, their personal wealth cannot be significantly altered by changes in the level of efficiency. Because public officials and bureau

THE FAMILY CIRCUS
By Bil Keane
1-26
©1998 Bil Keane, Inc.
Dist. by Cowles Synd., Inc.
BIL KEANE
"Daddy, could you buy a new metal detector? I dropped my quarter in the snow."

Just as the boy considers the quarter more important than the far greater cost of the metal detector, so too does the leader of a bureau often consider the bureau's goals more important than the costs, even if the latter are far greater.

managers spend other people's money, they are likely to be less conscious of cost than they would be with their own resources. Without a need to compare sales revenues to costs, there is no test with which to define economic inefficiency or measure it accurately, much less to eliminate it. The perverse incentive structure of a bureaucracy and the fact that market signals are missing are bound to affect its internal efficiency.

The empirical evidence is consistent with this view. Economies dominated by government control, like those of the former Soviet bloc, India, Syria, Nicaragua, and Nigeria (and many other African countries) have performed poorly. The level of output per unit of resource input in countries with numerous government enterprises is low. Similarly, when private firms are compared with government agencies providing the same goods or services, the private firms generally have been shown to provide them more economically.

Competition is a key to efficient production and low cost. Units of government can sometimes provide services on a more competitive basis by contracting with private firms or even with other units of government. For example, many cities contract with private firms to provide trash removal services. The city continues to finance the activity through taxes and to specify the level of service. But operational efficiency is greater because competition among potential contractors keeps the cost of the trash removal contracts down. This sort of competitive contracting has increased in recent decades. In the state of Illinois, more than 90 percent of municipalities contracted out their trash removal services. In the United States, 7 state governments were contracting out more than 100 services in 1998, while 14 states contracted out more than 50 services. Even the federal Internal Revenue Service has moved in this direction. The IRS recently awarded a $30.9 million contract to a private partnership to manage its inventory of office equipment and other supplies. Private, competitive firms can typically reduce costs, relative to government agency production.

ECONOMICS OF THE TRANSFER SOCIETY

As **Exhibit 6–4** illustrates, direct income transfers through the public sector have increased sharply during the past seven decades. In 1929 cash income transfers accounted for only 1.8 percent of national income; by 1997 the figure had risen to 16.8 percent. If in-kind benefits, such as food stamps, medical care, and housing, were included, the size of the transfer sector would have constituted well over 20 percent of national income.

The ideal distribution of income is largely a matter of personal preference. There is nothing in positive economics that tells us that one distribution of income is better than another. Some people may desire to enhance the living standards of those with low incomes. However, in some respects, income transfers to the poor are a public good. The contributions of any one individual will exert an insignificant impact on the living standards of the poor. Recognizing this point, even those who would willingly contribute to reduce the general level of poverty, have an incentive to become *free riders.* When many people become free riders, however, less than the desired amount of antipoverty effort will be voluntarily supplied. If everyone is required to contribute through the tax system, then the free-rider problem can be overcome. Under these circumstances, transfers directed to the poor may be consistent with economic efficiency.

However, there is also reason to believe that the rent-seeking model underlies a substantial portion of income transfers. In the United States, *means-tested transfers,* those directed toward the poor, constitute only about one-sixth of all transfers. No

EXHIBIT 6-4

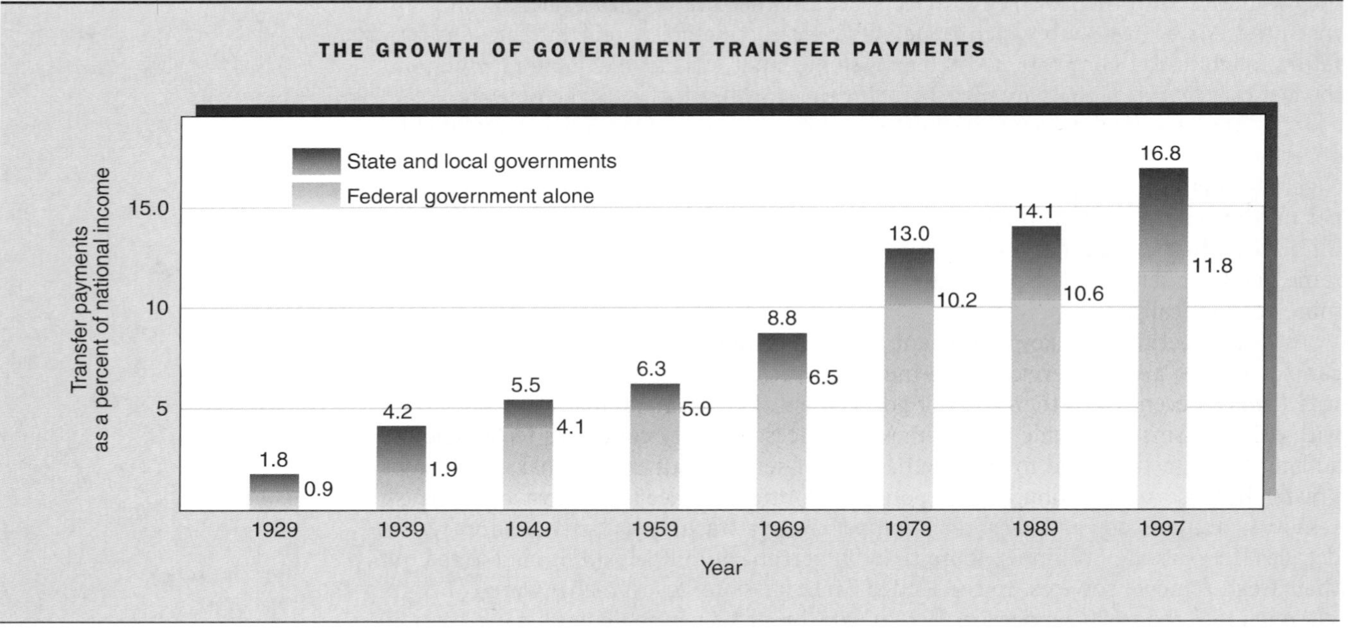

The government now taxes approximately 17 percent of national income away from some people and transfers it to others. Means-tested income transfers—those directed toward the poor—account for only about one-sixth of all income transfers.

SOURCE: Economic Report of the President, *1998, Tables B-83, B-84.*

income test is applied to the other five-sixths, and they are generally directed toward groups that are either well organized (like businesses and labor union interests) or easily identifiable (like the elderly and farmers). The recipients of these transfers often have incomes well above the average.

Within the framework of public-choice analysis, the relatively small portion of income transfers directed toward the poor is not surprising. There is little reason to believe that transfers to the poor will be particularly attractive to vote-seeking politicians. After all, in the United States, the poor are less likely to vote than middle- and upper-income recipients. They are also less likely to be well informed on political issues and candidates. They are not united. Neither are they a significant source of financial resources that exert a powerful influence on the political process.

Whatever the motivation for the income transfers, there are three major reasons why redistribution through the public sector will reduce the size of the economic pie. First, income redistribution weakens the link between productive activity and reward. When taxes take a larger share of one's income, the individual reward derived from hard work and productive service is reduced. The basic economic postulate suggests that when benefits allocated to producers are reduced (and benefits to nonproducers are raised), less productive effort will be supplied.

Second, as public policy redistributes a larger share of income, more resources will flow into wasteful rent-seeking activities. Resources used for lobbying and other means of rent seeking will not be available to increase the size of the economic pie.

Third, higher taxes to finance income redistribution and an expansion in rent seeking will induce taxpayers to focus less on income-producing activities, and more on actions to protect their income. More accountants, lawyers, and tax-shelter experts will be retained as people seek to limit the amount of their income that is redistributed to others. Like the resources allocated to rent seeking, resources allocated to protecting one's wealth from the reach of public policy will also be unavailable for productive activity. Therefore, the incentives generated by large-scale redistribution policies can be expected to reduce the size of the economic pie.

PUBLIC SECTOR VERSUS THE MARKET: A SUMMARY

Economic theory helps explain why both market forces and public-sector action sometimes break down—that is, why they sometimes fail to meet the criteria for ideal efficiency. The deficiencies of either sector will often be more or less decisive, depending on the type of economic activity. Nobel laureate Paul Samuelson has stated, "There are not rules concerning the proper role of government that can be established by *a priori* reasoning."[7] This does not mean, however, that economics has nothing to say about the *strength* of the case for either the market or the public sector in terms of specific classes of activities. Nor does it mean that social scientists have nothing to say about institutional arrangements for conducting economic activity. It merely indicates that each issue and type of activity must be considered individually.

When we consider the usefulness of government and the private sector in specific cases, it will help to remember two things. The first is the basic characteristic of government: its monopoly on the use of coercive force. It is a powerful tool indeed, for better and for worse. The second thing to remember is that individuals have two fundamental ways to inform and possibly influence an institution such as government or a private firm: exit and voice. Both exit and voice are quite useful in dealing with individuals, firms, and other groups in the private sector. We can speak, and if that doesn't work we can exit from a private arrangement by failing to renew it or by shifting to another alternative. Other buyers and sellers are available even if they do not have identical products in identical locations.

With government, we may be largely limited to voice. In a representative democracy, we can use voice to communicate our displeasure with a new tax or regulation, but exit is usually difficult. We have to move physically from the area of the government's authority. When government is at the local level, of course, exit is less costly. That is one reason why giving local government more powers is less dangerous than giving the same powers to a national government. Nonetheless, the ability to exit easily and shift to competing entities almost always gives individuals more control in the market than in the public sector.

When we make the necessary comparisons in individual situations, the case for government intervention is obviously stronger for some activities than for others. For example, if property rights cannot be well enforced so that an activity involves substantial external effects, market arrangements often result in economic inefficiency, and public-sector action should be considered; it may allow for greater efficiency. Similarly, when competitive pressures are weak and exit is more difficult for one party or the other, or when there is reason to expect consumers to be poorly informed, market failure may result. And again, government action should be examined. (See the Thumbnail Sketch for a summary of factors that influence the case for market or for public-sector action.)

[7]Paul A. Samuelson, "The Economic Role of Private Activity," in *The Collected Scientific Papers of Paul A. Samuelson,* vol. 2, ed. J. E. Stiglitz (Cambridge: MIT Press, 1966), p. 1423.

THUMBNAIL SKETCH

What Weakens the Case for Market-Sector Allocation versus Public-Sector Intervention, and Vice Versa?

These factors weaken the case for market-sector allocation:

1. Lack of competition
2. External costs and benefits
3. Public goods
4. Poor information

These factors weaken the case for public-sector intervention:

1. The power of special interests
2. The shortsightedness effect
3. Rent-seeking costs
4. Lack of signals and incentives to promote operational efficiency

The same analysis holds for the public sector. When there is a good reason to believe that special-interest influence will be strong, the case for government action to correct market failures is weakened. Similarly, the lack of a means to identify and weed out public-sector inefficiency weakens the case for government action. In many cases, the choice of proper institutions may be a choice among evils. For example, we might expect a lack of private-sector competition if a particular activity is left to the market, or perverse regulation due to the special-interest effect if it is turned over to the public sector. Understanding the shortcomings of both the market and the public sectors is important if we are to improve our current economic institutions.

IMPLICATIONS OF PUBLIC CHOICE: GETTING MORE FROM GOVERNMENT

It is important to distinguish between ordinary politics and constitutional rules. Constitutions establish the procedures that will be utilized to make political decisions. They also may reduce the negative results from the problems just discussed, by limiting the reach of the majority. They do so by placing certain matters (for example, the taking of private property without compensation, restrictions on freedom of speech or worship, and various restrictions on voting) beyond the reach of majority rule or normal legislative procedures.

Both bad news and good news flow from public-choice analysis. The bad news is that, for certain classes of economic activity, unconstrained democratic government will predictably be a source of economic waste and inefficiency. Not only does the invisible hand of the market sometimes fail to meet our ideal efficiency criteria; so, too, does political decision making. That makes the growth of government worrisome. But there is also some good news arising from public-choice theory: Properly structured constitutional rules can improve the expected result from government. So the study of how people behave when they make collective choices "in the world as it really is" suggests constructive alternatives for improving the government process.

Whether political organization leads to desirable or undesirable economic outcomes is dependent upon the structure of the political (constitutional) rules. In government as elsewhere, proper incentives are critical to good decision making. When the structure of the political rules harmonizes the self-interest of individual voters, politicians, and bureaucrats with the general welfare, government will promote economic prosperity. On the other hand, if the rules fail to bring about this harmony, political allocation will lead to both waste of resources and conflict among citizens. The challenge before us is to develop political economy institutions that are more consistent with economic efficiency and prosperity. Public-choice theory provides us with insight concerning how this objective might be achieved. Needless to say, this topic is one of the most exciting and potentially fruitful areas of study in economics.

LOOKING *Ahead*

Democratic governments are a creation of the interactions of human beings. Public-choice analysis helps us better understand these interactions and possible modifications of the rules that would improve the results achieved from government. Issues involving comparisons between market- and public-sector organization will be discussed repeatedly throughout this book. Public choice—the study of how the public sector works—is an integral and exciting aspect of economic analysis. It helps us to understand the "why" behind many of today's current events. Who said economics is the dismal science?

KEY POINTS

➤ In a representative democracy, government is controlled by voters who elect politicians to set policy and hire bureaucrats. All three classes of participants influence political outcomes.

➤ Other things constant, voters have a strong incentive to support the candidate who offers them the greatest gain relative to personal costs. But it is costly to obtain information. Because collective decisions break the link between the choice of the individual and the outcome of the issue, it is rational for voters to remain uninformed on many issues.

➤ Politicians have a strong incentive to follow a strategy that will enhance their chances of getting elected (and reelected). Political competition more or less forces them to focus on how their actions influence their support among voters.

➤ The distribution of the benefits and costs among voters influences how the political process works. When voters pay in proportion to the benefits they receive from a public-sector project, democratic decision making works quite well. Productive projects tend to be approved and counterproductive ones rejected.

➤ There is a strong incentive for politicians to support special-interest issues. Special-interest groups supply both financial and direct elective support to the politicians, while most other voters tend to be uninformed on special-interest issues.

➤ The shortsightedness effect is another potential source of conflict between good politics and sound economics. Both voters and politicians tend to support projects that promise substantial current benefits at the expense of difficult-to-identify future costs.

➤ Rent seeking moves resources away from productive activities. Widespread use of the taxing, spending, and regulating powers of government will encourage rent seeking. The output of economies with substantial amounts of rent seeking will fall below their potential.

➤ The economic incentive for operational efficiency is weak in the public sector. No individual or relatively small group of individuals can capture the gains derived from improved operational efficiency.

➤ A large and growing part of government is devoted to transferring income, most of which does not go to poor people. Transfers tend to reduce the size of the economic pie.

CRITICAL ANALYSIS QUESTIONS

1. Do you think that people who participate in the political process are motivated differently than when they participate in the private sector? Why or why not?

*2. "Government can afford to take a long view when it needs to, while a private firm has a short-term outlook. Corporate officers, for example, typically care about the next three to six months, not the next 50 to 100 years. Government, not private firms, should own things like forests, that take decades to develop." Evaluate this view.

3. "A democratic government is a corrective device used to remedy inefficiencies that arise when market allocation is not working well." Is this statement true or false? Explain.

4. What is rent seeking? When is it likely to be widespread? How does it influence economic efficiency? Explain.

*5. Does the democratic political process incorporate the invisible hand principle? Is the presence or absence of the invisible hand principle important? Why or why not?

*6. "The average person is more likely to make an informed choice when he or she purchases a personal computer than when he or she votes for a congressional candidate." Evaluate this statement.

7. Do you think special-interest groups exert much influence on local government? Why or why not? As a test, check the composition of the local zoning board in your community. How many real-estate agents, contractors, developers, and landlords are on the board? Are there any citizens without real-estate interests on the board?

*8. "Voters should simply ignore political candidates who play ball with special-interest groups, and vote instead for candidates who will represent all the people when they are elected. Government will work far better when this happens." Evaluate this view.

9. Do you think that advertising exerts more influence on the type of car chosen by a consumer than on the type of politician chosen by the same person? Explain your answer.

*10. "When an economic function is turned over to the government, social cooperation replaces personal self-interest." Is this statement true? Why or why not?

*11. What's wrong with this way of thinking? "Public policy is necessary to protect the average citizen from the power of vested interest groups. In the absence of government intervention, regulated industries, such as airlines, railroads, and trucking, would charge excessive prices, products would be unsafe, and the rich would oppress the poor. Government curbs the power of special-interest groups."

12. Do you think that the political process works to the advantage of the poor? Why or why not?

13. "Since government-operated firms do not have to make a profit, they can usually produce at a lower cost and charge a lower price than privately owned enterprises." Evaluate this view.

---

*Asterisk denotes questions for which answers are given in Appendix B.

PART 3

Core macroeconomics

Macroeconomics is about the growth and fluctuation in output, employment, and the level of prices for the entire economy. Gross domestic product (GDP) is the broadest and most widely used measure of output. As **Exhibit III-A** illustrates, real GDP—that is, GDP adjusted for inflation—has increased at an average annual rate of approximately 3 percent since 1950. Growth of output is highly important because it provides the basis for higher levels of consumption and standards of living.

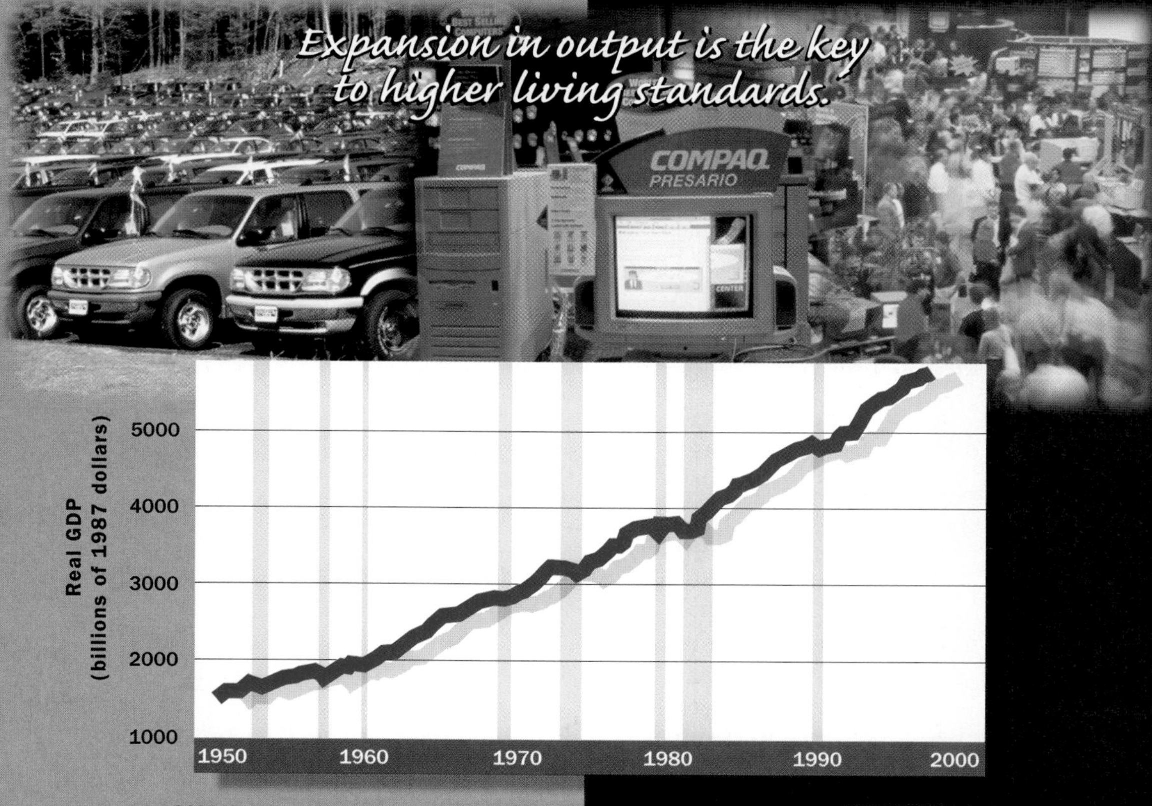

SOURCE: Economic Report of the President: 1999.
Shaded bars indicate periods of recession.

EXHIBIT III-A

FLUCTUATIONS IN OUTPUT

Like other countries, the United States has experienced fluctuations in output. **Exhibit III-B** indicates the periods of both expansion (rising real GDP) and recession (falling real GDP) since 1950. As the graph indicates, the length of both varies substantially, although the expansions have generally been longer. Since 1982, the U.S. economy has experienced two lengthy expansions interrupted only by a brief recession in 1990. What causes economic fluctuations? How might their intensity be reduced? Are recessions likely to be less common in the future? We will analyze these questions in Part III.

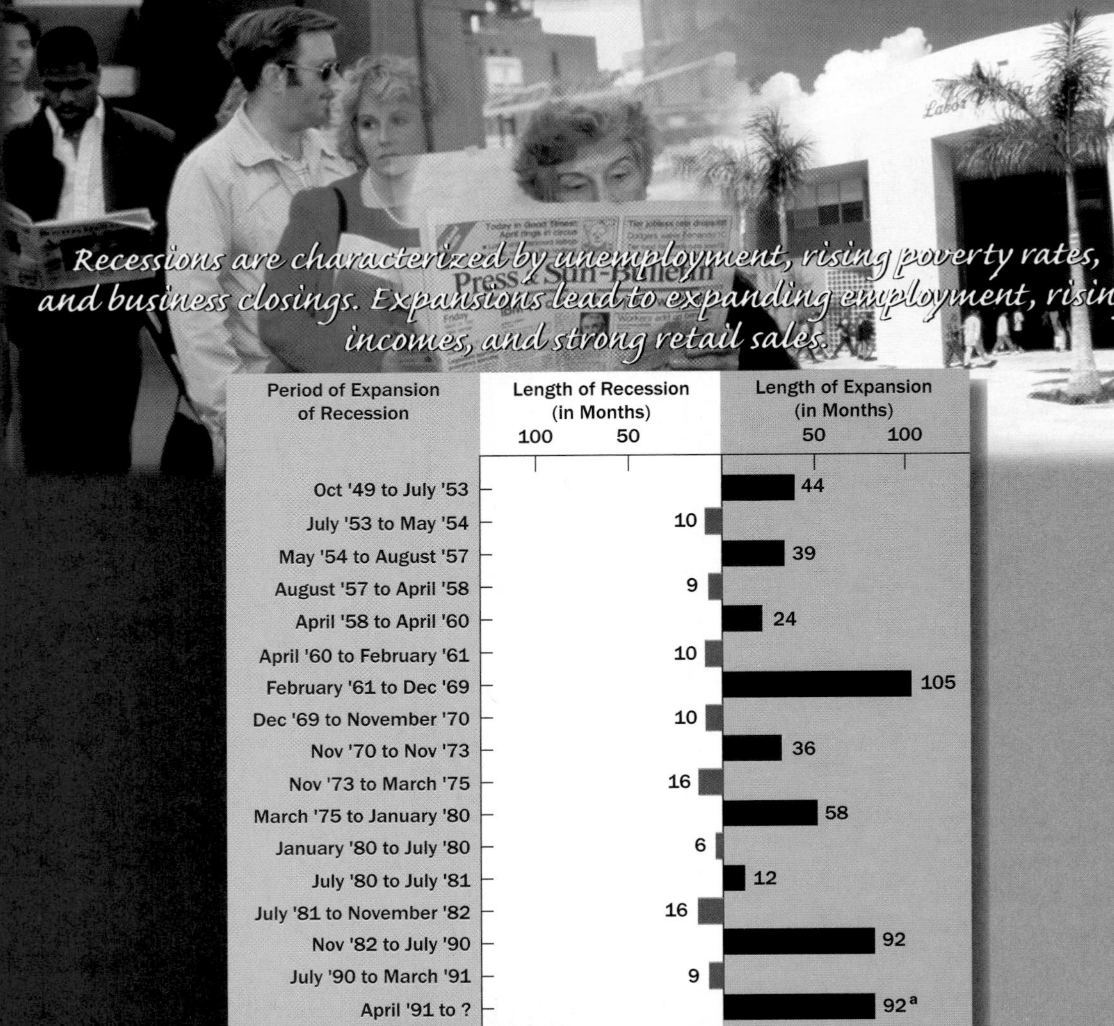

Recessions are characterized by unemployment, rising poverty rates, and business closings. Expansions lead to expanding employment, rising incomes, and strong retail sales.

EXHIBIT III-B

[a]*Through year-end 1998. This expansion is continuing.*
SOURCE: National Bureau of Economic Research

GROWTH OF OUTPUT

Exhibit III-C provides data on the growth of output during the last five decades. Even though there have been two lengthy expansions during the 1980s and 1990s, growth of real GDP has been less rapid than during the 1950s and 1960s. Why do economies grow? Has the long-term growth rate of the United States slowed? What can public policy do to encourage growth? These questions will be addressed in Part III.

SOURCE: Economic Report of the President, 1998, *and* 1999, *Table B-2. The data for the 1950s are for GNP, which was the primary measure of output at the time.*

EXHIBIT III-C

CHAPTER 7

It has been said that figures rule the world; maybe. I am quite sure that it is figures which show us whether it is being ruled well or badly.

Johann Wolfgang Goethe, 1830

Measurement is the making of distinction; precise measurement is making sharp distinctions.

Enrico Fermi[1]

Taking the Nation's Economic Pulse

CHAPTER FOCUS

- What is GDP? What items are included in GDP?
- How is GDP calculated? What are the major components of GDP?
- When making comparisons over time, why is it important to adjust nominal GDP for the effects of inflation?
- What do price indexes measure? How can they be used to adjust for changes in the general level of prices?
- Is GDP a good measure of output? What are its strengths and weaknesses?

[1]As quoted by Milton Friedman in *Economic Freedom: Toward a Theory of Measurement,* edited by Walter Block (Vancouver, B.C.: The Fraser Institute, 1991), p. 11.

Our society likes to keep score. The sports pages supply us with the win-loss records that reveal how well the various teams are doing. We also keep score on the performance of our economy. The scoreboard for economic performance is the *national income accounting system.* Just as a firm's accounting statement provides information on its performance, national income accounts supply performance information for the entire economy.

Simon Kuznets, the winner of the 1971 Nobel Prize in economics, developed the basic concepts of national income accounting during the 1920s and 1930s (see the Outstanding Economist feature). Through the years, these procedures have been modified and improved. In this chapter, we will explain how the flow of an economy's output (and income) is measured. We will also explain how changes in the quantity of goods and services produced are separated from changes that reflect merely inflation (higher prices). Finally, we will analyze the strengths and weaknesses of the measurement tools used to assess the performance of our national economy.

GDP—A MEASURE OF OUTPUT

Gross domestic product (GDP)
The market value of all final goods and services produced within a country during a specific period.

The* gross domestic product (GDP) *is the market value of final goods and services produced within a country during a specific time period, usually a year. GDP is the most widely used measure of economic performance. The GDP figures are closely watched both by policymakers and by those in the business and financial communities. In the United States, the numbers are prepared quarterly and released a few weeks following the end of each quarter.

GDP is a "flow" concept. By analogy, a water gauge measures the amount of water that flows through a pipe each hour. Similarly, GDP measures the market value of production that "flows" through the economy's factories and shops each year (or quarter).

OUTSTANDING ECONOMIST

Simon Kuznets (1901–1985)

Simon Kuznets provided the methodology for modern national income accounting and developed the first reliable national income measures for the United States. He is often referred to as the "father of national-income accounting."

A native Russian, he emigrated to the United States at the age of 21 and spent his academic career teaching at the University of Pennsylvania, Johns Hopkins University, and Harvard University.

WHAT COUNTS TOWARD GDP?

First and foremost, GDP is a measure of output. Thus, it cannot be arrived at merely by summing the totals on the nation's cash registers during a period. The key phrases in the definition of GDP—"market value" of "final goods and services" "produced" "within a country" "during a specific time period"—reveal a great deal about what should be included in and excluded from the calculation of GDP. Let's take a closer look at this issue.

Only Final Goods and Services Count. If output is to be measured accurately, all goods and services produced during the year must be counted once and only once. Most goods go through several stages of production before they end up in the hands of their ultimate users. To avoid double-counting, care must be taken to differentiate between **intermediate goods**—goods in intermediate stages of production—and **final market goods and services,** which are those purchased for final use rather than for resale or further processing.

Intermediate goods
Goods purchased for resale or for use in producing another good or service.

Final market goods and services
Goods and services purchased by their ultimate user.

Sales at intermediate stages of production are not counted by GDP because the value of the intermediate goods is embodied within the final-user good. Adding the sales price of both the intermediate good and the final-user good would exaggerate GDP. For example, when a wholesale distributor sells steak to a restaurant, the final purchase price paid by the patron of the restaurant for the steak dinner will reflect the cost of the meat. Double-counting would result if we included both the sale price of the intermediate good (the steak sold by the wholesaler to the restaurant) and the final purchase price of the steak dinner.

Exhibit 7–1 will help clarify the accounting method for GDP. Before the final good, bread, is in the hands of the consumer, it will go through several intermediate stages of production. The farmer produces a pound of wheat and sells it to the miller for 30 cents. The miller grinds the wheat into flour and sells it to the baker for 65 cents. The miller's actions have *added* 35 cents to the value of the wheat. The baker combines the flour with other ingredients, makes a loaf of bread, and sells it to the grocer for 90 cents. The baker has *added* 25 cents to the value of the bread. The grocer stocks the bread on the grocery shelves and provides a convenient location for consumers to shop. The grocer sells the loaf of bread for $1, *adding* 10 cents to the value of the final product. Only the final market value of the product—the $1 for the loaf of bread—is included in GDP. This price reflects the value added at each stage of production. The 30 cents *added* by the farmer, the 35 cents by the miller, the 25 cents by the baker, and the 10 cents by the grocer sum to the $1 purchase price.

Financial Transactions and Income Transfers Are Excluded Because They Do Not Involve Production. Remember, GDP is a measure of goods and services "produced." Purely financial transactions and income transfers merely transfer ownership from one party to another. They do not involve current production and therefore they should not be included in GDP. (*Note:* If a financial transaction involves a sales commission, the commission is included in GDP because it involves a service rendered during the current period.)

Thus, the purchases and sales of stocks, bonds, and U.S. securities are not included in GDP. Neither are private- and public-sector income transfers. If your aunt sends you $100 to help pay for your college expenses, your aunt has less wealth and you have more, but the transaction adds nothing to current production. Government income transfer payments, such as social security, welfare, and veterans' payments, are also omitted. The recipients of these transfers are not producing goods in return for the transfers. Therefore, it would be inappropriate to add them to GDP.

EXHIBIT 7-1

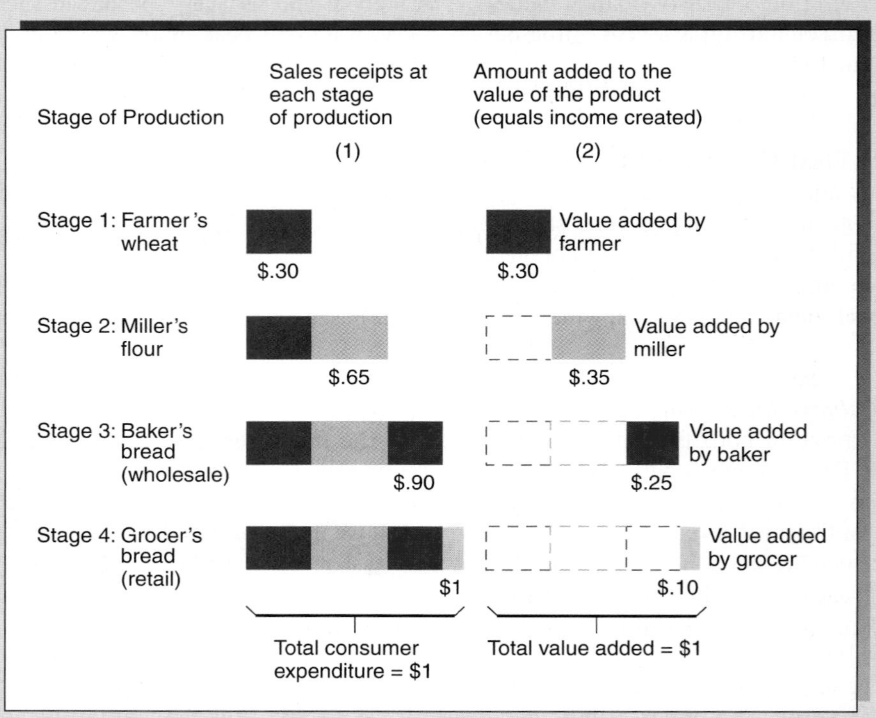

Most goods go through several stages of production. This chart illustrates both the market value of a loaf of bread as it passes through the various stages of production (column 1) and the amount added to the value by each intermediate producer (column 2). GDP counts only the market value of the final product. Of course, the amount added by each intermediate producer (column 2) sums to the market value of the final product.

GDP AND STAGES OF PRODUCTION

Stage of Production	Sales receipts at each stage of production (1)	Amount added to the value of the product (equals income created) (2)
Stage 1: Farmer's wheat	$.30	Value added by farmer $.30
Stage 2: Miller's flour	$.65	Value added by miller $.35
Stage 3: Baker's bread (wholesale)	$.90	Value added by baker $.25
Stage 4: Grocer's bread (retail)	$1	Value added by grocer $.10
	Total consumer expenditure = $1	Total value added = $1

Only Production Within the Country Is Counted. GDP counts only goods and services produced within the geographic borders of the country. When foreigners earn income within U.S. borders, it adds to the GDP of the United States. For example, the incomes of Canadian engineers and Mexican baseball players earned in the United States are included in the U.S. GDP. On the other hand, the earnings of Americans abroad—for example, an American college professor teaching in England—do not count toward the U.S. GDP because this income is not generated within the borders of the United States.

Only Goods Produced During the Current Period Are Counted. As the definition indicates, GDP is a measure of output "during the current period." Transactions involving the exchange of goods or assets produced during earlier periods are omitted because they do not reflect current production. For example, the purchase of "secondhand" goods, such as a used car or a home built five years ago, are not included in this year's GDP. Production of these goods was counted at the time they were produced and initially purchased. Resale of such items produced during earlier years merely changes the ownership of the goods or assets. It does not add to current production. Thus, it would be inappropriate to include them in current GDP. (*Note:* As in the case of financial transactions, sales commissions earned by those helping to arrange the sale of used cars, homes, or other assets are included in GDP because they reflect services provided during the current period.)

DOLLARS—THE COMMON DENOMINATOR FOR GDP

In elementary school, each of us was taught the difficulties of adding apples and oranges. Yet, this is precisely the nature of aggregate output. Literally millions of different commodities and services are produced each year. How can the production of apples, oranges, shoes, movies, roast beef sandwiches, automobiles, dresses, legal services, education, heart transplants, astrological services, and many other items be added together? Answer: The "market value" of each is added to GDP.

The vastly different goods and services produced in our modern world have only one thing in common: Someone pays a price for them. Therefore, when measuring output, units of each good are weighted according to their market value—the purchase price of the good or service. If a consumer pays $20,000 for a new automobile and $20 for a nice meal, production of the automobile adds 1,000 times as much to output as production of the meal. Similarly, production of a television set that is purchased for $1,000 will add 1/20 as much to output as the new automobile and 50 times the amount of the meal.

Each good produced increases output by the amount the purchaser pays for the good. The total spending on all goods and services produced during the year is then summed, in dollar terms, to obtain the annual GDP.

TWO WAYS OF MEASURING GDP

There are two ways of looking at and measuring GDP. First, the GDP of an economy can be reached by totaling the expenditures on goods and services produced during the year. National-income accountants refer to this method as the *expenditure approach.* ***Alternatively, GDP can be calculated by summing the income payments to the resource suppliers and the other costs of producing those goods and services.*** Production of goods and services is costly because the resources required for their production must be bid away from their alternative uses. These costs generate incomes for resource suppliers. Thus, this method of calculating GDP is referred to as the *resource cost-income approach.*

The prices used to weight the goods and services included in GDP reflect both the market value of the output and the income generated by the resources. From an accounting viewpoint, when a good is produced and sold, the total payments to the factors of production (including the producer's profit or loss) must be equal to the sales price generated by the good.[2] For example, consider a beauty shop operator who leases a building and equipment, purchases various cosmetic products, and combines these items with labor to provide hairdressing services for which customers pay $500 per day. The market value of the output, $500 per day, is added to GDP. Taking the operator's profit or loss into account, the $500 figure is also equal to the income resource owners receive from the provision of the service. Thus, GDP is a measure of both output and income.

The linkage between the market value of a good and the income (including profit and loss) of the resource suppliers is present for each good or service produced, and it is also present for the aggregate economy. This is a fundamental accounting identity.

Dollar flow of expenditures on final goods	= GDP =	Dollar flow of income (and indirect cost) of final goods

[2]In the national-income accounts, the terms *profit* and *corporate profit* are used in the accounting sense. Thus, they reflect *both* the rate of return on assets owned by a business firm (which is sometimes referred to as normal profit) *and* the firm's economic profit and loss, which was discussed in Chapter 3.

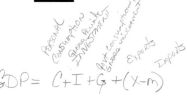

GDP is a measure of the value of the goods and services that were purchased by households, investors, governments, and foreigners. These purchasers valued the goods and services more than the purchase price; otherwise they would not have purchased them. ***GDP is also a measure of aggregate income.*** Production of the goods involves human toil, wear and tear on machines, use of natural resources, risk, managerial responsibilities, and other of life's unpleasantries. Resource owners have to be compensated with income payments in order to induce them to supply these resources.

Exhibit 7–2 summarizes the components of GDP for both the expenditure and resource cost-income approaches. Except for a few complicating elements that we will discuss in a moment, the revenues business firms derive from the sale of goods and services are paid directly to resource suppliers in the form of wages, self-employment income, rents, profits, and interest. We now turn to an examination of these components and the two alternative ways of deriving GDP.

DERIVING GDP BY THE EXPENDITURE APPROACH

When derived by the expenditure approach, there are four components of GDP: (1) personal consumption expenditures, (2) gross private domestic investment, (3) government consumption and gross investment, and (4) net exports to foreigners. The left side of **Exhibit 7–3** presents the values in 1998 for these four components. Later we will discuss the right side, which deals with the resource cost-income approach.

Personal consumption
Household spending on consumer goods and services during the current period. Consumption is a flow concept.

Consumption Purchases. **Personal consumption** purchases are the largest component of GDP; in 1998 they amounted to $5806 billion. Most consumption expenditures are for nondurable goods or services. Food, clothing, recreation, medical and legal services, and fuel are included in this category. These items are used up or consumed in a relatively short time. Durable goods, such as appliances and automobiles, comprise

There are two methods of calculating GDP. It can be calculated either by summing the expenditures on the "final-user" goods and services purchased by consumers, investors, governments, and foreigners (net exports) or by summing the income payments and direct cost items that accompany the production of goods and services.

EXHIBIT 7–2

TWO WAYS OF MEASURING GDP

EXPENDITURE APPROACH	RESOURCE COST-INCOME APPROACH
PERSONAL CONSUMPTION EXPENDITURES	AGGREGATE INCOME
+	Compensation of employees (wages and salaries)
GROSS PRIVATE DOMESTIC INVESTMENT	Income of self-employed proprietors
+	Rents
GOVERNMENT CONSUMPTION AND GROSS INVESTMENT	Profits
	Interest
+	+
NET EXPORTS OF GOODS AND SERVICES	NONINCOME COST ITEMS
=	Indirect business taxes
GDP	Depreciation
	+
	NET INCOME OF FOREIGNERS
	=
	GDP

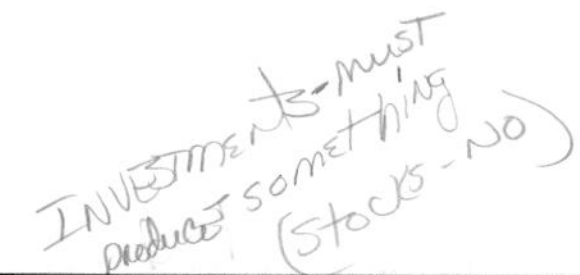

EXHIBIT 7-3

TWO WAYS OF MEASURING GDP—1998 DATA (BILLIONS OF DOLLARS)[a]

EXPENDITURE APPROACH			RESOURCE COST-INCOME APPROACH	
PERSONAL CONSUMPTION		$5,806	EMPLOYEE COMPENSATION	$4,980
Durable goods	$ 723		PROPRIETORS' INCOME	576
Nondurable goods	1,662		RENTS	162
Services	3,421		CORPORATE PROFITS	825
GROSS PRIVATE INVESTMENT		1,369	INTEREST INCOME	449
Fixed investment	1,309			
Inventories	60		INDIRECT BUSINESS TAXES	590
GOV. CONS. & GROSS INV.		1,488	DEPRECIATION (CAPITAL CONSUMPTION)[b]	908
Federal	521			
State and local	967		NET INCOME OF FOREIGNERS	19
NET EXPORTS		−154		
GROSS DOMESTIC PRODUCT		$8,509	GROSS DOMESTIC PRODUCT	$8,509

[a]*The left side shows the flow of expenditure and the right side the flow of income payments and indirect costs. Both procedures yield GDP.*

[b]*Includes $753 billion for the depreciation of privately owned capital and $155 billion for depreciation of government-owned assets.*

SOURCE: U.S. Department of Commerce. These data are also available in the Federal Reserve Bulletin, *which is published monthly.*

approximately one-eighth of all consumer purchases. These products are enjoyed over a longer period of time even though they are fully counted at the time they are purchased.

Gross Private Investment. The next item in the expenditure approach, **private investment,** is the production or construction of capital goods that provide a "flow" of future service. Unlike food or medical services, they are not immediately "used." Business plants and equipment are investment goods because they will help produce goods and services in the future. Similarly, a house is an investment good because it will also provide a stream of services long into the future. Increases in business inventories are also classified as investment because they will provide future consumer benefits.

Private investment
The flow of private-sector expenditures on durable assets (fixed investment) plus the addition to inventories (inventory investment) during a period. These expenditures enhance our ability to provide consumer benefits in the future.

Gross investment includes expenditures for both (1) the replacement of machinery, equipment, and buildings worn out during the year and (2) net additions to the stock of capital assets. Net investment is simply gross investment minus an allowance for **depreciation** and obsolescence of machinery and other physical assets during the year.

Depreciation
The estimated amount of physical capital (for example, machines and buildings) that is worn out or used up producing goods during the period.

Net investment is an important indicator of the economy's future productive capability. Substantial net investment indicates that the capital stock of the economy is growing, thereby enhancing the economy's future productive potential (shifting the economy's production-possibilities frontier outward). In contrast, a low rate of net investment, or even worse, negative net investment, implies a stagnating or even contracting economy. Of course, the impact of investment on future income will also be affected by the productivity of investment—whether the funds invested are channeled into wealth-creating projects. Other things the same, however, countries with a large net investment rate will tend to grow more rapidly than those with a low (or negative) rate of net investment. In 1998 gross private investment expenditures in the United States were $1369 billion, 16.1 percent of GDP. Of course, a large portion ($753 billion) of this figure was for replacement of private assets worn out during the year. Thus, net private investment was $616 billion, only 7 percent of GDP.

Inventory investment
Changes in the stock of unsold goods and raw materials held during a period.

Because GDP is designed to measure current production, allowance must be made for goods produced but not sold during the year—that is, for **inventory investment,** or changes during the year in the market value of unsold goods on shelves and in warehouses. If business firms have more goods on hand at the end of the year than they had at the beginning of the year, inventory investment will be positive. This inventory investment must be added to GDP. On the other hand, a decline in inventories would indicate that the purchases of goods and services exceeded current production. In this case, inventory *disinvestment* would be a subtraction from GDP. In 1998 the United States invested $60 billion in additional inventories.

Many goods possess both consumer- and investment-good characteristics. There is not always a clear distinction between the two. National accounting procedures have rather arbitrarily classified business purchases of final goods as private investment and considered household purchases, except housing, as personal consumption.

Government Consumption and Gross Investment. In 1998 federal, state, and local government consumption and investment summed to $1488 billion, approximately 17 percent of total GDP. The purchases of state and local governments exceeded those of the federal government by a wide margin. The government component includes both (a) expenditures on such items as office supplies, law enforcement, and the operation of veterans hospitals, which are "consumed" during the current period and (b) the purchase of long-lasting capital goods, such as missiles, highways, and dams for flood control. Remember, transfer payments are excluded from GDP because they do not involve current production. Thus, government purchases of consumption and investment goods are substantially less than total government expenditures.

Net exports
Exports minus imports.

Exports
Goods and services produced domestically but sold to foreigners.

Imports
Goods and services produced by foreigners but purchased by domestic consumers, investors, and governments.

Net Exports. The final item in the expenditure approach is **net exports,** or total exports minus imports. **Exports** are domestically produced goods and services sold to foreigners. **Imports** are foreign-produced goods and services purchased domestically. Remember, GDP is a measure of domestic production—output produced within the borders of a nation. Therefore, when measuring GDP by the expenditure approach, we must (1) add exports (goods produced domestically that were sold to foreigners) and (2) subtract imports (goods produced abroad that were purchased by Americans). For national-income accounting purposes, we can combine these two factors into a single entry:

$$\text{Net exports} = \text{Total exports} - \text{Total imports}$$

Net exports may be either positive or negative. When we sell more to foreigners than we buy from them, net exports are positive. In recent years, net exports have been negative, indicating we were buying more goods and services from foreigners than we were selling to them. In 1998 net exports were *minus* $154 billion.

Deriving GDP by the Resource Cost-Income Approach

The right side of Exhibit 7–3 illustrates how, rather than summing the flow of expenditures on final goods and services, we could reach GDP by summing the flow of costs incurred and income generated. Labor services play a very important role in the production process. It is therefore not surprising that employee compensation, $4980 billion in 1998, provides the largest source of income generated by the production of goods and services.

Self-employed proprietors undertake the risks of owning their own businesses and simultaneously provide their own labor services to the firm. Their earnings in 1998 contributed $576 billion to GDP, 7 percent of the total. Together, employees and self-employed proprietors accounted for approximately two-thirds of GDP.

Machines, buildings, land, and other physical assets also contribute to the production process. Rents, corporate profits, and interest are payments to persons who provide either the physical resources or the financial resources required to purchase physical assets. Rents are returns to resource owners who permit others to use their assets during a time period. Corporate profits are compensation earned by stockholders, who bear the risk of the business undertaking and who provide financial capital with which the firm purchases resources. Interest is a payment to parties who extend loans to producers.

Not all cost components of GDP result in an income payment to a resource supplier. In order to get to GDP, we need to account also for three other factors: indirect business taxes, the cost of depreciation, and the net income of foreigners.

Indirect Business Taxes. Taxes imposed on the sale of a good that increase the cost of the good to consumers are called **indirect business taxes.** The sales tax is a clear example. When you make a $1.00 purchase in a state with a 5 percent sales tax, the purchase actually costs you $1.05. The $1.00 goes to the seller to pay wages, rent, interest, and managerial costs. The 5 cents goes to the government. Indirect business taxes boost the market price of goods when GDP is calculated by the expenditure approach. Similarly, when looked at from the factor-cost viewpoint, taxes are an indirect cost of supplying the goods to the purchasers.

Indirect business taxes
Taxes that increase the business firm's costs of production and, therefore, the prices charged to consumers. Examples would be sales, excise, and property taxes.

Depreciation. Using machines to produce goods causes the machines to wear out. Depreciation of capital goods is a cost of producing current goods, but it is not a direct cost because it reflects what is lost to the producer when machines and facilities become less valuable. Depreciation does not involve a direct payment to a resource owner. It is an estimate, based on the expected life of the asset, of the decline in the asset's value during the year. In 1998 depreciation (sometimes called *capital consumption allowance*) of private and public sector capital amounted to $908 billion, approximately 11 percent of GDP.

Net Income of Foreigners. The sum of employee compensation, proprietors' income, rents, corporate profits, and interest yields **national income,** the income of Americans, regardless of whether that income was earned domestically or abroad. If depreciation and indirect business taxes—the two indirect cost components—are added to national income, the result will be **gross national product (GNP),** the income earned by Americans, regardless of whether the income is earned in the United States or abroad. Put another way, GNP counts the income that Americans earn abroad, but it omits the income foreigners earn in the United States.

Because GDP is a measure of domestic output, the net income earned by foreigners must be added when GDP is derived by the resource cost-income approach. The **net income of foreigners** is equal to the income foreigners earn in the United States minus the income that Americans earn abroad. If foreigners earn more income in the United States than Americans earn abroad, the net income of foreigners will be positive. In recent years, this has been the case. The net income of foreigners is generally

National income
The total income earned by the nationals (citizens) during a period. It is the sum of employee compensation, self-employment income, rents, interest, and corporate profits.

Gross national product (GNP)
The total market value of all final goods and services produced by the citizens of a country. It is equal to GDP minus the net income of foreigners.

Net income of foreigners
The income that foreigners earn by contributing labor and capital resources to the production of goods within the borders of a country minus the income the nationals of the country earn abroad.

small. In 1998, it was $19 billion, only about two-tenths of one percent of GDP. As Exhibit 7-3 indicates, when this figure is added to the other components, the sum is equal to GDP.

Relative Size of GDP Components

Exhibit 7–4 shows the average proportion of GDP accounted for by each of the components during 1996–1998. When the expenditure approach is used, personal consumption is by far the largest and most stable component of GDP. Consumption accounted for 68 percent of GDP during 1996–1998, compared to only 15 percent for private investment and 18 percent for government purchases. When GDP is measured by the resource cost-income approach, compensation to employees is the dominant component (58 percent of GDP). During 1996–1998, rents, corporate profits, and interest combined to account for 17 percent of GDP.

EXHIBIT 7–4

MAJOR COMPONENTS OF GDP IN THE UNITED STATES, 1996–1998

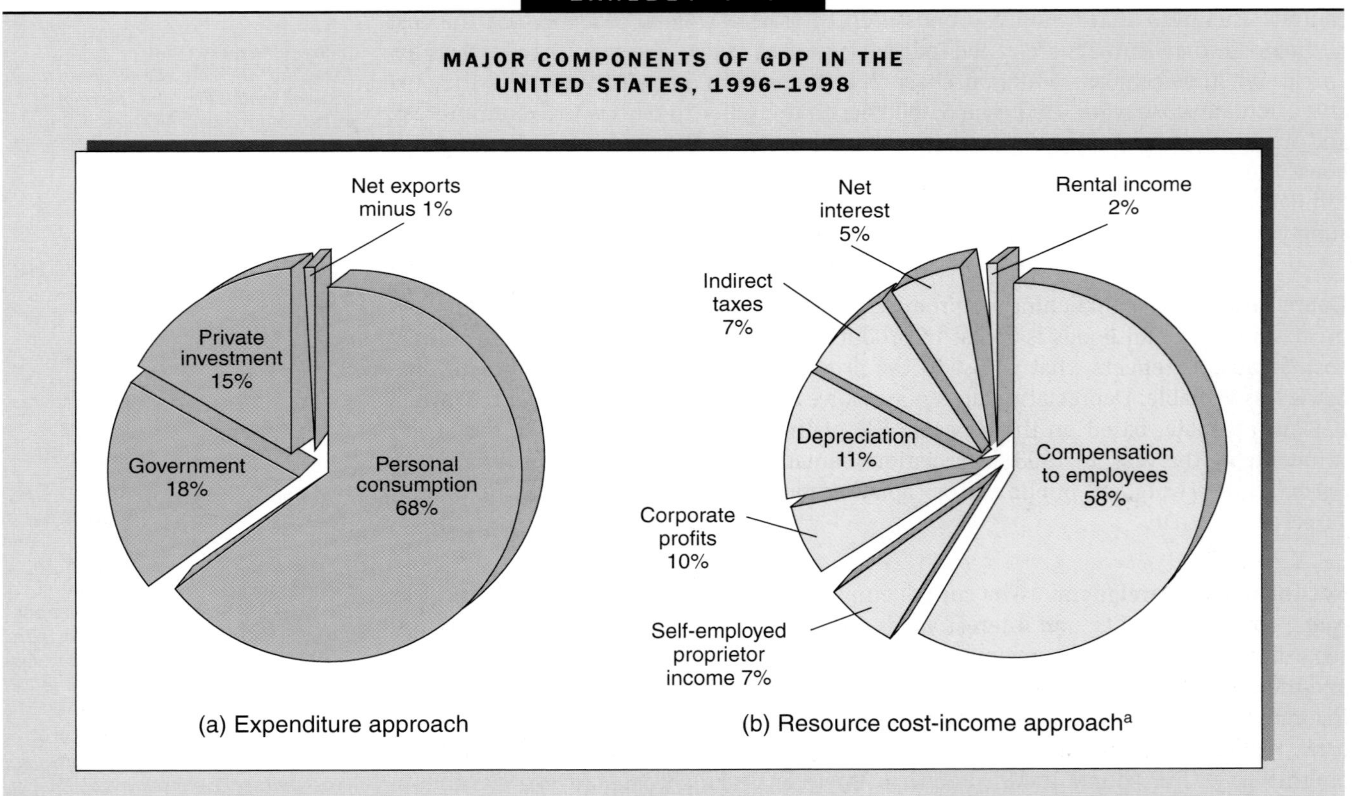

The relative sizes of the major components of GDP usually fluctuate within a fairly narrow range. The average proportion of each component during 1996–1998 is demonstrated here for both (a) the expenditure approach and (b) the resource cost-income approach.

[a]*The net income of foreigners was negligible.*

SOURCE: Economic Report of the President, 1999.

REAL AND NOMINAL GDP

GDP was developed in order to help us better assess what is happening to output (and income) over time. This is important because expansion in the production of goods and services that people value is the source of higher incomes and living standards. When comparing GDP across time periods, we confront a problem: The nominal value of GDP may increase as the result of either (1) expansion in the quantities of goods produced or (2) higher prices. Because only the former will improve our living standards, it is vitally important to distinguish between the two.

Economists use price indexes to adjust **nominal values** (or *money values,* as they are often called) for the effects of inflation—an increase in the general level of prices over time. Whenever economists use the term **real** (for example, *real GDP* or *real income*), this means that the data have been adjusted for the effects of inflation. When comparing data at different points in time, it is nearly always the real changes that are of most interest.

Nominal values
Values expressed in current dollars.

Real values
Values that have been adjusted for the effects of inflation.

What precisely is a price index, and how can it be used to adjust GDP and other figures for the effects of inflation? ***A price index measures the cost of purchasing a market basket (or "bundle") of goods at a point in time relative to the cost of purchasing the identical market basket during an earlier reference period.*** A base year (or period) is chosen and assigned a value of 100. As the cost of purchasing the reference bundle of goods rises relative to the base year, the price index increases proportionally. For example, if the cost of purchasing the reference bundle during the current period is 20 percent higher than during the base year, the current price index would be 120, compared to 100 for the base year.

TWO KEY PRICE INDEXES: THE CONSUMER PRICE INDEX AND THE GDP DEFLATOR

Price indexes indicate what is happening to the general level of prices. The two most widely used price indexes are the consumer price index (CPI) and the GDP deflator. Because the construction of the CPI is simpler, we will begin with it.

The* consumer price index (CPI) *is designed to measure the impact of price changes on the cost of the typical bundle of goods purchased by households. A bundle of 364 items that comprised the "typical bundle" purchased by urban consumers during the 1982–1984 base period provides the foundation for the CPI. The quantity of each good reflects the quantity actually purchased by the typical household during the base year. Every month, the Bureau of Labor Statistics surveys approximately 21,000 stores representative of the urban United States in order to derive the average price for each of the food items, consumer goods and services, housing, and property taxes included in the index. The cost of purchasing this 364-item market basket at current prices is then compared with the cost of purchasing the same market basket at base-year prices. The result is a measure of current prices compared to the 1982–1984 base-period prices. In 1998 the value of the CPI was 163.0, compared to the 100 during the 1982–1984 base period. This indicates the price level in 1998 was 63.0 percent higher than the price level of 1982–1984.

Consumer price index (CPI)
An indicator of the general level of prices. It attempts to compare the cost of purchasing the market basket bought by a typical consumer during a specific period with the cost of purchasing the same market basket during an earlier period.

The* GDP deflator *is a broader price index than the CPI. It is designed to measure the change in the average price of the market basket of goods included in GDP. In addition to consumer goods, the GDP deflator includes prices for capital goods and other goods and services purchased by businesses and governments. Therefore, in

GDP deflator
A price index that reveals the cost during the current period of purchasing the items included in GDP relative to the cost during a base year (currently, 1992). Because the base year is assigned a value of 100, as the GDP deflator takes on values greater than 100, it indicates that prices have risen.

addition to consumer goods, the bundle used to construct the GDP deflator will include such items as large computers, airplanes, welding equipment, and office space. The overall bundle is intended to be representative of those items included in GDP. Since 1995, the Department of Commerce has used the chain-link method to derive the GDP deflator. The cost of purchasing the typical bundle of goods included in this year's GDP is always compared with the cost of purchasing that same bundle at last year's prices. Because the chain-link procedure updates the typical bundle each year, it minimizes the impact of bias resulting from a failure to make allowance for the fact that buyers substitute away from more expensive goods. As a result, the GDP deflator is thought to yield a slightly more accurate measure of changes in the general level of prices than the CPI. As in the case of the CPI, a base year (currently 1992) is chosen for the GDP deflator and assigned a value of 100. As prices rise, the index increases. The year-to-year change in the index provides an estimate of the rate of inflation.

Exhibit 7–5 presents data for both the CPI and GDP deflator during the 1980s and 1990s. Even though they are based on different market baskets and procedures, the two measures of the annual rate of inflation are quite similar. Inspection of the annual rate of inflation as measured by each index indicates that the differences between these two alternative measures have been small, usually only a few tenths of a percentage point.

The CPI and GDP deflator were designed for different purposes. Choosing between the two depends on what we are trying to measure. If we want to determine how rising prices affect the money income of consumers, the CPI would be most appropriate because it includes only consumer goods. However, if we want an economywide

EXHIBIT 7–5

CONSUMER PRICE INDEX AND GDP DEFLATOR: 1981–1998

Year	CPI (1982–84 = 100)	Inflation Rate (percent)	GDP Deflator (1992 = 100)	Inflation Rate (percent)
1981	90.9	10.3	66.1	10.0
1982	96.5	6.2	70.2	6.2
1983	99.6	3.2	73.2	4.1
1984	103.9	4.3	75.9	3.7
1985	107.6	3.6	78.6	3.6
1986	109.6	1.9	80.6	2.5
1987	113.6	3.6	83.1	3.1
1988	118.3	4.1	86.1	3.6
1989	124.0	4.8	89.7	4.2
1990	130.7	5.4	93.6	4.3
1991	136.2	4.2	97.3	4.0
1992	140.3	3.0	100.0	2.8
1993	144.5	3.0	102.6	2.6
1994	148.2	2.6	105.1	2.4
1995	152.4	2.8	107.5	2.3
1996	156.9	3.0	109.5	1.9
1997	160.5	2.3	111.6	1.9
1998	163.0	1.5	112.7	1.0

SOURCE: Economic Report of the President, 1999

measure of inflation with which to adjust GDP data, clearly the GDP deflator is the appropriate index because it includes a broader set of goods and services.

USING THE GDP DEFLATOR TO DERIVE REAL GDP

We can use the GDP deflator together with **nominal GDP** to measure **real GDP:** GDP in dollars of constant purchasing power. If prices are rising, we simply deflate the nominal GDP during the latter period to account for the effects of inflation.

Nominal GDP
GDP expressed at current prices. It is often called money GDP.

Real GDP
GDP adjusted for changes in the price level.

Exhibit 7–6 illustrates how real GDP is measured and why it is important to adjust for price changes. Between 1992 and 1998, the nominal GDP of the United States increased from $6,244 billion to $8509 billion, an increase of 36.3 percent. However, a large portion of this increase in nominal GDP reflected inflation rather than an increase in real output. When making GDP comparisons across time periods, we generally do so in terms of the purchasing power of the dollar during the base year of the GDP deflator, currently 1992. The GDP deflator, the price index that measures changes in the cost of all goods included in GDP, increased from 100 in the 1992 base year to 112.7 in 1998. This indicates that prices rose by 12.7 percent between 1992 and 1998. To determine the real GDP for 1998 in terms of 1992 dollars, we deflate the 1998 nominal GDP for the rise in prices:

$$\text{Real GDP}_{98} = \text{Nominal GDP}_{98} \times \frac{\text{GDP deflator}_{92}}{\text{GDP deflator}_{98}}$$

Because prices were rising, the latter ratio is less than 1. Measured in terms of 1992 dollars, the real GDP in 1998 was $7550 billion, only 20.9 percent more than in 1992. So although money GDP (nominal GDP) expanded by 36.4 percent, real GDP increased by only 20.9 percent.

Data on both money GDP and price changes are essential for meaningful output comparisons between two time periods. By itself, a change in money GDP tells us nothing about what is happening to the rate of real production. For example, not even a doubling of money GDP would lead to an increase in real output if prices more than

EXHIBIT 7–6

CHANGES IN PRICES AND REAL GDP OF UNITED STATES, 1992–1998

	Nominal GDP (billions of dollars)	Price Index (GDP deflator, 1992 = 100)	Real GDP (billions of 1992 dollars)
1992	$6,244	100.0	$6,244
1998	8,509	112.7	7,550
Percent Increase	36.3	12.7	20.9

Between 1992 and 1998, nominal GDP increased by 36.3 percent. But when the 1998 GDP is deflated to account for price increases, we see that real GDP increased by only 20.9 percent.

SOURCE: U.S. Department of Commerce.

doubled during the time period. On the other hand, money income could remain constant while real GDP increased if there was a reduction in prices. Knowledge of both nominal GDP and the general level of prices is required for real income comparisons over time.

PROBLEMS WITH GDP AS A MEASURING ROD

GDP is not a perfect device for measuring current production and income. Some items that involve current production are excluded because their value is difficult to determine. The introduction of new products complicates the use of GDP as a measuring rod. Also, when production involves harmful "side effects" that are not fully registered in the market price of inputs, GDP will fail to accurately measure the level of output. These limitations are particularly important when GDP is used as an indicator of economic well-being, rather than as simply a measure of the rate of *market* output over time or across countries. Let us consider some of the major limitations of GDP.

NONMARKET PRODUCTION

The GDP fails to count household production because such production does not involve a market transaction. Because of this, the household services of millions of people are excluded. If you mow the yard, repair your car, paint your house, pick up relatives from school, or perform similar productive household activities, your labor services add nothing to GDP, because no market transaction is involved. Such nonmarket productive activities are sizable—10 percent or 15 percent of total GDP, perhaps more.

Furthermore, their exclusion results in some oddities in national-income accounting. Suppose, for example, that a woman marries her gardener, and, after the marriage, the spouse-gardener works for love rather than for money. GDP will decline because the services of the spouse-gardener no longer involve a market transaction and therefore will no longer contribute to GDP. If a family member decides to enter the labor force and hire someone to perform services previously provided by household members, there will be a double-barreled impact on GDP. It will rise as a result of (1) the market earnings of the new labor-force entrant plus (2) the amount paid to the person hired to perform the services that were previously supplied within the household.

The omission of many nonmarket productive activities makes comparisons over time and across countries at various stages of market development less meaningful. For example, compared to the situation 30 or 40 years ago, people are now more likely to eat out at a restaurant rather than prepare their own food; hire a lawn service rather than mow their own lawn; and purchase an automatic dishwasher rather than do the dishes by hand. These and many other similar changes involve the substitution of a market transaction, which adds to GDP, for self-provision, which is excluded. Because the share of total production provided within the household has declined relative to production that involves market transactions, current GDP, even in real dollars, is overstated relative to the earlier period.

Similarly, GDP comparisons overstate the output of developed countries when compared to that of underdeveloped countries. A larger share of the total production of underdeveloped countries originates in the household sector. For example, Mexican families are more likely than their U.S. counterparts to make their own clothing, raise and prepare their own food, provide their own child-rearing services, and even build their own homes. These productive labor services, originating in the household sector, are excluded from GDP. Therefore, GDP understates total output in Mexico even more than it does in the United States.

The Underground Economy

Some people attempt to conceal various economic activities in order to evade taxes or because the activities themselves are illegal. Economists refer to these unreported and therefore difficult to measure activities as the **underground economy.**

Underground economy
Unreported barter and cash transactions that take place outside recorded market channels. Some are otherwise legal activities undertaken to evade taxes. Others involve illegal activities, such as trafficking in drugs and prostitution.

Because cash transactions are difficult for government authorities to trace, they provide the lifeblood of the underground economy. This is why drug trafficking, smuggling, prostitution, and other illegal activities are generally conducted in cash. Not all underground economic activity is illegal. A large portion of the underground economy involves legal goods and services that go unreported to avoid taxes. The participants in this legal-if-reported portion of the underground economy are quite diverse. Taxicab drivers and waitresses may pocket fees and tips. Small-business proprietors may fail to ring up and report various cash sales. Craft and professional workers may fail to report cash income. Employees ranging from laborers to bartenders may work "off the books" and accept payment in cash in order to qualify for income-transfer benefits or evade taxes (or allow their employers to evade taxes).

Even though they are often productive, these unreported underground activities are not included in GDP. Estimates of the size of the underground economy in the United States range from 10 percent to 15 percent of total output. The available evidence indicates that the size of the underground economy is even larger in Western Europe (where tax rates are higher) and South America (where regulations often make it more costly to operate a business).

Leisure and Human Costs

GDP excludes leisure, a good that is valuable to each of us, and the human cost associated with the production of goods and services. Simon Kuznets, the "inventor" of GDP, believed that this omission substantially reduced the accuracy of GDP as a measure of economic well-being. One country might attain a $20,000 per capita GDP with an average workweek of 30 hours. Another might attain the same per capita GDP with a 50-hour workweek. The market output per person of the two countries would be identical. In terms of economic well-being, however, the first country would be better off because it "produces" more leisure, or sacrifices less human cost. GDP, though, does not reflect this fact.

The average number of hours worked per week in the United States has declined steadily over the years. The average nonagricultural production worker spent only 34.5 hours per week on the job in 1998, compared to more than 40 hours in 1947—a 14 percent reduction in weekly hours worked. Clearly, this reduction in the length of the workweek raised the American standard of living, even though it did not enhance GDP.

GDP also fails to take into account human costs. On average, jobs today are less physically strenuous and are generally performed in a safer, more comfortable environment than was true a generation ago. To the extent that working conditions have improved through the years, GDP figures understate the growth of real income.

Quality Variation and Introduction of New Goods

If GDP is going to measure accurately changes in real output, changes in the price level must be measured accurately. This is a difficult task in a dynamic world where new and improved products are constantly replacing old ones. Although statisticians attempt to make some allowance for quality improvements and new products, most believe that they are inadequate. Most economists believe that price indexes, including the GDP deflator, overestimate the rate of inflation by approximately 1 percent *annually.* If so, annual changes in output are underestimated by a similar amount.

Although the annual measurement error is relatively small, it can make a big difference over lengthy time periods. Consider the changes in the quality and availability of products during the last 25 years. Today, new automobiles are more fuel-efficient and generally safer than they were in the 1970s. Dental services are generally much less unpleasant than was true 25 years ago. Some commodities—compact disc players, video recorders, personal computers, and electronic mail, to name a few—simply were unavailable 25 years ago. When the bundle of goods available differs substantially between periods, the significance of income comparisons is reduced.

As **Exhibit 7–7** shows, per-capita real GDP in 1930 was only about one-fourth of the figure for 1998. Does this mean that, on average, Americans produced and consumed almost four times as much in 1998 as in 1930? Caution should be exercised before arriving at this conclusion. In the 1930s there were no jet planes, television programs, automatic dishwashers, personal computers, or videocassette players. In 1930 even a millionaire could not have purchased the typical bundle consumed by the average American in 1998.[3] On the other hand, in 1930 there were plenty of open spaces, trees, uncongested (but rough) roads, pure-water rivers, hiking trails, and areas with low crime rates. Thus, many goods were available in 1998 that were not available in 1930, and vice versa. Under such circumstances, comparative GDP statistics lose some of their precision.

Harmful Side Effects and Economic "Bads"

GDP makes no adjustment for harmful side effects that sometimes arise from production, consumption, and the events of nature. If they do not involve market transactions, economic "bads" are ignored in the calculation of GDP. Yet, in a modern industrial economy, production and consumption sometimes generate side effects that either detract from current consumption or reduce our future production possibilities. When property rights are defined imperfectly, air and water pollution are sometimes side effects of economic activity. For example, an industrial plant may pollute the air or water while producing goods. Automobiles may put harmful chemicals into the atmosphere while providing us with transportation. GDP makes no allowance for these negative side effects. In fact, expenditures on the cleanup of air and water pollution, should they be undertaken, will add to GDP.

Similarly, GDP makes no allowance for destructive acts of nature. Consider the impact of Hurricane Andrew, which left a path of destruction as it roared through South Florida during the fall of 1992. Numerous buildings, bridges, and homes were destroyed or damaged. Yet nothing was subtracted from GDP, because it makes no allowance for losses that operate outside of market channels. In fact, Andrew probably increased GDP in late 1992 and throughout 1993. Several hundred million dollars were poured into the reconstruction efforts that went on for more than a year. The cleanup

---

[3]The following quotation from the late Mancur Olson, longtime professor of economics at the University of Maryland, illustrates this point:

> *The price level has risen about eight times since 1932, so a $25,000 income then would be the "equivalent" of an income of $200,000 today—one could readily afford a Rolls-Royce, the best seats in the theater, and the care of the best physicians in the country. But the 1932 Rolls-Royce, for all its many virtues, does not embody some desirable technologies available today in the humblest Ford. Nor would the imposing dollar of 1932 buy a TV set or a home videocassette recorder. And if one got an infection, the best physicians in 1932 would not be able to prescribe an antibiotic.*

EXHIBIT 7-7

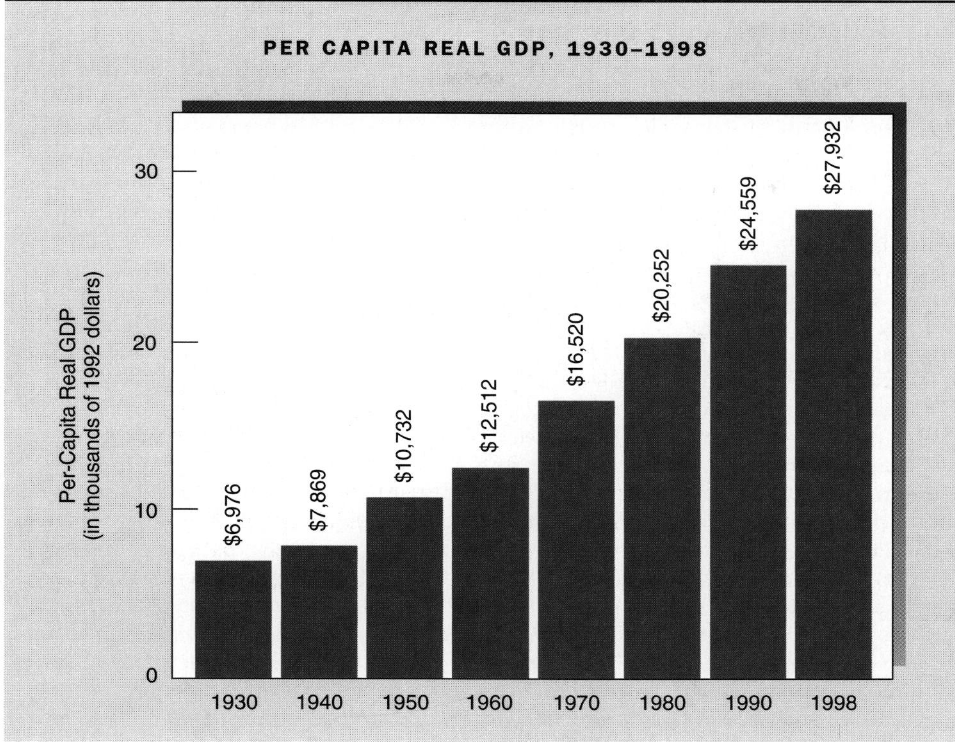

In 1998 per-capita real GDP was 2.2 times the 1960 level, 3.5 times the 1940 level, and 4 times the 1930 value. How meaningful are these numbers?

SOURCE: Derived from U.S. Department of Commerce data.

and replacement of items lost undoubtedly caused people to work longer and purchase more goods and services than otherwise would have been the case. Because GDP ignored the destruction, but counted the rebuilding activities, it tended to overstate the change in living standards during the period.

THE GREAT CONTRIBUTION OF GDP

While some of the shortcomings of GDP result in an understatement of economic well-being, the bias of others is in the opposite direction. It is much easier to point out the deficiencies than it is to determine the direction of the overall bias that they cause. Shortcomings aside, there is evidence that GDP per person is a broad indicator of the living standard available to people. As per-capita GDP in the United States has increased over time, the quality of most goods has increased while the amount of work time required for their purchase has declined. In many cases, the changes have been dramatic. (See the boxed feature, "The Time Cost of Goods: Today and Yesterday.") Like GDP, this indicates that our living standards have improved. Broad quality of life variables paint a similar picture. For example, life expectancy and both time and money spent on leisure activities have gone up, while illiteracy and infant mortality rates have gone down. Cross-country comparisons also show a strong positive relationship between per-capita GDP and various indicators of economic well-being.

When considering the significance of GDP, however, it is important to keep in mind what it was designed to measure. GDP is not a measure of economic welfare or happiness of the citizenry. It is not even primarily a measure of economic well-being.

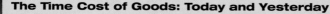

MEASURES OF ECONOMIC ACTIVITY

The Time Cost of Goods: Today and Yesterday

Many of you have heard stories from your parents or grandparents about how low prices were when they were young. A bottle of soda cost only a nickel, and a brand new car was less than $2,000. In this chapter you have learned that there is a difference between nominal and real values. When trying to figure out whether a good is now cheaper or more expensive, economists generally use a measure of the overall price level, such as the CPI or GDP deflator, to adjust the nominal prices of earlier periods. There is, however, an alternative way of looking at this issue: One might estimate how long an average person would have to work in order to earn enough to purchase various items. For example, just after telling you that a soda used to cost a nickel, your grandfather might have noted that he used to earn only 25 cents per hour. Thus, for an hour's worth of work, he could earn enough money to purchase five bottles of soda. Today, the price of a soda is approximately 60 cents. To earn the same real wage as your grandfather, you would only need to earn $3 per hour (exactly enough to purchase five sodas with your hour's wage).

Through time, the productivity of the average worker in America has increased substantially. This increased worker productivity is the key to higher real incomes and improved living standards. Using average wage rates, W. Michael Cox and Richard Alm of the Federal Reserve Bank of Dallas have computed the time of work required for the typical worker to purchase many common items. Their analysis shows that Americans today are able to acquire most goods with much less work time than was previously the case. Some examples are shown in the accompanying chart.

To purchase a new automobile in 1908 cost $850, which took the average worker 4,696 hours to earn. In 1955, a new automobile costing $3,030 took 1,638 hours of work to earn, and by 1997, a $17,995 new automobile cost a typical worker only 1,365 hours of work to earn. The time cost of a new car today is less than 30 percent of the time cost in 1908. Furthermore, the power, performance, and dependability of even the most economical 1997 model are lightyears advanced from the 1908 version.

The reductions in price have been particularly dramatic for technologically advanced products, such as computers, microwave ovens, calculators, and cellular phones. Cellular phones and computers now cost only a fraction of the time required for their purchase 15 years ago. In 1984, it took the average worker over 10 weeks of work to purchase a cellular phone, while today it takes slightly more than one 8-hour day. In 1901, spending on food, clothing, and shelter consumed 76 percent of the typical worker's paycheck. Because of greater productivity and higher real earnings, today the average worker spends only 38 percent of earnings on these items.

As worker productivity grows, real incomes increase, and the time cost required to purchase products falls. This process generates higher living standards and brings goods that used to be luxuries, costing weeks' or months' worth of a worker's salary, within the reach of most Americans. The next time you call home, remind your parents that in 1915, a 3-minute, coast-to-coast, long-distance telephone call cost more than two-weeks' worth of work at the average wage. Today, it costs only 1.8 minutes of work. Your parents will be happy to hear that, particularly if you are calling collect.

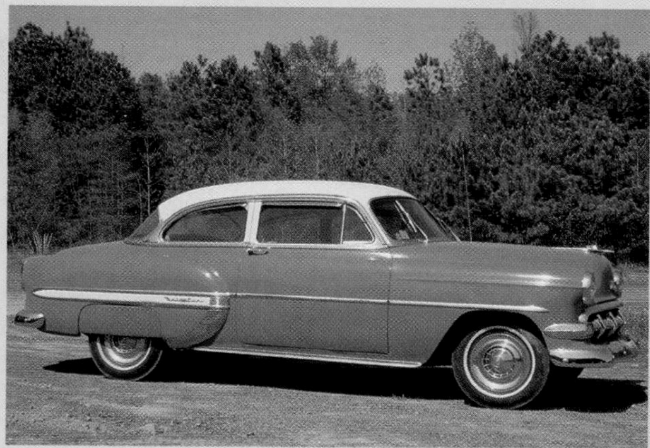

Is an automobile really more expensive than it was in 1955? You might be surprised to learn that in 1955 it took a typical worker 1638 hours of work time to purchase a car. Today, a vastly improved model can be purchased with only 1365 hours.

(continued)

CHART 1

THE COST OF PRODUCTS TO AN AVERAGE-WAGE WORKER IN MINUTES OR HOURS OF WORK

Item	Old Cost	Cost in 1997
Eggs (1 dozen)	80 minutes in 1919	5 minutes
Sugar (5 lbs.)	72 minutes in 1919	10 minutes
Coffee (1 lb.)	55 minutes in 1919	17 minutes
Bread (1 lb.)	13 minutes in 1919	4 minutes
Mattress and box spring (twin)	161 hours in 1929	24 hours
Refrigerator	3,162 hours in 1916	68 hours
Clothes washer and dryer	256 hours in 1956	52 hours
Automobile	4,696 hours in 1908	1,365 hours
Coast-to-coast airflight	366 hours in 1930	16 hours
Big Mac	27 minutes in 1940	9 minutes
Long-distance call (3 min.)	90 hours in 1915	1.8 minutes
Calculator	31 hours in 1972	46 minutes
Microwave oven	97 hours in 1975	15 hours
Cellular phone	456 hours in 1984	9 hours
Personal computer	435 hours in 1984	76 hours

SOURCE: W. Michael Cox and Richard Alm, "Time Well Spent: The Declining Real *Cost of Living in America,"* 1997 Annual Report of the Federal Reserve Bank of Dallas, *pp. 2–24. Also see Michael Cox,* Myths of Rich and Poor *(New York: Basic Books, 1999).*

Indeed, a number of things, such as leisure and household production, that obviously influence the well-being of people are omitted.

GDP was designed to measure the value of the goods and services produced in the market (or business) sector. In spite of its shortcomings and limitations, real GDP is a reasonably precise measure of the rate of output in the market sector and how that output rate is changing.

Adjusted for changes in prices, annual and quarterly GDP data provide the information required to track the performance level of the economy. These data allow us to compare the current output of goods and services relative to the rate of output in the recent past. This is a vitally important contribution. Without this information, policymakers would be less likely to adopt productive policies and business decision makers would be less able to determine the future direction of demand for their products. In the words of Kenneth Boulding, this contribution is significant enough to rank GDP as "one of the great inventions of the twentieth century, probably almost as significant as the automobile and not quite as significant as TV." [4]

---

[4]Kenneth Boulding, "Fun and Games with the Gross National Product—The Role of Misleading Indicators in Social Policy," in *The Environment Crisis,* ed. Harold W. Helfrich Jr. (New Haven, Conn.: Yale University Press, 1970), p. 157.

GDP is a measure of current production. It counts only goods and services produced during the year. Exchanges involving ownership rights to previously produced goods and assets are not included in GDP.

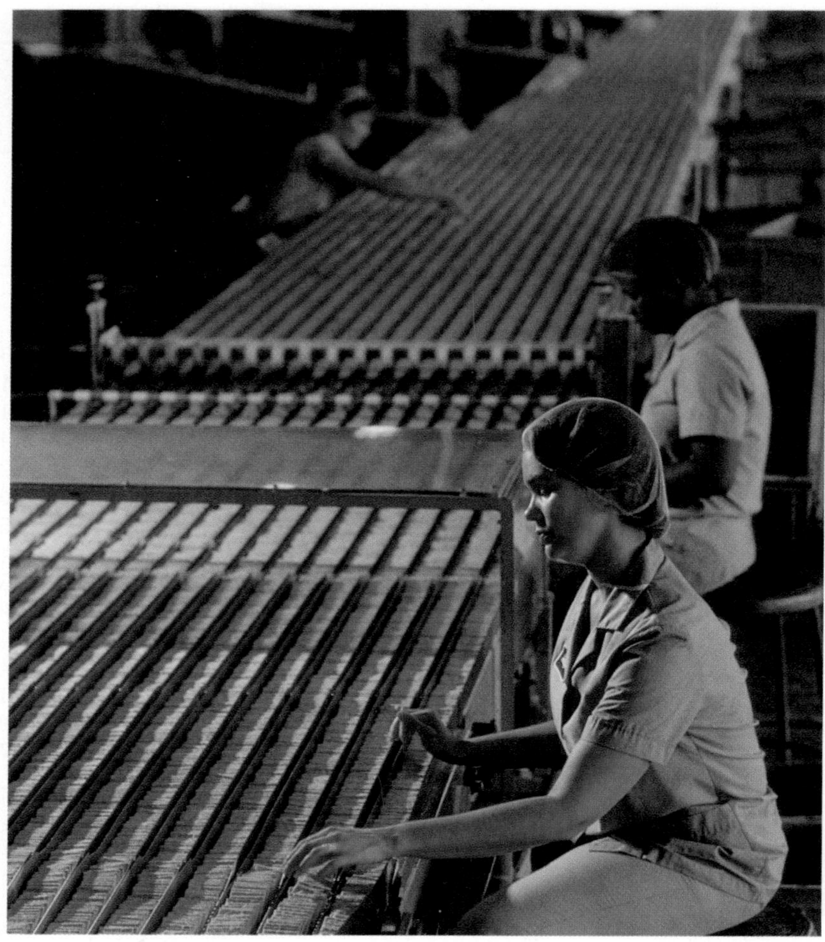

RELATED INCOME MEASURES

Exhibit 7–8 illustrates the relationship among five alternative measures of aggregate income. GDP, of course, is the most frequently quoted index of economic performance. The gross national product is a closely related figure that is designed to measure the income of a country's citizenry, regardless of whether earned at home or abroad. Thus, GNP excludes the net income of foreigners, the difference between the earnings of foreigners in the United States and the earnings of Americans abroad. Because this figure (net income of foreigners) is generally small, the difference between GDP and GNP is quite small for the United States and most other countries.

When the net income of foreigners, depreciation, and indirect business taxes are subtracted from GDP, the result is national income, the income earned by the domestic citizens (nationals) at its factor cost. As we previously noted, national income is also equal to the sum of employee compensation, interest, self-employment income, rents, and corporate profits.

Personal income
The total income received by domestic households and noncorporate businesses. It is available for consumption, saving, and payment of personal taxes.

Although national income represents the earnings of all resource owners, not all of this income is available for personal use. Exhibit 7-8 indicates the various adjustments to national income that must be made to derive **personal income,** which is the total of all income received by individuals and noncorporate businesses. As most workers know, the

EXHIBIT 7-8

FIVE ALTERNATIVE MEASURES OF INCOME

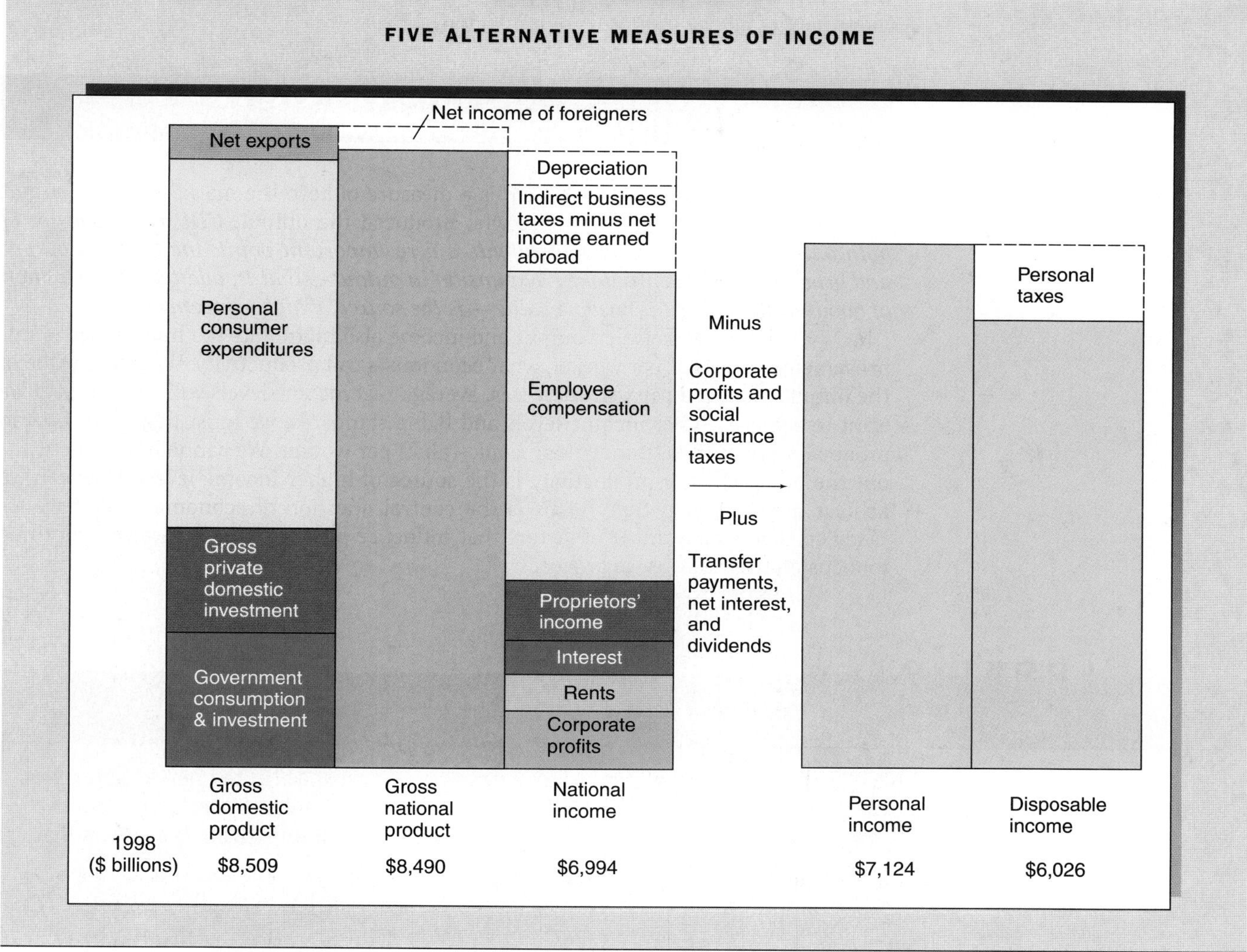

The bars illustrate the relationship among five alternative measures of national income. The alternatives range from the gross domestic product, which is the broadest measure of output, to disposable income, which indicates the funds available to households for either personal consumption or saving.

amount shown on your paycheck does not equal your salary. Personal taxes must be deducted. **Disposable income** is the income that is yours to do with as you please. It is simply personal income minus personal taxes.

Disposable income
The income available to individuals after personal taxes. It can be either spent on consumption or saved.

There are thus five alternative measures of domestic output and income:

1. Gross domestic product
2. Gross national product
3. National income
4. Personal income
5. Disposable income

Each of the five alternatives measures something different, but they are all closely related. Movement of one nearly always parallels movement of the other indicators. Because the five measures move together, economists often use only GDP or the terms *income, output,* or *aggregate production* when referring to the general movement of all five indicators of productive activity.

THE LINK BETWEEN OUTPUT AND INCOME

As we have stressed throughout, GDP is a measure of both the market value of output and the income generated by those who produced the output. ***GDP is a measure of both output and income. This highlights a very important point: Increases in output and growth of income are linked. Expansion in output—that is, additional production of goods and services that people value—is the source of higher income levels.***

The linkage between output and income also highlights the importance of improvements in output per worker, what economists call productivity. When the value of the output produced per year increases, average real income levels will rise. Thus, if we want to achieve higher income levels and living standards, we must figure out how to produce more output (things that people value) per worker. We cannot have one without the other. Greater productivity is the source of higher income levels. How can we achieve greater productivity? This is the central question of economics. We have already considered a number of factors that influence productivity, and we will continue to focus on this issue as we proceed.

LOOKING *Ahead*

GDP provides us with a measure of economic performance. In the next chapter, we will take a closer look at the path of real GDP in the United States and introduce other indicators of economic performance. Later, we will investigate the factors that underlie both the level of and fluctuations in real GDP.

KEY POINTS

➤ Gross domestic product (GDP) is a measure of the market value of final-user goods and services produced within the borders of a country during a specific time period, usually a year.

➤ Income transfers, purely financial transactions, and exchanges of goods and assets produced during earlier periods are not included in GDP because they do not involve current production.

➤ When derived by the expenditure approach, the four major components of GDP are (1) personal consumption, (2) gross private investment, (3) government consumption and gross investment, and (4) net exports.

➤ When derived by the resource cost-income approach, GDP equals (a) the direct income components (wages and salaries, self-employment income, rents, interest, and corporate profits), plus (b) indirect business taxes, depreciation, and the net income of foreigners.

➤ Price indexes measure changes in the general level of prices over time. They can be used to adjust nominal values for the effects of inflation. The two most widely used price indexes are the GDP deflator and the consumer price index (CPI).

➤ Real GDP_2 = Nominal $GDP_2 \times$ (GDP $deflator_1$/GDP $deflator_2$)

➤ GDP is an imperfect measure of current production. It excludes household production and the underground economy, fails to take leisure and human costs into account, and adjusts imperfectly for quality changes.

➤ Despite its limitations, GDP is vitally important because it is a reasonably accurate measure of short-term fluctuations in output and income.

➤ As the alternative ways of measuring GDP highlight, output and income are linked. Increases in output are the source of higher income levels.

CRITICAL ANALYSIS QUESTIONS

*1. Indicate how each of the following activities will affect this year's GDP:

a. The sale of a used economics textbook to the college bookstore
b. Smith's $500 doctor bill for setting her son's broken arm
c. Family lawn services provided by Smith's 16-year-old child
d. Lawn services purchased by Smith from the neighbor's 16-year-old child who has a lawn-mowing business
e. A $5,250 purchase of 100 shares of stock at $50 per share plus the sales commission of $250
f. A multibillion-dollar discovery of natural gas in Oklahoma
g. A hurricane that causes $10 billion of damage in Florida
h. $50,000 of income earned by an American college professor teaching in England

2. If a nation's gross investment exceeds its depreciation (capital consumption allowance) during the year, what has happened to the nation's stock of capital during the year? How will this affect future output? Is it possible for the net investment of a nation to be negative? Explain. What would negative net investment during a year imply about the nation's capital stock and future production potential?

*3. A large furniture retailer sells $100,000 of household furnishings from inventories built up last year. How does this sale influence GDP? How are the components of GDP affected?

4. Suppose a group of British investors finances the construction of a plant to manufacture skateboards in St. Louis, Missouri. How will the construction of the plant affect GDP? If the construction project is carried out with American workers, how will it affect GNP? Suppose the plant generates $100,000 in corporate profits this year. Will these profits contribute to GDP? Why or why not?

*5. Why might even real GDP be a misleading index of changes in output between 1950 and 1999 in the United States? Of differences in output between the United States and Mexico?

6. What are price indexes designed to measure? Outline how they are constructed. When GDP and other income figures are compared across time periods, explain why it is important to adjust for changes in the general level of prices.

*7. In 1982 the average hourly earnings of private nonagricultural workers were $8.49 per hour. By 1997 the average hourly earnings had risen to $12.26. In 1997 the CPI was 162.5, compared to 96.5 in 1982. What were the real earnings of private nonagricultural workers in 1997 measured in 1982 dollars?

8. Consider an economy with the following data:

	Nominal GDP (in trillions)	GDP deflator
1998	$8.5	120
1999	8.8	125

a. What was the 1999 GDP in constant 1998 dollars?
b. What was the growth rate of real GDP between 1998 and 1999?
c. What was the inflation rate between 1998 and 1999?

*9. How much do each of the following contribute to GDP?

a. Jones pays a repair shop $1,000 to have the engine of her automobile rebuilt.
b. Jones spends $200 on parts and pays a mechanic $400 to rebuild the engine of her automobile.
c. Jones spends $200 on parts and rebuilds the engine of her automobile herself.
d. Jones sells her four-year-old automobile for $5,000 and buys Smith's two-year-old model for $10,000.
e. Jones sells her four-year-old automobile for $5,000 and buys a new car for $10,000.

10. What is the difference between the consumer price index (CPI) and the GDP deflator? Which would be better to use if you want to measure whether your hourly earnings this year were higher than they were last year? Why?

*11. Indicate whether the following statements are true or false:

a. "For the economy as a whole, inventory investment can never be negative."
b. "The net investment of an economy must always be positive."
c. "An increase in GDP indicates that the standard of living of people has risen."

*12. How do the receipts and expenditures of a state-operated lottery affect GDP?

13. GDP does not count productive services, such as child care, food preparation, cleaning, and laundry, provided within the household. Why are these things excluded? Is GDP a sexist measure? Does it understate the productive contributions of women relative to men? Discuss.

*14. Indicate how each of the following will affect this year's GDP:

a. You suffer $10,000 of damage when you wreck your automobile.
b. You win $10,000 in a state lottery.
c. You spend $5,200 in January for 100 shares of stock ($5,000 for the stock and $200 for the sales commission) and sell the stock in August for $8,300 ($8,000 for the stock and $300 for the sales commission).
d. You pay $300 for this month's rental of your apartment.
e. You are paid $300 for computer services provided to a client.
f. You receive $300 from your parents.
g. You get a raise from $8 to $10 per hour and simultaneously decide to reduce your hours worked from 20 to 16 per week.
h. You earn $2,000 working in Spain as an English instructor.

15. "GDP counts the product of steel but not the disproduct of air pollution. It counts the product of automobiles but not the disproduct of 'blight' due to junkyards. It counts the product of cigarettes but not the disproduct of a shorter life expectancy due to cancer. Until we can come up with a more reliable index, we cannot tell whether economic welfare is progressing or regressing." Is this statement correct? Is this a fair criticism of GDP?

16. The accompanying chart presents 1994 data from the national-income accounts of the United States.

COMPONENT	(BILLIONS OF DOLLARS)
Personal consumption	$4,699
Employee compensation	4,008
Rents	159
Gov. consumption & investment	1,315
Imports	818
Depreciation	819
Corporate profits	527
Interest income	393
Exports	722
Gross private investment	1,014
Indirect business taxes	602
Self-employment income	415
Net income of Americans abroad	−9

a. Indicate the various components of GDP when it is derived by the expenditure approach. Calculate GDP using the expenditure approach.
b. Indicate the various components of GDP when it is derived by the resource cost-income approach. Calculate GDP using the resource cost-income approach.

*17. Fill in the blanks in the following table:

YEAR	NOMINAL GDP (IN BILLIONS)	GDP DEFLATOR (1992 = 100)	REAL GDP (BILLIONS OF 1992 DOLLARS)
1960	$ 526.6	23.3	a. ______
1970	$1,035.6	30.6	b. ______
1980	$2,784.2	c. ______	$4,611.9
1990	d. ______	93.6	$6,138.7
1992	$6,244.4	e. ______	$6,244.4
1994	$6,931.4	105.1	f. ______
1997	$8,110.9	111.6	g. ______

*Asterisk denotes questions for which answers are given in Appendix B.

CHAPTER 8

Prosperity is when the prices of the things that you sell are rising; inflation is when the prices of the things that you buy are rising. Recession is when other people are unemployed; depression is when you are unemployed.

Anonymous

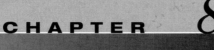

Economic Fluctuations, Unemployment, and Inflation

CHAPTER FOCUS

- What is a business cycle? How much economic instability has the United States experienced?
- Why do we experience unemployment? Are some types of unemployment worse than others?
- What do economists mean by full employment? How is full employment related to the natural rate of unemployment?
- What is the difference between anticipated and unanticipated inflation?
- What are some of the dangers that accompany inflation?

Measures of output, employment, and the level of prices are widely used to assess the performance of an economy. Key indicators, such as growth of real GDP, the rate of unemployment, and the inflation rate, are closely watched by investors, politicians, and the media. In this chapter, we will explain how several key economic indicators are derived and analyze their significance.

Changes in output, employment, and prices provide information on both the performance level and stability of the economy. This chapter focuses on economic performance and stability—how they are measured and what impact they have on our lives. As we proceed, we will develop a model of our economy that will help us better understand the causes of economic instability and the potential of government policy as a stabilizing force. The primary objectives of macroeconomic policy are rapid growth of output, a high level of employment, and stability in the general level of prices. There is widespread agreement concerning the desirability of these goals. However, there is considerable controversy with regard to how they can be achieved. In subsequent chapters, this issue will be analyzed in detail.

SWINGS IN THE ECONOMIC PENDULUM

During this century, the annual growth rate of real GDP in the United States has averaged approximately 3 percent. The rate of growth, however, has not been steady. During the Great Depression of the 1930s, economic growth plunged. Real GDP declined by 7.5 percent or more each year between 1930 and 1932. In 1933 it was almost 30 percent less than it was in 1929. The 1929 level of real GDP was not reached again until 1939. The Second World War was characterized by a rapid expansion of GDP, which was followed by a decline after the war. Real GDP did not reach its 1944 level again until 1953, although the output of consumer goods did increase significantly in the years immediately following the war.

As **Exhibit 8–1** illustrates, real GDP has continued to grow at an annual rate of approximately 3 percent from 1960 to 1998. Economic ups and downs have also continued. Real GDP grew rapidly throughout most of the 1960s, 1972–1973, 1976–1977, 1983–1988, and 1992–1998. Since 1960, there have been six periods (1960, 1970, 1974–1975, 1980, 1982, and 1991) of falling real GDP. Compared to the first half of this century, the growth of real GDP has been more stable during the last four decades. During this period, the annual fluctuations in real GDP have fallen within the range of *minus* 2 percent to *plus* 6 percent. This is a definite improvement.

A Hypothetical Business Cycle

Business cycle
Fluctuations in the general level of economic activity as measured by such variables as the rate of unemployment and changes in real GDP.

The economic record of the United States and other modern economies is characterized by both growth of real GDP and an instability in the pattern of that growth. Periods of economic expansion do not last forever. Inevitably, growth of real GDP has been followed by economic slowdown and contraction. Economists refer to these swings in the rate of output as the **business cycle.** Periods of growth in real output and other

EXHIBIT 8–1

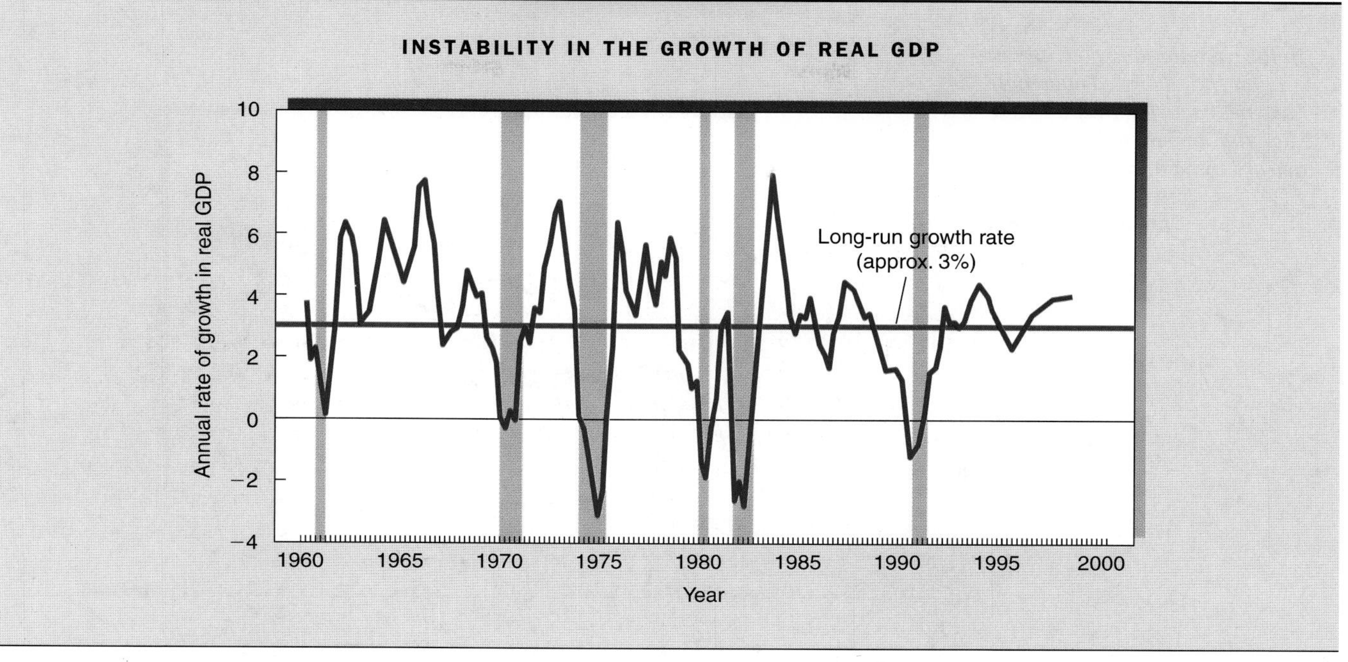

While real GDP fluctuates substantially, periods of positive growth outweigh the periods of declining real income. Since 1960, the U.S. growth rate of real GDP has averaged approximately 3.0 percent annually. Economists refer to periods of declining real GDP as recessions. The recessionary periods are shaded.

SOURCE: Economic Report of the President, *various issues.*

aggregate measures of economic activity followed by periods of decline are the distinguishing characteristics of business cycles.

Exhibit 8–2 illustrates a hypothetical business cycle. When most businesses are operating at capacity level and real GDP is growing rapidly, a *business peak,* or boom, is present. As aggregate business conditions slow, the economy begins the *contraction,* or recessionary, phase of a business cycle. During the contraction, the sales of most businesses fall, real GDP grows at a slow rate or perhaps declines, and unemployment in the aggregate labor market increases.

The bottom of the contraction phase is referred to as the *recessionary trough.* After the downturn reaches bottom, and economic conditions begin to improve, the economy enters the *expansion* phase of the cycle. Here business sales rise, GDP grows rapidly, and the rate of unemployment declines. The expansion eventually blossoms into another business peak. The peak, however, peters out and turns into a contraction, beginning the cycle anew.

The term **recession** is widely used to describe conditions during the contraction and recessionary trough phases of the business cycle—that is, a period during which real GDP declines. Many economists specify that a recession means a decline in real GDP for two or more successive quarters.[1] When a recession is prolonged and characterized by a sharp decline in economic activity, it is called a **depression.**

Recession
A downturn in economic activity characterized by declining real GDP and rising unemployment. In an effort to be more precise, many economists define a recession as two consecutive quarters in which there is a decline in real GDP.

Depression
A prolonged and very severe recession.

[1]See Geoffrey H. Moore, "Recessions," in *The Fortune Encyclopedia of Economics,* edited by David R. Henderson (New York: Time Warner Inc., 1993), for additional information on recessions in the United States.

EXHIBIT 8-2

BUSINESS CYCLE

In the past, ups and downs have often characterized aggregate business activity. Despite these fluctuations there has been an upward trend in real GDP in the United States and other industrial nations.

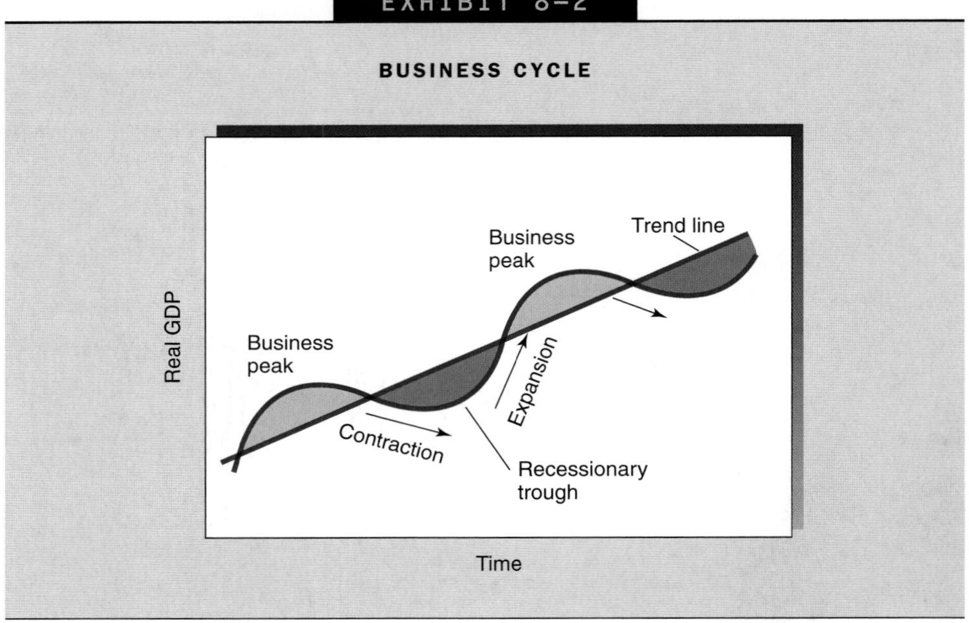

In one important respect, the term *business cycle* is misleading. *Cycle* generally implies that there is some regularity—like that indicated by the hypothetical business cycle of Exhibit 8–2—in the timing and duration of the activity. In the real world, as Exhibit 8–1 illustrates, this is not the case. The expansions and contractions last varying lengths of time, and the swings differ in terms of their magnitudes. For example, the recessions of 1961, 1982, and 1990 were followed by approximately eight years of uninterrupted growth of output. In contrast, the recession of 1980 was followed by an expansion that lasted only 12 months. The expansionary phase following the recessions of 1970 and 1974–1975 fell between these two extremes. ***In the real world, the observed fluctuations in real output are irregular and unpredictable.***

ECONOMIC FLUCTUATIONS AND THE LABOR MARKET

Civilian labor force
The number of persons 16 years of age and over who are either employed or unemployed. In order to be classified as unemployed, one must be looking for a job.

Fluctuations in real GDP influence the demand for labor and employment. In our modern world, people are busy with jobs, household work, school, and other activities. Exhibit 8–3 illustrates how economists classify these activities in relation to the **civilian labor force,** defined as the number of persons age 16 years and over who are either employed or seeking employment. The noninstitutional civilian adult population is grouped into two broad categories: (1) persons not in the labor force and (2) persons in the labor force. There are a variety of reasons why individuals may not currently be in the labor force. Some are retired. Others may be working in their own household or attending school. Still others may not be working as a result of illness or disability. Although many of these people are quite busy, their activities are outside the market labor force.

EXHIBIT 8–3

POPULATION, EMPLOYMENT, AND UNEMPLOYMENT, 1998

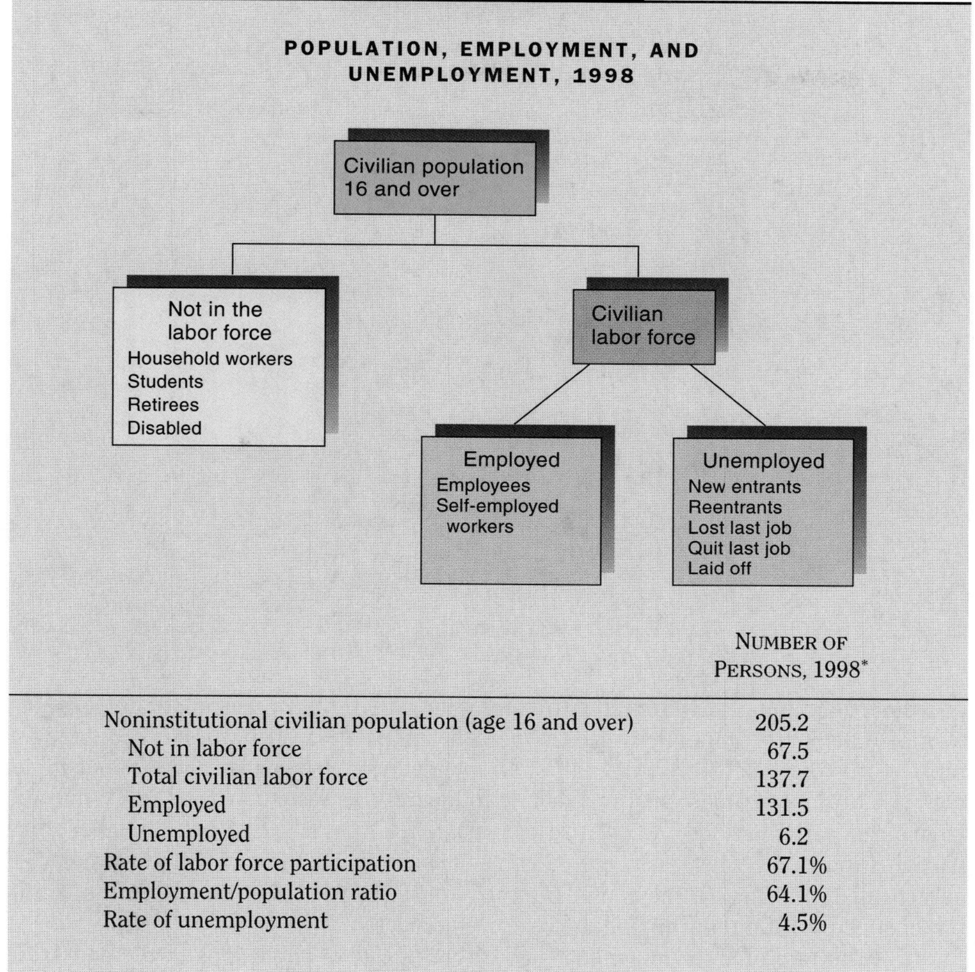

	Number of Persons, 1998*
Noninstitutional civilian population (age 16 and over)	205.2
Not in labor force	67.5
Total civilian labor force	137.7
Employed	131.5
Unemployed	6.2
Rate of labor force participation	67.1%
Employment/population ratio	64.1%
Rate of unemployment	4.5%

The accompaning diagram illustrates the alternative participation-status categories for the adult population.

**Data are measured in millions, except those expressed as percentages.* U.S. Department of Labor, Monthly Labor Review, *March, 1999.*

As Exhibit 8–3 illustrates, **unemployed** workers who are seeking work are included in the labor force along with employed workers. The **labor force participation rate** is the number of persons in the civilian labor force (including both the employed and the unemployed) as a percentage of the civilian population 16 years of age and over. In 1998, the population (16 years of age and over) of the United States was 205.2 million, 137.7 million of whom were in the labor force. Thus, the U.S. labor force participation rate was 67.1 percent (137.7 million divided by 205.2 million).

Unemployed
The term used to describe a person not currently employed who is either (1) actively seeking employment or (2) waiting to begin or return to a job.

Labor force participation rate
The number of persons in the civilian labor force 16 years of age or over who are either employed or actively seeking employment as a percentage of the total civilian population 16 years of age and over.

The labor force participation rate varies substantially across countries. For example, in 1996 the labor force participation rate was 67 percent in the United States, 65 percent in both Canada and Australia, and 64 percent in Sweden. In contrast, the labor force participation rate was only 53 percent in Germany and 48 percent in Italy. The percent of married women in the labor force is generally smaller in countries like Italy and Germany that have a low labor force participation rate.

In the United States, one of the most interesting labor force developments of the post–World War II era is the dramatic increase in the labor force participation rate

EXHIBIT 8–4

As the chart illustrates, the labor force participation rate for women has been steadily increasing for serveral decades, while the rate for men has been declining.

SOURCE: Monthly Labor Review *(variuos issues).*

LABOR FORCE PARTICIPATION OF MEN AND WOMEN, 1948–1998

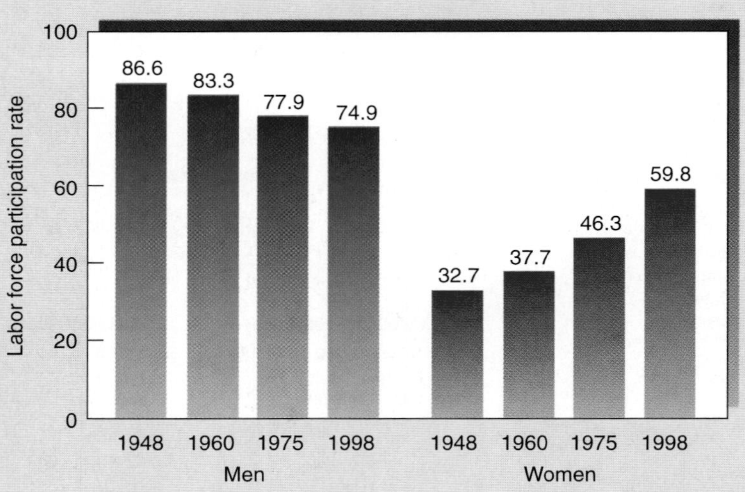

of women. Exhibit 8–4 illustrates this point. In 1998, 59.8 percent of adult women worked outside the home, up from 32.7 percent in 1948. Married women accounted for most of this increase. More than half of all married women now are in the labor force, compared to only 20 percent immediately following the Second World War. While the labor force participation of women rose, the rate for men fell. In 1998, the labor force participation rate of men was 74.9 percent, down from 83.3 percent in 1960 and 86.6 percent in 1948. Clearly, the composition of workforce participation within the family has changed substantially during the past five decades.

Rate of unemployment
The percentage of persons in the labor force who are unemployed. Mathematically, it is equal to

$$\frac{\text{Number of persons unemployed}}{\text{Number in the labor force}} \times 100$$

The **rate of unemployment** is a key barometer of conditions in the aggregate labor market. This notwithstanding, the term is often misunderstood. At the most basic level, it is important to note that unemployment is different from not working. As we have already indicated, there are several reasons—including household work, school attendance, retirement, and illness or disability—why a person may be neither employed nor looking for a job. These people, though not employed, are not counted in the unemployment tally.

Moreover, persons must either be employed or unemployed before they are counted as part of the labor force. The rate of unemployment is the number of persons unemployed expressed as a percentage of the labor force. In 1998 the rate of unemployment in the United States was 4.5 percent (6.2 million out of a labor force of 137.7 million). (See the Measures of Economic Activity box for information on how the Bureau of Labor Statistics derives the unemployment rate.)

Reasons for Unemployment

Not all people who are unemployed lost their last job. A dynamic economy will be characterized by considerable labor mobility as workers move (1) from contracting to expanding industries and (2) into and out of the labor force. Spells of unemployment often accompany such changes.

MEASURES OF ECONOMIC ACTIVITY

Deriving the Unemployment Rate

Each month, the Bureau of Labor Statistics (BLS) contacts a sample of 59,500 households that reflects the population characteristics of the United States. Specially trained interviewers pose identical questions designed to determine whether each of the approximately 100,000 adults in these households is employed, unemployed, or not in the labor force. Persons age 16 years and over are considered employed if they (1) worked at all (even as little as one hour) for pay or profit during the survey week, (2) worked 15 hours or more without pay in a family-operated enterprise during the survey week, or (3) have a job at which they did not work during the survey week because of illness, vacation, industrial disputes, bad weather, time off, or personal reasons.

People are considered unemployed if they (1) do not have a job, (2) are available for work, and (3) have actively looked for work during the past four weeks. Looking for work may involve any of the following activities: (1) registration at a public or private employment office, (2) meeting with prospective employers, (3) checking with friends or relatives, (4) placing or answering advertisements, (5) writing letters of application, or (6) being on a union or professional register. In addition, those not working are classified as unemployed if they are either waiting to start a new job within 30 days or waiting to be recalled from a layoff.

The BLS uses its survey data to calculate the unemployment rate and other employment-related statistics each month. States use the BLS survey and employment figures from industries covered by unemployment insurance to construct state and area employment statistics. These labor market figures are published by the U.S. Department of Labor in the *Monthly Labor Review* and *Employment and Earnings*.

The Department of Labor indicates five reasons why workers may experience unemployment. **Exhibit 8–5** indicates the share of unemployed workers in each of these five categories in 1998. Interestingly, 8.4 percent of the unemployed workers were first-time entrants into the work force and 34.3 percent were reentering after exiting for additional schooling, household work, or other reasons. Thus, 42.7 percent of

EXHIBIT 8–5

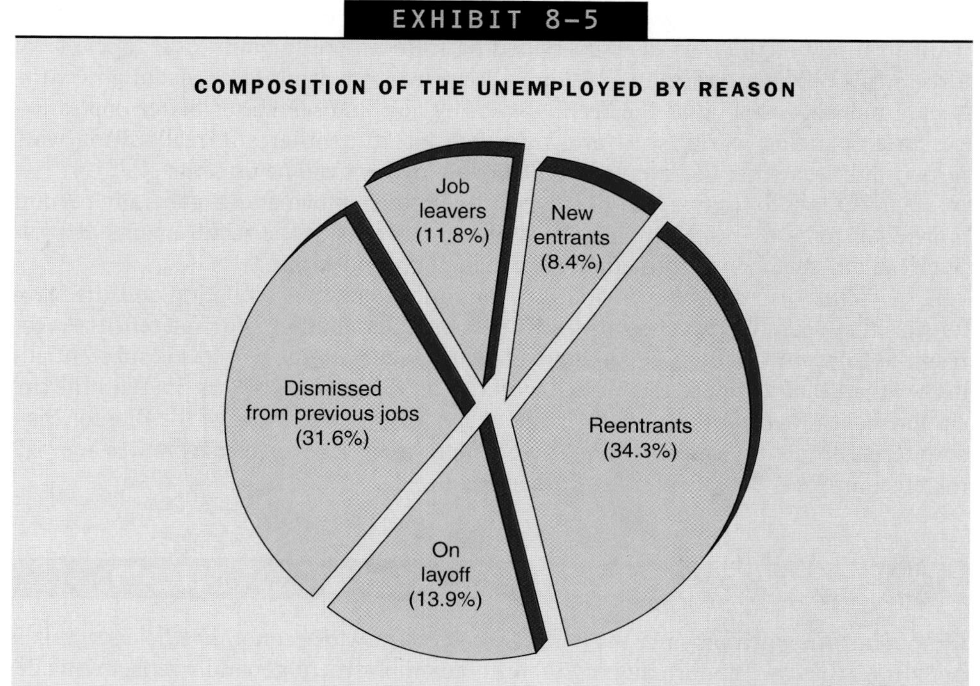

This chart indicates the various reasons why persons were unemployed in 1998. Less than one-third (31.6 percent) of the persons unemployed were terminated from their last job. More than two-fifths (42.7 percent) of the unemployed workers were either new entrants or reentrants into the labor force.

SOURCE: Monthly Labor Review, *March, 1999*

EXHIBIT 8–6

SOURCE: Monthly Labor Review, *March, 1999*

UNEMPLOYMENT RATE BY AGE AND SEX, 1998

Group	Civilian Rate of Unemployment, 1998 (percent)
Total, all workers	4.5
Men, Total	4.4
Ages 16–19	16.2
Ages 20–24	8.0
Ages 25 and over	3.2
Women, Total	4.6
Ages 16–19	12.9
Ages 20–24	7.7
Ages 25 and over	3.6

the unemployed workers were experiencing unemployment as the result of entry or reentry into the labor force. One out of every eight (11.8 percent) of the unemployed quit their last job. People laid off and waiting to return to their previous positions contributed 13.9 percent to the total. Workers dismissed from their last job accounted for less than one-third (31.6 percent) of the unemployed workers.

In a dynamic world where information, like most other things, is scarce and people are free to choose among jobs, some unemployment is inevitable. As new products are introduced and new technologies developed, some firms are expanding while others are contracting. Still other firms may be going out of business. This process results in the creation of new jobs and the disappearance of old ones. Similarly, at any point in time potential workers are switching from school (or nonwork) to the labor force, while others are retiring or taking a leave from the labor force. As long as workers are mobile—as long as they can voluntarily quit and search for better opportunities in a changing world, switching from one job to another and reallocating work responsibilities within the family—some unemployment will be present.

There is a positive side to job search and unemployment: It generally permits individuals to better match their skills and preferences with the requirements of a job. Such job moves enhance both employee productivity and earnings.

Young workers often switch jobs and move between schooling and the labor force as they search for a career path that best fits their abilities and preferences. As the result of this job switching, the unemployment rate of younger workers is substantially higher than that for more established workers. As **Exhibit 8–6** shows, in 1998 the unemployment rate of workers 20–24 years of age was more than twice the rate for their counterparts age 25 years and over. The unemployment rate for teenagers was approximately four times the rate of older workers.

THREE TYPES OF UNEMPLOYMENT

Although some unemployment is perfectly consistent with economic efficiency, this is not always the case. Abnormally high rates of unemployment generally reflect weak demand conditions for labor, counterproductive policies, and/or the inability or lack of incentive on the part of potential workers and potential employers to arrive at mutually advantageous agreements. To clarify matters, economists divide unemployment into three categories: frictional, structural, and cyclical. Let us take a closer look at each of these three classifications.

Frictional Unemployment

Unemployment that is caused by constant changes in the labor market is called **frictional unemployment.** It occurs because (a) employers are not fully aware of all available workers and their job qualifications and (b) available workers are not fully aware of the jobs being offered by employers. In other words, the basic cause of frictional unemployment is imperfect information. The number of job vacancies may match the number of persons seeking employment. The qualifications of the job seekers may even meet those required by firms seeking employees. Nonetheless, frictional unemployment will still occur because persons seeking jobs and firms hiring employees with the qualifications of the job seekers do not know about each other. Seeking to improve their options, both employers and employees will search for better alternatives.

Frictional unemployment
Unemployment due to constant changes in the economy that prevent qualified unemployed workers from being immediately matched up with existing job openings. It results from the scarcity of information and the search activities of both employers and employees for information that will help them make better employment choices.

Employers looking for a new worker seldom hire the first applicant who walks into their employment office. They want to find the "best available" worker to fill the opening. It is costly to hire workers who perform poorly. It is sometimes even costly to terminate their employment. So, employers search—they expend time and resources screening applicants in an effort to find the best qualified workers willing to accept their wage and employment conditions.

Similarly, job seekers search for their best option among the potential alternatives. They make telephone calls, respond to newspaper ads, submit to job interviews, use employment services, and so on. Pursuit of personal gain—the landing of a job that is more attractive than the current options of which they are aware—motivates job seekers to engage in job search activities.

As a job searcher finds out about more and more potential job opportunities, it becomes less likely that *additional search* will uncover a more attractive option. Therefore, the *marginal benefit* derived from job search declines with time spent searching for a job, because it becomes less likely that additional search will lead to a better position. The primary cost of job search is generally the opportunity cost of wages forgone as the result of failure to accept one's best current alternative. This cost will increase as better alternatives are found. Thus, the *marginal cost* of job search will rise with the length of one's job search time, primarily because still more search means forgoing wages on more attractive jobs discovered by prior search.

As the marginal benefit from additional search declines and marginal costs rise, eventually the rational job seeker will conclude that potential gain from additional search is not worth the cost. The best alternative resulting from the search process will be accepted. However, this process takes time, and during this time the job seeker is contributing to the frictional unemployment of the economy. It is important to note that, even though frictional unemployment is a side effect, the job search process typically leads to improved economic efficiency and a higher real income for employees (see the accompanying Myths of Economics box).

Changes that affect the costs and benefits of job search influence the level of unemployment. If, for example, the development of a computerized job listing system made it easier to acquire information about job openings quickly, frictional unemployment would tend to decline. On the other hand, a change that reduced the job seeker's cost of continued search would lead to more lengthy periods of search. For example, an increase in unemployment benefits would make it less costly to continue looking for a preferred job. Other things constant, this reduction in the cost of job search would

MYTHS OF ECONOMICS

"Unemployed resources would not exist if the economy were operating efficiently."

Nobody likes unemployment. Certainly, extended unemployment can be a very painful experience. Job search, however, performs an important labor market function: It leads to improvement in the match between worker skills and the requirements of jobs.

In a world of imperfect information, prospective employees will engage in job search in order to acquire information about employment opportunities and job requirements. In essence, job searchers are "shopping"—they are searching for information about the job opportunity that best fits their skills, earning capabilities, and preferences. Similarly, employers shop when they are seeking labor services. They, too, acquire information about available workers that will help them select employees whose skills and preferences match the demands of the job.

This shopping results in some unemployment, but it also provides both employees and employers with information that will help them make better choices. If the resources of an economy are going to be used effectively, the skills of workers must be matched with the jobs of employers. Waste will result if, for example, a person with high-level computer skills ends up working as a janitor while someone else with minimal computer skills is employed as a computer programmer. Job search improves the match between the skills and preferences of employees and the demands of various jobs. As workers search to find jobs for which their skills are well suited, they achieve higher wage rates and the economy is able to generate a larger output.

Perhaps thinking about the housing market will help the reader better understand why search time can be both beneficial and productive. As with the employment market, the housing market is characterized by both imperfect information and dynamic change. New housing structures are brought into the market; older structures depreciate and wear out. Families move from one community to another. In this dynamic world, it makes sense for renters from time to time to shop among the available accommodations, seeking the housing quality, price, and location that best fits their preferences and budgets. Similarly, landlords search among renters, seeking to rent their accommodations to those who value them most highly. Housing vacancies, a type of "frictional unemployment," occur. Is this indicative of inefficiency? No. It is the result of imperfect information and the search for a more efficient match on the part of both landlords and renters.

Of course, some types of unemployment, particularly cyclical unemployment, are indicative of inefficiency. However, this is not the case with frictional unemployment. The job searching (as well as the frictional unemployment that accompanies it) helps both job seekers and employers make better choices, and it leads to a more efficient match of applicants with job openings than would otherwise be possible. It is perfectly consistent with economic efficiency.

induce job seekers to expand their search time. As a result, the level of unemployment would be pushed upward.

STRUCTURAL UNEMPLOYMENT

Structural unemployment
Unemployment due to the structural characteristics of the economy that make it difficult for job seekers to find employment and for employers to hire workers. Although job openings are available, they generally require skills that differ from those of the unemployed workers.

In the case of **structural unemployment,** changes in the basic characteristics of the economy prevent the "matching up" of available jobs with available workers. It is not always easy to distinguish between frictional and structural unemployment. In each case, job openings and potential workers searching for jobs are present. The crucial difference between the two is that, with frictional unemployment, workers possess the requisite skills to fill the job openings; with structural unemployment, they do not. Essentially, the skills of a structurally unemployed worker have been rendered obsolete by changing market conditions and technology. Realistically, the structurally unemployed worker faces the prospect of either a career change or prolonged unemployment. For older workers in particular, these are bleak alternatives.

There are many causes of structural unemployment. Technological change is of course at the top of the list. The introduction of new products and production technologies can substantially alter the relative demand for workers with various skills. Changes of this type can affect the job opportunities of even highly skilled workers, particularly if their skills are not easily transferable to other industries and occupations. The "computer revolution" has dramatically changed the job opportunities of many workers. The alternatives available to workers with the skills required to operate and maintain high-tech equipment have improved substantially, while the prospects of those without such skills have, in some cases, deteriorated drastically.

Shifts in public sector priorities can also cause structural unemployment. As changing international conditions permitted the United States to reduce significantly defense expenditures in the early 1990s, these expenditure cuts resulted in reduced incomes and job prospects of workers in defense and related industries. Since the skills of many workers who lost their jobs in defense-related industries were not well suited for employment in expanding sectors of the economy, structural unemployment was a result.

Institutional factors that reduce the ability of employees to obtain skills necessary to fill existing job openings also increase structural unemployment. For example, minimum wage legislation may reduce the incentive of business firms to offer employment to low-skill workers, thereby contributing to structural unemployment.

Cyclical Unemployment

When there is a general downturn in business activity, **cyclical unemployment** arises. Because fewer goods are being produced, fewer workers are required to produce them. Employers lay off workers and cut back employment.

Cyclical unemployment
Unemployment due to recessionary business conditions and inadequate aggregate demand for labor.

Unexpected reductions in the general level of demand for goods and services are the major cause of cyclical unemployment. In a world of imperfect information, adjustments to unexpected declines in demand are often painful. When the demand for labor declines generally, workers will at first not know whether they are being laid off because of a specific shift in demand away from their previous employer or because of a general decline in demand. Similarly, they will not be sure whether their current bleak employment prospects are temporary or long-term. Workers will search for employment, hoping to find a job at or near their old wage rate. If their situation was merely the result of shifts among employers in demand, or if the downturn is brief, workers dismissed by employers cutting back output will generally be able to find jobs with employers who are expanding and hiring additional workers. The situation is different, however, when there is a general decline in demand. Many employers will be laying off workers and few will be hiring. Under these circumstances, most workers' search efforts will be fruitless and the duration of their unemployment will be abnormally long.

With time, unemployed workers will lower their expectations and many will be willing to accept employment at a lower wage. This adjustment process, however, will take time. During the adjustment period, an increase in the rate of unemployment is the expected result. As we proceed, we will investigate potential sources of cyclical unemployment and consider policy alternatives to reduce it.

EMPLOYMENT FLUCTUATIONS—THE HISTORICAL RECORD

Employment and output are closely linked over the business cycle. If we are going to produce more goods and services, we must either increase the number of workers or increase the output per worker. Although productivity, or output per worker, is the primary source of long-term economic growth, it changes slowly from year to year. Thus, rapid increases in output, such as those that occur during a strong business expansion, generally require an increase in employment. As a result, output and employment tend

EXHIBIT 8-7

UNEMPLOYMENT RATE, 1960–1998

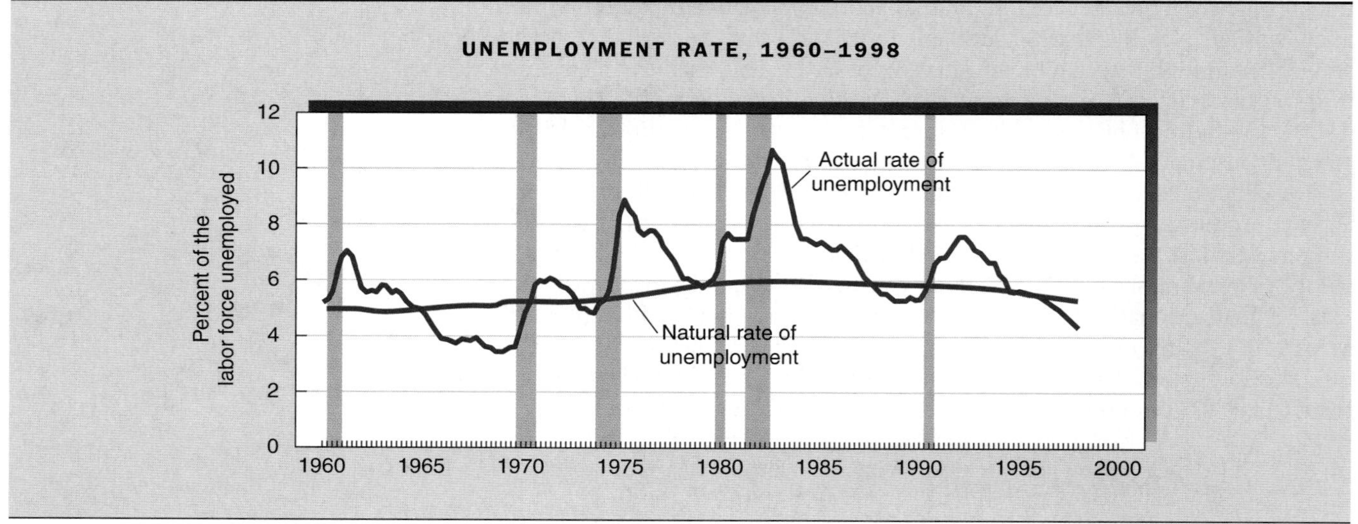

Here we illustrate the rate of unemployment during the 1960–1998 period. As expected, the unemployment rate rose rapidly during each of the six recessions (the shaded years indicate periods of recession). In contrast, soon after each recession ended, the unemployment rate began to decline as the economy moved to an expansionary phase of the business cycle. Also note that the actual rate of unemployment was substantially greater than the natural rate during and immediately following the recessions.

SOURCE: Economic Report of the President, 1998 *and Robert J. Gordon,* Macroeconomics *(Boston: Little Brown, 1990).*

to be positively related. Therefore, the unemployment rate generally increases when the economy dips into a recession.

The empirical evidence of **Exhibit 8–7** illustrates the inverse relationship between output and rate of unemployment. When output declines during a recession (indicated in shading), the unemployment rate generally rises. During the recession of 1960–1961, the rate of unemployment rose to approximately 7 percent. In contrast, it declined throughout the economic boom of the 1960s, only to rise again during the recession of 1970. During the recession of 1974–1975, the unemployment rate jumped to more than 9 percent. Similarly, it soared to nearly 11 percent during the severe recession of 1982 and to 7.6 percent during the aftermath of the 1991 recession. Conversely, it declined substantially during the expansions of the 1960s, 1976–1978, 1983–1989, and the post-1993 period.

Full employment
The level of employment that results from the efficient use of the labor force after allowance is made for the normal (natural) rate of unemployment due to information cost, dynamic changes, and the structural conditions of the economy. For the United States, full employment is thought to exist when between 94 and 95 percent of the labor force is employed.

The Concept of Full Employment

Full employment, a term widely used by economists and public officials alike, does not mean zero unemployment. As we have noted, in a world of imperfect information, both employees and employers will "shop" before they agree to accept a job or hire a new worker. Much of this shopping is efficient, since it leads to a better match between the skills of employees and the skills necessary to carry out productive tasks. Some unemployment is thus entirely consistent with the efficient operation of a dynamic labor market. ***Consequently, economists define full employment as the level of employment that results when the rate of unemployment is normal, considering both frictional and structural factors. In the United States, this figure is currently believed to be approximately 95 percent of the labor force.***

Closely related to the concept of full employment is the **natural rate of unemployment,** the amount of unemployment reflected by job shopping and imperfect information.

Natural rate of unemployment
The long-run average unemployment rate due to frictional and structural conditions of labor markets. This rate is affected both by dynamic change and by public policy. It is sustainable into the future. The current natural rate of unemployment in the United States is thought to be between 5 percent and 6 percent.

The natural rate of unemployment is not a temporary high or low; it is a rate that is sustainable into the future. Economists sometimes refer to it as the unemployment rate accompanying the economy's "maximum sustainable" rate of output.

The natural rate of unemployment, though, is not immutably fixed. It is influenced both by the structure of the labor force and by changes in public policy. For example, youthful workers experience more unemployment because they change jobs and move in and out of the labor force often (refer to Exhibit 8–6), so the natural rate of unemployment increases when youthful workers compose a larger proportion of the workforce. This is precisely what happened during the 1960s and 1970s. In 1958 youthful workers (ages 16 to 24) constituted only 15.6 percent of the labor force. As the postwar "baby boom" generation entered the labor market, youthful workers as a share of the labor force rose dramatically. By 1980 one out of every four workers was in the youthful-worker grouping. In contrast, prime-age workers (over age 25) declined from 84.4 percent of the U.S. workforce in 1958 to only 75.3 percent in 1980. Studies indicate that this increased representation of youthful workers pushed the natural rate of unemployment up by approximately 1.5 percent during the 1958–1980 period (see Exhibit 8–7.)

Public policies also affect the natural rate of unemployment. The natural rate is pushed upward by policies that (1) encourage workers to reject job offers and continue to search for employment, (2) prohibit employers from offering wage rates that would induce them to employ (and train) low-skill workers, and (3) reduce the employer's opportunity cost of using layoffs to adjust rates of production. These factors indicate that, for example, a higher legislated minimum wage and more attractive unemployment benefits will tend to increase the natural rate of unemployment.

Exhibit 8–7 illustrates the relationship between the *actual* unemployment rate and the *natural* unemployment rate during the past four decades. The actual unemployment rate fluctuates around the natural rate, in response to cyclical economic conditions. The actual rate generally rises above the natural rate during a recession and falls below the natural rate when the economy is in the midst of an economic boom. For example, the actual rate of unemployment was substantially above the natural rate during the recessions of 1974–1975 and 1982, while the reverse was the case during the economic booms of the 1960s and 1990s. As we proceed, we will often compare the actual and natural rates of unemployment. In a very real sense, macroeconomics studies why the actual and natural rates differ and attempts to discern the factors that cause the natural rate to change with the passage of time.

Without detracting from the importance of full employment—in the sense of maximum sustainable employment—we must not overlook another vital point. Employment is a means to an end. We use employment to produce desired goods and services. Full employment is an empty concept if it means employment at unproductive jobs. It is a meaningful concept only if it refers to productive employment that will generate goods and services desired by consumers at the lowest possible cost.

UNEMPLOYMENT AND MEASUREMENT PROBLEMS

The definition of unemployment is not without ambiguity. Remember that persons are counted as unemployed only if they are (1) available for and seeking work or (2) awaiting recall from a layoff. One can argue that the statistical definition of unemployment results both in (1) people being excluded even though they would prefer to be working (or working more) and (2) people being included who are not seriously seeking employment.

Discouraged workers
Persons who have given up searching for employment because they believe additional job search would be fruitless. Because they are not currently searching for work, they are not counted among the unemployed.

Consider individuals with job prospects that are so bleak they no longer consider it worthwhile to search for employment. Such persons are classified as **discouraged workers.** Even though many discouraged workers would be willing to accept employment if it were available, they are not counted as unemployed because they are not currently engaging in job search. As a result, the number unemployed may be understated. When the economy turns down, the number of workers in the discouraged category rises substantially. For example, during the 1991 recession, the Department of Labor estimated that there were one million discouraged workers (approximately 0.8 percent of the labor force) in the United States, up from 715,000 prior to the recession.

The method of classifying part-time workers may also result in an understatement of unemployment. Part-time workers who desire full-time employment are classified as employed rather than unemployed if they work as much as a single hour per week. Yet these people are certainly underemployed, if not unemployed.

On the other hand, some people who claim to be searching for work and are thus classified as unemployed are not seriously seeking employment. For example, an individual who rejects available employment because it is less attractive than the current combination of household work, continued job search, food stamps, and other government welfare programs is numbered among the unemployed. Since recipients of several government income-assistance programs are required to register for employment, many of them are classified as "unemployed" even though they may not be seriously searching for work. According to a study by Lawrence Summers and Kim Clark of Harvard University, these work-registration requirements push the official unemployment rate up by approximately 0.5 to 0.8 percent (600,000 to one million potential employees).[2]

The measurement of unemployment is also complicated by other factors. Unemployment insurance benefits tend to increase the measured unemployment rate by reducing the incentive of recipients to accept available jobs as long as they qualify for the benefits. If they are not otherwise gainfully employed, people engaged in criminal activities (for example, drug pushers, gamblers, and prostitutes) or working "off the books" in the underground economy may also be classified as unemployed. Although estimates are difficult to project, some researchers believe that as many as one million people fall into this category.

Employment/population ratio
The number of persons 16 years of age and over employed as civilians divided by the total civilian population 16 years of age and over. The ratio is expressed as a percentage.

As a result of these ambiguities, some economists argue that the **employment/population ratio**—the number of persons age 16 and over who are employed expressed as a percentage of the civilian population 16 years and over—is a more objective and meaningful indicator of job availability than is the rate of unemployment. Both the number employed and the population age 16 and over are well defined and readily measurable. Their measurement does not require a subjective judgment as to whether a person is actually "available for work" or "actively seeking employment." The rate of employment is relatively free of several defects that may distort the unemployment figures. For example, when a large number of discouraged job seekers stop

[2]Lawrence H. Summers and Kim B. Clark, "Labor Market Dynamics and Unemployment: A Reconsideration," *Brookings Papers on Economic Activity* 1 (1979): 13–60. Also see Lawrence H. Summers, *Understanding Unemployment* (Cambridge, Mass.: MIT Press, 1990).

looking for work, the rate of unemployment drops. The employment/population ratio, however, does not follow such a misleading course.

Which of the two figures should the wise observer follow? The answer is both. Our economy has been undergoing several structural changes that contribute to the diversity of the unemployed population and affect both the rate of unemployment and the employment/population ratio. Monitoring both of these variables will help one avoid invalid conclusions and more fully understand labor market conditions.

ACTUAL AND POTENTIAL GDP

If an economy is going to realize its potential, full employment is essential. When the actual rate of unemployment exceeds the natural rate, the actual output of the economy will fall below its potential. Some resources that could be productively employed will be underutilized.

The Council of Economic Advisers defines the **potential output** as: "The amount of output that could be expected at full employment. . . . It does not represent the absolute maximum level of production that could be generated by wartime or other abnormal levels of aggregate demand, but rather that which would be expected from high utilization rates obtainable under more normal circumstances."

Potential output
The level of output that can be achieved and sustained into the future, given the size of the labor force, expected productivity of labor, and natural rate of unemployment consistent with the efficient operation of the labor market. For periods of time, the actual output may differ from the economy's potential.

The concept of potential output encompasses two important ideas: (1) full utilization of resources, including labor, and (2) an output constraint. Potential output might properly be thought of as the maximum *sustainable* output level consistent with the economy's resource base, given its institutional arrangements. Estimates of the potential output level involve three major elements: the size of the labor force, the quality (productivity) of labor, and the natural rate of unemployment. Because these factors cannot be estimated with certainty, some variation exists in the estimated values of the potential rate of output for the U.S. economy. Relying on the projections of potential output developed by the Council of Economic Advisers, **Exhibit** 8–8 illustrates the relationship between the actual and potential output of the United States since 1960.

The relationship between actual and potential GDP reflects the business cycle. Note the similarity in the pattern of the actual real GDP data of Exhibit 8–8 and the hypothetical data of an idealized business cycle of Exhibit 8–2. Although the actual data of Exhibit 8–8 are irregular compared to the hypothetical data, periods of expansion and economic boom followed by contraction and recession are clearly observable. During the boom phase, actual output expands rapidly and may temporarily exceed the economy's long-run potential. In contrast, recessions are characterized by an actual real GDP that is less than potential. As we proceed, we will focus on how we can achieve the maximum potential output while minimizing economic instability.

EFFECTS OF INFLATION: AN OVERVIEW

Inflation is a continuing rise in the general level of prices, such that it costs more to purchase the typical bundle of goods and services that is produced or consumed or both. Of course, even when the general level of prices is stable, some prices will be rising and others will be falling. During a period of inflation, however, the impact of the rising prices will outweigh that of falling prices. Because of the higher prices (on average), a dollar will purchase less than it did previously. Inflation, therefore, might also be defined as a decline in the value (the purchasing power) of the monetary unit.

Inflation
A continuing rise in the general level of prices of goods and services. The purchasing power of the monetary unit, such as the dollar, declines when inflation is present.

How do we determine whether prices, in general, are rising or falling? Essentially, we answered that question in the preceding chapter when we indicated how a price index is constructed. When prices are rising, on average, the price index will also

EXHIBIT 8-8

ACTUAL AND POTENTIAL GDP

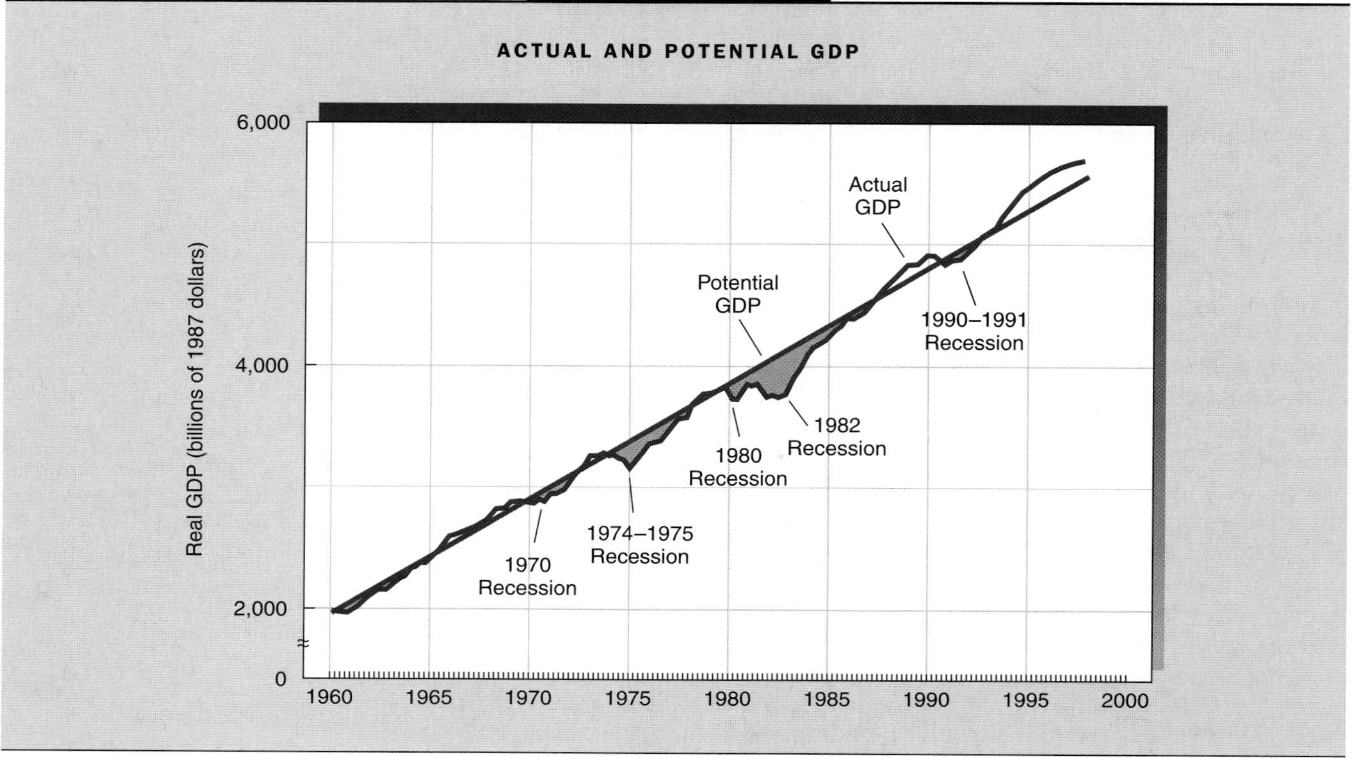

Here we illustrate both the actual and potential GDP. Note the gap (shaded area) between the actual and potential GDP during periods of recession.

SOURCE: U.S. Department of Commerce, Bureau of Economic Analysis.

rise. The annual inflation rate (i) is simply the percent change in the price index (PI) from one year to the next. Mathematically, the inflation rate (i) can be written as:

$$i = \frac{\text{This year's PI} - \text{Last year's PI}}{\text{Last year's PI}} \times 100$$

If the price index this year was 220, compared to 200 last year, the inflation rate would equal 10 percent:

$$\frac{220 - 200}{200} \times 100 = 10$$

The consumer price index (CPI) and the GDP deflator are the price indexes most widely used to measure the inflation rate in the United States. As we discussed in the preceding chapter, these two measures of the rate of inflation tend to follow a similar path. How rapidly has the general level of prices risen in the United States? Using the annual rate of change in the CPI, **Exhibit 8–9** presents a picture of the U.S. inflation rate since the early 1950s. During the 1950s and into the mid-1960s, the annual inflation rate was generally low. The average inflation rate during the 1953–1965 period was 1.3 percent. Beginning in the latter half of the 1960s, inflation began to accelerate upward, jumping to 12 percent or more during 1974, 1979, and 1980. During the

EXHIBIT 8-9

THE INFLATION RATE, 1953–1998

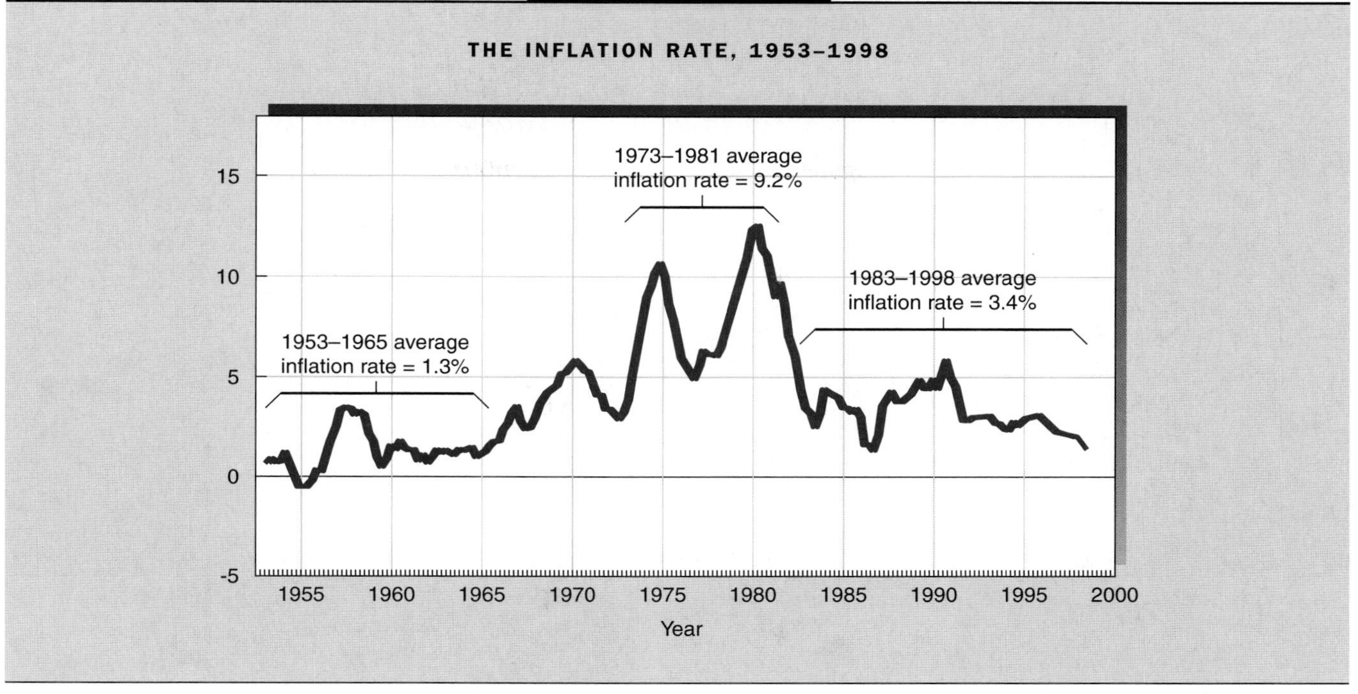

Here we present the annual rate of inflation for the last 45 years. Between 1953 and 1965, prices increased at an annual rate of only 1.3 percent. In contrast, the inflation rate averaged 9.2 percent during the 1973–1981 era, reaching double-digit rates during several years. Since 1982, the rate of inflation has been lower (the average annual rate was 3.4 percent during 1983–1998) and more stable.

SOURCE: Derived from computerized data supplied by FAME ECONOMICS. Also see Economic Report of the President *(published annually).*

1973–1981 period, the inflation rate averaged 9.2 percent. Price increases moderated again in the mid-1980s, as the inflation rate averaged 3.4 percent during 1983–1998.

The rate of inflation varies widely among countries. **Exhibit 8–10** provides data on the annual inflation rates during 1991–1997 for Canada, Germany, Japan, Singapore, and the United States—five countries with low rates of inflation. The annual inflation rate of these countries was generally less than 5 percent during this period; moreover, the year-to-year variation was relatively small. The inflation rate of these countries seldom changed by more than 1 or 2 percent from one year to the next.

Exhibit 8–10 also presents parallel inflation rate data for five high-inflation countries: Brazil, Democratic Republic of Congo, Romania, Turkey, and Venezuela. In contrast with the low-inflation countries, the inflation rate of the high-inflation countries was not only higher, it varied substantially more from one year to another. For example, consider the data for Brazil. The inflation rate of Brazil jumped from 440.9 percent in 1991 to 1,008.7 percent in 1992, to more than 2,000 percent during the next two years before receding to 66 percent in 1995 and eventually to 6.9 percent in 1997. (*Note:* An annual inflation rate of 2,000 percent indicates that the general level of prices is 20 times the level of just one year earlier!) The other countries in the high-inflation group also experienced wide fluctuations in the annual rate of inflation. The data of Exhibit 8-10 reflect a general pattern. ***High rates of inflation are almost always associated with substantial year-to-year swings in the inflation rate.***

EXHIBIT 8–10

VARIATION IN THE ANNUAL INFLATION RATE OF SELECTED COUNTRIES, 1991–1997

Country	1991	1992	1993	1994	1995	1996	1997
Low Inflation							
Canada	5.6	1.5	1.8	0.2	2.2	1.6	1.6
Germany	3.6	5.1	4.5	2.7	1.8	1.5	1.8
Japan	3.3	1.7	1.3	0.7	−0.1	0.1	1.7
Singapore	3.4	2.3	2.3	3.1	1.7	1.4	2.0
United States	4.2	3.0	3.0	2.6	2.8	2.9	2.3
High Inflation							
Brazil	440.9	1,008.7	2,148.4	2,075.9	66.0	15.8	6.9
Congo, Dem. Rep.	2,154.4	4,129.2	1,986.9	23,773.0	542.0	659.0	176.0
Romania	230.6	211.2	255.2	136.8	32.2	38.8	154.8
Turkey	66.0	70.1	66.1	106.3	88.1	80.4	85.7
Venezuela	34.2	31.4	38.1	60.8	59.9	99.9	50.0

SOURCE: International Monetary Fund, International Financial Statistics, *July 1998, and* International Financial Statistics Yearbook, *1997.*

The consumer price index was used to measure the inflation rate of each country.

Anticipated and Unanticipated Inflation

Unanticipated inflation
An increase in the general level of prices that was not expected by most decision makers.

Anticipated inflation
An increase in the general level of prices that was expected by most decision makers.

Before examining the effects of inflation, it is important that we distinguish between unanticipated and anticipated inflation. **Unanticipated inflation** is an increase in the price level that comes as a surprise, at least to most individuals. For example, suppose that, based on the recent past, most people anticipate an inflation rate of 3 percent. If the actual inflation rate turns out to be 10 percent, it will catch people off-guard. When the rate of inflation is high and variable, like the rates for the high-inflation countries of Exhibit 8–10, it will be virtually impossible for decision makers to anticipate future rates accurately, and long-range planning will be extremely difficult.

Anticipated inflation is a change in the price level that is widely expected. Decision makers are generally able to anticipate slow steady rates of inflation—such as those present in Canada, Germany, Japan, Singapore, and the United States during 1991–1997—with a high degree of accuracy.

Contrary to the satirical statement at the beginning of the chapter, inflation will affect the prices of things we sell as well as the prices of goods we buy. Both resource and product prices are influenced by inflation. Before we become too upset about inflation "robbing us of the purchasing power of our paychecks," we should recognize that inflation influences the size of those paychecks. The weekly earnings of employees would not have risen at an annual rate of 7 percent during the 1970s if the rate of inflation had not increased rapidly during that period. Wages are a price, also. Inflation raises both wages and prices.

Harmful Effects of Inflation

Simply because money income initially tends to rise with prices, it does not follow that there is no need to be concerned about inflation, particularly high rates of inflation.

Inflation causes problems! Our modern living standard is the result of gains from specialization, division of labor, and mass-production processes. Realization of gains from these sources is dependent upon trade and a smooth-functioning system of exchange. High and variable rates of inflation will generate uncertainty and weaken the link between income and productive activity. There are three major reasons why inflation will have a harmful impact on the economy.

1. ***Because unanticipated inflation alters the outcomes of long-term projects, such as the purchase of a machine or an investment in a business, it will increase the risks and retard the level of such productive activities.*** When the price level rises 15 percent one year, 40 percent the next year, and then increases again by 20 or 25 percent the following year, no one knows what to expect. Unanticipated changes of even 5 percent or 10 percent in the rate of inflation can often turn an otherwise profitable project into a personal economic disaster. Given the uncertainty that it creates, many decision makers will simply forgo capital investments and other transactions involving long-term commitments when the rate of inflation is highly variable and therefore unpredictable. As a result, mutually advantageous gains from trade will be lost and the efficiency of markets reduced.
2. ***Inflation distorts the information delivered by prices.*** Prices communicate important information concerning the relative scarcity of goods and resources. Some prices can be easily and regularly changed. But this will not be true for others—particularly those set by long-term contracts. For example, time delays will occur before the prices accompanying rental lease agreements, items sold in catalogs, mortgage interest rates, and collective bargaining contracts can be changed. Because some prices will respond quickly to inflationary policies while others will change more slowly, an unanticipated change in the rate of inflation will change *relative prices* as well as the *general price level.* The distorted relative prices will be a less reliable indicator of relative scarcity. As a result of these unreliable price signals, producers and resource suppliers will often make choices that they will later regret, and the allocation of resources will be less efficient than would be the case if the general level of prices was more stable.
3. ***People will respond to high and variable rates of inflation by spending less time producing and more time trying to protect themselves from inflation.*** Since the failure to anticipate accurately the rate of inflation can have a substantial effect on one's wealth, individuals will divert scarce resources from the production of desired goods and services to the acquisition of information on the future rate of inflation. The ability of business decision makers to forecast changes in prices becomes more valuable relative to their ability as managers and organizers of production. Speculative practices are encouraged as people try to outguess one another with regard to the future direction of prices. Funds flow into speculative investments, such as gold, silver, and art objects, rather than into productive investments (buildings, machines, and technological research) that expand the investor's ability to produce goods and services. Such practices are socially counterproductive. They reduce our production possibilities.

Although the initial effects of inflation can sometimes be positive, high and variable rates of inflation will inevitably exert a negative impact on real output and the level of prosperity. Economists have coined the term **stagflation** to describe the phenomenon of rapid inflation and sluggish economic growth. The 1970s were a period of stagflation in the United States. Two recessions (1974–1975 and 1979–1980) and sluggish growth accompanied the double-digit inflation rates of the 1970s.

Stagflation
A period during which an economy is experiencing both substantial inflation and either declining or slow growth in output.

WHAT CAUSES INFLATION?

We must acquire some additional tools before we can answer the question of what causes inflation in detail, but at this point we can outline a couple of theories. First, economists emphasize the link between aggregate demand and supply. If aggregate demand rises more rapidly than supply, prices will rise. Second, nearly all economists believe that a rapid expansion in a nation's stock of money causes inflation. The old saying is that prices will rise because "there is too much money chasing too few goods." The hyperinflation experienced by South American countries and, more recently, the countries of the former Soviet Union has mainly been the result of monetary expansion. Once we develop additional knowledge about the operation of our economy, we will consider this issue in more detail.

LOOKING *Ahead*

In this chapter, we have examined the historical record for real income, employment, and prices. Measurement problems and the side effects of economic instability were discussed. In the next chapter, we will begin to develop a macroeconomic model that will help us better understand both the sources of and potential remedies for economic instability.

KEY POINTS

➤ During the past century, real GDP in the United States has grown at an average annual rate of approximately 3 percent.

➤ Real GDP has also been characterized by cyclical movements. The four phases of the business cycle are *business expansion, peak (or boom), contraction,* and *recessionary trough.*

➤ A recession is defined as two successive quarters of declining real GDP. If a recession is quite severe, it is called a depression.

➤ There are three types of unemployment: (a) frictional unemployment, (b) structural unemployment, and (c) cyclical unemployment. In a world of imperfect information and dynamic change, some unemployment is inevitable.

➤ Full employment is the employment level consistent with the economy's natural rate of unemployment. Both full employment and the natural rate of unemployment are associated with the economy's maximum sustainable rate of output.

➤ The definition of *unemployed* involves some subjectivity. Some economists believe that the employment/population ratio is a more objective and accurate indicator of current labor market conditions.

➤ The concept of potential output encompasses two important ideas: (a) full utilization of resources and (b) a supply constraint that limits our ability to produce desired goods and services. Potential output is the maximum *sustainable* output level consistent with the economy's resource base and current institutional arrangements.

➤ Inflation is a general rise in the level of prices. It is important to distinguish between anticipated and unanticipated inflation. Unanticipated changes in the rate of inflation often alter the intended terms of long-term agreements and cause people to make choices that they will later regret.

➤ Inflation, particularly unanticipated inflation, has harmful effects. These include: (a) additional uncertainty accompanying time-dimension contracts, (b) distortion of relative prices, and (c) the shift of resources into activities designed to prevent inflation from eroding one's wealth.

CRITICAL ANALYSIS QUESTIONS

1. List the major phases of the business cycle and indicate how real GDP, employment, and unemployment change during these phases. Are the time periods of business cycles and the duration of the various phases relatively similar and therefore highly predictable?

*2. Explain why even an efficiently functioning economic system will have some unemployed resources.

3. Classify each of the following as employed, unemployed, or not in the labor force:
   a. Brown is not working; she applied for a job at Wal-Mart last week and is awaiting the result of her application.
   b. Martinez is vacationing in Florida during a layoff at a General Motors plant due to a model changeover, but he expects to be recalled in a couple of weeks.
   c. Green was laid off as a carpenter when a construction project was completed. He is looking for work but has been unable to find anything except an $8-per-hour job, which he turned down.
   d. West works 70 hours per week as a homemaker for her family of nine.
   e. Carson, a 17-year-old, works six hours per week as a route person for the local newspaper.
   f. Chang works three hours in the mornings at a clinic and for the last two weeks has spent the afternoons looking for a full-time job.

4. What is full employment? How are full employment and the natural rate of unemployment related? Indicate several factors that would cause the natural rate of unemployment to change. Is the actual rate of unemployment currently greater or less than the natural rate of unemployment? Why?

5. Carefully explain how both the rate of unemployment and the employment/population ratio are derived. If the rate of unemployment decreases, does the employment/population ratio necessarily increase? Why or why not? Which is the better indicator of employment opportunity? Why?

*6. "As the inflation proceeds and the real value of the currency fluctuates widely from month to month, all permanent relations between debtors and lenders, which form the ultimate foundation of capitalism, become so utterly disordered as to be almost meaningless; and the process of wealth-getting degenerates into a gamble and a lottery." Do you agree with this well-known economist's view? Why or why not? How high do you think the inflation rate would have to climb before these effects would become pronounced? Discuss.

*7. How are the following related to each other?
   a. Actual rate of unemployment
   b. Natural rate of unemployment
   c. Cyclical unemployment
   d. Potential GDP

*8. Use the following data to calculate (a) the labor force participation rate, (b) the rate of unemployment, and (c) the employment/population ratio:

Population	10,000
Labor force	6,000
Not currently working	4,500
Employed full-time	4,000
Employed part-time	1,500
Unemployed	500

*9. Persons are classified as unemployed if they are not currently working at a job and if they made an effort to find a job during the past four weeks. Does this mean that there were no jobs available? Does it mean that there were no jobs available that unemployed workers were qualified to perform? What does it mean?

*10. Indicate how an unanticipated 5 percent jump in the inflation rate will influence the wealth of the following:
   a. A person whose major asset is a house with a 30-year mortgage at a fixed interest rate.
   b. A family holding most of its wealth in long-term, fixed-yield bonds.

c. A retiree drawing a monthly pension.
d. A heavily indebted small-business owner.
e. The owner of an apartment complex with substantial outstanding debt at a fixed interest rate.
f. A worker whose wages are determined by a three-year union contract ratified three months ago.

11. Is the natural rate of unemployment fixed? Why or why not?

12. If a group of employees has a relatively low opportunity cost of job search, how will this affect their unemployment rate? How do you think the opportunity cost of job search of teenagers living with their parents compares with that of a prime earner with several dependents? How will this affect the unemployment rate of teenagers?

*13. How will each of the following affect a job seeker's decision to reject an available job offer and continue searching for a superior alternative?
a. The rumor that a major firm in the area is going to expand employment next month
b. The availability of food stamps
c. Optimism about the future of the economy

*14. "My money wage rose by 6 percent last year, but inflation completely erased these gains. How can I get ahead when inflation continues to wipe out my increases in earnings?" What's wrong with this way of thinking?

15. Suppose that the consumer price index at year-end 2000 was 150 and by year-end 2001 had risen to 160. What was the inflation rate during 2001?

16. Data for the nominal GDP and the GDP deflator (1990 = 100) in 1995 and 1996 for six major industrial countries are presented in the accompanying Table A.
a. Use the data provided to calculate the 1995 and 1996 real GDP of each country measured in 1990 prices. Place in the blanks provided.
b. Use the data for the GDP deflator to calculate the 1996 inflation rate of each country. Place in the blanks provided.
c. Which country had the highest growth rate of real GDP during 1996? Which had the lowest growth rate?
d. Indicate the countries that had the highest and the lowest inflation rates in 1996.
e. Which one of the countries had the most inflation during the 1990–1996 period?

TABLE A

Country	Nominal GDP (billions of local currency units)[a]		GDP Deflator (1990 = 100)		Real GDP (in 1990 currency units)		Inflation Rate
	1995	1996	1995	1996	1995	1996	1996
United States	7,253.8	7,576.1	115.0	117.2	______	______	______
Canada	776.3	797.8	107.6	109.0	______	______	______
Japan	482.9	500.4	104.6	104.7	______	______	______
Germany	3,459.6	3,540.0	118.7	119.9	______	______	______
France	7,662.4	7,865.5	111.5	112.8	______	______	______
United Kingdom	700.1	737.2	119.9	123.6	______	______	______

[a] *The data for Japan are in trillions of yen.*

Source: International Monetary Fund, International Financial Statistics Yearbook, *1997.*

17. The following Table B presents the 1996 population, employment, and unemployment data for several countries.
a. Calculate the number of people in the labor force in 1996 for each of the following countries: the United States, Canada, and Japan.
b. Calculate the 1996 labor force participation rate for each country and place it in the blanks provided. Which country had the highest rate of labor force participation? Which country had the lowest?
c. Calculate the rate of unemployment in 1996 for each country, and place it in the blanks provided. Which country had the highest rate of unemployment? Which had the lowest?

---

*Asterisk denotes questions for which answers are given in Appendix B.

TABLE B

Country	Population 16 Years and Over (in millions)	Number Employed (in millions)	Number Unemployed (in millions)	Rate of Labor Force Participation (percent)	Rate of Unemployment (percent)
United States	207.8	128.0	7.2	______	______
Canada	24.0	13.7	1.5	______	______
Japan	103.5	64.9	2.3	______	______
Germany	56.4	35.8	3.5	______	______
France	47.1	22.5	3.2	______	______
United Kingdom	47.4	26.2	2.3	______	______
Italy	49.4	20.6	2.8	______	______

CHAPTER 9

Macroeconomics is interesting . . . because it is challenging to reduce the complicated details of the economy to manageable essentials. Those essentials lie in the interactions among the goods, labor, and assets [loanable funds] markets of the economy.

Rudiger Dornbusch and Stanley Fischer[1]

An Introduction to Basic Macroeconomic Markets

CHAPTER FOCUS

- What is the circular flow of income? What are the major markets that coordinate macroeconomic activities?
- Why is the aggregate demand for goods and services inversely related to the price level?
- Why is an increase in the price level likely to expand output in the short run, but not in the long run?
- What determines the equilibrium level of GDP of an economy? When equilibrium is present, how will the actual rate of unemployment compare with the natural rate?
- What is the difference between the real interest rate and the money interest rate? Does inflation help borrowers relative to lenders?
- If equilibrium is present in the loanable funds and foreign exchange markets, how will this influence the leakages from and injections into the circular flow of income?

[1]Rudiger Dornbusch and Stanley Fischer, *Macroeconomics* (New York: McGraw-Hill, 1978).

As we have learned, the U.S. economy has historically grown at an annual rate of about 3 percent. This growth has improved the living standards of Americans. The growth, however, has not been steady. Although growth of real GDP during some years has increased more than the 3 percent average, during others it has fallen well below the average. During recessions, the size of the economy has actually declined. As we noted in Chapter 8, the U.S. economy has also experienced fluctuations in employment and the rate of inflation. The experience of other countries is similar. All countries have experienced short-term fluctuations in output and employment, and varying degrees of inflation.

It is one thing to describe these fluctuations and another to understand their causes. In this chapter, we will develop a simple macroeconomic model. As we proceed, this model will be used to explain why fluctuations in output, employment, and prices occur and to analyze what might be done to reduce them.

UNDERSTANDING MACROECONOMICS: OUR GAME PLAN

A model is like a road map; it illustrates relationships between things. The simple model developed in this chapter will help us better understand macroeconomic relationships. It will also help us analyze the impact of policy changes on important economic variables, such as output, employment, and the general level of prices.

Fiscal policy
The use of government taxation and expenditure policies for the purpose of achieving macroeconomic goals.

Monetary policy
The deliberate control of the money supply, and, in some cases, credit conditions, for the purposes of achieving macroeconomic goals.

Macroeconomic policy is usually divided into two components: fiscal policy and monetary policy. **Fiscal policy** entails the use of the government's taxation and spending policies in order to achieve macroeconomic goals. In the United States, fiscal policy is conducted by Congress and the president. It is thus a reflection of the political process. **Monetary policy** encompasses actions that alter the money supply. The direction of monetary policy is determined by a nation's central bank, the Federal Reserve System in the United States. Ideally, both monetary and fiscal policy are used to promote business stability, high employment, the growth of output, and a stable price level.

Money supply
The supply of currency, checking account funds, and traveler's checks. These items are counted as money because they are used as the means of payment for purchases.

Initially, as we develop our basic macroeconomic model, we will assume that monetary and fiscal policies are unchanged. Stated another way, we will proceed as if the government continues to maintain the current tax and spending policies and that the monetary policymakers maintain a constant **money supply**—that they follow policies that keep the amount of cash in our billfolds and deposits in our checking accounts constant. Of course, changes in government expenditures, taxes, and the money supply are potentially important. We will investigate their impact in detail in subsequent chapters. For now, though, things will go more smoothly if we simply assume that policymakers are holding government expenditures, taxes, and the supply of money constant.

FOUR KEY MARKETS: RESOURCES, GOODS AND SERVICES, LOANABLE FUNDS, AND FOREIGN EXCHANGE

Businesses generally purchase resources from households and use them to produce goods and services. In turn, households generally use a substantial portion of the income they earn from the sale of their productive services to purchase goods and services supplied by businesses. ***Thus, there is a circular flow of output and income between these two key sectors, businesses and households. This circular flow of income is coordinated by four key macroeconomic markets: (1) goods and services, (2) resources, (3) loanable funds, and (4) foreign exchange.*** Exhibit 9–1 illustrates both the circular flow of income between the household and business sectors and the interrelationships among the key macroeconomic markets. This is a very important exhibit. ***In essence, Exhibit 9–1 provides a visual representation of the macroeconomic model that we will develop and use to analyze the economy.***

EXHIBIT 9–1

FOUR KEY MARKETS AND THE CIRCULAR FLOW OF INCOME

Foreign exchange market
Exports
Imports
Goods and services market
Expenditures on national product
Consumption expenditures
Government purchases
Business investment expenditures
Government
Net capital flow
Business taxes
Net taxes
Borrowing for investment
Borrowing for budget deficit
Net savings
Businesses
Households
Loanable funds market
Resource payments
National income (wages+rents+interest+profits)
Resource market

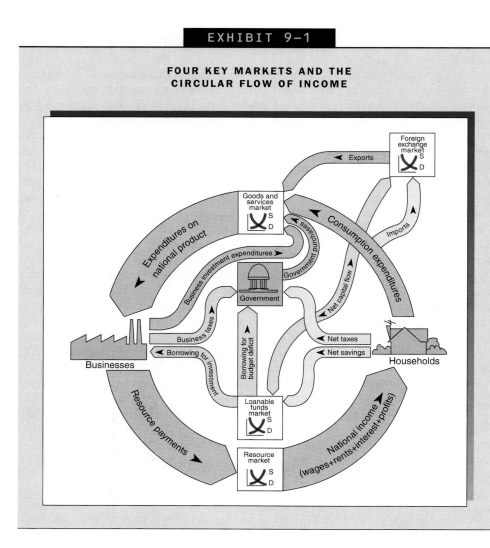

The circular-flow diagram presents a visual model of the economy. The circular flow of income is coordinated by four key markets. First, the resource market (bottom loop) coordinates the actions of businesses demanding resources and households supplying them in exchange for income. Second, the loanable funds market (lower center) brings the net saving of households plus the net inflow of foreign capital into balance with the borrowing of businesses and governments. Third, the foreign exchange market (top right) brings the purchases (imports) from foreigners into balance with sales (exports plus net inflow of capital) to them. Finally, the goods and services market (top loop) coordinates the demand (consumption, investment, government purchases, and net exports) for and supply of domestic production (real GDP).

Resource market
A highly aggregated market encompassing all resources (labor, physical capital, land, and entrepreneurship) that contribute to the production of current output. The labor market forms the largest component of this market.

Goods and services market
A highly aggregated market encompassing the flow of all final-user goods and services. The market counts all items that enter into GDP. Thus, real output in this market is equal to real GDP.

Loanable funds market
A general term used to describe the market arrangements that coordinate the borrowing and lending decisions of business firms and households. Commercial banks, savings and loan associations, the stock and bond markets, and insurance companies are important financial institutions in this market.

Saving
The portion of after-tax income that is not spent on consumption. Saving is a "flow" concept.

The bottom loop of this circular-flow diagram depicts the **resource market,** a highly aggregated market that includes the markets for labor services, natural resources, and physical capital. In the resource market, business firms demand resources because of their contribution to the production of goods and services. Households supply labor and other resources in exchange for income. The forces of demand and supply determine prices in the resource market. The payments to the suppliers of resources sum to national income.

The **goods and services market** comprises the top loop of the circular-flow diagram. In this market, sometimes referred to as the *product market,* businesses supply goods and services in exchange for sales revenue. As the arrows flowing into the goods and services market (top loop) indicate, there are four major sources of expenditures in this market: (1) household expenditures on consumption (and new housing), (2) business investment, (3) government purchases, and (4) net exports. The expenditures of households, business investors, governments, and foreigners (net exports) compose the aggregate (total) demand for domestic output. As the major demand components indicate, the goods and services market is a highly diverse market. It includes such items as ice cream, pizza, hairstyling, movie tickets, clothing, and television sets—goods purchased primarily by consumers. It also includes investment goods—machines, tools, and buildings. Finally, such items as highways, fire protection, and national defense, which are usually purchased by governments, are also part of the goods and services market.

There are two other key markets that will help direct the flow of income between the household and business sectors. The **loanable funds market** coordinates the actions of borrowers and lenders. The net **saving** of the household sector supplies funds to the loanable funds market. The demand for funds arises from businesses, to finance investment projects, and from government, to finance budget deficits. In an open economy, such as that of the United States, people also borrow from and lend to foreigners. Note the net inflow of capital from foreign economies into the loanable funds market in Exhibit 9–1. If the funds borrowed from foreigners exceed the loans to them, there will be a net inflow of funds, increasing supply relative to demand in the loanable funds market. On the other hand, if foreigners are net borrowers, there will be a net outflow of funds. As we discussed in Chapter 4, the interest rate is the price of loanable funds, and it will tend to bring the quantity of funds demanded by businesses and governments into balance with the quantity supplied by households (net saving) and foreigners (net capital inflow). When the borrowed funds are spent on investment goods and government purchases, they return to the circular flow.

Finally, the foreign exchange market coordinates transactions with foreigners. In our world of instant communications and shrinking transportation costs, trade between parties in different countries is common. When Americans purchase goods, services, and assets from foreigners, they will generate a demand for foreign exchange. On the other hand, the sale of items to foreigners will supply foreign exchange. The exchange rate—the price of one currency relative to another—will bring the purchases from foreigners into balance with the sales to them.

A major portion of the income earned by households will flow directly into the goods and services market in the form of consumption expenditures. However, households will not spend all their income on domestically produced products. Inspection of Exhibit 9-1 indicates that there are three forms of leakage from the circular flow of income: Households will use some of their income to purchase imports; some will be taxed away by the government; and some will be saved. Imports, net taxes, and net saving are leakage from the circular flow of income.

These leakages will tend to be channeled through the loanable funds and foreign exchange markets back into the circular flow. The loanable funds market will tend to direct the net saving of households toward the finance of business investment and government purchases. The foreign exchange market will tend to direct import expenditures toward either spending on exports or net capital inflow. As we proceed, we will investigate in more detail how the loanable funds and foreign exchange markets influence the leakages from and injections into the circular flow of income.

As we noted in Chapter 7, there are two ways of measuring gross domestic product (GDP), the aggregate domestic output of an economy. First, GDP can be measured by adding up the expenditures of consumers, investors, governments, and foreigners (net exports) on goods and services produced during the year. This method is equivalent to measuring the flow of output as it moves through the top loop—the goods and services market—of the circular-flow diagram. Alternatively, GDP can be measured by summing the income payments, both direct and indirect, received by the resource suppliers who produced the goods and services. This method uses the bottom loop—the resource market—to measure the flow of output.

AGGREGATE DEMAND FOR GOODS AND SERVICES

What goes on in the aggregate goods and services market is central to the health of an economy. Indeed, if we could keep our eye on just one market in an economy, we would choose the goods and services market. It is important to note that the "quantity" and "price" variables in this highly aggregated market differ from their counterparts in the market for a specific good. In the goods and services market, the "quantity" variable is output as measured by real GDP. The "price" variable is the price level as measured by a general price index (for example, the GDP deflator).

Just as the concepts of demand and supply enhance our understanding of markets for specific goods, they also contribute to our understanding of a highly aggregated market, such as the goods and services market. Because demand in the goods and services market aggregates together the purchases of consumers, investors, governments, and foreigners, it is called "aggregate demand." The **aggregate demand curve** indicates the various quantities of *domestically produced* goods and services that purchasers are willing to buy at different price levels. As **Exhibit 9–2** illustrates, the aggregate demand curve (*AD*) slopes downward to the right, indicating an inverse relationship between the amount of goods and services demanded and the price level.

Aggregate demand curve
A downward-sloping curve indicating an inverse relationship between the price level and the quantity of domestically produced goods and services that households, business firms, governments, and foreigners (net exports) are willing to purchase during a period.

WHY DOES THE AGGREGATE DEMAND CURVE SLOPE DOWNWARD?

Both the nature of the aggregate demand curve and the explanation for its downward slope differ substantially from that of the demand for a specific commodity, which we discussed previously in Chapter 3. The inverse relationship between price and the amount demanded of a specific commodity—television sets, for example—reflects the fact that consumers will substitute the good for other commodities when a price reduction makes the good less expensive relative to other goods. A price reduction in the aggregate goods and services market indicates that the level of prices has declined. On average, the prices of all goods are lower. When the prices of all goods produced domestically fall by the same proportion, there will be no incentive for *domestic* purchasers to substitute one good for another.

There are three major reasons why a reduction in the price level will lead to an increase in the aggregate quantity of goods and services demanded by purchasers.

As illustrated here, the quantity of goods and services purchased will increase (to Y_2) as the price level declines (to P_2). Other things constant, the lower price level will increase the wealth of people holding the fixed quantity of money, lead to lower interest rates, and make domestically produced goods cheaper relative to foreign goods. All these factors will tend to increase the quantity of goods and services purchased at the lower price level.

EXHIBIT 9-2

AGGREGATE DEMAND CURVE

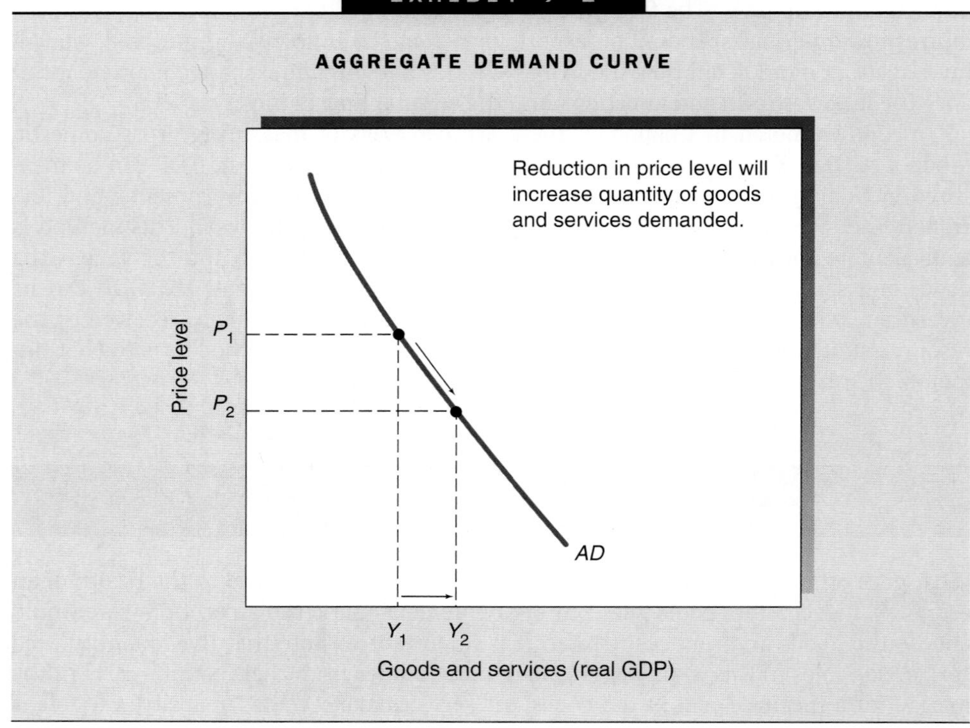

1. *A lower price level will increase the purchasing power of the fixed quantity of money.* As the level of prices declines, the purchasing power of the fixed quantity of money increases. For example, suppose that you have $2,000 in your bank account. Consider how a 20 percent reduction in the level of prices will influence your wealth and spending. At the lower price level, your $2,000 will buy more goods and services. In fact, your $2,000 will buy as much as $2,500 would have purchased at the previous higher level of prices. Other people are in an identical position. As the price level declines, the purchasing power of money and the real wealth of people holding fixed money balances increases. (*Note:* Remember we are assuming that the *nominal* supply of money is fixed.) Because of this increase in wealth, people will purchase more goods and services. Economists refer to this inverse relationship between the price level and the wealth of households and businesses holding a fixed supply of money as the **real balance effect.** It helps explain why a fall in the price level will lead to an increase in the quantity demanded of goods and services.

Real balance effect
The increase in wealth generated by an increase in the purchasing power of a constant money supply as the price level decreases. This wealth effect leads to an inverse relationship between price (level) and quantity demanded in the goods and services market.

2. *The interest rate effect: A lower price level will reduce the demand for money and lower the real interest rate, which will stimulate additional purchases during the current period.* When the average price of everything is lower, consumers and businesses will need less money to conduct their normal activities. Households will be able to get by just fine with a smaller money balance because, at the lower price level, they will be spending a smaller nominal amount on food, clothing, and other items regularly purchased. Similarly, businesses will need less money to pay employee wages, taxes, and other business expenses. At the lower price level, both consumers and businesses will attempt to reduce their money balances and shift more funds to interest-earning assets like bonds and savings deposits. This will channel more funds into the loanable funds market, placing downward pressure on interest rates.

What impact will a lower interest rate have on the demand for goods and services? A reduction in the interest rate will make it cheaper to purchase goods and services during the current period. Households can be expected to increase their purchases of interest-sensitive consumption goods, such as automobiles and consumer durables. Similarly, firms will expand their current investment expenditures on business expansion and new construction. Thus, the lower price level and accompanying reduction in the interest rate will encourage both households and businesses to demand a larger quantity of goods and services. This interest rate effect also contributes to the downward slope of the aggregate demand curve.

3. ***Other things constant, a lower price level will make domestically produced goods less expensive relative to foreign goods.*** At a lower price level, imports will decline as Americans find that many domestically produced goods are now cheaper than products produced abroad. At the lower price level, Americans will tend to purchase fewer Japanese automobiles, Korean textiles, Italian shoes, and other imports because these items are now more expensive relative to domestically produced goods. At the same time, foreigners will increase their purchases of American-made goods that are now relatively cheaper. Therefore, net exports (exports minus imports) will tend to rise.[2] This increase in net exports at the lower U.S. price level will directly increase the quantity demanded of domestically produced goods. This international-substitution effect provides a third reason for the downward slope of the aggregate demand curve.

THE DOWNWARD-SLOPING AGGREGATE DEMAND CURVE: A SUMMARY

The accompanying Thumbnail Sketch summarizes the reasons why a lower price level will increase the quantity demanded of domestically produced goods and services. A lower price level will (1) increase the purchasing power of the fixed money supply, (2) lower interest rates, and (3) reduce the price of domestically produced goods relative to goods produced abroad. Each of these factors will tend to increase the quantity demanded in the product market.

THUMBNAIL SKETCH

Why is the aggregate quantity demanded inversely related to the price level?

A decrease in the price level will raise aggregate quantity demanded because

1. The real wealth of persons holding money balances will increase when prices fall; this will encourage additional consumption.
2. A reduction in the demand for money balances at the lower price level will reduce interest rates, which will encourage current investment and consumption.
3. Net exports will expand (since the prices of domestic goods have fallen relative to foreign goods).

---

[2]An increase in exports and a decline in imports will place some upward pressure on the foreign exchange value of the currency. However, the lower interest rates (point 2 above) will result in an outflow of capital, which will place downward pressure on the foreign exchange value of the currency. Most economists believe that this latter effect will dominate. If it does, a depreciation in the nation's currency will stimulate net exports, which will also increase the quantity demanded of goods and services.

The effects would be just the opposite for a higher price level. At a higher price level, (1) the wealth of people holding the fixed supply of money would be less, (2) the demand for money would be greater, which would lead to higher interest rates, and (3) domestic goods would be more expensive relative to those produced abroad. Each of these factors would tend to reduce the quantity demanded of domestically produced goods. Therefore, even though the explanation differs, the quantity demanded in the aggregate goods and services market, like the quantity demanded for a specific product, will be inversely related to price.

AGGREGATE SUPPLY OF GOODS AND SERVICES

Aggregate supply curve
A curve indicating the relationship between the nation's price level and quantity of goods supplied by its producers. In the short run, it is probably an upward-sloping curve, but in the long run most economists believe the aggregate supply curve is vertical (or nearly so).

In light of our discussion of aggregate demand, it should come as no great surprise that the explanation of the general shape of the **aggregate supply curve** differs from that of the supply curve for a specific good. As we have already noted, an increase in price in the goods and services market indicates that the general level of prices has risen, rather than the price of one good relative to all other goods. Thus, the general shape of the aggregate supply (*AS*) curve is not a reflection of changes in the relative prices of goods.

When considering aggregate supply, it is particularly important to distinguish between the short run and the long run. In this context, the short run is the time period during which some prices, particularly those in labor markets, are set by prior contracts and agreements. Therefore, in the short run, households and businesses are unable to adjust these prices when unexpected changes occur, including unexpected changes in the price level. In contrast, the long run is a time period of sufficient duration that people have the opportunity to modify their behavior in response to price changes. We now consider both the short-run and long-run aggregate supply curves.

AGGREGATE SUPPLY IN THE SHORT RUN

The short-run aggregate supply* (SRAS) *curve indicates the various quantities of goods and services that domestic firms will supply in response to changing demand conditions that alter the level of prices in the goods and services market. As Exhibit 9–3 illustrates, the *SRAS* curve in the goods and services market slopes upward to the right. The upward slope reflects the fact that, in the short run, an unanticipated increase in the price level will, on average, improve the profitability of firms. They will respond with an expansion in output.

The *SRAS* curve is based on a specific expected price level, P_{100} in the case of Exhibit 9–3, and rate of inflation that generates that price level. When the expected price level is actually achieved, firms will earn normal profits and supply output Y_0. Why will an increase in the price level (to P_{105}, for example) enhance profitability, at least in the short run? Profit per unit equals price minus the producer's per-unit costs. ***Important components of producers' costs will be determined by long-term contracts.*** Interest rates on loans, collective bargaining agreements with employees, lease agreements on buildings and machines, and other contracts with resource suppliers will influence production costs during the current period. The prices incorporated into these long-term contracts at the time of the agreement are based on the expectation of price level (P_{100}) for the current period. These resource costs tend to be temporarily fixed. ***If an increase in demand causes the price level to rise unexpectedly during the current period, prices of goods and services will increase relative to the temporarily fixed***

EXHIBIT 9–3

SHORT-RUN AGGREGATE SUPPLY CURVE

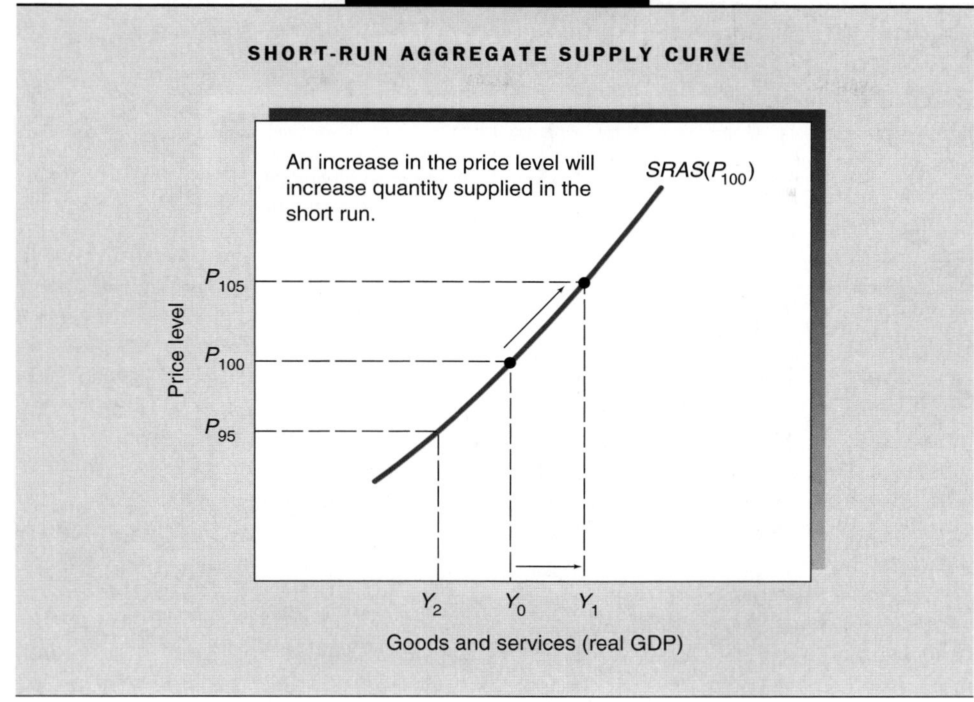

The short-run aggregate supply (SRAS) *curve shows the relationship between the price level and the quantity supplied of goods and services by domestic producers. In the short run, firms will generally expand output as the price level increases because the higher prices will improve profit margins since many components of costs will be temporarily fixed as the result of prior long-term commitments.*

components of costs. Profit margins will improve, and business firms will happily respond with an expansion in output (to Y_1***).***[3]

An unexpected reduction in the price level to P_{95} would exert just the opposite effect. It would decrease product prices relative to costs and thereby reduce profitability. In response, firms would reduce output to Y_2. Therefore, in the short run, there will be a direct relationship between amount supplied and the price level in the goods and services market.

Aggregate Supply in the Long Run

The long-run aggregate supply **(LRAS)** ***curve indicates the relationship between the price level and quantity of output after decision makers have had sufficient time to adjust their prior commitments where possible, or take steps to counterbalance them, in the light of any unexpected changes in market prices.*** A higher price level in the goods and services market will fail to alter the relationship between product and resource prices in the long run. Once people have time to fully adjust their prior commitments, competitive forces will restore the usual relationship between product prices and costs. Profit rates will return to normal, removing the incentive for firms to supply a larger rate of output. Therefore, as **Exhibit 9–4** illustrates, the *LRAS* curve is vertical.

[3]Other factors may also contribute to the positive relationship between the price level and output *in the short run.* In response to a general increase in demand, some firms may expand output without much of an increase in price because they believe that their current strong sales are only temporary and that a large price increase may drive their regular customers to rival suppliers. Other firms may expand output because they mistakenly believe that the demand for their product has increased relative to other products. In the long run, higher costs relative to product prices will make it impossible to sustain such expansions in output.

In the long run, a higher price level will not expand an economy's rate of output. Once people have time to adjust their prior long-term commitments, resource markets (and costs) will adjust to the higher level of prices and thereby remove the incentive of firms to supply a larger output at the higher price level. An economy's full employment rate of output —Y_F, the maximum output rate that is sustainable — is determined by the supply of resources, level of technology, and structure of institutions, factors that are insensitive to changes in the price level. The vertical LRAS *curve illustrates this point.*

EXHIBIT 9-4

LONG-RUN AGGREGATE SUPPLY CURVE

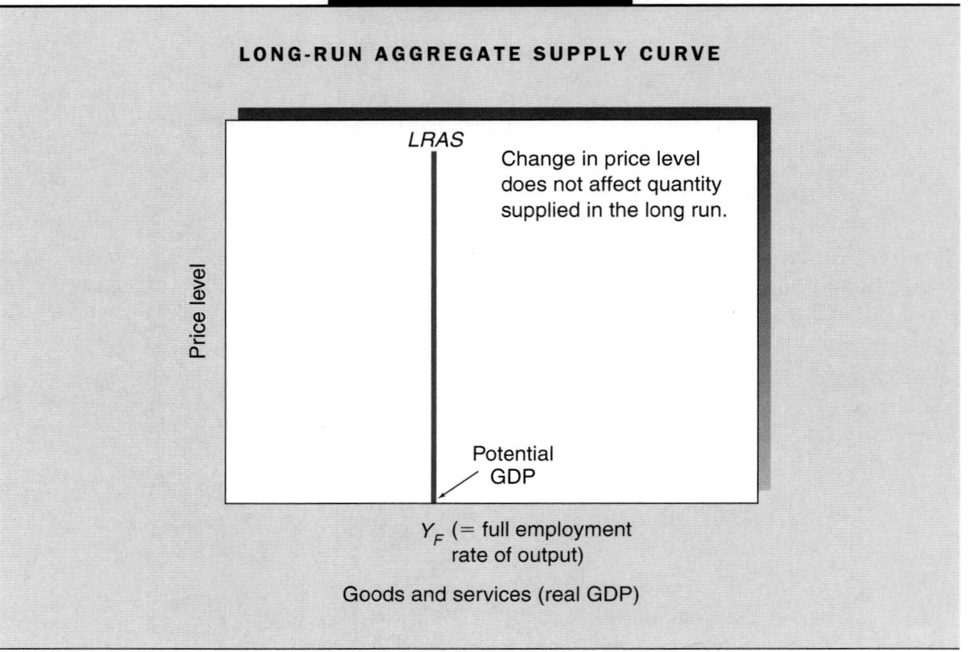

The forces that provide for an upward-sloping SRAS *curve are absent in the long run.* Costs that are temporarily fixed as the result of contractual agreements will eventually rise. With time, the long-term contracts will expire and be renegotiated. Once the contracts are renegotiated, resource prices will increase in the same proportion as product prices. A proportional increase in costs and product prices will leave the incentive to produce unchanged. Consider how a firm with a selling price of $20 and per-unit costs of $20 will be affected by the doubling of both product and resource prices. After the price increase, the firm's sales price will be $40, but so, too, will its per-unit costs. Thus, neither the firm's profit rate nor the incentive to produce is changed. Therefore, in the long run, an increase in the nominal value of the price level will fail to exert a lasting impact on aggregate output.

As we discussed in Chapter 2, at a point in time, the production possibilities of a nation are constrained by the supply of resources, level of technology, and institu-

THUMBNAIL SKETCH

Why is the short-run aggregate quantity supplied directly related to the price level?

➤ As the price level increases, profit margins will improve because *initially* the product prices of firms will rise relative to cost (important components of which are temporarily fixed by long-term contracts).

Why is the long-run aggregate supply curve vertical?

➤ Once people have the time to adjust fully to a new price level, the normal relationship between product prices and resource costs is restored.

➤ The sustainable potential output of an economy is determined by its quantity of resources, technology, and the efficiency of its institutional structures, not by the price level.

tional arrangements that influence the efficiency of resource use. The long-run aggregate supply curve is an alternative way to visualize the economy's production possibilities. Rather than focusing on the output of physical units, as does the production possibilities curve, the long-run aggregate supply curve focuses on the real dollar value of the units produced. The vertical long-run supply curve indicates that a change in the price level does not loosen the constraints that limit our production possibilities. For example, a doubling of prices will not improve technology. Neither will it expand the availability of productive resources, nor improve the efficiency of our economic institutions. Thus, there is no reason for a higher price level to increase our ability to produce goods and services. This is precisely what the vertical *LRAS* curve implies. The accompanying Thumbnail Sketch summarizes the factors that underlie both the short-run and long-run aggregate supply curves.

EQUILIBRIUM IN THE GOODS AND SERVICES MARKET

We are now ready to combine our analysis of aggregate demand and aggregate supply and consider how they act to determine the price level and rate of output. When a market is in **equilibrium,** there is a balance of forces such that the actions of buyers and sellers are consistent with one another. In equilibrium, buyers are willing to purchase all the units that sellers are willing to supply *at the current price.* Because the equilibrium price clears the market—all units produced are sold—some refer to it as the "market clearing price."

Equilibrium
A balance of forces permitting the simultaneous fulfillment of plans by buyers and sellers.

EQUILIBRIUM IN THE SHORT RUN

As **Exhibit 9–5** illustrates, short-run equilibrium is present in the goods and services market at the price level (*P*) where the aggregate quantity demanded is equal to the

EXHIBIT 9–5

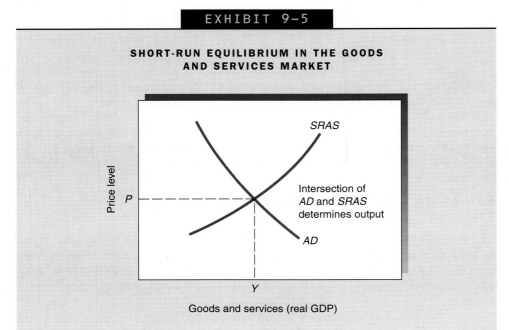

SHORT-RUN EQUILIBRIUM IN THE GOODS AND SERVICES MARKET

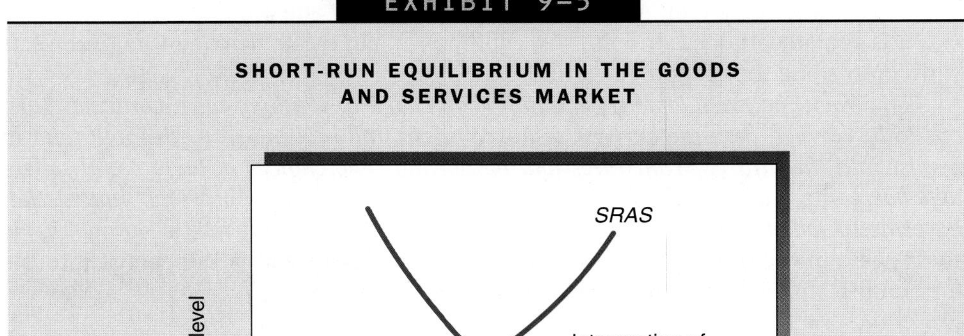

Short-run equilibrium in the goods and services market occurs at the price level (P) where AD and SRAS intersect. If the price level were lower than P, general excess demand in goods and services markets would push prices upward. Conversely, if the price level were higher than P, excess supply would result in falling prices.

aggregate quantity supplied. This occurs at the output rate (Y) where the *AD* and *SRAS* curves intersect. At this market clearing price (P), the amount that buyers want to purchase is just equal to the quantity that sellers are willing to supply during the current period.

If a price level of less than P were present, the aggregate quantity demanded would exceed the aggregate quantity supplied. Purchasers would be seeking to buy more goods and services than producers were willing to produce. This excess demand would place upward pressure on prices, causing the price level to rise toward P. On the other hand, at a price level greater than P, the aggregate quantity supplied would exceed the aggregate quantity demanded. Producers would be unable to sell all the goods produced. This would result in downward pressure (toward P) on prices. Only at the price level P would there be a balance of forces between the amount of goods demanded by consumers, investors, governments, and foreigners, and the amount supplied by domestic firms.

Equilibrium in the Long Run

In the short run, the goods and services market will gravitate toward a market clearing price—one that brings quantity demanded and quantity supplied into balance. ***However, a second condition is required for long-run equilibrium: Decision makers who agreed to long-term contracts influencing current prices and costs must have correctly anticipated the current price level at the time they arrived at the agreements.*** If this is not the case, buyers and sellers will want to modify the agreements when the long-term contracts expire. In turn, their modifications will affect costs, profit margins, and output.

Exhibit 9–6 illustrates a long-run equilibrium in the goods and services market. As in Exhibit 9–3, the subscripts attached to the *SRAS* and *AD* curves indicate the price level (an index of prices) that was anticipated by decision makers at the time they made decisions affecting the schedules. In this case, when buyers and sellers made their purchasing and production choices, they anticipated that the price level during the current period would be P_{100}, where the subscript 100 refers to an index of prices during an earlier base year. As the intersection of the *AD* and *SRAS* curves reveals, the P_{100} was actually attained. In long-run equilibrium, aggregate demand (*AD*) intersects with *SRAS* along the economy's vertical *LRAS*.

When the price level expectations embedded in the long-term contracts turn out to be correct, then the current resource prices and real interest rates will tend to persist into the future. Profit rates will be normal. The choices of buyers and sellers will harmonize, and neither will have reason to modify their previous contractual agreements when they come up for renegotiation. Thus, current rate of output (Y_F) is sustainable in the future. Long-run equilibrium is present and it will persist into the future until changes in other factors alter *AD* or *SRAS*.

Long-Run Equilibrium, Potential Output, and Full Employment

As we discussed in Chapter 8, potential GDP is equal to the economy's *maximum sustainable output* consistent with its resource base, current technology, and institutional structure. Potential GDP is neither a temporary high nor an abnormal low. When long-run equilibrium is present, the actual output achieved is equal to the economy's potential GDP.

The long-run equilibrium output rate (Y_F in Exhibit 9–6) also corresponds with the full employment of resources. When full-employment output is present, the

EXHIBIT 9-6

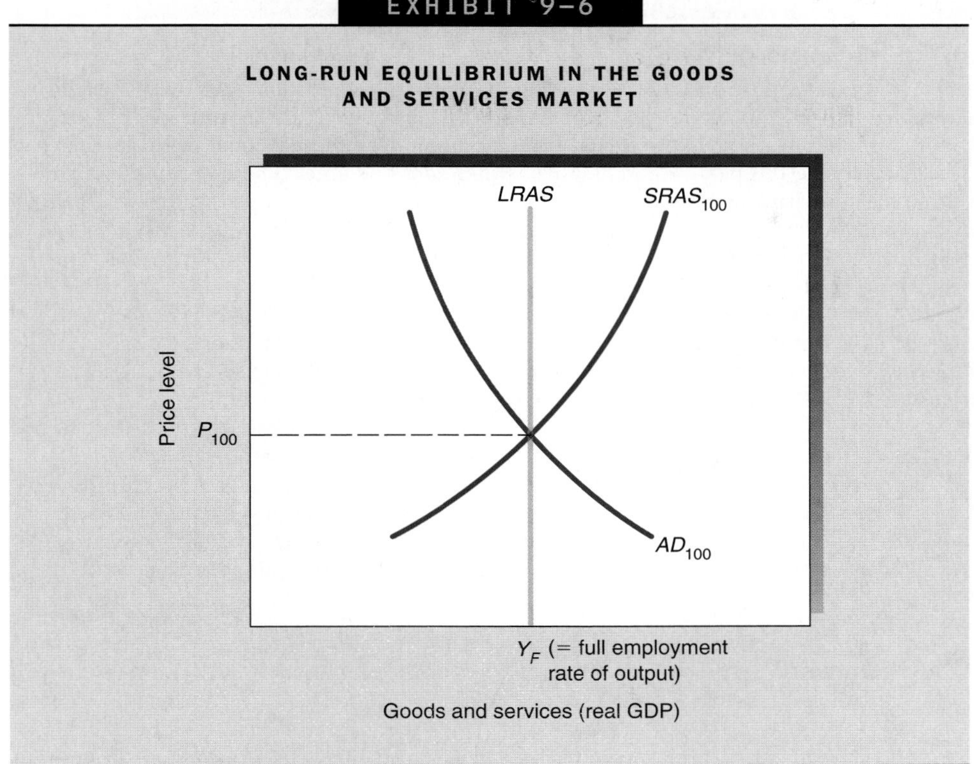

When the goods and services market is in long-run equilibrium, two conditions must be present. First, the quantity demanded must equal the quantity supplied at the current price level. Second, the price level anticipated by decision makers must equal the actual price level. The subscripts on the SRAS *and* AD *curves indicate that buyers and sellers alike anticipated the price level* P_{100}*, where the 100 represents an index of prices during an earlier base year. When the anticipated price level is actually attained, current output* (Y_F) *will equal the economy's potential* GDP *and full employment will be present.*

job-search time of unemployed workers will be normal, given the characteristics of the labor force and the institutional structure of the economy. Only frictional and structural unemployment will be present; cyclical unemployment will be absent.

When an economy is in long-run equilibrium, the *actual* rate of unemployment will be equal to the *natural* rate. Remember, the natural rate of unemployment reflects the normal job-search process of employees and employers, given the structure of the economy and the laws and regulations that affect the operation of markets. It is a rate that is neither abnormally high nor abnormally low; it can be sustained into the future. If long-run equilibrium is present, unemployment will be at its natural rate.(See the Measures of Economic Activity box, natural rate of unemployment.)

Summarizing, in long-run equilibrium, (a) output will be equal to its potential, (b) full employment will be achieved, and (c) the actual rate of unemployment will be equivalent to the natural rate of unemployment. It is this long-run maximum sustainable output that economists are referring to when they speak of "full employment output" or "potential GDP."

Adjustment When Output Differs from Long-Run Potential

What happens when changes in the price level catch buyers and sellers by surprise? When the actual price level differs from the level forecast by buyers and sellers, some decision makers will enter into agreements that they will later regret—agreements that they will want to change as soon as they have an opportunity to do so.

MEASURES OF ECONOMIC ACTIVITY

Natural Rate of Unemployment

The natural rate of unemployment is a theoretical concept and cannot be directly observed. The theory, however, indicates how it can be estimated. The natural rate of unemployment will be present when decision makers correctly anticipate the inflation rate. When the inflation rate of an economy is relatively constant—when it is neither increasing nor decreasing—buyers and sellers will be able to accurately anticipate it and adjust nominal prices, wages, and interest rates accordingly. ***Thus, the actual unemployment rate will tend to gravitate toward the economy's natural rate of unemployment when the inflation rate is constant for an extended period of time.***

A statistical equation that links the unemployment rate to the rate of inflation can be used to estimate the natural rate of unemployment. When the *change* in the inflation rate is set equal to zero within this equation, the results will provide an estimate for the natural rate of unemployment. ***Statistical estimates of this type indicate that the U.S. natural rate of unemployment in the late 1990s is approximately 5 percent.***

Over time, the natural rate is influenced by changes in the demographic composition of the labor force. Because younger workers are more likely than their older counterparts both to switch jobs and enter (and reenter) the labor force, the natural unemployment rate increases when youthful workers grow as a proportion of the labor force. This happened during the 1960s and 1970s, when the baby-boom generation—those born during the 15 years following the Second World War—entered the labor force. Researchers in this area estimate that the large influx of youthful workers during this period pushed the natural rate of unemployment up from approximately 5 percent in the late 1950s to nearly 7 percent in 1980. This situation reversed during the 1980s and 1990s as the baby boomers moved into their prime working years and the proportion of youthful workers as a share of the labor force fell. As a result, the natural rate of unemployment has declined during the last two decades, receding once again to the 5 percent or less level of the late 1950s.

Consider the situation when the price level *increases* more than was anticipated. Failing to foresee the price increase, lenders in the loanable funds market agree to interest rates that are lower than they are willing to accept once the general increase in prices (inflation) is taken into account. Similarly, anticipating a lower current price level, union officials and employees accept money-wage increases that end up creating lower real wages than were initially expected. In the short run, the atypically low interest rates and real wages reduce costs relative to product prices. Profit margins are abnormally high, and firms respond with a larger output. Employment expands. Unemployment falls below its natural rate.

But this abnormally large output and high level of employment are not sustainable. The "mistakes," based on a failure to predict the strength of current demand, will be recognized and corrected when contracts expire. Real wages and interest rates will increase and eventually reflect the higher price level and rate of inflation. Profit margins will return to normal. When these adjustments are completed, the temporarily large output rate and high employment level will decline and return to normal.

What will happen if product prices *decline or increase less* rapidly than decision makers anticipate? Anticipating a higher price level (a higher inflation rate than actually occurs), borrowers agree to interest rates that later *in real terms* prove to be unacceptably high. Similarly, employers agree to wage increases that result in higher real wages than expected, since the price level rises more slowly than people thought it would. The abnormally high interest and wage rates increase costs relative to product prices. As profit margins are squeezed, producers reduce output and lay off employees. The *actual rate* of unemployment rises above the *natural rate* of unemployment. Current output falls short of the economy's potential GDP.

Many economists think this is precisely what happened during 1982. After inflation rates of 13 percent in 1979 and 12 percent in 1980, price increases plummeted to 4 percent in 1982. This sharp reduction in the inflation rate caught many decision

The expected rate of inflation influences the prices incorporated into long-term contracts, such as collective bargaining agreements. If the actual price level differs from what was expected, output will differ from long-run equilibrium.

makers by surprise. Unable to pass along to consumers the large increases in money wages agreed to in 1980 and 1981, employers cut back production and laid off workers. The unemployment rate soared to 10.8 percent in late 1982, up from 7.6 percent in 1981. Eventually, new agreements provided for smaller money wage increases, or even wage reductions, in 1983 and 1984. Unemployment fell. Nevertheless, in 1982 unemployment was well above its natural rate. The necessary adjustments could not be made instantaneously.

In summary, an unexpected change in the price level (rate of inflation) will alter the rate of output in the short run. An unexpected increase in the price level will stimulate output and employment during the next year or two, while an unexpected decline in the price level will cause output and employment to fall in the immediate future.

RESOURCE MARKET

In addition to the aggregate goods and services market, the resource market, loanable funds market, and foreign exchange market help coordinate the circular flow of income between the household and business sectors. All four of these markets are interrelated—changes in one will have repercussions in the others. We will now turn to an analysis of the resource, loanable funds, and foreign exchange markets and their interrelation with the goods and services market.

The resource market is the place where labor, raw materials, machines, and other factors of production are bought and sold. Within the framework of our circular flow analysis, households supply resources in exchange for income, and business firms demand resources in order to produce goods and services (see Exhibit 9–1.) By far, the market for labor services is the largest component of the resource market. In the United States, the costs of labor make up approximately 70 percent of production costs.

Because of its size and importance, we will focus considerable attention on the labor market.

As in other markets, prices will coordinate the choices of buyers and sellers in the resource market. An increase in the price of labor and other resources will increase the cost of production and make it less profitable for firms to employ resources. As a result, businesses will demand less labor and other resources as their prices increase. Thus, the demand curve in the resource market will have the usual downward slope to the right. Although working and supplying resources generates income, it also requires one to give up something that is valuable: leisure—time for nonwork activities. Higher resource prices will make it more attractive to give up leisure and supply labor and other resources instead. Therefore, the quantity supplied of labor and other resources expands as resource prices increase.

As **Exhibit 9–7** illustrates, there will be a tendency to move toward a price that will clear the market and bring the amount demanded by business firms into balance with the amount supplied by resource owners. At this price (P_r), the choices of both buyers and sellers in the aggregate resource market harmonize—they are consistent with each other. If the market price were greater than P_r, an excess supply of resources would occur. In turn, this excess supply would push resource prices downward toward equilibrium. In contrast, if resource prices were below equilibrium (less than P_r), excess demand would place upward pressure on the price of resources. Market forces thus tend to move resource prices toward the price that clears the market—the price that brings amount demanded into equality with the amount supplied.

As we discussed in Chapter 4, the markets for resources and products are closely related. The demand for resources is directly linked to the demand for goods and services. In fact, the demand for resources is a *derived demand*—it stems from the demand for goods and services. An increase in demand in the goods and services

In general, as resource prices increase, the amount demanded by producers declines and the amount supplied by resource owners expands. In equilibrium, resource price brings the amount demanded into equality with the amount supplied in the aggregate-resource market. The labor market is a major component of the resource market.

EXHIBIT 9–7

EQUILIBRIUM IN THE RESOURCE MARKET

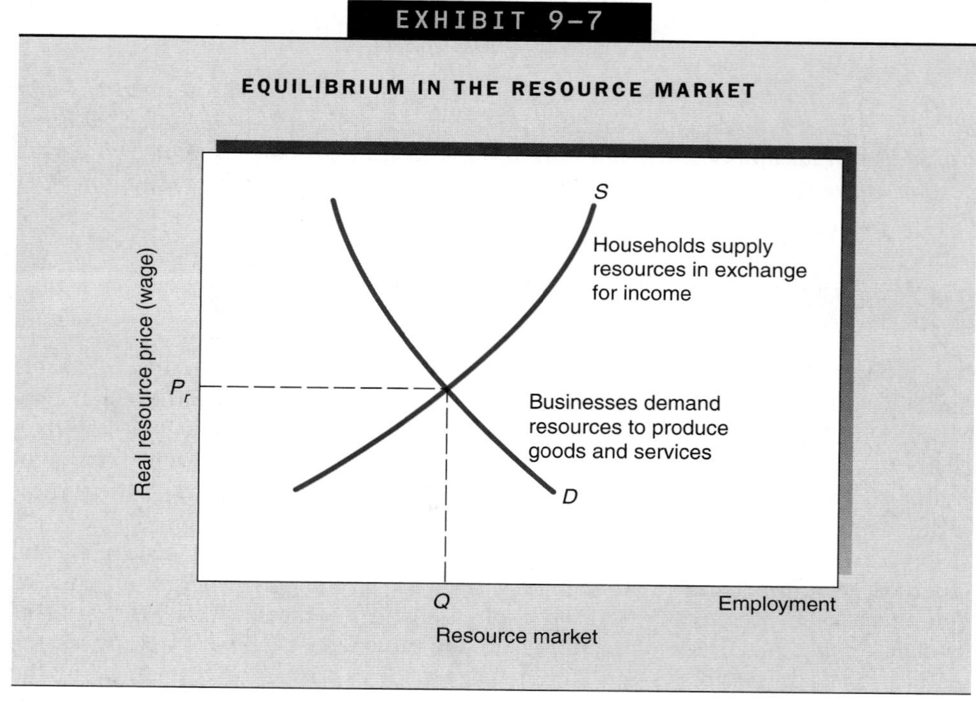

market will generate additional demand for resources. Similarly, a reduction in aggregate demand in the goods and services market will reduce the demand for resources.

The cost of producing goods and services is influenced directly by the price of resources. Other things remaining the same, an increase in resource prices will increase costs and squeeze profit margins in the goods and services market, causing the supply curve (*SRAS*) in the product market to shift to the left. Conversely, a reduction in resource prices will lower costs and improve profit margins in the goods and services market. An increase in aggregate supply (a shift to the right in *SRAS*) will result. As we analyze the macroeconomy, we will return again and again to the interrelations between these two markets.

When an economy is in long-run equilibrium, the price of resources relative to the price of goods and services will be such that business firms, on average, will be just able to cover their cost of production, including a competitive return on their investment. If this were not the case, producers would seek to either contract or expand output. For example, if the prices of resources were so high (relative to producers' prices) that firms were unable to cover their costs, many producers would cut back output or perhaps even discontinue production. Aggregate output would thereby be altered. Conversely, if resource prices were so low that firms were able to earn an above-market return, profit-seeking firms would expand output. New firms would begin production. Again, these forces would alter conditions in the goods and services market.

LOANABLE FUNDS MARKET

When we introduced the loanable funds market in Chapter 4, we indicated that borrowers demand loanable funds, while lenders supply them. In essence, borrowers are exchanging future income for purchasing power now. Most of us are impatient; we want things now rather than in the future. ***From the borrower's viewpoint, interest is the price paid for earlier availability (purchasing power now rather than in the future).***

Banks, savings and loan associations, and brokerage firms help coordinate saving and investment in the loanable funds market.

From the lender's viewpoint, interest is a premium received for waiting, for delaying possible expenditures into the future.

Other things constant, lower interest rates will make it less attractive to save and thereby supply funds to the loanable funds market. On the other hand, the lower rates will make it cheaper for businesses to undertake investment projects and for households to purchase "big ticket" items, such as houses and automobiles. Thus, the supply and demand curves in the loanable funds market have their usual shapes, and the interest rate will tend to bring the quantity of funds demanded by borrowers into equality with the quantity supplied by lenders.[4]

Money interest rate
The interest rate measured in monetary units. It overstates the real cost of borrowing during an inflationary period. When inflation is anticipated, an inflationary premium will be incorporated into the nominal value of this rate. The money interest rate is often referred to as the nominal interest rate.

Real interest rate
The interest rate adjusted for expected inflation; it indicates the real cost to the borrower (and yield to the lender) in terms of goods and services.

It is important to think of the interest rate in two ways. First, there is the **money interest rate,** the percentage of the amount borrowed that must be paid the lender in addition to the repayment of the principal. Money interest rates are those typically quoted in newspapers and business publications. Second, there is the **real interest rate,** which reflects the real burden to borrowers and the payoff to lenders in terms of command over goods and services.

The rate of inflation expected by borrowers and lenders will influence the attractiveness of various interest rates. Perhaps an example will illustrate this point and highlight the distinction between the money and real interest rate. Suppose that a borrower and lender—both anticipating that the general level of prices will be stable—agree to a 5 percent interest rate for a one-year loan of $1,000. After a year, the borrower must pay the lender $1,050—the $1,000 principal plus the 5 percent interest. Now, suppose during the year prices rose 5 percent as the result of inflation. Because of this, the $1,050 repayment after a year commands exactly the same purchasing power as the original $1,000 did when it was loaned. The lender receives nothing for making the purchasing power available to the borrower. In this case, the real interest return to the lender (and real cost to the borrower) is zero. Lenders are unlikely to continue making funds available at such bargain rates.

Inflation premium
A component of the money interest rate that reflects compensation to the lender for the expected decrease, due to inflation, in the purchasing power of the principal and interest during the course of the loan. It is determined by the expected rate of future inflation.

When inflation is present, people will come to anticipate it. Once borrowers and lenders expect a rate of inflation, 5 percent for example, they will build that rate into their loanable funds agreement. Lenders will demand (and borrowers will agree to pay) a higher money interest rate to compensate for the impact of inflation on the purchasing power of the loan proceeds. This premium for the expected decline in purchasing power of the dollar is called the **inflation premium.** It is equal to the expected rate of inflation. The relationship between the real and money interest rates is:

$$\text{Real interest rate} = \text{Money interest rate} - \text{Inflation premium}$$

Exhibit 9–8 illustrates how inflationary expectations influence money interest rates. Here we consider a situation where a 5 percent market rate of interest would emerge when borrowers and lenders anticipate stable prices. Because the expected rate of inflation is zero, there will be no inflation premium and, under these conditions, the money and real rates are equal. Consider how a persistent inflation rate of 5 percent will influence the choices of both borrowers and lenders. Compared to the zero inflation situation, a 10 percent interest return will be required to provide lenders with the same incentive to loan funds. Similarly, a 10 percent interest rate will provide borrowers with the same incentive to demand funds. Therefore, both the supply and demand curves will shift vertically by 5 percent to compensate for the expected rate of inflation. The money rate of interest will increase to 10 percent, 5 percent of which reflects an inflationary premium and 5 percent a real interest return.

[4]Of course, there are several different interest rates reflecting the time duration of the loan and the creditworthiness of the borrower.

EXHIBIT 9-8

INFLATION AND INTEREST RATES

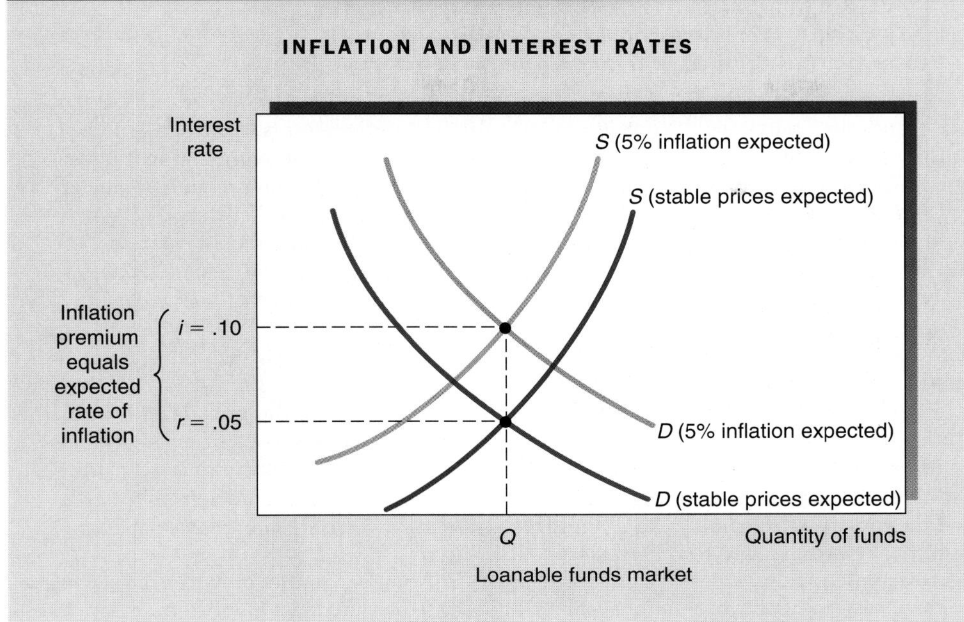

Suppose that when people expect the general level of prices to be stable (zero inflation) in the future, a 5 percent interest rate brings quantity demanded into balance with quantity supplied. Under these conditions, the money and real interest rates will be equal. When people expect prices to rise at a 5 percent rate, the money rate of interest (i) *will rise to 10 percent even though the real interest rate* (r) *remains constant at 5 percent.*

The money interest rate may be a misleading indicator of real (remember *real* always means adjusted for inflation) borrowing cost and lending return. The money interest will vary directly with the expected rate of inflation. The higher the expected rate of inflation, the greater the inflationary premium and therefore the larger the money rate of interest. However, it is the *real* interest rate—the money interest rate minus the inflationary premium—that reflects the true cost of borrowing and return to lending. (See the Myths of Economics box on inflation for further explanation.)

The circular-flow diagram (Exhibit 9–1) illustrates both the inflow and outflow to the loanable funds market. The net saving of households and net capital inflow from foreigners provide the inflow—the supply of funds—into the loanable funds market. The borrowing of businesses for investment projects and of governments for the finance of budget deficits leads to the outflow of funds. This borrowing generates the demand for loanable funds. Businesses and governments often borrow funds by issuing bonds that yield an interest rate. Issuing bonds is simply a method of demanding loanable funds. In turn, the purchasers of bonds are supplying loanable funds. It is important to note that there is an inverse relationship between bond prices and interest rates. ***Higher bond prices are the same thing as lower interest rates.*** (See the Applications in Economics box on bonds and interest rates for further explanation.)

In an open economy like that of the United States, domestic residents are also able to borrow from and lend to foreigners. When foreigners supply more loanable funds than they demand, there will be a net inflow of foreign capital that will supplement domestic saving. On the other hand, if foreigners are net borrowers, there will be a net outflow of capital from the domestic market. The real interest rate in the loanable funds market will move toward the rate that will bring the quantity of funds demanded into equality with the quantity supplied, *including the net inflow or outflow of capital.*

MYTHS OF ECONOMICS

"Because inflation erodes the burden of outstanding debt, it systematically helps borrowers at the expense of lenders."

Like most myths, this one has a grain of truth in it. Inflation does reduce the purchasing power of the proceeds paid by borrowers and received by lenders during the period while a loan is outstanding. But this is only part of the story. *Inflation also influences money interest rates* and therefore the amount paid by borrowers and received by lenders when funds are borrowed.

When higher rates of inflation are anticipated by decision makers, lenders will demand and borrowers will grant higher interest rates on loans because both parties will expect the value of the dollar to depreciate during the period that the loan is outstanding (see Exhibit 9–8). If borrowers and lenders accurately anticipate a rate of inflation, they will agree to a money interest rate that will be just high enough to compensate for the effects of inflation on the purchasing power of the loan proceeds during the period the loan is outstanding.

Of course, decision makers will not always be able to forecast the future rate of inflation accurately. Sometimes the rate of inflation will be higher than was expected, while in other instances it will be lower. There is no reason, however, to expect that these errors in forecasting future inflation rates will be systematic.

If the actual rate of inflation is higher than was expected, borrowers will tend to gain relative to lenders. For example, suppose borrowers and lenders expect a 3 percent future rate of inflation and therefore agree to an 8 percent interest rate on a loan—5 percent representing the real interest rate and 3 percent the inflation premium. If the actual rate of inflation turns out to be higher than 3 percent—6 percent, for example—the real amount paid by the borrower and received by the lender will decline. *When the actual rate of inflation is greater than was anticipated, borrowers gain relative to lenders.*

But the converse is true when the actual rate of inflation is less than expected. Suppose that after the borrower and lender agree to the 8 percent loan, the price level is stable while the loan is outstanding. In this case, the borrower ends up paying an 8 percent real interest rate, rather than the 5 percent that was anticipated. *When the actual rate of inflation is less than anticipated, lenders gain at the expense of borrowers.*

Thus, it is not inflation per se that produces redistributional effects, but rather the actual rate of inflation relative to the expected rate. ***Because there is no reason to believe that borrowers and lenders will systematically either underestimate or overestimate the future rate of inflation, there is no reason to believe that it will systematically help one relative to the other.***

In today's global financial markets, the flow of capital to the domestic loanable funds market will be directly related to the real interest rate. As **Exhibit 9–9** shows, when domestic demand is weak (D_1 for example) and the real interest rate low (r_1), capital will flow outward toward other markets where the rate of return is expected to be higher. In contrast, strong domestic demand (D_2 for example) for loanable funds and high real interest rates will lead to an inflow of capital.

Like the resource market, the loanable funds market is interrelated with the goods and services market. We previously indicated that the reduction in the interest rate that generally accompanies a lower price level when the supply of money is constant helps explain why the *AD* curve slopes downward to the right. In addition, the real interest rate may change for other reasons. When it does, it will affect the aggregate demand schedule. The real interest rate influences how households allocate their income between saving and current consumption. An increase in the interest rate will discourage current consumption by making it more attractive to save and more expensive to borrow. Thus, other things constant, higher interest rates will reduce current consumption and thereby reduce aggregate demand. Lower interest rates will exert the opposite effects. As we proceed, we will analyze in more detail the interrelationship between the loanable funds market and the goods and services market.

When an economy is in long-run equilibrium, the relationship between interest rates in the loanable funds market and prices in product and resource markets will be such that the typical firm is just able to earn normal returns on its investments. In other words, the typical producer's return to capital must equal the interest rate—that

APPLICATIONS IN ECONOMICS

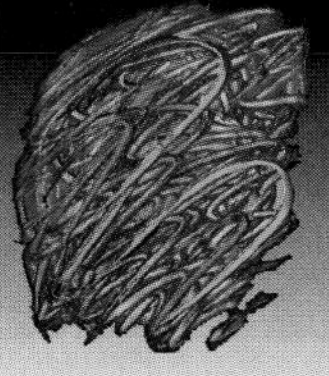

Bonds, Interest Rates, and Bond Prices

Bonds are simply IOUs issued by firms and governments. Issuing bonds is a method of borrowing money to finance economic activity. The entity issuing the bond promises to pay the bondholder the amount borrowed (called principal) plus a *fixed* interest rate (known as the coupon rate) while the bond is outstanding. The interest payments are generally made twice a year and the repayment of the principal is due at a designated future date, usually a set number of years (for example, five or ten) after the bond is issued.

Even though interest rates may change with the passage of time, *the bondholder will receive the fixed interest rate as a percentage of the original principal throughout the life of the bond.* Although bonds are issued for lengthy periods of time—the U.S. Treasury issues bonds for up to 30 years—they can be sold to another party prior to their maturity. Each day, sales of previously issued bonds comprise the majority of bonds bought and sold on the bond market.

When overall interest rates rise, the prices of outstanding bonds will fall, and vice versa. Suppose you bought a newly issued $1,000 bond that pays 8 percent per year in perpetuity (forever) on the $1,000 principal.[1] As long as you own the bond, you are entitled to a fixed return of $80 per year. Let us also assume that after you have held the bond for one year and have collected your $80 interest for that year, the market rate of interest for newly issued bonds like yours increases to 10 percent. How will this increase in the interest rate affect the market price of your bond? Because bond purchasers can now earn 10 percent interest if they buy newly issued bonds, they will be unwilling to pay more than $800 for your bond, which pays only $80 interest per year. After all, why would anyone pay $1,000 for a bond that yields only $80 interest per year when the same $1,000 will now purchase a bond that yields $100 (10 percent) per year? The increase in the interest rate to 10 percent will cause the *market price* of your $1,000 bond (which earns only 8 percent annually) to fall to $800. At that price, the new owners would earn the 10 percent market rate of interest. In this manner, rising market interest rates cause bond prices to decline.

On the other hand, falling interest rates will cause bond prices to rise. If the market interest rate had fallen to 6 percent, what would have happened to the market value of your bond? (*Hint:* $80 is 6 percent of $1,333.) ***Thus, bond prices and interest rates are inversely linked to each other.***

[1]Undated securities of this sort are available in the United Kingdom. They are called *consols.*

EXHIBIT 9-9

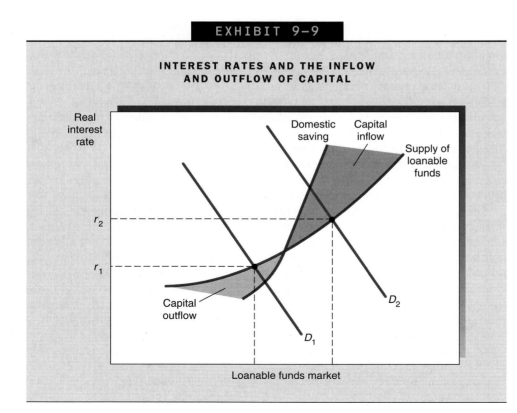

INTEREST RATES AND THE INFLOW AND OUTFLOW OF CAPITAL

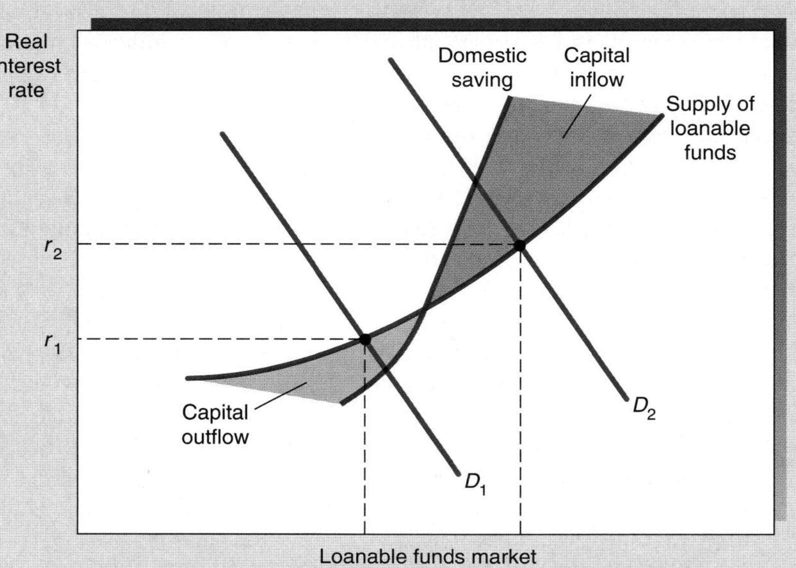

Demand and supply in the loanable funds market will determine the interest rate. When the demand for loanable funds is strong (like D_2), the real interest rate will be high (r_2) and there will be a net inflow of capital. In contrast, weak demand (like D_1) and low interest rates (like r_1) will lead to net capital outflow.

is, the opportunity cost of capital. Higher returns would induce producers to expand output, while lower returns would cause them to cut back on production.

FOREIGN EXCHANGE MARKET

Look back at Exhibit 9–1 and note the various transactions with foreigners. Households import some goods and services from foreigners, reducing the flow of spending into the product market. Businesses export some of the domestically produced goods to foreigners, which adds to the flow of spending into the product market. In addition, there is an inflow and outflow of capital in the loanable funds market. As we just discussed, the size and direction of this capital flow are dependent on the real interest rate.

International transactions generally require one of the trading partners to convert domestic currency to that of the other. As we noted in Chapter 4, this conversion takes place in the foreign exchange market, a market where the currency of one nation is traded for that of another. When Americans buy from foreigners and make investments abroad (an outflow of capital), they will require foreign currency for these purchases. Thus, these transactions generate a demand for foreign currency in the foreign exchange market. On the other hand, when Americans sell products and assets (including bonds) to foreigners, the transactions will generate a supply of foreign currency in exchange for dollars. Thus, the dollar demand for foreign currency emanates from Americans' purchases from foreigners, while the supply of foreign currency in exchange for dollars reflects Americans' sales to foreigners.

Exhibit 9–10 illustrates how the foreign exchange market will tend to bring the purchases from and sales to foreigners into balance. The dollar price of foreign currency is measured along the vertical axis. A reduction in the dollar price of foreign exchange—movement down the vertical axis—means that a dollar will buy more units of various foreign currencies. This will make it cheaper for Americans to purchase things from foreigners. Thus, we say that the dollar has **appreciated,** meaning that it will now buy more foreign goods than was previously true. As the dollar price for foreign exchange falls (movement down the vertical axis), Americans buy more from foreigners and therefore demand a larger quantity of foreign exchange for the purchases. Thus, the dollar demand for foreign currency will slope downward to the right. In contrast, an increase in the dollar price of foreign exchange—movement up the vertical axis—indicates that more dollars are required to purchase a unit of foreign currency. This makes foreign purchases more expensive for Americans and, therefore, it is referred to as a **depreciation** of the dollar. As the dollar depreciates, a unit of foreign currency will purchase a large quantity of dollars. This depreciation in the dollar will make American goods less expensive for foreigners. As the dollar depreciates (movement up the vertical axis), foreigners buy more from Americans and therefore supply more foreign currency in exchange for dollars. Thus, the supply curve for foreign exchange will slope upward to the right.

Appreciation
An increase in the value of a currency relative to foreign currencies. An appreciation increases the purchasing power of the currency over foreign goods.

Depreciation
A reduction in the value of a currency relative to foreign currencies. A depreciation reduces the purchasing power of the currency over foreign goods.

The forces of supply and demand in the foreign exchange market will move the exchange rate toward the equilibrium price (P in Exhibit 9–10). In equilibrium, the quantity demanded of foreign exchange will just equal the quantity supplied. When this is true, imports plus the outflow of capital for investment abroad will equal exports plus the inflow of capital from the investments of foreigners in the United States. Mathematically, when the exchange market is in equilibrium, the following relationship exists:

$$\text{Imports} + \text{Capital outflow} = \text{Exports} + \text{Capital inflow} \qquad (9\text{-}1)$$

This relationship can be rewritten in the following manner:

$$\text{Imports} - \text{Exports} = \text{Capital inflow} - \text{Capital outflow} \qquad (9\text{-}2)$$

The right side of Equation 9-2 is also called *net capital inflow.* Because it is a net fig-

EXHIBIT 9-10

FOREIGN EXCHANGE MARKET

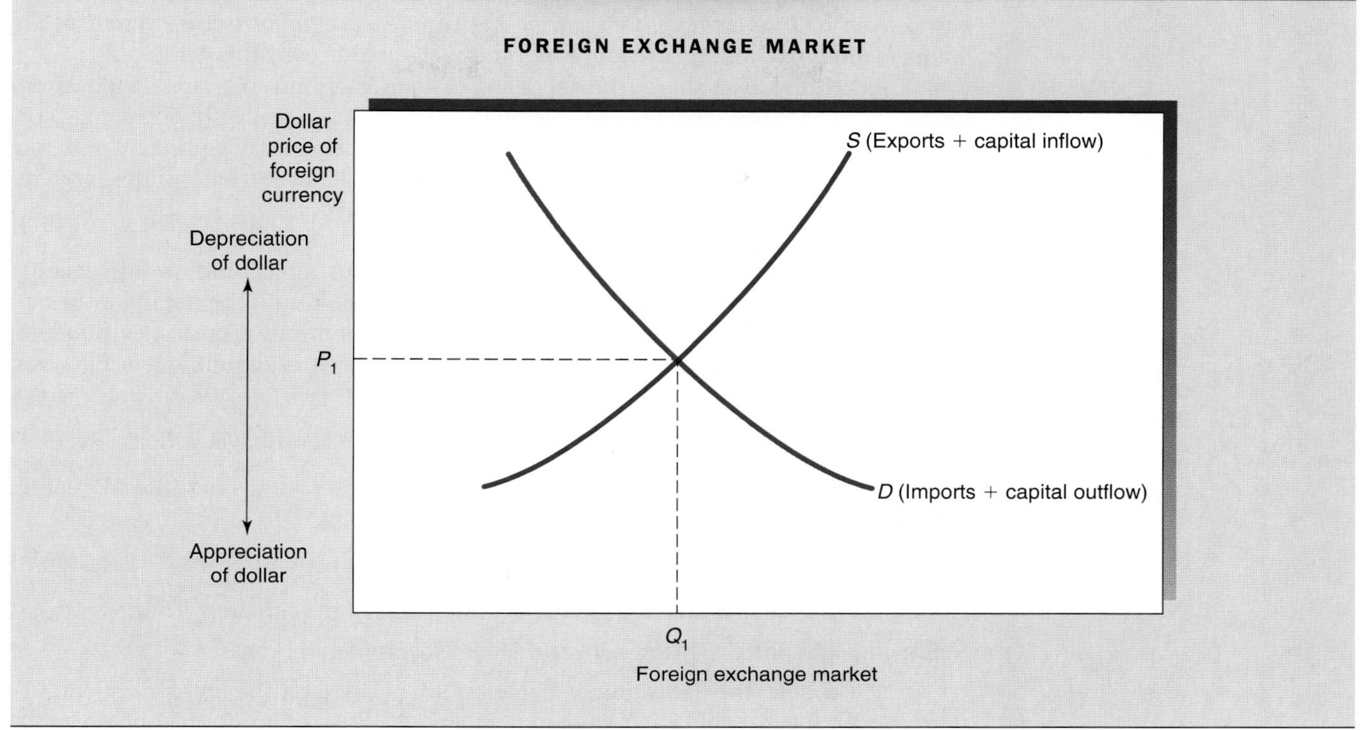

Americans demand foreign currencies in order to import goods and services and make investments abroad. Foreigners supply their currency in exchange for dollars in order to purchase American exports and undertake investments in the United States. The exchange rate will bring the quantity demanded into balance with the quantity supplied. This will also bring imports + capital outflow into equality with exports + capital inflow.

ure, it can be either positive (indicating an inflow of capital) or negative (indicating an outflow of capital).

A **trade deficit** is present when imports exceed exports. On the other hand, a **trade surplus** exists when exports exceed imports. There is an interesting implication of the relationship between the flow of trade and the flow of capital: When a trade deficit is present, there must be an inflow of capital. The reverse is also true: An inflow of capital implies a trade deficit. On the other hand, when a trade surplus (exports exceed imports) is present, there must also be an outflow of capital.

Trade deficit
The situation when a country's imports of goods and services are greater than its exports.

Trade surplus
The situation when a country's exports of goods and services are greater than its imports.

LEAKAGE AND INJECTIONS FROM THE CIRCULAR FLOW OF INCOME

If you look back at Exhibit 9–1, you will note that there are three leakages of the income received by households: saving, taxes, and imports. As the three arrows (other than the consumption of households) into the goods and services market indicate, there are also three injections of expenditures into the circular flow of income: investment, government purchases, and exports.

For macro equilibrium to be present, the flow of expenditures on goods and services (top loop of Exhibit 9–1) must equal the flow of income to resource owners

(bottom loop). This will be true if the injections (investment, government purchases, and exports) into the circular flow are equal to the leakages (saving, taxes, and imports) from it. Interestingly, this will be the case when equilibrium is present in the loanable funds and foreign exchange markets. Let's analyze why this is the case.

As Exhibit 9–1 shows, the net saving of households plus net capital inflow from foreigners provide the supply of loanable funds market. Business investment and government borrowing to finance budget deficits generate the demand. When the interest rate brings these two forces into balance, it means that the following relationship is present:

$$\text{Net saving} + \text{Net capital inflow} = \text{Investment} + \text{Budget deficit} \qquad (9\text{-}3)$$

The foreign exchange market brings imports plus capital outflow into equality with exports plus capital inflow (Equation 9-1 above). As a result, the net inflow of capital (capital inflow – capital outflow) is equal to imports minus exports (see Equation 9-2 above). Substituting imports minus exports for the net capital inflow in Equation 9-3 yields:

$$\text{Net saving} + \text{Imports} - \text{Exports} = \text{Investment} + \text{Budget deficit} \qquad (9\text{-}4)$$

Because the budget deficit is merely government purchases minus net taxes, Equation 9-4 can be rewritten as:

$$\text{Net saving} + \text{Imports} - \text{Exports} = \text{Investment} + \text{Government purchases} - \text{Taxes} \quad (9\text{-}5)$$

Finally, moving exports and taxes to the opposite sides of the equation yields:

$$\text{Net saving} + \text{Imports} + \text{Taxes} = \text{Investment} + \text{Government purchases} + \text{Exports} \quad (9\text{-}6)$$

Of course, the derivation of Equation 9-6 is based on the presence of equilibrium in both the loanable funds and foreign markets. When interest rates and exchange

THUMBNAIL SKETCH

Key Macro Market Relationships

1. Equilibrium in Foreign Exchange Market implies:

   Imports + Capital outflow = Exports + Capital inflow

2. Because *net* capital inflow is capital inflow minus capital outflow, the equation in 1 can be rewritten as:

   Imports – Exports = Net capital inflow

3. Equilibrium in Loanable Funds Market implies:

   Net saving + Net capital inflow = Investment + Budget deficit

4. Substituting the left side of the equation in 2 for net capital inflow yields:

   Net saving + Imports – Exports = Investment + Budget deficit

5. Because the budget deficit is government purchases minus taxes, the equation in 4 can be rewritten as:

   Net saving + Imports – Exports = Investment + Government purchases – Taxes

6. The equation in 5 can be rewritten as:

   Net saving + Imports + Taxes = Investment + Government purchases + Exports

Therefore, when the loanable funds and foreign exchange markets are in equilibrium, the leakages from the circular flow of income (saving + imports + taxes) and the injections into it (investment + government purchases + exports) will be equal.

rates bring these markets into equilibrium, they will also bring the leakage from (left side of Equation 9-6) and injection to (right side of Equation 9-6) the circular flow of income into balance. The accompanying Thumbnail Sketch provides a shorthand summary of the key relationships underlying this proposition.

LOOKING *Ahead*

We have now discussed all four basic macroeconomic markets: goods and services, resources, loanable funds, and foreign exchange. Like the legs of a chair, these four macroeconomic markets are dependent on each other. When an economy is in long-run equilibrium, the interrelationships among these four markets will be in harmony. The relationship among resource prices, interest rates, and product prices will be such that the firms will earn, on average, only a competitive rate of return. Correspondingly, the interest rates and exchange rates will bring the injections into the circular flow of income into balance with the leakages from it. When people correctly anticipate the current price level (rate of inflation), there are reasons to believe that market adjustments will move an economy toward long-run equilibrium.

However, we live in a world of dynamic change and unexpected events. How will the economy adjust to unanticipated economic shocks? The macro model developed in this chapter will help us address this question. Macroeconomics largely concerns tracing the impact of a change in one market through to other markets, particularly the goods and services market. In the following chapter, we will analyze how changing conditions influence the performance of an economy.

KEY POINTS

➤ The circular flow of income and expenditures highlights the significance of four key markets in the coordination of the macroeconomy: (a) goods and services, (b) resources, (c) loanable funds, and (d) foreign exchange.

➤ The aggregate demand curve indicates the various quantities of domestically produced goods and services purchasers are willing to buy at different price levels. It will slope downward to the right because consumers, investors, governments, and foreigners (net exports) will purchase a larger quantity at a lower price level.

➤ The aggregate supply (*AS*) curve indicates the various quantities of goods and services domestic suppliers will produce at different price levels. The short-run aggregate supply (*SRAS*) curve will slope upward to the right because a higher price level will improve profit margins when important cost components are temporarily fixed in the short run.

➤ In the long run, output is constrained by the economy's resource base, current technology, and efficiency of the existing institutions. A higher price level does not loosen these constraints. Thus, the long-run aggregate supply (*LRAS*) curve is vertical.

➤ Two conditions are necessary for long-run equilibrium in the goods and services market: (a) quantity demanded must equal quantity supplied, and (b) the *actual* price level must equal the price level decision makers *anticipated* when they made buying and selling decisions for the current period.

➤ When the economy is in long-run equilibrium, output will be at its maximum sustainable level. At this output level, full employment is present and the *actual rate* of unemployment will equal the *natural rate.*

➤ The aggregate demand/aggregate supply model reveals the determinants of the price level and real output.

In the short run, price and output will move toward an intersection of the aggregate demand (*AD*) and short-run aggregate supply (*SRAS*) curves. In the long run, price and output will gravitate to the levels represented by the intersection of *AD, SRAS,* and *LRAS.*

➤ When the economy is in long-run equilibrium, potential output will be achieved and full employment will be present (the actual rate of unemployment will equal the natural rate).

➤ It is important to distinguish between real and money interest rates. The real interest rate reflects the real burden to borrowers and the payoff to lenders in terms of command over goods and services. The real rate of interest is equal to the money rate of interest minus the inflation premium. The latter depends on the expected rate of inflation.

➤ When equilibrium is present in the loanable funds and foreign exchange markets, the injections (investment, government purchases, and exports) into the circular flow of income will equal the leakages (saving, taxes, and imports) from it.

➤ Macroeconomic equilibrium requires that equilibrium be achieved in all four key macroeconomic markets and that the interrelationships among these markets must be in harmony.

CRITICAL ANALYSIS QUESTIONS

1. In your own words, explain why aggregate demand is inversely related to the price level. Why does the explanation for the inverse relationship between price and quantity demanded for the aggregate demand curve differ from that of a demand curve for a specific good?

2. What are the major factors that influence our ability to produce goods and services in the long run? Why is the long-run aggregate supply curve vertical?

3. Why does the short-run aggregate supply curve slope upward to the right? If the prices of both (a) resources and (b) goods and services increased proportionally (by the same percent), would business firms be willing to expand output? Why or why not?

*4. Suppose prices had been rising at a 3 percent annual rate in recent years. A major union signs a three-year contract calling for increases in money wage rates of 6 percent annually. What will happen to the real wages of the union members if the price level is constant (unchanged) during the next three years? If other unions sign similar contracts, what will probably happen to the unemployment rate? Why? Answer the same questions under conditions in which the price level increases at an annual rate of 8 percent during the next three years.

5. What is the current money interest rate on 30-year government bonds? Is this also the real interest rate? Why or why not?

6. What is the natural rate of unemployment? Why might the actual rate of unemployment differ from the natural rate of unemployment? If the actual rate of unemployment is less than the natural rate, can this situation be sustained over a long period of time? Why or why not?

*7. In Chapter 3, we indicated the other things that are held constant when the supply and demand schedules for a specific good are constructed. What were they? What are the key "other things" held constant when the *AS, LRAS,* and *SRAS* schedules are constructed?

8. If the price level in the current period is higher than what buyers and sellers anticipated, what will tend to happen to real wages and the level of employment? How will the profit margins of business firms be affected? How will the actual rate of unemployment compare with the natural rate of unemployment? Will the current rate of output be sustainable in the future? Why or why not?

9. Suppose that you purchased a $5,000 bond that pays 6 percent interest annually and matures in five years. If the inflation rate in recent years has been steady at 3 percent annually, what is the estimated real rate of interest? If the inflation rate during the next five years remains steady at 3 percent, what real rate of return will you earn? If the inflation rate during the next five years is 6 percent, what will happen to your real rate of return?

*10. How are the following related to each other?
   a. The long-run equilibrium rate of output
   b. The potential real GDP of the economy
   c. The output rate resulting in the equality of the actual and natural rates of unemployment

11. Does inflation help debtors relative to lenders? Why or why not? Do you think that inflation will help people with low incomes relative to those with higher incomes? Explain. How will an unanticipated increase in the inflation rate influence the government's liability for the

national debt? Is the government helped by inflation? Discuss.

*12. If a bond pays $1,000 per year in perpetuity (each year in the future), what will be the market price of the bond when the long-term interest rate is 10 percent? What would it be if the interest rate were 5 percent?

*13. How are bond prices related to interest rates? Why are they related?

14. The following chart indicates the aggregate demand (*AD*) and short-run aggregate supply (*SRAS*) schedules of decision makers for the current period. Both buyers and sellers previously anticipated that the price level during the current period would be P_{105}.

a. Indicate the quantity of GDP that will be produced during this period.

b. Will it be a long-run equilibrium level of GDP? Why or why not?

c. What will be the relationship between the actual and natural rates of unemployment during the period? Explain your answer.

AD_{105}	PRICE LEVEL	$SRAS_{105}$
6,300	90	4,500
6,000	95	4,800
5,700	100	5,100
5,400	105	5,400
5,100	110	5,700
4,800	115	6,000

15. Consider an economy with the following aggregate demand (*AD*) and short-run aggregate supply (*SR*) schedules. Decision makers have previously made decisions anticipating that the price level during the current period would be P_{105}.

a. Indicate the quantity of GDP that will be produced during the period.

b. Is it a long-run equilibrium level of GDP? Why or why not?

c. How will the unemployment rate during the current period compare with this economy's natural rate of unemployment?

d. Will the current rate of GDP be sustainable into the future? Why or why not?

AD_{105}	PRICE LEVEL	$SRAS_{105}$
6,900	90	4,500
6,600	95	4,800
6,300	100	5,100
6,000	105	5,400
5,700	110	5,700
5,400	115	6,000

16. Show that when equilibrium is present in the loanable funds and foreign exchange markets, the leakages from the circular flow of income will just equal the injections into the circular flow.

*Asterisk denotes questions for which answers are given in Appendix B.

CHAPTER 10

We might as well reasonably dispute whether it is the upper or under blade of a pair of scissors that cuts a piece of paper, as whether value is governed by [demand] or [supply].

Alfred Marshall[1]

Working with Our Basic Aggregate Demand/Aggregate Supply Model

CHAPTER FOCUS

- What factors will cause shifts in aggregate demand? What factors will shift aggregate supply?
- How will the goods and services market adjust to changes in aggregate demand?
- How does the economy adjust to changes in aggregate supply?
- What are the causes of recessions and booms?
- Does a market economy have a self-correcting mechanism that will lead it to full employment?

[1]Alfred Marshall, *Principles of Economics,* 8th ed. (London: Macmillan, 1920), p. 348.

In Chapter 9, we focused on the equilibrium conditions in the four basic macroeconomic markets. Equilibrium is important, but we live in a dynamic world that continually wars against it. Markets are always being affected by unexpected changes, such as the discovery of a vastly improved computer chip, shifts in consumer confidence, a drought in Midwestern agricultural states, or changes in defense expenditures as the result of national security conditions. Consequently, equilibrium is continually disrupted. Thus, if we want to understand how the real world works, analysis of how macroeconomic markets adjust to dynamic change is of crucial importance.

We are now ready to consider how macroeconomic markets adjust to changes in aggregate demand and aggregate supply. As in the preceding chapter, we will continue to assume that the government's tax, spending, and monetary policies are unchanged. For now, we want to help the reader understand how macroeconomic markets work. Once this objective is achieved, we will be better able to understand both the potential and the limitations of macroeconomic policy.

ANTICIPATED AND UNANTICIPATED CHANGES

Anticipated change
A change that is foreseen by decision makers in time for them to adjust.

As we noted in the discussion of inflation in Chapter 8, it is important to distinguish between changes in the general level of prices that are anticipated and those that are unanticipated. This distinction is important in several areas of economics. **Anticipated changes** are foreseen by economic participants. Decision makers have time to adjust to them before they occur. For example, suppose that, under normal weather conditions, a new drought-resistant hybrid seed can be expected to expand the production of feed grain in the Midwest by 10 percent next year. As a result, buyers and sellers will plan for a larger supply and lower prices in the future. They will adjust their decision-making behavior accordingly.

Unanticipated change
A change that decision makers could not reasonably foresee. Thus, choices made prior to the event did not take the event into account.

In contrast, **unanticipated changes** catch people by surprise. Our world is characterized by dynamic change—new products are introduced, technological discoveries alter production costs, droughts reduce crop yields, demand expands for some goods and contracts for others. It is impossible for decision makers to foresee many of these changes.

Economics largely concerns how people respond and markets adjust to changing circumstances. As we will explain in a moment, there is good reason to expect that the adjustment process will differ depending on whether a change is anticipated.

FACTORS THAT SHIFT AGGREGATE DEMAND

The aggregate demand curve isolates the impact of the price level on the quantity demanded of goods and services. As we discussed in the previous chapter, a reduction in the price level will (1) increase the wealth of people holding the fixed quantity of money, (2) reduce the real rate of interest, and (3) make domestically produced goods cheaper compared to those produced abroad. All three of these factors will lead to an increase in the quantity of goods and services demanded at the lower price level.

The price level, however, is not the only factor that influences the demand for goods and services. When we constructed the aggregate demand curve, we assumed that several other factors affecting the choices of buyers in the goods and services market were constant. Changes in these "other factors" will shift the entire aggregate demand schedule, altering the amount purchased at each price level. Let us take a closer look at the major factors that will cause shifts in aggregate demand.

1. Changes in Real Wealth. Stock prices in the United States increased by more than 25 percent annually in the period 1995 to 1998. This stock market boom increased the real wealth of stockholders. In contrast, both stock prices and housing prices declined during 1990, reducing the real wealth of households.

How will changes in the wealth of households affect the demand for goods and services? As the real wealth of households increases—perhaps as the result of higher prices in stock, housing, and/or real estate markets—people will demand more goods and services. As **Exhibit 10–1** illustrates, this increase in wealth will shift the entire aggregate demand (AD) schedule to the right (from AD_0 to AD_1). More goods and services are purchased at each price level. Conversely, a reduction in wealth will reduce the demand for goods and services, shifting the AD curve to the left (to AD_2).

2. Changes in the Real Interest Rate. As we discussed previously, the major macroeconomic markets are closely related. A change in the real interest rate in the loanable funds market will influence the choices of consumers and investors in the goods and

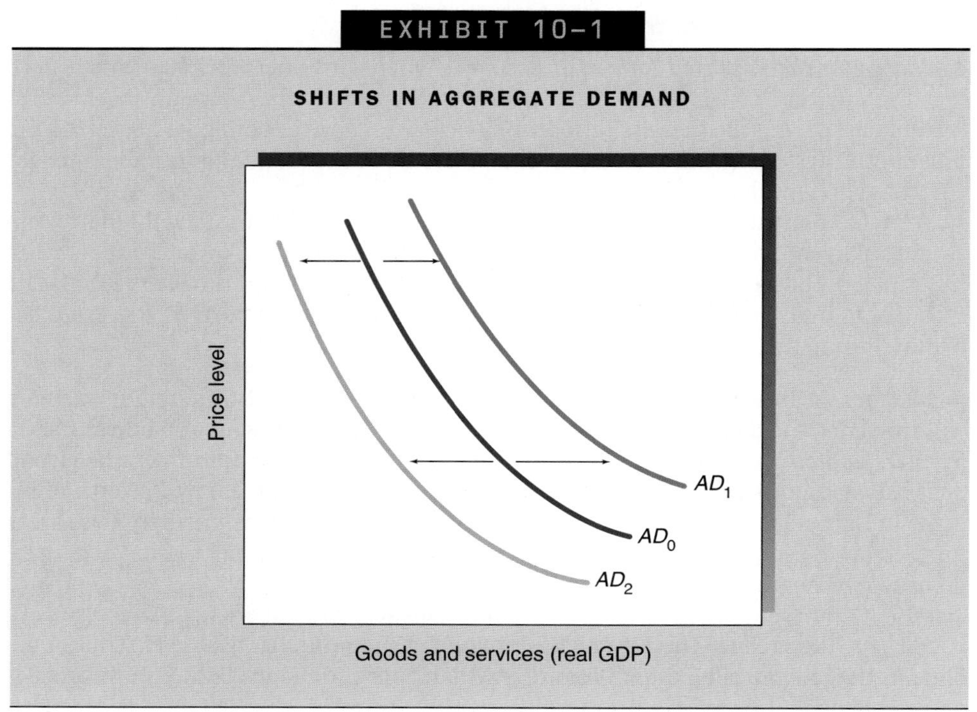

An increase in real wealth, such as would result from a stock market boom, for example, will increase aggregate demand, shifting the entire curve to the right (from AD_0 *to* AD_1*). In contrast, a reduction in real wealth decreases the demand for goods and services, causing* AD *to shift to the left (from* AD_0 *to* AD_2*).*

services market. A lower real interest rate makes it cheaper for consumers to buy major appliances, automobiles, and houses now rather than in the future. Simultaneously, a lower interest rate will also stimulate business spending on capital goods (investment). The interest rate influences the opportunity cost of all investment projects. If the firm must borrow, the real interest rate will contribute directly to the cost of an investment project. Even if the firm uses its own funds, it sacrifices real interest that could have been earned by loaning the funds to someone else. Therefore, a lower real interest rate reduces the opportunity cost of a project, regardless of whether it is financed with internal funds or by borrowing.

Because a reduction in the real interest rate makes both consumer and investment goods cheaper, both households and investors will increase their current expenditures in response. In turn, their additional expenditures will increase aggregate demand, shifting the entire schedule to the right. In contrast, a higher real interest rate makes current consumption and investment goods more expensive, which leads to a reduction in aggregate demand, shifting the *AD* curve to the left.

3. Change in the Expectations of Businesses and Households about the Future Direction of the Economy. What people think will happen in the future influences current purchasing decisions. Optimism concerning the future direction of the economy will stimulate current investment. Business decision makers know that an expanding economy will mean strong sales and improved profit margins. Investment today may be necessary if business firms are going to benefit fully from these opportunities. Similarly, consumers are more likely to buy big-ticket items, such as automobiles and houses, when they expect an expanding economy to provide them with both job security and rising income in the future. So increased optimism encourages additional current expenditures by both investors and consumers, increasing aggregate demand.

Of course, pessimism about the future state of the economy exerts just the opposite effect. When investors and consumers expect an economic downturn (a recession), they will cut back on their current spending for fear of becoming overextended. This pessimism leads to a decline in aggregate demand, shifting the *AD* schedule to the left.

4. Change in the Expected Rate of Inflation. When consumers and investors believe that the inflation rate is going to accelerate in the future, they have an incentive to spend more during the current period. "Buy now before prices go higher" becomes the order of the day. Thus, the expectation of an increase in the inflation rate will stimulate current aggregate demand, shifting the *AD* curve to the right.

In contrast, the expectation of a decline in the inflation rate will tend to discourage current spending. When prices are expected to stabilize (or at least increase less rapidly), the gain obtained by moving expenditures forward in time is reduced. The expectation of a reduction in the inflation rate will thus reduce current aggregate demand, shifting the *AD* curve to the left.

5. Changes in Income Abroad. Changes in the income of a nation's trading partners will influence the demand for the nation's exports. If the income of a nation's trading partners is increasing rapidly, the demand for exports will expand. In turn, the strong demand for exports will stimulate aggregate demand. For example, rapid growth of income in Europe, Canada, and Mexico increases the demand of consumers in these areas for U.S.-produced goods. This will cause U.S. exports to expand, increasing aggregate demand (shifting the *AD* schedule to the right).

Conversely, when a nation's trading partners are experiencing recessionary conditions, they reduce their purchases, including their purchases abroad. Thus, a decline in the income of a nation's trading partners tends to reduce both exports and aggregate demand.

Currently, approximately 12 percent of the goods and services produced in the United States are sold to purchasers abroad. The export sector is still larger for Canada, Mexico, and most Western European countries. The larger the size of the trade sector, the greater the potential importance of fluctuations in income abroad as a source of instability in aggregate demand. If the demand of foreign buyers does not rise and fall at the same time as domestic demand, however, the diversity of markets will reduce the magnitude of fluctuations in domestic demand.

6. Changes in Exchange Rates. As we previously explained, changes in exchange rates will influence the relative price of both imports and exports. An appreciation in the value of the dollar on the foreign exchange market will make it cheaper for Americans to purchase imported goods and more expensive for foreigners to purchase U.S. exports. As a result, U.S. imports will rise and exports will fall. Other things constant, the decline in net exports (exports − imports) will reduce aggregate demand (shift the *AD* schedule to the left).

Consider the impact of an increase in the foreign exchange value of the dollar relative to the Mexican peso, such as occurred during the Mexican financial crisis. In late 1994 and early 1995, the number of pesos that could be purchased with a dollar approximately doubled in just a few months. As a result of this appreciation of the dollar (and depreciation of the peso), Mexican imports were cheaper for American consumers. At the lower *dollar price,* Americans imported more goods from Mexico. Simultaneously, the depreciation of the peso made the prices of U.S. goods more expensive in terms of pesos. As a result, U.S. exports to Mexico fell. This reduction in net exports, reflecting the increase in imports from and reduction in exports to Mexico, placed some downward pressure on aggregate demand. More recently, an appreciation of the dollar relative to most Asian currencies exerted a similar impact. As the dollar appreciated (and the Asian currencies depreciated), net exports to Asian countries fell sharply during 1998, causing a reduction in aggregate demand in the United States.

A decline in the exchange rate value of the dollar will have just the opposite effect. When there is a reduction in the value of the dollar on the foreign exchange market, foreign-produced goods become more expensive for U.S. consumers, while U.S.–produced goods become cheaper for foreigners. As a result, net exports will increase and thereby stimulate aggregate demand (shifting *AD* to the right).[2]

The accompanying Thumbnail Sketch summarizes the major factors causing shifts in aggregate demand. Next, we will analyze how the goods and services market

THUMBNAIL SKETCH

What Factors Will Influence Aggregate Demand?

These factors will increase (decrease) aggregate demand (*AD*).[a]

1. An increase (decrease) in real wealth.
2. A decrease (increase) in the real rate of interest.
3. An increase in the optimism (pessimism) of businesses and consumers about future economic conditions.
4. An increase (decline) in the expected rate of inflation.
5. Higher (lower) real incomes abroad.
6. A reduction (increase) in the exchange rate value of the nation's currency.

[a]The important factors of macroeconomic policy will be considered later.

[2]Later, when discussing international finance, we will analyze the determinants of the exchange rate and consider how changes in exchange rates impact both trade and macroeconomic markets in more detail.

adjusts to changes in demand. The government's spending, taxing, and monetary policies also influence aggregate demand. Knowledge of how the goods and services market works will lay the foundation for the analysis of fiscal and monetary policies, topics that will be addressed in later chapters.

UNANTICIPATED CHANGES IN AGGREGATE DEMAND

How will unanticipated changes in aggregate demand influence price and output in the goods and services market? It will take time for decision makers to respond fully to unexpected changes. Initially, it may be unclear to decision makers whether a change—an increase in sales, for example—reflects a random occurrence or a real change in demand conditions. It will also take businesses some time to differentiate between temporary fluctuations and more permanent changes. Even after decision makers are convinced that market conditions have changed, time will be required for them to make new decisions and carry them out. In some cases, complete adjustment will also be delayed by the presence of long-term contracts. All these factors will reduce the speed of market adjustments to unexpected changes in demand conditions.

INCREASES IN AGGREGATE DEMAND

Part a of **Exhibit 10–2** illustrates how an economy that is initially in long-run equilibrium will adjust to an unanticipated increase in aggregate demand. Initially the economy is in long-run equilibrium at output Y_F and price level P_{100} (point E_1). Aggregate demand and aggregate supply are in balance. Decision makers have correctly anticipated the current price level, and the economy is operating at its full-employment level of output.

In response to an unanticipated increase in aggregate demand for goods and services (shift from AD_1 *to* AD_2*), prices will rise (to* P_{105}*) in the short run and output will temporarily exceed full-employment capacity (a). However, with the passage of time, prices in resource markets, including the labor market, will rise as the result of the strong demand. The higher resource prices will mean higher costs, which will reduce aggregate supply to* $SRAS_2$ *(b). In the long run, a new equilibrium at a higher price level (*P_{110}*) and an output consistent with the economy's sustainable potential will result. Thus, the increase in demand will expand output only temporarily.*

EXHIBIT 10–2

UNANTICIPATED INCREASE IN AGGREGATE DEMAND

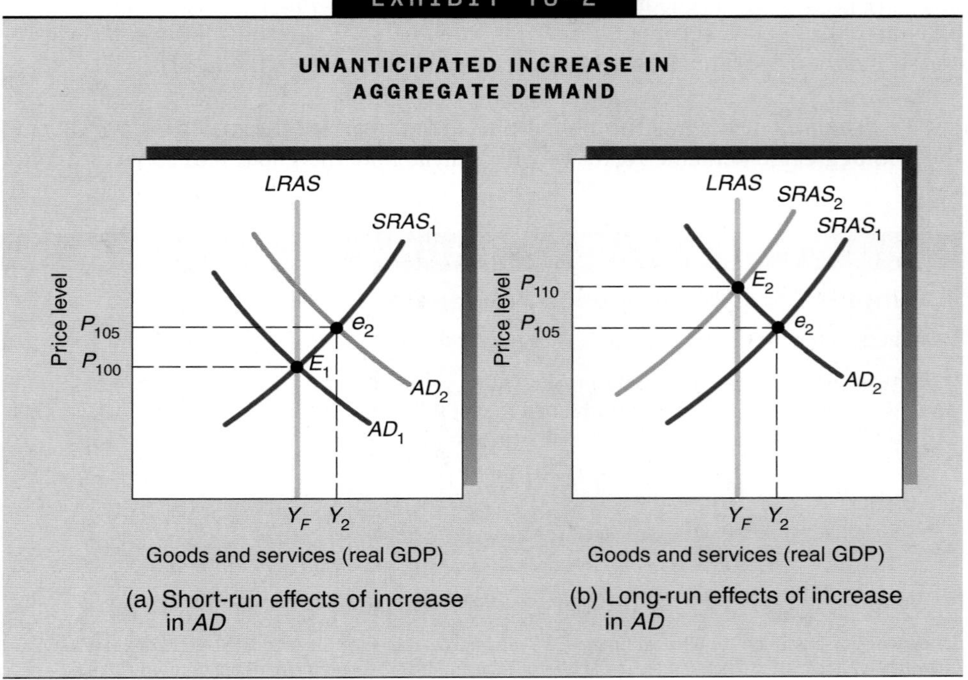

(a) Short-run effects of increase in *AD*

(b) Long-run effects of increase in *AD*

Consider what would happen if this equilibrium were disrupted by an unanticipated increase in aggregate demand (shift from AD_1 to AD_2) due to a stock market boom or the rapid growth of income abroad. An excess demand for goods and services would result at the initial price level (P_{100}). Responding to the strong sales and excess demand, businesses would increase their prices. Their profit margins would improve (since product prices increase relative to the cost of resources), and they would expand output along the *SRAS* curve. As part a of Exhibit 10–2 shows, the economy would move to a short-run equilibrium (e_2), at a larger output (Y_2) and higher price level (P_{105}). (Note: A short-run equilibrium is indicated with a lowercase *e*, while a capital *E* is used to designate a long-run equilibrium. This convention will be followed throughout the text.)

In the short run, output will deviate from full employment capacity when prices in the goods and services market deviate from the price level that people expected. This will occur when long-run equilibrium is disrupted by an unanticipated increase in aggregate demand. The strong demand will push the price level above the level decision makers expected. For a time, many wage rates, interest payments, rents, and other resource prices will continue to reflect the initial price level (P_{100}) and the previously weaker demand. Because markets do not adjust instantaneously, these resource prices, and therefore costs, will lag behind prices in the goods and services market. Thus, the higher price level will temporarily improve profit margins, which, in turn, will provide the incentive for business firms to expand both output and employment in the short run. As a result, the unemployment rate will drop below its natural rate, and output will temporarily exceed the economy's long-run potential output level.[3]

This is not the end of the story, however. The strong demand accompanying this high level of output will place upward pressure on prices in resource and loanable funds markets. With time, the strong demand conditions will push wages, other resource prices, and real interest rates upward. As part b of Exhibit 10–2 illustrates, the rising resource prices and costs will shift the short-run aggregate supply curve to the left (to $SRAS_2$). Eventually, a new long-run equilibrium (E_2) will be established at a higher price level (P_{110}) that is correctly anticipated by decision makers.

Thus, the increase in real GDP above the economy's long-run potential is temporary. It will last only until there is an opportunity to alter the temporarily fixed resource prices (and interest rates) upward in light of the new stronger demand conditions. As this happens, profit margins return to their normal level, output recedes to the economy's long-run potential, and unemployment returns to its natural rate.

Because an increase in aggregate demand does not alter the economy's productive capacity, it cannot permanently expand output (beyond Y_F). The expansion in demand temporarily expands output, but over the long term its major effect will be higher prices (inflation).

---

[3]Thoughtful students may wonder how output (and, by implication, the quantity of resources) can be increased, even temporarily, when real wages and resource prices more generally are declining. There are two reasons why this may be the case. First, in an inflationary environment, workers (and other resource suppliers) may be fooled, at least temporarily, by an increase in money wages (and resource prices) that is less rapid than the inflation rate. Responding to the higher money wages, workers may supply more labor even though their real wages have fallen. Although we have presented the analysis within the framework of a noninflationary environment, the basic linkage between real wages (costs) and *SRAS* still holds. A reduction in the real wage rate, even when it takes the form of a nominal wage increase that is less than the inflation rate, will reduce real costs, and thereby increase *SRAS*. Second, the resource base may temporarily expand in response to strong demand conditions because the cost of entering the labor force will decline during this boom phase of the business cycle. Potential new labor force entrants will be able to find jobs quickly during an economic expansion, causing the size of the labor force to grow rapidly. Conversely, the labor force will tend to shrink (or grow less rapidly) during a business contraction, when the cost of entering the labor force will be high.

Reductions in Aggregate Demand

How would the goods and services market adjust to an unanticipated reduction in aggregate demand? For example, suppose that decision makers become more pessimistic about the future or that an unexpected decline in income abroad reduces the demand for exports. **Exhibit 10–3** will help us analyze this issue.

Once again, we consider an economy that is in long-run equilibrium (E_1) at output Y_F and price level P_{100} (part a). Long-run equilibrium is disturbed by the reduction in aggregate demand: the shift from AD_1 to AD_2. As the result of the decline in demand, businesses will be unable to sell Y_F units of output at the initial price level of P_{100}. In the short run, business firms will both reduce output (to Y_2) and cut prices (to P_{95}) in response to the weak demand conditions. Because many costs of business firms are temporarily fixed, profit margins will decline. Predictably, firms will cut back on output and lay off workers, causing the unemployment rate to rise. The actual rate of unemployment will rise above the economy's natural rate of unemployment. Weak demand and excess supply will be widespread in resource markets. These forces will place downward pressure on resource prices.

If resource prices quickly adjust downward in response to weak demand and rising unemployment, then the decline in output to Y_2 ***will be brief.*** Lower resource prices will reduce costs and thereby increase aggregate supply (shift to $SRAS_2$). As part b of Exhibit 10–3 illustrates, the result will be a new long-run equilibrium (E_2) at the economy's full employment output rate (Y_F) and a lower price level (P_{90}). Lower interest rates may also play a role. Given the excess production capacity of many firms, weak demand for capital goods (investment) will reduce the demand for loanable funds and thereby place downward pressure on real interest rates. The lower rates will stimulate current spending, which will offset some of the reduction in demand and help direct the economy back to full employment equilibrium.

The short-run impact of an unanticipated reduction in aggregate demand (shift from AD_1 *to* AD_2*) will be a decline in output to* Y_2 *and a lower price level,* P_{95} *(a). Temporarily, profit margins will decline, output will fall, and unemployment will rise above its natural rate. In the long run, weak demand and excess supply in the resource market will lead to lower wage rates and resource prices. This will reduce costs, leading to an expansion in short-run aggregate supply (shift to* $SRAS_2$ *(b). However, this method of restoring equilibrium (*E_2*) may be both highly painful and quite lengthy.*

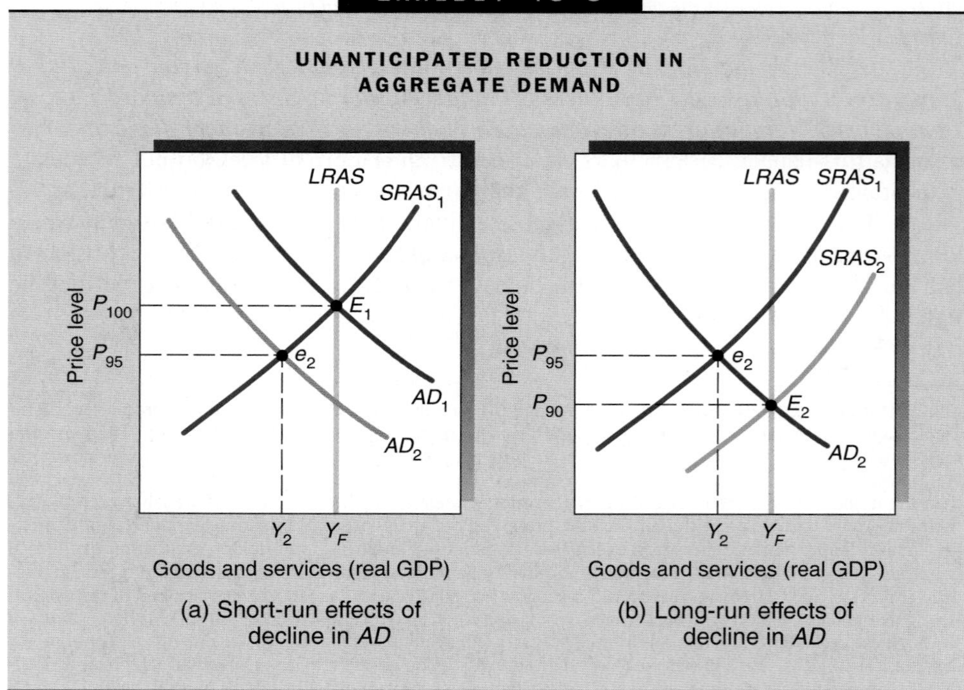

Resource prices and interest rates, however, may not adjust quickly. Long-term contracts and uncertainty as to whether the weak demand conditions are merely temporary will slow the adjustment process. In addition, individual workers and union officials may be highly reluctant to be the first to accept lower nominal wages. ***If resource prices are inflexible in a downward direction, as many economists believe, the adjustment process may be both lengthy and painful. Prolonged periods of economic recession—below-capacity output rates and abnormally high unemployment—may occur before the new long-run equilibrium is restored.***

SHIFTS IN AGGREGATE SUPPLY

What happens if aggregate demand stays the same but aggregate supply changes? The answer to this question depends on whether the aggregate supply change is long run or short run. By a long-run change in aggregate supply, we mean a change in the economy's long-run production possibilities (sustainable potential rate of output). For example, the discovery of a lower-cost source of energy would cause a long-run change in aggregate supply. In such a situation, both long-run (*LRAS*) and short-run (*SRAS*) aggregate supply would change.

In contrast, changes that temporarily alter the productive capability of an economy will shift the *SRAS* curve, but not the *LRAS*. A drought in California would be an example of such a short-run change. The drought will hurt in the short run, but it will eventually end, and output will return to the long-run normal rate. Changes that are temporary in nature will shift only *SRAS*. Let us now consider the major factors capable of shifting the *LRAS* and *SRAS* schedules.

CHANGES IN LONG-RUN AGGREGATE SUPPLY

Remember, the long-run aggregate supply curve indicates the maximum rate of sustainable output, given the current (1) resource base, (2) level of technology, and (3) institutional arrangements that affect productivity and efficiency of resource use. Changes in any of these three determinants of output would cause the *LRAS* curve to shift.

As part a of **Exhibit 10–4** illustrates, changes that increase the economy's productive capacity will shift the *LRAS* curve to the right. With the passage of time, net investment can expand the supply of physical capital, natural resources, and labor (human resources). Investment in physical capital can expand the supply of buildings, machines, and other physical assets. With the passage of time, changes in population and labor force participation may affect the supply of labor. Similarly, education, training, and skill-enhancing experience can improve the quality of the labor force, and thereby expand the supply of human resources.

Events that shift the long-run aggregate supply curve will make it possible to both produce *and sustain* a larger rate of output. Therefore, they will increase both *LRAS* and *SRAS*, causing both curves to shift to the right. On the other hand, a lasting reduction in the quantity (or quality) of resources will reduce both the current and long-term production capacity of the economy, shifting both *LRAS* and *SRAS* curves to the left.

Improvements in technology—the discovery of economical new products or less costly ways of producing goods and services—also permit us to squeeze a larger output from a specific resource supply. The enormous improvement in our living standards during the last 250 years is, to a large degree, the result of the discovery and adoption of technologically superior ways of transforming resources into goods and

Such factors as an increase in the stock of capital or an improvement in technology will expand the economy's potential output and shift the LRAS *to the right (a). Such factors as a reduction in resource prices, favorable weather, or a temporary decrease in the world price of an important imported resource would shift the* SRAS *to the right (b). Of course, changes that resulted in a decrease in either* LRAS *or* SRAS *would shift the respective schedules to the left.*

EXHIBIT 10-4

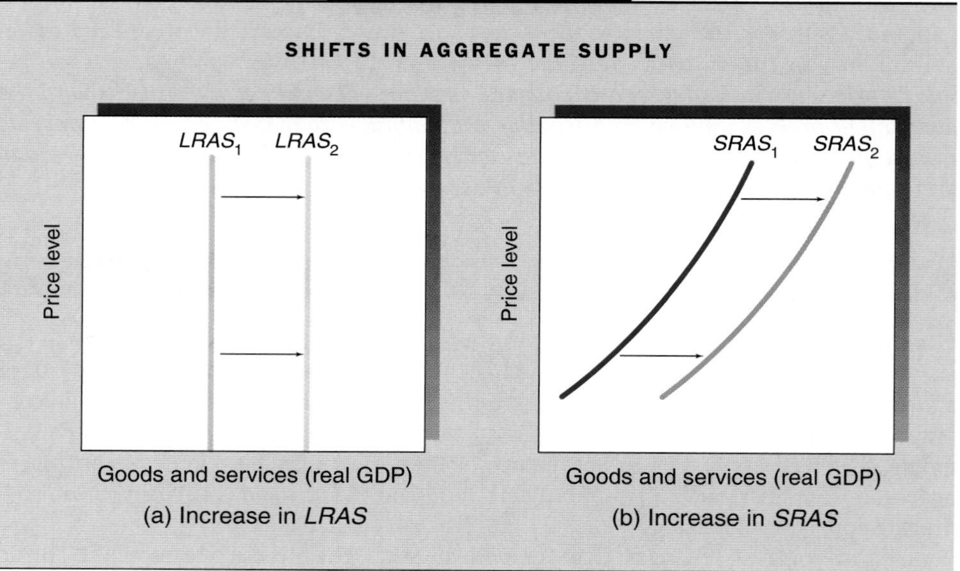

(a) Increase in *LRAS*

(b) Increase in *SRAS*

services. The development of the internal combustion engine, electricity, and nuclear power, has vastly altered our energy sources. The development of the railroad, the automobile, and the airplane dramatically changed both the cost and speed of transportation. More recently, the development of microcomputers, compact disc players, microwave ovens, video cameras and cassette players, and fax machines has vastly expanded our productive capacity and the ways in which we work and play. Improvements in technology enhance our **productivity** and thereby shift both *LRAS* and *SRAS* curves to the right.

Productivity
The average output produced per worker during a specific time period. It is usually measured in terms of output per hour worked.

Finally, institutional changes may also influence the efficiency of resource use and thereby alter the *LRAS* schedule. Public policy increases aggregate supply when it enhances economic efficiency by providing, for example, public goods at a low cost. In contrast, institutional arrangements sometimes promote waste and increase production costs. For example, studies indicate that minimum-wage legislation reduces employment and restricts the opportunity for training, particularly in the case of youthful workers. Such arrangements reduce aggregate supply.

The long-run growth trend of real GDP in the United States has been approximately 3 percent per year. This indicates that increases in the supply of resources and improvements in productivity have gradually expanded potential real output. Hence, the *LRAS* and *SRAS* curves have gradually drifted to the right at about a 3 percent annual rate, sometimes a little faster and sometimes a little slower.

Changes in Short-Run Aggregate Supply

Changes can sometimes influence current output without altering the economy's long-run capacity. When this is the case, the *SRAS* curve will shift even though *LRAS* is unchanged. What types of changes would do this?

1. Changes in Resource Prices. When we derived the *SRAS* schedule in Chapter 9, we noted explicitly that resource prices were being held constant. A change in resource prices will alter *SRAS* but not necessarily *LRAS*. A reduction in resource prices will

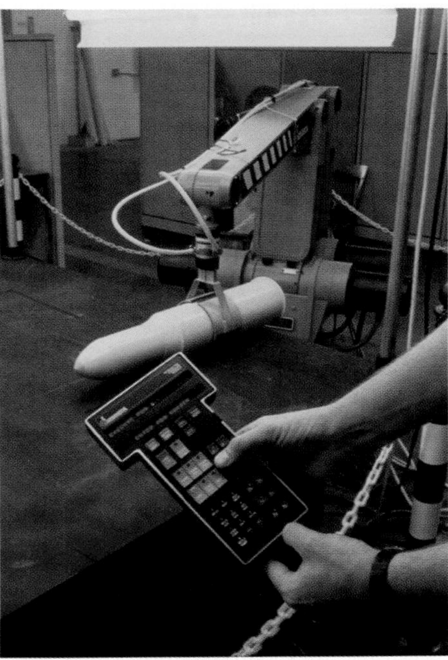

Net investment, technological advances, and improvements in institutional arrangements expand the productive capacity of an economy, shifting LRAS *to the right.*

lower costs and therefore shift the *SRAS* curve to the right, as illustrated in part b of Exhibit 10–4. However, unless the lower prices of resources reflect a long-term increase in the supply of resources, they will not alter *LRAS*. Conversely, an increase in the price of resources will increase costs, shifting the *SRAS* curve to the left. But unless the higher prices are the result of a long-term reduction in the size of the economy's resource base, they will not reduce *LRAS*.[4]

2. Changes in the Expected Rate of Inflation. As we previously noted, a change in the expected rate of inflation will influence current aggregate demand (*AD*) in the goods and services market. It will also alter *SRAS*. If sellers in the goods and services market expect the future rate of inflation to increase, their incentive to sell at a given price in the *current* period will be reduced. After all, goods that they do not sell today will be available for sale in the future at what they anticipate will be even higher prices (as the result of the increase in the rate of inflation). Therefore, an increase in the expected rate of inflation will reduce the *current* supply of goods, thereby shifting the *SRAS* curve to the left. Of course, a reduction in the expected rate of inflation will have just the opposite impact. When sellers scale back their expectations concerning future price increases, their incentive to sell in the current period is increased. Why wait, if the price is not going to increase very much in the future? Thus, a reduction in the expected rate of inflation will increase short-run aggregate supply (shift *SRAS* to the right).

[4]The definition of long-run aggregate supply helps clarify why a change in resource prices will affect short-run aggregate supply, but not long-run aggregate supply. When an economy is operating on its *LRAS* curve, the relationship between resource prices (costs) and product prices will reflect normal competitive market conditions. Because both profit and unemployment rates are at their normal levels, there is no tendency for resource prices to change relative to product prices when current output is equal to the economy's long-run potential. Therefore, when an economy is operating on its *LRAS* schedule, any change in resource prices will be matched by a proportional change in product prices, leaving the incentive to supply resources (and output) unchanged.

THUMBNAIL SKETCH

What Factors Will Influence Long-run and Short-run Aggregate Supply?

These factors will increase (decrease) long-run aggregate supply (*LRAS*).[a]

1. An increase (decrease) in the supply of resources.
2. An improvement (deterioration) in technology and productivity.
3. Institutional changes that increase (reduce) the efficiency of resource use.

These factors will increase (decrease) short-run aggregate supply (*SRAS*).[a]

1. A decrease (increase) in resource prices—that is, production costs.
2. A reduction (increase) in the expected rate of inflation.
3. Favorable (unfavorable) supply shocks, such as good (bad) weather or a reduction (increase) in the world price of an important imported resource.

[a]The important factors of macroeconomic policy will be considered later.

Supply shock
An unexpected event that temporarily either increases or decreases aggregate supply.

3. Supply Shocks. Various supply shocks may also alter current output without directly affecting the productive capacity of the economy. **Supply shocks** are surprise occurrences that temporarily increase or decrease current output. For example, adverse weather conditions, a natural disaster, or a temporary increase in the price of imported resources (for example, oil in the case of the United States) will reduce current supply, even though they do not alter the economy's long-term production capacity. They will thus decrease short-run aggregate supply (shift *SRAS* to the left) without directly affecting *LRAS*. On the other hand, favorable weather conditions or temporary reductions in the world price of imported resources will increase current output, even though the economy's long-run capacity remains unchanged.

The accompanying Thumbnail Sketch summarizes the major factors influencing both long-run and short-run aggregate supply. Of course, macroeconomic policy may also influence aggregate supply. As in the case of aggregate demand, we will consider the impact of macroeconomic policy on supply in subsequent chapters.

IMPACT OF CHANGES IN AGGREGATE SUPPLY

As we have previously stressed, the impact of changes in market conditions will be influenced by whether the changes are anticipated or unanticipated. When a change takes place slowly and predictably, decision makers will make choices based on the anticipation of the event. Such changes do not generally disrupt equilibrium conditions in markets.

ECONOMIC GROWTH AND ANTICIPATED SHIFTS IN LONG-RUN AGGREGATE SUPPLY

With the passage of time, net investment and improvements in technology and institutional efficiency will expand the sustainable rate of output. Such economic growth will shift the economy's *LRAS* curve to the right. When expansions in the productive capacity of an economy are persistent and predictable, they will be anticipated by decision makers. Thus, they need not disrupt macroeconomic equilibrium.

Exhibit 10–5 illustrates the impact of economic growth on the goods and services market. Initially, the economy is in long-run equilibrium at price level P_1 and

EXHIBIT 10–5

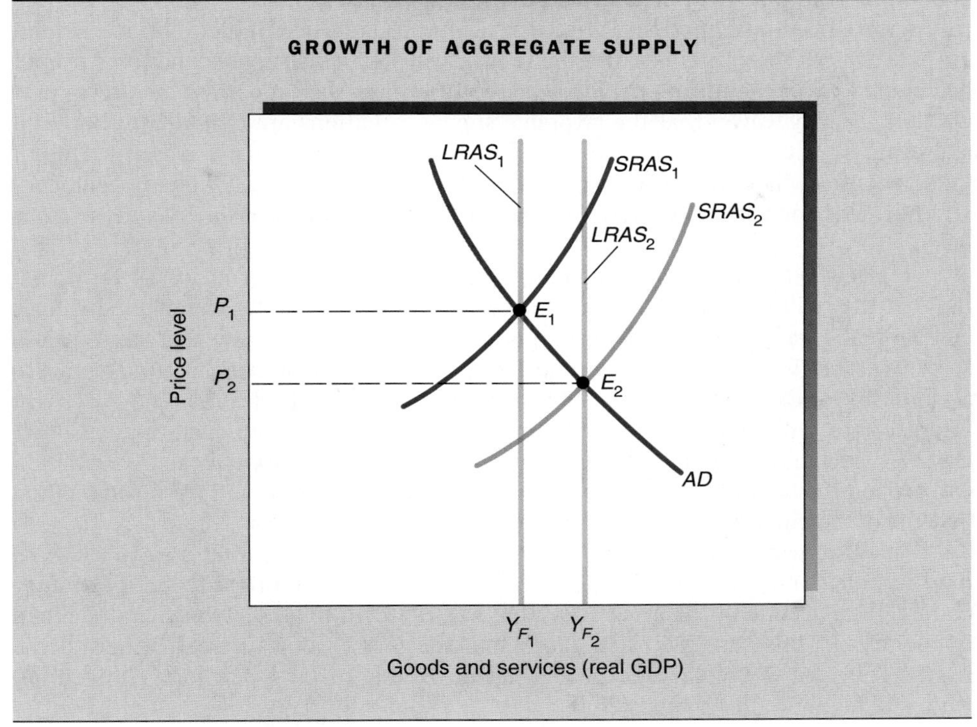

Here we illustrate the impact of economic growth due to capital formation or a technological advancement, for example. The full employment output of the economy expands from Y_{F_1} *to* Y_{F_2}*. Thus, both* LRAS *and* SRAS *increase (to* $LRAS_2$ *and* $SRAS_2$*). A sustainable, higher level of real output and real income is the result. If the money supply is held constant, a new long-run equilibrium will emerge at a larger output rate (*Y_{F_2}*) and lower price level (*P_2*).*

output Y_{F_1}. The growth expands the economy's potential output, shifting both the *LRAS* and *SRAS* curves to the right (to $LRAS_2$ and $SRAS_2$). Because these changes are gradual, decision makers have time to anticipate the changing market conditions and adjust their behavior accordingly.

When economic growth expands the economy's production possibilities, it will be possible to both produce and sustain a higher rate of real output (Y_{F_2}). The larger output rate can be achieved even while unemployment remains at its natural rate. If the money supply is held constant, the increase in aggregate supply will lead to a lower price level (P_2).

During the past 50 years, real output has expanded significantly in the United States and other countries. However, contrary to the presentation of Exhibit 10–5, the price level has generally not declined. This is because the monetary authorities have expanded the supply of money. As we will see later, an increase in the money supply stimulates aggregate demand (shifts *AD* to the right) and thereby pushes the price level upward.[5]

Unanticipated Changes in Aggregate Supply

In addition to changes that can be anticipated, *un*anticipated disturbances will often influence the level of prices and output in the aggregate goods and services market. Changes in the factors that influence the *SRAS* curve are particularly likely to be unanticipated. By their nature, supply shocks are unpredictable. We now turn to an analysis of unexpected changes in aggregate supply.

[5]In subsequent chapters, we will explain how stable prices can be achieved as real output increases.

Unanticipated Increases in *SRAS*. What would happen if highly favorable weather conditions or a temporary decline in the world market price of oil or some other critical imported resource increased the current output and income of a nation? **Exhibit 10–6** addresses this issue. Because the temporarily favorable supply conditions cannot be counted on in the future, they will not directly alter the economy's long-term production capacity. Given that the favorable supply conditions are temporary, short-run aggregate supply will increase (to $SRAS_2$), while *LRAS* will remain constant. Output (and income) will temporarily expand beyond the economy's full-employment constraints. This increase in current supply will place downward pressure on the price level.

How will households respond to their *temporarily* higher incomes? Recognizing that they will be unable to maintain their current high level of income, individuals will generally save a substantial portion of it for use at a future time that is not nearly so prosperous. This increased saving will expand the supply of loanable funds (shift to S_2 in part b of Exhibit 10–6), causing the real interest rate to decline. The lower real interest rate will stimulate investment and encourage the purchase of consumer durables, such as automobiles and appliances. In turn, the additional capital formation will expand the future resource base, which will make it possible to spread some of the benefits of the current high level of income into the future.

What would happen if the favorable conditions increasing supply reflected long-term factors? For example, suppose adoption of a new oil production technology resulted in a decline in the price of oil that was expected to be *permanent* rather than temporary. In this case, both the *LRAS* and the *SRAS* would increase (shift to the right). This case would parallel the analysis of Exhibit 10–5. A new long-run equilibrium at a higher output would result.

Unanticipated Decreases in *SRAS*. In recent decades, the U.S. economy has been jolted by several unfavorable supply-side factors. In 1973, and again in 1979, the United States and other oil-importing countries were hit with sharply higher oil prices as the

Here we illustrate the impact of an unanticipated, but temporary, increase in aggregate supply, such as might result from a bumper crop caused by highly favorable weather conditions. The increase in aggregate supply (shift to $SRAS_2$*) would lead to a lower price level (*P_{95}*) and an increase in current GDP to* Y_2*. Since the favorable supply conditions cannot be counted on in the future, the economy's long-run aggregate supply will not increase. Predictably, decision makers will save a large proportion of their temporarily higher real income, spreading the benefits into the future. Thus, the supply of loanable funds will increase. The real interest rate will fall to* r_2*, encouraging expenditures on interest-sensitive capital goods and consumer durables.*

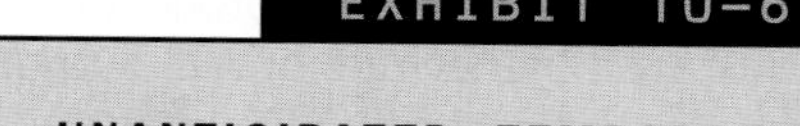

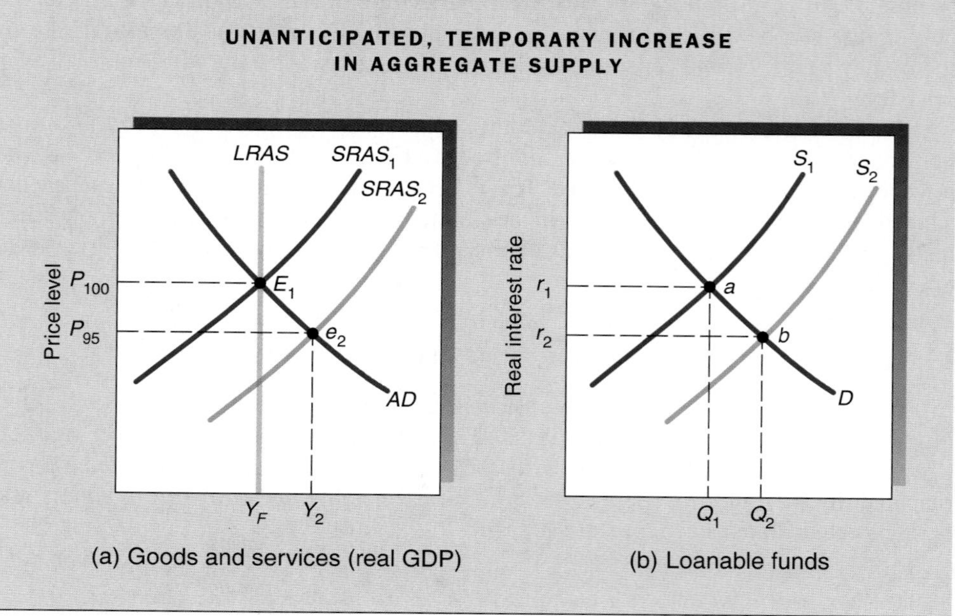

result of unstable conditions in the Middle East. During the summer of 1988, the most severe drought conditions in 50 years resulted in an extremely poor harvest in the U.S. agricultural belt. In August 1990, Iraq suddenly invaded Kuwait and threatened the oil fields of Saudi Arabia. Once again the world price of oil shot up, sharply increasing the cost of energy in the United States and other oil importing countries.

How do such unfavorable supply shocks influence macroeconomic markets? **Exhibit 10–7** illustrates the answer. Both an unfavorable harvest caused by adverse weather conditions and a higher world price of oil will reduce the supply of resources (from S_1 to S_2 in part a) in the domestic market. Resource prices will rise to P'_r. In turn, the higher resource prices will reduce short-run aggregate supply (the shift from $SRAS_1$ to $SRAS_2$ in part b) in the goods and services market. Because supply shocks of this type are generally unanticipated, initially they will reduce output and place upward pressure on prices (the rate of inflation) in the goods and services market.

If an unfavorable supply shock is expected to be temporary, as will generally be the case for a bad harvest, long-run aggregate supply will be unaffected. After all, unfavorable growing conditions for a year or two do not represent a permanent change in climate. Therefore, as normal weather patterns return with the passage of time, both supply and price conditions in the resource market will return to normal, permitting the economy to return to long-run equilibrium at output Y_F.

As in the case of the temporary increase in output, people will use the loanable funds market to smooth consumption in response to a temporary reduction in income. Believing that their lower incomes are temporary, households will reduce their current saving level (and dip into past savings) to maintain a current consumption level more consistent with their longer-term perceived opportunities. But when each household reduces its saving level, the supply of loanable funds decreases, causing an increase in the real interest rate. The higher real interest rate will allocate the available loanable funds to those willing to pay the most to maintain their current spending during the economic hard times. Of course, the higher real interest rate will also retard capital investment. A reduction in net investment and an accompanying decline in near-term economic growth are predictable side effects of a temporary reduction in aggregate supply.

EXHIBIT 10–7

EFFECTS OF ADVERSE SUPPLY SHOCK

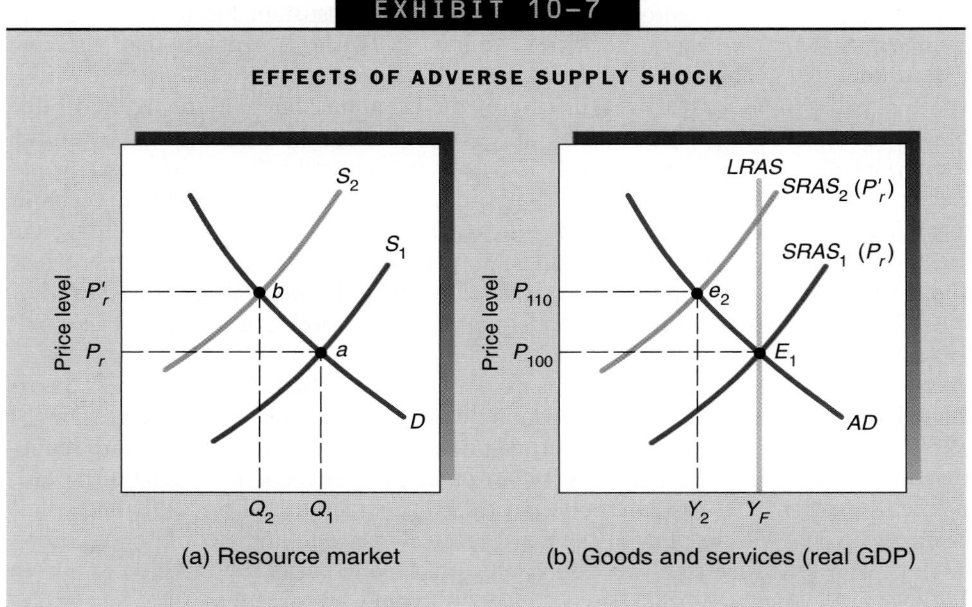

Suppose there is an unanticipated reduction in the supply of resources, perhaps as the result of a crop failure or sharp increase in the world price of a major imported resource, such as oil. Resource prices would rise from P_r *to* P'_r *(a). The higher resource prices would shift the* SRAS *curve to the left. In the short run, the price level would rise to* P_{110} *(b), and output would decline to* Y_2*. What happens in the long run depends on whether the reduction in the supply of resources is temporary or permanent. If it is temporary, resource prices will fall in the future, permitting the economy to return to its initial equilibrium (*E_1*). Conversely, if the reduced supply of resources is permanent, the productive potential of the economy will shrink (*LRAS *will shift to the left) and* e_2 *will become a long-run equilibrium.*

When an adverse supply-side factor is more permanent, the long-run supply curve would also shift to the left. For example, an increase in the price of oil imports that is expected to prevail for the next several years would reduce long-run as well as short-run aggregate supply. Under these circumstances, the economy would have to adjust to a lower level of real output. Regardless of whether the decline in aggregate supply is temporary or permanent, other things constant, the price level will rise. Similarly, output will decline, at least temporarily.

THE BUSINESS CYCLE REVISITED

It is interesting to view the business cycle within the framework of the aggregate demand/aggregate supply (*AD/AS*) model. This model indicates that unanticipated shifts in aggregate demand and aggregate supply underpin economic fluctuations. Such unexpected shifts lead to a misalignment between prices and costs because markets do not adjust instantaneously, and decision makers are not always able to anticipate accurately changes in the price level.

Recessions occur because prices in the goods and services market are low relative to costs of production (and resource prices). There are two reasons for this: (1) unanticipated reductions in aggregate demand and (2) unfavorable supply shocks. An unanticipated reduction in aggregate demand (illustrated by Exhibit 10–3a) leads to a lower than expected price level in the goods and services market. Given the weak demand and lower than expected prices, many firms will confront losses, which will force them to reduce output and, in some cases, terminate production. Correspondingly, an adverse supply shock (illustrated by Exhibit 10–7) leads to higher than expected resource prices and costs. This, too, will cause firms to incur losses and reduce output.

Correspondingly, economic booms—high rates of output that are unsustainable—occur when prices in the goods and services market are high relative to costs (and resource prices). The two causes of booms are: (1) unanticipated increases in aggregate demand and (2) favorable supply shocks. An unanticipated increase in aggregate demand (see Exhibit 10–2a) leads to a higher than expected price level in the goods and services market. The strong demand, high prices, and attractive profit margins induce firms to expand output to rates that are unsustainable in the long run. Similarly, a favorable supply shock (see Exhibit 10–6a) leads to lower than expected costs and unsustainable rates of output.

Exhibit 10–8 presents a picture of the economic fluctuations in the United States during the past 35 years. It is interesting to reflect on these figures within the framework of the *AD/AS* model. Real GDP grew substantially. This is what one would expect for an economy characterized by net investment and improvements in technology. Recessions were experienced during 1970, 1974–1975, 1979, 1982, and 1990–1991. As real output fell during these periods, the rate of unemployment rose above the natural rate (lower frame). (Note: Because the natural rate of unemployment is not directly observable, a range of estimates is provided in part b of Exhibit 10–8.)

The timing of the recessions is particularly interesting. The 1970 recession occurred as the Vietnam War was winding down. The more severe recession of 1974–1975 followed the doubling of crude oil prices (a supply shock) and sharp reduction in the rate of inflation (suggesting an unanticipated reduction in *AD*). The economic stagnation of 1979–1982 reflected these same factors. Oil prices doubled once again in 1978–1979, pushing costs up unexpectedly prior to and during the recession of 1979. The 1982 recession was associated with a reduction in the inflation rate from 12.5 percent in 1980 (and 13.3 percent in 1979) to only 3.8 percent in 1982, suggesting

EXHIBIT 10-8

EXPANSIONS, RECESSIONS, AND THE RATE OF UNEMPLOYMENT

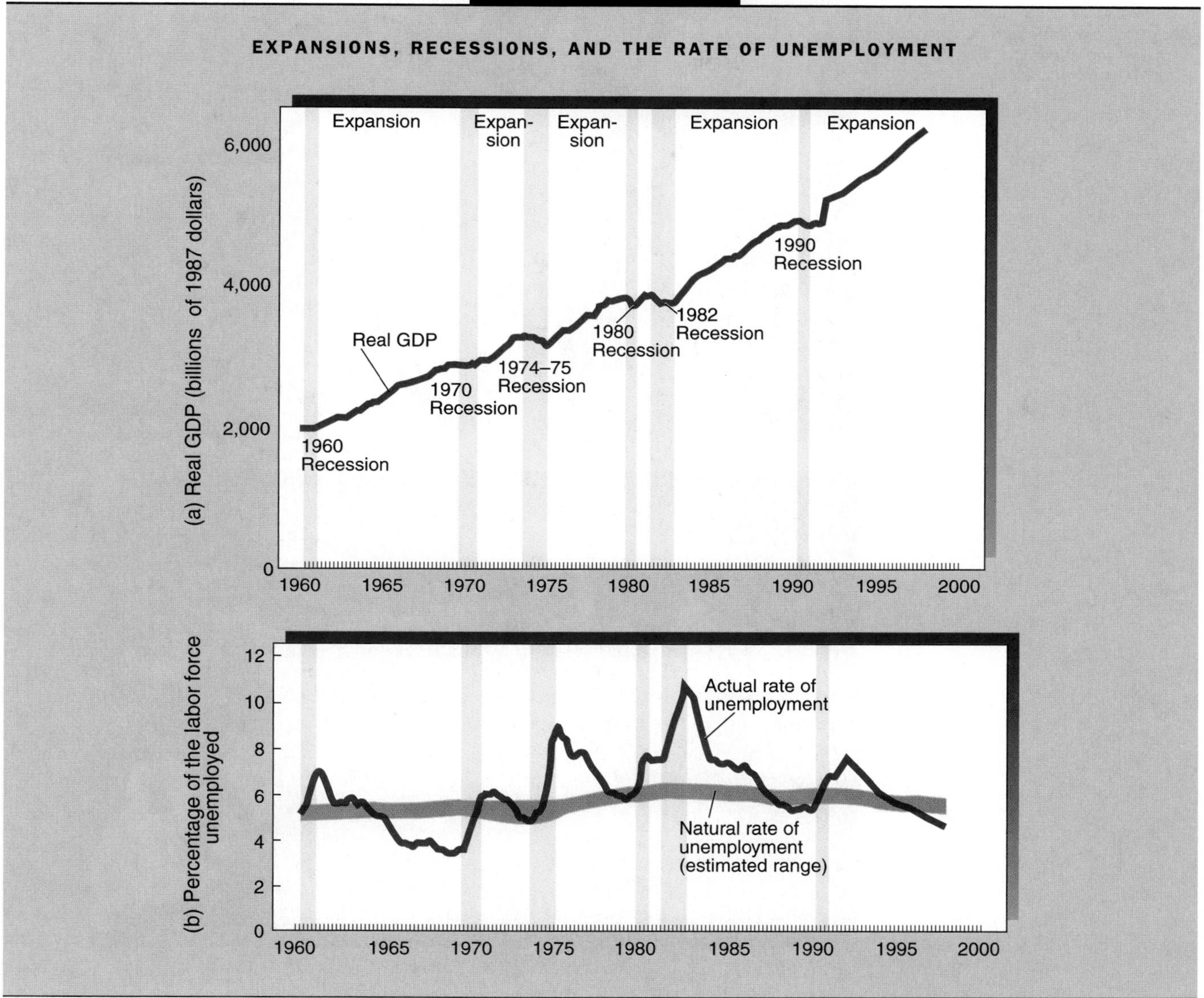

Here we illustrate the periods of expansion and contraction (recession) since 1960. Note how the reductions in real GDP (shaded periods) in the top graph are associated with increases in the rate of unemployment well above the natural rate (bottom graph). The AD/AS *model indicates that recessions are caused by unanticipated reductions in* AD *that are likely to accompany abrupt reductions in the inflation rate and/or adverse supply shocks that might occur, for example, when there is a large increase in the price of a key imported resource, such as crude oil.*

SOURCE: Derived from computerized data supplied by FAME ECONOMICS.

that there was an abrupt, and therefore unexpected, decline in aggregate demand during this period. Finally, the 1990 recession was associated with substantial reductions in defense expenditures following the collapse of communism and economic readjustments following the military buildup and war in Kuwait. Clearly, supply shocks and unanticipated changes in aggregate demand provided the underpinnings for these recessions.

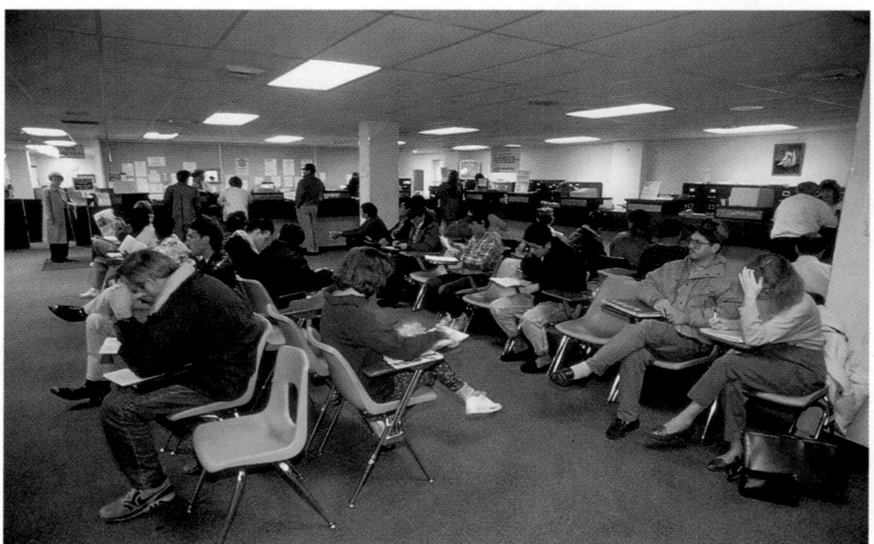

Plant closings, employee layoffs, and high rates of unemployment are indicative of economic recession. Unanticipated reductions in aggregate demand and/or adverse supply shocks are the primary causes of recession.

The distinction between long run and short run is vitally important within the framework of the *AD/AS* model. In the short run, expectations are fixed and output is determined by the intersection of *AD* and *SRAS*. In the long run, current economic conditions may cause people to alter their expectations concerning the future price level. As their expectations change, the short-run aggregate supply curve will shift. When an economy is in a recession, people will reduce their expectations with regard to the growth of real resource prices and the future level of prices (rate of inflation), which will shift *SRAS* to the right (Exhibit 10–3b illustrates this shift). Just the opposite will happen during an economic boom. The strong demand will cause people to expect a higher price level in the future, which will cause *SRAS* to shift to the left and output to recede to the long-run equilibrium rate (as illustrated in Exhibit 10–2b).

DOES A MARKET ECONOMY HAVE A SELF-CORRECTING MECHANISM?

In a dynamic world of changing demand conditions and supply shocks, economic ups and downs are inevitable. Are there market forces that will help stabilize an economy and cushion the effects of economic shocks? Does a market economy have a built-in mechanism that will prevent an economic downturn from plunging into a depression? There are three reasons to believe that the answer to both of these questions is yes.

1. Consumption demand is relatively stable over the business cycle. By far, consumption is the largest component of aggregate demand. As incomes fluctuate over the business cycle, there is good reason to expect that consumption spending will be considerably more stable than aggregate income. The **permanent income hypothesis,** developed by Nobel Prize–winning economist Milton Friedman, explains why. According to the permanent income hypothesis, the consumption of households is determined largely by their long-range expected, or permanent, income. Because temporary changes in income, such as those that occur over the business cycle, generally do not exert much impact on long-term expected income, these transitory increases or decreases do not exert a large impact on *current* consumption.[6]

Permanent income hypothesis
The hypothesis that consumption depends on some measure of long-run expected (permanent) income rather than on current income.

Therefore, when the incomes of many households increase rapidly during an economic expansion, a substantial amount of the above-normal gains in income will be allocated to saving. (Remember "saving"—without an "s" on the end—is income that is not spent on current consumption.) As a result, consumption demand will increase less rapidly than income during the expansion phase of the business cycle. Similarly, when experiencing a temporary decline in income during a recession, many households will reduce their current saving (and draw on their prior savings) in order to maintain a level of current consumption more consistent with their long-term earnings prospects (expected income). Thus, consumer demand will increase less than income during a boom and decline by a smaller amount than income during a recession. This relative stability of the large consumption component will help stabilize aggregate demand over the business cycle.

2. Changes in real interest rates will help to stabilize aggregate demand and redirect economic fluctuations. Real interest rates will tend to reflect business conditions. During an economic downturn, business demand for new investment projects and therefore loanable funds is generally quite weak. Because of this weak demand, real interest rates will generally fall during the contraction phase of the business cycle. In turn, the lower interest rates will both encourage current consumption and reduce the opportunity cost of investment projects. Both of these factors will help offset the decline in aggregate demand and thereby redirect output toward the full employment level.

---

[6]Perhaps a personal application will help explain why it is important to distinguish between temporary and long-term changes in income. Think for a moment how you would adjust your current spending on goods and services if an aunt left you a gift of $10,000 next month. No doubt you would spend some of the money almost immediately. Perhaps you would buy a new laptop or take a nice vacation. However, you would probably also use a significant portion of this temporary (one-time only) increase in income to pay bills or save for future education. Now, consider how you would alter your current spending if your aunt indicated you were to receive $10,000 per year for the next 30 years. Compared to the one-time gift, the annual gift for 30 years increases your long-term expected income by a much larger amount. In this case, you are likely to spend most of this year's $10,000 almost immediately. You might even borrow money to buy an automobile or make some major expenditures, and thereby expand your spending on goods and services this year by more than $10,000.

During an economic boom, many businesses will borrow in order to undertake capital spending projects needed to meet the strong demand for goods and services. Thus, during business booms, the demand for loanable funds will be strong, placing upward pressure on real interest rates. In turn, the higher real interest rates will make it more expensive to purchase consumer durables and undertake investment projects. This will restrain aggregate demand during a business expansion.

Thus, the movement of interest rates will exert a stabilizing influence on the economy. Lower real interest rates during recessionary periods of weak demand will help to stimulate current spending on goods and services. Correspondingly, higher real interest rates during business booms will help restrain aggregate demand and keep it in line with full employment equilibrium.

Interest-rate adjustments will also help to offset potential disturbances arising from changes in expectations. Suppose that consumers and business operators suddenly became more pessimistic and, as a result, reduced their current level of spending. Other things constant, a reduction in consumer spending implies an increase in saving, while a reduction in investment means weaker demand for loanable funds. Thus, the supply of loanable funds will increase relative to the demand. This will lead to lower real interest rates, which will help to offset the reduction in spending as the result of the increased pessimism.

Just the opposite would be the case if consumers and businesses suddenly became more optimistic. If they suddenly decide to spend more of their current income, their actions will reduce the supply of loanable funds relative to the demand, causing an increase in real interest rates. But the higher real interest rates will make current spending less attractive and thereby help to stabilize aggregate demand.

3. Changes in real resource prices will redirect economic fluctuations. Price adjustments in the resource market will also help keep the economy on an even keel. When the current output of an economy is less than its full employment potential, weak demand and slack employment in resource markets will place downward pressure on real resource prices. Under these conditions, real wages and other resource prices will decline (or increase at a very slow rate). In contrast, when an economy is operating beyond its full employment capacity—that is, when unemployment is less than the natural unemployment rate—strong demand will push the real price of labor and other resources up rapidly.

A Graphic Presentation of the Self-Correcting Mechanism

Exhibits 10-9 and 10-10 provide a graphic summary of the economy's self-corrective mechanism. **Exhibit 10–9** depicts the response of real interest rates and resource prices as market conditions change over the business cycle. When an economy is operating below its full employment potential (Y_F), both real interest rates and real resource prices will tend to decline. Both of these factors will help direct output toward long-run equilibrium (along the vertical *LRAS*). Similarly, when output exceeds the long-run sustainable level, rising real interest rates and resource prices will cause output to recede to the full employment level.

Exhibit 10–10 depicts the operation of the self-corrective mechanism within the framework of the *AD/AS* model. Part a illustrates the supply and demand conditions in the goods and services market for an economy initially operating beyond full-employment capacity, perhaps as the result of an unanticipated increase in aggregate demand. These are the conditions that one would expect when the

EXHIBIT 10–9

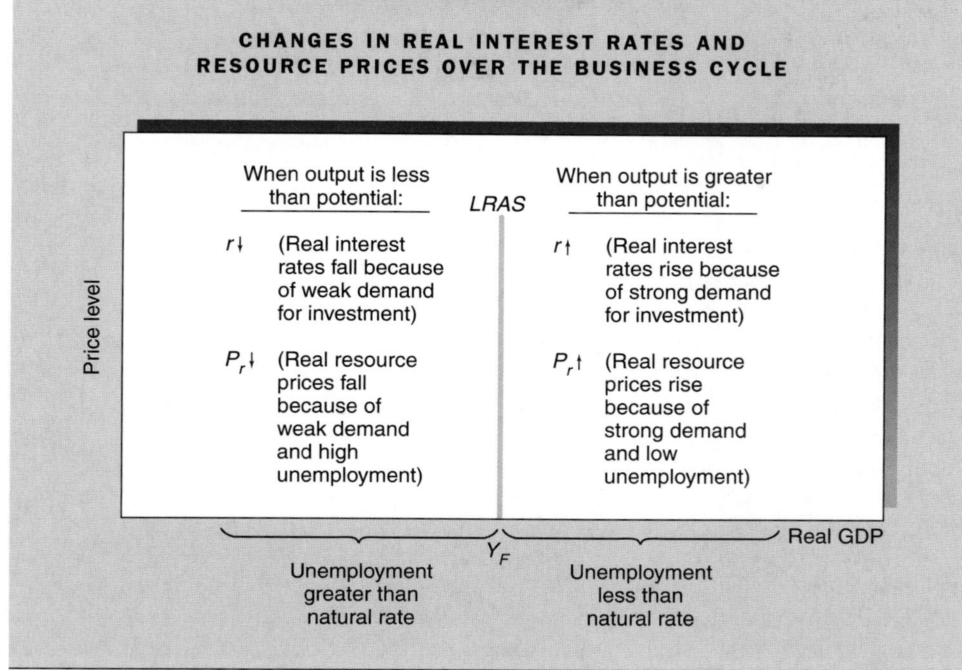
CHANGES IN REAL INTEREST RATES AND RESOURCE PRICES OVER THE BUSINESS CYCLE
When output is less than potential:
LRAS
When output is greater than potential:
r↓ (Real interest rates fall because of weak demand for investment)
r↑ (Real interest rates rise because of strong demand for investment)
Price level
P_r↓ (Real resource prices fall because of weak demand and high unemployment)
P_r↑ (Real resource prices rise because of strong demand and low unemployment)
Real GDP
Y_F
Unemployment greater than natural rate
Unemployment less than natural rate

When aggregate output is less than the economy's full employment potential (Y_F), weak demand for investment leads to lower real interest rates, while slack employment in resource markets will place downward pressure on wages and other resource prices (P_r). Conversely, when output exceeds Y_F, strong demand for capital goods and tight labor market conditions will result in rising real interest rates and resource prices.

expansionary phase of the business cycle results in an unsustainable economic boom. When these conditions are present, the strong demand for goods and services will lead to both a high level of employment and strong demand for investment funds by firms seeking to expand output capacity. As a result, the *actual rate* of unemployment will be less than the *natural rate.* However, the strong demand for both loanable funds (to finance investment) and resources will place upward pressure on real interest rates and resource prices, causing both to rise. The higher real interest rates will push up the cost of both investment projects and consumer durables, which will tend to retard the strong demand (shift from AD_1 to AD_2). At the same time, the rising cost of labor and other resources will push production costs upward, causing a reduction in short-run aggregate supply (shift to $SRAS_2$ in part a). As resource prices and costs rise, profit margins will decline to normal competitive rates, and output will recede to its long-run potential. ***Eventually, these forces—the higher real interest rates and resource prices—will direct the output of an over-employed economy back to long-run capacity.***

Part b of Exhibit 10–10 illustrates an economy that is initially in a recession. The initial short-run equilibrium (e_1 of part b) takes place at a rate of output (Y_1) well below the economy's full employment capacity. When current output is less than an economy's long-run potential, the demand for investment funds will be extremely weak. This weak demand for loanable funds will result in lower real interest rates, which lead to an increase in aggregate demand (shift to AD_2 in part b). At the same time, the abnormally high unemployment (initially the *actual rate* exceeds the *natural rate*) and weak demand for resources will place downward pressure on real wages and resource prices. Eventually, the excess supply in resource markets will induce suppliers to accept lower wage rates and prices for other resources. This reduction in the real price of resources will reduce costs and lead to an increase in short-run aggregate

EXHIBIT 10-10

THE ECONOMY'S SELF-CORRECTIVE MECHANISM

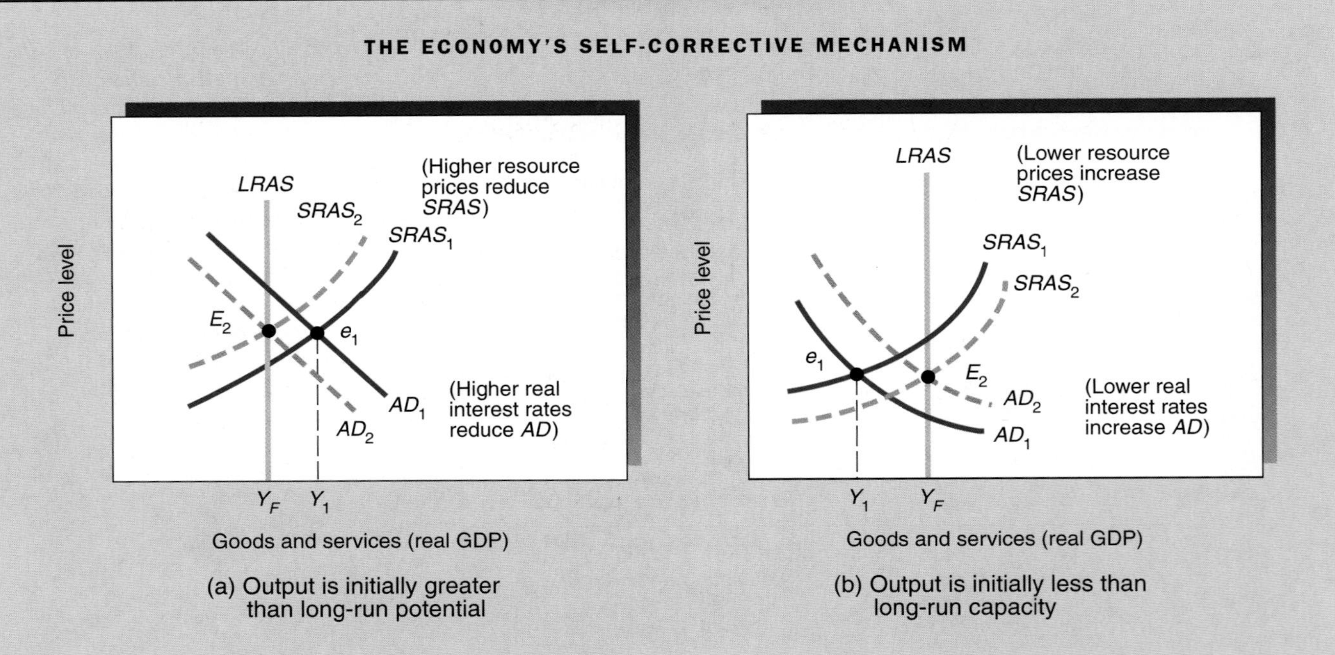

(a) Output is initially greater than long-run potential

(b) Output is initially less than long-run capacity

In the short run, output may either exceed or fall short of the economy's full-employment capacity (Y_F)*. If output is temporarily greater than the economy's potential (a), higher real interest rates and resource prices will lead to a lower but sustainable rate of output. The higher interest rates will reduce aggregate demand (shift from* AD_1 *to* AD_2)*. At the same time, the higher resource prices will increase production costs and therefore reduce short-run aggregate supply (shift to* $SRAS_2$ *[a]). These forces will direct output toward its full employment potential.*

When output is less than capacity (b), lower interest rates (reflecting the weak demand for investment funds) will stimulate aggregate demand (causing the shift to AD_2)*. In addition, lower resource prices (because of weak demand and abnormally high unemployment) will reduce production costs and thereby stimulate short-run aggregate supply (causing the shift to* $SRAS_2$)*. Thus, output will move toward the economy's full-employment capacity. However, this self-correction process may require considerable time. As we proceed, we will consider alternative methods of attaining full employment more rapidly.*

supply (shift to $SRAS_2$ in part b). ***With time, this combination of lower interest rates and resource prices will restore the economy's full employment rate of output (equilibrium*** E_2 ***of part b).***

The *AD/AS* model indicates that changes in real interest rates and real resource prices (wages) will redirect both an expansionary boom and a recessionary contraction. A boom will not continue to spiral upward. Neither will a contraction continue to plunge downward.

Exhibit 10–11 presents data on the estimated *real* interest rate (Aaa corporate bond rate minus the annual rate of inflation during the last three years) for the peaks and troughs of recent business cycles. Data are also presented for the annual rate of change in the *real* hourly compensation of nonfarm employees during the periods of expansion and recession. As our analysis predicts, real interest rates increased during economic expansions and receded during recessionary periods. The estimated real interest rate declined to 1.4 percent during the recession of 1970, down from 4.2 percent at the peak of the prior expansion. During the severe 1974–1975 recession, the real interest rate fell to 0.6 percent, compared to 5.9 percent at the peak of the 1971–1973

EXHIBIT 10-11

CHANGES IN REAL INTEREST RATES AND REAL WAGES OVER THE BUSINESS CYCLE

Expansions and Recessions	Estimated Real Interest Rate (at Peak for Expansion and at Trough for Recession)	Annual Percent Rate of Change in Real Compensation per Hour (Nonfarm Business Sector)
1966–1969 Expansion (Peak, December 1969)	4.2	2.9
1970 Recession (Trough, November 1970)	1.4	1.0
1971–1973 Expansion (Peak, November 1973)	5.9	2.2
1974–1975 Recession (Trough, March 1975)	0.6	−0.4
1976–1979 Expansion (Peak, December 1979)	3.9	1.8
1979–1982 Recession (Trough, November 1982)	1.7	−1.0
1983–1990 Expansion (Peak, July 1990)	4.4	0.5
1990–1991 Recession (Trough, March 1991)	3.3	−1.1

SOURCE: The real interest rate data were derived from the Federal Reserve Bulletin. *The estimated real interest rate is the corporate bond Aaa interest rate minus the expected rate of inflation. The average rate of inflation during the last three years was used to estimate the expected rate of inflation. The real compensation data are from the Department of Labor, Bureau of Labor Statistics. The shaded areas indicate the periods of recession.*

expansion. The real rate also declined during the 1979–1982 recessionary period and the 1990–1991 downturn.[7]

Real wages also followed the expected pattern. The hourly real compensation of nonfarm employees increased less rapidly during each recession than during the preceding (and subsequent) period of economic expansion. In fact, real hourly compensation actually declined during the 1974–1975, 1979–1982, and 1990–1991 recessions. Clearly, the observed pattern of change for both real interest rates and real wages is consistent with the view that they exert a stabilizing influence on the economy.

The Great Debate: How Rapidly Does the Self-Corrective Mechanism Work?

Following the Great Depression of the 1930s, many economists thought that market economies were inherently unstable. They argued that, unless monetary and fiscal policy were used to stimulate and guide the macroeconomy, prolonged recessions would result. Influenced by both a reevaluation of the 1930s and the experience of the last 60 years, most modern economists reject this stagnation view of market economies.[8] Today, there is a widespread consensus that market economies possess stabilizing forces.

What divides economists is disagreement about how rapidly the self-correcting forces work. This is a key issue. If the self-corrective process works slowly, then market economies will still experience prolonged periods of abnormally high unemployment and below-capacity output. Many economists believe this is the case. As a

[7]Officially, there were two recessions during the 1979–1982 stagnation: one of approximately 6 months' duration in 1980 and a second lasting approximately 18 months during 1981–1982. Because the economy recovered only briefly from the initial recession, the entire period was one economic stagnation.

[8]A detailed analysis of the forces causing and prolonging the Great Depression is presented in Chapter 15.

result, they have a good deal of confidence that discretionary monetary and fiscal policy can help promote stability and prosperity.

Conversely, other economists believe that the self-corrective mechanism of a market economy works reasonably well when monetary and fiscal policy follow a stable course. This latter group argues that macroeconomic policy mistakes are a major source of economic instability. Thus, they focus on the importance of stable, predictable monetary and fiscal policies, while relying mostly on the self-corrective mechanism of markets to keep the economy on track. We will return to this debate when we consider the impact of monetary and fiscal policy.

LOOKING *Ahead*

Modern macroeconomics reflects an evolutionary process. The Great Depression and the accompanying prolonged unemployment exerted an enormous impact on macroeconomics. John Maynard Keynes, the brilliant English economist, developed a theory that sheds light on the operation of an economy experiencing high rates of unemployment. The next chapter focuses on the Keynesian theory.

KEY POINTS

➤ It is important to distinguish between anticipated and unanticipated changes.

➤ An increase in aggregate demand involves a shift of the entire *AD* schedule to the right. Other than policy, major factors causing an increase in aggregate demand are (a) an increase in real wealth, (b) a lower real interest rate, (c) increased optimism on the part of businesses and consumers, (d) an increase in the expected rate of inflation, (e) higher real income abroad, and (f) a depreciation in the exchange rate. Conversely, if these factors change in the opposite direction, a decrease in aggregate demand will result.

➤ When long-run equilibrium is disrupted by an unanticipated increase in aggregate demand, output will temporarily increase beyond the economy's long-run capacity and unemployment will fall below its natural rate. However, as decision makers adjust to the increase in demand, resource prices will rise and output will recede to long-run capacity.

➤ An unanticipated reduction in aggregate demand will temporarily reduce output below capacity and push unemployment above its natural rate. Eventually, lower resource prices (and lower real interest rates) will direct the economy back to long-run equilibrium. However, the process may be both lengthy and painful, particularly if wages and prices are inflexible downward.

➤ It is important to distinguish between long-run and short-run aggregate supply. The following factors will increase *LRAS*: (a) increases in the supply of labor and capital resources, (b) improvements in technology and productivity, and (c) institutional changes improving the efficiency of resource use. Changes in resource prices, the expected rate of inflation, and supply shocks will cause shifts in short-run aggregate supply (*SRAS*).

➤ An increase in output due to economic growth (an increase in the economy's production capacity) will increase both short-run and long-run aggregate supply, permitting the economy to achieve and sustain a larger output level.

➤ When an economy in long-run equilibrium experiences an unanticipated favorable supply shock, output (and income) will temporarily rise above capacity and prices will decline. Lower real interest rates and a higher rate of capital formation are also predictable results.

➤ An adverse supply shock (decrease in *SRAS*) will reduce output and increase the price level. If the reduction in income is expected to be temporary, people will increase their borrowing (and reduce their saving) to maintain a consumption level more consistent with their longer-term income.

➤ Unanticipated reductions in aggregate demand and adverse supply shocks cause recessions. On the other hand, unanticipated increases in aggregate demand and favorable supply shocks lead to temporary expansions in output beyond the economy's maximum sustainable rate.

➤ Changes in real interest rates and resource prices provide a market economy with a self-corrective mechanism. During a recession, lower interest rates will stimulate aggregate demand, and lower resource prices (including wages) will increase short-run aggregate supply. Both of these forces will help direct output toward its full employment potential. Similarly, when current output exceeds potential GDP, higher real interest rates and rising real resource prices cause output to recede to the economy's potential capacity.

➤ There is considerable debate among economists concerning how rapidly the economy's self-corrective mechanism works.

CRITICAL ANALYSIS QUESTIONS

*1. Explain how and why each of the following factors would influence current aggregate demand in the United States:

a. Increased fear of recession
b. Increased fear of inflation
c. Rapid growth of real income in Canada and Western Europe
d. A reduction in the real interest rate
e. A higher price level (be careful)

*2. Indicate how each of the following would influence U.S. aggregate supply in the short run:

a. An increase in real wage rates
b. A severe freeze that destroys half the orange trees in Florida
c. An increase in the expected rate of inflation in the future
d. An increase in the world price of oil, a major import
e. Abundant rainfall during the growing season of agricultural states

3. Suppose that the key macroeconomic markets are initially in long-run equilibrium. How will an unanticipated reduction in aggregate demand affect real output, employment, and the price level in the short run? In the long run?

*4. When current output is less than full employment capacity, explain how the self-correcting mechanism will direct output toward the economy's long-run potential. Can you think of any reason why this mechanism might not work? Discuss.

5. What is the difference between an anticipated and an unanticipated increase in aggregate demand? Provide an example of each. Which is most likely to result in a temporary spurt in the growth of real output?

*6. Assume that both union and management representatives agree to wage increases because of their expectation that prices will rise 10 percent during the next year. Explain why the unemployment rate will probably increase if the actual rate of inflation next year is only 3 percent.

7. During the period 1980–1985, the exchange-rate value of the dollar increased sharply. How did this change influence aggregate demand, output, and the inflation rate during the 1980–1985 period? During the period 1986–1988, the exchange-rate value of the dollar fell. What impact did this decline have on aggregate demand, output, and inflation?

*8. When the actual output exceeds the long-run potential of the economy, how will the self-correcting mechanism direct the economy to long-run equilibrium? Why can't the above-normal output be maintained?

*9. Are the real wages of workers likely to increase more rapidly when the unemployment rate is high or when it is low? Why?

10. Suppose consumers and investors suddenly become more pessimistic about the future and therefore decide to reduce their consumption and investment spending. How will a market economy adjust to this increase in pessimism? What will happen to the real rate of interest?

11. "Unemployment benefits should replace 100 percent of an employee's earnings from his or her previous job when the employee is terminated or laid off through no fault of his or her own." Evaluate this statement. Do you think the idea expressed is a good one? How would such a practice affect the search time of the unemployed workers? What impact would it have on the unemployment rate?

*12. Suppose that an unexpectedly rapid growth in real income abroad leads to a sharp increase in the demand for U.S. exports. What impact will this change have on the price level, output, and employment in the short run? In the long run?

13. If the real interest rate increases, how will this affect the incentive of consumers and investors to purchase goods and services? How will it affect the *AD* curve?

14. Construct the *AD, SRAS,* and *LRAS* curves for an economy experiencing (a) full employment, (b) an economic boom, and (c) a recession.

15. As the result of changing international conditions, there was a decline in real national defense expenditures of approximately 15 percent between 1989 and 1991. What is the expected impact of this decline in defense expenditures on aggregate demand and output in the short run? If the United States is able to spend less on national defense in the future, how will this factor influence the standard of living of Americans? Discuss.

16. Consider an economy with the following aggregate demand (*AD*) and aggregate supply (*AS*) schedules. These schedules reflect the fact that, prior to the period in question, decision makers entered into contracts and made choices anticipating that the price level would be P_{105}.

AD_{105} (IN TRILLIONS)	PRICE LEVEL	$SRAS_{105}$ (IN TRILLIONS)
$5.1	95	$3.5
4.9	100	3.8
4.7	105	4.2
4.5	110	4.5
4.3	115	4.8

a. Indicate the quantity of GDP that will be produced and the price level that will emerge during this period.
b. Is the economy in long-run equilibrium? Why or why not?
c. How will the unemployment rate during the current period compare with this economy's natural rate of unemployment?
d. What will tend to happen to resource prices in the future? How will this affect the equilibrium rate of output?
e. Will the rate of GDP produced during this period be sustainable into the future? Why or why not?

17. Suppose that the price level that emerges from aggregate demand and aggregate supply conditions during the current period is lower than decision makers had anticipated.

a. Construct *AD, SRAS,* and *LRAS* schedules that reflect these conditions.
b. During the current period, how will the actual rate of unemployment compare with the natural rate? How will actual output compare with the economy's potential?
c. As the result of the current conditions, what will tend to happen to resource prices and interest rates? Why?

---

*Asterisk denotes questions for which answers are given in Appendix B.

CHAPTER 11

I believe myself to be writing a book on economic theory which will largely revolutionize — not, I suppose, at once but in the course of the next ten years — the way the world thinks about economic problems.

John Maynard Keynes[1]

Keynesian Foundations of Modern Macroeconomics

CHAPTER FOCUS

- What are the major components of the Keynesian model? What is the major factor that causes the level of output and employment to change?
- What was Keynes's explanation for the high rates of unemployment that persisted during the Great Depression?
- What determines the equilibrium level of output in the Keynesian model?
- What is the multiplier principle? Why is it important?
- Why do Keynesians believe market economies experience business instability?

[1]Letter from John Maynard Keynes to George Bernard Shaw, New Year's Day, 1935.

Modern macroeconomics is the product of an evolutionary process. Prior to the Great Depression of the 1930s, most economists thought market adjustments would automatically guide an economy to full employment within a relatively brief time. The presence of double-digit unemployment rates throughout the 1930s undermined the credibility of this view. The experience of the Great Depression also led to the development of a new theory, one designed to explain the persistently high unemployment levels of the period.

The new theory, developed by the English economist John Maynard Keynes (pronounced "canes"), provided a reasonable explanation for the widespread and prolonged unemployment of the 1930s.[2] It also exerted an enormous influence on the development of macroeconomics. Several basic concepts and much of the terminology we use today can be traced to Keynes. Modern macroeconomics is built on the foundation of Keynesian analysis. This chapter presents the Keynesian view and illuminates its influence on modern macroeconomic theory.

OUTSTANDING ECONOMIST

John Maynard Keynes (1883–1946)

Keynes might properly be referred to as the "father of macroeconomics." The son of a prominent nineteenth-century economist (John Neville Keynes), he earned a degree in mathematics from King's College, Cambridge, where he would later return and spend most of his career as an economist. His *General Theory of Employment, Interest, and Money,* published in 1936, revolutionized the way that economists think about macroeconomics. This work, written in the midst of the Great Depression, provided both a plausible explanation for the massive unemployment and a strategy for ending it. Keynes's message married an idea with a moment in time.

Keynes's work was both path-breaking and controversial. His view that governments should run budget deficits during a recession in order to stimulate demand and direct the economy back to full employment challenged the entrenched views of both policymakers and classical economists. Debate concerning the impact of budget deficits continues to this day.

Keynes correctly anticipated that his ideas would, with the passage of time, exert a powerful influence (see the chapter's opening quote). By the 1950s the Keynesian analysis was dominant in academic circles and by the 1960s, it formed the foundation for the macroeconomic policy of most Western nations. Keynes died rather suddenly in 1946, so he did not live to observe the enormous impact of his ideas on public policy.

The economic events of the 1970s tempered the confidence of macroeconomists in the basic analysis of Keynes. Nevertheless, his imprint is sure to endure. He revolutionized our way of thinking about macroeconomic issues.

---

[2]See the classic book by Keynes, *The General Theory of Employment, Interest, and Money* (London: Macmillan, 1936), for the presentation of this theory.

KEYNESIAN EXPLANATION OF THE GREAT DEPRESSION

Mainstream economists before the time of Keynes (often called **classical economists**) emphasized the importance of total production (aggregate supply) and paid little heed to aggregate demand. Classical economists adhered to **Say's Law,** named for nineteenth-century French economist J. B. Say. According to Say's Law, a general overproduction of goods relative to total demand is impossible, since supply (production) creates its own demand. The reasoning here is that the purchasing power necessary to buy (demand) desired products is generated by production. A farmer's supply of wheat generates income to meet the farmer's demand for shoes, clothes, automobiles, and other desired goods. Similarly, the supply of shoes generates the purchasing power with which shoemakers (and their employees) demand the farmer's wheat and other desired goods.

Classical economists
Economists from Adam Smith to the time of Keynes who focused their analyses on economic efficiency and production. With regard to business instability, they thought market prices and wages would decline during a recession quickly enough to bring the economy back to full employment within a short period of time.

Say's Law
The view that production creates its own demand. Demand will always be sufficient to purchase the goods produced because the income payments to the resource suppliers will equal the value of the goods produced.

Of course, producers might produce too much of some goods and not enough of others. But the pricing system would correct such imbalances. The prices of goods in excess supply would fall, and the prices of products in excess demand would rise. According to the classical view, deficient demand could never be a problem because the production of the goods would always generate a demand that was sufficient to purchase the goods produced.

According to the classical view, markets would always adjust and quickly direct the economy toward full employment, conditions parallel to those of long-run equilibrium of the aggregate demand/aggregate supply model developed in the preceding two chapters. If unemployment was temporarily high, wages would fall, which would reduce costs and lower prices until the excess supply of labor was eliminated. Similarly, market-determined interest rates would assure balance between saving and investment.

Before the Great Depression, the classical view seemed reasonable. But the depth and the prolonged duration of the decline during the 1930s challenged its validity and provided the foundation for what we now refer to as Keynesian economics. For those who are familiar only with the relative stability of the 1980s and 1990s, the depth

The Keynesian model was an outgrowth of the Great Depression. It provided an explanation for the widespread, prolonged unemployment of the 1930s.

of the economic decline during the 1930s is difficult to comprehend. *Real* GDP in the United States fell by more than 30 percent between 1930 and 1933. In 1933, 25 percent of the U.S. labor force was unemployed. The depressed conditions continued throughout the decade. In 1939, a decade after the plunge began, per capita income was still nearly 10 percent less than in 1929. Other industrial countries experienced similar conditions.

KEYNESIAN VIEW OF SPENDING AND OUTPUT

Keynes developed a theory that provided an explanation for prolonged depressed conditions like those of the 1930s. Rejecting the classical view, Keynes offered a completely new concept of output determination. ***Keynes believed that spending induced business firms to supply goods and services. From this, he argued that, if total spending fell (as it might, for example, if consumers and investors became pessimistic about the future or tried to save more of their current income), then business firms would respond by cutting back production. Less spending would thus lead to less output.***

Keynes and his followers rejected the classical view that wage and price reductions would eliminate unemployment. They argued that wages and prices were highly inflexible, particularly in a downward direction. Even when demand was weak, Keynesians believed that large business firms and powerful trade unions would resist price and wage reductions, and thereby retard movement toward full employment.

Keynes also introduced a different concept of equilibrium and a different mechanism for its achievement. ***In the Keynesian view, equilibrium takes place when the level of total spending is equal to current output. When this is the case, producers will have no reason to either expand or contract output.*** Keynesians believe that changes in output rather than changes in prices direct the economy to equilibrium. If total spending is less than full employment output, output will be cut back to the level of spending, and, most significantly, it will remain there until the level of spending changes. Therefore, if total spending is deficient, equilibrium output will be less than full employment output, and high rates of unemployment will continue. This is precisely what Keynes believed was happening during the 1930s.

The message of Keynes can be summarized as follows: Businesses will produce only the quantity of goods and services they believe consumers, investors, governments, and foreigners will plan to buy. If these planned aggregate expenditures are less than the economy's full employment output, output will fall short of its potential. When aggregate expenditures are deficient, there are no automatic forces capable of assuring full employment. Prolonged unemployment will persist. Against the background of the Great Depression, this was a compelling argument.

BASIC KEYNESIAN MODEL

The key to the basic Keynesian model is the concept of *planned* aggregate expenditures. As with aggregate demand, the four components of planned aggregate expenditures are consumption, investment, government purchases, and net exports. Before we develop the Keynesian model, however, it's useful to make a few assumptions in order to simplify the analysis. First, as with the *AD/AS* model developed in Chapters 9 and 10, we will assume there is a specific full employment level of output. Only the natural rate of unemployment is present when full employment capacity is attained. Second, following in the Keynesian tradition, we will assume that wages and prices are completely inflexible until full employment is reached. Once full employment is achieved, though, additional demand will lead only to higher prices. Strictly speaking, these polar assumptions will not hold in the real world. They may, however, approximate conditions in the short run. Finally, we will continue to assume that the government's taxing, spending, and monetary policies are constant.

Planned Consumption Expenditures

The most important component of planned aggregate expenditures is *planned* aggregate consumption (C). Keynes believed that current income is the primary determinant of consumption expenditures. As he stated:

> Men are disposed, as a rule and on the average, to increase their consumption as their income increases, but not by as much as the increase in their income.[3]

According to Keynes, disposable income is by far the major determinant of current consumption. If disposable income increases, consumers will increase their planned expenditures.

This positive relationship between consumption spending and disposable income is called the **consumption function.** Exhibit 11–1 illustrates this relationship for an economy. At low levels of aggregate income (less than $6 trillion), the consumption expenditures of households will exceed their disposable income. When income is low, households dissave—they either borrow or draw from their past savings to purchase consumption goods. Because consumption does not increase as rapidly as income, the slope of the consumption function will be less than 1. So the consumption schedule is

Consumption function
A fundamental relationship between disposable income and consumption, in which, as disposable income increases, current consumption expenditures rise, but by a smaller amount than the increase in income.

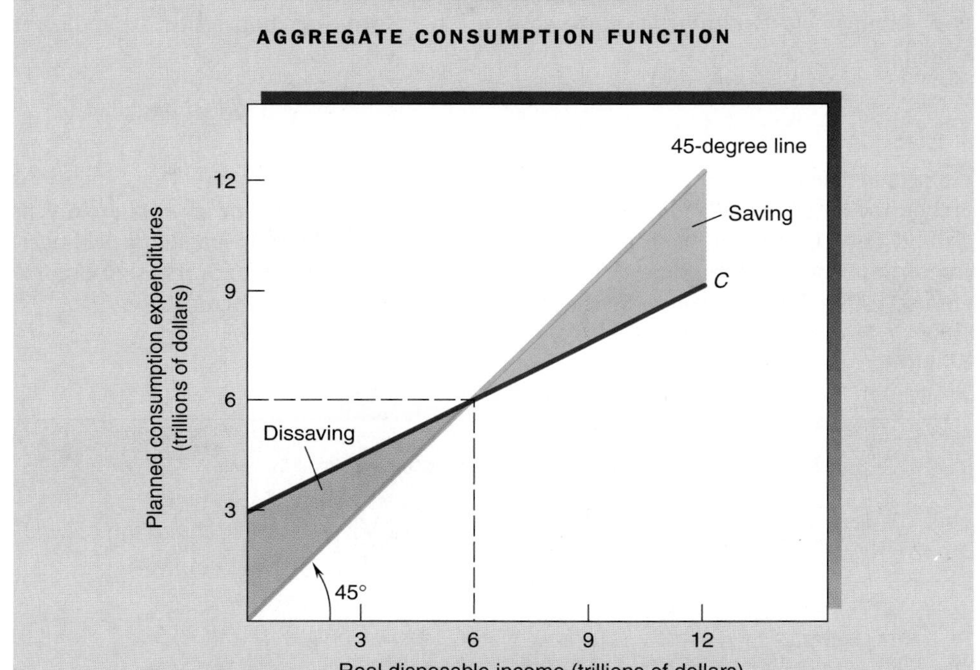

The Keynesian model assumes that there is a positive relationship between consumption and income. However, as income increases, consumption expands by a smaller amount. Thus, the slope of the consumption function (line C) is less than 1 (less than the slope of the 45-degree line).

[3]Keynes, *The General Theory of Employment, Interest, and Money,* p. 96.

flatter than the 45-degree line of Exhibit 11–1. As income increases, household aggregate income eventually equals and exceeds current consumption. For aggregate incomes above $6 trillion, saving increases as income rises.

Planned Investment Expenditures

Investment (I) encompasses (1) expenditures on fixed assets, such as buildings and machines, and (2) changes in the inventories of raw materials and final products not yet sold. Keynes argued that, in the short run, investment was best viewed as an **autonomous expenditure,** one independent of income. In the Keynesian model, planned investment does not change with the level of income. Instead, investment is primarily a function of current sales relative to plant capacity, expected future sales, and the interest rate. Changes in these latter factors would alter investment—they would cause the entire schedule to shift either upward or downward. But when focusing on the forces pushing an economy toward an equilibrium level of output, the basic Keynesian model postulates a constant level of planned investment expenditures.

Autonomous expenditures
Expenditures that do not vary with the level of income. They are determined by factors (such as business expectations and economic policy) that are outside the basic income-expenditure model.

Planned Government Expenditures

As with investment, planned government (G) expenditures in the basic Keynesian model are assumed to be independent of income. These expenditures need not change with the level of income. In the Keynesian model, government expenditures are a policy variable determined by the political process. Governments can, and often do, spend more than they receive in taxes. Perceiving government expenditures as autonomous of income allows us to focus more clearly on the stability characteristics of a private economy. Later, we will analyze how changes in government expenditures influence output and employment within the framework of the Keynesian aggregate expenditures model.

Planned Net Exports

Exports are dependent on spending choices and income levels abroad. These decisions are, by and large, unaffected by changes in a nation's domestic income level. Therefore, as **Exhibit 11–2** illustrates, exports remain constant (at $850 billion) when income changes. In contrast, increases in domestic income will induce consumers to purchase more foreign as well as domestic goods. So the level of imports increases as income rises.

EXHIBIT 11–2

INCOME AND NET EXPORTS

Total Output (Real GDP in Billions)	Planned Exports (Billions)	Planned Imports (Billions)	Planned Net Exports (Billions)
$7,600	$850	$650	$200
7,900	850	700	150
8,200	850	750	100
8,500	850	800	50
8,800	850	850	0

Because exports are determined by income abroad, they are constant at $850 billion. Imports increase as domestic income expands. Thus, planned net exports fall as domestic income increases.

Because exports remain constant and imports increase as aggregate income expands, net exports (*NX*) will decline as income expands (see Exhibit 11–2). Accordingly, the Keynesian model postulates a negative relationship between income and net exports.

Planned versus Actual Expenditures

It is important to distinguish between planned and actual expenditures. Planned expenditures reflect the choices of consumers, investors, governments, and foreigners, *given their expectations as to the choices of other decision makers.* Planned expenditures, though, need not equal actual expenditures. If purchasers spend a different amount on goods and services than business firms anticipate, the firms will experience unplanned changes in inventories. When this is the case, actual investment will differ from planned investment because inventories are a component of investment in our national income accounts.

Consider what would happen if the planned expenditures of consumers, investors, governments, and foreigners on goods and services were less than what business firms thought they would be. If this were the case, business firms would be unable to sell as much of their current output as they had anticipated. Their *actual* inventories would increase as they unintentionally made larger inventory investments than they *planned.* On the other hand, consider what would happen if purchasers bought more goods and services than businesses expected. The unexpected brisk sales would draw down inventories and result in less inventory investment than business firms planned. In this case, *actual* inventory investment would be less than they *planned.*

Actual and *planned* expenditures are equal only when purchasers buy the quantity of goods and services that business decision makers anticipated they would purchase. Only then will the plans of buyers and sellers in the goods and services market harmonize.

KEYNESIAN EQUILIBRIUM

Equilibrium is present in the Keynesian model when planned aggregate expenditures equal the value of current output. When this is the case, businesses are able to sell the total amount of goods and services that they produce. There are no unexpected changes in inventories. Thus, producers have no incentive to either expand or contract their output during the next period. In equation form, Keynesian macroequilibrium is attained when:

$$\underbrace{\text{Total output}}_{\text{Real GDP}} = \underbrace{\text{Planned } C + I + G + NX}_{\text{Planned aggregate expenditures}}$$

Keynesian Equilibrium—A Numeric Example

As an example of Keynesian macroeconomic equilibrium, let's take a look at the hypothetical economy described by **Exhibit 11–3.** To begin, let's focus on columns 1 and 2. At what level of total output is this economy in Keynesian macroeconomic equilibrium? Stop now and attempt to figure out the answer.

The answer is \$8,200 billion, because only there is total output exactly equal to planned aggregate expenditures. When real GDP is equal to \$8,200 billion, the planned expenditures of consumers, investors, governments, and foreigners (net exports) are precisely equal to the value of the output produced by business firms. To see

EXHIBIT 11–3

Note: *All figures are in billions of dollars. Column 2 equals the sum of columns 3 + 4 + 5.*

EXAMPLE OF KEYNESIAN MACROECONOMIC EQUILIBRIUM

Total Output (Real GDP) (1)	Planned Aggregate Expenditures (2)	Planned Consumption (3)	Planned Investment + Government Expenditures (4)	Planned Net Exports (5)	Tendency of Output (6)
$7,600	$7,900	$6,000	$1,700	$200	Expand
7,900	8,050	6,200	1,700	150	Expand
8,200	8,200	6,400	1,700	100	Equilibrium
8,500	8,350	6,600	1,700	50	Contract
8,800	8,500	6,800	1,700	0	Contract

this, note that only at $8,200 billion do columns 3 + 4 + 5 equal column 1. Because of this equality, the spending plans of purchasers mesh with the production plans of business decision makers. Given this balance, there is no reason for producers to change their plans.

What happens at other output levels? At any output other than equilibrium, the plans of producers and purchasers will conflict. If output is $7,900 billion, for example, planned aggregate expenditures will be $8,050 billion, $150 billion more than the current level of output. When expenditures (purchases) exceed output, inventories will decline. Under these circumstances, firms will expand their output in order to rebuild their inventories to normal levels. Therefore, when aggregate expenditures exceed current output, there will be a tendency for output to expand and move toward equilibrium.

At $8,500 billion, output will be greater than planned aggregate expenditures, and unwanted inventories will accumulate. Of course, business firms will not continue to produce goods they cannot sell, so they will reduce production during the subsequent period, moving the economy toward equilibrium.

Equilibrium at Less Than Full Employment

Because Keynesian equilibrium is dependent on equality between planned aggregate expenditures and output, it need not take place at full employment. If an economy is in Keynesian equilibrium, there will be no tendency for output to change even if output is well below full employment capacity.

To see this in our example, assume that full employment is at an output of $8,500 billion, in Exhibit 11–3. Given the current planned spending, the economy will fail to achieve full employment. The rate of unemployment will be high. In the Keynesian model, neither wages nor other resource prices will decline in the face of abnormally high unemployment and excess capacity. Therefore, output will remain at less than the full employment rate as long as insufficient spending prevents the economy from reaching its full potential.

This is precisely what Keynes thought was happening during the Great Depression. He believed that Western economies were in equilibrium at an employment

EXHIBIT 11–4

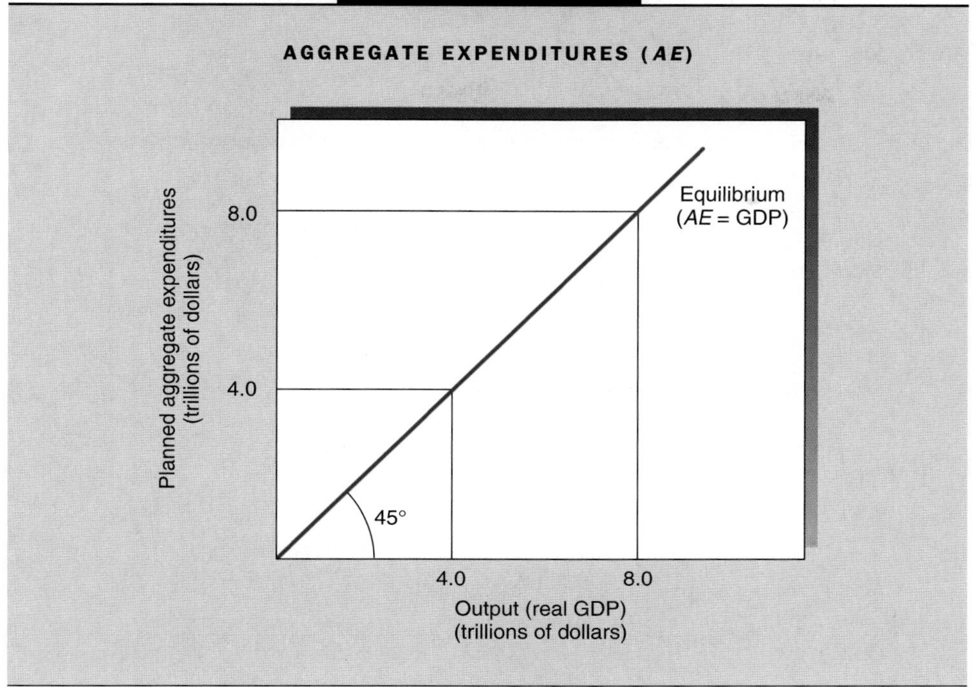

Aggregate expenditures will be equal to total output for all points along a 45-degree line from the origin. The 45-degree line thus maps out potential equilibrium levels of output for the Keynesian model.

rate substantially below capacity. Unless aggregate expenditures increased, therefore, the prolonged unemployment had to continue—as it did throughout that period.

Keynesian Equilibrium—A Graphic Presentation

The Keynesian analysis is presented graphically in **Exhibit 11–4**, where planned aggregate consumption, investment, government, and net export expenditures are measured on the y-axis and total output is measured on the x-axis. The 45-degree line that extends from the origin maps out all the points where aggregate expenditures *(AE)* are equal to total output (GDP).

Because aggregate expenditures equal total output for all points along the 45-degree line, the line maps out all possible equilibrium income levels. As long as the economy is operating at less than its full employment capacity, producers will produce any output along the 45-degree line they believe purchasers will buy. Producers, though, will supply a level of output only if they believe planned expenditures will be large enough to purchase it. Depending on the level of aggregate expenditures, each point along the 45-degree line is a potential equilibrium.

Using the data of Exhibit 11–3, **Exhibit 11–5** graphically depicts the Keynesian equilibrium. The $C + I + G + NX$ line indicates the total planned expenditures of consumers, investors, governments, and foreigners (net exports) at each income level. *Reflecting the consumption function,* the aggregate expenditure *(AE)* line is flatter than the 45-degree line. Remember, as income rises, consumption also increases, but by less than the increase in income. Therefore, as income expands, total expenditures increase by less than the expansion in income.

The equilibrium level of output will be $8.2 trillion, the point at which the total expenditures (measured vertically) are just equal to total output (measured

EXHIBIT 11–5

Here the data of Exhibit 11–3 are presented within the Keynesian graphic framework. The equilibrium level of output is $8.2 trillion because planned expenditures (C + I + G + NX) *are just equal to output at that level of income. At a lower level of income, $7.9 trillion, for example, unplanned inventory reduction would cause business firms to expand output (right-pointing arrow). Conversely, at a higher income level, such as $8.5 trillion, accumulation of inventories would lead to a reduction in future output (left-pointing arrow). Given current aggregate expenditures, only the $8.2 trillion output could be sustained. Note the $8.2 trillion equilibrium income level is less than the economy's potential of $8.5 trillion.*

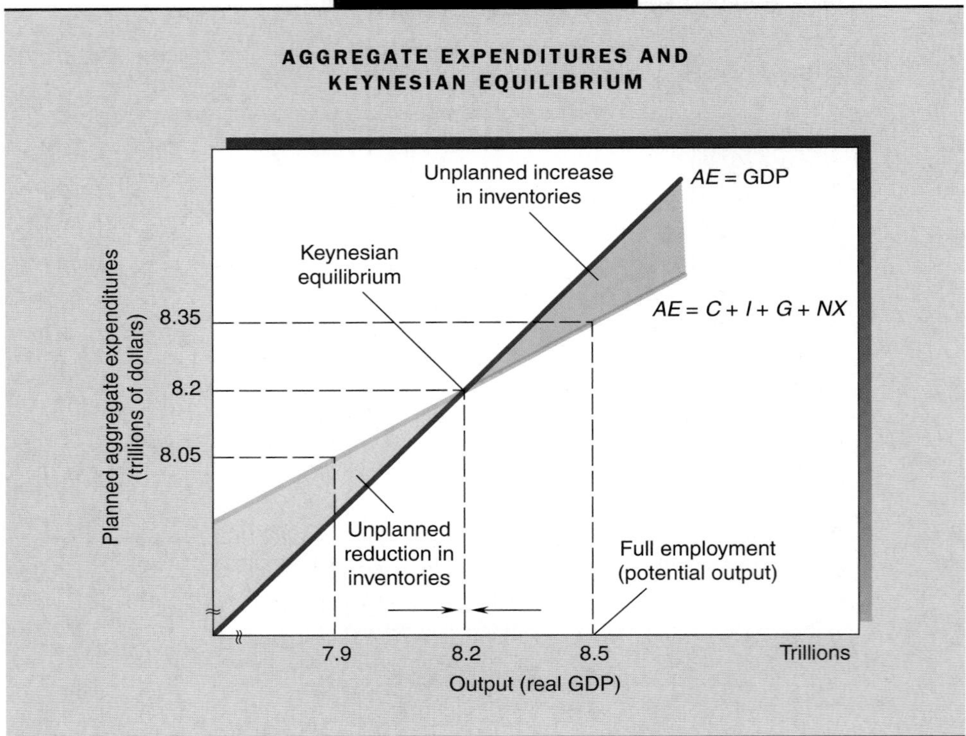

horizontally). Of course, the aggregate expenditures function $C + I + G + NX$ will cross the 45-degree line at the $8.2 trillion equilibrium level of output.

As long as the aggregate expenditures function remains unchanged, no other level of output can be sustained. When total output exceeds $8.2 trillion (for example, $8.5 trillion), the aggregate expenditure line lies below the 45-degree line. Remember that, when the $C + I + G + NX$ line is less than the 45-degree line, total spending is less than total output. Unwanted inventories will then accumulate, leading businesses to reduce their future production. Employment will decline. Output will fall back from $8.5 trillion to the equilibrium level of $8.2 trillion. Note that it is changes in output and employment, not price changes, that restore equilibrium in the Keynesian model.

In contrast, if total output is temporarily below equilibrium, there is a tendency for income to rise. Suppose output is temporarily at $7.9 trillion. At that output level, the $C + I + G + NX$ function lies above the 45-degree line. Aggregate expenditures exceed aggregate output. Businesses are selling more than they currently produce. Their inventories are falling. Excess demand is present. They will react to this state of affairs by hiring more workers and expanding production. Income will rise to the $8.2 trillion equilibrium level. Only at the equilibrium level, the point at which the $C + I + G + NX$ function crosses the 45-degree line, will the spending plans of consumers, investors, and governments, and foreigners sustain the existing output level into the future.

As Exhibit 11–5 illustrates, the economy's full employment potential income level is $8.5 trillion. At this income level, though, aggregate expenditures are insufficient to purchase the output produced. Given the aggregate expenditures function, output will remain below its potential. Unemployment will persist. Within the Keynesian model, equilibrium need not coincide with full employment.

Aggregate Expenditures, Output, and Employment

How could the economy reach its full employment capacity? According to the Keynesian model, it will not do so unless there is a change in the aggregate expenditures schedule. Because the Keynesian model assumes that prices are fixed until potential capacity is reached, wage and price reductions are ruled out as a feasible mechanism for directing the economy to full employment. Neither is the interest rate capable of stimulating demand and directing the economy to full employment.

If consumers, investors, governments, and foreigners could be induced to expand their expenditures, output would expand to full employment capacity. **Exhibit 11–6** illustrates this point. If additional spending shifted the aggregate expenditures schedule (*AE*) upward to AE_2, equilibrium output would expand to its potential capacity. At the higher level of expenditures, AE_2, total spending would equal output at $8.5 trillion.

What would happen if aggregate expenditures exceeded the economy's production capacity? For example, suppose aggregate expenditures rose to AE_3. Within the basic Keynesian model, aggregate expenditures in excess of output lead to a higher price

EXHIBIT 11–6

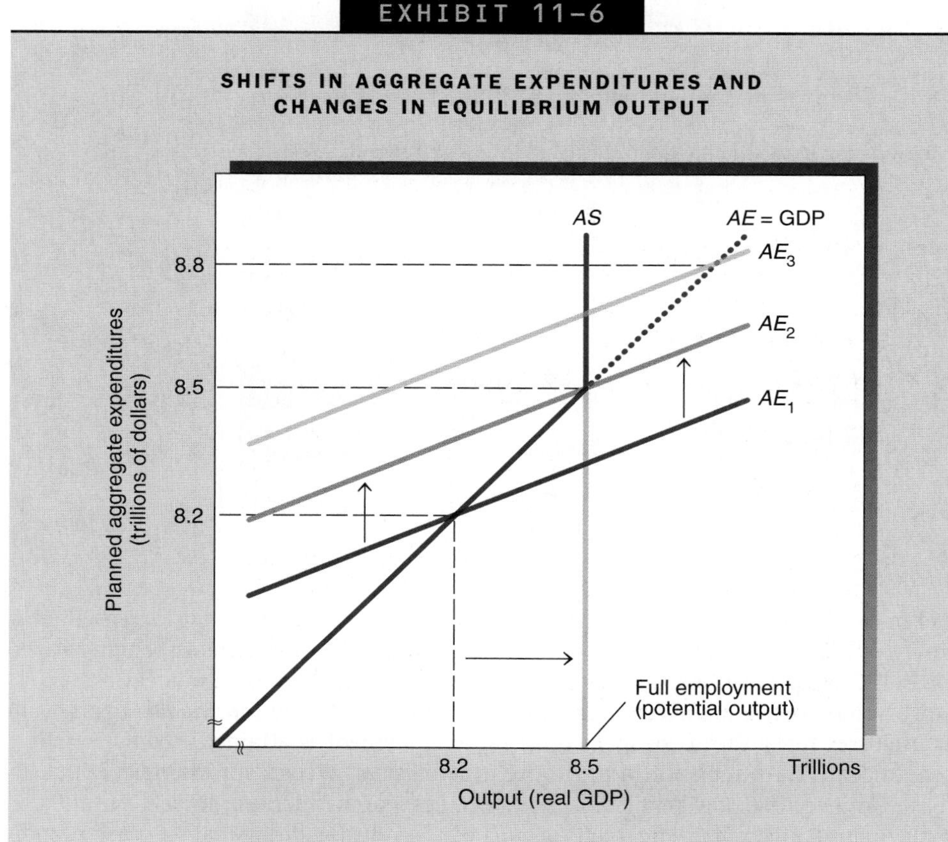

When equilibrium output is less than the economy's capacity, only an increase in expenditures (a shift in AE) will lead to full employment. If consumers, investors, governments, or foreigners would spend more and thereby shift the aggregate-expenditures schedule to AE_2, output would reach its full employment potential ($8.5 trillion). Once full employment is reached, further increases in aggregate expenditures, such as indicated by the shift to AE_3, would lead only to higher prices. Nominal output will expand (the dotted segment of the AE = GDP schedule), but real output will not.

APPLICATIONS IN ECONOMICS

Should Americans Spend or Save?

For several decades following the Second World War, many Keynesian economists worried that spending would be insufficient to promote full employment. Reflecting this view, several elements of the tax code (for example, the tax deductibility of interest expenditures) encouraged consumer spending and penalized saving. More recently, the emphasis has shifted to concern about the low savings rate of Americans. Because saving is necessary for investment, low rates of saving retard both capital formation and the growth of income.

Should Americans spend less and save more? From the Keynesian viewpoint, the answer is "It depends." During periods of high unemployment and excess capacity, Keynesians argue that an increase in consumption (and reduction in saving) would increase demand and help promote full employment. However, when an economy is already at full employment, additional consumption would be inflationary and, other things constant, a lower rate of saving (and capital formation) would retard growth.

level once the economy reaches full employment. Nominal output will increase, but it merely reflects higher prices, rather than additional real output. Total spending in excess of full employment capacity is inflationary within the Keynesian model.

Aggregate expenditures are the catalyst of the Keynesian model. Changes in expenditures make things happen. Until full employment is attained, supply is always accommodative. An increase in aggregate expenditures, caused, for example, by an increase in government expenditures, will thus lead to an increase in real output and employment. Once full employment is reached, however, additional aggregate expenditures lead merely to higher prices.

The Keynesian model implies that regulation of aggregate expenditures is the crux of sound macroeconomic policy. If we could assure aggregate expenditures large enough to achieve capacity output, but not so large as to result in inflation, the Keynesian view implies that maximum output, full employment, and price stability could be attained.

THE KEYNESIAN MODEL WITHIN THE *AD/AS* FRAMEWORK

The Keynesian model can also be presented within the now familiar aggregate demand/aggregate supply (*AD/AS*) framework of the previous two chapters. The only difference in the graphic analysis is that the short-run aggregate supply curve (*SRAS*) has a different shape than in previous chapters because of the assumptions of the Keynesian model. Take a look at **Exhibit 11–7.** Note that the *SRAS* is completely flat at the existing price level until full employment capacity is reached. This is because the Keynesian model assumes that, at less than full employment output levels, prices (and wages) are fixed because they are inflexible in a downward direction. In essence, firms have a horizontal supply curve when operating below normal capacity, so any change in aggregate demand will lead to a corresponding change in output. Economists sometimes refer to this horizontal segment as the *Keynesian range* of the aggregate supply curve.

What happens to the *SRAS* in Exhibit 11–7 when capacity is reached? In this situation, firms raise their prices to allocate the capacity output to those willing to pay the highest prices. Thus, the economy's *SRAS* is vertical at full employment capacity. So both *SRAS* and *LRAS* are vertical at the full employment rate of output (Y_F in Exhibit 11–7).

EXHIBIT 11–7

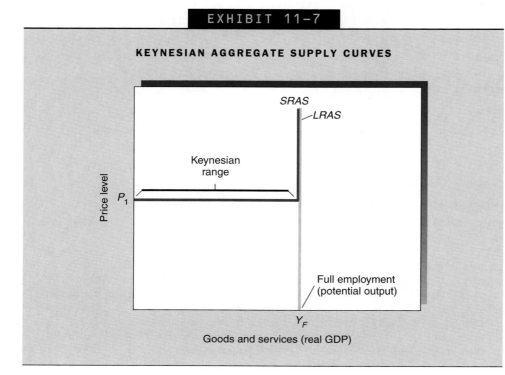

KEYNESIAN AGGREGATE SUPPLY CURVES

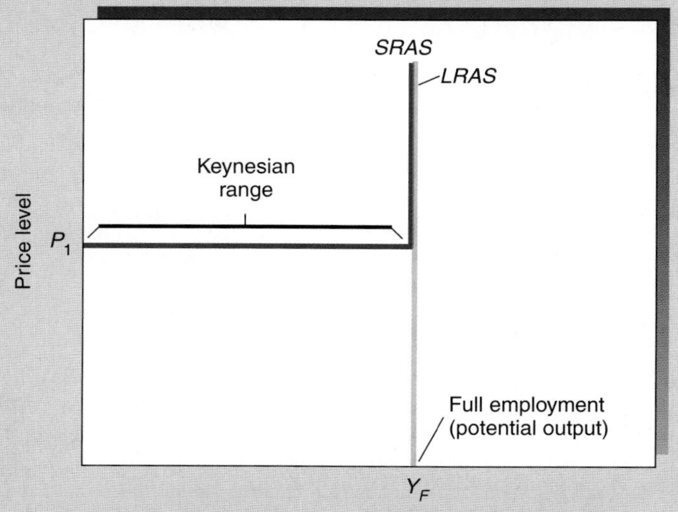

The Keynesian model implies a 90-degree, angle-shaped aggregate supply curve. Because the model postulates downward wage and price inflexibility, the SRAS *curve is flat for outputs less than potential GDP (Y_F). In this range, often referred to as the Keynesian range, output is entirely dependent on the level of aggregate demand. The Keynesian model implies that real output rates beyond full employment are unattainable. Thus, both* SRAS *and* LRAS *are vertical at the economy's full employment potential output.*

Part a of **Exhibit 11–8** illustrates the impact of a change in aggregate demand within the polar assumptions of the Keynesian model. When aggregate demand is less than AD_2 (for example, AD_1), the economy will languish below potential capacity. Because prices and wages are inflexible downward, below-capacity output rates (Y_1, for example) and abnormally high unemployment will persist unless there is an increase in aggregate demand. When output is below its potential, any increase in aggregate demand (for example, the shift from AD_1 to AD_2) brings previously idle resources into the productive process at an unchanged price level. In this range, the Keynesian analysis essentially turns Say's Law (supply creates an equivalent amount of demand) on its head. In the Keynesian range, an increase in demand creates its own supply. Of course, once the economy's potential output constraint (Y_F) is reached, additional demand would merely lead to higher prices rather than to more output. Because both the *SRAS* and *LRAS* curves are vertical at capacity output, an increase in aggregate demand to AD_3 fails to expand real output.

When constructing models, we often make polar assumptions to illustrate various points. The Keynesian model is no exception. In the real world, prices will not be completely inflexible. Similarly, in the short run, unanticipated increases in demand will not lead solely to higher prices. Nevertheless, the Keynesian model implies an important point that is illustrated more realistically by part b of Exhibit 11–8. The horizontal segment of the *SRAS* curve is an oversimplification intended to reinforce the

EXHIBIT 11–08

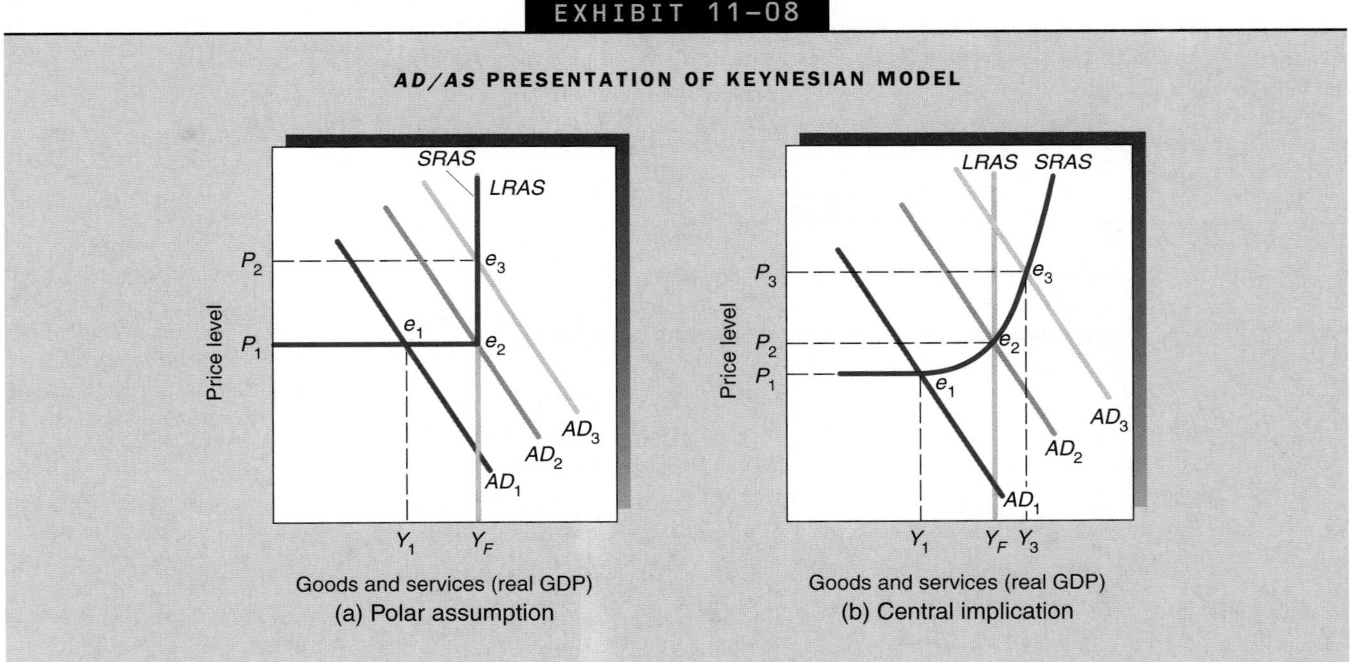

(a) Polar assumption

(b) Central implication

Part a illustrates the polar implications of the Keynesian model. When output is less than capacity (for example, Y_1*), an increase in aggregate demand such as illustrated by the shift from* AD_1 *to* AD_2 *will expand output without increasing prices. But, increases in demand beyond* AD_2*, such as a shift to* AD_3*, lead only to a higher price level (*P_2*). Part b relaxes the assumption of complete price inflexibility and short-run output inflexibility beyond* Y_F*. The* SRAS *curve therefore turns from horizontal to vertical more gradually. This would imply that unanticipated increases in aggregate demand would lead (1) primarily to increases in output when output is below capacity (for example,* Y_1*), and (2) primarily to increases in the price level when output is greater than capacity (for example,* Y_3*).*

idea that changes in aggregate demand exert little impact on prices and substantial impact on output when an economy is operating well below capacity. ***Therefore, under conditions like those of the 1930s—when idle factories and widespread unemployment are present—an increase in aggregate demand will generally exert its primary impact on output.***

On the other hand, the vertical segment of the aggregate supply curve is a simplifying assumption meant to illustrate the concept that there is an attainable output rate beyond which increases in demand will lead almost exclusively to price increases (and only small increases in real output). ***When aggregate demand is already quite strong (for example, AD_3), increases in aggregate demand will predictably exert their primary impact on prices rather than on output.***

THE MULTIPLIER

The multiplier occupies a central position in the Keynesian model. It focuses on the impact of changes in autonomous expenditures—spending unrelated to income that is determined by factors external to the basic income-expenditure model. Changes in autonomous expenditures—for example, an increase in the level of investment due to improved business expectations or an increase in net exports as the result of higher incomes abroad—will shift the entire aggregate expenditure schedule and generally lead to an expansion in income greater than the initial shift in expenditures. The **expenditure multiplier** is defined as the change in total income (equilibrium output) divided by the autonomous expenditure change that brought about the enlarged income.

Expenditure multiplier
The ratio of the change in equilibrium output to the independent change in investment, consumption, or government spending that brings about the change. Numerically, the multiplier is equal to 1 divided by *(1 − MPC) when the price level is constant.*

The multiplier principle builds on the point that one individual's expenditure becomes the income of another. As we previously discussed, consumption expenditures are directly related to income—an increase in income (or wealth) will lead to an increase in consumption. Predictably, income recipients will spend a portion of their additional earnings on consumption. In turn, their consumption expenditures will generate additional income for others who will also spend a portion of it.

Perhaps an example will illuminate the multiplier concept. Suppose that there were idle unemployed resources and that an entrepreneur decided to undertake a $1 million investment project. Because investment is a component of aggregate demand, the project will increase demand directly by $1 million. This is not the entire story, however. The investment project will require plumbers, carpenters, masons, lumber, cement, and many other resources. The incomes of the suppliers of these resources will increase by $1 million. What will they do with this additional income? Given the link between one's income and consumption, the resource suppliers will predictably spend a fraction of the additional income. They will buy more food, clothing, recreation, medical care, and thousands of other items. How will this spending influence the incomes of those who supply these additional consumption products and services? Their incomes will increase, also. After setting aside (saving) a portion of this additional income, these persons will also spend some of their additional income on current consumption. Their consumption spending will result in still more additional income for other product and service suppliers.

The term *multiplier* is also used to indicate the number by which the initial investment would be multiplied to obtain the total summation of the increases in income. If the $1 million investment resulted in $4 million of additional income, the multiplier would be 4. The total increase in income would be four times the amount of the initial increase in spending. Similarly, if total income increased by $3 million, the multiplier would be 3.

The Size of the Multiplier

Marginal propensity to consume (MPC)
Additional current consumption divided by additional current disposable income.

The size of the multiplier depends on the proportion of the additional income that households choose to spend on consumption.[4] Keynes referred to this fraction as the **marginal propensity to consume (MPC).** Mathematically:

$$\text{MPC} = \frac{\text{Additional consumption}}{\text{Additional income}}$$

For example, if your income increases by $100 and you therefore increase your current consumption expenditures by $75, your marginal propensity to consume is 3/4, or 0.75.

Exhibit 11–9 illustrates why the size of the multiplier is dependent on the MPC. Suppose the MPC is equal to 3/4, indicating that consumers spend 75 cents of each additional dollar earned. Continuing with our previous example, we know that a $1 million investment would initially result in $1 million of additional income in round 1. Because the MPC is 3/4, consumption would increase by $750,000 (the other $250,000 would flow into saving), contributing that amount to income in round 2. The recipients of the round 2 income of $750,000 would spend three-fourths of it on current consumption. Hence, their spending would increase income by $562,500 in round 3. Exhibit 11–9 illustrates the additions to income through other rounds. In total, income would increase by $4 million, given an MPC of 3/4. The multiplier is 4.

If the MPC had been greater, income recipients would have spent a larger share of their additional income on current consumption during each round. Thus, the additional income generated in each round would have been greater, increasing the

EXHIBIT 11–9

THE MULTIPLIER PRINCIPLE

Expenditure Stage	Additional Income (Dollars)	Additional Consumption (Dollars)	Marginal Propensity to Consume
Round 1	1,000,000	750,000	3/4
Round 2	750,000	562,500	3/4
Round 3	562,500	421,875	3/4
Round 4	421,875	316,406	3/4
Round 5	316,406	237,305	3/4
Round 6	237,305	177,979	3/4
Round 7	177,979	133,484	3/4
Round 8	133,484	100,113	3/4
Round 9	100,113	75,085	3/4
Round 10	75,085	56,314	3/4
All Others	225,253	168,939	3/4
Total	4,000,000	3,000,000	3/4

[4]For the purposes of simplicity when calculating the size of the multiplier, we will assume that all additions to income are either (1) spent on domestically produced goods or (2) saved. This assumption means that we are ignoring the impact of taxes and spending on imports as income expands via the multiplier process. At the conclusion of our analysis, we will indicate the significance of this assumption.

EXHIBIT 11–10

A HIGHER MPC MEANS A LARGER MULTIPLIER

MPC	Size of Multiplier
9/10	10
4/5	5
3/4	4
2/3	3
1/2	2
1/3	1.5

size of the multiplier. There is a precise relationship between the expenditure multiplier and the MPC. The expenditure multiplier, M, is:

$$M = \frac{1}{1 - \text{MPC}}$$

Exhibit 11–10 indicates the size of the multiplier for several different values of MPC.

Real-World Significance of the Multiplier

Within the framework of the Keynesian model, the multiplier is important because it explains why even small changes in investment, government, or consumption spending can trigger much larger changes in output. The multiplier magnifies the fluctuations in output and employment that emanate from autonomous changes in spending.

There are both positive and negative sides to the amplified effects. On the negative side, the multiplier principle indicates that a small reduction in investment expenditures, perhaps due to a decline in business optimism, can be an important source of economic instability. As a result, many Keynesian economists believe that the stability of a market economy is quite fragile and constantly susceptible to even modest disruptions. On the positive side, the multiplier principle illustrates the potential of macroeconomic policy to stimulate output even if it is able to exert only a small impact on autonomous expenditures.

In evaluating the significance of the multiplier, it is important to keep three points in mind. ***First, in addition to saving, leakages in the form of taxes and spending on imports will also reduce the size of the multiplier.*** In order to keep things simple, we assumed that all income was either saved or spent on domestically produced goods throughout our analysis. Like saving, taxes and imports will siphon some of the additional income away from spending on domestic goods and services. These leakages from the flow of spending will dampen the effects of the multiplier. Therefore, the actual multiplier will be somewhat smaller than the simple expenditure multiplier of our analysis.

Second, it takes time for the multiplier to work. In the real world, several weeks or perhaps even months will be required for each successive round of spending. Only a fraction of the multiplier effect will be observed quickly. Most researchers

APPLICATIONS IN ECONOMICS

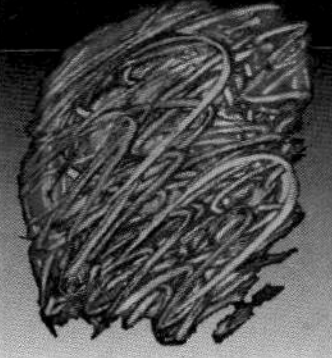

Sports Stadiums, Development Subsidies, and the Multiplier

Arguing that they will promote economic development and employment, many local governments have constructed or heavily subsidized sports stadiums, civic and art centers, and even hotels. The multiplier concept is often used in support of such projects. Proponents buttress their case by claiming, for example, that a $100 million project will promote additional spending of three or four times this amount, and thereby generate additional income and tax revenue for the financing of the project.

The construction of BOB (Bank One Ballpark) is typical of such projects. This nearly 50,000-seat stadium is used by the Arizona Diamondbacks major league baseball team. Opening in 1998, the facility cost $360 million, three-fourths of which was financed with taxpayer funds generated by a 1/4 cent increase in the local sales tax.

Does the multiplier enhance the attractiveness of projects like BOB? When thinking about this question, it is important to keep two points in mind. First, the multiplier applies only for shifts in expenditures—that is, spending that otherwise would not have taken place. Economists refer to spending of this type as "exogenous expenditures." Clearly, the $360 million spent on the stadium substantially overstates the net increase in expenditures. The tax increase (and government borrowing) drained approximately $270 million from local taxpayers. If these funds had not been used to finance BOB, taxpayers would have purchased more food, housing, recreation, health care, and numerous other items in the local economy. This reduction in spending is a partial offset against the increased spending resulting from the stadium construction.

Second, if the multiplier is going to work its magic and expand real income, resources that would have otherwise been unemployed must be brought into the production process. Unless this is the case, the expansion in demand will merely lead to higher prices. At the time of BOB's construction, the rate of unemployment in Phoenix and other areas of the country was very low. Given these conditions, a large portion of any increased demand derived from the stadium construction would merely push prices upward, rather than expanding employment and real income.

What about the spending of people attending the games? Again, a substantial portion of this spending will be replacement in nature. If people did not spend their income on major league baseball, most would spend it on other things—basketball and football games, movies, other forms of entertainment, and eating out, for example. The composition of spending is affected, but there is little, if any, impact on the level of expenditures. Of course, there will be some increase in local spending generated by those attending games from out of town. This spending will generate a multiplier effect for the local economy. However, Diamondback fans in the Phoenix area may follow the team to other cities, and, as a result, spend less in the local economy. This would, at least partially, offset the additional spending in the Phoenix area by those from out of town.

Rhetoric aside, local government spending projects for sports, entertainment, and the arts are generally more about rent-seeking than economic development. All of us would like to have others help pay for things we enjoy, or things that will increase the value of assets we own. As the public choice model highlights, rent-seeking is an important motivation for public sector action. Viewed from this perspective, exaggerated claims of multiplier effects by proponents seeking to gain through public sector action are an expected occurrence.

Do government expenditures on projects like the construction of the Bank One Ballpark in Phoenix, Arizona, exert a multiplier effect?

believe that only about one-half the total multiplier effect will be felt during the first six months following a change in expenditures.

Third, the multiplier implies that the additional spending brings idle resources into production, leading to additional real output rather than to increased prices. When unemployment is widespread, this is a realistic assumption. However, when there is an absence of abundant idle resources, the multiplier effect will be dampened by an increase in the price level.

THE KEYNESIAN VIEW OF THE BUSINESS CYCLE

Keynesian economists believe that a market economy, if left to its own devices, is unstable and likely to experience prolonged periods of recession. The Keynesian view emphasizes the destabilizing potential of autonomous changes in expenditures powered by the multiplier and changes in optimism. Suppose there is an increase in aggregate demand triggered by what appears to be a relatively minor disruption—for example, higher incomes abroad, an increase in consumer optimism, or a burst of business optimism generated by a new innovation. Keynesians believe that such changes will often lead to an expansion in output that will have a tendency to feed on itself. The initial increase in demand, *magnified by the multiplier,* will lead to an expansion in employment and a rapid growth of income. In turn, the higher incomes will lead to additional consumption and strong business sales. Inventories will decline, and businesses will expand output (to rebuild inventories) and move investment projects forward as they become more optimistic about the future. Unemployment will decline to a low level as the economy experiences a boom.

Can this expansionary phase continue indefinitely? The answer is no. Eventually, full employment capacity will be reached. Constrained by the availability of both labor and machines, the growth rate of the economy will slow. The slower growth will dampen the optimism of business decision makers and cause them to cut back on fixed investments. Again, the multiplier will magnify the impact of the change in demand. Thus, the reduction in investment and increased pessimism about the future will often lead to a sharp reduction in output. As the economy plunges into a recession, inventories will rise as businesses are unable to sell their goods because of the low level of demand. Workers will be laid off. The ranks of unemployed workers will grow. Bankruptcies will become more common.

This is what Keynes perceived was happening in the 1930s. Consumers were not spending because their incomes had fallen and they were extremely pessimistic about the future. Similarly, businesses were not producing because there was little demand for their products. Investment had come to a complete standstill because underutilized resources and capacity were abundantly available.

Wide fluctuation in private investment is the villain of Keynesian business cycle theory. An economic expansion accelerates into a boom because investment, amplified by the multiplier, stimulates other sectors of the economy. At the first sign of a slowdown, though, investment plans are sharply curtailed. Eventually, machines will wear out and the capital stock will decline to a level consistent with the current level of income. At that point, *additional* investment will be necessary for replacement purposes. The new investment will stimulate additional output and employment, and start the cycle anew. ***Keynesian economists believe that the recessionary phase is likely to be quite lengthy and they have little confidence that either lower interest rates or falling resource prices will be able to reverse the tide of the falling incomes.***

EVOLUTION OF MODERN MACROECONOMICS

MAJOR INSIGHTS OF KEYNESIAN ECONOMICS

Keynesian economics and the aggregate expenditure (*AE*) model dominated the thinking of macroeconomists for three decades following the Second World War. Three major insights of the Keynesian model stand out.

1. ***Changes in output, as well as changes in prices, play a role in the macroeconomic adjustment process, particularly in the short run.*** The classical model emphasized the role of prices in directing an economy to macroeconomic equilibrium. Keynesian analysis highlights the importance of changes in output.
2. ***The responsiveness of aggregate supply to changes in demand will be directly related to the availability of unemployed resources.*** Keynesian analysis emphasizes that, when idle resources are present, output will be highly responsive to changes in aggregate demand. Conversely, when an economy is operating at or near its capacity, output will be much less sensitive to changes in demand. So the *SRAS* curve is relatively flat when an economy is well below capacity and relatively steep when the economy is operating near and beyond capacity (see Exhibit 11–8).
3. ***Fluctuations in aggregate demand are an important potential source of business instability.*** Abrupt changes in demand are a potential source of both recession and inflation. Policies that effectively stabilize aggregate demand—that minimize abrupt changes in demand—will substantially reduce economic instability.

DIMINISHED POPULARITY OF THE *AE* MODEL

As we have stressed, both Keynesian economics and the *AE* model were an outgrowth of the Great Depression. Keynesian analysis provides an explanation for what happened during the 1930s. However, other explanations are also possible. Many economists believe misguided economic policies, particularly monetary policy, contributed to the depth and duration of the Great Depression. According to this view, markets were unable to restore full employment within a reasonable length of time during the 1930s because policies were inadvertently adopted that not only hampered recovery, but actually depressed economic conditions. This monetary view of the business cycle will be presented in Chapters 14 and 15.

In recent years, the popularity of the Keynesian aggregate expenditure model has diminished. There are two major reasons for this. First, the *AE* model is unable to explain the simultaneous occurrence of inflation and high unemployment. In the *AE* model, aggregate expenditures are either too low (resulting in recession) or too high (leading to inflation). Because the model fails to incorporate expectations, it is unable to explain the simultaneous presence of both high unemployment and inflation, such as occurred during the 1970s.

The second factor contributing to the decline of the aggregate expenditure model is the stability of recent years. The *AE* model was designed to explain lengthy recessions—equilibrium at less than full employment—and the fragile nature of business stability. This played well in the aftermath of the Great Depression. But it is less relevant today. During the last 16 years (1983–1998), the United States has experienced only nine months of recession. Just as the classical model appeared to have little relevance to the 1930s, a model stressing the recession-prone nature of a market economy seems out of place today. Of course, this may change—it is way too early to pronounce the death of the business cycle. As long as the current stability continues, however, there is likely to be more emphasis on long-run growth and less on economic fluctuations.

The Hybrid Nature of Modern Macroeconomics

Modern macroeconomics is a hybrid, reflecting elements of both classical and Keynesian analysis as well as some unique insights drawn from other areas of economics. As we discussed in the previous chapter, various shocks (unanticipated changes in *AD* or *AS*) can disrupt full employment equilibrium and lead either to recessionary unemployment or to an inflationary boom in the short run. Furthermore, macroeconomic markets do not adjust instantaneously. In the short run, incorrect perceptions of the current price level and "sticky" wages and prices may lead to output levels that differ from long-run equilibrium. This is reflective of the Keynesian view.

However, modern analysis also indicates that changes in real wages and interest rates will act as a stabilizing force, directing a market economy toward full employment. When an economy is operating below its potential during a recession, falling real wages and interest rates will help restore full employment. Similarly, rising real wages and interest rates will tend to retard an economic boom. These long-run implications of modern analysis are reflective of the classical view.

Economic conditions during the past several decades are consistent with the modern view. We continue to experience economic ups and downs, short-run disequilibrium conditions resulting from various shocks. But economic downturns do not spiral downward and result in prolonged periods of stagnation. The self-corrective characteristics of a market economy are more potent than was previously thought.

In addition, modern macroeconomics indicates that the impact of economic change is more complex than either the earlier classical or Keynesian economists realized. When analyzing the impact of a change, it makes a difference whether the change is anticipated or unanticipated. It is also important whether people expect the change to be temporary or permanent. Today, both Keynesians and non-Keynesians integrate these factors into their analysis.

Several key elements of modern macroeconomics are more easily visualized within the framework of the multimarket *AD/AS* model we developed in Chapters 9 and 10. The *AD/AS* model also makes it easier to understand and distinguish between long-run and short-run conditions. In essence, the classical model is a long-run equilibrium model, while the Keynesian aggregate expenditure model is a short-run excess-capacity model. The *AD/AS* model incorporates and highlights the importance of both the short and long runs. The *AD/AS* model is more flexible, and it can be used to address a broader range of topics than either the classical or Keynesian models. As a result, it will be our primary tool as we seek to develop more depth in our understanding of macroeconomic issues.

Looking Ahead

Although Keynes emphasized that a market economy might fail to reach automatically its potential capacity, he argued that governments could use their tax and expenditure policies to stabilize aggregate demand and assure full employment. Keynes and his followers forced a reluctant economics profession to think seriously about macroeconomic policy. Turning next to this issue, we will begin by considering the potential of fiscal policy as a tool with which to promote full employment, stable prices, and the growth of real output.

KEY POINTS

➤ Classical economists believed production created an equivalent amount of current demand (Say's Law) and that flexible wages, prices, and interest rates would assure full employment. The Great Depression undermined the credibility of the classical view.

➤ The concept of planned aggregate expenditures ($C + I + G + NX$) is central to the Keynesian analysis. In the Keynesian model, as income expands, consumption increases, but by a lesser amount than the income increase. Both planned investment and government expenditures are independent of income in the Keynesian model. Planned net exports decline as income increases.

➤ The Keynesian model postulates that business firms will produce the amount of goods and services they believe consumers, investors, governments, and foreigners (net exports) plan to buy. Thus, equilibrium is present when planned total expenditures are equal to output.

➤ When total expenditures are less than current output, business firms will accumulate unplanned additions to inventories that will cause them to cut back on future output and employment. On the other hand, when total expenditures are greater than output, inventories will fall and businesses will respond with an expansion in output in an effort to restore inventories to their normal levels. Aggregate expenditures must equal current output (AE = GDP) for equilibrium to occur.

➤ Keynesian equilibrium need not occur at the full employment level of output.

➤ Changes in aggregate expenditures are the catalyst of the Keynesian model. When an economy is operating below full employment capacity, increases in aggregate expenditures lead to an expansion in both output and employment. Once capacity is reached, further expansions in expenditures lead only to higher prices.

➤ The Keynesian model implies that maintaining aggregate expenditures at the level consistent with full employment and stable prices is the primary function of sound macroeconomic policy.

➤ The expenditure multiplier indicates that independent changes in planned investment, government expenditures, and consumption will cause income (and output) to increase by some multiple of the initial increase in spending. The multiplier is the number by which the initial change in spending is multiplied to obtain the total amplified increase in income. The size of the multiplier increases with the marginal propensity to consume.

➤ In evaluating the importance of the multiplier, one should remember that (a) taxes and spending on imports will dampen the size of the multiplier; (b) it takes time for the multiplier to work; and (c) the amplified effect on real output will be valid only when the additional spending brings idle resources into production without price changes.

➤ According to the Keynesian view of the business cycle, upswings and downswings tend to feed on themselves. During a downturn, business pessimism, declining investment, and the multiplier principle combine to plunge the economy farther toward recession. During an economic upswing, business and consumer optimism and expanding investment interact with the multiplier principle to propel the economy to an inflationary boom. The theory suggests that a market-directed economy, left to its own devices, will tend to fluctuate between economic recession and inflationary boom.

➤ While modern macro analysis incorporates elements of both Keynesian and classical economics, it also highlights the role of expectations and the importance of distinguishing between market adjustments in the long and short runs.

CRITICAL ANALYSIS QUESTIONS

1. What determines the equilibrium rate of output in the Keynesian model? Explain why an equilibrium level of output will continue to persist. What did Keynes think had happened during the prolonged, high level of unemployment of the Great Depression?

*2. How will each of the following factors influence the consumption schedule?

a. The expectation that consumer prices will rise more rapidly in the future
b. Pessimism about future employment conditions
c. A reduction in income taxes
d. An increase in the interest rate
e. A decline in stock prices
f. A redistribution of income from older workers (age 45 and over) to younger workers (under 35)
g. A redistribution of income from the wealthy to the poor

3. What is the major reason for fluctuations in output within the framework of the Keynesian model? What is necessary for maintenance of full employment?

*4. What is the multiplier principle? What determines the size of the multiplier? Does the multiplier principle make it more or less difficult to stabilize the economy? Explain.

5. In the Keynesian *AE* model, why does an increase in aggregate spending lead to an equal increase in real GDP as long as output is at less than full employment capacity? What does this imply about the shape of the aggregate supply curve?

6. Widespread acceptance of the Keynesian aggregate expenditure *(AE)* model took place during and immediately following the Great Depression. Can you explain why? The aggregate expenditure model declined in popularity when many economies experienced both high rates of unemployment and inflation during the 1970s. Was this surprising? Explain.

*7. What role do declining real wages and resource prices play in the restoration of full employment in the Keynesian model? If output is currently below the full employment rate, what will direct the economy to full employment in the Keynesian model?

8. Suppose that individuals suddenly decided to spend less on consumption and save more of their current income. Compare and contrast this change within the framework of the Keynesian *AE* and the *AD/AS* models.

*9. "Historically, interest rates have generally been higher during periods of economic boom than during recessions. This indicates that higher interest rates stimulate additional investment." Evaluate this view.

10. How would an increase in income abroad influence the equilibrium level of output at home within the framework of the Keynesian *AE* model? Would the results differ within the framework of the *AD/AS* model? Explain.

11. Economists often state that the Keynesian *AE* model has its greatest relevance in the short run, while the classical model is most relevant to the long run. In what sense is this true?

*12. In recent years, approximately 35 percent of the income of Canadians has been spent on imports. In the United States, spending on imports constitutes about 12 percent of income. Would you expect the size of the multiplier to be larger or smaller in Canada than in the United States? Explain.

13. The rate of output and planned expenditures for an economy are indicated in the accompanying table.

Total Output (Real GDP in billions)	Planned Aggregate Expenditures (in billions)
$5,000	$5,250
5,500	5,500
6,000	5,750
6,500	6,000
7,000	6,250

a. If the current output rate were $5,000 billion, what would tend to happen to business inventories, future output, and employment?
b. If the current output rate were $6,500 billion, what would tend to happen to inventories, future output, and employment?
c. What is the equilibrium rate of income of this economy?
d. If the economy's full employment rate of output were $6,000 billion, would the rate of unemployment be high, low, or normal, assuming the current planned demand persisted into the future?
e. What would happen if there was an autonomous increase in investment of $250 billion?

*Asterisk denotes questions for which answers are given in Appendix B.

CHAPTER 12

In the early stages of the Keynesian revolution, macroeconomists emphasized fiscal policy as the most powerful and balanced remedy for demand management. Gradually, shortcomings of fiscal policy became apparent. The shortcomings stem from timing, politics, macroeconomic theory, and the deficit itself.[1]

Paul Samuelson, Nobel Laureate

Fiscal Policy

CHAPTER FOCUS

- How does fiscal policy affect aggregate demand? How does it affect aggregate supply?
- What is the Keynesian view of fiscal policy? How do the crowding-out and new classical models modify the basic Keynesian analysis?
- How difficult is it to time fiscal policy properly? Why is proper timing important?
- Is there a synthesis view of fiscal policy? What are its major elements?
- Are there supply-side effects of fiscal policy?

[1]Paul A. Samuelson and William D. Nordhaus, *Economics*, 15th ed. (New York: McGraw-Hill, 1995), p. 644.

As we indicated in Chapter 9, fiscal policy involves the use of the government's spending and taxing authority. As the basic aggregate demand and aggregate supply model has been used to analyze the economy, we have previously assumed that the government's fiscal policy remained unchanged. We are now ready to relax this assumption and investigate the impact of fiscal policy on output, prices, and employment.

There is some disagreement among economists with regard to both how fiscal policy works and its potential to improve the performance of a market economy. In fact, views on this topic have changed in recent decades. This chapter will cover four alternative fiscal policy models—the Keynesian, crowding-out, new classical, and supply-side perspectives. We will consider how and why views toward these models have changed in recent decades. The basic AD-AS macroeconomic model will be used to illustrate each of the fiscal policy perspectives.

Because we want to isolate the impact of changes in fiscal policy from changes in monetary policy, we will continue to assume that the monetary authorities maintain a constant supply of money. We will begin our analysis of monetary policy in the following chapter.

BUDGET DEFICITS AND SURPLUSES

Fiscal policy is reflected through the government's spending, taxing, and borrowing policies. It is one of the major tools that might be used to help promote the goals of full employment, price stability, and rapid economic growth. When the supply of money is constant, government expenditures must be financed with either: (1) taxes and other revenues derived from the sale of services or assets or (2) borrowing. When government revenues from taxes and sales are equal to government expenditures (including both purchases of goods and services and transfer payments), the government has a **balanced budget.** The budget need not be in balance, however. A **budget deficit** is present when total government spending exceeds total government revenue from all sources. When a budget deficit is present, the government must borrow funds to finance the excess of its spending relative to revenue. It borrows by issuing interest-bearing bonds that become part of what we call the national debt, the total amount of outstanding government bonds. Conversely, a **budget surplus** is present when the government's revenues exceed its total expenditures. The surplus allows the government to reduce its outstanding debt.

Balanced budget
A situation in which current government revenue from taxes, fees, and other sources is just equal to current government expenditures.

Budget deficit
A situation in which total government spending exceeds total government revenue during a specific time period, usually one year.

Budget surplus
A situation in which total government spending is less than total government revenue during a time period, usually a year.

The federal budget is much more than a mere revenue and expenditure statement of a large organization. Of course, its sheer size means that it exerts a substantial influence on the economy. Its importance, though, stems from its position as a policy variable. The federal budget is the primary tool of fiscal policy. In contrast with private organizations that are directed by the pursuit of income and profit, the federal government can alter its budget with an eye toward influencing the future direction of the economy.

Changes in the size of the federal deficit or surplus are often used to gauge whether fiscal policy is adding additional demand stimulus or imposing additional demand restraint. It is important to note, however, that changes in the size of the deficit may arise from two different sources. ***First, changes in the size of the deficit may merely reflect the state of the economy.*** During a recession, tax revenues generally fall and expenditures on transfer programs increase as the result of the weak economic conditions. This will shift the budget toward a deficit even if there is no change in fiscal policy. Just the opposite will happen during the expansion phase of the business cycle. Tax revenue will increase and transfer payments decline as the result of the rapid growth of income. This will shift the budget toward a surplus (or smaller deficit) during a strong economic expansion. ***Second, changes in the deficit may reflect*** **discretionary fiscal policy.** Policymakers may institute deliberate changes in tax laws or spending on government programs in order to alter the size of the budget deficit (or surplus). When we speak of "changes in fiscal policy," we are referring to changes of this type—deliberate changes in government expenditures or tax policy or both that are designed to affect the size of the budget deficit or surplus.

Discretionary fiscal policy
A change in laws or appropriation levels that alters government revenues and/or expenditures.

KEYNESIAN VIEW OF FISCAL POLICY

Prior to the 1960s, the desirability of a balanced federal budget was widely accepted among business and political leaders. Keynesian economists, though, were highly critical of this view. Keynesians argued that the federal budget should be used to promote a level of aggregate demand consistent with the full employment rate of output.

How might policymakers use the budget to stimulate aggregate demand? First, an increase in government purchases of goods and services will directly increase aggregate demand. As the government spends more on highways, flood control projects, education, and national defense, for example, these expenditures will increase demand in the goods and services market. Second, changes in tax policy will also influence aggregate demand. For example, a reduction in personal taxes will increase the current disposable income of households. As their after-tax income rises, individuals will spend more on consumption. In turn, this increase in consumption will stimulate aggregate demand. Similarly, a reduction in business taxes increases after-tax profitability, which will stimulate both business investment and aggregate demand.

When an economy is operating below its potential capacity, the Keynesian model suggests that government should institute **expansionary fiscal policy.** In other words, the government should either increase its purchases of goods and services or cut taxes or both. Of course, this policy will increase the government's budget deficit. In order to finance the enlarged budget deficit, the government will have to borrow from either private domestic sources or foreigners.[2]

Expansionary fiscal policy
An increase in government expenditures and/or a reduction in tax rates such that the expected size of the budget deficit expands.

Exhibit 12–1 illustrates the case for expansionary fiscal policy when an economy is experiencing abnormally high unemployment caused by deficient aggregate demand. Initially, the economy is operating at e_1. Output is below potential capacity, Y_F, and unemployment exceeds its natural rate. As we have previously discussed, if there is no change in policy, abnormally high unemployment and excess supply in the resource market would eventually reduce real wages and other resource prices. The

[2]Alternatively, the government could borrow from its central bank—the Federal Reserve Bank in the United States. However, as we will see in the following chapter, this method of financing a budget deficit would expand the money supply. Since we want to differentiate between fiscal and monetary effects, we must hold the supply of money constant. So for now, we assume that the government deficit must be financed by borrowing from private sources.

EXHIBIT 12-1

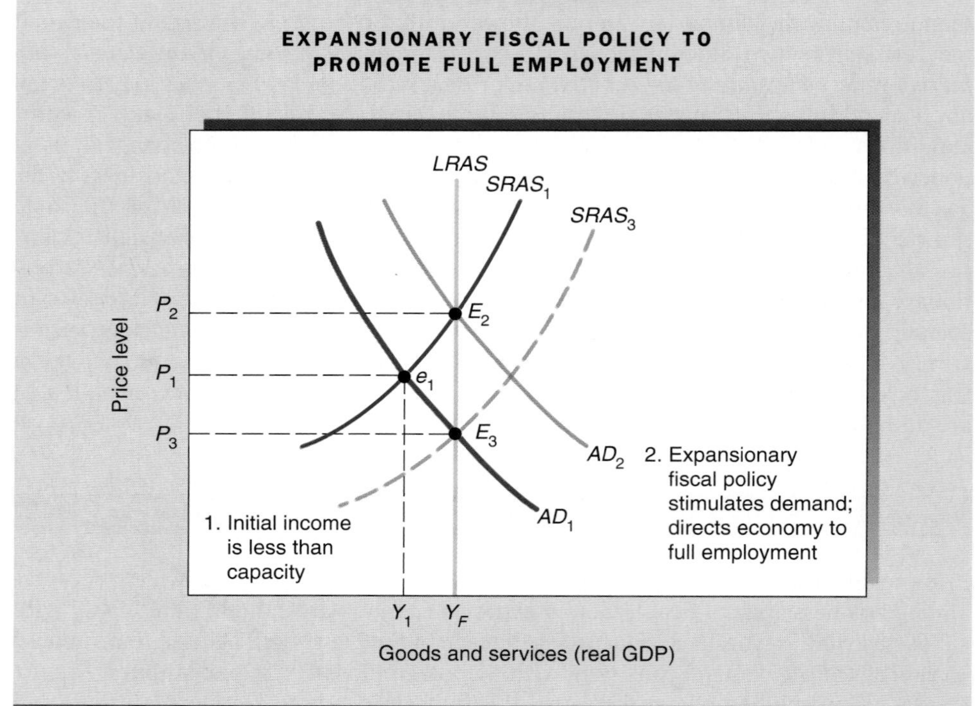

Here we illustrate an economy operating in the short run at Y_1*, below its potential capacity of* Y_F*. There are two routes to a long-run full employment equilibrium. First, policymakers could wait for lower wages and resource prices to reduce costs, increase supply to* $SRAS_3$*, and restore equilibrium at* E_3*. Keynesians believe this market-adjustment method will be slow and uncertain. Alternatively, expansionary fiscal policy could stimulate aggregate demand (shift to* AD_2*) and guide the economy to* E_2*.*

accompanying lower costs would increase aggregate supply (shift to $SRAS_3$) and guide the economy to a full employment equilibrium (E_3) at a lower price level (P_3). In addition, lower real interest rates resulting from weak business demand for investment funds may help stimulate aggregate demand and restore full employment.

As we noted in the previous chapter, Keynesians believe that wages and prices are inflexible—particularly in a downward direction. Thus, they have little confidence in the ability of lower wages and falling interest rates to restore full employment in the midst of a recession. Keynesians recommend government action—a shift to a more expansionary fiscal policy in order to speed up the movement toward full employment equilibrium. Keynesians advocate more government spending or a reduction in taxes or both—that is, a deliberate increase in the budget deficit—as a means of stimulating aggregate demand. Furthermore, they argue that the multiplier process will magnify the initial increase in spending. Suppose that the government holds taxes constant and increases its spending on highways and school construction by $10 billion. The additional spending will enhance the incomes of those undertaking the construction by $10 billion. As these individuals use a portion of this income to buy consumer goods, this will provide additional demand stimulus. Thus, Keynesians expect that the total increase in aggregate demand will be substantially greater than the initial $10 billion increase in government purchases.

When an economy is operating below its potential capacity, the Keynesian prescription calls for expansionary fiscal policy—a deliberate change in expenditures and/or taxes that will increase the size of the government's budget deficit. An appropriate dose of expansionary fiscal policy, if timed properly, would stimulate aggregate demand (shift the curve to AD_2 in Exhibit 12–1) and guide the economy to full employment equilibrium (E_2).

The Keynesian view also provides a fiscal policy remedy for inflation. Suppose that an economy is experiencing an inflationary economic boom as the result of excessive aggregate demand. As **Exhibit 12–2** illustrates, in the absence of a change in policy, the strong demand (AD_1) would push up wages and other resource prices. In time, the higher resource prices would increase costs, reduce aggregate supply (from $SRAS_1$ to $SRAS_3$), and lead to a higher price level (P_3). The basic Keynesian model, however, indicates that **restrictive fiscal policy** could be used to reduce aggregate demand (shift to AD_2) and guide the economy to a noninflationary equilibrium (E_2). A reduced level of government purchases would diminish aggregate demand directly. Alternatively, higher taxes on households and businesses could be used to dampen consumption and private investment. The restrictive fiscal policy—a spending reduction and/or an increase in taxes—would shift the government budget toward a surplus (or smaller deficit). ***The Keynesian analysis suggests that a shift toward a more restrictive fiscal policy is the proper prescription with which to combat inflation generated by excessive aggregate demand.***

Restrictive fiscal policy
A reduction in government expenditures and/or an increase in tax rates such that the expected size of the budget deficit declines (or the budget surplus increases).

The Keynesian revolution challenged the view that a responsible government should constrain spending within the bounds of its revenues. Rather than balancing the budget annually, the Keynesian view stressed the importance of* countercyclical policy, *that is, policy designed to "counter" or offset fluctuations in aggregate demand. When an economy is threatened by a recession, the government should shift to a more expansionary fiscal policy, increasing spending or reducing taxes in a manner that will increase the size of the budget deficit. On the other hand, fiscal policy should become more restrictive—the budget should be shifted toward a smaller deficit or larger surplus—in response to a threat of inflation. According to the Keynesian view, fluctuations in aggregate demand are the major source of economic disturbances. Moreover,

Countercyclical policy
A policy that tends to move the economy in an opposite direction from the forces of the business cycle. Such a policy would stimulate demand during the contraction phase of the business cycle and restrain demand during the expansion phase.

EXHIBIT 12–2

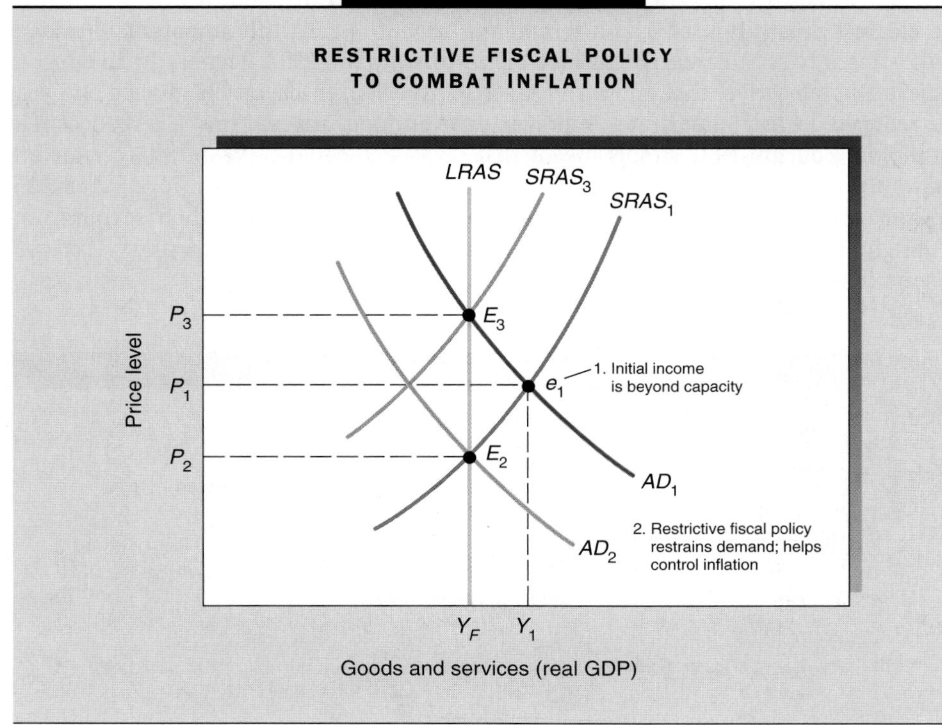

Strong demand such as AD_1 *will temporarily lead to an output rate beyond the economy's long-run potential* (Y_F)*. If maintained, the high level of demand will lead to long-run equilibrium* (E_3) *at a higher price level. However, restrictive fiscal policy could restrain demand to* AD_2 *(or better still, prevent demand from expanding to* AD_1 *in the first place) and thereby guide the economy to a noninflationary equilibrium* (E_2)*.*

wise use of fiscal policy can help stabilize and maintain demand at or near the full employment rate of output.

Temporary versus Permanent Changes in Taxes

The potency of a change in tax policy is influenced by whether the change is expected to be temporary or permanent. Why does this matter? Suppose that the government announces that taxes will be cut by $500 per household. A permanent $500 tax reduction would add substantially to the wealth and financial resources of households. As a result, they are likely to spend a large portion of the $500 increase in their annual disposable income. By way of comparison, suppose that the government announces a one-year-only tax cut of $500 per household. This temporary tax cut will increase the wealth of households by a much smaller amount than a $500 tax reduction that is expected to remain in place for several years. Because the temporary tax cut exerts a smaller impact on household wealth, people will increase their current spending by a lesser amount. Thus, the demand stimulus effect of a temporary tax cut will be substantially less than would be the case for a permanent reduction in taxes.

Experience with temporary changes in taxes is consistent with this view. Changes of this type have been largely ineffective. The 10 percent personal income tax surcharge imposed by the Johnson administration in 1968 illustrates this point. This one-year-only tax increase was designed to cool an overheated economy during the Vietnam War. It failed to do so. Given the limited restraint imposed by the temporary tax increase, the inflation rate continued to rise.

Hoping to stimulate the economy during the 1974–1975 recession, President Ford and Congress agreed to a temporary tax cut. Taxpayers were granted a partial rebate of their 1974 tax payments and rates were reduced for the balance of 1975. By the time the legislation was passed, the recovery was already underway. Nonetheless, studies indicate that the demand stimulus effects of the rebates were modest, at best.

Perhaps the 1992 withholding reduction of the Bush administration provides the clearest illustration of why a temporary tax cut is relatively impotent. President Bush wanted to stimulate a sluggish economy prior to the 1992 election. In an effort to achieve this objective, the amount of taxes withheld from paychecks during the year was reduced. Legislated tax rates, however, were left unchanged. Thus, the reduction in withholding during 1992 simply meant that taxpayers would confront a larger tax bill (or would receive a smaller refund) when they filed their returns prior to April 15, 1993. Of course, taxpayers were well aware of this fact and planned their spending accordingly. Predictably, the demand stimulus accompanying this temporary "tax cut" was minimal.

OUTSTANDING ECONOMIST

Paul Samuelson (1915–)

The first American to win the Nobel Prize in Economics, Paul Samuelson played a central role in the development and acceptance of Keynesian economics in the 1950s and 1960s. Through the years, his views regarding the effectiveness of fiscal policy have gradually changed (see chapter opening quote). A professor of economics at MIT for more than four decades, Samuelson's *Collected Scientific Papers* encompass five lengthy volumes.[1]

[1]Paul Samuelson, *Collected Scientific Papers of Paul Samuelson* (Cambridge: MIT Press, 1966).

FISCAL POLICY AND THE CROWDING-OUT EFFECT

By the early 1960s, the Keynesian view was widely accepted both by economists and by policymakers. At that time, it was generally believed that changes in the size of the budget deficit exerted a powerful impact on aggregate demand and output. More recently, however, economists have noted that there are secondary effects that tend to weaken the potency of fiscal policy.

When the government borrows funds to finance an enlarged deficit, typically it will do so by issuing additional bonds. As we previously discussed, issuing bonds is simply a means of demanding loanable funds. The total demand for loanable funds will increase as government borrowing competes with private borrowing for the available supply of funds. Thus, the additional government borrowing to finance a larger deficit will increase the demand for loanable funds and thereby place upward pressure on the real interest rate.

What impact will a higher real interest rate have on private spending? Consumers will reduce their purchases of interest-sensitive goods, such as automobiles and consumer durables. More important, a higher interest rate will increase the opportunity cost of investment projects. Businesses will postpone spending on plant expansions, heavy equipment, and capital improvements. Residential housing construction and sales will also be hurt. Thus, the higher real interest rates caused by the larger deficit will retard private spending. Economists refer to this squeezing out of private spending by a deficit-induced increase in the real interest rate as the **crowding-out effect.**

Crowding-out effect
A reduction in private spending as a result of higher interest rates generated by budget deficits that are financed by borrowing in the private loanable funds market.

The crowding-out effect suggests that budget deficits will exert less impact on aggregate demand than the basic Keynesian model implies. Because financing the deficit pushes up interest rates, budget deficits will tend to retard private spending, particularly spending on investment. This reduction in private spending as the result of higher interest rates will at least partially offset additional spending emanating from the deficit. Thus, the crowding-out effect implies that the impact of a budget deficit on demand, output, and employment may not be very potent.

Furthermore, the crowding-out effect implies that the budget deficit will change the composition of aggregate demand. As the higher interest rates accompanying the deficits crowd out private investment, the output of capital goods will decline. As a result, the future stock of capital (for example, heavy equipment, other machines, and buildings) will be smaller than would otherwise have been the case. To the extent that budget deficits crowd out private investment, they will reduce the supply of capital available to future workers and thereby reduce their productivity and income.

Although most all economists accept the logic of the crowding-out effect, many Keynesians would argue that it is unlikely to be very important during a recession, particularly a serious one. Remember, the magnified effects of the multiplier are dependent on the drawing of previously unemployed resources into the production process. During normal times, an autonomous increase in demand is likely to lead primarily to higher prices, without much impact on real output and employment. But, when widespread unemployment is present during a serious recession, an autonomous increase in government purchases may well exert a substantial multiplier effect on output, employment, and real income. If the incomes of households increase, they will save more, which will permit the government to finance its enlarged deficit without much upward pressure on interest rates. In addition, when applied during a recession, the demand stimulus may improve business profit expectations and thereby stimulate additional private investment.

The implications of the crowding-out analysis are symmetrical. Restrictive fiscal policy will "crowd in" private spending. If the government increases taxes and/or cuts back on expenditures and thereby reduces its demand for loanable funds, the real interest rate will decline. The lower real interest rate will stimulate additional private investment and consumption. So the fiscal policy restraint will be at least partially offset by an expansion in private spending. ***As the result of this crowding in, restrictive fiscal policy may not be very effective as a weapon against inflation.***

The Crowding-Out Effect in a World of Global Financial Markets

Suppose the United States increases government spending or cuts taxes or both, shifting the federal budget toward a larger deficit. As the crowding-out effect stresses, the government's increase in demand for loanable funds will place upward pressure on real interest rates. How will foreigners respond to this situation? The higher real interest yields on bonds and other financial assets will attract funds from abroad. In turn, this inflow of financial capital will increase the supply of loanable funds and thereby moderate the rise in real interest rates in the United States.[3]

How will this inflow of financial capital influence the crowding-out effect? At first glance, the crowding-out effect would appear to be weakened because the inflow of funds will moderate the upward pressure on domestic interest rates. Closer inspection, though, reveals this will not be the case. Foreigners cannot buy more U.S. bonds and financial assets without "buying" more dollars. Thus, additional bond purchases will increase the demand for U.S. dollars (and supply of foreign currencies) in the foreign exchange market—the market that coordinates exchanges of the various national currencies. As foreigners demand more dollars in order to increase their financial investments in the United States, their actions will cause an appreciation in the foreign exchange value of the dollar. The appreciation of the dollar will make imports cheaper for Americans. Simultaneously, it will make U.S. exports more expensive for foreigners. Predictably, the United States will import more and export less. Thus, net exports will decline (or net imports increase), causing a reduction in aggregate demand. Therefore, while the inflow of capital from abroad will moderate the increase in the interest rate and the crowding out of private domestic investment, it will also reduce net exports and thereby retard aggregate demand.

Exhibit 12–3 summarizes the crowding-out view of budget deficits in an open economy. As larger budget deficits push up real interest rates, the higher financial returns will attract an inflow of foreign capital. This capital inflow will moderate both the rise in real interest rates and the reduction in domestic private investment. However, it will also increase the foreign exchange demand for the dollar, causing it to appreciate. In turn, the appreciation of the dollar will reduce both net exports and aggregate demand. ***Thus, while the inflow of capital from abroad modifies the form of the crowding-out effect, it does not alter the major point: Budget deficits will trigger secondary effects in other markets that will largely, if not entirely, offset the stimulus effects of the deficits.***

Furthermore, our analysis indicates that budget deficits and trade deficits—an excess of imports relative to exports—will tend to be linked. When budget deficits push up interest rates and thereby attract an inflow of foreign capital, they will simultaneously cause a nation's currency to appreciate. In turn, imports will increase relative to exports in response to the appreciation.

---

[3]For students who are unsure about the demand for and supply of loanable funds, this would be a good time to review the topic within the framework of our basic macro model outlined by Exhibit 9–1. As this exhibit indicates, household saving and the inflow of financial capital from abroad supply loanable funds. In turn, private investment and borrowing by the government to finance budget deficits generates the demand for these funds.

EXHIBIT 12-3

VISUAL PRESENTATION OF THE CROWDING-OUT EFFECT IN AN OPEN ECONOMY

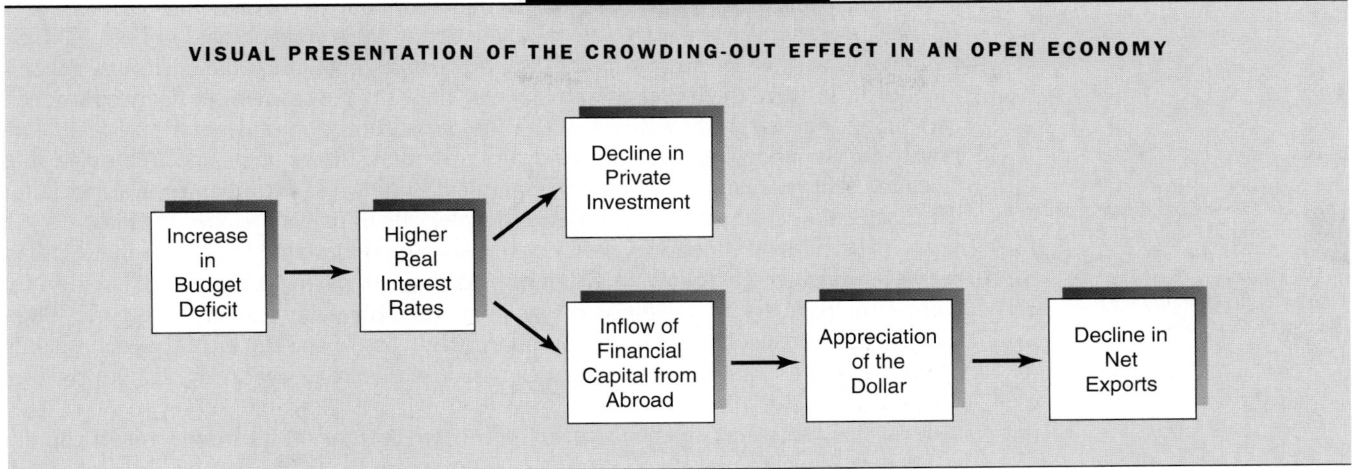

An increase in government borrowing to finance an enlarged budget deficit will place upward pressure on real interest rates. This will retard private investment and thereby aggregate demand. In an open economy, the higher interest rates will also attract an inflow of capital from abroad. As foreigners demand more dollars to buy U.S. bonds and other financial assets, the dollar will appreciate. In turn, the appreciation of the dollar will cause net exports to fall. Thus, the higher interest rates will trigger reductions in both private investment and net exports, which will weaken the expansionary impact of a budget deficit.

NEW CLASSICAL VIEW OF FISCAL POLICY

Some economists stress still another possible offsetting secondary effect that may weaken the impact of budget deficits on aggregate demand. Rather than spending more, households may save more so they will be better able to pay the higher future taxes implied by the larger outstanding debt. Until now, we have implicitly assumed that the current saving decisions of taxpayers are unaffected by the higher future taxes implied by budget deficits. Some economists argue that this is an unrealistic view. Robert Lucas (University of Chicago), the 1995 Nobel laureate, Thomas Sargent (University of Minnesota), and Robert Barro (Harvard University) have been leaders among a group of economists arguing that taxpayers will reduce their current consumption and increase their saving in anticipation of the higher future taxes implied by the debt financing. Because this position has its foundation in classical economics, these economists and their followers are referred to as **new classical economists.**

New classical economists
Modern economists who believe there are strong forces pushing a market economy toward full employment equilibrium and that macroeconomic policy is an ineffective tool with which to reduce economic instability.

In the basic Keynesian model, a reduction in current taxes financed by borrowing increases the current disposable income of households. Given their additional disposable income, households increase their current consumption. New classical economists argue that this analysis is incorrect because it ignores the impact of the higher future tax liability implied by the budget deficit and the interest payments required to service the additional debt. ***New classical economists stress that debt financing simply substitutes higher future taxes for lower current taxes. Thus, budget deficits merely affect the timing of the taxes.***

A mere change in the timing of taxes will not alter the wealth of households. Therefore, there is no reason to believe that current consumption will change when current taxes are cut and government debt and future taxes are increased by an equivalent amount. According to the new classical view, households will reduce their current consumption in response to additional government debt (and the higher taxes that the debt implies) just as surely as if the equivalent amount of current taxes had been levied. In essence, households will simply save the reduction in their current taxes so they will have the income with which to pay the higher future taxes implied by the additional government debt. In turn, the increase in saving will allow the government to finance its deficit without an increase in the interest rate. Thus, the substitution of debt for taxes will leave private consumption, aggregate demand, and real interest rates unchanged. This view that taxes and debt financing are essentially equivalent is known as **Ricardian equivalence,** after the nineteenth-century economist, David Ricardo, who initially developed the idea.

Ricardian equivalence
The view that a tax reduction financed with government debt will exert no impact on current consumption and aggregate demand because people will fully recognize the higher future taxes implied by the additional debt.

Perhaps an illustration will help explain the underlying logic of the new classical view. Consider the following alternative methods of paying a $1,000 tax liability: (1) a one-time payment of $1,000 or (2) payments of $100 each year in the future. When the interest rate is 10 percent, the opportunity cost of a $100 liability each year is $1,000. Therefore, just as the first option reduces current wealth by $1,000, so, too, does the second.

Now let us consider the impact of the two options on future income. If you dip into your savings to make a one-time $1,000 payment, your future interest income will be reduced by $100 each year in the future (assuming a 10 percent interest rate). Just as the second option reduces your future net income by $100 each year, so, too, does the first. In both cases, current wealth is reduced by $1,000. Similarly, in both cases the flow of future net income is reduced by $100 each year. Because of this, the new classical economists believe the two options are essentially the same.

Exhibit 12–4 illustrates the implications of the new classical view as to the potency of fiscal policy. Suppose the fiscal authorities issue $50 billion of additional debt in order to cut taxes by an equal amount. The government borrowing increases the demand for loanable funds (D_1 shifts to D_2 in part b of Exhibit 12–4) by $50 billion. If the taxpayers did not recognize the higher future taxes implied by the debt, they would expand consumption in response to the lower taxes and the increase in their current

New classical economists emphasize that budget deficits merely substitute future taxes for current taxes. If households did not anticipate the higher future taxes, aggregate demand would increase to AD_2. However, demand remains unchanged at AD_1 when households fully anticipate the future increase in taxes (a). Simultaneously, the additional saving to meet the higher future taxes will increase the supply of loanable funds to S_2 and permit the government to borrow the funds to finance its deficit without pushing up the real interest rate (b). In this model, fiscal policy exerts no effect. The real interest rate, real GDP, and level of employment all remain unchanged.

EXHIBIT 12–4

NEW CLASSICAL VIEW—HIGHER EXPECTED FUTURE TAXES CROWD OUT PRIVATE SPENDING

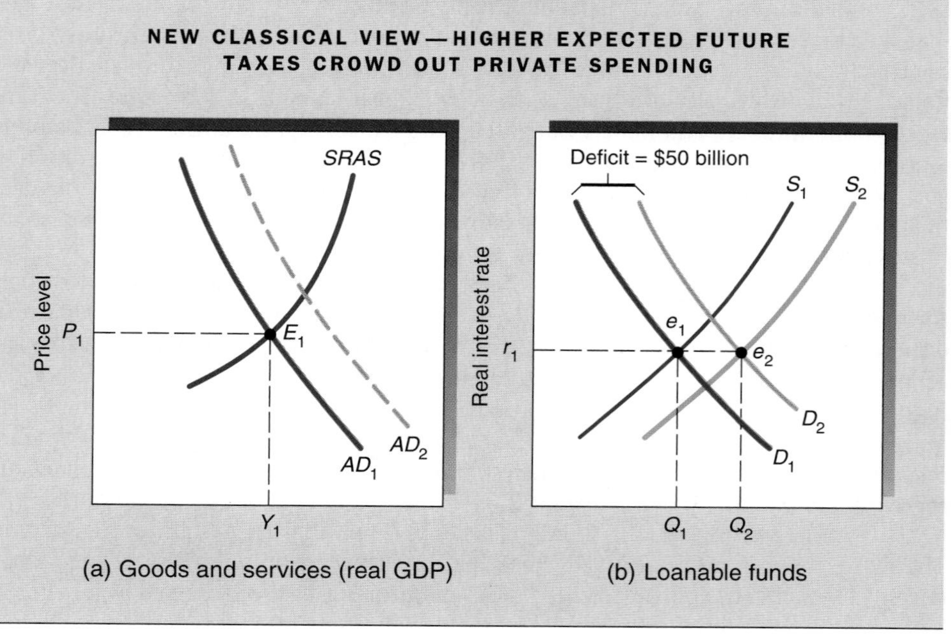

(a) Goods and services (real GDP)

(b) Loanable funds

disposable income. Under such circumstances, aggregate demand in the goods and services market would expand to AD_2. In the new classical model, though, this will not be the case. Recognizing the higher future taxes, taxpayers will maintain their initial level of consumption spending and use the tax cut to increase their savings in order to generate the additional income required to pay the future taxes implied by the $50 billion of additional debt. Because consumption is unchanged, aggregate demand also remains constant (at AD_1). At the same time, the additional saving (to pay the implied increase in future taxes) allows the government to finance its deficit without an increase in the real interest rate. In this polar case, fiscal policy exerts no demand stimulus. In fact, it does not change much of anything. Output, employment, the price level, and even the real interest rate all remain constant.

The new classical view might be summarized as follows: The substitution of government debt for current taxes will fail to alter either the wealth or permanent income of the taxpaying households. Households will continue to maintain the same level of consumption even if the government cuts taxes and increases its outstanding debt. Thus, budget deficits will not stimulate aggregate demand. Neither will they affect output and employment. Similarly, the real interest rate is unaffected by deficits since people will save more in order to pay the higher future taxes. According to the new classical view, fiscal policy is completely impotent.

This new classical theory of fiscal policy is controversial.[4] Critics argue that it is unrealistic to expect that taxpayers will anticipate all or even most of the future taxes implied by additional government debt. In addition, even if people did anticipate the higher future taxes, in our world of limited life spans, many would recognize that they will not be around to pay, at least not in full, the future tax liability implied by debt financing. Many economists reject the new classical view of fiscal policy, at least in its pure form. Nonetheless, the significance of the new classical theory and its implications with regard to fiscal policy continue to provide one of the lively topics of debate in modern macroeconomics.

FISCAL POLICY: PROBLEMS OF PROPER TIMING

If fiscal policy is going to reduce economic instability, changes in policy must inject stimulus during a recession and restraint during an inflationary boom. But proper timing of fiscal policy is not an easy task. Because forecasting a forthcoming recession or boom is a highly imperfect science, there is usually a time lag between when a change in policy is needed and when its need is widely recognized by policymakers.

In addition, there is generally a lag between the time when the need for a fiscal policy change is recognized and the time when it is actually instituted. Discretionary fiscal policy requires changes in tax laws and government expenditure programs. The time required for such changes is likely to be quite lengthy. This will be particularly true for a political structure like that of the United States, with a number of checks and balances built into the system.[5] Congressional committees must meet, hear testimony,

[4]See Robert J. Barro, "Are Government Bonds Net Wealth?" *Journal of Political Economy* (November–December 1974): pp. 1095–1117; Robert J. Barro, "The Ricardian Approach to Budget Deficits," *Journal of Economic Perspectives* (spring 1989): pp. 37–44; Alan S. Blinder, "Keynes after Lucas," *American Economic Review* (May 1987): pp. 130–136; James M. Buchanan, "Barro on the Ricardian Equivalence Theorem," *Journal of Political Economy* (April 1976): pp. 337–342; and Gerald P. O'Driscoll, Jr., "The Ricardian Nonequivalence Theorem," *Journal of Political Economy* (February 1977): pp. 207–210.

[5]The time required for the institution of a change in fiscal policy may be shorter under a parliamentary political system, such as that of Canada or the United Kingdom. This is highly likely to be the case if a single party has a parliamentary majority.

and draft legislation. Key legislators may choose to delay action if they can use their positions to obtain special favors for their constituencies. A majority of the lawmakers must be convinced that a proposed action is in the interest of the country, and the details of the policy must be arranged such that they will also believe that their own districts and supporters will not be disadvantaged. All these things take time.

Finally, still another factor adds to the complexity of fiscal policymaking: Even after a policy is adopted, it may be six to twelve months before its major impact is felt. If government expenditures are going to be increased, time will be required for competitive bids to be submitted and new contracts granted. Contractors may be unable to begin work right away. Although a tax reduction will generally exert demand stimulus more quickly, it will take time for these effects to work their way through the economy.

Macroeconomic policymaking is a little bit like lobbing a ball at a moving target that sometimes changes directions unpredictably. In order to institute fiscal policy

EXHIBIT 12-5

WHY PROPER TIMING OF FISCAL POLICY IS DIFFICULT

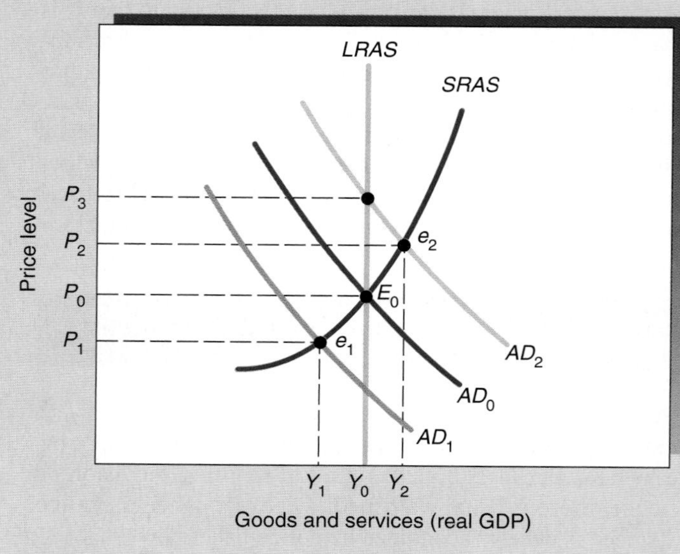

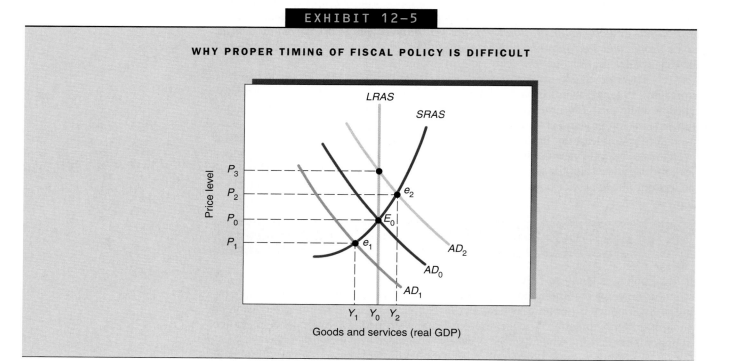

Here we consider an economy that experiences shifts in AD that are not easy to forecast. Initially, the economy is in long-run equilibrium (E_0) at price level P_0 and output Y_0. At this output, only the natural rate of unemployment is present. However, an investment slump and business pessimism result in an unanticipated decline in aggregate demand (to AD_1). Output falls and unemployment increases. After a time, policymakers institute expansionary fiscal policy seeking to shift aggregate demand back to AD_0. By the time fiscal policy begins to exert its primary effect, though, private investment has recovered and decision makers have become increasingly optimistic about the future. So aggregate demand is already, on its own accord, shifting back to AD_0. Thus, the expansionary fiscal policy overshifts aggregate demand to AD_2 rather than AD_0. Prices rise as the economy is now overheated. Unless the expansionary fiscal policy is reversed, wages and other resource prices will eventually increase, shifting SRAS to the left, thus pushing the price level still higher (to P_3). Alternatively, suppose an investment boom disrupts the initial equilibrium. The increase in investment shifts aggregate demand to AD_2, placing upward pressure on prices. Policymakers respond by increasing taxes and cutting government expenditures. By the time the restrictive fiscal policy exerts its primary impact, though, investment returns to its normal rate. As a result, the restrictive fiscal policy overshifts aggregate demand to AD_1 and throws the economy into a recession. Since fiscal policy does not work instantaneously, and since dynamic factors are constantly influencing private demand, proper timing of fiscal policy is not an easy task.

in a manner that will help stabilize the economy, policymakers need to know what economic conditions are going to be six, twelve, or eighteen months in the future. Unfortunately, our ability to forecast future economic conditions is limited. Therefore, in a world characterized by dynamic change and unpredictable events, some policy errors are inevitable.

Exhibit 12–5 illustrates the implications of the difficulties involved in the proper timing of fiscal policy. Suppose that policymakers attempt to use expansionary fiscal policy to stimulate aggregate demand during an economic downturn. If inability to forecast a recession and delays accompanying the adoption of a policy change take a substantial period, the economy's self-corrective mechanism may already have restored full employment by the time the fiscal stimulus begins to exert its primary impact. If so, the fiscal stimulus will cause excessive demand and inflation. Similarly, restrictive fiscal policy to cool an overheated economy may cause a recession if aggregate demand declines prior to the fiscal restraint.

In the real world, a discretionary change in fiscal policy is like a two-edged sword—it has the potential to do harm as well as good. If timed correctly, it will reduce economic instability. If timed incorrectly, however, the fiscal change will increase rather than reduce economic instability.

AUTOMATIC STABILIZERS

Fortunately, there are a few fiscal programs that tend automatically to apply demand stimulus during a recession and demand restraint during an economic boom. Programs of this type are called **automatic stabilizers.** They are automatic in that, without any new legislative action, they tend to increase the budget deficit (or reduce the surplus) during a recession and increase the surplus (or reduce the deficit) during an economic boom.

Automatic stabilizers
Built-in features that tend automatically to promote a budget deficit during a recession and a budget surplus during an inflationary boom, even without a change in policy.

The major advantage of automatic stabilizers is that they institute countercyclical fiscal policy without the delays associated with policy changes that require legislative action. Thus, they minimize the problem of proper timing. When unemployment is rising and business conditions are slow, these stabilizers automatically reduce taxes and increase government expenditures, giving the economy a shot in the arm. On the other hand, automatic stabilizers help to apply the brakes to an economic boom, increasing tax revenues and decreasing government spending. Three of these built-in stabilizers deserve specific mention: unemployment compensation, corporate profit tax, and progressive income tax.

Unemployment Compensation. When an economy begins to dip into a recession, government payments for unemployment benefits will increase as the number of laid-off and unemployed workers expands. Simultaneously, the receipts from the employment tax that finances the system will decline because employment falls during a recession. Therefore, this program will automatically run a deficit during a business slowdown. In contrast, during an economic boom, the tax receipts from the program will increase because more people are now working, and the amount paid out in benefits will decline since fewer people are unemployed. Thus, the program will automatically tend to run a surplus during good times. So without any change in policy, the unemployment compensation program has the desired countercyclical effect on aggregate demand.[6]

---

[6]Although unemployment compensation has the desired countercyclical effect on demand, it also reduces the incentive to accept available employment opportunities. Research in this area indicates that the existing unemployment compensation system increases the length of job search by unemployed workers and thereby increases the long-run natural (normal) unemployment rate.

Corporate Profit Tax. Tax studies show that the corporate profit tax is the most countercyclical of all the automatic stabilizers. This results because corporate profits are highly sensitive to cyclical conditions. During a recession, corporate profits decline sharply, and so too do corporate tax payments. In turn, the decline in tax revenues will enlarge the size of the budget deficit. In contrast, when the economy is expanding, corporate profits typically increase much more rapidly than wages, income, or consumption. This increase in corporate profits will result in a rapid increase in the "tax take" from the business sector during the expansion phase of the business cycle. Thus, corporate tax payments will go up during an expansion and fall rapidly during a contraction, even though no new legislative action has been instituted.

Progressive Income Tax. When income grows rapidly, the average personal income tax liability of individuals and families increases. With rising incomes, more people will find their income above the "no tax due" cutoff. Others will be pushed into a higher tax bracket. Therefore, during an economic expansion, revenue from the personal income tax increases more rapidly than income. Other things constant, the budget moves toward a surplus (or smaller deficit), even though the economy's tax rate structure is unchanged. On the other hand, when income declines, many individuals will be taxed at a lower rate or not at all. Income tax revenues will fall more rapidly than income, automatically enlarging the size of the budget deficit during a recession.

FISCAL POLICY AS A STABILIZATION TOOL: A MODERN SYNTHESIS

During the 1960s the basic Keynesian view was widely accepted. Fiscal policy was thought to be highly potent. Furthermore, it was widely believed that political decision makers, with the assistance of their economic advisors, were fully capable of instituting discretionary fiscal policy changes in a manner that would help stabilize the economy. During the 1970s and 1980s, both the operation of fiscal policy and its efficacy as a stabilization tool were analyzed and hotly debated among professional economists. A synthesis view has emerged from that debate. Most macroeconomists—both Keynesian and non-Keynesian—now accept the following three elements of the modern synthesis view.

1. ***Proper timing of discretionary fiscal policy is both difficult to achieve and of crucial importance.*** Given our limited ability to forecast turns in the business cycle and the political delays that inevitably accompany a change in fiscal policy, the effectiveness of discretionary fiscal policy as a stabilization tool is highly questionable. Therefore, most macroeconomists now place less emphasis on fiscal policy. (*Note:* The chapter opening quotation from Paul Samuelson, a long-time Keynesian, highlights this point.)
2. ***Automatic stabilizers reduce the fluctuation of aggregate demand and help to direct the economy toward full employment.*** Since they are not dependent on legislative action, automatic stabilizers are able consistently to shift the budget toward a deficit during a recession and toward a surplus during an economic boom. Thus, they add needed stimulus during the recession and act as a restraining force during an inflationary boom. Although some question their potency, most all would agree that they exert a stabilizing influence.
3. ***Fiscal policy is much less potent than the early Keynesian view implied.*** The current debate among macroeconomists concerning the impact of fiscal policy during normal times is not whether crowding out takes place, but rather how it takes

place. The crowding-out and new classical models highlight this point. Both models indicate that there are side effects of budget deficits that will substantially, if not entirely, offset their impact on aggregate demand. In the crowding-out model, higher real interest rates and a decline in net exports as the result of currency appreciation reduce private demand and offset the expansionary effects of budget deficits. In the new classical model, higher anticipated future taxes lead to the same result. Both models indicate that fiscal policy will exert little, if any, impact on current aggregate demand, employment, and real output during normal economic times.

SUPPLY-SIDE EFFECTS OF FISCAL POLICY

Thus far, we have focused on the potential demand-side effects of fiscal policy. However, when fiscal changes alter tax rates, they influence the incentive of people to work, invest, and use resources efficiently. Thus, tax changes may also influence aggregate supply. In the past, macroeconomists have often ignored the impact of changes in tax rates, thinking they were of little importance. In recent years, **supply-side economists** have challenged this view.[7] The supply-side argument provided the foundation for the substantial reduction in marginal tax rates in the United States and several other countries during the 1980s.

Supply-side economists
Modern economists who believe that changes in marginal tax rates exert important effects on aggregate supply.

From a supply-side viewpoint, the marginal tax rate is of crucial importance. As we discussed in Chapter 4, the marginal tax rate determines the breakdown of one's additional income between tax payments on the one hand and personal income on the other. A reduction in marginal tax rates increases the reward derived from added work, investment, saving, and other activities that become less heavily taxed. People shift into these activities away from leisure (and leisure-intensive activities), tax shelters, consumption of tax-deductible goods, and other forms of tax avoidance. Supply-side economists believe that these substitutions both enlarge the effective resource base and improve the efficiency with which the resources are applied.

The source of the supply-side effects accompanying a change in tax rates is fundamentally different from the source of the demand-side effects. A change in tax policy affects aggregate demand through its impact on disposable income and the flow of expenditures. ***In contrast, changes in tax rates, particularly marginal tax rates, will affect aggregate supply through their impact on the relative attractiveness of productive activity in comparison to leisure and tax avoidance.***

Exhibit 12–6 graphically depicts the impact of a supply-side tax cut, one that reduces marginal tax rates. The lower marginal tax rates increase aggregate supply as the new incentive structure encourages taxpayers to earn additional income and use resources more efficiently. If the tax change is perceived as long term, both long- and short-run aggregate supply (*LRAS* and *SRAS*) will increase. Real output and income expand.

Of course, the increase in real income will also increase demand (shift to AD_2). If the lower marginal rates are financed by a budget deficit, depending on the strength of the crowding-out effect and the anticipation of higher future taxes (new classical theory), aggregate demand may increase by more than aggregate supply. If this is the case, the price level will rise.

---

[7]See Dwight Lee, ed., *Taxation and the Deficit Economy* (San Francisco: Pacific Institute, 1986); and Lawrence Lindsey, *The Growth Experiment: How the New Tax Policy Is Transforming the U.S. Economy* (New York: Basic Books, 1989) for additional information on supply-side economics.

EXHIBIT 12-6

Here we illustrate the supply-side effects of a reduction in marginal tax rates. The lower marginal tax rates increase the incentive to earn and use resources efficiently. Since these effects are long-run as well as short-run, both LRAS *and* SRAS *increase (shift to the right). Real output expands. If the lower tax rates are financed by a budget deficit, aggregate demand may expand by a larger amount than aggregate supply, leading to an increase in the price level.*

TAX RATE EFFECTS AND SUPPLY-SIDE ECONOMICS

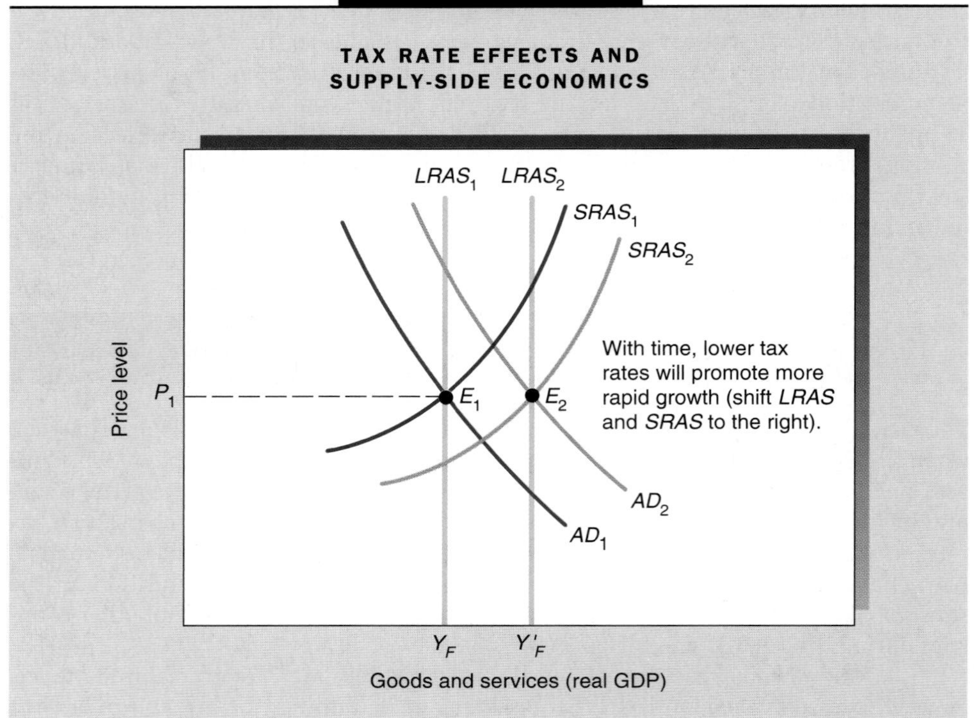

Supply-side economics should not be viewed as a short-run countercyclical tool. It will take time for changing market incentives to move resources out of tax-motivated investments and into higher-yield activities. The full positive effects of lower marginal tax rates will not be observed until labor and capital markets have time to adjust fully to the new incentive structure. ***Clearly, supply-side economics is a long-run, growth-oriented strategy.***

Why High Tax Rates Tend to Retard Output

There are three major reasons why high tax rates are likely to retard the growth of output. First, high marginal tax rates discourage work effort and reduce the productive efficiency of labor. When marginal tax rates soar to 55 percent or 60 percent, individuals get to keep less than half of what they earn—and when the payoff from working declines, people tend to work less. Some (for example, those with a working spouse) will drop out of the labor force. Others will simply work fewer hours. Still others will decide to take more lengthy vacations, forgo overtime opportunities, retire earlier, or forget about pursuing that promising but risky business venture. In some cases, high tax rates will even drive highly productive citizens to other countries where taxes are lower. High tax rates will also result in inefficient utilization of labor. Some individuals will substitute less-productive activities that are not taxed (for example, do-it-yourself projects) for work opportunities yielding taxable income.

Second, high tax rates will adversely affect the rate of capital formation and the efficiency of its use. When tax rates are high, foreign investment will be repelled and domestic investors will search for investment projects abroad where taxes are lower. In addition, domestic investors will direct more of their time and effort into hobby businesses (for example, collecting antiques, raising horses, or giving golf lessons) that provide both enjoyable activities and tax-shelter benefits. This process will divert investment resources away from projects with a higher rate of return but fewer tax-avoidance benefits. As the result of the tax-shelter benefits, individuals will often be able to gain even though the "investments" reduce the value of resources. Scarce capital is wasted and resources are channeled away from their most productive uses.

Third, high marginal tax rates encourage individuals to substitute less-desired tax-deductible goods for more-desired nondeductible goods. Here the inefficiency stems from the fact that individuals do not bear the full cost of tax-deductible purchases. High marginal tax rates make tax-deductible expenditures cheap for persons in high tax brackets. Since the personal cost, but not the cost to society, is cheap, taxpayers confronting high marginal tax rates will spend more money on pleasurable, tax-deductible items, such as plush offices, Hawaiian business conferences, and various fringe benefits (for example, a company luxury automobile, business entertainment, and a company retirement plan). Because such tax-deductible purchases reduce their taxes, people will often buy such goods even though they do not value them as much as the cost of producing them.

How Important Are Supply-Side Effects?

Just as economists were divided during the 1970s and 1980s with regard to the demand-side potency of fiscal policy, division currently exists with regard to the importance of the supply-side fiscal incentive effects. Critics of supply-side economics stress that the rate reductions of the 1980s were associated with a modest growth rate of output, a significant reduction in the real tax revenue of the federal government, and large budget deficits. These outcomes do not indicate that the supply-side effects are highly potent. Defenders of the supply-side position respond by noting that the rate reductions of both the 1960s and the 1980s resulted in impressive growth and lengthy economic expansions. Furthermore, supply-side economists stress that the supply response in the top brackets—where lower rates have the largest incentive effects—has been substantial.[8] As **Exhibit 12–7** shows, the share of taxes paid by high-income taxpayers actually increased in both the 1960s and 1980s when the top marginal tax rates were reduced.

It is important to keep in mind that supply-side effects often take place over lengthy time periods. Several European countries—including Belgium, Denmark, France, Germany, Netherlands, and Sweden—confront a "brain drain" problem, an exodus of high-skill (and therefore high-income) business and professional workers. While supply-side effects of this type do not dramatically alter year-to-year growth rates, they can exert a significant impact on income levels with the passage of time.

There is evidence that countries with high marginal tax rates (for example, 50 percent or more) do less well than those with lower rates (say, 40 percent or less).[9] Related to this point, it is interesting to compare the experience of the United Kingdom with that of France and Germany. The UK reduced its top marginal tax rate from 83

---

[8]Martin Feldstein and Daniel Feenberg of the National Bureau of Economic Research estimate that high-income taxpayers reported 8.5 percent less income in 1993 than they would have if their rates had not been increased during that year. See Martin Feldstein and Daniel Feenberg, *The Effect of Increased Tax Rates on Taxable Income and Efficiency: Preliminary Analysis of the 1993 Tax Rate Increases* (Cambridge, Mass.: National Bureau of Economic Research, 1995). In a related study, Feldstein estimated that the economy suffered a deadweight loss (less output and fewer gains from trade) of approximately $2 for every $1 of revenue generated by the 1993 rate increases. See Martin Feldstein, *Tax Avoidance and the Deadweight Loss of the Income Tax* (Cambridge, Mass.: National Bureau of Economic Research, 1996).

[9]See Alvin Rabushka, "Taxation, Economic Growth, and Liberty," *Cato Journal* (spring–summer 1987): pp. 121–148, for evidence on this point.

The accompanying graph indicates the share of the personal income tax paid by the top one-half percent of earners during 1960–1996. There were three major reductions in the top marginal tax rate during this period. First, the Kennedy-Johnson tax cut reduced the top rate from 91 percent in 1963 to 70 percent in 1965. During the Reagan administration, the top rate was reduced from 70 percent in 1980 to 50 percent in 1982. In 1986, the top rate was sliced still further to approximately 30 percent. Interestingly, the share of the tax bill paid by these "super-rich" earners increased following each of these tax cuts. Perhaps surprising to some, these high-income taxpayers paid a smaller portion of the tax bill when inflation pushed more and more taxpayers into high tax brackets during the 1970s and when rates were increased again (to 39.6 percent) during the Bush and Clinton years. This suggests that, at least for this group of high-income recipients, there were strong supply-side effects associated with the changes in marginal rates.

EXHIBIT 12-7

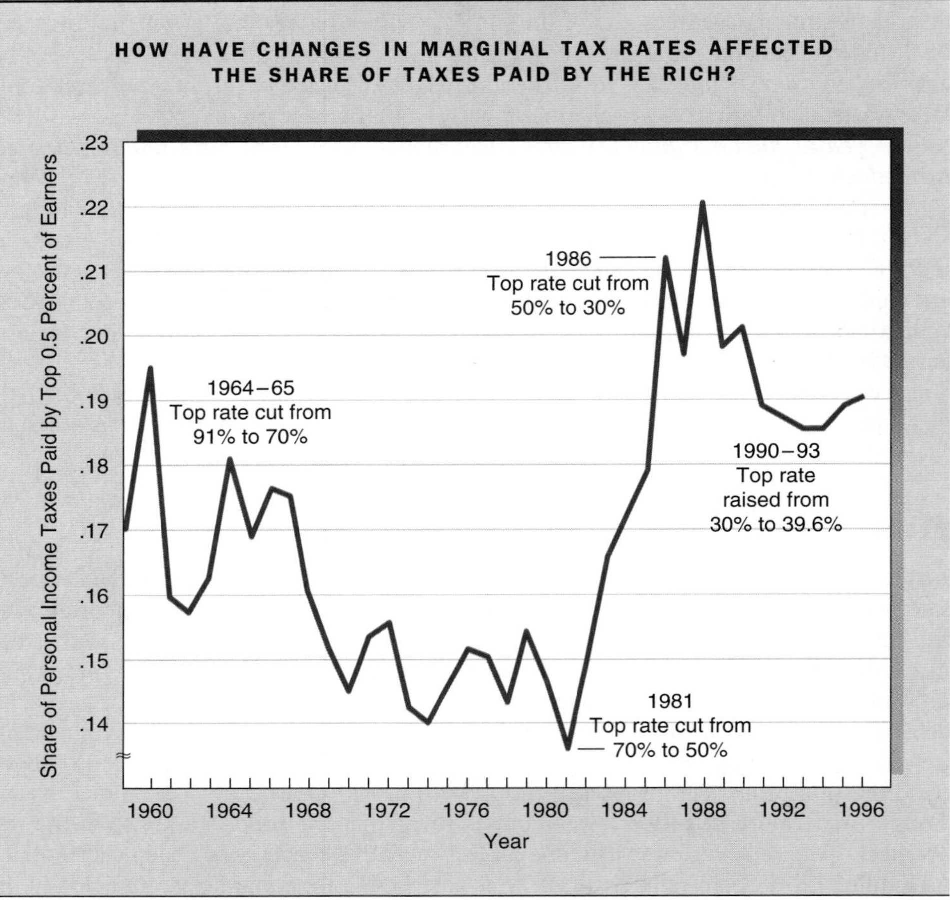

percent in 1979 to 40 percent in 1985, a rate that has been maintained since that time. In contrast, the top rate has been persistently high—55 percent or more—in both France and Germany. During the 1970s, the UK was considered the "basket case" of Western Europe, while both France and Germany achieved impressive growth rates. During the last 15 years, these positions have reversed. The UK economy is doing well. Investment has grown rapidly, particularly during the period following the tax cuts of the early 1980s, and the rate of unemployment has been contained to single-digit levels. In contrast, the growth of the French and German economies has languished during the last decade, and their unemployment rates have persistently exceeded 10 percent. Of course, tax policy alone is not responsible for these role reversals, but there is reason to believe that it has played at least a minor role.

FISCAL POLICY: A CLOSER LOOK AT THE EMPIRICAL EVIDENCE

The accompanying Thumbnail Sketch summarizes the major implications of the alternative theories with regard to the impact of expansionary fiscal policy. In general, the

THUMBNAIL SKETCH

Impact of Expansionary Fiscal Policy—A Summary of Four Models

1. **Basic Keynesian model:** An increase in government spending and/or a reduction in taxes will be magnified by the multiplier process and lead to a substantial increase in aggregate demand. When an economy is operating below capacity, real output and employment will also increase substantially.
2. **Crowding-out model:** Expansionary fiscal policy will exert little or no impact on aggregate demand and employment because borrowing to finance the budget deficit will push up interest rates and crowd out private spending, particularly investment. In an open economy, the higher interest rates will lead to an inflow of capital, a currency appreciation, and a decline in net exports.
3. **New classical model:** Expansionary fiscal policy will exert little or no impact on aggregate demand and employment because households will anticipate the higher future taxes implied by the debt and reduce their spending (and increase their saving) in order to pay them. Like current taxes, debt (future taxes) will crowd out private spending.
4. **Supply-side model:** A reduction in marginal tax rates will increase the incentive to earn (produce) and improve the efficiency of resource use, leading to an increase in aggregate supply (real output) in the long run.

effects of restrictive fiscal policy would be just the opposite. As we previously mentioned, economists use changes in the size of the deficit, rather than the absolute amount of a deficit or surplus, to determine whether fiscal policy is shifting toward expansion or restriction. An increase in the size of the deficit relative to GDP indicates that fiscal policy is becoming more expansionary. Conversely, a reduction in the size of the deficit as a share of GDP would imply a more restrictive fiscal policy.

Exhibit 12–8 presents data on federal expenditures and revenues as a share of GDP during the last four decades. In general, the data indicate that the budget deficits as a percentage of GDP expanded during recessions (shaded portions of Exhibit 12–8) and contracted during business expansions. For example, expenditures increased and revenues fell as a share of GDP during the recessions of 1970, 1974–1975, 1982, and 1990. Thus, there were substantial increases in the size of the deficit during and immediately following each of these recessions. In contrast, the budget deficit shrank as a share of GDP during the expansions of 1971–1973, 1976–1979, the late 1980s, and 1993–1998. This pattern of deficits and surpluses indicates that fiscal policy was countercyclical—that it added stimulus during recessions and moved toward restraint during periods of expansion.

However, this pattern is primarily the result of automatic stabilizers rather than discretionary changes in fiscal policy. The timing of discretionary changes has been mixed. The 1964 tax cut stimulated a sluggish economy, but as inflation began to heat up and the economy approached full employment during 1967–1968, fiscal policy remained highly expansionary. As a share of GDP, budget deficits were quite large during both 1967 and 1968. These deficits contributed to the inflation of the late 1960s. As we previously mentioned, the temporary tax rebate of the Ford administration during the 1974–1975 recession was a case of too little, too late. The economy was already on its way to recovery by the time the tax cut was passed.

Taxes were cut and expenditures increased during the recession of 1982. However, supply-side economics rather than countercyclical fiscal policy provided the underpinnings for the tax legislation during the Reagan era. Furthermore, expenditures continued to increase and deficits remained at high levels during the recovery from the 1982 recession.

EXHIBIT 12-8

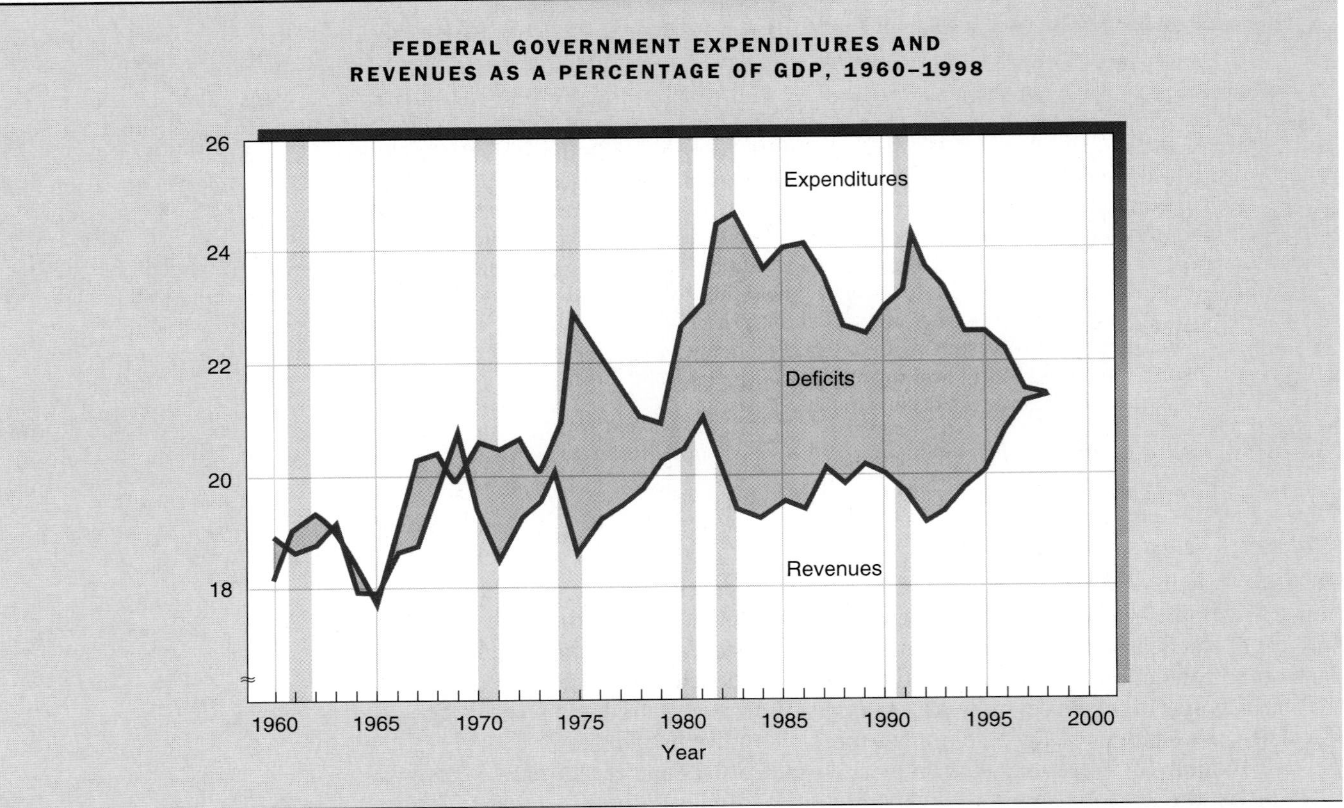

Since 1960 the federal budget deficit as a percentage of GDP has generally increased during recessions and declined during periods of economic expansion. (The shaded bars indicate periods of recession.)

SOURCE: Economic Report of the President, 1998, *tables B–1 and B–79.*

Deficits and Interest Rates

There are major differences among fiscal policy models with regard to the predicted impact of budget deficits on interest rates. The crowding-out model indicates that deficits will increase the demand for loanable funds and thereby place upward pressure on the real rate of interest. In an open economy, however, the increase in domestic interest rates will be moderated by an inflow of financial capital from abroad. The new classical model implies that the higher expected future taxes will stimulate additional saving and thereby permit the government to expand its borrowing at an unchanged interest rate.

What does the empirical evidence indicate? Several studies have investigated the year-to-year (and quarter-to-quarter) relationship between budget deficits and interest rates. The results are mixed. A Congressional Budget Office survey of 24 studies found that only a few indicated that there was a significant positive short-term link between budget deficits and real interest rates. The majority of the studies found no statistically significant relationship.[10] Seemingly, these findings would buttress the new

[10]Congressional Budget Office, "Deficits and Interest Rates: Empirical Findings and Selected Bibliography," Appendix A in *The Economic Outlook* (February 1984): pp. 99–102. Also see Charles Plosser, "The Effects of Government Financing Decisions on Asset Returns," *Journal of Monetary Economics* (May 1982); and Paul Evans, "Do Large Deficits Produce High Interest Rates?" *American Economic Review* (March 1985).

classical view that deficits exert little impact on interest rates. They must, however, be interpreted with caution. When an economy dips into a recession, the budget deficit will tend to rise as the result of the recessionary conditions. At the same time, the demand for investment funds is weakened, which will place downward pressure on interest rates. Thus, recessionary business conditions tend to generate both *larger* budget deficits and *lower* real interest rates. Clearly, this phenomenon makes it more difficult to determine the independent impact of budget deficits on interest rates.

Although the year-to-year linkage between budget deficits and real interest rates is weak, there is evidence that rising and persistently large deficits push the real interest rate upward. As Exhibit 12–8 shows, the size of the deficit was persistently larger during the 1980s than during the latter half of the 1970s. Correspondingly, the exhibit illustrates that there was clearly an upward trend in the size of the deficit as a share of the economy during the 1960–1990 period.

How did these long-term changes affect the economy? **Exhibit 12–9** addresses this question. This exhibit presents data for real interest rates over lengthy periods of both large and small deficits. Budget deficits averaged 5.1 percent of GDP during the five years (1983–1987) subsequent to the recession of 1982 compared with 2.9 percent during the five years (1976–1980) following the 1974–1975 recession. During the latter period of large budget deficits, the real interest rate averaged 7.5 percent, nearly four times the comparable figure for the earlier period of lower budget deficits.[11]

Exhibit 12–9 also presents the average real interest rate for the 1960–1974 period (when budget deficits averaged only 0.9 percent of GDP) and the 1981–1994 period (during which the deficits averaged 4 percent of GDP). Once again, the real rate of interest was much higher (6.1 percent compared to 2.4 percent) during the period of larger budget deficits. Thus, while the year-to-year data indicate a loose relationship between budget deficits and interest rates, these figures suggest that over a more lengthy period, persistently large budget deficits do lead to higher interest rates just as the crowding-out model implies.

Deficits, Consumption, and Investment

Higher interest rates will cause private investors to forgo some projects that would have been profitable at a lower rate of interest. Thus, the crowding-out model predicts that there will be a reduction in private investment as budget deficits push interest rates upward. In contrast, the new classical model predicts that households will increase their saving in response to larger budget deficits. In turn, the higher rate of saving will permit the budget deficit to be financed without either an increase in interest rates or a reduction in investment.

Clearly, the data of Exhibit 12–9 are more supportive of the crowding-out model. During the 1983–1987 period of large deficits, personal consumption as a percentage of GDP rose to 65.0, up from 62.3 during 1976–1980. Correspondingly, gross investment as a percentage of GDP declined from 17.5 percent in 1976–1980 to 16.7 percent during 1983–1987. Contrary to the new classical view, there was no evidence that the large budget deficits of the 1980s led to an increase in the saving rate. In fact, the increase in consumption as a share of GDP implies just the opposite. The pattern was the same when the 1981–1994 period was compared with the 1960–1974 period.

[11]Of course, the real interest rate is the money interest rate minus the expected rate of inflation. Because the expected rate of inflation cannot be directly observed, it must be approximated. The actual inflation rate was used as a proxy for the expected rate in the calculations of Exhibit 12–9. The derived real interest rate was equal the Aaa corporate bond rate minus the actual rate of inflation as measured by the GDP deflator. Annual data were used to make all the calculations.

EXHIBIT 12-9

BUDGET DEFICITS AND CHANGES IN PERSONAL CONSUMPTION, INVESTMENT, AND NET EXPORTS AS A SHARE OF GDP

			Component as a Percentage of GDP				
Time Period	Federal Deficit % of GDP	Real Interest Rate[a]	Personal Consumption	Gross Private Investment	Net Foreign Investment	Gross Investment Less Net Foreign Investment	Net Exports
1976–1980	2.9	1.9	62.3	17.5	0.0	17.5	−0.8
1983–1987	5.1	7.5	65.0	16.7	2.6	14.1	−2.6
Differential[b]	+2.2	+5.6	+2.2	−0.8	+2.6	−3.4	−1.8
1960–1974	0.9	2.4	62.0	15.7	−0.5	16.2	0.2
1981–1994	4.0	6.1	65.8	15.3	1.6	13.7	−1.6
Differential[b]	+3.1	+3.7	+3.8	−0.4	+2.1	−2.5	−1.8

[a]*The real interest rate was derived by subtracting the annual inflation rate as measured by the GDP deflator from the Aaa corporate bond rate.*

[b]*Later period minus earlier period. As the data of the first column indicate, the federal deficits were larger during the later period.*

Source: Derived from the Economic Report of the President, 1996, *Tables B-1, B-3, B-28, and B-73.*

The larger budget deficits of the latter period were associated with higher personal consumption and lower investment as a share of GDP.

Appreciation of the Dollar, Capital Inflow, and Net Exports

What impact did the persistently large deficits of the early and mid-1980s have on the foreign exchange value of the dollar? As interest rates rose during this period, foreign capital poured into the United States, just as the crowding-out model implies. In 1980 the financial investments of Americans abroad were slightly greater than the investments of foreigners in the United States. Thus, there was a small outflow of capital. As the deficits rose during the 1980s, the situation changed dramatically. By 1984 the United States was experiencing an inflow of capital from abroad equal to 2.1 percent of GDP. For the 1983–1987 period, net foreign investment averaged 2.6 percent of GDP, up from zero during 1976–1980. And, just as the crowding-out analysis predicts, this large inflow of capital pushed up the foreign exchange value of the dollar. Between 1980 and 1985, the U.S. dollar appreciated by more than 50 percent (relative to the currencies of our major trading partners) on the foreign exchange market. This appreciation of the dollar made imports cheaper for Americans (and American goods more expensive for foreigners). Predictably, net exports declined sharply.

Look at what happened to the investment spending of Americans. The investment expenditures of Americans (gross investment less net foreign investment) fell from 17.5 percent of GDP in 1976–1980 to 14.1 percent in 1983–1987. Thus, as the size of the budget deficit increased substantially during the 1983–1987 period,

As a share of GDP, government expenditures fell and tax revenues increased during the 1990s. This combination substantially reduced the budget deficit (see Exhibit 12–8). Reduction in national defense spending from 6.5 percent to 4.3 percent of GDP between 1990 and 1997 was the primary reason for the lower expenditures, while the sustained expansion was primarily responsible for the increase in revenues.

Americans increased their current consumption and substantially reduced their domestically financed capital formation.

Exhibit 12–9 also presents capital inflow and trade data for the 1960–1974 and 1981–1994 periods. Once again, there was a substantial increase in net foreign investment and a reduction in net exports during the period when the deficits were large. This pattern is highly consistent with the crowding-out model.

CURRENT VIEW OF FISCAL POLICY

During the last four decades, we have pretty much come full circle with regard to fiscal policy. In the 1960s, most economists thought that fiscal policy was highly potent and that it could be used successfully to smooth the business cycle. Few now adhere to that view. There is now much greater awareness of both political and economic factors that make the proper timing of fiscal policy changes difficult. Confidence in the ability of Congress and the president to institute fiscal policy in a countercyclical manner has waned. In addition, the higher interest rates, reductions in investment, and inflow of foreign capital accompanying the growth of budget deficits indicate that the offsetting secondary factors—particularly those highlighted by the crowding-out model—are quite significant. Thus, most economists now believe that fiscal policy exerts only a modest impact on aggregate demand, at least during normal times.

In the 1990s, the focal point of fiscal policy shifted to the long run. Both economists and policymakers expressed concern that large budget deficits were reducing the rate of capital formation and leading to an unhealthy reliance on the inflow of foreign capital. In contrast with earlier recessions, Congress and the Bush administration agreed to a tax increase and budget accord designed to reduce the budget deficit during the 1990–1991 recession. The Clinton administration increased taxes in 1993. At the same time, the Democratic-controlled Congress defeated a 1993 "demand stimulus" package. Later, the Clinton administration and a Republican-controlled Congress combined forces to reduce both government expenditures and budget deficits as a share of GDP during the 1994–1998 period. To a large degree, the lower deficits of the 1990s reflect sustained economic expansion and lower defense spending in the aftermath of the Cold War rather than a major shift in fiscal policy. Nonetheless, it is clear that fiscal policy is viewed much differently in the 1990s than it was in the 1970s.

LOOKING *Ahead*

If fiscal policy is now less important, the significance of monetary policy—the other major stabilization weapon—is elevated.[12] We are now ready to integrate the monetary system into our analysis. Chapter 13 will focus on the operation of the banking system and the factors that determine the supply of money. In Chapter 14, we will analyze the impact of monetary policy on real output, interest rates, and the price level.

KEY POINTS

➤ The federal budget is the primary tool of fiscal policy. Discretionary fiscal policy encompasses deliberate changes in the government's spending and tax policies designed to alter the size of the budget deficit and thereby influence the overall level of economic activity.

➤ According to the Keynesian view, fluctuations in aggregate demand are the major source of economic instability. Policies that help to maintain aggregate demand at a level consistent with the economy's full employment capacity will reduce economic instability.

➤ Rather than balancing the budget annually, Keynesian analysis indicates that fiscal policy should reflect business cycle conditions. During a recession, fiscal policy should become more expansionary (a larger deficit should be planned). During an inflationary boom, fiscal policy should become more restrictive (shift toward a budget surplus).

➤ The crowding-out model indicates that expansionary fiscal policy will lead to higher real interest rates and less private spending, particularly for investment. In an open economy, the higher interest rates will also lead to an inflow of capital, appreciation of the dollar, and a reduction in net exports. The crowding-out theory implies that these secondary effects will largely offset the demand stimulus effects of expansionary fiscal policy. The secondary effects of restrictive fiscal policy will also render it impotent.

➤ The new classical model stresses that substitution of debt for tax financing changes the timing, but not the level, of taxes. According to this view, the higher expected future taxes implied by the bond financing of the deficit will lead to more saving and less private spending, which will offset the expansionary effects of the deficit.

➤ Changes in fiscal policy must be timed properly if they are going to exert a stabilizing influence on an economy. The ability of policymakers to time fiscal policy changes in a countercyclical manner is reduced by (a) our limited ability to forecast future macroeconomic conditions, (b) predictable delays in the institution of policy changes, and (c) a time lag between when a policy change is instituted and when it will exert its primary impact.

➤ The problem of proper timing is reduced in the case of automatic stabilizers—programs that apply stimulus during a recession and restraint during a boom even though no legislative action has been taken.

➤ A modern synthesis concerning the impact of fiscal policy as a stabilization tool has emerged. The major points of the synthesis view are: (1) Proper timing of discretionary fiscal policy is both difficult to achieve and crucially important; (2) automatic stabilizers reduce the fluctuation of aggregate demand and thereby help to promote economic stability; and (3) fiscal policy is much less potent than the early Keynesian view implied.

➤ When fiscal policy changes marginal tax rates, it influences aggregate supply by altering the relative attractiveness of productive activity compared to leisure and tax avoidance. Other things constant, lower marginal tax rates will increase aggregate supply. Supply-side economics

[12]With regard to this point, the current view of Paul Samuelson is again revealing. In the 1995 edition of *Economics* (now coauthored with William D. Nordhaus), Samuelson wrote, "Fiscal policy is no longer a major tool of stabilization policy in the United States. Over the foreseeable future, stabilization policy will be performed by Federal Reserve monetary policy" (p. 645).

should be viewed as a long-run strategy, not a countercyclical tool.

➤ Difficulties involved in the proper timing of discretionary policy changes and concern about the impact of budget deficits on interest rates and capital formation have reduced the importance of fiscal policy as a stabilization tool and induced policymakers to move toward a balanced budget during the 1990s.

CRITICAL ANALYSIS QUESTIONS

1. Suppose that you are a member of the Council of Economic Advisers. The president has asked you to prepare a statement on the question "What is the proper fiscal policy for the next 12 months?" Prepare such a statement, indicating (a) the current state of the economy (that is, unemployment rate, growth in real income, and rate of inflation) and (b) your fiscal policy suggestions. Should the budget be in balance? Explain the reasoning behind your suggestions.

*2. What is the crowding-out effect? How does it modify the implications of the basic Keynesian model with regard to fiscal policy? How does the new classical theory of fiscal policy differ from the crowding-out model?

3. Why is proper timing of discretionary changes in fiscal policy difficult? Do you think political factors as well as economic factors limit the use of fiscal policy as a stabilization tool? Why or why not?

*4. What are automatic stabilizers? Explain their major advantage.

5. Outline the supply-side view of fiscal policy. How does this view differ from the various demand-side theories? Explain why a supply-side economist would probably favor a reduction in tax rates financed by the elimination of various tax-deductible items (interest expense, medical expenditures, and state and local taxes, for example).

6. According to the Keynesian view, what fiscal policy actions should be taken if the unemployment rate is high and current GDP is well below the economy's sustainable output rate?

7. In the early 1990s, many argued that the large deficits were reducing the long-term rate of economic growth. Use the major fiscal policy models developed in this chapter to analyze this view. Is the argument correct? Why or why not?

*8. "If we set aside our reluctance to use fiscal policy as a stabilization force, it is quite easy to achieve full employment and price stability. When output is at less than full employment, we run a budget deficit. If inflation is a problem, we run a budget surplus. Quick implementation of proper fiscal policy will stabilize the economy." Evaluate this view.

9. "Budget deficits may stimulate aggregate demand and output in the short run, but since they divert funds away from capital formation and toward current consumption, they will retard the growth of output in the long run."

a. Explain why you either agree or disagree with the statement.
b. Would a proponent of the crowding-out theory agree with this view? Why or why not?
c. Would a new classical economist agree with it? Why or why not?

*10. Some people argue that the growth of output and employment in the 1980s was the result of the large budget deficits. As one politician put it, "Anyone could create prosperity if he wrote $200 billion of hot checks every year." Evaluate this view. If demand stimulus created the prosperity, what would you expect to happen to the rate of inflation? Did this happen during the 1980s?

11. As a share of GDP, the budget deficit decreased steadily during 1993–1998. What factors accounted for the reduction in the deficit during the period? Do you think a change in views toward fiscal policy played any role? Why or why not? Did the deficit reduction exert a positive or negative impact on the economy? Discuss.

12. If deficits tend to be larger during a recession, how will this affect the relationship between budget deficits and real interest rates?

*13. "If the marginal propensity to consume (MPC) is 0.75, a $10 billion increase in government expenditures will stimulate $40 billion of additional expenditures ($10 billion times the multiplier of 4), while a $10 billion tax increase will reduce spending by only $30 billion ($7.5 billion times the multiplier of 4). Thus, a $10 billion increase in both government expenditures and taxes will stimulate aggregate output by $10 billion." Evaluate this statement.

*14. If the impact on tax revenues is the same, does it make any difference whether the government cuts taxes by (a) reducing marginal tax rates or (b) increasing the personal exemption allowance? Explain.

15. Professor Paul Samuelson is widely recognized as the leading American Keynesian economist of this century. Look at his statement at the beginning of this chapter. Use the analysis of the chapter to explain precisely what Samuelson means when he states, "The shortcomings [of fiscal policy] stem from timing, politics, macroeconomic theory, and the deficit itself." Discuss the significance of this statement.

---

*Asterisk denotes questions for which answers are given in Appendix B.

CHAPTER 13

Money is whatever is generally accepted in exchange for goods and services — accepted not as an object to be consumed but as an object that represents a temporary abode of purchasing power to be used for buying still other goods and services.

Milton Friedman[1]

Money and the Banking System

CHAPTER FOCUS

- What is money? How is the money supply defined?
- What is a fractional reserve banking system? How does it influence the ability of banks to create money?
- What are the major functions of the Federal Reserve System?
- What are the major tools with which the Federal Reserve controls the supply of money?
- How are financial innovations and other changes affecting the nature of money? What will money be like in the future?

[1]Milton Friedman, *Money Mischief: Episodes in Monetary History* (New York: Harcourt Brace Jovanovich, 1992), p. 16.

The simple macroeconomic model we have developed thus far has four major markets: (1) goods and services, (2) resources, (3) loanable funds, and (4) foreign exchange. When people make exchanges in any of these markets, they generally use money. Money is used to purchase all types of goods, services, physical assets such as houses, and financial assets such as stocks and bonds.

This chapter focuses on the nature of money, how the banking system works, and how the **central bank**—the Federal Reserve System in the United States—controls the supply of money. Money and monetary policy play an important role in the operation of an economy. Reflecting this importance, the next two chapters will focus primarily on how monetary policy works and the impact that it has on the level of prices, output, employment, and the business cycle.

Central bank
An institution that regulates the banking system and controls the supply of money of a country.

WHAT IS MONEY?

Money is the item that is commonly used as a means of payment for goods, services, assets, and outstanding debt. (See the chapter opening quotation of Professor Friedman.) Paradoxically, most modern money has no intrinsic worth. Nonetheless, most of us would like to have more of it. Why? Because money is an asset that performs three basic functions: It serves as a medium of exchange, it provides a means of storing value for future use, and it is used as an accounting unit.

Medium of Exchange

Money is one of the most important inventions in human history because of its role as a **medium of exchange.** Money simplifies and reduces the costs of transactions. This reduction in transaction cost permits us to realize the enormous gains from specialization, division of labor, and mass-production processes that underlie our modern standard of living. Without money, exchange would be complicated, time-consuming, and enormously costly. Think what it would be like to live in a barter economy—one without money, where goods were traded for goods. If you wanted to buy a pair of jeans, for example, you would have to first find someone willing to sell you the jeans who was also willing to purchase your labor services or something else you were willing to supply. Such an economy would be highly inefficient.

Medium of exchange
An asset that is used to buy and sell goods or services.

Money oils the wheels of trade and makes it possible for each of us to specialize in the supply of those things that we do best while purchasing (and consuming) a broad cross section of goods and services consistent with our individual preferences. People simply sell their productive services or assets for money and, in turn, use the money to buy the goods and services they want. For example, if a farmer wants to exchange a cow for electricity and medical services, the cow is sold for money, which is then used to buy the electricity and the medical services. Money permits a society to escape cumbersome barter procedures.

Store of Value

Money is a financial asset—a method of storing value and moving purchasing power from one time period to another. There are some disadvantages of money as a **store of value.** Many methods of holding money do not yield an interest return. During a time of inflation, the purchasing power of money will decline, imposing a cost on those who are holding wealth in the form of money.

Store of value
An asset that will allow people to transfer purchasing power from one period to the next.

Money is not the only way of storing value. Other assets, such as food products, land, houses, stocks, or bonds, might be used to store value for the future. *Money, however, has one big advantage—because of its use as a medium of exchange, money is the most* ***liquid of all assets.*** It can be easily and quickly transformed into other goods at a low transaction cost and without an appreciable loss in its nominal value. In contrast, it will take time to locate an acceptable buyer for a house, a plot of land, or an office building. Thus, these assets are illiquid. While stocks and bonds are quite liquid—they can usually be sold quickly for only a small commission—they are not readily acceptable as a direct means of payment. Money provides readily available purchasing power for dealing with an uncertain future. Thus, most people hold some of their wealth in the form of money.

Liquid asset
An asset that can be easily and quickly converted to purchasing power without loss of value.

Unit of Account

Money also serves as a **unit of account.** Just as we use yards or meters to measure distance, units of money are used to measure the exchange value and costs of goods, services, assets, and resources. The value (and cost) of movie tickets, CD recorders, labor services, automobiles, houses, and numerous other items is measured in units of money. Money serves as a common denominator for the expression of both costs and value. If consumers are going to spend their income wisely, they must be able to compare the costs of a vast array of goods and services. Prices measured in units of money help them make such comparisons. Similarly, sound business decisions require cost and revenue comparisons among vastly different productive services. Resource prices and accounting procedures measured in money units facilitate this task.

Unit of account
The units of measurement used by people to post prices and keep track of revenues and costs.

WHY IS MONEY VALUABLE?

At various times in the past, societies have used gold, silver, beads, seashells, cigarettes, precious stones, and other commodities as money. When commodities are used as money, people will employ scarce resources—resources that could be used to produce valuable goods and services—trying to produce more of the thing that is used as money. Because of this, the opportunity cost of commodity-based money is high.

If a society uses something as money that costs little or nothing to produce, more scarce resources are available for the production of desired goods and services. Thus, most modern nations use **fiat money,** money that has little or no intrinsic value. A dollar bill is just a piece of paper. Checking account deposits are nothing more than accounting numbers. Coins have some intrinsic value as metal, but in most cases this value is considerably less than their value as money.

Fiat money
Money that has neither intrinsic value nor the backing of a commodity with intrinsic value; paper currency is an example.

Why is fiat money valuable? To a degree, its value is based on the confidence of the people who use it. People are willing to accept fiat money because they know it can be used to purchase real goods and services. Governments issuing fiat money often designate it as "legal tender," meaning it is acceptable for payment of debts.

The main thing that makes money valuable, however, is the same thing that generates value for other commodities: Demand relative to supply. People demand

Money is the item commonly used to buy and sell things. During the Second World War, prisoners of war used cigarettes as money in POW camps.

money because it reduces the cost of exchange. When the supply of money is limited relative to the demand, money will be valuable.

The value of a unit of money—a dollar, for example—is measured in terms of what it will buy. Its value, therefore, is inversely related to the level of prices. An increase in the level of prices and a decline in the purchasing power of a unit of money are the same thing. If the purchasing power of money is to remain stable over time, the supply of money must be controlled. Assuming a constant rate of use, if the supply of money grows more rapidly than the real output of goods and services, prices will rise. In layman's terms, there is "too much money chasing too few goods."

When government authorities rapidly expand the supply of money, it becomes less valuable in exchange and is virtually useless as a store of value. The rapid growth in the supply of money in Germany following the First World War provides a dramatic illustration of this point. During the period 1922–1923, the supply of German marks increased by 250 percent *per month* for a time. The German government was printing money almost as fast as the printing presses would run. Since money became substantially more plentiful in relation to goods and services, it quickly lost its value. As a result, an egg cost 80 billion marks and a loaf of bread 200 billion. Workers picked up their wages in suitcases. Shops closed at the lunch hour to change price tags. The value of money had eroded. More recently (in the 1980s and 1990s), Argentina, Bolivia, Brazil, Israel, Yugoslavia, Russia, and Ukraine (and several other countries of the former Soviet Union) have experienced this same cycle of rapid growth in the money supply (to pay for government expenditures) and hyperinflation.

THE SUPPLY OF MONEY

How is the supply of money defined? There is no straightforward, single answer to this question. Economists and policy makers have developed several alternative measures. We will briefly describe the two most widely used of these money supply measures.

The M1 Money Supply

Above all else, money is a medium of exchange. The narrowest definition of the money supply, **M1,** focuses on this function. Based on its role as a medium of exchange, it is clear that currency (including both coins and paper bills) and checkable deposits should be included in the supply of money. Deposits that can be drawn from by writing a check are called **transaction accounts.** There are two general categories of transaction accounts. First, there are **demand deposits,** non-interest-earning deposits with banking institutions that are available for withdrawal ("on demand") at any time without restrictions. Demand deposits are usually withdrawn by writing a check. Second, there are **other checkable deposits** that earn interest but carry some restrictions on their transferability. Interest-earning checkable deposits generally either limit the number of checks written each month or require the depositor to maintain a substantial minimum balance ($1,000, for example). Like currency and demand deposits, interest-earning checkable deposits are available for use as a medium of exchange. Traveler's checks are also a means of payment. They can be freely converted to cash at parity (equal value). ***Thus, the M1 money supply comprises (1) currency in circulation, (2) checkable deposits (both demand deposits and interest-earning checkable deposits), and (3) traveler's checks.***

M1 (money supply)
The sum of (1) currency in circulation (including coins), (2) checkable deposits maintained in depository institutions, and (3) traveler's checks.

Transaction accounts
Accounts, including demand deposits and interest-earning checkable deposits, against which the account holder is permitted to transfer funds for the purpose of making payment to a third party.

Demand deposits
Non-interest-earning checking deposits that can be either withdrawn or made payable on demand to a third party. Like currency, these deposits are widely used as a means of payment.

Other checkable deposits
Interest-earning deposits that are also available for checking.

As **Exhibit 13–1** shows, the total M1 money supply in the United States was $1,092 billion at year-end 1998. Demand and other checkable deposits accounted for approximately two-thirds of the M1 money supply. This large share reflects the fact that most of the nation's business is conducted by check.

EXHIBIT 13–1

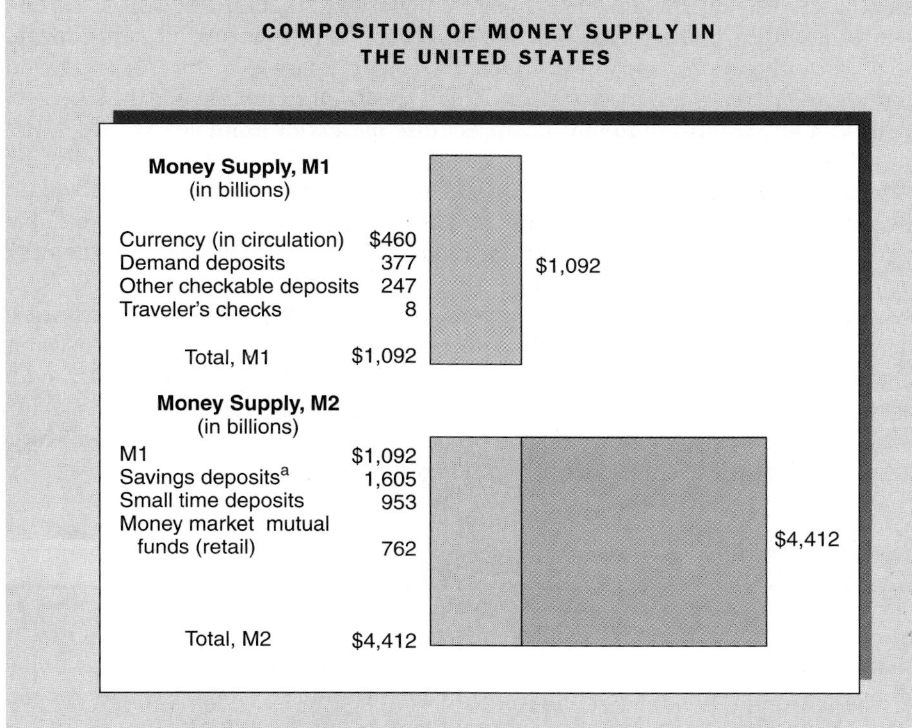

COMPOSITION OF MONEY SUPPLY IN THE UNITED STATES

Money Supply, M1 (in billions)	
Currency (in circulation)	$460
Demand deposits	377
Other checkable deposits	247
Traveler's checks	8
Total, M1	$1,092

Money Supply, M2 (in billions)	
M1	$1,092
Savings deposits[a]	1,605
Small time deposits	953
Money market mutual funds (retail)	762
Total, M2	$4,412

The size and composition (as of December 1998) of the two most widely used measures of the money supply are shown. M1, the narrowest definition of the money supply, is comprised of currency, checking deposits, and traveler's checks. M2, which contains M1 plus the various savings components indicated, is four times the size of M1.

[a]*Including money market deposit accounts.*
SOURCE: Federal Reserve Bulletin, *March 1999.*

The Broader M2 Money Supply

M2 (money supply)
Equal to M1 plus (1) savings deposits, (2) time deposits (accounts of less than $100,000) held in depository institutions, and (3) money market mutual fund shares.

Depository institutions
Businesses that accept checking and savings deposits and use a portion of them to extend loans and make investments. Banks, savings and loan associations, and credit unions are examples.

Money market mutual funds
Interest-earning accounts offered by brokerage firms that pool depositors' funds and invest them in highly liquid short-term securities. Since these securities can be quickly converted to cash, depositors are permitted to write checks (which reduce their share holdings) against their accounts.

In modern economies, several financial assets can easily be converted into checking deposits or currency; therefore, the line between money and "near monies" is often blurred. Broader definitions of the money supply include various assets that can be easily converted to checking account funds and cash. The most common broad definition of the money supply is **M2.** It includes all the items included in M1 plus (1) savings deposits (including money market deposit accounts), (2) time deposits of less than $100,000 at all **depository institutions,** and (3) money market mutual funds.

Although the non-M1 components of the M2 money supply are not generally used as a means of making payment, they can be easily and quickly converted to currency or checking deposits for such use. For example, if you maintain funds in a savings account, you can easily transfer them to your checking account for use as a means of payment. **Money market mutual funds** are interest-earning accounts offered by brokerage firms that pool depositors' funds and invest them in highly liquid short-term securities. Because these securities can be quickly converted to cash, depositors are permitted to write checks (which reduce their share holdings) against these accounts.

Many economists—particularly those who stress the store-of-value function of money—prefer the broader M2 definition of the money supply to the narrower M1 concept. As Exhibit 13–1 shows, at year-end 1998 the M2 money supply was $4,412 billion, approximately four times the M1 money supply. Other definitions of the money supply have been developed for specialized purposes, but the M1 and M2 definitions are the most important and most widely used.

Credit Cards versus Money

Credit
Funds acquired by borrowing.

It is important to distinguish between money and credit. Money is a financial asset that provides the holder with future purchasing power. **Credit** is liability acquired when one borrows funds. This distinction sheds light on a question students frequently ask: "Because credit cards are often used to make purchases, why aren't credit card expenditures part of the money supply?" In contrast with money, credit cards are not purchasing power. They are merely a convenient means of arranging a loan. When you use your Visa or MasterCard to buy a compact disc player, for example, you are not really paying for the player. Instead, you are taking out a loan from the institution issuing your card, and that institution is paying for the player. Payment is not made by you until you write a check to settle your credit card bill and thereby reduce your money balances. Thus, credit card purchases are not money; they are not an asset representing future purchasing power.

Although credit cards are not money, their use will influence the amount of money people will want to hold. Credit cards make it possible for people to buy things throughout the month and then pay for them with a single transaction at the end of the month. This makes it possible for people to conduct their regular business affairs with less money than would otherwise be needed. Thus, widespread use of credit cards will tend to reduce the average quantity of money people hold.

THE BUSINESS OF BANKING

Federal Reserve System
The central bank of the United States; it carries out banking regulatory policies and is responsible for the conduct of monetary policy.

We must understand a few things about the business of banking before we can explain the factors that influence the supply of money. The banking industry in the United States operates under the jurisdiction of the **Federal Reserve System,** the nation's central bank. Not all banks belong to the Federal Reserve, but under legislation enacted in

Money is an asset; it is part of the wealth of the people who hold it. In contrast, credit card purchases create a liability. They are merely a convenient method of arranging a short-term loan.

1980, only a nominal difference exists between member and nonmember banks. We will discuss the Federal Reserve System in detail later in this chapter.

The banking system is an important component of the capital market. Like other private businesses, banks are profit-seeking operations. Banks provide services (for example, safekeeping of funds and checking-account services) and pay interest in order to attract both checking and savings depositors. ***They help to bring together people who want to save for the future with those who want to borrow in order to undertake investment projects.*** Income derived from loans in support of investment projects is the primary source of revenue for banks.

When deciding whether to fund a project, bankers have a strong incentive to judge both the project's expected profitability and the borrower's creditworthiness. Borrowers may be unable to repay their loans if the funds are channeled into unprofitable investments. In turn, lenders who finance business failures may lose all or part of their funds. Efficient allocation of investment funds is an important source of economic growth. Profitable business projects increase the value of resources and promote economic growth; unprofitable projects have the opposite effect. An efficiently operating capital market, of which the banking system is an integral part, will extend loans and provide financial support for projects that are more likely to be winners—that is, profitable rather than unprofitable.

Savings and loan associations
Financial institutions that accept deposits in exchange for shares that pay dividends. Historically, these funds have been channeled into residential mortgage loans. Under banking legislation adopted in 1980, S&Ls are permitted to offer a broad range of services similar to those of commercial banks.

Credit unions
Financial cooperative organizations of individuals with a common affiliation (such as an employer or a labor union). They accept deposits, including checkable deposits, pay interest (or dividends) on them out of earnings, and channel funds primarily into loans to members.

Commercial banks
Financial institutions that offer a wide range of services (for example, checking accounts, savings accounts, and extension of loans) to their customers. Commercial banks are owned by stockholders and seek to operate at a profit.

In the United States, the banking system consists of savings and loan institutions, credit unions, and commercial banks. **Savings and loan associations** accept deposits in exchange for shares that pay dividends. **Credit unions** are cooperative financial organizations of individuals with a common affiliation (such as an employer) that accept deposits, pay interest (or dividends) on them, and generate earnings primarily through the extension of loans to members. **Commercial banks** offer a wide range of services—including checking and savings accounts and extension of loans—and are owned by stockholders. Under legislation passed in 1980, all these depository institutions are authorized to offer both checking and savings accounts and to extend a wide variety of loans to customers.

All these depository institutions are now under the jurisdiction of the Federal Reserve System, which applies similar regulations and offers similar services (for example, check clearing and access to borrowing from the Fed) to each. ***Therefore, when we speak of the banking industry, we are referring to not only commercial banks, but savings and loan associations and credit unions as well.***

The consolidated balance sheet of commercial banking institutions (**Exhibit 13–2**) illustrates the major banking functions. It shows that the major liabilities of banks are transaction (checking), savings, and time deposits. *From the viewpoint of a bank,* these are liabilities because they represent an obligation of the bank to its depositors. Outstanding interest-earning loans comprise the major class of banking assets. In addition, most banks own sizable amounts of interest-earning securities—bonds issued by either governments or private corporations.

EXHIBIT 13–2

Banks provide services and pay interest to attract transaction (checking), savings, and time deposits (liabilities). Most of the deposits are invested and loaned out, providing interest income for the bank. Banks hold a portion of their assets as reserves (either cash or deposits with the Fed) to meet their daily obligations toward their depositors.

SOURCE: Federal Reserve Bulletin, *March 1999.*

FUNCTIONS OF COMMERCIAL BANKING INSTITUTIONS

CONSOLIDATED BALANCE SHEET OF COMMERCIAL BANKING INSTITUTIONS, YEAR-END 1998 (BILLIONS OF DOLLARS)

ASSETS		LIABILITIES	
Vault cash	$ 36	Transaction deposits	$ 665
Reserves at the Fed	9	Savings and time deposits	2,656
Loans outstanding	3,316	Borrowings	985
U.S. government securities	793	Other liabilities	560
Other securities	443	Net worth	421
Other assets	690		
Total	$5,287		$5,287

The banking industry (commercial banks, savings and loan associations, and credit unions) plays an important role in the loanable funds market. In addition to providing checking services that facilitate convenient payment, banks act as an intermediary between borrowers and lenders, helping to channel funds toward profitable investment projects.

Banking differs from most businesses in that a large portion of its liabilities are payable on demand. However, even though it would be possible for all depositors to demand the money in their checking accounts on the same day, the probability of this occurring is generally quite remote. Typically, while some individuals are making withdrawals, others are making deposits. These transactions tend to balance out, eliminating sudden changes in demand deposits.

Thus, banks maintain only a fraction of their assets in reserves to meet the requirements of depositors. As Exhibit 13–2 illustrates, **bank reserves**—vault cash plus reserve deposits with the Federal Reserve—were only $45 billion at year-end 1998, compared to transaction (checking) deposits of $665 billion. Thus, on average, banks were maintaining less than 10 percent of their assets in reserve against the checking deposits of their customers.

Bank reserves
Vault cash plus deposits of the bank with Federal Reserve banks.

Fractional Reserve Goldsmithing

Economists often like to draw an analogy between our current banking system and the goldsmiths of the past. In the past, gold was used as the means of making payments. It was money. People would store their money with a goldsmith for safekeeping, just as many of us open a checking account for safety reasons. Gold owners received a certificate granting them the right to withdraw their gold anytime they wished. If they wanted to buy something, they would go to the goldsmith, withdraw gold, and use it as a means of making a payment. Thus, the money supply was equal to the amount of gold in circulation plus the gold deposited with goldsmiths.

The day-to-day deposits of and requests for gold were always only a fraction of the total amount of gold deposited. A major portion of the gold simply "lay idle in the goldsmiths' vaults." Taking notice of this fact, goldsmiths soon began loaning gold to local merchants. After a time, the merchants would pay back the gold, plus pay interest for its use. What happened to the money supply when a goldsmith extended loans to local merchants? The deposits of persons who initially brought their gold to the goldsmith were not reduced. Depositors could still withdraw their gold anytime they wished (as long as they did not all try to do so at once). In addition, the merchants were now able to use the gold they borrowed from the goldsmith as a means of payment. ***As goldsmiths lent gold, they increased the amount of gold in circulation, thereby increasing the money supply.***

It was inconvenient to make a trip to the goldsmith every time one wanted to buy something. Because the certificates were redeemable in gold, they began to circulate as a means of payment. The depositors were pleased with this arrangement because it eliminated the need for a trip to the goldsmith every time something was exchanged for gold. As long as they had confidence in the goldsmith, sellers were glad to accept the certificates as payment.

As gold certificates began to circulate, the daily withdrawals and deposits with goldsmiths declined even more. Local goldsmiths would keep about 20 percent of the total gold deposited with them so they could meet the current requests to redeem the gold certificates in circulation. The remaining 80 percent of their gold deposits would be loaned out to merchants, traders, and other citizens. Therefore, 100 percent of the gold certificates was circulating as money; that portion of gold that had been loaned out, 80 percent of the total deposits, was also circulating as money. The total money supply, gold certificates plus gold, was now 1.8 times the amount of gold that had been originally deposited with the goldsmith. Because the goldsmiths issued loans and kept only a fraction of the total gold deposited with them, they were able to increase the money supply.

As long as the goldsmiths held enough reserves to meet the current requests of the depositors, everything went along smoothly. Most gold depositors probably did not even realize that the goldsmiths did not have their actual gold and that of other depositors, precisely designated as such, sitting in the "vaults."

Goldsmiths derived income from loaning gold. The more gold they loaned, the greater their total income. Some goldsmiths, trying to increase their income by extending more and more interest-earning loans, depleted the gold in their vaults to imprudently low levels. If an unexpectedly large number of depositors wanted their gold, these imprudent goldsmiths would be unable to meet their requests. As this happened, the system of fractional reserve goldsmithing would tend to break down.

Fractional Reserve Banking

Fractional reserve banking
A system that permits banks to hold reserves of less than 100 percent against their deposits.

In principle, our modern banking system is very similar to goldsmithing. The United States has a **fractional reserve banking** system. Banks are required to maintain only a fraction of their deposits in the form of cash and other reserves. Just as the early goldsmiths did not have enough gold to pay all their depositors simultaneously, neither do our banks have enough reserves (vault cash and deposits with Federal Reserve banks) to pay all their depositors simultaneously. (Note: As Exhibit 13–2 illustrates, the vault cash plus the reserves held with the Federal Reserve are less than 10 percent of the transaction—that is, checking—deposits of commercial banks.) The early goldsmiths expanded the money supply by issuing loans. So do present-day bankers. The amount of gold held in reserve to meet the requirements of depositors limited the ability of the goldsmiths to expand the money supply. The amount of cash and other **required reserves** limits the ability of present-day banks to expand the money supply.

Required reserves
The minimum amount of reserves that a bank is required by law to keep on hand to back up its deposits. Thus, if reserve requirements were 15 percent, banks would be required to keep \$150,000 in reserves against each \$1 million of deposits.

However, there are also important differences between modern banking and early goldsmithing. Today, the actions of individual banks are regulated by a central bank. The central bank is supposed to follow policies designed to promote a healthy economy. It also acts as a lender of last resort. If all depositors in a specific bank suddenly attempted to withdraw their funds simultaneously, the central bank would intervene and supply the bank with enough funds to meet the demand.

HOW BANKS CREATE MONEY BY EXTENDING LOANS

Under a fractional reserve system, an increase in reserves will permit banks to extend additional loans and thereby create additional transaction (checking) deposits. Since transaction deposits are money, the extension of the additional loans expands the supply of money. To enhance our understanding of this process, let us consider a banking system without a central bank, one in which only currency acts as a reserve against deposits. Initially, we will assume that all banks are required by law to maintain vault currency equal to at least 20 percent of the checking accounts of their depositors. This proportion—the percent of reserves that must be maintained against checkable transaction deposits—is called the **required reserve ratio.** The required reserve ratio in our example is 20 percent.

Required reserve ratio
A percentage of a specified liability category (for example, transaction accounts) that banking institutions are required to hold as reserves against that type of liability.

Suppose you found $1,000 that your long-deceased uncle had apparently hidden in the basement of his house. How much would this newly found $1,000 of currency expand the money supply? You take the bills to the First National Bank, open a checking account of $1,000, and deposit the cash with the banker. First National is now required to keep an additional $200 in vault cash, 20 percent of your deposit. However, it received $1,000 of additional cash, so after placing $200 in the bank vault, First National has $800 of **excess reserves,** reserves over and above the amount it is required by law to maintain. Given its current excess reserves, First National can now extend an $800 loan. Suppose it loans $800 to a local citizen to help pay for a car. At the time the loan is extended, the money supply will increase by $800 as the bank adds the funds to the checking account of the borrower. No one else has less money. You still have your $1,000 checking account, and the borrower has $800 for a new car.

Excess reserves
Actual reserves that exceed the legal requirement.

When the borrower buys a new car, the seller accepts a check and deposits the $800 in a bank, Citizen's State Bank. What happens when the check clears? The temporary excess reserves of the First National Bank will be eliminated when it pays $800 to the Citizen's State Bank. But when Citizen's State Bank receives $800 in currency, it will now have excess reserves. It must keep 20 percent, an additional $160, as required reserves against the $800 checking account deposit of the automobile seller.

The remaining $640 could be loaned out. Because Citizen's State, like other banks, is in business to make money, it will be quite happy to "extend a helping hand" to a borrower. When the second bank loans out its excess reserves, the deposits of the person borrowing the money will increase by $640. Another $640 has now been added to the money supply. You still have your $1,000, the automobile seller has an additional $800, and the new borrower has just received an additional $640. Because you found the $1,000 and deposited it in the bank, the money supply has increased by $1,440 ($800 + $640).

Of course, the process can continue. **Exhibit 13–3** follows the potential creation of money resulting from the initial $1,000 through several additional stages. When the reserve requirement is 20 percent, the money supply can expand to a maximum of $5,000, the initial $1,000 plus an additional $4,000 in demand deposits that can be created by extending new loans.

The multiple by which new reserves increase the stock of money is referred to as the **deposit expansion multiplier.** The amount by which additional reserves can increase the supply of money is determined by the ratio of required reserves to deposits. In fact, the **potential deposit expansion multiplier** is merely the reciprocal of the required reserve ratio (r). Mathematically, the potential deposit expansion multiplier is equal to $1/r$. In our example, the required reserves are 20 percent, or one-fifth of the total deposits. So the potential deposit expansion multiplier is 5. If only 10 percent reserves were required, the potential deposit expansion multiplier would be 10, the

Deposit expansion multiplier
The multiple by which an increase (decrease) in reserves will increase (decrease) the money supply. It is inversely related to the required reserve ratio.

Potential deposit expansion multiplier
The maximum potential increase in the money supply as a ratio of the new reserves injected into the banking system. It is equal to the inverse of the required reserve ratio.

EXHIBIT 13-3

CREATING MONEY FROM NEW RESERVES

Bank	New Cash Deposits: Actual Reserves	New Required Reserves	Potential Demand Deposits Created by Extending New Loans
Initial deposit (Bank A)	$1,000.00	$ 200.00	$ 800.00
Second stage (Bank B)	800.00	160.00	640.00
Third stage (Bank C)	640.00	128.00	512.00
Fourth stage (Bank D)	512.00	102.40	409.60
Fifth stage (Bank E)	409.60	81.92	327.68
Sixth stage (Bank F)	327.68	65.54	262.14
Seventh stage (Bank G)	262.14	52.43	209.71
All others (other banks)	1,048.58	209.71	838.87
Total	$5,000.00	$1,000.00	$4,000.00

When banks are required to maintain 20 percent reserves against demand deposits, the creation of $1,000 of new reserves will potentially increase the supply of money by $5,000.

reciprocal of one-tenth. ***The lower the percentage of the reserve requirement, the greater is the potential expansion in the money supply resulting from the creation of new reserves. The fractional reserve requirement places a ceiling on potential money creation from new reserves.***

The Actual Deposit Multiplier

Will the introduction of the new currency reserves necessarily have a full deposit expansion multiplier effect? The answer is no. The actual deposit multiplier will generally be less than the potential for two reasons.

First, the deposit expansion multiplier will be reduced if some persons decide to hold the currency rather than deposit it in a bank. For example, suppose the person who borrowed the $800 in the preceding example spends only $700 and stashes the remaining $100 away for a possible emergency. Only $700 can then end up as a deposit in the second stage and contribute to the excess reserves necessary for expansion. The potential of new loans in the second stage and in all subsequent stages will be reduced proportionally. When currency remains in circulation, outside the banks, it reduces the size of the deposit expansion multiplier.

Second, the actual deposit multiplier will be less than its maximum potential when banks fail to use all the new excess reserves to extend loans. Banks, though, have a strong incentive to loan out or invest most of their new excess reserves. Idle excess reserves do not earn interest. Because banks are in business to earn income, they will maintain only a very small portion of their assets—mostly currency needed for daily transactions—in the form of excess reserves. In recent years, excess reserves have accounted for less than 1 percent of the total reserves of banks.

Currency leakages and idle excess bank reserves will result in a deposit expansion multiplier that is less than its potential maximum. However, because people generally keep most of their money in bank deposits (rather than currency) and the excess reserves of banks are typically small, the injection of new reserves into the system can be counted on to expand the supply of money by a multiple of the additional reserves.

THE FEDERAL RESERVE SYSTEM

Most countries have a central banking authority that controls the money supply and conducts monetary policy. As we previously noted, the central bank of the United States is the Federal Reserve System. In the United Kingdom, the central bank is the Bank of England; in Canada, it is the Bank of Canada; in Japan, it is the Bank of Japan. Central banks are responsible for the conduct of their nation's monetary policy.

STRUCTURE OF THE FED

The major purpose of the Federal Reserve System (and other central banks) is to regulate the money supply and provide a monetary climate that is in the best interest of the entire economy. Congress has instructed the Federal Reserve, or the Fed, as it is often called, to conduct monetary policy in a manner that promotes both full employment and price stability. Unlike commercial banks, the Federal Reserve is not a profit-making institution. The earnings of the Fed, over and above its expenses, belong to the Treasury.

Exhibit 13–4 illustrates the structure of the Fed. There are three major centers of decision making within the Federal Reserve: (1) the Board of Governors, (2) the district and regional banks, and (3) the Federal Open Market Operations Committee.

EXHIBIT 13–4

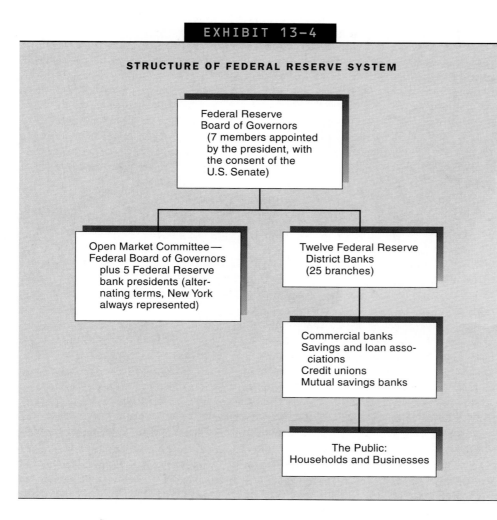

STRUCTURE OF FEDERAL RESERVE SYSTEM

Federal Reserve Board of Governors (7 members appointed by the president, with the consent of the U.S. Senate)

Open Market Committee— Federal Board of Governors plus 5 Federal Reserve bank presidents (alternating terms, New York always represented)

Twelve Federal Reserve District Banks (25 branches)

Commercial banks
Savings and loan associations
Credit unions
Mutual savings banks

The Public: Households and Businesses

The Board of Governors of the Federal Reserve System is at the center of the banking system in the United States. The board sets the rules and regulations for all depository institutions. The seven members of the Board of Governors also serve on the Federal Open Market Committee, a 12-member board that establishes Fed policy with regard to the buying and selling of government securities, the primary mechanism used to control the money supply in the United States.

Board of Governors. The Board of Governors is the decision-making center of the Fed. This powerful board consists of seven members, each appointed to a staggered 14-year term by the president with the advice and consent of the Senate. The president designates one of the seven members as chair for a four-year term. (See Outstanding Economist: Alan Greenspan.) The Board of Governors establishes the rules and regulations applicable to all depository institutions. It sets the reserve requirements and regulates the composition of the asset holdings of depository institutions. The board is the rule maker, and often the umpire, of the banking industry.

Federal Reserve District Banks. There are 12 Federal Reserve District banks with 25 regional branches spread throughout the nation. **Exhibit 13–5** shows the regions covered by each of the 12 district banks. These district and regional banks operate under the supervision of the Board of Governors. Federal Reserve banks are bankers' banks; they provide banking services for commercial banks. Private citizens and corporations do not bank with the Fed.

The district banks are primarily responsible for the monitoring of the commercial banks in their region. They audit the books of depository institutions regularly

EXHIBIT 13–5

THE TWELVE FEDERAL RESERVE DISTRICTS

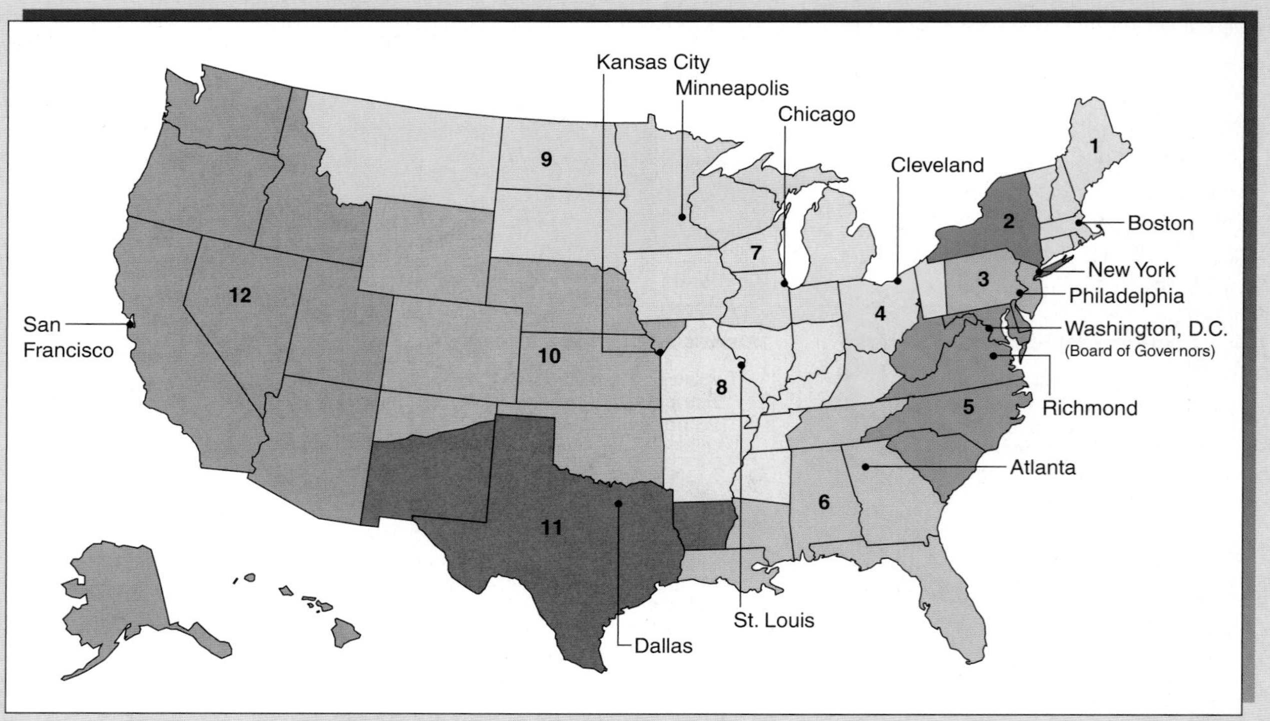

The map indicates the 12 Federal Reserve districts and the city in which the district bank is located. These district banks monitor the commercial banks in their region and assist them with the clearing of checks. If you look at any dollar bill, it will identify the Federal Reserve district bank that initially issued the currency. The Board of Governors of the Fed is located in Washington, D.C.

OUTSTANDING ECONOMIST

Alan Greenspan

A highly successful Wall Street economist and financial analyst, Greenspan served as chair of the Council of Economic Advisers (1974–1977) during the Ford administration. In 1987, President Reagan appointed him to a four-year term as chairman of the Fed's Board of Governors. Later, he was reappointed to that position by both Presidents Bush and Clinton. The Fed chairman directs the staff, presides over Board meetings, and testifies frequently before Congress. Because of the importance of monetary policy and the power of the position, the Fed chairman is often said to be the second most influential person—next to the president—in the United States. As the result of the low rate of inflation and the lengthy economic expansion (except for the brief 1990 recession), Greenspan is given high marks for his tenure as chairman.

in order to assure their compliance with reserve requirements and other regulations of the Fed. The district banks also play an important role in the clearing of checks through the banking system. Most depository institutions, regardless of their Fed membership status, maintain deposits with Federal Banks. As a result, the clearing of checks through the Federal Reserve System becomes merely an accounting transaction. The district and regional banks handle approximately 85 percent of all check-clearing services of the banking system.

Federal Open Market Committee (FOMC). The **Federal Open Market Committee** is a powerful committee that determines the Fed's policy with respect to the purchase and sale of government bonds. As we shall soon see, this is the Fed's most frequently used method of controlling the money supply in the United States. This important policy-making arm of the Fed is made up of (1) the seven members of the Board of Governors, (2) the president of the New York District Bank, and (3) four (of the remaining eleven) additional presidents of the Fed's District Banks, who rotate on the committee. Although they do not always have a vote, all 12 Federal Reserve district bank presidents participate in the FOMC meetings, held every five to eight weeks.

Federal Open Market Committee (FOMC)
A 12-member board that establishes Fed policy with regard to the buying and selling of government securities, the primary mechanism used to control the money supply in the United States.

The Independence of the Fed

Like the Supreme Court, the Federal Reserve operates with considerable independence from both Congress and the executive branch of government. Several factors contribute to this independence. The lengthy terms—14 years—protect the seven members of the Fed's Board of Governors from political pressures. Because their terms are staggered—a new governor is appointed only every two years—even two-term presidents are well into their second term before they are able to appoint a majority of the Fed's governing board. The Fed's earnings on its financial assets, mostly government bonds, provide it with substantially more funding than is needed to cover its operating costs. Thus, it is not dependent on Congress for funding allocations. The Fed does not even have to undergo audits from the General Accounting Office, a government agency that audits the books of most government operations. This independence of the Fed is designed to reduce the likelihood that political pressures will adversely affect its ability to follow a stable, noninflationary monetary policy.

Does the independence of a central bank affect policy? There is considerable variation in the independence of central banks. Like the Fed, the German Bundesbank was largely insulated from the political authorities. (Note: With the development of a

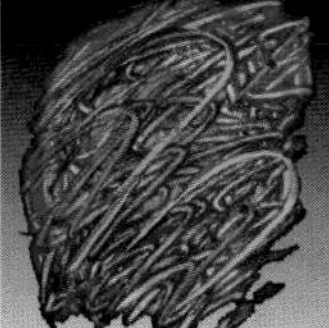

APPLICATIONS IN ECONOMICS

The Introduction of a New Currency—The Euro

If you have ever traveled in Europe, you know that as you go from country to country, you have to exchange currencies in order to do business. This will soon be changing. Eleven European nations (Austria, Belgium, Finland, France, Germany, Ireland, Italy, Luxembourg, Netherlands, Portugal, and Spain) are in the process of moving toward a single European currency, the euro. This new currency will be managed by a new central bank, the European Central Bank (ECB).

As of January 1, 1999, the exchange rate between the euro and the currencies of these 11 countries was fixed. The actual euro currency will not be introduced until 2002. Prior to that time, individuals and businesses are permitted, but not required, to make payment in euros. Banks now offer both checking and savings accounts in euros. During this transition period, prices will be quoted in both euros and domestic currency. The euro will trade in foreign exchange markets; many employees, particularly those working for large corporations, will receive their paychecks in euros; debit and credit cards can be used to make payment in euros. Thus, for three years (1999–2001) the euro will exist as a sort of "virtual money" operating alongside existing national currencies.

The relationship between the ECB and the former central banks of the 11 countries is much like that between the Board of Governors of the Fed and the District Federal Reserve banks. The ECB sets policy; the national central banks are expected to carry it out. The ECB, located in the Eurotower in Frankfurt, is directed by a 6-member executive committee and a 17-member council comprised of the six executive committee members plus the central bank governor from each of the 11 euro countries. On paper, the ECB is largely independent of political forces—some have called it the world's most independent central bank. Its prime objective laid out in the Maastricht Treaty is price stability. The current target rate of inflation is 2 percent or less. The euro is expected not only to reduce transactions costs within the monetary union, but also to challenge the dollar and the yen for use in international markets. It will be interesting to follow the development of this new currency. One thing is certain—credibility is an important element influencing the choice of currency. Thus, it will be vitally important for the euro to get off to a good start—to begin establishing a record of price stability along with sound economic growth.

European currency, the Bundesbank will soon be replaced with a European central bank.) In other instances, central banks are directly beholden to political officials. The central banks of many Latin American countries fit into this category. Studies of this topic indicate that when a country's central bank is strongly influenced by political considerations, the bank is more likely to follow inflationary policies.

How the Fed Controls the Money Supply

The Fed has three major means of controlling the money stock: (1) establishing reserve requirements for depository institutions, (2) buying and selling U.S. government securities in the open market, and (3) setting the interest rate at which it will loan funds to commercial banks and other depository institutions. We will analyze in detail how each of these tools can be used to regulate the amount of money in circulation.

Reserve Requirements The Federal Reserve System requires banking institutions (including credit unions and savings and loan associations) to maintain reserves against the demand deposits of their customers. The reserves of banking institutions are composed of (1) currency held by the bank (vault cash) and (2) deposits of the bank with the Federal Reserve System. A bank can always obtain additional currency by drawing on its deposits with the Federal Reserve. So both cash-on-hand and the bank's deposits with the Fed can be used to meet the demands of depositors. Both therefore count as reserves.

Exhibit 13–6 indicates the required reserve ratio—the percentage of each deposit category that banks are required to keep in reserve (that is, in the form of either vault cash or deposits with the Fed). As of December 1998, the reserve requirement for transaction accounts was set at 3 percent for amounts up to $46.5 million and 10 percent for amounts in excess of $46.5 million. Currently, banks are not required to keep reserves against their savings and time deposits.

Why are commercial banks required to maintain assets in the form of reserves? One reason is to prevent imprudent bankers from overextending loans and thereby placing themselves in a poor position to deal with any sudden increase in withdrawals by depositors. The quantity of reserves needed to meet such emergencies is not left totally to the judgment of individual bankers. The Fed sets the rules.

The Fed's control over reserve requirements, however, is important for another reason. By altering reserve requirements, the Fed can alter the money supply. The law does not prevent commercial banks from holding reserves over and above those required by the Fed, but, as we previously noted, banking institutions will want to hold interest-earning assets (like loans to customers and bonds) rather than excess reserves. Because reserves draw no interest, profit-seeking banks will shave their excess reserves to a low level. As a result, an increase in reserve requirements will typically force banks to reduce their outstanding loans and investments. As the volume of loans (and other forms of credit) extended by banks declines, so, too, will the money supply. ***Thus, an increase in the reserve requirements will reduce the supply of money.***

A reduction in reserve requirements will have the opposite impact. When the Fed reduces the reserve requirements, it creates additional excess reserves for banks. Predictably, profit-seeking banks will use a large portion of these newly created excess reserves to extend additional loans and undertake other investments. As they do so, their actions will expand the supply of money. ***Thus, lower reserve requirements increase the capacity of banks to lend and, as they extend additional loans, the money supply increases.***

In recent years, the Fed has seldom used its regulatory power over reserve requirements to alter the supply of money. Why? For one thing, changes in reserve requirements can be disruptive of banking operations. A change in the required reserve ratio may force many banks to sell securities quickly or call in loans even if there has been no change in the level of their deposits. Furthermore, reserve requirement changes are a blunt instrument—small changes in reserve requirements can sometimes lead to large changes in the money supply. The magnitude and timing of a

EXHIBIT 13-6

REQUIRED RESERVE RATIO OF BANKING INSTITUTIONS

	Transaction Accounts	
	$0–$46.5[a] million	Over $46.5[a] million
Required reserves as a percent of deposits	3%	10%

Banking institutions are required to maintain 3 percent reserves against transaction-account deposits of up to $46.5 million and 10 percent reserves for transaction deposits over $46.5 million (in effect December 1998).

[a]*The $46.5 million dividing point is adjusted each year by 80 percent of the change in total transaction-account deposits in all banking institutions.*

SOURCE: Federal Reserve Bulletin, *March 1999.*

change in the money stock resulting from a change in reserve requirements are difficult to predict with precision. For these reasons, the Fed has usually preferred to use other monetary tools.

Open market operations
The buying and selling of U.S. government securities (national debt) by the Federal Reserve.

Open Market Operations The most common tool used by the Fed to alter the money supply is **open market operations**—the buying and selling of U.S. securities on the open market. As we indicated earlier, Fed policy in this area is conducted by the Federal Open Market Committee (FOMC). This committee meets every five or six weeks to map out the Fed's policy. Open market operations can be undertaken easily and quietly. Because they influence the money supply either directly or through their impact on bank deposits, open market operations are less disruptive than changes in reserve requirements.

Unlike individuals, businesses, and even other government agencies, the Fed can write a check without funds in its account. When the Fed buys things, it creates money. The primary thing that the Fed buys is the national debt—bonds that were originally issued by the U.S. Treasury and sold to private parties in order to finance budget deficits.

If the Fed wanted to expand the money supply, it would merely instruct its bond traders at the New York Federal Reserve Bank to buy bonds. (Note: Because of its location near major financial markets, the New York bank handles the Fed's bond trading.) ***When the Fed purchases U.S. securities, it injects "new money" into the economy in the form of additional currency in circulation and deposits with commercial banks.***

Let us consider a hypothetical case. Suppose the Fed purchases $10,000 of U.S. securities from Maria Valdez. The Fed receives the securities and Valdez receives a check for $10,000. If she merely cashes the check drawn on the Federal Reserve, the amount of currency in circulation would expand by $10,000, increasing the money supply by that amount. If, as is more likely to be the case, she deposits the funds in her checking account at City Bank, the supply of checking-account money will increase by $10,000 and new bank reserves are created. City Bank is required to maintain additional reserves of only a fraction of Valdez's $10,000 deposit. Assuming a 10 percent required reserve ratio, City Bank can now extend new loans of up to $9,000 while maintaining its initial reserve position. As the new loans are extended, they too will contribute to a further expansion in the money supply. Part of the new loans will eventually be deposited in other banks, and they also will be able to extend additional loans. As the process continues, the money supply expands by a multiple of the securities purchased by the Fed.

Open market operations can also be used to reduce the money stock. ***If the Fed wants to reduce the money stock, it sells some of its current holdings of government securities.*** When the Fed sells securities, the buyer pays for them with a check drawn on a commercial bank. As the check clears, both the buyer's checking deposits and the reserves of the bank on which the check was written will decline. Thus, the action will reduce the money supply both directly (by reducing checking deposits) and indirectly (by reducing the quantity of reserves available to the banking system).

Monetary base
The sum of currency in circulation plus bank reserves (vault cash and reserves with the Fed). It reflects the stock of U.S. securities held by the Fed.

The Fed's purchase and sale of U.S. securities influence the size of the **monetary base.** The monetary base is equal to the reserves of commercial banks (vault cash and reserve deposits with the Fed) plus the currency in circulation. As **Exhibit 13–7** illustrates, the monetary base provides the foundation for the money supply of the United States. Of course, the currency in circulation ($468 billion in December 1998) contributes directly to the money supply. In turn, the bank reserves ($45 billion in December 1998) underpin the checking deposits ($624 billion). Fed purchases of U.S. securities increase the monetary base. Some of the proceeds (received by those selling bonds to the Fed) will circulate as currency. Each new dollar of currency in circulation

EXHIBIT 13–7

MONETARY BASE AND MONEY SUPPLY

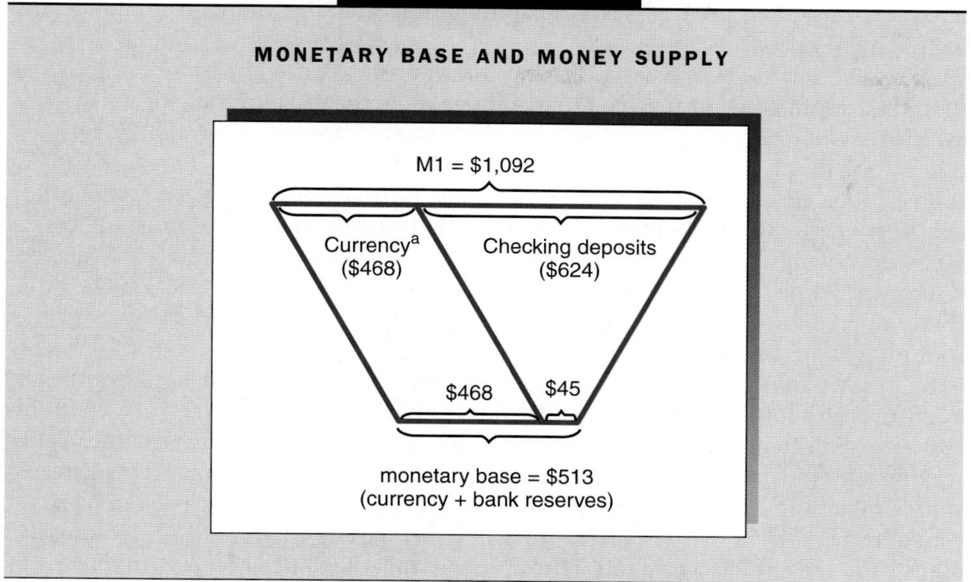

The monetary base (currency plus bank reserves) provides the foundation for the money supply. The currency in circulation contributes directly to the money supply, while the bank reserves provide the underpinnings for checking deposits. Fed actions that alter the monetary base will affect the money supply.

[a]*Traveler's checks are included in this category.*

will increase the money supply by exactly $1. In addition, many of those receiving proceeds from bond sales to the Fed will deposit the funds in a bank. When this happens, bank reserves increase and most of the additional reserves will be used to extend loans, causing additional expansion in the money supply.

By how much will the money supply change as the Fed injects and withdraws reserves through open market operations? Given the reserve requirements present in the late 1990s (see Exhibit 13–6), an increase in the monetary base could potentially expand the money supply (M1) by a multiple of 10 or more. However, leakages in the form of additional currency in circulation and increases in excess bank reserves will result in an actual deposit expansion multiplier that is substantially less than the potential. Exhibit 13–7 shows that the M1 money supply was approximately twice the size of the monetary base in 1998. This suggests that changes in the monetary base as the result of the Fed's open market operations will change the M1 money supply by about $2 for every $1 change in the monetary base.

Discount Rate—The Cost of Borrowing from the Fed When banking institutions borrow from the Federal Reserve, they must pay interest on the loan. The interest rate that banks pay on loans from the Federal Reserve is called the **discount rate.** Borrowing from the Fed is a privilege, not a right. The Fed does not have to loan funds to banking institutions. Banks borrow from the Fed primarily to meet temporary shortages of reserves. They are most likely to borrow from the Fed for a brief period of time while they are making other adjustments in their loan and investment portfolios that will permit them to meet their reserve requirement.

Discount rate
The interest rate the Federal Reserve charges banking institutions for borrowing funds.

An increase in the discount rate makes it more expensive for banking institutions to borrow from the Fed. Borrowing is discouraged, and banks are more likely to build up their reserves to ensure that they will not have to borrow from the Fed. ***An increase in the discount rate is thus restrictive. It tends to discourage banks from shaving their excess reserves to a low level.***

In contrast, a reduction in the discount rate is expansionary. At the lower interest rate, it costs banks less if they have to turn to the Fed to meet a temporary emergency. Therefore, as the cost of borrowing from the Fed declines, banks are more likely to reduce their excess reserves to a minimum, extending more loans and increasing the money supply.

The general public has a tendency to overestimate the importance of a change in the discount rate. Many people think an increase in the discount rate means their local banker will (or must) charge them a higher interest rate for a loan.[2] This is not necessarily so. Reserves acquired through transaction and time deposits are the major source of loanable funds for commercial banks. Borrowing from the Fed amounts to less than one-tenth of 1 percent of the available loanable funds of commercial banks. Since borrowing from the Fed is such a negligible source of funds, a 0.5 percent change in the discount rate has something less than a profound impact on the availability of credit and the supply of money. Certainly, it does not necessarily mean that your local bank will alter the rate at which it will lend to you.

Federal funds market
A loanable funds market in which banks seeking additional reserves borrow short-term (generally for seven days or less) funds from banks with excess reserves. The interest rate in this market is called the federal funds rate.

If a bank has to borrow to meet its reserve requirements, it need not turn to the Fed. Instead, it can go to the **federal funds market.** In this market, banks with excess reserves extend short-term (sometimes for as little as a day) loans to other banks seeking additional reserves. If the interest rate in the federal funds market is lower or approximately the same as the discount rate, banks seeking additional reserves will generally borrow from the federal funds market rather than the Fed. The federal funds rate and the discount rate tend to move together. If the federal funds rate is significantly higher than the discount rate, banks will attempt to borrow heavily from the Fed. Typically, when this happens, the Fed will raise its discount rate, removing the incentive for banks to borrow from it rather than from the federal funds market.

Controlling the Money Supply—A Summary

Exhibit 13–8 summarizes the monetary tools of the Federal Reserve. ***If the Fed wants to follow an expansionary policy, it can decrease reserve requirements, purchase additional U.S. securities, and/or lower the discount rate. If it wants to reduce the money stock, it can increase the reserve requirements, sell U.S. securities, and/or raise the discount rate.*** Because the Fed typically seeks only small changes in the money stock (or its rate of increase), it typically uses only one or two of these tools at a time to accomplish a desired objective.

FRANK AND ERNEST® by Bob Thaves

SOURCE: Frank and Ernest reprinted by permission of Newspaper Enterprise Association, Inc.

[2]The discount rate is also sometimes confused with the prime interest rate, the rate at which banks loan money to low-risk customers. The two rates are different. A change in the discount rate will not necessarily affect the prime interest rate.

EXHIBIT 13-8

SUMMARY OF MONETARY TOOLS OF THE FEDERAL RESERVE

Federal Reserve Policy	Expansionary Monetary Policy	Restrictive Monetary Policy
1. Reserve requirements	*Reduce reserve requirements,* because this will create additional excess reserves and induce banks to extend additional loans, which will expand the money supply.	*Raise reserve requirements,* because this will reduce the excess reserves of banks, causing them to make fewer loans; as the outstanding loans of banks decline, the money stock will be reduced.
2. Open market operations	*Purchase additional U.S. securities,* which will expand the money stock directly, and increase the reserves of banks, inducing bankers in turn to extend more loans; this will expand the money stock indirectly.	*Sell previously purchased U.S. securities,* which will reduce both the money stock and excess reserves; the decline in excess reserves will indirectly lead to an additional reduction in the money supply.
3. Discount rate	*Lower the discount rate,* which will encourage more borrowing from the Fed; banks will tend to reduce their reserves and extend more loans because of the lower cost of borrowing from the Fed if they temporarily run short on reserves.	*Raise the discount rate,* thereby discouraging borrowing from the Fed; banks will tend to extend fewer loans and build up their reserves so they will not have to borrow from the Fed.

The Fed and the Treasury

Many students have a tendency to confuse the Federal Reserve with the U.S. Treasury, probably because both sound like monetary agencies. The Treasury is a budgetary agency. If there is a budgetary deficit, the Treasury will issue U.S. securities as a method of financing the deficit. Newly issued U.S. securities are almost always sold to private investors (or government trust funds). Bonds issued by the Treasury to finance a budget deficit are seldom purchased directly by the Fed. In any case, the Treasury is primarily interested in obtaining funds so it can pay Uncle Sam's bills. Except for nominal amounts, mostly coins, the Treasury does not issue money. Borrowing—the public sale of new U.S. securities—is the primary method used by the Treasury to cover any excess of expenditures in relation to revenues from taxes and other sources.

Whereas the Treasury is concerned with the revenues and expenditures of the government, the Fed is concerned primarily with the availability of money and credit for the entire economy. The Fed does not issue U.S. securities. It merely purchases and sells government securities issued by the Treasury as a means of controlling the economy's money supply. Unlike the Treasury, the Fed can purchase government bonds by writing a check on itself without having deposits, gold, or anything else to back it up. In doing so, the Fed creates money out of thin air. The Treasury does not have this power. The Fed does not have an obligation to meet the financial responsibilities of the U.S. government. That is the domain of the Treasury. Although the two agencies cooperate with each other, they are distinctly different institutions established for different purposes (see accompanying Thumbnail Sketch).

THUMBNAIL SKETCH

What are the Differences between the U.S. Treasury and the Federal Reserve Banking System?

U.S. Treasury

1. Concerned with the finances of the federal government
2. Issues bonds to the general public to finance the budget deficits of the federal government
3. Does not determine the money supply

Federal Reserve

1. Concerned with the monetary climate for the economy
2. Does not issue bonds
3. Determines the money supply—primarily through its buying and selling of bonds issued by the U.S. Treasury

It is important to recognize that the buying and selling of bonds by the Treasury and by the Fed have different effects on the supply of money. The key point here is that the Treasury and the Fed handle revenues collected from the selling of bonds in a different manner. When the Treasury issues and sells bonds, it does so to pay for federal government expenditures. After all, the Treasury issues the bonds in order to generate the required revenue for its spending. The people who buy the bonds from the Treasury have less money, but when the Treasury spends, the recipients of its spending will have more money. Thus, Treasury borrowing and spending does not change the supply of money.

In contrast, when the Fed sells bonds, it, in effect, takes the revenues and holds them, keeping them out of circulation. Because this money is out of circulation and can no longer be used for the purchase of goods and services, the money supply shrinks. On the other hand, if the Fed later wishes to increase the money supply, it can buy bonds, which will increase the availability of bank reserves and the money supply.

AMBIGUITIES IN THE MEANING AND MEASUREMENT OF THE MONEY SUPPLY

In the past, economists have generally used the *growth rate* of the money supply (either M1 or M2) to gauge the direction of monetary policy. A rapid growth rate of the money supply was indicative of expansionary monetary policy—a policy that was adding stimulus to the economy. Conversely, slow growth, or a decline, in the money stock implied a more restrictive monetary policy.

Both the history of money and recent developments in financial markets are causing many economists to reconsider the significance of growth rate figures. Historically, major shifts in the nature of money (for example, the shift from precious metals to a fiat currency) have substantially influenced the lives of people. Financial innovations continue to affect our methods of payment and the meaning of the various money supply measures.

Throughout most of the 1970s, M1 was comprised almost entirely of currency and demand deposits. At the time, regulations virtually prohibited banks from offering their customers interest-earning checking accounts. Increased competition from mutual funds led to the repeal of the regulatory restraints in 1980, and, as **Exhibit 13–9** illustrates, this repeal was followed by rapid growth of interest-earning checking deposits. In turn, growth of these deposits pushed up the growth rate of the M1 money supply. The growth of M1 during the 1980s, however, was deceptive. To a degree, it reflected a change in the nature of the M1 money supply. Interest-earning checking accounts are less costly to hold than currency and demand deposits. In essence, interest-earning checking accounts are partly medium-of-exchange money and partly savings. As a result, the M1 money supply of the 1980s is not precisely comparable with the figures for earlier years.

Another innovation has influenced the M1 money supply in the 1990s. Beginning in 1994, a number of banks began to encourage customers to move deposits from interest-earning checking accounts into money market deposit accounts. Each of these accounts provides customers with similar services. However, because interest-earning checking deposits are included in M1 but money market deposits are not, this shift reduced the size of the M1 money supply figures. It was largely responsible for the decline in the M1 money supply during the period 1995–1997 (see Exhibit 13–9). As with the introduction of interest-earning checking during the 1980s, these shifts distorted the M1 money supply statistics and reduced their comparability across time periods.

Other structural changes and financial innovations—some of which are already present and others of which are likely to develop in the near future—are altering the nature of money, and therefore the usefulness of money growth figures (both M1 and M2), as an indicator of monetary policy. Let's consider three of these factors.

1. ***Widespread use of the U.S. dollar outside of the United States.*** The U.S. dollar is widely used in other countries (see Applications in Economics box, "The Foreign Holdings of U.S. Dollars"). To a degree, this has been true for a long time. However, a number of countries have recently relaxed legal restraints limiting the domestic use of foreign currencies (and the maintenance of foreign currency bank accounts).[3] As noted earlier, the currency component of the M1 money supply was

[3]The number of countries where it is legal for citizens to maintain a foreign currency bank account rose from 38 in 1985 to 62 in 1995. See James Gwartney, Robert Lawson, and Walter Block, *Economic Freedom of the World: 1975–1995* (Washington, D.C.: Cato Institute, 1996), p. 81.

EXHIBIT 13-9

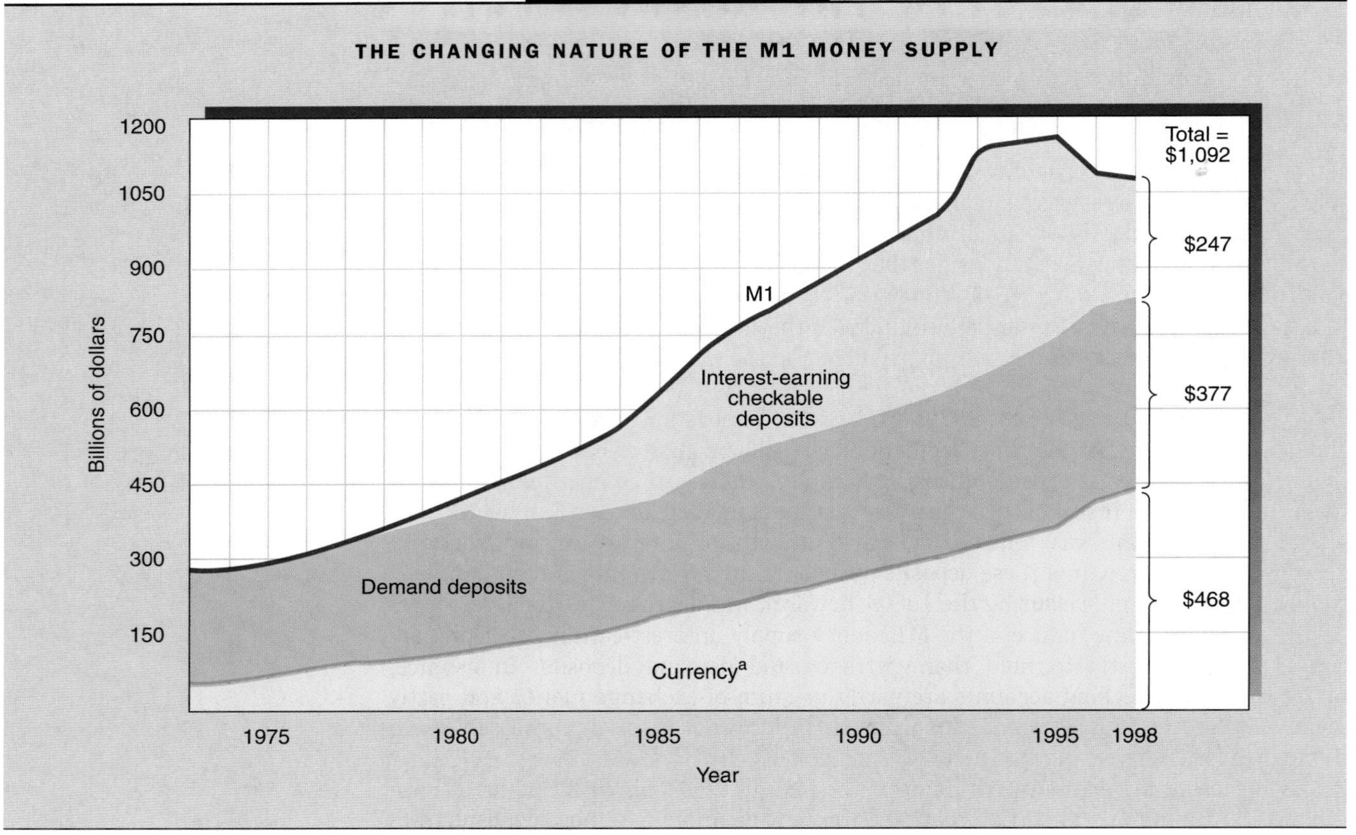

As the result of deregulation during the 1980s, interest-earning checkable deposits grew rapidly and they now account for approximately one quarter of the M1 money supply. Since the opportunity cost of holding these other checkable deposits is less than for other forms of money, strictly speaking, the money supply today is not exactly comparable to the money supply prior to 1980.

[a] *Traveler's checks are included in this category.*

SOURCE: Federal Reserve Bulletin, *March 1999.*

approximately $460 billion at year-end 1998. According to a recent study by the Federal Reserve, more than one-half and perhaps as much as two-thirds of this currency is held overseas. The movement of these funds abroad (and our inability to measure it with any degree of precision) substantially reduces the reliability of the M1 money supply figures. (Note: There is also some impact on M2. However, since the currency component is a much smaller proportion of M2 than M1, the distortion of M2 is less severe.)

2. ***The increasing availability of low-fee stock and bond mutual funds.*** Until recently, financial investors were generally required to pay a substantial start-up, or load, fee when purchasing stock and bond mutual funds. This reduced their attractiveness relative to the various savings instruments included in the M2 money supply. No-load stock and bond mutual funds—that is, funds without an initial fee—are now increasingly available. Because stock and bond mutual fund investments are not counted in any of the monetary aggregates, movement of funds from various

APPLICATIONS IN ECONOMICS

The Foreign Holdings of U.S. Dollars

If you have traveled to Mexico, Eastern Europe, or South America lately, you probably noticed that many merchants were willing to accept U.S. dollars as a means of payment. Recent studies indicate that between \$200 billion and \$250 billion—more than half of the U.S. currency supply—is held abroad.

Why do foreigners want to hold dollars? People in many countries, particularly those with a history of hyperinflation or political instability or both, do not have much faith in their domestic currency. They believe that the U.S. dollar and several other currencies (particularly the German mark and Japanese yen) with a history of relatively stable value are safer ways to store value for the future. Currently, dollars are widely held and, in some cases, used as a means of exchange in Russia (and several other countries of the former Soviet Union), Argentina, Bolivia, Mexico, and other Latin American countries.

How do these holdings of dollars by foreigners affect the U.S. economy? Foreigners acquired the dollars by providing goods and services to Americans. In effect, Americans got valuable goods and services by simply issuing pieces of paper—dollar bills. The dollars held abroad are very much like an interest-free loan to the U.S. government and, indirectly, the taxpayers of the United States. If foreigners were not willing to hold these dollars at a zero interest rate, the U.S. Treasury would have to issue more bonds (perhaps as much as \$250 billion more) and pay interest to the bondholders. As a result, the annual interest costs of the federal government would be between \$15 billion and \$20 billion higher.

M2 components (money market mutual funds, for example) will distort the M2 money supply figures.[4]

3. ***Debit cards and electronic money.*** Financial innovators are currently developing a more convenient and versatile debit card. A card of this type would transfer funds from the cardholder's bank account to that of the seller. If more and more businesses accept payment via debit cards in the future, Americans will have less reason to hold currency. As less money is held in the form of currency (and more as bank deposits), the money supply will grow rapidly unless the Fed takes offsetting actions. Like other changes in the nature of money, innovations in this area will reduce the future reliability of the money supply data, particularly the M1 figures, as indicators of monetary policy.

   Finally, there is the expected development of electronic money (see Applications in Economics box, "Will Electronic Money Alter Your Future?"). It is difficult to forecast the nature of changes in this area. However, if individuals and businesses can economically and safely use electronic cash, instead of checking deposits and currency, it will clearly change the nature of money and the meaning of the monetary aggregates. If, as is anticipated, these electronic deposits can safely be maintained outside of the banking system, they may also change the major functions of the banking system.

Exhibit 13–10 presents data on the annual growth rates of both M1 and M2. Reflecting the factors we have just discussed, the M1 money supply has recently shown more variability than the M2 figures. When using money supply growth rates as an indicator of monetary policy, most analysts now rely on M2 (rather than M1). We will follow this convention. However, we should keep in mind that future innovative changes

[4]For additional information on this topic, see Sean Collins and Cheryl L. Edwards, "Redefining M2 to Include Bond and Equity Mutual Funds," Federal Reserve Bank of St. Louis *Review*, November/December 1994, pp. 7–30; Kenneth N. Daniels and Neil B. Murphy, "The Impact of Technological Change on the Currency Behavior of Households: An Empirical Cross-Section Study," *Journal of Money, Credit, and Banking* 26 (November 1994): 867–874; and John V. Duca, "Should Bond Funds Be Included in M2?" *Journal of Banking and Finance* 19 (April 1995): 131–152.

APPLICATIONS IN ECONOMICS

Will Electronic Money Alter Your Future?

Consider a world where your "paycheck" is deposited in an electronic cash account accessible through your personal computer, but protected with a personal code. With the touch of a few computer keys, you can transfer funds to pay your monthly utility bill, mortgage and auto loan payments, and other regular expenditures. You can also shop on the Internet and use your deposits to pay for magazines, financial advice, and numerous consumer goods. Your funds can also be used to purchase stocks, bonds, mutual funds, and other financial investments. Like your paycheck, earnings from (or future sales of) these investments can be automatically deposited into your electronic cash account. If you want to withdraw some electronic cash, you merely insert a card and load it with transferable purchasing power, which is widely accepted by restaurants, recreation facilities, retail stores, and other business establishments. If you want to give or receive funds from family or friends, you simply merge their "cash cards" with yours and the funds will be added to one card and subtracted from the other. In effect, your electronic money allows you to do anything you can currently do with currency or checking deposits—and you can do it faster, safer, and more conveniently.

Many think that this world, or something very much like it, is only a few years away. If true, it will certainly change the nature of money and reduce the importance of the banking system. It may even limit the ability of central banks to conduct monetary policy.

EXHIBIT 13-10

THE GROWTH RATE OF THE M1 AND M2 MONEY SUPPLY: 1970–1998

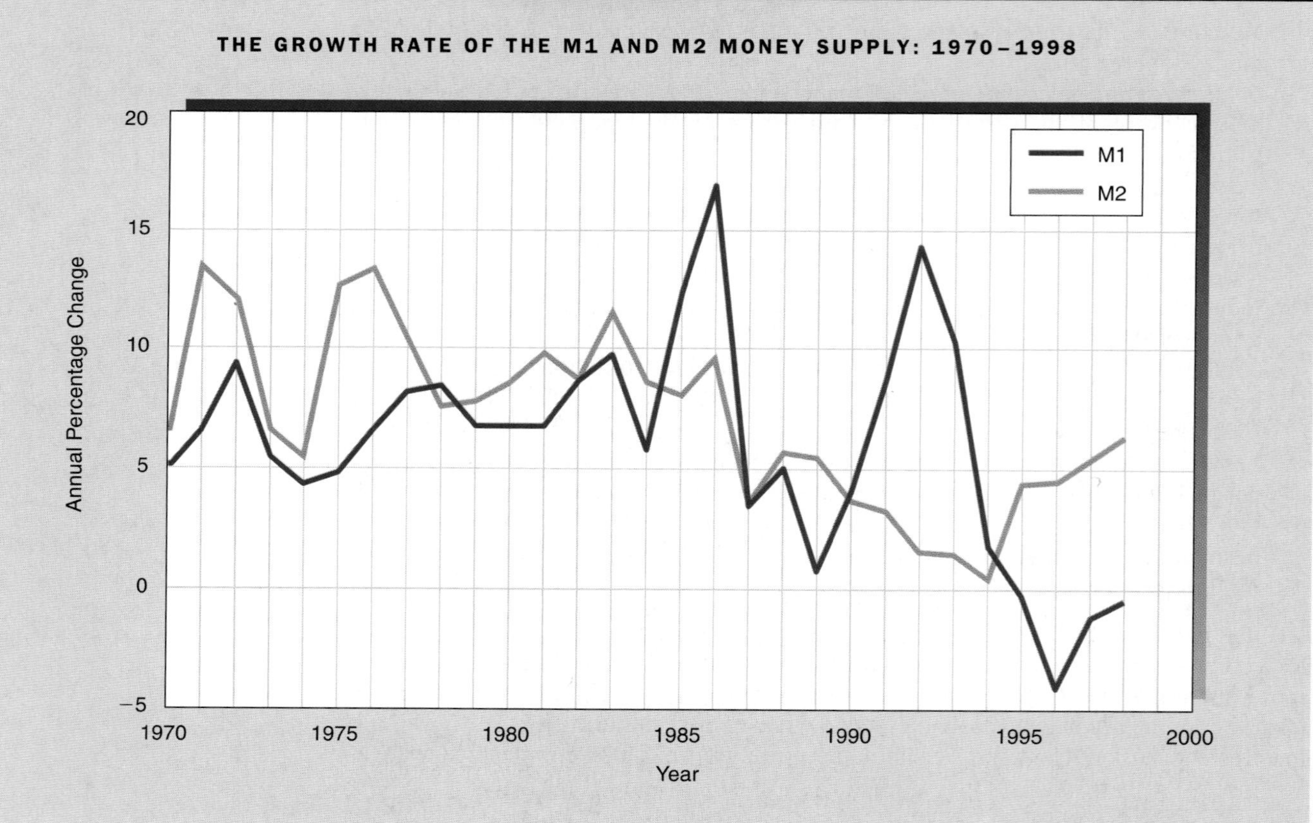

Here we present the annual growth rates for both the M1 and M2 money supply figures. Since the mid-1980s, the variability of the M1 supply has been much greater than that for M2. To a large degree, the greater variability of M1 reflects regulatory changes and innovations in financial markets that have changed the nature of M1.

SOURCE: Economic Report of the President, *1998, Table B-69.*

are likely to alter the nature of money and therefore the reliability of the money supply figures (including those for M2) as an indicator of monetary policy.

BANK RUNS, BANK FAILURES, AND DEPOSIT INSURANCE

In recent years, banking systems in several countries have experienced difficulties. The source of the problems has varied. Sometimes, it has involved the extension of foreign currency loans to businesses that derived most of their revenues in the domestic currency. A substantial unfavorable change in the exchange rate can make loans of this type virtually impossible to repay. In other cases, loans were extended on the basis of political rather than economic considerations. This was particularly true in countries like Indonesia, where there are many government-owned banks and even the private banks are subject to political pressure.

Compared to other businesses, banks are more vulnerable to failure (and abuse) and the consequences of failure exert a larger impact on the economy. The vulnerability of banks reflects the fact that their liabilities to depositors are current, while many of the assets are illiquid. This means that if a significant share of depositors lose confidence and withdraw their funds, it will quickly lead to problems. In turn, when a bank fails, it affects not only the owners and employees, but the depositors as well. These secondary effects can undermine the operation of an economy.

The U.S. economy has had its share of banking problems. Between 1922 and 1933, more than 10,000 banks (one-third of the total) failed. Most of these failures were the result of "bank runs," panic withdrawals as people lost confidence in the banking system. Remember, under a fractional reserve system, banks do not have a sufficient amount of reserves to redeem the funds of all (or even most) depositors seeking to withdraw their funds at the same time.

If loss of confidence leads to a bank run, even technically solvent banks will often be unable to satisfy all depositors seeking to make withdrawals under a fractional reserve banking system.

Federal Deposit Insurance Corporation (FDIC)
A federally chartered corporation that insures the deposits held by commercial banks and thrift institutions.

The bank failures of the 1920s and 1930s led to the establishment of the **Federal Deposit Insurance Corporation (FDIC)** in 1934. The FDIC guarantees the deposits of banking customers up to some limit—currently $100,000 per account. Even if the bank should fail, the depositors will be able to get their money (up to the $100,000 limit). Member banks pay an insurance premium to the FDIC for each dollar on deposit, and the FDIC uses these premiums to reimburse depositors with funds in a bank that fails. The FDIC restored confidence in the banking system and brought bank runs to a halt. As a result, bank failures were extremely rare during the 1940–1980 period.

After declining to only a trickle—less than 15 per year during the 1940–1980 period, the number of bank failures increased sharply during the 1980s, soaring to more than 200 per year between 1986 and 1988. In contrast with the earlier wave of bank failures, the bank failures of the 1980s were generally the result of loan defaults (rather than bank runs). When banks finance investments that turn sour, borrowers are often unable to repay their loans. The bank loses funds when borrowers default. Banks that extend a high percentage of such bad loans will eventually fail.

Why were there so many commercial bank failures and loan defaults during the 1980s? There were several contributing factors. The inflation of the 1970s pushed up both nominal interest rates and the cost of funds. This increase in the cost of funds really put the squeeze on depository institutions that used short-term deposits to finance long-term loans *previously issued at lower interest rates.* This factor was particularly important in the savings and loan industry.[5] Economic instability in oil markets was also a contributing factor. Bad loans extended to oil interests as the price of oil soared during the 1970s turned sour when oil prices collapsed during the 1980s.

Paradoxically, many economists believe that the structure of the FDIC's premium system also contributed to the bank failures of the 1980s. Unlike the premiums charged by private insurers, the FDIC charges banks a single premium on deposits, regardless of the riskiness of the bank's loan portfolio. This premium structure encourages banks to undertake riskier investments (for example, junk bonds and loans to businesses with low credit ratings) that yield a higher interest return. Moreover, because their accounts are fully insured (up to $100,000), depositors have little incentive to investigate the riskiness of outstanding loans and the financial security of depository institutions. Thus, banks willing to pay slightly higher interest rates are able to attract substantial deposits from healthier financial institutions. Essentially, the deposit insurance system creates what economists refer to as a **moral hazard problem,** the tendency of an insured party to undertake more risk as the result of the protection provided by the insurance. In the 1980s, the moral hazard problem encouraged a type of "reverse bank run"—the movement of funds from low-risk to high-risk depository institutions. With time, these actions increased both the number of bank failures and the liability of the FDIC.

Moral hazard problem
The tendency of a party with insurance protection against an unfavorable event to engage in behavior that makes it more likely that the event will occur.

Economists have been in the forefront of those urging reform in the deposit insurance system so that the premiums charged banking institutions for the insurance will reflect the riskiness of their asset portfolio. In essence, the single-rate system provides an implicit subsidy to banks that make risky (or imprudent) investments at the expense of healthy institutions. Removal of this implicit subsidy would encourage banks to evaluate loan applications more carefully, extend fewer risky loans, and follow sounder banking practices.

---

[5]In the 1970s, long-term, fixed-interest-rate mortgages provided the primary source of income for S&Ls. Unsurprisingly, income from these assets failed to keep up with rising interest costs of the period.

LOOKING *Ahead*

In this chapter, we focused on the banking industry and the mechanics of monetary policy. We are now ready to analyze the impact of monetary policy on output, growth, and prices. How do Fed policies influence the economy? Have they exerted a stabilizing influence? These topics and related issues will be considered in the next two chapters.

KEY POINTS

➤ Money is a financial asset that is widely accepted as a medium of exchange. It also provides a means of storing purchasing power into the future and is used as a unit of account. Without money, exchange would be both costly and tedious. Money derives its value from its scarcity (supply) relative to its usefulness (demand).

➤ Economists use alternative measures of the money supply to judge the conduct of monetary policy. The narrowest definition of the money supply (M1) includes only (a) currency in the hands of the public, (b) checkable deposits (both demand and interest-earning) held in depository institutions, and (c) traveler's checks.

➤ The broader M2 money supply includes M1 plus (a) savings deposits, (b) time deposits (of less than $100,000), and (c) money market mutual funds shares.

➤ Banking is a business. Banks provide their depositors with safekeeping of money, check-clearing services on demand deposits, and interest payments on time deposits. Banks derive most of their income from the extension of loans and investments in interest-earning securities.

➤ Under legislation adopted in 1980, savings and loan associations and credit unions are permitted to provide essentially the same services as commercial banks. The Federal Reserve System now imposes similar regulation on all these depository institutions. In essence, they are all part of an integrated banking system.

➤ Under a fractional reserve banking system, banks are required to maintain only a fraction of their deposits in the form of reserves (vault cash or deposits with the Fed). Excess reserves may be invested or loaned to customers. When banks extend additional loans, they create additional deposits and thereby expand the money supply.

➤ The Federal Reserve System is a central banking authority designed to provide a stable monetary framework for the entire economy. The Fed is a banker's bank. The structure of the Fed is designed to insulate it from political pressures so that it will have greater freedom to follow policies more consistent with economic stability.

➤ The Fed has three major tools with which to control the money supply.

a. ***Establishment of the required reserve ratio.*** When the Fed lowers the required reserve ratio, it creates excess reserves and allows banks to extend additional loans, expanding the money supply. Raising the reserve requirements has the opposite effect.

b. ***Open market operations.*** When the Fed buys U.S. securities, the money supply will expand because bond buyers will acquire money and bank reserves will increase, placing banks in a position to expand the money through the extension of additional loans. When the Fed sells securities, the money supply will contract because bond buyers are giving up money in exchange for securities and the reserves available to banks will decline (causing them to extend fewer loans).

c. ***The discount rate.*** An increase in the discount rate is restrictive because it discourages banks from borrowing from the Fed to extend new loans. A reduction in the discount rate is expansionary because it makes borrowing from the Fed less costly.

➤ The Federal Reserve and the U.S. Treasury are distinct agencies. The Fed is concerned primarily with the money supply and the establishment of a stable monetary climate, while the Treasury focuses on budgetary matters—tax revenues, government expenditures, and the financing of government debt.

➤ Historically, the rate of change of the money supply has been used to judge the direction and intensity of monetary policy. However, recent financial innovations and other structural changes (for example, the widespread use of U.S. currency in other countries) have blurred the meaning of money and reduced the reliability of the various money supply measures. In the computer age, continued change in this area is likely.

CRITICAL ANALYSIS QUESTIONS

*1. What is meant by the statement, "This asset is illiquid"? List some things that you own, ranking them from most liquid to most illiquid.

2. What determines whether or not a financial asset is included in the M1 money supply? Why are interest-earning checkable deposits included in M1, while interest-earning savings accounts and Treasury bills are not?

*3. What makes money valuable? Does money perform an economic service? Explain. Could money perform its function better if there were twice as much of it? Why or why not?

4. "People are poor because they don't have very much money. Yet, central bankers keep money scarce. If people had more money, poverty could be eliminated." Evaluate this view. Do you think it reflects sound economics?

5. Why can banks continue to hold reserves that are only a fraction of the demand deposits of their customers? Is your money safe in a bank? Why or why not?

*6. Suppose you withdraw $100 from your checking account. How does this transaction affect (a) the supply of money, (b) the reserves of your bank, and (c) the excess reserves of your bank?

7. Explain how the creation of new bank reserves would cause the money supply to increase by some multiple of the newly created reserves.

*8. How will the following actions affect the money supply?

a. A reduction in the discount rate
b. An increase in the reserve requirements
c. Purchase by the Fed of $100 million of U.S. securities from a commercial bank
d. Sale by the U.S. Treasury of $100 million of newly issued bonds to a commercial bank
e. An increase in the discount rate
f. Sale by the Fed of $200 million of U.S. securities to a private investor

9. What's wrong with this way of thinking? "When the government runs a budget deficit, it simply pays its bills by printing more money. As the newly printed money works its way through the economy, it waters down the value of paper money already in circulation. Thus, it takes more money to buy things. Budget deficits are the major cause of inflation."

*10. If the Federal Reserve does not take any offsetting action, what would happen to the supply of money if the general public decided to increase its holdings of currency and decrease its checking deposits by an equal amount?

11. If market interest rates on short-term loans (including the federal funds rate) are declining, does a reduction in the discount rate indicate that the Fed is trying to increase the money supply? What will happen to the amount of reserves borrowed from the Fed if it does not reduce its discount rate? Explain.

*12. If the Fed wants to expand the money supply, why is it more likely to do so by purchasing bonds rather than by lowering reserve requirements?

*13. Are the following statements true or false?

a. "You can never have too much money."
b. "When you deposit currency in a commercial bank, cash goes out of circulation and the money supply declines."
c. "If the Fed would create more money, Americans would achieve a higher standard of living."

14. "The bank failures of the 1980s are a replay of the 1920s and 1930s." Evaluate this statement.

15. How has the nature of the M1 money supply changed in recent years? How have these changes influenced the usefulness of M1 as an indicator of monetary policy? Why do many analysts prefer to use M2 rather than M1 when comparing the monetary policy of the 1990s with that of earlier periods?

16. Why do foreigners often hold U.S. dollars? How does the holding of dollars by foreigners affect the welfare of Americans?

*17. Suppose that the Federal Reserve purchases a bond for $100,000 from Donald Truck, who deposits the proceeds in the Manufacturer's National Bank.

a. What will be the impact of this transaction on the supply of money?

b. If the reserve requirement ratio is 20 percent, what is the maximum amount of additional loans that the Manufacturer's Bank will be able to extend as the result of Truck's deposit?
c. Given the 20 percent reserve requirement, what is the maximum increase in the quantity of checkable deposits that could result throughout the entire banking system as the result of the Fed's action?
d. Would you expect this to happen? Why or why not? Explain.

18. Suppose that the reserve requirement is 10 percent and the balance sheet of the People's National Bank looks like the accompanying example.

ASSETS		LIABILITIES	
Vault Cash	$ 20,000	Checking deposits	$200,000
Deposits at Fed	30,000	Net worth	15,000
Securities	45,000		
Loans	120,000		

a. What are the required reserves of People's National Bank? Does the bank have any excess reserves?
b. What is the maximum loan that the bank could extend?
c. Indicate how the bank's balance sheet would be altered if it extended this loan.
d. Suppose that the required reserves were 20 percent. If this were the case, would the bank be in a position to extend any additional loans? Explain.

*19. Suppose that the reserve requirements are 10 percent and that the Federal Reserve purchases $2 billion of additional securities on a given day.
a. How will this transaction affect the M1 money supply?
b. If the brokerage firm that sold the bonds to the Fed deposits the proceeds of the sale into its account with City Bank, what is the maximum amount of additional loans that City Bank will be able to extend as the result of this deposit?
c. If additional loans are extended throughout the banking system and the proceeds are always redeposited back into a checking account, by how much will the M1 money supply increase if banks use all their additional reserves to extend new loans?
d. Suppose that banks use all their additional reserves to extend new loans but that 10 percent of the loan proceeds (and the additional funds of the brokerage firm) are held as currency rather than being redeposited into a checking account. When this is the case, by how much will the Fed's action increase the money supply?
e. Suppose that banks use 5 percent of their additional reserves to build up their excess reserves and that 10 percent of the proceeds of new loans (and the initial bond sale) end up circulating as currency rather than being redeposited into a checking account. By how much will the Fed's action increase the money supply? Indicate the size of both the potential and actual money deposit multiplier in this case.
f. Why is the actual money deposit multiplier generally less than the potential multiplier?

20. How would the following influence the growth rates of the M1 and M2 money supply figures over time?
a. An increase in the quantity of U.S. currency held overseas
b. A shift of funds from interest-earning checking deposits to money market mutual funds
c. A reduction in the holdings of currency by the general public because debit cards have become more popular and widely accepted
d. The shift of funds from money market mutual funds into stock and bond mutual funds because the fees to invest in the latter have declined

*Asterisk denotes questions for which answers are given in Appendix B.

CHAPTER 14

The conventional wisdom once held that money doesn't matter. Now there is wide agreement that monetary policy can significantly affect real economic activity in the short run, though only price level in the long run.

Daniel L. Thornton and David C. Wheelock[1]

Modern Macroeconomics: Monetary Policy

CHAPTER FOCUS

- What are the determinants of the demand for money? How is the supply of money determined?
- How does monetary policy affect interest rates, output, and employment?
- Can monetary policy stimulate real GDP in the short run? Can it do so in the long run?
- Does it make any difference whether people quickly anticipate the effects of a change in monetary policy? Why?
- Does an increase in the stock of money cause inflation?

[1]Daniel L. Thornton and David C. Wheelock, "Editor's Introduction," *Federal Reserve Bank of St. Louis: Review* (May/June 1995): vii.

In the preceding chapter we noted that many consider the chairman of the Federal Reserve System to be the second most important person—next to the president—in the United States. Why is this so? Along with other members of the Fed's Board of Governors and Federal Open Market Committee, the Fed chairman is in charge of monetary policy. Monetary policy exerts a powerful impact on the economy. The central objective of monetary policy is the establishment of a stable environment so the economy can achieve high levels of both output and employment. Price stability—a persistently low rate of inflation—is crucial for the achievement of this objective. When conducted appropriately, monetary policy provides the foundation for economic prosperity. In contrast, the consequences of inappropriate monetary policy are often disastrous.

As we have used the aggregate demand/aggregate supply model up to this point, we have assumed that the supply of money was constant. We will now relax this assumption. The previous chapter outlined the tools the Fed has to alter the supply of money. This chapter will focus on how monetary policy works—how changes in the supply of money affect interest rates, output, and prices.

IMPACT OF MONETARY POLICY

Like the modern view of fiscal policy, the modern view of monetary policy is the product of an evolutionary process. In the aftermath of the Great Depression and Keynesian Revolution, there was a great debate concerning the importance of monetary policy. During the 1950s and 1960s, most Keynesians argued that monetary policy could be used to control inflation, but that it was often ineffective as a means of stimulating aggregate demand. It was popular to draw an analogy between monetary policy and the workings of a string. Like a string, monetary policy could be used to pull (hold back) price increases and thereby control inflation. However, just as one cannot push with a string, according to this popular view, monetary policy could not be used to push (stimulate) aggregate demand.

Monetarists
A group of economists who believe that (1) monetary instability is the major cause of fluctuations in real GDP and (2) rapid growth of the money supply is the major cause of inflation.

Beginning in the late 1950s, this position was hotly contested by Milton Friedman, later a Nobel laureate, and a group of economists, subsequently called **monetarists.** In contrast with the Keynesians of that era, the monetarists argued that changes in the stock of money exerted a powerful influence on output (in the short run), as well as prices (in the long run). Indeed, the monetarists charged that erratic monetary policy was the primary source of both business instability and inflation. Milton Friedman summarized the monetarist position in his 1967 presidential address to the American Economic Association when he stated,

> Every major contraction in this country has been either produced by monetary disorder or greatly exacerbated by monetary disorder. Every major inflation has been produced by monetary expansion.[2]

[2]Milton Friedman, "The Role of Monetary Policy," *American Economic Review* (March 1968): 12.

OUTSTANDING ECONOMIST

Milton Friedman (1912-)

The 1976 recipient of the Nobel Prize, Friedman is widely regarded as the most influential spokesman for a free market economy in the twentieth century. With the assistance of other monetarists, he eventually convinced even his critics that monetary policy exerts a strong impact on the economy. Friedman maintains that business fluctuations are the result of monetary instability. His popular books *Capitalism and Freedom* (1962) and *Free to Choose* (1980), coauthored with his wife, Rose, are classical treatises in support of economic freedom. After spending years at the University of Chicago, he is currently on the faculty at Stanford University. Now in his eighties, he continues to be an active scholar and writer.

A modern view of monetary policy emerged from this debate. While minor disagreements remain, both modern Keynesians and monetarists now agree that monetary policy produces an important impact on our economy.[3] The following sections present the modern consensus view with regard to how monetary policy affects the economy.

Demand and Supply of Money

Why do individuals and businesses want to hold cash and checking-account money rather than bonds, stocks, automobiles, buildings, and consumer durables? When considering this question, one must not confuse (1) the desire to hold money balances with (2) the desire for more wealth (or income). Of course, all of us would like to have more wealth, but we may be perfectly satisfied with our holdings of money in relation to our holdings of other goods, *given our current level of wealth.* When we say people want to hold more (or less) money, we mean that they want to restructure their wealth toward larger (smaller) money balances.

People hold money for a variety of reasons. As we discussed in the previous chapter, money provides us with instant purchasing power. At the most basic level, we hold money so we can conduct transactions. Households hold money balances so they can pay for the weekly groceries, the monthly house payment, gasoline for the car, lunch for the kids, and other items purchased regularly. Businesses demand money so they can meet the weekly payroll, pay the utility bills, purchase supplies, and conduct other transactions. Most individuals also hold money so they will be in a better position to deal with the uncertainties of the real world—an unexpected repair bill, an accident, or a medical emergency, for example. Economists refer to this as the *precautionary motive* for holding money. In addition, money is an asset—a means of storing value. Some may hold money as a method of storing purchasing power for future use.

Higher interest rates make it more costly to hold money. Consider the cost of holding $1,000 in the form of currency and demand deposits (which do not earn interest) rather than in interest-earning bonds, for example. If the interest rate is 10 percent, it will cost you $100 to hold an additional $1,000 of non-interest-earning money. In contrast, if the interest rate is 1 percent, the cost of holding the $1,000 money balance will be only $10. Even if you maintain money balances in an interest-earning

[3]The evolution of the views of Paul Samuelson, who might properly be regarded as the father of American Keynesian economics, best illustrates the change in the Keynesian view with regard to the relative importance of monetary and fiscal policy. Commenting on the 12th edition of his classic text in 1985, Samuelson stated: "In the early editions of the book, fiscal policy was top banana. In later editions that emphasis changed to equality. In this edition we've taken a stand that monetary policy is most important."

checking account, higher interest returns are generally available if you are willing to tie up the funds in a bond or some other less liquid form of savings. Thus, the opportunity cost of holding money is directly related to the nominal interest rate.

Demand for money
A curve that indicates the relationship between the interest rate and the quantity of money people want to hold. Because higher interest rates increase the opportunity cost of holding money, the quantity demanded of money will be inversely related to the interest rate.

A curve that outlines the relationship between the interest rate (measured on the y-axis) and the quantity of money (measured on the x-axis) is called the* demand for money.** As part a of **Exhibit 14–1** illustrates, ***there is an inverse relationship between the interest rate and the quantity of money demanded. This inverse relationship reflects the fact that higher interest rates make it more costly to hold money instead of interest-earning assets like bonds. Therefore, as interest rates rise, individuals and businesses will try to manage their affairs with smaller money balances.

Like other demand curves, the demand curve for money is constructed holding other things constant. The demand for money balances will generally increase with the nominal value of transactions. If wages and prices increase, more money will be required by households to purchase the costlier weekly market basket, and more money will be required by businesses to pay the larger wage bill. Similarly, if prices remain constant, while the quantity of goods bought and sold increases, larger money balances will be required to conduct the larger volume of business. In essence, as nominal GDP increases as the result of either higher prices or the growth of real output, the demand for money balances will also increase—that is, the entire demand for money schedule will shift to the right. Conversely, a decline in nominal GDP will decrease the demand for money, shifting the schedule to the left.

With the passage of time, changes in institutional factors will also influence the demand schedule for money. Both evidence and logic indicate that changes in institutional arrangements have reduced the demand for money in recent years. The widespread use of general-purpose credit cards makes it easier for households to reconcile their bills with their receipt of income. Readily available short-term loans have reduced the need to maintain substantial cash balances for emergencies. These changes have gradually reduced the demand for money (shifting the entire schedule to the left).

As we discussed in the previous chapter, the quantity of money available to the economy is determined by the monetary authorities, the Fed in the case of the United

The demand for money is inversely related to the money interest rate (a). The supply of money is determined by the monetary authorities (the Fed) through their open market operations, discount-rate policy, and reserve requirements (b).

EXHIBIT 14–1

DEMAND AND SUPPLY OF MONEY

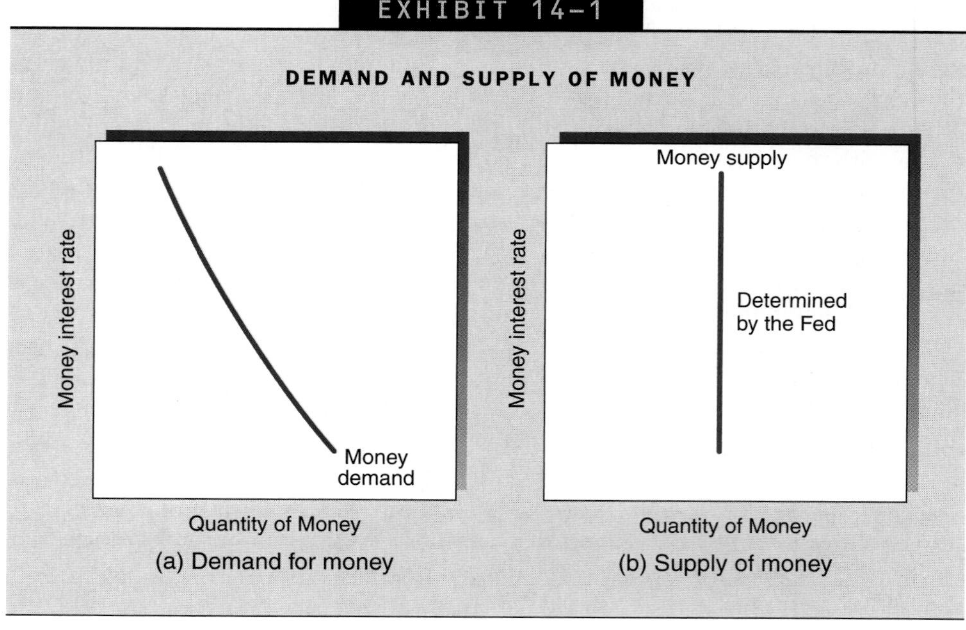

EXHIBIT 14–2

MONEY SUPPLY, MONEY DEMAND, AND EQUILIBRIUM

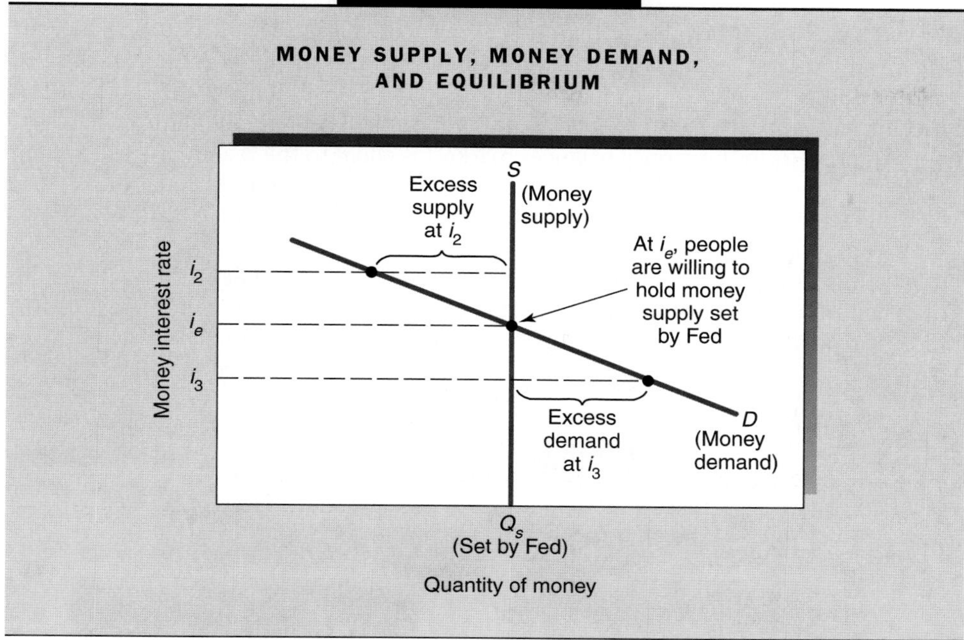

The money interest rate will tend to gravitate toward equilibrium i_e, where the quantity of money demanded by households and businesses will equal the quantity of money supplied by the Fed.

States. The Fed can use its control over reserve requirements, the discount rate, and especially open market operations to set the supply of money at whatever level it wants. Changes in the interest rate do not alter the Fed's ability to determine the supply of money. Therefore, as Exhibit 14–1 (part b) illustrates, the money supply schedule is vertical. The vertical supply curve reflects that the quantity of money is determined by Fed policy and it is not affected by changes in the interest rate.

Equilibrium between Money Demand and Money Supply

Exhibit 14–2 brings the money demand and money supply together and illustrates how they determine the equilibrium rate of interest. The money interest rate will move toward i_e, where the quantity of money demanded by households and businesses is just equal to the quantity supplied by the Fed. At the equilibrium interest rate, people are willing to hold the stock of money the Fed has supplied to the economy.

At an above equilibrium interest rate, i_2 for example, people would not want to hold as much money as the Fed has supplied. Accordingly, they would try to reduce their money balances. They might do so by using some of their money balances to buy bonds. This increase in demand for bonds would drive bond prices up and interest rates down. (Remember: Higher bond prices imply lower interest rates.) As a result, the money interest rate would move toward the i_e equilibrium. On the other hand, at a below equilibrium money interest rate, i_3 for example, an excess demand for money would be present. Excess money demand indicates that people would like to hold a larger quantity of money than the Fed has supplied. Under these circumstances, they might sell bonds in an effort to get their hands on more money. In turn, their sale of bonds would reduce bond prices and place upward pressure on interest rates, causing them to move toward i_e. Therefore, only the equilibrium interest rate i_e would tend to persist into the future.

Transmission of Monetary Policy

Expansionary monetary policy
A shift in monetary policy designed to stimulate aggregate demand. Bond purchases, creation of additional bank reserves, and an increase in the growth rate of the money supply are generally indicative of a shift to a more expansionary monetary policy.

How will a change in the money supply affect the economy? As we previously noted, the Fed typically uses open market operations to control the supply of money. If the Fed wants to shift to a more **expansionary monetary policy,** it will buy bonds. Exhibit 14–3 illustrates the impact on the economy. Initially, we consider the situation where the money interest (i_1 in the money balances market) is equal to the real interest rate (r_1 in the loanable funds market). This indicates that the expected rate of inflation is zero. When the Fed purchases bonds in order to increase the money supply (shift from S_1 to S_2 in part a), it bids up bond prices and injects additional reserves into the banking system. Profit-seeking banks will not let the additional reserves lay idle—they will seek to attract additional loan customers so that the available reserves can be fully invested in interest-earning assets. This combination of factors—higher bond prices and additional reserves that the banks will use to extend loans—will increase the supply of

When the Fed shifts to a more expansionary monetary policy, it will generally buy additional bonds. This will supply the banking system with additional reserves. Both the Fed's bond purchases and the banks' use of the additional reserves to extend new loans will increase the supply of loanable funds (shift from S_1 to S_2, part b) and place downward pressure on the real rate of interest. As the real interest rate falls (to r_2), aggregate demand increases (to AD_2 in part c). Since the effects of the monetary expansion were unanticipated, the expansion in AD leads to both an increase in current output (to Y_2) and higher prices (inflation) in the short run.

EXHIBIT 14–3

TRANSMISSION OF MONETARY POLICY

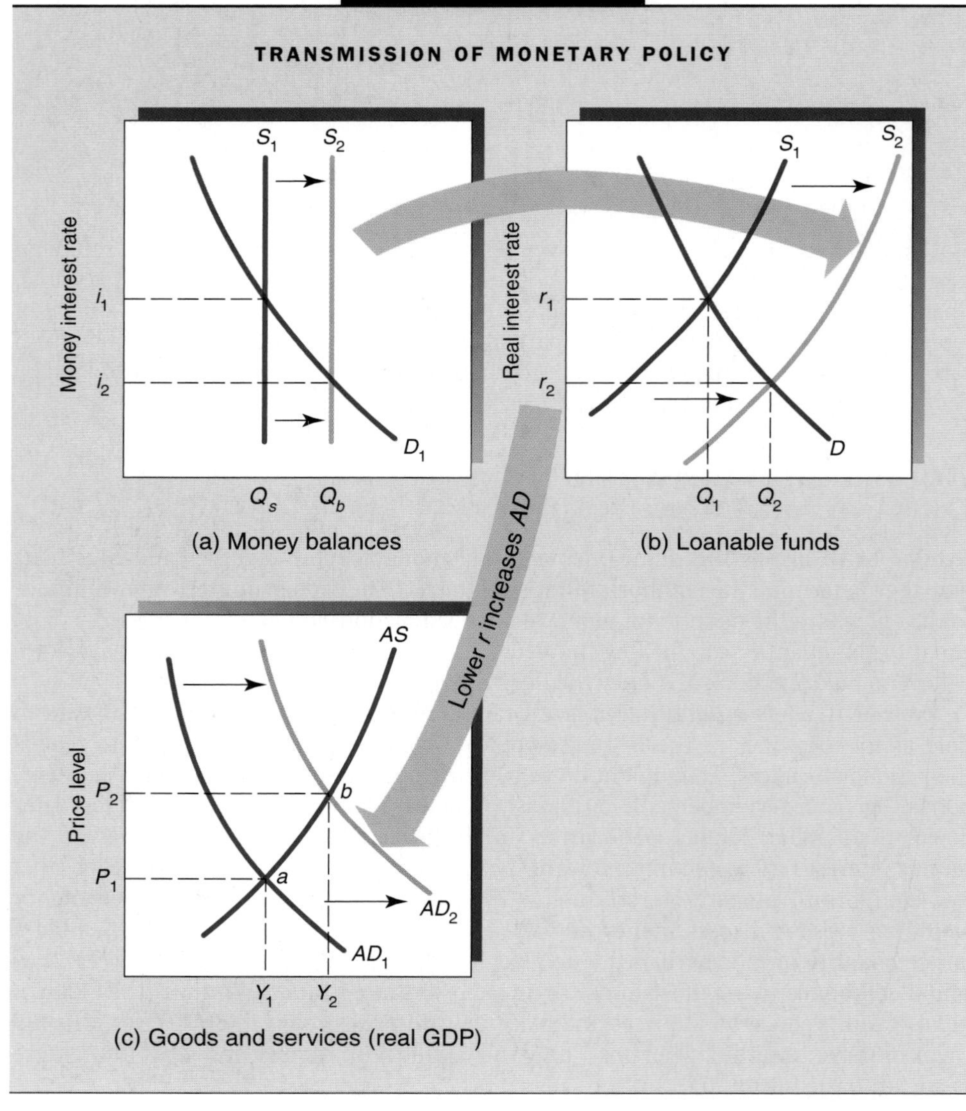

(a) Money balances

(b) Loanable funds

(c) Goods and services (real GDP)

loanable funds (shift to S_2 as shown in part b of Exhibit 14–3). In the short run, the real interest rate will fall to r_2.

How will the Fed's bond purchases, creation of additional bank reserves, and lower real interest rate influence the demand for goods and services? As part c of Exhibit 14–3 illustrates, aggregate demand will increase (shift from AD_1 to AD_2). Economists stress the importance of three factors that contribute to this increase in aggregate demand.[4]

1. ***The lower real interest rate will make current investment and consumption cheaper relative to future spending.*** At the lower interest rate, entrepreneurs will undertake some investment projects they otherwise would have forgone. Spending by firms on structures and equipment will increase. Similarly, consumers will decide to expand their purchases of automobiles and consumer durables, which can now be enjoyed with smaller monthly payments.
2. ***The lower interest rate may also lead to an outflow of capital, which will cause the dollar to depreciate and thereby stimulate the net export component of aggregate demand.*** As domestic interest rates fall, both domestic and foreign investors will shift some of their financial investments to other countries where rates of return are more attractive. As investors shift funds abroad, they will supply dollars and demand foreign currencies in the foreign exchange market. This will cause the dollar to depreciate. In turn, the depreciation in the exchange-rate value of the dollar will make imports more expensive for Americans and U.S. exports cheaper for foreigners. As a result, U.S. imports will decline and exports will expand. This increase in net exports will also stimulate aggregate demand.
3. ***The lower interest rates will tend to increase asset prices—for example, the prices of stocks, houses, and other structures—which will also stimulate current demand.*** As the prices of real and financial assets rise, household wealth increases, which will stimulate additional consumption. Perhaps more important, the higher prices of houses and other physical assets will make new construction of these assets more profitable. The increased profitability will induce entrepreneurs to undertake additional construction in these areas, which will expand both investment and aggregate demand.

The accompanying Thumbnail Sketch outlines the complex sequence of events through which Fed bond purchases expand the money supply and stimulate aggregate demand. This sequence is sometimes referred to as the interest rate transmission mechanism of monetary policy.[5]

Unanticipated Expansionary Monetary Policy

As we have previously discussed, modern macroeconomic analysis stresses the importance of whether a change is anticipated or unanticipated. If people do not anticipate the increase in aggregate demand accompanying an expansionary monetary policy,

[4]See the *Federal Reserve Bank of St. Louis: Review* (May/June 1995), and the *Journal of Economic Perspectives* (fall 1995) for additional details on how changes in monetary policy affect aggregate demand.

[5]There is also a more direct route through which expansionary monetary policy may stimulate aggregate demand. When the Fed expands the supply of money, it will create an "excess supply of money" *at the initial money interest rate.* People may respond by directly increasing their purchases of goods and services in an effort to reduce their money balances to desired levels. Obviously, this will increase aggregate demand. This direct path is most relevant when the government expands the supply of money by paying its bills with newly created currency. Because the money supply of the United States is generally expanded via open market operations, we have focused on the transmission of monetary policy through the interest rate. The implications of both the direct and indirect paths are identical—both indicate that expansionary monetary policy will stimulate aggregate demand.

THUMBNAIL SKETCH

Transmission of Monetary Policy—A Summary

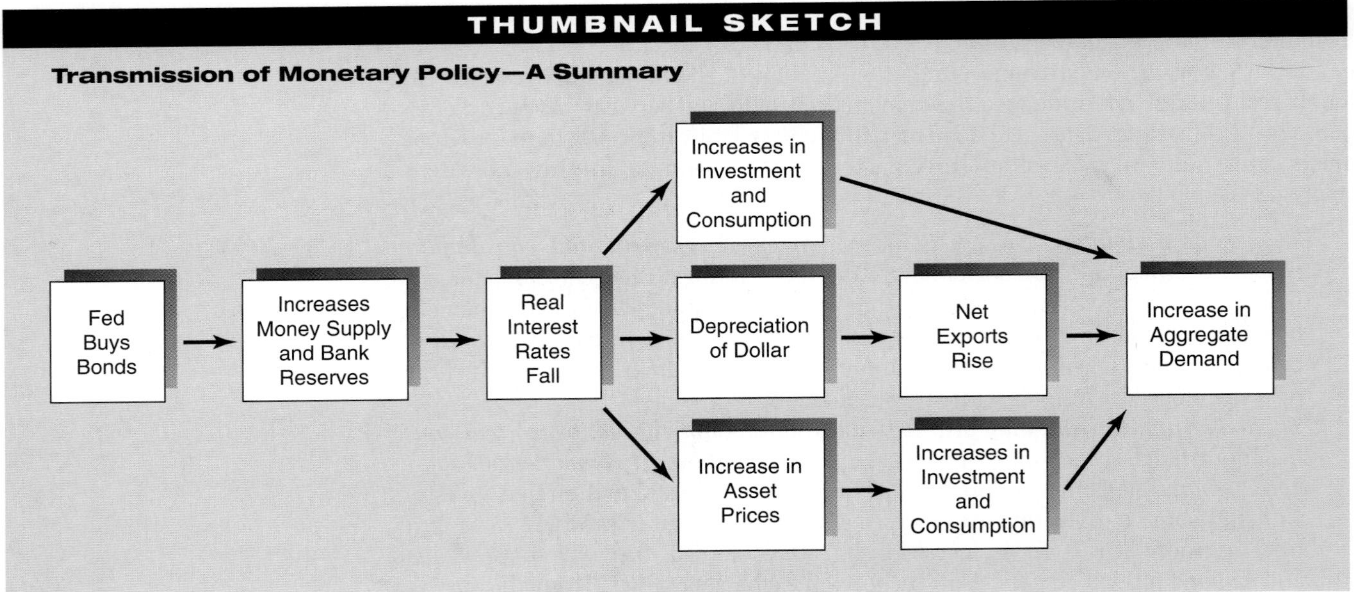

costs will rise less than prices in the short run. Profit margins will improve. Businesses will respond with an expansion in the output of goods and services (as illustrated by the increase in real output from Y_1 to Y_2 in part c of Exhibit 14–3).

Modern analysis indicates that an unexpected increase in the supply of money will reduce the real rate of interest, thereby triggering an increase in the demand for goods and services. In turn, the increase in aggregate demand will expand real output and employment in the short run.

EXHIBIT 14–4

EFFECTS OF EXPANSIONARY MONETARY POLICY

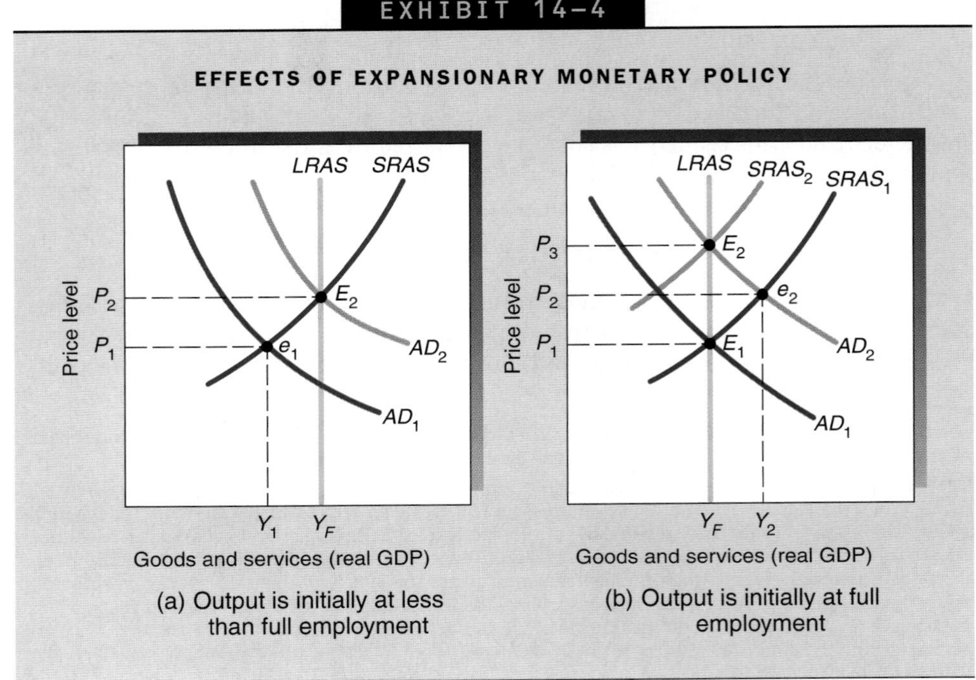

(a) Output is initially at less than full employment

(b) Output is initially at full employment

If the impact of an increase in aggregate demand accompanying expansionary monetary policy is felt when the economy is operating below capacity, the policy will help direct the economy to a long-run full-employment equilibrium (a). In this case, the increase in output from Y_1 to Y_F will be long term. In contrast, if the demand-stimulus effects are imposed on an economy already at full employment (b), they will lead to excess demand and higher product prices. Output will temporarily increase (to Y_2). However, in the long run, the strong demand will push up resource prices, shifting short-run aggregate supply to $SRAS_2$. The price level will rise to P_3 and output will recede (to Y_F) from its temporary high.

Part a of **Exhibit 14–4** illustrates the potential of expansionary monetary policy to direct a recessionary economy to full employment. Consider an economy initially at output Y_1, below full employment capacity (Y_F). Expansionary monetary policy will increase aggregate demand (to AD_2). Real output will expand (to Y_F). In essence, the expansionary monetary policy provides an alternative to the economy's self-corrective mechanism. In the absence of demand stimulus, declining resource prices and real interest rates will eventually restore full employment. But many economists believe that expansionary monetary policy can hasten the return to full-employment equilibrium.

How would a shift to expansionary monetary policy influence output and the price level if the economy were already at full employment? Although this is generally not a desirable strategy, nonetheless it is interesting to analyze the outcome. As part b of Exhibit 14–4 illustrates, the monetary expansion will increase aggregate demand, causing product prices to rise relative to costs, important components of which are temporarily fixed by long-term contracts. The shift in demand will *temporarily* push real output to Y_2, beyond the economy's long-run capacity of Y_F. Output and employment will expand. However, the high rates of output (Y_2) and employment will not be sustainable. Eventually, long-term contracts based on the previously weaker demand (AD_1) will expire. New agreements will reflect the stronger demand. Resource prices will rise, shifting *SRAS* upward to the left. Eventually, long-run equilibrium (E_2) will result at a higher price level (P_3). Output will recede to Y_F. Thus, when an economy is already at full employment, an unexpected shift to a more expansionary monetary policy will temporarily increase output, but in the long run it merely leads to higher prices. Hence, the wisdom of such a shift is highly questionable.

UNANTICIPATED RESTRICTIVE MONETARY POLICY

Restrictive monetary policy
A shift in monetary policy designed to reduce aggregate demand and place downward pressure on the general level of prices (or the rate of inflation). Bond sales, a decline in bank reserves, and a reduction in the growth rate of the money supply are generally indicative of a restrictive monetary policy.

Suppose the Fed moves toward a more **restrictive monetary policy.** It would generally do so by selling bonds to the general public, which will reduce both the supply of money and the reserves of banks. **Exhibit 14–5** illustrates the impact of the more

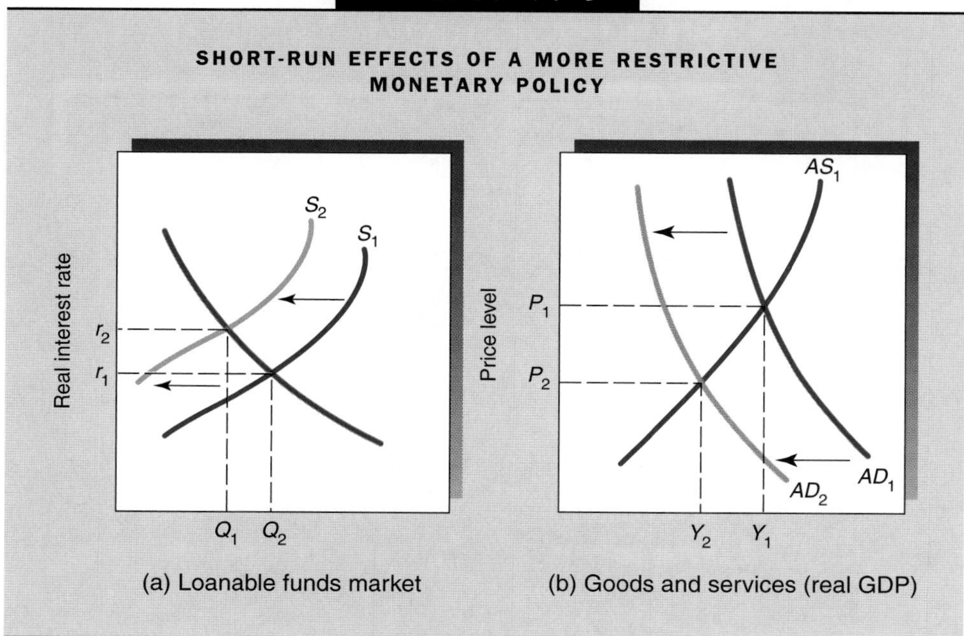

When the Fed shifts to a more restrictive policy, it sells bonds, which reduces the reserves available to banks, decreases the supply of loanable funds, and places upward pressure on interest rates (a). The higher interest rates will decrease aggregate demand (shift to AD_2 in b). When the reduction in aggregate demand is unanticipated, real output will decline (to Y_2) and downward pressure on prices will result.

restrictive monetary policy on the loanable funds and goods and services markets. The Fed's sale of bonds reduces bond prices and drains reserves from the banking system (reducing the ability of banks to extend loans). As a result, the supply of loanable funds will decline, causing the real interest rate to rise (from r_1 to r_2 in frame a of Exhibit 14–5). The higher real interest rates will tend to reduce current spending on both investment and consumer durables. They are also likely to cause an inflow of capital and appreciation in the exchange-rate value of the dollar. In turn, this appreciation of the dollar will encourage imports and discourage exports, leading to a reduction in net exports (and aggregate demand). The higher interest rates may also reduce the prices of housing and other assets, thereby discouraging new construction. All these factors will tend to reduce aggregate demand in the goods and services market (shift from AD_1 to AD_2 in part b of Exhibit 14–5).

The unexpected decline in the demand for goods and services will place downward pressures on prices, squeeze profit margins, and reduce output in the goods and services market. As part b of Exhibit 14–5 illustrates, the price level will decline (to P_2) and output will fall (to Y_2) as the result of the restrictive monetary policy.

The appropriateness of a restrictive policy depends on the initial state of the economy. **Exhibit 14–6** illustrates this point. When an economy is experiencing upward pressure on prices as the result of strong demand, restrictive policy is an effective weapon against inflation. Suppose that, as illustrated by part a of Exhibit 14–6, an economy is temporarily operating at e_1 and Y_1, beyond its full employment real GDP of Y_F. Strong aggregate demand is placing upward pressure on prices. The problem is inflation, not recession. Under these circumstances, restrictive policy makes good sense. It would help control the inflation. If the proper dosage is timed correctly, restrictive policy would retard aggregate demand (to AD_2) and direct the economy to a noninflationary, long-run equilibrium at P_2 and Y_F (that is, E_2).

As part b of Exhibit 14–6 illustrates, however, an unanticipated shift to restrictive policy would be damaging if applied to an economy in full-employment

EXHIBIT 14–6

EFFECTS OF RESTRICTIVE MONETARY POLICY

The stabilization effects of restrictive monetary policy depend on the state of the economy when the policy exerts its primary impact. Restrictive monetary policy will reduce aggregate demand. If the demand restraint comes during a period of strong demand and an overheated economy, then it will limit or even prevent the occurrence of an inflationary boom (a). In contrast, if the reduction in aggregate demand takes place when the economy is at full employment, then it will disrupt long-run equilibrium, reduce output, and result in a recession (b).

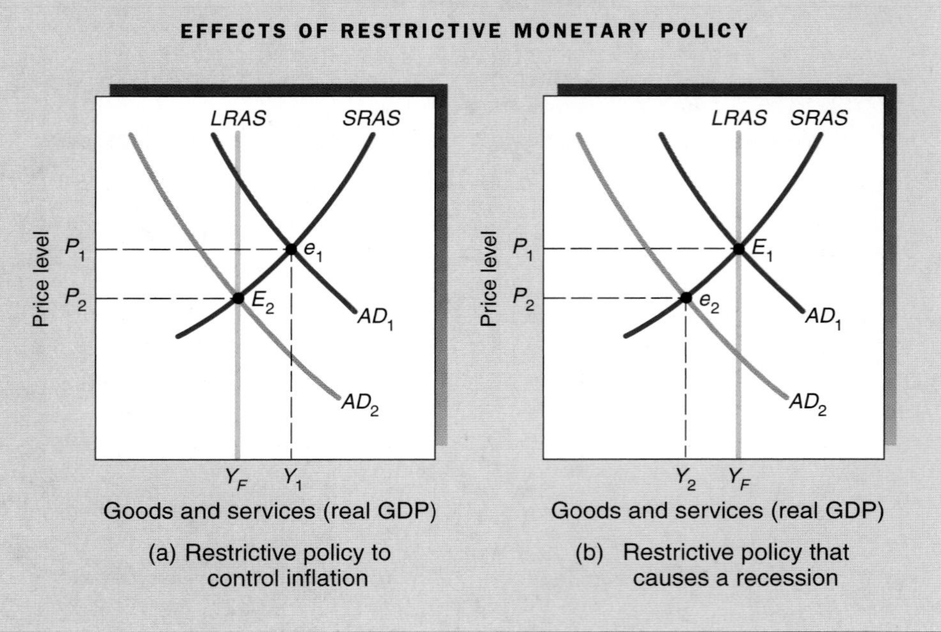

(a) Restrictive policy to control inflation

(b) Restrictive policy that causes a recession

equilibrium. If the output of an economy is at full employment (or worse still, at less than full employment), a shift to restrictive policy would reduce aggregate demand (shift to AD_2) and throw the economy into a recession. Real GDP would decline from Y_F to Y_2. Output would fall below the economy's full employment capacity, and unemployment would rise above the natural rate of unemployment.

Proper Timing

As with fiscal policy, monetary policy must be properly timed if it is to help stabilize an economy. Exhibits 14–4 and 14–6 emphasize this point. When an economy is operating below its long-run capacity, expansionary monetary policy can stimulate demand and push the output of the economy to its sustainable potential (part a of Exhibit 14–4). Similarly, if properly timed, restrictive monetary policy can help control (or prevent) inflation (part a of Exhibit 14–6).

If it is timed improperly, however, monetary policy can be destabilizing. Expansionary monetary policy is a source of inflation if the effects of the policy are felt when the economy is already at or beyond its capacity (part b of Exhibit 14–4). Similarly, if the effects of a restrictive policy come when an economy is operating at its potential GDP, recession is the likely outcome (part b of Exhibit 14–6). Worse still, the impact of restrictive policy may be disastrous if imposed on an economy already in the midst of a recession.

Proper timing of monetary policy is not an easy task. While the Fed can institute policy changes rapidly, there may be a substantial time lag before the change in policy will exert a significant impact on aggregate demand. Economists who have studied this issue estimate that this impact lag will be five or six months at a minimum. Some economists, particularly monetarists, estimate that the primary impact of a change in monetary policy on output and employment is often as much as 12 to 18 months after the change is instituted. In terms of its impact on the price level and rate of inflation, the estimated impact lag is even longer, perhaps as much as 36 months. Given our limited ability to forecast the future, such lengthy time lags clearly reduce the potential effectiveness of discretionary monetary policy as a stabilization tool.

MONETARY POLICY IN THE LONG RUN

Since the middle of the eighteenth century, economists have argued that excessive money growth leads to inflation. Nearly a hundred years ago, Englishman Alfred Marshall and American Irving Fisher formalized the **quantity theory of money** in support of this view. ***The quantity theory indicates that an increase in the supply of money will cause a proportional increase in the price level.***

Quantity theory of money
A theory that hypothesizes that a change in the money supply will cause a proportional change in the price level because velocity and real output are unaffected by the quantity of money.

The quantity theory of money can be more easily understood once we recognize that there are two ways of viewing GDP. As the *AD-AS* model shows, nominal GDP is the sum of the price, P, times the output, Y, of each final-product good purchased during the period. In aggregate, P represents the economy's price level, while Y indicates real income or real GDP. There is also a second way of visualizing GDP. When the existing money stock, M, is multiplied by the number of times, V, that money is used to buy final products, this, too, yields the economy's nominal GDP. Therefore,

$$PY = \text{GDP} = MV$$

Velocity of money
The average number of times a dollar is used to purchase final goods and services during a year. It is equal to GDP divided by the stock of money.

The **velocity of money** (V) is simply the average number of times a dollar is used to purchase a final product or service during a year. Velocity is equal to nominal GDP divided by the size of the money stock. For example, in 1998 GDP was equal to

\$8,509 billion, while the M1 money supply was \$1,093 billion. On average, each dollar in the M1 money supply was used 7.8 times to purchase final-product goods and services included in GDP. The velocity of the M1 money stock therefore was 7.8. The velocity of the M2 money stock can be derived in a similar manner. In 1998, the M2 money stock was \$4,401 billion. Thus, the velocity of M2 was 1.9 (\$8,509 billion divided by \$4,401 billion).

The concept of velocity is closely related to the demand for money. When decision makers conduct a specific amount of business with a smaller amount of money, their demand for money balances is reduced. Each dollar, though, is being used more often—the velocity of money has increased. Thus, for a given income level, when the demand for money declines, the velocity of money increases.

When considering the behavior of prices, output, money, and velocity over time, we can write the quantity theory equation in terms of growth rates:

$$\text{Rate of inflation} + \text{Growth rate of real output} = \text{Growth rate of the money supply} + \text{Growth rate of velocity}$$

Equation of exchange
MV = PY, *where* M *is the money supply,* V *is the velocity of money,* P *is the price level, and* Y *is the output of goods and services produced.*

The $MV = PY$ relationship is simply an identity, or a tautology. Economists refer to it as the **equation of exchange,** because it reflects both the monetary and real sides of each final-product exchange. The quantity theory of money, though, postulates that Y and V are determined by factors other than the amount of money in circulation. Classical economists believed that real output Y was determined by such factors as technology, the size of the economy's resource base, and the skill of the labor force. These factors were thought to be insensitive to changes in the money supply. Similarly, the velocity of money was thought to be determined primarily by institutional factors, such as the organization of banking and credit, the frequency of income payments, the rapidity of transportation, and the communication system. These factors would change quite slowly. Thus, classical economists thought that, for all practical purposes, both Y and V were constant (or changed only by small amounts) over periods of two, three, or four years. If both Y and V are constant, then the $MV = PY$ relationship indicates that an increase in the money supply will lead to a proportional increase in the price level. Correspondingly, an increase in the growth rate of the money supply can be expected to cause a similar increase in the rate of inflation.

Long-Run Implications of Modern Analysis

What does modern analysis indicate with regard to the validity of the quantity theory of money? In addressing this question, it will be helpful to focus on the dynamic long-run implications of the *AD-AS* model. Thus far, we have used comparative statics to analyze monetary policy. Within this framework, an increase in the supply of money is reflective of more expansionary policy. In the real world, however, shifts in monetary policy generally involve changes in the *growth rate* of the money supply. An increase in money growth suggests a move toward a more expansionary monetary policy, while a reduction in the growth rate of the money supply implies a shift to a more restrictive policy. Similarly, in a comparative static framework, an increase in the price level implies inflation. However, inflation is a dynamic concept—a rate of increase in prices, not a once-and-for-all movement to a higher price level.

In order to both add realism and analyze the long-run implications more fully, this section will recast the prior static analysis into a dynamic framework. We will begin with a simple dynamic case. Suppose that the real GDP of an economy is growing at a 3 percent annual rate and that the monetary authorities are expanding the money supply by 3 percent each year. In addition, let's assume that the velocity of money is constant. This would imply that the 3 percent annual increase in output would lead to a 3 percent annual increase in the demand for money. Under these circumstances, the 3 percent monetary growth would be consistent with stable prices (zero inflation). Initially, we will assume that the economy's real interest rate is 4 percent. Because the inflation rate is zero, the nominal rate of interest is also equal to 4 percent. **Exhibits 14–7** and **14–8** illustrate an economy initially (Period 1) characterized by these conditions.

What will happen if the monetary authorities permanently increase the growth rate of the money supply from 3 percent to 8 percent annually (see part a of Exhibit 14–7, beginning in Period 2)?[6] In the short run, the expansionary monetary policy will reduce the real interest rate and stimulate aggregate demand (shift to AD_2 in part b of Exhibit 14–7), just as we previously explained (Exhibits 14–3 and 14–4). For a time,

[6]In the preceding chapter, we noted the difficulties involved in the measurement of the money supply (both M1 and M2). Changes in the growth rate of the money supply may not always be indicative of a shift in monetary policy. More generally, the example presented in the text assumes that the Fed has shifted to a more expansionary monetary policy—one that will lead to an increase in the rate of inflation—regardless of whether the monetary aggregates as currently measured reflect this shift.

EXHIBIT 14–7

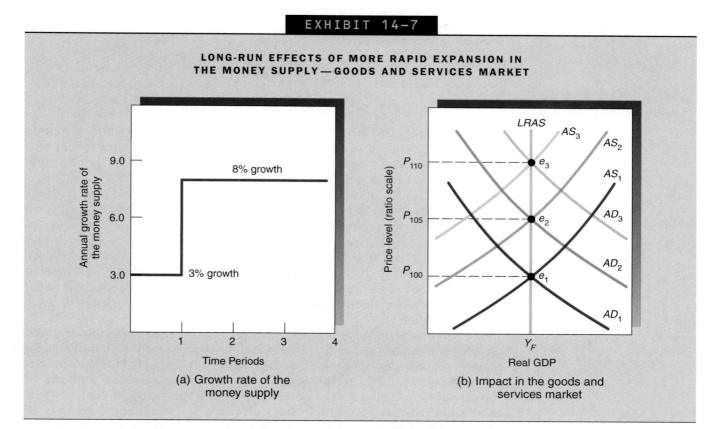

LONG-RUN EFFECTS OF MORE RAPID EXPANSION IN THE MONEY SUPPLY—GOODS AND SERVICES MARKET

(a) Growth rate of the money supply

(b) Impact in the goods and services market

Here we illustrate the long-term impact of an increase in the annual growth rate of the money supply from 3 to 8 percent. Initially, prices are stable (P_{100}) when the money supply is expanding by 3 percent annually. The acceleration in the growth rate of the money supply increases aggregate demand (shift to AD_2). At first, real output may expand beyond the economy's potential (Y_F). However, abnormally low employment and strong demand conditions will create upward pressure on wages and other resource prices, shifting aggregate supply to AS_2. Output will return to its long-run potential, and the price level will increase to P_{105} (e_2). If the more rapid monetary growth continues in subsequent periods, AD and AS will continue to shift upward, leading to still higher prices (e_3 and points beyond). The net result of this process is sustained inflation.

When prices are stable, supply and demand in the loanable funds market are in balance at a real and nominal interest rate of 4 percent. If more rapid monetary expansion leads to a long-term 5 percent inflation rate (see Exhibit 14–7), borrowers and lenders will build the higher inflation rate into their decision making. As a result, the nominal interest rate (i) will rise to 9 percent—the 4 percent real rate plus a 5 percent inflationary premium.

EXHIBIT 14–8

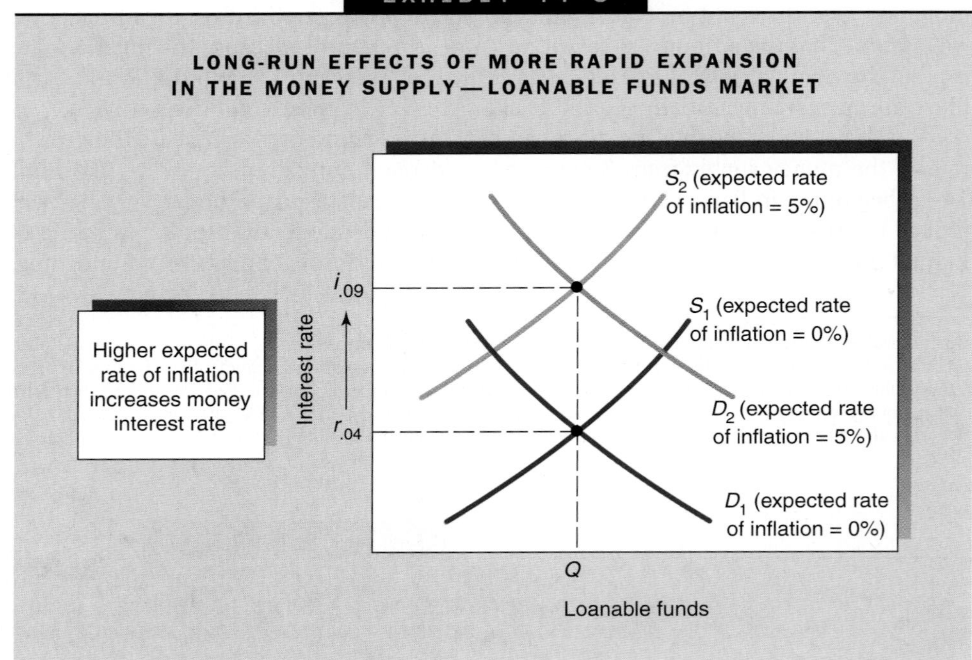

real output may exceed the economy's potential. However, as they confront strong demand conditions, many resource suppliers (who previously committed to long-term agreements) will want to modify these agreements in light of the strong demand conditions. With the passage of time, more and more resource suppliers (including labor represented by union officials) will have the opportunity to alter their prior contracts. As this happens, wages and other resource prices will increase. As they do, costs will rise and profit margins will recede to normal levels. The higher costs will reduce aggregate supply (shift to AS_2). As the rapid monetary growth continues in subsequent periods (periods 3, 4, and so on), both AD and AS will shift upward. The price level will rise to P_{105}, P_{110}, and on to still higher levels as the money supply continues to grow more rapidly than the monetary growth rate consistent with stable prices. The continuation of the expansionary monetary policy leads to a higher and higher price level—that is, a sustained inflation.

Suppose an inflation rate of 5 percent eventually emerges from the more rapid growth rate (8 percent rather than 3 percent) of the money supply. With the passage of time, more and more people will adjust their decision making in light of the persistent 5 percent inflation. In the resource market, both buyers and sellers will eventually incorporate the expectation of the 5 percent inflation rate into long-term contracts, such as collective bargaining agreements. Once this happens, resource prices and costs will rise as rapidly as prices in the goods and services market. ***When the inflation rate is anticipated fully, it will fail to either reduce real wages or improve profit margins. Unemployment will return to its natural rate.***

Exhibit 14–8 illustrates the adjustments in the loanable funds market once borrowers and lenders expect the 5 percent inflation rate. When lenders anticipate a 5 percent annual increase in the price level, a 9 percent interest rate will be necessary to provide them with as much incentive to supply loanable funds as 4 percent interest provided *when stable prices were expected.* Thus, the supply of loanable funds will shift vertically by the 5 percent expected rate of inflation. Simultaneously, borrowers who were willing to pay 4 percent interest on loans when they expected stable prices will be willing to pay 9 percent when they expect prices to increase by 5 percent annually. The demand for loanable funds will therefore also increase (shift vertically) by the expected rate of inflation. Once borrowers and lenders anticipate the higher (5 percent) inflation rate, the equilibrium money interest rate will rise to 9 percent. Of course, the real interest rate is equal to the money interest rate (9 percent) minus the expected rate of inflation (5 percent). In the long run, a 4 percent real interest rate will emerge with inflation, just as it did with stable prices.[7] Inflation, then, will fail to reduce the real interest rate in the long run.

The long-run implications of modern analysis are consistent with those of the earlier quantity theory of money. ***In the long run, the major consequence of rapid money growth is inflation. While an unanticipated shift to a more expansionary policy may exert a positive impact on output and employment in the short run, this will not be the case in the long run. Rapid monetary growth will neither reduce unemployment nor stimulate real output in the long run.***

MONETARY POLICY WHEN EFFECTS ARE ANTICIPATED

Thus far, we have assumed that decision makers come to anticipate the effects of monetary policy only after they begin to occur. For example, we assumed that borrowers and lenders began to anticipate a higher inflation rate only after prices began to rise more rapidly. Similarly, resource suppliers anticipated the inflation only after it had begun.

What if enough decision makers in the market catch on to the link between expansionary monetary policy and an increase in the inflation rate? Suppose borrowers and lenders start paying attention to the money-supply figures and other monetary policy indicators. Observing a shift toward a more expansionary monetary policy, they revise upward their expectation of the future inflation rate. Lenders become more reluctant to supply loanable funds. Simultaneously, borrowers increase their demand for loanable funds at existing rates of interest because they also anticipate a higher rate of future inflation and they want to buy now before prices rise. Under these circumstances, a reduction in supply and an increase in demand for loanable funds will quickly push up the money interest rate. If borrowers and lenders quickly and accurately forecast the future rate of inflation accompanying the monetary expansion, the real interest rate will decline for only a short period of time, if at all.

If buyers and sellers in the goods and services market also anticipate a shift to a more expansionary monetary policy, they too may anticipate its inflationary consequences. As buyers anticipate future price increases, many will buy now rather than later. Current aggregate demand will rise. Similarly, expecting an acceleration in the inflation rate, sellers will be reluctant to sell except at premium prices. Current aggregate supply will fall. This combination of factors will quickly push prices of goods and services upward.

Simultaneously, if buyers and sellers in the resource market believe that more rapid monetary growth will lead to a higher rate of inflation, they too will build this

[7]Higher rates of inflation are generally associated with an increase in the variability of the inflation rate. Thus, greater risk (the possibility of either a substantial gain or loss associated with a sharp change in the inflation rate) accompanies exchange in the loanable funds market when inflation rates are high. This additional risk may result in higher real interest rates than would prevail at lower rates of inflation. The text discussion does not introduce this consideration.

EXHIBIT 14–9

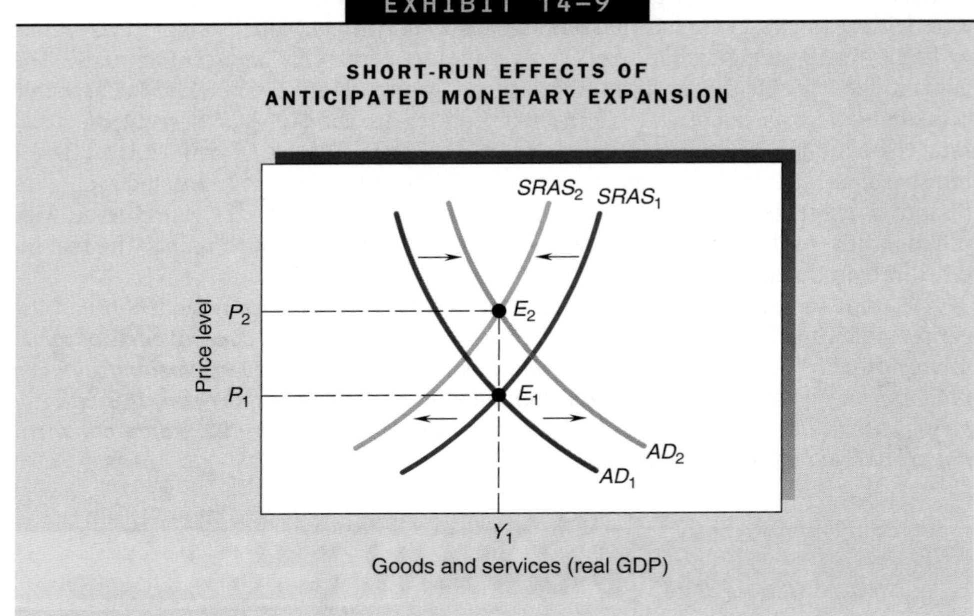

When decision makers fully anticipate the effects of monetary expansion, the expansion does not alter real output even in the short run. Suppliers, including resource suppliers, build the expected price rise into their decisions. The anticipated inflation leads to a rise in nominal costs (including wages), causing aggregate supply to decline (shift to $SRAS_2$*). While nominal wages, prices, and interest rates rise, their real counterparts are unchanged. The result: inflation without any change in real output (*Y_1*).*

Escalator clause
A contractual agreement that periodically and automatically adjusts money wage rates upward as the price level rises. They are sometimes referred to as cost-of-living adjustments or COLAs.

view into long-run contracts. Union officials will demand and employers will pay an inflationary premium for future money wages, based on their expectation of inflation. Alternatively, they may write an **escalator clause** (sometimes called cost-of-living adjustments) into their collective bargaining agreements. Such provisions will automatically raise money wages when the inflation transpires. If decision makers in the resource market correctly anticipate the inflation, real resource prices will not decline once prices accelerate upward.

As **Exhibit 14–9** illustrates, when individuals correctly anticipate the effects of expansionary monetary policy *prior to their occurrence,* the short-run impact of monetary policy is much like its impact in the long run. The price level will increase, pushing up money income (P_2Y_1), but real income (Y_1) will be unchanged. Nominal interest rates will rise, but real interest rates will be unchanged. Thus, when the effects of expansionary monetary policy are fully anticipated, they exert little impact on real economic activity.

Are people likely to anticipate the effects of monetary policy? This is a topic of hot debate among economists, and we will consider it in more detail in the next chapter. Because the effects of monetary policy differ substantially depending on whether they are anticipated, the question is clearly a very important one.

INTEREST RATES AND MONETARY POLICY

Can the Fed control interest rates? How quickly will a shift in monetary policy exert a significant impact on output and prices in the goods and services market? These two questions are linked. Let us begin with the interest rate question. In order to simplify matters, we have proceeded as if there were only a single interest rate in the loanable funds market. In the real world loanable funds market, of course, there are numerous interest rates reflecting loans of differing risk and time length. For example, there are short-term interest rates, such as those for federal funds, Treasury bills, and savings deposits. In addition, there are longer-term rates, such as those for home mortgages and long-term bonds.

When the Fed moves toward a more expansionary policy—when it purchases bonds and injects additional reserves into the system—there is an immediate impact on short-term interest rates, like the rate in the federal funds market—the market where banks with excess reserves extend short-term loans to banks with insufficient reserves. As the federal funds rate declines, so too will other short-term interest rates—for example, the rates on savings deposits, three-month Treasury bills, and bank certificates of deposit (CDs).

However, the impact of the expansionary monetary policy on long-term interest rates, such as home mortgages and ten-year bonds, will be more modest and less predictable. There are two reasons for this: First, the long-term rates are influenced more by real factors, such as the demand for investment funds, than by monetary factors. Second, to the extent that monetary factors influence long-term interest rates, they operate primarily through their impact on the expected rate of inflation. The expected long-term future rate of inflation is an important component of long-term nominal interest rates. If people expect a higher future rate of inflation as the result of the shift to a more expansionary policy, long-term rates may rise rather than fall. Thus, although a shift in Fed policy is able to exert a substantial impact on short-term interest rates rather quickly, its impact on longer-term rates is both less certain and likely to occur with a substantially longer time lag. Because the long-term rates are most relevant for the investment decisions of businesses and households, the ambiguity concerning the impact of monetary policy on these rates is particularly important.

Short-Term Interest Rates, Velocity of Money, and Time Lag of Monetary Policy

Furthermore, the impact of the change in short-term nominal interest rates on the velocity of money adds an additional complication. A reduction in the short-term rates will reduce the opportunity cost of holding money balances. Predictably, the velocity of money will decline, which will tend to dampen the initial stimulus effects of the monetary expansion. Of course, if the more expansionary monetary policy persists, a combination of lower real interest rates—particularly short-term rates—and more readily available credit will eventually stimulate aggregate demand (see Exhibit 14–3). With time, the additional demand will place upward pressure on prices, which will also serve to increase both the expected rate of inflation and nominal interest rates, including short-term nominal rates. When this happens—and several quarters may pass before it does—the higher short-term nominal interest rates will increase the velocity of money and amplify the demand-stimulus effects of the policy. It is at this point in time that the primary effects of the expansionary monetary policy will be most potent.

The same forces are also present in the case of a shift to a more restrictive monetary policy. When the Fed shifts to a more restrictive policy, it typically drains reserves from the banking system, which will quickly place upward pressure on the federal funds rate and other short-term interest rates. The restrictive policy, however, will generally exert less impact on longer-term interest rates. If people perceive that inflation is less of a threat as the result of the more restrictive monetary policy, this factor will place downward pressure on long-term interest rates, which will at least partially offset the restraining effects emanating from the increase in the short-term rates.

At the same time, the higher short-term rates will increase the opportunity cost of holding money and, as a result, its velocity. This increase in the velocity of money will promote additional spending, which will, *for a time,* tend to dampen the restrictive effects of the policy. Of course, the restrictive policy, if continued, will eventually begin to retard inflation and lower nominal interest rates (including short-term rates), which will reduce the velocity of money. Once this happens, and many months may pass before it does, the restrictive policy will be highly potent—it will substantially reduce aggregate demand, output, and prices.

All these factors suggest that the linkage between a change in monetary policy and a change in output and prices is likely to be both lengthy and variable. When there is a shift in monetary policy, the potency of the short-run effects may differ substantially from the potency of the policy shift over a longer period of time. Obviously, these factors will complicate the job of monetary policy makers and make it more difficult for them to institute changes in a manner that will exert a stabilizing influence on the economy.

Money Supply and the Federal Funds Rate

Throughout, we have used shifts in the money supply to indicate the direction of changes in monetary policy. In recent years, however, the Fed has often used interest rates—particularly the federal funds rate—as a means of instituting changes in monetary policy. If the Fed wants to shift toward a more expansionary policy, it may announce that it is reducing its target for the federal funds interest rate. The Fed controls this rate through its open market operations. In order to achieve the lower rate, it will buy more bonds and thereby inject additional reserves into the system, which will place downward pressure on the federal funds rate. Of course, the Fed's buying of bonds will also increase the money supply. Therefore, even though the news media and others may highlight the change in the fed funds rate, the impact on the economy will be the same as for an increase in the money supply. On the other hand, when the Fed shifts to a more restrictive policy, it may seek to increase the fed funds rate. However, the Fed achieves this objective through its sale of bonds, which will reduce the reserves available to the banking system. Again, the result will be the same as for a reduction in the money supply.

Dangers of Using Interest Rates as an Indicator of Monetary Policy

Are interest rates indicative of Fed policy? For example, do low interest rates indicate that the Fed is following an expansionary policy? Here, it is vitally important to distinguish between the short run and the long run. When the Fed shifts to a more expansionary policy, it generally injects additional reserves into the banking system. In the short run, this will place downward pressure on interest rates—particularly for short-term rates. However, think what would happen if the Fed continued on a highly expansionary course, seeking to push interest rates down over a long period of time. In the long run, the monetary expansion will lead to inflation. As people come to expect the inflation, nominal interest rates will rise instead of fall. Once the inflation is anticipated fully, even real interest rates will return to their normal level.

Paradoxically, while expansionary monetary policy can reduce interest rates in the short run, in the long run the result will be just the opposite. A persistent expansionary monetary policy will lead to inflation and higher nominal interest rates. Similarly, a shift to a more restrictive policy will increase interest rates in the short run. But when pursued over a lengthy time period, restrictive policy will lead to deflation (falling prices) and low interest rates.

Thus, interest rates are often a misleading gauge of monetary policy. In the United States, interest rates were high during the 1970s, a period of expansionary monetary policy and inflation. On the other hand, interest rates were relatively low during the 1960s and 1990s, periods of more restrictive monetary policy. During the Great Depression, interest rates fell to less than 1 percent. But this was not indicative of expansionary monetary policy. To the contrary, it was reflective of a highly restrictive monetary policy that was causing deflation and the expectation of a falling price level. Internationally, the picture is the same. The highest interest rates in the world are found in countries experiencing hyperinflation—Argentina and Brazil in the 1980s and Russia in the 1990s, for example. In the late 1990s, several interest rates in Japan fell below 1 percent. Like the United States during the Great Depression, the low Japanese interest rates are reflective of a highly restrictive monetary policy, one that has led to a falling price level and the expectation of deflation.

EFFECTS OF MONETARY POLICY—A SUMMARY

The accompanying Thumbnail Sketch summarizes the theoretical implications of our analysis. The impact of monetary policy on major economic variables is indicated for three alternatives: (1) the short run when the effects are unanticipated, (2) the short

THUMBNAIL SKETCH

What is the Impact of Monetary Policy?

<table>
<tr><th></th><th>Short-Run Effects When Policy Is Unanticipated (1)</th><th>Short-Run Effects When Policy Is Anticipated[a] (2)</th><th>Long-Run Effects (3)</th></tr>
<tr><td>Impact of Expansionary Monetary Policy on</td><td></td><td colspan="2"></td></tr>
<tr><td>Inflation rate</td><td>Only a small increase, particularly if excess capacity is present.</td><td colspan="2">Increase</td></tr>
<tr><td>Real output and employment</td><td>Increase, particularly if excess capacity is present.</td><td colspan="2">No change</td></tr>
<tr><td>Money interest rate</td><td>Short-term rates will probably decline.</td><td colspan="2">Increase</td></tr>
<tr><td>Real interest rate</td><td>Decrease</td><td colspan="2">No change</td></tr>
<tr><td>Impact of Restrictive Monetary Policy on</td><td></td><td colspan="2"></td></tr>
<tr><td>Inflation rate</td><td>Only a small decrease</td><td colspan="2">Decrease</td></tr>
<tr><td>Real output and employment</td><td>Decrease, particularly if economy at less than capacity.</td><td colspan="2">No change</td></tr>
<tr><td>Money interest rate</td><td>Short-term rates will probably increase.</td><td colspan="2">Decrease</td></tr>
<tr><td>Real interest rate</td><td>Increase</td><td colspan="2">No change</td></tr>
</table>

[a]Beginning from long-run equilibrum

run when the effects are anticipated, and (3) the long run. Note that the impact of monetary policy in the latter two cases is the same. When decision makers quickly anticipate the effects of monetary policy, the adjustment process speeds up, and therefore the short-run effects are identical to the long-run effects. Under these circumstances, only nominal variables (money interest rates and the inflation rate) are affected. Real variables (real GDP, employment, and the real interest rate) are unaffected.

Five major predictions flow from our analysis:

1. ***An unanticipated shift to a more expansionary (restrictive) monetary policy will temporarily stimulate (retard) output and employment.*** As Exhibits 14–3 and 14–4 illustrate, an increase in aggregate demand emanating from an unanticipated increase in the money supply will lead to a short-run expansion in real output and employment. Conversely, as Exhibit 14–5 shows, an unanticipated move toward a more restrictive monetary policy reduces aggregate demand and retards real output.
2. ***The stabilizing effects of a change in monetary policy are dependent upon the state of the economy when the effects of the policy change are observed.*** If the effects of an expansionary policy come when the economy is operating at less than capacity, then the demand stimulus will push the economy toward full employment. However, if the demand stimulus comes when the economy is operating at or beyond capacity, it will contribute to an acceleration in the inflation rate. Correspondingly, restrictive policy will help to control inflation if the demand-restraining effects are felt when output is beyond the economy's long-run capacity. On the other hand, restrictive policy will result in recession if the reduction in demand comes when the economy is at or below long-run capacity.
3. ***Persistent growth of the money supply at a rapid rate will cause inflation.*** Although the short-run effects of expansionary monetary policy may be primarily on output, particularly if excess capacity is present, a persistent expansion in the money supply at a rate greater than the growth of real output will cause inflation. The more rapid the sustained growth rate of the money supply (relative to real output), the higher the accompanying rate of inflation.
4. ***Money interest rates and the inflation rate will be directly related.*** As the inflation rate rises, money interest rates will eventually increase because both borrowers and lenders will begin to expect the higher rate of inflation and build it into their decision making. Conversely, as the inflation rate declines, a reduction in the expected rate of inflation will eventually lead to lower money interest rates. Therefore, when monetary expansion leads to an acceleration in the inflation rate, it will also result in an increase in nominal interest rates.
5. ***There will be only a loose year-to-year relationship between shifts in monetary policy and changes in output and prices.*** It takes time for markets to adjust to changing demand conditions. Some prices in both product and resource markets are set by long-term contracts. Obviously price responses in these markets will take time. In some cases, people may anticipate the effects of a policy change and adjust quickly; in others, the reaction to a policy change may take more time. Differences in this area will weaken the year-to-year relationship between monetary indicators and important economic variables.

   In addition, a monetary policy shift will initially exert a far greater impact on short-term interest rates than on longer-term rates. Movements in the short-term nominal rates are likely to cause changes in the velocity of money that will tend to dampen the initial effects of a monetary policy shift. This, too, will tend to weaken the year-to-year link between changes in monetary policy and changes in output and prices. Therefore, even though our analysis indicates that monetary policy does influence output and prices, the year-to-year relationships are likely to be weak.

TESTING THE MAJOR IMPLICATIONS OF MONETARY THEORY

Is the real world consistent with our analysis? The next four exhibits provide evidence on this topic. Our analysis indicates that a shift to a more expansionary monetary policy will initially stimulate output, while a shift to monetary restriction will retard it. **Exhibit 14–10** shows the relationship between changes in the growth rate of the money supply and real output since 1960 for the United States. Because the introduction of interest-earning checking accounts changed the nature of M1 (and affected its growth rate) during the 1980s, the M2 money-supply measure is used here. Of course, factors other than monetary policy (for example, supply shocks, fiscal policy, or

EXHIBIT 14–10

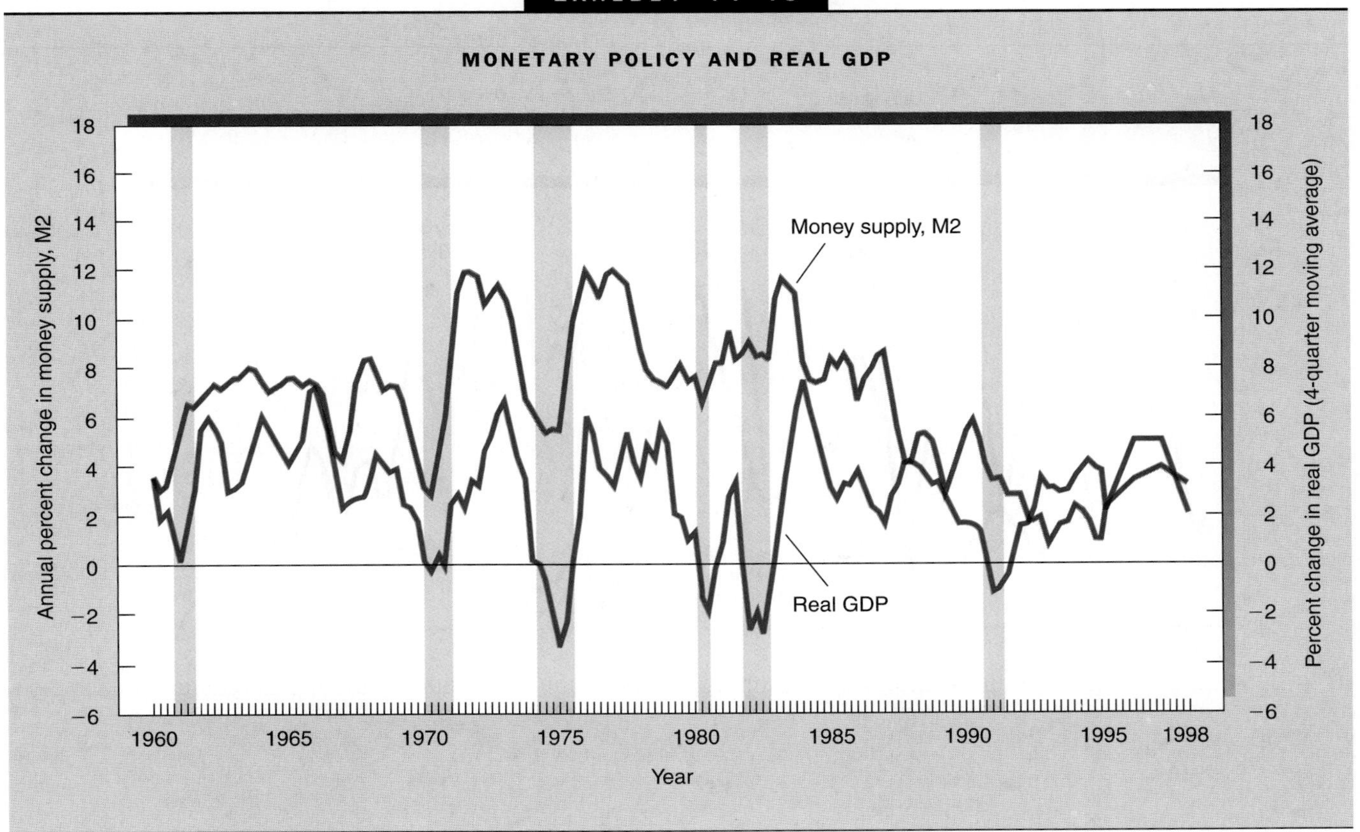

Sharp declines in the growth rate of the money supply, such as those of 1968–1969, 1973–1974, 1977–1978, and 1988–1991, have generally preceded reductions in real GDP and periods of recession (indicated by shading). Conversely, periods of sharp acceleration in the growth rate of the money supply, such as 1971–1972 and 1976, have often been followed by a rapid growth of GDP. The monetary authorities have generally increased the growth rate of the money supply during recessions. Note that the growth rate of the money supply has been slower and more stable during the last decade.

SOURCE: Derived from computerized data supplied by FAME ECONOMICS. Also see Economic Report of the President *(published annually).*

changes in incomes abroad) will influence the growth of output. Thus, the relationship between changes in the money supply and the growth of real GDP will be fairly loose. However, close inspection of the data reveals that periods of sharp acceleration in the growth rate of the money supply were generally associated with an acceleration in the growth rate of real GDP. For example, an acceleration in the growth rate of the money supply during 1961–1964, 1971–1972, 1976, and 1983 was associated with an increase in the growth rate of real GDP during each of the periods. The converse was also true: Periods of sharp deceleration in the growth rate of the money supply were generally associated with (or followed by) economic recession. A decline in the growth rate of the money supply preceded the recessions of 1960, 1970, and 1974–1975. Similarly, a sharp decline in the growth rate of the money stock from 12 percent in 1976–1977 to less than 8 percent in 1978–1979 preceded the back-to-back recessions and sluggish growth of 1979–1982. Most recently, the recession and sluggish growth of 1989–1991 was preceded by a substantial deceleration in the growth rate of the money supply. Hence, just as our theory predicts, there does appear to be a relationship between shifts in monetary policy and changes in real GDP.

EXHIBIT 14-11

EFFECT OF CHANGES IN MONEY SUPPLY ON INFLATION

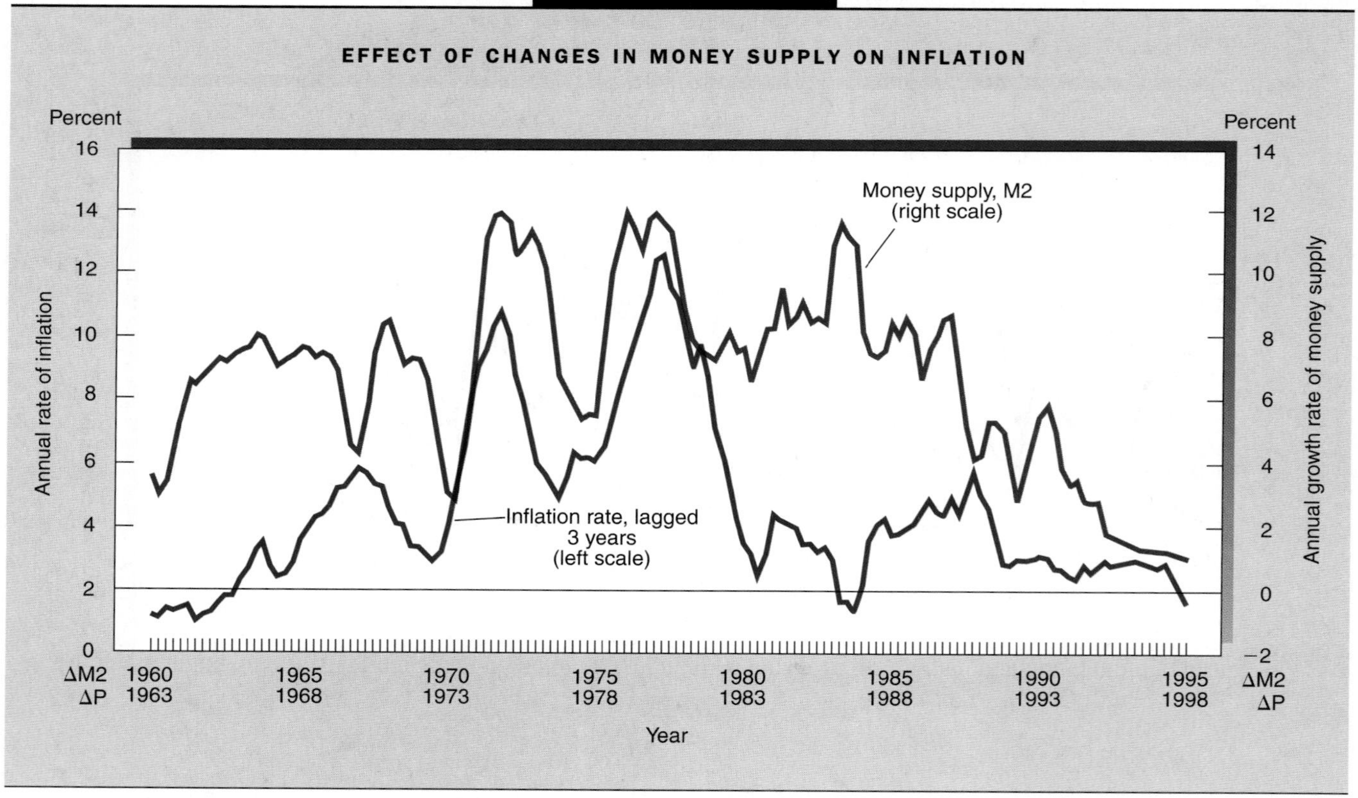

Here we illustrate the relationship between the rate of growth in the money supply (M2) and the annual inflation rate three years later. While the two are not perfectly correlated, the data do indicate that periods of monetary acceleration (for example: 1971–1972 and 1975–1976) tend to be associated with an increase in the inflation rate about three years later. Similarly, a slower growth rate of the money supply, like that of the 1990s, is generally associated with a reduction in the rate of inflation.

SOURCE: Derived from computerized data supplied by FAME ECONOMICS. Also see Economic Report of the President *(published annually). The consumer price index was used to measure the rate of inflation.*

Exhibit 14–11 presents a graphic picture of the relationship between monetary policy and the inflation rate for the United States. Although our theory indicates that persistent, long-term growth of the money supply will be closely associated with inflation, it also indicates that time is required for a monetary expansion (or contraction) to alter demand relationships and impact prices. Most economists believe that the time lag between shifts in monetary policy and observable changes in the level of prices is often two or three years. Reflecting these views, Exhibit 14–11 compares the current money supply (M2) data with the inflation rate three years in the future. Once again, though the linkage is far from tight, it definitely exists. Most noticeably, the rapid monetary acceleration during 1971–1972 was followed by a similar acceleration in the inflation rate during 1973–1974. Similarly, the sharp monetary contraction of 1974–1975 was accompanied by not only the recession of 1974–1975, but also a sharp deceleration in the inflation rate during 1976–1977. However, as monetary policy again shifted toward expansion in 1976–1977, the double-digit inflation rates of 1979–1980 were soon to follow.

During the 1980–1986 period, the linkage between monetary growth and the inflation rate a few years later appeared to weaken. To some degree this may reflect the financial innovations and changing nature of money during this period. There is some evidence that the relationship is once again becoming more predictable now that the transition period to interest-earning checking accounts has been completed. During

EXHIBIT 14–12

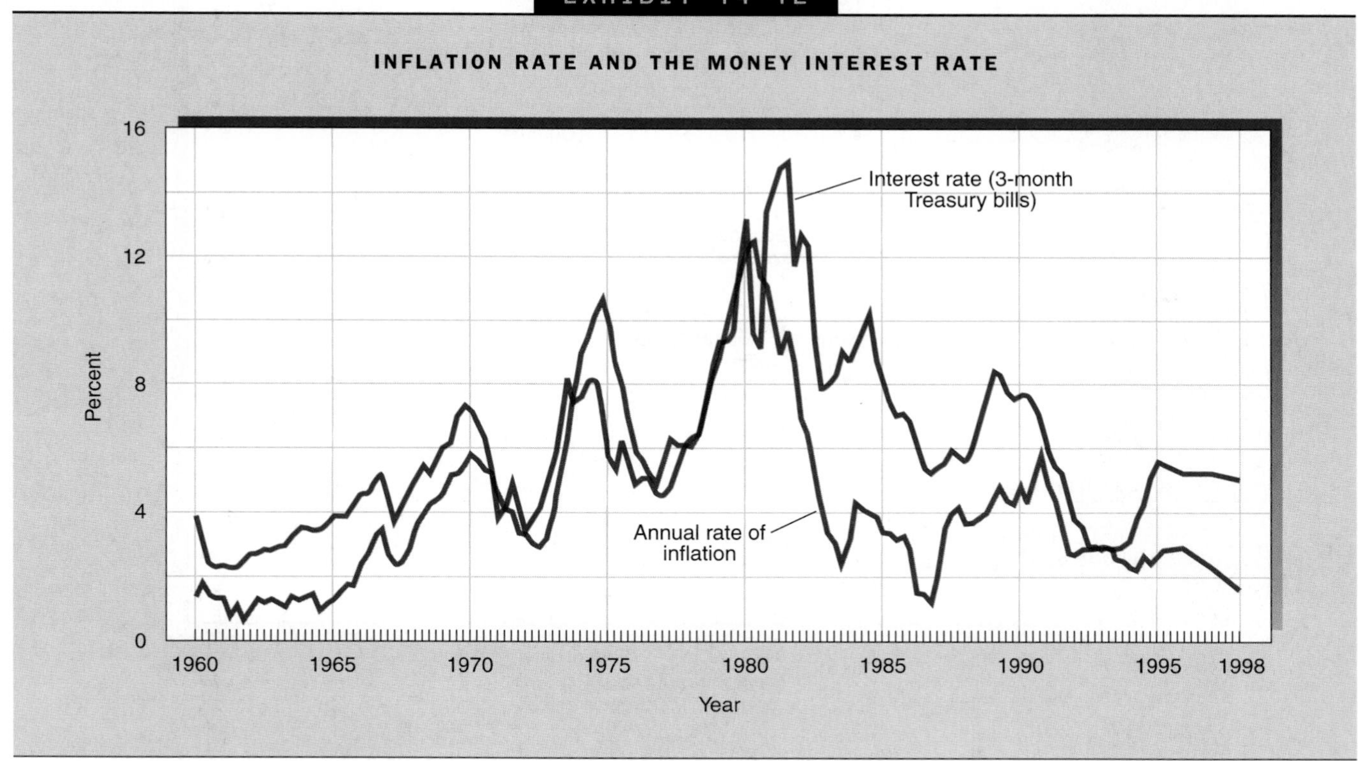

The expectation of inflation (a) reduces the supply and (b) increases the demand for loanable funds, causing money interest rates to rise (see Exhibit 14–8). Note how the short-term money rate of interest has tended to increase when the inflation rate accelerates (and decline as the inflation rate falls).

SOURCE: Derived from computerized data supplied by FAME ECONOMICS. Also see Economic Report of the President *(published annually). The consumer price index was used to measure the rate of inflation.*

the 1987–1993 period, the annual growth rate of the money supply (M2) decelerated from approximately 8 percent to less than 2 percent. With a lag, the inflation rate followed a similar path during this period. Furthermore, the low rate of money growth during the 1990s (the average money growth rate has been approximately 3 percent during this period) has been associated with low rates of inflation.

Exhibit 14–12 shows the relationship between the inflation rate (change in CPI) and the nominal interest rate. Because our measure of inflation is the annual rate

EXHIBIT 14–13

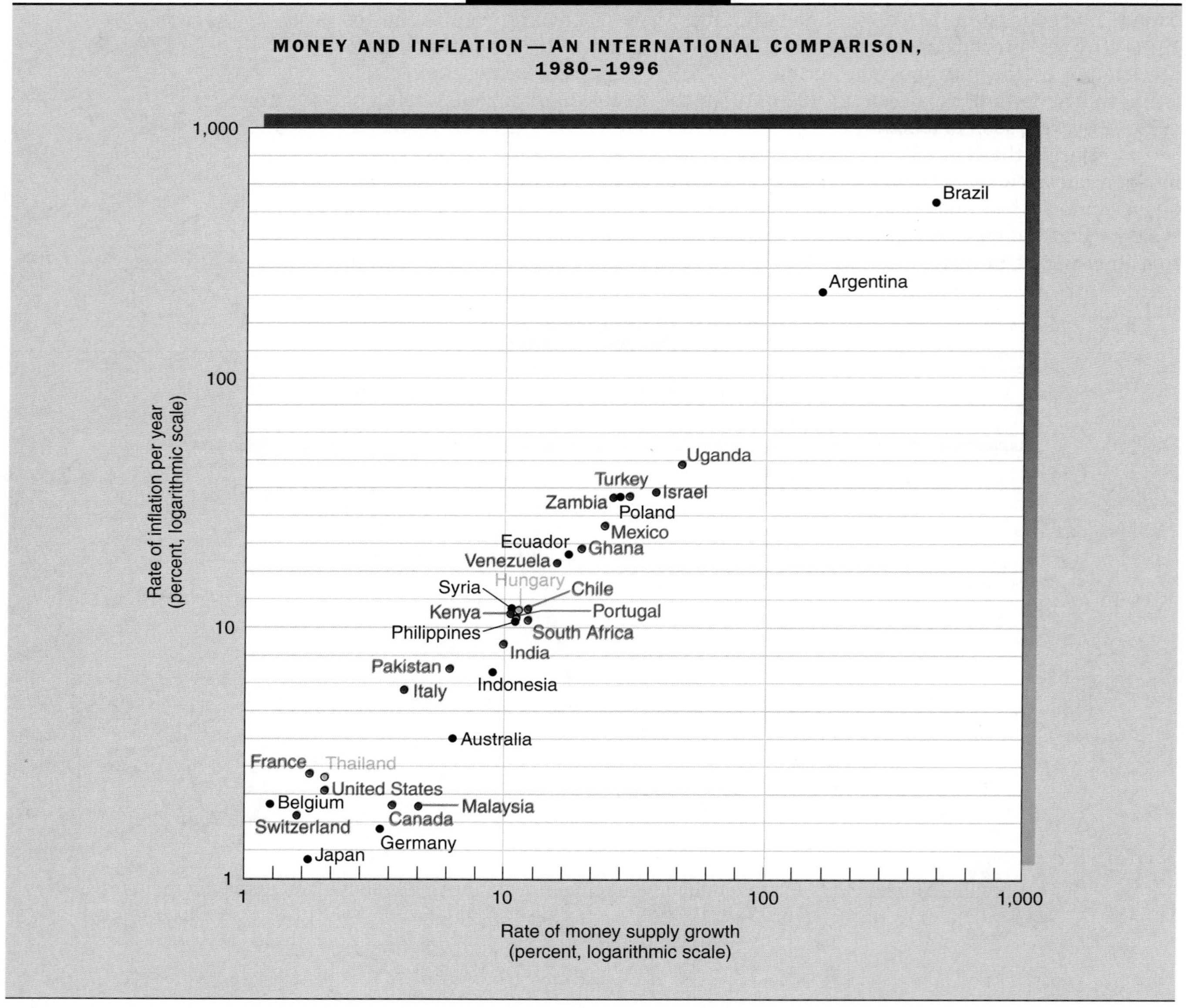

The relationship between the average annual growth rate of the money supply and the rate of inflation is shown here for the 1980–1996 period. Clearly, there is a close relationship between the two. Higher rates of money growth lead to higher rates of inflation.

Note: The money supply data are the actual growth rate of the money supply minus the growth rate of real GDP.

SOURCES: International Monetary Fund, International Financial Statistics Yearbook, 1997 *and* International Financial Statistics *(December 1998).*

of change in the price level, we will compare it with a short-term nominal interest rate—the three-month Treasury bill rate. Our theory implies that nominal interest rates will tend to rise with the rate of inflation. The empirical evidence indicates that is indeed the case. As the inflation rate rose significantly during the late 1960s, so also did the nominal rate of interest. During the 1970s, sharp increases in the inflation rate, particularly during 1977–1980, were accompanied by substantial increases in the nominal interest rate. Similarly, as the inflation rate decelerated from the double-digit levels of the late 1970s, the money interest rate also plunged during the 1980–1987 period. Later, a modest increase in the inflation rate during 1988–1990 resulted in a similar modest increase in short-term interest rates. Finally, as the inflation rate declined to its lowest level in 20 years in 1993, so did nominal interest rates. These data provide strong evidence that, just as our theory predicts, the choices of borrowers and lenders are strongly influenced by the inflation rate and expectations concerning its path in the future.

A major implication of our analysis is that rapid growth rates in the money supply over long periods of time will be associated with high rates of inflation. **Exhibit 14–13** presents data on the annual growth rate of the money supply (adjusted for the growth rate of the nation's output) and the rate of inflation for a diverse set of countries during the 1980–1996 period. The results clearly illustrate the linkage between monetary policy and inflation. Countries with single-digit rates of money growth—for example, Belgium, Japan, Switzerland, and the United States—experienced single-digit rates of inflation. Similarly, countries with rates of money growth in the 15 percent to 45 percent range experienced rates of inflation in this same range. The data for Hungary, Chile, Ecuador, Ghana, and Mexico illustrate this point. Finally, look at the data for Argentina and Brazil. The average annual rate of money growth of both countries was exceedingly high—200 percent and up—during this period. Predictably, the hyper money growth led to hyperinflation.

Just as economic theory indicates, money growth and inflation are closely linked in the long run. Persistently low rates of money growth lead to low rates of inflation. Similarly, high rates of money growth lead to high rates of inflation. When considered over a lengthy time period, this linkage between money growth and inflation is one of the more consistent empirical relations in all economics.

LOOKING Ahead

As we discussed in this chapter, theory indicates that the impact of monetary policy will be influenced by whether economic agents anticipate its effects. Thus far, we have said little about how decision makers form expectations about the future. The next chapter will consider this important issue.

KEY POINTS

➤ The quantity of money people want to hold is inversely related to the money rate of interest, because higher interest rates make it more costly to hold money instead of interest-earning assets like bonds. The supply of money is vertical because it is determined by the Fed. The money interest rate will gravitate toward the rate where the quantity of money people want to hold is just equal to the stock of money the Fed has supplied.

➤ The impact of a shift in monetary policy is generally transmitted through interest rates, exchange rates, and asset prices.

➤ When instituting a more expansionary monetary policy, the Fed generally buys bonds, which will both increase bond prices and create additional bank reserves, placing downward pressure on real interest rates. In the short run, an *unanticipated* shift to a more expansionary policy will stimulate aggregate demand and thereby increase output and employment.

➤ When instituting a more restrictive monetary policy, the Fed sells bonds, which will depress bond prices and drain reserves from the banking system. An unanticipated shift to a more restrictive monetary policy will increase real interest rates and reduce aggregate demand, output, and employment in the short run.

➤ The quantity theory of money postulates that the velocity of money is constant (or approximately so) and that real output is independent of monetary factors. When these assumptions hold, an increase in the stock of money will lead to a proportional increase in the price level.

➤ In the long run, the primary impact of monetary policy will be on prices rather than on real output. When expansionary monetary policy leads to rising prices, decision makers eventually anticipate the higher inflation rate and build it into their choices. As this happens, money interest rates, wages, and incomes will reflect the expectation of inflation, so real interest rates, wages, and output will return to their long-run normal levels.

➤ When the effects of expansionary monetary policy are anticipated prior to their occurrence, the short-run impact of an increase in the money supply is similar to its impact in the long run. Nominal prices and interest rates rise, but real output remains unchanged.

➤ While the Fed can strongly influence short-term interest rates, its impact on long-term rates is much more limited. Interest rates can be a misleading indicator of monetary policy. In the long run, expansionary monetary policy leads to inflation and high interest rates, rather than low interest rates. Similarly, restrictive monetary policy when pursued over a lengthy time period leads to low inflation and low interest rates.

➤ The empirical evidence indicates that changes in monetary policy influence real GDP in the short run.

➤ Both the U.S. experience and international comparisons strongly indicate that persistent, rapid growth in the money supply is closely linked with inflation. Countries with low (high) rates of growth in the money supply tend to experience low (high) rates of inflation.

CRITICAL ANALYSIS QUESTIONS

1. Why do people hold money? How will an increase in the interest rate influence the amount of money that people will want to hold?

*2. How would each of the following influence the quantity of money that you would like to hold?
   a. An increase in the interest rate on checking deposits
   b. An increase in the expected rate of inflation
   c. An increase in income
   d. An increase in the differential interest rate between money market mutual funds and checking deposits

*3. What is the opportunity cost of the following: (a) obtaining a $100,000 house, (b) holding the house during the next year, (c) obtaining $1,000, and (d) holding the $1,000 in your checking account during the next year?

4. Historically, shifts toward more expansionary monetary policy have often been associated with increases in real output. Why? Would a more expansionary policy increase the long-term growth rate of real GDP? Why or why not?

5. What impact will an unanticipated increase in the money supply have on the real interest rate, real output, and employment in the short run? How will expansionary monetary policy affect the economy when the effects are widely anticipated? Why does it make a difference whether the effects of monetary policy are anticipated?

6. How rapidly has the money supply (M1) grown during the past 12 months? How rapidly has M2 grown? Do you think the monetary authorities should increase or decrease the growth rate of the money supply during the next year? Why? (The data necessary to answer this question for the United States are available in the *Federal Reserve Bulletin*.)

*7. If the Fed shifts to a more restrictive monetary policy, it will generally sell bonds in the open market. How will this action influence each of the following? Briefly explain each of your answers.
   a. The reserves available to banks
   b. Real interest rates
   c. Household spending on consumer durables
   d. The exchange rate value of the dollar
   e. Net exports

f. The prices of stocks and real assets like apartment or office buildings
g. Real GDP

8. Will a budget deficit be more expansionary if it is financed by borrowing from the Federal Reserve or from the general public? Explain.

9. Political officials often call on the monetary authorities to expand the money supply more rapidly so that interest rates can be reduced. Will expansionary monetary policy reduce interest rates in the short run? Will it do so in the long run? Explain. The highest interest rates in the world are found in countries that expand the supply of money rapidly. Can you explain why?

*10. Many economists believe that there is a "long and variable time lag" between when a change in monetary policy is instituted and when the change exerts its primary impact on output, employment, and prices. If true, how does this long and variable time lag affect the ability of policy makers to use monetary policy as a stabilization tool?

*11. "Historically, when interest rates are high, the inflation rate is high. High interest rates are a major cause of inflation." Evaluate this statement.

*12. If the supply of money is constant, how will an increase in the demand for money influence aggregate demand?

13. a. What is the quantity theory of money?
b. Is the quantity theory of money valid?
c. Is it a complete theory with regard to the impact of shifts in monetary policy on the economy? Why or why not?

*14. The accompanying chart presents data on the money supply, price level, and real GDP for three countries during the 1993–1996 period.
a. Fill in the missing data.
b. Which country followed the most expansionary monetary policy (highest average rate of growth in the money supply) between 1993 and 1996?
c. Which country experienced the highest average annual rate of inflation during the 1993–1996 period?
d. Which country experienced the most rapid increase in real output during the 1993–1996 period?

*Asterisk denotes questions for which answers are given in Appendix B.

	Money Supply (in billions of local currency)	GDP Deflator (1990 = 100)	Nominal GDP (in current currency units)	Real GDP (in 1990 currency units)	Percent Rate of Change	
					Money Supply	Price Level
United States						
1993	1,231	109.7	6,553	_____	X	X
1994	1,232	112.2	6,936	_____	_____	_____
1995	1,221	115.0	7,254	_____	_____	_____
1996	1,238	117.2	7,576	_____	_____	_____
Chile						
1993	1,629	157.3	18,454	_____	X	X
1994	1,892	179.2	21,918	_____	_____	_____
1995	2,313	201.1	26,702	_____	_____	_____
1996	2,687	208.2	29,645	_____	_____	_____
Venezuela						
1993	409	205.0	5,454	_____	X	X
1994	981	334.1	8,632	_____	_____	_____
1995	1,367	505.5	13,504	_____	_____	_____
1996	1,349	1,068.8	28,091	_____	_____	_____

SOURCE: International Monetary Fund, International Financial Yearbook, 1997.

CHAPTER 15

Unfortunately, policymakers cannot act as if the economy is an automobile that can quickly be steered back and forth. Rather, the procedure of changing aggregate demand is much closer to that of a captain navigating a giant super-tanker. Even if he gives a signal for a hard turn, it takes a mile before he can see a change, and ten miles before the ship makes the turn.

Robert J. Gordon[1]

Stabilization Policy, Output, and Employment

CHAPTER FOCUS

- Historically, how much has real output fluctuated? Are economic fluctuations becoming more or less severe?
- Can active use of discretionary macroeconomic policy moderate the business cycle?
- Why is proper timing of changes in macroeconomic policy both crucially important and difficult to achieve?
- How are expectations formed? Do expectations influence how macroeconomic policy works?
- What is the modern view of stabilization policy?
- Did perverse macroeconomic policy cause the Great Depression?

[1]Robert J. Gordon, *Macroeconomics* (Boston: Little, Brown, 1978), p. 334.

In previous chapters we have analyzed the impact of both fiscal and monetary policy on output, employment, and prices. We have also noted that the initial impact of policy changes often differs from the impact over a more lengthy time period. We now want to consider the potential of macro policy as a stabilization tool. Can active management of fiscal and/or monetary policy reduce economic instability? What types of fiscal and monetary policy are best for the economy? This chapter will focus on the tools that enhance and the factors that limit the achievement of a stable economic environment. We will also consider alternative theories about how expectations are formed and investigate their implications with regard to how macroeconomic policy works. We will begin by taking a look at the magnitude of economic fluctuations during this century.

ECONOMIC FLUCTUATIONS—THE HISTORICAL RECORD

Wide fluctuations in the general level of business activity—in income, employment, and the price level—make personal economic planning extremely difficult. Such changes can cause even well-devised investment plans to go awry. The tragic stories of unemployed workers begging for food and newly impoverished investors jumping out of windows during the Great Depression vividly portray the enormous personal and social costs of economic instability and the uncertainty that it generates.

Historically, substantial fluctuations in real output have occurred. **Exhibit 15–1** illustrates the growth record of real GDP in the United States during the past 90 years. Prior to the Second World War, double-digit swings in real GDP during a single year were not uncommon. Real GDP rose by more than 10 percent annually during the First World War, during an economic boom in 1922, during a mid-1930s recovery, and again during the Second World War. In contrast, output fell at an annual rate of 5 percent or more during the 1920–1921 recession, in the depression years of 1930–1932 and 1938, and again following the Second World War. Since 1950, economic ups and downs have been more moderate. Nevertheless, substantial fluctuations are still observable.

PROMOTING ECONOMIC STABILITY—ACTIVIST AND NONACTIVIST VIEWS

There is widespread agreement concerning the goals of macroeconomic policy. Economists of almost all persuasions believe that the performance of a market economy would be improved if economic fluctuations were minimal, the general level of prices stable, and employment maintained at a high level (unemployment at the natural rate).

EXHIBIT 15–1

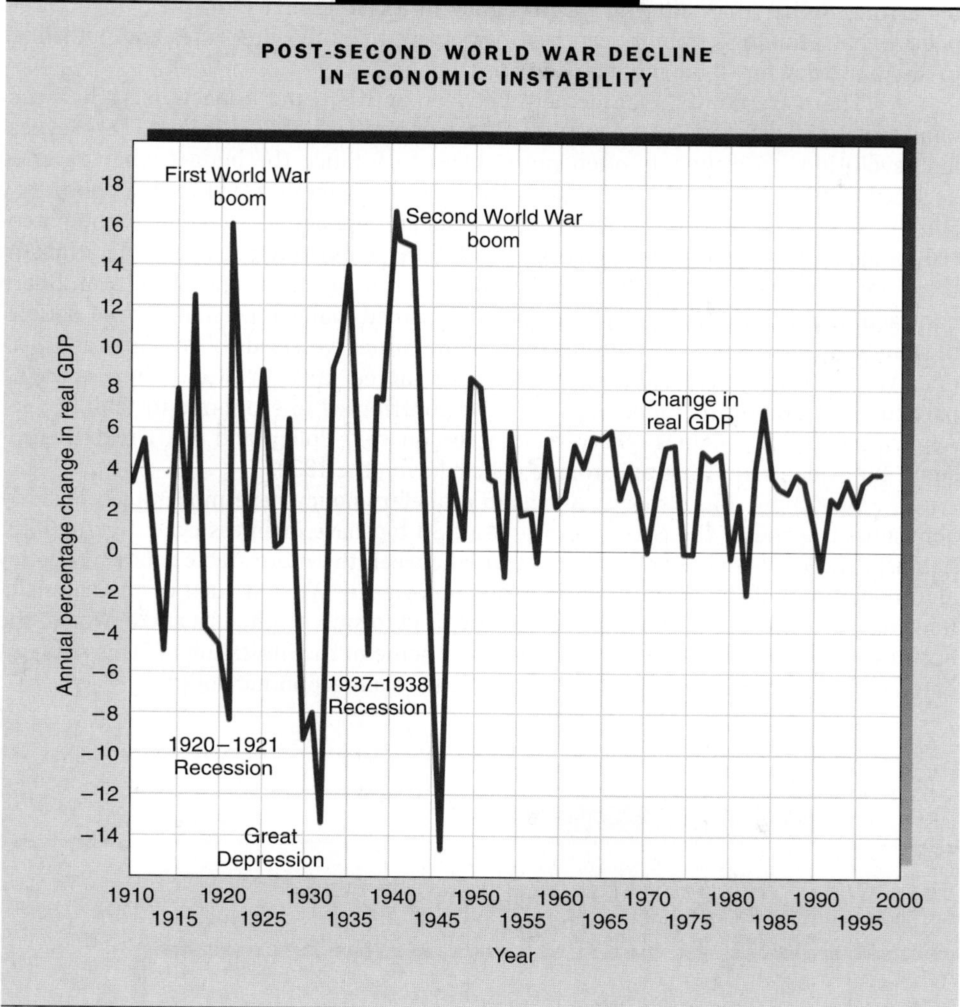

Prior to the conclusion of the Second World War, the United States experienced double-digit increases in real GDP in 1918, 1922, 1935–1936, and 1941–1943. In contrast, real output fell by 5 percent or more in 1920–1921, 1930–1932, 1938, and 1946. As illustrated here, fluctuations in real GDP have moderated during the last four decades. Most economists believe that more appropriate macro policy—particularly monetary policy—deserves much of the credit (see Exhibit 15–2).

SOURCES: Historical Statistics of the United States, *p. 224; and* Economic Report of the President, 1999.

How to achieve these goals is, however, a hot topic of debate among macroeconomists. Many economists argue that the major macroeconomic goals can best be achieved through the active use of discretionary monetary and fiscal policy. The proponents of an **activist strategy** believe that macro policy can be used successfully to speed the adjustment process and reduce the swings of the business cycle. Activists often argue that the economy's self-corrective mechanism works slowly. Therefore, when economic shocks disrupt equilibrium, policy makers will be able to manage demand in a manner that will keep the economy on track and minimize the adverse consequences of unexpected shocks.

Activist strategy
Deliberate changes in monetary and fiscal policy in order to inject demand stimulus during a recession and apply restraint during an inflationary boom and thereby, it is hoped, minimize economic instability.

In contrast with activists, **nonactivists** argue that discretionary use of monetary and fiscal policy in response to changing economic conditions is likely to do more harm than good. According to the nonactivist view, the economy's self-corrective mechanism, if not stifled by perverse macro policy, will prevent prolonged periods of economic decline and high unemployment. Nonactivists charge that erratic policy, particularly the instability of monetary policy, is a major source of economic fluctuations. They note that the really serious cases of economic instability, such as the Great

Nonactivist strategy
The maintenance of the same monetary and fiscal policy—that is, no change in money growth, tax rates, or expenditures—during all phases of the business cycle.

Depression of the 1930s and the inflation of the 1970s, were primarily the result of policy errors. Rather than altering macro policy in a discretionary manner, nonactivists believe that economic stability can best be achieved by following rules and guidelines that will provide for stable monetary and fiscal policy.

There are points of agreement between activists and nonactivists. Both recognize that policy errors have contributed to economic instability. Prior to the Keynesian revolution, governments often raised taxes to balance the budget when revenue declined during a recession. Of course, modern analysis implies that such a policy may add to the severity of a recession. Both activists and nonactivists recognize the potential dangers of monetary instability. As **Exhibit 15–2** illustrates, extreme gyrations in the money supply characterized monetary policy prior to the Second World War. Sharp contractions in the money supply often accompanied major recessions, while double-digit money growth was observed during the inflationary periods of the First and Second World Wars. Activists and nonactivists agree that erratic policy changes, particularly those in the monetary area, have contributed to economic instability. (See Applications in Economics, "Perverse Macroeconomic Policy and the Great Depression," for evidence on the tragic role of policy during the 1930s.)

As Exhibit 15–2 shows, swings in monetary policy have moderated considerably since the end of the Second World War. So too have business cycle fluctuations. Activists and nonactivists agree that the link between the more stable monetary policy and moderation of the business cycle is no coincidence. We now turn to an analysis of how macroeconomic policy might be actively used to smooth the ups and downs of the business cycle. As we proceed, we will consider some of the limitations of this strategy. Later, we will also present the nonactivist view of macroeconomic policy.

EXHIBIT 15–2

POST–SECOND WORLD WAR DECLINE IN MONETARY INSTABILITY

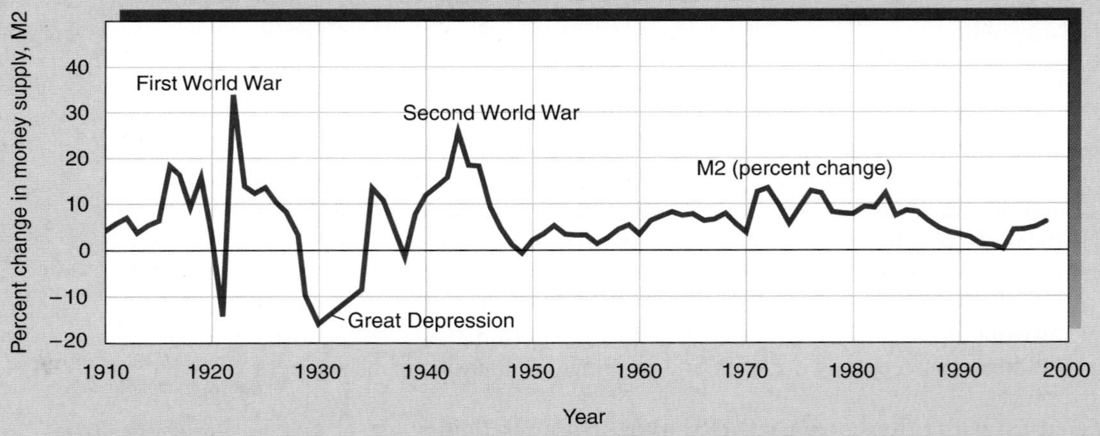

Prior to 1950, monetary policy was characterized by wide swings. Huge increases (15 percent or more) in the supply of money (M2) for a year or two were often followed by sharp contractions. Since the end of the Second World War, the fluctuations in the supply of money have declined, as the monetary authorities followed a more stable course.

SOURCE: Economic Report of the President, 1999; *and Robert J. Gordon,* Macroeconomics *(Glenview, Ill.: Scott Foresman, 1990).*

APPLICATIONS IN ECONOMICS

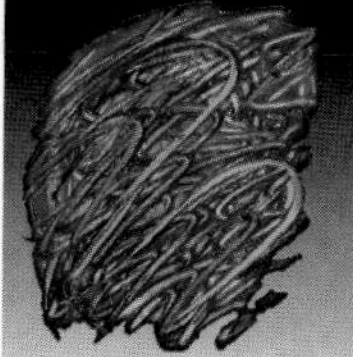

Perverse Macroeconomic Policy and the Great Depression

As we previously discussed, the Great Depression exerted an enormous impact both on economic thought and on economic institutions. Table 1 presents data that illustrate both the severity and length of the economic contraction. For four successive years (1930–1933), real output fell. Unemployment soared to nearly one-quarter of the workforce in 1932 and 1933. Although recovery did take place during 1934–1937, the economy again fell into the depth of depression in 1938. Ten years after the catastrophe began, real GDP was virtually the same as it had been in 1929.[1]

Armed with knowledge of how monetary and fiscal policies work, one can clearly see that at least the severity of the calamity was the result of perverse macroeconomic policy. Three important factors contributed to the economic collapse of the 1930s.

1. ***A sharp reduction in the supply of money during 1930–1933 reduced aggregate demand and real output.*** The supply of money expanded slowly but steadily throughout the 1920s.[2] As Table 1 shows, monetary policy suddenly shifted in 1930. The money supply fell by 6.9 percent during 1930, by 10.9 percent in 1931, and by 4.7 percent in 1932. As banks failed and the money supply collapsed, the Fed failed to inject new reserves into the system. Neither did it act as a lender of last resort. The quantity of money in 1933 was 27 percent less than in 1929! A sudden shift to a restrictive monetary policy will reduce both aggregate demand and real output. A drastic reduction in the money supply, such as that of the early 1930s, is likely to result in a drastic reduction in output. This is precisely what happened. Real output plunged. By 1933, real GDP was 29 percent lower than the 1929 level.

2. ***A large tax increase in the midst of a severe recession made a bad situation worse.*** Prior to the Keynesian revolution, the dominant view was that the federal budget should be balanced. Reflecting the ongoing economic downturn, the federal budget ran a deficit in 1931, and an even larger deficit was shaping up for 1932. Assisted by the newly elected Democratic majority in the House of Representatives, the Republican Hoover administration passed the largest peacetime tax-rate increase in the history of the United States. At the bottom of the income scale, marginal tax rates were raised from 1.5 percent to 4 percent in 1932. At the top of the scale, tax rates were raised from 25 percent to 63 percent. As our prior analysis of fiscal policy suggests, a huge tax increase in the midst of a severe recession will further reduce aggregate demand and the incentive to earn. Table 1 shows the degree to which this happened. As tax rates

TABLE 1

THE ECONOMIC RECORD OF THE GREAT DEPRESSION

Year	Real GDP in 1989 Dollars (billions)	Implicit GDP Deflator (1929 = 100)	Unemployment Rate	Changes in the Money Suppply (M1)
1929	821.8	100.0	3.2	+1.0
1930	748.9	96.8	8.7	−6.9
1931	691.3	88.0	15.9	−10.9
1932	599.7	77.6	23.6	−4.7
1933	587.1	76.0	24.9	−2.9
1934	632.6	82.4	21.7	+10.0
1935	681.3	84.8	20.1	+18.2
1936	777.9	84.8	16.9	+13.9
1937	811.4	89.6	14.3	+4.7
1938	778.9	87.2	19.0	−1.3
1939	840.7	86.4	17.2	+12.1

SOURCE: Economic Report of the President: 1993 *(Washington, D.C.: U.S. Government Printing Office, 1993); and Bureau of the Census,* The Statistical History of the United States from Colonial Times to the Present *(New York; Basic Books, 1976).*

(continued)

Perhaps the most catastrophic example of inappropriate stabilization policy was that of the Great Depression. A sharp reduction in the supply of money, a huge tax increase, and protectionist trade policies turned a recession into the worst depression in U.S. history.

were increased in 1932, real GDP fell by 13.3 percent. Unemployment rose from 15.9 percent in 1931 to 23.6 percent in 1932.

3. ***Tariff increases retarded international exchange.*** Concerned about low agricultural prices, an influx of imports, rising unemployment, and declining tax revenues, Congress adopted various trade restraints. Tariffs (taxes on imported goods) on a wide range of products were increased substantially in early 1930.[3] Other countries promptly responded by increasing their tariffs, further reducing the volume of trade between nations. As the flow of trade diminished, so too did the mutual gains trading partners derive from specialization and exchange.

When discussing the Great Depression, historians often stress the role of the 1929 stock market crash. Since the stock market crash diminished the wealth of many, it was a contributing factor to the reduction in aggregate demand and output. However, the severity of the Great Depression was the result of disastrous macroeconomic policy, not an inevitable consequence of a stock market crash. The experience following the October 1987 crash illustrates this point. In just a few days, the stock market lost a third of its value in 1987, just as it did in 1929. But that is where the parallel ends. In contrast with the response to the 1929 crash, in 1987 the Fed moved quickly to supply reserves to the banking system. The money supply did not fall. Tax rates were not increased. And even though there was a lot of political rhetoric about "the need to protect American businesses," trade barriers were not raised. In short, sensible policies were followed subsequent to the crash of 1987. Continued growth and stability were the result. Inadvertently, perverse macroeconomic policies were followed subsequent to the crash of 1929. Economic disaster was the result.

---

[1]See Robert J. Samuelson, "Great Depression," in *The Fortune Encyclopedia of Economics*, ed. David R. Henderson (New York: Warner Books, 1993), for an interesting and informative commentary on this time period.

[2]From 1921 through 1929, the money stock expanded at an annual rate of 2.7 percent, slightly less rapidly than the growth in the output of goods and services. Thus, the 1920s were a decade of price stability, even of slight deflation.

[3]The high-tariff policy was ineffective as a revenue measure. Even though the taxes on imported goods were increased by approximately 50 percent, imports declined so sharply that tariff revenues fell from $602 million in 1929 to $328 million in 1932.

THE CONDUCT OF DISCRETIONARY STABILIZATION POLICY

Macroeconomic policy reduces instability only if it injects stimulus and applies restraint at the proper phase of the business cycle. Proper timing is the key to effective stabilization policy. But how can policy makers know whether they should be stimulating aggregate demand or applying the economic brake?

Of course, economic indicators, such as the growth of real GDP and the rate of unemployment, provide policy makers with information on the current state of the economy. However, this is not exactly what policy makers need. Because it takes time for macroeconomic policy to work, policy makers really need to know about the future—where the economy is going to be six to twelve months from now. They need to know whether a business recession or an inflationary boom is around the corner. If they do not know where the economy is going, a policy change may fail to exert its primary impact quickly enough to offset a downturn or restrain future inflation.

How can policy makers find out where the economy is going in the future and when a turn in the macroeconomic road is about to occur? The two most widely used sources of information on the future direction of the economy are the index of leading economic indicators and economic forecasting models.

Index of Leading Indicators

The **index of leading indicators** is a composite statistic based on 10 key variables that generally turn down prior to a recession and turn up before the beginning of a business expansion (see Measures of Economic Activity, "Index of Leading Indicators"). **Exhibit 15–3** illustrates the path of the index during the 1950–1998 period. Two or three consecutive monthly declines in the index are considered a warning that the economy is about to dip into a recession. This index has forecast each of the eight recessions since 1950. On four occasions, the downturn occurred eight to eleven months prior to a recession, providing policy makers with sufficient lead time to modify policy, particularly monetary policy. There has been significant variability, however, in the lead time of the index. Sometimes it is exceedingly short—the index declined just five months prior to the recession of 1954. In other instances it has been quite lengthy, as when it turned

Index of leading indicators
An index of economic variables that historically has tended to turn down prior to the beginning of a recession and turn up prior to the beginning of a business expansion.

EXHIBIT 15–3

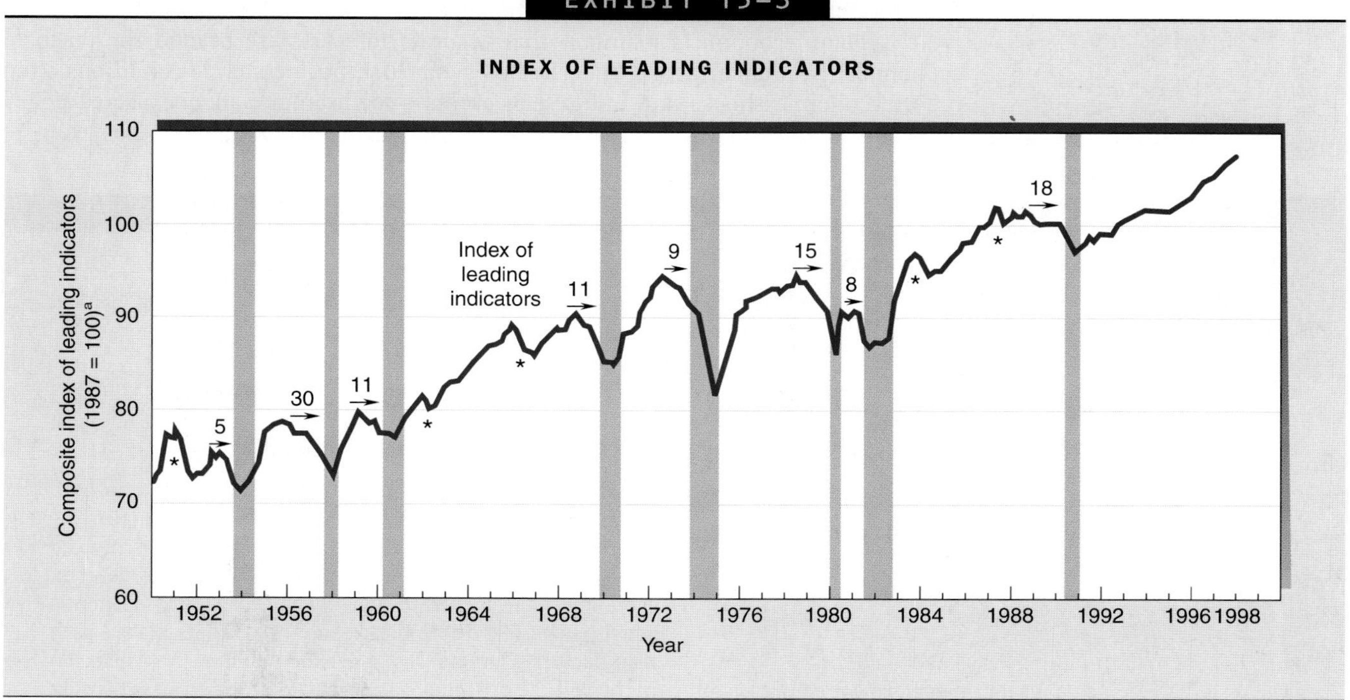

The shaded periods represent business recessions. The index of leading indicators forecast each of the eight recessions during the 1950–1993 period. As the arrows show, however, the time lag between when the index turned down and when the economy fell into a recession varied. In addition, on five occasions (1950–1951, 1962, 1966, 1984, and 1987), the index forecast a recession that did not occur.

[a]*The arrows indicate the number of months that the downturn in the index preceded a recession. An asterisk (*) indicates a false signal of a recession.*

SOURCE: Conference Board, Business Cycle Indicators.

down 30 months prior to the recession of 1957–1958 and 18 months prior to the 1990–1991 recession.

A downturn in the index is not always an accurate indicator of the future. On five occasions (1950–1951, 1962, 1966, 1984, and 1987), a decline in the index of leading indicators forecast a future recession that did not materialize. This has given rise to the quip that the index has accurately forecast thirteen of the last eight recessions.

Forecasting Models

Economists have developed highly complex econometric (statistical) models to improve the accuracy of macroeconomic forecasts. In essence, these models use past data on economic interrelationships to project how currently observed changes will influence the future path of key economic variables, such as real GDP, employment, and the price level. The most elaborate of these models use hundreds of variables and equations to simulate the various sectors and macroeconomic markets. Powerful, high-speed computers are employed to analyze the effects of various policy alternatives and attempt to predict the future.

To date, the record of computer forecasting models is mixed. When economic conditions are relatively stable (for example, when the growth of real GDP and the rate of inflation follow a steady trend), the models have generally provided accurate forecasts for both aggregate economic variables and important subcomponents of the economy. Unfortunately, however, they have generally missed the major turns in the economic road. For example, none of the major computer models forecast either the 1982 recession or the sharp decline in the inflation rate during the period 1982–1984.

Many economists maintain that accurate forecasts are beyond the reach of economics. Two major factors underlie this view. First, business cycle conditions often reflect economic shocks and unforeseen events—for example, an unexpected policy

MEASURES OF ECONOMIC ACTIVITY

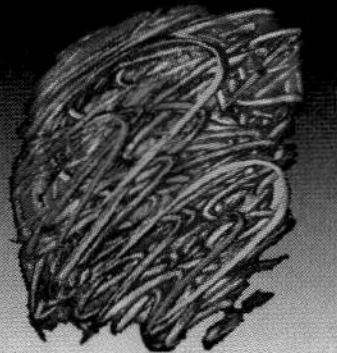

Index of Leading Indicators

History indicates that no single indicator is able to forecast accurately the future direction of the economy. However, several economic variables do tend to reach a high or low prior to the peak of a business expansion or the trough of an economic recession. Such variables are called leading economic indicators.

To provide more reliable information on the future direction of the economy, economists have devised an index of 10 such indicators:

1. Length of the average workweek in hours
2. Initial weekly claims for unemployment compensation
3. New orders placed with manufacturers
4. Percentage of companies receiving slower deliveries from suppliers
5. Contracts and orders for new plants and equipment
6. Permits for new housing starts
7. Interest rate spread, 10-year Treasury bonds less Fed funds rate
8. Index of consumer expectations
9. Change in the index of stock prices (500 common stocks)
10. Change in the money supply (M2)

The variables included in the index were chosen both because of their tendency to lead (or predict) turns in the business cycle and because they are available frequently and promptly. In some cases, it is easy to see why a change in an economic indicator precedes a change in general economic activity. Consider the indicator of "new orders placed with manufacturers" (measured in constant dollars). An expansion in the volume of orders is generally followed by an expansion in manufacturing output. Similarly, manufacturers will tend to scale back their future production when a decline in new orders signals the probability of weak future demand for their products. The index of leading indicators is published by the Conference Board in *Business Cycle Indicators*.

change, discovery of a new resource or technology, abnormal weather, or political upheaval in an important oil-exporting nation. There is no reason to believe that economists or anyone else will be able to predict such changes accurately and consistently. Thus, while economic theory helps to predict the implications of unforeseen events, it cannot foretell what those events will be and when they might occur. Second, the critics of forecasting models argue that the future will differ from the past because people will often make different choices as the result of what they learned from previous events. Therefore, forecasting models based on past relationships—including elaborate computer models—will never be able to generate consistently accurate predictions.

Market Signals and Discretionary Monetary Policy

Some economists believe that information supplied by certain markets can also provide policy makers with an early warning of the need to institute a change in policy. For example, since they fluctuate daily and are determined in auction markets, changes in commodity prices often foretell future changes in the general price level. An increase in a broad index of commodity prices implies that money is plentiful (relative to demand). This suggests the Fed should shift toward a more restrictive policy in order to offset future inflation. In contrast, falling commodity prices indicate that deflation is a potential future danger, in which case the Fed might want to shift toward a more expansionary policy.

Exchange rates also provide policy makers with information about the relative scarcity of money and fear of inflation. Because exchange rates, to a degree, reflect the willingness of foreigners to hold U.S. dollars, a decline in the exchange-rate value of the dollar (the value of the dollar relative to other currencies) often implies a fear of higher inflation and a reluctance to hold dollars. This would signal the need to shift to a more restrictive policy. Conversely, an increase in the exchange-rate value of the dollar is a strong vote of confidence in the future purchasing power of the dollar. This provides the Fed with some leeway to move toward a more expansionary policy.

Commodity prices, exchange rates, and other market signals can help us judge the early effects and likely future impact of current policies. They are best used as a supplement to, rather than as a substitute for, other economic indicators and forecasting devices.

Discretionary Policy—The Activist View

Activists recognize that it is difficult to institute countercyclical macroeconomic policy. However, they believe that the index of leading indicators, forecasting models, sensitive market variables, and other economic indicators provide policy makers with an early warning system. Thus, they are able to alter policy in a manner that will smooth business ups and downs. Responding to the early signals, policy makers can initially undertake moderate changes. With the passage of time, more substantial changes can be instituted if more comprehensive information indicates they are needed.

The following scenario outlines the essentials of the activist view. Suppose the economy were about to dip into a recession. Prior to the recession, the index of leading indicators would almost surely alert policy makers to the possibility of a downturn. This would permit them to shift toward macroeconomic stimulus, expanding the money supply more rapidly. Initially, the shift toward macroeconomic stimulus could be applied in moderate doses, which could easily be reversed in the future if necessary. On the other hand, if the signs of a downturn became more pronounced and current business conditions actually weakened, additional stimulus could be injected. Perhaps a tax reduction or a speedup in government expenditures might be used to supplement the more expansionary monetary policy.

Policy makers can constantly monitor the situation, adjusting their actions as additional information becomes available. If the weakness persists, the expansionary policy can be continued. Conversely, when the signs point to a strong recovery, policy makers can move toward restraint and thereby head off potential inflationary pressure. According to the activist view, policy makers are more likely to keep the economy on track when they are free to apply stimulus or restraint based on forecasting devices and current economic indicators.

Lags and the Problem of Timing

Discretionary changes in both monetary and fiscal policy must be timed appropriately if they are going to exert a stabilizing influence on the economy. There are three time lags that make proper timing difficult. First, there is the **recognition lag,** the time period between a change in economic conditions and recognition of the change by policy makers. It generally takes a few months to gather and tabulate reliable information on the recent performance of the economy in order to determine whether it has dipped into a recession or whether the inflation rate has accelerated, and so forth.

Recognition lag
The time period after a policy change is needed from a stabilization standpoint but before the need is recognized by policy makers.

Second, even after the need for a policy change is recognized, there is generally an additional time period before the policy change is instituted. Economists refer to this delay as **administrative lag.** In the case of monetary policy, the administrative lag is generally quite short. The Federal Open Market Committee meets monthly and is in a position to institute a change in monetary policy quickly. This is a major advantage of monetary policy. For discretionary fiscal policy, the administrative lag is likely to be much longer. Congressional committees must meet. Legislation must be proposed and debated. Congress must act, and the president must consent. Each of these steps takes time.

Administrative lag
The time period after the need for a policy change is recognized but before the policy is actually implemented.

Finally, there is the **impact lag,** the time period between the implementation of a macro policy change and when the change exerts its primary impact on the economy. Although the impact of a change in tax rates is generally felt quickly, the expansionary effects of an increase in government expenditures are usually much less rapid. It will take time for the submission of competitive bids and the letting of new contracts. Several months may pass before work on a new project actually begins. The impact lag in the case of monetary policy is likely to be even longer. The time period between a shift in monetary policy, a change in interest rates, and, in turn, a change in the level of spending may be quite lengthy.

Impact lag
The time period after a policy change is implemented but before the change begins to exert its primary effects.

Economists who have studied this topic, including Milton Friedman and Robert Gordon, conclude that the combined duration of these time lags is generally 12 to 18 months in the case of monetary policy, and even longer in the case of fiscal policy. This means that, if a policy is going to exert the desired effect at the proper time, policy makers cannot wait until a problem develops before they act. Rather, they must correctly forecast the future direction of the economy and act before there is a contraction in real GDP or an observable increase in the rate of inflation. Given our ability to forecast the future, nonactivists argue that proper timing of discretionary policy changes is unrealistic. Furthermore, even if forecasting were a more precise science, the time lags accompanying changes in monetary and fiscal policies are long and variable. This also reduces the viability of discretionary policy as a stabilization tool.

Exhibit 15–4 presents a graphic illustration of the difference between the views of the activists and nonactivists. When the economy begins to dip into a recession, activists argue that policy makers can reasonably be expected to recognize the danger and shift to a more expansionary policy at point *B*. If the demand-stimulus

EXHIBIT 15-4

TIME LAGS AND EFFECTS OF DISCRETIONARY POLICY

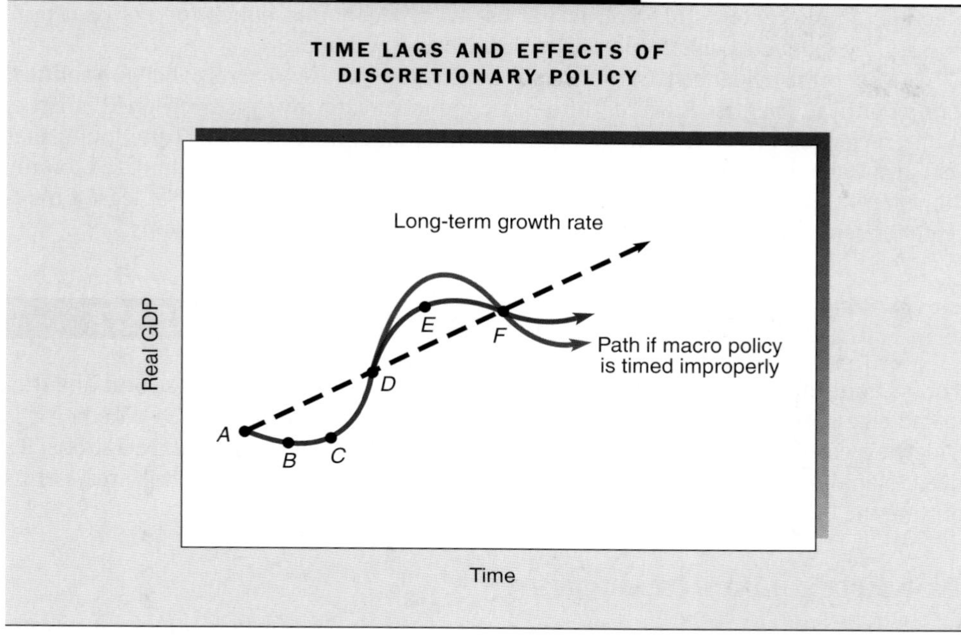

Beginning with A, we illustrate the path of a hypothetical business cycle. If a forthcoming recession can be recognized quickly and a more expansionary policy instituted at point B, the policy may add stimulus at point C and help to minimize the magnitude of the downturn. Activists believe that discretionary policy is likely to achieve this outcome. However, if delays result in the adoption of the expansionary policy at C and if it does not exert its major impact until D, the demand stimulus will exacerbate the inflationary boom. In turn, an anti-inflationary strategy instituted at E may exert its primary effects at F, just in time to increase the severity of a recession beyond F. Nonactivists fear that improper timing of discretionary macro policy will exert such destabilizing effects.

effects are felt quickly (before the economy gets to point *C*), the shift to the more expansionary macro policy will help to minimize the decline in output accompanying the business downturn.

In contrast, nonactivists believe that policy makers are unlikely to act so quickly, and, even if they did, the time lags accompanying changes in monetary and fiscal policies are likely to make their actions ineffective. The shift to the more expansionary policy will not come until point *C*, according to this reasoning, and its effects will not be significant until point *D*. In this case, the expansionary policy will contribute to the severity of the inflationary boom (beyond point *D*). Similarly, a subsequent shift to an anti-inflationary policy may begin to exert its major impact at point *F*, just in time to make an oncoming recession worse (beyond point *F*). Therefore, nonactivists believe that discretionary policy shifts are likely to be destabilizing rather than stabilizing.

Politics and the Timing of Policy Changes

Public-choice analysis has led to an increased awareness of another potential pitfall of discretionary policy-making: Macro policy may be used to pursue political objectives rather than stabilization. In a democracy, macro policy will be designed by elected representatives, an elected president, and officials (such as the Board of Governors of the Federal Reserve) who are appointed by the elected president. Like other policy choices, macro policy provides political entrepreneurs with a potential tool for furthering their political objectives. Predictably, discretionary macro policy choices will be influenced by political considerations. It is naive to expect otherwise.

The nature of the political process, particularly the shortsightedness effect, provides politicians with little incentive to look beyond the next election. Expansionary policies 12 to 18 months prior to an election can generally stimulate output and employment, getting the economy in great shape by election day. Because demand-stimulus policies generally affect output before they begin to exert a major impact on the price level, the inflationary effects of such a policy may be minimal prior to the election. To the extent that politicians use macroeconomic policy for political purposes, they reduce its effectiveness as a stabilization weapon.

Is there evidence that politicians have sought to use macro policy for political gain? Political scientist Edward Tufte has conducted extensive research on this issue. While reviewing evidence from 90 elections in 27 different countries, Tufte found that real disposable income accelerated in 77 percent of the election years compared to only 46 percent of the years without an election.[2] This suggests that there is at least a moderate tendency to follow more expansionary policies prior to major elections.

HOW ARE EXPECTATIONS FORMED?

Throughout this text, we have carefully differentiated between anticipated and unanticipated changes. A change may exert a very different impact, depending on whether it is widely expected or catches people by surprise. Given the importance of expectations, we need to analyze how they are formed. There are two general theories in this area. Let us outline the essentials of each.

Adaptive-expectations hypothesis
The hypothesis that economic decision makers base their future expectations on actual outcomes observed during recent periods. For example, according to this view, the rate of inflation actually experienced during the past two or three years would be the major determinant of the rate of inflation expected for the next year.

ADAPTIVE EXPECTATIONS

The simplest theory concerning the formation of expectations is that people rely on the past to predict future trends. According to this theory, which economists call the **adaptive-expectations hypothesis,** decision makers believe that the best indicator of the future is what has happened in the recent past. For example, individuals would expect the price level to be stable next year if stable prices had been present during the past two or

According to the adaptive-expectations hypothesis, the actual occurrence during the most recent period (or set of periods) determines people's future expectations. Thus, the expected future rate of inflation (b) lags behind the actual rate of inflation (a) by one period as expectations are altered over time.

EXHIBIT 15-5

ADAPTIVE-EXPECTATIONS HYPOTHESIS

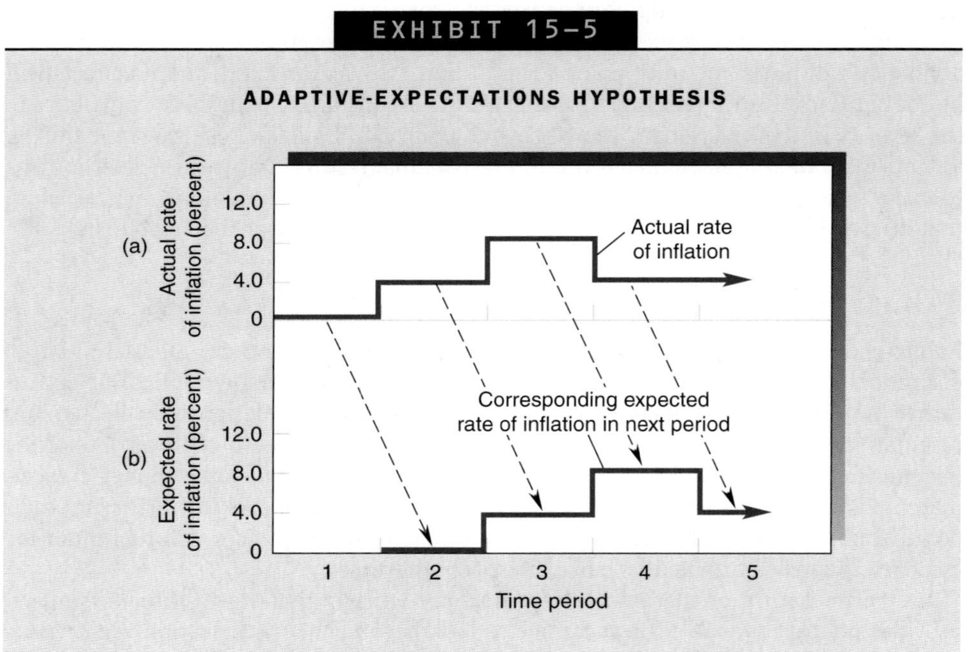

[2]Edward R. Tufte, *Political Control of the Economy* (Princeton: Princeton University Press, 1978).

three years. Similarly, if prices had risen at an annual rate of 4 or 5 percent during the past several years, people would expect similar increases next year.

Exhibit 15–5 presents a graphic illustration of the adaptive-expectations hypothesis. In period 1, prices were stable (part a). Therefore, on the basis of the experience of period 1, decision makers assume that prices will be stable in period 2 (part b). However, the actual rate of inflation in period 2 jumps to 4 percent. Continuation of the 4 percent inflation rate throughout period 2 (the periods may range from six months to two or three years in length) causes decision makers to change their expectations. Relying on the experience of period 2, they anticipate 4 percent inflation in period 3. When their expectations turn out to be incorrect (the actual rate of inflation during period 3 is 8 percent), they again alter their expectations accordingly. Then, during period 4, the actual rate of inflation declines to 4 percent, less than the expected rate. Again, decision makers adjust their expectations as to the rate of inflation in period 5.

Of course, one would not expect the precise mechanical link between past occurrences and future expectations outlined in Exhibit 15–5. Rather than simply using the inflation rate of the immediate past period, people may use a weighted average of recent inflation rates when forming their expectations. It is the structure, however, that is important. With adaptive expectations, decision makers will always expect the next period to be pretty much like the recent past.

Rational Expectations

The idea that people form their expectations about the future on the basis of all available information, including knowledge about policy changes and how they affect the economy, is called the **rational-expectations hypothesis.** According to this view, rather than merely assuming the future will be pretty much like the immediate past, people also consider the expected effects of changes in policy. Based on their understanding of economic policy, people alter their expectations with regard to the future when the government, for example, runs a larger deficit or expands the supply of money more rapidly.

Rational-expectations hypothesis
The hypothesis that economic decision makers weigh all available evidence, including information concerning the probable effects of current and future economic policy, when they form their expectations about future economic events (such as the probable future inflation rate).

Perhaps an example will help clarify the rational-expectations hypothesis. Suppose prices had increased at an annual rate of 3 percent during each of the past three years. In addition, assume that decision makers believe there is a relationship between the growth rate of the money supply and rising prices. They note that the money stock has expanded at a 12 percent annual rate during the last nine months, up from the 4 percent rate of the past several years. According to the rational-expectations hypothesis, they will integrate the recent monetary acceleration into their forecast of the future inflation rate. Thus, they may project an increase in the inflation rate, perhaps to the 6 percent to 10 percent range. In other words, they will expect the future inflation rate to respond to the more rapid growth of the money supply. In contrast, the adaptive-expectations hypothesis implies that people would expect the inflation rate for the next period to be the same as that for the last period (or the last several periods).

The rational-expectations hypothesis does not assume that forecasts will always be correct. We live in a world of uncertainty. Even rational decision makers will err. But they will learn from their past mistakes; they will not continue to make the same types of errors. Thus, the rational-expectations hypothesis assumes that the errors of decision makers will tend to be random. For example, sometimes decision makers may overestimate the increase in the inflation rate caused by monetary expansion, and at other times they may underestimate it. But because they learn from prior experience, people will not continue to make systematic errors year after year.

OUTSTANDING ECONOMIST

Robert Lucas (1937–)

The 1995 Nobel laureate, Robert Lucas is generally given credit for the introduction of the rational-expectations theory into macroeconomics. His technical work in this area has substantially altered the way economists think about macroeconomic policy. He is a long-time professor of economics at the University of Chicago.

Major Differences between Adaptive and Rational Expectations

The adaptive and rational expectations theories differ in two major respects: (1) how quickly people adjust to a change and (2) the likelihood of systematic forecasting errors. If the adaptive expectations theory is correct, people will adjust more slowly. When a more expansionary policy leads to inflation, for example, there will be a significant time lag before people come to expect the inflation and incorporate it into their decision making. In contrast, the rational expectations theory implies that people will begin to anticipate more inflation as soon as they observe a move toward a more expansionary policy, perhaps even before there is an actual increase in the rate of inflation. Therefore, with rational expectations, the time lag between a shift in policy and a change in expectations is likely to be brief.

Systematic errors will occur with adaptive expectations. For example, when the inflation rate is rising, decision makers will systematically tend to underestimate the future rate of inflation. In contrast, when the rate of inflation is falling, individuals will tend systematically to overestimate its future rate. With rational expectations, the errors will be random. People will be as likely to overestimate as to underestimate the future rate of inflation.

How Macro Policy Works: The Implications of Adaptive and Rational Expectations

From the viewpoint of macro policy, does it make any difference how quickly people alter their expectations and whether errors are random or systematic? The *AD/AS* model can be used to address this question. Suppose that there is a shift to a more expansionary macro policy—an increase in the money growth rate, for example. As part a of **Exhibit 15–6** illustrates, the policy shift will stimulate aggregate demand and place upward pressure on the price level (or the inflation rate in the dynamic case). Under adaptive expectations, people will initially fail to anticipate the higher prices. Therefore, as we have previously discussed, output will temporarily increase to Y_2, beyond the economy's long-run potential. Correspondingly, employment will expand and unemployment will recede below the economy's natural rate. When the effects of expansionary policy are unanticipated, both output and employment increase in the short run. Of course, the output rate beyond the economy's capacity will be unsustainable. Eventually, strong demand for resources and the expectation of a higher price level (or rate of inflation) will push resource prices up also. Thus, the high level of output and employment will only be temporary. When decision makers adjust slowly, however, it may be possible to maintain the higher rate of output for a year or two, perhaps even a little longer.

EXHIBIT 15–6

EXPECTATIONS AND THE SHORT-RUN EFFECTS OF DEMAND STIMULUS

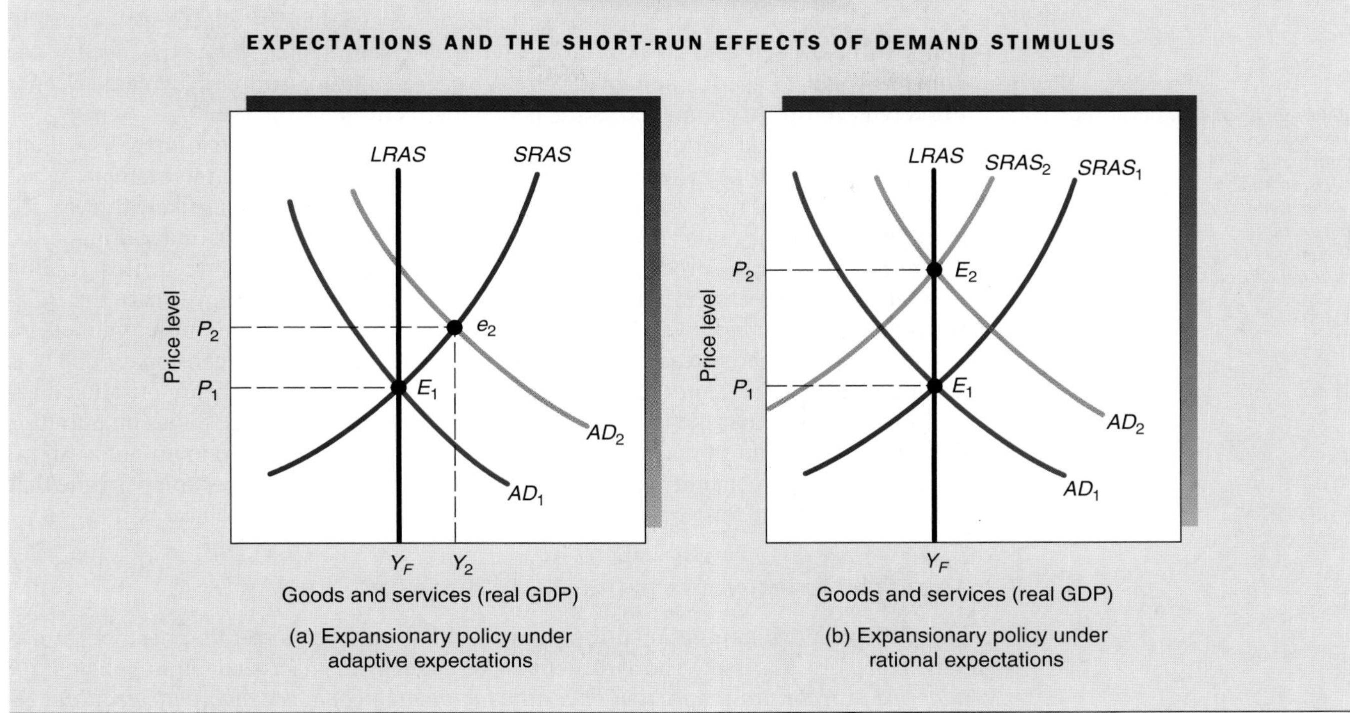

Under adaptive expectations, anticipation of inflation will lag behind its actual occurrence. As a result, a shift to a more expansionary policy will increase aggregate demand and lead to a temporary increase in real GDP from Y_F *to* Y_2, *(a). In contrast, under rational expectations, decision makers will quickly anticipate the inflationary impact of a demand-stimulus policy. Thus, resource prices and production costs will rise as rapidly as prices. While aggregate demand shifts upward, so too will short-run aggregate supply (shift to* $SRAS_2$*) (b). With rational expectations, the demand-stimulus policy will increase prices without altering real output even in the short run.*

Part b of Exhibit 15–6 illustrates the impact of expansionary macroeconomic policy under rational expectations. Remember with rational expectations, decision makers will quickly begin to anticipate the probable effects of the more expansionary policy—stronger demand and a rising rate of inflation, for example—and alter their choices accordingly. Agreements specifying future wage rates and resource prices will quickly make allowance for an expected increase in the price level. These agreements may even incorporate escalator clauses providing for automatic increases in nominal wages as the general level of prices rises. When buyers and sellers in the resource market anticipate fully and adjust quickly to the effects of the demand-stimulus policies, wage rates and resource prices will rise as rapidly as product prices. Hence, the short-run aggregate supply curve will shift upward (to $SRAS_2$) as rapidly as the aggregate demand curve. When people quickly and accurately anticipate the inflationary effects of the more expansionary policy, the result will merely be an increase in the general level of prices (move from E_1 to E_2 in part b of Exhibit 15–6). Neither real output nor employment will expand.

The implications are symmetrical for restrictive policy. Under adaptive expectations a shift to a more restrictive policy will reduce both aggregate demand and real output. Under rational expectations, however, the weaker demand and lower prices will be anticipated quickly. Thus, there will also be downward pressure on resource prices and costs, which will make it possible to maintain the initial level of output, even though the general price level has fallen.

The proponents of rational expectations believe that the effects of a change in policy will be widely and quickly anticipated by decision makers. Once this occurs, the policy will fail to exert a systematic impact on real output and employment. Economists refer to this phenomenon as the **policy-ineffectiveness theorem.**

Policy-ineffectiveness theorem
The proposition that any systematic policy will be rendered ineffective once decision makers figure out the policy pattern and adjust their decision making in light of its expected effects. The theorem is a corollary of the theory of rational expectations.

As we noted, rational-expectations theory does not imply that forecasts will always be correct. But the errors will be random. This means that, for example, when there is a shift to a more expansionary macro policy, people will be as likely to overestimate the inflationary side effects as to underestimate them. If people underestimate the future rate of inflation, product prices will rise relative to costs (resource prices) leading to a temporary increase in output. However, if decision makers overestimate the inflationary side effects, costs will increase relative to product prices and output will fall. As we noted, when the increase in inflation accompanying a more expansionary policy is accurately forecast, real output will remain unchanged. Thus, the theory of rational expectations implies that the impact of a shift in monetary and/or fiscal policy on output is unpredictable. A shift in macro policy is as likely to cause a reduction in output as an increase. This unpredictability explains why proponents of rational expectations argue that macro policy should follow a steady course and focus on long-range objectives.

Policy Implications: A Summary

Thus, the adaptive- and rational-expectations theories have quite different implications with regard to the likely short-run effects of changes in macroeconomic policy. ***With adaptive expectations, there will be a time lag before people anticipate the eventual effects of a shift to a more expansionary policy. Therefore, policies that stimulate demand and place upward pressure on the general level of prices will temporarily***

THUMBNAIL SKETCH

Expectations and the Impact of Shifts in Macro Policy

	Under Adaptive Expectations (1)	Under Rational Expectations (2)
Impact in the Short Run		
Shift to a More Expansionary Policy	Higher prices (inflation); increase in output	Higher prices (inflation); no change in output
Shift to a More Restrictive Policy	Lower prices (deflation); reduction in output	Lower prices (deflation) no change in output
Impact in the Long Run		
Shift to a More Expansionary Policy	Higher prices (inflation); no change in output	Higher prices (inflation); no change in output
Shift to a More Restrictive Policy	Lower prices (deflation); no change in output	Lower prices(deflation) no change in output

Note: Price stability was initially assumed to be present. If inflation was initially present, the shift to a more restrictive policy would reduce the rate of inflation rather than lead to deflation.

increase output and employment. In contrast, when the inflationary side effects of expansionary policies are anticipated quickly, as the rational-expectations theory implies, the primary impact of the demand stimulus will be an increase in the price level.

While the implications of the two expectations theories differ with regard to the short-run effects of policy changes, their long-run implications are identical. Like rational expectations, the adaptive-expectations theory indicates that decision makers will eventually anticipate the long-run effects of more expansionary policy. As this happens, output will recede to the economy's long-run potential. Therefore, both theories imply that the long-run effects of a more expansionary macro policy will be inflation, rather than sustainable increases in output. The accompanying Thumbnail Sketch summarizes the implications of both adaptive and rational expectations regarding how a change in macro policy will impact the price level (inflation) and real output in both the long and short runs.

NONACTIVIST STABILIZATION POLICY

Timing problems, the public choice perspective, and the theory of rational expectations provide the foundation for the nonactivist view of macro policy. While nonactivists often arrive at their position from different paths, they have two major points in common. They believe that (1) discretionary policy changes will increase rather than reduce economic instability and (2) greater stability would result if stable, predictable policies based on predetermined rules or guidelines were followed.

Nonactivists recommend that policy makers choose a long-run policy path (for example, a low, stable rate of inflation and no change in tax rates or real government expenditures) and inform the public of this choice. This course should then be pursued regardless of cyclical ups and downs. As policy makers stay on course, they will gain credibility. The public will develop confidence in the future stability of the policy. Uncertainty will be reduced, thereby increasing the efficiency of private decision making. Nonactivists are confident this strategy would result both in less instability and in more rapid growth than Western economies have experienced in the past.

NONACTIVIST MONETARY POLICY

Suppose we are going to adopt a nonactivist strategy. What rules or guidelines would we choose? Nonactivists believe that monetary policy should focus on achieving either (1) a stable growth rate of the money supply or (2) a stable price-level rule.

Monetary Growth Rule. The most widely advocated nonactivist monetary policy is the constant money growth rule long championed by Milton Friedman. Under this plan, the money supply would be expanded continuously at an annual rate (3 percent, for example) that approximates the long-run growth of the U.S. economy. When real output is growing rapidly (for example, 5 percent annually), the supply of money would decline relative to real GDP. Thus, monetary policy would automatically exert a restraining influence during a period of rapid growth. In contrast, during a recession, the constant money growth rate would exceed the growth of real output, offsetting any tendency toward a downward spiral.

Nonactivists note that monetary policy has often followed a stop-and-go pattern. Many times, after expanding the money supply and causing inflation, policy makers have slammed on the monetary brakes and thrown the economy into a recession (see Exhibit 15–1). The nonactivists believe that monetary instability is the major source of economic instability. Rather than responding to forecasts and current economic indicators, the Fed, they say, would be a more stabilizing force if it simply increased the supply of money, month after month, at a low (noninflationary) constant rate.

The experience of the 1980s highlighted a potential drawback of the monetary rule approach. The introduction of interest-earning checking deposits drastically changed the nature of the M1 money supply during the 1980s. As the interest-earning checking accounts were legalized and more people began using them, the M1 money supply grew rapidly and fluctuated substantially. But this growth was not indicative of a highly expansionary monetary policy. The inflation rate declined sharply during the early 1980s and was relatively constant during the remainder of the decade. When the nature of money is changing, steady money growth may fail to yield monetary and price stability.

Furthermore, as people shift their savings among financial instruments, the shifts influence the growth of the various money supply measures. This can result in conflicting signals. For example, the M1 money supply expanded at a 12 percent annual rate during 1992–1993, suggesting that monetary policy was highly expansionary. During the same period, the annual growth of the M2 money supply was only 1.5 percent, indicating that monetary policy was quite restrictive. Technological developments in the financial sector have substantially reduced the usefulness of the money supply figures as an indicator of monetary policy. In a dynamic world, changes in this area are almost sure to continue. (See pages 341–345 on measurement problems and the future of money.)[3]

Price Level Rule. The shortcomings of money supply figures as an indicator of monetary policy have enhanced the attractiveness of price-level targeting. Under this approach, the monetary authorities would directly target a broad price index, such as the GDP deflator or consumer price index. The advocates of a price-level rule argue that, in the long run, monetary policy cannot determine real output, employment, interest rates, or other real variables. What it can and does determine is the level of prices. Therefore, why not require that the monetary authorities maintain a persistently low rate of inflation and hold them accountable for their actions? Under this plan, if the general price index were rising, the monetary authorities would have an incentive to institute more restraint. Conversely, if the price level were falling, a move toward expansion would be in order. The proponents of this rule argue that it would reduce both instability arising from monetary sources and the uncertainty of time-dimension transactions (for example, loan agreements and other long-term contracts).

New Zealand adopted the price-level rule in 1990. Although the Central Bank of New Zealand is fully responsible for monetary policy, it is legally required to maintain the inflation rate within a narrow range, currently between zero and 2 percent. If the central bank fails to meet this target, the bank's governor is subject to dismissal. This structure requires the central bank to focus on a well-defined target (a low rate of inflation) that is achievable with monetary policy and holds it accountable for failure to meet the objective. To date, the policy has been highly successful. Prior to 1990, New Zealand had the highest and most variable inflation rate among the high-income industrial nations. In contrast, its rate of inflation has been low (between 0.1 percent and

[3]In recent years, economists have generally placed more confidence in the M2 money supply figures. But there are no assurances that future financial innovations will not also alter the nature of the M2 and undermine its use as a gauge of monetary policy. In fact, evidence of such changes is already present. In response to recent reductions in the start-up cost of stock and bond mutual funds, many individuals shifted funds from various savings instruments that are part of the M2 money supply to the mutual funds, which are not. These shifts reduced both the growth rate of the M2 money supply during 1994–1995 and the reliability of these figures as an indicator of monetary policy.

2.7 percent) since the legislation took effect. Other countries appear to be moving in this direction. The new European Central Bank has committed itself to the achievement of price stability. Several other central banks have also set targets and designated price stability as their primary objective.

Nonactivist Fiscal Policy

In the area of fiscal policy, the simplest rule would require that the budget be balanced annually. Because revenues and expenditures fluctuate over the business cycle, however, a balanced budget rule would require tax increases and/or expenditure reductions during a recession. The opposite changes would be required during a period of rapid growth. Such changes are inconsistent with the nonactivist pursuit of stable (unchanged) policies.

In theory, the proper nonactivist fiscal strategy is a balanced budget *over the business cycle.* Under this plan, the same tax rates and expenditure policies would remain in effect during both booms and recessions. Surpluses would result during periods of prosperity, while deficits would accrue during recessions. Unfortunately, this rule is an elastic-band constraint. At any point in time, it is difficult to assess if current tax and expenditure policy will balance the budget over the cycle. Thus, nonactivists, particularly those with a public-choice persuasion, recognize that a "balance the budget over the business cycle" rule is unlikely to impose a steady course on policy makers.

Some nonactivists believe that a constitutional amendment limiting both government spending and budget deficits is a necessary ingredient for stable fiscal policy. Pressure from special interest groups and the short time horizon of political officials elected for limited terms biases the political process toward expansionary fiscal policy (increased spending and debt). Because of this, some nonactivists argue that a supramajority (for example, 60 percent) should be required for congressional approval for either (1) deficit-financed government spending or (2) rapid increases (more rapid than the growth of national income) in federal spending.

It is one thing to favor a general strategy and another to develop a workable program for implementation. Clearly, the nonactivists have not yet arrived at a detailed fiscal policy program that would command wide acceptance among even the proponents of nonactivism.

EMERGING CONSENSUS VIEW

Stabilization is an area of continuing debate among economists. Nonetheless, a consensus view does appear to be emerging in several areas. The following are the major elements of the consensus view.

1. ***Monetary policy should focus on price stability—the attainment of persistently low rates of inflation.*** Achievement of this objective will reduce uncertainty, improve the efficiency of markets, and promote full employment. When monetary authorities achieve this objective, they have done their job well.
2. ***Demand stimulus policies cannot reduce the rate of unemployment below the natural level—at least not for long.*** In the 1960s and 1970s, many economists thought that there was a trade-off between inflation and unemployment. While recognizing demand stimulus policies would lead to some inflation, many believed that they would also reduce the unemployment rate. Expectations theories highlight the error of this view. Once people come to expect inflation, the inflation-unemployment trade-off dissipates. While the adaptive-expectations

theory implies that an unanticipated shift to a more expansionary policy can temporarily reduce the unemployment rate, the rational-expectations theory indicates that even the temporary reduction is questionable. Given the uncertainty of the short-run trade-off and clear absence of a long-lasting trade-off, most economists now believe that stimulating inflation in an effort to reduce unemployment is both destabilizing and short-sighted. (See Application 3, "The Phillips Curve: Is There a Trade-off between Inflation and Unemployment?" for an in-depth view of this issue.)

3. ***Wide swings in both monetary and fiscal policy should be avoided.*** Given our limited forecasting ability and knowledge about how quickly changes in monetary and fiscal policy impact the economy, policy makers should not attempt to respond to every turn in the economic road. Major changes in tax policy, budget deficits, and the money supply *in response to business cycle conditions* are likely to increase rather than reduce instability. More stability will result if the policy makers adopt a long-range strategy and stick with it.
4. ***Use of discretionary fiscal policy as an effective stabilization tool is impractical, particularly in countries like the United States.*** Proper timing is essential for the effective use of stabilization policy. Given the checks and balances built into the U.S. political structure, it is unrealistic to expect speedy changes in fiscal policy. The crowding-out effect creates additional uncertainty with regard to the potency of fiscal policy. These shortcomings have caused even long-time Keynesians like Paul Samuelson to conclude that fiscal policy is an impractical stabilization tool.

THE RECENT STABILITY OF THE U.S. ECONOMY

The focus of stabilization policy has changed dramatically during the last four decades. In the 1960s, it was widely believed that macro policy—particularly fiscal policy—could be effectively used both to smooth the ups and downs of the business cycle and to promote a high level of employment. Tempered by both the integration of expectations into macroeconomic analysis and the instability of the 1970s, the objectives of stabilization policy have been less ambitious in recent years. Rather than trying to control output and employment, the focus has shifted to the achievement of price stability.

Paradoxically, movement toward price stability has led to a rather dramatic reduction in economic fluctuations. **Exhibit 15–7** illustrates this point. From 1910 to 1959, the U.S. economy was in recession 32.8 percent of the time. Between 1960 and 1982, recession was present 22.8 percent of the time. By way of comparison, 1983–1998 was an unprecedented period of economic stability. Over this 192-month period, the economy was in recession only eight months—4.2 percent of the time.

Interestingly, this period was one of considerable political change. After 12 years of Republican presidents, a Democratic president was elected in 1992. In contrast, Republicans in 1994 gained control of both branches of Congress for the first time in nearly 50 years. There was additional upheaval—the collapse of communism, the 1987 stock market crash, the 1990–1991 Gulf War, a defense build-up in the early 1980s followed by a sharp reduction in the 1990s, and even the impeachment of a president in 1998. In the midst of all this change, the economy stayed on track.

What accounts for the recent stability? Perhaps luck played a role—there were no major wars. Most economists, however, would give the major credit to monetary policy. Compared to earlier periods (see Exhibit 15–2), monetary policy was much more stable. Under the leadership of first Paul Volcker and later Alan Greenspan, the

EXHIBIT 15-7

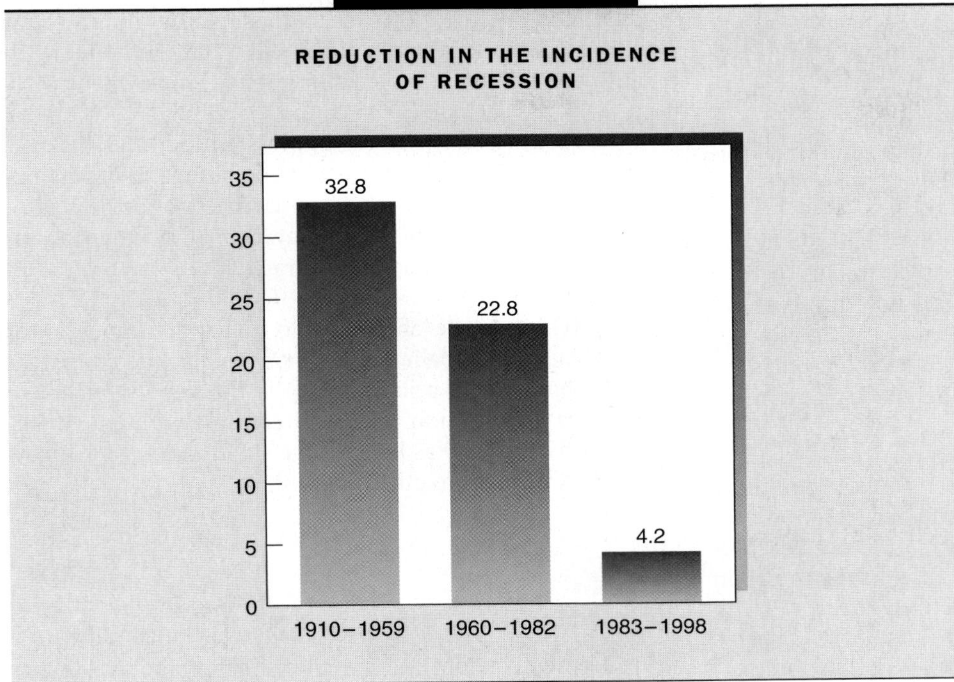

The U.S. economy was in recession 32.8 percent of the time during the 1910–1959 period and 22.8 percent of the time between 1960 and 1982, but only 4.2 percent of the time during 1983–1998.

SOURCES: R.E. Lipsey and D. Preston, Source Book of Statistics Relating to Construction *(1966); and New York: National Bureau of Economic Research.*

Fed avoided wide swings in the rate of inflation. During this entire 1983–1998 period, the inflation rate (as measured by the GDP deflator) remained in a narrow range between 1.1 percent and 4.3 percent. Even more impressive, the year-to-year change in the inflation rate never exceeded 1.2 percent. In essence, the Fed followed policies consistent with a low and stable rate of inflation, and these policies led to economic stability. This is consistent with the model we have developed. Unexpected price changes, whether caused by macro policy or external events, lead to economic booms and busts. Fed policy has avoided such swings in recent years.

Does this mean that there will be less instability in the future? Of course, disturbances arising from wars, financial turbulence, and policy errors can be expected in the future. However, there is some reason for optimism. The recent record suggests that when functioning in a low inflation–stable price environment, the self-corrective characteristics of a market economy work pretty well.

LOOKING *Ahead*

Following up on the topic of economic stability, the next chapter will analyze the determinants of economic growth. Why do some economies grow more rapidly than others? What can policy do to promote high and sustainable rates of economic growth? These questions and related issues will be addressed in the following chapter.

KEY POINTS

➤ Historically, the United States has experienced substantial swings in real output. Prior to the Second World War, year-to-year changes in real GDP of 5 percent to 10 percent were experienced on several occasions. During the last five decades, the fluctuations of real output have been more moderate.

➤ While stable growth, price-level stability, and full employment are widely recognized as desirable, there is considerable disagreement concerning how these objectives can be achieved. Activists believe that discretionary use of macro policy can contribute to the achievement of these goals, while nonactivists argue that steady, more passive policies are better.

➤ After a change in policy has been undertaken, there will be a time lag before it exerts a major impact on economic activity. This means the policy makers need to forecast economic conditions several months in the future in order to institute policy changes effectively.

➤ The index of leading indicators and other forecasting tools provide policy makers with information about the likely future economic conditions. Activists argue that policy makers can initially respond with caution to signals indicating the need for a policy change and then act more aggressively if the situation merits it. Activists are confident that discretionary monetary and fiscal policy can be used effectively to promote economic stability.

➤ Nonactivists believe that a market economy's self-corrective mechanism works quite well if it is not short-circuited by perverse macroeconomic policy. Furthermore, they argue that the problems of proper timing and political considerations undermine the effectiveness of discretionary macro policy as a stabilization tool. Rather than reacting to cyclical conditions, nonactivists favor steady, predictable policies.

➤ There are two major theories as to how expectations are formed. According to the adaptive-expectations hypothesis, individuals form their expectations about the future on the basis of data from the recent past. The rational-expectations hypothesis assumes that people use all pertinent information, including data on the conduct of current policy, in forming their expectations about the future.

➤ With adaptive expectations, an unanticipated shift to a more expansionary policy will temporarily stimulate output and employment. In contrast, with rational expectations, expansionary policy will not generate a systematic change in output. Both expectations theories indicate that sustained expansionary policies will lead to inflation without permanently increasing output and employment.

➤ Analysis of the Great Depression indicates that the severity and length of the economic plunge, if not its onset, were the result of perverse macroeconomic policy—a sharp contraction in the money supply, a huge tax increase, and a sharp rise in tariff rates.

➤ While debate about macro policy continues, most economists now believe that monetary policy consistent with approximate price stability is the key ingredient of effective stabilization policy. In contrast with the 1960s, use of fiscal policy as an effective stabilization tool is now thought to be impractical.

CRITICAL ANALYSIS QUESTIONS

1. The chair of the Council of Economic Advisers has requested that you write a short paper indicating how economic policy can be used to stabilize the economy and achieve a high level of economic growth during the next five years. Be sure to make specific proposals. Indicate why your recommendations will work. You may submit your paper to your instructor.

*2. How does economic instability during the past four decades compare with instability prior to the Second World War? Is there any evidence that stabilization policy has either increased or decreased economic stability during recent decades?

3. Evaluate the effectiveness of monetary and fiscal policy during the past three years. Has it helped to promote stable prices, rapid growth, and high employment? Do you think policy makers have made mistakes during this period? If so, indicate why.

4. State in your own words the adaptive-expectations hypothesis. How does the theory of rational expectations differ from that of adaptive expectations?

*5. Why do many nonactivists favor a monetary rule such as expansion of the money supply at a constant annual rate? What are some of the practical problems with a monetary rule? Do you think a monetary rule could be devised that would reduce economic instability? Why or why not?

6. Compare and contrast the impact of an unexpected shift to a more expansionary monetary policy under both rational and adaptive theories of expectations. Are the implications of the two theories different in the short run? Are the long-run implications different? Explain.

7. What is the index of leading indicators? Why is it useful to macro policy makers?

8. What are some of the practical problems that limit the effectiveness of discretionary monetary and fiscal policy as stabilization tools?

9. Many central banks now indicate that their primary objective is to keep inflation at a persistently low rate. If the rate of inflation is persistently low, will this help reduce the instability of the business cycle? Why or why not?

10. "The Great Depression indicates that the self-correcting mechanism of a market economy is weak and unreliable." Evaluate this statement.

---

*Asterisk denotes questions for which answers are given in Appendix B.

CHAPTER 16

Certain fundamental principles — formulating sound monetary and fiscal policies, removing domestic price controls, opening the economy to international market forces, ensuring property rights and private property, creating competition, and reforming and limiting the role of government — are essential for a healthy market economy.

Economic Report of the President, 1991

Economic Growth

CHAPTER FOCUS

- Why is economic growth important?
- How does per-capita income vary among nations?
- How does sustained economic growth change income levels and the lives of people?
- What are the major sources of economic growth?
- What impact do the role and size of government have on economic growth?
- Does economic freedom enhance growth?

The previous chapter focused on economic stability. This one will analyze economic growth. Throughout history, most of the world's population has struggled 50, 60, and 70 hours per week just to obtain the basic necessities of life—food, clothing, and shelter. During the last two centuries, sustained economic growth has changed that situation for most people in North America, Europe, Oceania, and Japan. Rising incomes and improvements in the standard of living have not always been present in Western countries. According to Phelps Brown, the real income of English building-trade workers was virtually unchanged between 1215 and 1798, a period of nearly six centuries.[1] In other parts of Europe, workers experienced a similar stagnation of real earnings throughout much of this period.

Low incomes and widespread poverty are still the norm in most countries—particularly those of South and Central America, Africa, and South-Central Asia. Why have income levels in some countries grown rapidly, while they have continued to stagnate in others? What are the key ingredients of economic growth? What can governments do to enhance growth? We have already considered several aspects of these questions. We are now prepared to pull together the lessons of basic economics and address the topic of economic growth and sources of prosperity in a more comprehensive manner.

THE IMPORTANCE OF ECONOMIC GROWTH

Economic growth is important because it is a necessary ingredient for higher incomes and living standards. Remember, there are two ways of measuring GDP. It can be measured by summing either (1) the expenditures on all the output produced during a period or (2) the incomes received by those who supplied the resources required to produce the output. Thus, GDP is a measure of both output and income. This fact highlights a very important point: Growth of output is necessary for the growth of income. Without more output, it will be impossible to achieve more income.

Economic growth expands the productive capacity of an economy. The impact of growth can be shown within the framework of the production possibilities concept discussed in Chapter 2. Suppose that a country experienced economic growth during the 1990s. Thus, it will be possible to produce a larger quantity of both consumer and capital goods in 2000 than was true in 1990. As **Exhibit 16–1** (frame a) shows, the growth during the decade will shift the economy's production possibilities curve outward (from AA to BB).

Exhibit 16–1 (frame b) also illustrates the impact of economic growth within the framework of the *AD/AS* model. The long-run aggregate supply indicates the

[1]Phelps Brown, *A Century of Pay: The Course of Pay and Production in France, Germany, Sweden, the United Kingdom, and the United States* (London: Macmillan, 1968).

EXHIBIT 16–1

ECONOMIC GROWTH, PRODUCTION POSSIBILITIES, AND AGGREGATE SUPPLY

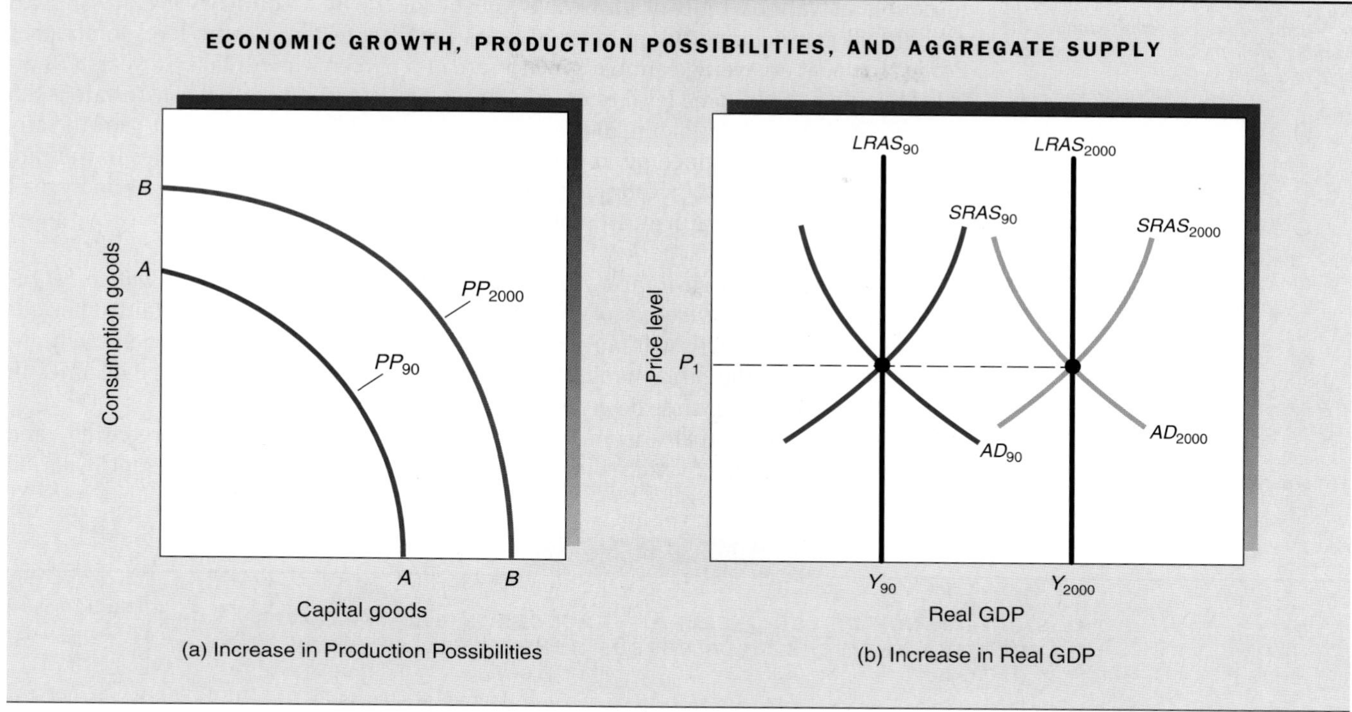

Economic growth expands the sustainable output rate of an economy. This can be illustrated by either an outward shift in the production possibilities curve (frame a) or an increase in long-run aggregate supply (shift from $LRAS_{90}$ *to* $LRAS_{2000}$ *in frame b). If monetary policy maintains the initial price level* (P_1)*, equilibrium real GDP will increase from* Y_{90} *to* Y_{2000}*.*

economy's maximum sustainable rate of output. As the economy grows, the LRAS curve will move to the right. Therefore, the growth during the 1990s will cause the LRAS curve to shift from $LRAS_{90}$ to $LRAS_{2000}$. Assuming that monetary policy maintains the initial price level, the equilibrium level of output will expand from Y_{90} to Y_{2000}.

When a nation's GDP is increasing more rapidly than its population, per-capita GDP—that is, GDP per person—will also expand. Growth of per-capita GDP means more goods and services per person. Typically, this leads to a higher standard of living for most people, as well as improvement in life expectancy, literacy, and health.

IMPACT OF SUSTAINED ECONOMIC GROWTH

There is a tendency to think that a 1 percent or 2 percent difference in growth is of little consequence. However, when sustained over a lengthy period, seemingly small differences in growth can exert a huge impact. If the income per person in Country A grows at an annual rate of 3.5 percent, per-capita income will double every 20 years. In contrast, if the growth rate of Country B is 1.75 percent, it will take 40 years for per-capita income to double. If the two countries start with the same income level, after 40 years the income of Country A will be twice that of Country B. The principle of compound return is at work here.

Rule of 70
If a variable grows at a rate of x *percent per year, 70/*x *will approximate the number of years required for the variable to double.*

The **rule of 70** makes it easy to figure how many years it will take for income to double at various rates of growth. If you divide 70 by a country's average growth rate, it will approximate the number of years required for an income level to double.[2] For example, at an average annual growth rate of 5 percent, it will take 14 years (70 divided by 5) for the income level to double. As we just noted, when the growth rate is 3.5 percent, income will double in 20 years (70 divided by 3.5). At a 1 percent growth rate, it will take 70 years for income to double. (*Note:* The rule of 70 also applies to the rate of return on savings and investments. Thus, when maintained over a long period, small differences in rates of return can make a big difference in the value of your savings or investment at the end of a period.)

Differences in sustained growth rates over two or three decades will substantially alter the relative incomes of countries. Nations that experience sustained periods of rapid economic growth will move up the income ladder and eventually achieve high-income status. On the other hand, nations that grow slowly or experience declines in real GDP per capita will slide down the economic ladder.

Using the actual income figures for Hong Kong, Japan, Argentina, and Venezuela, **Exhibit 16–2** vividly illustrates how sustained growth over a lengthy period

EXHIBIT 16–2

THE SIGNIFICANCE OF LONG-TERM DIFFERENCES IN GROWTH RATES: ARGENTINA AND VENEZUELA VERSUS HONG KONG AND JAPAN

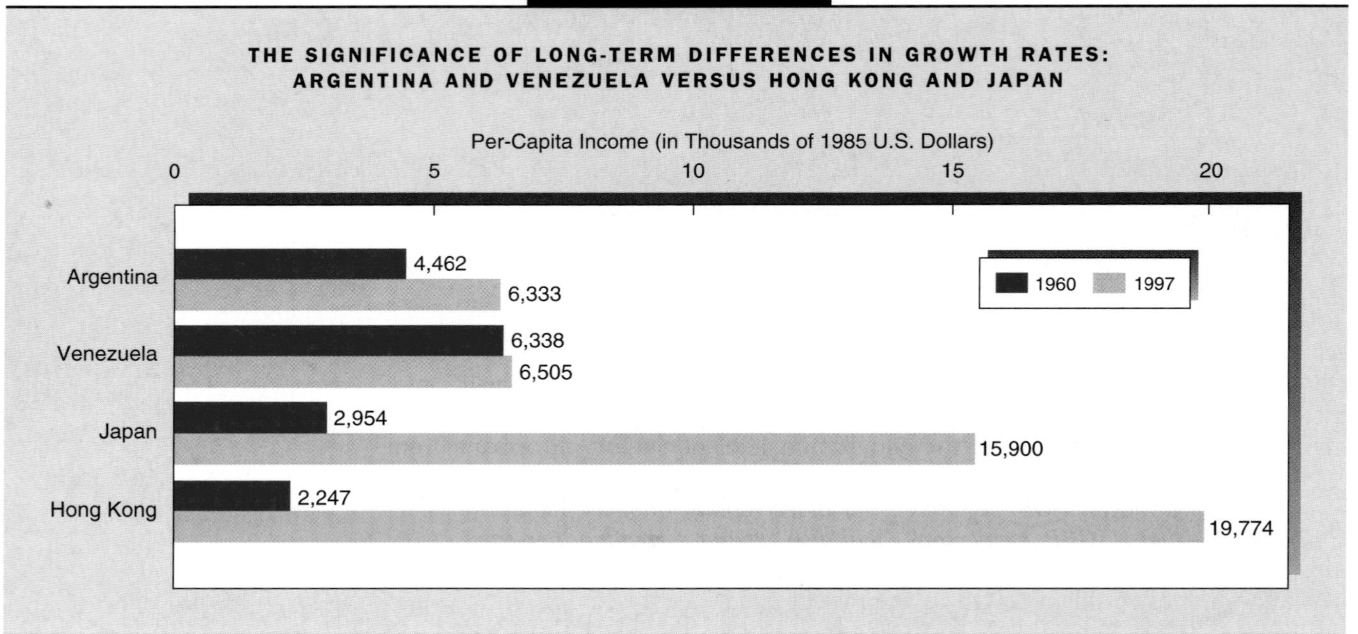

The graph illustrates the 1960 and 1997 per-capita GDP figures for Argentina, Venezuela, Japan, and Hong Kong. During the 1960–1997 period, the per-capita growth rates of Hong Kong and Japan were 6.0 percent and 4.7 percent, respectively, compared to growth rates of 1 percent for Argentina and 0.1 percent for Venezuela. Note how the more rapid growth rates of the two Asian nations drastically altered their relative incomes compared to those of the two Latin American countries.

SOURCE: Robert Summers and Alan Heston, Penn World Tables *(Cambridge: National Bureau of Economic Research, 1994). These data were through 1992. They were updated to 1997 by the authors.*

[2]Sometimes this rule is called the rule of 72, rather than 70. While 70 yields more accurate estimates for growth rates of less than 5 percent, 72 yields slightly more accurate estimates when the annual rate of growth exceeds 5 percent.

influences relative incomes. Look at the figures for 1960. *Measured in 1985 dollars,* the per-capita GDP of Hong Kong was $2,247 in 1960, substantially less than the comparable figures of both Argentina ($4,462) and Venezuela ($6,338). Between 1960 and 1997, however, the per-capita real GDP of Hong Kong expanded at a 6.0 percent annual rate, far greater than the rates of 1 percent for Argentina and 0.1 percent for Venezuela. Now look at the 1997 figures for these three countries. In 1997, per-capita GDP of Hong Kong was $19,774—more than three times the figures of Argentina and Venezuela. The Japanese figures illustrate the same point. Between 1960 and 1997, the per-capita growth rate of Japan was 4.7 percent, well above the rates for both Argentina and Venezuela. Even though GDP per capita of Japan was lower than the comparable figures for the Latin American countries in 1960, Japan's higher rate of growth over a 37-year period dramatically changed the picture.

Observing the income differences between the wealthy industrial nations and **less developed countries (LDCs),** some have argued that the rich are consistently getting richer while the poor are getting poorer. Is this true? Which countries are growing most rapidly? Which are falling behind?

Less-developed countries (LDCs)
Low-income countries generally characterized by rapid population growth and an agriculture-household sector that dominates the economy. Sometimes these countries are referred to as developing countries.

Exhibit 16–3 presents data on the growth of per-capita GDP for (a) high-growth LDCs, (b) high-income industrial economies, and (c) LDCs with the worst growth records. Only seven countries—China, South Korea, Taiwan, Singapore, Thailand, Ireland, and Hong Kong—with a population of 2 million or more were able to achieve a growth rate of real per-capita GDP of 4 percent or more during 1980–1998. Interestingly, all except Ireland had been classified as LDCs at the beginning of the period. Again, all except Ireland were in Asia. Several of these countries—particularly South Korea and Thailand—are now experiencing serious recession. However, even after taking this into account, their

EXHIBIT 16–3

THE GROWTH OF PER-CAPITA GDP (1980–1998) OF HIGH-INCOME INDUSTRIAL COUNTRIES, HIGH-GROWTH LDCs, AND LOW-GROWTH LDCs

High-Growth LDCs[a]	Growth of Per-Capita GDP, 1980–1998	High-Income Industrial Countries	Growth of Per-Capita GDP, 1980–1998	Low-Growth LDCs[b]	Growth of Per-Capita GDP, 1980–1998
China	8.2	Japan	2.3	Congo (Zaire)	−5.3
South Korea	6.4	United Kingdom	1.9	Togo	−4.1
Taiwan	5.4	Germany	1.8	Niger	−3.9
Singapore	5.4	United States	1.8	Haiti	−3.6
Thailand	4.9	Australia	1.8	Nicaragua	−3.0
Ireland	4.3	Italy	1.7	Madagascar	−3.0
Hong Kong	4.2	France	1.5	Cameroon	−2.8
		Netherlands	1.5	Côte d'Ivoire	−2.6
		Canada	1.1	Zambia	−2.3
		Switzerland	0.7	Romania	−2.2

The growth of LDCs is characterized by diversity. A number of LDCs (left above) are growing more rapidly than the high-income countries, but others (right above) are falling farther and farther behind.

[a]*LDCs with a growth rate of 4 percent or more during 1980–1998.*
[b]*LDCs with a negative growth rate of 2 percent or less during 1980–1998.*

SOURCE: Derived from World Bank, World Tables, *CD-Rom. Only countries with a population of 2 million or more are included in this table. In a few cases, the 1998 data were unavailable. When this was true, the growth rate was for the 1980–1997 period.*

long-term growth is highly impressive. In these high-growth economies, per-capita income has increased sharply and living standards improved dramatically in recent decades.

Among the high-income industrial economies, Japan—another country with current economic difficulties—had the highest annual growth rate (2.3 percent) during the 1980–1998 period. The growth rates of the United Kingdom, Germany, Australia, the United States, Italy, and the Netherlands were bunched within a narrow range between 1.5 percent and 1.9 percent. The growth of Canada and Switzerland lagged behind. Most of the other smaller high-income economies (not included in the exhibit) also had growth rates between 1 percent and 2 percent during the period.

APPLICATIONS IN ECONOMICS

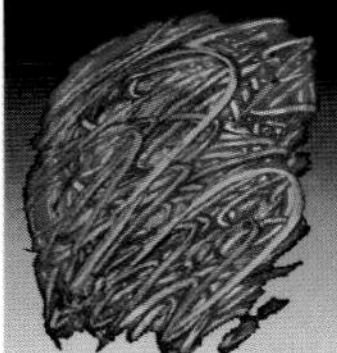

China: Is It a Special Case?

Some may be surprised to find China among the high-growth countries of Exhibit 16–3. After all, isn't China a centrally planned socialist economy that has generally followed policies inconsistent with growth and prosperity?

Following the 1978 Communist Party Congress, China began to introduce reforms that have dramatically changed the structure of the economy. ***Today, there are essentially two Chinese economies: (1) agriculture, small businesses, and "special economic zones," and (2) the state enterprises. The first is now a relatively free economy, while the second continues to be centrally planned.***

Initially, China took several important steps toward economic liberalization of the agricultural sector. The collective farms were dismantled and replaced with what the Chinese refer to as a contract responsibility system. Under this organizational form, individual families are permitted to lease land for up to 15 years in exchange for supplying the state with a fixed amount of production at a designated price (which is generally below the market price). Amounts produced above the required quota belong to the individual farmers and may be either directly consumed or sold at a free market price.

Even though the legal ownership remains with the state, this system of long-term land leases provides farmers with something akin to a private property right. This is particularly true since renewal of the lengthy leases is now virtually automatic. Because the state quota is relatively low—approximately 15 percent—and the farmers are permitted to keep all production above the fixed quota, the effective marginal tax rate is zero. Clearly, this provides a strong incentive for farmers to expand output. Markets play a key role in the allocation of agricultural products. Currently, more than 85 percent of the grain (rice, wheat, and barley) output is produced privately and sold at market-determined prices.[1]

Success in agriculture encouraged reforms in other sectors. Restrictions on the operation of small-scale service and retail businesses were relaxed in the 1980s. Private restaurants, stores, and repair shops sprang up and began to compete with state-operated enterprises. By the mid-1980s, Chinese cities were teeming with sidewalk vendors, restaurants, small retail businesses, and hundreds of thousands of individuals providing personal services.

At the same time, China has established so-called special economic zones. Approximately 20 percent of the Chinese labor force now works in these zones. In these areas, people are permitted to establish businesses, engage in trade with foreigners, maintain bank accounts in foreign currencies, and undertake investment without having to obtain government approval. Taxes in the special zones are generally quite low. During the past decade these zones attracted substantial investment from abroad, which has contributed to the growth of the Chinese investment rate. Economic activity in these regions has also made a sizable contribution to the growth of the trade sector, which has tripled as a share of the economy since 1980.

Although the moves toward liberalization have contributed substantially to China's recent growth, there may also be a second factor at work: The growth-rate data of China are probably exaggerated. Clearly, this was the case for the former Soviet Union and the countries of Eastern Europe during the 1970s and 1980s. Since centrally planned economies do not rely on product prices to allocate goods and services, output is measured by the physical quantities of goods produced and inputs used. These factors may be a highly unreliable indicator of the value of what is actually being produced. As China has moved away from a command/barter economy in recent years toward greater reliance on markets, some productive activities that were not counted (or were counted only at a depressed level) are now being counted as part of GDP. This will tend to exaggerate the growth of GDP. Thus, the growth estimates of China should be interpreted with caution.

---

[1]Other reforms also enhanced the development of markets in agricultural products. Restrictions on individual stock breeding, household sideline occupations, transport of agricultural goods, and trade fairs (marketplaces) were removed. Farmers were permitted to own tractors and trucks, and even hire laborers to work in their leased fields. Such economic activities were prohibited prior to 1978.

Thus, per-capita incomes of the high-growth economies were expanding at three to four times the rate of the typical high-income industrial economy.

Unfortunately, there is another group of LDCs that not only has failed to grow, but has regressed. The nations in Exhibit 16–3 (right side) experienced declines in per-capita GDP of 2 percent or more during 1980–1998. Per-capita GDP fell at an annual rate of 3 percent or more in Congo (formerly Zaire), Haiti, Togo, Nicaragua, Madagascar, and Niger. This implies that the per-person income level of these countries in 1998 was only about half the income level of 1980. The per-capita GDP of Côte d'Ivoire, Cameroon, Romania, and Zambia also declined substantially between 1980 and 1998.

The growth picture of LDCs is clearly one of diversity. The fastest-growing countries in the world are LDCs. These rapidly growing countries have closed the income gap relative to their wealthier counterparts.[3] At the same time, other LDCs are doing very poorly and falling farther and farther behind.[4]

SOURCES OF ECONOMIC GROWTH

Why have some countries grown rapidly, while others have experienced economic stagnation and even reductions in income? It is tempting to argue that natural resources are the key ingredient of economic growth. Of course, other things constant, countries with abundant natural resources do have an advantage. It is clear, though, that natural resources are neither a necessary nor sufficient condition for economic growth. Other than its harbor, Hong Kong has practically no natural resources. Japan likewise has few natural resources, and it imports almost all of its industrial energy supply. Nonetheless, as Exhibit 16–2 illustrates, both Hong Kong and Japan have grown rapidly during the past several decades and have achieved high levels of income. In contrast, Argentina has a great deal of fertile land and several other natural resources, and Venezuela is one of the most oil-rich countries in the world. Yet these countries, along with other resource-rich countries like Ghana, Kenya, and Bolivia, are poor, and they have been growing slowly, if at all. Natural resources can help promote economic prosperity, but clearly they are not the primary determinant of growth.

Economic growth is a complex process. Several factors contribute to it, and they are often interrelated. Much as the performance of an athletic team reflects the joint output of the team members, economic growth is jointly determined by several factors. And just as one or two weak players can substantially reduce overall team performance, a counterproductive policy in one or two key areas can substantially harm the overall performance of an economy. Although economics cannot provide us with a precise recipe for economic growth, it does reveal the important sources of such growth: (1) investment in physical and human capital, (2) technological advances, and (3) institutions and policies consistent with efficient economic organization.

INVESTMENT IN PHYSICAL AND HUMAN CAPITAL

Machines can have a substantial impact on a person's ability to produce. Even Robinson Crusoe on an uninhabited island can catch more fish with a net than he can with his hands. Farmers working with modern tractors and plows can cultivate many more

---

[3]In fact, the income levels of two of the high-growth countries—Hong Kong and Singapore—have risen so much that they are no longer classified as less developed.

[4]For additional analysis of the diversity of growth rates among LDCs, see Stephen L. Parente and Edward C. Prescott, "Changes in the Wealth of Nations," *Quarterly Review: Federal Reserve Bank of Minneapolis* (spring 1993): 3–16.

acres than could their great-grandparents, who probably worked with hoes. Similarly, education and training that improve the knowledge and skills of workers can vastly improve their productivity. For example, a cabinetmaker, skilled after years of training and experience, can build cabinets far more rapidly and efficiently than a neophyte.

Investment in both physical capital (machines) and human capital (knowledge and skills) can expand the productive capacity of a worker. In turn, people who produce more goods and services valued by others will tend to have higher incomes. Economics suggests that, other things constant, countries using a larger share of their resources to produce tools, machines, and factories will tend to grow more rapidly. Allocation of more resources to education and training will also tend to enhance economic growth.

Of course, investment is not a free lunch; an opportunity cost is involved. When more resources are used to produce machines and factories and develop skills, fewer resources are available for production of current-consumption goods. Economics is about trade-offs. It does, however, indicate that people who save and invest more will be able to produce more in the future.

Technological Progress

Technological advancement
The introduction of new techniques or methods of production that enable a greater output per unit of input.

Technological advancement—the adoption of new, improved techniques or methods of production—enables workers to produce more output with the same amount of resources. Clearly, improved technology—the result of using brainpower to discover economical new products and/or less costly methods of production—has substantially enhanced our production possibilities. During the last 250 years, the substitution of power-driven machines for human labor; the development of miracle grains, fertilizer, and new sources of energy; and improvements in transportation and communication have vastly improved living standards around the world. Technological improvements continue to change our lives. Consider the impact of computers, compact disc players, word processors, microwave ovens, video cameras and cassette players, and fax machines. Development and improvement of these and other products during the past two decades has vastly changed the way many people work and play.

Invention
The discovery of a new product or process, often facilitated by the knowledge of engineering and scientific relationships.

Innovation
The successful introduction and adoption of a new product or process; the economic application of inventions.

Obviously, technological progress encompasses **invention,** the discovery of new products or processes. But, it also includes **innovation,** the practical and effective adoption of new techniques. Compared to scientific inventions, it is easy to overlook the highly significant role of innovators in the adoption and dissemination of technological improvements. Many innovators were not even involved in the invention of the products for which they are now famous. Henry Ford played a minor role in the invention and development of the automobile. His contribution was an innovative one—the adoption of mass-production techniques that enabled the low-cost production of reliable automobiles. Ray Kroc, the developer of the McDonald's fast-food chain, did not invent anything. In fact, he was not even involved in the operation of the first McDonald's restaurant. But he recognized a good idea when he saw it. Kroc was an innovator. He franchised the business, trained operators of McDonald's, and in the process changed the eating habits of a nation. Inventions are important, but without innovators, inventions are merely ideas waiting to be exploited.

Modern technology is available to all nations—rich and poor alike. Poor nations do not have to invest in research and development—they can emulate (or import at a low cost) the proven technologies of the developed countries. Thus, the opportunity to grow by adopting improved technology is greater in poor developing countries than it is in high-income, developed nations. This factor helps explain why countries like South Korea, Taiwan, Hong Kong, Singapore, and even Ireland that were relatively poor just a few years ago dominate the list of the world's fastest-growing economies (see Exhibit 16–3 for evidence on this point).

Henry Ford was the central figure in the development of the automobile in the United States. He started not only Ford, but also the company that eventually became General Motors. His major contribution was an innovation: the assembly line shown here. As a source of economic progress, innovations are even more important than inventions.

However, as in the case of natural resources, it is important to keep the contribution of technology in perspective. If technology were the primary factor limiting the creation of wealth, most low-income countries would be growing more rapidly than developed nations. This is not the case. Many poor countries continue to stagnate even though the proven technologies of high-income industrial countries are readily available to them.

Institutional Environment and Economic Efficiency

Following the approach outlined in a classic article by Nobel laureate Robert Solow, traditional models of economic growth have stressed the importance of inputs.[5] In fact, the growth of output has often been attributed to the growth of the human capital and physical capital inputs, plus an unexplained residual that was credited to improvements in technology. Clearly, investment in capital goods, education, and technology are important. By themselves, however, they do not necessarily produce economic growth. The experience of the formerly centrally planned economies illustrates this point. These economies had both very high rates of capital formation and rapid improvements in schooling levels. Despite this growth of inputs, their economic performance was unimpressive. Slow growth and poor living standards eventually led to their collapse.

The last decade has seen a renewal of interest in the effects of institutions and policies on economic growth. Building on the work of Peter Bauer and Douglass C. North, this "new growth theory" stresses the importance of an economic environment that is consistent with the development and efficient use of resources.[6] Proponents of

[5]Robert Solow, "A Contribution to the Theory of Economic Growth," *Quarterly Journal of Economics* 70, no. 1 (February 1956): 65–94.

[6]See Peter T. Bauer, *Dissent on Development: Studies and Debates in Development Economics* (Cambridge: Harvard University Press, 1972); and Douglass C. North, *Institutions, Institutional Change, and Economic Performance* (Cambridge: Cambridge University Press, 1990).

OUTSTANDING ECONOMIST

Douglass C. North (1920–)

A 1993 recipient of the Nobel Prize in Economics, he is best known for his application of both economic theory and statistical analysis to topics in the field of economic history. A professor at Washington University in St. Louis, his work indicates that the development of both patent laws and the corporation as a legal entity were important sources of economic growth during the 17th and 18th centuries. His analysis of the linkage between institutional change and economic progress has played an important role in the development of the new growth theory.

the new growth theory, such as Robert Barro of Harvard and Gerald Scully of the University of Texas, argue that inappropriate institutions and policies can cause growth to fall well below its potential.[7] Furthermore, the more recent approach stresses that when nations establish a sound environment, people will develop their skills (human capital), and investors—both foreign and domestic—will supply the necessary physical capital. In many ways, this recent view is a return to the approach of Adam Smith, who also stressed the importance of policies and institutions.

INSTITUTIONS AND POLICIES CONDUCIVE TO ECONOMIC GROWTH

Policy can influence growth, either for good or ill, in many ways. The task is thus to try to exploit as many as possible of these avenues for good.

Arnold C. Harberger[8]

What types of institutions and policies will promote economic growth? Of course, numerous factors are of some significance, but economic theory suggests a few that are vitally important. We have already discussed some of them; others will be considered in

THUMBNAIL SKETCH

Sources of Economic Growth	Key Institutions and Policies That Enhance Efficiency and Growth
1. Investment in physical and human capital	1. Secure property rights and political stability
2. Advancements in technology	2. Competitive markets
3. Institutions and policies that improve economic efficiency	3. Stable money and prices
	4. Free trade
	5. Open capital markets
	6. Avoidance of high marginal tax rates

[7]See Robert Barro and Xaviar Sala-I-Martin, *Economic Growth* (New York: McGraw-Hill, 1995); and Gerald Scully, *Constitutional Environments and Economic Growth* (Princeton: Princeton University Press, 1992).

[8]Arnold C. Harberger, *Economic Policy and Economic Growth* (San Francisco: International Center for Economic Growth, 1985), p. 8.

more detail as we proceed. The accompanying Thumbnail Sketch lists six primary ingredients for the creation of an environment that promotes economic efficiency and growth. Let us consider each of them.

Security of Property Rights and Political Stability

As we have previously discussed, private ownership provides legal protection against those who would use violence, theft, and fraud to take things that do not belong to them. Most important is the incentive structure that emanates from private ownership. ***When the property rights of all citizens—including the vitally important property right to their labor—are clearly defined and securely enforced, production and trade replace plunder as the means of acquiring wealth. When property ownership rights are well defined and enforced, people get ahead by helping and cooperating with others.*** Employers, for example, have to provide prospective employees and other resource suppliers with at least as good a deal as they can get elsewhere. To succeed, business owners will have to develop and provide potential customers with goods and services that they value highly (relative to cost). Moreover, private owners have an incentive to practice wise maintenance and conservation. An owner who fails to maintain the owned assets properly will see the value of those assets, and thus the owner's wealth, decline.

Throughout history, people have searched for and established other forms of ownership that they thought would be more humanitarian or more productive. These experiences have ranged from unsuccessful to disastrous. To date, we do not know of any institutional arrangement that provides individuals with as much freedom and incentive to use resources productively and efficiently as does private ownership.[9]

A volatile political climate undermines the security of property rights. Historically, some governments have confiscated physical and financial assets, imposed punitive taxes, and used regulations to punish those out of favor with the current political regime. Countries with a history like this will find it difficult to restore confidence and reestablish the security of property rights.

Unfortunately, the political climate of many poor, less-developed countries is highly unstable. In some cases, prejudice, injustice, and highly unequal wealth status create a fertile environment for political upheaval. In other instances, political corruption and a history of favoritism to a ruling class provide the seeds for unrest. Regardless of its source, one thing is clear: Potential political upheaval that reduces the security of property rights will repel capital investment and retard economic growth. In recent years, this factor has contributed to the dismal economic performance of several nations, including the Democratic Republic of Congo, Haiti, Nicaragua, Russia, and several other countries of the former Soviet Union (see Exhibit 16–3).

Competitive Markets

As Adam Smith stressed long ago, when competition is present, even self-interested individuals will tend to promote the general welfare. Conversely, when competition is weakened, business firms have more leeway to raise prices and pursue their own objectives and less incentive to innovate and develop better ways of doing things. Such policies as free entry into businesses and occupations, and freedom of exchange with

[9]For evidence that a legal system that protects property rights, enforces contracts, and relies on rule-of-law principles for the settlement of disputes among parties promotes economic growth, see Stephen Knack and Philip Keefer, "Institutions and Economic Performance: Cross-Country Tests Using Alternative Institutional Measures," *Economics and Politics* 7 (1995): 207–227.

foreigners, will enhance competition and thereby help to promote economic progress. In contrast, such policies as business subsidies, price controls, entry restraints, and trade restrictions stifle competition and conflict with economic progress.

Competition is a disciplining force for both buyers and sellers. In a competitive environment, producers must provide goods at a low cost and serve the interests of consumers since they will have to woo them away from other suppliers. Firms that develop improved products and figure out how to produce them at a low cost will succeed. Sellers that are unwilling or unable to provide consumers with quality goods at competitive prices will be driven from the market. This process leads to improvement in both products and production methods, while directing resources toward projects where they are able to produce more value. It is a powerful stimulus for economic progress.

Stable Money and Prices

A stable monetary environment provides the foundation for the efficient operation of a market economy. In contrast, monetary and price instability make both the price level and relative prices unpredictable, generate uncertainty, and undermine the security of contractual exchanges. When prices increase 20 percent one year, 50 percent the next year, 15 percent the year after that, and so on, individuals and businesses are unable to develop sensible long-term plans. The uncertainty will reduce the attractiveness of time-dimension exchanges, particularly investment decisions. Rather than deal with the uncertainties that accompany double-and triple-digit inflation rates, citizens will save less, while many investors and business decision makers will move their activities to countries with a more stable environment. Foreigners will invest elsewhere, and citizens will often go to great lengths to get their savings (potential funds for investment) out of the country. As a result, potential gains from capital formation and business activities will be lost.

International Trade and an Open Economy

In the absence of trade barriers, producers in various countries will be directed toward those areas where they have a comparative advantage, and the competition from abroad will help keep domestic producers on their toes. International trade allows the residents of each country to use more of their resources to supply goods they can produce at a low cost, while using the proceeds from these sales to purchase goods that could be produced domestically only at a high cost. As a result, the trading partners are each able to produce a larger output and purchase a wider variety of products at more economical prices than would otherwise be possible.

Policies that retard international trade stifle this process and thereby retard economic progress. Obviously, tariffs (taxes on imported goods) and quotas fall into this category because they limit the ability of domestic citizens to trade with people in other countries. So, too, do exchange-rate controls. When a nation fixes the exchange-rate value of its currency above the market level, the country's export products will be unattractive to foreigners. But if domestic citizens sell less to foreigners, they will have less foreign currency with which to buy from foreigners. Thus, exchange-rate controls will reduce the volume of international trade and thereby retard economic progress.

Open Capital Market

If investment is going to increase the wealth of a nation, capital must be channeled into productive projects. When the value of the additional output derived from an investment exceeds the cost of the investment, the project will increase the value of the resources, and thereby create wealth. In contrast, if the value of the additional output is less than the cost of the investment, undertaking the project will reduce the wealth of the nation. If a nation is going to realize its potential, it must have a mechanism capable of attracting savings and channeling them into wealth-creating projects. A competitive capital market performs this function.

When a nation's capital market is integrated with the world capital market, it will be able to attract savings (financial capital) from throughout the world at the cheapest possible price (interest rate). Similarly, its citizens will have access to the most attractive investment opportunities regardless of where those opportunities are located.

In a competitive capital market, private investors have a strong incentive to evaluate projects carefully and allocate their funds toward those projects expected to yield the highest rates of return. In turn, profitable projects will tend to increase the wealth not only of the investor but also of the nation.

When governments fix interest rates, they hamper the ability of the capital market to bring savers and investors together and channel funds into wealth-creating projects. Worse still, when the fixing of interest rates is combined with inflationary monetary policy, negative real interest rates will result. In turn, the negative rates will lead to capital flight as domestic investors seek positive returns abroad and foreign investors completely shun the country's potential investment projects. Such policies undermine capital markets, while retarding both investment and economic growth.

Without a capital market, it will be virtually impossible to consistently allocate saving into wealth-creating projects. If investment funds are allocated by governments rather than by the capital market, political clout rather than the expected rate of return will determine which projects are undertaken. And when politics replaces economic considerations, predictably more unprofitable and counterproductive investments will be undertaken. The experience of Eastern Europe and the former Soviet Union highlights this point. For four decades (1950–1990), the investment rates (as a share of GDP) of these countries were among the highest in the world. These countries channeled approximately one-third of GDP into investment. But even these high rates of investment did little to improve living standards. Without the direction of a capital market, the investment funds were often channeled toward political and military projects favored by the planners rather than toward projects that would increase the future availability of consumer goods.

Avoidance of High Marginal Tax Rates

When high marginal tax rates take a large share of the fruits generated by productive activities, the incentive of individuals to work and undertake business projects is reduced. High tax rates may also drive a nation's most productive citizens to other countries (where taxes are lower) and discourage foreigners from financing domestic investment projects. In short, economic theory indicates that high marginal tax rates will retard productive activity, capital formation, and economic growth.

The most detailed study of the impact of high marginal tax rates on the economic growth of LDCs has been conducted by Alvin Rabushka of Stanford University.[10] Rabushka found that the countries that kept marginal tax rates low (or applied high marginal rates only at exceedingly high income thresholds) generally experienced more rapid economic growth. He summarized his findings as follows:

> Good economic policy, including tax policy, fosters economic growth and rising prosperity. In particular, low marginal income tax rates, or high thresholds

[10]See Alvin Rabushka, "Taxation, Economic Growth, and Liberty," *Cato Journal* (spring–summer 1987): 121–148.

for medium-and high-rate tax schedules, appear consistent with higher growth rates. The key in any system of direct taxation is to maintain low tax rates or high (income) thresholds.[11]

High taxes on employment can also reduce economic efficiency. A large gap between the employer's cost of hiring a worker and the employee's take-home pay will reduce employment in the formal economy. Such policies tend to drive workers into the "informal," or underground, economy, where the legal structure is less certain and property rights less secure. This reduces the gains from investment and trade, and thereby retards economic growth.

THE SIZE OF GOVERNMENT AND ECONOMIC GROWTH

The preceding section makes it clear that various functions of government are vitally important for the smooth operation of markets and the efficient allocation of resources. These activities might be called the core functions of government. Although there is room for debate concerning the precise activities that comprise these core functions, two general categories emerge: (1) activities that protect persons and their property from plunder and (2) provision of a limited set of public goods that for various reasons markets may find it difficult to provide.

As governments undertake and provide these core functions, they will enhance economic growth. It is easy to identify a number of these core functions. Certainly, the establishment and operation of legal and police systems capable of maintaining secure property rights, enforcing contracts, and resolving disputes among parties would be included. So, too, would a stable monetary regime that would facilitate the operation of markets and business planning across time periods. In addition, government provision of some public goods, such as roads and national defense to protect the citizenry from intrusions by foreigners, are also likely to promote economic growth. Public sector expenditures that expand educational opportunity and the development of human capital may also be beneficial.

However, as government continues to grow and more and more resources are allocated by political rather than market forces, four major factors suggest that the beneficial effects on economic growth will wane and eventually become negative.

1. ***Higher taxes and/or additional borrowing will impose an increasing burden of deadweight losses on the economy, as the size of government expands.*** When government takes more and more of the earnings of workers, their incentive to invest, to take risks, and to undertake productivity-enhancing activities decreases. Like taxes, borrowing will crowd out private investment and will also lead to higher future taxes. Thus, even if the productivity of government expenditures did not decline, the disincentive effects of taxation and borrowing required to shift resources from the private sector to the public sector will increase with the size of government as a share of the economy.
2. ***As government grows relative to the market sector, diminishing returns will reduce the rate of return derived from government activity.*** A government that concentrates on those functions for which it is best suited (for example, the core

[11]Alvin Rabushka, "Taxation and Liberty in the Third World" (Paper presented at conference on Taxation and Liberty, Santa Fe, New Mexico, September 26–27, 1985).

functions previously mentioned), and performs these functions well, enables the efficient operation of markets, thus enhancing economic growth. As it expands into other areas, such as the provision of infrastructure and education, the government may continue to improve performance and promote growth. If the expansion in government continues, however, expenditures are channeled into areas where government is less and less productive. As the government becomes larger and undertakes more activities for which it is ill-suited, economic growth is retarded. For example, this is likely to result when governments become involved in the provision of private goods—goods for which the consumption benefits accrue to individual consumers. Goods like food, housing, medical service, and child care fall into this category. There is no reason to expect that governments will either allocate or provide such goods more efficiently than the market sector.

3. ***The political process is much less dynamic than the market process. Compared to the market, there is less incentive to discover and undertake productive actions (and to refrain from counterproductive activities) in the government sector.*** In the market sector, profit provides decision makers with a strong incentive to keep cost low, discover better ways of doing things, and adopt improved technologies quickly. On the other hand, losses impose swift and sure punishment on those that have high cost and/or use resources unproductively. Thus, market dynamics are constantly channeling resources toward uses that are more highly valued. There is

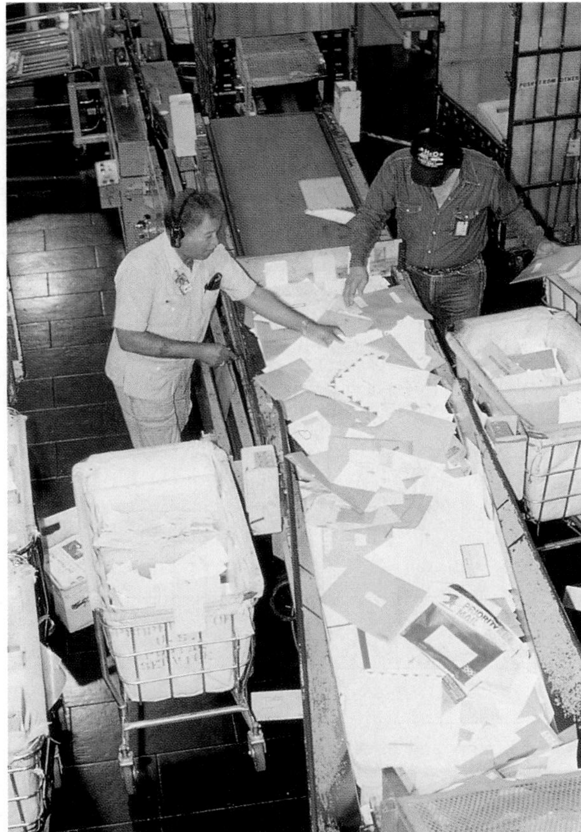

Are government enterprises innovative? Can they be counted on to deliver quality service at a reasonable price?

no similar mechanism that performs this function effectively in the public sector. Thus, adjustment to change is much slower in the public sector. By way of comparison with markets, the required time for the weeding out of errors (for example, bad investments) and adjusting to changing circumstances, new information, and improved technologies is more lengthy for governments. This is a major shortcoming as it relates to economic growth. To a large degree, growth is a discovery process. As entrepreneurs discover new and improved technologies, better methods of production, and opportunities that were previously overlooked, they are able to combine resources into goods and services that are more highly valued.[12]

4. ***As government grows, it invariably becomes more heavily involved in the redistribution of income and regulatory activism. In turn, these activities will encourage wasteful rent-seeking.*** As we discussed in Chapter 6, government income transfers and discriminatory regulations will induce individuals to shift resources away from wealth-creating activities toward the pursuit of government favors. This shift will retard economic growth and lead to income levels well below the economy's potential.[13]

In summary, while government activities that focus on the areas where it has a comparative advantage will enhance growth, continued growth of government will eventually exert a negative impact on the economy. **Exhibit 16–4** illustrates the implications with regard to the expected relationship between the size of government and economic growth, *assuming that governments undertake activities based on their rate of return.* As the size of government, measured on the horizontal axis, expands from zero (complete anarchy), initially the growth rate of the economy—measured on the vertical axis—increases. The A to B range of the curve illustrates this situation. As

If governments undertake activities in the order of their productivity, at first government expenditures would promote economic growth (moves from A to B above), but additional expenditures would eventually retard growth (moves along the curve to the right of B).

EXHIBIT 16–4

THE SIZE OF GOVERNMENT–GROWTH CURVE

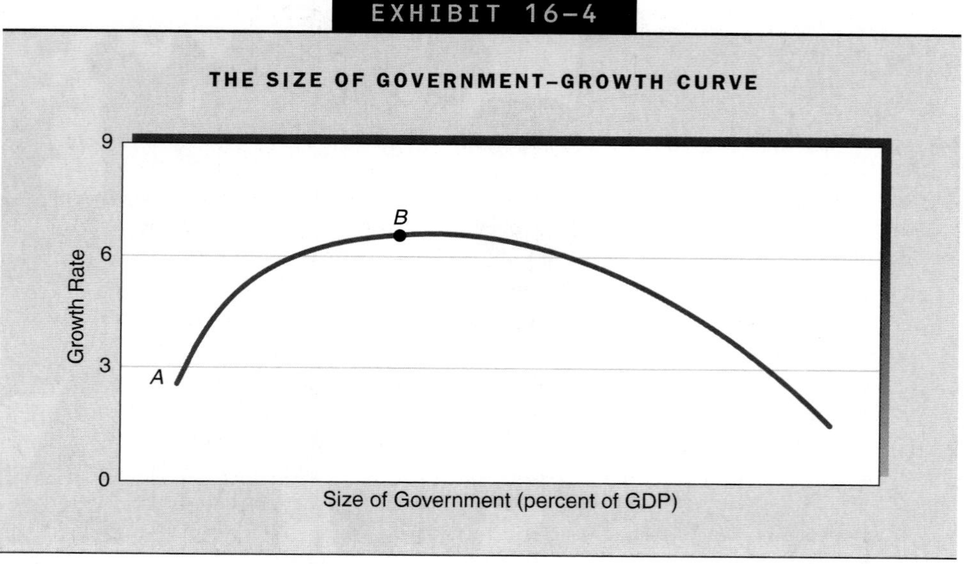

[12]Israel Kirzner and Joseph Schumpeter have contributed the classic literature on this topic. See Kirzner, *Competition and Entrepreneurship* (Chicago, IL: University of Chicago Press, 1973); and Schumpeter, *The Theory of Economic Development* (1912). Translated by R. Opie, 1934. Reprinted 1961.

[13]See Gordon Tullock, "The Welfare Costs of Tariffs, Monopolies, and Theft," *Western Economic Journal* 5 (1967): 224–232; and Anna Kreuger, "The Political Economy of the Rent-Seeking Society," *American Economic Review* 64 (1974): 291–303, for additional details and analysis of the harmful side effects of rent seeking.

EXHIBIT 16–5

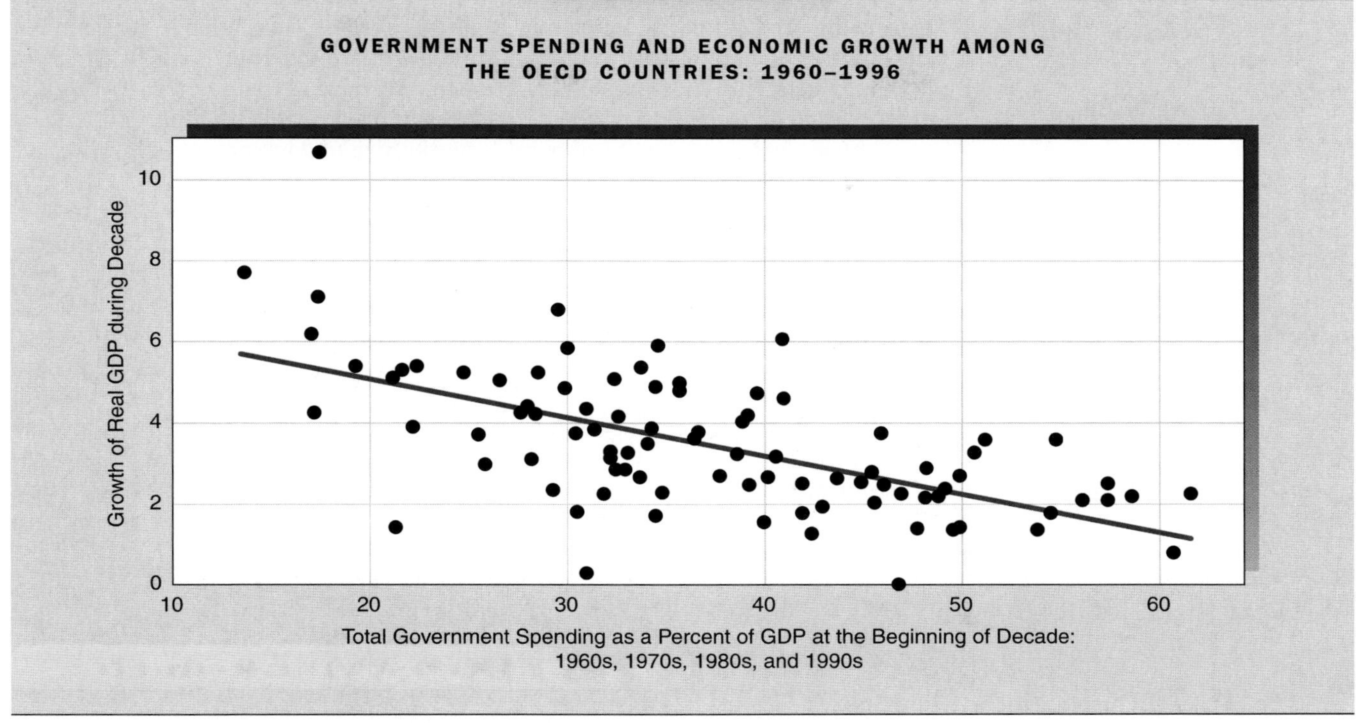

Here we show the relationship between size of government at the beginning of the decade and growth of real GDP during the decade. These data indicate that a 10 percent increase in government expenditures as a share of GDP reduces the annual rate of growth by about 1 percent.

government continues to grow as a share of the economy, expenditures are channeled into less-productive (and later counterproductive) activities, causing the rate of economic growth to diminish and eventually decline.[14] The range of the curve beyond B illustrates this point.[15] Thus, our analysis indicates that there is a set of activities and size of government that will maximize economic growth. Expansion of government beyond (and outside of) these functions will retard economic growth.

How large is the growth-maximizing size of government? This is a complex and difficult question. However, several researchers have addressed this topic. **Exhibit 16–5** presents data for OECD countries on size of government at the beginning of the decade (measured on the x-axis) and growth of real GDP *during the decade* (measured on the y-axis). The exhibit contains four dots for each of the 23 OECD members—one for each of the four decades—for a total of 92 dots. Each dot represents a country's total government spending *at the beginning of the decade* and its accompanying growth of real GDP *during that decade.* As the plot illustrates, there is a clearly observable negative relationship between size of government and long-term growth of real GDP.

[14]For the development of a formal model with the characteristics we have outlined here, see Robert J. Barro, "Government Spending in a Simple Model of Endogenous Growth," *Journal of Political Economy* 98 (1990): S103–S125.

[15]In the real world, governments may not undertake activities based on their rate of return and comparative advantage. Many governments that are small relative to the size of the economy fail to focus on the core activities that are likely to enhance economic growth. Thus, one would expect that the relationship between size of government and economic growth will be a loose one. The empirical evidence is consistent with this view.

The "best fit" line drawn through the points indicates that a 10 percentage point increase in government expenditures as a share of GDP leads to approximately a 1 percentage point reduction in economic growth. During this period, government expenditures as a share of GDP ranged from a low of around 15 percent to a high of more than 60 percent. There was no evidence that the size of the government was too small in any of these countries. Put another way, the evidence indicates that all of these countries were to the right of point B on the size of government–growth curve of Exhibit 16–4.[16]

While Exhibit 16–5 utilizes data across countries, time series data for specific countries have also been used to investigate the link between size of government and growth. Edgar Peden estimates that for the United States, the "maximum productivity growth occurs when government expenditures represent about 20% of GDP." Gerald Scully estimates that the growth-maximizing size of government (combined federal, state, and local) is "between 21.5 percent and 22.9 percent of gross national product (GNP)." Although the methodology of these studies differs, they do have one thing in common: They all indicate that size of government in high-income industrial countries is too large to maximize economic growth.[17] Given the long-term significance of relatively small differences in growth rates, this has important implications. This is an exciting area that is sure to attract additional research in the future.

ECONOMIC FREEDOM AND GROWTH

Since the time of Adam Smith, economists have generally argued that freer economies are likely to be more productive. Is this really true? Economic freedom is complex and multidimensional. Therefore, it is very difficult to measure. Beginning in the mid-1980s, the Fraser Institute began work on a special project designed to develop a cross-country measure of economic freedom. Several leading scholars, including Nobel laureates Milton Friedman and Douglass North, participated in the endeavor. This eventually led to the development of an index of economic freedom that covered approximately 100 countries.[18]

This index—now published by a network of institutes in nearly 50 countries—is based on the premise that personal choice, freedom of exchange, and protection of private property are the central ingredients of economic freedom. Various components were assembled and used to measure the consistency of the legal structure and policies of various countries with sound money, reliance on markets, avoidance of takings and discriminatory taxes, and freedom of international exchange. In order to achieve a high economic freedom rating, governments had to do some things but

[16]The findings presented here are from James Gwartney, Robert Lawson, and Randall Holcombe, *The Size and Functions of Government and Economic Growth* (Washington: Joint Economic Committee of the U.S. Congress, 1998). These authors also found that the OECD countries with largest *increases* in size of government between 1960 and 1996 had the largest *reductions* in economic growth during this period.

[17]See Edgar Peden, "Productivity in the United States and Its Relationship to Government Activity: An Analysis of 57 Years, 1929–1986," *Public Choice* 69 (1991): 153–173; and Gerald Scully, *What Is the Optimal Size of Government in the United States?* (Dallas, TX: National Center for Policy Analysis, 1994).

[18]See James Gwartney, Robert Lawson, and Walter Block, *Economic Freedom of the World: 1975–1995* (Vancouver: Fraser Institute 1996); and James Gwartney and Robert Lawson, *Economic Freedom of the World: 1997 Report* (Vancouver: Fraser Institute, 1997).

refrain from doing others. They had to create a stable monetary environment and allow individuals to choose for themselves. But they also had to keep taxes low, allow most production to take place in the private sector, and refrain from creating barriers to both domestic and international trade. **Exhibit 16–6** indicates the 10 most free and 10 least free economies in the world as measured by the 1997 Fraser index (because of ties, there are 12 in each category).

In many respects, this index reflects the factors listed in the Thumbnail Sketch (page 412) that are most likely to enhance economic efficiency and growth. If secure property rights, monetary stability, free trade, and reliance on markets really matter, this index should be closely correlated with prosperity and growth. **Exhibit 16–7** indicates that this is indeed the case. Clearly, countries with more economic freedom in 1995 also had both a higher average per-capita GDP and more rapid average growth rates during 1985–1996.

Although the data of Exhibit 16–7 are not adjusted for other factors, such as initial income level, demographic factors, investment, and years of schooling,

EXHIBIT 16–6

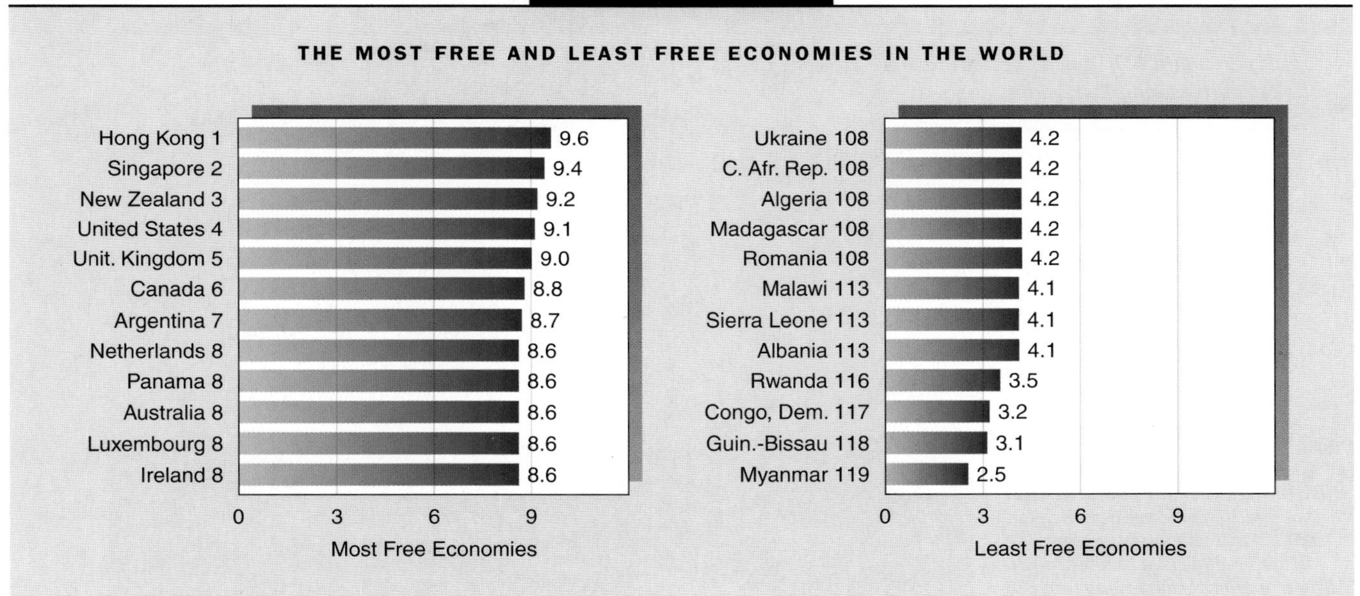

The Fraser Institute was able to assemble the required data to rate the economic freedom of 119 economies in 1997. The summary ratings presented here are based on data for 25 different components designed to identify the consistency of institutions and policies with economic freedom. Among the components incorporated into the index were: government consumption as a share of GDP, government enterprises as a share of the economy, standard deviation of the inflation rate, freedom to use alternative currencies, rule of law, mean tariff rate, exchange rate controls, and capital market controls. Countries that permitted their citizens to engage more freely in trade and that relied more fully on markets (rather than on government expenditures and regulations) to allocate goods received higher ratings. The ten most free economies in 1997 are indicated on the left. Hong Kong, Singapore, New Zealand, the United States, and the United Kingdom head this list. The ten least free are presented on the right. Myanmar, Guinea-Bissau, the Democratic Republic of Congo (formerly Zaire), and Rwanda were rated the least free. It is important to note that this index was designed to measure economic freedom, rather than political freedom, civil liberties, or degree of democracy.

SOURCE: James Gwartney and Robert Lawson, Economic Freedom of the World: 1998–1999 Interim Report *(Vancouver: Fraser Institute, 1998).*

EXHIBIT 16-7

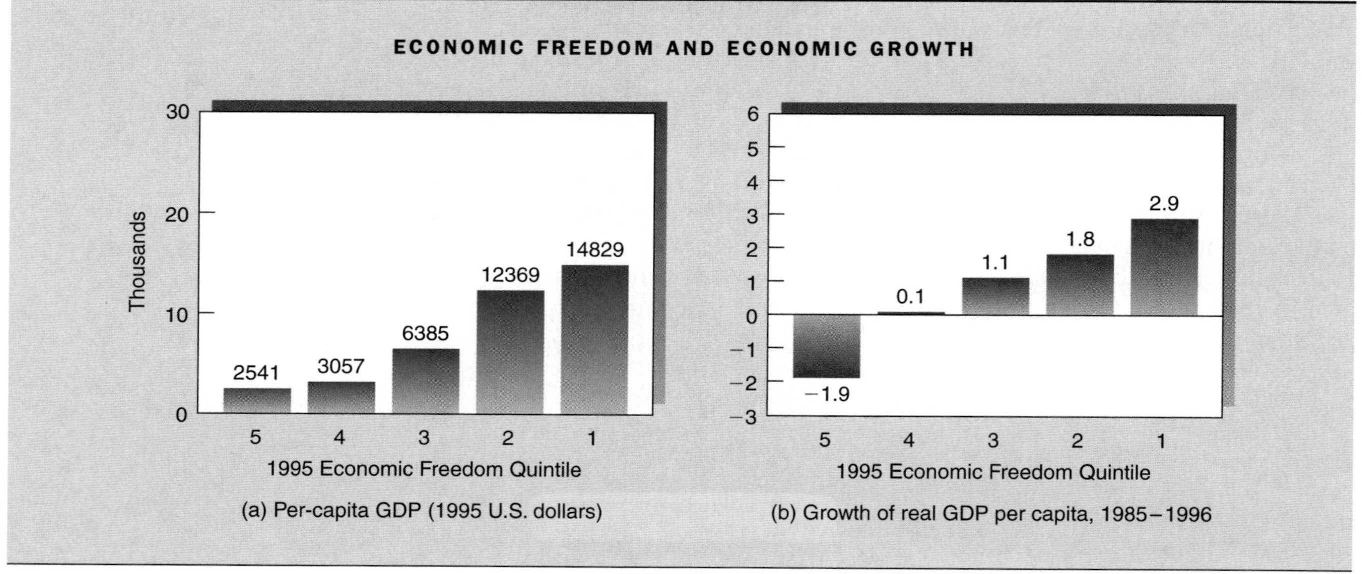

Both per-capita GDP and its growth rate are positively linked with economic freedom.

SOURCE: James Gwartney and Robert Lawson, Economic Freedom of the World: 1997 Annual Report *(Vancouver: Fraser Institute, 1997), p. 34.*

Despite recent problems accompanying the Asian financial crisis, Hong Kong is still a modern economic miracle. Even though its income per person fell in 1998, it was still almost 9 times the figure for 1960 (see Exhibit 16–2). The economy of Hong Kong is one of the most free—if not the freest—in the world. Will it remain that way, now that it is once again united with China?

more comprehensive analysis indicates that even after these factors are taken into consideration, countries with more economic freedom tend to grow more rapidly.[19] This indicates that, like additional capital equipment and improved technology, sound institutions and policies also enhance economic growth.

IS THE GROWTH TREND OF THE U.S. CHANGING?

In the previous chapter, we noted the unprecedented stability of the U.S. economy during the last 15 years. The growth record has been much less impressive. In fact, there is substantial concern about an apparent slowdown in economic growth among most all the high-income industrial countries during the last 25 years. During this period, the growth of both income and productivity has slowed throughout Europe, North America, and Japan.

Exhibit 16–8 presents the U.S. growth figures for both real GDP and productivity (output per hour worked) during the last four decades. As these data show, the growth of real GDP has fallen each decade since the 1960s. Even though the economy has continually expanded in the 1990s, the 2.5 percent average annual rate of growth is nonetheless well below the 4.4 percent figure achieved during the 1960s. The slowdown in productivity is even more pronounced. The growth of output per hour worked during the last two decades—1.2 percent in the 1980s and 1.5 percent during the 1990s—is less than half the comparable figure for the 1960s.

Despite this record, there is some reason for optimism. Several factors favorable to economic growth are now present. The persistent low rate of inflation has reduced the uncertainty accompanying long-term projects. The international trade sector has doubled as a share of the economy since 1980. The size of government as a share of the economy has declined slightly during the 1990s, primarily because of reductions in defense expenditures following the collapse of communism and the end of the Cold War. Even demographic factors are now positive. The baby-boom generation now ranges in age from 40 to 55 years. This is precisely the life-cycle period where education and experience generally combine to generate both peak earnings and high savings rates.

There is some evidence that these favorable factors may now be exerting a positive impact on economic growth. During 1995–1998, the average growth rate of real GDP was 3.5 percent, still below the rate of the 1960s, but better than the rates of the 1970s and 1980s. After stagnating throughout most of 1987–1995, productivity has also improved during the last three years. Are the favorable figures of the last three or four years the beginning of a sustained period of more rapid growth? Or are they merely a temporary upturn in the midst of long-term secular decline? At this point, it is too early to tell. But one can be sure that economists and others will be monitoring these figures closely during the next few years. The quality of our long-range economic future may well depend on them.

---

[19]For a comprehensive analysis indicating that economic freedom enhances growth, see John W. Dawson, "Institutions, Investment, and Growth: New Cross-Countries and Panel Data Evidence," *Economic Inquiry* 36 (October 1998): 603–619; Stephen T. Easton and Michael Walker, "Income, Growth, and Economic Freedom," *American Economic Review* 87, no. 2 (May, 1997): 328–332; and James Gwartney, Randall Holcombe, and Robert Lawson, "Economic Freedom and the Environment for Economic Growth," *Journal of Institutional and Theoretical Economics* (forthcoming).

The average growth rate of real GDP has fallen during each of the last three decades. The growth of productivity per hour worked during the 1980s and 1990s was less than half the rate achieved during the 1960s. Unless these trends are reversed, the income of Americans will grow more slowly in the future.

SOURCE: Economic Report of the President, *1999, Tables B-2 and B-50.*

EXHIBIT 16-8

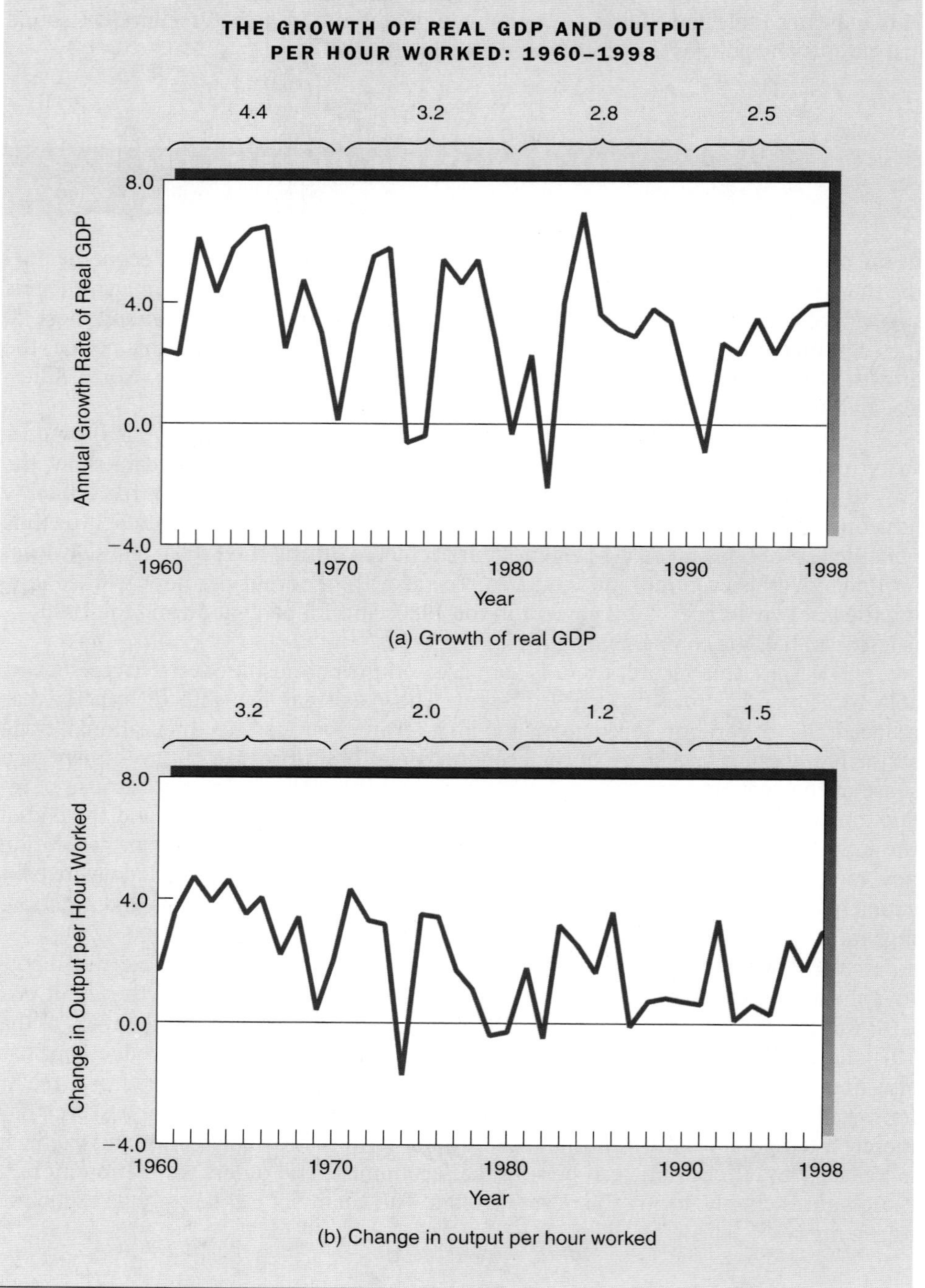

LOOKING *Ahead*

International trade and global financial markets exert an increasingly important impact on our lives. As was noted in this chapter, both international trade and financial markets capable of directing capital toward productive projects are key ingredients of prosperity. The next two chapters will focus on these topics.

KEY POINTS

➤ Economic growth increases the production possibilities of an economy. Within the *AD/AS* model, growth is indicated by a shift to the right in the long-run aggregate supply (LRAS) curve.

➤ When real GDP expands more rapidly than population, per-capita real GDP increases. The growth of per-capita real GDP means more goods and services per person, which typically leads to higher living standards and improvements in life expectancy, literacy, and health.

➤ Even seemingly small differences in growth rates sustained over two or three decades will substantially alter the relative incomes. For example, if Country A and Country B have the same initial income but the growth rate of A is 2 percent greater than that of B, after 35 years the income level of Country A will be twice that of B.

➤ The growth picture of LDCs is clearly one of diversity. Over the last several decades, the fastest-growing countries in the world have been LDCs. These rapidly growing countries have closed the income gap relative to their wealthier counterparts. At the same time, other LDCs are doing very poorly and falling farther and farther behind.

➤ Contrary to a popular view, the availability of domestic natural resources is not the major determinant of growth. Countries such as Japan and Hong Kong have impressive growth rates without such resources, while many resource-rich nations continue to stagnate.

➤ Economic growth is a complex process. Economists stress the importance of three major sources of economic progress: (1) investment in physical and human capital, (2) technological advances, and (3) institutional and policy changes that improve the efficiency of economic organization.

➤ The following are important for the efficiency of economic organization: (a) secure property rights and political stability, (b) competitive markets, (c) monetary stability, (d) freedom to trade with foreigners, (e) a capital market that directs investment toward productive projects, and (f) avoidance of high tax rates.

➤ When governments focus on the provision of (a) a legal and enforcement structure that protects people and their property from aggression by others and (b) a limited set of public goods, they promote economic growth. However, when governments expand into activities for which they are ill-suited, they deter growth. The empirical evidence indicates that the governments of most, if not all, industrial countries are larger than the growth-maximizing size.

➤ More economic freedom is present when people are permitted to choose for themselves, trade freely with others in both domestic and international markets, and live in an environment where property rights are secure and money has a stable value. Countries with more economic freedom tend to grow more rapidly.

CRITICAL ANALYSIS QUESTIONS

1. Imagine you are an economic advisor to the president of a less-developed country. You have been asked to suggest policies to promote economic growth and a higher standard of living for the citizens. Outline your suggestions and discuss their rationale.

2. What can government do to promote economic growth? Is the role of government important? Why or why not? As the size of government increases as a share of the economy, how is the growth rate of real GDP likely to be affected? Explain.

*3. "Without aid from the industrial nations, poor countries are caught in the poverty trap. Because they are poor, they are unable to save and invest; and, lacking investment, they remain poor." Evaluate this view.

4. Discuss the importance of the following as determinants of economic growth: (a) natural resources, (b) physical capital, (c) human capital, (d) technical knowledge, (e) economic policy.

5. Evaluate each of the following policies in terms of its impact on the growth and prosperity of a nation.

a. Adoption of a regulation that would limit foreign ownership of domestic businesses
b. Imposition of a surtax on the corporate profits of foreign firms operating in the country
c. Legislation limiting the number of hours any employee can work during a week to 32
d. Adoption of a minimum wage equal to 75 percent of the country's average hourly wage
e. Legislation requiring employers to provide health care for all of their employees
f. Legislation requiring employers to provide one year of severance pay to any employee who is dismissed from employment

*6. How did the growth rate of productivity (output per hour worked) change during the 1973–1994 period? Why is productivity important? The large baby-boom generation is currently between the ages of 40 and 55 years. Does this influence the economywide level of productivity? Why or why not?

*7. Do you think that the absence of international trade barriers would be more important for a small country like Costa Rica than for a larger country like Mexico? Explain.

8. "Since government-operated firms do not have to make a profit, they can usually produce at a lower cost and charge a lower price than privately owned enterprises." Evaluate this view.

9. "Governments can promote economic growth by using taxes and subsidies to direct investment funds toward high-tech, heavy manufacturing, and other growth industries that will enhance the future income of the nation." Evaluate this view.

10. More than 200 years ago, Adam Smith argued that the wealth of nations was dependent upon gains from (a) specialization and trade, (b) expansion in the size of the market, and (c) the discovery of better (more productive) ways of doing things. Explain why you either agree or disagree with Smith's view.

11. "The institutional environment is the key to economic growth. If a nation creates an environment conducive for economic growth, people will supply and develop the resources and technology." Evaluate this view. Is the proper economic environment more important than the supply of resources? Why or why not?

---

*Asterisk denotes questions for which answers are given in Appendix B.

International economics

More than one-fifth of the worldwide output is produced in one country and exported to another country, twice the figure of 1960. In the United States, both the exports and imports have tripled *as a share of the economy* since 1960. Lower costs of both transpo tion and communications have contributed substan to the growth of international trade. Lower tariffs more liberal trade policies have also played a role.

The rapid grow of internationa trade is chang our lives. The world is becoming a global village.

DIFFERENCES AMONG COUNTRIES IN THE SIZE OF THE TRADE SECTOR

Here we illustrate the size of the trade sector as a share of the economy for various countries rouped by size. Data are presented for both 1970 and 997. Smaller, less populous countries (like Singapore, ong Kong, and Ireland) generally have larger trade sectors as a share of total output. Note the general increase trade between 1970 and 1997.

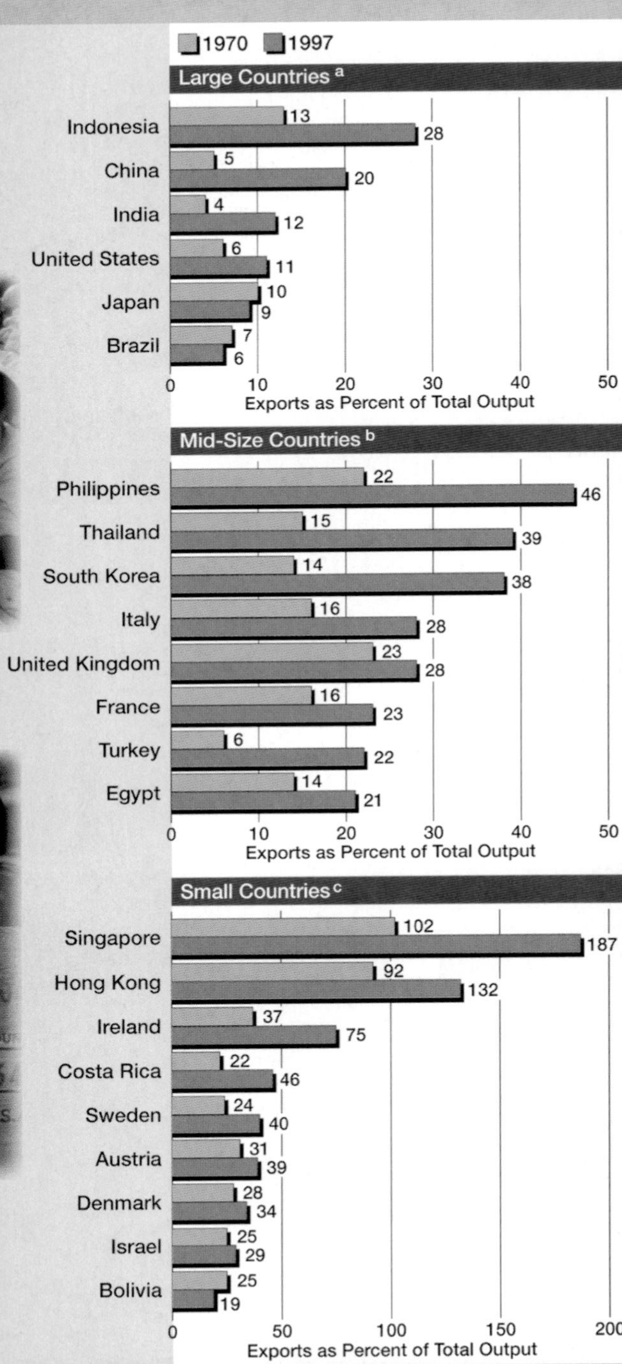

[a]*Population more than 120 million.*
[b]*Population between 40 and 65 million.*
[c]*Population less than 10 million.*
SOURCE: World Bank, World Development Report *(various years).*

EXHIBIT IV-A

THE MAJOR IMPORT AND EXPORT PRODUCTS OF THE UNITED STATES

Economic theory indicates that trade and specialization permit both the United States and its trading partners to achieve a larger output and a higher consumption level than would otherwise be possible. Domestic producers of export products, such as computers, aircraft, wheat, corn, and soybeans, gain from sales to foreigners at attractive prices. Domestic consumers of import products, such as petroleum, clothing, shoes, and electronic equipment, and agricultural products, such as coffee, bananas, and kiwi gain from the purchase of these goods from foreigners at low prices. Furthermore, competition in worldwide markets for automobiles, semiconductors, telecommunications equipment, and industrial machines enhances economic efficiency. International trade and competition help promote prosperity.

EXHIBIT IV-B

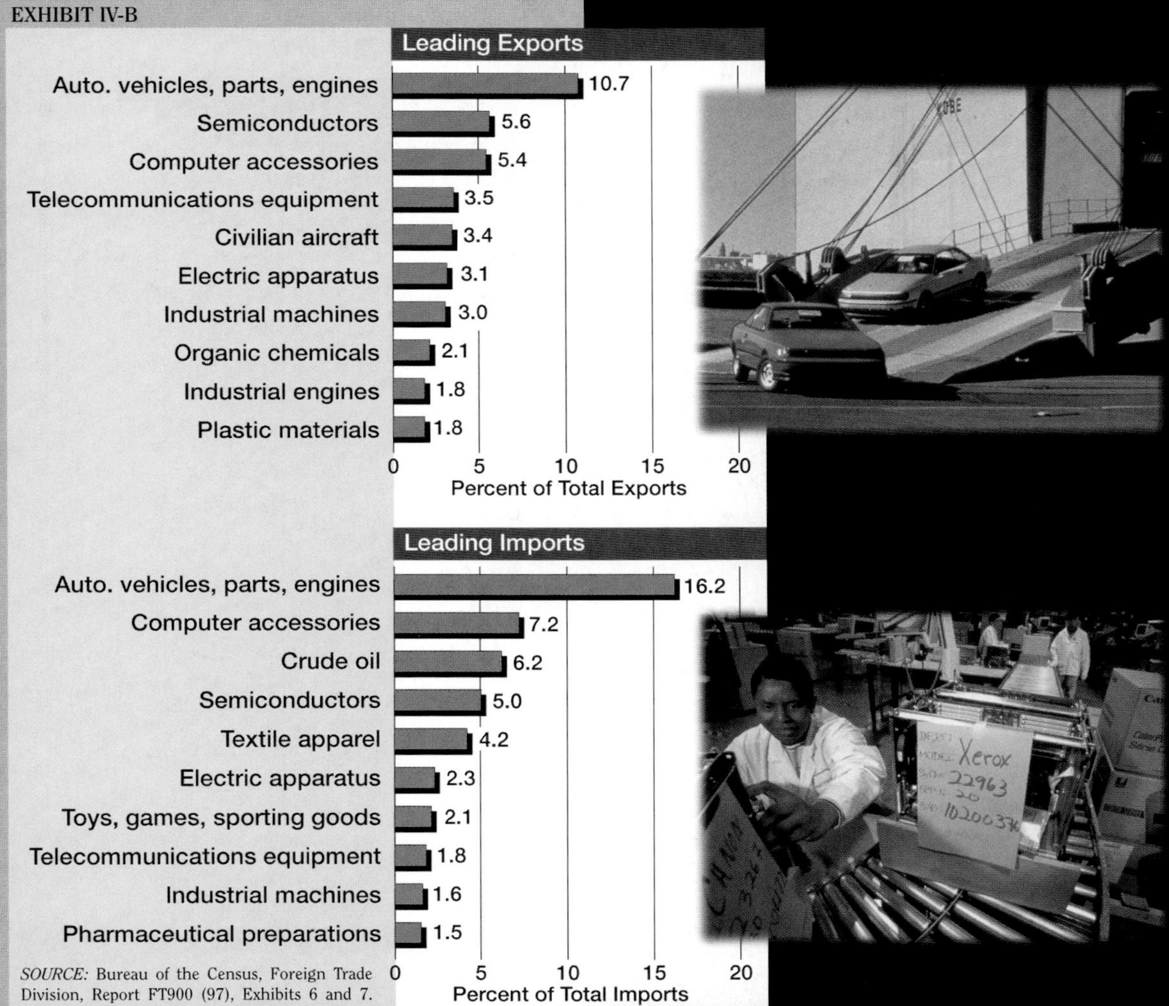

SOURCE: Bureau of the Census, Foreign Trade Division, Report FT900 (97), Exhibits 6 and 7.

Thirty percent of the new autos sold in the United States are produced by a foreign manufacturer. United States computer firms, such as Apple, Compaq, Dell, Gateway, and IBM, sell a large share of their output abroad.

THE MAJOR TRADING PARTNERS OF THE UNITED STATES

The major trading partners of the United States are Canada, Japan, and Mexico. In 1997, 42 percent of all United States trade was with these three countries. During the last decade, trade with Mexico has expanded rapidly.

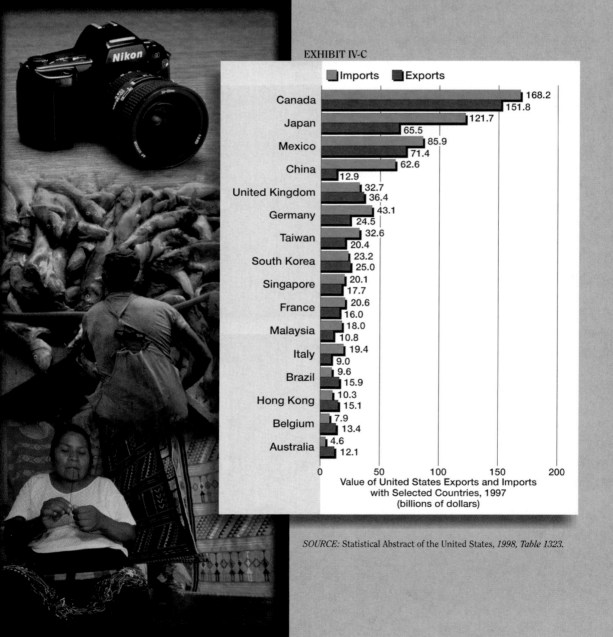

EXHIBIT IV-C

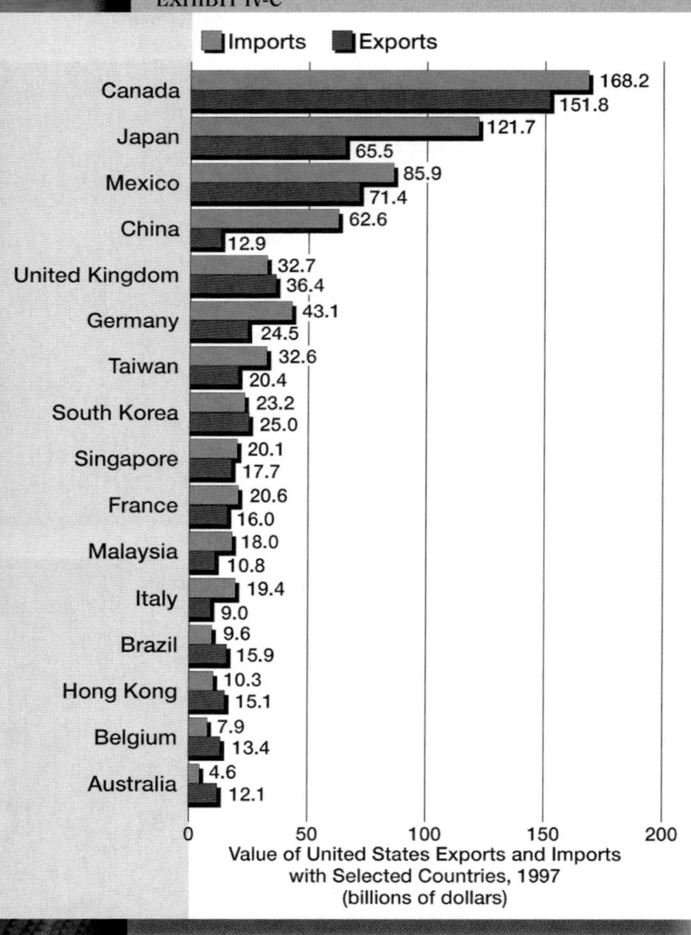

SOURCE: Statistical Abstract of the United States, *1998, Table 1323.*

TRADE GENERATES FOREIGN EXCHANGE TRANSACTIONS

Although the same general principles apply to trade among individuals, business firms, and nations, the latter generally involves the exchange of one currency for another. Thus, this section will analyze the impact of both international trade and the operation of the foreign exchange market.

CHAPTER 17

Free trade consists simply in letting people buy and sell as they want to buy and sell. It is protection [trade restrictions] that requires force, for it consists in preventing people from doing what they want to do.

Henry George[1]

Gaining from International Trade

CHAPTER FOCUS

- How has the magnitude of international trade changed in recent decades?
- Under what conditions can a nation gain from international trade?
- What impact do trade restrictions have on an economy?
- Do trade restrictions create jobs? Does trade with low-wage countries depress wage rates in high-wage countries like the United States?
- Why do nations adopt trade restrictions?
- How does the economic record of countries that impose trade restrictions compare with the record of those that follow more liberal trade policies?

---

[1]Henry George, *Protection or Free Trade* (1886; New York: Robert Schalkenbach Foundation, 1980), p. 47.

We live in a shrinking world. The breakfast of many Americans includes bananas from Honduras, coffee from Brazil, or hot chocolate made from Nigerian cocoa beans. Americans often drive a car produced by a Japanese or European manufacturer that consumes gasoline refined from petroleum extracted in Saudi Arabia or Venezuela. Similarly, many Americans work for companies that sell a substantial amount of their products to foreigners. Spurred by cost reductions in transportation and communications, the volume of international trade has grown rapidly in recent decades. Approximately 21 percent of the world's total output is now sold in a country other than that in which it was produced—double the figure of four decades ago.

Perhaps surprising to some, most international trade is not between the governments of the nations involved but rather between individuals and business firms that happen to be located in different countries. Why do people engage in international trade? The expectation of gain provides the answer. Domestic producers are often able to sell their products to foreigners at attractive prices, while domestic consumers sometimes find that the best deals are available from foreign suppliers. Like other voluntary exchange, international trade results because both the buyer and the seller expect to gain and generally do. If both parties did not expect to gain, they would not agree to the exchange.

CROSS COUNTRY DIFFERENCES IN THE SIZE OF THE TRADE SECTOR

The size of the trade sector varies substantially among nations. Some of the difference is due to size of country. For industries in which economies of scale are important, the domestic market of a less-populated country may not be large enough to support cost-efficient firms. Therefore, in small countries, firms in such industries will tend to export a larger share of their output, and consumers will be more likely to purchase goods produced abroad. As a result, the size of the trade sector as a share of the economy tends to be inversely related to the population of the country.

Even among countries of similar size, there is considerable variation in the size of the trade sector. (See Illustrated Exhibit IV-A at the beginning of this section for evidence on this point.) Among the countries with a large population (120 million or more), the trade sector is largest in Indonesia. In 1997, exports accounted for 28 percent of the Indonesian output, compared to 20 percent for China, 12 percent for India, and 11 percent for the United States. The trade sectors of Japan and Brazil were even smaller: 9 percent and 6 percent, respectively. Among the mid-size countries (population between 40 million and 65 million), the trade sectors of Thailand, Philippines, and South Korea are quite large, while those of Egypt, Turkey, and France are small. As a share of domestic output, Singapore and Hong Kong have the largest international trade sectors in the world. Both import large quantities of raw materials and unfinished goods and manufacture them into products that are often exported abroad. Therefore, the gross exports of these two vibrant trade centers actually exceed their gross domestic product.

THE TRADE SECTOR OF THE UNITED STATES

As **Exhibit 17–1** illustrates, the size of the trade sector of the United States has grown rapidly during the last several decades. In 1960, total exports of goods and services accounted for less than 4 percent of the U.S. economy, while imports summed to nearly 5 percent. By 1980, both exports and imports were approximately 7 percent of the economy. Since 1980 the size of the trade sector *as a share of the economy* has approximately doubled. In 1998, exports accounted for 13 percent of total output, while imports summed to 16.1 percent.[2]

Who are the major trading partners of Americans? Canada, Japan, and Mexico head the list. In 1997, approximately 42 percent of U.S. exports were sold to purchasers in these three countries. Canadians purchased 22 percent of U.S. exports, while Mexicans purchased 11 percent, and Japanese 10 percent. These three countries also supplied approximately 42 percent of the U.S. imports—19 percent by Canadians, 14 percent by Japanese, and 10 percent by Mexicans. The nations of the European Union (particularly Germany, the United Kingdom, France, and Italy), China (including Hong Kong), and several other smaller Asian countries (Taiwan, South Korea, Singapore, and Malaysia) are also major trading partners of the United States. (See Illustrated Exhibit IV-C for additional details.)

EXHIBIT 17–1

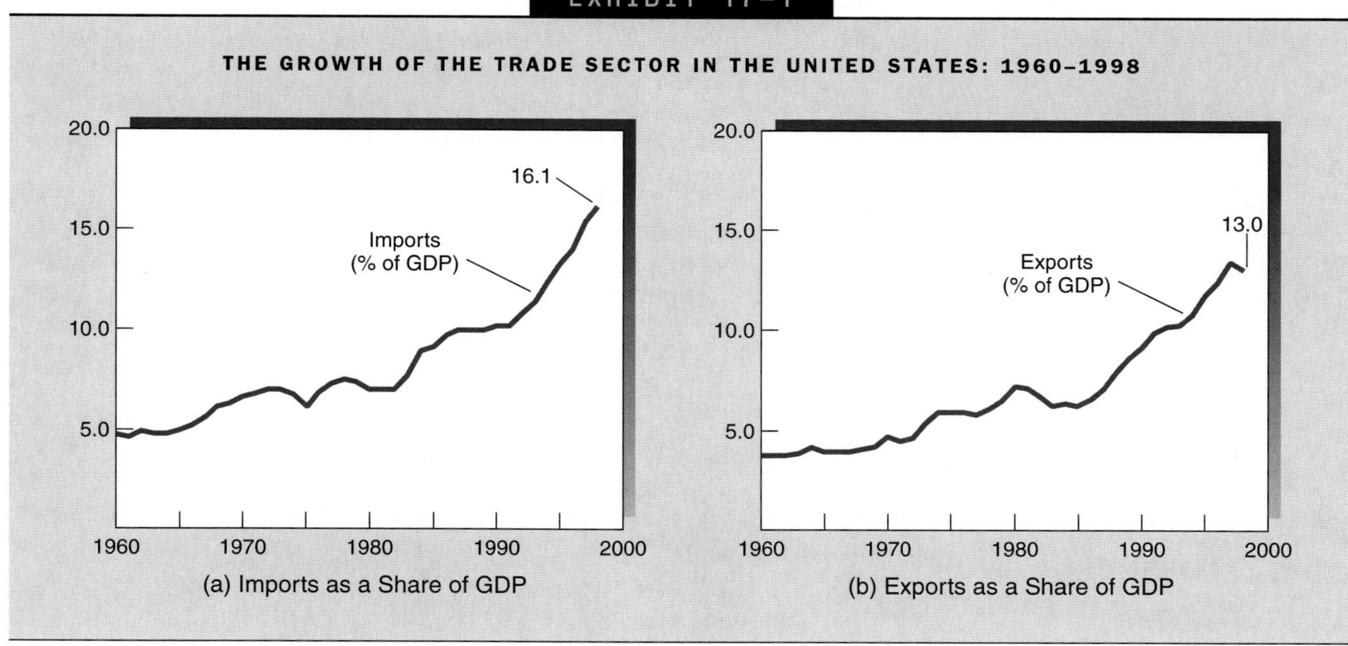

During the past several decades, international trade has grown more rapidly than total output. The growth of the trade sector has been exceedingly rapid since 1980. Imports rose from 7 percent of GDP in 1980 to 16.1 percent in 1998. During the same period, exports rose from 7 percent to 13 percent of GDP.

SOURCE: Economic Report of the President, 1998, *Table B-2. The figures are based on data for real imports, exports, and GDP.*

[2]These calculations are based on the real values of exports, imports, and GDP. If the nominal figures had been used to make the calculations, the size of the trade sector would be slightly smaller in recent years.

What are the leading imports and exports of the United States? The U.S. both imports and exports a substantial quantity of capital goods, such as automobiles, computers, semiconductors, telecommunications equipment, and industrial machines. The markets for these items are worldwide. Producers in the United States sell substantial quantities abroad, while, at the same time, many U.S. consumers purchase these goods from foreign manufacturers. Civilian aircraft, electrical equipment, chemicals, and plastics are also among the leading export products of the United States, while crude oil, textiles, toys, sporting goods, and pharmaceutical products are major imports. (See Illustrated Exhibit IV-B for additional details.)

Clearly, the impact of international trade differs across industries. In some industries, domestic producers find it very difficult to compete with their rivals abroad. For example, approximately 90 percent of the shoes purchased by Americans and nearly two-thirds of the radio and television sets, watches, and motorcycles are produced abroad. Imports also supply a high percentage of the clothing and textile products, paper, cut diamonds, and VCRs consumed in the United States. On the other hand, a large proportion of the aircraft, power-generating equipment, scientific instruments, construction equipment, and fertilizers produced in the United States is exported to purchasers abroad.

GAINS FROM SPECIALIZATION AND TRADE

If a foreign country can supply us with a commodity cheaper than we ourselves can make it, [we had] better buy it of them with some part of our own industry, employed in a way in which we have some advantage.

Adam Smith[3]

Comparative advantage
The ability to produce a good at a lower opportunity cost than others can produce it. Relative costs determine comparative advantage.

As we discussed in Chapter 2, the law of **comparative advantage** explains why a group of individuals, regions, or nations can gain from specialization and exchange. Trading partners can gain if each specializes in the production of the goods for which it is a low-opportunity-cost producer and trades for those goods for which it is a high-opportunity-cost producer. Specialization in the area of one's comparative advantage minimizes the cost of production and leads to maximum joint output.

International trade leads to mutual gain because it allows the residents of each country to: (1) specialize more fully in the production of those things that they do best, and (2) import goods when foreigners are willing to supply them at a lower cost than domestic producers. Labor-force skills and resource endowments differ substantially across countries. These differences influence costs. Therefore, a good that is quite costly to produce in one country may be economically produced in another. For example, the warm, moist climate of Brazil, Colombia, and Guatemala enhances the economical production of coffee. Countries like Saudi Arabia and Venezuela with rich oil fields can produce petroleum cheaply. Countries with an abundance of fertile land, like Canada and Australia, are able to produce products like wheat, feed grains, and beef at a low cost. In contrast, land is scarce in Japan, a nation with a highly skilled labor force. The Japanese, therefore, specialize in manufacturing, using their comparative advantage to produce cameras, automobiles, and electronic products for export. With international trade, the residents of each country can gain by specializing in the production

[3]Adam Smith, *An Inquiry into the Nature and Causes of the Wealth of Nations* (1776; Cannan's ed., Chicago: University of Chicago Press, 1976), pp. 478–479.

of goods that they can produce economically and using the proceeds to import goods that would be expensive to produce domestically.

Because failure to comprehend the principle of mutual gains from trade is often a source of "fuzzy thinking," we will take the time to illustrate the principle in detail. To keep things simple, we will consider a case involving only two countries, the United States and Japan, and two products, food and clothing. Furthermore, we will assume that labor is the only resource used to produce these products. In addition, since we want to illustrate that gains from trade are nearly always possible, we are going to assume that Japan has an **absolute advantage**—that the Japanese workers are more efficient than the Americans—in the production of both commodities. **Exhibit 17–2** illustrates this situation. Perhaps due to their prior experience or higher skill level, Japanese workers can produce three units of food per day, compared with only two units per day for U.S. workers. Similarly, Japanese workers are able to produce nine units of clothing per day, compared to one unit of clothing per day for U.S. workers.

Absolute advantage
A situation in which a nation, as the result of its previous experience and/or natural endowments, can produce more of a good (with the same amount of resources) than another nation.

Let us consider the following question: Can two countries gain from trade if one of them can produce both goods with fewer resources? Perhaps surprising to some, the answer is yes. As long as *relative* production costs of the two goods differ between Japan and the United States, gains from trade will be possible. Consider what would happen if the United States shifted three workers from the clothing industry to the food industry. This reallocation of labor would allow the United States to expand its food output by six units (two units per worker), while clothing output would decline by three units (one unit per worker). Suppose Japan reallocates labor in the opposite direction. When Japan moves one worker from the food industry to the clothing industry, Japanese clothing production expands by nine units while food output declines by three units. The exhibit shows that this reallocation of labor *within* the two countries has increased their joint output by three units of food and six units of clothing.

The source of this increase in output is straightforward: Aggregate output expands because the reallocation of labor permits each country to specialize more fully in the production of those goods that it can produce at a *relatively* low cost. Our old friend, the opportunity-cost concept, reveals the low-cost producer of each good. If Japanese workers produce one additional unit of food, they sacrifice the production of three units of clothing. Therefore, in Japan the opportunity cost of one unit of food is three units of clothing. On the other hand, one unit of food in the United States can be produced at an opportunity cost of only one-half unit of clothing. American workers

EXHIBIT 17–2

GAINS FROM SPECIALIZATION AND TRADE

	Output per Worker Day		Potential Change in Output[a]	
Country	Food (1)	Clothing (2)	Food (3)	Clothing (4)
United States	2	1	+6	−3
Japan	3	9	−3	+9
Change in Total Output			+3	+6

[a]*Change in output if the United States shifts three workers from the clothing to the food industry and if Japan shifts one worker from the food to the clothing industry.*

Columns 1 and 2 indicate the daily output of either food or clothing of each worker in the United States and Japan. If the United States moves 3 workers from the clothing industry to the food industry, it can produce 6 more units of food and 3 fewer units of clothing. Similarly, if Japan moves 1 worker from food to clothing, clothing output will increase by 9 units while food output will decline by 3 units. With this reallocation of labor, the United States and Japan are able to increase their aggregate output of both food (3 additional units) and clothing (6 additional units).

are therefore the low-opportunity-cost producers of food, even though they cannot produce as much food per day as the Japanese workers. Simultaneously, Japan is the low-opportunity-cost producer of clothing. The opportunity cost of producing a unit of clothing in Japan is only one-third unit of food, compared to two units of food in the United States. The reallocation of labor illustrated in Exhibit 17–2 expanded joint output because it moved resources in both countries toward areas where they had a comparative advantage.

As long as the relative costs of producing the two goods differ in the two countries, gains from specialization and trade will be possible. When this is the case, each country will find it cheaper to trade for goods that can be produced only at a high opportunity cost. For example, both countries can gain if the United States trades food to Japan for clothing at a trading ratio greater than one unit of food equals one-half unit of clothing (the U.S. opportunity cost of food) but less than one unit of food equals three units of clothing (the Japanese opportunity cost of food). Any trading ratio between these two extremes will permit the United States to acquire clothing more cheaply than it could be produced within the country and simultaneously permit Japan to acquire food more cheaply than it could be produced domestically.

How Trade Expands Consumption Possibilities

Because trade permits nations to expand their joint output, it also allows each nation to expand its consumption possibilities. The production-possibilities concept can be used to illustrate this point. Suppose that there were 200 million workers in the United States and 50 million in Japan. Given these figures and the productivity of workers indicated in Exhibit 17–2, the production-possibilities curves for the two countries are presented in **Exhibit 17–3.** If the United States used all of its 200 million workers in the food industry, it could produce 400 million units of food per day—two units per worker—and zero units of clothing (point N). Alternatively, if the United States used all its workers to produce clothing, daily output would be 200 million units of clothing

Here we illustrate the daily production possibilities of a U.S. labor force of 200 million workers and a Japanese labor force of 50 million workers, given the cost of producing food and clothing presented in Exhibit 17-2. In the absence of trade, consumption possibilities will be restricted to points such as U.S.$_1$ *in the United States and* J$_1$ *in Japan along the production possibilities curve of each country.*

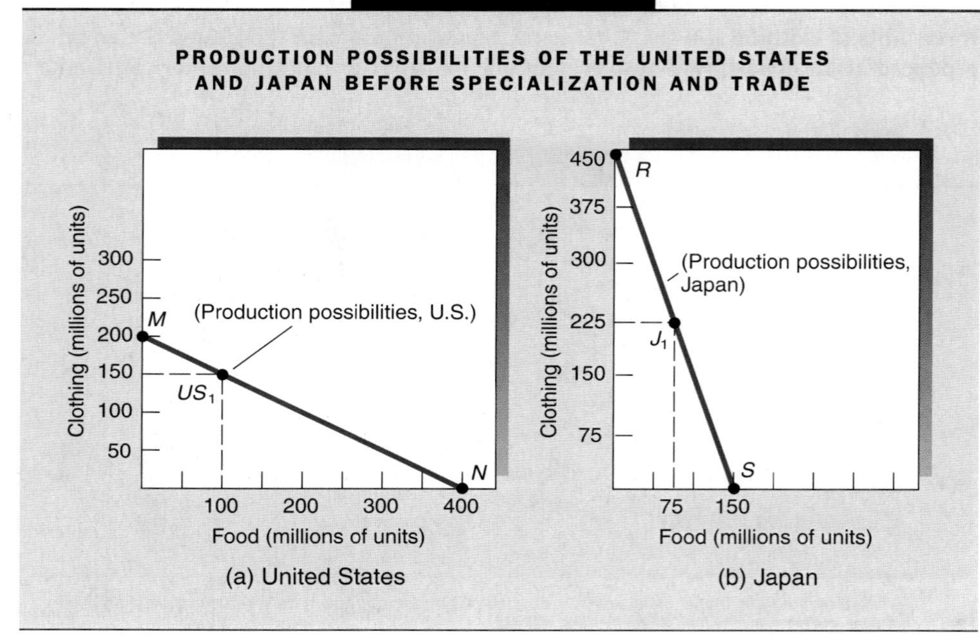

and no food (point M). Intermediate output combinations along the production-possibilities line (MN) intersecting these two extreme points also could be achievable. For example, the United States could produce 150 million units of clothing and 100 million units of food (point US_1).

Part b of Exhibit 17–3 illustrates the production possibilities of the 50 million Japanese workers. Japan could produce 450 million units of clothing and no food (R), 150 million units of food and no clothing (S), or various intermediate combinations, like 225 million units of clothing and 75 million units of food (J_1). The slope of the production-possibilities constraint reflects the opportunity cost of food relative to clothing. Because Japan is the high-opportunity-cost producer of food, its production-possibilities constraint is steeper than the constraint for the United States.

In the absence of trade, the consumption of each country is constrained by the country's production possibilities. Trade, however, expands the consumption possibilities of both. As we previously indicated, both countries can gain from specialization if the United States trades food to Japan at a price greater than one unit of food equals one-half unit of clothing but less than one unit of food equals three units of clothing. Suppose that they agree on an intermediate price of one unit of food equals one unit of clothing. As part a of **Exhibit 17–4** illustrates, when the United States specializes in the production of food (where it has a comparative advantage) and trades food for clothing (at the price ratio where one unit of food equals one unit of clothing), it can consume

EXHIBIT 17–4

CONSUMPTION POSSIBILITIES WITH TRADE

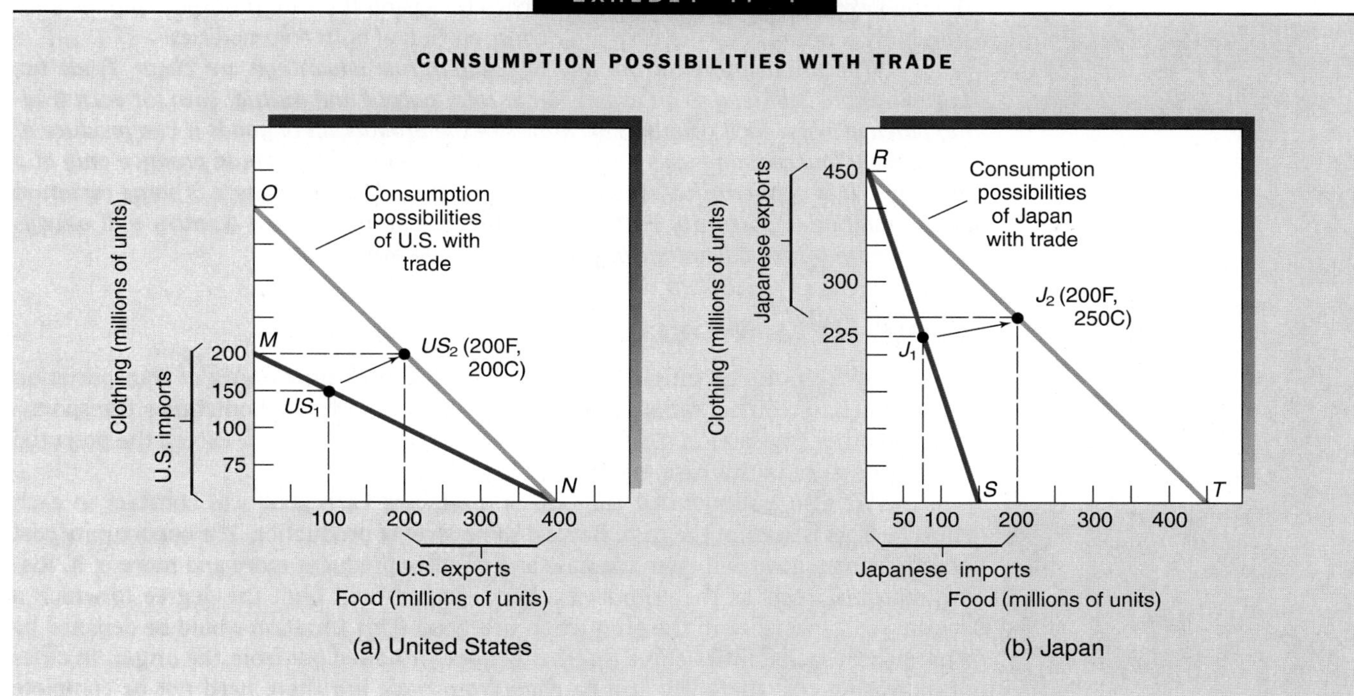

With specialization and trade, the consumption possibilities of a country can be expanded. If the United States can trade one unit of clothing for one unit of food, it can specialize in the production of food and consume along the ON *line (rather than its original production-possibilities constraint,* MN*). Similarly, when Japan is able to trade one unit of clothing for one unit of food, it can specialize in the production of clothing and consume any combination along the line* RT*. For example, with specialization and trade, the United States could increase its consumption from* US_1 *to* US_2*, gaining 50 million units of clothing and 100 million units of food. Simultaneously, Japan could increase consumption from* J_1 *to* J_2*, a gain of 125 million units of food and 25 million units of clothing.*

along the line *ON*. If the United States insisted on self-sufficiency, it would be restricted to consumption possibilities like US_1 (100 million units of food and 150 million units of clothing) along its production-possibilities constraint of *MN*. With trade, however, the United States can achieve such combinations as US_2 (200 million units of food and 200 million units of clothing) along the line *ON*. Trade permits the United States to expand its consumption of both goods.

Simultaneously, Japan is able to expand its consumption of both goods when it is able to trade clothing for food at the one-to-one price ratio. As part b of Exhibit 17–4 illustrates, Japan can specialize in the production of clothing and consume along the constraint *RT* when it can trade one unit of clothing for one unit of food. Without trade, consumption in Japan would be limited to points like J_1 (75 million units of food and 225 million units of clothing) along the line *RS*. With trade, however, it is able to consume combinations like J_2 (200 million units of food and 250 million units of clothing) along the constraint *RT*.

Look what happens when Japan specializes in clothing and the United States specializes in food. Japan can produce 450 million units of clothing, export 200 million to the United States (for 200 million units of food), and still have 250 million units of clothing remaining for domestic consumption. Simultaneously, the United States can produce 400 million units of food, export 200 million to Japan (for 200 million units of clothing), and still have 200 million units of food left for domestic consumption. After specialization and trade, the United States is able to consume at the point of US_2 and Japan at point J_2, consumption levels that would otherwise be unattainable. Specialization and exchange permit the two countries to expand their joint output, and, as a result, both countries can increase their consumption of both commodities.

The implications of the law of comparative advantage are clear: Trade between nations will lead to an expansion in total output and mutual gain for each trading partner when each country specializes in the production of goods it can produce at a relatively low cost and uses the proceeds to buy goods that it could produce only at a high cost. It is comparative advantage that matters. As long as there is some variation in the relative opportunity cost of goods across countries, each country will always have a comparative advantage in the production of some goods.

Some Real-World Considerations

In order to keep things simple, we ignored the potential importance of transportation costs, which, of course, reduce the potential gains from trade. Sometimes transportation and other transaction costs, both real and artificially imposed, exceed the potential for mutual gain. In this case, exchange does not occur.

We also assumed that the cost of producing each good was constant in each country. This is seldom the case. Beyond some level of production, the opportunity cost of producing a good will often increase as a country produces more and more of it. Rising marginal costs as the output of a good expands will limit the degree to which a country will specialize in the production of a good. This situation would be depicted by a production-possibilities curve that was convex, or bowed out from the origin. In cases of increasing cost there will still be gains from trade but there need not be complete specialization.

Additional Sources of Gain from International Trade

In addition to the gains derived from specialization in areas of comparative advantage, there are two other important sources of gains from international trade.

1. Gains from Economies of Scale and Expansion in the Size of the Market. ***International trade allows both domestic producers and consumers to gain from reductions in per-unit costs that often accompany large-scale production, marketing, and distribution.*** Trade expands the potential size of the market available to both domestic and foreign firms. When economies of scale are important in an industry, successful domestic firms will be able to produce larger outputs and achieve lower costs than would be possible if they were unable to sell abroad. This point is particularly important for small countries. For example, textile manufacturers in Malaysia, Taiwan, and South Korea would have much higher costs if they could not sell abroad. The domestic textile markets of these countries are too small to support large, low-cost firms in this industry. With international trade, however, textile firms in these countries operate at a large scale and compete quite effectively in the world market.

International trade also benefits domestic consumers by permitting them to purchase from large-scale producers abroad. The aircraft industry provides a vivid illustration of this point. Given the huge design and engineering costs, the domestic market of almost all countries would be substantially less than the quantity required for the efficient production of jet planes. With international trade, however, consumers around the world are able to purchase planes economically from large-scale producers like Boeing.

2. Gains from More Competitive Markets. ***International trade promotes competition in domestic markets and allows consumers to purchase a wide variety of goods at economical prices.*** Competition from abroad helps keep domestic producers on their toes. It forces them to improve the quality of their products and keep costs low. At the same time, the variety of goods that are available from abroad provides consumers with a much broader array of choices than would be available in the absence of international trade.

The recent experience of the U.S. automobile industry illustrates this point. Faced with stiff competition from Japanese firms, U.S. automobile manufacturers worked hard to improve the quality of their vehicles. As a result, the reliability of the

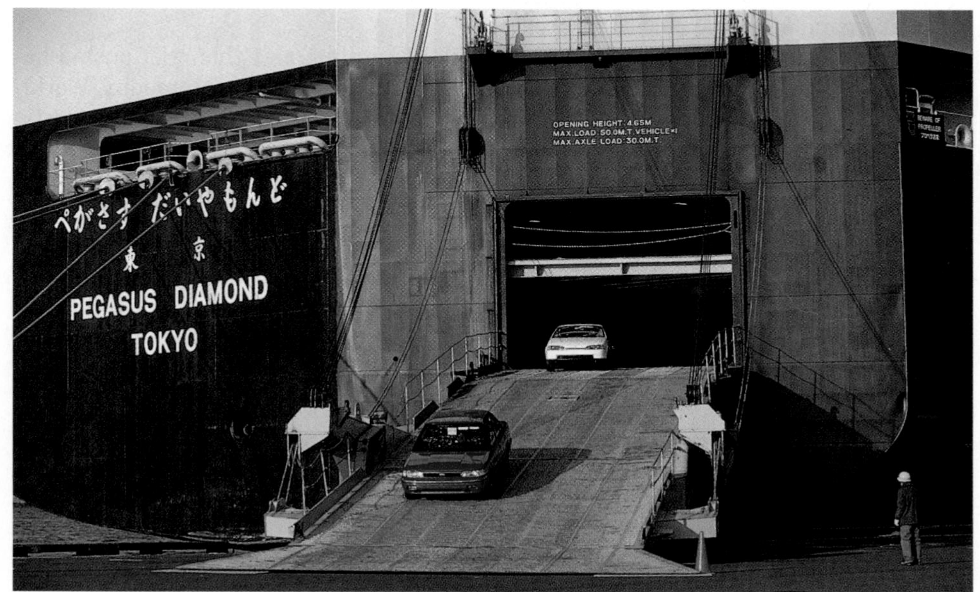

More than one-fifth of the world's output is produced in one country and sold in another. The gains from specialization, division of labor, and adoption of mass-production methods that accompany international trade allow the trading partners to achieve a larger output and higher living standards than would otherwise be the case.

automobiles and light trucks available to American consumers—including those vehicles produced by domestic manufacturers—is almost certainly higher than would have been the case in the absence of competition from abroad.

EXPORT-IMPORT LINK

Doubts about the merits of international trade often result from a failure to consider all the consequences. Why are other nations willing to export their goods to the United States? So they can obtain dollars. Yes, but why do they want dollars? Would foreigners be willing to continue exporting oil, radios, watches, cameras, automobiles, and thousands of other valuable products to Americans in exchange for pieces of paper? If so, Americans could all be semiretired, spending only an occasional workday at the dollar printing-press office! Of course, foreigners are not so naive. They trade goods for dollars so they can use the dollars to buy U.S. goods and purchase ownership rights to U.S. assets.

Exports, broadly perceived to include goods, services, and assets, provide the buying power that makes it possible for a nation to import. If a nation did not export goods, it would not have the foreign currency that is required for the purchase of imports. Similarly, if a nation did not import goods, foreigners would not have the purchasing power to buy that nation's export products. Therefore, if imports decline, so will the demand for the nation's exports. Exports and imports are closely linked.

SUPPLY, DEMAND, AND INTERNATIONAL TRADE

How does international trade affect prices and output levels in domestic markets? Supply and demand analysis will help us answer this question. Given our modern transportation and communication networks, the market for many commodities is worldwide. When a product can be transported long distances at a low cost (relative to its value), the domestic price of the product is in effect determined by the forces of supply and demand in the worldwide market.

Using soybeans as an example, **Exhibit 17–5** illustrates this relationship between the domestic and world markets for an internationally traded commodity. Worldwide market conditions determine the price of soybeans. In an open economy, domestic producers are free to sell and domestic consumers are free to buy the product at the world market price (P_w). At this price, U.S. producers will supply Q_p, while U.S. consumers will purchase Q_c. Reflecting their comparative advantage, U.S. soybean producers will export $Q_p - Q_c$ units at the world market price.

Let us compare the open-economy outcome with the situation in the absence of trade. If U.S. producers were not allowed to export soybeans, the domestic price would be determined by the domestic supply (S_d) and demand (D_d) only. A lower "no-trade" price (P_n) would emerge. Who are the winners and losers as the result of free trade in soybeans? Clearly, soybean producers gain. Free trade allows domestic producers to sell a larger quantity (Q_p rather than Q_n). As a result, the net revenues of soybean producers will rise by $P_w bcP_n$. On the other hand, domestic consumers of soybeans will have to pay a higher price under free trade. Consumers will lose (1) because they have to pay P_w rather than P_n for the Q_c units they purchase, and (2) because they lose the consumer surplus on the $Q_n - Q_c$ units now purchased at the higher price. Thus, free trade imposes a net cost of $P_w acP_n$ on consumers. As can be seen in Exhibit 17-5, how-

EXHIBIT 17–5

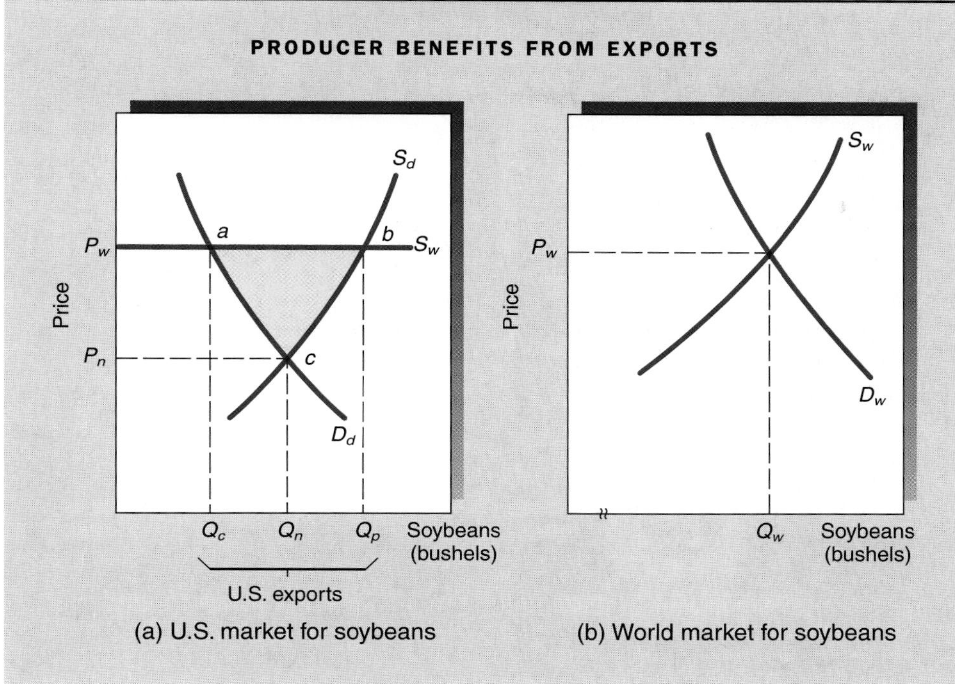

The price of soybeans and other internationally traded commodities is determined by the forces of supply and demand in the world market (b). If U.S. soybean producers were prohibited from selling to foreigners, the domestic price would be P_n *(a). Free trade permits the U.S. soybean producers to sell* Q_p *units at the higher world price (*P_w*). The quantity* $Q_p - Q_c$ *is exported abroad. Compared to the no-trade situation, the producers' gain from the higher price (*P_wbcP_n*) exceeds the cost imposed on domestic consumers (*P_wacP_n*) by the triangle* abc.

ever, the gains of producers outweigh the losses to consumers by the triangle *abc*. Free trade leads to a net welfare gain.

When one focuses only on an export product, it appears that free trade benefits producers relative to consumers—but this ignores the secondary effects. How will foreigners generate the dollars they need to purchase the export products of the United States? If foreigners do not sell goods to Americans, they will not have the purchasing power necessary to purchase goods from Americans. U.S. imports—that is, the purchase of goods from low-cost foreign producers—provide foreigners with the dollar purchasing power necessary to buy U.S. exports. In turn, the lower prices in the import-competitive markets will benefit the U.S. consumers who appeared at first glance to be harmed by the higher prices (compared to the no-trade situation) in export markets.

Exhibit 17–6 illustrates the impact of imports, using shoes as an example. In the absence of trade, the price of shoes in the domestic market would be P_n, the intersection of the domestic supply and demand curves. However, the world price of shoes is P_w. In an open economy, many U.S. consumers would take advantage of the low shoe prices available from foreign producers. At the lower world price, U.S. consumers would purchase Q_c units of shoes, importing $Q_c - Q_p$ from foreign producers.

Compared to the no-trade situation, free trade in shoes results in lower prices and an expansion in domestic consumption. The lower prices lead to a net consumer gain of P_nabP_w. Domestic producers lose P_nacP_w in the form of lower sales prices and reductions in output. However, the net gain of consumers exceeds the net loss of producers by *abc*.

For an open economy, international competition directs the resources of a nation toward the areas of competitive advantage. When domestic producers have a comparative advantage in the production of a good, they will be able to compete effectively

EXHIBIT 17-6

CONSUMER BENEFITS FROM IMPORTS

In the absence of trade, the domestic price of shoes would be P_n. *Since many foreign producers have a comparative advantage in the production of shoes, international trade leads to lower prices. At the world price* P_w, *U.S. consumers will demand* Q_c *units, of which* $Q_c - Q_p$ *are imported. Compared to the no-trade situation, consumers gain* $P_n abP_w$, *while domestic producers lose* $P_n acP_w$. *A net gain of* abc *results.*

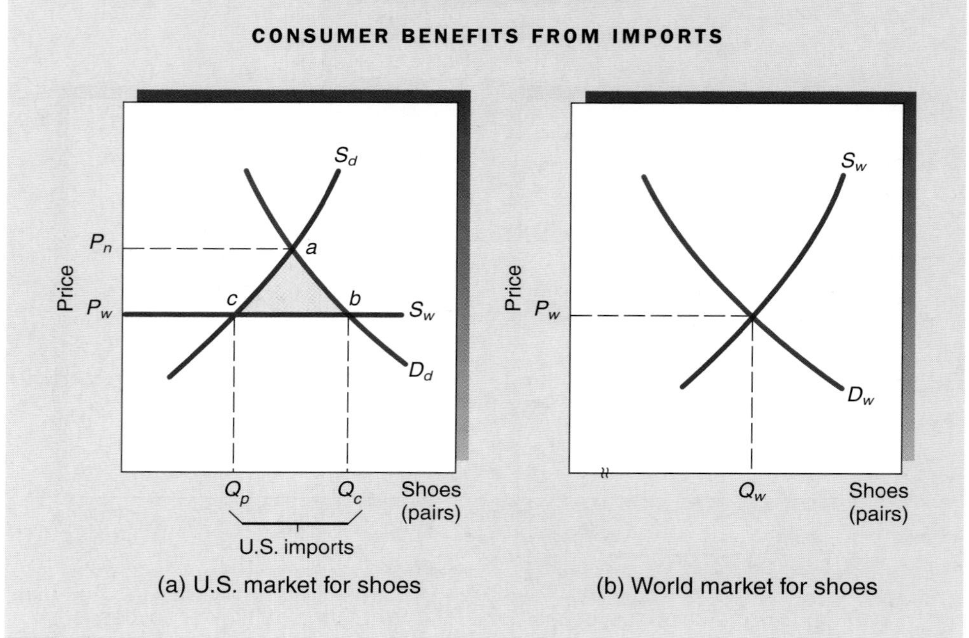

(a) U.S. market for shoes

(b) World market for shoes

in the world market and profit from the export of goods to foreigners. In turn, the exports will generate the purchasing power necessary to buy goods that foreigners can supply more economically.

International trade and specialization result in lower prices (and higher domestic consumption) for imported products and higher prices (and lower domestic consumption) for exported products. More important, trade permits the residents of each nation to concentrate on the things they do best (produce at a low cost), while trading for those they do least well. The result is an expansion in both output and consumption compared to what could be achieved in the absence of trade.

The pattern of U.S. exports and imports is consistent with this view. The United States is a nation with a technically skilled labor force, fertile farmland, and substantial capital formation. Thus, we export computers, aircraft, power-generating equipment, scientific instruments, and land-intensive agricultural products—items we are able to produce at a comparatively low cost. Simultaneously, we import substantial amounts of petroleum, textile (clothing) products, shoes, coffee, and diamonds—goods costly for us to produce. Clearly, trade permits us to gain by specializing in those areas in which our comparative advantage is greatest.

ECONOMICS OF TRADE RESTRICTIONS

Despite the potential benefits from free trade, almost all nations have erected trade barriers. Tariffs, quotas, and exchange-rate controls are the most commonly used trade-restricting devices. Let us consider how various types of trade restrictions influence the economy.

Economics of Tariffs

A **tariff** is nothing more than a tax on imports from foreign countries. As **Exhibit 17–7** shows, average tariff rates of between 30 percent and 50 percent of product value were often levied prior to 1945. The notorious Smoot-Hawley trade bill of 1930 pushed the average tariff rate upward to 60 percent. Many economists believe that this legislation was a major contributing factor to the length and severity of the Great Depression. During the past 50 years, the tariff rates of the United States have declined substantially. In 1997, the average tariff rate on imported goods was only 2.2 percent.

Tariff
A tax levied on goods imported into a country.

Exhibit 17–8 illustrates the impact of a tariff on automobiles. In the absence of a tariff, the world market price of P_w would prevail in the domestic market. At that price, U.S. consumers purchase Q_1 units. Domestic producers supply Q_{d1}, while foreigners supply $Q_1 - Q_{d1}$ units to the U.S. market. When the United States levies a tariff, t, on automobiles, Americans can no longer buy cars at the world price. U.S. consumers now have to pay $P_w + t$ to purchase an automobile from foreigners. At that price, domestic consumers demand Q_2 units (Q_{d2} supplied by domestic producers and $Q_2 - Q_{d2}$ supplied by foreigners). The tariff results in a higher price and lower level of domestic consumption.

The tariff benefits domestic producers and the government at the expense of consumers. Since they do not pay the tariff, domestic producers will expand their output in response to the higher (protected) market price. In effect, the tariff acts as a subsidy to domestic producers. Domestic producers gain the area S (Exhibit 17–8) in the form of additional net revenues. The tariff raises revenues equal to the area T for the government. The areas U and V represent costs imposed on consumers that do not benefit either producers or the government. Simply put, U and V represent a *deadweight loss* (loss of efficiency).

As a result of the tariff, resources that could have been used to produce goods that U.S. firms produce efficiently (compared to producers abroad) are diverted into the

EXHIBIT 17–7

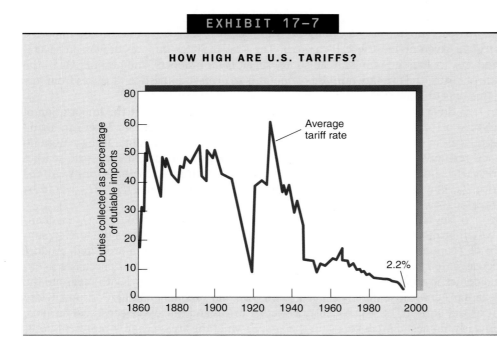

HOW HIGH ARE U.S. TARIFFS?

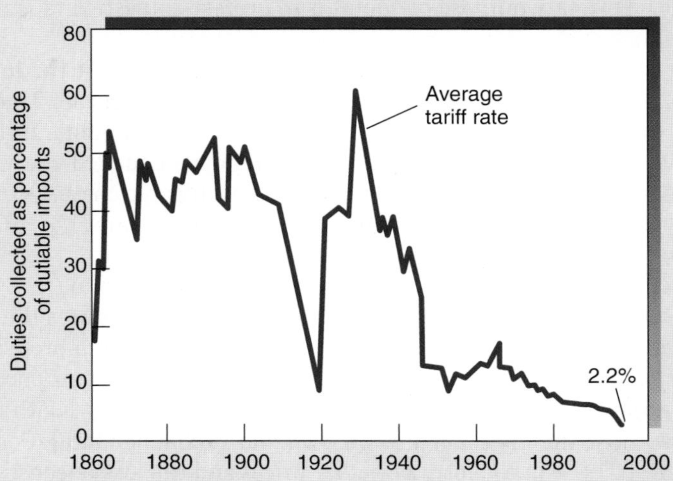

Tariff rates in the United States fell sharply during the period from 1935 to 1950. Subsequently, after rising slightly during the 1950s, they have trended downward since 1960. In 1997, the average tariff rate on merchandise imports was 2.2 percent.

EXHIBIT 17–8

IMPACT OF A TARIFF

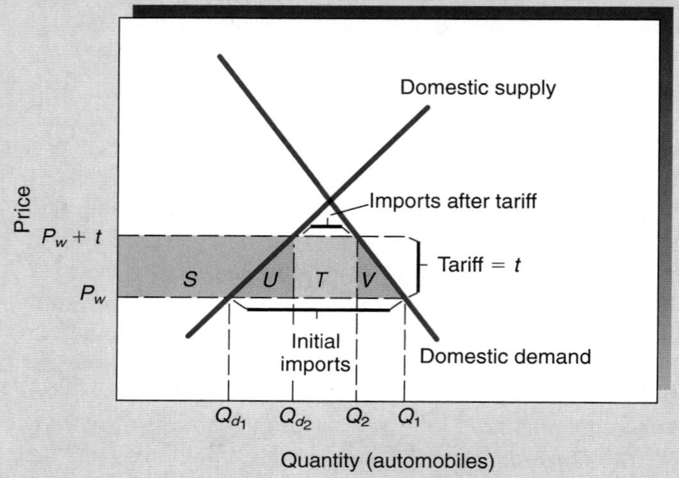

Price
$P_w + t$
P_w
Domestic supply
Imports after tariff
Tariff = t
S U T V
Initial imports
Domestic demand
Q_{d_1} Q_{d_2} Q_2 Q_1
Quantity (automobiles)

Here we illustrate the impact of a tariff on automobiles. In the absence of the tariff, the world price of automobiles is P_w: *U.S. consumers purchase* Q_1 *units* (Q_{d1}) *from domestic producers plus* $Q_1 - Q_{d1}$ *from foreign producers). The tariff makes it more costly for Americans to purchase automobiles from foreigners. Imports decline and the domestic price increases. Consumers lose the sum of the areas* S + U + T + V *in the form of higher prices and a reduction in consumer surplus. Producers gain the area* S *and the tariff generates* T *tax revenues for the government. The areas* U *and* V *are deadweight losses due to a reduction in allocative efficiency.*

production of automobiles. Thus, we end up producing less in areas where we have a comparative advantage and more in areas where we are a high-cost producer. Potential gains from specialization and trade go unrealized.

Economics of Quotas

Import quota
A specific limit or maximum quantity (or value) of a good permitted to be imported into a country during a given period.

An **import quota,** like a tariff, is designed to restrict foreign goods and protect domestic industries. A quota places a ceiling on the amount of a product that can be imported during a given period (typically a year). The United States imposes quotas on several products, including brooms, steel, shoes, sugar, dairy products, and peanuts. As in the case of tariffs, the primary purpose of quotas is to protect domestic industries from foreign competition.

Since 1953 the United States has imposed a quota to limit the importation of peanuts to 1.7 million pounds per year, approximately two peanuts per American. Using peanuts as an example, **Exhibit 17–9** illustrates the impact of a quota. If there were no trade restraints, the domestic price of peanuts would be equal to the world market price (P_w). Under those circumstances, Americans would purchase Q_1 units. At the price P_w, domestic producers would supply Q_{d1}, and the amount $Q_1 - Q_{d1}$ would be imported from foreign producers.

Now consider what happens when a quota limits imports to $Q_2 - Q_{d2}$, a quantity well below the free-trade level of imports. Since the quota reduces the foreign supply of peanuts to the domestic market, the price of the quota-protected product increases (to P_2). At the higher price, U.S. consumers will reduce their purchases to Q_2, and domestic producers will happily expand their production to Q_{d2}. With regard to the welfare of consumers, the impact of a quota is similar to that of a tariff. Consumers lose the area $S + U + T + V$ in the form of higher prices and the loss of consumer surplus. Similarly, domestic producers gain the area S, while the areas U and V represent deadweight losses from allocative inefficiency.

EXHIBIT 17-9

IMPACT OF A QUOTA

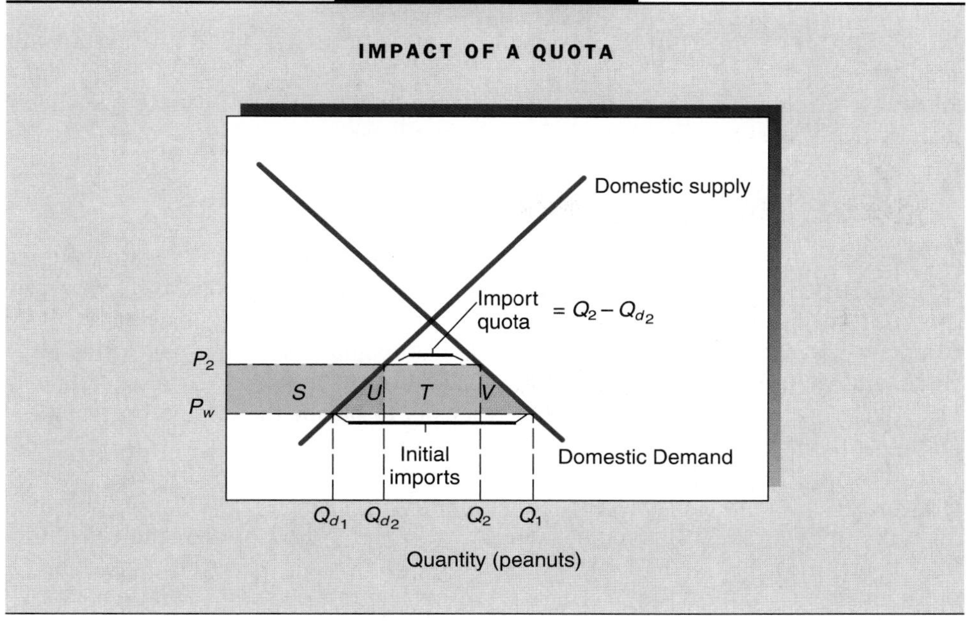

Here we illustrate the impact of a quota, such as the one the United States imposes on peanuts. The world market price of peanuts is P_w. *If there were no trade restraints, the domestic price would also be* P_w, *and the domestic consumption would be* Q_1. *Domestic producers would supply* Q_{d1} *units, while* $Q_1 - Q_{d1}$ *would be imported. A quota limiting imports to* $Q_2 - Q_{d2}$ *would push up the domestic price to* P_2. *At the higher price, the amount supplied by domestic producers increases to* Q_{d2}. *Consumers lose the sum of the area* S + U + T + V, *while domestic producers gain the area* S. *In contrast with tariffs, quotas generate no revenue for the government. The area* T *goes to foreign producers who are granted permission to sell in the U.S. market.*

However, there is a big difference between tariffs and quotas with regard to the area *T*. Under a tariff, the U.S. government would collect revenues equal to *T*, representing the tariff rate multiplied by the number of units imported. With a quota, however, these revenues will go to the foreign producers, who are granted import permits to sell in the U.S. market. Clearly, this right to sell at a premium price (since the domestic price exceeds the world market price) is extremely valuable. Thus, foreign producers will compete for the permits. They will hire lobbyists, make political contributions, and engage in other rent-seeking activities in an effort to secure the right to sell at a premium price in the U.S. market.

In many ways, quotas are more harmful than tariffs. With a quota, foreign producers are prohibited from selling additional units regardless of how much lower their costs are relative to those of domestic producers. In contrast with a tariff, a quota brings in no revenue for the government. While a tariff transfers revenue from U.S. consumers to the Treasury, quotas transfer these revenues to foreign producers. Obviously, this politically granted privilege creates a strong incentive for foreign producers to engage in wasteful rent-seeking activities. Thus, by rewarding both domestic producers with higher prices and foreign producers with valuable import permits, quotas generate two strong interest groups supportive of their continuation. As a result, removal of a quota is often even more difficult to achieve than a tariff reduction.

Other Nontariff Barriers to Trade

In order to avoid the imposition of other types of trade barriers, such as tariffs and quotas, foreign firms will sometimes agree to limit their exports to a country. Even though they are almost always the result of political pressure, agreements of this type are called **voluntary export restraints (VERs).** Japanese auto manufacturers have agreed to a VER on exports to the United States. The economic impact of a VER is similar to that of a quota. The higher selling price of the product that is caused by the VER

Voluntary export restraint (VER)
An agreement by foreign firms to limit their own exports.

creates a gain for both foreign and domestic producers, but hurts domestic consumers by more than an offsetting amount.

Other types of barriers, such as licensing requirements and product quality standards, are also used by governments to restrict trade. These barriers make it difficult and more costly for firms to import products into the country. Again these policies hurt domestic consumers but benefit domestic producers.

Exchange-Rate Controls as a Trade Restriction

Many countries, particularly less-developed countries, fix the exchange-rate value of their currency above the market rate and impose restrictions on exchange-rate transactions. At the official (artificially high) exchange rate, the country's export goods will be extremely expensive to foreigners. As a result, foreigners will purchase goods elsewhere, and the country's exports will be small. In turn, the low level of exports will make it extremely difficult for domestic residents to obtain the foreign currency required for the purchase of imports. Such exchange-rate controls both reduce the volume of trade and lead to black-market currency exchanges. Indeed, a large black-market premium indicates that the country's exchange-rate policy is substantially limiting the ability of its citizens to trade with foreigners. The greater the black-market premium, the larger the expected decline in the size of the country's international trade sector as the result of the exchange-rate controls.

WHY DO NATIONS ADOPT TRADE RESTRICTIONS?

> ***Protective tariffs are as much applications of force as are blockading squadrons, and their objective is the same—to prevent trade. The difference between the two is that blockading squadrons are a means whereby nations seek to prevent their enemies from trading; protective tariffs are a means whereby nations attempt to prevent their own people from trading.***
>
> *Henry George*[4]

Physical obstacles, like bad roads and stormy weather, that increase transaction costs will retard the gains from trade. Tariffs, quotas, exchange-rate controls, and other human-made trade restrictions have similar effects. Henry George compared tariffs and other trade restrictions to a blockade (see quotation above). Both the blockade imposed by an enemy and a self-imposed blockade in the form of trade restrictions will retard the gains from specialization and exchange.

If trade restrictions promote inefficiency and reduce the potential gains from exchange, why do nations adopt them? Several factors play a role. First, there are some partially valid arguments for the protection of specific industries under certain circumstances. Second, economic illiteracy plays a role. Failing to comprehend the implications of the law of comparative advantage and the linkage between imports and exports, many people wrongly believe that trade restrictions increase employment and help keep the wages of Americans high. (See the accompanying Myths of Economics box on these topics.) Finally, and most important, trade restrictions reflect the political power of concentrated interests. We will now take a look at each of these factors.

---

[4]George, *Protection or Free Trade,* p. 47.

Partially Valid Arguments for Restrictions

There are three major, at least partially valid, arguments for protecting certain domestic industries from foreign competitors: the national-defense, infant-industry, and antidumping arguments.

National-Defense Argument. According to the national-defense argument, certain industries—aircraft, petroleum, and weapons, for example—are vital to national defense and therefore should be protected from foreign competitors so that a domestic supply of necessary materials would be available in case of an international conflict. Would we want to be entirely dependent on Arabian or Russian petroleum? Would complete dependence on French aircraft be wise? Many Americans would answer no, even if trade restrictions were required to prevent such dependence by preserving domestic industries.

Although the national-defense argument has some validity, it is often abused. Relatively few industries are truly vital to our national defense. If a resource is important for national defense, often it would make more sense to stockpile the resource during peacetime rather than follow protectionist policies to preserve a domestic industry. Furthermore, it is important to recognize that a strong economy capable of producing large volumes of the goods necessary to sustain a large war effort is itself part of a strong defense. Because the national-defense argument is often used by special interests to justify protection for their industry at the expense of the economy in general, the merits of each specific case must be carefully evaluated.

Infant-Industry Argument. Advocates of the infant-industry argument hold that new domestic industries should be protected from older, established foreign competitors. As the new industry matures, it will be able to stand on its own feet and compete effectively with foreign producers, at which time protection can be removed.

The infant-industry argument has a long and often notorious history. Alexander Hamilton used it to argue for the protection of early U.S. manufacturing. Although it is an argument for only temporary protection, the protection, once granted, is generally difficult to remove. For example, a century ago, this argument was used to gain tariff protection for the newly emerging steel industry in the United States. With time, the steel industry developed and became very powerful, both politically and economically. Despite this maturity, the tariffs remained. To this day, legislation continues to provide the steel industry with various protections that limit competition from abroad.

Anti-Dumping Argument. In some cases, **dumping,** the sale of goods abroad at a price below their cost (and below their price in the domestic market of the exporting nation), merely reflects the exporter's desire to penetrate a foreign market. In other instances, dumping may be prompted by export subsidies of foreign governments. At various times, it has been alleged that Argentina has dumped textiles, Korea has dumped steel, and Canada has dumped radial tires into the U.S. market. Dumping is illegal. The Trade Agreements Act of 1979 provides for special antidumping *duties* (tariffs) when a good is sold in the United States at a price lower than that found in the domestic market of the exporting nation.

Dumping
The sale of a good by a foreign supplier in another country at a price below that charged by the supplier in its home market.

Dumping generally benefits domestic consumers and imposes costs on domestic producers of goods for which the imports are good substitutes. The lower prices of the "dumped" goods permit consumers to obtain the goods more economically. Simultaneously, the lower prices make it more difficult for domestic producers of the goods to compete. Predictably, domestic producers (and their employees) are the major source of the charge that dumping is unfair.

MYTHS OF ECONOMICS

"Trade restrictions that prohibit foreign producers from selling their goods at lower prices than domestic producers will increase employment and protect American jobs."

Many people sincerely believe that trade restrictions increase employment and "save American jobs." This fallacious belief stems from a failure to consider the secondary effects of import restrictions on export industries. Tariffs, quotas, exchange-rate controls, and other trade restrictions may result in more employment *in industries shielded by the restraints,* but they will *destroy jobs in other industries.*

Remember, the sales from foreigners to us (our imports) provide them with the purchasing power required to buy from us (our exports). If foreigners are unable to sell as much to Americans, then they will have fewer dollars with which to buy from Americans. Therefore, a secondary effect accompanies trade restrictions: The demand for American export goods declines. As a result, output and employment in export industries will be smaller, offsetting any jobs saved in protected industries. Most noneconomists fail to recognize the link between a decline in imports due to trade restrictions and a decline in exports because foreigners have acquired fewer dollars. Thus, it is easy to see why this myth is so widely believed.

When trade restraints are lowered (or there is discussion about lowering them), predictably many workers and business officials in import-competitive industries will charge that jobs will be lost to foreign competitors. In contrast, the additional jobs in the export industries do not yet exist. No one will be saying, "I will not be employed next year if the trade restraints are not lowered." Because the jobs (and employees) in the import-competitive industries are highly visible, while the future jobs in the exporting industries are invisible, reducing trade restraints is very difficult.

Actually, the focus on jobs is misleading. After all, it is income and high productivity, not jobs, that are the sources of prosperity. The shift from less- to more-productive jobs is not without cost, but it is necessary if workers and the economy are going to reach their full potential. In essence, import restraints direct resources away from areas where domestic producers have a comparative advantage and into areas where domestic producers are relatively inefficient. Since fewer of our resources are used to produce things that we are good at (as indicated by our ability to compete effectively) and more resources are squandered attempting to produce things that we do poorly (as evidenced by our inability to compete in the world market), the per-capita output and income of Americans is lower than would be the case in the absence of the restraints.

Consider the following: If import restrictions are a good idea, why don't we use them to restrict trade among the 50 states? After all, think of all the jobs that are lost when, for example, Michigan "imports" oranges from Florida, apples from Washington, wheat from Kansas, and cotton from Georgia. All these products could be produced in Michigan. However, the residents of Michigan generally find it cheaper to "import" these commodities rather than produce them domestically. Michigan gains by using its resources to produce and "export" automobiles (and other goods it can produce economically) and then using the sales revenue to "import" goods that would be expensive to produce in Michigan.

Most people recognize that free trade among the 50 states is a major source of prosperity for each of the states. Similarly, most recognize that "imports" from other states do not destroy jobs—at least not for long. The source of gains from trade among nations is exactly the same as that from trade among people in different states. Free trade among the 50 states promotes prosperity; so, too, does free trade among nations.

Of course, sudden removal of trade barriers might harm producers and workers in protected industries. It may be costly to quickly transfer the protected resources to other, more productive activities. Gradual removal of the barriers would minimize this shock effect and the accompanying cost of relocation.

Economists generally emphasize two points with regard to dumping. First, dumping can, in a few instances, be used as a weapon to gain monopoly power. For example, if the foreign firm temporarily cuts its price below cost, it might eliminate domestic competition and later raise its price to a higher level after the domestic competitors have been driven from the market. However, this is usually not a feasible strategy. After all, domestic producers might reenter the market if the price rises in the future. In addition, alternative foreign suppliers limit the monopoly power of a producer attempting this strategy.

Second, the law of comparative advantage indicates that a country (as a whole) can gain from the purchase of foreign-produced goods when they are cheaper than domestic goods. This is true regardless of whether the low price of foreign goods reflects comparative advantage, subsidies by foreign governments, or poor business practices. Unless the foreign supplier is likely to monopolize the domestic market, there is little reason to believe that dumping harms the economy receiving the goods.

Special Interests and the Politics of Trade Restrictions

Protectionism is a politician's delight because it delivers visible benefits to the protected parties while imposing the costs as a hidden tax on the public.

Murray L. Weidenbaum[5]

Although trade restrictions arise from multiple sources, as Professor Weidenbaum points out, there is no question as to the primary reason for their adoption. ***Trade restrictions provide highly visible, concentrated benefits for a small group of people, while imposing widely dispersed costs that are often difficult to identify on the general citizenry.*** As we discussed in Chapter 6, ***politicians have a strong incentive to favor issues of this type, even if they conflict with economic efficiency.***

Trade restrictions almost always benefit producers (and resource suppliers) at the expense of consumers. In general, the former group—investors and workers in a specific industry—are well organized, and the "jobs saved" and "high wages protected" in these industries are often highly visible (refer again to the Myths of Economics box on trade restrictions). Thus, organized interest groups that benefit from trade restrictions frequently provide contributions and other resources to politicians willing to support trade restrictions favorable to their industry. In contrast, consumers, who will pay higher prices for the products of a protected industry, are an unorganized group. Most of them will not associate the higher product prices with the trade restrictions. However, it has been estimated that the average U.S. family pays at least $1,000 more per

The U.S. tariff code is complex, lengthy (the schedule fills 3,825 pages), and costly to administer. High tariffs are imposed on some products (for example, textiles, apparel, tobacco, and footwear), while low tariffs are imposed on others. Highly restrictive quotas limit the import of other goods (peanuts and sugar, for example). This system of targeted trade restrictions encourages wasteful rent-seeking. Many politicians benefit from this system because it permits them to provide protectionist policies in exchange for campaign contributions from interest groups wanting to restrict competition from foreign rivals.

---

[5]Personal correspondence with the authors. Professor Weidenbaum is a former chairman of the President's Council of Economic Advisers and long-time director of the Center for the Study of American Business of Washington University.

year for the products it buys because of trade restrictions. Similarly, potential workers and investors in export industries harmed by the restrictions are often unaware of their impact. Thus, most of the people harmed by trade restrictions are likely to be uninformed and thus unconcerned about trade policy.

Predictably, well-organized special interests favoring trade restrictions will generally have more political clout than those harmed by the restrictions. As a result, politicians will often be able to gain more votes by supporting trade restrictions that benefit organized interest groups than they could gain from the support of consumers and exporters. In the case of trade restrictions, sound economics often conflicts with a winning political strategy.

EMPIRICAL EVIDENCE ON THE IMPACT OF TRADE RESTRICTIONS

Our analysis indicates that countries imposing trade barriers will fail to realize their full economic potential. Countries use various means—tariffs, quotas, exchange-rate controls, and licensing requirements, for example—to restrain international trade. It is not always easy to determine the extent to which each country is restricting trade. Taxes on international trade are generally substantially lower in high-income industrial nations than in less-developed countries (LDCs). Similarly, while exchange-rate controls are a negligible restrictive factor in developed countries, they are a major factor restricting trade in several less-developed countries. Among LDCs, considerable variation exists in the height of trade barriers. Some LDCs impose exceedingly high tariffs. Others impose exchange-rate controls. When a country both imposes high tariffs and fixes the value of its currency at unrealistic rates (relative to convertible currencies like the dollar and yen), its international trade will be retarded substantially.

More than 80 less-developed countries were analyzed in a recent study. **Exhibit 17–10** presents data for the 10 with the lowest trade barriers.[6] The trade sectors of these 10 countries are large, given the size of their population. Their tariff rates are low and the exchange-rate value of their currency is pretty much in line with market forces (a low black-market exchange-rate premium provides evidence on this point). Data are also provided for the 10 LDCs that follow the most restrictive trade policies. For this latter group, the size of the trade sector is small (given the size of the country), tariffs are high, and the black-market exchange-rate premium for the conversion of the domestic currency is often high. As we previously discussed, a high black-market premium indicates that the country has imposed tight exchange-rate controls, which will restrain international trade.

The average size of the trade sector of the low-restriction countries (72.7 percent of GDP) was more than three times the average for the nations imposing substantial trade barriers. Compared to the low-restriction countries, the average tax (tariff) rate imposed on international trade was nine times higher in 1995 (and four times higher in 1980) for the high-restriction countries. Similarly, the black-market exchange-rate premium for the domestic currency was substantially higher in the high-restriction countries in both 1980 and 1995.

Look at the growth of per-capita GDP for the two groups. The average annual growth rate of per-capita GDP during the 1980–1997 period was positive for all of the countries that followed more liberal trade policies. Seven of the 10 achieved per-capita

[6]The empirical data presented in this section are part of a larger study undertaken by one of the authors. See James Gwartney and Robert Lawson, *Economic Freedom of the World: 1997 Annual Report* (Washington, D.C.: Cato Institute, 1997).

EXHIBIT 17-10

ECONOMIC GROWTH OF LESS-DEVELOPED COUNTRIES WITH LOW AND HIGH TRADE RESTRICTIONS: 1980–1997

	Size of Trade Sector as a Percentage of GDP, 1995[a]	Average Tax Rate on International Trade		Black-Market Exchange-Rate Premium		Growth of Per-Capita GDP, 1980–1997
		1980	1995	1980	1995	
Low Trade Restrictions[b]						
Singapore	166.0%	0.5	0.1	0	0	5.4
Hong Kong	148.9	0.5	0.3	0	0	4.7
Panama	94.0	3.1	1.4	0	0	0.5
Malaysia	90.6	7.7	2.1	0	0	4.0
Ireland	71.8	3.0	1.5	0	0	4.2
Taiwan	43.3	3.6	2.0	1	0	5.9
South Korea	33.7	4.1	2.0	5	0	7.5
Portugal	30.5	2.1	0.1	2	0	2.8
Indonesia	25.6	2.9	2.2	2	2	4.8
Greece	21.8	3.2	0.1	7	0	1.3
Average	72.7%	3.1	1.1	2	0	4.1
High Trade Restrictions[b]						
Rwanda	6.6%	13.3	14.6	67	105	−3.4
India	11.4	15.5	12.7	5	8	3.0
Burundi	14.8	18.1	13.6	45	44	−1.7
Iran	16.2	17.0	5.6	164	115	1.0
Bangladesh	18.3	13.4	12.1	111	28	2.4
Cameroon	20.1	11.0	7.7	2	1	−0.9
Sierra Leone	23.7	13.3	7.7	62	2	−3.5
Madagascar	27.4	8.5	8.5	51	2	−1.8
Dominican Republic	27.8	9.2	12.2	37	2	−0.4
Syria	37.5	7.1	4.0	35	301	0.4
Average	20.4%	12.6	9.9	58	61	−0.5

[a]*The size of the trade sector is equal to one-half of exports plus imports as a percentage of GDP. As Illustrated Exhibit IV-A shows, the size of the trade sector tends to be inversely related to the population of a country. Given population, the trade sector is generally large in countries with low trade restrictions and small in countries with high trade restrictions.*

[b]*More than 100 countries were rated on the basis of three international trade factors: (1) tariff rates, (2) black-market exchange rate, and (3) the actual size of the trade sectors relative to the expected size given the country's population, geographic size, and location. The less-developed countries in this table are the ten highest and ten lowest rated in the area of international trade. See James Gwartney and Robert Lawson,* Economic Freedom of the World: 1997 Annual Report *(Washington, D.C.: Cato Institute, 1997).*

growth of 4 percent or more. The average annual growth of per-capita GDP of the low-restriction countries was 4.1 percent. In contrast, the average growth rate of the 10 countries with high trade restrictions was *minus* 0.5 percent. Per-capita GDP declined during 1980–1997 in six of the ten countries that imposed substantial restrictions on international trade. Only two of the countries with high trade restrictions—Bangladesh and India—were able to achieve a growth rate in excess of 1 percent. Just as our theory implies, these data indicate that trade barriers are harmful to the economic health of a country.[7]

REDUCTIONS IN TRADE RESTRICTIONS

General Agreement on Tariffs and Trade (GATT)
An organization formed following the Second World War to set the rules for the conduct of international trade and reduce barriers to trade among nations.

World Trade Organization (WTO)
The new name given to GATT in 1994; it is currently responsible for monitoring and enforcing the multilateral trade agreements among the 133 member countries.

North American Free Trade Agreement (NAFTA)
A comprehensive trade agreement between the United States, Mexico, and Canada that went into effect in 1994. Tariff barriers will continue to be phased out under the agreement until 2004.

Although vulnerable to special-interest politics, reductions in trade restrictions have not been totally ignored. The major industrial nations established the **General Agreement on Tariffs and Trade (GATT)** organization shortly following the Second World War. For five decades, GATT played a central role in the multilateral tariff reductions and the relaxation (or elimination) of quotas. The average tariff rates of GATT members fell from approximately 40 percent in 1947 to less than 5 percent in 1997. When the most recent round of trade negotiations—the Uruguay Round—was completed at year-end 1993, GATT was given a new name: the **World Trade Organization (WTO).** This organization of 133 countries is now responsible for the monitoring and enforcement of the trade agreements developed through GATT.

In 1988, the United States and Canada negotiated a trade agreement designed to reduce barriers limiting both trade and the flow of capital between the two countries. A few years later, the United States, Canada, and Mexico finalized the **North American Free Trade Agreement (NAFTA),** which took effect in 1994. As the result of NAFTA, tariffs on the shipment of most products among the three countries will be eliminated by 2004. The agreement will also remove limits on financial investments, liberalize trade in services such as banking, and establish uniform legal requirements for the protection of intellectual property. Preliminary analysis suggests that the agreement has had significant positive effects on the trade among the three nations. Pushed along by both NAFTA and unilateral Mexican tariff reductions, trade between the United States and Mexico has increased sharply during the last decade. In 1997, U.S. exports to (and imports from) Mexico were approximately 1 percent of GDP, more than double the figure of a decade earlier. Trade between the United States and Canada has also increased as a share of the economy during the last decade.

Compared with Canada, the free trade agreement with Mexico was—and continues to be—much more controversial. As we have discussed, trade flows among nations are determined by comparative advantage, *not* relative wage rates. Nonetheless, many Americans and Canadians fear that competition from low-wage workers will adversely affect their earnings (see the Myths of Economics box on free trade with low-wage countries). Political candidate Ross Perot argued that NAFTA would lead to massive job losses because many U.S. firms would find it difficult to compete with lower-wage Mexican rivals.[8] In line with economic theory, these losses have not materialized. In fact, the growth of both output and employment in the United States has been quite strong during the post-NAFTA period. Certainly the reduced trade barriers have resulted and will continue to result in some reallocations of resources as each country adjusts and moves toward areas of comparative advantage. Although these adjustments are sometimes painful, economic theory indicates that they will lead to stronger and more prosperous North American economies.

---

[7]For additional evidence that trade restrictions retard economic growth, see Robert Barro, "Economic Growth in a Cross-Section of Countries," *Quarterly Journal of Economics* (May 1991): 407–443; David M. Gould, Roy J. Ruffin, and Graeme L. Woodbridge, "The Theory and Practice of Free Trade," *Economic Review—Federal Reserve Bank of Dallas* (fourth quarter 1993): 1–16; and Michael Michaely, Demetris Papageorgiou, and Armeane M. Choksi, eds., *Liberalizing Foreign Trade: Lessons of Experience in the Developing World* (Cambridge, Mass.: Basil Blackwell, 1991).

[8]The colorful Perot often argued his point by telling his audiences that "the sucking sound that you hear is American jobs going south."

APPLICATIONS IN ECONOMICS

Tomatoes, Regulations, and Trade Restrictions[9]

In 1995–1996, Florida tomato growers complained to the Clinton administration and Congress that the import of cheap tomatoes from Mexico was driving them out of business. Blaming the North American Free Trade Agreement (NAFTA) for their plight, they sought to have Congress declare "winter vegetables" a separate industry so they would qualify for greater protection. They also filed an antidumping suit with the Commerce Department seeking the imposition of higher tariffs on Mexican tomatoes.

When these strategies failed, the growers asked Congress to pass special package and labeling legislation. While the hard, unripe Florida tomatoes are shipped in solid-tray boxes, the Mexican tomatoes are ripened on the vine, hand-packaged, and shipped in cushioned cartons. At least some consumers believe that this procedure makes the tomatoes tastier. This issue aside, the Florida growers wanted legislation that would require all growers to use the hard-tray cartons. Of course, this would make it difficult for the riper Mexican tomatoes to be shipped without being battered or bruised. Interestingly, the problems of the Florida growers had little to do with NAFTA. The major factor contributing to the increased competitiveness of the Mexican-grown tomatoes was the sharp reduction in the exchange rate of the peso relative to the dollar during 1994–1995.

This case illustrates why it is so difficult to maintain freedom of exchange in international markets. Rather than simply argue for trade restraints, organized interest groups often support regulations that they say will be "safer," or "more convenient," or "facilitate inspection." Of course, such regulations also just happen to give the special-interest groups a competitive edge over their rivals. This is true in all countries. Japan, in particular, has been charged with the use of such diversionary tactics.

Neither is Mexico blameless. For example, the Mexican government attempted to impose cumbersome labeling and inspection procedures in an effort to reduce the competitiveness of American tires in the Mexican market. Mexico continues to prohibit American express delivery firms, such as United Parcel Service, from using large trucks south of the border. Consumers are the losers when restrictions of this type are imposed. Unfortunately, since consumers are disorganized and generally unaware they are being harmed, support of well-organized interest groups is often politically attractive.

[1]This feature is based on an article by Helene Cooper and Bruce Ingersoll, "With Little Evidence, Florida Growers Blame Tomato Woes on NAFTA," *Wall Street Journal,* April 3, 1996, p. 1.

MYTHS OF ECONOMICS

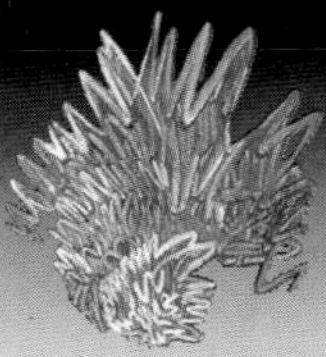

"Free trade with low-wage countries, such as China and India, would cause the wages of U.S. workers to fall."

Many Americans believe that if it were not for trade restrictions, the wages of American workers would fall to the level of workers in less-developed countries. How can U.S. labor compete with workers in China or India who are willing to work for $1 per hour or less? The fallacy of this argument stems from a misunderstanding of the source of high wages and ignorance of the law of comparative advantage. After all, average wages differ substantially between U.S. states despite more than 200 years of free trade!

High hourly wages do not necessarily mean high per-unit labor cost. Labor productivity must also be considered. For example, suppose a U.S. steel worker receives an hourly wage rate of $20 and a steel worker in India receives only $2 per hour. Given the skill level of the workers and the capital and production methods used in the two countries, however, the U.S. worker produces 20 times as many tons of steel per worker-hour as the Indian worker. Because of the higher productivity per worker-hour, labor cost per unit of output is actually lower in the United States than in India!

Labor in the United States possesses a high skill level and works with large amounts of capital equipment. These factors contribute to the high productivity per worker, which is the source of the high wages. Similarly, low productivity per worker-hour is the foundation of the low wages in such countries as India and China.

When analyzing the significance of wage and productivity differentials across countries, one must remember that gains from trade emanate from comparative advantage, not absolute advantage (see Exhibits 17-2, 17-3, and 17-4). The United States cannot produce everything cheaper than China or India merely because U.S. workers are more productive and work with more capital than workers in China and India. Neither can the Chinese and Indians produce everything cheaper merely because their wage rates are low compared to those of U.S. workers. When resources are directed by relative prices and the principle of comparative advantage, both high-wage and low-wage countries gain from the opportunity to specialize in those activities that, relatively speaking, they do best.

The comparative advantage of low-wage countries is likely to be in the production of labor-intensive goods, such as wigs, rugs, toys, textiles, and assembled manufactured products. On the other hand, the comparative advantage of the United States lies in the production of high-tech manufacturing products and other goods produced economically by a well-educated labor force. Trade permits both high- and low-wage countries to reallocate their resources away from productive activities in which they are inefficient (relative to foreign producers) toward activities in which they are highly efficient. The net result is an increase in output and consumption opportunities for both trading partners.

If foreigners, even low-wage foreigners, will sell us a product cheaper than we ourselves could produce it, we can gain by using our resources to produce other things. Perhaps an extreme example will illustrate the point. Suppose a foreign producer, perhaps a Santa Claus (who was able to hire workers at low wages), was willing to supply us with free winter coats. Would it make sense to enact a tariff barrier to keep out the free coats? Of course not. Resources that were previously used to produce coats could now be freed to produce other goods. Output and the availability of goods would expand. The real wage of U.S. workers would rise. It makes no more sense to erect trade barriers to keep out cheap foreign goods than to keep out the free coats of a friendly, foreign Santa Claus.

FALLING TRADE BARRIERS IN OTHER COUNTRIES

The reduction in trade barriers and growth of the trade sector in the United States reflects a worldwide trend. No doubt influenced by the economic success of relatively open economies like those of Hong Kong and Singapore, many LDCs unilaterally reduced their trade barriers during the late 1980s and early 1990s. Among Latin American countries, Chile began moving toward freer trade policies in the early 1980s. Spurred by the rapid economic growth of Chile during the latter half of the 1980s, other Latin American countries followed suit. Mexico cut its tariff rates by more than 50 percent during the late 1980s. In 1991 Argentina cut its average tariff level from 18 percent to 11 percent. Brazil, Bolivia, Colombia, Ecuador, Peru, and Venezuela have also made substantial cuts in their tariff rates and reduced other trade barriers in the

1990s.[9] Exchange-rate controls have also been relaxed or eliminated throughout much of Latin America during the past five years. In other parts of the world, even some of the most "protectionist" countries—including Pakistan, the Philippines, and Turkey—have cut their tariffs or relaxed restrictive quotas or both in the 1990s.

LOOKING *Ahead*

As the result of recent financial turbulence in several Asian and Latin American countries, focus has now shifted away from trade restrictions and toward the development of more stable financial arrangements. There are many similarities between trade within national borders and trade across national boundaries. However, there is also a major difference. In addition to the exchange of goods for money, trade across national borders generally involves the exchange of national currencies. The next chapter deals with the foreign exchange market and other dimensions of international finance.

KEY POINTS

➤ The volume of international trade has grown rapidly in recent decades. Over 20 percent of the world's output is sold outside the country in which it was produced. The size of the trade sector is generally larger in countries with a smaller population.

➤ Comparative advantage rather than absolute advantage is the source of gains from trade. As long as the relative production costs of goods differ among nations, all nations will be able to gain from trade. Specialization and trade allow trading partners to maximize their joint output and expand their consumption possibilities.

➤ Exports and imports are closely linked. The exports of a nation are the primary source of purchasing power used to import goods. When a nation restricts imports, it simultaneously limits the ability of foreigners to acquire the purchasing power necessary to buy the nation's exports.

➤ Relative to the no-trade alternative, international exchange and specialization result in lower prices for products that are imported and higher domestic prices for products that are exported. However, the net effect is an expansion in the aggregate output and consumption possibilities available to a nation.

➤ Import restrictions, such as tariffs and quotas, reduce foreign supply and cause the price to rise for domestic consumers. Thus, such restrictions are subsidies to producers (and workers) in protected industries at the expense of (a) consumers and (b) producers (and workers) in export industries. Jobs protected by import restrictions are offset by jobs destroyed in export industries.

➤ National-defense, infant-industry, and antidumping arguments can be used to justify trade restrictions for specific industries under certain conditions. It is clear, though, that the power of special-interest groups and voter ignorance about the harmful effects of trade restrictions are the major explanations for real-world policies.

➤ Both high-wage and low-wage countries gain from trade. If a low-wage country can supply a good to the United States cheaper than the United States can produce it, the United States can gain by purchasing the good from the low-wage country and using U.S. resources to produce other goods for which the United States has a comparative advantage. Free trade with low-wage

[9]See Susan Hickok, "Recent Trade Liberalization in Developing Countries: The Effects of Global Trade and Output," *Quarterly Review: Federal Reserve Bank of New York* (autumn 1993): 6–19.

countries does not result in wage rates equalizing or massive outflows of jobs, because these wage differences reflect productivity differences.

➤ There is substantial variation among LDCs with regard to the imposition of trade restrictions. LDCs that have low tariff rates, a freely convertible currency, and large trade sectors (relative to the size of their population) have generally outperformed those with restrictive trade policies.

CRITICAL-ANALYSIS QUESTIONS

*1. "Trade restrictions limiting the sale of cheap foreign goods in the United States are necessary to protect the prosperity of Americans." Evaluate this statement made by an American politician.

2. Suppose as the result of the Civil War that the United States had been divided into two countries and that through the years high trade barriers had grown up between the two. How might the standard of living in the "divided" United States have been affected? Explain.

*3. Can both of the following statements be true? Why or why not?

a. "Tariffs and import quotas promote economic inefficiency and reduce the real income of a nation. Economic analysis suggests that nations can gain by eliminating trade restrictions."

b. "Economic analysis suggests that there is good reason to expect that trade restrictions will exist in the real world."

4. "The average American is hurt by imports and helped by exports." Do you agree or disagree with this statement? How do imports and exports affect the welfare of and prices paid by the average American consumer? How do they affect the welfare of domestic corporations and producers producing the goods?

*5. "An increased scarcity of a product benefits producers and harms consumers. In effect, tariffs and other trade restrictions increase the domestic scarcity of products by reducing the supply from abroad. Such policies benefit domestic producers of the restricted product at the expense of domestic consumers." Evaluate this statement.

*6. The United States uses an import quota to maintain the domestic price of sugar well above the world price. Analyze the impact of the quota. Use supply-and-demand analysis to illustrate your answer. To whom do the gains and losses of this policy accrue? How does the quota affect the efficiency of resource allocation in the United States? Why do you think Congress is supportive of this policy?

7. Suppose that it costs American textile manufacturers $20 to produce a shirt, while foreign producers can supply the same shirt for $15.

a. Would a tariff of $6 per shirt help American manufacturers compete with foreign manufacturers?

b. Would a subsidy of $6 per shirt to domestic manufacturers help them compete?

c. Is there any difference between the tariff and a direct subsidy to the domestic manufacturer?

*8. "Getting more Americans to realize that it pays to make things in the United States is the heart of the competitiveness issue." (This is a quote from an American business magazine.)

a. Would Americans be better off if more of them paid higher prices in order to "buy American" rather than purchase from foreigners? Would U.S. employment be higher? Explain.

b. Would Californians be better off if they bought only goods produced in California? Would the employment in California be higher? Explain.

*9. It is often alleged that Japanese producers receive subsidies from their government that permit them to sell their products at a low price in the U.S. market. Do you think we should erect trade barriers to keep out cheap Japanese goods if the source of their low price is governmental subsidies? Why or why not?

10. How do tariffs and quotas differ? Can you think of any reason why foreign producers might prefer a quota rather than a tariff? Explain your answer.

11. What's wrong with this economic experiment? A researcher hypothesizes that higher tariffs on imported automobiles would cause total employment in the United States to increase. Automobile tariffs are raised, and the following year employment in the U.S. auto industry increases by 50,000. The researcher concludes that the higher tariffs created 50,000 jobs.

*12. Does international trade cost American jobs? Does interstate trade cost your state jobs? What is the major effect of international and interstate trade?

13. "The United States is suffering from a huge excess of imports. Cheap foreign products are driving American

firms out of business and leaving our economy in shambles." Evaluate this statement from an American politician.

14. Do you think the United States will benefit as trade barriers with Mexico are reduced? Will Mexico benefit? Will trade with a low-wage country like Mexico push wages down in a high-wage country like the United States? Why or why not?

*15. "Tariffs not only reduce the volume of imports, they also reduce the volume of exports." Is this statement true or false? Explain your answer.

16. Answer the following questions and carefully compare and contrast your answers.

a. Would the people of Europe be better off if there were dangerous rivers with no bridges that ran along the borders between countries? Why or why not?

b. Would the people of Europe be better off if there were sizable tariffs (taxes on imports), import quotas, and other regulations that limited foreigners from selling goods cheaply in the domestic market of another country? Why or why not?

c. If foreigners were "dumping" their goods—if they were selling in another country at a price below their production costs—would your answer to part b have been different?

17. Suppose that a very high tariff were placed on steel imported into the U.S. How would that affect employment in the U.S. auto industry? (Hint: Think about how higher steel prices will impact the cost of producing automobiles.)

---

*Asterisk denotes questions for which answers are given in Appendix B.

CHAPTER 18

Currencies, like tomatoes and football tickets, have a price at which they are bought and sold. An exchange rate is the price of one currency in terms of another, such as the price of a French franc in U.S. dollars or German marks.

Gary Smith[1]

International Finance and the Foreign Exchange Market

CHAPTER FOCUS

- What determines the exchange-rate value of the dollar relative to other currencies?
- What information is included in the balance-of-payments accounts of a nation? Will the balance-of-payments accounts of a country always be in balance?
- How do monetary and fiscal policies influence the exchange-rate value of a nation's currency?
- Will a healthy economy run a balance-of-trade surplus? Does a balance-of-trade deficit indicate that a nation is in financial trouble?
- How have international financial arrangements changed in recent years? How are they likely to change in the future?

[1]Gary Smith, *Macroeconomics* (New York: W. H. Freeman, 1985), p. 514.

Trade across national boundaries is complicated by the fact that nations generally use different currencies to buy and sell goods in their respective domestic markets. The British use pounds, the Japanese yen, the Mexicans pesos, and so on. Therefore, when a good or service is purchased from a seller in another country, it is generally necessary for someone to convert one currency to another. This adds to the complexity of international exchange. This complication could be avoided if the trading partners used a common currency. This is precisely what 11 European nations have decided to do. They are in the process of phasing in a common currency, the euro. If things go as planned, trade among the citizens of these nations will be conducted in euros by 2002.

Most exchanges across national boundaries, however, still involve currency conversions. If you travel in Europe, Asia, or South America, you will generally have to convert your dollars to another currency in order to purchase items. What determines the value of one currency relative to another? What is the role of the foreign exchange market? How do exchange-rate regimes differ across countries? How do these differences influence international trade? This chapter will investigate these issues and related topics.

FOREIGN EXCHANGE MARKET

Foreign exchange market
The market in which the currencies of different countries are bought and sold.

We have previously discussed the **foreign exchange market,** the market where the currencies of different countries are bought and sold. We now want to consider this market in more detail and analyze the factors that cause changes in exchange rates. Suppose you own a sporting goods shop in the United States and are preparing to place an order for athletic shoes. You can purchase them from either a domestic or foreign manufacturer. If you decide to purchase the shoes from a British firm, either you will have to change dollars into pounds at a bank and send them to the British producer, or the British manufacturer will have to go to a bank and change your dollar check into pounds. In either case, purchasing the British shoes will involve an exchange of dollars for pounds.

The British producer has offered to supply the shoes for 20 pounds per pair. How can you determine whether this price is high or low? To compare the price of the British-supplied shoes with the price of those produced domestically, you must know the **exchange rate** between the dollar and the pound. ***The exchange rate is one of the most important prices of an economy because it enables consumers in one country to translate the prices of foreign goods into units of their own currency. Specifically, the dollar price of a foreign good is determined by multiplying the foreign product price by the exchange rate (the dollar price per unit of the foreign currency).*** For example, if it takes $1.50 to obtain 1 pound, then the British shoes priced at 20 pounds would cost $30 (20 times the $1.50 price of the pound).

Exchange rate
The domestic price of one unit of foreign currency. For example, if it takes $1.50 to purchase one English pound, the dollar-pound exchange rate is 1.50.

Suppose the exchange rate is $1.50 = 1 pound and that you decide to buy 200 pairs of athletic shoes from the British manufacturer at 20 pounds ($30) per pair. You will need 4,000 pounds in order to pay the British manufacturer. If you contact an

American bank that handles foreign exchange transactions and write the bank a check for $6,000 (the $1.50 exchange rate multiplied by 4,000), it will supply the 4,000 pounds. The bank will typically charge a small fee for handling the transaction.

Where does the American bank get the pounds? The bank obtains the pounds from British importers who want dollars to buy things from Americans. ***Note that the U.S. demand for foreign currencies (such as the pound) is generated by the demand of Americans for things purchased from foreigners. On the other hand, the U.S. supply of foreign exchange reflects the demand of foreigners for things bought from Americans.***

Exhibit 18–1 presents data on the exchange rate—the cents required to purchase a German mark, Japanese yen, British pound, and Canadian dollar—during 1990–1998. An index of the exchange-rate value of the dollar against ten major currencies is also shown. Under the flexible rate system present in most industrial countries, the exchange rate between currencies changes from day to day and even from hour to hour. Thus, the annual exchange-rate data given in Exhibit 18–1 are really averages for each year.

An **appreciation** in the value of a nation's currency means that fewer units of the currency are now required to purchase one unit of a foreign currency. For example, in 1998, only 56.8 cents were required to purchase a German mark, down from 69.8 cents in 1995.[2] ***As the result of this appreciation in the value of the dollar relative to the mark, German goods became less expensive to Americans.*** The direction of change in the prices that Germans paid for American goods was just the opposite. An appreciation of the U.S. dollar relative to the mark is the same thing as a depreciation in the mark relative to the dollar.

Appreciation
An increase in the value of a domestic currency relative to foreign currencies. An appreciation increases the purchasing power of the domestic currency for foreign goods.

EXHIBIT 18–1

FOREIGN EXCHANGE RATES, 1990–1998

	U.S. Cents per Unit of Foreign Currency				Index of Exchange-Rate Value of the Dollar (Ten Currencies)[a]
Year	German Mark	Japanese Yen	British Pound	Canadian Dollar	
1990	61.9	0.690	178.41	85.7	89.1
1991	60.2	0.743	176.74	87.3	89.3
1992	64.0	0.789	176.63	82.7	86.6
1993	60.4	0.900	150.16	77.5	93.2
1994	61.7	0.979	153.19	73.2	91.3
1995	69.8	1.064	157.85	72.9	84.3
1996	66.4	0.919	156.07	73.3	87.3
1997	57.6	0.826	163.76	72.2	96.4
1998	56.8	0.763	165.73	67.4	98.8

[a]*March 1973 = 100. In addition to the currencies listed above, the index includes the Belgian franc, French franc, Italian lira, Netherlands guilder, Swedish krona, and Swiss franc.*

SOURCE: Council of Economic Advisers, Economic Report of the President *(Washington, D.C.: U.S. Government Printing Office, 1999).*

[2]Because an appreciation means a lower price of foreign currencies, some may think it looks like a depreciation. Just remember that a lower price of the foreign currency means that one's domestic currency will buy more units of the foreign currency and thus more goods and services from foreigners.

Depreciation
A reduction in the value of a domestic currency relative to foreign currencies. A depreciation reduces the purchasing power of the domestic currency for foreign goods.

When a **depreciation** occurs, it will take more units of the domestic currency to purchase a unit of foreign currency. Between 1993 and 1998, the dollar depreciated against the British pound (see Exhibit 18–1). In 1993, it took 150.16 cents to purchase a British pound; by 1998, the figure had risen to 165.73. As the number of cents required to purchase a British pound rose, British goods became more expensive for Americans.

The ten-currency index of the dollar's exchange-rate value presented in Exhibit 18–1 provides evidence on what is happening to the dollar's general exchange-rate value.[3] An increase in the index implies an appreciation in the dollar, while a decline is indicative of a depreciation in the dollar. After depreciating between 1993 and 1995, the dollar appreciated by approximately 17 percent during 1995–1998. Frequently, people will use the terms "strong" and "weak" when referring to the exchange-rate value of a currency. A strong currency is one that has appreciated substantially in value, while a weak currency is one that has declined in value on the foreign exchange market.

DETERMINANTS OF EXCHANGE RATE

Flexible exchange rates
Exchange rates that are determined by the market forces of supply and demand. They are sometimes called floating exchange rates.

What determines the exchange rate between two currencies? Under a system of **flexible exchange rates,** also called *floating exchange rates,* the value of currencies in the foreign exchange market is determined by market forces. Just as the forces of supply and demand determine other prices, so do they determine the exchange-rate value of currencies in the absence of government intervention.

The exchange-rate system in effect since 1973 might best be described as a managed flexible rate system. It is flexible because all the major industrial countries allow the exchange-rate value of their currencies to float. But the system is also "managed" because the major industrial nations have from time to time attempted to alter supply and demand in the foreign exchange market by buying and selling various currencies. Compared to the total size of this market, however, these transactions have been relatively small. Thus, the exchange-rate value of major currencies like the U.S. dollar, British pound, Japanese yen, and the new European euro is determined primarily by market forces. Several countries link their currency to major currencies, such as the U.S. dollar, English pound, or Japanese yen. As we proceed, we will investigate alternative methods of linking currencies and analyze the operation of different regimes.

DEMAND, SUPPLY, AND EQUILIBRIUM PRICE IN THE FOREIGN EXCHANGE MARKET

To simplify our explanation of how the exchange rate is determined, let us assume that the United States and Great Britain are the only two countries in the world. When Americans buy and sell with each other, they use dollars. Therefore, American sellers will want to be paid in dollars. Similarly, when the British buy and sell with each other, they use pounds. As a result, British sellers will want to be paid in pounds.

If Americans want to buy from British sellers, they will need to acquire pounds. ***In our two-country world, the demand for pounds in the exchange-rate market originates from the demand of Americans for British goods, services, and assets***

[3]In the construction of this index, the exchange rate of each currency relative to the dollar is weighted according to the proportion of U.S. trade with the country. For example, the index weights the U.S. dollar–Japanese yen exchange rate more heavily than the U.S. dollar–Swiss franc exchange rate because the volume of U.S. trade with Japan exceeds the volume of trade with Switzerland.

(both real and financial). For example, when U.S. residents purchase men's suits from a British manufacturer, travel in the United Kingdom, or purchase the stocks, bonds, or physical assets of British business firms, they demand pounds from (and supply dollars to) the foreign exchange-rate market to pay for these items.

The supply of foreign exchange (pounds in our two-country case) originates from sales by Americans to foreigners. When Americans sell goods, services, or assets to the British, for example, the British buyers will supply pounds (and demand dollars) in the exchange-rate market in order to acquire the dollars required to pay for the items purchased from Americans.[4]

Exhibit 18–2 illustrates the demand and supply curves of Americans for foreign exchange—British pounds in our two-country case. The demand for pounds is downward sloping because a lower dollar price of the pound—meaning a dollar will buy more pounds—makes British goods cheaper for American importers. The goods produced by one country are generally good substitutes for the goods of another country. This means that when foreign (British) goods become cheaper, Americans will increase their expenditures on imports (and therefore the quantity of pounds demanded will increase). Thus, as the dollar price of the pound declines, Americans will both buy more of the lower-priced (in dollars) British goods and demand more pounds, which are required for the purchases.

Similarly, the supply curve for pounds is dependent on the sales by Americans to the British (that is, the purchase of American goods by the British). An increase in

EXHIBIT 18–2

EQUILIBRIUM IN FOREIGN EXCHANGE MARKET

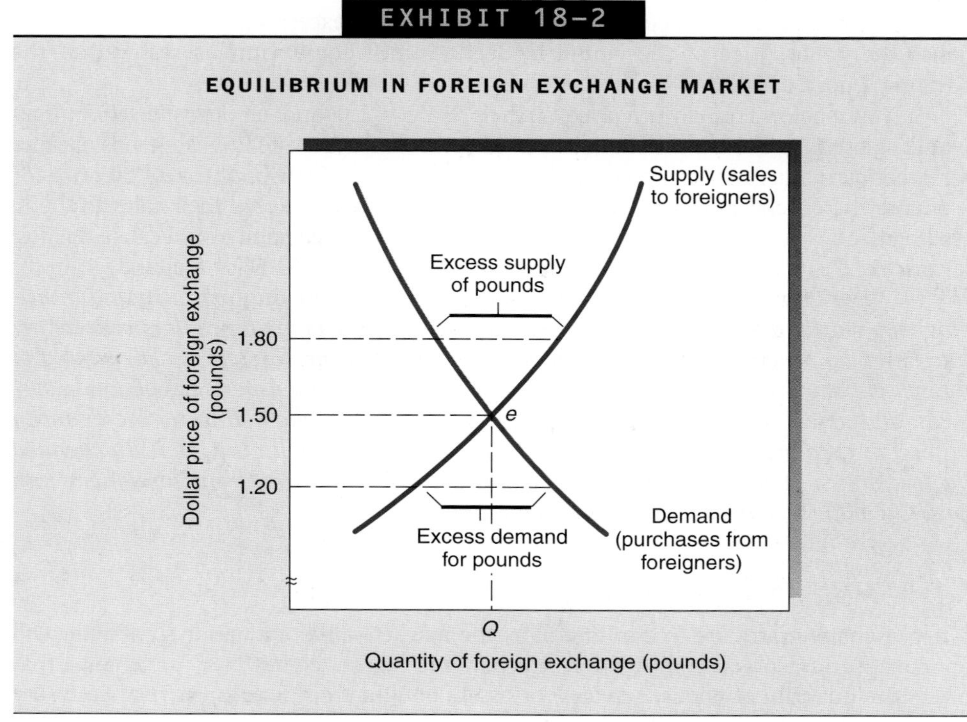

The dollar price of the pound is measured on the vertical axis. The horizontal axis indicates the flow of pounds to the foreign exchange market. The equilibrium exchange rate is $1.50 = 1 pound. At the equilibrium price, the quantity demanded of pounds just equals the quantity supplied. A higher price of pounds, such as $1.80 = 1 pound, would lead to an excess supply of pounds, causing the dollar price of the pound to fall. On the other hand, a lower price—for example, $1.20 = 1 pound—would result in an excess demand for pounds, causing the pound to appreciate.

[4]We analyze the foreign exchange market in terms of the demand for and supply of foreign currencies. Alternatively, this analysis could be done in terms of the supply of and demand for dollars. Since one currency is traded for another, the same actions that generate a demand for foreign exchange simultaneously generate a supply of dollars. Correspondingly, the same exchanges that create a supply of foreign currencies simultaneously generate a demand for dollars in the foreign exchange market.

the dollar price of the pound means that a pound will purchase more dollars and more goods priced in dollars. Thus, the price (in pounds) of American goods, services, and assets to British purchasers declines. The British will purchase more from Americans and therefore supply more pounds to the foreign exchange market as the dollar price of the pound rises. Because of this, the supply curve for pounds tends to slope upward to the right.

As Exhibit 18–2 shows, equilibrium is present at the dollar price of the pound that brings the quantity demanded and quantity supplied of pounds into balance, \$1.50 = 1 pound in this case. ***The market-clearing price of \$1.50 per pound not only equates demand and supply in the foreign exchange market, it also equates (1) the value of U.S. purchases of items supplied by the British with (2) the value of items sold by U.S. residents to the British.*** Demand and supply in the currency market are merely the mirror images of these two factors.

What would happen if the price of the pound were above equilibrium—\$1.80 = 1 pound, for example? At the higher dollar price of the pound, British goods would be more expensive for Americans. Americans would cut back on their purchases of shoes, glassware, textile products, financial assets, and other items supplied by the British. Reflecting this reduction, the quantity of pounds demanded by Americans would decline. Simultaneously, the higher dollar price of the pound would make U.S. exports cheaper for the British. For example, an \$18,000 American automobile would cost British consumers 12,000 pounds when 1 pound trades for \$1.50, but it would cost only 10,000 pounds when 1 pound exchanges for \$1.80. If the dollar price of the pound were \$1.80, the British would supply more pounds to the foreign exchange market than Americans demand. As can be seen in Exhibit 18–2, this excess supply of pounds would cause the dollar price of the pound to decline until equilibrium is restored at the \$1.50 = 1 pound price.

At a below-equilibrium price, such as \$1.20 = 1 pound, an opposite set of forces would be present. The lower dollar price of the pound would make English goods cheaper for Americans and American goods more expensive for the British. At the \$1.20 price for a pound, the purchases of Americans from the British would exceed their sales to them, leading to an excess demand for pounds. In turn, the excess demand would cause the dollar price of the pound to rise until equilibrium was restored at \$1.50 = 1 pound.

The implications of the analysis are general. In our multicountry and multicurrency world, the demand for foreign currencies in exchange for dollars reflects the purchases by Americans of goods, services, and assets from foreigners. The supply of foreign currencies in exchange for dollars reflects the sales by Americans of goods, services, and assets to foreigners. The equilibrium exchange rate will bring the quantity of foreign exchange demanded by Americans into equality with the quantity supplied by foreigners. It will also bring the purchases by Americans from foreigners into equality with the sales by Americans to foreigners.

Changes in Exchange Rates

When exchange rates are free to fluctuate, the market value of a nation's currency will appreciate and depreciate in response to changing market conditions. Any change that alters the quantity of goods, services, or assets bought from foreigners relative to the quantity sold to foreigners will also alter the exchange rate. What types of change will alter the exchange-rate value of a currency?

Changes in Income. An increase in domestic income will encourage the nation's residents to spend a portion of their additional income on imports. When the income of a nation grows rapidly, the nation's imports tend to rise rapidly as well. As **Exhibit 18–3** illustrates, an increase in imports also increases the demand for foreign exchange (the pound in our two-country case). As the demand for pounds increases, the dollar price of the pound rises (from $1.50 to $1.80). This depreciation of the dollar reduces the incentive of Americans to import British goods and services, while increasing the

American consumer purchases an auto from a Japanese manufacturer.

American vacationer buys a ticket on British Airways.

Foreign student pays tuition to Harvard.

Foreign investor purchases a bond from a U.S. corporation.

How will each of these transactions influence the demand for and supply of foreign currencies in exchange for the dollar?

EXHIBIT 18–3

GROWTH OF INCOME AND GROWTH OF IMPORTS

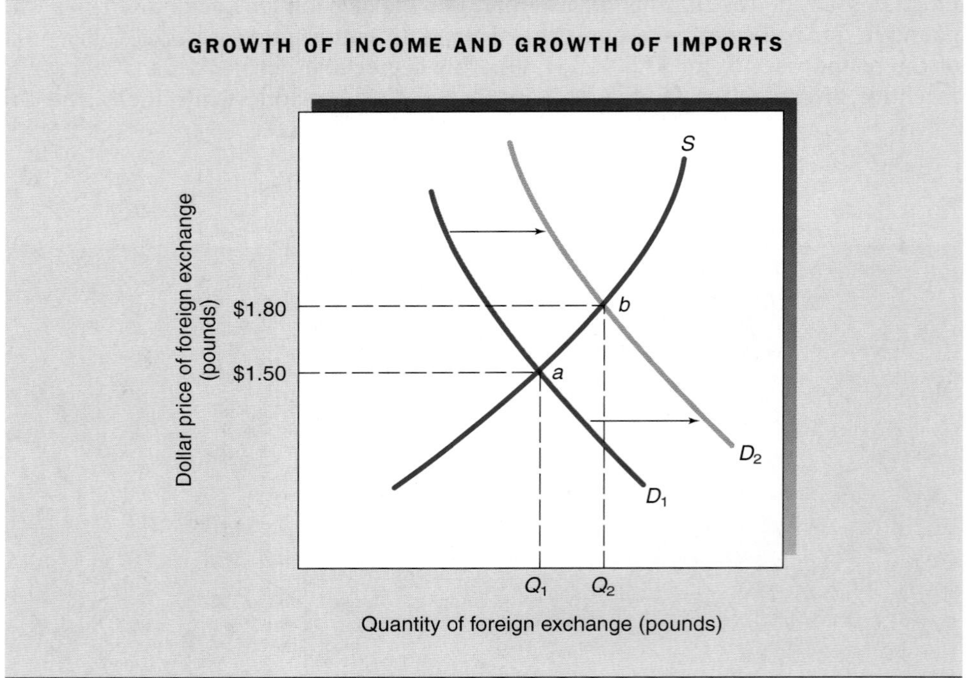

Other things constant, if incomes grow in the United States, U.S. imports will grow. The increase in the imports will increase the demand for pounds, causing the dollar price of the pound to rise (from $1.50 to $1.80).

incentive of the British to purchase U.S. exports. These two forces will restore equilibrium in the foreign exchange market at a new, higher dollar price of the pound.

Just the opposite takes place when the income of a trading partner (Great Britain in our example) increases. Rapid growth of income abroad will lead to an increase in U.S. exports, causing the supply of foreign exchange (and demand for dollars) to increase. This will cause the dollar to appreciate—the dollar price of the pound will fall.

What will happen if both countries are growing? Other things constant, it is the relative growth rate that matters. A country that grows more rapidly than its trading partners will increase its imports relative to exports, which will cause the exchange-rate value of its currency to fall. Correspondingly, sluggish growth of income relative to one's trading partners will lead to a decline in imports relative to exports. ***Paradoxical as it may seem, sluggish growth relative to one's trading partners will tend to cause a nation's currency to appreciate.***

Differences in Rates of Inflation. Other things constant, domestic inflation will cause the value of a nation's currency to depreciate in the foreign exchange market, whereas deflation will result in appreciation. Suppose prices in the United States rise by 50 percent while our trading partners are experiencing stable prices. The domestic inflation will cause U.S. consumers to increase their demand for imported goods (and foreign currency). In turn, the inflated domestic prices will cause foreigners to reduce their purchases of U.S. goods, thereby reducing the supply of foreign currency to the exchange market. As **Exhibit 18–4** illustrates, the exchange rate will adjust to this set of circumstances. The dollar will depreciate relative to the pound.

EXHIBIT 18-4

INFLATION WITH FLEXIBLE EXCHANGE RATES

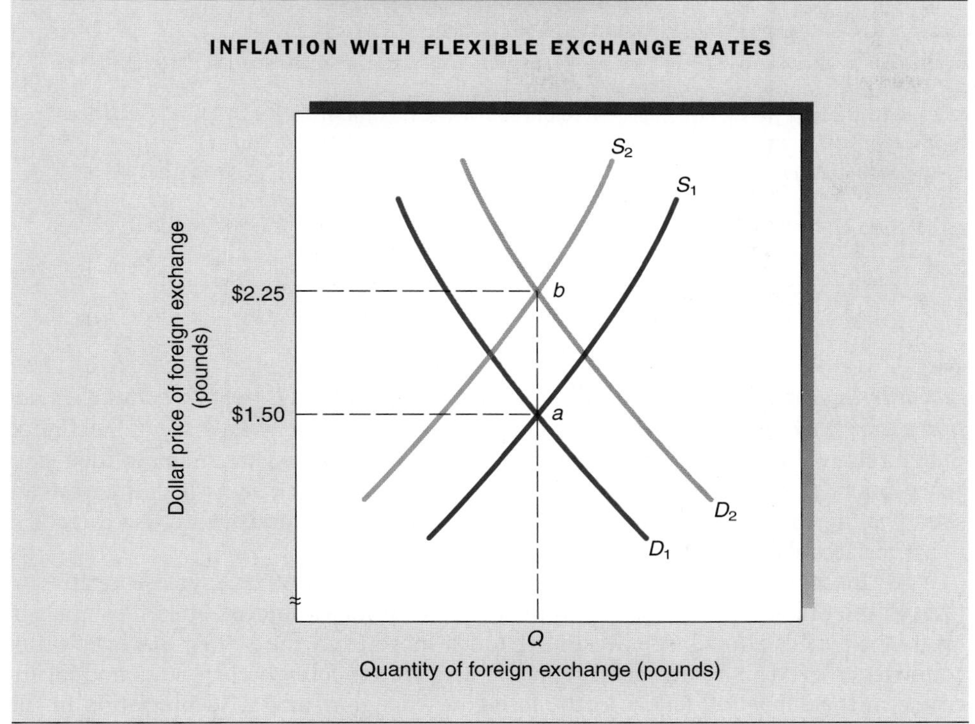

If prices were stable in Britain while the price level increased 50 percent in the United States, the U.S. demand for British products (and pounds) would increase, whereas U.S. exports to Britain would decline, causing the supply of pounds to fall. These forces would cause the dollar to depreciate relative to the pound.

Exchange-rate adjustments permit nations with even high rates of inflation to engage in trade with countries experiencing relatively stable prices.[5] A depreciation in a nation's currency in the foreign exchange market compensates for the nation's inflation rate. For example, if inflation increases the price level in the United States by 50 percent, and the value of the dollar in exchange for the pound depreciates (such that the value of the foreign currency increases 50 percent), then the prices of American goods measured in pounds are unchanged to British consumers. Thus, when the exchange-rate value of the dollar changes from $1.50 = 1 pound to $2.25 = 1 pound, the depreciation in the dollar restores the original prices of U.S. goods to British consumers even though the price level in the United States has increased by 50 percent.

When domestic prices are increasing more rapidly than those of one's trading partners, the value of the domestic currency will tend to depreciate in the foreign exchange market. On the other hand, if a nation's inflation rate is lower than that of its trading partners, then its currency will tend to appreciate.

Changes in Interest Rates. Financial investments will be quite sensitive to changes in real interest rates—that is, interest rates adjusted for the expected rate of inflation. International loanable funds will tend to move toward areas where the expected real rate of return (after compensation for differences in risk) is highest. ***Thus, increases in***

[5]However, high rates of inflation are likely to cause greater variability in the foreign exchange value of a currency across time periods. In turn, this increased variability of the exchange rate will generate uncertainty and reduce the volume of international trade—particularly transactions involving a time dimension. Thus, exchange-rate instability is generally harmful to the health of an economy.

THUMBNAIL SKETCH

What Factors Cause a Nation's Currency to Appreciate or Depreciate?

These Factors Will Cause a Nation's Currency to Appreciate:

1. Slow growth of income (relative to trading partners) that causes imports to lag behind exports.
2. A rate of inflation that is lower than that of one's trading partners.
3. Domestic real interest rates that are higher than real interest rates abroad.

These Factors Will Cause a Nation's Currency to Depreciate:

1. Rapid growth of income (relative to trading partners) that stimulates imports relative to exports.
2. A rate of inflation that is higher than that of one's trading partners.
3. Domestic real interest rates that are lower than real interest rates abroad.

real interest rates relative to a nation's trading partners will tend to cause that nation's currency to appreciate. For example, if real interest rates rise in the United States relative to Britain, British citizens will demand dollars (and supply their currency, pounds) in the foreign exchange market to purchase the high-yield American assets. The increase in demand for the dollar and supply of pounds will cause the dollar to appreciate relative to the British pound.

In contrast, when real interest rates in other countries increase relative to rates in the United States, short-term financial investors will move to take advantage of the higher yields abroad. As investment funds move from the United States to other countries, there will be an increase in the demand for foreign currencies and an increase in the supply of dollars in the foreign exchange market. A depreciation in the dollar relative to the currencies of the countries with the higher real interest rates will be the result. The accompanying Thumbnail Sketch summarizes the major forces that cause a nation's currency to appreciate or depreciate when exchange rates are determined by market forces.

BALANCE OF PAYMENTS

Balance of payments
A summary of all economic transactions between a country and all other countries for a specific time period, usually a year. The balance-of-payments account reflects all payments and liabilities to foreigners (debits) and all payments and obligations received from foreigners (credits).

Just as countries calculate their gross domestic product (GDP) so that they have a general idea of their domestic level of production, most countries also calculate their balance of international payments in order to keep track of their transactions with other nations. The **balance of payments** summarizes the transactions of the country's citizens, businesses, and governments with foreigners. It provides information on the nation's exports, imports, earnings of domestic residents on assets located abroad, earnings on domestic assets owned by foreigners, international capital movements, and official transactions by central banks and governments.

Balance-of-payments accounts are kept according to the principles of basic bookkeeping. Any transaction that creates a demand for foreign currency (and a supply of the domestic currency) in the foreign exchange market is recorded as a debit, or minus, item. Imports are an example of a debit item. Transactions that create a supply of foreign currency (and demand for the domestic currency) on the foreign exchange market are recorded as a credit, or plus, item. Exports are an example of a credit item. ***Because the foreign exchange market will bring quantity demanded and quantity supplied into balance, it will also bring the total debits and total credits into balance.***

Balance-of-payments transactions can be grouped into three basic categories: current account, capital account, and official reserve account. Let us take a look at each of these components.

CURRENT-ACCOUNT TRANSACTIONS

All payments (and gifts) related to the purchase or sale of goods and services and income flows during the designated period are included in the **current account.** In general, there are four major types of current-account transactions: the exchange of merchandise goods, the exchange of services, income from investments, and unilateral transfers.

Current account
The record of all transactions with foreign nations that involve the exchange of merchandise goods and services, current income derived from investments, and unilateral gifts.

Merchandise Trade Transactions. The export and import of merchandise goods compose the largest portion of a nation's balance-of-payments account. When U.S. producers export their products, foreigners will supply their currency in exchange for dollars in order to pay for the U.S.-produced goods. Because U.S. exports generate a supply of foreign exchange and demand for dollars in the foreign exchange market, they are a credit (plus) item. In contrast, when Americans import goods, they will demand foreign currencies and supply dollars in the foreign exchange market. Thus, imports are a debit (minus) item.

As Exhibit 18–5 shows, the United States exported $679.3 billion of merchandise goods in 1997, compared to imports of $877.3 billion. The difference between the value of a country's merchandise exports and the value of its merchandise imports is known as the **balance of merchandise trade** (or *balance of trade*). If the value of a country's merchandise exports falls short of the value of its merchandise imports, it is said to have a balance-of-trade deficit. In contrast, the situation where a nation exports more than it imports is referred to as a trade surplus. In 1997, the United States ran a merchandise-trade deficit of $198.0 billion (line 3 of Exhibit 18–5).

Balance of merchandise trade
The difference between the value of merchandise exports and the value of merchandise imports for a nation. The balance of merchandise trade is only one component of a nation's total balance of payments. Also called simply balance of trade *or* net exports.

Other things constant, a U.S. merchandise-trade deficit implies that Americans are supplying more dollars to the exchange market in order to purchase foreign-made goods than foreigners are demanding for the purchase of American goods. If the merchandise-trade deficit were the only factor influencing the value of the dollar on the exchange market, one could anticipate a decline in the foreign exchange value of the U.S. currency. However, several other factors also affect the supply of and demand for the dollar on the exchange market.

Service Exports and Imports. The export and import of *invisible services,* as they are sometimes called, also exert an important influence on the foreign exchange market. The export of insurance, transportation, and banking services generates a supply of foreign exchange and demand for dollars just as the export of merchandise does. A Mexican business that is insured with an American company will supply pesos and demand dollars with which to pay its premiums. Similarly, when foreigners travel in the United States or transport cargo on American ships, they will supply foreign exchange and demand dollars with which to pay for these services. Thus, these service exports are credit items.

On the other hand, the import of services from foreigners generates a demand for foreign currency and supply of dollars in the exchange market. Therefore, service imports are entered into the balance-of-payments accounts as debit items. Travel abroad by U.S. citizens, the shipment of goods on foreign carriers, and the purchase of other services from foreigners are all debit items, since they create a demand for foreign exchange.

These service transactions are substantial. As Exhibit 18-5 illustrates, in 1997, U.S. service exports were $258.3 billion, compared with service imports of $170.5 billion. Thus, the United States ran an $87.8 billion surplus on its service trade transactions (line 6 of Exhibit 18-5). When we add the balance of service exports and imports to the balance of merchandise trade, we obtain the **balance on goods and services.** In 1997, the United States ran a $110.2 billion deficit (the sum of the $198.0 billion merchandise-trade deficit and the $87.8 billion service surplus) in the goods and services account.

Balance on goods and services
The exports of goods (merchandise) and services of a nation minus its imports of goods and services.

EXHIBIT 18-5

U.S. BALANCE OF PAYMENTS, 1997 (IN BILLIONS OF DOLLARS)

	DEBITS	CREDITS	BALANCE: DEFICIT (−) OR SURPLUS (+)
CURRENT ACCOUNT			
1. U.S. merchandise exports		+679.3	
2. U.S. merchandise imports	−877.3		
3. Balance of merchandise trade (1 + 2)			−198.0
4. U.S. service exports		+258.3	
5. U.S. service imports	−170.5		
6. Balance on service trade (4 + 5)			+87.8
7. Balance on goods and services (3 + 6)			−110.2
8. U.S. investment income on U.S. assets abroad		+241.8	
9. Foreign income on foreign assets in the U.S.	−247.1		
10. Net investment income (8 + 9)			−5.3
11. Net unilateral transfers	−39.7		−39.7
12. Balance on current account (7 + 10 + 11)			**−155.2**
CAPITAL ACCOUNT			
13. Foreign investment in the U.S. (capital inflow)		+717.6	
14. U.S. investment abroad (capital outflow)	−577.2[a]		
15. Balance on capital account (13 + 14)			**+140.4**
16. Official Reserve Account Balance			+14.8
17. Total (12 + 15 + 16)			0.0

[a]*Statistical discrepancy is included in this figure.*

SOURCE: Survey of Current Business, *U.S. Department of Commerce, October 1998.*

Income from Investments. In the past, Americans have made substantial investments in stocks, bonds, and real assets in other countries. As these investments abroad generate income, dollars will flow from foreigners to Americans. The income of Americans from their investments abroad supplies foreign currency (and creates a demand for dollars) in the foreign exchange market. Thus, it enters as a credit item on the current account.

Correspondingly, foreigners hold substantial investments in the United States. As these investments earn dividends, interest, and rents, they earn income for foreigners. This income of foreigners leads to an outflow of dollars. As foreigners convert their dollar earnings to their domestic currency, the demand for foreign currency (and supply of dollars) increases in the foreign exchange market. Thus, the income of foreigners from their investments in the United States is a debit item in the balance-of-payments accounts.

As Exhibit 18-5 shows, in 1997 Americans earned $241.8 billion from investments abroad, while foreigners earned $247.1 billion from their investments in the United States. On balance, Americans earned $5.3 billion less on their investments abroad than foreigners earned on their investments in the United States. This $5.3 billion net outflow of investment income added to the deficit on current-account transactions.

Unilateral Transfers. Monetary gifts to foreigners, such as U.S. aid to a foreign government or private gifts from U.S. residents to their relatives abroad, generate a demand for foreign currencies and supply dollars in the exchange market. Thus, these gifts are debit items in the balance-of-payments accounts. Monetary gifts to Americans from foreigners are credit items. Gifts in kind are more complex. When products are given to foreigners, goods flow abroad, but there is no offsetting influx of foreign currency—that is, a demand for dollars. Balance-of-payments accountants handle such transactions as though the United States had demanded the foreign exchange and supplied the dollars with which to purchase the direct grants made to foreigners. So these items are also entered as debits. Because the U.S. government and private U.S. citizens gave $39.7 billion more to foreigners than we received from them, this net unilateral transfer was entered as a debit item on the current account in 1997.

Balance on Current Account. The difference between (1) the value of a country's current exports and earnings from investments abroad and (2) the value of its current imports and the earnings of foreigners on their domestic assets (plus net unilateral transfers to foreigners) is known as the **balance on current account.** Current-account transactions involve only current exchanges of goods and services and current income flows (and gifts). They do not involve changes in the ownership of either real or financial assets. The current-account balance provides a summary of all current-account transactions. As with the balance of trade, when the value of the current-account debit items (import-type transactions) exceeds the value of the credit items (export-type transactions), we say that the country is running a current-account deficit. Alternatively, if the credit items are greater than the debit items, the country is running a current-account surplus. In 1997, the United States ran a current-account deficit of $155.2 billion.

Balance on current account
The import-export balance of goods and services, plus net investment income earned abroad, plus net private and government transfers. If the value of the nation's export-type items exceeds (is less than) the value of the nation's import-type items plus net unilateral transfers to foreigners, a current-account surplus (deficit) is present.

Capital-Account Transactions

In contrast with current-account transactions, **capital-account** transactions focus on changes in the ownership of real and financial assets. These transactions are composed of (1) direct investments by Americans in real assets abroad (or by foreigners in the United States) and (2) loans to and from foreigners. When foreigners make investments in the United States—for example, by purchasing stocks, bonds, or real assets from Americans—their actions will supply foreign currency and generate a demand for dollars in the foreign exchange market. Thus, these capital inflow transactions are a credit.

Capital account
The record of transactions with foreigners that involve either (1) the exchange of ownership rights to real or financial assets or (2) the extension of loans.

On the other hand, capital outflow transactions are recorded as debits. For example, if a U.S. investor purchases a shoe factory in Mexico, the Mexican seller will want to be paid in pesos. The U.S. investor will supply dollars (and demand pesos) on the foreign exchange market. Since U.S. citizens will demand foreign currency (and supply dollars) when they invest in stocks, bonds, and real assets abroad, these transactions enter into the balance-of-payments accounts as a debit. In 1997, foreign investments in the United States (capital inflow) summed to $717.6 billion, while U.S. investments abroad (capital outflow) totaled $577.2 billion.[6] Since the capital inflow exceeded the outflow, the United States ran a $140.4 billion capital-account surplus in 1997.

Official Reserve Account

Special drawing rights (SDRs)
Supplementary reserves, in the form of accounting entries, established by the International Monetary Fund (also called paper gold*). Like gold and foreign currency reserves, they can be used to make payments on international accounts.*

International Monetary Fund (IMF)
An international banking organization, with more than 180 member nations, designed to oversee the operation of the international monetary system. Although it does not control the world supply of money, it does hold currency reserves for member nations and makes currency loans to national central banks.

Governments maintain official reserve balances in the form of foreign currencies, gold, and **special drawing rights (SDRs)** with the **International Monetary Fund (IMF),** a special bank that was established in order to facilitate international transactions. Countries running a deficit on their current- and capital-account balances can draw on their reserves. Similarly, countries running a surplus can build up their reserves of foreign currencies and reserve balances with the IMF. Under the current (primarily) flexible rate system, changes in the exchange rate are generally relied on to balance the amount of goods, services, and assets purchased from foreigners and the amount sold to foreigners. Therefore, these official reserve transactions are usually quite modest relative to the total of all international transactions.

Balance of Payments Must Balance

The sum of the debit and credit items of the balance-of-payments accounts must balance. Thus, the following identity must hold:

$$\begin{matrix}\text{Current-Account} \\ \text{Balance}\end{matrix} + \begin{matrix}\text{Capital-Account} \\ \text{Balance}\end{matrix} + \begin{matrix}\text{Official Reserve Account} \\ \text{Balance}\end{matrix} = 0$$

However, the specific components of the accounts need not balance. For example, the debit and credit items of the current account need not be equal. Specific components may run either a surplus or a deficit. Nevertheless, since the balance of payments as a whole must balance, a deficit in one area implies a surplus in another. For example, if a nation is experiencing a current-account deficit, it must experience an offsetting surplus on the sum of its capital-account and official reserve account balances.

A current-account deficit means that, in aggregate, the citizens of a nation are buying more goods and services from foreigners than they are selling to foreigners. Under a pure flexible rate system, this excess of expenditures relative to receipts is paid for by borrowing from and selling assets to foreigners. The current system is not a pure flexible rate system; if it were, there would be no official reserve transactions. However, the official reserve transactions are generally small. In 1997, the United States ran a $155.2 billion current-account deficit and a $140.4 billion capital-account surplus. The difference between these two figures—a $14.8 billion deficit—was exactly offset by a $14.8 billion surplus in the official reserve account. Thus, the deficits and surpluses of the current-, capital-, and official reserve accounts summed to zero as is shown in Exhibit 18-5 (line 17).

Under a pure flexible rate system, official reserve transactions are zero. When this is the case, a capital-account surplus (inflow of capital) implies a current-account deficit. Similarly, a capital-account deficit (outflow of capital) implies a current-account surplus. ***With flexible exchange rates, changes in the net inflow of capital will***

[6] The statistical discrepancy is also included in the investments abroad category. This item was quite large ($99.7 billion debit) in 1997. International transactions—particularly those conducted in cash—can be difficult to monitor. As we noted when discussing the money supply, 60 percent or more of the U.S. currency supply circulates abroad. Because this "outflow" of currency is not included in balance-of-payments accounts, such movements would contribute to the statistical discrepancy. Illegal drug trade may also increase the size of this item.

influence the current-account balance. If a nation is experiencing an increase in net foreign investment, perhaps as the result of higher real interest rates, this increase in the capital-account surplus will enlarge the current-account deficit. In contrast, capital flight (outflow of capital) will move the current account toward a surplus.

MACROECONOMIC POLICY IN AN OPEN ECONOMY

During the post–Second World War period, there has been a dramatic increase in international trade and in the flow of investment capital across national boundaries. This increasing mobility of both goods and capital influences the effects of macroeconomic policy, even in a country such as the United States with a relatively small trade sector. We now live in a global economy. No country can conduct its macroeconomic policy in isolation.

Throughout this text, we have focused on the impact of macroeconomic policy within the framework of an open economy. However, we have paid little attention to the impact of macroeconomic policy on exchange rates and on the components of a nation's balance-of-payments accounts. We now turn to these issues.

MACROECONOMIC POLICY AND THE EXCHANGE RATE

Because monetary and fiscal policies exert an impact on income growth, inflation, and real interest rates, they will also influence exchange rates. These two major macropolicy tools differ with regard to their impact on the foreign exchange market. Thus, we will consider them separately.

Monetary Policy and the Exchange Rate. Suppose the United States began to follow a more expansionary monetary policy. How would this policy influence the foreign exchange market? *When the effects are not fully anticipated,* a shift to a more expansionary monetary policy will lead to more rapid economic growth, an increase in the inflation rate, and lower real interest rates.[7] As we previously discussed, each of these factors will increase the demand for foreign exchange, causing the dollar to depreciate (see prior Thumbnail Sketch). The rapid growth of income will stimulate imports. Similarly, the increase in the U.S. inflation rate (relative to our trading partners) will make U.S. goods less competitive abroad, causing a decline in exports. Simultaneously, the lower real interest rate will encourage the flow of capital abroad. ***Thus, the expected short-run effect of an unanticipated shift to a more expansionary monetary policy is a depreciation in the exchange-rate value of the dollar.***

The expected outcome of an unanticipated switch to a more restrictive monetary policy will be just the opposite. The restrictive monetary policy will retard economic growth, reduce the rate of inflation, and push real interest rates upward. Exports will grow relative to imports. Investment funds from abroad will be drawn by the high real interest rates in the United States. Foreigners will demand more dollars with

[7]As we previously noted when considering monetary policy, the impact of a policy change is dependent on whether the effects of the change are anticipated or unanticipated. Neither growth nor the real interest rate will change if people fully anticipate the effects of the change in monetary policy on the price level. In this chapter, we assume for simplicity that the price-level effects accompanying a shift in monetary policy are not fully anticipated. Clearly, this is more likely to be true in the short run than in the long run.

which to purchase goods, services, and real assets in the United States. The increase in the supply of foreign currencies and strong demand for the dollar in the foreign exchange market will cause the dollar to appreciate.

Fiscal Policy and the Exchange Rate. Fiscal policy tends to generate conflicting influences on the foreign exchange market. Suppose the United States unexpectedly shifts toward a more restrictive fiscal policy, planning a budget surplus or at least a smaller deficit. Just as with restrictive monetary policy, the restrictive fiscal policy will tend to cause a reduction in aggregate demand, an economic slowdown, and a decline in the rate of inflation. These factors will discourage imports and stimulate exports, placing upward pressure on the exchange-rate value of the dollar. However, restrictive fiscal policy will also mean less government borrowing, which will reduce real interest rates in the United States. The lower real interest rates will cause financial capital to flow from the United States. This will increase the supply of dollars in the foreign exchange market, and thereby place downward pressure on the exchange-rate value of the U.S. dollar.

Which of these two effects is likely to dominate? When answering this question, one must consider the mobility of capital relative to trade flows. ***Financial capital is highly mobile. Investors can and do quickly shift their funds from one country to another in response to changes in interest rates. In contrast, importers and exporters often enter into long-term contracts when buying and selling goods. Thus, they are likely to respond more slowly to changing market conditions. Consequently, to the extent that a more restrictive fiscal policy places downward pressure on interest rates, the outflow of capital is likely to dominate in the short run.*** At least a temporary depreciation in the nation's currency is the most likely outcome.

The analysis of expansionary fiscal policy is symmetrical. To the extent that larger budget deficits stimulate aggregate demand and domestic inflation, they will encourage imports, which will place downward pressure on the exchange-rate value of a nation's currency. However, the increased borrowing to finance larger budget deficits will push real interest rates up and draw foreign investment to the United States, causing the dollar to appreciate. In the short run, the latter outcome is more likely.

Macroeconomic Policy and the Current Account

How does macroeconomic policy affect a nation's balance on the current account? It is important to remember that the current- and capital-account balances must sum to zero under a pure flexible rate system. Thus, any deficit on the current (capital) account must be exactly offset by a capital (current) account surplus of equal size. Because unanticipated shifts in macroeconomic policy influence both the demand for imports and real interest rates, clearly they will exert an impact on both current-account and capital-account balances.

Monetary Policy and Current Account. Suppose that the Federal Reserve suddenly increases the growth rate of the money supply. How will this shift to a more expansionary monetary policy influence the U.S. balance on the current account? As we just indicated, the more rapid money growth will stimulate income, place upward pressure on the inflation rate, and reduce real interest rates. Think how this combination of factors will affect the current and capital accounts. The growth of income and higher domestic prices will stimulate imports, retard exports, and thus cause the current account to shift toward a larger deficit (or smaller surplus). At the same time, the lower domestic interest rates will encourage investors, both domestic and foreign, to shift funds from

THUMBNAIL SKETCH

How Will Monetary and Fiscal Policy Affect the Exchange-Rate and Balance-of-Payments Components?

A. The Impact of Unanticipated Shift in Monetary Policy:

	Expansionary Monetary Policy	Restrictive Monetary Policy
Exchange rate[a]	Depreciates.	Appreciates.
Real interest rates	Decline.	Increase.
Flow of capital	Capital outflow.	Capital inflow.
Current account	Shifts toward a surplus.	Shifts toward a deficit.

B. The Impact of Unanticipated Shift in Fiscal Policy:

	Expansionary Fiscal Policy	Restrictive Fiscal Policy
Exchange rate[a]	Uncertain, but the interest rate effect is likely to cause appreciation.	Uncertain, but the interest rate effect is likely to cause depreciation.
Real interest rates	Increase.	Decline.
Flow of capital	Capital inflow.	Capital outflow.
Current account	Shifts toward a deficit.	Shifts toward a surplus.

[a]Value of domestic currency

the United States to other countries where they can earn a higher rate of return. Predictably, this outflow of capital will cause a capital-account deficit and depreciation in the foreign exchange value of the dollar. In turn, the dollar depreciation will encourage exports, discourage imports, and act as a partial offset to the direct effects of the more rapid income growth. Because capital is far more mobile than goods in international markets, the outflow of capital effect will generally dominate in the short run. For a time, therefore, the shift to a more expansionary monetary policy will tend to cause an outflow of capital that will shift the capital account toward a deficit (or smaller surplus) and the current account toward a surplus (or smaller deficit).

Now consider the impact of an unanticipated shift to a more restrictive monetary policy on a nation's current-account balance. The restrictive policy will tend to slow growth and inflation, which will reduce the demand for imports. However, it will also increase real interest rates, leading to an inflow of capital and appreciation in the nation's currency. In the short run, the inflow of capital will generally dominate. Thus, the expected result of the more restrictive monetary policy is higher interest rates, an inflow of capital, a shift toward a capital-account surplus (or smaller deficit), and a shift toward a current-account deficit in the short run.

Fiscal Policy and Current Account. What impact will large budget deficits have on a nation's current account? Expansionary fiscal policy will tend to stimulate aggregate demand and push domestic interest rates upward (the *crowding-out effect*). The increase in aggregate demand will encourage the purchase of imports, and thereby shift the current account toward a deficit (or smaller surplus). Simultaneously, the higher real interest rates will both attract investment by foreigners and help keep domestic capital at home. Predictably, there will be a net capital inflow, which will shift the capital account toward a surplus.

When fiscal policy is expansionary, both the increase in imports due to the demand stimulus and the increase in the net capital inflow as the result of the higher interest rates will shift the current account toward a deficit and the capital account toward a surplus. In this way, large budget deficits will also tend to result in large current-account deficits.

Once again, the analysis is symmetrical. A shift to a more restrictive fiscal policy—for example, a reduction in the size of a budget deficit—will retard demand and reduce interest rates. As the result of the decline in aggregate demand, imports will tend to fall, shifting a nation's current account toward a surplus (or smaller deficit). Simultaneously, the low interest rates will lead to a net capital outflow, which will shift the capital account toward a deficit. Thus, restrictive fiscal policy will tend to cause a current-account surplus and a capital-account deficit. The accompanying Thumbnail Sketch summarizes the expected impacts of unanticipated shifts in monetary and fiscal policy.

MACROECONOMIC POLICY, EXCHANGE RATES, CAPITAL FLOWS, AND CURRENT-ACCOUNT DEFICITS

We are now in a position to consider the empirical evidence with regard to the impact of recent macroeconomic policy on the flow of capital and the foreign exchange value of the dollar. **Exhibit 18–6** provides data on the exchange rate, current-account balance, and net foreign investment (capital-account balance) during the last 25 years. This graphic illustrates several important points. First, the impact of the shift toward a more restrictive monetary policy and more expansionary fiscal policy during the first half of the 1980s is clearly visible. Responding to the double-digit inflation rates of 1979–1980, the Federal Reserve reduced the rate of money growth and pushed real interest rates upward in the early 1980s. The U.S. inflation rate plunged from the double-digit levels of 1979–1980 to 3.2 percent in 1983. At the same time, fiscal policy was expansionary. Increases in defense expenditures coupled with a reduction in tax rates led to a substantial increase in the federal budget deficit during the early 1980s.

Our analysis indicates that this policy combination—a more restrictive monetary policy coupled with expansionary fiscal policy—will cause higher real interest rates, an inflow of capital, currency appreciation, and a current-account deficit (see the prior Thumbnail Sketch). This is precisely what happened. In the early 1980s, real interest rates rose to historic highs. In turn, the higher interest rates led to a sharp increase in net foreign investment in the United States (frame c of Exhibit 18–6). This inflow of capital increased the demand for the dollar, causing it to appreciate sharply during 1981–1985 (frame a). The inflow of capital and appreciation of the dollar led to a dramatic increase in the current-account deficit (frame b). The annual current account of the United States shifted from a small surplus in 1981 to a deficit of more than 3 percent of GDP in the mid-1980s. These outcomes—an inflow of capital, appreciation of the dollar, and expansion in the size of the current-account deficit—are precisely what our model predicts.

APPLICATIONS IN ECONOMICS

The J-Curve Effect

As a market adjusts to a change in price, time often plays an important role. There is reason to believe that this will be true in the foreign exchange market. The impact of a currency depreciation on a current-account deficit can be broken down into a *price effect* and a *quantity effect*. A 10 percent depreciation in the dollar means that import prices increase by 10 percent in terms of dollars. Of course, this increase in the dollar price of imports will discourage purchases. However, the 10 percent depreciation also means that, *for a given quantity sold,* foreigners will earn 10 percent more dollars. Therefore, unless Americans reduce the *quantity* of their imports by more than 10 percent, their *expenditures* on imports will increase in response to a depreciation in the dollar. Similarly, the depreciation will make U.S. exports 10 percent cheaper to foreigners. Unless foreigners increase their *quantity* purchased by more than 10 percent, their demand for dollars in the exchange market will *decrease* as the result of the depreciation.

Since American and foreign-produced goods are excellent substitutes for one another, there is good reason to expect that both the U.S. demand for imports and foreign demand for U.S. exports will be highly elastic in the long run.[1] However, this may not be true in the short run. When the dollar depreciates, it will take time for American consumers to substitute away from the more expensive imports and for foreign consumers to adjust their consumption, purchasing more of the now cheaper American exports. Therefore, initially, the increase in the quantity of exports may be less than the 10 percent reduction in price. If this is the case, for a time the depreciation will actually cause the current-account deficit to worsen—the dollar expenditures on imports will rise while the dollar sales of exports will decline. With time, this situation will reverse as the U.S. demand for imports and foreign demand for U.S. exports become more elastic. Eventually, the quantity effects will dominate, and a depreciation will reduce the current-account deficit.

Economists refer to this time path of adjustment as the **J-curve effect.** A nation's current-account deficit will initially widen (slide down the hook of the "J") before it shrinks (moves up the stem of the "J") as the result of a currency depreciation. This occurs because the short-run domestic demand for imports and foreign demand for exports are inelastic. Thus, the depreciation initially increases import expenditures relative to export sales. However, in the long run, the demand for both imports and exports is elastic. Therefore, the depreciation of a nation's currency will eventually shrink the nation's current-account deficit.[2]

The J-curve effect explains why there is sometimes a substantial time lag—perhaps two or three years—between the depreciation of a nation's currency and a reduction in the current-account deficit. This was the case for the sharp reduction in the exchange-rate value of the dollar in 1985. It was nearly three years later before this depreciation began to reduce the size of the current-account deficit. (See frames b and c of Exhibit 18–6.)

[1]When demand is elastic, the quantity purchased is highly responsive to a change in price. Therefore, a change in price will cause total expenditures to change in the opposite direction. Correspondingly, *inelastic* means that the quantity purchased will be relatively unresponsive to a change in price. When this is the case, an increase in price will cause total expenditures to change in the same direction.

[2]See Jeffrey A. Rosensweig and Paul D. Koch, "The U.S. Dollar and the 'Delayed J-Curve,'" Federal Reserve Bank of Atlanta, *Economic Review,* July–August 1988, pp. 2–15, for an interesting article on the J-curve effect as it applies to the trade imbalances of the United States during the 1980s.

J-curve effect
The tendency of a nation's current-account deficit to widen initially before it shrinks in response to an exchange-rate depreciation. This tendency results because the short-run demand for both imports and exports is often inelastic, even though the long-run demand is almost always elastic.

Second, as real interest rates adjusted and the capital inflow slowed, the dollar depreciated sharply during 1986–1988. This dollar depreciation stimulated exports and discouraged imports, causing the current-account deficit to shrink during 1988 and 1989. As real GDP fell during the 1990 recession, the current account moved in balance. (Remember, slow growth of income will reduce imports relative to exports.)

Third, the strong expansion of the 1990s once again stimulated imports relative to exports, shifting the current account toward a deficit and the capital account toward a surplus. During 1997–1998, financial instability in both Latin America and Asia caused many investors to look for a safe haven. Dollar investments in U.S. stocks and bonds fit this bill. Thus, net foreign investment in the United States increased, pushing the exchange-rate value of the dollar upward. Predictably, these factors—an inflow of capital and appreciation of the dollar—resulted in a continuation of the sizable current-account deficits in the late 1990s.

EXHIBIT 18-6

THE EXCHANGE RATE, CURRENT-ACCOUNT BALANCE, AND NET FOREIGN INVESTMENT

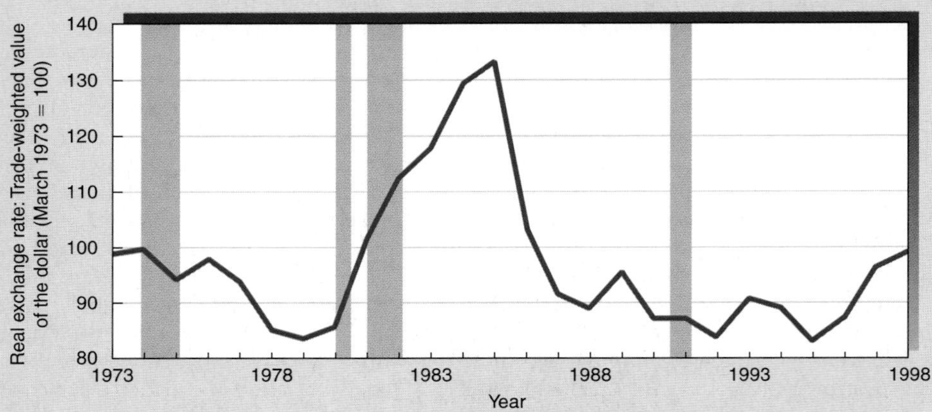

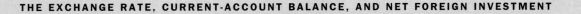

(a) Exchange-rate value of the dollar (compared with ten currencies)

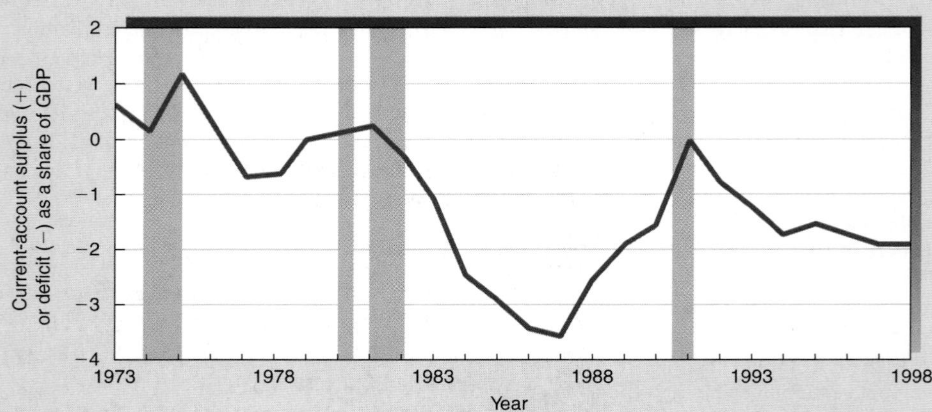

(b) Current-account balance as a share of GDP

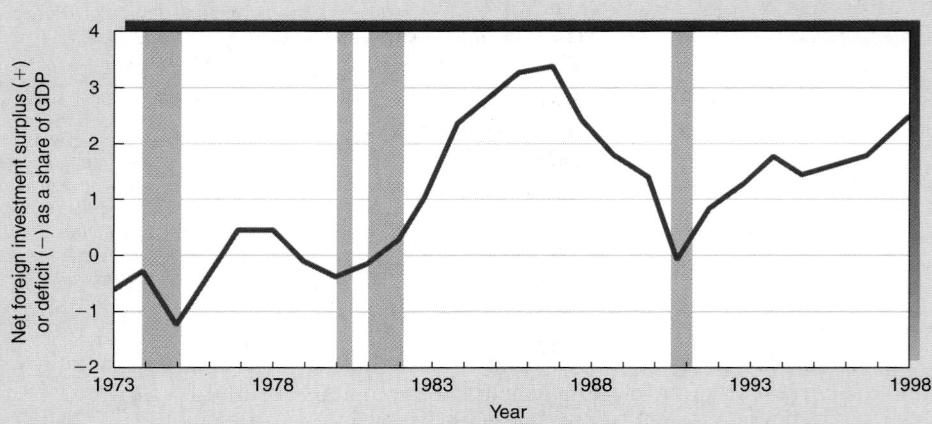

(c) Net foreign investment as a share of GDP

Note: Data are given in billions of dollars.

SOURCE: Economic Report of the President, *1999, Tables B-1, B-24, B-103, and B-110.*

Here we illustrate the relationship between the exchange rate, the current-account deficit, and net foreign investment (capital inflow). The shaded areas represent recessions.

As we have stressed throughout, the flow of capital and the current-account balance are closely related. Exhibit 18–6 clearly illustrates this point. A small capital inflow during 1977–1978 was associated with a current-account deficit of approximately the same size. When there was a small outflow of capital during 1979–1980, the current account moved to a surplus. The surge in the inflow of capital during 1982–1986 was accompanied by an equally large increase in the current-account deficit. As the capital inflow slowed during the late 1980s, the current-account deficit shrank. Later, as the inflow of capital resumed during the expansion of the 1990s, the current-account deficit widened once again. Clearly, the sizes of these two variables—net foreign investment and the current-account deficit—are closely linked.

HOW DO CURRENT-ACCOUNT DEFICITS AFFECT AN ECONOMY?

There is a tendency to think that current-account and trade surpluses are good and deficits bad. This is certainly understandable. The term *deficit* generally suggests something bad—things like excessive spending relative to income or an overdraft at the bank. In the balance-of-payments area, however, this is not always true.

What precisely is a current-account deficit? The current account measures mainly trade in goods and services. The other two current-account categories—net income from investments abroad and unilateral transfers—are generally small. Because trade in goods and services dominates current-account transactions, trade deficits and current-account deficits are closely related. Countries with large trade deficits almost always run substantial current-account deficits. Both of these deficits generally reflect that the country is importing more goods and services than it is exporting. In contrast, trade (and current-account) surpluses imply that sales of goods and services to foreigners (exports) exceed purchases from them (imports).

It is not obvious that a trade surplus is preferable to a deficit. After all, a nation that is running a trade deficit is getting more goods and services from others than it is supplying to them. What is so bad about that? Similarly, a trade surplus implies that a nation is supplying more goods and services for foreigners to consume than it is receiving from them. Is this something that people will want to continue to do?

A nation's trade deficit or surplus is an aggregation of the voluntary choices of businesses and individuals. In contrast with a budget deficit of an individual, business, or government, there is no legal entity that is responsible for the trade deficit. As Herbert Stein, a former chairman of the president's Council of Economic Advisers, once put it: "The trade deficit does not belong to any individual or institution. It is a pure-statistical aggregate, like the number of eggs laid in the U.S. or the number of bald-headed men living here."[8]

How long can a nation continue to run a current-account deficit? Perhaps surprising to some, the answer is a long time. A current-account deficit is not like business losses or an excess of household spending relative to income—conditions that eventually force decision makers to change their ways. The United States ran a current-account (trade) deficit almost every year from 1800 to 1875. On the other hand, it consistently ran current-account surpluses from 1946 to 1976. The trade accounts of other countries have followed similar lengthy periods of both deficits and surpluses.

Current-account deficits and the flow of capital. Under a pure flexible rate system, a current-account deficit implies a capital-account surplus. But it is equally true

[8]Herbert Stein, "Leave the Trade Deficit Alone," *Wall Street Journal,* March 11, 1987.

to say that a capital account surplus—that is, an inflow of foreign capital—implies a current-account deficit. In a global economy where capital moves rather freely across borders, countries with the most attractive investment environments will experience an inflow of capital. If the investments of foreigners in a country exceed those of the domestic investors abroad, foreigners will have to fill this gap. Under a flexible rate system, foreigners pay for their excess of capital purchases relative to capital sales with an excess of exports relative to imports. Thus, countries that attract a net inflow of foreign capital also tend to run current-account deficits. (see frames b and c of Exhibit 18–6.)

Are current-account deficits and an inflow of foreign capital bad? The prudent answer is: it depends on why the capital inflow is occurring and how it is used. Low-income countries often find it difficult to finance even attractive investment opportunities from their current domestic saving. When this is the case, investment funds from abroad can help them increase both their rate of capital formation and economic growth. As long as the inflow of capital is channeled into profitable investment, it enhances the growth and prosperity of a nation. Examples of this abound. Prior to 1985, Singapore ran large current-account deficits financed with an inflow of capital. Propelled by a high investment rate, it has achieved rapid growth for more than two decades and is now running a large current-account surplus. During the 1970s, South Korea ran large current-account deficits and capital-account surpluses. Like Singapore, Korea used the inflow of capital to achieve high rates of both capital formation and growth. Both economic theory and real-world experiences indicate that an inflow of capital can—if directed into profitable investments—play a positive role in the development of an economy.

Correspondingly, a current-account surplus is not always indicative of strength. For example, a country would run a current-account surplus and capital-account deficit if its profitable domestic investment alternatives were insufficient to absorb its current savings. Since domestic investors would be drawn to the more attractive investment opportunities abroad, such countries would experience an outflow of capital. In recent years, Japan has been in this position.

The current-account deficit of the United States. As part b of Exhibit 18–6 illustrates, the United States has persistently run sizable current-account deficits since 1982. The large budget deficits throughout much of this period may well have increased real interest rates and thereby contributed to both the inflow of foreign capital and the current-account deficits. However, if this were the case, the inflow of funds from abroad would have moderated both the upward pressure on interest rates and the reduction in domestic investment. When considering the significance of the current-account deficit, one should remember that the United States has a system of secure property rights, a stable monetary and political environment, and a rapidly growing labor force (compared with Europe and Japan). This makes it an attractive country in which to invest. On the other hand, the saving rate of the United States is low compared to our major trading partners. To a large degree, the U.S. current-account deficit reflects this combination of factors—an attractive domestic investment environment and a low saving rate.

INTERNATIONAL FINANCE AND EXCHANGE-RATE REGIMES

There are three major types of exchange-rate regimes: (1) flexible rates, (2) fixed rate, unified currency, and (3) pegged exchange rates. We have already explained how a flexible rate system works. We will now consider the operation of the other two.

Fixed Rate, Unified Currency System

Obviously, the 50 states of the United States have a unified currency, the dollar. In Panama, both the U.S. dollar and the Panamian balboa (available only in coins) are fully interchangeable at a one-to-one rate and equally acceptable as a means of payment. For all practical purposes, Panama has adopted the dollar as its currency. Almost two decades ago, Hong Kong linked its currency with the U.S. dollar. In 1991, Argentina did the same. Both Hong Kong and Argentina have **currency boards** that have the power to create currency only in exchange for a specific quantity of U.S. dollars (one peso = $1 in Argentina and 7.8 HK dollars = $1 in Hong Kong). Thus, the United States, Panama, Hong Kong, and Argentina have a unified currency regime.

Currency board
An entity that (a) issues a currency with a fixed designated value relative to a widely accepted currency (for example, the U.S. dollar), (b) promises to continue to redeem the issued currency at the fixed rate, and (c) maintains bonds and other liquid assets denominated in the other currency that provide 100 percent backing for all currency issued.

Beginning in 1999, 11 countries of the European Union (EU)—Belgium, Germany, Spain, France, Ireland, Italy, Luxembourg, Netherlands, Austria, Portugal, and Finland—adopted a common currency, the euro. Although the currencies of these countries will continue to circulate until 2002, each of their values is now linked to the euro at a fixed rate. Thus, these countries now have a unified currency system. In turn, the value of the euro relative to other currencies, such as the dollar and yen, is determined by market forces (flexible exchange rates).

The distinguishing characteristic of a fixed rate, unified currency regime is the presence of only one central bank with the power to expand and contract the supply of money. For the dollar, that central bank is the Federal Reserve System; for the euro, it is the European Central Bank. Those linking their currency at a fixed rate to the dollar or the euro are no longer in a position to conduct monetary policy. For example, the former central banks of the countries now using the euro no longer have the power to create money. In essence, they are now branches of the European Central Bank, much like the regional and district Federal Reserve banks are branches of the Fed.

The adoption of a currency board provides a method of unifying one currency with another that has greater credibility in international financial markets. This attribute is particularly attractive for countries like Argentina with a long history of monetary expansion and hyperinflation. ***A currency board does two things. First, it issues domestic currency at a fixed rate in exchange for a designated foreign currency.***

The symbol for the euro looks like the Greek letter epsilon, but with two center horizontal lines. This was chosen because of Greece's historical significance in European history, as well as the letter e being the first letter of the word "Europe." The two center lines are intended to represent stability. How will the euro influence future financial arrangements?

Second, the foreign currency is then invested in bonds denominated in that currency. This means that the money issued by the currency board is backed 100 percent by the foreign currency. Therefore, the holders of the money issued by the currency board know that it will always have sufficient funds to exchange the domestic currency for the foreign one at the fixed rate.

If domestic citizens are buying more (imports) from foreigners than they are selling to them (exports), the amount of the domestic currency exchanged for the foreign one will increase. This will cause the domestic money supply to fall, which will place downward pressure on the price level (rate of inflation). In turn, the lower level of prices will encourage exports relative to imports, and thereby automatically keep the value of the two currencies in line. Countries that adopt the currency board approach are no longer in a position to conduct monetary policy. Instead, they essentially accept the monetary policy of the nation to which their currency is tied. They also accept the exchange-rate fluctuations of that currency relative to other currencies outside of the unified zone.

A pure gold standard system, where each country sets the value of its currency in terms of gold and fully backs its domestic money supply with gold, is also a fixed rate, unified system. In this case, the world supply of gold (rather than a central bank) determines the total supply of money. If a country were importing more than it was exporting, its supply of gold would fall, which would reduce the domestic supply of money. This would place downward pressure on the domestic price level and bring the payments to and receipts from foreigners back into balance. Things would change in the opposite direction if a country were exporting more than it was importing. International financial arrangements approximated those of a gold standard during the period between the American Civil War and the establishment of the Federal Reserve System in 1913.

Fixed exchange rate
An exchange rate that is set at a determined amount by government policy.

Between 1944 and 1971, most of the world operated under a system of **fixed exchange rates,** where each nation fixed the price of its currency relative to others. In essence, this was a quasi-unified system. It was unified in the sense that the value of one currency was fixed relative to others over lengthy time periods. But it was not a fully unified system because the countries continued to exercise control over monetary policy. Nations maintained reserves with the International Monetary Fund, which could be drawn on when payments to foreigners exceeded receipts from them. This provided each with some leeway in its conduct of monetary policy. However, countries running persistent payment deficits would eventually deplete their reserves. This constrained the country's monetary independence and provided its policy makers with an incentive to keep monetary policy approximately in line with that of its trading partners. Under this fixed exchange-rate regime, nations confronting balance-of-payments problems often imposed tariffs, quotas, and other trade barriers in an effort to keep their payments and receipts in balance. Various restrictions on the convertibility of currencies were also common. These problems eventually led to the demise of the system.

Pegged Exchange Rates

Pegged exchange-rate system
A commitment to use monetary and fiscal policy to maintain the exchange-rate value of the domestic currency at a fixed rate or within a narrow band relative to another currency (or bundle of currencies).

A **pegged exchange-rate system** is one where a country commits itself to the maintenance of a specific exchange rate (or exchange-rate range) relative to another, stronger currency (such as the U.S. dollar) or a bundle of currencies. In contrast with the currency board approach, however, countries adopting the pegged exchange rate continue to conduct monetary policy. Thus, an excess of payments (imports) relative to receipts (exports) does not force the country to reduce its domestic money supply.

In order for a pegged rate system to be effective, a country must follow a monetary policy consistent with the fixed rate. Maintenance of the pegged rate requires the country to give up monetary independence. A nation can either (1) follow an independent monetary policy and allow its exchange rate to fluctuate or (2) tie its monetary policy to the maintenance of the fixed exchange rate. It cannot, however, maintain the convertibility of its currency at the fixed exchange rate while following a monetary policy more expansionary than that of the country to which the domestic currency is tied. Attempts to do so will lead to a financial crisis—a situation where falling foreign currency reserves eventually force the country to forgo the pegged exchange rate.

This is precisely what happened in Mexico. During 1989–1994, Mexico sought to peg the value of the peso to the U.S. dollar. At the same time, Mexico expanded its domestic money supply much more rapidly than the United States. This led to a higher rate of inflation in Mexico than in the United States. Responding to the different inflation rates, more and more people shifted away from the Mexican peso and toward the dollar. By December 1994, Mexico's foreign exchange reserves were virtually depleted. As a result, it could no longer maintain the fixed exchange rate with the dollar. Mexico devalued its currency, triggering a crisis that affected several other countries following similar policies.

More recently, much the same thing happened in Brazil and several Asian countries (Thailand, South Korea, Indonesia, and Malaysia). As in Mexico, these countries sought to maintain fixed exchange rates (or rates within a narrow band), while following monetary and fiscal policies that were inconsistent with the fixed rate. As their reserves declined, they were forced to abandon their exchange-rate pegs. This was extremely disruptive to these economies. Imports suddenly became much more expensive and therefore less affordable. Businesses (including banks) that had borrowed money in dollars (or some other foreign currency) were unable to repay their loans as the result of the sharp decline in the exchange-rate value of the domestic currency. These economies experienced sharp economic declines during 1997–1998.

THE FUTURE

Currently, international financial arrangements are in a state of flux. The recent failures of pegged rate systems have created a vacuum. Many countries are reluctant either to (a) give up their monetary policy independence as the currency board approach requires or (b) adopt a purely flexible exchange rate. Both economic theory and real-world experience indicate that either of these two approaches will work reasonably well. On the other hand, the pegged exchange approach is something like a time bomb. Pushed by political considerations, monetary policy makers in most countries are unable to follow a course consistent with the maintenance of pegged rates.

As the relative size of international exchange continues to grow, so too will the demand for currency of stable value. During the past decade, there has been a dramatic increase in the number of countries where citizens are free to use and maintain bank accounts in any currency they choose, including those issued by other governments. In most areas of the world, the U.S. dollar is the preferred foreign currency. As a result, more than half the currency issued by the Federal Reserve circulates in other countries.[9] The legalization of foreign currencies is an important structural change. The availability of competitive currencies reduces the incentive of the domestic monetary authorities to inflate. If they do, more and more people will shift to the dollar and

[9]If this currency did not circulate outside of the United States, it would be necessary for the U.S. government to have a larger quantity of interest-bearing debt outstanding. When foreigners hold dollars, in essence they are extending an interest-free loan to the U.S. government. Thus, the circulation of dollars abroad is advantageous to the United States.

other, more stable currencies. In essence, the use of a foreign currency provides citizens with an alternative to the uncertainties accompanying an unstable domestic monetary regime.

The shape of financial and exchange-rate regimes is likely to change substantially in the years immediately ahead. Much of Europe has already moved toward a unified currency. As the euro gains credibility, the four EU members (Denmark, Greece, Sweden, and the United Kingdom) that have not yet adopted the euro are likely to do so. So too are several Eastern European countries, either through a currency board arrangement or by directly joining the monetary union. It would not be surprising to see a similar trend in North and South America. Brazil, Mexico, and several other countries in the Americas may well seek currency stability through some form of linkage with the dollar. A substantial share of international trade is also conducted in Japanese yen. In the future, the dollar, euro, and yen—perhaps along with two or three other currencies—may well emerge as the dominant currencies used throughout the world for domestic as well as international trade. These developments make this an exciting time to follow international finance.

KEY POINTS

- Because countries generally use different currencies, international trade usually involves the conversion of one currency to another. The currencies of different countries are bought and sold in the foreign exchange market. The exchange rate is the price of one national currency in terms of another.

- The dollar demand for foreign exchange arises from the purchase (import) of goods, services, and assets by Americans from foreigners. The supply of foreign currency in exchange for dollars arises from the sale (export) of goods, services, and assets by Americans to foreigners. The equilibrium exchange rate will bring these two forces into balance.

- With flexible exchange rates, the following will cause a nation's currency to appreciate: (1) rapid growth of income abroad (and/or slow domestic growth), (2) low inflation (relative to trading partners), and (3) rising domestic real interest rates (and/or falling rates abroad). The reverse of these conditions will cause a nation's currency to depreciate.

- The balance-of-payments accounts provide a summary of transactions with foreigners. Transactions like imports that generate a demand for foreign currencies (and supply of the domestic currency) in the foreign exchange market are recorded as debit items. Transactions like exports that create a supply of foreign currencies (and demand for the domestic currency) are recorded as credit items.

- The foreign exchange market will bring the quantity demanded of foreign exchange into balance with the quantity supplied. This will also bring the total debits and total credits of the balance-of-payments accounts into balance.

- There are three major balance-of-payments components: (1) current account, (2) capital account, and (3) official reserve account. The balances of these three components must sum to zero, but the individual components of the accounts need not be in balance. Therefore, a deficit in one area implies an offsetting surplus in other areas. Under a pure flexible rate system, there will not be any official reserve account transactions. Under these circumstances, a current-account deficit implies a capital-account surplus (and vice versa).

- An unanticipated shift to a more restrictive monetary policy will raise the real interest rate, reduce the rate of inflation, and, at least temporarily, reduce aggregate demand and the growth of income. These factors will all cause the nation's currency to appreciate. In turn, the currency appreciation along with the inflow of capital will result in a current-account deficit. In contrast, the effects of a more expansionary monetary policy will be just the opposite: lower interest rates, an outflow of capital, currency depreciation, and a shift toward a current-account surplus.

- An unanticipated shift to a more expansionary fiscal policy will tend to increase real interest rates, lead to an inflow of capital, and cause the nation's current account to shift toward a deficit. The effects of a shift to a more restrictive fiscal policy will be just the opposite: lower interest rates, an outflow of capital, and movement toward a current-account surplus.

- Under a flexible exchange-rate system, an inflow of capital implies a current-account deficit. Correspondingly, an outflow of capital implies a current-account surplus. Whether a country runs a current-account deficit or surplus is largely dependent upon the attractiveness of domestic investment opportunities relative to the nation's saving rate.

➤ There are three major types of exchange-rate regimes: (1) flexible rates, (2) fixed rate, unified currency, and (3) pegged exchange rates. Eleven nations of the European Union have recently adopted a unified currency system. Countries can also use a currency board to unify their currency with another. The currencies of Hong Kong, Argentina, and Panama are unified with the U.S. dollar. In order to be effective, pegged rate systems require that a nation follow a monetary policy consistent with the maintenance of the pegged rate. Political pressure often makes this difficult to do.

CRITICAL ANALYSIS QUESTIONS

1. If the dollar depreciates relative to the Japanese yen, how will this affect your ability to purchase a Honda Accord? How will this change influence the quantity of Hondas purchased by Americans? How will it affect the dollar expenditures of Americans on Hondas?

2. How do flexible exchange rates bring about balance in the exchange-rate market? Do they lead to a balance between merchandise exports and imports? Explain.

3. "If a trade deficit means that we are getting more items from abroad than we are sending to foreigners, why is it considered a bad thing?" Answer this question.

*4. The accompanying chart indicates an actual newspaper quotation of the exchange rate of various currencies. On February 2, did the dollar appreciate or depreciate against the British pound? How did it fare against the French franc?

	U.S. Dollar Equivalent	
	February 1	February 2
British pound	1.755	1.746
French franc	0.1565	0.1575

*5. Suppose the exchange rate between the United States and Mexico freely fluctuates in the open market. Indicate which of the following would cause the dollar to appreciate (or depreciate) relative to the peso.

a. An increase in the quantity of drilling equipment purchased in the United States by Pemex, the Mexican oil company, as a result of a Mexican oil discovery
b. An increase in the U.S. purchase of crude oil from Mexico as a result of the development of Mexican oil fields
c. Higher real interest rates in Mexico, inducing U.S. citizens to move their financial investments from U.S. to Mexican banks
d. Lower real interest rates in the United States, inducing Mexican investors to borrow dollars and then exchange them for pesos
e. Inflation in the United States and stable prices in Mexico
f. An increase in the inflation rate from 2 percent to 10 percent in both the United States and Mexico
g. An economic boom in Mexico, inducing Mexicans to buy more U.S.-made automobiles, trucks, electric appliances, and television sets
h. Attractive investment opportunities, inducing U.S. investors to buy stock in Mexican firms

6. Explain why a current-account balance and a capital-account balance must sum to zero under a pure flexible rate system.

7. "A nation cannot continue to run a deficit on its current account. A healthy, growing economy will not persistently expand its indebtedness to foreigners. Eventually, the trade deficits will lead to national bankruptcy." Evaluate this view.

8. In recent years, a substantial share of the domestic capital formation in the United States has been financed by foreign investors. Is this inflow of capital from abroad indicative that the U.S. economy is in poor health? How might the United States go about reducing its current-account deficit?

*9. Suppose that the United States were running a current-account deficit. How would each of the following changes influence the size of the current-account deficit?

a. A recession in the United States
b. A decline in the attractiveness of investment opportunities in the United States
c. An improvement in investment opportunities abroad

10. Several politicians have suggested that the federal government should run a sizable budget surplus during the next decade in order to "save social security." If the

federal government does run a large surplus, what is the expected impact on interest rates, the inflow of capital, the current-account deficit, and the foreign exchange value of the dollar? Explain the reasoning underlying your answer.

*11. If foreigners have confidence in the U.S. economy and therefore move to expand their investments in the United States, how will the U.S. current-account balance be affected? How will the exchange-rate value of the dollar be affected?

12. Is a trade surplus indicative of a strong, healthy economy? Why or why not?

13. What is the J-curve effect? According to the J-curve effect, how will a depreciation in a nation's currency affect its current-account balance?

*14. "Changes in exchange rates will automatically direct a country to a current-account balance under a flexible exchange-rate system." Is this statement true or false?

*15. In recent years, many American political figures have been highly critical of the fact that U.S. imports from Japan have consistently exceeded U.S. exports to Japan.

a. Under a flexible exchange-rate system, is there any reason to expect that the imports from a given country will tend to equal the exports to that country?

b. Can you think of any reason why the United States might persistently run a trade deficit with a country such as Japan?

c. If Japan purchased substantially more American goods, would this significantly reduce the current-account deficit the United States has been running? Why or why not?

---

*Asterisk denotes questions for which answers are given in Appendix B.

PART 5

Applications and Special Topics in Economics

Economics has a lot to say about current issues and real world events. Why are unemployment rates substantially higher in Europe than in the United States? Why were the rates of both inflation and unemployment so high during the 1970s? Why does the current social security system face problems and what might be done to minimize them? Do labor unions increase the wages of workers? Is the world in danger of running out of natural resources? How can we best protect the environment? This section will focus on these topics and several other current issues.

APPLICATION 1 UNEMPLOYMENT RATES: THE UNITED STATES VERSUS EUROPE

APPLICATION 2 HOW DO BUDGET DEFICITS AND THE NATIONAL DEBT AFFECT FUTURE GENERATIONS?

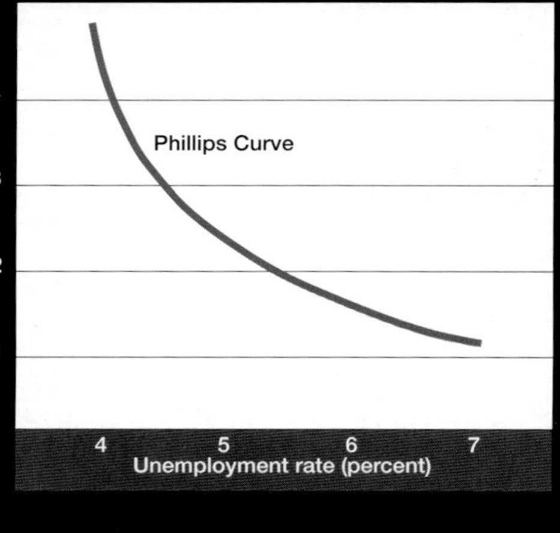

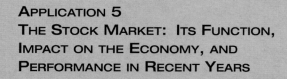

APPLICATION 3
THE PHILLIPS CURVE — THE DREAM AND THE REALITY

APPLICATION 4
SOCIAL SECURITY: THE NATURE OF THE PROBLEM AND THE ALTERNATIVES FOR DEALING WITH IT

APPLICATION 5
THE STOCK MARKET: ITS FUNCTION, IMPACT ON THE ECONOMY, AND PERFORMANCE IN RECENT YEARS

Economics helps us better understand the real world.

APPLICATION 1

If work does not pay, people will be reluctant to work.
OECD Jobs Strategy Report[1]

Labor Markets and Unemployment Rates: A Cross-Country Analysis

APPLICATION FOCUS

- Why are unemployment rates substantially higher in Europe than in the United States?
- How do the structure of labor markets and level of unemployment benefits influence the rate of unemployment?
- How have the United Kingdom and New Zealand altered the structure of their labor markets?

[1]OECD, *OECD Jobs Strategy: Making Work Pay* (Paris: OECD, 1997), p. 7.

As we push toward the millennium, concern about persistently high rates of unemployment is widespread in Europe, Canada, and Australia. Unemployment in these three areas has remained at double-digit levels throughout most of the 1990s. At the same time, however, the unemployment rate in the United States has declined to its lowest level in nearly three decades. The U.S. rate is approximately one-half the rate of the European Union (EU). Although the Japanese unemployment rate has been rising in the 1990s, it is still substantially lower than that of the EU. Why is the unemployment rate so much higher in Europe than in the United States and Japan? Why do the Canadian and Australian unemployment rates look much like those of Europe? Does the structure of labor markets make any difference? This application will address these issues.

CROSS-COUNTRY VARIATIONS IN UNEMPLOYMENT RATES

Exhibit A1–1 shows the standardized unemployment rates during 1986–1990 and 1991–1998 for the five most populous European countries, plus Australia, Canada, Japan, and the United States.[2] These countries are all members of the Organization for Economic Cooperation and Development (OECD). They are perhaps the nine most important market economies in the world. During 1991–1998, the unemployment rate averaged 10.6 percent in Italy, 11.6 percent in France, and a whopping 20.9 percent in Spain. For the European Union as a whole, the average unemployment rate during 1991–1998 was 10.4 percent, compared to 5.9 percent for the United States and 3 percent for Japan. During the last 2 years, Germany—like France, Italy, and Spain—has also experienced double-digit rates of unemployment.

These high unemployment rates are not the result of recession. The nine economies of Exhibit A1–1 expanded in the 1990s and the inflation rate of each has been low and stable—neither rising nor falling. Under these circumstances, unemployment will move toward the natural rate, the lowest sustainable unemployment rate consistent with the economy's institutional structure. Thus, there is reason to believe that the high rates of unemployment are a long-term rather than temporary phenomenon.

Employment growth in Europe has also lagged well behind that of the United States and Japan. Total employment for the 15 European Union countries in 1997 was only 2.3 percent higher than the figure for 1980. Employment actually declined in Italy during the 1980–1997 period. The total growth of employment in Germany, France,

[2]This section borrows freely from Edward Bierhanzl and James Gwartney, "Regulation, Unions, and Labor Markets," *Regulation* (summer 1998): 40–53.

EXHIBIT A1-1

THE STANDARDIZED UNEMPLOYMENT RATES OF NINE MAJOR INDUSTRIAL ECONOMIES: 1986–1998

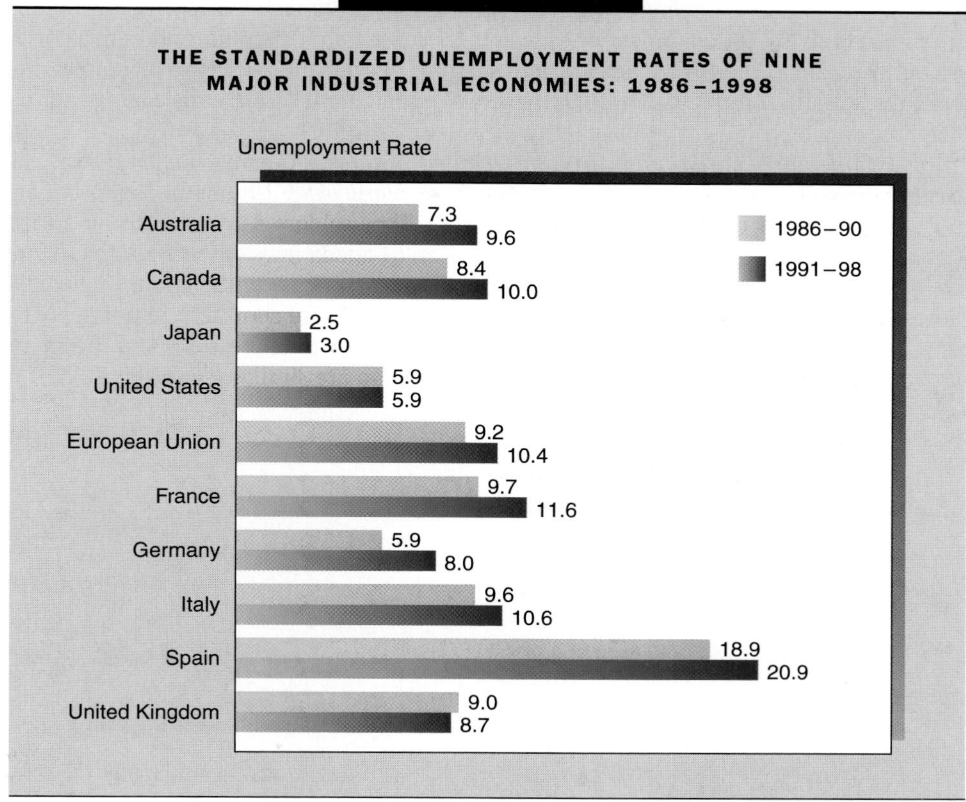

Since the mid-1980s, the unemployment rates of Australia, Canada, and the major European economies have been persistently higher than the rates for the United States and Japan.

SOURCE: OECD, *OECD Economic Outlook* (December 1998).

the United Kingdom, and Spain was 5 percent or less during this same period. By way of comparison, employment grew by 18.5 percent in Japan and by 29.5 percent in the United States.

THE STRUCTURE OF LABOR MARKETS

Labor market structural characteristics and policies differ substantially among countries. Compared to the United States and Japan, the labor markets of Europe, Australia, and Canada are characterized by (1) higher rates of unionization, (2) greater regulation, and (3) more generous unemployment assistance.[3] Let us look at the cross-country data and consider how each of these factors will influence the rate of unemployment.

[3]For additional information on this topic, see Charles Bean, "European Unemployment: A Survey," *Journal of Economic Literature,* 1995, no. 2:573–619; Sveinbjorn Blondal and Mark Pearson,"Unemployment and Other Nonemployment Benefits," *Oxford Review of Economic Policy,* 1995, no. 1:136–169; OECD, *Implementing the OECD Jobs Strategy: Member Countries' Experience* (Paris: OECD, 1997); OECD, *Making Work Pay: Taxation, Benefits, Employment and Unemployment* (Paris: OECD, 1997); and Horst Siebert, "Labor Market Rigidities: At the Root of Unemployment in Europe," *Journal of Economic Perspectives,* 1997, no. 3:37–54.

Centralized Wage-Setting

Exhibit A1–2 indicates both the percentage of the nonfarm labor force that is unionized and the share of employees whose wages are set by collective bargaining. Among the nine countries, the unionization rate is highest for Italy, Australia, and Canada; it is lowest for France, the United States, and Spain. However, the structure of unions differs substantially across countries. Therefore, membership is often a misleading indicator of the role of unions in the wage-setting process.

Collective bargaining in the United States, Canada, and Japan is decentralized—it takes place at the company or plant level. Unions in Japan are almost exclusively of the "company union" variety. They seldom set wages for an entire industry. Although unions in the United States and Canada may operate across an entire industry, the bargaining process is nearly always between a union and a single employer, or, in some cases, a single plant of the employer. These contracts do not apply to other firms. Under these circumstances, the union density (membership) and the share of workers whose wages are set by collective bargaining are similar (see Exhibit A1–2).

EXHIBIT A1–2

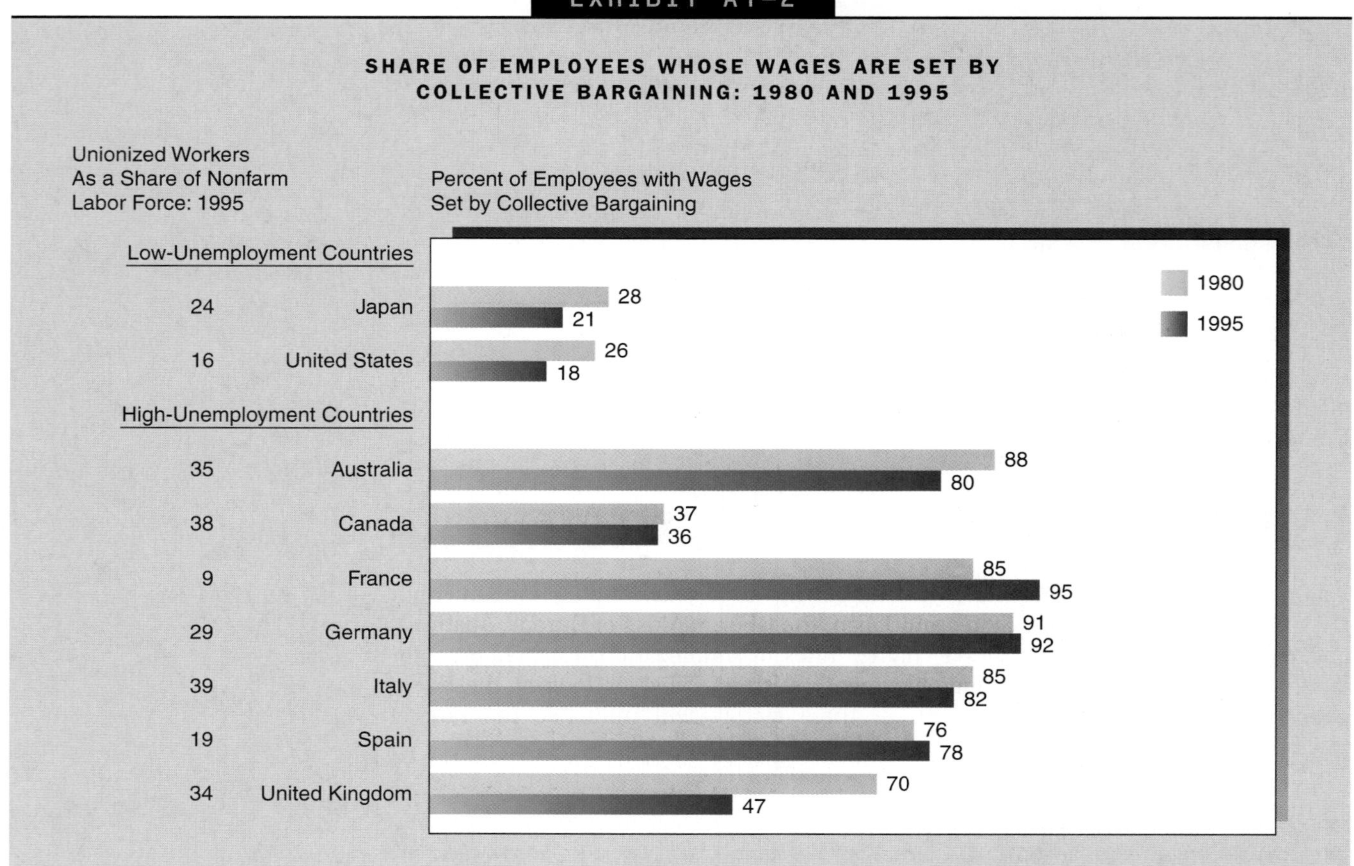

Centralized collective bargaining agreements that set wages for all workers in an industry and/or occupation are far more common in Australia and the major European economies than in the United States, Canada, and Japan.

SOURCES: OECD, Employment Outlook *(July 1994), Table 5.7; OECD,* Employment Outlook *(July 1997), Table 3.3; and OECD,* Country Surveys *(various issues).*

In contrast, the wage-setting process is highly centralized throughout most of Europe as well as in Australia. Negotiations between a union (or federation of unions) and an association of employers set the wages for all or most all workers in various industries, occupations, and/or regions. Statutory legislation extends these agreements to both nonunion employees and nonassociation employers who neither participated in the bargaining process nor agreed to the wage contracts. Sometimes political officials are also actively involved in the wage-setting process.

Therefore, as Exhibit A1–2 shows, the share of employees whose wages are set by collective bargaining in Australia and the populous countries of Europe (except for the United Kingdom in recent years) is far greater than union membership. For example, while union members were only 9 percent of the French labor force in 1995, collective bargaining set the wages for 95 percent of the employees. In Spain, Australia, Italy, and Germany, the pattern was the same. In all of these countries, highly centralized "agreements" set the wages of most workers—both union and nonunion—within various industry and occupational categories. This explains why the proportion of employees whose wages are set by collective bargaining is so much higher than union workers as a share of the workforce.

Does it make any difference whether wages are set at the firm level or for an entire industry, occupation, or region? Economic theory indicates that it does. When union members (and unionized firms) compete with nonunion workers and firms, market forces continue to play an important role. If the unionized workers push wages significantly above the competitive level, it will be more difficult for their employers to compete effectively with nonunion rivals. Thus, higher wages for union members would lead to employment reductions in the unionized sector. This will temper the bargaining process.

In contrast, the discipline of market forces is eroded when the wages for all workers and firms in an industry, an occupation, and a region are set centrally. A union that can set the wages of all firms in an industry will have considerable monopoly power. As wages are pushed up, the costs of both union and nonunion employers will rise. There will be less opportunity for nonunion firms to expand and hire workers willing to work at a lower wage. Of course, market forces will not be totally absent. Higher wages will encourage the substitution of capital for labor and make it more difficult for domestic firms to compete in international markets. Some firms will move production operations to other countries, where the services of workers of similar skill are available at a lower cost. The predictable result will be high rates of unemployment (and slow rates of employment growth) like that experienced by European countries during the last two decades.

Centralized wage-setting will have fewer adverse effects in small countries with labor forces that are relatively homogeneous in skills and education. In large countries with regional differences in cost-of-living and greater diversity among labor force participants, centrally determined wage rates will predictably lead to a substantial excess supply of workers in some areas and excess demand in others. In fact, unions and employers in high-wage regions can use the centralized wage-setting process to foist higher costs on rival firms and workers in regions where wages, reflecting educational and skill levels, would normally be lower. By pushing wages up in those regions, lower-wage and lower-skill workers are priced out of the market and rendered less competitive. The incentive for capital to move toward the low-wage regions is thus reduced.

Northern and southern Italy illustrate the significance of this strategy. Workers in southern Italy generally have fewer skills and less education than their counterparts in the North. With centralized labor contracts, however, wages in the various job categories are the same in both regions. As a result, workers in the South are less competitive and the incentive for capital to move toward that region is substantially

In Europe and Australia, union contracts often set the wages for all workers—both union and nonunion—in industry and occupational categories. The wages of more than three out of four employees are set by unions in Europe, compared to one in five in the United States.

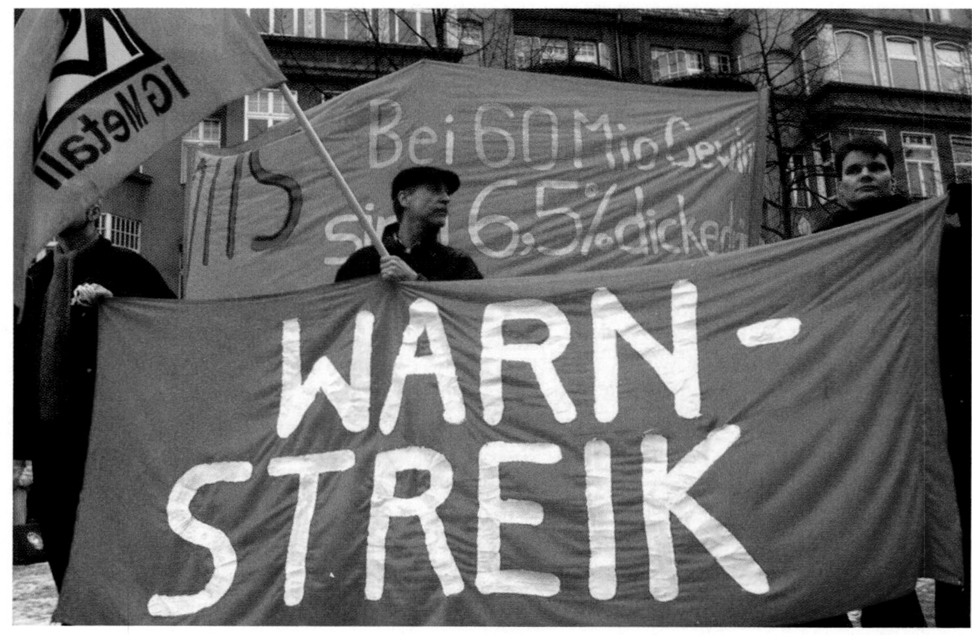

reduced. Obviously, the northern workers and their union representatives find this arrangement highly attractive. In the South, however, the results are disastrous. In recent years, unemployment rates in southern Italy have ranged between 20 percent and 30 percent—three or four times the rates of the North. Centralized wage-setting has also reduced the competitiveness of low-skill workers in several regions of Spain. As in Italy, the policy has led to both a high overall rate of unemployment and substantial regional disparity.

Regulation of Dismissal and Mandated Severance Pay

Severance pay
Pay by an employer to an employee upon the termination of employment with the firm.

European labor markets are also characterized by laws mandating various periods of prior notification and/or months of **severance pay** for the dismissal of a worker. Exhibit A1–3 presents data on the restrictiveness of dismissal regulations in various countries. The graph indicates the number of months of severance pay plus one-half the months of prior notification required for a no-fault dismissal of an employee. Since these mandates generally vary with seniority of the employee, the figures are the average for two workers, one with 4 years and another with 20 years of seniority.

The sum of the months of severance pay and prior notification required for a dismissal are relatively short in the United States, Japan, and Canada.[4] In contrast, they are quite lengthy in Italy and Spain. For example, Italian employers are required to give a dismissed worker with 4 years of seniority 1.1 months of notification and 3.5 months of severance pay. If the worker has 20 years of seniority, prior notification of 2.2 months and severance pay of 18 months are required. In

[4]Although there is no general notification requirement in the United States, employers with 100 or more full-time employees are required to give 60-day notice to employees dismissed as the result of a plant closing or mass layoff.

EXHIBIT A1-3

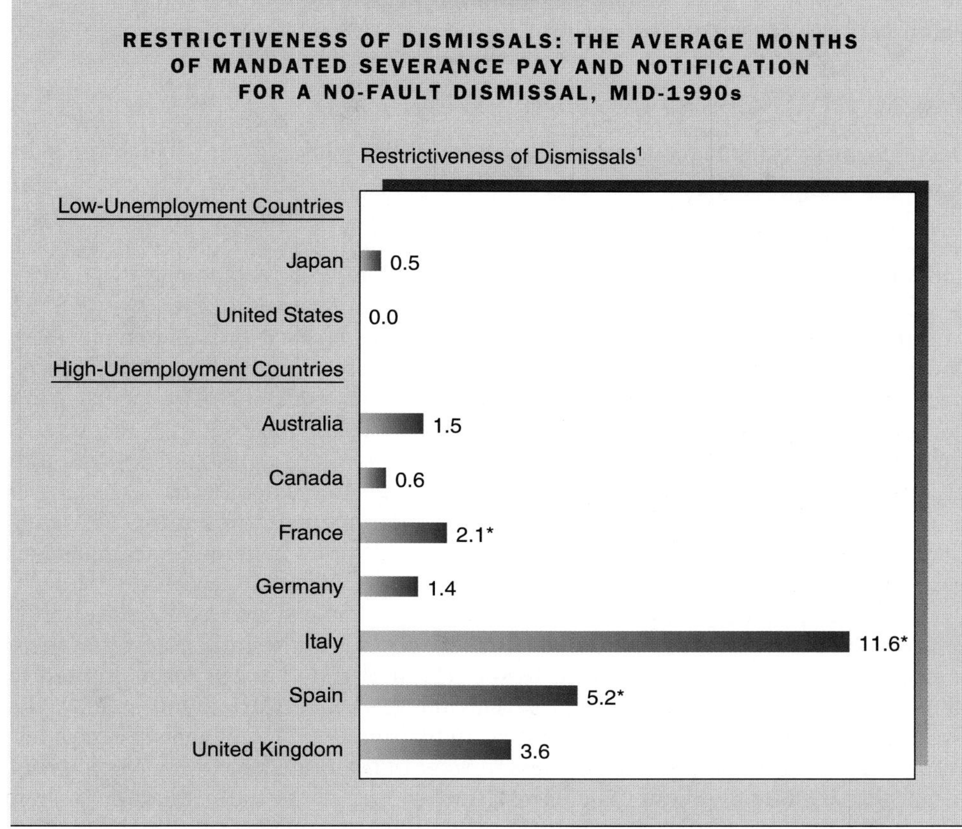

In Europe and Australia, government regulations generally require employers to give dismissed employees substantial prior notification and pay them severance pay for lengthy periods of time. These dismissal regulations are particularly restrictive in Italy and Spain.

[1]The average months of mandated severance pay plus ½ of the average months of mandated notification for the no-fault dismissal of a worker (average for workers with 4 years and 20 years of employment).
*Indicates that collective dismissals required approval from political authorities.
SOURCES: OECD, OECD Jobs Study: Evidence and Explanations *(1994), Part II, Table 6.5; and OECD,* Country Surveys *(various issues).*

addition, several European countries require political approval for mass layoffs. Employers in Italy, Spain, and France must convince various political officials that a business necessity is present before they are permitted to reduce their workforce by a sizable amount.

Proponents argue that regulations mandating notification and severance pay will help protect workers against arbitrary dismissal and provide them with greater job security. However, regulations that make it more costly to dismiss workers also make it more costly to hire them. When dismissal costs are high, employers will be reluctant to add workers during periods of strong demand because it will be costly to dismiss them if future conditions are less favorable. Thus, firms will often find that it is cheaper to expand output—particularly if the expansion is expected to be temporary—by using more capital, contracting out, or hiring part-time workers not covered by the dismissal regulations.

Furthermore, restrictive dismissal policies reduce the competition between workers with jobs and those seeking employment. They make it more expensive for employers to substitute current job seekers for established workers. In essence, the restrictions will make it extremely difficult for new entrants to find jobs and acquire labor-force experience. Thus, one of the expected side effects is high unemployment among youthful workers seeking employment. The data are consistent with this view. The unemployment rates of countries with the most restrictive dismissal policies are extremely high in the age category (15 to 24 years) where new labor-force entrants are most likely. The unemployment rate among 15- to 24-year-olds in 1996 was 42 percent in Spain, 34 percent in Italy, and 27 percent in Greece, another European country with highly restrictive dismissal policies.

Impact of Unemployment Benefits

Unemployment benefits reduce the opportunity cost of job search and thereby encourage more lengthy "spells" of unemployment. When set at a high level, they can become an attractive source of income in comparison to work. The generosity of the benefit levels may also influence unemployment in more subtle ways. Employers in seasonal and other industries offering erratic employment will often be able to pay lower wages because the benefits provide employees with income supplements when they are not working. In essence, the benefits subsidize businesses offering unstable employment and encourage the expansion of such employment.[5] More generous benefits tend to reduce the political repercussions of high unemployment rates. This is particularly important when the government is an active participant in the wage-setting process, as is the case throughout much of Europe. When the benefit levels are high, political officials will have less reason to resist the wage demands of unions even if the higher wages mean fewer jobs and higher rates of unemployment in the future. Therefore, there are good reasons to expect that countries with more generous unemployment benefits will experience higher unemployment.

Replacement rate
The share of previous earnings replaced by unemployment benefits.

Unemployment benefit systems are highly complex. Interestingly, the initial **replacement rate** among the major industrial countries is quite similar. However, there is considerable variation with regard to the length of time persons are permitted to draw benefits. The shortest duration periods for the benefits are found in Italy, the United States, the United Kingdom, Canada, and Japan, where the benefits for most unemployed workers expire in a year or less.[6] (*Note:* In the United States, unemployment benefits expire after 26 weeks.) In contrast, unemployed workers are permitted to draw benefits for two years or more in Spain, France, Germany, and Australia.

The replacement rate often varies with previous level of earnings, family size and situation, previous length of employment, and duration of unemployment. The OECD has calculated the replacement rate of member countries for recipients at two different income levels, three family situations, and three time periods of unemployment. The average replacement rates for these 18 different categories provide a reasonably good "index of generosity" for the unemployment system of each country.[7]

As **Exhibit A1–4** shows, the unemployment benefits are generally more attractive (and less restrictive with regard to eligibility) in Europe, Australia, and Canada

---

[5]In several countries, including the United States, employers with more erratic employment patterns are required to pay a higher payroll tax for unemployment insurance. However, the higher tax is generally insufficient to cover the additional benefits paid to the workers laid off or dismissed by these firms.

[6]Italy uses mandated severance pay (see Exhibit A1–3) as a substitute for unemployment compensation. Until recently, only a token unemployment compensation system was present in Italy.

[7]The OECD figures cover the replacement rate for the first year of unemployment, years 2 and 3, and years 4 and 5. Because the benefits will expire after 6 months or 1 year in many countries, this average replacement rate for most countries is substantially lower than the initial replacement rate. For example, unemployment benefits initially replace 60 percent of earnings in the United States. However, since the benefits can only be drawn for 6 months, the average replacement rate over the 5-year time period is much lower than the initial figure.

EXHIBIT A1-4

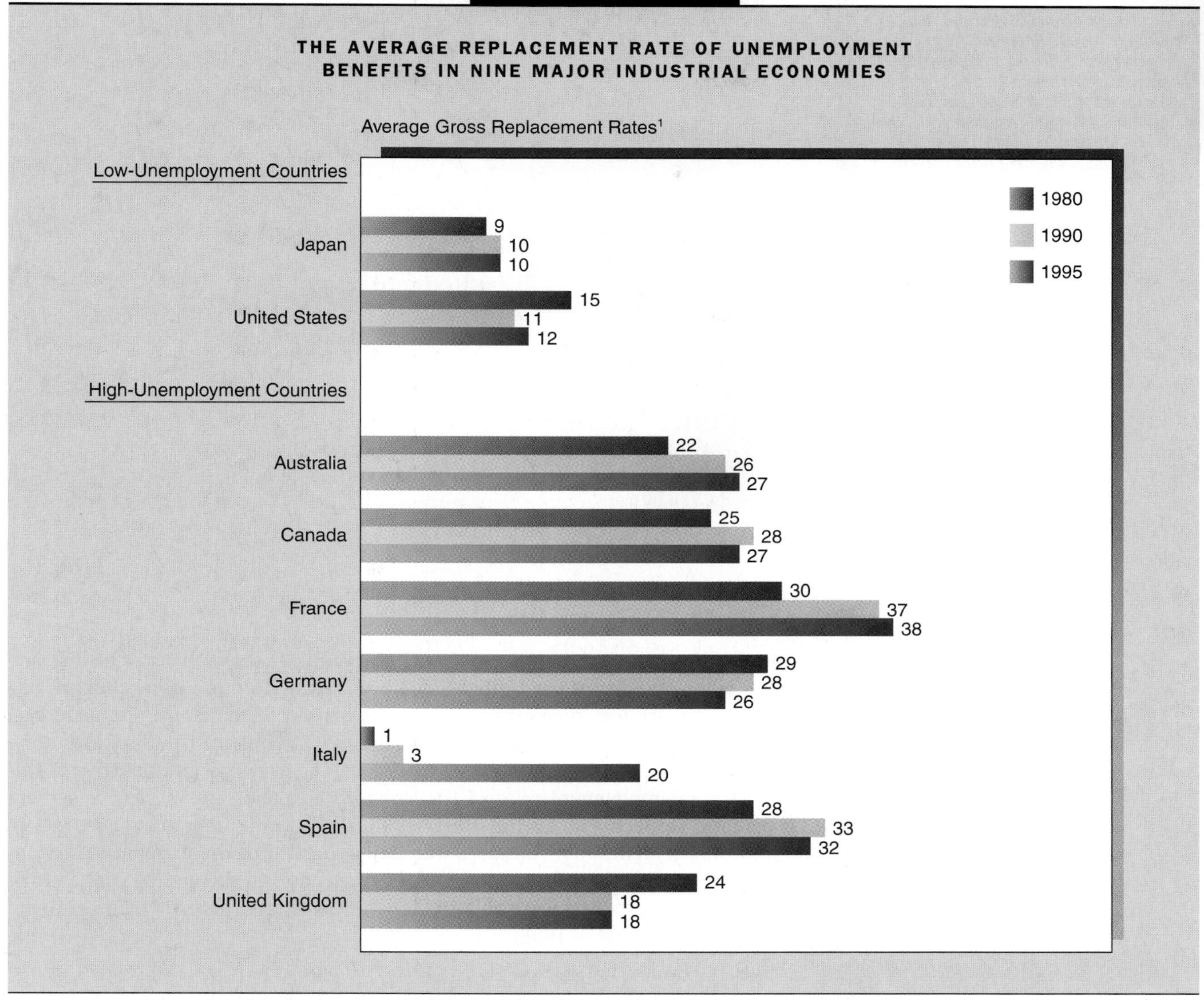

Compared to Japan and the United States, unemployment benefits in Australia, Canada, and Europe replace a larger proportion of an unemployed worker's lost earnings. How will this influence the natural rate of unemployment?

[1]*Average for two earnings levels (2/3 average and average earnings), three family situations (single, married with dependent spouse, and married with working spouse), and three duration periods (1 year, 1 to 3 years, and 3 to 5 years).*

SOURCES: OECD, OECD Jobs Strategy: Making Work Pay *(1997), Figure 2; and OECD,* Implementing the OECD Jobs Strategy: Member Countries' Experience, *Table 5.*

than in the United States and Japan. The average replacement rates of the United States and Japan generally range from one-half to one-third the replacement rates of the European countries, Australia, and Canada. Predictably, the higher unemployment benefit levels of these latter countries will encourage more lengthy periods of job search and thereby push the unemployment rate up.

Business is brisk in this German unemployment office. Compared to the United States and Japan, unemployment benefits are more generous in Europe and Australia. Higher unemployment benefits reduce the opportunity cost of job search and thereby tend to lengthen spells of unemployment. This pushes unemployment rates upward.

Pulling It Together

Compared to the five most populous European countries, as well as Australia and Canada, the labor markets of the United States and Japan are more decentralized, dismissal regulations are less restrictive, and unemployment benefits are less generous. Economic theory indicates that each of these factors will enhance the flexibility of labor markets and help keep unemployment rates low. The evidence is supportive of this view. While the unemployment rates of the United States and Japan were 5.9 percent and 3.0 percent, respectively, during 1991–1998, the average unemployment rate of the seven more interventionist countries was 11.3 percent. For the European Union as a whole, the unemployment rate averaged 10.4 percent during this period. None of the more regulated labor markets were able to do better than an 8 percent average rate of unemployment during 1991–1998.

LABOR MARKET REFORMS IN THE UNITED KINGDOM AND NEW ZEALAND

If a country moved toward a more liberal labor market, would it make any difference? The recent experience of the United Kingdom and New Zealand sheds light on this issue. These two countries have recently adopted significant reforms designed to protect the rights of workers and make their labor markets more competitive.

In the United Kingdom, the reforms focused on promotion of democratic decision making and the protection of workers' rights. The Employment Act of 1980 required secret ballot approval prior to the establishment of a closed shop. Later, legislation was adopted (1) requiring worker approval every 5 years for the continuation of a closed shop and (2) making strike action to establish a closed shop unlawful. Nonunion members were also granted legal protection against dismissal and discriminatory actions as the result of their nonunion status. Union members were given the right to join the union of their choice and granted protection against unions seeking to discipline them for failure to support a strike. These changes both weakened the monopoly power of unions and led to a more decentralized wage-setting process. Union membership in the United Kingdom fell from 50 percent of the workforce in 1980 to 34 percent in 1995. More important, centralized bargaining became less commonplace. The share of employees having their wages set by collective bargaining contracts fell from 70 percent in 1980 to 47 percent in 1995. The labor market reforms were supplemented with less-generous unemployment benefits. As Exhibit A1–4 indicates, the average replacement rate in the United Kingdom fell from 24 percent in 1980 to 18 percent in 1990 and 1995.

In New Zealand, the Employment Contracts Act of 1991 restructured the labor market even more rapidly than the English reforms. This act allowed all employees to "choose whether or not to associate with other employees for advancing the employees' collective employment interests." Employees were granted the right to negotiate labor contracts, with or without the assistance of an agent. Most significantly, while rights to strike and lockout were explicitly recognized, these weapons were permitted only at the expiration of labor contracts and then only after employee approval was obtained at the *enterprise* level. This effectively changed the wage-setting process in New Zealand from a centralized to a decentralized system. As in the United Kingdom, union membership fell and the share of employees having their wages set by union contracts declined from 67 percent in 1990 to 31 percent in 1995.

How have the labor markets of these two countries reacted to economic liberalization? In the United Kingdom, the economy expanded rapidly throughout most of the 1980s and the unemployment rate declined. Following the recession in the early 1990s, the economy rebounded nicely and by 1998, the rate of unemployment in the United Kingdom had fallen to 6.3 percent, the lowest rate achieved since the 1970s. In New Zealand, the results have been similar. New Zealand's rate of unemployment fell from 10.3 percent in 1992 to 6.4 percent during 1996–1998. The unemployment rates of both countries are now significantly lower than the rates of similarly situated countries that have followed more interventionist policies. The UK unemployment rate stands in stark contrast to the double-digit rates of the other populous European countries. New Zealand's unemployment rate is well below that of Australia, a country that continues to rely on centralized wage-setting processes.

LABOR MARKETS IN THE UNITED STATES AND CANADA

Comparisons between the United States and Canadian labor markets are quite revealing. Although the Canadian labor market is less regulated and more decentralized than those of the major European economies, it is clearly less liberal than that of the United States. Compared to the United States, the share of employees with wages set by collective bargaining is greater, dismissal regulations are more restrictive, and unemployment benefits are more generous in Canada. Furthermore, the Canadian labor market has been drifting toward the European model. Union membership has been increasing as a share of the labor force in Canada, while it has been declining in the United States. During the last decade, Canada has enacted legislation making it more difficult for employers to dismiss workers and reduce the size of their workforce. According to the OECD, the average replacement rate of Canada's unemployment benefit system has risen from 20 percent in 1970 to 25 percent in 1980 and 28 percent in 1990.

These factors show up in the unemployment statistics. During the 1960s and 1970s, the Canadian average unemployment rate was virtually the same as that of the

United States. This is no longer true. During the 1980s, the Canadian average rate of unemployment was about 2 percent greater than the rate of the United States, and in the 1990s the gap has widened to 4 percent (see Exhibit A1–1).

KEY POINTS

➤ During the last decade, the major European economies, Australia, and Canada have persistently experienced double-digit unemployment rates. In recent years, the unemployment rate of the European Union has been about twice that of the United States.

➤ When used in large and diverse labor markets, a centralized wage-setting process will push wage rates above market levels in various regions and skill categories. This will tend to cause higher rates of unemployment. Similarly, regulations that make it more costly to dismiss workers will also make employers more reluctant to hire employees. This will lead to sluggish employment growth and high rates of unemployment, particularly for youthful workers seeking to enter the workforce. High unemployment benefits will reduce the opportunity cost of job search, and thereby cause more lengthy spells of unemployment.

➤ Compared to the United States and Japan, the labor markets of Europe, Australia, and Canada are characterized by centralized wage-setting processes, more restrictive dismissal regulations, and high unemployment benefit replacement rates. There is reason to believe that these policies have contributed to the high unemployment rates of these economies.

➤ Recent reforms in the United Kingdom and New Zealand have increased the competitiveness of labor markets. The rates of unemployment in both countries have declined and are now significantly lower than the rates of similarly situated countries that have followed more restrictive labor market practices.

CRITICAL ANALYSIS QUESTIONS

*1. Compared to the situation where a union is able to organize only a portion of the firms in an industry, how does the ability to set wages for an entire industry influence the power of a labor union? What does this suggest about the relative strength of unions in Europe versus those in the United States and Japan?

2. Explain why unemployment compensation is an indirect subsidy to employers with a less stable workforce. Is it a good idea to subsidize this type of unemployment? Why or why not?

3. Suppose that legislation was passed requiring all employers in the United States to pay dismissed workers one week of severance pay for every year they were employed by the firm. What impact would this have on (a) the dismissal rate of employees, (b) the productivity of employees, and (c) the unemployment rate of youthful workers? Discuss.

4. Do you think that the United States should move toward the European labor market model characterized by more extensive collective bargaining, greater government regulation, and more generous unemployment benefits? Why or why not?

---

*Asterisk denotes questions for which answers are given in Appendix B.

APPLICATION 2

The attractiveness of financing spending by debt issue to the elected politicians should be obvious. Borrowing allows spending to be made that will yield immediate political payoffs without the incurring of any immediate political cost.

James Buchanan[1]

How Do Budget Deficits and the National Debt Affect Future Generations?

APPLICATION FOCUS

- How large is the national debt? Will the debt have to be paid off?
- Who owns the national debt?
- How are future generations affected by the national debt?
- How does the national debt of the United States compare with those of other countries?
- Why have budget deficits been smaller in the 1990s? Is the era of large budget deficits over?

[1]James Buchanan, *The Deficit and American Democracy* (Memphis: P. K. Steidman Foundation, 1984).

Concern about the federal budget deficit and the national debt has fluctuated considerably over the last half century. Deficit spending was a hot topic in the 1950s, as Keynesian economists challenged the reigning orthodoxy—the view that the federal budget should be balanced annually. By the 1960s, the Keynesians had clearly won the debate in both the academic and political arenas. Thus, no one paid much attention as the federal government incurred a string of budget deficits during the 1960s and 1970s. As larger and larger deficits pushed the national debt upward in the 1980s, the topic once again moved to center stage. Recently, however, lower defense expenditures and the lengthy economic expansion of the 1990s have wiped out the budget deficits and now there is widespread discussion concerning what to do with future budget surpluses. What precisely is the national debt? How do budget deficits and the national debt influence the lives of people? Will the "era of budget surpluses" be long-lasting? This application addresses these topics and related issues.

BUDGET DEFICITS AND THE NATIONAL DEBT

When the federal government uses debt rather than taxes and user charges to pay for its expenditures, the U.S. Treasury fills this gap by borrowing in the loanable funds market. When borrowing funds, the Treasury generally issues interest-bearing bonds. These bonds compose the national debt. In effect, the national debt consists of outstanding loans from financial investors to the general fund of the U.S. Treasury.

The federal budget deficit and the national debt are directly related. The deficit is a "flow" concept (like water running into a bathtub), while the national debt is a "stock" figure (like the amount of water in the tub at a point in time). In essence, the **national debt** represents the cumulative effect of all the prior budget deficits and surpluses. A budget deficit increases the size of the national debt by the amount of the deficit. Conversely, a budget surplus allows the federal government to pay off bondholders and thereby reduces the size of the national debt.

National debt
The sum of the indebtedness of the federal government in the form of outstanding interest-earning bonds. It reflects the cumulative impact of budget deficits and surpluses.

The creditworthiness of an organization is dependent upon the size of its debt relative to its income base. Therefore, when analyzing the significance of budget deficits and the national debt, one must consider their size relative to the entire economy. **Exhibit A2–1** presents data for the 1950–1998 period for both the federal budget deficit and the national debt as a percentage of GDP. Since the defense effort during the Second World War was financed substantially with debt rather than with taxes, the national debt was quite large at the end of the war. Following the war, the combination of economic growth and small budget deficits reduced the size of the national debt as a percentage of GDP. During the 1950–1974 period, budget deficits averaged less than 1 percent of GDP. Historically, real output in the United States has grown at an annual rate of approximately 3 percent. When the budget deficit as a percent of GDP is less than the growth of real output, the federal debt will decline relative to the size of the economy. This is precisely what happened during the 1950–1974 period. Budget

EXHIBIT A2-1

BUDGET DEFICITS AND THE NATIONAL DEBT AS A PERCENTAGE OF GDP

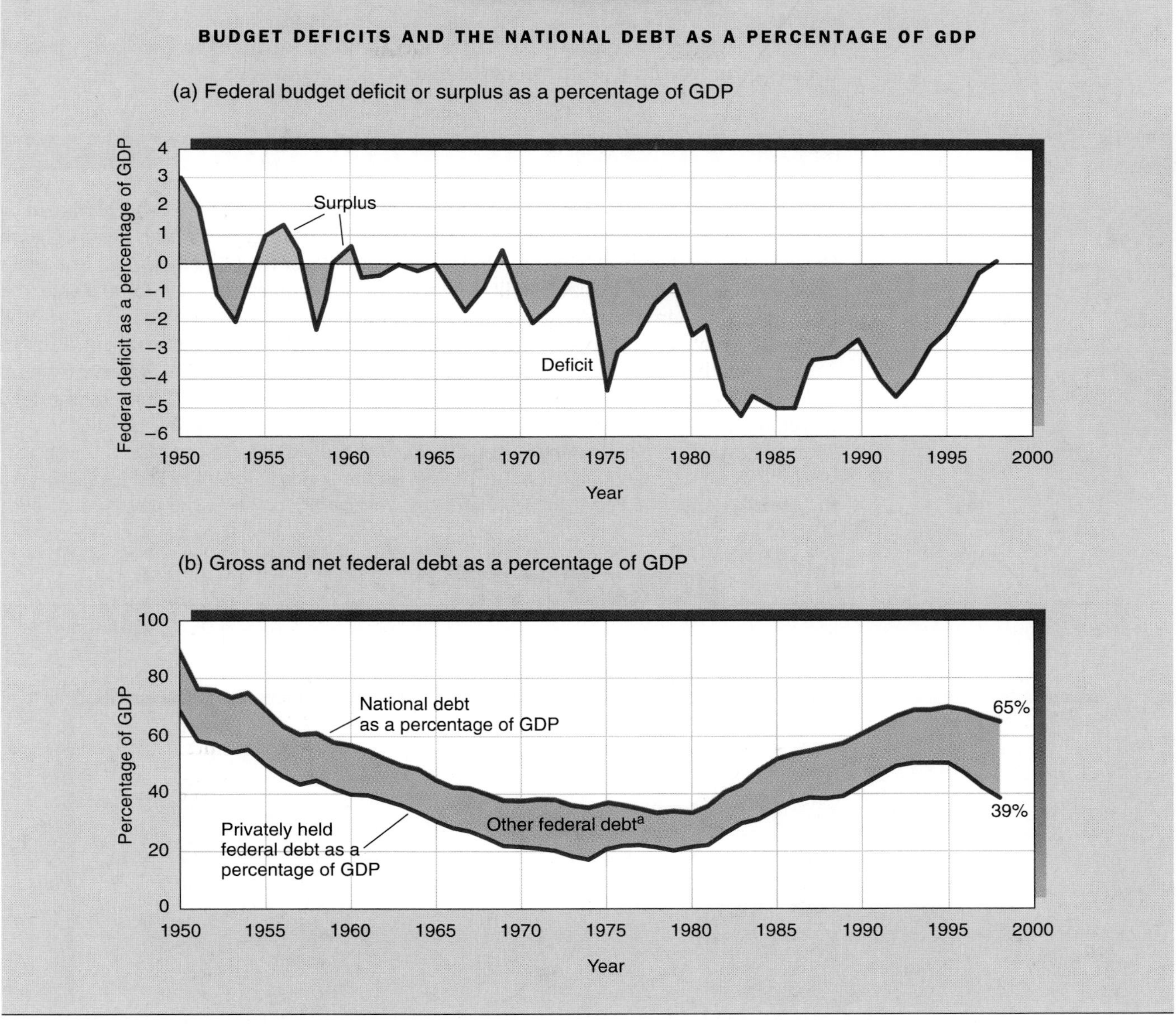

Throughout most of the 1950s and 1960s, federal budget deficits were small as a percentage of GDP, and occasionally the government ran a budget surplus (a). During this period, the national debt declined as a proportion of GDP (b). During 1974–1995, budget deficits were quite large, causing the national debt to increase as a percentage of GDP. During the last few years, the national debt has fallen as a share of the economy.

[a] *Federal debt held by U.S. government agencies and Federal Reserve banks.*

deficits were present, and they pushed up the nominal national debt (from $256.7 billion at year-end 1950 to $492.7 billion at the end of 1974). But GDP grew even more rapidly. By 1974 the national debt had fallen to 34 percent of GDP, down from 89 percent in 1950 (and 127 percent in 1946).

This situation was reversed in the mid-1970s. During the period 1974–1995, federal budget deficits averaged nearly 4 percent of GDP (part a of Exhibit A2–1). When the budget deficit as a percentage of GDP exceeds the growth of real GDP, the national debt will increase relative to the size of the economy. Pushed along by the large budget deficits of the 1980s and early 1990s, the national debt expanded to 68 percent of GDP in 1995, up from 34 percent in 1974. As the economy expanded in the 1990s, budget deficits shrunk and the debt/GDP ratio fell to 65 percent in 1998.

WHO OWNS THE NATIONAL DEBT?

As **Exhibit A2–2** illustrates, nearly one-third (31.7 percent) of the national debt is held by agencies of the federal government. For example, social security trust funds are often used to purchase U.S. bonds. When the debt is owned by a government agency, it is little more than an accounting transaction indicating that one government agency (for example, the Social Security Administration) is making a loan to another (the U.S. Treasury). Even the interest payments in this case represent little more than an internal government transfer.

Another 8.3 percent of the public debt is held by the Federal Reserve System. When the Fed purchases U.S. securities, it creates money. The bonds held by the Fed, therefore, are indicative of prior government expenditures that have been paid for with "printing-press" money—money created by the central bank. As in the case of the securities held by government agencies, the interest on the bonds held by the Fed is returned to the Treasury after the Fed has covered its costs of operation. Thus, the government both

EXHIBIT A2–2

WHO OWNS THE NATIONAL DEBT?

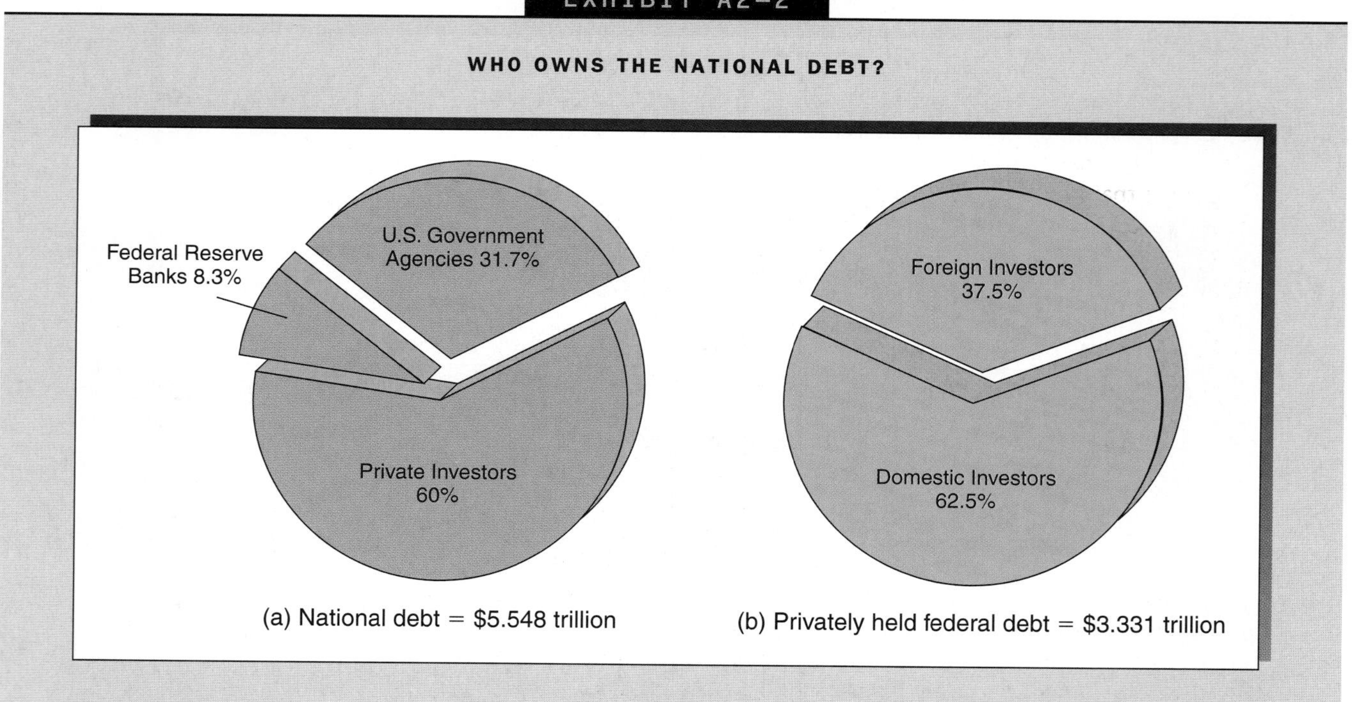

Of the $5.548 trillion national debt, 40 percent is held by government agencies (primarily the social security trust fund) and Federal Reserve banks. Of the $3.331 trillion privately held federal debt, 62.5 percent is held by domestic investors and 37.5 percent by foreigners.

SOURCE: Federal Reserve Bulletin, *January 1999.*

pays and receives the interest on the bonds held by government agencies and the Federal Reserve (minus Fed expenses). These bonds do not represent a net interest obligation.

In contrast, **privately held government debt** imposes a net interest burden on the federal government. In the case of the privately held debt—that is, the bonds held by individuals, insurance companies, mutual funds, and other investors—the federal government will have to impose taxes to meet the future interest payments on these bonds. Thus, it is important to distinguish between (1) the total national debt and (2) privately held government debt. Only the latter imposes a net interest obligation on the federal government. The privately held debt comprises only three-fifths of the national debt. Of the privately held debt, 62.5 percent is owned by domestic investors and 37.5 percent by foreigners. The portion owned by foreigners is sometimes referred to as **external debt.**

Privately held government debt
The portion of the national debt owed to domestic and foreign investors. It does not include bonds held by agencies of the federal government or the Federal Reserve.

External debt
The portion of the national debt owed to foreign investors.

Part b of Exhibit A2–1 presents data on the size of the privately held federal debt as a percentage of GDP for the 1950–1998 period. Like the overall national debt, the privately held federal debt as a share of GDP declined during the 1950–1974 period and rose during the 1975–1995 period, prior to the slight reduction during the last few years. In 1998, the privately held federal debt stood at 39 percent of GDP, up from 20 percent in 1974.

CONCERNS ABOUT THE NATIONAL DEBT

How Does Debt Financing Influence Future Generations?

Laypeople, politicians, and economists have debated about the burden of the national debt for many years.[2] Opponents of debt financing often charge that we are mortgaging the future of our children and grandchildren—that debt financing permits us to consume today, then send the bill to future generations. In the 1960s and 1970s, the overwhelming bulk of the national debt was held by domestic investors. During this era, Keynesians argued that there was little reason for concern because "We owe it to ourselves." Today, new classical economists take the position that debt affects the timing, but not the magnitude, of taxes. Like Keynesians, they are unconcerned about debt financing.

When considering our ability to shift the cost of government onto future generations, one must keep two points in mind. First, in the case of domestically held debt, our children and grandchildren will indeed pay the taxes to service the debt, but they will also receive the interest payments. Admittedly, those paying the taxes and receiving the interest payments will not always be the same people. Some will gain and others will lose. But both those who gain and those who lose will be members of the future generation.

Second, debt financing of a government activity cannot push the opportunity cost of the resources used by government onto future generations. If current GDP is $9 trillion and the federal government spends $2 trillion on goods and services, then only $7 trillion will be available for consumption and investment by individuals, businesses, and state and local governments. This will be true regardless of whether the federal government finances its expenditures with taxes or debt. When the government builds a highway, constructs an antimissile defense system, or provides police protection, it draws resources with alternative uses away from the private sector. This cost is incurred in the present; it cannot be avoided through debt financing.

---

[2]See Richard H. Fink and Jack High, eds., *A Nation in Debt: Economists Debate the Federal Budget Deficit* (Frederick, MD: University Publications of America, 1987), for an excellent set of readings summarizing this debate.

If the opportunity cost of resources occurs during the current period, does this mean that the welfare of future generations is unaffected by debt financing? Not necessarily. Debt financing influences future generations primarily through its potential impact on saving and capital formation. If lots of factories, machines, houses, technical knowledge, and other productive assets are available to future generations, then their productive potential will be high. Alternatively, if fewer productive assets are passed along to the next generation, then their productive capability will be less. Thus, the true measure of how government debt influences future generations involves knowledge of its impact on capital formation.

The impact of budget deficits on capital formation is a complex issue. Consider an economy operating at its normal productive capacity. Holding government expenditures constant, how would the substitution of debt financing for current taxation influence capital formation? As our discussion of fiscal-policy models implies, economists differ in their responses to this question. We will consider two major theories: the traditional view that budget deficits reduce future capital stock and the opposing new classical view that such deficits exert no significant future impact.

Traditional View: Budget Deficits Reduce Future Capital Stock. Most economists embrace the traditional view that budget deficits will retard private investment and thereby reduce the welfare of future generations. Suppose that the government substitutes borrowing for current taxation. For example, consider what would happen if the government cut the current taxes of each household by $100 and borrowed the funds to replace the lost revenues. As a result, the after-tax income of each household increases by $100. Of course, the households may save some of the $100 addition to their disposable income, but they are also likely to spend some of it on consumption goods, according to the traditional view. If they do not save all the $100, the additional government borrowing will increase the demand for loanable funds relative to the supply and thereby push real interest rates upward.[3] In turn, the higher real interest rates will retard private investment, which will reduce the physical capital available to future generations. To the extent future generations work with less capital (fewer productivity-enhancing tools and machines), their productivity and wages will be lower than would have been the case had the budget deficits not crowded out private investment.

In addition, the higher interest rates will attract foreign investors. But investments in the United States will require dollars. As foreigners increase their investments in the United States, they will demand dollars in the foreign exchange market. This strong demand will cause the dollar to appreciate relative to other currencies. In turn, the appreciation in the exchange-rate value of the dollar will make U.S. exports more expensive to foreigners and foreign goods cheaper for Americans. These relative price changes will retard exports and stimulate imports. Predictably, net exports will decline.

The inflow of capital from abroad will dampen both the increase in interest rates and the reduction in domestic investment. However, it will also increase the asset holdings of foreigners in the United States. The returns to these assets will generate income for foreigners rather than Americans. Therefore, compared to the situation where

[3]Alternatively, one could approach this topic from the viewpoint of how households value the government bonds relative to the future tax liability implied by the bonds. If bondholders recognize the asset value of the government bonds while taxpayers fail to recognize fully the accompanying tax liability, then the general populace will have an exaggerated view of its true wealth position. Wealth is an important determinant of consumption. When people think they are wealthier, they will consume more and save less than they would if they had fully recognized their future tax liability. Of course, the increase in consumption and reduction in savings would place upward pressure on the real rate of interest. This is simply an alternative way of viewing the substitution of government debt for current taxation.

government was financed with current taxation, future generations of Americans will inherit both a smaller stock of physical capital and less income from that capital (because the share owned by foreigners has increased). Succeeding generations will be less well-off as a result.

In summary, the traditional view argues that the substitution of debt financing for current taxation will increase current consumption, push up real interest rates, and retard private investment. In addition, the higher real interest rates will lead to an increase in net foreign investment, appreciation in the exchange-rate value of the dollar, and a decline in net exports (imports will increase relative to exports). According to the traditional view, budget deficits will retard the growth rate of capital formation, particularly that owned by Americans, and reduce national income and future living standards of Americans.

New Classical View: Budget Deficits Exert Little Impact on Future Capital Stock. Not all economists accept the traditional view of budget deficits. An alternative theory, most closely associated with Robert Barro of Harvard University, encompasses the new classical perspective of fiscal policy.[4] This new classical view stresses that additional debt implies an equivalent amount of future taxes. If, as the new classical model assumes, individuals fully anticipate the added future tax liability accompanying the debt, current consumption will be unaffected when governments substitute debt for taxes. According to this view, when future taxes (debt) are substituted for current taxes, people will save the reduction in current taxes so that they will have the required income to pay the higher future taxes implied by the additional debt. Continuing with our previous example, the new classical theory implies that households receiving a $100 reduction in current taxes financed by issuing bonds (that imply higher future taxes) will save all the $100 increase in their current disposable income. This increase in saving, triggered by the anticipation of the higher future taxes, allows the additional government debt to be financed without an increase in the real rate of interest. Since there is no increase in interest rates, private investment is unaffected. Neither is there an influx of foreign capital. Under these circumstances, the substitution of debt for taxes exerts little or no impact on either capital formation or the welfare of future generations.

Empirical Evidence on the Impact of the Deficit. What does the empirical evidence indicate with regard to the validity of the two theories? Empirical studies have found little, if any, relationship between year-to-year changes in the budget deficit and real interest rates. New classical economists argue that these findings are supportive of their theory.

However, the experience with the large budget deficits subsequent to 1980 would appear to support the traditional theory. As the size of the budget deficit increased substantially during the 1980s, Americans increased their current consumption expenditures and substantially reduced their domestically financed capital formation. Simultaneously, there was an inflow of net foreign investment and a reduction in net exports (imports increased relative to exports). This pattern is precisely what the traditional theory predicts will happen when debt financing is substituted for current taxation. (See Exhibit 12–9 on page 314 for evidence on these points.) Empirical work on the linkage between (1) the budget deficit on the one hand and (2) interest

[4]See Robert Barro, "Are Government Bonds Net Wealth?" *Journal of Political Economy* 82 (November–December 1974): 1095–1117; and "The Ricardian Approach to Budget Deficits," *Journal of Economic Perspectives* 2 (spring 1989).

rates, consumption, and inflow of capital on the other is continuing. At this point, however, the bulk of the evidence appears to be consistent with the traditional view.

Dependence on Foreign Investors

As we noted, nearly two-fifths of the privately held federal debt is now owned by foreigners. Studies indicate that foreigners own approximately 5 percent of the domestic capital assets of the United States. How does foreign investment affect the U.S. economy? When considering a possible burden emanating from foreign investment, one must keep an eye on both sides of the transaction. The inflow of foreign capital leads to lower interest rates and a higher level of investment than would take place in its absence. An increase in machines, structures, and other capital assets, even if financed by foreign investment, will increase the productivity and wages of American workers. Of course, the inflow of investment funds also enlarges the future profit and interest claims of foreigners. However, if the funds are invested wisely, the projects will generate returns (future income) that provide an offset against the future income claims of foreigners. On the other hand, if the funds are squandered on low-return projects, the wealth of investors will be reduced. But this would be equally true for projects financed solely with domestic funds.

Doesn't this inflow of capital from abroad make the United States more dependent on foreign creditors? In the analysis of this issue, it is important to keep the nature of the foreign investment in mind. Substantial portions of the funds supplied by foreigners are in the form of risk capital—investments in stocks, land, physical structures, and business ventures. Such investments do not involve a contractual repayment commitment. Others are invested in bonds, both corporate and government. These investments are almost entirely fixed-interest-rate obligations. As long as the investment project is profitable, U.S. citizens as well as foreigners will gain as the result of undertaking the project.

What would happen if foreigners suddenly decided to take their "money" home and quit financing investments in the United States? It is not obvious why literally tens of thousands of foreign investors would be any more likely to "sell out" suddenly than would tens of thousands of domestic investors. But even if they did, market adjustments would exert a stabilizing effect. Remember, the "money" of foreigners is in the form of stocks, bonds, and physical assets. If foreigners suddenly tried to sell these assets, falling prices would create some real bargains for domestic investors. Domestic investors would gain and foreign investors would lose. Similarly, if foreigners cut back their financial investments in the United States, real interest rates would rise. But the higher real interest rates would make U.S. investments more attractive and thereby help deter any outflow of funds.

Finally, the vulnerability accompanying foreign investment almost certainly lies with the foreign investor rather than with the recipient country. It is much easier for a government to expropriate the property of a foreigner than it is for an investor to exercise much control over the policies of a foreign government. History illustrates the vulnerability of the foreign investor. The United States expropriated the property of Germans and Japanese during the Second World War. Several Middle Eastern countries expropriated the property of foreign investors when they nationalized their domestic oil industries in the 1950s and 1960s. Under Fidel Castro, the Cuban government expropriated the assets of foreigners. Foreign investment is a hostage to the domestic policies of the recipient country. A major reason why investment in the United States is attractive to foreigners is the confidence they have that the U.S. government will not abuse its superior position.

DEBT FINANCING IN OTHER COUNTRIES

How large is the government debt in other countries? **Exhibit A2–3** provides data on net government debt as a share of GDP for several high-income industrial nations. Among the industrial nations, the net public debt/GDP ratio in 1998 was lowest, 16 percent, for Australia. The parallel figure for Japan was 30 percent. The debt/GDP ratios were similar for the United States, the United Kingdom, France, and Germany; all were in the 39 percent to 47 percent range.

Among industrial countries, the debt/GDP ratio was highest for Belgium and Italy. In both countries, the outstanding government debt exceeded GDP. Of course, a large outstanding debt means high interest payments for debt service. As a share of the economy, interest payments on government debt in Italy and Belgium are about five times the level in the United States. The governments of Belgium and Italy tax away approximately 7.5 percent of the GDP generated by their citizens just to make the interest payments on outstanding debt.

As the size of a nation's debt gets larger and larger, eventually global credit markets will apply some discipline. Countries with large debt/GDP ratios will have to pay higher real interest rates in order to induce investors to purchase their bonds. At

EXHIBIT A2–3

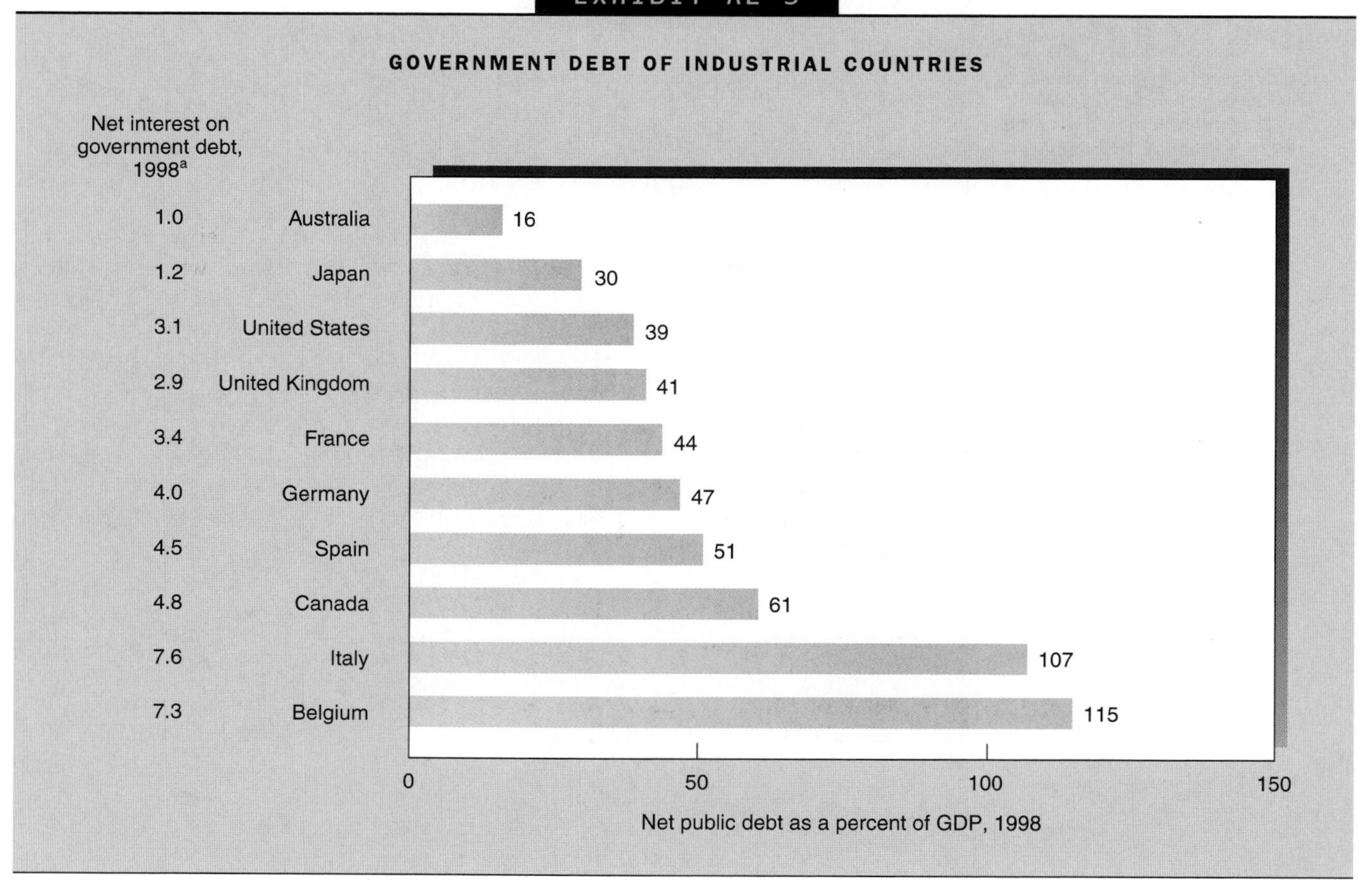

[a]*As a percent of GDP*

SOURCE: OECD Economic Outlook *(December 1998), Annex Tables 30 and 35.*

some point, countries will be more or less forced to bring spending more closely in line with revenues in order to maintain the confidence of investors. This is what happened to Belgium in 1994. Loss of investor confidence led to a sharp decline in the foreign exchange value of the Belgian franc. In order to maintain creditworthiness, the Belgian government was forced to take some drastic steps. Spending on social programs—including social security, health care, and child benefits—was substantially reduced. Continuing discipline will be required if Belgium is going to regain the full confidence of investors.

HOW DOES THE SOCIAL SECURITY SYSTEM INFLUENCE THE NATIONAL DEBT?

As conventionally measured, the budget deficit includes the revenues and expenditures of government trust funds, including the social security trust fund. Until recently, the net revenue flowing into this fund was small relative to the size of the budget. Therefore, it really did not make much difference whether it was included in or excluded from budget deficit calculations. All this began to change during the latter half of the 1980s. Under legislation passed in 1983, the social security trust fund is currently running approximately a $100 billion surplus. As a result, the inclusion of social security

Would budget surpluses encourage capital formation and help reduce the burden accompanying the retirement of the baby-boom generation? Can you explain both the traditional and new classical responses to this question?

in the unified budget calculation makes the deficit appear smaller or the surplus appear larger than would otherwise be the case. For example, if the $99 billion surplus of the social security system had not been included in the 1998 budget calculation, the federal government would have run a $29 billion deficit rather than a $70 billion surplus.

More is at stake here than just a definitional issue. The surplus of the social security system was planned in order to set funds aside for the increase in the share of the population that will draw social security benefits when the baby boom generation begins to retire in the years following 2015. The current social security surpluses are intended to increase the national saving rate and stimulate additional investment, and thereby help to finance the retirement benefits of the baby boomers. Using these funds to finance current government expenditures completely undermines this strategy.

Given the future demands of the social security system, many economists argue that the federal government should balance its operating budget—that is, its budget exclusive of the social security system. This would imply a surplus at least equal to the annual surplus of the social security system. (For additional discussion of this topic, see Application 4, "Social Security: The Nature of the Problem and the Alternatives for Dealing with It.")

POLITICAL ECONOMY, DEMOGRAPHICS, AND DEBT FINANCING

Why were budget deficits relatively small—except during periods of war—prior to 1960? Why did the United States run perpetual deficits during the 1960–1990 period? Why have deficits shrunk during the 1990s? These are complex questions, and there is reason to believe the answers lie in politics and demographics as well as economics.

Prior to 1960, almost everyone—including the leading figures of both political parties—thought that the government should balance its budget except perhaps during times of war. In essence, there was widespread implicit agreement—much like a constitutional rule—that the federal budget should be balanced. The Keynesian analysis changed opinions, first among economists and later among others, including political officials. In essence, the Keynesian view eroded the discipline that emanated from the implicit balanced-budget concept.

Released from that constraint, politicians consistently spent more than they were willing to tax during the period 1960–1990.[5] From a public choice viewpoint, the political attractiveness of spending compared to taxation is not surprising. Spending provides political officials with a means to buy the favor of various interest groups and voting blocs. However, government expenditures must be financed in some manner. Borrowing provides an alternative to current taxation. Because they push the taxes into the future, deficits are less visible to people than is current taxation. Thus, borrowing allows politicians to supply voters with immediate benefits without having to impose a parallel visible cost in the form of higher taxes or user charges.

Furthermore, it was widely believed that budget deficits stimulated demand, output, and employment during the 1960s and 1970s. This also contributed to the deficit spending of that era. By 1990, however, both the stagflation—slow growth and high unemployment—of the 1970s and the integration of expectations into macroeconomic analysis tempered views with regard to the potential of expansionary fiscal policy. Rather than increasing spending and cutting taxes during the 1990 recession, both

[5]See James M. Buchanan and Richard Wagner, *Democracy in Deficit: The Political Legacy of Lord Keynes* (New York: Academic Press, 1977), for a detailed account of the changes wrought by the Keynesian revolution.

Congress and the president sought to reduce the size of the deficit. The proponents of this prescription charged that large deficits were causing high interest rates, which were slowing the economic recovery.

While disenchantment with Keynesian demand stimulus policies contributed to the smaller deficits of the 1990s, there was another factor at work. Demographics were highly favorable to both rapid income growth and lower levels of government spending. During the 1990s, the baby boomers moved into their prime earning years. This helped to reduce the budget deficit in several ways. First, as a larger and larger share of the workforce moves into the peak earning years of life, the growth of income is enhanced and the rate of unemployment reduced. Second, peak earning years are also high-saving years. During the 1990s, a record amount of funds flowed into the bond market, placing downward pressure on interest rates. In turn, the lower interest rates reduced the government's interest cost on its outstanding debt. Finally, the number of taxpayers relative to retirees held steady during this period. These favorable factors helped to reduce the deficit during the 1990s and they are likely to continue through at least the first decade of the new millennium.

However, this situation will begin to shift again around 2015, as the baby boomers begin to move into the retirement phase of life. When this happens, there will be upward pressure on government expenditures for health care and social security, while income growth is likely to slow because of a shrinking share of the workforce in the prime working years of life. Unless major structural changes are undertaken prior to that time, there will likely be strong pressure for larger budget deficits when the baby boomers begin to retire. Therefore, while debt financing may temporarily fade into the background, it will almost surely reemerge as a major issue in the future.

KEY POINTS

➤ The national debt is the sum of the outstanding bonds of the U.S. Treasury. Budget deficits increase the national debt, while surpluses reduce it. The national debt reflects the cumulative effect of all prior budget deficits and surpluses.

➤ Two-fifths of the national debt is owned by U.S. government agencies and Federal Reserve banks. For this portion of the debt, the government both pays and receives the interest (except for the expenses of the Fed). Only the privately held federal debt—the portion of the national debt owned by domestic and foreign investors—generates a net interest obligation for the government.

➤ When considering the impact of the national debt on future generations, one must keep two points in mind. First, the future generations that pay the tax liability accompanying the debt will also receive the interest income implied by the debt. Second, the opportunity cost of resources used by the government is incurred during the current period regardless of how the government activity is financed.

➤ Budget deficits affect future generations through their impact on capital formation.

➤ According to the traditional view, the substitution of debt financing for taxes will increase real interest rates and reduce the rate of capital formation—particularly capital owned by Americans. Thus, the traditional view indicates that future generations are adversely affected.

➤ In contrast with the traditional view, the new classical theory argues that people will increase their saving in anticipation of the higher future taxes implied by additional debt. In the new classical model, the substitution of debt for taxes leaves interest rates, consumption, and investment unaffected.

➤ A large national debt relative to the size of an economy leads to a large tax burden just to pay the interest on the debt. Several countries have larger government debt to GDP ratios than the United States.

➤ Inclusion of social security in the budget calculations makes the deficit appear smaller or the surplus larger than would be true if these funds were omitted.

➤ Sustained economic growth and favorable demographic factors moved the federal budget to surplus in 1998. As the baby-boom generation moves into the retirement phase of their life beginning in 2015, large budget deficits are likely to reemerge.

CRITICAL ANALYSIS QUESTIONS

*1. Does the national debt have to be paid off at some time in the future? What will happen if it is not?

2. Do we owe the national debt to ourselves? Does this mean the size of the national debt is of little concern? Why or why not?

3. "The national debt is a mortgage against the future of our children and grandchildren. We are forcing them to pay for our current consumption of goods and services." Evaluate this statement.

*4. When government bonds are held by foreigners, the interest income from the bonds goes to foreigners rather than to Americans. Would Americans be better off if we prohibited the sale of bonds to foreigners?

5. How is the social security system currently influencing the size of the budget deficit? If it is not reformed, how will social security influence the budget deficit in the years following 2020? Is this a cause for concern? Why or why not?

*6. Would you predict that government expenditures would be higher or lower if taxes (and user charges) were required for the finance of all expenditures? Why? Do you think the government would spend funds more or less efficiently if it could not issue debt? Why?

7. "If the government is spending $20 billion to maintain and improve highways, these costs are incurred during the current period regardless of whether they are financed with taxes or debt." Evaluate this statement.

*8. Does an increase in the national debt increase the supply of money (M1)? Can the money supply increase when the U.S. Treasury is running a budget surplus?

9. Suppose that the federal government ran a sizable budget surplus during the next decade. Compared to balancing the budget, how would this surplus affect interest rates, saving, and investment? Compare and contrast the traditional view and the new classical view.

---

*Asterisk denotes questions for which answers are given in Appendix B.

APPLICATION 3

Inflation does give a stimulus . . . when it starts from a condition that is noninflationary. If the inflation continues, people get adjusted to it. But when people get adjusted to it, when they expect rising prices, the mere occurrence of what has been expected is no longer stimulating.

Sir John R. Hicks[1]

The Phillips Curve: Is There a Trade-off between Inflation and Unemployment?

APPLICATION FOCUS

- What is the Phillips curve?
- Does inflation reduce the unemployment rate?
- Why were the early views about the Phillips curve wrong?
- How did belief in the inflation-unemployment trade-off affect macro policy in the 1960s and 1970s? How did later rejection of the trade-off view affect policy in the 1980s and 1990s?

[1]J. R. Hicks, "Monetary Theory and Keynesian Economics," in *Monetary Theory*, ed. R. W. Clower (Harmondsworth: Penguin, 1969), p. 260.

In an influential article published in 1958, the British economist A. W. Phillips noted that in the United Kingdom there had been an inverse relationship between the rate of change in wages and the unemployment rate for nearly a century.[2] When wages were rising rapidly, unemployment was low. Correspondingly, wage rates rose more slowly when the unemployment rate was high. Others noted that a similar inverse relationship was present between inflation and unemployment during the post–Second World War period in the United States. Because it is based on Phillips's earlier work, a curve indicating the relationship between the rate of inflation and the rate of unemployment is known as the **Phillips curve.**

Phillips curve
A curve that illustrates the relationship between the rate of change in prices (or money wages) and the rate of unemployment.

The views of economists and policy makers with regard to the Phillips curve and the potential of demand stimulus to reduce the rate of unemployment have changed twice during the last four decades. Beginning in the early 1960s, several influential economists argued that there was a trade-off between inflation and unemployment—that a lower rate of unemployment could be achieved if we were willing to tolerate a little more inflation. By the end of the 1960s, there was widespread acceptance of this view. However, both the experience of the 1970s and important developments in economic theory led to another shift in views. By the 1980s, the perceived inflation-unemployment trade-off had lost most of its luster. As views shifted on this topic, so too did macroeconomic policy. This application focuses on the Phillips curve and analyzes the impact of changing views on the topic.

EARLY VIEWS ABOUT THE PHILLIPS CURVE

Phillips did not draw any policy implications from his analysis, but others did. As early as 1959, Paul Samuelson and Robert Solow (each of whom would later win a Nobel Prize in economics) argued that we could trade a little more inflation for less unemployment. Samuelson and Solow told the American Economic Association,

> In order to achieve the nonperfectionist's goal of high enough output to give us no more than 3 percent unemployment, the price index might have to rise by as much as 4 to 5 percent per year. That much price rise [inflation] would seem to be the necessary cost of high employment and production in the years immediately ahead.[3]

The view that expansionary macroeconomic policy could be used to lower the rate of unemployment and achieve a more rapid rate of real economic growth grew in popularity during the 1960s. There was some basis for the view. **Exhibit A3–1,** taken from the 1969 *Economic Report of the President,* illustrates that there was an inverse

[2]A. W. Phillips, "The Relationship between Unemployment and the Rate of Change of Money Wages in the United Kingdom, 1861–1957," *Economica* 25 (1958): 238–299.

[3]Paul A. Samuelson and Robert Solow, "Our Menu of Policy Changes," *American Economic Review* (May 1960).

EXHIBIT A3–1

THE PHILLIPS CURVE—BEFORE THE INFLATION OF THE 1970s

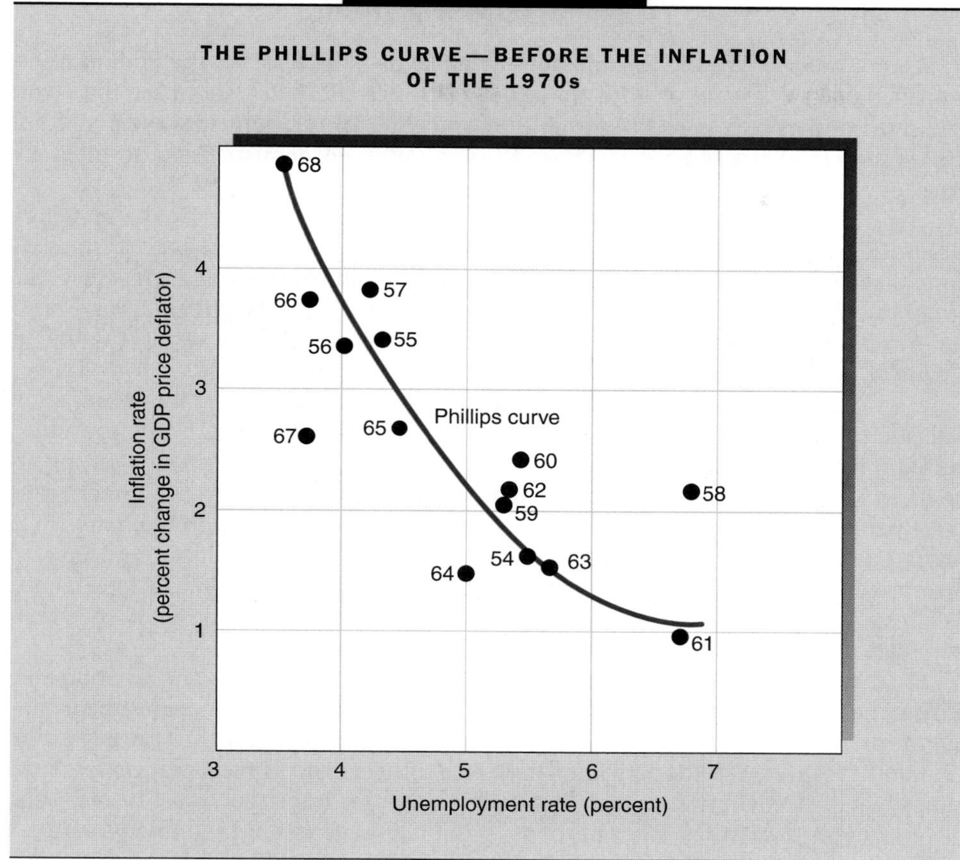

This exhibit is from the 1969 Economic Report of the President, *prepared by the president's Council of Economic Advisers. Each dot on the diagram indicates, as a coordinate point on the graph, the inflation rate and unemployment rate for the year. The report stated that the chart "reveals a fairly close association of more rapid price increases with lower rates of unemployment." Economists refer to this link as the Phillips curve. In the 1960s it was widely believed that policy makers could pursue expansionary macroeconomic policies and thereby permanently reduce the unemployment rate. More recent experience has caused most economists to reject this view.*

SOURCE: Economic Report of the President, 1969, *p. 95. The Phillips curve is fitted to the points to illustrate the relationship.*

relationship between inflation and unemployment during the 1954–1968 period. At the time, most economists thought the inflation-unemployment relationship was stable. In other words, they believed that expansionary policies would lead to some inflation, but would also lead to a long-lasting lower rate of unemployment.[4]

Influenced by the Phillips curve analysis, both monetary and fiscal policy were more expansionary during the latter half of the 1960s. For a while, it seemed that the demand-stimulus policies were yielding the expected result. As Exhibit A3–1 shows, the higher inflation rates of the late 1960s were associated with lower rates of unemployment. However, things began to change in the 1970s. As the inflation rate rose from 3 percent in the late 1960s to double-digit levels during 1974–1975, the rate of unemployment rose from less than 4 percent to more than 8 percent. As high rates of inflation continued in the latter half of the 1970s, so too did the high rates of unemployment. In contrast with the predictions of the early Phillips curve proponents, the United States experienced high rates of both inflation and unemployment throughout most of the 1970s.

[4]Not all economists accepted the view that there was a trade-off between inflation and unemployment. At the height of its popularity, the theoretical underpinning of the alleged trade-off was independently challenged by both Edmund Phelps and Milton Friedman. See Edmund S. Phelps, "Phillips Curves, Expectations of Inflation and Optimal Employment over Time," *Economica* 3 (1967): 254–281; and Milton Friedman, "The Role of Monetary Policy," *American Economic Review* (May 1968): 1–17.

Error of Early Phillips Curve Proponents: Failure to Consider Expectations

What went wrong? Why did the inflation-unemployment forecasts of the Phillips curve proponents prove so faulty? With the benefit of hindsight, it is easy to see the error: The early Phillips curve proponents failed to integrate expectations into their analysis. Building on the work of an early paper by John Muth, economists began to integrate expectations into their analysis during the 1970s.[5]

How do expectations affect the Phillips curve analysis? Suppose the monetary authorities unexpectedly shift to a more expansionary policy. As our basic macroeconomic model indicates, the more expansionary policy will stimulate aggregate demand. When the increase in demand is unanticipated, the initial effects will be upward pressure on prices and increases in both output and employment. As a result, the unemployment rate will fall.

There are two reasons why an unanticipated increase in the rate of inflation will stimulate employment and reduce the rate of unemployment. First, the unexpected inflation will reduce the real wages of workers employed under long-term contracts and thereby stimulate employment. Union wage contracts and other wage agreements often determine money-wage rates over periods ranging from one to three years. Unanticipated inflation means that the impact of strong demand and upward pressure on prices has not been fully factored into long-term money-wage agreements. As a result, an unexpected increase in the inflation rate will reduce the employee's real-wage rate and the employer's real-wage costs.

Suppose that employees and employers anticipate a 4 percent inflation rate during the next year. From this, they concur on a collective bargaining agreement calling for money wages of $10 during the current year and $10.40 for the year beginning 12 months from now. If the actual inflation rate this year equals the 4 percent expected rate, the $10.40 money-wage rate 12 months from now translates to a $10 real-wage rate *at today's price level.* What happens to the real-wage rate if the inflation rate exceeds the expected rate of 4 percent? If actual inflation during the next 12 months is 8 percent, for example, the real-wage rate one year from now will fall to $9.63 at current prices. The higher the actual inflation rate is, the lower the real wages of the employees. Unanticipated inflation tends to reduce the real-wage rates of employees whose money wages are fixed by long-term contracts. At the lower real-wage rate, firms will hire more workers and employment will expand.

There is a second reason why underestimation of the inflation rate will tend to expand employment. Misled by inflation, some job seekers will quickly accept job offers on the basis of a mistaken belief that the offers are particularly good ones in relation to the market for their labor services. When people underestimate the extent to which inflation has increased both prices and money wages, many job seekers will fail to recognize how much nominal wages have increased in their skill category. Unaware of just how much their money-wage opportunities have improved, they will tend to accept offers that are not as good as they think they are (relative to jobs that could be found with additional search). Unemployed workers thus shorten their search time, which lowers the unemployment rate.

To summarize, unanticipated (or underestimated) inflation reduces the real-wage rate of workers whose money wages are determined by long-term contracts and reduces the search time of job seekers. Both of these factors will expand employment and reduce the unemployment rate below its natural rate.

---

[5]The leading contributors to the integration of expectations in macroeconomics are Robert Barro of Harvard, Robert Lucas of the University of Chicago, and Thomas Sargent of the University of Minnesota.

However, once the importance of expectations is considered, it is clear that the lower rate of unemployment will only be temporary. With time, people will anticipate the higher rate of inflation and adjust their decision making accordingly. The adaptive expectations theory implies that there will be a significant time lag—perhaps one to three years—before people are able to anticipate and adjust to the higher rate of inflation. The rational expectations theory indicates that many will foresee the effects of policy changes and therefore alter their choices more quickly. Both theories of expectations, however, imply that individuals will eventually anticipate the higher rate of inflation and adjust their behavior in light of it.

Once the higher rate of inflation is anticipated, workers and their union representatives will demand and employers will agree to money-wage increases that reflect the higher current and expected future inflation rate. Similarly, job seekers will become fully aware of the extent that inflation has increased (and continues to increase) their money-wage alternatives. As they do so, their search time will return to normal. ***Once decision makers fully anticipate the higher rate of inflation and reflect it in their choices, the inflation rate will neither depress real-wage rates nor reduce the search time of job seekers. As this happens, both real output and unemployment will return to their natural (long-run) rates.***

Exhibit A3–2 uses our aggregate-demand/aggregate-supply (*AD/AS*) model to illustrate the implications of adaptive expectations with regard to the Phillips curve analysis. Beginning from a position of stable prices and long-run equilibrium (point *A*), part a of Exhibit A3–2 illustrates the impact of an unanticipated increase in aggregate demand. Initially the demand stimulus will increase output (to Y_2) and employment. The unemployment rate will recede below the economy's natural rate. The strong demand and tight resource markets will place upward pressure on resource prices. *For a time,* the economy will experience both rising prices and an output beyond full-employment capacity (point *B*). This high level of output, however, will not be long-lasting. People will eventually anticipate the rising prices (inflation). When this happens, resource prices and costs will rise (from their temporary low levels) relative to product prices, causing the *SRAS* curve to shift to the left. As the previous relationship between resource prices and product prices is restored, output will recede to the economy's full-employment level (point *C*). If the rising prices continue at the same rate, they will be anticipated by decision makers. When this is the case, both the *AD* and *SRAS* curves will continually shift upward (the dotted curves of part a). The price level will steadily increase, but output and employment will remain at the full-employment level.

Part b of Exhibit A3–2 illustrates the same case within the Phillips curve framework. Because initially stable prices are present and the economy is in long-run equilibrium, unemployment is equal to its natural rate (point *A*). We assume that the economy's natural rate of unemployment is 5 percent. The condition of long-run equilibrium implies that the stable prices are both anticipated and observed. Under adaptive expectations, an unanticipated shift to a more expansionary policy will temporarily increase output and reduce unemployment. It will also place upward pressure on prices. Suppose that demand-stimulus policies lead to 4 percent inflation and a reduction in the unemployment rate from 5 percent to 3 percent (moving from *A* to *B* along the short-run Phillips curve PC_1). Although point *B* is attainable, it will not be sustainable. After a period of time, decision makers will begin to anticipate the 4 percent rate of inflation. Workers and their union representatives will take the higher expected rate of inflation into account in their job search and collective bargaining decision making. Once the 4 percent rate of inflation is anticipated, the economy will confront a new, higher short-run Phillips curve (PC_2). The rate of unemployment will return to the long-run natural rate of 5 percent, even though prices will continue to rise at an annual rate of 4 percent (point *C*).

EXHIBIT A3–2

AD/AS MODEL, ADAPTIVE EXPECTATIONS, AND PHILLIPS CURVE

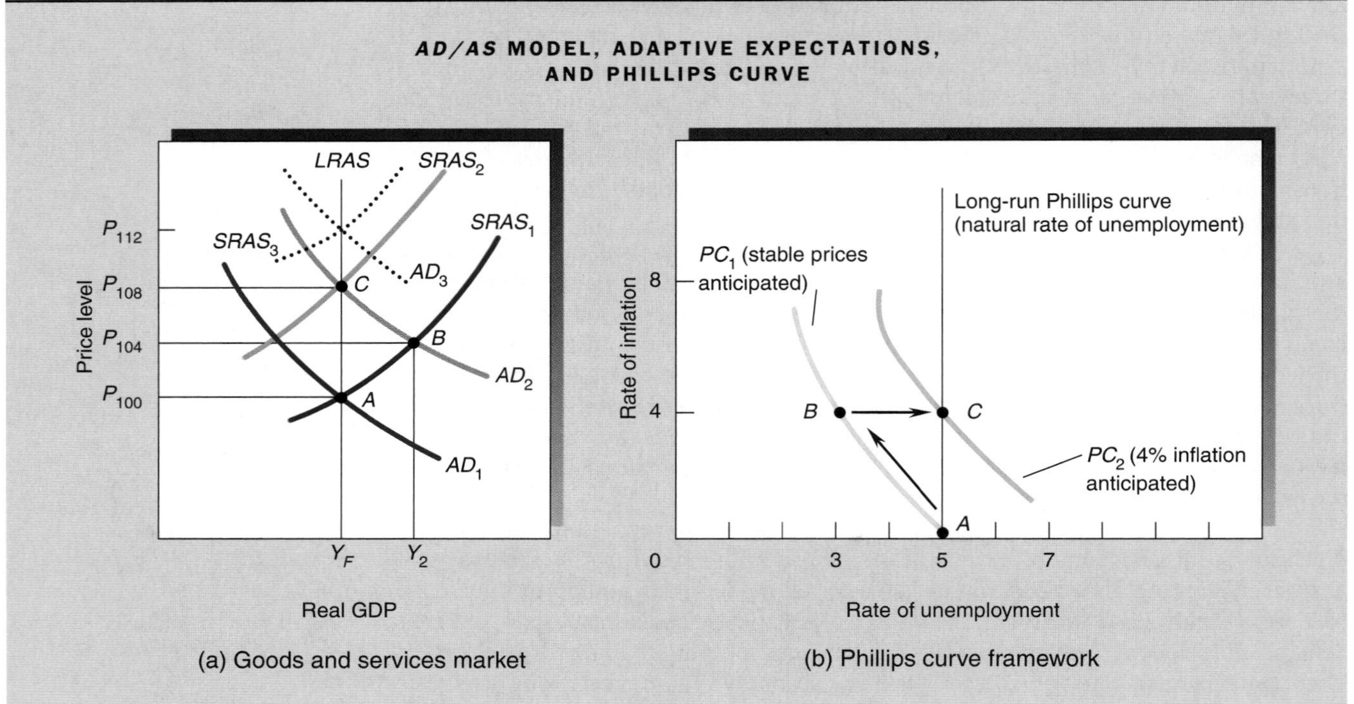

(a) Goods and services market

(b) Phillips curve framework

When stable prices are observed and *anticipated, both full-employment output and the natural rate of unemployment will be present (*A *in both panels). With adaptive expectations, a shift to a more expansionary policy will increase prices, expand output beyond its full-employment potential, and reduce the unemployment rate below its natural level (move from* A *to* B *in both panels). Decision makers, though, will eventually anticipate the rising prices and incorporate them into their decision making. When this happens, the* SRAS *curve shifts to the left, output recedes to the economy's full-employment potential, and unemployment returns to the natural rate (move from* B *to* C *in both panels). As the inflationary policy continues and decision makers anticipate it, both the* AD *and* SRAS *curves will continually shift upward (dotted* AD *and* SRAS *curves in panel a) without leading to an increase in output and employment. Inflation fails to expand output and reduce the unemployment rate when it is anticipated. Thus, the long-run Phillips curve is vertical at the natural rate of unemployment.*

The moves from point A to point B in both panels of Exhibit A3–2 are simply alternative ways of representing the same phenomenon—a temporary increase in output and reduction in unemployment as the result of an unanticipated increase in aggregate demand. Similarly, the moves from point B to point C in the two panels both represent the return of output to its long-run potential and unemployment to its natural rate, once decision makers anticipate fully the observed rate of inflation.

What would happen if the macro planners attempted to keep the unemployment rate low (below its natural rate) by shifting to a still more expansionary policy? As **Exhibit A3–3** illustrates, this course of action would accelerate the inflation rate to still higher levels. For a time, people may continue to anticipate only the 4 percent rate of inflation. If so, the higher 8 percent rate of inflation will lead to another temporary reduction in unemployment (movement from C to D). Of course, once the 8 percent rate persists for a while, it too will be fully anticipated. The short-run Phillips curve will again shift to the right (to PC_3), unemployment will return to its long-run natural rate, and inflation will continue at a rate of 8 percent (point E).

EXHIBIT A3–3

EXPECTATIONS AND SHIFTS IN THE PHILLIPS CURVE

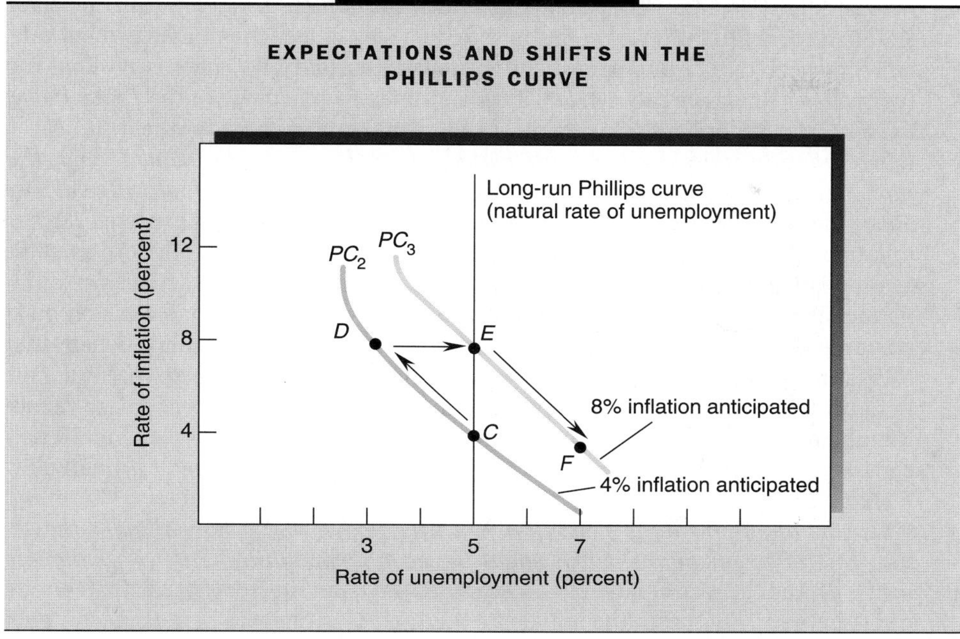

Continuing with the example of Exhibit A3–2, part b, point C *illustrates an economy experiencing 4 percent inflation that was anticipated by decision makers. Because the inflation was anticipated, the natural rate of unemployment is present. With adaptive expectations, demand-stimulus policies that result in a still higher rate of inflation (8 percent, for example) would once again temporarily reduce the unemployment rate below its long-run, normal level (move from* C *to* D *along* PC_2*). After a time, however, decision makers would come to anticipate the higher inflation rate, and the short-run Phillips curve would shift still farther to the right to* PC_3 *(move from* D *to* E*). Once the higher rate is anticipated, if macro planners try to decelerate the rate of inflation, unemployment will temporarily rise above its long-run natural rate (for example, move from* E *to* F*).*

Once decision makers anticipate a high rate of inflation (for example, the 8 percent rate), what will happen if macro planners shift to a more restrictive policy designed to bring the inflation under control? Suppose that wage rates are based on agreements that anticipated a continuation of the 8 percent inflation rate (point *E* of Exhibit A3–3). If the actual inflation rate falls to 4 percent when 8 percent inflation was expected, the real wages of workers will exceed the real wage present when the actual and expected rates of inflation were equal at 8 percent. The more the actual inflation rate falls short of the expected rate, the higher the real wages of workers will be. Similarly, the search time of job seekers will increase when they overestimate the impact of inflation on money-wage rates. Unaware that the attractive money-wage offers they seek are unavailable, job hunters will lengthen their job search. In the short run, rising unemployment will be a side effect of the higher real wages and more lengthy job searches.

As Exhibit A3–3 illustrates, an anticipated shift to a more restrictive policy designed to reduce the inflation rate will cause abnormally high unemployment (the move from *E* to *F* along PC_3) and economic recession. The abnormally high unemployment rate will continue until a lower rate of inflation convinces decision makers to alter their inflationary expectations downward and revise long-term contracts accordingly.

EXPECTATIONS AND THE MODERN VIEW OF THE PHILLIPS CURVE

Expectations substantially alter the naive Phillips curve view of the 1960s. Three major points follow from the integration of expectations into the Phillips curve analysis.

1. ***Demand stimulus will lead to inflation without permanently reducing unemployment below the natural rate.*** Once people fully anticipate the inflationary side

effects of expansionary policies, resource prices will rise, profit margins will return to normal levels, and unemployment will return to its natural rate. An unanticipated shift to a more expansionary policy may temporarily reduce the unemployment rate, but the lower rate of unemployment will not be sustainable. There is no long-run (permanent) trade-off between inflation and unemployment. Like the *LRAS* curve, the long-run Phillips curve is vertical at the natural rate of unemployment.

2. ***When inflation is greater than anticipated, unemployment falls below the natural rate. Conversely, when inflation is less than expected, unemployment will rise above the natural rate.*** It is the *difference* between the actual and expected rates of inflation that influences unemployment, not the magnitude of inflation, as some economists previously thought. When people underestimate the actual rate of inflation, abnormally low unemployment will occur. Conversely, when decision makers expect a higher rate of inflation than what actually occurs—when they overestimate the inflation rate—unemployment will rise above its natural rate. Equal changes in the actual and expected inflation rates, though, will fail to reduce the unemployment rate. If actual inflation rates of 5 percent, 10 percent, 20 percent, or even higher are accurately anticipated, they will fail to reduce unemployment below its natural rate.[6]
3. ***When the inflation rate is steady—when it is neither rising nor falling—the actual rate of unemployment will equal the economy's natural rate of unemployment.*** If the inflation rate of an economy is constant (or approximately so), decision makers will come to anticipate the rate. This rate will be reflected in both long-term contracts and the job search of workers. Once this happens, unemployment will return to its natural rate. In fact, the natural rate of unemployment is sometimes defined as the unemployment rate present when the inflation rate is neither rising nor falling.

EXPECTATIONS, INFLATION, AND UNEMPLOYMENT: THE EMPIRICAL EVIDENCE

Integration of expectations into the Phillips curve analysis helps clarify the U.S. data on inflation and unemployment during the last several decades. After nearly 20 years of low inflation (and moderate monetary and fiscal policy) following the Second World War, decision makers, accustomed to relative price stability, expected low rates of inflation. As a result, the shift toward expansionary policies in the mid-1960s caught people by surprise.[7] Therefore, as Exhibit A3–1 shows, these policies initially reduced the unemployment rate.

Contrary to the popular view of the 1960s, though, the abnormally low unemployment rate could not be sustained. **Exhibit A3–4,** which is an updated version of

[6]Empirically, higher rates of inflation are generally associated with greater variability in the inflation rate. Erratic variability increases economic uncertainty. It is likely to inhibit business activity, reduce the volume of mutually advantageous exchange, and cause the level of employment to fall. Thus, higher, more variable inflation rates may actually increase the rate of unemployment.

[7]The following data are indicative of the shift toward more expansionary macroeconomic policies beginning in the mid-1960s. Between 1965 and 1980, the M1 money supply grew at an annual rate of 6.3 percent, compared to only 2.5 percent during the previous 15 years. Similarly, perpetual federal deficits replaced balanced budgets. During the 1950–1965 period, there were eight budget deficits and seven surpluses. On average, the federal budget was approximately in balance during this 15-year period. In contrast, there was only one year of budget surplus and annual deficits averaged 1.5 percent of GDP during the 1965–1980 period.

EXHIBIT A3–4

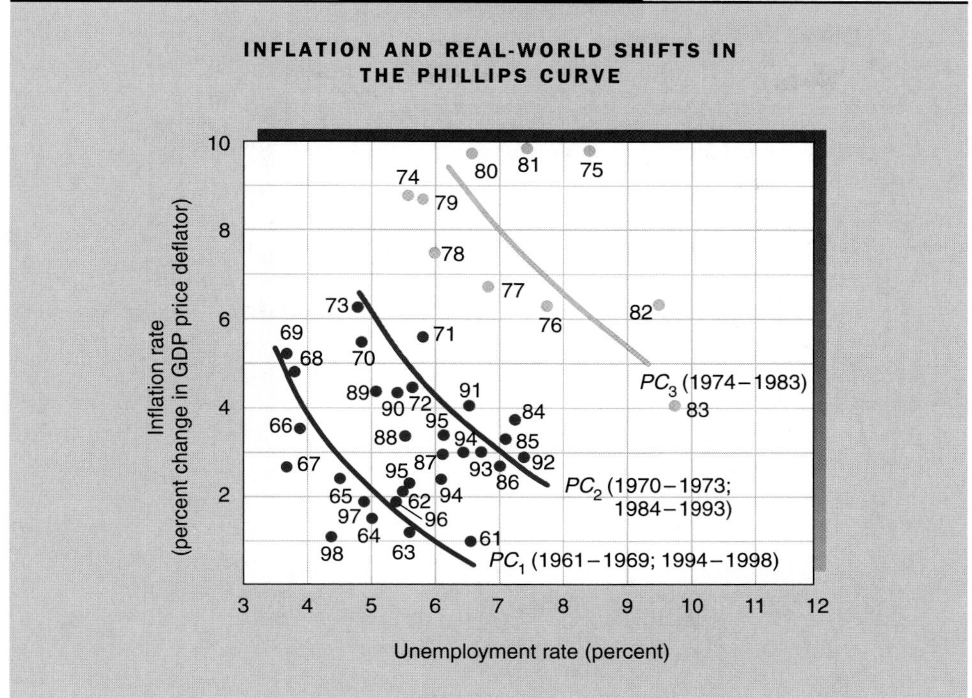

While the 1961–1969 unemployment-inflation data mapped Phillips curve PC$_1$ *(see Exhibit A3–1), as demand-stimulus policies led to higher inflation rates, the Phillips curve shifted outward to* PC$_2$ *(for the 1970–1973 period) and* PC$_3$ *(for the 1974–1983 period). Just as our theories of expectations indicate, the high rates of inflation failed to reduce permanently the rate of unemployment. Similarly, as lower rates of inflation were achieved and eventually anticipated, the Phillips curve shifted inward. By 1994–1998, the position of the Phillips curve was similar to its position during the 1960s.*

SOURCE: Economic Report of the President, 1999.

Exhibit A3–1, makes this point clear. Just as our theory predicts, the inflation-unemployment conditions worsened substantially as the expansionary policy persisted. The Phillips curve consistent with the 1970–1973 data (PC_2) was well to the right of PC_1. During the 1974–1983 period, still higher rates of inflation were observed. As inflation rates in the 6 percent to 10 percent range became commonplace in the latter half of the 1970s, the Phillips curve once again shifted upward, to PC_3.

As monetary policy tightened in 1981–1983 and the Reagan administration promised to bring inflation under control, the inflation rate decelerated sharply. Just as our theory predicts, initially the unemployment rate soared, to 9.7 percent in 1982 and 9.6 percent in 1983, when macroeconomic policy shifted toward restraint. As the restraint continued, the inflation rate declined from the high rates of the late 1970s to the 2.5 percent to 4.5 percent range during 1984–1993. Soon after the decline in inflation, people scaled their expectations for the inflation rate downward, and the Phillips curve shifted inward (from PC_3 to PC_2). As low rates of inflation were maintained, the 1994–1998 Phillips curve appears to be in a position quite similar to that of the 1960s.

The modern view indicates that it is the difference between the actual and expected rates of inflation that will influence the rate of unemployment. Abrupt changes in the inflation rate are less likely to be correctly anticipated. **Exhibit A3–5** presents data on changes in the annual rate (12-month moving average) of inflation and the rate of unemployment. As the graph shows, there were sharp reductions in the rate of inflation during 1975, 1981–1982, and 1991. For example, the inflation rate fell from 12.4 percent in 1974 to 6.9 percent in 1975, a drop of more than 5 percentage points. Decision makers are likely to underestimate the magnitude of such sharp reductions in the inflation rate. When this is the case, the actual rate of inflation will be less than the

EXHIBIT A3–5

CHANGES IN THE RATE OF INFLATION AND UNEMPLOYMENT

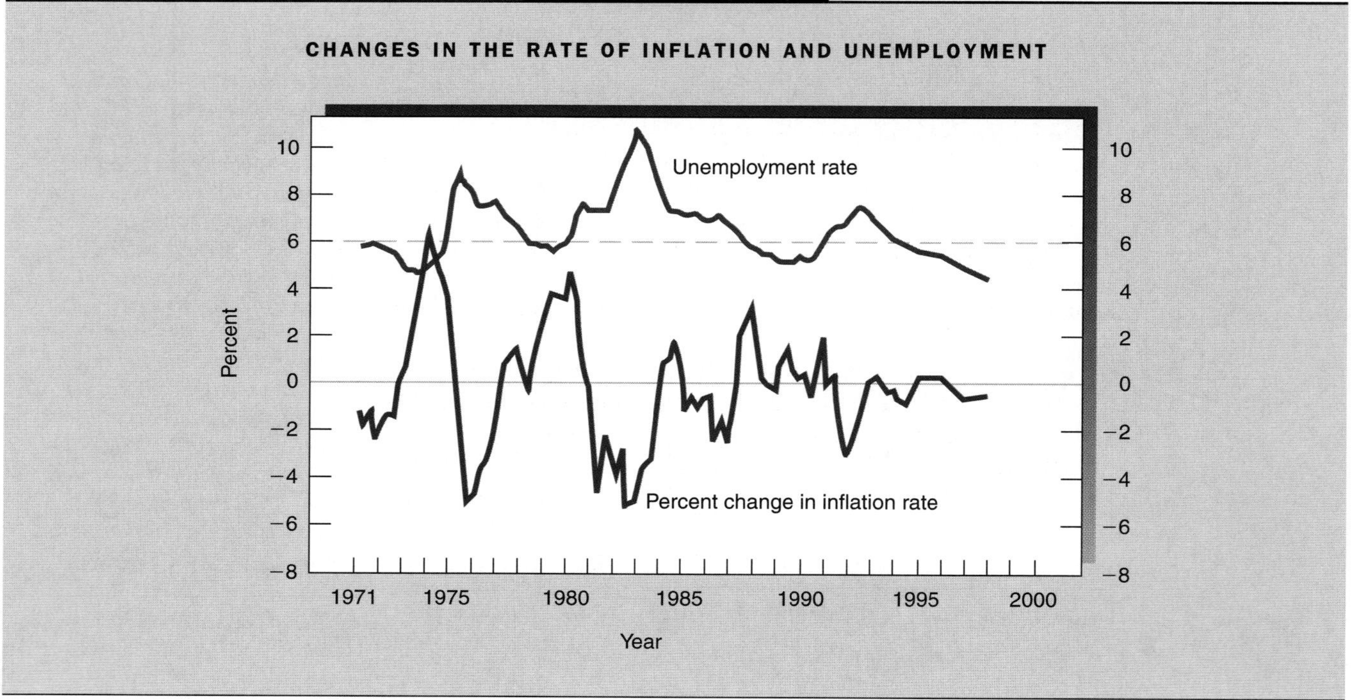

Here we illustrate the relationship between changes *in the rate of inflation (this year's inflation rate minus the rate during the preceding year) and the rate of unemployment. Note how the sharp reductions in the rate of inflation during 1975, 1981–1982, and 1991 were associated with recession and substantial increases in the unemployment rate. In contrast, the low and steady inflation rates of 1992–1998 led to low rates of unemployment.*

SOURCE: Economic Report of the President, 1999.

expected rate. Under these circumstances, our analysis indicates that unemployment will rise above its natural rate. As Exhibit A3–5 shows, the unemployment rate rose substantially in response to the steep declines in the rate of inflation during 1975, 1981–1982, and again in 1991. In contrast, during the period 1993–1998, the year-to-year differences in the inflation rate were quite small. The unemployment rate declined during this period of low (and steady) inflation. By the late 1990s, most observers estimated that unemployment in the United States was approximately equal to the natural rate.

THE PHILLIPS CURVE AND MACRO POLICY

The evolution of views with regard to the Phillips curve illustrates how ideas—even when they are wrong—can influence policy. As we noted, in the 1960s and 1970s, most economists thought that there was a trade-off between inflation and unemployment. If a little inflation would stimulate output and reduce the unemployment rate, why not follow this course? After all, inflation only influences the nominal value of things, whereas changes in real output and employment affect real incomes and living standards. Arguments along these lines provided the foundation for the more expansionary macro policy of the 1970s.

By 1980, however, things were shifting the other way. Both the experience of the 1970s and the integration of expectations into numerous areas of economics, including the Phillips curve analysis, had convinced many economists that the earlier view of the Phillips curve was fallacious. In the 1980s most believed that even if a trade-off did exist between inflation and unemployment, it would not last long. Thus, attempting to exploit the questionable trade-off would be shortsighted.

Once again, there was an impact on policy. Key monetary policy makers, such as Fed Chairmen Paul Volcker and Alan Greenspan, sought to achieve low and steady rates of inflation. In contrast with earlier recessions, Congress did not attempt to enlarge the budget deficit and stimulate the economy during the 1990 recession. In fact, taxes were increased and spending restrained in an effort to reduce the size of the deficit. Rather than demand stimulus, macro policy has focused on price stability and deficit reduction since the mid-1980s.

Interestingly, the pursuit of more expansionary policies during the era when most believed in the inflation-unemployment trade-off led to higher rates of both inflation and unemployment. **Exhibit A3–6** highlights this point. The average annual rate of inflation rose during the 1970s, but so too did the average rate of unemployment. As the dream of the inflation-unemployment trade-off dissipated, policy

EXHIBIT A3–6

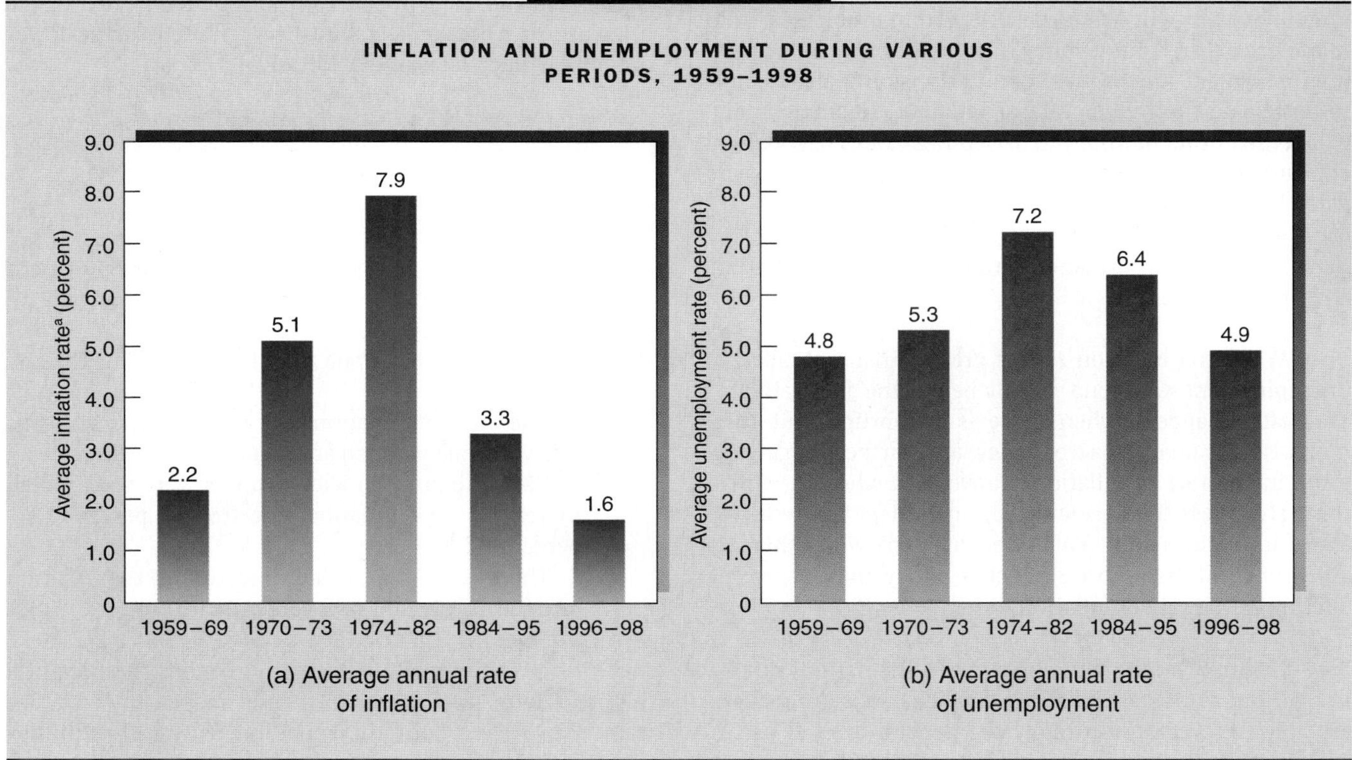

When more expansionary policies were pursued during the 1970–1973 and 1974–1982 periods, higher rates of both inflation and unemployment occurred. In contrast, lower rates of unemployment have accompanied the lower inflation rates of the more recent periods. There is no conflict between price stability and low unemployment.

[a] *Measured by the changes in the GDP deflator.*

SOURCE: Economic Report of the President, 1999. *The GDP deflator was used to measure the rate of inflation.*

makers—particularly those in the monetary area—shifted their emphasis toward the achievement of price stability. Paradoxically, as they did so, the unemployment rate fell.[8]

There are two important lessons to be learned from the Phillips curve era. First, expansionary macro policy will not reduce the rate of unemployment, at least not for long. Efforts to use it in this manner will lead to higher rates of both inflation and unemployment. Second, macro policy, particularly monetary policy, can achieve persistently low rates of inflation. In turn, the stable and predictable price-level environment will help promote low rates of unemployment. There is no inconsistency between low (and stable) rates of inflation and low rates of unemployment.

KEY POINTS

➤ The Phillips curve indicates the relationship between the unemployment rate and inflation rate. Prior to the late 1970s, it was widely believed that higher inflation would lower the rate of unemployment.

➤ Integration of expectations into the Phillips curve analysis indicates that any trade-off between inflation and unemployment will be short-lived. An unanticipated shift to a more expansionary policy may temporarily reduce the unemployment rate, but as soon as decision makers come to anticipate the higher rate of inflation, unemployment will return to its natural rate. Even high rates of inflation will fail to reduce unemployment once they are anticipated by decision makers.

➤ There is no permanent trade-off between inflation and unemployment.

➤ When the inflation rate is greater than anticipated, unemployment will tend to fall below the natural rate. This often happens when there is an abrupt shift to a more expansionary macro policy and an accompanying jump in the rate of inflation. Conversely, when the inflation rate is less than anticipated, unemployment will rise above its natural rate. This often happens when there is an abrupt shift to a more restrictive policy and a sharp reduction in the rate of inflation.

➤ Unemployment will move toward the natural rate—its minimum sustainable rate—when decision makers are able to forecast accurately the general level of prices and integrate it into their decision making. Because predictably low rates of inflation will be easier for people to forecast accurately, they will lead to low rates of unemployment.

➤ The early inflation-unemployment trade-off view helped promote the more expansionary macro policy of the 1970s. In contrast, the rejection of the inflation-unemployment trade-off during the 1980s created an environment more conducive to price stability. In turn, the increase in price-level stability contributed to the lower unemployment rates of the 1990s.

CRITICAL ANALYSIS QUESTIONS

1. How would you expect the actual unemployment rate to compare with the natural unemployment rate in the following cases?
   a. Prices are stable and have been stable for the last four years.
   b. The current inflation rate is 3 percent, and this rate was widely anticipated more than a year ago.
   c. Expansionary policies lead to an unexpected increase in the inflation rate from 3 percent to 7 percent.
   d. There is an unexpected reduction in the inflation rate from 7 percent to 2 percent.

*2. Prior to the mid-1970s, many economists thought a higher rate of unemployment would reduce the inflation rate. Why? How does the modern view of the Phillips curve differ from the earlier view?

[8]Youthful workers generally have higher rates of unemployment than their older counterparts. Therefore, as we noted in Chapter 8, the natural rate of unemployment will tend to rise when youthful workers comprise a larger share of the labor force. Youthful workers rose as a share of the labor force during the 1970s and declined during the 1990s. This factor also contributed to the higher unemployment rates during the earlier time period and lower rates of more recent years.

3. If policy makers think that demand stimulus policies will reduce the unemployment rate, how is this likely to influence macro policy? Would you expect acceptance of this view to lead to a more or less expansionary macro policy prior to major elections, such as those for president in the United States? Why or why not?

4. How did integration of expectations into the Phillips curve analysis and rejection of the view that higher inflation will reduce the unemployment rate affect macro policy in the 1990s?

*5. Explain what happens to real wages, the job-search time of workers, and the unemployment rate when unanticipated inflation occurs. What happens when the inflation is anticipated?

---

*Asterisk denotes questions for which answers are given in Appendix B.

APPLICATION 4

The federal government's handling of [social security] pension monies is very different from that of private pension plans.

Mark Weinberger[1]

Social Security: The Nature of the Problem and the Alternatives for Dealing with It

APPLICATION FOCUS

- Why is social security headed for problems?
- Will the Social Security Trust Fund lighten the tax burden of future generations?
- How does the social security system impact young workers and women?
- What are the alternatives to the current system?

[1]Mark Weinberger, *Social Security: Facing the Facts* (Washington, D.C.: Cato Institute, 1996), p. 2.

The social security program in the United States is officially known as Old Age and Survivors Insurance (OASI). It offers protection against the loss of income that usually accompanies old age or the death of a breadwinner. In spite of its official title, social security is not based on principles of insurance. Private insurance and pension programs invest the current payments of customers in buildings, farms, or other real assets. Alternatively, they buy stocks and bonds that finance the development of real assets. These real assets generate income that allows the pension fund (or insurance company) to fulfill its future obligations to its customers.

Social security does not follow this saving-and-investment model. Instead, most of the funds flowing into the system are paid out to current retirees and survivors in the program. In essence, the social security system is an intergenerational income-transfer program. Most of the taxes collected from the present generation of workers are paid out to current beneficiaries.

The social security retirement program is financed by a payroll tax of 6.2 percent levied on both the employee and the employer. (Additional payroll taxes finance

EXHIBIT A4-1

WORKERS PER SOCIAL SECURITY BENEFICIARY

1950

1998

2025

In 1950, there were 16 workers per social security beneficiary. By 1998, the figure had fallen to only 3.1. By 2025, there will be only 2 workers per retiree. As the worker/beneficiary ratio falls under a pay-as-you-go system, either taxes must be increased or benefits reduced (or both).

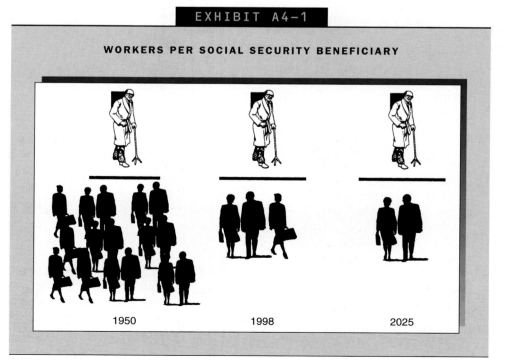

SOURCE: 1995 Annual Report of the Board of Trustees of the Federal Old Age and Survivors Insurance and Disability Insurance Trust Funds *(Washington, D.C.: Government Printing Office, 1995), p. 122.*

Medicare and disability programs, which are sometimes considered part of the social security program.) Therefore, the total tax for the social security retirement program is equal to 12.4 percent of employee earnings. In 1998, the tax applied to all employee earnings up to $65,400. Thus, employees earning $65,400 or more paid $8,110 (counting both employee and employer payments) in social security taxes to finance the OASI retirement program that year.

When the program began in 1935, the nation had lots of workers and few eligible retirees. As **Exhibit A4–1** illustrates, there were 16 workers for every social security beneficiary as recently as 1950. That ratio has declined sharply through the years. As a result, higher and higher taxes per worker have been required just to maintain a constant level of benefits. In 1998, there were 3.1 workers per retiree. By 2025, there will be only two workers per social security beneficiary.

Today's retirees typically receive real benefits of three or four times the amount they paid into the system, equivalent to a rate of return of more than 20 percent—far better than they could have done had they invested the funds privately. In contrast, studies indicate the workers now paying for these large benefits will not do nearly as well. For example, those now at age 35 can expect to earn a real rate of return of about 2 percent on their social security tax dollars, substantially less than what they could earn from personal investments. For two-earner couples just entering the labor force, the expected return from social security taxes is negative. ***Thus, social security has been a good deal for current and past retirees. It is not, however, a very good deal for younger workers. Workers now entering the labor force would be better off if they could invest their social security tax dollars privately.***

WHY IS SOCIAL SECURITY HEADED FOR PROBLEMS?

During the 15 years following the Second World War, the birthrate in the United States was very high. The baby boomers are now in their prime working years and their large numbers are an important factor explaining why the revenues from the social security tax currently exceed the expenditures. However, when these baby boomers move into the retirement phase of their life, the situation is going to change dramatically.

As we previously noted, the number of workers per social security retiree will fall from the current 3.1 level to only 2.0 in 2025. As **Exhibit A4–2** shows, there are now approximately 25 million persons age 70 and over in the United States. By 2030, the number of septuagenarians will soar to 47.8 million. This increase will be particularly sharp beginning around 2010. The medical expenditures of persons 70 years and over are considerably higher than those of persons a few years younger. Thus, these demographic changes will place strong pressure on the Medicare program as well as the social security retirement system.

Exhibit A4–3 shows how these demographic factors will influence the expenditures and tax revenues of the current pay-as-you-go social security retirement system. The current surplus of revenues from the payroll tax relative to retirement benefits will dissipate around 2014. The deficits will grow larger and larger as the number of beneficiaries relative to workers continues to grow throughout the 2020s and 2030s.

Between 2000 and 2030, the number of persons age 70 years and over will almost double. The medical expenses of persons in this age group are particularly high. Thus, this will place strong pressure on both the social security and Medicare programs.

SOURCES: Bipartisan Commission on Entitlement and Tax Reform, Final Report to the President *(Washington, D.C.: Government Printing Office, 1995), p. 13; and* 1995 Annual Report of the Board of Trustees of the Federal Old Age and Survivors Insurance and Disability Insurance Trust Funds, *p. 21.*

EXHIBIT A4-2

THE INCREASE IN THE NUMBER OF PEOPLE AGE 70 AND OVER

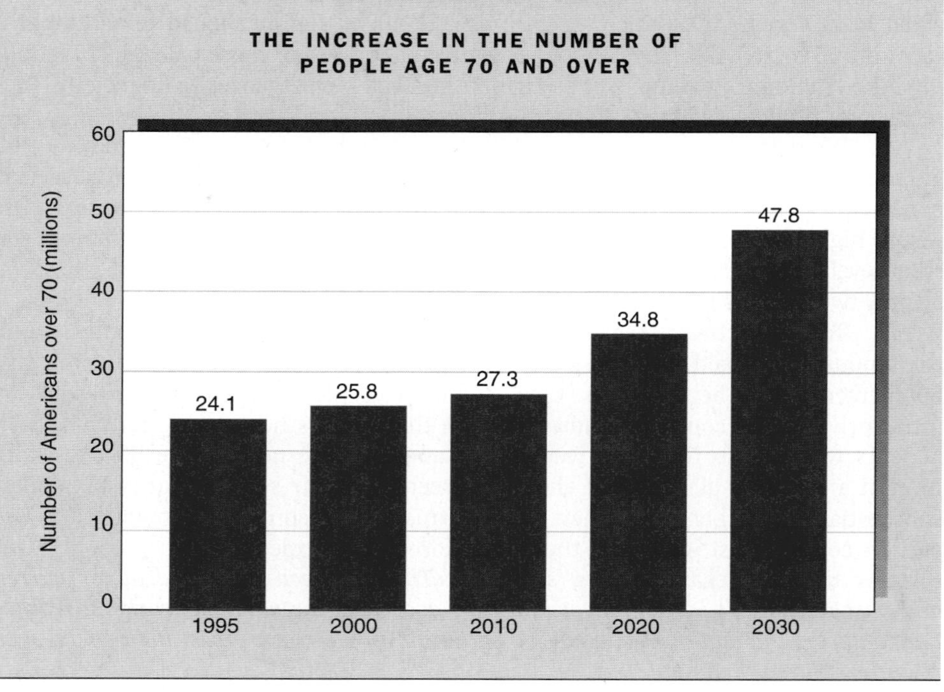

Given current payroll taxes and retirement benefit levels, the system will run larger and larger deficits during the 2014–2030 period.

SOURCE: Bipartisan Commission on Entitlement and Tax Reform, Final Report to the President *(Washington, D.C.: Government Printing Office, 1995), p. 22.*

EXHIBIT A4-3

THE FORTHCOMING DEFICIT BETWEEN PAYROLL TAX REVENUES AND BENEFIT EXPENDITURES

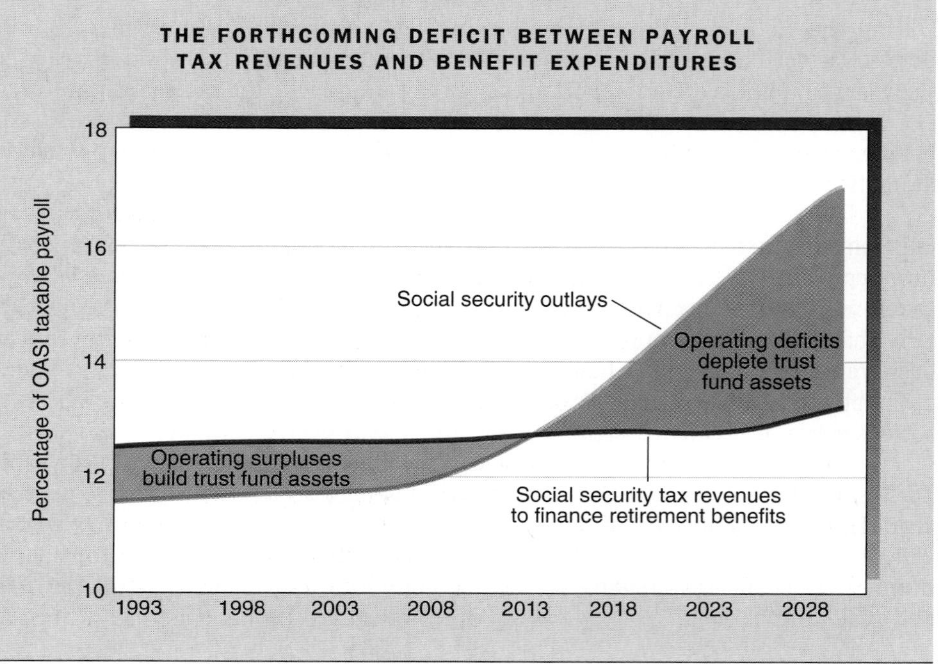

WILL THE TRUST FUND LIGHTEN THE FUTURE TAX BURDEN?

Since the mid-1980s, the revenues derived from the payroll tax have exceeded the benefits paid to current retirees. Currently, only about 80 percent of the revenues are required for the payments to current beneficiaries. Thus, the system is running a substantial surplus—about $100 billion per year. A sizable surplus is expected in the decade ahead. Under current law, the surplus is channeled into the Social Security Trust Fund (SSTF). The trust funds are used to purchase U.S. Treasury bonds.

The original idea was to build up the SSTF while the baby boomers were in the workforce and then draw on these funds later to help pay for the baby boomers' retirement benefits. If other elements of the federal budget were in balance, the social security surplus would reduce real interest rates and increase private sector investment. In turn, the higher rate of capital formation would promote economic growth and thereby make it easier to provide the benefits to the baby boomers during their retirement years. However, throughout the 1980s and most of the 1990s, the federal government ran large deficits. In essence, the surplus of the social security retirement system was used to finance current government operations. During the next decade, the social security retirement system will run a sizable surplus, expanding the size of the trust fund. Somewhere around 2014, however, the surplus will dissipate as the baby boomers begin to retire. After 2014, large deficits are projected "as far as the eye can see."

Will enlarging the trust fund make it easier to deal with the retirement of the baby boomers? Some are surprised to learn that there is little reason to believe that it will. Unlike the bonds, stocks, and physical assets held by a private insurance company, the SSTF bonds will not generate a stream of future income for the federal government. Neither are they a "pot of money" set aside for the payment of future benefits. Instead the trust fund bonds are an IOU from one government agency—the Treasury—to another—the Social Security Administration. The assets of the trust funds are a liability of the Treasury. ***Thus, no matter how many bonds are in the trust fund, their net asset value to the federal government is zero!***

THE REAL SOCIAL SECURITY PROBLEM

The real crisis faced by the pay-as-you-go system will arise around 2014 when the revenues from the payroll tax will begin to fall short of the benefits promised to retirees. As **Exhibit A4–4** illustrates, there only four ways to deal with this situation: (1) reduce benefits, (2) raise taxes and/or cut other government expenditures in order to inject additional funds into the system, (3) borrow from the general public, or (4) reform the system in a manner that will increase the rate of return earned by (or for) workers and future retirees. The presence of SSTF bonds will not change these alternatives. Of course, the SSTF bonds represent funds borrowed by the Treasury from the social security system. This makes the claim on these funds by future social security recipients more legitimate.

However, the presence of the bonds will not make it any easier to deal with future social security deficits. Remember, the federal government is both the payee and recipient of the interest and principal represented by the SSTF bonds. In order to redeem the bonds and thereby provide the social security system with funds to cover future deficits, the federal government will have to raise taxes, cut other expenditures, or borrow from the public. These options will not change with the depletion of the trust fund, an event expected to occur around 2032.

EXHIBIT A4-4

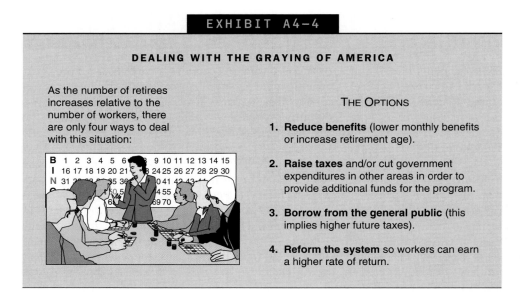

DEALING WITH THE GRAYING OF AMERICA

As the number of retirees increases relative to the number of workers, there are only four ways to deal with this situation:

THE OPTIONS

1. **Reduce benefits** (lower monthly benefits or increase retirement age).
2. **Raise taxes** and/or cut government expenditures in other areas in order to provide additional funds for the program.
3. **Borrow from the general public** (this implies higher future taxes).
4. **Reform the system** so workers can earn a higher rate of return.

The problem is not depletion of the trust funds. Instead it is the burden of soaring social security deficits on the economy beginning in about 15 years. It will not be easy to cover these deficits. If benefits are reduced, current beneficiaries and persons near retirement will—quite correctly—feel that a commitment made to them has been broken. At the same time, it will be difficult to cover the gap with tax increases and expenditure cuts. As the baby boomers retire, approximately a 50 percent increase in the payroll tax or a 30 percent increase in the personal income tax will be needed to cover the social security deficits. Tax increases of this magnitude are likely to retard economic growth, which will further aggravate the problem. Neither will it be easy to cut other expenditures. Defense spending has already been sliced substantially and the growth of the elderly population is sure to place upward pressure on Medicare spending, another major federal program. Finally, a major increase in borrowing will place upward pressure on interest rates, slowing both capital formation and economic growth. In addition, borrowing means higher future taxes just to cover the interest cost. Thus, it merely delays the problem.

REFORM ALTERNATIVES

There is increasing awareness that a pay-as-you-go system is ill-suited for the demographics of the future. In the past, when each generation was larger than its successor, it was possible to keep the taxes imposed on current workers low while still providing substantial benefits to retirees. However, the era of successively larger generations is over. This makes pay-as-you-go less attractive.

Previously, political considerations essentially ruled out major structural reform. Given the severity of the problem and unattractiveness of other alternatives, reform may now be more feasible. What type of reform would minimize the most harmful side effects accompanying the retirement of the baby boomers and subsequent generations? Several ideas have been put forth. We will consider two of the most widely discussed proposals.

Government Investment in the Stock Market

In 1999, President Clinton presented a social security plan that called for the investment of a portion of the SSTF in the stock market. Historically, the real rate of return on stocks has been about 7 percent, compared to 2 percent for government bonds. If the government could earn 7 percent rather than 2 percent on these funds, this would help make the system solvent for a longer period of time. The president's plan would cover the social security deficit for about 6 years.

The plan is not entirely new. States have invested employee retirement funds in the stock and bond markets for many years. With a few exceptions, it has worked out reasonably well. The rate of return earned by most state plans has exceeded the return on government bonds. However, the state employee retirement funds are small compared to the SSTF. Fed Chairman Alan Greenspan and others have expressed concern about the plan's impact on financial markets. In the past, the federal government has stayed out of the stock market. Many believe that this is one reason why U.S. financial markets have worked so well. If the federal government had sizable holdings, several temptations would arise. For example, would the government try to offset a downturn in the stock market with a stock buying spree? As government investment funds fell due to a shrinkage in the size of the SSTF, might this not trigger a collapse in stock prices? Might the government use the investment funds to favor some firms (perhaps those whose officers provided large political contributions) and penalize other, less politically favored firms?

The record of government-directed funds in other countries has been poor. Funds managed by the governments of Malaysia and Singapore earned 6.2 percent and 3.2 percent, respectively, during 1980–1997. Most other governments have done worse. Since 1980, funds invested by the governments of Ecuador, Egypt, Venezuela, and Peru have all earned negative returns for their citizens.[2]

Use of Payroll Taxes to Fund Personal Retirement Accounts

For those concerned about potential abuse accompanying government investment, it would be preferable to channel a portion of the payroll tax into personal retirement accounts managed by individuals. There are various ways such plans might work, but one possibility would be to allow individuals to fund their own retirement by channeling a portion of their payroll tax into a personal retirement saving account. As these retirement accounts grow, individuals could be allowed to allocate more and more of their payroll tax into them in exchange for the receipt of lower social security benefits. Rather than the government managing these funds, individuals would be permitted to choose among various stock and bond mutual funds.

In essence, this plan recognizes that social security is both a redistributional program and a mandated savings plan. For a time, people would have to continue funding the redistributional part of the program. But those willing to set aside funds for their own retirement could in effect "buy out" of the mandated saving portion of the system. Because individuals would have a property right to the funds channeled into their personal retirement accounts, the adverse incentive effects accompanying taxation would be largely avoided.

---

[2]See Peter J. Ferrara and Michael Tanner, *A New Deal for Social Security* (Washington, D.C.: Cato Institute, 1998), for evidence on this point.

Basically, there is only one way that we can simultaneously protect and improve the retirement benefits of the baby boomers and subsequent generations without increasing the tax burden on working Americans: Encourage more savings, investment, and ownership of capital by future retirees. Allowing workers to begin channeling some of their payroll tax into retirement accounts in exchange for lower social security benefits would be a step in that direction.

Some of the elderly may want to accumulate wealth by working a few extra years. Current tax treatment discourages this alternative. The working elderly are still liable for the payroll tax even though their payments add nothing to their benefit levels. If social security retirees earn more than $15,500, they confront the payroll tax, a 15 percent initial income tax liability, and a 50 cent reduction in their social security benefits for every additional dollar they earn. This combination hits them with nearly a 60 percent marginal tax rate—higher than the rate imposed on millionaires. Removal of roadblocks like this would also help future retirees provide for a better retirement.

Making Private Social Security an Option: The Experience of Chile and Other Countries

In recent years, several countries have adopted privatized social security plans. In 1993, Peru privatized its social security system. A year later, Argentina and Colombia did likewise. Still more recently, Mexico, Bolivia, and El Salvador have adopted privatized social retirement systems. The reforms in each of these countries were patterned after the system of Chile. Chile's pioneering plan was first adopted in 1980. The basics of the Chilean plan are (1) a defined contribution system and (2) privately owned and managed investment accounts. Let us consider this plan in more detail.

Workers in Chile were given an option: They could continue with the government social security program or contribute a minimum of 10 percent of their wages (up to 20 percent if they wanted earlier retirement or greater retirement benefits) into an approved private investment fund. These funds would contract to deliver retirement and insurance benefits in place of the social security program. In 1995, there were 21 alternative private "Pension Fund Administration" (AFP) companies competing for the retirement contributions of Chileans. Each AFP is a management firm with investment and operating policies regulated by the government. Each is a separate legal entity from the portfolio of stocks and bonds it manages. It receives a management fee, but has no claim on the portfolio that it manages. So if an AFP were to go bankrupt—although none has since the plan began—the holdings would remain to finance the future benefits to workers.

Ninety percent of all workers chose to leave the government system even though they had paid into it for years. They were issued "recognition bonds" that reflected the value of their previous contributions. The government pledged to buy back these bonds, with interest, from each worker upon retirement. Workers may either spend this supplemental money in retirement or use it to purchase annuities that pay a fixed amount until death.

Employers paid more than half of the payroll tax under the old Chilean system, but the current system requires no contribution from them. Instead, they were required in 1981 to provide an 18 percent raise to workers. From the raise, workers paid their own contributions.

While the Chilean plan forces employees to save, it also provides them with a property right to the funds in their retirement account. From the viewpoint of individual workers, the contributions represent earnings and an investment backed by private assets. Thus, the adverse incentive effects are minimal—substantially less than those accompanying pay-as-you-go tax plans. Furthermore, the retirement funds are clearly an asset paid for by individual workers, rather than a political favor granted by politicians. This enhances the economic and political freedom of workers. As part owners of the private economy, workers have an incentive to oppose inefficient regulations or excessive taxes placed on "business" that would hurt the economy and reduce their retirement funding. This change has helped to depoliticize the economy, as well as the pension system.

The Chilean plan has worked well for both the participants and the economy. During the first 17 years of the plan, the average rate of return earned by the contributions has been 12 percent. The contributions into the plan have led to higher rates of both saving and investment. In the 1990s, Chile's saving rate has averaged 26 percent of GDP, up from 20 percent prior to the adoption of the plan. In turn, the additional saving has stimulated capital formation and helped to strengthen the economy. Since 1985, Chile's per-capita GDP has grown at an annual rate of 5 percent. It is now one the fastest-growing economies in the world.

The Latin American countries that have moved toward private systems are much less developed than the United States. Among the high-income industrial economies, the United Kingdom has made the most dramatic moves toward privatization. Since 1986, the United Kingdom has permitted employees and self-employed workers to channel 4.6 percentage points of their payroll tax into private retirement accounts. In exchange for their participation in the private plans, employees accept a lower level of government retirement benefits. The private option has been quite popular. Approximately 73 percent of British workers now have a private plan.

Exhibit A4–5 provides information on the real rate of return earned by various private plans around the world. All of these plans have performed reasonably

EXHIBIT A4–5

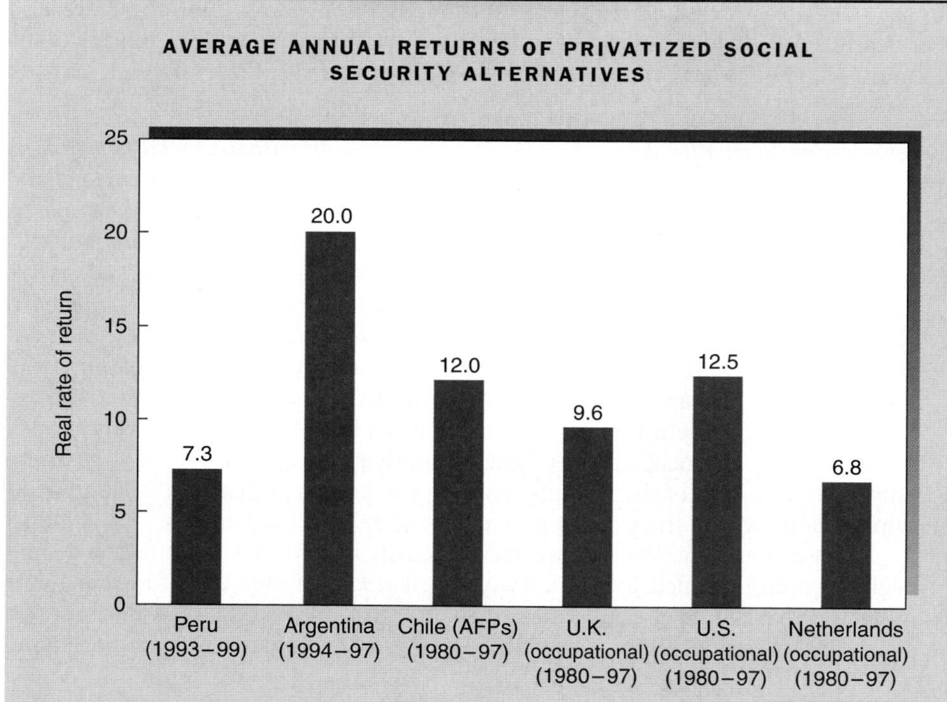

Several countries have either privatized their social security systems or provided private alternatives. The rate of return on the private alternatives is shown here. In the United States, prior to 1983, county, municipal, and state government employees were permitted to opt out of the traditional social security system. The investment rate of return of these alternative plans has been much higher than the rate earned by the social security trust fund.

SOURCE: Peter J. Ferrara and Michael Tanner, A New Deal for Social Security *(Washington, D.C.: Cato Institute, 1998), p. 150.*

well—several have earned double-digit real returns for their beneficiaries. These returns certainly compare favorably with the less than 2 percent real returns that future retirees in the United States can expect.

It is also interesting to note the experience of one group that is not part of the current social security system. Prior to 1983, county, municipal, and state government employees were permitted to opt out of the traditional social security system. More than one million state and local government employees are still participating in these retirement plans. The rate of return on the funds invested in these plans averaged 12.5 percent during 1980–1997, far higher than the returns earned by the Social Security Trust Fund.

Critics argue that private plans are more risky and that some investors will make bad decisions, leading to a higher poverty rate among the elderly. To a degree, these charges have some validity. There is certainly no assurance that individual investors will not make some bad choices. However, mutual funds provide a mechanism whereby even small, novice investors can hold a diverse portfolio of stocks and bonds while still keeping administrative costs low. Furthermore, the historical evidence indicates that when held over a lengthy time period, a diverse holding of stocks is a low-risk investment. Still, it can be expected to yield much higher returns than government bonds. (See the following application with regard to these points.) Given these factors, consideration of private investment options is likely to be an integral part of the social security debate in the years immediately ahead.

SOCIAL SECURITY AND FAIRNESS ISSUES

Social security reform is being seriously considered for several reasons. The most important is the future financial difficulties that are sure to plague the system as the number of retirees increases relative to the number of workers. But there are also other reasons to consider reform. The system exerts a discriminatory impact—one that most would consider unfair—on several different groups. Let's take a closer look at this issue.

1. ***Generations born after World War II would be better off without social security.*** As we mentioned earlier, social security has been a very good deal for current and previous retirees. Most earned a higher rate of return than would have been possible from private investments. But this will not be true for the baby-boom and subsequent generations. If tax payments into social security are viewed as an "investment" and the promised benefits a return, under current law, persons born between 1945 and 1964 will earn a rate of return of about 1.8 percent on their social security taxes. This is less than half of what they could earn on inflation-proof Treasury bonds and approximately one-fourth of the stock market's historical return (7 percent). To put this in perspective, if the baby boomers had been permitted to invest their social security taxes into private investment accounts earning only 5 percent, each of them would have, on average, more than $200,000 in additional wealth beyond the amount provided by social security benefits.[3]

   Furthermore, their future social security benefits are risky. As the system begins running a deficit in just a few years, it is conceivable their future benefits might be reduced. Is it fair to force people into a retirement plan that does so poorly? After paying high taxes while working, is the dependency accompanying

[3]These figures are from the Federal Reserve Bank of Cleveland, *Economic Trends* (March 1999): 12–13.

THE WIZARD OF ID

social security fair? People are giving more thought to questions like these as reform becomes a viable possibility.

2. ***Social security discriminates against middle-income recipients.*** The social security payroll tax does not apply beyond the $65,400 annual income threshold. Thus, the average payroll tax rates of persons with incomes above the cutoff are lower than for those with incomes below the cutoff. On the benefit side, the formula favors those with low incomes. In contrast, middle-income recipients pay high taxes, while receiving very little in additional benefits. Social security retirement benefits are linked to each worker's lifetime base earnings—the worker's average annual earnings for his or her 35 highest-earning years. (*Note:* The income figures are adjusted for inflation.) However, as base earnings rise, the increase in retirement benefits is far less than proportional.[4] In fact, increases in average annual earnings beyond approximately $32,000 lead to only a 15 percent increase in benefit levels. Thus, middle earners in this $32,000 to $65,000 range get virtually nothing for the additional payroll taxes they paid during their working years.[5]
3. ***Social security discriminates against married women in the workforce.*** This is not the intent, but nonetheless, it is the result. The problem arises because individuals are permitted to draw benefits based on either their own earnings or 50 percent of their spouse's earnings. But they cannot draw both. In the case of many working married women, the benefits based on the earnings of their spouses are approximately equal to, or in some cases greater than, benefits based on their own earnings. Thus, these married women derive virtually nothing from the payroll taxes paid during their working years.
4. ***Political dependency results from the system.*** The current social security system makes every group of retirees dependent on politics and politicians. Even though individuals pay throughout their working years, the current system does not give

[4]The annual retirement benefits are equal to: 90 percent of the first $5,244 of base earnings; 32 percent of base earnings between $5,244 and $31,620, and 15 percent of base earnings above $31,620. Therefore, as base earnings rise, benefits fall *as a percentage of average earnings* (and payroll taxes paid) during one's lifetime. For example, the retirement benefits of persons with base annual earnings of $10,000 sum to 62 percent of their average working-year earnings. In contrast, the retirement benefits of those with base earnings of $60,000 are only 29 percent of their average preretirement earnings. These figures are based on the 1996 formula.

[5]Compared to the poor, middle- and high-income recipients tend to live longer and therefore draw retirement benefits over a more lengthy time period. This will partially offset their lower annual benefit levels per dollar of social security taxes paid during working years.

them a clearly defined property right to future benefits. For many, this too is a fairness question. Why should Americans, high- and low-wage alike, have to beg, demand, or lobby politicians to get benefits that they were forced to pay for earlier? That is especially frustrating for those who believe that they could have purchased greater benefits more cheaply through mutual funds or other private investmentS.

Historically, social security has been viewed as almost a sacred program. Nonetheless, it now confronts several problems. The lives of today's students will be strongly affected by how these problems are dealt with in the years immediately ahead.

KEY POINTS

➤ Social security does not follow the saving-and-investment model. Most of the funds flowing into the system are paid out to current retirees and survivors under the program.

➤ While the current tax revenues exceed the payments to retirees, this will change dramatically as the baby boomers begin to move into the retirement phase of life. Beginning around 2014, the system's current surplus will shift to a deficit, which will persist for several decades.

➤ The current surplus of the social security system is used to purchase U.S. Treasury bonds. Because the federal government is both the payee and recipient of these bonds, their net asset value to the federal government is zero. They will not reduce the level of future taxes needed to cover the social security deficit when the baby boomers begin to retire.

➤ The major problem resulting from the current system is the fact that huge increases in taxes (or reductions in spending) will be required to cover the future deficits. Large tax increases would be likely to cause a slowdown in the rate of economic growth.

➤ Several potential reforms, including government investment in the stock market and moving toward privatization through personal retirement accounts, are currently under consideration. Reforms are also being considered for reasons of fairness.

CRITICAL ANALYSIS QUESTIONS

1. Is the social security system based on the same principles as private insurance? Why or why not?

*2. Why does the social security system face a crisis? Will the surplus that is currently being built up in the Social Security Trust Fund help to avert higher future taxes and/or benefit reductions when the baby boomers retire? Why or why not?

3. Do you think workers should be permitted to invest all or part of their social security contribution in private investment funds? What are the advantages and disadvantages of a private option system? If given the opportunity, would you choose the private option or stay with the current system? Why?

4. The social security payroll tax is split equally between the employee and the employer. Would it make any difference if the entire tax was imposed on employees? Would employees be helped if all the tax was imposed on employers? (*Hint:* You may want to consult Chapter 4, pages 107–109.)

5. In early 1999, President Clinton proposed that the government should invest part of the Social Security Trust Fund in the stock market. Do you think this is a good idea? Why or why not?

---

*Asterisk denotes questions for which answers are given in Appendix B.

APPLICATION 5

In investing money, the amount of interest you want should depend on whether you want to eat well or sleep well.

J. Kenfield Morley[1]

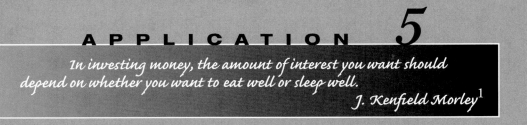

The Stock Market: What Does It Do and How Has It Performed?

APPLICATION FOCUS

- What is the economic function of the stock market?
- How are stock prices related to the interest rate?
- Why has the stock market risen so much since 1982?
- Is the stock market too high? Is it a bubble that will burst?
- How will the retirement of the baby-boomers' generation affect stock prices?

---

[1]As quoted in Burton G. Malkiel, *A Random Walk Down Wall Street* (New York: Norton Company, 1990), p. 287.

The market for corporate shares is called the stock market. The extremely rapid rise of stock prices in recent years has often been front page news. On the whole, investors in American stocks have done exceedingly well and this has been true over a long period. Since 1802, the returns of stock holdings have averaged 7 percent, corrected for inflation. That means that, on average, stock investments have doubled in value every 10 years.

In the 1980s and 1990s, the returns have been even higher. The Standard and Poor's 500 Index indicates the performance of the broad stock market. This index factors in the value of dividends as if they were reinvested in the market. Thus, it provides a measure of the rate of return received by investors in the form of both dividends and changes in share prices. As **Exhibit A5-1** illustrates, the S&P 500 stocks generated a 15 percent average annual rate of return during 1983–1998. Even after adjustment for inflation, the returns averaged 11.7 percent during this period.

EXHIBIT A5-1

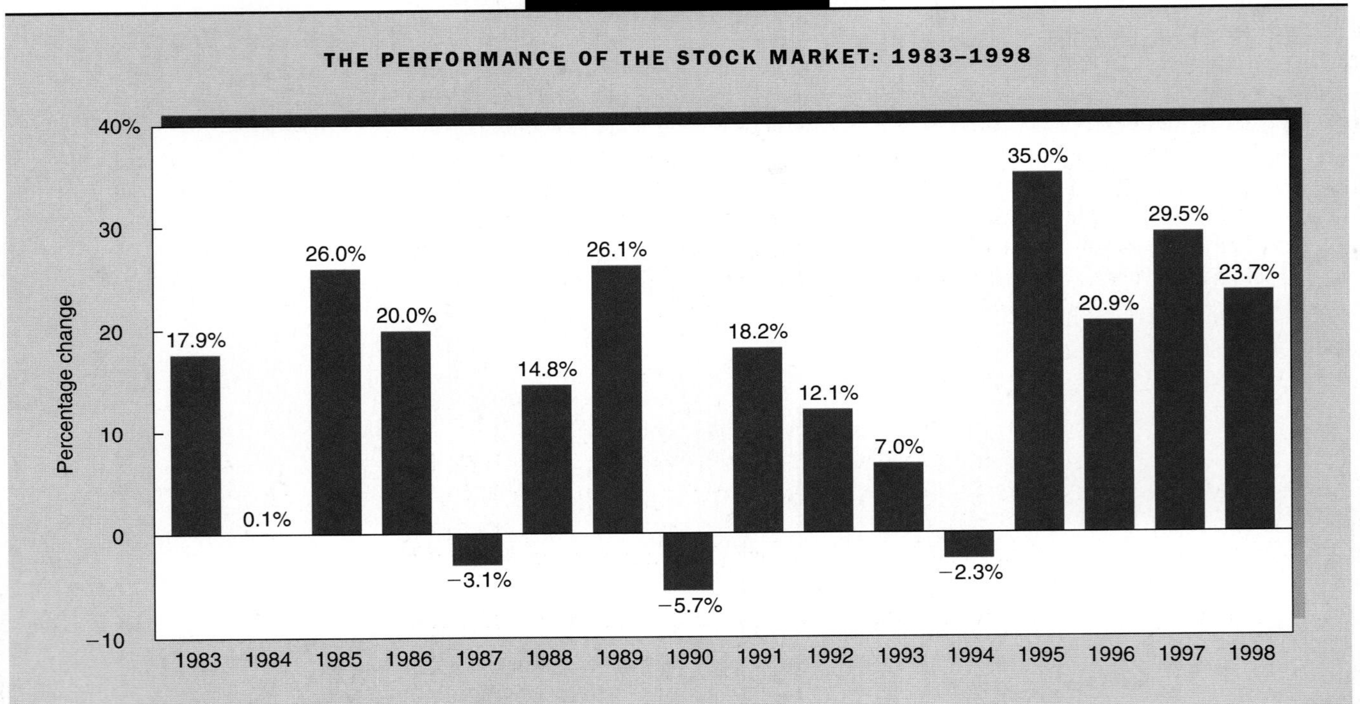

During the last 16 years, the broad S&P 500 stock index indicates that stock investors earned a 15 percent average annual rate of return. Double-digit returns were earned during 11 of the 16 years, while the returns were negative during only 3 of the years.

SOURCE: Standard and Poor's.

The prices of individual stocks can rise and fall spectacularly. Those who buy and sell stocks, especially when they try to outguess market changes, can gain or lose huge sums of money in a very short time. Is the stock market simply a giant casino? Or does it perform functions that are critical for the growth of an economy? Why has the market performed so well during the last 16 years? Will this trend continue or can we expect a downturn or even a stock market crash in the near future? How do changes in factors like the interest rate and the number of people currently in certain age categories affect the demand for stocks? This application addresses these questions and related issues.

THE ECONOMIC FUNCTIONS OF THE STOCK MARKET

The stock market performs several important functions in a modern economy. That is true even though a few active traders in the market treat it much like a casino. Those who constantly buy and sell, trying to predict the movement of each stock price and to outguess others in the market, are gambling. Most will probably lose over time, because buying and selling is itself costly. Traders looking for quick profits face a difficult task. They must frequently be right about price changes, just to break even over time. Yet it is very difficult to outguess the others in the market.

Most participants in the stock market have little special expertise. Only a few are willing to take the time to obtain detailed information on a large number of firms. Nonetheless, the stock market provides them with a means through which they can share in the profits (and the risks) of large businesses. Investment fund managers and other advisors offer, for a fee, to manage their investments. Savers have found the stock market to be an excellent place to invest their savings in order to build wealth over time. At the same time, firms seeking funds have found new stock issues to be an excellent method to identify others willing to share the risks and the opportunities that accompany their business activities. Investors and firms seeking investment capital can gain from the exchange of savings for ownership shares. For the economy as a whole, the stock market channels investment funds into profitable activities. It rewards the choice and recognition of successful business strategies. It also disciplines business decision makers who use resources in a wasteful or destructive manner. Let us look at each of these stock market functions more closely.

HOW THE STOCK MARKET WORKS FOR SAVERS AND INVESTORS

A large and rapidly growing number of savers invest as a long-term strategy. For them the stock market has been an excellent place to build wealth. Today it is possible for investors to buy shares of ownership in a wide variety of firms and hold them over long periods of time. Such a strategy can substantially reduce risk, although the stock market has no guaranteed returns.

One source of risk for a stock market investor is the fact that individual stocks can rise and fall unpredictably. Investing in any one firm is risky. But investors can reduce their risk of losses by holding a diverse **portfolio,** or collections of stocks, with small amounts of many stocks. The increases in some stock prices tend to balance out the decreases in others. That way, swings in the value of any one stock do not matter so much. The fees of stockbrokers have fallen over time. For example, trades that might have cost hundreds of dollars 15 years ago can now be made for as little as $8. An investor can economically purchase a very small ownership share in any listed firm.

Portfolio
All the stocks, bonds, or other securities held by an individual or corporation for investment purposes.

Holding shares in 20 firms from independent industries will reduce the variability of the investor's returns by about 70 percent. ***Holding shares of many firms in unconnected industries helps to reduce portfolio risk.***

Equity mutual fund
A corporation that pools the funds of investors, including small investors, and uses them to purchase a bundle of stocks.

One way an individual investor can easily purchase an interest in many firms at one time is to purchase stock in an **equity mutual fund,** a corporation that buys and holds shares of stock in many firms. A popular form of fund in recent years has been the index fund, which holds a portfolio mirroring one or another of the many stock indexes, such as the S&P 500 Index or the Dow Jones Industrials. These mutual funds do very little trading and as a result have low operating costs. They have had better yields than most of the more actively managed mutual funds—those trading more often in search of greater gains. Mutual funds with diverse holdings offer relatively low risks. As **Exhibit A5-2** shows, the combined holdings of equity mutual funds summed to approximately $3 trillion in 1998. That was about 20 percent of all publicly traded U.S. stocks. Moreover, stock ownership through these mutual funds has been growing rapidly in recent years.

A second source of risk facing investors is the fact that nearly all stocks in the market may rise or fall together, when expectations about the entire economy change. Such change can be sudden. For example, on October 19, 1987, the stocks listed in the Dow Jones Industrial Average lost more than 22 percent of their value in just one trading day. But as **Exhibit A5-3** shows, holding stocks for a longer period reduces the risk of large losses. For example, stocks in the S&P Index held for one year beginning in any month between 1950 and 1996 lost 38.9 percent in the worst case. A gain of 61 percent was the best case. But the index stocks held over any 10 years brought a small positive return of 0.5 percent in the worst case. In the best case 10-year period, the return was

EXHIBIT A5-2

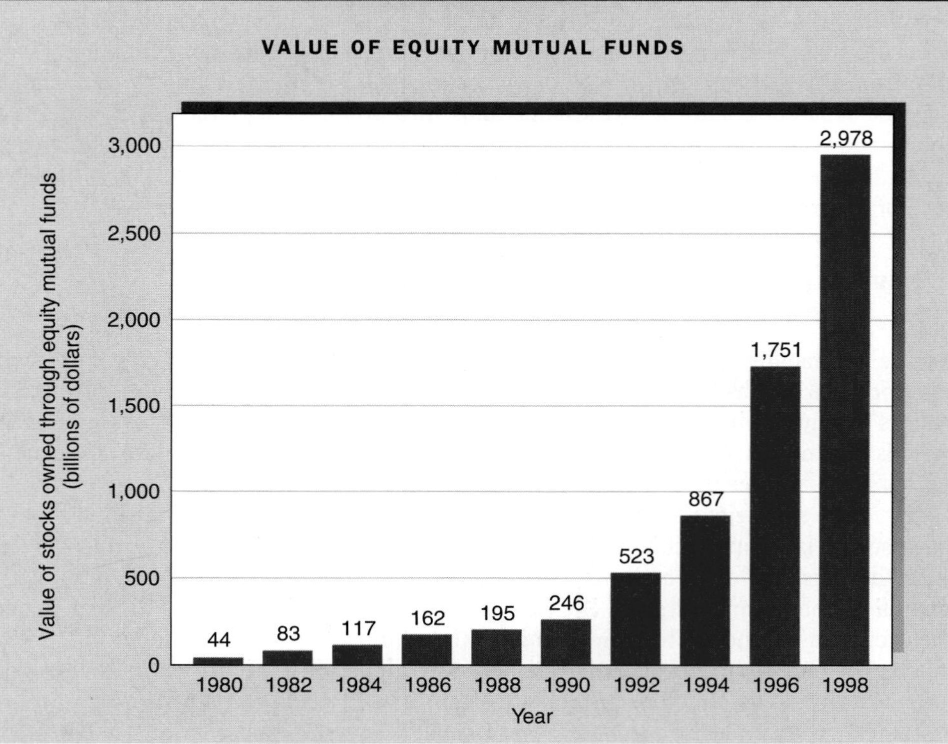

The amount of money that people put into U.S. equity mutual funds, in order to hold shares in the ownership of stocks, rose dramatically in the 1990s. Purchasing shares in a mutual fund is a simple way for an individual to buy and hold an interest in a large variety of stocks with one purchase.

SOURCE: Investor Company Institute <www.ici.org>.

EXHIBIT A5-3

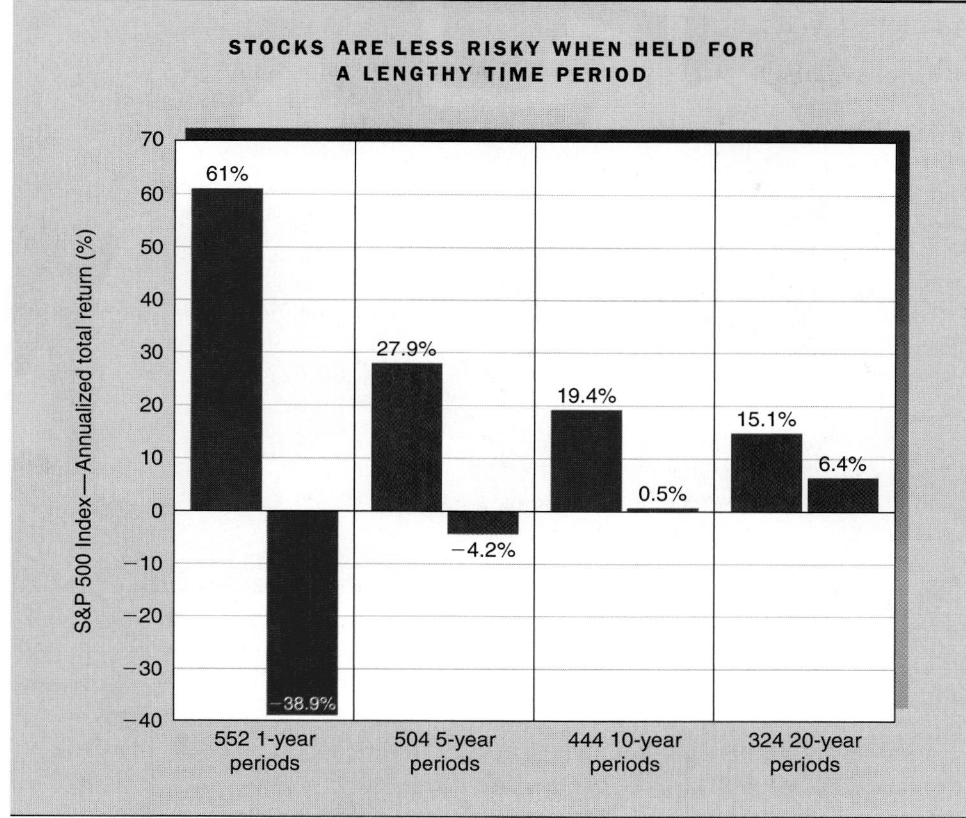

This graphic highlights the best and the worst annualized performance for each holding period from 1950 to 1996. It shows that there is less risk of a low or negative return when a portfolio of stocks (S&P 500) is held for a longer period of time.

SOURCE: Ibbotson Associates and Merrill Lynch, published in the Merrill Lynch newsletter, Insights and Strategies *3, no. 4 (1998): 1. The analysis uses "rolling time periods." The first rolling 1-year period, for example, begins on January 1, 1950, and ends on December 31, 1950. The second 1-year period begins on February 1, 1950, and ends on January 31, 1951. Similarly, the rolling 5-year periods run from January 1950 through December 1954, February 1950 through January 1955, and so on.*

19.4 percent. Over any 20-year period, 6.4 percent was the worst return, while 15.1 percent was the best. Clearly, holding a portfolio of stocks for a longer period greatly reduces the risk of very low or negative returns to the investor, although it similarly reduces the chance of very large returns.

Two decades ago, the high historical rate of return on stocks was thought to reflect their greater risk relative to bonds and other investments like savings accounts. Stocks are risky when held for a relatively short time or when only small numbers of stocks are held in one's portfolio. ***However, when a diverse set of stocks is held over a lengthy time period, historically stocks have yielded a high rate of return and the variation of that return has been relatively small. The development of stock mutual funds makes it possible for even small investors to hold a diverse portfolio, add to it regularly, and still keep transaction costs low.***

The development of equity mutual funds has both reduced the risk of stock investments and attracted large amounts of funds into the market, helping to push prices upward. Currently, many Americans are reaching retirement with substantially more wealth than they expected just a few years ago. In early 1999, U.S. households owned \$11 trillion in stocks, up from \$7.2 trillion at the end of 1996. More than four in every ten households now own stock, either directly or through an equity mutual fund. The wealth of these households has increased substantially as their stock holdings have risen in value.

Are stocks riskier than bonds? If held for only a short time—1 to 3 years, for example—stocks are more risky. However, when held over lengthy periods like 20 or 30 years, historically the rate of return on stocks has been both higher and less variable than that of bonds. What does this imply with regard to where persons saving for their retirement while in their 20s and 30s should place their funds?

How the Stock Market Works for Corporations

To raise money to develop new products or expand output, a corporation has several options. It can use retained earnings (profits earned but not paid out to stockholders), it can borrow money, or it can sell stock. In borrowing, it promises to repay to the lender a specific amount, including principal and interest. But when it sells stock, it is selling a share of ownership in the firm. The buyer of the stock is purchasing a fractional share in the firm's future net revenues.

Newly issued stocks are sold through specialized firms to the public. A firm that issues new stock sells it in the ***primary market.*** When news reports tell us about how stock prices are changing, they are referring to ***secondary markets,*** where previously issued stocks are traded. Secondary markets make it easy to buy and sell listed stock. That is important to the primary market. The initial buyers want to know that their stocks will be easy to sell later. Entry is more attractive when exit will be easy. That helps the corporation that issues new stock to sell it for a higher price.

Primary market
Market where financial institutions aid in the sale of new securities.

Secondary Market
Market where financial institutions aid in the buying and selling of existing securities.

A stock exchange is a secondary market. It is a place where stockbrokers come to arrange trades for buyers and sellers. The largest and best known stock market is the New York Stock Exchange, where more than 2,500 stocks are traded. There are other such markets in the United States, as well as in London, Tokyo, and other trading centers around the world.

The expectation of future dividends paid from profits and gain derived from increases in share prices are the major reasons why people buy the stock of a corporation. Periodically, the firm's board of directors determines when the firm will provide dividend payments to its shareholders. A firm that earns greater profits can provide more dividend income to owners of its stock over time.

However, sometimes a firm will not pay out its profits as dividends. Instead it retains those earnings to invest in the firm. If its investments are good, they will increase the firm's future profits. The prospect of greater future profits raises the value of the stock. A good investment is simply one that increases stock value by more than the amount of the forgone dividend. In general, stockholders are happy either with profits now or with a rising stock price. Microsoft, for example, has made many stockholders rich even though it has never paid a dividend. It has used its large profits to invest even more in hiring people and increasing its ability to produce larger profits in the future. In fact, stocks in many new firms, especially those investing in high technology, rise in value before they ever earn a profit. The stock price increase is strictly due to expected future profits.

Either dividend payments or rising stock values will increase the stockholder's wealth. Of course, if the firm does not invest wisely, then future earnings will decline, as will the price of the stock. The value of a firm's stock rises (falls) when investors come to expect future profits to rise (fall). ***Thus when investors believe that a new investment by a corporation is wise—that it will increase future earnings—the stock price will rise. When a new management decision seems unwise to investors, many will sell, driving the stock price down.***

It pays for a stockholder, and especially a large stockholder such as a fund manager, to be alert to whether the firm's decisions are good ones. Those who spot a corporation's problems early can sell part or all of their stock in that firm before others notice and lower the price by selling their own stock. Those who first notice decisions that will be profitable can gain by increasing their holdings of the stock. Stockholder alertness benefits the corporation, too. The firm's board of directors can utilize the price changes resulting from investor vigilance to reward good management decisions. They often do so by tying the compensation of the top corporate officers to stock performance. How? Rather than paying these officers entirely in the form of salaries, boards of directors can integrate **stock options** into the compensation package of top executives. When good decisions drive the stock price up, the executives' options will have substantial value. On the other hand, if bad decisions cause the stock price to fall, then the options will have little or no value.

Stock options
The option to buy a specified number of shares of the firm's stock at a designated price. The designated price is generally set so that the options will be quite valuable if the firm's shares increase in price, but of little value if their price falls. Thus, when used to compensate top managers, stock options provide a strong incentive to follow policies that will increase the value of the firm.

Of course, luck can enter also, as when demand rises or falls in the firm's product market. Some boards of directors make the option price dependent on the firm's performance relative to competing firms. If the firm does well compared to others in the same market, then the reward grows. Because a firm's directors also are normally stockholders, the stock market automatically disciplines them, too. Their own rewards are larger when they choose successful corporate managers and effectively motivate them.

How the Stock Market Works for the Economy

We have seen how the stock market benefits stockholders and helps discipline corporate decision makers to be more efficient. As it does so, it is providing both information and the incentives needed to build prosperity. The secondary market in a corporation's shares constantly sends signals to the listed corporation's board of directors and managers. Changing stock prices reward good decisions and penalize bad ones. This provides executives and managers with an incentive to follow policies that increase the firm's value. In order to achieve this objective, the firm must generate an income stream that is worth more than the cost of its assets. Put another way, it must undertake productive projects.

STOCK PRICES AND THE INTEREST RATE

Underlying today's price of a firm's stock is the present value of the firm's expected future net earnings, or profit. What those future profits are worth to an investor today depends on three things: (1) the expected size of future net earnings, (2) when these earnings will be achieved, and (3) how much the investor discounts the future income. The last depends on the interest rate. As we noted in an earlier chapter, the present-value procedure can be used to determine the current value of any future income (or cost) stream. If D represents dividends (and gains from a higher stock price) earned in various years in the future (indicated by the subscripts) and i represents the discount or interest rate, the present value of the future income stream[2] is

$$PV = \frac{D_1}{(1+i)} + \frac{D_2}{(1+i)^2} + \cdots + \frac{D_n}{(1+i)^n}$$

A higher interest rate reduces the present value of future returns from holding shares of a stock. And that is true even if the size of future returns is not affected by changes in the interest rate. Stock analysts often stress that lower interest rates are good for the stock market. This should not be surprising because the lower rates of interest will increase the value of future income (and capital gains). For example, when the interest rate is 12.5 percent, the discounted value of $100 of future income to be received each year in perpetuity is $800 ($100 divided by 0.125). But when the interest rate is 5 percent, the discounted value of this same income stream is $2,000 ($100 divided by 0.05). Other things constant, lower interest rates will increase stock values.

THE STOCK MARKET SINCE 1982: WHAT CAUSED THE DRAMATIC RISE?

In March 1982, the daily closings of the Dow Jones Industrials averaged 812. Seventeen years later, on March 29, 1999, the Dow closed at 10,006. Other stock indexes showed similar increases. What factors explain this 12-fold increase in the value of stocks? Because stock prices depend on the changing expectations of millions of investors, no one can say exactly what caused the strong increase. However, most observers believe the following four factors played an important role.

- **Interest rates and inflation fell.** The interest rate on 10-year Treasury bonds stood at 13.00 percent in 1982. By March 1999, the 10-year bond rate had fallen to 5.15 percent. The lower structure of interest rates in the late 1990s compared to the early 1980s reflected a rather dramatic change in the inflationary environment. In the 2 years prior to 1982, prices had risen 10.7 percent annually; but in the 2 years prior to March 1999, prices rose only 2.5 percent annually.

  As we just noted, lower interest rates will tend to increase the discounted value of future income derived from stock ownership. In addition, there are two other reasons why lower rates of inflation and interest will tend to boost stock values. First, a lower rate of inflation will reduce the tax burden accompanying capital gains. The United States taxes nominal capital gains. Therefore, if stock prices rise with the general price level, investors will have to pay taxes on the inflation-

---

[2]For a specific annual income stream in perpetuity, the present value is equal simply to R/i, where R is the annual revenue stream and I is the interest rate. For example, if the interest rate is 5 percent, the PV of a $100 annual income stream in perpetuity is equal to $100/0.05, or $2,000.

ary as well as the real increases in stock values. Stability in the general level of prices, however, will eliminate the tax on the phantom inflationary gains. Second, low and stable rates of inflation reduce the uncertainty of investment and other long-term contracts. This will help both the economy and the stock markets.

- **Corporate earnings were higher.** Profits were four times larger in the 2 years prior to 1999 than in the 2 years prior to 1982. The 1990s were especially profitable. Per-share operating profits of the Dow Industrials grew 19 percent per year between 1991 and 1997. There were several reasons for this growth of profits. First, shareholders, especially pension fund and other fund managers with large stock holdings, had begun to insist that firms seek greater earnings. More corporations became willing to sell unprofitable divisions, to merge and grow, or to downsize and lay off managers and workers. Those and other painful measures were taken as shareholders insisted on and got greater productivity and profits.

  Second, boards of directors themselves, representing shareholders, more often insisted that their fellow directors hold a significant share of their wealth in the corporation's stock. They also increased the proportion of top managers' compensation paid in the form of stock options rather than salary. These measures tied the managers' rewards more closely to those of stockholders.

  Third, stockholders encouraged firms to take advantage of technological advances that allowed greater productivity. For example, new computerized systems gave managers updated information that helped firms adjust more quickly and operate more efficiently with smaller inventories. This reduced capital requirements and meant that when buyer demands changed, outdated inventories were smaller. Computers also reduced waste by allowing better fuel and industrial process management. Quicker response times and less waste increased productivity and profits.

  Fourth, greater productivity increased the firms' ability to compete internationally. The firms represented in the Dow Jones Industrial Average made 35 percent of their sales abroad in 1988. By 1999 they raised that figure to 40 percent. As lower transportation costs and reduced trade barriers expanded world trade, U.S. firms were well positioned to expand their market share.
- **The improving U.S. economy drew investment funds from abroad.** Lower tax rates, persistently low rates of inflation, and the general strength of the U.S. economy have attracted substantial investment funds from abroad during the last 15 years. In turn, this inflow of funds into the U.S. stock market has helped push stock prices higher. As **Exhibit A5-4** shows, foreign holdings of U.S. stocks amounted to $76 billion in 1982. By 1998, the figure had risen to $1.1 trillion. U.S. corporations represented a growing share of the world's stock value. The U.S. stock market rose to 53 percent of world market value in 1999, up from 29 percent in 1988.
- **Mutual funds expanded their holdings dramatically.** Stock mutual funds make it possible for even small investors to maintain a diverse portfolio of stocks. These funds have become increasingly attractive, particularly to long-term investors planning for their retirement. The recent growth of these funds has also been propelled by the movement of the baby-boom generation into the prime-earning and high-saving years of life. As the baby boomers and others have channelled record amounts into retirement plans, the pool of funds invested in stock mutual funds has grown to record levels (see Exhibit A5-2). In 1996 and 1997, stock funds gained $15 billion to 20 billion *per month.* While the flow of funds into stock mutuals slowed in 1998, it still amounted to between $10 billion and $12 billion per month. This strong demand for stocks purchased through mutual funds has boosted stock prices.

In 1982, foreign holdings of U.S. stocks amounted to $76 billion. By 1998, they had risen to more than $1 trillion. This strong demand by foreigners helped to raise U.S. stock prices to record levels.

SOURCE: Department of Commerce, Bureau of Economic Analysis.

EXHIBIT A5-4

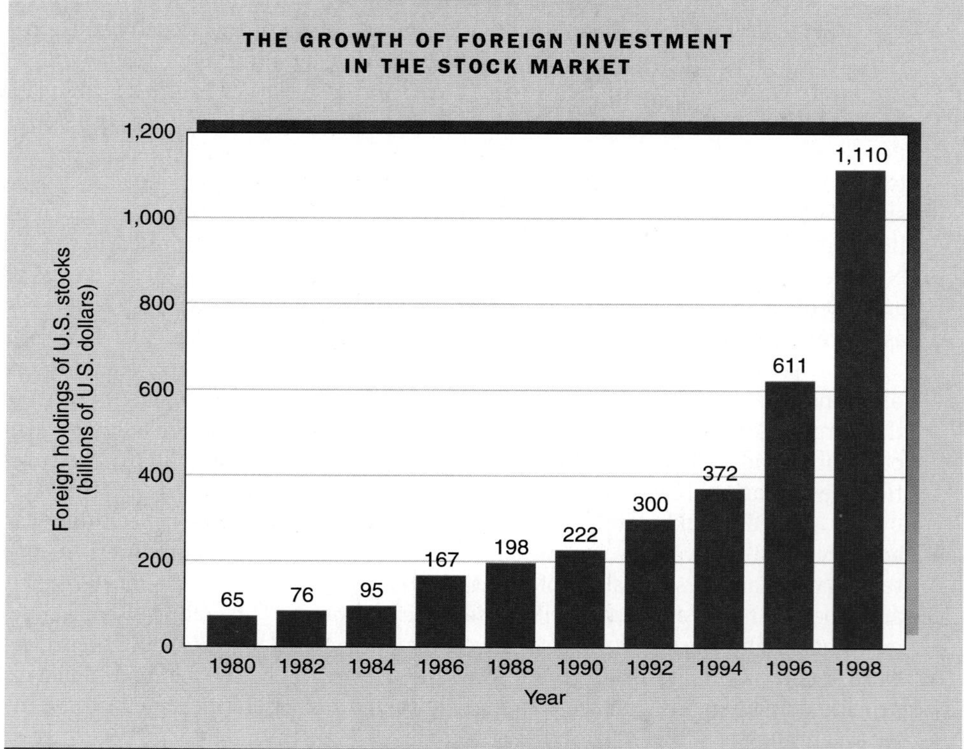

IS THE STOCK MARKET TOO HIGH — IS IT A BUBBLE THAT WILL BURST?

The economic factors listed above helped to fuel the strong rise in stock indexes since 1982. Will they continue to push many stock prices higher? Or will these factors weaken and lead to a long-lasting collapse in stock prices? Since expectations about future earnings and stock prices drive current stock prices, no one can answer these questions with certainty. In fact, as we write, there are prominent stock market experts on both sides of this issue. Some are forecasting a continued increase in stock prices, while others predict a major correction if not impending doom.

What insights can be derived from the factors that drove stock prices up? How are these factors likely to change in the future?

Inflation and Interest Rates. Most analysts expect the rate of inflation to continue at low levels, with perhaps a slight decline. This would help keep interest rates low. Thus, the danger of a stock market collapse due to higher inflation and rising interest rates would appear to be small. On the other hand, future stock prices are unlikely to receive much of an additional boost from lower interest rates and less inflation.

Corporate Earnings. Will future corporate profits be higher in general? This is a key question. Experts differ in their forecasts, and no one can be sure of their answers. Technological advances continue and may even accelerate in the future. Stockholders continue to reward firms that are willing to try new systems and new approaches. One

EXHIBIT A5-5

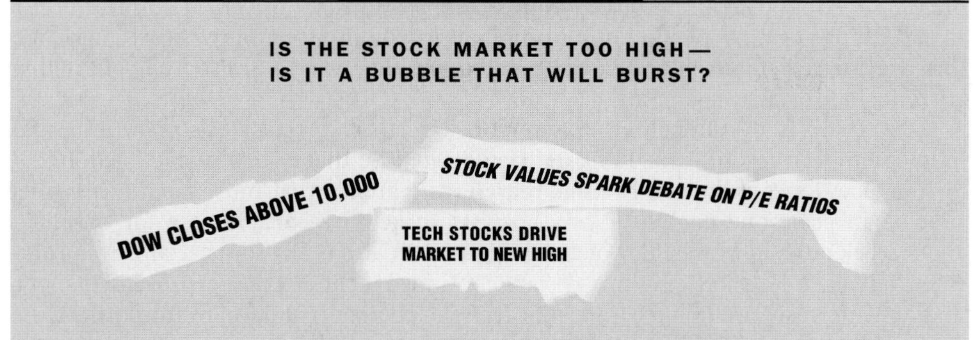

IS THE STOCK MARKET TOO HIGH—
IS IT A BUBBLE THAT WILL BURST?
DOW CLOSES ABOVE 10,000
STOCK VALUES SPARK DEBATE ON P/E RATIOS
TECH STOCKS DRIVE
MARKET TO NEW HIGH

Lower interest rates, higher corporate profits, increased inflow of foreign capital, and a huge flow of savings into stock mutual funds helped push the U.S. stock market to record highs again and again throughout 1993–1999.

indication of this is the fact that technology stocks continue to do well in the stock market, even when their current and past earnings are unimpressive. There is certainly the possibility that productivity and corporate earnings will continue to rise. Optimism about continuing increases seems plausible, but future stock price gains from this source are certainly not guaranteed.

Stock Investments from Abroad. The inflow of foreign funds into the U.S. stock market depends not only on conditions in the investment market here, but also on the situation in other nations. Continuing prosperity abroad means greater demand for stocks. But if prosperity abroad occurs, will foreign stock markets also offer better investment conditions? Greater unification of markets in Europe is occurring. Will this lead to larger or smaller European investments in the United States? If Asian markets improve strongly, will that divert demand from the U.S. stock market? Or will demand in all markets be stimulated by the rising prosperity? No one really knows whether foreigners will continue to pour money into the U.S. stock market.

Mutual Fund Investments. American workers now have much more faith in the stock market. Will they continue to pour large quantities of savings into the stock market? It seems quite possible that this can continue for some years, but once again, the future is uncertain. Continued enthusiasm may bring more new stock market investors. After all, fewer than half of all Americans currently own stock. But enthusiasm for putting savings into stocks could decline. Also, members of the baby-boom generation will begin to move into the retirement phase of life in the near future. As they do, will they sell their stock investments to finance retirement? Or will they continue to work at least part-time? Working would help delay the sale of their stocks, keeping demand stronger. Will they try to consume most of what they have saved? That would speed the selling of their stocks and tend to reduce stock prices. Most current retirees, though, try to keep much of their wealth intact. That helps insure them against poverty in an old age of uncertain length. It also allows them to pass along large portfolios to their children. If the baby boomers follow this path, then their children will be more wealthy and may demand even more stocks.

Concluding Thoughts

No one knows for sure where the U.S. stock market will go in the future. Most economists adhere to the **random walk theory** of the stock market. According to this theory, current stock prices already reflect the best known information about the future state

Random walk theory
The theory that current stock prices already reflect known information about the future. Therefore, the future movement of stock prices will be determined by surprise occurrences. This will cause them to change in a random fashion.

of corporate earnings, the health of the economy, and other factors that influence stock prices. Therefore, the future direction of stock prices will be driven by surprise occurrences, things that people do not currently anticipate. By their very nature, these factors are unpredictable. If they were predictable, they would already be reflected in current stock prices.

There is no compelling reason to believe that current stock prices must fall from the high levels of early 1999 and stay down. The theory that a level near 10,000 for the Dow Jones Industrial Average represents a bubble that must burst has limited support in economic analysis. Many analysts make a reasonable case for optimism about stock price increases. But of course this result also is far from certain. Some analysts do make a plausible case that despite continued technological improvements, productivity increases are unlikely to justify even the current high level of stock prices.

In summary, expert analysts disagree on the future course of stock prices for one fundamental reason: No one can predict the future course of savers and investors. But there are some lessons from history. Stocks have been a good long-term investment in the past. This is unlikely to change. Thus, persons investing for the long term are likely to do well if they have a substantial portion of their funds invested in a diverse bundle of stocks.

KEY POINTS

➤ The stock market has allowed many Americans without special business skills and without making specific business decisions to participate in the risks and opportunities of corporate America. Many have prospered as a result. Real returns for the past two centuries have been 7 percent per year.

➤ Buying and selling individual stocks without specialized knowledge, for a quick profit, is very risky. But holding a diverse portfolio of unrelated stocks and holding them for long periods of time greatly reduces the risk of investing in the stock market.

➤ Vigilant investors and investment fund managers, as they buy and sell stocks for their own portfolios, generate price changes that help to allocate capital efficiently and to discipline corporate decision makers in ways that benefit consumers and stockholders in general.

➤ The U.S. stock market's dramatic rise in value since 1982 has resulted from lower inflation and interest rates, rising corporate earnings, increased purchases by foreign investors, and increased stock purchases through mutual funds.

➤ Stock prices reached levels in early 1999 that were very high by historic standards. Economic analysis suggests that optimists who think stock price levels will rise significantly in the near future can make a plausible case. But pessimists can do the same for their view. In fact, investor expectations about an uncertain future determine current prices, and no one can forecast future stock prices with precision or certainty.

CRITICAL ANALYSIS QUESTIONS

*1. A friend just inherited $50,000. She informs you of her investment plans and asks for your advice. "I want to put it into the stock market and use it for my retirement in 30 years. What do you think is the best plan that will provide high returns at a relatively low risk?" What answer would you give? Explain.

2. What risks are faced by those who put a large part of their savings into the stock market? What can they do to reduce that risk while keeping their money in the market?

*3. Microsoft stock rose from less than $10 in 1995 to nearly $100 in early 1999. Microsoft has made sizable profits, but never paid a dividend. Why were people willing to pay such a high price knowing that they might not get dividends for many years?

4. In the late 1980s and through the 1990s, as U.S. stocks became more expensive, foreign investors bought more and more of them. Explain why.

*5. The stocks of some corporations that have never made a profit or paid a dividend, especially those in high-technology industries, have risen in price. What causes investors to be willing to buy these stocks?

6. New firms without proven track records are more risky than mature firms. Why are investors still willing to bid up their prices?

7. If an investment advisor gives you some hot new stock tip, is it likely to be a "sure thing"? Why or why not?

*Asterisk denotes questions for which answers are given in Appendix B.

APPENDIX A

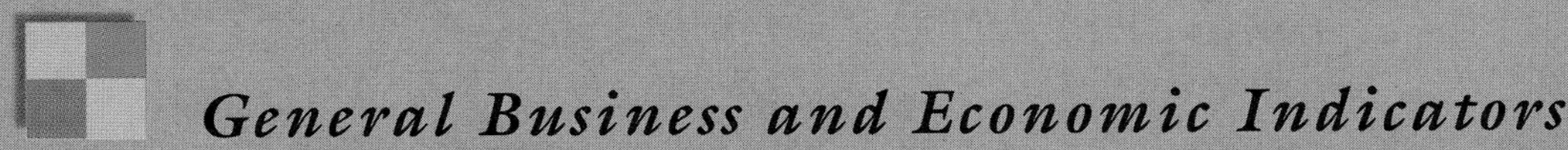

General Business and Economic Indicators

SECTION 1

GROSS DOMESTIC PRODUCT AND ITS COMPONENTS

Year	Personal Consumption Expenditures	Gross Private Domestic Investment	Government Consumption and Gross Investment	Net Exports	Gross Domestic Product (GDP)
1959	318.1	78.8	112.0	−1.7	507.2
1960	332.2	78.8	113.2	2.4	526.6
1961	342.6	77.9	120.9	3.4	544.8
1962	363.4	87.9	131.4	2.4	585.2
1963	383.0	93.4	137.7	3.3	617.4
1964	411.4	101.7	144.4	5.5	663.0
1965	444.3	118.0	153.0	3.9	719.1
1966	481.9	130.4	173.6	1.9	787.8
1967	509.5	128.0	194.6	1.4	833.6
1968	559.8	139.9	212.1	−1.3	910.6
1969	604.7	155.0	223.8	−1.2	982.2
1970	648.1	150.2	236.1	1.2	1,035.6
1971	702.5	176.0	249.9	−3.0	1,125.4
1972	770.7	205.6	268.9	−8.0	1,237.3
1973	851.6	242.9	287.6	0.6	1,382.6
1974	931.2	245.6	323.2	−3.1	1,496.9
1975	1,029.1	225.4	362.6	13.6	1,630.6
1976	1,148.8	286.6	385.9	−2.3	1,819.0
1977	1,277.1	356.6	416.9	−23.7	2,026.9
1978	1,428.8	430.8	457.9	−26.1	2,291.4
1979	1,593.5	480.9	507.1	−24.0	2,557.5
1980	1,760.4	465.9	572.8	−14.9	2,784.2
1981	1,941.3	556.2	633.4	−15.0	3,115.9
1982	2,076.8	501.1	684.8	−20.5	3,242.1
1983	2,283.4	547.1	735.7	−51.7	3,514.5
1984	2,492.3	715.6	796.6	−102.0	3,902.4
1985	2,704.8	715.1	875.0	−114.2	4,180.7
1986	2,892.7	722.5	938.5	−131.5	4,422.2
1987	3,094.5	747.2	992.8	−142.1	4,692.3
1988	3,349.7	773.9	1,032.0	−106.1	5,049.6
1989	3,594.8	829.2	1,095.1	−80.4	5,438.7
1990	3,839.3	799.7	1,176.1	−71.3	5,743.8
1991	3,975.1	736.2	1,225.9	−20.5	5,916.7
1992	4,219.8	790.4	1,263.8	−29.5	6,244.4
1993	4,459.2	876.2	1,283.4	−60.7	6,558.1
1994	4,717.0	1,007.9	1,313.0	−90.9	6,947.0
1995	4,953.9	1,043.2	1,356.4	−83.9	7,269.6
1996	5,215.7	1,131.9	1,405.2	−91.2	7,661.6
1997	5,493.7	1,256.0	1,454.6	−93.4	8,110.9
1998	5,805.6	1,368.7	1,487.5	−151.2	8,510.7

NOTE: These figures are in billions of current dollars.

SOURCES: Economic Report of the President, *1999, Table B-1; and* Survey of Current Business, *March 1999, Table 1.1.*

SECTION 1 (continued)

REAL GROSS DOMESTIC PRODUCT

REAL GROSS DOMESTIC PRODUCT, 1959–1998

YEAR	1992 PRICES (BILLIONS OF DOLLARS)	ANNUAL REAL RATE OF GROWTH	REAL GDP PER CAPITA (1992 DOLLARS)
1959	2,210.2	7.4	12,478
1960	2,262.9	2.4	12,519
1961	2,314.3	2.3	12,595
1962	2,454.8	6.1	13,156
1963	2,559.4	4.3	13,520
1964	2,708.4	5.8	14,112
1965	2,881.1	6.4	14,825
1966	3,069.2	6.5	15,612
1967	3,147.2	2.5	15,835
1968	3,293.9	4.7	16,408
1969	3,393.6	3.0	16,739
1970	3,397.6	0.1	16,566
1971	3,510.0	3.3	16,900
1972	3,702.3	5.5	17,637
1973	3,916.3	5.8	18,479
1974	3,891.2	−0.6	18,192
1975	3,873.9	−0.4	17,936
1976	4,082.9	5.4	18,721
1977	4,273.6	4.7	19,400
1978	4,503.0	5.4	20,226
1979	4,630.6	2.8	20,571
1980	4,615.0	−0.3	20,265
1981	4,720.7	2.3	20,524
1982	4,620.3	−2.1	19,896
1983	4,803.7	4.0	20,499
1984	5,140.1	7.0	21,744
1985	5,323.5	3.6	22,320
1986	5,487.7	3.1	22,801
1987	5,649.5	2.9	23,264
1988	5,865.2	3.8	23,934
1989	6,062.0	3.4	24,504
1990	6,136.3	1.2	24,549
1991	6,079.4	−0.9	24,060
1992	6,244.4	2.7	24,447
1993	6,389.6	2.3	24,750
1994	6,610.7	3.5	25,357
1995	6,761.7	2.3	25,691
1996	6,994.8	3.4	26,338
1997	7,269.8	3.9	27,138
1998	7,552.1	3.9	28,012

SOURCES: Economic Report of the President, *1999, Table B-1; and* Survey of Current Business, *March 1999, Table 1.2.*

SECTION 2

PRICES AND INFLATION

PRICE INDEXES: 1959–1998

	GDP DEFLATOR		CONSUMER PRICE INDEX	
YEAR	INDEX (1992 = 100)	ANNUAL PERCENTAGE CHANGE	INDEX (1982–84 = 100)	PERCENTAGE CHANGE (DEC. TO DEC.)
1959	23.0	1.0	29.1	1.7
1960	23.3	1.4	29.6	1.4
1961	23.5	1.2	29.9	0.7
1962	23.8	1.3	30.2	1.3
1963	24.1	1.2	30.6	1.6
1964	24.5	1.5	31.0	1.0
1965	25.0	2.0	31.5	1.9
1966	25.7	2.8	32.4	3.5
1967	26.5	3.2	33.4	3.0
1968	27.6	4.4	34.8	4.7
1969	28.9	4.7	36.7	6.2
1970	30.5	5.3	38.8	5.6
1971	32.1	5.2	40.5	3.3
1972	33.4	4.2	41.8	3.4
1973	35.3	5.6	44.4	8.7
1974	38.5	9.0	49.3	12.3
1975	42.1	9.4	53.8	6.9
1976	44.6	5.8	56.9	4.9
1977	47.4	6.5	60.6	6.7
1978	50.9	7.3	65.2	9.0
1979	55.2	8.5	72.6	13.3
1980	60.3	9.2	82.4	12.5
1981	66.0	9.4	90.9	8.9
1982	70.2	6.3	96.5	3.8
1983	73.2	4.3	99.6	3.8
1984	75.9	3.8	103.9	3.9
1985	78.5	3.4	107.6	3.8
1986	80.6	2.6	109.6	1.1
1987	83.1	3.1	113.6	4.4
1988	86.1	3.7	118.3	4.4
1989	89.7	4.2	124.0	4.6
1990	93.6	4.3	130.7	6.1
1991	97.3	4.0	136.2	3.1
1992	100.0	2.8	140.3	2.9
1993	102.6	2.6	144.5	2.7
1994	105.1	2.4	148.2	2.7
1995	107.5	2.3	152.4	2.5
1996	109.5	1.9	156.9	3.3
1997	111.6	1.9	160.5	1.7
1998	112.7	1.0	163.0	1.6

SOURCES: Economic Report of the President, *1999, Tables B-3, B-60, and B-63; and* Survey of Current Business, *March 1999, Table 7.1.*

SECTION 3

POPULATION AND EMPLOYMENT

Population and Labor Force

Year	Civilian Noninstitutional Population Age 16+ (Millions)	Civilian Labor Force (Millions)	Civilian Labor Force Participation Rate (Percent)	Civilian Employment/ Population Ratio (Percent)
1959	115.3	68.4	59.3	56.0
1960	117.2	69.6	59.4	56.1
1961	118.8	70.5	59.3	55.4
1962	120.2	70.6	58.8	55.5
1963	122.4	71.8	58.7	55.4
1964	124.5	73.1	58.7	55.7
1965	126.5	74.5	58.9	56.2
1966	128.1	75.8	59.2	56.9
1967	129.9	77.3	59.6	57.3
1968	132.0	78.7	59.6	57.5
1969	134.3	80.7	60.1	58.0
1970	137.1	82.8	60.4	57.4
1971	140.2	84.4	60.2	56.6
1972	144.1	87.0	60.4	57.0
1973	147.1	89.4	60.8	57.8
1974	150.1	91.9	61.3	57.8
1975	153.2	93.8	61.2	56.1
1976	156.2	96.2	61.6	56.8
1977	159.0	99.0	62.3	57.9
1978	161.9	102.3	63.2	59.3
1979	164.9	105.0	63.7	59.9
1980	167.7	106.9	63.8	59.2
1981	170.1	108.7	63.9	59.0
1982	172.3	110.2	64.0	57.8
1983	174.2	111.6	64.0	57.9
1984	176.4	113.5	64.4	59.5
1985	178.2	115.5	64.8	60.1
1986	180.6	117.8	65.3	60.7
1987	182.8	119.9	65.6	61.5
1988	184.6	121.7	65.9	62.3
1989	186.4	123.9	66.5	63.0
1990	189.2	125.8	66.5	62.8
1991	190.9	126.3	66.2	61.7
1992	192.8	128.1	66.4	61.5
1993	194.8	129.2	66.3	61.7
1994	196.8	131.1	66.6	62.5
1995	198.6	132.3	66.6	62.9
1996	200.6	133.9	66.8	63.2
1997	203.1	136.3	67.1	63.8
1998	205.2	137.7	67.1	64.1

SOURCE: Economic Report of the President, *1999, Table B-35.*

SECTION 3 (continued)

POPULATION AND EMPLOYMENT

Year	Unemployment Rates: All Workers	Both Sexes, Age 16 to 19	Men Age 20+	Women Age 20+
1959	5.5	14.6	4.7	5.2
1960	5.5	14.7	4.7	5.1
1961	6.7	16.8	5.7	6.3
1962	5.5	14.7	4.6	5.4
1963	5.7	17.2	4.5	5.4
1964	5.2	16.2	3.9	5.2
1965	4.5	14.8	3.2	4.5
1966	3.8	12.8	2.5	3.8
1967	3.8	12.9	2.3	4.2
1968	3.6	12.7	2.2	3.8
1969	3.5	12.2	2.1	3.7
1970	4.9	15.3	3.5	4.8
1971	5.9	16.9	4.4	5.7
1972	5.6	16.2	4.0	5.4
1973	4.9	14.5	3.3	4.9
1974	5.6	16.0	3.8	5.5
1975	8.5	19.9	6.8	8.0
1976	7.7	19.0	5.9	7.4
1977	7.1	17.8	5.2	7.0
1978	6.1	16.4	4.3	6.0
1979	5.8	16.1	4.2	5.7
1980	7.1	17.8	5.9	6.4
1981	7.6	19.6	6.3	6.8
1982	9.7	23.2	8.8	8.3
1983	9.6	22.4	8.9	8.1
1984	7.5	18.9	6.6	6.8
1985	7.2	18.6	6.2	6.6
1986	7.0	18.3	6.1	6.2
1987	6.2	16.9	5.4	5.4
1988	5.5	15.3	4.8	4.9
1989	5.3	15.0	4.5	4.7
1990	5.6	15.5	5.0	4.9
1991	6.8	18.7	6.4	5.7
1992	7.5	20.1	7.1	6.3
1993	6.9	19.0	6.4	5.9
1994	6.1	17.6	5.4	5.4
1995	5.6	17.3	4.8	4.9
1996	5.4	16.7	4.6	4.8
1997	4.9	16.0	4.2	4.4
1998	4.5	14.6	3.7	4.1

SOURCE: Economic Report of the President, *1999, Tables B-35 and B-42.*

SECTION 4

MONEY SUPPLY, INTEREST RATES, AND FEDERAL FINANCES

	Money Supply Data				Interest Rate
Year	Money Supply M1 (Billions)	Annual Change in M1	Money Supply M2 (Billions)	Annual Change in M2	AAA Corporate Bonds
1959	140.0	—	297.8	—	4.38
1960	140.7	0.5	312.4	4.9	4.41
1961	145.2	3.2	335.5	7.4	4.35
1962	147.8	1.8	362.7	8.1	4.33
1963	153.3	3.7	393.2	8.4	4.26
1964	160.3	4.6	424.7	8.0	4.40
1965	167.8	4.7	459.2	8.1	4.49
1966	172.0	2.5	480.2	4.6	5.13
1967	183.3	6.6	524.8	9.3	5.51
1968	197.4	7.7	566.8	8.0	6.18
1969	203.9	3.3	587.9	3.7	7.03
1970	214.4	5.1	626.5	6.6	8.04
1971	228.3	6.5	710.3	13.4	7.39
1972	249.2	9.2	802.3	13.0	7.21
1973	262.9	5.5	855.5	6.6	7.44
1974	274.2	4.3	902.4	5.5	8.57
1975	287.4	4.8	1,017.0	12.7	8.83
1976	306.4	6.6	1,152.8	13.4	8.43
1977	331.3	8.1	1,271.5	10.3	8.02
1978	358.4	8.2	1,368.0	7.6	8.73
1979	382.9	6.8	1,475.8	7.9	9.63
1980	408.9	6.8	1,601.1	8.5	11.94
1981	436.8	6.8	1,756.2	9.7	14.17
1982	474.7	8.7	1,910.9	8.8	13.79
1983	521.2	9.8	2,127.7	11.3	12.04
1984	552.3	6.0	2,312.3	8.7	12.71
1985	619.9	12.2	2,497.7	8.0	11.37
1986	724.4	16.9	2,734.0	9.5	9.02
1987	749.7	3.5	2,832.7	3.6	9.38
1988	787.0	5.0	2,996.4	5.8	9.71
1989	794.2	0.9	3,161.0	5.5	9.26
1990	825.8	4.0	3,279.6	3.8	9.32
1991	897.3	8.7	3,379.9	3.1	8.77
1992	1,025.0	14.2	3,434.7	1.6	8.14
1993	1,129.9	10.2	3,487.5	1.5	7.22
1994	1,150.7	1.8	3,503.0	0.4	7.96
1995	1,128.7	−1.9	3,651.2	4.2	7.59
1996	1,082.8	−4.1	3,826.1	4.8	7.37
1997	1,076.0	−0.6	4,046.4	5.8	7.26
1998	1,092.3	1.5	4,412.3	9.0	6.53

SOURCE: Economic Report of the President, *1999, Tables B-69 and B-73.*

SECTION 4 (continued)

MONEY SUPPLY, INTEREST RATES, AND FEDERAL FINANCES

	Federal Budget Totals (Billions of Dollars)			National Debt	
Year	Fiscal Year Outlays	Fiscal Year Receipts	Surplus (+) or Deficit (−)	Billions of Dollars	As a Percent of GDP
1959	92.1	79.2	−12.8	287.5	58.5
1960	92.2	92.5	0.3	290.5	56.1
1961	97.7	94.4	−3.3	292.6	55.1
1962	106.8	99.7	−7.1	302.9	53.4
1963	111.3	106.6	−4.8	310.3	51.9
1964	118.5	112.6	−5.9	316.1	49.4
1965	118.2	116.8	−1.4	322.3	46.9
1966	134.5	130.8	−3.7	328.5	43.6
1967	157.5	148.8	−8.6	340.4	41.9
1968	178.1	153.0	−25.2	368.7	42.5
1969	183.6	186.9	3.2	365.8	38.6
1970	195.6	192.8	−2.8	380.9	37.8
1971	210.2	187.1	−23.0	408.2	37.9
1972	230.7	207.3	−23.4	435.9	37.0
1973	245.7	230.8	−14.9	466.3	35.7
1974	269.4	263.2	−6.1	483.9	33.6
1975	332.3	279.1	−53.2	541.9	34.9
1976	371.8	298.1	−73.7	629.0	36.3
1977	409.2	355.6	−53.7	706.4	35.8
1978	458.7	399.6	−59.2	776.6	35.1
1979	504.0	463.3	−40.7	829.5	33.2
1980	590.9	517.1	−73.8	909.1	33.4
1981	678.2	599.3	−79.0	994.8	32.6
1982	745.8	617.8	−128.0	1,137.3	35.4
1983	808.4	600.6	−207.8	1,371.7	40.1
1984	851.9	666.5	−185.4	1,564.7	41.0
1985	946.4	734.1	−212.3	1,817.5	44.3
1986	990.5	769.2	−221.2	2,120.6	48.5
1987	1,004.1	854.4	−149.8	2,346.1	50.9
1988	1,064.5	909.3	−155.2	2,601.3	52.5
1989	1,143.7	991.2	−152.5	2,868.0	53.6
1990	1,253.2	1,032.0	−221.2	3,206.6	56.4
1991	1,324.4	1,055.0	−269.4	3,598.5	61.4
1992	1,381.7	1,091.3	−290.4	4,002.1	65.1
1993	1,409.4	1,154.4	−255.0	4,351.4	67.2
1994	1,461.7	1,258.6	−203.1	4,643.7	67.8
1995	1,515.7	1,351.8	−163.9	4,921.0	68.4
1996	1,560.5	1,453.1	−107.5	5,181.9	68.6
1997	1,601.2	1,579.3	−21.9	5,369.7	67.2
1998	1,652.6	1,721.8	69.2	5,478.7	65.2

SOURCE: Economic Report of the President, *1999, Tables B-78 and B-79.*

SECTION 5

SIZE OF GOVERNMENT AS A SHARE OF GDP, 1959–1998

	Federal, State, and Local Government				
Year	Expenditures (% of GDP)	Revenues (% of GDP)	Purchases of Goods and Services (% of GDP)	Non-Defense Purchases of Goods and Services (% of GDP)	Transfer Payments to Persons (% of GDP)
1959	23.0	25.4	22.1	11.1	5.4
1960	23.1	26.4	21.5	11.1	5.6
1961	24.0	26.5	22.2	11.6	6.2
1962	24.1	26.6	22.5	11.8	5.9
1963	24.1	27.1	22.3	12.2	5.9
1964	23.7	26.1	21.8	12.5	5.7
1965	23.4	26.0	21.3	12.7	5.7
1966	24.2	26.7	22.0	12.7	5.8
1967	26.1	27.2	23.3	13.1	6.5
1968	26.8	28.7	23.3	13.2	6.9
1969	26.9	29.9	22.8	13.4	7.1
1970	28.3	28.9	22.8	14.0	8.1
1971	28.7	28.4	22.2	14.3	8.8
1972	28.5	29.5	21.7	14.2	9.0
1973	28.0	29.6	20.8	14.0	9.2
1974	29.3	30.2	21.6	14.8	10.1
1975	31.6	28.7	22.2	15.4	11.6
1976	30.6	29.5	21.2	14.8	11.4
1977	29.9	29.8	20.6	14.4	10.9
1978	28.7	29.6	20.0	14.1	10.4
1979	28.4	29.8	19.8	13.9	10.4
1980	30.2	30.0	20.6	14.3	11.4
1981	30.6	30.6	20.3	13.8	11.6
1982	32.5	30.0	21.1	14.0	12.4
1983	32.4	29.3	20.9	13.7	12.4
1984	31.1	29.3	20.4	13.2	11.5
1985	31.4	29.7	20.9	13.5	11.5
1986	31.6	29.7	21.2	13.7	11.6
1987	31.4	30.5	21.2	13.7	11.4
1988	30.7	30.0	20.4	13.4	11.3
1989	30.5	30.2	20.1	13.5	11.3
1990	31.4	30.1	20.5	14.0	11.8
1991	32.1	30.1	20.7	14.2	12.2
1992	33.1	30.0	20.2	14.2	13.6
1993	32.7	30.2	19.6	14.1	13.8
1994	31.9	30.6	18.9	13.9	13.6
1995	31.8	30.9	18.7	13.9	13.8
1996	31.3	31.5	18.3	13.8	13.8
1997	30.5	31.9	17.9	13.7	13.5
1998	29.8	32.5	17.5	13.5	13.3

SOURCES: Calculated from Economic Report of the President, *1999, Tables B-1, B-83, and B-84, and* Survey of Current Business, *March 1999, Tables 1.1 and 3.7.*

SECTION 6

BASIC ECONOMIC DATA FOR 58 COUNTRIES

	Population 1997 (Millions)	Real GNP per Capita 1997 (in 1997 Dollars)	Average Annual Growth Rate of Real GDP 1990–1997	Annual Growth Rate of Money Supply 1980–1996	Average Annual Inflation Rate 1980–1996	Gross Investment as a Share of GDP 1990–1997[1]
High-Income Countries						
Australia	19	20,170	3.7	12.0	6.0	20.8
Austria	8	21,980	1.6	6.9	3.3	23.3
Belgium	10	22,370	1.2	9.7	3.7	18.3
Canada	30	21,860	2.1	8.1	4.5	18.7
Denmark	5	22,740	2.3	8.5	4.4	19.0
Finland	5	18,980	1.1	8.7	4.9	18.1
France	59	21,860	1.3	6.1	4.7	18.9
Germany	82	21,300	2.5	6.8	2.8	22.9
Hong Kong	7	24,540	5.3	15.7	7.7	30.6
Italy	57	20,060	1.1	8.6	7.8	18.5
Japan	126	23,400	1.4	6.4	1.7	30.1
Netherlands	16	21,340	2.3	5.6	2.5	20.4
Singapore	3	29,000	8.5	12.9	2.3	34.9
Spain	39	15,720	1.6	10.2	7.6	21.9
Sweden	9	19,030	0.9	6.3	6.1	15.9
Switzerland	7	26,320	−0.1	6.6	3.2	22.5
United Kingdom	59	20,520	1.9	16.0	5.3	16.1
United States	268	28,740	2.5	6.3	4.1	16.5
Africa						
Botswana	2	8,220	5.2	17.6	11.2	27.8
Cameroon	14	1,980	0.1	3.6	7.9	—
Côte d'Ivoire	15	1,640	3.0	6.0	6.3	10.8
Ghana	18	1,790	4.3	40.4	37.8	14.0
Kenya	28	1,110	2.0	18.3	15.3	20.1
Mauritius	1	9,360	5.1	18.5	7.7	28.9
Nigeria	118	880	2.7	22.8	29.6	9.5
South Africa	38	7,490	1.5	14.9	13.1	17.1
Tanzania	31	685	2.9	27.2	29.0	22.5
Zambia	9	890	−0.5	51.9	155.0	23.6
Asia and Pacific						
Bangladesh	124	1,050	4.5	16.9	8.1	14.2
China	1227	3,570	11.9	27.0	10.1	38.5
India	961	1,650	5.9	17.0	9.4	24.3
Indonesia	200	3,450	7.5	25.1	8.8	32.8
Malaysia	21	10,920	8.7	14.8	3.6	38.5
Pakistan	137	1,590	4.4	15.5	8.5	19.2
Philippines	73	3,670	3.3	18.8	12.5	23.1
South Korea	46	13,500	7.2	18.1	6.2	36.8
Taiwan	22	13,150	6.4	15.9	4.4	22.4
Thailand	61	6,590	7.5	18.3	4.6	40.3

SECTION 6 (continued)

BASIC ECONOMIC DATA FOR 58 COUNTRIES

	Population 1997 (Millions)	Real GNP per Capita 1997 (in 1997 Dollars)	Average Annual Growth Rate of Real GDP 1990–1997	Annual Growth Rate of Money Supply 1980–1996	Average Annual Inflation Rate 1980–1996	Gross Investment as a Share of GDP 1990–1997[1]
South/Central America						
Argentina	36	9,950	4.5	207.7	194.6	17.0
Brazil	164	6,240	3.1	431.3	399.5	21.7
Chile	15	12,080	7.2	26.5	17.3	25.2
Colombia	38	6,720	4.5	29.5	23.8	19.7
Dominican Republic	8	4,540	5.0	25.9	19.1	25.0
Guatemala	11	3,840	4.1	18.1	14.2	14.9
Mexico	95	8,120	1.8	47.8	46.1	22.7
Peru	25	4,390	6.0	191.3	228.7	20.2
Venezuela	23	8,530	1.9	29.7	33.4	17.2
Middle East/Mediterranean						
Egypt	60	2,940	3.9	19.5	15.3	21.5
Greece	11	13,080	1.8	18.4	16.7	20.5
Iran	61	5,530	6.0	21.9	22.0	26.7
Israel	6	16,960	6.4	34.9	54.2	23.6
Syria	15	2,990	6.9	17.9	17.5	23.1
Turkey	64	6,430	3.6	71.8	57.4	23.8
Eastern Europe						
Bulgaria	8	3,860	−3.5	—	—	16.7
Hungary	10	7,000	−0.4	14.0	15.8	22.7
Poland	39	6,380	3.9	53.0	57.5	19.1
Romania	23	4,290	0.0	36.1	—	27.1
Russia	147	4,190	−9.0	83.4[2]	288.3[2]	26.5

[1]*When the most recent data were unavailable, investment figures from one to two years before 1990 were used to derive an eight-year average. In the case of Russia, only 1992–97 data were available.*
[2]*Derived on the basis of 1993–97 data only.*

SOURCES: World Bank, World Development Report, *1998/99; International Monetary Fund,* International Financial Statistics Yearbook, *1998;* and Statistical Yearbook of the Republic of China, *1998.*

APPENDIX B

Answers to Selected Critical Analysis Questions

CHAPTER 1 The Economic Approach

2. Production of scarce goods always involves a cost; there are no free lunches. When the government provides goods without charge to consumers, other citizens (taxpayers) will bear the cost of their provision. Thus, provision by the government affects how the costs will be covered, not whether they are incurred.
4. For most taxpayers, the change will reduce the after-tax cost of raising children. Other things constant, one would predict an increase in the birth rate.
5. False. Intentions do not change the impact of the policy. If the policy runs counter to sound economics, it will lead to a counterproductive outcome even if that was not the intention of the policy. Bad policies are often advocated by people with good intentions.
7. Raising the price of new cars by requiring safety devices, which customers would not have purchased if given the choice, slows the rate of sales for new cars. Thus the older, less safe cars are driven longer, partially offsetting the safety advantage provided by the newer, safer cars. Also, drivers act a bit differently—they may take more risks—when they believe the safety devices will provide protection should they have an unexpected accident. In fact, economist Gordon Tullock says that the greatest safety device of all might be a dagger built into the center of the steering wheel, pointed directly at the driver's chest!
8. Money has nothing to do with whether an individual is economizing. Any time a person chooses, in an attempt to achieve a goal, he or she is economizing.
9. Positive economics can help one better understand the likely effects of alternative policies. This will help one choose alternatives that are less likely to lead to disappointing results.
10. Association is not causation. It is likely that a large lead, near the end of the game, caused the third team to play more, rather than the third team causing the lead.

CHAPTER 2 Some Tools of the Economist

2. This is an opportunity cost question. Even though the productivity of painters has changed only slightly, rising productivity in other areas has led to higher wages in other occupations, thereby increasing the opportunity cost of being a house painter. Since people would not supply house painting services unless they were able to meet their opportunity costs, higher wages are necessary to attract house painters from competitive (alternative) lines of work.
4. The statement reflects the "exchange is a zero sum game" view. This view is false. No private business can force customers to buy. Neither can a customer force a business to sell. Unless both buyer and seller believe the exchange is in their interest, they will not enter into the exchange. Mutual gain provides the foundation for voluntary exchange.
8. Yes. This question highlights the incentive of individuals to conserve for the future when they have private ownership rights. The market value of the land will increase in anticipation of the future harvest, as the trees grow and the expected day of harvest moves closer. Thus, with transferable private property, the tree farmer will be able to capture the value added by his planting and holding the trees for a few years, even if the actual harvest does not take place until well after his death.
9. In general, it sanctions all forms of competition except for the use of violence (or the threat of violence), theft, or fraud.
11. If the food from land, now and in the future, is worth more than the housing services from the same land, then developers will not be able to bid the land away

from farmers. However, comparative advantage determines the efficient use of a resource; thus, even the best farmland, if situated in the right location, may be far more valuable for buildings. Other, poorer land can always be made more productive by the use of different (and more costly) farming techniques, irrigation, fertilizer, and so on. Physical characteristics alone do not determine the value or the most valuable use of a resource, including land.

12. Those who get tickets at the lower price gain, while those who are prevented from offering a higher price to ticket holders may not get a ticket even though both the buyer and some ticket holders would have gained from the exchange at the higher price. Ticket holders may simply break the law, or may sell at the regulated price only to buyers willing to provide them with other favors. Price controls, if they are effective, always reduce the gains from trade.

CHAPTER 3 Supply, Demand, and the Market Process

1. Choices a and b would increase the demand for beef; c and d would affect primarily the supply of beef, rather than the demand; e leads to a change in quantity demanded, not a change in demand.
4. a. Reductions in the supply of feed grains and hay led to sharply higher prices. b. The higher feed grain and hay prices increased the cost of maintaining a cattle herd and thereby caused many producers to sell (an increase in current supply), depressing cattle prices in 1998. c. The reduction in the size of cattle herds led to a smaller future supply and higher cattle prices in 1989.
8. True. "Somebody" must decide who will be the business winners and losers. Neither markets nor the political process leaves the determination of winners and losers to chance. Under market organization, business winners and losers are determined by the decentralized choices of millions of consumers who use their dollar votes to reward firms that provide preferred goods at a low cost and penalize others who fail to do so. Under political decision making, the winners and losers are determined by political officials who use taxes, subsidies, regulations, and mandates to favor some businesses and penalize others.
10. a. Profitable production increases the value of resources owned by people and leads to mutual gain for resource suppliers, consumers, and entrepreneurs. b. Losses reduce the value of resources, which reduces the well-being of at least some people. There is no conflict.
12. In the absence of trade restrictions, modest price increases in France will attract wheat from other regions, minimizing the effects in the drought region and resulting in slightly higher prices worldwide.
15. a. Demand would increase, rising vertically by $3 per meal—the added per-meal cost previously paid separately. b. Both price and quantity will rise in response to the rise in demand.

CHAPTER 4 Supply and Demand: Applications and Extensions

4. Agreement of both buyer and seller is required for an exchange. Price ceilings push prices below equilibrium and thereby reduce the quantity sellers are willing to offer. Price floors push prices above equilibrium and thereby reduce the quantity consumers wish to buy. Both decrease the actual quantity traded in the market.
6. a. Decreases; b. Increases; c. Decreases; d. Increases.

11. The deadweight loss is the loss of the potential gains of buyers and sellers emanating from trades that are squeezed out by the tax. It is an excess burden because even though the exchanges that are squeezed out by the tax impose a cost on buyers and sellers, they do not generate tax revenue (since the trades do not take place).
14. The employment level of low-skill workers with large families would decline. Some would attempt to conceal the presence of their large family in order to get a job.

CHAPTER 5 The Economic Role of Government

1. When payment is not demanded for services, potential customers have a strong incentive to attempt a "free ride." However, when the number of nonpaying customers becomes such that the sales revenues of sellers are diminished (and in some cases eliminated), the sellers' incentive to supply the good is thereby reduced (or eliminated).
4. The anti-missile system is a public good for the residents of Washington, D.C. Strictly speaking, none of the other items is a public good since each could be provided to some consumers (paying customers, for example) without being provided to others.

CHAPTER 6 The Economics of Collective Decision Making

2. Corporate officers, while they surely care about the next few months and the profits during that time, care also about the value of the firm and its stock price. If the stock price rises sufficiently in the next few months—as it will if investors believe that current investments in future-oriented projects (planting new trees, for example) are sound—then the officers will find their jobs secure even if current profits do not look good. Rights to the profits from those (future) trees are saleable now in the form of the corporation's stock. There is no such mechanism to make the distant fruits of today's investments available to the political entrepreneurs who might otherwise fight for the future-oriented project. Only if the project appeals to today's voters, and they are willing to pay today for tomorrow's benefits, will the program be a political success. In any case, the wealth of the political entrepreneur is not directly enhanced by his or her successful fight for the project.
5. The invisible hand principle is present only when the self-interest of individuals is consistent with the general welfare. Both the special interest effect and the shortsightedness effect indicate that this will not always be the case, even when political choices are made democratically.
6. True. Since each individual computer customer both decides the issue (what computer, if any, will be purchased) and bears the consequences of a mistaken choice, each has a strong incentive to acquire information needed to make a wise choice. In contrast, each voter recognizes that one vote, even if mistaken, will not decide the congressional election. Thus, each has little incentive to search for information to make a better choice.
8. It is difficult for the voter to know what a candidate will do once elected, and the rationally ignorant voter is usually unwilling to spend the time and effort required to understand issues because the probability that any single vote will decide the issue is exceedingly small. Special interest voters, on the other hand, will

know which candidate has promised them the most on their issue. Also, the candidate who is both competent and prepared to ignore special interests will have a hard time getting these facts to voters without financial support from special interest groups. Each voter has an incentive to be a "free rider" on the "good government" issue. Controlling government on behalf of society as a whole is a public good, requiring much private activity. Like other public goods, it tends to be underproduced.

10. No. The government is merely an alternative form of organization. Government organization does not permit us to escape either scarcity or competition. It merely affects the nature of the competition. Political competition (voting, lobbying, political contributions, taxes, and politically determined budgets) replaces market competition. Neither is there any reason to believe that government organization modifies the importance of personal self-interest.
11. When the welfare of a special interest group conflicts with that of a widely dispersed, unorganized majority, the legislative political process can reasonably be expected to work to the benefit of the special interest.

CHAPTER 7 Taking the Nation's Economic Pulse

1. a, c, f, g, and h will exert no impact on GDP; b and d will increase GDP by the amount of the expenditure; and e will increase GDP by $250 (the commission on the transaction).
3. Since the furniture was produced last year, the sale does not affect GDP this year. It reduces inventory investment by $100,000 and increases consumption by $100,000, leaving GDP unchanged.
5. The reliability of GDP comparisons over long periods of time is reduced because the leisure and human costs may change substantially between the two years, and because the types of goods available for consumption during the two years may be vastly different. Likewise, GDP may not be a good index of output differences between countries (for example, the United States and Mexico) for the same reasons. In addition, there may be substantial differences between countries in the production of (a) economic "bads," (b) goods in the household sector, and (c) the size of the underground economy.
7. $7.28
9. a. $1,000; b. $600; c. $200; d. 0; e. $10,000
11. a. False. Inventory investment indicates whether the holdings of unsold goods are rising or falling. A negative inventory investment (economists refer to this as disinvestment) means that inventories were drawn down during the period. b. False. If gross investment is less than the depreciation of capital goods during the period, net investment would be negative. Net investment in the United States was negative for several years during the Great Depression of the 1930s. c. Not necessarily. Rather, it may be the result of an increase in prices, population, or hours worked.
12. Neither the receipts nor the expenditures on payouts would count toward GDP because they are merely transfers—they do not involve production. However, expenditures on operations, administration, and government-provided goods and services from lottery proceeds would add to GDP.
14. a. 0; b. 0; c. $500; d. $300; e. $300; f. 0; g. 0; h. 0
17. a. $2,260.1 billion; b. $3,384.3 billion; c. 60.4. (You should be able to easily calculate the others.)

CHAPTER 8 Economic Fluctuations, Unemployment, and Inflation

2. Job seekers do not know which employers will offer them the more attractive jobs. They find out by searching. Job search is "profitable" and consistent with economic efficiency as long as the marginal gain from search exceeds the marginal cost of searching.
6. One of the most harmful side effects of inflation is the uncertainty it creates with regard to time dimension contracts. As the statement indicates, it tends to undermine the ability of markets to allocate goods and resources to those who value them the most. In effect, it encourages speculation rather than production. The well-known economist who made the statement referred to in the question was John Maynard Keynes. See *The Economic Consequences of Peace* (New York: Harcourt Brace, 1920), pages 235–236.
7. When the actual unemployment rate is equal to the natural rate of unemployment, cyclical unemployment is absent and potential GDP is at its sustainable rate. When the actual unemployment rate is greater (less) than the natural rate of unemployment, cyclical unemployment is positive (negative) and potential GDP is less (greater) than its sustainable rate.
8. a. 60 percent; b. 8.3 percent; c. 55 percent
9. No. No. It means that there were now jobs available at wage rates acceptable to the potential workers who were unemployed. Thus, they continued to search for more attractive opportunities.
10. The inflation will tend to increase the wealth of a and e because it will increase the nominal value of their assets and reduce their real liabilities. It will hurt b, c, and f because their income will rise less rapidly than prices. With regard to d, it depends on whether his indebtedness is at a fixed or variable interest rate. If it is fixed, the inflation will reduce his real indebtedness, but if it is variable (tied to an interest rate that can be expected to increase with the inflation rate), his interest cost will rise with inflation.
13. Each will encourage additional search.
14. The wages people earn are also prices (prices for labor services) and, like other prices, they usually rise as the general level of prices increases. The statement ignores this factor. It implicitly assumes that money wages are unaffected by inflation—that they would have increased by the same amount (6 percent) even if prices would have been stable. Generally, this will not be the case.

CHAPTER 9 An Introduction to Basic Macroeconomic Markets

4. If the inflation rate unexpectedly falls from 3 percent to zero, the real wages of union members will rise. If other unions have similar contracts, the unemployment rate will increase because employment costs have risen relative to product prices. Profit margins will be cut and producers will respond by reducing output and laying off workers. In contrast, if the inflation rate rises to 8 percent, profit margins will improve, producers will expand their output, and the unemployment rate will decline.
7. The key things held constant when constructing the demand and supply schedules for a specific good are demand (consumer income, prices of related goods, consumer preferences, expected future price of the good, and number of consumers) and supply (resource prices, technology, and expected future price of the good). Changes in these factors shift the relevant schedule.

The key things held constant when constructing the aggregate schedules are *AD* (money supply, the government's tax and spending policies, real wealth, real income of one's trading partners, consumer preferences, and the expected future price level); *LRAS* (size of resource base, technology, and institutional structure of the economy); and *SRAS* (factors held constant in the *LR* plus resource prices and the expected price level). Again, changes in these factors will shift the schedules indicated.

10. They are all equal.
12. $10,000; $20,000
13. Inversely; an increase in interest rates is the same thing as a reduction in bond prices.

CHAPTER 10 Working with Our Basic Aggregate Demand/Aggregate Supply Model

1. Choice a would decrease *AD*; b, c, and d would increase it; and e would leave it unchanged. For the "why" part of the question, see the Factors That Shift Aggregate Demand section at the beginning of the chapter.
2. a, b, c, and d will reduce *SRAS;* e will increase it.
4. When an economy is operating at less than full employment, weak demand in resource markets will tend to reduce (a) the real rate of interest and (b) resource prices relative to product prices and thereby restore normal profit and the incentive of firms to produce the long-run potential output level. If resource prices and the real interest rate were inflexible downward, the self-correcting mechanism would not work.
6. At the lower than expected inflation rate, *real* wages (and costs) will increase relative to product prices. This will squeeze profit margins and lead to reductions in output and employment, causing the unemployment rate to rise.
8. Tightness in resource markets will result in rising resource prices relative to product prices, causing the *SRAS* to shift to the left. Profit margins will decline, output rate will fall, and long-run equilibrium will be restored at a higher price level. The above-normal output cannot be maintained because it reflects input prices that people would not have agreed to and output decisions they would not have chosen if they had anticipated the current price level (and rate of inflation). Once they have a chance to correct these mistakes, they do so; and output returns to the economy's long-run potential.
9. Real wages will tend to increase more rapidly when the unemployment rate is low because a tight labor market (strong demand) will place upward pressure on wages.
12. The increase in demand for exports will increase aggregate demand. In the short run, this unanticipated expansion in demand will tend to increase output and employment, while exerting modest upward pressure on the price level. In the long run, the primary impact will be a higher price level, with no change in output and employment.

CHAPTER 11 Keynesian Foundations of Modern Macroeconomics

2. a. Increase current consumption, as the expectation of rising future prices will induce consumers to buy now.
   b. Decrease current consumption, as people will attempt to save more for hard times.

c. Increase current consumption, as the result of an expansion in disposable income.
d. May have little effect. However, the tendency will be toward a reduction in consumption, since households have an incentive to save more at the higher interest rate.
e. Decrease consumption, as failing stock prices will reduce the wealth of consumers.
f. and g. Increase consumption, as the young and the poor typically have a higher marginal propensity to consume than the elderly and wealthy.

4. It is the concept that a change in one of the components of aggregate demand—investment, for example—will lead to a far greater change in the equilibrium level of income. Since the multiplier equals 1/1 − MPC, its size is determined by the marginal propensity to consume. The multiplier makes stabilizing the economy more difficult, since relatively small changes in aggregate demand have a much greater impact on equilibrium income.
7. None. The Keynesian model assumes that wages and prices are inflexible downward. It will take an increase in aggregate expenditures to restore full employment.
9. The statement fails to recognize that association does not imply a direction of causation. The investment demand conditions differ during periods of boom and recession. During an expansionary boom, investment demand is strong. In turn, the strong investment demand pushes interest rates up, not vice versa. Similarly, during a recession, weak investment demand leads to lower interest rates. Thus, it is the fluctuations in investment demand (shifts of the schedule) that explain the pattern of interest rates over the business cycle.
12. You would expect the multiplier to be smaller in Canada because Canadians would be expected to spend a larger share of their additions to income on imports, rather than domestic goods. This will reduce the size of the multiplier.

CHAPTER 12 Fiscal Policy

2. The crowding-out effect is the theory that budget deficits will lead to higher real interest rates, which retard private spending. The crowding-out effect indicates that fiscal policy would not be nearly so potent as the simple Keynesian model implies. The new classical theory indicates that anticipation of higher future taxes (rather than higher interest rates) will crowd out private spending when government expenditures are financed by debt.
4. Automatic stabilizers are built-in features (unemployment compensation, corporate profit tax, progressive income tax) that tend automatically to promote a budget deficit during a recession and a budget surplus (or smaller deficit) during an inflationary boom. Automatic stabilizers have the major advantage of providing needed restraint, or stimuli, without congressional approval—which, in turn, minimizes the problem of proper timing.
8. This statement depicts the views of many economists three decades ago. Today, most economists recognize that it is naive. Given our limited ability to accurately forecast future economic conditions, timing of fiscal policy is more difficult than was previously thought. Political considerations—remember, the government is merely an alternative form of social organization, not a corrective device—reduce the likelihood that fiscal policy will be used as a stabilization tool. Changes in interest rates and private spending may offset fiscal actions and thereby reduce the potency of fiscal policy. All factors considered, it is clear that the use of fiscal policy to stabilize the economy is both difficult and complex.

10. There is a major defect in this view. If the budget deficits stimulated demand and thereby output and employment, we would have expected the inflation rate to accelerate. This was not the case; in fact, the inflation rate declined. The failure of the inflation rate to accelerate during the expansion of the 1980s strongly suggests that factors other than demand stimulus were at work.
13. This is an accurate statement of what economists refer to as the balanced budget multiplier. It is correct under very restrictive assumptions. However, it ignores the secondary effects in the loanable funds market. If the taxes of consumers rise by $10 billion and consumers reduce their spending by only $7.5 billion, then a $2.5 billion reduction in the supply of loanable funds is implied. This will place upward pressure on the real interest rate, which, under normal circumstances, will crowd out $2.5 billion dollars of private spending. Thus, when the secondary effects are considered, the validity of the statement is highly questionable.
14. Yes. Only the lower rates would increase the incentive to earn marginal income and thereby stimulate aggregate supply.

CHAPTER 13 Money and the Banking System

1. A liquid asset is one that can easily and quickly be transformed into money without experiencing a loss of its market value. Assets such as high-grade bonds and stocks are highly liquid. In contrast, illiquid assets cannot be easily and quickly converted to cash without some loss of their value. Real estate, a family-owned business, business equipment, and artistic works are examples of illiquid assets.
3. Money is valuable because of its scarcity relative to the availability of goods and services. The use of money facilitates (reduces the cost of) exchange transactions. Money also serves as a store of value and a unit of account. Doubling the supply of money, holding output constant, would simply cause its purchasing power to fall without enhancing the services that it performs. In fact, fluctuations in the money supply would create uncertainty as to its future value and reduce the ability of money to serve as a store of value, accurate unit of account, and medium of exchange for time-dimension contracting.
6. a. No change; currency held by the public increases, but checking deposits decrease by an equal amount. b. Bank reserves decrease by $100. c. Excess reserves decrease by $100, minus $100 multiplied by the required reserve ratio.
8. Answers b, e, and f will reduce the money supply; a and c will increase it; if the Treasury's deposits (or the deposits of persons who receive portions of the Treasury's spending) are considered part of the money supply, then d will leave the money supply unchanged.
10. While the transformation of deposits into currency does not directly affect the money supply, it does reduce the excess reserves of banks. The reduction in excess reserves will cause banks to reduce their outstanding loans and thereby shrink the money supply. Therefore, an increase in the holding of currency relative to deposits will tend to reduce the supply of money.
12. There are two major reasons. First, the money supply can be altered quietly via open market operations, while a reserve requirement change focuses attention on Fed policy. Second, open market operations are a fine-tuning method, while a reserve requirement change is a blunt instrument. Generally, the Fed prefers quiet, marginal changes to headline-grabbing, blunt changes that are more likely to disrupt markets.
13. a. False; statements of this type often use money when they are really speaking about wealth (or income).

b. False; the checking deposit also counts as money. In addition, the deposit increases the reserves of the receiving bank, and thereby places it in a position to extend additional loans that would increase the money supply.

c. False; only an increase in the availability of goods and services valued by people will improve our standard of living. Without an additional supply of goods and services, more money will simply lead to a higher price level.

17. a. Money supply increases by $100,000; b. $80,000; c. $500,000; d. no; there will be some leakage in the form of additional currency holdings by the public and additional excess reserve holdings by banks.

19. a. Money supply will increase by $2 billion; b. $1.8 billion; c. $20 billion; d. approximately $10.5 billion; e. approximately $8.51 billion; the potential money multiplier was 10, but the actual multiplier was only 4.255; f. the leakages in the form of currency held by the public and additions to bank reserves cause the actual money multiplier to be less than the potential multiplier.

CHAPTER 14 Modern Macroeconomics: Monetary Policy

2. Choices a and c would increase your incentive to hold money deposits; b and d would reduce your incentive to hold money.

3. a. The cost of obtaining the house is $100,000, but

   b. the cost of holding it is the interest forgone on the $100,000 sales value of the house.

   c. the cost of obtaining $1,000 is the amount of goods one must give up in order to acquire the $1,000. For example, if a pound of sugar sells for 50 cents, the cost of obtaining $1,000 in terms of sugar is 2,000 pounds.

   d. As in the case of the house, the cost of holding $1,000 is the interest forgone.

7. a. bank reserves will decline; b. real interest rates will rise; c. spending on consumer durables will fall; d. dollar will appreciate because the higher interest rates will attract bond purchases by foreigners; e. exports will decline because the appreciation of the dollar will make U.S. goods more expensive for foreigners; f. the higher real interest rates will tend to reduce real asset prices; and g. real GDP will fall.

10. If the time lag is long and variable (rather than short and highly predictable), it is less likely that policy makers will be able to time changes in monetary policy so that they will exert a *countercyclical* impact on the economy. The policy makers will be more likely to make mistakes and thereby exert a destabilizing influence.

11. Association does not reveal causation. Decision makers—including borrowers and lenders—will eventually anticipate a high rate of inflation and adjust their choices accordingly. As the expected rate of inflation increases, the demand for loanable funds will increase and the supply will decrease. This will lead to higher nominal interest rates. Thus, economic theory indicates that the causation tends to run the opposite direction from that indicated by the statement.

12. Aggregate demand will decline as individuals and businesses reduce spending in an effort to build up their money balances (demand more money).

14. Real GDP: U.S. (5,974; 6,182; 6,308; 6,464); Chile (11,732; 12,231; 13,278; 14,191); Venezuela (2,660; 2,584; 2,671; 2,628); Percent rate of change in money supply: U.S. (0.1; −0.9; 1.4); Chile (16.1; 22.3; 16.2); Venezuela (139.9; 38.3; −1.3); Percent rate of change in price level: U.S. (2.3; 2.5; 1.9); Chile (13.9; 12.2; 3.5); Venezuela (63.0; 51.3; 111.4); b. Venezuela; c. Venezuela; d. Chile.

CHAPTER 15 Stabilization Policy, Output, and Employment

2. Compared with earlier periods, the United States has experienced less economic instability during the last four decades. There is reason to believe that a more stable monetary policy has contributed to the increase in stability. See text Exhibits 15-1 and 15-2.
5. Nonactivists think that a monetary rule would result in less instability from monetary sources. The changing nature of money may reduce the stabilizing effects of a monetary rule.

CHAPTER 16 Economic Growth

3. A few years ago, many believed that this view was essentially true. However, this is no longer the case. Foreign aid has played an insignificant role in the progress of most of the high-growth LDCs. In some cases, it has adversely affected economies. In the past, aid has disrupted markets and retarded the incentive of producers in less-developed countries. Furthermore, attractive investment alternatives will draw investment from abroad even if domestic saving is inadequate. Thus, the efficacy of aid as a tool to promote economic growth is highly questionable.
6. Productivity fell during 1973–1994. Productivity growth is important because it is the source of higher earnings. Without the growth of productivity, there can be no growth of earnings per hour worked. Persons age 40 to 55 years are generally at or near the peak of their life-cycle productivity. The combination of education, training, and experience enhances productivity during these years. When a larger proportion of the population is in this age bracket, it will also enhance the economy-wide level of productivity.
7. Yes. Trade barriers limit the ability of both businesses and consumers to benefit from economies associated with an expansion in the size of the market. This limitation will be more restrictive for small countries (like Costa Rica) than for larger countries (like Mexico) because the latter will often have sizable domestic markets.

CHAPTER 17 Gaining from International Trade

1. Availability of goods and services, not jobs, is the source of economic prosperity. When a good can be purchased cheaper abroad than it can be produced at home, a nation can expand the quantity of goods and services available for consumption by specializing in the production of those goods for which it is a low-cost producer and trading them for the cheap (relative to domestic costs) foreign goods. Trade restrictions limiting the ability of Americans to purchase low-cost goods from foreigners stifle this process and thereby reduce the living standard of Americans.
3. Statements a and b are not in conflict. Since trade restrictions are typically a special interest issue, political entrepreneurs can often gain by supporting them even when they promote economic inefficiency.
5. True. The primary effect of trade restrictions is an increase in domestic scarcity. This has distributional consequences, but it is clear that as a whole, a nation will be harmed by the increased domestic scarcity accompanying the trade restraints.
6. The quota reduces the supply of sugar to the domestic market and drives up the domestic price of sugar. Domestic producers benefit from the higher prices at the expense of domestic consumers (see Exhibit 17-9). Studies indicate that the quota expanded the gross income of the 11,000 domestic sugar farmers by approximately $130,000 per farm in the mid-1980s, at the expense (in the form of higher prices of

sugar and sugar products) of approximately $6 per year to the average domestic consumer. Since the program channels resources away from products for which the United States has a comparative advantage, it reduces the productive capacity of the United States. Both the special interest nature of the issue and rent-seeking theory explain the political attractiveness of the program.

8. a. No. Americans would be poorer if we used more of our resources to produce things for which we are a high opportunity-cost producer and less of our resources to produce things for which we are a low opportunity-cost producer. Employment might either increase or decrease, but the key point is that it is the value of goods produced, not employment, that generates income and provides for the wealth of a nation. The answer to b is the same as a.
9. In thinking about this issue, consider the following points. Suppose the Japanese were willing to give products such as automobiles, electronic goods, and clothing to us free of charge. Would we be worse off if we accepted the gifts? Should we try to keep the free goods out? What is the source of real income—jobs or goods and services? If the gifts make us better off, doesn't it follow that partial gifts would also make us better off?
12. While trade reduces employment in import-competing industries, it expands employment in export industries. On balance, there is no reason to believe that trade either promotes or destroys jobs. The major effect of trade is to permit individuals, states, regions, and nations to generate a larger output by specializing in the things they do well and trading for those things that they would produce only at a high cost. A higher real income is the result.
15. True. If country A imposes a tariff, other countries will sell less to A and therefore acquire less purchasing power in terms of A's currency. Thus, they will have to reduce their purchases of A's export goods.

CHAPTER 18 International Finance and the Foreign Exchange Market

4. On February 2, the dollar appreciated against the pound and depreciated against the franc.
5. Answers a and g would cause the dollar to appreciate; b, c, d, e, and h would cause the dollar to depreciate; f would leave the exchange rate unchanged.
9. Each of the changes would reduce the size of the current account deficit.
11. The current account balance will move toward a larger deficit (or smaller surplus) and the dollar will appreciate.
14. False. Flexible exchange rates bring the sum of the current and capital accounts into balance, but they do not necessarily lead to balance for either component.
15. a. No. The exchange rate will bring the sum of the current and capital accounts into balance, but it will not bring about either an overall merchandise trade balance or a trade balance with a specific country.
    b. Compared to the United States, Japan has a high savings rate. High-income countries with high savings rates tend to invest substantially abroad. In order to pay for these investments, Japan must run a current account surplus. Its trading partners—particularly those with a low saving rate like the United States—will do the opposite. In addition, Japan is a major importer of natural resources and raw materials, two product areas where the United States does not generally have a comparative advantage. Because the United States is generally not a low-cost producer of the primary products imported by the Japanese, the United States tends to export less goods and services to Japan than it imports.

c. Americans will not want to hold the additional yen. They can be expected to use them to purchase additional foreign-produced goods, including goods supplied by the Japanese. Clearly, the trade deficit with Japan is only a part of the total current account deficit.

APPLICATION 1 Labor Markets and Unemployment Rates: A Cross-Country Analysis

1. The ability to organize only a portion of the firms in an industry leaves the organized firms in competition with the unorganized firms. When organized firms pay higher wages, they find it harder to compete with nonunion firms due to higher costs. This restricts the ability of the union to raise wages in the organized firms. Because competition from nonunion firms is less prevalent in Europe than in the United States, European unions are better able to increase the wages of union members than their counterparts in the United States.

APPLICATION 2 How Do Budget Deficits and the National Debt Affect Future Generations?

1. No. Both private corporations and governments can, and often do, have continual debt outstanding. Borrowers can continue to finance and refinance debt as long as lenders have confidence in their ability to pay. This will generally be the case as long as the interest liability is small relative to income (or the potential tax base).
4. No. Remember, trade is a positive-sum game. Bonds are sold to foreigners because they are offering a better deal (acceptance of a lower interest rate) than is available elsewhere. Prohibiting the sale of bonds to foreigners would result in higher real interest rates and less investment, both of which would adversely affect Americans.
6. Lower; voters do not enjoy paying taxes and, therefore, voter dissatisfaction places a restraint on higher taxes, which would also restrain expenditures if the budget had to be balanced. More efficient; the restraint of tax increases would tighten the budget constraint and make the reality of opportunity cost more visible to both voters and politicians.
8. No. Yes.

APPLICATION 3 The Phillips Curve: Is There a Trade-Off between Inflation and Unemployment?

2. Economists in the mid-1970s thought inflation would reduce unemployment; they failed to recognize that decision makers would eventually come to anticipate the inflation. The modern view of the Phillips curve incorporates expectations into the analysis.
5. With unanticipated inflation, real wages fall because many workers, who did not anticipate the inflation, accepted explicit and implicit contracts at wage rates they would have found unacceptable had they correctly anticipated the magnitude of the price increase. Job search time will decline because many workers will accept jobs at money wage rates they would have rejected if they had been fully aware of how much inflation had increased money wages. Both of these

factors will temporarily reduce the unemployment rate. When the inflation is anticipated, it will be fully reflected in long-term wage agreements. Thus, the inflation will fail to reduce real wage rates. Similarly, job search time will be normal because workers will recognize how much inflation has increased the money wages of potential jobs. Thus, anticipated inflation fails to reduce the unemployment rate.

APPLICATION 4 Social Security: The Nature of the Problem and the Alternatives for Dealing with It

2. The pay-as-you-go social security system will face a crisis sometime around 2014 when the inflow of tax revenue will be insufficient to cover the promised benefits. While the Social Security Trust Fund has bonds, they are merely an IOU from the Treasury to the Social Security Administration. In order to redeem these bonds and provide additional funds to finance social security benefits, the federal government will have to raise taxes (or pay the interest on additional Treasury bonds it sells), or cut other expenditures, or both. Thus, the presence of the SSTF bonds does not do much to alleviate the crisis.

APPLICATION 5 The Stock Market: What Does It Do and How Has It Performed?

1. History shows that in the U.S. stock market, a relatively low risk with fairly high returns can be gained by holding a diverse portfolio of stocks in unrelated industries, for a period of 20 years or more. Mutual funds are an option that allows a person to purchase a diverse portfolio while keeping commission costs low.
3. High profits now and the expectation of higher profits in the future have driven up the price of the stock, despite the lack of dividend payment in the first years of the firm. Investors are equally happy with high dividends or the equivalent in rising stock value due to the firm's retaining of its profits for further investment.
5. Investors are buying such a stock for its rising value (price), which reflects expected future earnings and dividends.

Absolute advantage A situation in which a nation, as the result of its previous experience and/or natural endowments, can produce more of a good (with the same amount of resources) than another nation.

Activist strategy Deliberate change in monetary and fiscal policy in order to inject demand stimulus during a recession and apply restraint during an inflationary boom and thereby, it is hoped, minimize economic instability.

Adaptive-expectations hypothesis The hypothesis that economic decision makers base their future expectations on actual outcomes observed during recent periods. For example, according to this view, the rate of inflation actually experienced during the past two or three years would be the major determinant of inflation expected for the next year.

Administrative lag The time period after the need for a policy change is recognized but before the policy is actually implemented.

Aggregate demand curve A downward-sloping curve indicating an inverse relationship between the price level and the quantity of domestically produced goods and services that households, business firms, governments, and foreigners (net exports) are willing to purchase during a period.

Aggregate supply curve A curve indicating the relationship between the nation's price level and quantity of goods supplied by its producers. In the short run, it is probably an upward-sloping curve, but in the long run most economists believe the aggregate supply curve is vertical (or nearly so).

Anticipated change A change that is foreseen by decision makers in time for them to adjust.

Anticipated inflation An increase in the general level of prices that was expected by most decision makers.

Appreciation An increase in the value of a currency relative to foreign currencies. An appreciation increases the purchasing power of the currency over foreign goods.

Asymmetric-information problem A problem arising when either buyers or sellers have important information about the product that is not possessed by the other side in potential transactions.

Automatic stabilizers Built-in features that tend automatically to promote a budget deficit during a recession and a budget surplus during an inflationary boom, even without a change in policy.

Autonomous expenditures Expenditures that do not vary with the level of income. They are determined by factors (such as business expectations and economic policy) that are outside the basic income-expenditure model.

Average tax rate (ATR) Tax liability divided by taxable Income. It is the percentage of income paid in taxes.

Balance of merchandise trade The difference between the value of merchandise exports and the value of merchandise imports for a nation. The balance of merchandise trade is only one component of a nation's total balance of payments. Also called simply balance of trade or net exports.

Balance of payments A summary of all economic transactions between a country and all other countries for a specific time period, usually a year. The balance-of-payments account reflects all payments and liabilities to foreigners (debits) and all payments and obligations received from foreigners (credits).

Balance on current account The import-export balance of goods and services, plus net investment income earned abroad, plus net private and government transfers. If the value of the nation's export-type items exceeds (is less than) the value of the nation's import-type items plus net unilateral transfers to foreigners, a current-account surplus (deficit) is present.

Balance on goods and services The exports of goods (merchandise) and services of a nation minus its imports of good and services.

Balanced budget A situation in which current government revenue from taxes, fees, and other sources is just equal to current government expenditures.

Bank reserves Vault cash plus deposits of the bank with Federal Reserve banks.

Black market A market that operates outside the legal system, either by selling illegal goods or by selling goods at illegal prices or terms.

Budget deficit A situation in which total government spending exceeds total government revenue during a specific time period, usually one year.

Budget surplus A situation in which total government spending is less than total government revenue during a time period, usually a year.

Business cycle Fluctuations in the general level of economic activity as measured by such variables as the rate of unemployment and changes in real GDP.

Capital account The record of transactions with foreigners that involve either (1) the exchange of ownership rights to real or financial assets or (2) extension of loans.

Capital formation The production of buildings, machinery, tools, and other equipment that will enhance the ability of future economic participants to produce. The term can also be applied to efforts to upgrade the knowledge and skill of workers and thereby increase their ability to produce in the future.

Capitalism An economic system based on private ownership of productive resources and allocation of goods according to the signals provided by market prices.

Central bank An institution that regulates the banking system and controls the supply of money of a country.

Ceteris paribus A Latin term meaning "other things constant," used when the effect of one change is being described, recognizing that if other things changed, they also could affect the result. Economists often describe the effects of one change, knowing that in the real world, other things might change and have their effects, too.

Choice The act of selecting among alternatives.

Civilian labor force The number of persons 16 years of age and over who are either employed or unemployed. In order to be classified as unemployed, one must be looking for a job.

Classical economists Economists from Adam Smith to the time of Keynes who focused their analyses on economic efficiency and production. With regard to business instability, they thought market prices and wages would decline during a recession quickly enough to bring the economy back to full employment within a short period of time.

Collective decision making The method of organization that relies on public-sector decision making (voting, political bargaining, lobbying, and so on) to resolve basic issues.

Commercial banks Financial institutions that offer a wide range of services (for example, checking accounts, savings accounts, and extension of loans) to their customers. Commercial banks are owned by stockholders and seek to operate as a profit.

Comparative advantage The ability to produce a good at a lower opportunity cost than others can produce it. Relative costs determine comparative advantage.

Complements Products that are usually consumed jointly (for example, peanut butter and jelly). They are related such that a decrease in the price of one will cause an increase in demand for the other.

Consumer price index (CPI) An indicator of the general level of prices. It attempts to compare the cost of purchasing the market basket bought by a typical consumer during a specific period with the cost of purchasing the same market basket during an earlier period.

Consumer surplus The difference between the maximum price consumers are willing to pay and the price they actually pay. It is the net gain derived by the buyers of the good.

Consumption function A fundamental relationship between disposable income and consumption, in which, as disposable income increases, current consumption expenditures rise, but by a smaller amount than the increase in income.

Countercyclical policy A policy that tends to move the economy in an opposite direction from the forces of the business cycle. Such a policy would stimulate demand during the contraction phase of the business cycle and restrain demand during the expansion phase.

Credit Funds acquired by borrowing.

Credit unions Financial cooperative organizations of individuals with a common affiliation (such as an employer or a labor union). They accept deposits, including checkable deposits, pay interest (or dividend) on them out of earnings, and channel funds primarily into loans of members.

Crowding-out effect A reduction in private spending as a result of higher interest rates generated by budget deficits that are financed by borrowing in the private loanable funds market.

Currency board An entity that (a) issues a currency with a fixed designated value relative to a widely accepted currency (for example, the U.S. dollar) (b) promises to continue to redeem the issued currency at the fixed rate, and (c) maintains bonds and other liquid assets denominated in the other currency that provide 100 percent backing for all currency issued.

Current account The record of all transactions with foreign nations that involve the exchange of merchandise goods and services, current income derived from investments, and unilateral gifts.

Cyclical unemployment Unemployment due to recessionary business conditions and inadequate aggregate demand for labor.

Deadweight loss A loss of gains from trade resulting from the imposition of a tax. It imposes a burden of taxation over and above the burden associated with the transfer of revenues to the government.

Demand deposits Non-interest-earning checking deposits that can be either withdrawn or made payable on demand to a third party. Like currency, these deposits are widely used as a means of payment.

Demand for money A curve that indicates the relationship between the interest rate and the quantity of money people want to hold. Because higher interest rates increase the opportunity cost of holding money, the quantity demanded of money will be inversely related to the interest rate.

Deposit expansion multiplier The multiple by which in increase (decrease) in reserves will increase (decrease) the money supply. It is inversely related to the required reserve ratio.

Depository institutions Businesses that accept checking and savings deposits and use a portion of them to extend loans and make investments. Banks, savings and loan associations and credit unions are examples.

Depreciation A reduction in the value of a domestic currency relative to foreign currencies. A depreciation reduces the purchasing power of the domestic currency for foreign goods.

Depression A prolonged and very severe recession.

Discount rate The interest rate the Federal Reserve charges banking institutions for borrowing funds.

Discouraged workers Persons who have given up searching for employment because they believe additional job search would be fruitless. Because they are not currently searching for work, they are not counted among the unemployed.

Discretionary fiscal policy A change in laws or appropriate levels that alters government revenues and/or expenditures.

Disposable income The income available to individuals after personal taxes. It can be either spent on consumption or saved.

Division of labor A method that breaks down the production of a commodity into a series of specific tasks, each performed by a different worker.

Dumping The sale of a good by a foreign supplier in another country at a price below that charged by the supplier in its home market.

Economic efficiency Economizing behavior. When applied to a community, it implies that (1) an activity should be undertaken if the sum of the benefits to the individuals exceeds the sum of their costs and (2) no activity should be undertaken if the costs borne by the individuals exceed the benefits.

Economic good A good that is scarce. The desire for economic goods exceeds the amount that is freely available from nature.

Economic Theory A set of definitions, postulates, and principles assembled in a manner that makes clear the "cause-and-effect" relationship of economic data.

Economizing behavior Choosing with the objective of gaining a specific benefit at the least possible cost. A corollary of economizing behavior implies that, when choosing among items of equal cost, individuals will choose the option that yields the greatest benefit.

Employment/population ratio The number of persons 16 years of age and over employed as civilians divided by the total civilian population 16 years of age and over. The ratio is expressed as a percentage.

Entrepreneur A profit-seeking decision maker who decides which projects to undertake and how they should be undertaken. A successful entrepreneur's actions will increase the value or resources.

Equation of exchange MV = PY, where M is the money supply, V is the velocity of money, P is the price level, and Y is the output of goods and services provided.

Equilibrium A state of balance between conflicting forces, such as supply and demand.

Equity mutual fund A corporation that pools the funds of investors, including small investors, and uses them to purchase a bundle of stocks.

Escalator clause A contractual agreement that periodically and automatically adjusts money usage rates upward as the price level rises. They are sometimes referred to as cost-of-living adjustments or COLAs.

Excess burden of taxation Another term for deadweight loss. It reflects losses that occur when beneficial activities are forgone because they are taxed.

Excess reserves Actual reserves that exceed the legal requirement.

Exchange rate The domestic price of one unit of foreign currency. For example, if it takes $1.50 to purchase one English pound, the dollar-pound exchange rate is 1.50.

Exit The ability to withdraw from an economic relationship with another person or organization.

Expansion monetary policy A shift in monetary policy designed to stimulate aggregate demand. Bond purchases, creation of additional bank reserves, and an increase in the growth rate of the money supply are generally indicative of a shift to a more expansionary monetary policy.

Expansionary fiscal policy An increase in government expenditures and/or a reduction in tax rates such that the expected size of the budget deficit expands.

Expenditure multiplier The ratio of the change in equilibrium output to the independent change in investment, consumption, or government spending that brings about the change. Numerically, the multiplier is equal to 1 divided by (1-MPC) when the price level is constant.

Exports Goods and services produced domestically but sold to foreigners.

External debt The portion of the national debt owed to foreign investors.

Externalities The side effects or spillover effects, of an action that influence the well-being of nonconsenting parties. The nonconsenting parties may be either helped (by external benefits) or harmed (by external costs).

Fallacy of composition Erroneous view that what is true for the individual (or the part) will also be true for the group (or the whole).

Federal Deposit Insurance Corporation (FDIC) A federally chartered corporation that insures the deposits held by commercial banks and thrift institutions.

Federal funds market A loanable fund market in which banks seeking additional reserves borrow short-term (generally for seven days or less) funds from banks with excess reserves. The interest rate in this market is called the federal funds rate.

Federal Open Market Committee (FOMC) A 120-member board that establishes Fed policy with regard to the buying and selling of government securities, the primary mechanism used to control the money supply in the United States.

Federal Reserve System The central bank of the United States; it carries out banking regulatory policies and is responsible for the conduct of monetary policy.

Final market goods and services Goods and services purchased by their ultimate user.

Fiscal policy The use of government taxation and expenditure policies for the purpose of achieving macroeconomic goals.

Fixed exchange rate An exchange rate that is set at a determined amount by government policy.

Flat money Money that has neither intrinsic value nor the backing of a commodity with intrinsic value; paper currency is an example.

Flexible exchange rates Exchange rates that are determined by the market forces of supply and demand. They are sometimes called floating exchange rates.

Foreign exchange market The market in which the currencies of different countries are bought and sold.

Fractional reserve banking A system that permits banks to hold reserves of less than 100 percent against their deposits.

Free rider One who receives the benefit of a good without contributing to its costs. Public goods and commodities that generate external benefits offer people the opportunity to become free riders.

Frictional unemployment Unemployment due to constant changes in the economy that prevent qualified unemployed workers from being immediately matched up with existing job openings. It results from the scarcity of information and the search activities of both employers and employees for information that will help them make better employment choices.

Full employment The level of employment that results from the efficient use of the labor force after allowance is made for the normal (natural) rate of unemployment due to information cost, dynamic changes, and the structural conditions of the economy. For the United States, full employment is thought to exist when between 94 and 95 percent of the labor force is employed.

GDP deflator A price index that reveals the cost of purchasing the items included in GDP during the period relative to the cost of purchasing these same items during a base year (currently, 1992). Because the base year is assigned a value of 100, as the GDP deflator takes on values greater than 100, it indicates that prices have risen.

General Agreement on Tariffs and Trade (GATT) An organization formed following the Second World War designed to set the rules for the conduct of international trade and reduce barriers to trade among nations.

Goods and services market A highly aggregated market encompassing the flow of all final-user goods and services. The market counts all items that enter into GDP. Thus, real output in this market is equal to real GDP.

Gross domestic product (GDP) The market value of all final goods and services produced within a country during a specific period.

Gross national product (GNP) The total market value of all final goods and services produced by the citizens of a country. It is equal to GDP minus the net income of foreigners.

Impact lag The time period after a policy change is implemented but before the change begins to exert its primary effects.

Imports Goods and services produced by foreigners but purchased by domestic consumers, investors, and government.

Import quota A specific limit or maximum quantity (or value) of a good permitted to be imported into a country during a given period.

Index of leading indicators An index of economic variables that historically has tended to turn down prior to the beginning of a business expansion.

Indirect business taxes Taxes that increase the business firm's costs of production and, therefore, the prices charged to consumers. Examples would be sales, excise, and property taxes.

Inflation A continuing rise in the general level of prices of goods and services. The purchasing power of the monetary unit, such as the dollar, declines when inflation is present.

Inflation premium A component of the money interest rate that reflects compensation to the lender for the expected decrease, due to inflation, in the purchasing power of the principal and interest during the course of the loan. It is determined by the expected rate of future inflation.

Innovation The successful introduction and adoption of a new product or process. The economic application of inventions and marketing techniques.

Intermediate goods Goods purchased for resale for use in producing another good or service.

International Monetary Fund (IMF) An international banking organization, with more than 180 member nations, designed to over see the operation of the international monetary system. Although it does not control the world supply of money, it does hold currency reserves for member nationals and makes currency loans to national central banks.

Invention The creation of a new product or process, often facilitated by the knowledge of engineering and scientific relationships.

Inventory investment Changes in the stock of unsold goods, and raw materials held during a period.

Invisible hand principle The tendency of market prices to direct individuals pursuing their own interests into productive activities that also promote the economic well-being of the society.

J-curve effect The tendency of a nation's current-account deficit to widen initially before it shrinks to an exchange-rate depreciation. This tendency results because the short-run demand for both imports and exports is often inelastic, even though the long-run demand is almost always elastic.

Labor force participation rate The number of persons in the civilian labor force 16 years of age or over who are either employed or actively seeking employment as a percentage of the total civilian population 16 years of age and over.

Laffer curve A curve illustrating the relationship between the tax rate and tax revenue. Tax revenue will be low for both very high and very low tax rates. Thus, when tax rates are quite high, a reduction in the tax rate can increase tax revenue.

Law of comparative advantage A principle that states that individuals, firms, regions, or nations can gain by specializing in the production of goods that they produce cheaply (that is, at a low opportunity cost) and exchanging those goods for other desired goods for which they are a high-opportunity-cost producer.

Law of demand A principle that states there is an inverse relationship between the price of a good and the amount of it buyers are willing to purchase. As the price of a product increases, other things constant, consumers will purchase less of the product.

Law of supply A principle that states there is a direct relationship between the price of a good and the amount of it offered for sale. As the price of a product increases, other things constant, producers will increase the amount of the product supplied to the market.

Less-developed countries (LDCs) Low-income countries generally characterized by rapid population growth and an agriculture-household sector that dominates the economy. Sometimes these countries are referred to as developing countries.

Liquid asset An asset that can be easily and quickly converted to purchasing power without loss of value.

Loanable funds market A general term used to describe the broad market that coordinates the borrowing and lending decisions of business firms and households. Commercial banks, savings and loan associations, the stock and bond markets, and insurance companies are important financial institutions in this market.

Logrolling The exchange between politicians of political support on one issue for political support on another issue.

Long run A time period of sufficient length to enable decision makers to adjust fully to a market change.

Loss Deficit of sales revenue relative to the opportunity cost of production. Losses are a penalty imposed on those who misuse resources in lower-valued uses as judged by buyers in the market.

M1 (money supply) The sum of (1) currency in circulation (including co ins), (2) checkable deposits maintained in depository institution, and (3) traveler's checks.

M2 (money supply) Equal to M1 plus (1) savings deposits, (2) time deposits (accounts of less than $100,000) held in depository institutions, and (3) money market mutual fund shares.

Macroeconomics The branch of economics that focuses on how human behavior affects outcomes in highly aggregated markets, such as the markets for labor or consumer products.

Marginal Term used to describe the effects of a change in the current situation. For example, the marginal cost is the cost of producing an additional unit of a product, given the producer's current facility and production rate.

Marginal propensity to consume (MPC) Additional current consumption divided by additional current disposable income.

Marginal tax rate (MTR) Additional tax liability divided by additional taxable income. It is the percentage of an extra dollar of income that must be paid in taxes. It is the marginal tax rate that is relevant in personal decision making.

Market An abstract concept that encompasses the trading arrangements of buyers and sellers that underlie the forces of supply and demand.

Market organization A method of organization that allows unregulated prices and the decentralized decisions of private property owners to resolve the basic economic problems of consumption, production, and distribution.

Medium of exchange An asset that is used to buy and sell goods or services.

Microeconomics The branch of economics that focuses on how human behavior affects the conduct of affairs within narrowly defined units, such as individual households or business firms.

Middleman A person who buys and sells, or who arranges trades. A middleman reduces transaction costs.

Minimum wage Legislation requiring that workers be paid at least the state minimum hourly rate of pay.

Monetarists A group of economists who believe that (1) monetary instability is the major cause of fluctuations in real GDP and (2) rapid growth of the money supply is the major cause of inflation.

Monetary base The sum of currency in circulation plus bank reserves (vault cash) and reserves with the Fed. It reflects the stock of U.S. securities held by the Fed.

Monetary policy The deliberate control of the money supply, and, in some cases, credit conditions, for the purposes of achieving macroeconomic goals.

Money interest rate The interest rate measured in monetary units. It overstates the real cost of borrowing during an inflationary period. When inflation is anticipated, an inflationary premium will be incorporated into the nominal value of this rate. The money interest rate is often referred to as the nominal interest rate.

Money market mutual funds Interest-earning accounts offered by brokerage firms that pool depositors' funds and invest them in highly liquid short-term securities. Since these securities can be quickly converted to cash, depositors are permitted to write checks (which reduce their share holdings) against their accounts.

Money supply The supply of currency, checking account funds, and traveler's checks. These items are counted as money because they are used as the means of payment for purchases.

Moral hazard problem The tendency of a party with insurance protection against an unfavorable event to engage in behavior that makes it more likely that the event will occur.

National debt The sum of the indebtedness of the federal government in the form of outstanding interest-earning bonds. It reflects the cumulative impact of budget deficits and surpluses.

National income The total income earned by the nationals (citizens) during a period. It is the sum of employee income, rents, interest, and corporate profits.

Natural rate of unemployment The long-run average unemployment rate due to frictional and structural conditions of labor markets. This rate is affected both by dynamic change and by public policy. It is sustainable into the future. The current natural rate of unemployment in the United States is thought to be between 5 percent and 6 percent.

Net exports Exports minus imports.

Net income of foreigners The income that foreigners earn by contributing labor and capital resources to the production of goods within the borders of a country minus the income the nationals of the country earn abroad.

New classical economists Modern economists who believe there are strong forces pushing a market economy toward full employment equilibrium and that macroeconomic policy is an ineffective tool with which to reduce economic stability.

Nominal GDP GDP expressed at current prices. It is often called money GDP.

Nominal values Values expressed in current dollars.

Nonactivist strategy The maintenance of the same monetary and fiscal policy – that is, no change in money growth, tax rates, or expenditures during all phases of the business cycle.

Normative economics Judgments about "what ought to be" in economic matters. Normative economic views cannot be proved false, because they are based on value judgments.

North American Free Trade Agreement (NAFTA) A comprehensive trade agreement between the United States, Mexico, and Canada that went into effect in 1994. Tariff barriers will continue to be phased out under the agreement until 2004.

Open market operations The buying and selling of U.S. government securities (national debt) by the Federal Reserve.

Opportunity cost The highest valued alternative that must be sacrificed as a result of choosing among alternatives.

Opportunity cost of production The total economic cost of producing a good or service. The cost component includes the opportunity cost of all resources, including those owned by the firm. The opportunity cost is equal to the value of the production of other goods sacrificed as the result producing the good.

Other checkable deposits Interest-earning deposits that are also available for checking.

Pegged exchange-rate system A commitment to use monetary and fiscal policy to maintain the exchange-rate value of the domestic currency at a fixed rate or within a narrow band relative to another currency (or bundle of currencies).

Permanent income hypothesis The hypothesis that consumption depends on some measure of long-run expected (permanent) income rather than on current income.

Personal consumption Household spending on consumer goods and services during the current period. Consumption is a flow concept.

Personal income The total income received by domestic households and noncorporate businesses. It is available for consumption, saving, and payment of personal taxes.

Phillips curve A curve that illustrates the relationship between the rate of change in prices (or money wages) and the rate of unemployment.

Policy-ineffectiveness theorem The proposition that any systematic policy will be rendered ineffective once decision makers figure out the policy pattern and adjust their decision making in light of its expected effects. The theorem is a corollary of the theory of rational expectations.

Pork-barrel legislation A package of spending projects benefiting local areas at federal expense. The projects typically have costs that exceed benefits, but are intensely desired by the residents of the district getting the benefits without having to pay much of the costs.

Positive economics The scientific study of "what is" among economic relationships.

Potential deposit expansion multiplier The maximum potential increase in the money supply as a ratio of the new reserves injected into the banking system. It is equal to the inverse of the required reserve ratio.

Potential output The level of output that can be achieved and sustained into the future, given the size of the labor force, expected productivity of labor, and natural rate of unemployment consistent with the efficient operation of the labor market. For periods of tie, the actual output may differ from the economy's potential.

Price ceiling A legally established maximum price that sellers may charge for a good or resource.

Price controls Government-mandated prices they may be either greater or less than the market equilibrium price.

Price floor A legally established minimum price that buyers must pay for a good or resource.

Private investment The flow of private-sector expenditures on durable assets (fixed investment) plus the addition to inventories (inventory investment) during a period. These expenditures enhance our ability to provide consumer benefits in the future.

Private property rights Property rights that are exclusively held by an owner, or group of owners, and that can be transferred to others at the owner's discretion.

Privately held government debt The portion of the national debt owed to domestic and foreign investors. It does not include bonds held by agencies of the federal government or the Federal Reserve.

Producer surplus The difference between the minimum supply price and the actual sales price. It measures the net gains to producers and resource suppliers from market trade. It is not the same as profit.

Production possibilities curve A curve that outlines all possible combinations of total output that could be produced, assuming (1) the utilization of a fixed amount of production resources, (2) full and efficient use of those resources, and (3) a specific state of technical knowledge. The slope of the curve indicates the rate at which one product can be traded off to produce more of the other.

Productivity The average output produced per worker during a specific time period. It is usually measured in terms of output per hour worked.

Profit An excess of sales revenue relative to the opportunity cost of production. The cost component includes the opportunity cost of all resources, including those owned by the firm. Therefore, profit accrues only when the value of the good produced is greater than the value of other goods that could have been produced with those same resources.

Progressive tax A tax in which the average tax rate rises with income. Persons with higher incomes will pay a higher percentage of their income in taxes.

Property rights The right to use, control, and obtain the benefits from a good or service.

Public choice analysis The study of decision making as it affects the formation and operation of collective organizations, such as governments. In general, the principles and methodology of economics are applied to political science topics.

Public goods Jointly consumed goods that are not diminished when one person enjoys their consumption. When consumed by one person, they are also made available to others. National defense, flood control dams, and scientific theories are all public goods.

Quantity theory of money A theory that hypothesizes that a change in the money supply will cause a proportional change in the price level because velocity and real output are unaffected by the quantity of money.

Random walk theory The theory that current stock prices already reflect known information about the future. Therefore, the future movement of stock prices will be determined by surprise occurrences. This will cause them to change in a random fashion.

Rate of unemployment The percentage of persons in the labor force who are unemployed. Mathematically, it is equal to number of persons unemployed divided by number in the labor force x 100.

Rational ignorance effect Voter ignorance resulting from the fact that people perceive their individual votes as unlikely to be decisive. Therefore, they rationally have little incentive to seek the information needed to cast an informed vote.

Rational-expectations hypothesis The hypothesis that economic decision makers weigh all available evidence, including information concerning the probable effects of current and future economic policy, when they form their expectations about future economic events (such as the probable future inflation rate).

Rationing An allocation of a limited supply of a good or resource to users who would like to have more of it. Various criteria, including charging a price, can be utilized to allocate the limited supply. When price performs the rationing function, the good or resource is allocated to those willing to give up the most "other things" in order to obtain ownership rights.

Real balance effect The increase in wealth generated by an increase in the purchasing power of a constant money supply as the price level decreases. This wealth effect leads to an inverse relationship between price (level) and quantity demanded in the goods and services market.

Real interest rate The interest rate adjusted for expected inflation; it indicates the real cost to the borrower (and yield to the lender) in terms of goods and services.

Real values Values that have been adjusted for the effects of inflation.

Recession A downturn in economic activity characterized by declining real GDP and rising unemployment. In an effort to be more precise, economists define a recession as two consecutive quarters in which there is a decline in real GDP.

Recognition lag The time period after a policy change is needed from a stabilization standpoint but before the need is recognized by policy makers.

Regressive tax A tax in which the average tax rate falls with income. Persons with higher incomes will pay a lower percentage of their income in taxes.

Rent seeking Actions by individuals and interest groups designed to restructure public policy in a manner that will either directly or indirectly redistribute more income to themselves.

Repeat-purchase item An item purchased often by the same buyer.

Replacement rate The share of previous earnings replaced by unemployment benefits.

Required reserves The minimum amount of reserves that a bank is required by law to keep on hand to back up its deposits. Thus, if reserve requirements were 15 percent, banks would be required to keep $150,000 in reserves against each $1 million of deposits.

Resource An input used to produce economic goods. Land, labor, skills, natural resources, and capital are examples. Our history is a record of our struggle to transform available, but limited, resources into things that we would like to have—economic goods.

Restrictive fiscal policy A reduction is government expenditures and/or an increase in tax rates such that the expected size of the budget deficit declines (or the budget surplus increases).

Restrictive monetary policy A shift in monetary policy designed to reduce aggregate demand and place downward pressure on the general level of prices (or the rate of inflation). Bond sales, a decline in bank reserves, and a reduction in the growth rate of the money supply are generally indicative of a restrictive monetary policy.

Ricardian equivalence The view that a tax reduction financed with government debt will exert no impact on current consumption and aggregate demand because people will fully recognize the higher future taxes implied by the additional debt.

Saving The portion of after-tax income that is not spent on consumption. Saving is a "flow" concept.

Savings and loan associations Financial institutions that accept deposits in exchange for shares that pay dividend. Historically, these funds have been channeled into residential mortgage loans. Under banking legislation adopted in 1980, S&Ls are permitted to offer a broad range of services similar to those of commercial banks.

Say's Law The view that production creates its own demand. Demand will always be sufficient to purchase the good produced because the income payments to the resource suppliers will equal the value of the goods purchased.

Scarcity Fundamental concept of economics that indicates that a good is less freely available than consumers would like.

Scientific thinking Development of a theory from basic postulates and the testing of the implications of that theory as to their consistency with events in the real world. Good theories are consistent with and help explain real-world events. Theories that are inconsistent with the real world are invalid and must be rejected.

Secondary effects Economic consequences of an economic change that are not immediately identifiable but are felt only with the passage of time.
Severance pay Pay by an employer to an employee upon the termination of employment with the firm.
Shortage A condition in which the amount of a good offering for sale by producers is less than the amount demanded by buyers at the existing price. An increase in price would eliminate the shortage.
Short run A time period of insufficient length to permit decision makers to adjust fully to a change in market conditions. For example, in the short run, producers will have time to increase output by using more labor and raw materials, but they will not have time to expand the size of their plants or to install additional heavy equipment.
Shortsightedness effect Misallocation of resources that results because public-sector action is biased (1) in favor or proposals yielding clearly defined current benefits in exchange for difficult-to-identify future costs and (2) against proposals with clearly identified current costs but yielding less concrete and less obvious future benefits.
Socialism A system of economic organization in which (1) the ownership and control of the basic means of production rest with the state, and (2) resource allocation is determined by centralized planning rather than market forces.
Special drawing rights (SDRs) Supplementary reserves, in the form of accounting entries, established by the International Monetary Fund (also called paper gold). Like gold and foreign currency reserves, they can be used to make payments on international accounts.
Special interest issue An issue that generates substantial individual benefits to a small minority while imposing a small individual cost on many other voters. In total, the net cost to the majority might either exceed or fall short of the net benefits to the special-interest group.
Stagflation A period during which an economy is experiencing both substantial inflation and either declining or slow growth in output.
Stock options The option to buy a specified number of shares of the firm's stock at a designated price. The designate price is generally set so that the options will be quite valuable if the firm's shares increase in price, but of little value if their price falls. Thus, when used to compensate top managers, stock options provide a strong incentive to follow policies that will increase the value of the firm.
Store of value An asset that will allow people to transfer purchasing power from one period to the next.
Structural unemployment Unemployment due to the structural characteristics of the economy that make it difficult for job seekers to find employment and for employers to hire workers. Although job openings are available, they generally require skills that differ from those of the unemployed workers.
Substitutes Products that serve similar purposes. They are related such that an increase in the price of one will cause an increase in demand for the other (for example, hamburgers and tacos, butter and margarine, Chevrolets and Fords).
Supply shock An unexpected event that temporarily either increases or decreases aggregate supply.
Supply-side economics Modern economists who believe that changes in marginal tax rates exert important effects on aggregate supply.
Surplus A condition in which the amount of a good offered for sale by producers is greater than the amount that buyers will purchase at the existing price. A decline in price would eliminate the surplus.
Tariff A tax levied on goods imported into a country.
Tax base The level or quantity of the economic activity that is taxed (e.g., gallons of gasoline). Because they make the activity less attractive, higher tax rates reduce the level of the tax base.
Tax incidence The manner in which the burden of a tax is distributed among economic units (consumers, producers, employees, and so on). The actual tax burden does not always fall on those who are statutorily assigned to pay the tax.
Tax rate The per-unit amount of the tax or the percentage rate at which the economic activity is taxes.
Technological advancement The introduction of new techniques or methods of production that enable a greater output per unit of light.
Technology The technological knowledge available at any given time. The level of technology establishes the relationship between inputs and the maximum output they can generate.
Trade deficit The situation when a country's imports of goods and services are greater than its exports.
Trade surplus The situation when a country's exports of goods and services are greater than its imports.
Transaction accounts Accounts, including demand deposits and interest-earning checkable deposits, against which the account holder is permitted to transfer funds for the purpose of making payment to a third party.
Transaction costs The time, effort, and other resources needed to search out, negotiate and consummate an exchange.
Unanticipated change A change that decision makers could not reasonably foresee. Thus, choices made prior to the event did not take the event into account.
Unanticipated inflation An increase in the general level of prices that was not expected by most decision makers.
Underground economy Unreported barter and cash transactions that take place outside recorded market channels. Some are otherwise legal activities undertaken to evade taxes. Others involve illegal activities, such as trafficking in drugs and prostitution.
Unemployed The term used to describe a person not currently employed who is either (1) actively seeking employment or (2) waiting to begin or return to a job.
Unit of account The units of measurement used to people to post prices and keep track of revenues and costs.
Utility The benefit or satisfaction expected from a choice or course of action.

Velocity of money The average number of times a dollar is used to purchase final goods and services during a year. It is equal to GDP divided by the stock of money.

Voice The ability to communicate complaints, desires and suggestions to decision makers who may be private buyers, sellers, or decision makers in government.

Voluntary export restraint (VER) An agreement by foreign firms to limit their own exports.

World Trade Organization (WTO) The new name given to GATT in 1994; it is currently responsible for monitoring and enforcing the multilateral trade agreements among the 133 member countries.

LITERARY CREDITS

Exhibit 15-3 "Measures of Economic Activity: Index of Leading Indicators" from BUSINESS CYCLE INDICATORS published by The Conference Board. Reprinted by permission of The Conference Board.

P. 377 Chart from *International Financial Statistics Yearbook: 1997.* Reprinted by permission of International Monetary Fund.

Exhibit A4-5 From A NEW DEAL FOR SOCIAL SECURITY by Peter J. Ferrar and Michael Tanner, 1998, p. 150. Reprinted by permission of The Cato Institute.

PHOTO CREDITS

P. 1 Left	© Bill Bachmann/The Image Works
P. 1 Top right	© Jeff Greenberg/The Image Works
P. 1 Bottom right	© Steven Rubin/The Image Works
P. 2 Left	© Robert Brenner/PhotoEdit
P. 2 Center	© Jonathan Nourok/PhotoEdit
P. 2 Right	© L. Rorke/The Image Works
P. 3 Left	© Karim Shamsi-Basha/ The Image Works
P. 3 Center	© Gary A. Conner/PhotoEdit
P. 3 Right	© Bob Daemmrich/ The Image Works
P. 4	© Tony Freeman/PhotoEdit
P. 11	Library of Congress
P. 13	© Myrleen Ferguson/PhotoEdit
P. 35	Photo courtesy of the Hoover Institution
P. 33	© Phil Sears
P. 39 Left	© David Young-Wolff/PhotoEdit
P. 39 Right	© Leo Snider/The Image Works
P. 46 Left	© Jeff Greenberg/PhotoEdit
P. 46 Top right	© James Nubile/The Image Works
P. 46 Bottom right	© Wesley Bocxe/The Image Works
P. 53 Top left	© Steven Rubin/The Image Works
P. 53 Top right	© David Young-Wolff/PhotoEdit
P. 53 Bottom left	© Paul Conklin/PhotoEdit
P. 53 Bottom right	© Steven Rubin/The Image Works
P. 54 Top	© Bob Daemmrich/The Image Works
P. 54 Bottom left	© John Neubauer/PhotoEdit
P. 54 Bottom right	© David Young-Wolff/PhotoEdit
P. 56	© PhotoDisc
P. 69	Stock Montage
P. 77	© PhotoDisc
P. 100	© John Griffin/The Image Works
P. 104	© Richard Hutchings/PhotoEdit
P. 124	© Corbis/Bettman
P. 129	© David Young-Wolff/PhotoEdit
P. 137 Left	© Bob Daemmrich/The Image Works
P. 137 Right	© Bob Daemmrich/The Image Works
P. 140	© Bill Aron/PhotoEdit
P. 141	© Tony Freeman/PhotoEdit
P. 145	Photo courtesy of George Mason University
P. 146 Left	© Tom Prettyman/PhotoEdit
P. 146 Center	© Bob Daemmrich/The Image Works
P. 146 Right	© Bob Daemmrich/The Image Works
P. 163 Left	© William Johnson/Stock, Boston
P. 163 Center	© Michael Newman/PhotoEdit
P. 163 Right	© Bonnie Kamin/PhotoEdit
P. 164 Left	© Rob Crandall/Stock, Boston
P. 164 Center	© Steven Rubin/The Image Works
P. 164 Right	© Will Hart/PhotoEdit
P. 165	© Gary Wagner/Stock, Boston
P. 168	Photo courtesy of Harvard University
P. 184 Left	© Archive Photos
P. 184 Right	© Reuters/Archive Photos
P. 186	© Mark Godfrey/The Image Works
P. 229	© Steve Skjold/PhotoEdit
P. 231	© 1998 Don Couch Photography
P. 253 Left	© Tony Freeman/PhotoEdit
P. 253 Right	© Spencer Grant/PhotoEdit
P. 260 Top	© David Young-Wolff/PhotoEdit
P. 260 Bottom	© Rob Crandall/Stock, Boston
P. 270	Photo by British Information Services
P. 271	© Corbis/Bettman
P. 286	© Vince Laforet/AllSport
P. 298	© Donna Coveney/Institute Professor Emeritus, MIT
P. 315	© Kevin Horan/Stock, Boston
P. 322	© Corbis/Bettman
P. 325 Top	© Mary M. Steinbacher/PhotoEdit
P. 325 Bottom	© David Young-Wolff/PhotoEdit
P. 327	© Robert Brenner/PhotoEdit
P. 333	© Matt Mendelsohn/Corbis
P. 334	© AFP/Corbis
P. 340 Top	© John Neubauer/PhotoEdit
P. 340 Bottom	© Sandra Baker/Liaison International
P. 345	©Underwood & Underwood/Corbis/ Bettman
P. 353	Photo courtesy of the University of Chicago
P. 384	© Corbis/Bettman
P. 392	Photo courtesy of the University of Chicago
P. 411	© Walter Edwards/National Geographic Society Image Collection
P. 417	©Bob Daemmrich/Stock, Boston
P. 422	© Jane Tyska/Stock, Boston
P. 427 Top left	© Tony Freeman/PhotoEdit
P. 427 Top right	© Jeff Greenberg/PhotoEdit
P. 427 Bottom	© Charles Gupton/Stock, Boston
P. 428 Top	© A. Ramey/PhotoEdit
P. 428 Bottom	© J. Nordell/The Image Works
P. 429 Top	© Paul Conklin/PhotoEdit

P. 429 Bottom © Mark Richards/PhotoEdit
P. 430 Top © David Young-Wolff/PhotoEdit
P. 430 Center © Spencer Grant/PhotoEdit
P. 430 Bottom © Jeff Greenberg/PhotoEdit
P. 431 © Tony Freeman/PhotoEdit
P. 435 © Lisa Quinones/Black Star
P. 445 © Mark Richards/PhotoEdit
P. 449 © Spencer Grant/PhotoEdit
P. 466 © Michelle Bridwell/PhotoEdit
P. 467 Top © John Neubauer/PhotoEdit
P. 467 Bottom © Richard Pasley/Stock, Boston
P. 468 © 1999 Don Couch Photography
P. 484 © Christian Vioujard/Liaison Agency
P. 489 Left © Bruno Barbey/Magnum/PNI
P. 489 Right © Steven Rubin/The Image Works
P. 490 Top © Gary Conner/PhotoEdit
P. 490 Bottom © J. Pickerell/The Image Works
P. 496 © AP Photo/Hans Edinger
P. 500 © AP Photo/Hans Edinger
P. 512 © Kevin Horan/Stock, Boston
P. 548 © Joseph Giannetti/Stock, Boston/PNI

CARTOON CREDITS

P. 10 SHOE reprinted by permission of Tribune Media Services.
P. 12 FAMILY CIRCUS reprinted by special permission of King Features Syndicate.
P. 15 HI AND LOIS reprinted by special permission of King Features Syndicate.
P. 37 From The *Wall Street Journal.* Reprinted by permission of Cartoon Features Syndicate.
P. 107 © John Trever, *Albuquerque Journal.* Reprinted by permission.
P. 131 © Dana Fradon, *The New Yorker* Collection, 1991, from cartoonbank.com. All Rights Reserved.
P. 156 FAMILY CIRCUS reprinted by special permission of King Features Syndicate.
P. 280 TOLES © *The Buffalo News.* Reprinted with permission of Universal Press Syndicate.
P. 338 FRANK & ERNEST © 1988 Bob Thaves. Newspaper Enterprise Association.
P. 541 WIZARD OF ID reprinted by permission of Johnny Hart and Creators Syndicate, Inc.

INDEX

Year	Population and Labor Force				Money Supply (M2)	
	Civilian Noninstitutional Population Age 16+ (Millions)	Civilian Labor Force Participation Rate (Percent)	Rate of Unemployment (Percent)	Civilian Employment/ Population Ratio (Percent)	Money Supply M2 (Billions)	Annual Change in M2
1959	115.3	59.3	5.5	56.0	297.8	-
1960	117.2	59.4	5.5	56.1	312.4	4.9
1961	118.8	59.3	6.7	55.4	335.5	7.4
1962	120.2	58.8	5.5	55.5	362.7	8.1
1963	122.4	58.7	5.7	55.4	393.2	8.4
1964	124.5	58.7	5.2	55.7	424.7	8.0
1965	126.5	58.9	4.5	56.2	459.2	8.1
1966	128.1	59.2	3.8	56.9	480.2	4.6
1967	129.9	59.6	3.8	57.3	524.8	9.3
1968	132.0	59.6	3.6	57.5	566.8	8.0
1969	134.3	60.1	3.5	58.0	587.9	3.7
1970	137.1	60.4	4.9	57.4	626.5	6.6
1971	140.2	60.2	5.9	56.6	710.3	13.4
1972	144.1	60.4	5.6	57.0	802.3	13.0
1973	147.1	60.8	4.9	57.8	855.5	6.6
1974	150.1	61.3	5.6	57.8	902.4	5.5
1975	153.2	61.2	8.5	56.1	1,017.0	12.7
1976	156.2	61.6	7.7	56.8	1,152.8	13.4
1977	159.0	62.3	7.1	57.9	1,271.5	10.3
1978	161.9	63.2	6.1	59.3	1,368.0	7.6
1979	164.9	63.7	5.8	59.9	1,475.8	7.9
1980	167.7	63.8	7.1	59.2	1,601.1	8.5
1981	170.1	63.9	7.6	59.0	1,756.2	9.7
1982	172.3	64.0	9.7	57.8	1,910.9	8.8
1983	174.2	64.0	9.6	57.9	2,127.7	11.3
1984	176.4	64.4	7.5	59.5	2,312.3	8.7
1985	178.2	64.8	7.2	60.1	2,497.7	8.0
1986	180.6	65.3	7.0	60.7	2,734.0	9.5
1987	182.8	65.6	6.2	61.5	2,832.7	3.6
1988	184.6	65.9	5.5	62.3	2,996.4	5.8
1989	186.4	66.5	5.3	63.0	3,161.0	5.5
1990	189.2	66.5	5.6	62.8	3,279.6	3.8
1991	190.9	66.2	6.8	61.7	3,379.9	3.1
1992	192.8	66.4	7.5	61.5	3,434.7	1.6
1993	194.8	66.3	6.9	61.7	3,487.5	1.5
1994	196.8	66.6	6.1	62.5	3,503.0	0.4
1995	198.6	66.6	5.6	62.9	3,651.2	4.2
1996	200.6	66.8	5.4	63.2	3,826.1	4.8
1997	203.1	67.1	4.9	63.8	4,046.4	5.8
1998	205.2	67.1	4.5	64.1	4,412.3	9.0

Source: *Economic Report of the President,* 1999.